MARKETING

AN INTRODUCTION FOURTH CANADIAN EDITION

GARY ARMSTRONG
UNIVERSITY OF NORTH CAROLINA

PHILIP KOTLER
NORTHWESTERN UNIVERSITY

VALERIE TRIFTS
DALHOUSIE UNIVERSITY

LILLY ANNE BUCHWITZ
WILFRID LAURIER UNIVERSITY

CONTRIBUTING AUTHOR
PAUL FINLAYSON
RYERSON UNIVERSITY

Pearson Canada
Toronto

Library and Archives Canada Cataloguing in Publication

Marketing: an introduction / Gary Armstrong ... [et al.] ; contributing author, Paul Finlayson.—4th Canadian ed.

Includes bibliographical references and index.

ISBN 978-0-13-254984-4

1. Marketing—Textbooks.   I. Armstrong, Gary

| HF5415.M295 2011 | 658.8 | C2010-906785-1 |

ISBN 978-0-13-254984-4

Vice-President, Editorial Director: Gary Bennett
Editor-in-Chief: Nicole Lukach
Acquisitions Editor: Nick Durie
Marketing Manager: Leigh-Anne Graham
Developmental Editor: Victoria Naik
Project Managers: Cheryl Jackson, Avinash Chandra
Production Editor: Deborah Cooper-Bullock
Copy Editor: Eleanor Gasparik
Proofreader: Deborah Cooper-Bullock
Compositor: Debbie Kumpf
Photo and Permissions Researcher: Debbie Henderson
Art Director: Julia Hall
Cover and Interior Designer: Miguel Angel Acevedo
Cover Image: Opus House Inc./Sonya Thursby

2 3 4 5   (CR)   15 14 13 12

Printed and bound in the United States of America.

Brief Contents

Contents

6   Understanding Consumer and Business Buyer Behaviour   201

PART 3: DESIGNING A CUSTOMER-DRIVEN MARKETING STRATEGY AND
MARKETING MIX   244

7   Segmentation, Targeting, and Positioning   245

8 Developing and Managing Products and Services 287

11 Marketing Channels: Retailing and Wholesaling 403

About the Authors

GARY ARMSTRONG is Crist W. Blackwell Distinguished Professor Emeritus of Undergraduate Education in the Kenan-Flagler Business School at the University of North Carolina at Chapel Hill. He holds undergraduate and masters degrees in business from Wayne State University in Detroit, and he received his Ph.D. in marketing from Northwestern University. Dr. Armstrong has contributed numerous articles to leading business journals. As a consultant and researcher, he has worked with many companies on marketing research, sales management, and marketing strategy.

But Professor Armstrong's first love has always been teaching. His long-held Blackwell Distinguished Professorship is the only permanent endowed professorship for distinguished undergraduate teaching at the University of North Carolina at Chapel Hill. He has been very active in the teaching and administration of Kenan-Flagler's undergraduate program. His administrative posts have included chair of marketing, associate director of the undergraduate business program, director of the business honors program, and many others. Through the years, he has worked closely with business student groups and has received several campus-wide and Business School teaching awards. He is the only repeat recipient of the school's highly regarded Award for Excellence in Undergraduate Teaching, which he received three times. Most recently, Professor Armstrong received the UNC Board of Governors Award for Excellence in Teaching, the highest teaching honour bestowed by the sixteen-campus University of North Carolina system.

PHILIP KOTLER is S. C. Johnson & Son Distinguished Professor of International Marketing at the Kellogg School of Management, Northwestern University. He received his master's degree at the University of Chicago and his Ph.D. at M.I.T., both in economics. Dr. Kotler is author of *Marketing Management* (Pearson Prentice Hall), now in its 13th edition and the world's most widely used marketing textbook in graduate schools of business worldwide. He has authored dozens of other successful books and has written more than 100 articles in leading journals. He is the only three-time winner of the coveted Alpha Kappa Psi award for the best annual article in the *Journal of Marketing*.

Professor Kotler was named the first recipient of two major awards: the Distinguished Marketing Educator of the Year Award given by the American Marketing Association and the Philip Kotler Award for Excellence in Health Care Marketing presented by the Academy for Health Care Services Marketing. His numerous other major honours include the Sales and Marketing Executives International Marketing Educator of the Year Award; The European Association of Marketing Consultants and Trainers Marketing Excellence Award; the Charles Coolidge Parlin Marketing Research Award; and the Paul D. Converse Award, given by the American Marketing Association to honour "outstanding contributions to science in marketing." In a recent *Financial Times* poll of 1000 senior executives across the world,

Professor Kotler was ranked as the fourth "most influential business writer/guru" of the 21st century.

Dr. Kotler has served as chairman of the College on Marketing of the Institute of Management Sciences, a director of the American Marketing Association, and a trustee of the Marketing Science Institute. He has consulted with many major U.S. and international companies in the areas of marketing strategy and planning, marketing organization, and international marketing. He has travelled and lectured extensively throughout Europe, Asia, and South America, advising companies and governments about global marketing practices and opportunities.

VALERIE TRIFTS is an associate professor in marketing at Dalhousie University School of Business in Halifax. She received her undergraduate business degree from the University of Prince Edward Island, her MBA from Saint Mary's University, and her Ph.D. in marketing from the University of Alberta. Her primary research interests are in the area of consumer information search and decision-making. Specifically, she is interested in how firms can benefit from strategically providing their customers with information about competitors, as well as exploring individual difference variables that influence search behaviour. She integrates her research into a variety of courses she has taught, including introduction to marketing, consumer behaviour, Internet marketing, and marketing research at both the undergraduate and graduate levels. Her research has been published in *Marketing Science* and the *Journal of Consumer Psychology*, presented at numerous academic conferences, and funded by the Social Sciences and Humanities Research Council of Canada.

LILLY ANNE BUCHWITZ is an author, teacher, and expert in the field of Internet marketing and advertising who became an academic after 15 years in the professional world of high-tech product marketing and Internet services. In the early days of the Internet, she was the marketing manager for the Open Text Index, one of the original Internet search engines developed by Canadian software company Open Text; she became somewhat notorious for developing paid search advertising in 1996. She later worked for the Internet start-up that became About.com, helped launch Internet advertising network DoubleClick in Canada, and was the Internet marketing manager for Chapters Online. Her professional activities eventually led her to teaching and research in the still-developing field of Internet advertising, and she recently completed her Ph.D. in marketing at Bristol Business School, University of the West of England. She is currently working on turning her dissertation, "Exploring the Life Cycle of Advertising on a New Mass Medium: A Comparison of the Histories of Internet and Radio Advertising," into a book. She has undergraduate degrees in English literature and education from McGill University, and an MBA from Wilfrid Laurier University. She began her university teaching career at the University of New Brunswick in their emerging e-commerce program in St. John, as well as in their business education program in Beijing, China. Later, she taught marketing communications and Internet marketing at Brock University in St. Catharines, and then spent three years in the capital of Silicon Valley, as an Assistant Professor at San Jose State University. She is currently an instructor in the School of Business and Economics at Wilfrid Laurier University in Waterloo.

Preface

THE FOURTH CANADIAN EDITION OF *MARKETING: AN INTRODUCTION*: CREATING MORE VALUE FOR YOU!

The fourth Canadian edition of Marketing: An Introduction makes learning and teaching marketing more effective, easier, and more enjoyable than ever. Its streamlined approach strikes a careful balance between depth of coverage and ease of learning. The fourth Canadian edition's brand new design enhances student understanding. And when combined with MyMarketingLab, our online homework and personalized study tool, *Marketing: An Introduction* ensures that you will come to class well prepared and leave class with a richer understanding of basic marketing concepts, strategies, and practices.

MARKETING: CREATING CUSTOMER VALUE AND RELATIONSHIPS

Top marketers all share a common goal: putting the consumer at the heart of marketing. Today's marketing is all about creating customer value and building profitable customer relationships. It starts with understanding consumer needs and wants, deciding which target markets the organization can serve best, and developing a compelling value proposition by which the organization can attract, keep, and grow targeted consumers. If the organization does these things well, it will reap the rewards in terms of market share, profits, and customer equity. In the fourth Canadian edition of *Marketing: An Introduction*, you'll see how *customer value*—creating it and capturing it—drives every good marketing strategy.

FIVE MAJOR VALUE THEMES

The text is built around the five major themes described below. These themes and the many related key concepts are brought to life through cases and examples that have been written just for this edition by Canadian authors. In this fourth Canadian edition, you'll find many stories about Canadian companies, such as The Running Room and RIM, and real Canadians working in fields such as marketing research and music marketing. Each chapter also considers international marketing, both in terms of what Canadian companies are doing abroad and what interesting marketing activities foreign companies are engaging in.

The fourth Canadian edition of *Marketing: An Introduction* builds on five major value themes:

1. ***Creating value for customers in order to capture value from customers in return.*** Today's outstanding marketing companies understand the marketplace and customer needs, design value-creating marketing strategies, develop integrated marketing programs that deliver value and satisfaction, and build strong customer relationships. In return, they capture value from customers in the form of sales, profits, and customer equity. This innovative customer value framework is introduced in a five-step marketing process model, which details how marketing creates customer value and captures value in return. The framework is carefully explained and integrated throughout the text.

2. ***Building and managing strong brands to create brand equity.*** Well-positioned brands with strong brand equity provide the basis upon which to build profitable customer relationships. Today's marketers must position their brands powerfully and manage them well. The fourth Canadian edition provides a deep focus on brands with expanded coverage of brand strategy and management in Chapter 9.

3. ***Measuring and managing return on marketing.*** Marketing managers must ensure that their marketing dollars are being well spent. In the past, many marketers spent freely on big, expensive marketing programs, often without thinking carefully about the financial returns on their spending. But all that has changed—measuring and managing return on marketing investments has become an important part of strategic marketing decision-making. The fourth Canadian edition specifically addresses return on marketing investment.

4. ***Harnessing new marketing technologies.*** New digital and other high-tech marketing developments are dramatically changing consumers and marketers, and the ways in which they relate to one another. The fourth Canadian edition thoroughly explores the new technologies impacting marketing, from "Web 3.0" to new-age digital marketing and from online technologies to the exploding use of social networks and customer-generated marketing.

5. ***Marketing in a socially responsible way around the globe.*** As technological developments make the world an increasingly smaller place, marketers must be good at marketing their brands globally and in socially responsible ways. The fourth Canadian edition integrates global marketing and social responsibility topics throughout the text, including a revised Chapter 3 dedicated to sustainable marketing.

NEW IN THE FOURTH CANADIAN EDITION

We've thoroughly revised the fourth Canadian edition of *Marketing: An Introduction* to reflect the major trends and forces impacting marketing in this era of customer value and relationships. Here are just some of the major changes you'll find in this edition.

☐ New **ScanLife™ barcodes** enable students to link to Pearson Canada's unique Study on the Go content directly from their smartphones.

☐ Throughout the fourth Canadian edition, you will find important new coverage of the rapidly **changing nature of customer relationships** with companies and brands. Today's marketers aim to create deeper consumer involvement and a sense of community surrounding a brand—to make the brand a meaningful part of consumers' conversations and their lives. New relationship-building tools include everything from websites, blogs, in-person events, and video sharing to online communities and social networks such as Facebook, YouTube, Twitter, or a company's own social networking sites.

☐ New coverage in every chapter shows how companies are dealing with **marketing and the turbulent economy** in the aftermath of the recent worldwide economic meltdown. Starting with a major new section in Chapter 1 and continuing with discussions and examples integrated throughout the text, the fourth Canadian edition shows how, now more than ever, marketers must focus on creating customer value and sharpening their value propositions to serve the needs of today's more frugal consumers.

☐ A revised Chapter 3 pulls marketing together under an important new **sustainable marketing** framework. Additional discussions throughout the fourth Canadian edition show how sustainable marketing calls for socially and environmentally responsible actions that meet both the immediate and the future needs of customers, the company, and society as a whole.

☐ Increasingly, marketing is taking the form of two-way conversations between consumers and brands. The fourth Canadian edition contains new material on the exciting trend toward **consumer-generated marketing**, by which marketers invite consumers to play a more active role in providing customer insights (Chapter 5), shaping new products (Chapter 8), developing or passing along brand messages (Chapter 12), interacting in customer communities (Chapters 6, 12, and 14), and other developments.

☐ This edition provides new and expanded discussions of new **marketing technologies**, from "Web 3.0" in Chapter 1 to neuromarketing in Chapter 6 to RFID in Chapter 11 to the new-age digital marketing and online technologies in Chapters 1, 6, 12, and 14.

☐ In line with the text's emphasis on **measuring and managing return on marketing**, we've added end-of-chapter financial and quantitative marketing exercises that let students apply analytical thinking to relevant concepts in each chapter and link chapter concepts to the text's innovative Appendix 3, Marketing by the Numbers.

☐ The fourth Canadian edition provides refreshed and expanded coverage of the explosive developments in **integrated marketing communications** and **direct and online marketing**. It tells how marketers are incorporating a host of new digital and direct approaches to build and create more targeted, personal, and interactive customer relationships. No other text provides more current or encompassing coverage of these exciting developments.

☐ An expanded discussion of **branding** (Chapter 9) provided better coverage of how brands are effectively developed and managed, and a restructured **pricing** chapter (Chapter 10) provides improved coverage of pricing strategies and tactics in an uncertain economy.

REAL VALUE THROUGH REAL MARKETING

Marketing: An Introduction features in-depth, real-world examples and stories that show concepts in action and reveal the drama of modern marketing. In the fourth Canadian edition, every chapter contains an opening vignette and Marketing@Work stories that provide fresh and relevant insights into real marketing practices. Learn how:

☐ The Running Room's obsession with creating the very best customer experience has resulted in avidly loyal customers and astronomical growth.

☐ Nike's customer-focused mission and deep sense of customer brand community have the company sprinting ahead while competitors are gasping for breath.

☐ Bullfrog Power shows how an innovative new company can address issues related to sustainability while stretching a limited marketing budget through the use of powerful public relations techniques.

☐ When it comes to sustainability, no company in the world is doing more good these days than Wal-Mart. That's right—big, bad Wal-Mart.

☐ Biotherm Homme, a division of Montreal-based L'Oréal, targets the fast-growing male grooming products segment of the cosmetics market.

☐ Google innovates at the speed of light—it's part of the company's DNA.

☐ Canadian brewery Sleeman branded itself as "Notoriously good since 1834," and targets individuals 25 and older who are looking for a "notoriously good evening."

☐ McDonald's, the quintessentially all-American company, now sells more burgers and fries outside the United States than within.

☐ Amazon.com has become one of the best-known names on the Web and has been viewed as the model for business in the digital age.

Beyond these features, each chapter is packed with countless real, relevant, and timely examples that reinforce key concepts. No other text brings marketing to life like the fourth Canadian edition of *Marketing: An Introduction*.

VALUABLE LEARNING AIDS

A wealth of chapter-opening, within-chapter, and end-of-chapter learning devices help students to learn, link, and apply major concepts:

☐ ***Chapter-opening Content.*** The new, more active and integrative opening spread in each chapter features a brief Previewing the Concepts section that includes chapter concepts, an outline of chapter content and learning objectives, and an opening vignette—an engaging, deeply developed, illustrated, and annotated marketing story that introduces the chapter material and sparks student interest.

☐ ***Marketing@Work highlights.*** Each chapter contains two highlight features that provide an in-depth look at real marketing practices of large and small companies.

☐ ***Reviewing the Concepts.*** A summary at the end of each chapter reviews major chapter concepts and links them to chapter objectives.

☐ ***Key Terms.*** A helpful listing of chapter key terms by order of appearance with page numbers facilitates easy reference.

☐ ***Talk About Marketing.*** This section contains discussion questions that require students to think about, discuss, defend, and apply the concepts in the chapter.

☐ ***Think Like a Marketing Manager.*** A very short case gives a real-world example of one of the concepts in the chapter in action, followed by application questions.

☐ ***Marketing Ethics.*** Situation descriptions and questions at the end of each chapter highlight important issues in marketing ethics and social responsibility.

☐ ***Marketing Technology.*** Application exercises at the end of each chapter facilitate discussion of important and emerging marketing technologies in this digital age.

☐ ***Marketing by the Numbers.*** An exercise at the end of each chapter lets students apply analytical and financial thinking to relevant chapter concepts and links the chapter to Appendix 3, Marketing by the Numbers.

☐ ***Video Case.*** Short vignettes with discussion questions at the end of every chapter are to be used with the set of mostly new 4- to 7-minute videos that accompany the fourth Canadian edition.

☐ ***Marketing by the Numbers.*** An innovative Appendix 3 provides you with a comprehensive introduction to the marketing financial analysis that helps to guide, assess, and support marketing decisions.

The fourth Canadian edition of Marketing: An Introduction provides an effective and enjoyable total package for moving you down the road to learning marketing!

STUDY ON THE GO

Featured at the end of each chapter, you will find a unique barcode providing access to Study on the Go, an unprecedented mobile integration between text and online content. Students link to Pearson's unique Study on the Go content directly from their smartphones, allowing them to study whenever and wherever they wish! Go to one of the sites listed on the right to see how you can download an app to your smartphone for free. Once the app is installed, your phone will scan the code and link to a website containing Pearson's Study on the Go content, including the popular study tools Glossary Flashcards, Audio Summaries, and Quizzes, which can be accessed anytime.

ScanLife
http://get.scanlife.com/

NeoReader
http://get.neoreader.com/

QuickMark
http://www.quickmark.com.tw/

COMPREHENSIVE CASE: CANADA GOOSE®

Canada Goose Inc. is a privately held outerwear manufacturer based in Toronto. Their outdoor gear is considered by many to be amongst the warmest and most fashionable cold weather outerwear in the world. We've used Canada Goose as our comprehensive case in the fourth edition. This case material can be found in three key areas of the text:

1. *Canada Goose Mini Cases.* At the end of each chapter is a short case about the company that illustrates how they employ the topics covered in that chapter.

2. *Appendix 1 – General Company Information: Canada Goose.* This appendix tells the story of Canada Goose and illustrates how their marketing strategy has been a key element of their success.

3. *Appendix 2 – The Marketing Plan: An Introduction.* Our second appendix contains a sample marketing plan that helps you to see how marketing concepts translate into real-life marketing strategies.

CANADA GOOSE® MINI CASE

RUFFLED FUR: KEEPING TRUE TO THE BRAND

Canada Goose's brand mantra is "Ask Anyone Who Knows™." The message is clear: If you understand the quality of fabric, down, and overall construction necessary to create an effective warm coat, you'll go with Canada Goose. However, in staying true to its message of value and utility, Canada Goose has faced some complex ethical choices.

For example, consider the fur-trimmed hood featured in many of its jacket designs. When investigating the best natural hood trim for its winter jackets, Canada Goose learned from Inuit experts that coyote fur was the most functional and practical way to keep people warm. However, in many of Canada Goose's markets, environmentalists and animal activists are against the use of fur under all circumstances. How could Canada Goose explain its decision to use real fur to these individuals?

For Canada Goose, the answer was to honour the "true users" segment of its customer makeup by providing the best cold-weather outerwear by using the most environmentally sustainable materials available. This meant rejecting the use of fake fur, which is a petroleum-based product and has little functional value for providing warmth. Canada Goose delved deep into the science of fabrics and warmth and, with the aid of a researcher with a Ph.D., discovered that coyote fur has unique characteristics that lead to unparalleled efficacy at keeping the wearer's neck and face warm.

There was no doubt that if Canada Goose was to uphold its commitment to create the best cold-weather outdoor gear, then coyote fur was the best product. The company wanted, however, to assure its customers that the fur was not coming from "fur farms." Instead, it decided that it would purchase all fur through audited auctions.

"There will always be critics," said vice-president of marketing Kevin Spreekmeester. "But we felt that coyote fur was the right way to go. Coyote fur is more environmentally sustainable than a petroleum-based fake fur, coyote fur actually protects your face from frostbite and faux fur is not functional—it's simply an aesthetic, and we need to be loyal to our customers who expect us to provide the most effective cold weather materials."

To read more about Canada Goose's fur policy, visit the frequently asked questions section of its website at www.canada-goose.com/faq/.

QUESTIONS

1. Whether you agree or disagree with fur being used on the hoods, what do you think of the way Canada Goose has approached this issue?
2. Is "sustainability" simply a new marketing "flavour of the month," or does it have an ethical meaning for you? Discuss.
3. How closely related is corporate social responsibility to public relations? If public relations are about keeping good relations with the public and the public respects "socially responsible" organizations, can the two directives lead to the same point?

Appendix 2
The Marketing Plan: An Introduction

As a marketer, you'll need a good marketing plan to provide direction and focus for your brand, product, or company. With a detailed plan, any business will be better prepared to launch a new product or build sales for existing products. Non-profit organizations also use marketing plans to guide their fundraising and outreach efforts. Even government agencies put together marketing plans for initiatives such as building public awareness of proper nutrition and stimulating area tourism.

THE PURPOSE AND CONTENT OF A MARKETING PLAN

Unlike a business plan, which offers a broad overview of the entire organization's mission, objectives, strategy, and resource allocation, a marketing plan has a more limited scope. It serves to document how the organization's strategic objectives will be achieved through specific marketing strategies and tactics, with the customer as the starting point. It is also linked to the plans of other departments within the organization. Suppose a marketing plan calls for selling 200 000 units annually. The production department must gear up to make that many units; the finance department must arrange funding to cover the expenses; the human resources department must be ready to hire and train staff; and so on. Without the appropriate level of organizational support and resources, no marketing plan can succeed.

Although the exact length and layout will vary from company to company, a marketing plan usually contains the sections described in Chapter 2. Smaller businesses may create shorter or less formal marketing plans, whereas corporations frequently require highly structured marketing plans. To guide implementation effectively, every part of the plan must be described in considerable detail. Sometimes a company will post its marketing plan on an internal website, which allows managers and employees in different locations to consult specific sections and collaborate on additions or changes.

THE ROLE OF RESEARCH

Marketing plans are not created in a vacuum. To develop successful strategies and action programs, marketers need up-to-date information about the environment, the competition, and the market segments to be served. Often, analysis of internal data is the starting point for assessing the current marketing situation, supplemented by marketing intelligence and research investigating the overall market, the competition, key issues, and threats and opportunities. As the plan is put into effect, marketers use a variety of research techniques to measure progress toward objectives and to identify areas for improvement if results fall short of projections.

Finally, marketing research helps marketers learn more about their customers' requirements, expectations, perceptions, and satisfaction levels. This deeper understanding provides a foundation for building competitive advantage through well-informed segmenting, targeting, and positioning decisions. Thus, the marketing plan should outline what marketing research will be conducted and how the findings will be applied.

575

TEACHING AND LEARNING SUPPORT

A successful marketing course requires more than a well-written book. Today's classroom requires a dedicated teacher and a fully integrated teaching package. A total package of teaching and learning supplements extends this edition's emphasis on effective teaching and learning. The aids on the following page support *Marketing: An Introduction.*

Instructor's Resource CD-ROM (ISBN-13: 978-0-13-216578-5). This is the one-stop shop for all your supplement needs. The CD-ROM contains the entire Instructor's Resource Manual, TestGen, PowerPoint Presentations, Personal Response System "Clicker" Questions, and Image Library.

Instructor's Resource Manual. This invaluable resource not only includes chapter-by-chapter teaching strategies, it also features notes about the PowerPoint slides and the video cases. This supplement is available on the Instructor's Resource CD-ROM and through Pearson Education Canada's online catalogue at http://vig.pearsoned.ca.

Pearson MyTest. This computerized test bank includes up to 110 multiple-choice and true/false questions, plus essay and short-answer questions. All questions include the correct answer and are linked to a learning objective from the chapter. The MyTest is available through MyMarketingLab at www.pearsoned.ca/mymarketinglab.

PowerPoint® Presentations. PowerPoint slides are available with this edition, with a minimum of 25 slides per chapter. The PPTs can be accessed on the Instructor's Resource CD-ROM. The Express set is also available to instructors through Pearson Education Canada's online catalogue at http://vig.pearsoned.ca.

Image Library. Includes figures, tables, and photos from the text.

Personal Response System Questions. These questions are designed to be used in conjunction with "clickers" from an outside vendor. They are a great way to increase student participation, especially in large introductory courses.

MyMarketingLab. This online platform contains an eText, and lots of multimedia tutorials, animations, concept maps, videos, MP3 audio downloads, quizzes, study plans, and cases. MyMarketingLab is robust enough to administer an online course, helpful for students as a study tool, and can be used as a testing platform for course marks.

Technology Specialists. Pearson's Technology Specialists work with faculty and campus course designers to ensure that Pearson technology products, assessment tools, and online course materials are tailored to meet your specific needs. This highly qualified team is dedicated to helping schools take full advantage of a wide range of educational resources, by assisting in the integration of a variety of instructional materials and media formats. Your local Pearson Education sales representative can provide you with more details on this service program.

CourseSmart. CourseSmart is a new way for instructors and students to access textbooks online anytime from anywhere. With thousands of titles across hundreds of courses, CourseSmart helps instructors choose the best textbook for their class and give their students a new option for buying the assigned textbook as a lower cost eTextbook. For more information, visit www.coursesmart.com.

ACKNOWLEDGMENTS

Writing a textbook, even when it is a new edition of a previous work, is a long, long process that requires a hard-working and dedicated team of people. On behalf of Gary Armstrong, Philip Kotler, and Lilly Anne Buchwitz, I would like to acknowledge the incredible team of editors, writers, and designers at Pearson without whom you would not be holding this book in your hands: Gary Bennett, editor-in-chief; Nick Durie, acquisitions editor; Victoria Naik, senior developmental editor; Cheryl Jackson, project manager; Deborah Cooper-Bullock, production editor; Eleanor Gasparik, copy editor; Miguel Acevedo, designer; and Leigh-Anne Graham, marketing manager. I would also like to thank Paul Finlayson, the author of the Canada Goose mini cases and Appendix 1 and 2 for his contributions to the text. Dani Reise, president and CEO of Canada Goose, and Kevin Spreekmeester, vice-president global marketing at Canada Goose, deserve a very special thanks for all of their help in providing information for the Comprehensive Case material.

There were many marketing instructors and professors at schools across Canada who provided valuable comments and suggestions for this edition. In particular, I would like to thank:

Jack Brown, *Georgian College*

Brahm Canzar, *John Abbot College*

Sungchul Choi, *University of Northern British Columbia*

George Dracopoulos, *Vanier College*

Ian Fisher, *Sheridan College*

Bob Graves, *Grant MacEwan University*

Don Hill, *Langara College*

Tom Jopling, *British Columbia Institute of Technology*

Yuanfang Lin, *University of Alberta*

Brad MacDonald, *Nova Scotia Community College*

Sherry McEvoy, *Fanshawe College*

David Moulton, *Douglas College*

Diana Serafini, *Dawson College*

Finally, we owe many thanks to our families for their constant support and encouragement. To them, we dedicate this book.

Valerie Trifts

MARKETING

AFTER STUDYING THIS CHAPTER, YOU SHOULD BE ABLE TO

 define marketing and outline the steps in the marketing process

 explain the importance of understanding customers and the marketplace, and identify the five core marketplace concepts

 identify the key elements of a customer-driven marketing strategy and discuss the marketing management orientations that guide marketing strategy

 discuss customer relationship management and identify strategies for creating value *for* customers and capturing value *from* customers in return

 describe the major trends and forces that are changing the marketing landscape in this age of relationships

Marketing: Creating and Capturing Customer Value

PREVIEWING THE CONCEPTS

You're about to begin an exciting journey toward learning about marketing. In this chapter, we start with the question, What *is* marketing? Simply put, marketing is managing profitable customer relationships. The aim of marketing is to create value *for* customers and to capture value *from* customers in return. Next, we discuss the five steps in the marketing process—from understanding customer needs, to designing customer-driven marketing strategies and integrated marketing programs, to building customer relationships and capturing value for the firm. Finally, we discuss the major trends and forces affecting marketing in this age of customer relationships. Understanding these basic concepts, and forming your own ideas about what they really mean to you, will give you a solid foundation for all that follows.

Let's start with a good story about marketing in action at the Running Room, one of Canada's most successful specialty retailers. The secret to the Running Room's success? It's really no secret at all. Customer service is an essential component of the company philosophy and is what keeps the Running Room competitive. In return, customers reward the Running Room with their brand loyalty and buying dollars. You'll see this theme of creating customer value in order to capture value in return repeated throughout the first chapter and throughout the text.

RUNNING ROOM: A PASSION FOR CREATING CUSTOMER VALUE AND RELATIONSHIPS

Perhaps no Canadian retailer has experienced growth quite as remarkable as that of the Running Room. Founded in Edmonton in 1984 by John Stanton, who was looking to purchase quality running shoes from someone knowledgeable about the sport, the Running Room has grown to over 100 locations across Canada and a handful in the United States. While exact sales numbers are not available for this family-owned business, some analysts estimate sales of over $100 million annually.

Expansion to the U.S. market was one growth strategy of the company, but not its primary one. In 2004, Stanton announced the opening of the Walking Room, which allowed the company to grow into smaller Canadian markets, such as Sudbury, Ontario, and Fredericton, New Brunswick, which would not have been financially feasible for the Running Room alone. While expecting its new stores to cater to seniors and older boomers no longer able to handle the physical stress of running, the company soon found out that the new combined Running Room/Walking Room stores were attracting younger customers in their 20s and 30s who wanted to become more active. "A lot of younger people today work harder and longer, and they do that work in front of computers. As a result, they're more sedentary. They're looking at doing something active, but running can be intimidating," says Stanton. "Dealing with walkers of all ages was a huge learning curve for us. We discovered we weren't talking to walkers who would eventually become runners. Walkers made it clear to us that walking was their sport and that they had no intention of ever becoming runners."

In a recent interview with the *Calgary Herald*, John Stanton was asked about the major reason his business was expanding:

> I think everybody is concerned about childhood obesity and the aging baby boomer, and the burden that our health-care system is under. People know they have to get fit and be active. The primary thing we try to do is to show people through our Learn To Run programs and training clinics that when you engage in exercise there's a natural transition to healthy eating, and pretty soon you start to take control of your own life just by the simple thing of going for a run. If someone's overweight, walking is sometimes a great option for them to get started. It's less daunting. The number one thing I've found that keeps people from exercising is fear of embarrassment.... By putting people in a group environment, it's like kids joining a soccer team, a ball team or a hockey team. All of a sudden you start having fun and enjoying it and it continues. That's what we've been able to do.

So, what factors led to the company's success? The Running Room's reputation has been built upon product innovation, quality, and the knowledge of the sport of running. Its private label products have been developed to provide customers with the best in style, functionality, fabric innovations, and reasonable price, and have been developed with the input of customers and staff alike. The company even created a new clothing line for walkers, who require heavier, looser clothing in contrast to the close-fitting spandex garments favoured by runners. Even packs had to be specially designed for walkers. Runners may carry a nutrient bar, but walkers want room for more substantial snacks. While quality merchandise is one factor contributing to the company's success (judging by the rate at which runners and walkers alike purchase the products), it is not the main reason behind the explosive growth. In fact, the Running Room's success can be summed up in one word: *relationships*. The deep connections cultivated among the owner/company, its customers, and the broader community are the driving force behind the Running Room's success.

The Running Room has managed to create customer value and relationships in a number of ways. Service has always been an essential component of the company philosophy and is what keeps it competitive. All employees are considered Team Members, and all are runners. Who else but a runner is knowledgeable about the needs of runners, as well as the products that cater to those needs? The Running Room philosophy is that if you're out there running on the same roads as the customers, you can relate to their exact needs. The Running Room is truly a store for runners by runners. Yet, when the company opened the combined Running Room/Walking Room outlets, it had to overcome its own brand image to deal with the potential intimidation walkers may feel on entering a running store. The solution was to give equal prominence to the Walking Room brand on the exterior signs of the new combined stores. In-store signage also clearly differentiates walking and running gear.

In addition to its in-store service, the Running Room offers an incredible number of clinics such as Walking, Learn to Run, Marathon, Half Marathon, 10K Training, Personal Best, and For Women Only Running Clinics. The tremendous success of these clinics is evident from the over 600 000 clinic graduates to date. The Running Room clinic program is committed to a lifestyle of fitness. The various programs meet the needs of those just getting into a fitness routine and of those contemplating a marathon. In addition, there is the Running Room

Running Club, which has no membership fee and allows all levels of runners to run in a group setting twice weekly. The Running Room Running Club really adds a social component to running since you get an opportunity to run with a variety of people and receive some great coaching on running techniques and training methods.

Finally, the Running Room and its owner, John Stanton, are actively involved in building strong relationships in the community. The Running Room sponsors and helps organize and promote more than 400 walks, runs, and events that annually raise millions of dollars for local charities and non-profit organizations. For example, the Running Room hosts clinics all across Canada for runners wishing to compete in the Scotiabank Toronto Waterfront Marathon, which is expected to raise more than $2.5 million in 2010 for Canadian charities. It partnered with Weight Watchers Canada to promote the country's first Walk-It Challenge, which saw over 7000 Canadians from coast-to-coast take their first steps toward physical activity. Stanton himself takes part in several of these events, from participating as the "pace bunny" in Halifax's Scotiabank Blue Nose Marathon to holding Q&A online forums on the *Globe and Mail* website.

The company's hands-on approach and deep customer focus has led to some wonderful personal success stories, including the following:

☐ The Calgary writer, whose long-time dream to finish a marathon alongside her husband finally came through—she first completed 16 weeks of marathon training offered by the Running Room.

☐ Sudbury, Ontario, native Kandis Stoughton, who completed the 2010 Boston Marathon, known to be one of the most challenging marathons to even qualify for—her passion for running began with a 5k clinic offered by the Running Room.

☐ Darrel Wilkins of New Brunswick, who quit smoking after 33 years and has become an accomplished marathoner with over 10 races behind him, including the Boston Marathon—the path to his success began with a 5k clinic offered by the Running Room.

Personal achievements such as these have come as a result of the company's deep commitment to building lasting relationships not only with customers and community but also between customers. "We believe that the Running Room philosophy and our in-store environment are unlike any other retail business in North America. While we offer clothing, shoes, products and accessories for walkers and runners, we also help people to change their lives through fitness activities," said Stanton. "Through the Running Room and Walking Room, people can gain a tremendous sense of belonging that comes from walking or running alongside people who share similar goals: improving wellness, while having fun and adventure exploring our cities on foot. The Running Room becomes very important to our customers, because their well-being is very important to us."[1]

TODAY'S successful companies have one thing in common: Like the Running Room, they are strongly customer focused and heavily committed to marketing. These companies share a passion for understanding and satisfying customer needs in well-defined target markets. They motivate everyone in the organization to help build lasting customer relationships based on creating value.

Customer relationships and value are especially important in today's tough economic times, when more frugal consumers are cutting back and spending more carefully. "The challenge facing us is not just one of consumers being more-value conscious," says one marketing consultant. "It's how we gain ... a renewed relationship with consumers who have less inclination to listen to [companies with whom] they do not have strong and valued relationships."[2]

WHAT IS MARKETING? 🔘

Marketing, more than any other business function, deals with customers. Although we will soon explore more-detailed definitions of marketing, perhaps the simplest definition is this one: *Marketing is managing profitable customer relationships.* The twofold goal of marketing is to attract new customers by promising superior value and to keep and grow current customers by delivering satisfaction.

For example, Wal-Mart has become the world's largest retailer—and the world's second-largest *company*—by delivering on its promise, "Save money. Live better." Nintendo surged ahead in the video games market with the promise that "Wii would like to play," backed by its wildly popular Wii console and growing list of popular games and accessories for all ages. And Apple fulfills its motto to "Think Different" with dazzling, customer-driven innovation that captures customer imaginations and loyalty. Its incredibly successful iPod grabs more than 70 percent of the music player market; its iTunes music store is now the world's number-two music store—online or offline (Wal-Mart is number one).[3]

Sound marketing is critical to the success of every organization. Large for-profit firms such as Procter & Gamble, Google, Research In Motion, Honda, and Marriott use marketing. But so do not-for-profit organizations such as universities, hospitals, museums, symphony orchestras, and even churches.

You already know a lot about marketing—it's all around you. Marketing comes to you in the good old traditional forms: You see it in the abundance of products at your nearby shopping mall and in the advertisements that fill your TV screen, spice up your magazines, or stuff your mailbox. But in recent years, marketers have assembled a host of new marketing approaches, everything from imaginative websites and online social networks to interactive TV and your cellphone. These new approaches do more than just blast out messages to the masses. They reach you directly and personally. Today's marketers want to become a part of your life and to enrich your experiences with their brands—to help you to *live* their brands.

At home, at school, where you work, and where you play, you see marketing in almost everything you do. Yet, there is much more to marketing than meets the consumer's casual eye. Behind it all is a massive network of people and activities competing for your attention and purchases. This book will give you a complete introduction to the basic concepts and practices of today's marketing. In this chapter, we begin by defining marketing and the marketing process.

MARKETING DEFINED

What *is* marketing? Many people think of marketing only as selling and advertising. And no wonder—every day we are bombarded with TV commercials, direct-mail offers, sales calls, and email pitches. However, selling and advertising are only the tip of the marketing iceberg.

Today, marketing must be understood not in the old sense of making a sale—"telling and selling"—but in the new sense of *satisfying customer needs.* If the marketer understands consumer needs; develops products that provide superior customer value; and prices, distributes, and promotes them effectively, these products will sell easily. In fact, according to management guru Peter Drucker, "The aim of marketing is to make selling unnecessary."[4] Selling and advertising are only part of a larger "marketing mix"—a set of marketing tools that work together to satisfy customer needs and build customer relationships.

Broadly defined, marketing is a social and managerial process by which individuals and organizations obtain what they need and want through creating and exchanging value with others. In a narrower business context, marketing involves building profitable, value-laden exchange relationships with customers. Hence, we define **marketing** as the process by which companies create value for customers and build strong customer relationships in order to capture value from customers in return.[5]

Marketing
The process by which companies create value for customers and build strong customer relationships in order to capture value from customers in return.

THE MARKETING PROCESS

Figure 1.1 presents a simple five-step model of the marketing process. In the first four steps, companies work to understand consumers, create customer value, and build strong customer relationships. In the final step, companies reap the rewards of creating superior customer value. By creating value *for* consumers, they in turn capture value *from* consumers in the form of sales, profits, and long-term customer equity.

In this chapter and the next, we will examine the steps of this simple model of marketing. In this chapter, we will review each step but focus more on the customer relationship steps—understanding customers, building customer relationships, and capturing value from customers. In Chapter 2, we'll look more deeply into the second and third steps—designing marketing strategies and constructing marketing programs.

UNDERSTANDING THE MARKETPLACE AND CUSTOMER NEEDS (LO2)

As a first step, marketers need to understand customer needs and wants and the market place within which they operate. We now examine five core customer and marketplace concepts: (1) *needs, wants, and demands;* (2) *market offerings (products, services, and experiences);* (3) *value and satisfaction;* (4) *exchanges and relationships;* and (5) *markets.*

CUSTOMER NEEDS, WANTS, AND DEMANDS

The most basic concept underlying marketing is that of human needs. Human **needs** are states of felt deprivation. They include basic *physical* needs for food, clothing, warmth, and safety; *social* needs for belonging and affection; and *individual* needs for knowledge and self-expression. These needs were not created by marketers; they are a basic part of the human makeup.

Wants are the form human needs take as they are shaped by culture and individual personality. A Canadian *needs* food but *wants* a breakfast sandwich and a large double-double from Tim Hortons. Wants are shaped by one's society as well as by marketing programs. They are described in terms of objects that will satisfy needs. When backed by buying power, wants become **demands**. Given their wants and resources, people demand products with benefits that add up to the most value and satisfaction.

Needs
States of felt deprivation.

Wants
The form human needs take as shaped by culture and individual personality.

Demands
Human wants that are backed by buying power.

FIGURE 1.1 A simple model of the marketing process

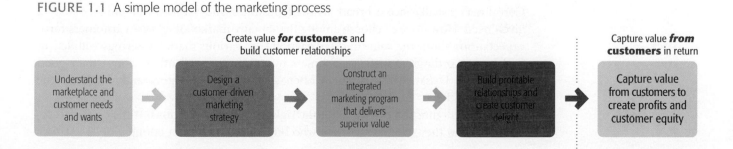

Outstanding marketing companies go to great lengths to learn about and understand their customers' needs, wants, and demands. They conduct consumer research and analyze mountains of customer data. Their people at all levels—including top management—stay close to customers. For example, Procter & Gamble CEO A. G. Lafley is known for actually going into customers' homes to undertake his own ethnographic research to ensure that customers' needs are well understood. And at the Running Room, founder John Stanton uses online forums such as the Globe and Mail discussion board to build more personal connections with customers.[6]

MARKET OFFERINGS—PRODUCTS, SERVICES, AND EXPERIENCES

Market offerings
Some combination of products, services, information, or experiences offered to a market to satisfy a need or want.

Consumers' needs and wants are fulfilled through **market offerings**—some combination of products, services, information, or experiences offered to a market to satisfy a need or want. Market offerings are not limited to physical *products*. They also include *services*—activities or benefits offered for sale that are essentially intangible and do not result in the ownership of anything. Examples include banking, airline, hotel, tax preparation, and home repair services.

More broadly, market offerings also include other entities, such as *persons, places, organizations, information*, and *ideas*. For example, EarthShare powerfully markets the idea that individuals and organizations can be involved in creating a healthy and sustainable environment.

Marketing myopia
The mistake of paying more attention to the specific products a company offers than to the benefits and experiences produced by these products.

Many sellers make the mistake of paying more attention to the specific products they offer than to the benefits and experiences produced by these products. These sellers suffer from **marketing myopia**. They are so taken with their products that they focus only on existing wants and lose sight of underlying customer needs.[7] They forget that a product is only a tool to solve a consumer problem. A manufacturer of quarter-inch drill bits may think that the customer needs a drill bit. But what the customer *really* needs is a quarter-inch hole. These sellers will have trouble if a new product comes along that serves the customer's need better or less expensively. The customer will have the same *need* but will *want* the new product.

Smart marketers look beyond the attributes of the products and services they sell. By orchestrating several services and products, they create *brand experiences* for consumers. For example, you don't just watch a NASCAR race, you immerse yourself in the exhilarating, high-octane NASCAR experience. Similarly, Hewlett-Packard (HP) recognizes that a personal computer is much more than just a collection of wires and electrical components. It's an intensely personal user experience. As noted in a recent HP ad, "There is hardly anything that you own that is *more* personal. Your personal computer is your backup brain. It's your life.... It's your astonishing strategy, staggering proposal, dazzling calculation. It's your autobiography, written in a thousand daily words."[8]

CUSTOMER VALUE AND SATISFACTION

Consumers usually face a broad array of products and services that might satisfy a given need. How do they choose among these many market offerings? Customers form expectations about the value and satisfaction that various market offerings will deliver and buy accordingly. Satisfied customers buy again and tell others about their good experiences. Dissatisfied customers often switch to competitors and disparage the product to others.

Marketers must be careful to set the right level of expectations. If they set expectations too low, they may satisfy those who buy but fail to attract enough buyers. If they raise expectations too high, buyers will be disappointed. Customer value and customer satisfaction are key building blocks for developing and managing customer relationships. We will revisit these core concepts later in the chapter.

EXCHANGES AND RELATIONSHIPS

Marketing occurs when people decide to satisfy needs and wants through exchange relationships. **Exchange** is the act of obtaining a desired object from someone by offering something in return. In the broadest sense, the marketer tries to bring about a response to some market offering. The response may be more than simply buying or trading products and services. A political candidate, for instance, wants votes, a church wants membership, an orchestra wants an audience, and a social action group wants idea acceptance.

Marketing consists of actions taken to build and maintain desirable exchange *relationships* with target audiences involving a product, service, idea, or other object. Beyond simply attracting new customers and creating transactions, the company wants to retain customers and grow its business. Marketers want to build strong relationships by consistently delivering superior customer value. We will expand on the important concept of managing customer relationships later in the chapter.

Exhibit 1.1 Market offerings are not limited to physical products. EarthShare powerfully markets the idea that individuals and organizations can be involved in creating a healthy and sustainable environment.

Exchange
The act of obtaining a desired object from someone by offering something in return.

Market
The set of all actual and potential buyers of a product or a service.

MARKETS

The concepts of exchange and relationships lead to the concept of a market. A **market** is the set of all actual and potential buyers of a product. These buyers share a particular need or want that can be satisfied through exchange relationships.

Marketing means managing markets to bring about profitable customer relationships. However, creating these relationships takes work. Sellers must search for buyers, identify their needs, design good market offerings, set prices for them, promote them, and store and deliver them. Activities such as consumer research, product development, communication, distribution, pricing, and service are core marketing activities.

Although we normally think of marketing as being carried on by sellers, buyers also carry on marketing. Consumers do marketing when they search for products and interact with companies and obtain information and make their purchases. In fact, today's digital technologies, from websites and online social networks to cellphones, have empowered consumers and made marketing a truly interactive affair. Thus, in addition to customer relationship management, today's marketers must also deal effectively with *customer-managed relationships*. Marketers are no longer asking only "How can we reach our customers?" but also "How should our customers reach us?" and even "How can our customers reach each other?"

Figure 1.2 shows the main elements in a marketing system. Marketing involves serving a market of final consumers in the face of competitors. The company and competitors research the market and interact with consumers to understand their needs. Then they create and send their market offerings and messages to consumers, either directly or through marketing intermediaries. All the parties in the system are affected by major environmental forces (demographic, economic, physical, technological, political/legal, and social/cultural).

Each party in the system adds value for the next level. All of the arrows represent relationships that must be developed and managed. Thus, a company's success at building profitable relationships depends not only on its own actions but also on how well the entire system serves the needs of final consumers. Wal-Mart cannot fulfill its promise of low prices unless its suppliers provide merchandise at low costs. And Ford cannot deliver a high-quality car-ownership experience unless its dealers provide outstanding sales and service.

DESIGNING A CUSTOMER-DRIVEN MARKETING STRATEGY L03

Marketing management
The art and science of choosing target markets and building profitable relationships with them.

Once it fully understands consumers and the marketplace, marketing management can design a customer-driven marketing strategy. We define **marketing management** as the art and science of choosing target markets and building profitable relationships with them. The marketing manager's aim is to find, attract, keep, and grow target customers by creating, delivering, and communicating superior customer value.

To design a winning marketing strategy, the marketing manager must answer two important questions: *What customers will we serve (what's our target market)?* and *How can we serve these customers best (what's our value proposition)?* We will discuss these marketing strategy concepts briefly here, and then look at them in more detail in the next chapter.

SELECTING CUSTOMERS TO SERVE

The company must first decide *who* it will serve. It does this by dividing the market into segments of customers (*market segmentation*) and selecting which segments it will go after (*target marketing*). Some people think of marketing management as finding as many customers as possible and increasing demand. But marketing managers know that they cannot serve all customers in every way. By trying to serve all customers, they may

FIGURE 1.2 A modern marketing system

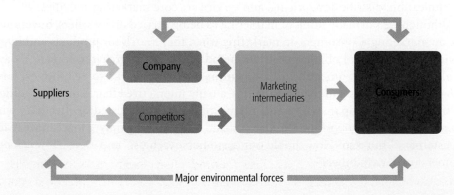

not serve any customers well. Instead, the company wants to select only customers that it can serve well and profitably. For example, Holt Renfrew stores profitably target affluent professionals; Dollarama stores profitably target families with more modest means.

Ultimately, marketing managers must decide which customers they want to target and on the level, timing, and nature of their demand. Simply put, marketing management is *customer management* and *demand management.*

CHOOSING A VALUE PROPOSITION

The company must also decide how it will serve targeted customers—how it will *differentiate and position* itself in the marketplace. A brand's *value proposition* is the set of benefits or values it promises to deliver to consumers to satisfy their needs. At TELUS, "The future is friendly," whereas Nokia is "Connecting people." The diminutive Smart car suggests that you "Open your mind to the car that challenges the status quo," whereas Infiniti "Makes luxury affordable." And a recent joint advertisement by Kraft and Campbell features a tomato-soup-and-grilled-cheese-sandwich combo that "Warms hearts without stretching budgets."

Such value propositions differentiate one brand from another. They answer the customer's question "Why should I buy your brand rather than a competitor's?" Companies must design strong value propositions that give them the greatest advantage in their target markets. For example, the Kraft/Campbell value proposition positions the companies' brands strongly against more expensive eating-out alternatives in today's budget-strapped economy.

Exhibit 1.2 Value propositions: Smart car suggests that you "Open your mind to the car that challenges the status quo."

MARKETING MANAGEMENT ORIENTATIONS

Marketing management wants to design strategies that will build profitable relationships with target consumers. But what *philosophy* should guide these marketing strategies? What weight should be given to the interests of customers, the organization, and society? Very often, these interests conflict.

There are five alternative concepts under which organizations design and carry out their marketing strategies: the *production, product, selling, marketing,* and *societal marketing concepts.*

The Production Concept   The **production concept** holds that consumers will favour products that are available and highly affordable. Therefore, management should focus on improving production and distribution efficiency. This concept is one of the oldest orientations that guides sellers.

The production concept is still a useful philosophy in some situations. For example, computer maker Lenovo dominates the highly competitive, price-sensitive Chinese PC market through low labour costs, high production efficiency, and mass distribution. However, although useful in some situations, the production concept can lead to marketing myopia. Companies adopting this orientation run a major risk of focusing too narrowly

Production concept
The idea that consumers will favour products that are available and highly affordable and that the organization should therefore focus on improving production and distribution efficiency.

on their own operations and of losing sight of the real objective—satisfying customer needs and building customer relationships.

The Product Concept The **product concept** holds that consumers will favour products that offer the most in quality, performance, and innovative features. Under this concept, marketing strategy focuses on making continuous product improvements.

Product quality and improvement are important parts of most marketing strategies. However, focusing *only* on the company's products can also lead to marketing myopia. For example, some manufacturers believe that if they can "build a better mousetrap, the world will beat a path to their door." But they are often rudely shocked. Buyers may be looking for a better solution to a mouse problem, but not necessarily for a better mousetrap. The better solution might be a chemical spray, an exterminating service, a house-cat, or something else that works even better than a mousetrap. Furthermore, a better mousetrap will not sell unless the manufacturer designs, packages, and prices it attractively; places it in convenient distribution channels; brings it to the attention of people who need it; and convinces buyers that it is a better product.

The Selling Concept Many companies follow the **selling concept**, which holds that consumers will not buy enough of the firm's products unless the company undertakes a large-scale selling and promotion effort. The selling concept is typically practised with unsought goods—those that buyers do not normally think of buying, such as insurance or blood donations. These industries must be good at tracking down prospects and selling them on product benefits.

Such aggressive selling, however, carries high risks. It focuses on creating sales transactions rather than on building long-term, profitable customer relationships. The aim often is to sell what the company makes rather than making what the market wants. It assumes that customers who are coaxed into buying the product will like it. Or, if they don't like it, they will possibly forget their disappointment and buy it again later. These are usually poor assumptions.

The Marketing Concept The **marketing concept** holds that achieving organizational goals depends on knowing the needs and wants of target markets and delivering the desired satisfactions better than competitors do. Under the marketing concept, customer focus and value are the *paths* to sales and profits. Instead of a product-centred "make and sell" philosophy, the marketing concept is a customer-centred "sense and respond" philosophy. The job is not to find the right customers for your product but to find the right products for your customers.

Figure 1.3 contrasts the selling concept and the marketing concept. The selling concept takes an *inside-out* perspective. It starts with the factory, focuses on the company's existing products, and calls for heavy selling and promotion to obtain profitable sales. It focuses

Product concept
The idea that consumers will favour products that offer the most quality, performance, and features and that the organization should therefore devote its energy to making continuous product improvements.

Selling concept
The idea that consumers will not buy enough of the firm's products unless it undertakes a large-scale selling and promotion effort.

Marketing concept
The marketing management philosophy that holds that achieving organizational goals depends on knowing the needs and wants of target markets and delivering the desired satisfactions better than competitors do.

FIGURE 1.3 The selling and marketing concepts contrasted

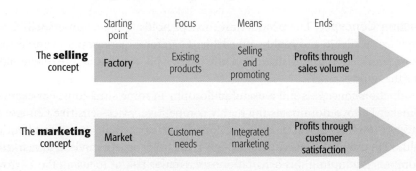

primarily on customer conquest—getting short-term sales with little concern about who buys or why.

In contrast, the marketing concept takes an *outside-in* perspective. As Herb Kelleher, Southwest Airlines' colourful founder, puts it, "We don't have a marketing department; we have a customer department." The marketing concept starts with a well-defined market, focuses on customer needs, and integrates all the marketing activities that affect customers. In turn, it yields profits by creating lasting relationships with the right customers based on customer value and satisfaction.

Implementing the marketing concept often means more than simply responding to customers' stated desires and obvious needs. Customer-driven companies research current customers deeply to learn about their desires, gather new product and service ideas, and test proposed product improvements. Such customer-driven marketing usually works well when a clear need exists and when customers know what they want.

Exhibit 1.3 Customer-driving marketing: Even 20 years ago, how many consumers would have thought to ask for now-commonplace products such as cellphones, personal digital assistants, notebook computers, iPods, and digital cameras. Marketers must often understand customer needs even better than customers themselves do.

In many cases, however, customers don't know what they want or even what is possible. For example, even 20 years ago, how many consumers would have thought to ask for now-commonplace products such as notebook computers, iPhones, digital cameras, 24-hour online buying, and satellite navigation systems in their cars? Such situations call for customer-driving marketing—understanding customer needs even better than customers themselves do and creating products and services that meet existing and latent needs, now and in the future. As an executive at 3M puts it, "Our goal is to lead customers where they want to go before they know where they want to go."

The Societal Marketing Concept The **societal marketing concept** questions whether the pure marketing concept overlooks possible conflicts between consumer *short-run wants* and consumer *long-run welfare*. Is a firm that satisfies the immediate needs and wants of target markets always doing what's best for consumers in the long run? The societal marketing concept holds that marketing strategy should deliver value to customers in a way that maintains or improves both the consumer's *and society's* well-being. It calls for *sustainable marketing*, socially and environmentally responsible marketing that meets the present needs of consumers and businesses while also preserving or enhancing the ability of future generations to meet their needs.

Consider today's flourishing bottled water industry. You may view bottled water companies as offering a convenient, tasty, and healthy product. Its packaging suggests "green" images of pristine lakes and snow-capped mountains. Yet making, filling, and shipping billions of plastic bottles generates huge amounts of carbon dioxide emissions that contribute substantially to global warming. Further, the plastic bottles pose a substantial recycling and solid waste disposal problem. Thus, in satisfying short-term consumer wants, the bottled water industry may be causing environmental problems that run against society's long-run interests.[9]

As Figure 1.4 shows, companies should balance three considerations in setting their marketing strategies: company profits, consumer wants, *and* society's interests. Johnson & Johnson does this well. Its concern for societal interests is summarized in a company document called "Our Credo," which stresses honesty, integrity, and putting people before profits. Under this credo, Johnson & Johnson would rather take a big loss than ship a bad batch of one of its products.

Societal marketing concept
The idea that a company's marketing decisions should consider consumers' wants, the company's requirements, consumers' long-run interests, and society's long-run interests.

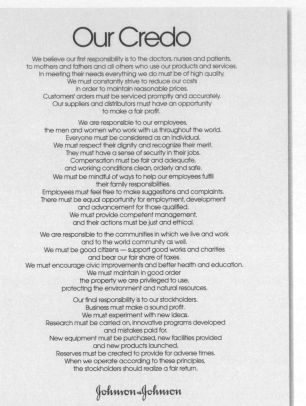

Exhibit 1.4 The societal marketing concept: The Johnson & Johnson Credo stresses putting people before profits.

Johnson & Johnson management has learned that doing what's right benefits both consumers and the company. Says former CEO Ralph Larsen, "The Credo should not be viewed as some kind of social welfare program ... it's just plain good business. If we keep trying to do what's right, at the end of the day we believe the marketplace will reward us." And the company stands behind this credo with action. For example, as the founding corporate sponsor of Safe Kids Canada, Johnson & Johnson continues to show its dedication to being a world leader in child care. Thus, over the years, Johnson & Johnson's dedication to consumers and community service has made it one of North America's most admired companies *and* one of the most profitable.[10]

PREPARING AN INTEGRATED MARKETING PLAN AND PROGRAM

The company's marketing strategy outlines which customers the company will serve and how it will create value for these customers. Next, the marketer develops an integrated marketing program that will actually deliver the intended value to target customers. The marketing program builds customer relationships by transforming the marketing strategy into action. It consists of the firm's *marketing mix*, the set of marketing tools the firm uses to implement its marketing strategy.

The major marketing mix tools are classified into four broad groups, called the *four Ps* of marketing: product, price, place, and promotion. To deliver on its value proposition, the firm must first create a need-satisfying market offering (product). It must decide how much it will charge for the offering (price) and how it will make the offering available to target consumers (place). Finally, it must communicate with target customers about the offering and persuade them of its merits (promotion). The firm must blend all of these marketing mix tools into a comprehensive *integrated marketing program* that communicates and delivers the intended value to chosen customers. We will explore marketing programs and the marketing mix in much more detail in later chapters.

FIGURE 1.4 The considerations underlying the societal marketing concept

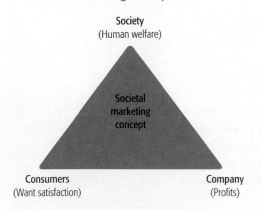

BUILDING CUSTOMER RELATIONSHIPS LO4

The first three steps in the marketing process—understanding the marketplace and customer needs, designing a customer-driven marketing strategy, and constructing marketing programs—all lead up to the fourth and most important step: building profitable customer relationships.

CUSTOMER RELATIONSHIP MANAGEMENT

Customer relationship management is perhaps the most important concept of modern marketing. Some marketers define customer relationship management narrowly as a customer data management activity (a practice called *CRM*). By this definition, it involves managing detailed information about individual customers and carefully managing customer "touchpoints" to maximize customer loyalty. We will discuss this narrower CRM activity in Chapter 5 when dealing with marketing information.

Most marketers, however, give the concept of customer relationship management a broader meaning. In this broader sense, **customer relationship management** is the overall process of building and maintaining profitable customer relationships by delivering superior customer value and satisfaction. It deals with all aspects of acquiring, keeping, and growing customers.

Relationship Building Blocks: Customer Value and Satisfaction The key to building lasting customer relationships is to create superior customer value and satisfaction. Satisfied customers are more likely to be loyal customers and to give the company a larger share of their business.

CUSTOMER VALUE Attracting and retaining customers can be a difficult task. Customers often face a bewildering array of products and services from which to choose. A customer buys from the firm that offers the highest **customer-perceived value**—the customer's evaluation of the difference between all the benefits and all the costs of a market offering relative to those of competing offers. Importantly, customers often do not judge values and costs "accurately" or "objectively." They act on perceived value.

To some consumers, "value" might mean sensible products at affordable prices, especially in the aftermath of the recent downward economic spiral. To other consumers, however, value might mean paying more to get more. For example, despite the challenging economic environment, GE recently introduced its new Profile washer-and-dryer set, which retails for more than US$2500. Profile ads feature stylish machines in eye catching colours, such as cherry red. But the ads also focus on down-to-earth practicality. They position the Profile line as a revolutionary new "clothes care system," with technology that allocates the optimal amount of soap and water per load and saves money by being gentle on clothes, extending garment life. Compared with less expensive appliances, are Profile washers and dryers worth the much higher price? It's all a matter of personal value perceptions. To many consumers, the answer is no. But to the target segment of style-conscious, affluent buyers, the answer is yes.[11]

CUSTOMER SATISFACTION Customer satisfaction depends on the product's perceived performance relative to a buyer's expectations. If the product's performance falls short of expectations, the customer is dissatisfied. If performance matches expectations, the customer is satisfied. If performance exceeds expectations, the customer is highly satisfied or delighted.

Outstanding marketing companies go out of their way to keep important customers satisfied. Most studies show that higher levels of customer satisfaction lead to greater customer loyalty, which in turn results in better company performance. Smart companies aim to delight customers by promising only what they can deliver, and then delivering more than they promise. Delighted customers not only make repeat purchases, they also become willing marketing partners and "customer evangelists" who spread the word about their good experiences to others (see Marketing@Work 1.1).[12]

Customer relationship management
The overall process of building and maintaining profitable customer relationships by delivering superior customer value and satisfaction.

Customer-perceived value
The customer's evaluation of the difference between all the benefits and all the costs of a market offering relative to those of competing offers.

Customer satisfaction
The extent to which a product's perceived performance matches a buyer's expectations.

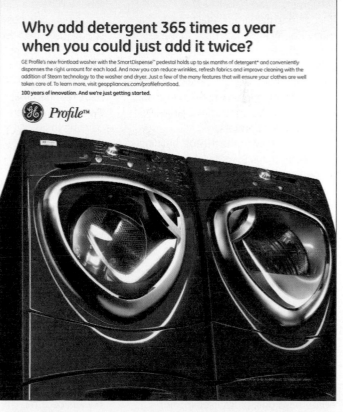

Why add detergent 365 times a year when you could just add it twice?

GE Profile's new frontload washer with the SmartDispense™ pedestal holds up to six months of detergent* and conveniently dispenses the right amount for each load. And now you can reduce wrinkles, refresh fabrics and improve cleaning with the addition of Steam technology to the washer and dryer. Just a few of the many features that will ensure your clothes are well taken care of. To learn more, visit geappliances.com/profilefrontload.
100 years of innovation. And we're just getting started.

GE *Profile*™

Exhibit 1.5 Perceived value: To some customers, "value" might mean paying more to get more. For example, are GE's Profile Harmony washers and dryers worth the higher price? To the target segment of style-conscious, affluent buyers, the answer is yes.

MARKETING@WORK 1.1

iRobot's Roomba: The Power of Customer Delight

When you were a child, you probably didn't like it much when your mother made you vacuum around the house. You probably still don't much like vacuuming—it's a thankless, seemingly never-ending task. But there's one group of people who don't mind vacuuming at all. In fact, they're absolutely delighted about it. They are the folks who own an iRobot Roomba, the cute little robotic vacuum that zips around rooms, avoiding furniture and other obstacles, tirelessly sniffing up dirt, dust, and dog hair.

People love their little Roombas. They name them, talk to them, and even buy a second Roomba so that the first one won't be lonely. Many Roomba owners spend more time watching their little pet-like robots than they would spend vacuuming a room themselves. Recognizing the strong attachments that many Roomba owners have to these personable little machines, iRobot does all it can to involve its customers in everything from product development to technical support, turning them into an army of Roomba consumer evangelists and marketing partners.

iRobot began in the 1990s, building devices for the U.S. military—small robots called PackBots now used to diffuse improvised explosive devices (IEDs) in Iraq or explore caves in Afghanistan. Based on this advanced technology, the company introduced its first Roomba in 2002. Made up of more than 100 plastic parts, motors, controllers, sensors, brushes, and a dustbin, the 4.5-kilogram Roomba uses a sophisticated algorithm to scoot around a room, even going under tables, chairs, sofas, and beds. When it runs into obstacles, it figures out how to clean around them. And when its rechargeable battery begins to lose its charge, the Roomba finds its way to its home base unit, plugs itself in, and recharges automatically. Owners can even program more expensive models to clean at certain times of the day or days of the week, even when no one is home.

In the summer of 2002, iRobot negotiated distribution deals with key retailers such as Brookstone, and Roomba sales took off. Soon, the company began getting calls from major chains such as Target, Kohl's, and Linens 'N Things. iRobot's factory churned out 50 000 units just to meet that year's holiday demand.

Then the real fun began. As iRobot received Roombas back for servicing, customer-service reps noted that many owners were customizing and humanizing their little robotic assistants. In fact, before consumers sent in their Roombas for repair, they would sometimes etch their names on the machines to be sure of getting their own robots back. "Somehow, they grow attached to the squad, disk-shaped sweepers and worry that a new robot will have a different personality," comments one observer. Rather than selling just a high-tech household appliance, it seems that iRobot had invented a new kind of family pet. Reps reported that owners were often painting their Roombas, dressing them, turning them on to entertain their friends, and referring to them by name and gender. The most popular name was Rosie, after the robotic maid on the classic animated TV series, *The Jetsons*.

Before long, delighted Roomba owners became iRobot's best marketing partners. An independent website sprang up,

MyRoomBud.com, offering RoomBud costumes that transform a Roomba from "just a naked vacuum" into a lovable character such as "Roobit the Frog," "Mooba the Cow," or "RoomBette La French Maid." The site even lets Roomba enthusiasts print out official-looking birth certificates for their newly adopted robotic pets.

Smitten Roomba owners by the hundreds began posting video clips of their Roombas in action on YouTube. One mounted a camera on his Roomba to create a RoombaCam. Other Roomba customers created the Roomba Review website, featuring news, chats, product reviews, and hacker information.

Noting all of this customer enthusiasm and delight, iRobot developed programs to strengthen and organize the growing sense of community among Roomba owners. For example, it opened its programmatic interface, encouraging owners, amateur robotics enthusiasts, and

Exhibit 1.6: Delighting customers: People love their pet-like little Roombas. They name them, talk to them, and even buy a second Roomba so that the first one won't be lonely. Recognizing this, iRobot has turned customers into an army of Roomba consumer evangelists.

others to develop their own programs and uses for the Roomba. It also offered an iRobot Create programmable robot for educators, students, and developers to program customized behaviours, sounds, and movements and to add their own additional electronics. These actions turned Roomba owners into a community of amateur tinkerers and hobbyists. Customers themselves began to develop improved features that iRobot would later adopt.

By monitoring interactions with and among enthusiastic Roomba customers, iRobot was able to discover product problems and additional customer needs. Complaints that animal hair often clogged the machines led the company to introduce the Roomba for Pets model, featuring easy-to-clean brushes that make removing pet hair easier. For customers who wanted a robotic "floor mopper," iRobot introduced the Scooba floor washer, another personable little gizmo that preps, washes, scrubs, and

squeegees tile, linoleum, and hardwood floors "so that you don't have to!" For customers who complained about cleaning gutters, iRobot developed the Looj Gutter Cleaning Robot. The Verro Pool Cleaning Robot "gets pools deep-down clean from floor to waterline—just drop it in and let it go!" And the iRobot Dirt Dog, with its high-capacity sweeper bin, cleans up heavy-duty messes in workshops, garages, and basements and on patios and decks. Customers are now clamouring for a Roomba lawn mower!

Based on interactions with its customer community, iRobot has also continued to improve the original Roomba. Even smarter Roombas can now free themselves from almost any jam, including rug tassels and power cords, reducing the need to prep a room before unleashing the little sniffer. New models also feature a built-in voice tutorial for new users that explains the Roomba's features right out of the box.

Thus, iRobot has discovered the power of customer delight. More than that, it's working to harness that power by partnering with its satisfied-customer community to improve current products, develop new ones, and help spread the word to new customers. Last year, the company's sales reached nearly US$310 million, up almost 63 percent over the previous two years. With the help of its delighted customers, iRobot is filling the vacuum and really cleaning up.

Sources: Based on information found in Paul Gillin, "Cleaning Up with Customer Evangelists," *BtoB*, August 13, 2007, p. 10; Faith Arner, "How the Roomba Was Realized," *BusinessWeek*, October 6, 2003, p. 10; Anita Slomski, "Robots Can Already Perform Surgery and Track Your Meds. Now, New Models Aim to Provide Therapy and Support," *Washington Post*, March 10, 2009, p. F1; "iRobot Corporation," *Hoover's Company Records*, August 1, 2009, p. 132607; and www.myroombud.com, accessed November 2009.

For companies interested in delighting customers, exceptional value and service become part of the overall company culture. For example, year after year, The Ritz-Carlton ranks at or near the top of the hospitality industry in terms of customer satisfaction. Its passion for satisfying customers is summed up in the company's credo, which promises that its luxury hotels will deliver a truly memorable experience—one that "enlivens the senses, instills well-being, and fulfills even the unexpressed wishes and needs of our guests."

Check into any Ritz-Carlton hotel around the world, and you'll be amazed by the company's fervent dedication to anticipating and meeting even your slightest need. Without ever asking, they seem to know that you want a king-size bed, a non-allergenic pillow, and breakfast with decaffeinated coffee in your room. Each day, hotel staffers—from those at the front desk to those in maintenance and housekeeping—discreetly observe and record even the smallest guest preferences. Then, every morning, each hotel reviews the files of all new arrivals who have previously stayed at a Ritz-Carlton and prepares a list of suggested extra touches that might delight each guest.

Once they identify a special customer need, the Ritz-Carlton employees go to legendary extremes to meet it. For example, to serve the needs of a guest with food allergies, a Ritz-Carlton chef in Bali located special eggs and milk in a small grocery store in another country and had them delivered to the hotel. In another case, when the hotel's laundry service failed to remove a stain on a guest's suit before the guest departed, the hotel manager travelled to the guest's house and personally delivered a reimbursement check for the cost of the suit. As a result of such customer-service heroics, an amazing 95 percent of departing guests report that their stay has been a truly memorable experience. More than 90 percent of The Ritz-Carlton's delighted customers return.[13]

Exhibit 1.7 Customer satisfaction: The Ritz-Carlton's passion for satisfying customers is summed up in its credo, which promises a truly memorable experience—one that "enlivens the senses, instills well-being, and fulfills even the unexpressed wishes and needs of our guests."

Exhibit 1.8 Building customer relationships: Harley-Davidson sponsors the Harley Owners Group (H.O.G.), which gives Harley owners "an organized way to share their passion and show their pride." The worldwide club now numbers more than 1500 local chapters and 1 million members.

However, although a customer-centred firm seeks to deliver high customer satisfaction relative to competitors, it does not attempt to *maximize* customer satisfaction. A company can always increase customer satisfaction by lowering its price or increasing its services. But this may result in lower profits. Thus, the purpose of marketing is to generate customer value profitably. This requires a very delicate balance: The marketer must continue to generate more customer value and satisfaction but not "give away the house."

Customer Relationship Levels and Tools Companies can build customer relationships at many levels, depending on the nature of the target market. At one extreme, a company with many low-margin customers may seek to develop *basic relationships* with them. For example, Procter & Gamble (P&G) does not phone or call on all of its Tide consumers to get to know them personally. Instead, P&G creates relationships through brand-building advertising, sales promotions, and its Tide Total Care Network website (www.tide.ca). At the other extreme, in markets with few customers and high margins, sellers want to create *full partnerships* with key customers. For example, P&G customer teams work closely with Wal-Mart, Safeway, and other large retailers. In between these two extremes, other levels of customer relationships are appropriate.

Beyond offering consistently high value and satisfaction, marketers can use specific marketing tools to develop stronger bonds with consumers. For example, many companies offer *frequency marketing programs* that reward customers who buy frequently or in large amounts. Airlines offer frequent-flyer programs, hotels give room upgrades to their frequent guests, and supermarkets give patronage discounts to "very important customers."

Other companies sponsor *club marketing programs* that offer members special benefits and create member communities. For example, Harley-Davidson sponsors the Harley Owners Group (H.O.G.), which gives Harley riders a way to share their common passion of "making the Harley-Davidson dream a way of life." H.O.G. membership benefits include a quarterly *HOG* magazine, the *H.O.G.* Touring Handbook, a roadside assistance program, a specially designed insurance program, theft reward service, a travel centre, and a "Fly & Ride" program, enabling members to rent Harleys while on vacation. The worldwide club now numbers more than 1500 local chapters and more than 1 million members.[14]

THE CHANGING NATURE OF CUSTOMER RELATIONSHIPS

Significant changes are occurring in the ways in which companies are relating to their customers. Yesterday's big companies focused on mass marketing to all customers at arm's length. Today's companies are building deeper, more direct, and lasting relationships with more carefully selected customers. Here are some important trends in the way companies and customers are relating to one another.

Relating with More Carefully Selected Customers Few firms today still practise true mass marketing—selling in a standardized way to any customer who comes along. Today, most marketers realize that they don't want relationships with every customer.

Instead, they target fewer, more profitable customers. "Not all customers are worth your marketing efforts," states one analyst. "Some are more costly to serve than to lose." Adds another marketing expert, "If you can't say who your customers *aren't*, you probably can't say who your customers *are*."[15]

Many companies now use customer profitability analysis to pass up or weed out losing customers and to target winning ones for pampering. One approach is to pre-emptively screen out potentially unprofitable customers. Progressive Insurance does this effectively. It asks prospective customers a series of screening questions to determine whether they are right for the firm. If they're not, Progressive will likely tell them, "You might want to go to Allstate." A marketing consultant explains, "They'd rather send business to a competitor than take on unprofitable customers." Screening out unprofitable customers lets Progressive provide even better service to potentially more profitable ones.[16]

Exhibit 1.9 Weeding out unprofitable customers: American Express recently sent a letter to some of its members that offered them $300 in exchange for paying off their balances and closing out their accounts.

But what should the company do with unprofitable customers that it already has? If it can't turn them into profitable ones, it may even want to dismiss customers that are too unreasonable or that cost more to serve than they are worth. "Like bouncers in glitzy nightspots," says another consultant, "executives will almost certainly have to 'fire' [those] customers." For example, American Express recently sent letters to some of its members, offering them $300 in exchange for paying off their balances and closing out their accounts. Reading between the lines, the credit card company was dumping unprofitable customers.

Relating More Deeply and Interactively Beyond choosing customers more selectively, companies are now relating with chosen customers in deeper, more meaningful ways. Rather than relying only on one-way, mass-media messages, today's marketers are incorporating new, more interactive approaches that help build targeted, two-way customer relationships.

New technologies have profoundly changed the ways in which people relate to one another. New tools for relating include everything from email, websites, blogs, cellphones, and video sharing to online communities and social networks such as MySpace, Facebook, YouTube, and Twitter.

This changing communications environment also affects how companies and brands relate to consumers. The new communications approaches let marketers create deeper consumer involvement and a sense of community surrounding a brand—to make the brand a meaningful part of consumers' conversations and lives. "Becoming part of the conversation between consumers is infinitely more powerful than handing down information via traditional advertising," says one marketing expert. Says another, "Brands that engage in two-way conversation with their customers create stronger, more trusting relationships. People today want a voice and a role in their brand experiences. They want co-creation."[17]

However, at the same time that the new technologies create relationship-building opportunities for marketers, they also create challenges. They give consumers greater power and control. Today's consumers have more information about brands than ever before, and they have a wealth of platforms for airing and sharing their brand views with other consumers. Thus, the marketing world is now embracing not just customer relationship management, but also **customer-managed relationships**.

Greater consumer control means that, in building customer relationships, companies can no longer rely on marketing by *intrusion*. Instead, marketers must practise marketing by *attraction*—creating market offerings and messages that involve consumers rather than interrupt them. Hence, most marketers now augment their mass-media marketing efforts with a rich mix of direct marketing approaches that promote brand–consumer interaction.

Customer-managed relationships Marketing relationships in which customers, empowered by today's new digital technologies, interact with companies and with each other to shape their relationships with brands.

For example, many brands are creating dialogues with consumers via their own or existing *online social networks*. To supplement their marketing campaigns, companies now routinely post their latest ads and made-for-the-Web videos on video sharing sites. They join social networks. Or they launch their own blogs, online communities, or consumer-generated review systems, all with the aim of engaging customers on a more personal, interactive level.

Take Twitter, for example. Organizations ranging from Dell, West 49, Lululemon, and Dalhousie University to the Edmonton Oilers and Tourism P.E.I. have opened Twitter accounts. They use "tweets" to start conversations with Twitter's more than 6 million registered users, address customer-service issues, research customer reactions, and drive traffic to relevant articles, websites, contests, videos, and other brand activities. For example, Dell monitors Twitter-based discussions and responds quickly to individual problems or questions, and Lululemon has close to 30 000 customers following the company's tweets. One marketer notes that companies can "use Twitter to get the fastest, most honest research any company ever heard—the good, bad, and ugly—and it doesn't cost a cent."[18]

Despite their rapid growth in recent years, most marketers are still learning how to use the social media effectively. The problem is to find unobtrusive ways to enter consumers' social conversations with engaging and relevant brand messages. Marketing has "historically been an exposure and intrusion practice—get in someone's face and talk about the attributes of the brand," says a social media analyst. "That approach works less and less effectively all the time, and it is absolutely fatal in the social arena."[19] Moreover, simply posting a humorous video, creating a social network page, or hosting a blog isn't enough. Successful social network marketing means making relevant and genuine contributions to consumer conversations. "Nobody wants to be friends with a brand," says one online marketing executive. "Your job [as a brand] is to be part of other friends' conversations."[20]

As a part of the new customer control and dialogue, consumers themselves are now creating brand conversations and messages on their own. And increasingly, companies are even *inviting* consumers to play a more active role in shaping brand messages and ads. For

Exhibit 1.10 Online social networks: Many organizations are creating dialogues via their own or existing networks. Tourism P.E.I. uses Twitter to promote events such as local golf tournaments and music festivals to visitors and Islanders alike.

example, Frito Lay, Southwest, Visa, Heinz, and many other companies have run contests for consumer-generated commercials that have been aired on national television.[21]

Exhibit 1.11 Harnessing consumer-generated marketing: When H. J. Heinz invited consumers to submit homemade ads for its ketchup brand on YouTube, it received more than 8000 entries—some very good but most only so-so or even downright dreadful.

> For the 2007 Super Bowl, Frito-Lay's Doritos brand launched a "Crash the Super Bowl" contest in which it invited 30-second ads from consumers and ran the two best during the game. One of the fan-produced ads, which showed a supermarket checkout girl getting frisky with a shopper, was judged in one poll as 67 percent more effective than the average Super Bowl ad. The other selected ad, showing a young driver eating Doritos and flirting with a pretty girl, cost only $12.79 to produce (the cost of four bags of chips) but was judged 45 percent more effective. Doritos has been running the "Crash the Super Bowl" challenge ever since. Last year it offered a cool US$1 million to any fan who could generate a Doritos commercial that took the top spot on the *USA Today* Super Bowl Ad Meter. Consumers submitted nearly 2,000 entries. One of the consumer-generated ads—titled "Free Doritos" and featuring a vending-machine-shattering snow globe—claimed No. 1 on the *USA Today* Ad Meter, and Doritos gladly paid out the prize. A second consumer-created ad took the No. 5 spot. It was "the best million dollars the Doritos brand has ever spent," says the brand's marketing vice president.

However, harnessing consumer-generated content can be a time-consuming and costly process, and companies may find it difficult to glean even a little gold from all the garbage. For example, when H. J. Heinz invited consumers to submit homemade ads for its ketchup brand on its YouTube page, it ended up sifting through more than 8000 entries, of which it posted nearly 4000. Some of the amateur ads were very good—entertaining and potentially effective. Most, however, were so-so at best, and others were downright dreadful. In one ad, a contestant chugs ketchup straight from the bottle. In another, the would-be filmmaker brushes his teeth, washes his hair, and shaves his face with Heinz's product.

Consumer-generated marketing, whether invited by marketers or not, has become a significant marketing force. Through a profusion of consumer-generated videos, blogs, and websites, consumers are playing an increasing role in shaping their own brand experiences and those of other consumers. Beyond creating brand conversations, on their own or by invitation, customers are having an increasing say about everything from product design, usage, and packaging to pricing and distribution.[22]

Consumer-generated marketing
Brand exchanges created by consumers themselves–both invited and uninvited–by which consumers are playing an increasing role in shaping their own brand experiences and those of other consumers.

PARTNER RELATIONSHIP MANAGEMENT

When it comes to creating customer value and building strong customer relationships, today's marketers know that they can't go it alone. They must work closely with a variety of marketing partners. In addition to being good at *customer relationship management*, marketers must also be good at **partner relationship management**. Major changes are occurring in how marketers partner with others inside and outside the company to jointly bring more value to customers.

Partners Inside the Company Traditionally, marketers have been charged with understanding customers and representing customer needs to different company departments. The old thinking was that marketing is done only by marketing, sales, and customer-support people. However, in today's more connected world, every functional area can interact with customers, especially electronically. The new thinking is that—no

Partner relationship management
Working closely with partners in other company departments and outside the company to jointly bring greater value to customers.

matter what your job in a company—you must understand marketing and be customer focused. The late David Packard, co-founder of Hewlett-Packard, wisely said, "Marketing is far too important to be left only to the marketing department."[23]

Today, rather than letting each department go its own way, firms are linking all departments in the cause of creating customer value. Rather than assigning only sales and marketing people to customers, they are forming cross-functional customer teams. For example, Procter & Gamble assigns "customer development teams" to each of its major retailer accounts. These teams—consisting of sales and marketing people, operations specialists, market and financial analysts, and others—coordinate the efforts of many P&G departments toward helping the retailer be more successful.

Marketing Partners Outside the Firm Changes are also occurring in how marketers connect with their suppliers, channel partners, and even competitors. Most companies today are networked companies, relying heavily on partnerships with other firms.

Marketing channels consist of distributors, retailers, and others who connect the company to its buyers. The *supply chain* describes a longer channel, stretching from raw materials, to components, to final products that are carried to final buyers. For example, the supply chain for PCs consists of suppliers of computer chips and other components, the computer manufacturer, and the distributors, retailers, and others who sell the computers.

Through *supply chain management*, many companies today are strengthening their connections with partners all along the supply chain. They know that their fortunes rest not just on how well they perform. Success at building customer relationships also rests on how well their entire supply chain performs against competitors' supply chains. These companies don't just treat suppliers as vendors and distributors as customers. They treat both as partners in delivering customer value. On the one hand, for example, Lexus works closely with carefully selected suppliers to improve quality and operations efficiency. On the other hand, it works with its franchise dealers to provide top-grade sales and service support that will bring customers in the door and keep them coming back.

CAPTURING VALUE FROM CUSTOMERS

The first four steps in the marketing process outlined in Figure 1.1 involve building customer relationships by creating and delivering superior customer value. The final step involves capturing value in return in the form of current and future sales, market share, and profits. By creating superior customer value, the firm creates highly satisfied customers who stay loyal and buy more. This, in turn, means greater long-run returns for the firm. Here, we discuss the outcomes of creating customer value: customer loyalty and retention, share of market and share of customer, and customer equity.

CREATING CUSTOMER LOYALTY AND RETENTION

Good customer relationship management creates customer delight. In turn, delighted customers remain loyal and talk favourably to others about the company and its products. Studies show big differences in the loyalty of customers who are less satisfied, somewhat satisfied, and completely satisfied. Even a slight drop from complete satisfaction can create an enormous drop in loyalty. Thus, the aim of customer relationship management is to create not just customer satisfaction, but customer delight.

When the economy tightens, customer loyalty and retention become even more important. There are fewer customers and less spending to go around, so firms must work to hang on to the customers they have. It's five times cheaper to keep an old customer than to acquire a new one. "When wallets tighten up, focusing on [customer] loyalty and retention simply makes sense from an economic standpoint."[24]

The recent economic recession has put strong pressures on customer loyalty. For example, a U.K. study showed that 88 percent of the British public admit that they are no longer buying their favourite brands. One-third of shoppers are now visiting cheaper stores to do their weekly shopping and 50 percent are now buying private label products at the supermarket. Even more staggering, 37 percent say that the economic downturn has weakened the trust they have in leading brands.[25] Thus, companies today must shape their value propositions even more carefully and treat their profitable customers well.

Companies are realizing that losing a customer means losing more than a single sale. It means losing the entire stream of purchases that the customer would make over a lifetime of patronage. For example, here is a dramatic illustration of **customer lifetime value:**

Exhibit 1.12 Customer lifetime value: To keep customers coming back, Stew Leonard's has created the "Disneyland of dairy stores." Rule #1—The customer is always right. Rule #2—If the customer is ever wrong, reread Rule #1.

Stew Leonard, who operates a highly profitable four-store supermarket, says that he sees US$50,000 flying out of his store every time he sees a sulking customer. Why? Because his average customer spends about $100 a week, shops 50 weeks a year, and remains in the area for about 10 years. If this customer has an unhappy experience and switches to another supermarket, Stew Leonard's has lost US$50,000 in revenue. The loss can be much greater if the disappointed customer shares the bad experience with other customers and causes them to defect. To keep customers coming back, Stew Leonard's has created what *The New York Times* has dubbed the "Disneyland of Dairy Stores," complete with costumed characters, scheduled entertainment, a petting zoo, and animatronics throughout the store. From its humble beginnings as a small dairy store in 1969, Stew Leonard's has grown at an amazing pace. It's built 29 additions onto the original store, which now serves more than 300,000 customers each week. This legion of loyal shoppers is largely a result of the store's passionate approach to customer service. Rule #1: At Stew Leonard's—The customer is always right. Rule #2: If the customer is ever wrong, reread rule #1![26]

Stew Leonard is not alone in assessing customer lifetime value. Lexus, for example, estimates that a single satisfied and loyal customer is worth more than US$600 000 in lifetime sales.[27] And the estimated lifetime value of a young mobile phone consumer is US$26 000. In fact, a company can lose money on a specific transaction but still benefit greatly from a long-term relationship. This means that companies must aim high in building customer relationships. Customer delight creates an emotional relationship with a brand, not just a rational preference. And that relationship keeps customers coming back.

Customer lifetime value
The value of the entire stream of purchases that the customer would make over a lifetime of patronage.

GROWING SHARE OF CUSTOMER

Beyond simply retaining good customers to capture customer lifetime value, good customer relationship management can help marketers to increase their **share of customer**—the share they get of the customer's purchasing in their product categories. Thus, banks want to increase "share of wallet." Supermarkets and restaurants want to get more "share of stomach." Car companies want to increase "share of garage," and airlines want greater "share of travel."

To increase share of customer, firms can offer greater variety to current customers. Or they can create programs to cross-sell and upsell in order to market more products and services to existing customers. For example, Amazon.com is highly skilled at leveraging relationships with its 88 million customers to increase its share of each customer's

Share of customer
The portion of the customer's purchasing that a company gets in its product categories.

purchases. Originally an online bookseller, Amazon.com now offers customers music, videos, gifts, toys, consumer electronics, office products, home improvement items, lawn and garden products, apparel and accessories, jewellery, tools, and even groceries. In addition, based on each customer's purchase history, previous product searches, and other data, the company recommends related products that might be of interest. This recommendation system influences up to 30 percent of all sales.[28] In these ways, Amazon.com captures a greater share of each customer's spending budget.

BUILDING CUSTOMER EQUITY

We can now see the importance of not just acquiring customers, but of keeping and growing them as well. One marketing consultant puts it this way: "The only value your company will ever create is the value that comes from customers—the ones you have now and the ones you will have in the future. Without customers, you don't have a business."[29] Customer relationship management takes a long-term view. Companies want not only to create profitable customers but also to "own" them for life, earn a greater share of their purchases, and capture their customer lifetime value.

What Is Customer Equity? The ultimate aim of customer relationship management is to produce high *customer equity*.[30] **Customer equity** is the total combined customer lifetime values of all of the company's current and potential customers. As such, it's a measure of the future value of the company's customer base. Clearly, the more loyal the firm's profitable customers, the higher the firm's customer equity. Customer equity may be a better measure of a firm's performance than current sales or market share. Whereas sales and market share reflect the past, customer equity suggests the future. Consider Cadillac:[31]

Customer equity
The total combined customer lifetime values of all of the company's customers.

> In the 1970s and 1980s, Cadillac had some of the most loyal customers in the industry. To an entire generation of car buyers, the name "Cadillac" defined luxury. Cadillac's share of the luxury car market reached a whopping 51 percent in 1976. Based on market share and sales, the brand's future looked rosy. However, measures of customer equity would have painted a bleaker picture. Cadillac customers were getting older (average age 60) and average customer lifetime value was falling. Many Cadillac buyers were on their last car. Thus, although Cadillac's market share was good, its customer equity was not. Compare this with BMW. Its more youthful and vigorous image didn't win BMW the early market share war. However, it did win BMW younger customers with higher customer lifetime values. The result: In the years that followed, BMW's market share and profits soared while Cadillac's fortunes eroded badly. Thus, market share is not the answer. We should care not just about current sales but also about future sales. Customer lifetime value and customer equity are the name of the game. Recognizing this, in recent years, Cadillac has attempted to make the Caddy cool again by targeting a younger generation of consumers with new high-performance models and more vibrant advertising. The average consumer aspiring to own a Cadillac is now about 36 years old.

Exhibit 1.13 To increase customer lifetime value and customer equity, Cadillac is cool again. Its ad campaigns target a younger generation of consumers.

Building the Right Relationships with the Right Customers Companies should manage customer equity carefully. They should view customers as assets that need to be managed and maximized. But not all customers, not even all loyal customers, are good investments. Surprisingly, some loyal customers can be unprofitable, and some disloyal customers can be profitable. Which customers should the company acquire and retain?

The company can classify customers according to their potential profitability and manage its relationships with them accordingly. Figure 1.5 classifies customers into one of four relationship groups, according to their profitability and projected loyalty.[32] Each group requires a different relationship management strategy. "Strangers" show low potential profitability and little projected loyalty. There is little fit between the company's offerings and their needs. The relationship management strategy for these customers is simple: Don't invest anything in them.

"Butterflies" are potentially profitable but not loyal. There is a good fit between the company's offerings and their needs. However, like real butterflies, we can enjoy them for only a short while and then they're gone. An example is stock market investors who trade shares often and in large amounts but who enjoy hunting out the best deals without building a regular relationship with any single brokerage company. Efforts to convert butterflies into loyal customers are rarely successful. Instead, the company should enjoy the butterflies for the moment. It should create satisfying and profitable transactions with them, capturing as much of their business as possible in the short time during which they buy from the company. Then, it should cease investing in them until the next time around.

"True friends" are both profitable and loyal. There is a strong fit between their needs and the company's offerings. The firm wants to make continuous relationship investments to delight these customers and nurture, retain, and grow them. It wants to turn true friends into "true believers," who come back regularly and tell others about their good experiences with the company.

"Barnacles" are highly loyal but not very profitable. There is a limited fit between their needs and the company's offerings. An example is smaller bank customers who bank regularly but do not generate enough returns to cover the costs of maintaining their accounts. Like barnacles on the hull of a ship, they create drag. Barnacles are perhaps the most problematic customers. The company might be able to improve their profitability by selling them more, raising their fees, or reducing service to them. However, if they cannot be made profitable, they should be "fired."

The point here is an important one: Different types of customers require different relationship management strategies. The goal is to build the *right relationships* with the *right customers.*

FIGURE 1.5 Customer relationship groups

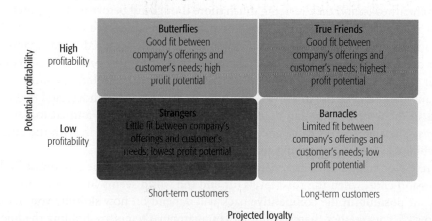

THE CHANGING MARKETING LANDSCAPE (L05)

Every day, dramatic changes are occurring in the marketplace. Richard Love of Hewlett-Packard observes, "The pace of change is so rapid that the ability to change has now become a competitive advantage." Yogi Berra, the legendary New York Yankees catcher and manager, summed it up more simply when he said, "The future ain't what it used to be." As the marketplace changes, so must those who serve it.

In this section, we examine the major trends and forces that are changing the marketing landscape and challenging marketing strategy. We look at five major developments: the uncertain economic environment, the digital age, rapid globalization, the call for more ethics and social responsibility, and the growth of not-for-profit marketing.

THE UNCERTAIN ECONOMIC ENVIRONMENT

Beginning in 2008, world economies experienced a stunning economic meltdown, unlike anything since the Great Depression of the 1930s. The stock market plunged and trillions of dollars of market value simply evaporated. The financial crisis left shell-shocked consumers short of both money and confidence as they faced losses in income, a severe credit crunch, declining home values, and rising unemployment. "The bad news keeps coming, fast and furious," said one analyst at the time. "Houses are worth less, home-equity lines of credit are being suspended, jobs are at risk, wages aren't keeping up with inflation, and energy prices continue to soar, eating away at disposable income."[33]

The faltering and uncertain economy caused many consumers to rethink their spending priorities and cut back on their buying. After a decade of overspending, "frugality has made a comeback," announced one analyst. "A new sense of back-to-basics frugality and common sense has taken hold," said another.[34] In the aftermath of the meltdown, consumers are now spending less and more wisely. More than just a temporary change, the economic downturn will likely affect consumer buying attitudes and spending behaviour for many years to come (see Marketing@Work 1.2).

In response, companies in all industries—from discounters such as Zellers to luxury brands such as Lexus—have tightened their budgets and aligned their marketing strategies with the new economic realities. More than ever, marketers are emphasizing the *value* in their value propositions. They are focusing on value-for-the-money, practicality, and durability in their product offerings and marketing pitches. "Value is the magic word," says a P&G marketing executive. "In these economic times, people are doing the math in their heads, and they're being much more thoughtful before making purchases. Now, we're going to be even more focused on helping consumers see value."[35]

In adjusting to the new economy, companies might be tempted to cut marketing budgets deeply and slash prices in an effort to coax cash-strapped customers into opening their wallets. However, although cutting costs and offering selected discounts can be important marketing tactics in a down economy, smart marketers understand that making cuts in the wrong places can damage long-term brand images and customer relationships. The challenge is to balance the brand's value proposition with the current times while also enhancing its long-term equity.

"A recession creates winners and losers just like a boom," notes one economist. "When the recession ends, when the road levels off and the world seems full of promise once more, your position in the competitive pack will depend on how skilfully you manage right now."[36] Thus, rather than slashing prices, many marketers are holding the line on prices and are instead explaining why their brands are worth it. And rather than cutting their marketing budgets in the difficult times, companies such as Wal-Mart and McDonald's have maintained or actually increased their marketing spending. In fact, a

MARKETING@WORK 1.2

The New Era of Consumer Frugality

Frugality has made a comeback. Beaten down by the recent economic turmoil, North Americans are showing an enthusiasm for thriftiness not seen in decades. This behavioural shift isn't simply about spending less. The new frugality emphasizes stretching every dollar. It means bypassing the fashion mall for the discount chain store, buying second-hand clothes and furniture, or trading down to store brands. Consumers are clipping more coupons and swiping their credit cards less. Says one analyst:

> A shift in behaviour has taken place. Consumers across all income segments are responding to the economy by reining in spending, postponing big purchases, and trading down when possible. Above all else, they're seeking out the best value for their money. Marketers must take a different tack to reach these increasingly pragmatic consumers: Forego the flash and prove your product's worth.

Frugality is likely to be more than a fad. "It is a whole reassessment of values," says one retailing consultant. "We've just been shopping until we drop, and consuming and buying it all, and replenishing before things wear out. People are learning again to say, 'No, not today.'" Even people who can afford to indulge themselves are doing so more sparingly, and then bargain hunting to offset the big purchases.

The frugality trend is evident in where cash registers are ringing and where they are not. In the face of an overall drop in retail sales, Wal-Mart is thriving, whereas Abercrombie & Fitch is struggling. Likewise, as casual dining chains such as Red Lobster see fewer customers, McDonald's is serving more, including people who have given up $4 Starbucks drinks in favour of the fast-food chain's coffee. And despite the economic recession, Tim Hortons has become one of the most profitable franchises in Canada and continues to expand in the United States. Tellingly, Wal-Mart said recently that it has seen a jump this year in shoppers from households earning $65 000 or more.

The housing bust, credit crunch, and stock-market plunge ate away at the retirement savings and confidence of consumers who for years operated on a buy-now, pay-later philosophy, chasing bigger homes, bigger cars, and better brands. The new economic realities are forcing families to bring their spending in line with their incomes and to rethink priorities. However, it's difficult to predict how long the pullback will last, particularly among generations of consumers who have never seen such a sharp economic downturn. "This is scary stuff, and confidence is such an elusive thing," says one economist. As several consumer surveys indicate, "it seems like this trend towards spending less is only going to continue," says a consumer behaviour researcher. "It doesn't require a lost job or decimated retirement account to make shopping for new things seem wasteful."

What does the new era of frugality mean to marketers? Whether it's for everyday products or expensive luxuries, marketers must clearly spell out their value propositions: what it is that makes their brands worth a customer's hard-earned money. "The saying has always been, 'Sell the sizzle, not the steak.' Well, I think there's been too much sizzle," says one luxury goods marketer. "Image alone doesn't sell anymore—consumers want to know what they're getting for their money."

Even diamond marketer De Beers has adjusted its long-standing "A diamond is forever" value proposition to these more frugal times. A recent ad headlined "Here's to Less" makes that next diamond purchase seem—what else—downright practical:

> Our lives are filled with things. We're overwhelmed by possessions we own but do not treasure. Stuff we buy but never love. To be thrown away in weeks rather than passed down for generations. Perhaps we will be different now. Perhaps now is an opportunity to reassess what really matters. After all, if everything you ever bought her disappeared overnight, what would she truly miss? A diamond is forever.

Sources: Portions adapted from Dan Sewell, "New Frugality Emerges," *Washington Times*, December 1, 2008; with quotes, extracts, and other information from Elizabeth A. Sullivan, "Austerity Marketing," *Marketing News*, October 15, 2008, pp. 12–14; Noreen O'Leary, "Squeeze Play," *Adweek*, January 12, 2009, pp. 8–9; and http://iamfrugal.blogspot.com/, accessed October 2009.

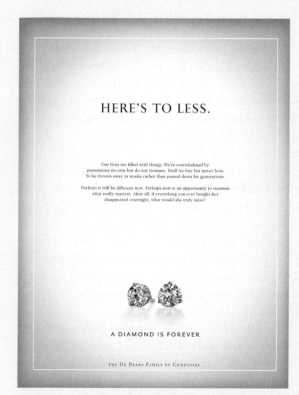

Exhibit 1.14 The new consumer frugality: Today, marketers in all industries must clearly spell out their value propositions. Even diamond marketer De Beers has adjusted its long-standing "a diamond is forever" promise to these more frugal times. This ad makes buying a diamond seem downright practical.

recent survey of more than 650 marketers at companies in a variety of industries found that, despite the down economy, half of the companies surveyed were holding firm on their marketing budgets or planning increases.[37] The goal is to build market share and strengthen customer relationships at the expense of competitors who are cutting back.

A troubled economy can present opportunities as well as threats. For example, the fact that 40 percent of consumers say they are eating out less poses threats for many full-service restaurants. However, it presents opportunities for fast-food marketers. For instance, a Seattle McDonald's franchise operator recently took on Starbucks in its hometown with billboards proclaiming "Large is the new grande" and "Four bucks is dumb." Playing on its cheap-eats value proposition, McDonald's worldwide sales grew 7.2 percent in the fourth quarter last year and earnings grew 11 percent, while Starbucks earnings dropped 96 percent.[38]

THE DIGITAL AGE

The recent technology boom has created a digital age. The explosive growth in computer, communications, information, and other digital technologies has had a major impact on the ways companies bring value to their customers. Now, more than ever before, we are all connected to one another and information anywhere in the world. Where it once took days or weeks to receive news about important world events, we now learn about them as they are occurring through live satellite broadcasts and news websites. Where it once took weeks to correspond with others in distant places, they are now only moments away by cellphone, email, or webcam.

The digital age has provided marketers with exciting new ways to learn about and track customers and to create products and services tailored to individual customer needs. It's helping marketers to communicate with customers in large groups or one-to-one. Through Web videoconferencing, marketing researchers at a company's headquarters in Vancouver can look in on focus groups in Halifax or Paris without ever stepping onto a plane. With only a few clicks of a mouse button, a direct marketer can tap into online data services to learn anything from what car you drive to what you read to what flavour of ice cream you prefer. Or, using today's powerful computers, marketers can create their own detailed customer databases and use them to target individual customers with offers designed to meet their specific needs.

Digital technology has also brought a new wave of communication, advertising, and relationship-building tools—ranging from online advertising, video sharing tools, cellphones, and video games to Web widgets and online social networks. The digital shift means that marketers can no longer expect consumers to always seek them out. Nor can they always control conversations about their brands. The new digital world makes it easy for consumers to take marketing content that once lived only in advertising or on a brand website with them wherever they go and to share it with friends. More than just add-ons to traditional marketing channels, the new digital media must be fully integrated into the marketer's customer-relationship-building efforts.

The most dramatic digital technology is the **Internet**. The number of Internet users worldwide now stands at more than 1.4 billion and will reach an estimated 3.4 billion by 2015. People now spend twice as much time surfing the Web as they do watching TV—an average of 32.7 hours per week. On a typical day, 58 percent of adults check their email, 49 percent Google or use another search engine to find information, 36 percent get the news, 19 percent keep in touch with friends on social networking sites such as Facebook and LinkedIn, and 16 percent watch a video on a video-sharing site such as YouTube. And by 2020, many experts believe, the Internet will be accessed primarily via a mobile device operated by voice, touch, and even thought or "mind-controlled human-computer interaction."[39]

Whereas *Web 1.0* connected people with information, the next generation *Web 2.0* has connected people with people, employing a fast-growing set of new Web technologies such as blogs, social-networking sites, and video-sharing sites. *Web 3.0,* starting now, puts all of these information and people connections together in ways that will make our Internet experience more relevant, useful, and enjoyable.[40]

In Web 3.0, small, fast, customizable Internet applications, accessed through multifunction mobile devices, "will bring you a virtual world you can carry in your pocket. We will be carrying our amusements with us— best music collections, video collections, instant news access—all tailored to our preferences and perpetually updatable. And as this cooler stuff [evolves], we won't be connecting to this new Web so much as walking around inside it."[41] The interactive, community-building nature of these new Web technologies makes them ideal for relating with consumers.

Online marketing is now the fastest-growing form of marketing. These days, it's hard to find a company that doesn't use the Web in a significant way. In addition to the click-only dot-coms, most traditional brick-and-mortar companies have now become click-and-mortar companies. They have ventured online to attract new customers and build stronger relationships with existing ones. Canada has one of the highest Internet penetration rates in the world: roughly 85 percent of the population has Internet access and a large percentage of them are shopping online.[42] Business-to-business online commerce is also booming. It seems that almost every business has set up shop on the Web.

Thus, the technology boom is providing exciting new opportunities for marketers. We will explore the impact of digital marketing technologies in future chapters, especially Chapter 14.

Exhibit 1.15 Web 3.0—the third coming of the Web—"will bring you a virtual world you can carry in your pocket."

RAPID GLOBALIZATION

As they are redefining their customer relationships, marketers are also taking a fresh look at the ways in which they relate with the broader world around them. In an increasingly smaller world, companies are now connected *globally* with their customers and marketing partners.

Today, almost every company, large or small, is touched in some way by global competition. A neighbourhood florist buys its flowers from Mexican nurseries, and a large U.S. electronics manufacturer competes in its home markets with giant Korean rivals. A fledgling Internet retailer finds itself receiving orders from all over the world at the same time that a Canadian consumer-goods producer introduces new products into emerging markets abroad.

North American firms have been challenged at home by the skilful marketing of European and Asian multinationals. Companies such as Honda, Nokia, Nestlé, and Samsung have often outperformed their North American counterparts. Similarly Canadian companies in a wide range of industries have developed truly global operations, making and selling their products worldwide. Research In Motion, with corporate offices in North America, Europe, and Asia, now sells a wide variety of BlackBerry smartphones in countries around the globe. British Columbia–based Lululemon, a yoga-inspired athletic apparel company, manufactures its products in seven countries and has over 100 retail locations in Canada, the United States, Australia, and Hong Kong. Today, companies are not only trying to sell more of their locally produced goods in international markets, they also are buying more supplies and components abroad.

Exhibit 1.16 Companies in a wide range of industries have developed truly global operations. The Waterloo, Ontario, based company Research In Motion® (RIM), with corporate offices in North America, Europe, and Asia, now sells a wide variety of BlackBerry® smartphones in countries around the globe.

Thus, managers in countries around the world are increasingly taking a global, not just local, view of the company's industry, competitors, and opportunities. They are asking: What is global marketing? How does it differ from domestic marketing? How do global competitors and forces affect our business? To what extent should we "go global"? These issues will be discussed throughout the text.

SUSTAINABLE MARKETING—THE CALL FOR MORE SOCIAL RESPONSIBILITY

Marketers are re-examining their relationships with social values and responsibilities and with the very Earth that sustains us. As the worldwide consumerism and environmentalism movements mature, today's marketers are being called to develop *sustainable marketing* practices. Corporate ethics and social responsibility have become hot topics for almost every business. And few companies can ignore the renewed and very demanding environmental movement. Every company action can affect customer relationships:[43]

> There is an unwritten contract today between customers and the brands they buy. First, they expect companies to consistently deliver what they advertise. Second, they expect the companies they do business with to treat them with respect and to be honourable and forthright.... Everything a company does affects the brand in the eyes of the customer. For example, Celestial Seasonings incurred customers' wrath by ignoring its advertised corporate image of environmental stewardship when it poisoned prairie dogs on its property. By contrast, Google's decision to use solar energy for its server farms reinforces what Google stands for and strengthens the Google brand.

The social-responsibility and environmental movements will place even stricter demands on companies in the future. Some companies resist these movements, budging only when forced by legislation or organized consumer outcries. More forward-looking companies, however, readily accept their responsibilities to the world around them. They view sustainable marketing as an opportunity to do well by doing good. They seek ways to profit by serving the best long-run interests of their customers and communities.

Some companies—such as Patagonia, Ben & Jerry's, Timberland, and others—are practising "caring capitalism," setting themselves apart by being civic-minded and responsible. They are building social responsibility and action into their company value and mission statements. For example, when it comes to environmental responsibility, outdoor gear marketer Patagonia is "committed to the core." "Those of us who work here share a strong commitment to protecting undomesticated lands and waters," says the company's website. "We believe in using business to inspire solutions to the environmental crisis." Patagonia backs these words with actions. Each year it pledges at least 1 percent of its sales or 10 percent of its profits, whichever is greater, to the protection of the natural environment.[44] We will revisit the topic of sustainable marketing in greater detail in Chapter 3.

THE GROWTH OF NOT-FOR-PROFIT MARKETING

In recent years, marketing also has become a major part of the strategies of many not-for-profit organizations, such as universities, hospitals, museums, zoos, symphony orchestras, and even churches. The nation's not-for-profits face stiff competition for support and membership. Sound marketing can help them to attract membership and support.[45] Consider the marketing efforts of the American Society for the Prevention of Cruelty to Animals:

> The American Society for the Prevention of Cruelty to Animals (ASPCA) gets its funding from more than 1 million active supporters. However, like many not-for-profits, attracting new donors is tricky—that is until Canadian singer-songwriter Sarah McLachlan came

along and created what many in not-for-profit circles call "The Ad." Produced by a small 12-person Canadian firm, Eagle-Com, the two-minute television commercial features heart-breaking photographs of dogs and cats scrolling across the screen while McLachlan croons the haunting song "Angel" in the background (see the "The Ad" at www.youtube.com/watch?v=Iu_JqNdp2As). McLachlan appears only momentarily to ask viewers to share her support for the ASPCA. The heart-rending commercial has tugged at viewers' heart strings and opened their wallets. This one ad has attracted 200,000 new donors and raised roughly $30 million for the organization since it started running in early 2007. That makes it a landmark in nonprofit fund-raising, where such amounts are virtually unimaginable for a single commercial. The donations from the McLachlan commercial have enabled the ASPCA to buy prime-time slots on national networks like CNN, which in turn has generated more income. The ASPCA is now rolling out new McLachlan ads to further bolster its fund-raising efforts.[46]

Government agencies have also shown an increased interest in marketing. For example, both the Canadian military and Royal Canadian Mounted Police have marketing plans to attract recruits to their different services, and various government agencies are now designing *social marketing campaigns* to encourage energy conservation and concern for the environment or to discourage smoking, excessive drinking, and drug use. According to *Strategy* magazine, public sector advertising is annually among the top three categories of television advertising in English Canada.[47]

SO, WHAT IS MARKETING? PULLING IT ALL TOGETHER

At the start of this chapter, Figure 1.1 presented a simple model of the marketing process. Now that we've discussed all of the steps in the process, Figure 1.6 presents an expanded model that will help you pull it all together. What is marketing? Simply put, marketing is the process of building profitable customer relationships by creating value for customers and capturing value in return.

The first four steps of the marketing process focus on creating value for customers. The company first gains a full understanding of the marketplace by researching customer needs and managing marketing information. It then designs a customer-driven marketing strategy based on the answers to two simple questions. The first question is "What consumers will we serve?" (market segmentation and targeting). Good marketing companies know that they cannot serve all customers in every way. Instead, they need to focus their resources on the customers they can serve best and most profitably. The second marketing strategy question is "How can we best serve targeted customers?" (differentiation and positioning). Here, the marketer outlines a value proposition that spells out what values the company will deliver to win target customers.

With its marketing strategy decided, the company now constructs an integrated marketing program—consisting of a blend of the four marketing mix elements, or the four *P*s—that transforms the marketing strategy into real value for customers. The company develops product offers and creates strong brand identities for them. It prices these offers to create real customer value and distributes the offers to make them available to target consumers. Finally, the company designs promotion programs that

Exhibit 1.17 Not-for-profit marketing: A single two-minute TV commercial—"The Ad"—has attracted 200 000 new donors and raised roughly US$30 million for the ASPCA since it started running in early 2007.

communicate the value proposition to target consumers and persuade them to act on the market offering.

Perhaps the most important step in the marketing process involves building value-laden, profitable relationships with target customers. Throughout the process, marketers practise customer relationship management to create customer satisfaction and delight. In creating customer value and relationships, however, the company cannot go it alone. It must work closely with marketing partners both inside the company and throughout the marketing system. Thus, beyond practising good customer relationship management, firms must also practise good partner relationship management.

The first four steps in the marketing process create value *for* customers. In the final step, the company reaps the rewards of its strong customer relationships by capturing value *from* customers. Delivering superior customer value creates highly satisfied customers who will buy more and will buy again. This helps the company to capture customer lifetime value and greater share of customer. The result is increased long-term customer equity for the firm.

Finally, in the face of today's changing marketing landscape, companies must take into account three additional factors. In building customer and partner relationships, they must harness marketing technology, take advantage of global opportunities, and ensure that they act in an ethical and socially responsible way.

Figure 1.6 provides a good road map to future chapters of the text. Chapters 1 and 2 introduce the marketing process, with a focus on building customer relationships and

FIGURE 1.6 An expanded model of the marketing process

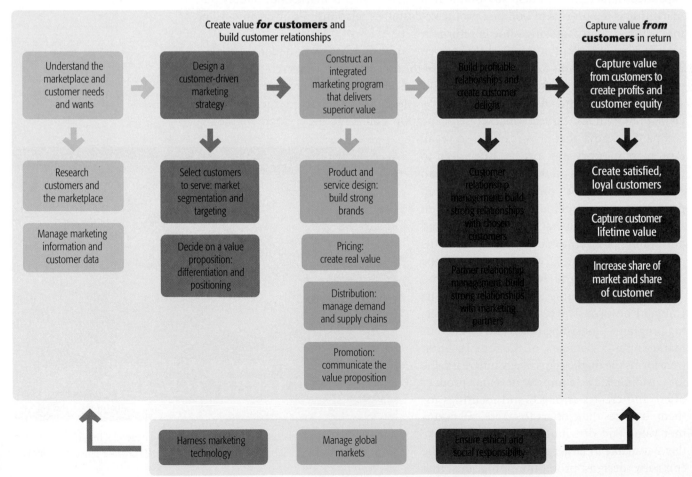

capturing value from customers. Chapter 3 focuses on understanding the impact marketing has on society and the ethical concerns associated with marketing practice. Chapters 4, 5, and 6 address the first step of the marketing process—understanding the marketing environment, managing marketing information, and understanding consumer and business buyer behaviour. In Chapter 7, we look more deeply into the two major marketing strategy decisions: selecting which customers to serve (segmentation and targeting) and deciding on a value proposition (differentiation and positioning). Finally, Chapters 8 through 14 discuss the marketing mix variables, one by one.

CANADA GOOSE® MINI CASE

FOCUSING ON THE "TRUE USER"

Canada Goose is a private, Canadian, family-owned company. It was started over 50 years ago in Toronto by Canada Goose's current president and CEO Dani Reiss's grandfather. At that time, the company went by the name Metro Sportswear and manufactured lumber jackets, shirts, and other types of outerwear.

By 2000, the company was focused on its own brand and all its products came together under the Canada Goose name, with the familiar Arctic disc logo patch we see today. Canada Goose products are currently sold in over 40 countries, and the company has been named one of Canada's fastest-growing private companies by *Profit* magazine.

"We sell to fashion stores, women's stores, men's stores, sporting goods stores, ski shops, industrial shops and street wear stores, Reiss said. "There aren't many brands that can do that."

As its name indicates, Canada Goose takes its nationality very seriously. It is the only Canadian outerwear brand that manufactures in Canada. The Canadian core of the company's brand also extends deeply into the Canadian North, where Canada Goose tests its products and sponsors northern people and northern-based athletic events, such as dogsled racing and the Arctic Winter Games.

Canada Goose says authenticity and natural organic growth are at the core of its brand. While the company prides itself on its commitment to quality and practicality, its coats have become popular outside the "true outdoor user" category and are enthusiastically sported by celebrities and trendsetters in North America, Europe, and many other countries in other continents.

Canada Goose insists the company's marketing strategy isn't about branding for the sake of branding. Explains Reiss, "We believe in creating warm, beautiful outdoor gear using the best and most advanced technologies, and we believe that if we stick to this our market will continue to grow. We are the Land Rover of the apparel world in that when you make the best, most functional products, they become aspirational and iconic."

QUESTIONS

1. What does Canada Goose believe defines value for its customers?
2. How does Canada Goose show it is "customer driven"?
3. This chapter discusses five major changes in the marketplace landscape. Which of these do you feel Canada Goose seems to be responding to? How is it responding?
4. Give one example from above of how Canada Goose is moving toward capturing customer equity.
5. Is talking about "authenticity" branding?

REVIEWING THE CONCEPTS

1. Define marketing and outline the steps in the marketing process.

Marketing is the activity, set of institutions, and processes for creating, communicating, delivering, and exchanging offerings that have value for customers, clients, partners, and society at large.

The marketing process involves five steps. The first four steps create value *for* customers. First, marketers need to understand the marketplace and customer needs and wants. Next, marketers design a customer-driven marketing strategy with the goal of getting, keeping, and growing target customers. In the third step, marketers construct a marketing program that actually delivers superior value. All of these steps form the basis for the fourth step, building profitable customer relationships and creating customer delight. In the final step, the company reaps the rewards of strong customer relationships by capturing value *from* customers.

2. Explain the importance of understanding customers and the marketplace, and identify the five core marketplace concepts.

Outstanding marketing companies go to great lengths to learn about and understand their customers' needs, wants, and demands. This understanding helps them to design want-satisfying market offerings and build value-laden customer relationships by which they can capture customer lifetime value and greater share of customer. The result is increased long-term customer equity for the firm.

The core marketplace concepts are needs, wants, and demands; market offerings (products, services, and experiences); value and satisfaction; exchange and relationships; and markets. Wants are the form taken by human needs when shaped by culture and individual personality. When backed by buying power, wants become demands. Companies address needs by putting forth a value proposition, a set of benefits that they promise to consumers to satisfy their needs. The value proposition is fulfilled through a market offering, which delivers customer value and satisfaction, resulting in long-term exchange relationships with customers.

3. Identify the key elements of a customer-driven marketing strategy and discuss the marketing management orientations that guide marketing strategy.

To design a winning marketing strategy, the company must first decide *who* it will serve. It does this by dividing the market into segments of customers (*market segmentation*) and selecting which segments it will cultivate (*target marketing*). Next, the company must decide *how* it will serve targeted customers (how it will *differentiate and position* itself in the marketplace).

Marketing management can adopt one of five competing market orientations. The *production concept* holds that management's task is to improve production efficiency and bring down prices. The *product concept* holds that consumers favour products that offer the most in quality, performance, and innovative features; thus, little promotional effort is required. The *selling concept* holds that consumers will not buy enough of the organization's products unless it undertakes a large-scale selling and promotion effort. The *marketing concept* holds that achieving organizational goals depends on determining the needs and wants of target markets and delivering the desired satisfactions more effectively and efficiently than competitors do. The *societal marketing concept* holds that generating customer satisfaction *and* long-run societal well-being through sustainable marketing strategies are the keys to both achieving the company's goals and fulfilling its responsibilities.

4. Discuss customer relationship management and identify strategies for creating value *for* customers and capturing value *from* customers in return.

Broadly defined, *customer relationship management* is the process of building and maintaining profitable customer relationships by delivering superior customer value and satisfaction. The aim of customer relationship management is to produce high *customer equity*, the total combined customer lifetime values of all of the company's current and potential customers. The key to building lasting relationships is the creation of superior *customer value* and *satisfaction*.

Companies want not only to acquire profitable customers but also to build relationships that will keep them and grow "share of customer." Different types of customers require different customer relationship management strategies. The marketer's aim is to build the *right relationships* with the *right customers*. In return for creating value *for* targeted customers, the company captures value *from* customers in the form of profits and customer equity.

In building customer relationships, good marketers realize that they cannot go it alone. They must work closely with marketing partners inside and outside the company. In addition to being good at customer relationship management, they must also be good at *partner relationship management.*

5. **Describe the major trends and forces that are changing the marketing landscape in this age of relationships.**

Dramatic changes are occurring in the marketing arena. The recent economic meltdown has left many consumers short of both money and confidence, creating a new age of consumer frugality. More than ever, marketers must now emphasize the *value* in their value propositions. The challenge is to balance a brand's value proposition with the current times while also enhancing its long-term equity.

The boom in computer, telecommunications, information, transportation, and other technologies has created exciting new ways to learn about and relate to individual customers. It has also allowed new approaches by which marketers can target consumers more selectively and build closer, two-way customer relationships.

In an increasingly smaller world, many marketers are now connected *globally* with their customers and marketing partners. Today, almost every company, large or small, is touched in some way by global competition. Today's marketers are also re-examining their ethical and societal responsibilities. Marketers are being called upon to take greater responsibility for the social and environmental impact of their actions. Finally, in recent years, marketing also has become a major part of the strategies of many not-for-profit organizations, such as universities, hospitals, museums, zoos, symphony orchestras, and even churches.

Pulling it all together, as discussed throughout the chapter, the major new developments in marketing can be summed up in a single word: *relationships.* Today, marketers of all kinds are taking advantage of new opportunities for building relationships with their customers, their marketing partners, and the world around them.

KEY TERMS

Consumer-generated marketing   21
Customer equity   24
Customer lifetime value   23
Customer relationship management   15
Customer satisfaction   15
Customer-managed relationships   19
Customer-perceived value   15
Demands   7

Exchange   9
Market   9
Market offerings   8
Marketing   7
Marketing concept   12
Marketing management   10
Marketing myopia   8
Needs   7

Partner relationship management   21
Product concept   12
Production concept   11
Selling concept   12
Share of customer   23
Societal marketing concept   13
Wants   7

TALK ABOUT MARKETING

1. Form a small group of three or four students. Have each member of the group talk to five other people, varying in age from young adult to very old, about their automobiles. Ask them what value means to them with regard to an automobile and how the manufacturer and dealer create such value. Discuss your findings with your group and write a brief report of what you learned about customer value.

2. *Maclean's* is Canada's only weekly current affairs magazine. With over 2.8 million readers, *Maclean's* has managed to create considerable customer equity for this product. What is *customer equity*? Using the customer relationship groups in Figure 1.5, explain which group best describes *Maclean's* subscribers. Discuss other products or services that *Maclean's* could offer to grow its share of customer.

3. Compare and contrast the five different marketing management orientations. For what types of products might it be most appropriate to adopt each of these orientations? Is one orientation necessarily always the "right" one and the others "wrong"? Explain.

4. Research the following brands and try to determine the value proposition offered by each.
   a. Enterprise Rent-A-Car
   b. Lexus automobiles
   c. Gain laundry detergent
   d. iPhone

5. Browse the Canadian Marketing Association's job board at http://www.marketing-jobs.ca to learn about careers in marketing. Interview someone who works in one of the marketing jobs described here and ask him or her the following questions:

   a. What does your job entail?
   b. How did you get to this point in your career? Is this what you thought you'd be doing when you grew up? What influenced you to get into this field?
   c. What education is necessary for this job?
   d. What advice can you give to marketing students?
   e. Add one additional question that you create.

   Write a brief report of the responses to your questions, and explain why you would or would not be interested in working in this field.

THINK LIKE A MARKETING MANAGER

West 49 is a leading Canadian specialty retailer of fashion, apparel, footwear, accessories, and equipment related to the youth action sports lifestyle. The company's stores, which are primarily mall-based, carry a variety of high-performance, premium brand name and private label products that fulfill the lifestyle needs of identified target markets, primarily tweens and teens. As of January 2010, the company operated 136 stores in nine provinces under the banners West 49, Billabong, Off the Wall, Amnesia/Arsenic, and D-Tox. In addition to its private label brand, West 49 carries a wide range of products catering to skateboard, snowboard, and surfing enthusiasts, including brands such as DC, Quiksilver, Vans, Hurley, Roxy, and C1RCA.

West 49 has been very successful at reaching the very loyal, but often difficult to market to, skateboarding segment. The company sponsors a number of up-and-coming skateboarders and features profiles of each of them on the company website (www.west49.com). It also provides Canadian boarding enthusiasts with a skateboard park locator, tips and tricks for newbies, and advice on how to get sponsored. Visit the West 49 website and answer the following questions.

QUESTIONS

1. Suppose you are the marketing manager at West 49. How would you describe your value proposition?
2. What specific elements of its website help create customer loyalty? What other ways could the company build relationships with its customers?

MARKETING ETHICS

Did you drive a car today? Use a laptop computer? Buy a product in a store? If so, you emitted carbon dioxide (CO_2) and created a carbon footprint. All of us do that every day. Individuals and companies emit carbon dioxide in everyday activities. Many consumers feel bad about doing this; others expect companies to take action. What's the answer? Reducing carbon emissions is one solution, but another one is to offset your carbon emissions by purchasing carbon offsets and renewable energy certificates (RECs)—forms of "emission trading." Individual consumers do this, and companies are flocking to purchase carbon offsets for themselves or to offer them to their customers, resulting in an estimated US$100 million annual market. And experts predict exponential growth over the next few years. Airlines routinely offer flyers the option of paying a few extra dollars to offset their carbon emissions. For example, in partnership with Zerofootprint, Air Canada has launched the "carbon offset program" for individual and corporate travellers. Since it began in 2007, Air Canada customers have contributed nearly $250 000, resulting in over 150 000 tonnes of CO_2 offset: roughly equivalent to planting over 3000 trees or taking 3700 cars off the road for a year!

QUESTIONS

1. Learn more about carbon offsets and discuss four examples of how businesses are using them. In your opinion, are these companies embracing the societal marketing concept?
2. One criticism of carbon offsetting is that companies are not really helping the environment by changing their own behaviour. Instead, they're merely buying "environmental pardons." Do you think carbon offsets are a responsible solution to environmental concerns? Why or why not? Write a brief essay debating this issue.

MARKETING TECHNOLOGY

In only a few short years, *consumer-generated marketing* has increased exponentially. It's also known as *consumer-generated media* and *consumer-generated content*. More than 100 million websites contain user-generated content. You may be a contributor yourself if you've ever posted something on a blog, reviewed a product at Amazon.com, uploaded a video on YouTube, or sent a video from your mobile phone to a news website, such as CNN.com or FoxNews.com. This force has not gone unnoticed by marketers, and with good reason. Nielsen, the TV ratings giant, found that most consumers trust consumer opinions posted online. As a result, savvy marketers encourage consumers to generate content. For example, Coke has more than 3.5 million fans on Facebook, mothers can share information at Pampers Village (www.pampers.com), and Doritos scored a touchdown with consumer-created advertising during the past

several Super Bowls. Apple even encourages iPhone users to develop applications for its device. However, consumer-generated marketing is not without problems—just check out the Diet Coke/Mentos videos or search "I hate (insert company name)" in any search engine!

QUESTIONS

1. Find two examples (other than those discussed in the chapter) of marketer-supported consumer-generated content, along with two examples of consumer-generated content that is not officially supported by the company whose product is involved. Provide the Web link to each and discuss how the information impacts your attitude toward the companies involved.
2. Discuss the advantages and disadvantages of consumer-generated marketing.

MARKETING BY THE NUMBERS

How much are you worth to a given company if you continue to purchase its brand for the rest of your life? Many marketers are grappling with that question, but it's not easy to measure. Calculating customer lifetime value can be very complicated. Intuitively, however, it can be a fairly simple net present value calculation. To determine a basic customer lifetime value, each stream of profit is discounted back to its present value (PV) and then summed. The basic equation for calculating net present value (NPV) is

$$NPV = \sum_{t=0}^{n} \frac{C_t}{(1+r)^t}$$

Where,

t = time of the cash flow
N = total customer lifetime
r = discount rate
C_t = net cash flow (the profit) at time t (The initial cost of acquiring a customer would be a negative profit at time 0.)

NPV can be calculated easily on most financial calculators or by using one of the calculators available on the Internet, such as the one found at www.investopedia.com/calculator/NetPresentValue.aspx. For more discussion of the financial and quantitative implications of marketing decisions, see Appendix 3, Marketing by the Numbers.

QUESTIONS

1. Assume that a customer shops at a local grocery store, spending an average of $150 a week, and that the retailer earns a 5 percent margin. Using the calculator found at the website given above, determine the customer lifetime value if this shopper remains loyal over a 10-year lifespan, assuming a 5 percent annual interest rate and no initial cost to acquire the customer.
2. Discuss how a business can increase a customer's lifetime value.

VIDEO CASE

Visit MyMarketingLab at www.pearsoned.ca/ mymarketinglab to view the video for this chapter.

HARLEY-DAVIDSON

Few brands engender such intense loyalty as that found in the hearts of Harley-Davidson owners. Why? Because the company's marketers spend a great deal of time thinking about customers. They want to know who customers are, how they think and feel, and why they buy a Harley. That attention to detail has helped build Harley-Davidson into a $5 billion company with more than 900 000 Harley Owners Group (H.O.G.) members, the largest company-sponsored owners' group in the world.

Harley sells much more than motorcycles. The company sells a feeling of independence, individualism, and freedom. These strong emotional connections have made Harley-Davidson ownership much more of a lifestyle than only a product consumption experience. To support that lifestyle, Harley-Davidson recognizes that its most important marketing tool is the network of individuals who ride Harleys. For this reason, Harley-Davidson engages its customer base through company-sponsored travel adventures, events, and other things such as clothes and accessories both for riders and for those who simply like to associate with the brand.

After viewing the video featuring Harley-Davidson, answer the following questions about managing profitable customer relationships.

QUESTIONS

1. How does Harley-Davidson build long-term customer relationships?

2. What is Harley-Davidson's value proposition?

3. Relate the concept of customer equity to Harley-Davidson. How does Harley-Davidson's strategy focus on the right relationships with the right customers?

END-OF-CHAPTER CASE

THE SELF-SERVE SOCIETY

It is now possible to buy an airline ticket online from your home in Toronto, and then check in at an automated kiosk at Pearson International and fly to Vancouver. For your return flight, you can check in at the Fairmont Vancouver Airport Hotel by using the self-serve kiosk and fly back to Toronto—all without ever having to speak to another human being. There was a time not too long ago when this kind of technology was only in the realm of science fiction, but today it is becoming more and more commonplace.

For better or worse, self-service technology is here. The irony of the airline example is obvious—the travel and hospitality industry, traditionally based on high levels of personal customer service, is now indicating that they'd rather have customers fend for themselves. From an overall marketing perspective, how far can we go with the technology and at what cost to relationship building?

One of the pioneers of self-serve technology was Interac, an organization created in the mid-1980s as a co-operative venture among five Canadian financial institutions: Royal Bank, CIBC, Scotiabank, TD Bank, and La Confédération des caisses Desjardins du Québec. It is the network that allows Canadians to access funds (called Shared Cash Dispensing, or SCD) from automated bank machines (ABMs) across the country. By 1986, the association had grown to 10 members, including the Bank of Montreal and Credit Union Central. Based on the success of the initial service, the association then launched Interac Direct Payment (IDP), Canada's national debit card service, and today, IDP has surpassed cash as the preferred payment method for Canadians. A report by the Strategic Council for the Interac Association showed that 85 percent of Canadians use a bank card to make automated transactions. In 2002, Canadians used the Interac service 2.4 billion times at 40 000 ABMs and other self-serve locations. And at 54.3 transactions per capita (compared with only 27.5 per capita in the United States), Canada leads the world in the use of debit payments and automated bank machines.

Who would have guessed that ABMs would be so pervasive? And today, banks aren't the only ones offering self-service. The technology is now available at gas stations, movie theatres, and libraries. In some provinces, consumers can even use self-serve kiosks to renew their drivers' licences and automobile licence stickers.

Famous Players Theatres uses 1000 self-serve ticket dispensers across Canada in their theatres. According to Andrew Sherbin, manager of corporate affairs for Famous Players Theatres, "Guests appreciate the convenience." Approximately one-third of the theatre chain's customers use the self-serve kiosks, and that percentage is increasing.

One company behind the self-serve revolution is The Kiosk Factory in Toronto, an innovative designer and builder of high-quality kiosks and interactive point-of-purchase displays. It specializes in solving problems associated with customer service, customer access, and information presentation. The products and technology offered range from heavy-duty kiosks for demanding public environments such as theatres and malls to high-visibility, interactive point-of-sale displays for retailers.

The company's success and the growth of the self-serve society are based on a simple fact: "People don't like lines," states Robert Machen, vice-president of customer-facing technology at Hilton Hotels. And pilot projects of automated check-in services at hotels in New York and Chicago have also helped reduce lineup times.

Other applications of the company's technology are available in Ontario's electric power plants, where the company has installed shop-floor database access kiosks. Other installations include health education kiosks in public health centres, student access kiosks for Canadian and U.S. universities, library book checkout machines for Canadian and U.S. libraries, and historical exhibits in Toronto's Old Fort York. The company also builds a custom simulator housing for the Air and Space Museum in Washington, D.C.

What are the future possibilities for this technology? Could fast-food providers such as McDonald's ever go self-serve? The concept could be as simple as turning the cash register around. By reducing the number of items available to the customer and reorganizing the cash register facade, anyone could order their own Happy Meal. Could Starbucks or Second Cup be candidates for self-serve? Julian Bowron of the Kiosk Factory thinks so. "By our estimates, the vast majority—75 percent—of people would settle for a narrower range of menu options in exchange for speed." So an automated self-serve line could be the next new thing at your favourite coffee shop.

How about the grocery store? Loblaws has installed self-serve checkout lanes in many of its stores. You simply pass your packages over the bar-code scanner, which reads the codes on your packages. You can even check out fresh produce by weighing the items and using a keypad on the self-service screen to identify the type of produce. The machine then calculates the cost of your purchases and communicates it to you. Your final step is to swipe your credit/debit card or insert cash in the checkout machine, and then you're away in less time than it would take to use the typical checkout service. Self-serve checkout has also appeared in Home Depot and Ikea stores in Canada.

Many experts agree that the self-serve society will expand much further in the coming years, not because of the availability of technology, but because it provides a level of independence for the consumer. However, this seems to conflict with our desire for customer service. On the one hand is the self-serve revolution where consumers are willing to make sacrifices for quicker service, and on the other hand are consumers who demand excellent one-to-one service from retailers.

QUESTIONS

1. Does the marketing concept apply to organizations that rely on self-service for a high proportion of transactions?

2. Is it possible for self-serve–based organizations to create customer value? If so, what value(s) can be created?

3. How do companies with significant levels of self-service exemplify a new model of connecting with customers, as explained in this chapter?

4. Consider the position of a company such as The Kiosk Factory. What is the next industry that you would target for integrating self-serve technology?

AFTER STUDYING THIS CHAPTER, YOU SHOULD BE ABLE TO

 explain company-wide strategic planning and its four steps

 discuss how to design business portfolios and develop growth strategies

 explain marketing's role in strategic planning and how marketing works with its partners to create and deliver customer value

 describe the elements of a customer-driven marketing strategy and mix, and the forces that influence it

list the marketing management functions, including the elements of a marketing plan, and discuss the importance of measuring and managing return on marketing investment

Company and Marketing Strategy: Partnering to Build Customer Relationships

PREVIEWING THE CONCEPTS

In the first chapter, we explored the marketing process by which companies create value for consumers in order to capture value from them in return. In this chapter, we dig deeper into steps two and three of the marketing process—designing customer-driven marketing strategies and constructing marketing programs. First, we look at the organization's overall strategic planning, which guides marketing strategy and planning. Next, we discuss how, guided by the strategic plan, marketers partner closely with others inside and outside the firm to create value for customers. We then examine marketing strategy and planning—how marketers choose target markets, position their market offerings, develop a marketing mix, and manage their marketing programs. Finally, we look at the important step of measuring and managing return on marketing investment.

First, let's look at Nike. During the past several decades, Nike has built the Nike swoosh into one of the world's best-known brand symbols. Nike's outstanding success results from much more than just making and selling good sports gear. It's based on a customer-focused mission and strategy through which Nike creates valued brand experiences and deep brand community with its customers.

NIKE'S MISSION: CREATING VALUED BRAND EXPERIENCES AND DEEP BRAND COMMUNITY

The Nike "swoosh"—it's everywhere! Just for fun, try counting the swooshes whenever you pick up the sports pages or watch a pickup basketball game or tune into a televised golf match. Through innovative marketing, Nike has built the ever-present swoosh into one of the best-known brand symbols on the planet.

Some 45 years ago, when young CPA Phil Knight and college track coach Bill Bowerman co-founded the company, Nike was just a brash, young upstart in the athletic footwear industry. In 1964, the pair chipped in $500 apiece to start Blue Ribbon Sports. In 1970, Bowerman cooked up a new sneaker tread by stuffing a piece of rubber into his wife's waffle iron. The Waffle Trainer quickly became the nation's bestselling training shoe. In 1972, the company became Nike, named after the Greek goddess of victory. And by 1979, Nike had sprinted ahead of the competition, owning 50 percent of the U.S. running shoe market.

During the 1980s, Nike revolutionized sports marketing. To build its brand image and market share, Nike lavishly outspent its competitors on big-name endorsements, splashy promotional events, and big budget, in-your-face "Just Do It" ads. Nike gave customers much more than just good athletic gear. Whereas competitors stressed technical performance, Nike built customer relationships. Beyond shoes, apparel, and equipment, Nike marketed a way of life, a genuine passion for sports, and a just-do-it attitude. Customers didn't just *wear* their Nikes, they *experienced* them. As the company stated on its Web page, "Nike has always known the truth—it's not so much the shoes but where they take you."

Nike powered its way through the early 1990s, moving aggressively into a dozen new sports, including baseball, golf, skateboarding, wall climbing, bicycling, and hiking. The still-brash young company slapped its familiar swoosh logo on everything from sunglasses and soccer balls to batting gloves and golf clubs. It seemed that things couldn't be going any better.

In the late 1990s, however, Nike stumbled and its sales slipped. As the company grew larger, its creative juices seemed to run a bit dry. Its ads began to look like just more of the same and its ho-hum new sneaker designs collected dust on retailer shelves as buyers seeking a new look switched to competing brands. Looking back, Nike's biggest obstacle may have been its own incredible success. As sales approached the US$10 billion mark, the swoosh may have become too common to be cool. Instead of being *anti*-establishment, Nike *was* the establishment, and its hip, once-hot relationship with customers cooled. Nike needed to rekindle its meaning to consumers.

To turn things around, Nike returned to its roots: new-product innovation and a focus on customer relationships. Its newly minted mission: Nike wants "to bring inspiration and innovation to every athlete* in the world (*if you have a body, you are an athlete)." With its deep pockets, as in the past, Nike can outspend most competitors on marketing by a wide margin. But this time around, the sports marketer set out to create a new kind of customer relationship—a deeper, more involving one. Now, Nike no longer just talks *at* its customers through media ads and celebrity endorsers. Instead, it uses cutting-edge marketing tools to interact *with* customers to build brand experiences and deep brand community.

Nike still invests hundreds of millions of dollars each year on creative advertising. However, it now spends less than one-third of its US$650 million annual promotion budget on television and other traditional media, down 55 percent from 10 years ago. These days, behind the bright lights, Nike has developed a host of innovative new relationship-building approaches.

Using community-oriented, digitally led, social-networking tools, Nike is now building communities of customers who talk not only with the company about the brand, but with each other. "Nike's latest masterstroke is social networking, online and off," says one Nike watcher. Whether customers come to know Nike through ads, in-person events at a Niketown store, a local Nike running club, or at one of the company's many community websites, more and more people are bonding closely with the Nike brand experience. Consider this example:

> Twice a week, 30 or more people gather at a local Nike store and go for an evening run. Afterward the members of the Niketown running club chat in the store over refreshments. Nike's staff keeps track of their performances and hails members who have logged more than 100 miles. The event is a classic example of up-close-and-personal relationship building with core customers.
>
> Nike augments such events with an online social network aimed at striking up meaningful long-term interactions with even more runners. The Nike+ running website lets customers with iPod-linked Nike shoes monitor their performances—the distance, pace, time, and calories burned during their runs. Runners can upload and track their own performances over time, compare them with those of other runners, and even participate in local or worldwide challenges.
>
> Talk about brand involvement. Nike+ can be the next best thing to your own personal trainer or jogging buddy. The Nike+ website offers a "Nike Coach" that provides advice and training routines to help you prepare for competitive races. When running, if you have earphones, at the end of every mile a friendly voice tells you how far you've gone and then counts down the final metres. If you hit the wall while running, the push of a button brings up a personally

selected "power song" that gives you an extra boost and gets you going again. Back home again, after a quick upload of your running data, Nike+ charts and helps you analyze your run.

In a little more than two years, Nike+ members have logged more than 116 million miles on the site. Collectively, the Nike+ community has run the equivalent of 4600 trips around the world or 240 journeys to the moon and back. Last September, a million runners competed virtually in a global "Human Race" 10k, posting their times on Nike+, comparing themselves with runners worldwide, and seeing how their cities or countries performed. A San Francisco "Women's Marathon" featured 20 000 participants, plus 3000 who competed in their hometowns and posted their times at Nike+. The long-term goal is to have 15 percent of the world's 100 million runners using the system.

Thanks to efforts such as Nike+, Nike has built a new kinship and sense of community with and between its customers. More than just something to buy, Nike products have once again become a part of customers' lives and times. As a result, Nike is once again achieving stunning results. Over the past five years, Nike's global sales have surged nearly 75 percent and profits have quadrupled. In 2008, as the faltering economy had most sports apparel and footwear competitors gasping for breath, Nike raced ahead. It's global sales jumped 14 percent, and Nike captured a highest-ever 50 percent share of the global running shoe market.

In fact, Nike views uncertain economic times as "an incredible opportunity" to take advantage of its strong brand. As in sports competition, the strongest and best-prepared athlete has the best chance of winning. With deep customer relationships comes powerful competitive advantage. And Nike is once again very close to its customers. As one writer notes, "Nike is blurring the line between brand and experience."[1]

Exhibit 2.1 Nike has built the swoosh into one of the world's best-known brand symbols, signifying the very close bond between customers and the Nike brand.

LIKE Nike, outstanding marketing organizations employ strongly customer-driven marketing strategies and programs that create customer value and relationships. These marketing strategies and programs, however, are guided by broader company-wide strategic plans, which must also be customer focused. Thus, to understand the role of marketing, we must first understand the organization's overall strategic planning process.

COMPANY-WIDE STRATEGIC PLANNING: DEFINING MARKETING'S ROLE 🔘

Each company must find the game plan for long-run survival and growth that makes the most sense given its specific situation, opportunities, objectives, and resources. This is the focus of **strategic planning**—the process of developing and maintaining a strategic fit between the organization's goals and capabilities and its changing marketing opportunities.

Strategic planning sets the stage for the rest of the planning in the firm. Companies usually prepare annual plans, long-range plans, and strategic plans. The annual and long-range plans deal with the company's current businesses and how to keep them going. In contrast, the strategic plan involves adapting the firm to take advantage of opportunities in its constantly changing environment.

At the corporate level, the company starts the strategic planning process by defining its overall purpose and mission (see Figure 2.1). This mission is then turned into detailed supporting objectives that guide the whole company. Next, headquarters decides what portfolio of businesses and products is best for the company and how much support to give each one. In turn, each business and product develops detailed marketing and other departmental plans that support the company-wide plan. Thus, marketing planning occurs at the business-unit, product, and market levels. It supports company strategic planning with more detailed plans for specific marketing opportunities.

Strategic planning
The process of developing and maintaining a strategic fit between the organization's goals and capabilities and its changing marketing opportunities.

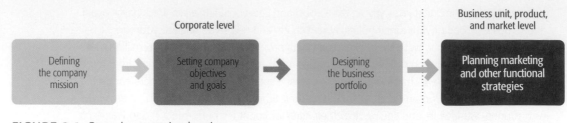

FIGURE 2.1 Steps in strategic planning

DEFINING A MARKET-ORIENTED MISSION

An organization exists to accomplish something, and this purpose should be clearly stated. Forging a sound mission begins with the following questions: What is our business? Who is the customer? What do consumers value? What *should* our business be? These simple-sounding questions are among the most difficult the company will ever have to answer. Successful companies continuously raise these questions and answer them carefully and completely.

Many organizations develop formal mission statements that answer these questions. A **mission statement** is a statement of the organization's purpose—what it wants to accomplish in the larger environment. A clear mission statement acts as an "invisible hand" that guides people in the organization.

Some companies define their missions myopically in product or technology terms ("We make and sell furniture" or "We are a chemical-processing firm"). But mission statements should be *market oriented* and defined in terms of satisfying basic customer needs. Products and technologies eventually become outdated, but basic market needs may last forever. Indigo Books & Music's mission isn't simply to sell books and music. Its mission is "to provide booklovers and those they care about with the most inspiring retail and online environments in the world for books and life-enriching products and services." Likewise, Under Armour's mission isn't just to make performance sports apparel, it's "to make all athletes better through passion, science, and the relentless pursuit of innovation." Table 2.1 provides several other examples of product-oriented versus market-oriented business definitions.[2]

Mission statement

A statement of the organization's purpose—what it wants to accomplish in the larger environment.

Exhibit 2.2 Indigo Books & Music's mission is "to provide booklovers and those they care about with the most inspiring retail and online environments in the world for books and life-enriching products and services."

TABLE 2.1   Market-Oriented Business Definitions

Company	Product-Oriented Definition	Market-Oriented Definition
Disney	We run theme parks.	We create fantasies—a place where dreams come true and America still works the way it's supposed to.
Google	We provide the world's best online search engine.	We help you organize the world's information and make it universally accessible and useful.
Home Depot	We sell tools and home repair and improvement items.	We empower consumers to achieve the homes of their dreams.
Kraft	We make consumer food and drink products.	We help people around the world eat and live better.
Nike	We sell athletic shoes and apparel.	We bring inspiration and innovation to every athlete* in the world. (*If you have a body, you are an athlete.)
Revlon	We make cosmetics.	We sell lifestyle and self-expression; success and status; memories, hopes, and dreams.
Ritz-Carlton Hotels & Resorts	We rent rooms.	We create the Ritz-Carlton experience—one that enlivens the senses, instills well-being, and fulfills even the unexpressed wishes and needs of our guests.
Wal-Mart	We run discount stores.	We deliver low prices every day and give ordinary folks the chance to buy the same things as rich people. "Save Money. Live Better."

Mission statements should be meaningful and specific yet motivating. They should emphasize the company's strengths in the marketplace. Too often, mission statements are written for public relations purposes and lack specific, workable guidelines. Says marketing consultant Jack Welch:[3]

> Few leaders actually get the point of forging a mission with real grit and meaning. [Mission statements] have largely devolved into fat-headed jargon. Almost no one can figure out what they mean. [So companies] sort of ignore them or gussy up a vague package deal along the lines of: "our mission is to be the best fill-in-the-blank company in our industry." [Instead, Welch advises, CEOs should] make a choice about how your company will win. Don't mince words! Remember Nike's old mission, "Crush Reebok"? That's directionally correct. And Google's mission statement isn't something namby-pamby like "To be the world's best search engine." It's "To organize the world's information and make it universally accessible and useful." That's simultaneously inspirational, achievable, and completely graspable.

Finally, a company's mission should not be stated as making more sales or profits—profits are only a reward for creating value for customers. Instead, the mission should focus on customers and the customer experience the company seeks to create. Thus, McDonald's mission isn't "to be the world's best and most profitable quick-service restaurant," it's "to be our customers favourite place and way to eat." If McDonald's accomplishes this customer-focused mission, profits will follow (see Marketing@Work 2.1).

SETTING COMPANY OBJECTIVES AND GOALS

The company needs to turn its mission into detailed supporting objectives for each level of management. Each manager should have objectives and be responsible for reaching them. For example, Kohler makes and markets familiar kitchen and bathroom fixtures—everything from bathtubs and toilets to kitchen sinks. But Kohler also offers a breadth of other products and services, including furniture, tile and stone, and even small engines and backup power systems. It also owns resorts and spas in the United States and

MARKETING@WORK 2.1

McDonald's: On a Customer-Focused Mission

More than half a century ago, Ray Kroc, a 52-year-old salesman of milk-shake-mixing machines, set out on a mission to transform the way Americans eat. In 1955, Kroc discovered a string of seven restaurants owned by Richard and Maurice McDonald. He saw the McDonald brothers' fast-food concept as a perfect fit for America's increasingly on-the-go, time-squeezed, family-oriented lifestyles and bought the small chain for US$2.7 million. In 1967, McDonald's expanded internationally, opening its first restaurant outside the United States in Richmond, British Columbia.

From the start, Kroc preached a motto of QSCV—quality, service, cleanliness, and value. These goals became mainstays in McDonald's customer-focused mission statement. Applying these values, the company perfected the fast-food concept—delivering convenient, good-quality food at affordable prices.

McDonald's grew quickly to become the world's largest fast-feeder. The fast-food giant's more than 32 000 restaurants worldwide (including 1400 in Canada) now serve 58 million customers each day, racking up system-wide sales of more than US$60 billion annually. The Golden Arches are one of the world's most familiar symbols, and other than Santa Claus, no character in the world is more recognizable than Ronald McDonald.

In the mid-1990s, however, McDonald's fortunes began to turn. The company appeared to fall out of touch with both its mission and its customers. Consumers were looking for fresher, better-tasting food and more contemporary atmospheres. They were also seeking healthier eating options. In a new age of health-conscious consumers and $5 lattes at Starbucks, McDonald's seemed a bit out of step with the times. One analyst sums it up this way:

McDonald's was struggling to find its identity amid a flurry of new competitors and changing consumer tastes. The company careened from one failed idea to another. It tried to keep pace by offering pizza, toasted deli sandwiches, and the Arch Deluxe, a heavily advertised new burger that flopped. It bought into non-burger franchises like Chipotle and Boston Market. It also tinkered with its menu, no longer toasting the buns, switching pickles, and changing the special sauce on Big Macs. None of it worked. All the while, McDonald's continued opening new restaurants at a ferocious pace, as many as 2,000 a year. The new stores helped sales, but customer service and cleanliness declined because the company couldn't hire and train good workers fast enough. Meanwhile, McDonald's increasingly became a target for animal-rights activists, environmentalists, and nutritionists, who accused the chain of contributing to the nation's obesity epidemic with "super size" French fries and sodas as well as Happy Meals that lure kids with the reward of free toys.

While McDonald's remained the world's most visited fast-food chain, the once-shiny Golden Arches lost some of their lustre. Sales growth slumped, and its market share fell by more than 3 percent between 1997 and 2003. In 2002, the company posted its first-ever quarterly loss. In the face of changing customer value expectations, the company had lost sight of its fundamental value proposition. "We got distracted from the most important thing: hot, high-quality food at a great value at the speed and convenience of McDonald's," says current CEO Jim Skinner. The company and its mission needed to adapt.

In early 2003, a troubled McDonald's announced a turnaround plan—what it now calls its "Plan to Win." At the heart of this plan was a new mission statement that refocused the company on its customers. According to the analyst,

The company's mission was changed from "being the world's best quick-service restaurant" to "being our customers' favourite place and way to eat." The Plan to Win lays out where McDonald's wants to be and how it plans to get there, all centered on five basics of an exceptional customer experience: people, products, place, price, and promotion. While the five Ps smack of corny corporate speak, company officials maintain that they have profoundly changed McDonald's direction and priorities. The plan, and the seemingly simple shift in mission, forced McDonald's and its employees to focus on quality, service, and the restaurant experience rather than simply providing the cheapest, most convenient option to customers. The Plan to Win—which barely fits on a single sheet of paper—is now treated as sacred inside the company.

Under the Plan to Win, McDonald's got back to the basic business of taking care of customers. It halted rapid expansion, and instead poured money back into improving the food, service, atmosphere, and marketing at existing outlets.

Exhibit 2.3: McDonald's new mission—"being our customers' favourite place and way to eat"—coupled with its Plan to Win, got the company back to the basics of creating exceptional customer experiences.

McDonald's has redecorated its restaurants with clean, simple, more-modern interiors and amenities such as live plants, wireless Internet access, and flat-screen TVs showing cable news. Play areas in some new restaurants feature video games and even stationary bicycles with video screens. To make the customer experience more convenient, McDonald's stores now open earlier to extend breakfast hours and stay open longer to serve late-night diners—more than one-third of McDonald's restaurants are now open 24 hours a day.

A reworked menu now provides more choice and variety, including healthier options such as Chicken McNuggets made with white meat, Chicken Selects whole-breast strips, low-fat "milk jugs," apple slices, and a line of Premium Salads. Within only a year of introducing its Premium Salads, McDonald's became the world's largest salad seller. The

company also launched a major multi-faceted education campaign—themed "it's what i **eat** and what i **do** ... i'm lovin' it"—that underscores the important interplay between eating right and staying active.

McDonald's rediscovered dedication to customer value sparked a remarkable turnaround. Since announcing its Plan to Win, McDonald's sales have increased by more than 50 percent and profits have more than quadrupled. In 2008, when the stock market lost one-third of its value—the worst loss since the Great Depression—McDonald's stock gained nearly 6 percent, making it one of only two companies in the Dow Jones industrial average whose share price rose during that year (the other was Wal-Mart). In the fourth quarter of that year, McDonald's same-store sales increased 5 percent; by comparison, Starbucks' same-store sales decreased 10 percent. Through 2009, as the economy and the

restaurant industry as a whole continued to struggle, McDonald's outperformed its competitors by a notable margin.

Thus, McDonald's now appears to have the right mission for the times. Once again, when you think McDonald's you think value—whether it's a college student buying a sandwich for a buck or a working mother at the drive-through grabbing a breakfast latte that's a dollar cheaper than a latte from Starbucks. And that has customers and the company alike humming the chain's catchy jingle, "I'm lovin' it."

Sources: Extracts based on information found in Andrew Martin, "At McDonald's, the Happiest Meal Is Hot Profits," *New York Times,* January 11, 2009; and Jeremy Adamy, "McDonald's Seeks Ways to Keep Sizzling," *Wall Street Journal,* March 10, 2009, p. A1. Also see "McDonald's Delivers Another Year of Strong Results in 2008," McDonald's press release, January 26, 2009, accessed at www.mcdonalds.com; and other financial information and facts accessed at http://www.aboutmcdonalds.com/mcd/investors.html, October 2009.

Scotland. Kohler ties this diverse product portfolio together under the mission of "contributing to a higher level of gracious living for those who are touched by our products and services."

This broad mission leads to a hierarchy of objectives, including business objectives and marketing objectives. Kohler's overall objective is to build profitable customer relationships by developing efficient yet beautiful products that embrace the "essence of gracious living." It does this by investing heavily in research and design (R&D). R&D is expensive and requires improved profits to plow back into research programs. So improving profits becomes another major objective for Kohler. Profits can be improved by increasing sales or reducing costs. Sales can be increased by improving the company's share of domestic and international markets. These goals then become the company's current marketing objectives.

Marketing strategies and programs must be developed to support these marketing objectives. To increase its market share, Kohler might increase its products' availability and promotion in existing markets and expand business via acquisitions. For example, Kohler intends to boost its production capacity in Thailand to better serve the Asian market. It is also setting up new facilities in India and China. In addition, Kohler's Hospitality Group opened a Kohler Waters Spa in the Chicago area and the Interiors Group acquired furniture manufacturer Mark David.[4]

Exhibit 2.4 Kohler's overall objective is to build profitable customer relationships by developing efficient yet beautiful products that embrace the "essence of gracious living."

These are Kohler's broad marketing strategies. Each broad marketing strategy must then be defined in greater detail. For example, increasing the product's promotion may require more salespeople, advertising, and public relations efforts; if so, both requirements will need to be spelled out. In this way, the firm's mission is translated into a set of objectives for the current period.

DESIGNING THE BUSINESS PORTFOLIO

Business portfolio
The collection of businesses and products that make up the company.

Guided by the company's mission statement and objectives, management now must plan its **business portfolio**—the collection of businesses and products that make up the company. The best business portfolio is the one that best fits the company's strengths and weaknesses to opportunities in the environment. Business portfolio planning involves two steps. First, the company must analyze its *current* business portfolio and decide which businesses should receive more, less, or no investment. Second, it must shape the *future* portfolio by developing strategies for growth and downsizing.

ANALYZING THE CURRENT BUSINESS PORTFOLIO

Portfolio analysis
The process by which management evaluates the products and businesses that make up the company.

The major activity in strategic planning is business **portfolio analysis**, whereby management evaluates the products and businesses that make up the company. The company will want to put strong resources into its more profitable businesses and phase down or drop its weaker ones.

Management's first step is to identify the key businesses that make up the company, called *strategic business units* (SBUs). An SBU can be a company division, a product line within a division, or sometimes a single product or brand. The company next assesses the attractiveness of its various SBUs and decides how much support each deserves. When designing a business portfolio, it's a good idea to add and support products and businesses that fit closely with the firm's core philosophy and competencies.

The purpose of strategic planning is to find ways in which the company can best use its strengths to take advantage of attractive opportunities in the environment. So most standard portfolio analysis methods evaluate SBUs on two important dimensions—the attractiveness of the SBU's market or industry, and the strength of the SBU's position in that market or industry. The best-known portfolio-planning method was developed by the Boston Consulting Group, a leading management consulting firm.[5]

Growth-share matrix
A portfolio-planning method that evaluates a company's strategic business units (SBUs) in terms of its market growth rate and relative market share. SBUs are classified as stars, cash cows, question marks, or dogs.

The Boston Consulting Group Approach   Using the now-classic Boston Consulting Group (BCG) approach, a company classifies all its SBUs according to the **growth-share matrix,** as shown in Figure 2.2. On the vertical axis, *market growth rate* provides a measure of market attractiveness. On the horizontal axis, *relative market share* serves as a measure of company strength in the market. The growth-share matrix defines four types of SBUs:

Stars. Stars are high-growth, high-share businesses or products. They often need heavy investments to finance their rapid growth. Eventually their growth will slow down, and they will turn into cash cows.

Cash Cows. Cash cows are low-growth, high-share businesses or products. These established and successful SBUs need less investment to hold their market share. Thus, they produce a lot of cash that the company uses to pay its bills and support other SBUs that need investment.

Question Marks. Question marks are low-share business units in high-growth markets. They require a lot of cash to hold their share, let alone increase it. Management

FIGURE 2.2 The BCG growth-share matrix

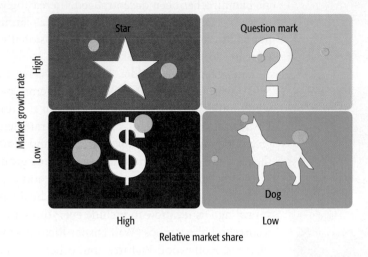

has to think hard about which question marks it should try to build into stars and which should be phased out.

Dogs. Dogs are low-growth, low-share businesses and products. They may generate enough cash to maintain themselves but do not promise to be large sources of cash.

The 10 circles in the growth-share matrix represent a company's 10 current SBUs. The company has two stars, two cash cows, three question marks, and three dogs. The areas of the circles are proportional to the SBU's dollar sales. This company is in fair shape, although not in good shape. It wants to invest in the more promising question marks to make them stars and to maintain the stars so that they will become cash cows as their markets mature. Fortunately, it has two good-sized cash cows. Income from these cash cows will help finance the company's question marks, stars, and dogs. The company should take some decisive action concerning its dogs and its question marks.

Once it has classified its SBUs, the company must determine what role each will play in the future. One of four strategies can be pursued for each SBU. The company can invest more in the business unit to *build* its share. Or it can invest just enough to *hold* the SBU's share at the current level. It can *harvest* the SBU, milking its short-term cash flow regardless of the long-term effect. Finally, the company can *divest* the SBU by selling it or phasing it out and using the resources elsewhere.

As time passes, SBUs change their positions in the growth-share matrix. Many SBUs start out as question marks and move into the star category if they succeed. They later become cash cows as market growth falls, then finally die off or turn into dogs toward the end of their life cycles. The company needs to add new products and units continuously so that some of them will become stars and, eventually, cash cows that will help finance other SBUs.

Problems with Matrix Approaches The BCG and other formal methods revolutionized strategic planning. However, such centralized approaches have limitations: They can be difficult, time-consuming, and costly to implement. Management may find it difficult to define SBUs and measure market share and growth. In addition, these approaches focus on classifying *current* businesses but provide little advice for *future* planning.

Because of such problems, many companies have dropped formal matrix methods in favour of more customized approaches that better suit their specific situations. Moreover, unlike former strategic-planning efforts that rested mostly in the hands of

Exhibit 2.5 Managing the business portfolio: Most people think of Disney as theme parks and wholesome family entertainment but over the past two decades, it's become a sprawling collection of media and entertainment businesses that requires big doses of the famed "Disney Magic" to manage.

Product/market expansion grid
A portfolio-planning tool for identifying company growth opportunities through market penetration, market development, product development, or diversification.

FIGURE 2.3 The product/market expansion grid

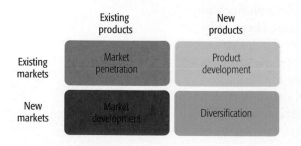

senior managers at company headquarters, today's strategic planning has been decentralized. Increasingly, companies are placing responsibility for strategic planning in the hands of cross-functional teams of divisional managers who are close to their markets.

For example, consider The Walt Disney Company. Most people think of Disney as theme parks and wholesome family entertainment. But in the mid-1980s, Disney set up a powerful, centralized strategic planning group to guide the company's direction and growth. Over the next two decades, the strategic planning group turned The Walt Disney Company into a huge and diverse collection of media and entertainment businesses. The sprawling Disney grew to include everything from theme resorts and film studios (Walt Disney Pictures, Touchstone Pictures, Hollywood Pictures, and others) to media networks (ABC plus Disney Channel, ESPN, A&E, History Channel, and a half-dozen others) to consumer products and a cruise line.

The newly transformed Disney company proved hard to manage and performed unevenly. Recently, Disney disbanded the centralized strategic planning unit, decentralizing its functions to Disney division managers. As a result, Disney reclaimed its position at the head of the world's media conglomerates. And despite recently facing "the weakest economy in our lifetime," Disney's sound strategic management of its broad mix of businesses has helped it fare better than its rival media companies.[6]

Developing Strategies for Growth and Downsizing   Beyond evaluating current businesses, designing the business portfolio involves finding businesses and products the company should consider in the future. Companies need growth if they are to compete more effectively, satisfy their stakeholders, and attract top talent. "Growth is pure oxygen," states one executive. "It creates a vital, enthusiastic corporation where people see genuine opportunity." At the same time, a firm must be careful not to make growth itself an objective. The company's objective must be to manage "profitable growth."[7]

Marketing has the main responsibility for achieving profitable growth for the company. Marketing needs to identify, evaluate, and select market opportunities and lay down strategies for capturing them. One useful device for identifying growth opportunities is the **product/market expansion grid**, shown in Figure 2.3.[8] We apply it here to performance sports apparel maker Under Armour. Only 13 years ago, Under Armour introduced its innovative line of comfy, moisture-wicking shirts and shorts. Since then, it has grown rapidly in its performance-wear niche. In the five years ending in 2007, Under Armour grew at a blistering 65 percent annual rate. And even as retail sales slumped across the board in last year's down economy, Under Armour's sales grew by nearly 20 percent. Looking forward, the company must look for new ways to keep growing.[9]

First, Under Armour might consider whether the company can achieve deeper **market penetration**—making more sales without changing its original product. It can spur growth through

Exhibit 2.6 Growth: Under Armour has grown at a blistering rate under its multi-pronged growth strategy.

marketing mix improvements—adjustments to its product design, advertising, pricing, and distribution efforts. For example, Under Armour offers an ever-increasing range of styles and colours in its original apparel lines. And it recently boosted its promotion spending in an effort to drive home its "performance and authenticity" positioning. Following a blockbuster US$4.4 million 2008 Super Bowl ad, Under Armour this year launched its largest-ever advertising campaign—themed "Athletes Run." The company also added direct-to-consumer distribution channels, including its own retail stores, website, and toll-free call centre. Direct-to-consumer sales grew 47 percent last year and now account for more than 11 percent of total revenues.

Second, Under Armour might consider possibilities for **market development**—identifying and developing new markets for its current products. Under Armour could review new *demographic markets*. For instance, the company recently stepped up its emphasis on women consumers: The "Athletes Run" campaign includes a 30-second "women's only" spot. Under Armour could also pursue new *geographical markets*. For example, the brand has announced its intentions to expand internationally, bringing its products to more athletes throughout the world.

Third, Under Armour could consider **product development**—offering modified or new products to current markets. Last year, in an effort to transform itself from a niche player to a mainstream brand, Under Armour entered the US$19 billion athletic footwear market with a line of cross-trainer shoes. This year, it introduced high-performance running shoes. Although this puts the company into direct competition with sports heavyweights such as Nike and Adidas, it also offers promise for big growth. In fact, in this year's troubled economy, Under Armour expects that most of its growth will come from its new line of running shoes.

Finally, Under Armour might consider **diversification**—starting up or buying businesses outside of its current products and markets. For example, it could move into non-performance leisurewear or begin making and marketing Under Armour fitness equipment. When diversifying, companies must be careful not to overextend their brands' positioning.

Companies must not only develop strategies for *growing* their business portfolios but also strategies for **downsizing** them. There are many reasons that a firm might want to abandon products or markets. The firm may have grown too fast or entered areas where it lacks experience. This can occur when a firm enters too many international markets without the proper research or when a company introduces new products that do not offer superior customer value. The market environment might change, making some of the company's products or markets less profitable. For example, in difficult economic times, many firms prune out weaker, less-profitable products and markets to focus their

Market penetration
A strategy for company growth by increasing sales of current products to current market segments without changing the product.

Market development
A strategy for company growth by identifying and developing new market segments for current company products.

Product development
A strategy for company growth by offering modified or new products to current market segments.

Diversification
A strategy for company growth through starting up or acquiring businesses outside the company's current products and markets.

Downsizing
Reducing the business portfolio by eliminating products or business units that are not profitable or that no longer fit the company's overall strategy.

more limited resources on the strongest ones. Finally, some products or business units simply age and die.

When a firm finds brands or businesses that are unprofitable or that no longer fit its overall strategy, it must carefully prune, harvest, or divest them. Weak businesses usually require a disproportionate amount of management attention. Managers should focus on promising growth opportunities, not fritter away energy trying to salvage fading ones.

PLANNING MARKETING: PARTNERING TO BUILD CUSTOMER RELATIONSHIPS (L03)

The company's strategic plan establishes what kinds of businesses the company will operate and its objectives for each. Then, within each business unit, more detailed planning takes place. The major functional departments in each unit—marketing, finance, accounting, purchasing, operations, information systems, human resources, and others—must work together to accomplish strategic objectives.

Marketing plays a key role in the company's strategic planning in several ways. First, marketing provides a guiding *philosophy*—the marketing concept—that suggests that company strategy should revolve around building profitable relationships with important consumer groups. Second, marketing provides *inputs* to strategic planners by helping to identify attractive market opportunities and by assessing the firm's potential to take advantage of them. Finally, within individual business units, marketing designs *strategies* for reaching the unit's objectives. Once the unit's objectives are set, marketing's task is to help carry them out profitably.

Customer value is the key ingredient in the marketer's formula for success. However, as we noted in Chapter 1, marketers alone cannot produce superior value for customers. Although marketing plays a leading role, it can be only a partner in attracting, keeping, and growing customers. In addition to *customer relationship management*, marketers must also practise *partner relationship management*. They must work closely with partners in other company departments to form an effective internal *value chain* that serves the customer. Moreover, they must partner effectively with other companies in the marketing system to form a competitively superior external *value delivery network*. We now take a closer look at the concepts of a company value chain and a value delivery network.

PARTNERING WITH OTHER COMPANY DEPARTMENTS

Value chain

The series of internal departments that carry out value-creating activities to design, produce, market, deliver, and support a firm's products.

Each company department can be thought of as a link in the company's internal **value chain**.[10] That is, each department carries out value-creating activities to design, produce, market, deliver, and support the firm's products. The firm's success depends not only on how well each department performs its work, but also on how well the various departments coordinate their activities.

For example, Wal-Mart's goal is to create customer value and satisfaction by providing shoppers with the products they want at the lowest possible prices. Marketers at Wal-Mart play an important role. They learn what customers need and stock the stores' shelves with the desired products at unbeatable low prices. They prepare advertising and merchandising programs and assist shoppers with customer service. Through these and other activities, Wal-Mart's marketers help deliver value to customers.

However, the marketing department needs help from the company's other departments. Wal-Mart's ability to offer the right products at low prices depends on the purchasing department's skill in developing the needed suppliers and buying from them at low cost. Wal-Mart's information technology department must provide fast and accurate information about which products are selling in each store. And its operations people must provide effective, low-cost merchandise handling.

A company's value chain is only as strong as its weakest link. Success depends on how well each department performs its work of adding customer value and on how well the activities of various departments are coordinated. At Wal-Mart, if purchasing can't obtain the lowest prices from suppliers, or if operations can't distribute merchandise at the lowest costs, then marketing can't deliver on its promise of unbeatable low prices.

Ideally then, a company's different functions should work in harmony to produce value for consumers. But, in practice, departmental relations are full of conflicts and misunderstandings. The marketing department takes the consumer's point of view. But when marketing tries to develop customer satisfaction, it can cause other departments to do a poorer job *in their terms*. Marketing department actions can increase purchasing costs, disrupt production schedules, increase inventories, and create budget headaches. Thus, the other departments may resist the marketing department's efforts.

Exhibit 2.7 The value chain: Wal-Mart's ability to help you "Save money. Live Better." by offering the right products at lower prices depends on the contributions of people in all of the company's departments.

Yet marketers must find ways to get all departments to "think consumer" and to develop a smoothly functioning value chain. Jack Welch, the highly regarded former GE CEO, emphasized that all GE people, regardless of their department, have an impact on customer satisfaction and retention. Another marketing expert puts it this way: "True market orientation does not mean becoming marketing-driven; it means that the entire company obsesses over creating value for the customer and views itself as a bundle of processes that profitably define, create, communicate, and deliver value to its target customers.... Everyone must do marketing regardless of function or department."[11] Thus, whether you're an accountant, operations manager, financial analyst, IT specialist, or human resources manager, you need to understand marketing and your role in creating customer value.

PARTNERING WITH OTHERS IN THE MARKETING SYSTEM

In its quest to create customer value, the firm needs to look beyond its own internal value chain and into the value chains of its suppliers, distributors, and, ultimately, its customers. Consider McDonald's. People do not swarm to McDonald's only because they love the chain's hamburgers. Consumers flock to the McDonald's *system*, not just to its food products. Throughout the world, McDonald's finely tuned value delivery system delivers a high standard of QSCV—quality, service, cleanliness, and value. McDonald's is effective only to the extent that it successfully partners with its franchisees, suppliers, and others to jointly create "our customers' favourite place and way to eat."

More companies today are partnering with the other members of the supply chain—suppliers, distributors, and, ultimately, customers—to improve the performance of the customer **value delivery network**. For example, cosmetics maker L'Oréal knows the importance of building close relationships with its extensive network of suppliers, who supply everything from polymers and fats to spray cans and packaging to production equipment and office supplies:

Value delivery network
The network made up of the company, suppliers, distributors, and, ultimately, customers who partner with each other to improve the performance of the entire system.

> L'Oréal is the world's largest cosmetics manufacturer, with 25 brands ranging from Maybelline and Kiehl's to Lancôme and Redken. The company's supplier network is crucial to its success. As a result, L'Oréal treats suppliers as respected partners. On the one hand, it expects a lot from suppliers in terms of design innovation, quality, and socially responsible actions. The

Exhibit 2.8 The value delivery system: L'Oréal builds long-term supplier relationships based on mutual benefit and growth. It "wants to make L'Oréal a top performer and one of the world's most respected companies. Being respected also means being respected by our suppliers."

Marketing strategy
The marketing logic by which the company hopes to create customer value and achieve profitable customer relationships.

company carefully screens new suppliers and regularly assesses the performance of current suppliers. On the other hand, L'Oréal works closely with suppliers to help them meet its exacting standards. Whereas some companies make unreasonable demands of their suppliers and "squeeze" them for short-term gains, L'Oréal builds long-term supplier relationships based on mutual benefit and growth. According to the company's supplier Web site, it treats suppliers with "fundamental respect for their business, their culture, their growth, and the individuals who work there. Each relationship is based on ... shared efforts aimed at promoting growth and mutual profits that make it possible for suppliers to invest, innovate, and compete." As a result, more than 75 percent of L'Oréal's supplier-partners have been working with the company for 10 years or more, and the majority of them for several decades. Says the company's head of purchasing, "The CEO wants to make L'Oréal a top performer and one of the world's most respected companies. Being respected also means being respected by our suppliers."[12]

Increasingly in today's marketplace, competition no longer takes place between individual competitors. Rather, it takes place between the entire value delivery networks created by these competitors. Thus, carmaker Toyota's performance against Ford depends on the quality of Toyota's overall value delivery network versus Ford's. Even if Toyota makes the best cars, it might lose in the marketplace if Ford's dealer network provides more customer-satisfying sales and service.

MARKETING STRATEGY AND THE MARKETING MIX ⬤LO4

The strategic plan defines the company's overall mission and objectives. Marketing's role and activities are shown in Figure 2.4, which summarizes the major activities involved in managing a customer-driven marketing strategy and the marketing mix.

Consumers stand in the centre. The goal is to create value for customers and build profitable customer relationships. Next comes **marketing strategy**—the marketing logic by which the company hopes to create this customer value and achieve these profitable relationships. The company decides which customers it will serve (segmentation and targeting) and how (differentiation and positioning). It identifies the total market, then divides it into smaller segments, selects the most promising segments, and focuses on serving and satisfying the customers in these segments.

Guided by marketing strategy, the company designs an integrated *marketing mix* made up of factors under its control—product, price, place, and promotion (the four *P*s). To find the best marketing strategy and mix, the company engages in marketing analysis, planning, implementation, and control. Through these activities, the company watches and adapts to the actors and forces in the marketing environment. We will now look briefly at each activity. Then, in later chapters, we will discuss each one in more depth.

FIGURE 2.4 Managing marketing strategies and the marketing mix

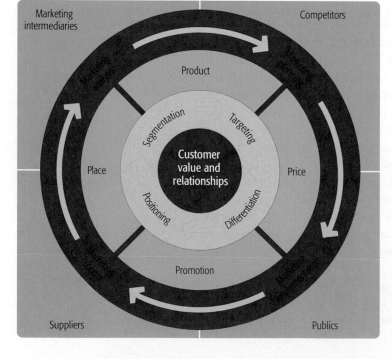

CUSTOMER-DRIVEN MARKETING STRATEGY

As we emphasized throughout Chapter 1, to succeed in today's competitive marketplace, companies need to be customer centred. They must win customers from competitors, and then keep and grow them by delivering greater value. But before it can satisfy customers, a company must first understand their needs and wants. Thus, sound marketing requires careful customer analysis.

Companies know that they cannot profitably serve all consumers in a given market—at least not all consumers in the same way. There are too many different kinds of consumers with too many different kinds of needs. And most companies are in a position to serve some segments better than others. Thus, each company must divide up the total market, choose the best segments, and design strategies for profitably serving chosen segments. This process involves *market segmentation, market targeting, differentiation,* and *positioning.*

Market Segmentation The market consists of many types of customers, products, and needs. The marketer has to determine which segments offer the best opportunities. Consumers can be grouped and served in various ways based on geographic, demographic, psychographic, and behavioural factors. The process of dividing a market into distinct groups of buyers who have different needs, characteristics, or behaviours, and who might require separate products or marketing programs is called **market segmentation.**

Every market has segments, but not all ways of segmenting a market are equally useful. For example, Tylenol would gain little by distinguishing between low-income and high-income pain reliever users if both respond the same way to marketing efforts. A **market segment** consists of consumers who respond in a similar way to a given set of marketing efforts. In the car market, for example, consumers who want the biggest, most comfortable car regardless of price make up one market segment. Consumers who care mainly about price and operating economy make up another segment. It would be difficult to make one car model that was the first choice of consumers in both segments. Companies are wise to focus their efforts on meeting the distinct needs of individual market segments.

Market Targeting After a company has defined market segments, it can enter one or many of these segments. **Market targeting** involves evaluating each market segment's attractiveness and selecting one or more segments to enter. A company should target segments in which it can profitably generate the greatest customer value and sustain it over time.

A company with limited resources might decide to serve only one or a few special segments or "market niches." Such "nichers" specialize in serving customer segments that major competitors overlook or ignore. For example, Ferrari sells only 1500 of its very high-performance cars in the United States each year, but at very high prices—from an eye-opening $229 500 for its Ferrari F430 F1 Spider convertible to an astonishing more than $2 million for its FXX super sports car, which can be driven only on race tracks. Most nichers aren't quite so exotic. WhiteWave, maker of Silk Soymilk, has found its niche as North America's largest soymilk producer. And although Logitech is only a fraction the size of giant Microsoft, through skilful niching, it dominates the PC mouse market, with Microsoft as its runner-up (see Marketing@Work 2.2).

Alternatively, a company might choose to serve several related segments—perhaps those with different kinds of customers but with the same basic wants. Abercrombie & Fitch, for example, targets college students, teens, and kids with the same upscale, casual clothes and accessories in three different outlets: the original Abercrombie & Fitch, Hollister, and Abercrombie. Or a large company might decide to offer a complete range of products to serve all market segments.

Market segmentation
Dividing a market into distinct groups of buyers who have different needs, characteristics, or behaviours, and who might require separate products or marketing programs.

Market segment
A group of consumers who respond in a similar way to a given set of marketing efforts.

Market targeting
The process of evaluating each market segment's attractiveness and selecting one or more segments to enter.

MARKETING@WORK 2.2

Nicher Logitech: The Little Mouse that Roars

Among the big tech companies, market leader Microsoft is the king of the jungle. When giant Microsoft looms, even large competitors quake. But when it comes to dominating specific market niches, overall size isn't always the most important thing. For example, in its own corner of the high-tech jungle, Logitech International is the little mouse that roars. In its niches, small but mighty Logitech is the undisputed market leader.

Logitech focuses on what it calls "personal peripherals"—interface devices for PC navigation, Internet communications, home-entertainment systems, and gaming and wireless devices. Logitech's rapidly expanding product portfolio now includes everything from cordless mice and keyboards, gaming controllers, and remote controls to webcams, PC speakers, headsets, notebook stands, and cooling pads. But it all started with computer mice.

Logitech makes every variation of mouse imaginable. Over the years, it has flooded the world with more than 1 billion computer mice of all varieties, mice for left- and right-handed people, wireless mice, travel mice, mini mice, 3-D mice, mice shaped like real mice for children, and even an "air mouse" that uses motion sensors to let you navigate your computer from a distance.

In the PC mouse market, Logitech competes head-on with Microsoft. At first glance it looks like an unfair contest. Microsoft's more than US$60 billion in sales is 25 times bigger than Logitech's US$2.4 billion. But when it comes to mice and other peripherals, Logitech has a depth of focus and knowledge that no other company in the world—including Microsoft—can match. Whereas mice and other interface devices are pretty much a sideline for software maker Microsoft—almost a distraction—they are the main attraction for Logitech. As a result, each new Logitech device is a true work of

both art and science. Logitech's mice, for example, receive raves from designers, expert reviewers, and users alike.

A *BusinessWeek* analyst gives us a behind-the-scenes look at Logitech's deep design and development prowess:

> One engineer, given the moniker "Teflon Tim" by amused colleagues, spent three months scouring the Far East to find just the right nonstick coatings and sound-deadening foam. Another spent hours taking apart wind-up toys. Others poured over the contours of luxury BMW motorcycles, searching for designs to crib. They were members of a most unusual team that spent thousands of hours during

the past two years on a single goal: to build a better mouse. The result: Logitech's revolutionary MX Revolution, the next-generation mouse that hit consumer electronics shelves about two years ago. It represented the company's most ambitious attempt yet to refashion the lowly computer mouse into a kind of control center for a host of PC applications. The sheer scope of the secret mission—which crammed 420 components, including a tiny motor, into a palm-sized device that usually holds about 20—brought together nearly three dozen engineers, designers, and marketers from around the globe.

Exhibit 2.9: Nichers: In its own corner of the high-tech jungle, Logitech is a little mouse that roars, with giant Microsoft as its runner-up.

Part of Logitech's product-development strategy is defensive. Once content to design mice and other peripherals for PC makers to slap their own names on, Logitech over the past half-decade has increasingly focused on selling its branded add-on equipment directly to consumers. Nearly 90 percent of Logitech's annual sales now come from retail. That forces Logitech to deliver regular improvements and new devices to entice new shoppers and purchases.

"We think of mice as pretty simple," says one industry analyst, "but there's a pretty aggressive technology battle going on to prove what the mouse can do." One of Logitech's latest feats of cutting-edge wizardry is its MX Air, which promises to change the very definition of the computer mouse as we know it. More like an airborne remote control than a traditional mouse, you can surf the Web, play games, and control your home theatre PC from up to 9 metres away. There's also a cool-factor at play. Wielding the MX Air is like holding a work of art.

And at Logitech, it's not just about mice anymore. Logitech now applies its cool-factor to create sleek, stylish, and functional devices that not only enhance your PC experience, but also help you get the most out of everything from Internet navigation to all of the new gadgets in today's digital home. For example, Logitech's family of Harmony advanced universal remote controls helps even technology challenged novices tame the complexities of their home-entertainment systems.

Breeding mice and other peripherals has been very good for nichier Logitech. For example, thanks to its dedication to creating the next best mouse, Logitech has dominated the world mouse market, with giant Microsoft as its runner-up. And although Logitech isn't nearly as big as Microsoft, pound for pound it's even more profitable. Over the past six years, despite tough economic times for the PC and consumer electronics industries, Logitech's sales and profits have more than doubled. Looking ahead, as Logitech forges forward in its personal peripherals niche, Logitech is well positioned to weather the recent economic storms and emerge stronger than ever.

"Our business is about the last inch between people and content and technology," explains Logitech CEO Guerrino De Luca. Nobody spans that last inch better than Logitech. The next time you navigate your PC, watch or listen to downloaded Web audio or video content, or pick up an entertainment-system remote, it's a pretty good bet that you'll have your hand on a Logitech device. It's also a good bet that you'll really like the way it works and feels. "The goal [is] passing the 'ooooh' test," says a Logitech project leader, "creating a visceral experience that communicates both performance and luxury."

Sources: Lisa Johnston and John Laposky, "Logitech Intros Accessories, Ships Billion Mouse," *TWICE*, December 15, 2008, p. 84; Cliff Edwards, "Here Comes Mighty Mouse," *BusinessWeek*, September 4, 2006, p. 76; Cliff Edwards, "The Mouse that Soars," *BusinessWeek*, August 20, 2007, p. 22; "Logitech International S.A.," *Hoover's Company Records*, March 1, 2009, p. 42459; "Haig Simonian, "Logitech Warns of Gloom Ahead," FT.com, January 21, 2009; http://ir.logitech.com/overview.cfm?cl=us.en; and annual reports and other information from http://ir.logitech.com/overview.cfm?cl=us.en and www.logitech.com, accessed October 2009.

Most companies enter a new market by serving a single segment, and if this proves successful, they add more segments. For example, Nike started with innovative running shoes for serious runners. Large companies eventually seek full market coverage. Nike now makes and sells a broad range of sports products for just about anyone and everyone, with the goal of "helping athletes at every level of ability reach their potential."[13] It has different products designed to meet the special needs of each segment it serves.

Market Differentiation and Positioning After a company has decided which market segments to enter, it must decide how it will differentiate its market offering for each targeted segment and what positions it wants to occupy in those segments. A product's *position* is the place the product occupies relative to competitors' products in consumers' minds. Marketers want to develop unique market positions for their products. If a product is perceived to be exactly like others on the market, consumers would have no reason to buy it.

Positioning is arranging for a product to occupy a clear, distinctive, and desirable place relative to competing products in the minds of target consumers. As one positioning expert puts it, positioning is "why a shopper will pay a little more for your brand."[14]

Thus, marketers plan positions that distinguish their products from competing brands and give them the greatest advantage in their target markets.

Wal-Mart promises "Save Money. Live Better."; Canadian Tire is "for days like today"; YouTube let's you "Broadcast Yourself." You can "Feel Better" with Tylenol; and with Excedrin, "The Pain Stops. You Don't." And at Burger King, you can "Have it your way," whereas people at McDonald's say "I'm lovin' it." Such deceptively simple statements form the backbone of a product's marketing strategy. For example, Burger King

Positioning
Arranging for a product to occupy a clear, distinctive, and desirable place relative to competing products in the minds of target consumers.

Exhibit 2.10 Positioning: Burger King builds its entire worldwide marketing campaign around its "Have it your way" positioning.

Differentiation

Actually differentiating the market offering to create superior customer value.

Marketing mix

The set of controllable, tactical marketing tools—product, price, place, and promotion—that the firm blends to produce the response it wants in the target market.

designs its entire worldwide integrated marketing campaign—from television and print commercials to its websites—around the "Have it your way" positioning.

In positioning its product, the company first identifies possible customer value differences that provide competitive advantages upon which to build the position. The company can offer greater customer value either by charging lower prices than competitors or by offering more benefits to justify higher prices. But if the company *promises* greater value, it must then *deliver* that greater value. Thus, effective positioning begins with **differentiation**—actually *differentiating* the company's market offering so that it gives consumers more value. Once the company has chosen a desired position, it must take strong steps to deliver and communicate that position to target consumers. The company's entire marketing program should support the chosen positioning strategy.

DEVELOPING AN INTEGRATED MARKETING MIX

After deciding on its overall marketing strategy, the company is ready to begin planning the details of the marketing mix, one of the major concepts in modern marketing. The **marketing mix** is the set of controllable, tactical marketing tools that the firm blends to produce the response it wants in the target market. The marketing mix consists of everything the firm can do to influence the demand for its product. The many possibilities can be collected into four groups of variables known as "the four *P*s": *product, price, place*, and *promotion*. Figure 2.5 shows the marketing tools under each *P*.

FIGURE 2.5 The four *P*s of the marketing mix

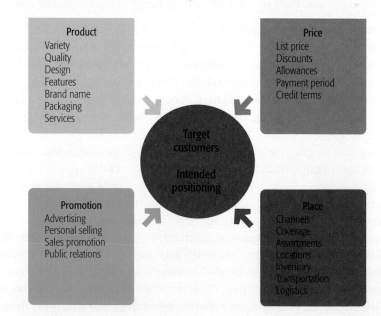

Product means the goods-and-services combination the company offers to the target market. Thus, a Ford Escape consists of nuts and bolts, spark plugs, pistons, headlights, and thousands of other parts. Ford offers several Escape models and dozens of optional features. The car comes fully serviced and with a comprehensive warranty that is as much a part of the product as the tailpipe.

Price is the amount of money customers must pay to obtain the product. Ford calculates suggested retail prices that its dealers might *charge* for each Escape. But Ford dealers rarely charge the full sticker price. Instead, they negotiate the price with each customer, offering discounts, trade-in allowances, and credit terms. These actions adjust prices for the current competitive and economic situations and bring them into line with the buyer's perception of the car's value.

Place includes company activities that make the product available to target consumers. Ford partners with a large body of independently owned dealerships that sell the company's many different models. Ford selects its dealers carefully and supports them strongly. The dealers keep an inventory of Ford automobiles, demonstrate them to potential buyers, negotiate prices, close sales, and service the cars after the sale.

Promotion means activities that communicate the merits of the product and persuade target customers to buy it. Ford Motor Company spends more than US$2 billion each year on advertising to tell consumers about the company and its many products.[15] Dealership salespeople assist potential buyers and persuade them that Ford is the best car for them. Ford and its dealers offer special promotions—sales, cash rebates, low-financing rates—as added purchase incentives.

An effective marketing program blends all of the marketing mix elements into an integrated marketing program designed to achieve the company's marketing objectives by delivering value to consumers. The marketing mix constitutes the company's tactical tool kit for establishing strong positioning in target markets.

Some critics think that the four Ps may omit or underemphasize certain important activities. For example, they ask, "Where are services?" Just because they don't start with a P doesn't justify omitting them. The answer is that services, such as banking, airline, and retailing services, are products too. We might call them *service products*. "Where is packaging?" the critics might ask. Marketers would answer that they include packaging as just one of many product decisions. As Figure 2.5 suggests, many marketing activities that might appear to be left out of the marketing mix are subsumed under one of the four Ps. The issue is not whether there should be four, six, or ten Ps so much as what framework is most helpful in designing integrated marketing programs.

There is another valid concern, however. It holds that the four Ps concept takes the seller's view of the market, not the buyer's view. From the buyer's viewpoint, in this age of customer value and relationships, the four Ps might be better described as the four Cs:[16]

Four *Ps*	Four *Cs*
Product	Customer solution
Price	Customer cost
Place	Convenience
Promotion	Communication

Thus, whereas marketers see themselves as selling products, customers see themselves as buying value or solutions to their problems. And customers are interested in more than just the price; they are interested in the total costs of obtaining, using, and disposing of a product. Customers want the product and service to be as conveniently available as possible. Finally, they want two-way communication. Marketers would do well to think through the four Cs first and then build the four Ps on that platform.

MANAGING THE MARKETING EFFORT **LO5**

In addition to being good at the *marketing* in marketing management, companies also need to pay attention to the *management*. Managing the marketing process requires the four marketing management functions shown in Figure 2.6—*analysis, planning, implementation*, and *control*. The company first develops company-wide strategic plans and then translates them into marketing and other plans for each division, product, and brand. Through implementation, the company turns the plans into actions. Control consists of measuring and evaluating the results of marketing activities and taking corrective action where needed. Finally, marketing analysis provides information and evaluations needed for all of the other marketing activities.

MARKETING ANALYSIS

Managing the marketing function begins with a complete analysis of the company's situation. The marketer should conduct a **SWOT analysis**, by which it evaluates the company's overall strengths (S), weaknesses (W), opportunities (O), and threats (T) (see Figure 2.7). Strengths include internal capabilities, resources, and positive situational factors that may help the company to serve its customers and achieve its objectives. Weaknesses include internal limitations and negative situational factors that may interfere with the company's performance. Opportunities are favourable factors or trends in the external environment that the company may be able to exploit to its advantage. And threats are unfavourable external factors or trends that may present challenges to performance.

The company should analyze its markets and marketing environment to find attractive opportunities and identify environmental threats. It should analyze company strengths and weaknesses as well as current and possible marketing actions to determine which opportunities it can best pursue. The goal is to match the company's strengths to attractive opportunities in the environment, while eliminating or overcoming the weaknesses and minimizing the threats. Marketing analysis provides inputs to each of the other marketing management functions. We discuss marketing analysis more fully in Chapter 4.

SWOT analysis
An overall evaluation of the company's strengths (S), weaknesses (W), opportunities (O), and threats (T).

FIGURE 2.6 Managing marketing: analysis, planning, implementation, and control

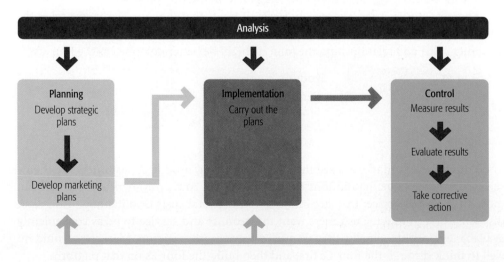

FIGURE 2.7 SWOT analysis: strengths (S), weaknesses (W), opportunities (O), and threats (T)

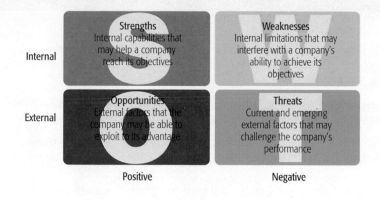

Internal	**Strengths** Internal capabilities that may help a company reach its objectives	**Weaknesses** Internal limitations that may interfere with a company's ability to achieve its objectives
External	**Opportunities** External factors that the company may be able to exploit to its advantage	**Threats** Current and emerging external factors that may challenge the company's performance
	Positive	Negative

MARKETING PLANNING

Through strategic planning, the company decides what it wants to do with each business unit. Marketing planning involves deciding on marketing strategies that will help the company attain its overall strategic objectives. A detailed marketing plan is needed for each business, product, or brand. What does a marketing plan look like? Our discussion focuses on product or brand marketing plans.

Table 2.2 outlines the major sections of a typical product or brand marketing plan. (See Appendix 2 for a sample marketing plan.) The plan begins with an executive summary that quickly reviews major assessments, goals, and recommendations. The main section of the plan presents a detailed SWOT analysis of the current marketing situation as well as potential threats and opportunities. The plan next states major objectives for the brand and outlines the specifics of a marketing strategy for achieving them.

A *marketing strategy* consists of specific strategies for target markets, positioning, the marketing mix, and marketing expenditure levels. It outlines how the company intends to create value for target customers in order to capture value in return. In this section, the planner explains how each strategy responds to the threats, opportunities, and critical issues spelled out earlier in the plan. Additional sections of the marketing plan lay out an action program for implementing the marketing strategy, along with the details of a supporting *marketing budget*. The last section outlines the controls that will be used to monitor progress, measure return on marketing investment, and take corrective action.

MARKETING IMPLEMENTATION

Planning good strategies is only a start toward successful marketing. A brilliant marketing strategy counts for little if the company fails to implement it properly. **Marketing implementation** is the process that turns marketing *plans* into marketing *actions* to accomplish strategic marketing objectives. Whereas marketing planning addresses the *what* and *why* of marketing activities, implementation addresses the *who, where, when,* and *how*.

Many managers think that "doing things right" (implementation) is as important as, or even more important than, "doing the right things" (strategy). The fact is that both are critical to success, and companies can gain competitive advantages through effective implementation. One firm can have essentially the same strategy as another, yet win in the marketplace through faster or better execution. Still, implementation is difficult—it is often easier to think up good marketing strategies than it is to carry them out.

Marketing implementation
The process that turns marketing strategies and plans into marketing actions to accomplish strategic marketing objectives.

TABLE 2.2 Contents of a Marketing Plan

Section	Purpose
Executive summary	Presents a brief summary of the main goals and recommendations of the plan for management review, helping top management to find the plan's major points quickly. A table of contents should follow the executive summary.
Current marketing situation	Describes the target market and company's position in it, including information about the market, product performance, competition, and distribution. This section includes ☐ A *market description* that defines the market and major segments, and then reviews customer needs and factors in the marketing environment that may affect customer purchasing. ☐ A *product review* that shows sales, prices, and gross margins of the major products in the product line. ☐ A review of *competition* that identifies major competitors and assesses their market positions and strategies for product quality, pricing, distribution, and promotion. ☐ A review of *distribution* that evaluates recent sales trends and other developments in major distribution channels.
Threats and opportunities analysis	Assesses major threats and opportunities that the product might face, helping management to anticipate important positive or negative developments that might have an impact on the firm and its strategies.
Objectives and issues	States the marketing objectives that the company would like to attain during the plan's term and discusses key issues that will affect their attainment. For example, if the goal is to achieve 15 percent market share, this section looks at how this goal might be achieved.
Marketing strategy	Outlines the broad marketing logic by which the business unit hopes to create customer value and relationships and the specifics of target markets, positioning, and marketing expenditure levels. How will the company create value for customers in order to capture value from customers in return? This section also outlines specific strategies for each marketing mix element and explains how each responds to the threats, opportunities, and critical issues spelled out earlier in the plan.
Action programs	Spells out how marketing strategies will be turned into specific action programs that answer the following questions: *What* will be done? *When* will it be done? *Who* will do it? *How* much will it cost?
Budgets	Details a supporting marketing budget that is essentially a projected profit-and-loss statement. It shows expected revenues (forecasted number of units sold and the average net price) and expected costs of production, distribution, and marketing. The difference is the projected profit. Once approved by higher management, the budget becomes the basis for materials buying, production scheduling, personnel planning, and marketing operations.
Controls	Outlines the control that will be used to monitor progress and allow higher management to review implementation results and spot products that are not meeting their goals. It includes measures of return on marketing investment.

In an increasingly connected world, people at all levels of the marketing system must work together to implement marketing strategies and plans. At Black & Decker, for example, marketing implementation for the company's power tools, outdoor equipment, and other products requires day-to-day decisions and actions by thousands of people both inside and outside the organization. Marketing managers make decisions about target segments, branding, packaging, pricing, promoting, and distributing. They talk with engineering about product design, with manufacturing about production and inventory levels, and with finance about funding and cash flows. They also connect with outside people, such as advertising agencies, to plan ad campaigns and the news media to obtain publicity support. The sales force urges Home Depot, Lowe's, and other retailers to advertise Black & Decker products, provide ample shelf space, and use company displays.

MARKETING DEPARTMENT ORGANIZATION

The company must design a marketing organization that can carry out marketing strategies and plans. If the company is very small, one person might do all of the research, selling, advertising, customer service, and other marketing work. As the company expands, a marketing department emerges to plan and carry out marketing activities. In large companies, this department contains many specialists. They have product and market managers, sales managers and salespeople, market researchers, advertising experts, and many other specialists.

To head up such large marketing organizations, many companies have now created a *chief marketing officer* (or CMO) position. The CMO heads up the company's entire marketing operation and represents marketing on the company's top management team. The CMO position puts marketing on equal footing with other C-level executives, such as the chief executive officer (CEO) and the chief financial officer (CFO).[17]

Modern marketing departments can be arranged in several ways. The most common form of marketing organization is the *functional organization*. Under this organization, different marketing activities are headed by a functional specialist—a sales manager, advertising manager, marketing research manager, customer-service manager, or new-product manager. A company that sells across the country or internationally often uses a *geographic organization*. Its sales and marketing people are assigned to specific countries, regions, and districts. Geographic organization allows salespeople to settle into a territory, get to know their customers, and work with a minimum of travel time and cost. Companies with many very different products or brands often create a *product management organization*. Using this approach, a product manager develops and implements a complete strategy and marketing program for a specific product or brand.

For companies that sell one product line to many different types of markets and customers that have different needs and preferences, a *market* or *customer management organization* might be best. A market management organization is similar to the product management organization. Market managers are responsible for developing marketing strategies and plans for their specific markets or customers. This system's main advantage is that the company is organized around the needs of specific customer segments. Many companies develop special organizations to manage their relationships with large customers. For example, companies such as Procter & Gamble and Black & Decker have large teams, or even whole divisions, set up to serve large customers such as Wal-Mart, Safeway, or Home Depot.

Large companies that produce many different products flowing into many different

Exhibit 2.11 Marketers must continually plan their analysis, implement their plans, and control activities.

geographic and customer markets usually employ some *combination* of the functional, geographic, product, and market organization forms.

Marketing organization has become an increasingly important issue in recent years. More and more, companies are shifting their brand management focus toward *customer management*—moving away from managing just product or brand profitability and toward managing customer profitability and customer equity. They think of themselves not as managing portfolios of brands but as managing portfolios of customers.

MARKETING CONTROL

Marketing control

The process of measuring and evaluating the results of marketing strategies and plans and taking corrective action to ensure that objectives are achieved.

Because many surprises occur during the implementation of marketing plans, marketers must practise constant **marketing control**—the process of measuring and evaluating the results of marketing strategies and plans and taking corrective action to ensure that objectives are attained. Marketing control involves four steps. Management first sets specific marketing goals. It then measures its performance in the marketplace and evaluates the causes of any differences between expected and actual performance. Finally, management takes corrective action to close the gaps between its goals and its performance. This may require changing the action programs or even changing the goals.

Operating control involves checking ongoing performance against the annual plan and taking corrective action when necessary. Its purpose is to ensure that the company achieves the sales, profits, and other goals set out in its annual plan. It also involves determining the profitability of different products, territories, markets, and channels. *Strategic control* involves looking at whether the company's basic strategies are well matched to its opportunities. Marketing strategies and programs can quickly become outdated, and each company should periodically reassess its overall approach to the marketplace.

MEASURING AND MANAGING RETURN ON MARKETING INVESTMENT

Marketing managers must ensure that their marketing dollars are being well spent. In the past, many marketers spent freely on big, expensive marketing programs, often without thinking carefully about the financial returns on their spending. They believed that marketing produces intangible outcomes, which do not lend themselves readily to measures of productivity or return. But in today's more constrained economy, all that is changing:

> For years, corporate marketers have walked into budget meetings like neighbourhood junkies. They couldn't always justify how well they spent past handouts or what difference it all made. They just wanted more money—for flashy TV ads, for big-ticket events, for, you know, getting out the message and building up the brand. But those heady days of blind budget increases are fast being replaced with a new mantra: measurement and accountability. "Marketers have been pretty unaccountable for many years," notes one expert. "Now they are under big pressure to estimate their impact. Another analyst puts in more bluntly: "Marketing needs to stop fostering 'rock star' behaviour and focus on rock-steady results."[18]

According to a recent study, as finances have tightened, marketers see return on marketing investment as the second biggest issue after the economy. "Increasingly, it is important for marketers to be able to justify their expenses," says one marketer. "We need to get smarter as a community as we assess how effective our brand [strategies are]."[19]

Return on marketing investment (or marketing ROI)

The net return from a marketing investment divided by the costs of the marketing investment.

In response, marketers are developing better measures of *return on marketing investment*. **Return on marketing investment** (or **marketing ROI**) is the net return from a marketing investment divided by the costs of the marketing investment. It measures the profits generated by investments in marketing activities.

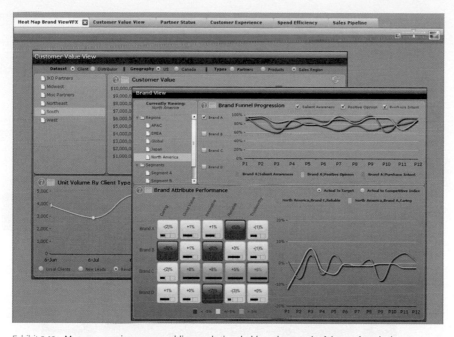

Exhibit 2.12 Many companies are assembling marketing dashboards—meaningful sets of marketing performance measures in a single display used to set and adjust their marketing strategies.

Marketing returns can be difficult to measure. In measuring financial ROI, both the R and the I are uniformly measured in dollars. But there is as of yet no consistent definition of marketing ROI. "It's tough to measure, more so than for other business expenses," says one analyst. "You can imagine buying a piece of equipment ... and then measuring the productivity gains that result from the purchase," he says. "But in marketing, benefits like advertising impact aren't easily put into dollar returns. It takes a leap of faith to come up with a number."[20]

One recent survey found that although two-thirds of companies have implemented return on marketing investment programs in recent years, only one-quarter of companies report making good progress in measuring marketing ROI. Another survey of chief financial officers (CFOs) reported that 93 percent of those surveyed are dissatisfied with their ability to measure return on marketing. The major problem is figuring out what specific measures to use and obtaining good data on these measures.[21]

A company can assess return on marketing in terms of standard marketing performance measures, such as brand awareness, sales, or market share. Many companies are assembling such measures into *marketing dashboards*—meaningful sets of marketing performance measures in a single display used to monitor strategic marketing performance. Just as automobile dashboards present drivers with details on how their cars are performing, the marketing dashboard gives marketers the detailed measures they need to assess and adjust their marketing strategies.[22]

Increasingly, however, beyond standard performance measures, marketers are using customer-centred measures of marketing impact, such as customer acquisition, customer retention, customer lifetime value, and customer equity. These measures capture not just current marketing performance but also future performance resulting from stronger customer relationships. Figure 2.8 views marketing expenditures as investments that produce returns in the form of more profitable customer relationships.[23] Marketing investments result in improved customer value and satisfaction, which in turn increase customer attraction and retention. This increases individual customer lifetime values and the firm's overall customer equity. Increased customer equity, in relation to the cost of the marketing investments, determines return on marketing investment.

FIGURE 2.8 Return on marketing investment

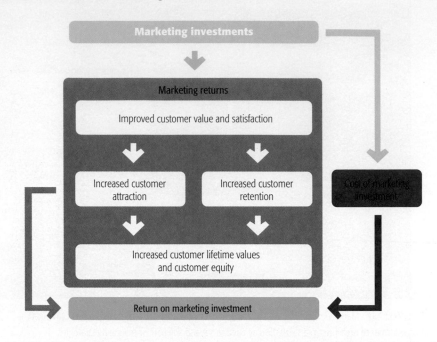

Source: Adapted from Roland T. Rust, Katherine N. Lemon, and Valerie A. Zeithaml, "Return on Marketing: Using Consumer Equity to Focus Marketing Strategy," *Journal of Marketing,* January 2004, p. 112.

Regardless of how it's defined or measured, the return on marketing investment concept is here to stay. "The marketing accountability revolution must continue," says one marketer. In today's demanding business environment, companies must know the impact of their marketing investments." Adds another, "You gotta be accountable."[24]

BUILDING PARTNERSHIPS AND COMMUNITY THROUGH NON-TRADITIONAL MARKETING

In the winter outerwear marketplace, Canada Goose needs to carefully and continually adjust its market strategy so that it can reach its core customer base and encourage customer purchases.

Canada Goose competes in the worldwide winter outerwear market, a market dominated by bold, aggressive retailers and a market that invests hundreds of millions of dollars in marketing research. However, Canada Goose has at its core a strategic imperative that its brand and marketing strategy should not be driven by focus groups, but by a faith that there is a market for the most functional, durable, attractive, and effective cold-weather gear that is made in Canada.

With its primary focus on the authentic "true user," Canada Goose is clearly dedicated to ensuring that form is driven by function. But who are these true users? They are outdoor guides, dog mushers, Arctic tourists, and anyone whose job or activity puts them outside for long periods of time during the winter. Even celebrities who sport the Canada Goose coats say that it is the coats' utility that has won them over. For example, actors Maggie Gyllenhaal and Matt Damon have often been seen wearing theirs on the streets of Boston and New York, and Hayden Christensen was photographed wearing his Canada Goose parka at the 2010 Vancouver Olympics.

Many brands, such as Billabong, have started off as niche, exclusive, true-user brands and moved later into the mainstream, where they often are able to leverage the credibility from their previous true users to convince more mainstream customers to adopt their brands. Instead of following this path, Canada Goose has made the strategic decision to continue to design for true users, and it has successfully marketed the authenticity of its products around the world.

QUESTIONS

1. Should Canada Goose focus on market penetration or market development? What would the latter strategy do to its brand?
2. What makes up Canada Goose's value chain?
3. What partners does Canada Goose have in its value chain?
4. Give an example of what might happen to Canada Goose if it introduced a line of lower-end coats. What would the influence be on the other Ps? More importantly, what effect would the line have on the overall brand?
5. What could happen to Canada Goose's brand perception if customers perceived that the company was trying to reach out of its core base, the "true user" customer segment?

REVIEWING THE CONCEPTS

1. Explain company-wide strategic planning and its four steps.

Strategic planning sets the stage for the rest of the company's planning. Marketing contributes to strategic planning, and the overall plan defines marketing's role in the company.

Strategic planning involves developing a strategy for long-run survival and growth. It consists of four steps: (1) defining the company's mission, (2) setting objectives and goals, (3) designing a business portfolio, and (4) developing functional plans. The company's mission should be market oriented, realistic, specific, motivating, and consistent with the market environment. The mission is then transformed into detailed *supporting goals and objectives*, which in turn guide decisions about the *business portfolio*. Then each business and product unit must develop *detailed marketing plans* in line with the company-wide plan.

2. Discuss how to design business portfolios and develop growth strategies.

Guided by the company's mission statement and objectives, management plans its *business portfolio*, or the collection of businesses and products that make up the company. The firm wants to produce a business portfolio that best fits its strengths and weaknesses to opportunities in the environment. To do this, it must analyze and adjust its *current* business portfolio and develop growth and downsizing strategies for adjusting the *future* portfolio. The company might use a formal portfolio-planning method. But many companies are now designing more-customized portfolio-planning approaches that better suit their unique situations.

3. Explain marketing's role in strategic planning and how marketing works with its partners to create and deliver customer value.

Under the strategic plan, the major functional departments—marketing, finance, accounting, purchasing, operations, information systems, human resources, and others—must work together to accomplish strategic objectives. Marketing plays a key role in the company's strategic planning by providing a *marketing concept philosophy* and *inputs* regarding attractive market opportunities. Within individual business units, marketing designs *strategies* for reaching the unit's objectives and helps to carry them out profitably.

Marketers alone cannot produce superior value for customers. Marketers must practise *partnerrelationship management*, working closely with partners in other departments to form an effective *value chain* that serves the customer. And they must partner effectively with other companies in the marketing system to form a competitively superior *value delivery network*.

4. Describe the elements of a customer-driven marketing strategy and mix, and the forces that influence it.

Consumer value and relationships are at the centre of marketing strategy and programs. Through market segmentation, targeting, differentiation, and positioning, the company divides the total market into smaller segments, selects segments it can best serve, and decides how it wants to bring value to target consumers in the selected segments. It then designs an *integrated marketing* mix to produce the response it wants in the target market. The marketing mix consists of product, price, place, and promotion decisions (the four Ps).

5. List the marketing management functions, including the elements of a marketing plan, and discuss the importance of measuring and managing return on marketing investment.

To find the best strategy and mix and put them into action, the company engages in marketing analysis, planning, implementation, and control. The main components of a *marketing plan* are the executive summary, current marketing situation, threats and opportunities, objectives and issues, marketing strategies, action programs, budgets, and controls. To plan good strategies is often easier than to carry them out. To be successful, companies must also be effective at *implementation*—turning marketing strategies into marketing actions.

Marketing departments can be organized in one or a combination of ways: *functional marketing organization*, *geographic organization*, *product management organization*, or *market management organization*. In this age of customer relationships, more and more companies are now changing their organizational focus from product or territory management to customer relationship management. Marketing organizations carry out *marketing control*, both operating control and strategic control.

Marketing managers must ensure that their marketing dollars are being well spent. In a tighter economy, today's marketers face growing pressures to show that they are adding value in line with their costs. In response, marketers are developing better measures of *return on marketing investment*. Increasingly, they are using customer-centred measures of marketing impact as a key input into their strategic decision-making.

KEY TERMS

Business portfolio 50
Differentiation 60
Diversification 53
Downsizing 53
Growth-share matrix 50
Market development 53
Market penetration 53
Market segment 57
Market segmentation 57

Market targeting 57
Marketing control 66
Marketing implementation 63
Marketing mix 60
Marketing strategy 56
Mission statement 46
Portfolio analysis 50
Positioning 59
Product development 53

Product/market expansion grid 52
Return on marketing investment
  (or marketing ROI) 66
Strategic planning 45
SWOT analysis 62
Value chain 54
Value delivery network 55

TALK ABOUT MARKETING

1. Explain why it is important for all departments of an organization—marketing, accounting, finance, operations management, human resources, and so on—to "think consumer." Why is it important that even people who are not in marketing understand it?

2. Imagine you are a team of marketing managers at a large consumer packaged-goods company, and you're planning the launch of a new line of shampoo. With which departments in your company will you need to work to plan the launch, and what role will each department play?

3. Discuss how TELUS might use the processes of market segmentation, market targeting, and market positioning. How is TELUS differentiated from its competitors?

4. In a small group, develop a SWOT analysis for a business in your community. From that analysis, recommend a marketing strategy and marketing mix for this business Go to www.pg.com to learn about the brands offered by P&G. Select one product category in which P&G offers multiple brands. What is P&G's positioning for each brand in that product category? Then, visit a store and record the prices of each brand, using a common basis such as price per millilitre. Write a brief report on what you learn. Are there meaningful positioning differences between the brands? Are any price differences you find justified?

THINK LIKE A MARKETING MANAGER

Apple markets several lines of personal electronic devices, including computers, iPod music and video players, and, most recently, iPhones and iPads. Spend some time on Apple's website and learn more about its products, and then think like a marketing manager to answer the following questions.

QUESTIONS

1. Which of Apple's products are its stars, cash cows, question marks, and dogs?
2. Which of the four market growth strategies in the product/market expansion grid have you observed Apple using?
3. How does Apple employ the elements of the marketing mix—product, price, place (distribution), and promotion?
4. The iPhone was available in the United States in June 2007 but was not available in Canada until a year later. Similarly, Apple released the iPad in the United States in April 2010 but international consumers, who were only able to pre-order the product on May 10, were still faced with an "undetermined" launch date. What can you infer about Apple's international growth strategy?

MARKETING ETHICS

Ever felt like everything happens at once? Well, sometimes it does: The car breaks down, the kids are sick, the dog needs to go to the vet, and then, to top it off, the electric bill is past due again. Rather than having your kids suffer and letting the electric company cut off your lights, simply stop by and get a payday loan. Sounds easy, doesn't it? For many Canadians, payday loans have become a necessary alternative to traditional bank loans, and the trend is growing. Edmonton-based The Cash Store Financial Services Inc., with 415 stores across Canada, and Money Mart, with over 350 stores, announced record profits in 2008, with plans for future market expansion. The Canadian Payday Loan Association, which represents 20 payday loan companies, maintains that its members provide a valuable service to cash-strapped consumers, but consumer advocate groups disagree, arguing that these firms prey on those who can least afford their services—low-income families who do not qualify for low-interest bank loans. In fact, according to Credit Canada, a non-profit credit counselling service, Canadians are now carrying in excess of $1 trillion in personal debt. Provincial governments across the nation are now enacting legislation to protect consumers from excessive interest rates charged by many of these services.

QUESTIONS

1. What are the current and emerging external factors (i.e., opportunities and threats) contributing to the growth of payday loan companies in Canada?
2. Visit www.apaydayloan.ca and answer the following questions: What are they offering consumers? Do you see any problems with the service they provide? Explain. Click on the online loan application link and calculate the cost of borrowing $500 for one month. Do the cost of borrowing and the annualized interest rate surprise you? What are the implications for consumer debt in Canada? In your opinion, are payday loan companies offering a legitimate service to consumers or are they merely loan sharks in disguise?

MARKETING TECHNOLOGY

Mobile marketing is touted as the next "big thing," offering the promise of connecting with consumers on the most personal medium—their cellphones. Technological advances are letting marketers send not only text messages to cellphones but also video messages. In Japan, QR Codes (quick response codes) originally developed for manufacturing purposes are now placed on outdoor, print, and other media advertisements so that consumers can snap pictures of them and be taken directly to mobile websites. Although not yet widely practised, some marketers are now dabbling in mobile marketing. For example, Jaguar used a mobile campaign and sold over 1100 XFs in one month. Visa used mobile marketing in China to encourage consumers to pass on video commercials to their friends via mobile phones. Although there are still technical roadblocks stifling rapid expansion of this marketing method, some experts claim that marketers had better jump on this bandwagon or risk being left behind.

QUESTIONS

1. Visit the Mobile Marketing Association's website at www.mmaglobal.com and click on "Resources" and

then "Case Studies" on the left. Discuss one case study and describe the factors you think made that application of mobile marketing a success.

2. The rapid advance in mobile technology poses opportunities as well as threats for marketers. Discuss both the opportunities and threats for marketers.

MARKETING BY THE NUMBERS

Appendix 3, Marketing by the Numbers, discusses other marketing profitability metrics beyond the return on marketing investment (marketing ROI) measure described in this chapter. The text on the right is a profit-and-loss statement for a business. Review Appendix 3 and answer the questions below.

QUESTIONS

1. Calculate the net marketing contribution (NMC) for this company.
2. Calculate both marketing return on sales (or marketing ROS) and marketing return on investment (or marketing ROI) as described in Appendix 3. Is this company doing well?

Net Sales		$800,000,000
Cost of goods sold		(375,000,000)
Gross Margin		$425,000,000
Marketing Expenses		
Sales expenses	$70,000,000	
Promotion expenses	30,000,000	
		(100,000,000)
General and Administrative Expenses		
Marketing salaries and expenses	$10,000,000	
Indirect overhead	60,000,000	70,000,000
Net profit before income tax		$255,000,000

VIDEO CASE

Visit MyMarketingLab at www.pearsoned.ca/mymarketinglab to view the video for this chapter.

LIVE NATION

Live Nation may not be a household name, but if you've been to a concert in the past few years, chances are you've purchased a Live Nation product. In fact, Live Nation has been the country's largest concert promoter for many years, promoting as many as 29 000 events annually. Through very savvy strategic planning, Live Nation is shaking up the structure of the music industry.

A recent $120 million deal with Madonna illustrates how this concert promoter is diving into other businesses as well. Under this deal, Live Nation will become Madonna's record label, concert promoter, ticket vendor, and merchandise agent. Similar deals have been reached with other performers such as Jay-Z and U2.

However, contracting with artists is only part of the picture. Live Nation is partnering with other corporations as well. A venture with Citigroup will expand its reach to potential customers through a leveraging of database tech-

nologies. Joining forces with ticket reseller powerhouses such as StubHub will give Live Nation a position in the thriving business of secondary ticket sales.

After viewing the video featuring Live Nation, answer the following questions about the role of strategic planning.

QUESTIONS

1. What is Live Nation's mission?
2. Based on the product/market expansion grid, provide support for the strategy that Live Nation is pursuing.
3. How does Live Nation's strategy provide better value for customers?

END-OF-CHAPTER CASE

APPLE'S MARKETING STRATEGY FOR THE IPHONE

The Apple iPhone has gone through several generations since it was first introduced in January 2007, but it was during the period between the second generation, or "2G," and the release of the iPhone 3G in June 2008 that Apple had to completely rethink the product's marketing strategy.

The iPhone 3G was launched into the market with the advertising tagline, "Twice as fast. Half the price." Apple CEO Steve Jobs unveiled the new iPhone in his keynote speech at the Apple Worldwide Developers Conference (WWDC) in San Francisco, California. Immediately, the marketing world was abuzz about the possibilities, because the new iPhone would allow third parties to develop, market, and sell mobile applications that can be run on the iPhone. Apple did not permit this in the earlier versions of the product; in fact, it actively discouraged it, but enthusiastic techies nevertheless hacked into their own iPhones and eagerly created and shared applications to run on it.

Apple listened, considered, and changed its marketing strategy. The development and launch of the iPhone as a product resulted in the re-organization of Apple's strategic business units. As Apple CEO Steve Jobs said at WWDC 2008, "There's three parts to Apple now. The first part of course is the Mac. The second part is our music businesses, the iPod, and iTunes; and the third part is now the iPhone."

The iPhone 3G still offered the basic functions of a phone, an iPod, and Internet access, but several new features were added: a scientific calculator, contacts search feature, maps with GPS, support for more languages, and an application store. The application store offered optional features such as games, finance, health and fitness, and entertainment options—in other words, software applications, some of which were designed, built, and marketed by companies other than Apple.

The Apple website introduced the iPhone 3G this way: "Introducing iPhone 3G. With fast 3G wireless technology, GPS mapping, support for enterprise features like Microsoft Exchange, and the new App Store, iPhone 3G puts even more features at your fingertips. And like the original iPhone, it combines three products in one—a revolutionary phone, a widescreen iPod, and a breakthrough Internet device with rich HTML email and a desktop-class web browser. iPhone 3G. It redefines what a mobile phone can do—again." The marketing strategy for the 3G also targeted three distinct market segments: enterprise (global address lookup, remote wiping of a lost phone, network security features); software developers; and consumers.

With software developers now comprising a distinct market segment for the iPhone, the third generation of the product included a developer kit, to allow third-party individuals and companies to develop iPhone apps—a 180-degree change in strategy from the first generation of the iPhone. In the first three months after announcing its new software developer program, the company saw over 250 000 downloads of the software development kit, and 4000 people were selected as beta testers of the new applications—consumers who were able to download these new software features to their iPhone, use them, and provide feedback to Apple.

Software developers weren't the only ones excited about the new iPhone. Major corporations decided to purchase the iPhone 3G for their employees. Randy Brooks, senior vice-president, IT strategy & architecture, The Walt Disney Company, says the company manages roughly 55 000 desktop and laptop computers around the world, which run 15 000 different business applications. "We've been testing the beta release for the last couple of months, and the software is definitely there." Business applications include seamless integration with Microsoft Exchange so the company can push email and calendaring functions to its employees. They can also use, share, and collaborate by using Word and Excel on their iPhones. Managers and employees can look up other employees anywhere in the world, and access business applications and documents from anywhere. "We believe the iPhone is an enterprise-class mobile computing platform. It has the ability to pack the power of a laptop into the size of a smartphone."

These third-party applications were quickly developed for business use and consumer use, and today most banks offer their own iPhone apps for their customers to access their accounts through their phone. FedEx developed an app for customers to check their shipments, and more and more marketers are following suit. Many marketers believe that mobile phone apps are the wave of the future and that we'll move away quickly from the idea of software being created only to run on a certain type of computer.

Marketers are also buzzing about the new possibilities for mobile marketing that the new iPhone opens up. For the past couple of years, the model of mobile marketing that most marketers and advertisers were envisioning was one similar to television or Internet advertising; that is, sponsors would pay to have their message delivered through the same device that delivers the content. Content on mobile devices was thought of as text, email, and voice messages. But now that model is changing, and marketers are talking about a new kind of mobile marketing, one that's "experiential" in nature.

One technology products expert believes Apple's long-term marketing strategy for the iPhone is to position its software not as a secret operating system accessible only to Apple developers, but more like content—and it's long been believed that on the Internet, content is king. The introduction of iPhone applications was a major shift in product marketing strategy, and it has turned into a revolution. The App Store is now a section of iTunes, and iPhone owners can choose from thousands of apps.

Sources: Apple website at www.apple.com; video of Steve Jobs's keynote speech at WWDC 2008, available on Apple's website; Abbey Klaassen, "New iPhone Also Brings New Way of Mobile Marketing," *Advertising Age,* June 16, 2008, at www.adage.com.

QUESTIONS

1. What information about their target market should marketers of iPhone web apps research before they begin developing applications?

2. Write a brief description (profile) of the typical customer in each of the three market segments Apple has targeted with the new iPhone. What types of marketing programs and tactics should Apple employ for each segment? Choose one target market segment, and write an outline of a marketing plan for it.

3. Some countries are considering deploying iPhones to their troops. What types of applications would soldiers use their iPhones for? What types of security precautions would the military demand of Apple before making these decisions?

4. How has the iPhone evolved since the 3G? Has there been another shift in strategy?

This home is

bullfrog**powered**™

with 100%
green electricity.

www.bullfrogpower.com

AFTER STUDYING THIS CHAPTER, YOU SHOULD BE ABLE TO

1. define *sustainable marketing* and discuss its importance

2. identify the major social criticisms of marketing

3. define *consumerism* and *environmentalism*, and explain how they affect marketing strategies

4. describe the principles of sustainable marketing

5. explain the role of ethics in marketing

Sustainable Marketing Social Responsibility and Ethics

PREVIEWING THE CONCEPTS

In this chapter, we'll examine the concepts of sustainable marketing, meeting the needs of consumers, businesses, and society—now and in the future—through socially and environmentally responsible marketing actions. We'll start by defining sustainable marketing and then look at some common criticisms of marketing as it impacts individual consumers and public actions that promote sustainable marketing. Finally, we'll see how companies themselves can benefit from proactively pursuing sustainable marketing practices that bring value not just to individual customers but also to society as a whole. You'll see that sustainable marketing actions are more than just the right thing to do; they're also good for business.

First, let's look at an example of sustainable marketing in action. When it comes to socially and environmentally responsible practices, few companies meet the standard set by Bullfrog Power.

BULLFROG POWER: THE SUSTAINABLE COMPANY

You switch on a light or leave your computer up and running without thought of the negative impact each action may have on the environment. Bullfrog Power wants to change this. With an understanding that conventional electricity generation is a leading source of carbon dioxide, the primary greenhouse gas linked to climate change, as well as other emissions that contribute to poor air quality, Bullfrog provides consumers and businesses with an easy way to green their electricity and reduce their impact on the environment. It has successfully overcome a huge marketing challenge in the process: It had to convince potential customers to pay a premium for something they can't see or touch. Despite the fact that it uses relatively low-key marketing focused on building strong customer relationships, Bullfrog was named *Marketing Magazine's* Marketer of the Year in 2008. It seems to have taken a page out of marketing guru Seth Godin's book: "In a field of black and white Holsteins, a purple cow gets all the attention!"

Bullfrog Power is Canada's 100 percent green electricity provider. The Toronto-based company was founded in 2005. Today it stands out as the only company providing 100 percent renewable electricity to Prince Edward Island, Nova Scotia, New Brunswick, Ontario, Alberta, and British Columbia residents and businesses. When homes and businesses sign on for Bullfrog Power, Bullfrog's generators inject renewable electricity onto the grid to match the amount of power the home or business uses; the electricity is not injected directly into the facility. Across Canada, Bullfrog's electricity comes exclusively from wind and hydro facilities that have been certified as low impact by Environment Canada—instead of from polluting sources such as coal, oil, natural gas, and nuclear.

Bullfrog is working hard to build its customer base of both end consumers and businesses. Its business and organizational clients include such firms as Wal-Mart Canada, BMO Financial Group, Toronto's City Hall, and Mountain Equipment Co-op, to name a few.

Bullfrog has excelled by living by strong brand values. Its mission is to provide Canadians with easy and practical 100 percent renewable energy solutions for their homes, businesses, and transportation. The organization believes businesses can serve a vital function as community leaders in promoting and fostering responsible environmental action. It is a "double bottom line" company that maintains a dual focus on environmental responsibility and profitability. The company has pledged to donate 10 percent of profits to organizations that support sustainability. Bullfrog not only delivers green power on behalf of its customers, it empowers them to be change agents in the world. Bullfrog and its clients hope to demonstrate that change can come through collective action. The more people who sign up with Bullfrog, the more demand grows for renewable power generation.

Bullfrog's brand values have resonated with many Canadians. Thus, it has been able to rely on grassroots marketing, word-of-mouth endorsements, and the Web to spread its message. "Word of mouth is an extremely powerful form of communication," says Tom Heintzman, Bullfrog's president. "To a large measure, we divest ourselves of the brand and put it in the hands of our customers." All of Bullfrog's communications are done in-house to ensure that it remains true to its brand.

It's not surprising that Bullfrog is a strong believer in relationship marketing. "Interpersonal contact is a really important part of our brand," says Heintzman, who communicates frequently with clients via the Bullfrog e-buzz newsletter. Bullfrog also works hard to add extra value for its business clients. Its website features a Green Directory—an easy-to-search source of companies that support 100 percent green electricity.

Bullfrog's website, www.bullfrogpower.com, has proven to be a powerful tool. First, it makes it easy for consumers and businesses alike to sign up for its green electricity service. People just fill in a simple-to-complete online form in a few minutes. Bullfrog also provides a toll-free number on the screen if people need help with the process.

Bullfrog uses social media to strengthen its relationships. You can see Bullfrog featured in a number of video clips on YouTube, and it maintains an up-to-date page on Facebook where it talks about its activities. Bullfrog also uses more traditional tools to market its service, including national newspapers such as the *Globe and Mail*, but it has put a distinctive Bullfrog stamp on this use of traditional media by using information-rich content to explain its service and how customers can make changes.

Public relations are also a big part of Bullfrog's communication mix. Its people do a lot of public speaking to help bring home their message. The Bullfrog team can also be seen at many events linked to environmental initiatives—it is involved in over 700 different events a year. For example, an event called the Bullfrog Bash featured supporter Gord Downie of The Tragically Hip. Finally, Bullfrog uses a lot of outdoor signage. Its simple yet powerful signs featuring a leaping frog and the phrase "bullfrogpowered" seem to be everywhere, from front lawns, to ATMs, to beer cases, and on the websites and newsletters of countless customers and partners. As the Bullfrog story illustrates, a focus on sustainability and strong marketing can go hand-in-hand to build value for multiple stakeholders.[1]

RESPONSIBLE marketers such as Bullfrog Power discover what consumers want and respond with market offerings that create value for buyers in order to capture value in return. The *marketing concept* is a philosophy of customer value and mutual gain. Not all marketers follow the marketing concept, however. In fact, some companies use questionable marketing practices that serve their own rather than consumers' or society's interests. Responsible marketers must consider whether their actions are *sustainable* in the longer run.

Consider the sale of sport-utility vehicles (SUVs). These large vehicles meet the immediate needs of many drivers in terms of capacity, power, and utility. However, SUV sales involve larger questions of consumer safety and environmental responsibility. For example, in accidents, SUVs are more likely to kill both their own occupants and the occupants of other vehicles. Research shows that SUV occupants are three times more likely to die from their vehicle rolling than are occupants of sedans. Moreover, gas-guzzling SUVs use more than their fair share of the world's energy and other resources and contribute disproportionately to pollution and congestion problems, creating costs that must be borne by both current and future generations.[2]

This chapter examines *sustainable* marketing and the social and environmental effects of private marketing practices. First, we address this question: What is sustainable marketing and why is it important?

SUSTAINABLE MARKETING LO1

Sustainable marketing calls for socially and environmentally responsible actions that meet the present needs of consumers and businesses while also preserving or enhancing the ability of future generations to meet their needs. Figure 3.1 compares the sustainable marketing concept with other marketing concepts we studied in Chapters 1 and 2.[3]

The *marketing concept* recognizes that organizations thrive from day to day by determining the current needs and wants of target group customers and fulfilling those needs and wants more effectively and efficiently than competitors do. It focuses on meeting the company's short-term sales, growth, and profit needs by giving customers what they want now. However, satisfying consumers' immediate needs and desires doesn't always serve the future best interests of either customers or the business.

For example, McDonald's early decisions to market tasty but fat- and salt-laden fast foods created immediate satisfaction for customers and sales and profits for the company. However, critics assert that McDonald's and other fast-food chains contributed to a longer-term national obesity epidemic, damaging consumer health and burdening the national health system. In turn, many consumers began looking for healthier eating options, causing a slump in fast-food industry sales and profits. Beyond issues of ethical behaviour and social welfare, McDonald's was also criticized for the sizable environmental footprint of its vast global operations, everything from wasteful packaging and solid waste creation to inefficient energy use in its stores. Thus, McDonald's strategy was not sustainable in terms of either consumer or company benefit.

Whereas the *societal marketing concept* identified in Figure 3.1 considers the future welfare of consumers and the *strategic planning concept* considers future company needs,

Sustainable marketing
Socially and environmentally responsible marketing that meets the present needs of consumers and businesses while also preserving or enhancing the ability of future generations to meet their needs.

FIGURE 3.1 Sustainable marketing

Exhibit 3.1   Sustainable marketing: McDonald's Plan to Win strategy has both created sustainable value for customers and positioned the company for a profitable future.

the *sustainable marketing concept* considers both. Sustainable marketing calls for socially and environmentally responsible actions that meet both the immediate and future needs of customers and the company.

For example, as we discussed in Chapter 2, in recent years, McDonald's has responded with a more sustainable "Plan to Win" strategy of diversifying into salads, fruits, grilled chicken, low-fat milk, and other healthy fare. Also, after a seven-year search for healthier cooking oil, McDonald's phased out traditional artery-clogging trans fats without compromising the taste of its french fries. And the company launched a major multi-faceted education campaign—called "it's what i eat and what i do ... i'm lovin' it"—to help consumers better understand the keys to living balanced, active lifestyles.

The McDonald's Plan to Win strategy also addresses environmental issues. For example, it calls for food-supply sustainability, reduced and environmentally sustainable packaging, reuse and recycling, and more responsible store designs. McDonald's has even developed an environmental scorecard that rates its suppliers' performance in areas such as water use, energy use, and solid waste management.

McDonald's more sustainable strategy is benefiting the company as well as its customers. Since announcing its Plan to Win strategy, McDonald's sales have increased by more than 50 percent and profits have more than quadrupled. And for the past four years, the company has been included in the Dow Jones Sustainability Index, recognizing its commitment to sustainable economic, environmental, and social performance. Thus, McDonald's is well positioned for a sustainably profitable future.[4]

Truly sustainable marketing requires a smooth-functioning marketing system in which consumers, companies, public policy–makers, and others work together to ensure socially and environmentally responsible marketing actions. Unfortunately, however, the marketing system doesn't always work smoothly. The following sections examine several sustainability questions: What are the most frequent social criticisms of marketing? What steps have private citizens taken to curb marketing ills? What steps have legislators and government agencies taken to promote sustainable marketing? What steps have enlightened companies taken to carry out socially responsible and ethical marketing that creates sustainable value for both individual customers and society as a whole?

SOCIAL CRITICISMS OF MARKETING LO2

Marketing receives much criticism. Some of this criticism is justified; much is not. Social critics claim that certain marketing practices hurt individual consumers, society as a whole, and other business firms.

MARKETING'S IMPACT ON INDIVIDUAL CONSUMERS

Consumers have many concerns about how well the marketing system serves their interests. Surveys usually show that consumers hold mixed or even slightly unfavourable attitudes toward marketing practices. Consumer advocates, government agencies, and other critics have accused marketing of harming consumers through high prices, deceptive practices, high-pressure selling, shoddy or unsafe products, planned obsolescence, and poor service to disadvantaged consumers. Such questionable marketing practices are not sustainable in terms of long-term consumer or business welfare.

High Prices   Many critics charge that the marketing system causes prices to be higher than they would be under more "sensible" systems. Such high prices are hard to swallow, especially when the economy takes a downturn. Critics point to three factors—*high costs of distribution, high advertising and promotion costs,* and *excessive markups.*

HIGH COSTS OF DISTRIBUTION   A long-standing charge is that greedy channel intermediaries mark up prices beyond the value of their services. Critics charge that there are too many intermediaries, that intermediaries are inefficient, or that they provide unnecessary or duplicate services. As a result, distribution costs too much, and consumers pay for these excessive costs in the form of higher prices.

How do resellers answer these charges? They argue that intermediaries do work that would otherwise have to be done by manufacturers or consumers. Markups reflect services that consumers themselves want—more convenience, larger stores and assortments, more service, longer store hours, return privileges, and others. In fact, they argue, retail competition is so intense that margins are actually quite low. For example, after taxes, supermarket chains are typically left with barely 1 percent profit on their sales. If some resellers try to charge too much relative to the value they add, other resellers will step in with lower prices. Low-price stores such as Wal-Mart, Costco, and other discounters pressure their competitors to operate efficiently and keep their prices down. In fact, in the wake of the recent recession, only the most efficient retailers have survived profitably.

HIGH ADVERTISING AND PROMOTION COSTS   Modern marketing is also accused of pushing up prices to finance heavy advertising and sales promotion. For example, a few dozen tablets of a heavily promoted brand of pain reliever sell for the same price as 100 tablets of less-promoted brands. Differentiated products—cosmetics, detergents, toiletries—include promotion and packaging costs that can amount to 40 percent or more of the manufacturer's price to the retailer. Critics charge that much of the packaging and promotion adds only psychological value to the product rather than functional value.

Marketers respond that advertising does add to product costs, but that it also adds value by informing potential buyers of the availability and merits of a brand. Brand name products may cost more, but branding gives buyers assurances of consistent quality. Moreover, consumers can usually buy functional versions of products at lower prices. However, they *want* and are willing to pay more for products that also provide psychological benefits—that make them feel wealthy, attractive, or special. Also, heavy advertising and promotion may be necessary for a firm to match competitors' efforts—the business would lose "share of mind" if it did not match competitive spending.

At the same time, companies are cost conscious about promotion and try to spend their money wisely. Today's increasingly more frugal consumers are demanding genuine value for the prices they pay. The continuing shift toward buying store brands and generics suggests that when it comes to value, consumers want action, not just talk.

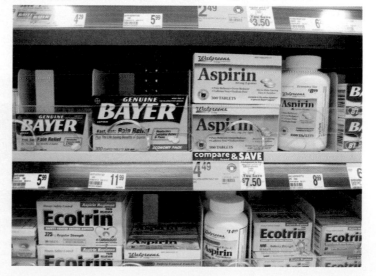

Exhibit 3.2   A heavily promoted brand of Aspirin sells for much more than a virtually identical non-branded or store-branded product. Critics charge that promotion adds only psychological value to the product rather than functional value.

EXCESSIVE MARKUPS   Critics also charge that some companies mark up goods excessively. They point to the drug industry, where a pill costing five cents to make may cost the consumer $2 to buy. They point to the pricing tactics of funeral homes that prey on the confused emotions of bereaved relatives and to the high charges for auto repair and other services.

Marketers respond that most businesses try to deal fairly with consumers because they want to build customer relationships and repeat business and that most consumer abuses are unintentional. When shady marketers do take advantage of consumers, they should be reported to Better Business Bureaus or to the provincial Consumer Affairs office. Marketers sometimes respond that consumers often don't understand the reasons for high markups. For example, pharmaceutical markups must cover the costs of purchasing, promoting, and distributing existing medicines plus the high research and development costs of formulating and testing new medicines. As pharmaceuticals company GlaxoSmithKline states in its ads, "Today's medicines finance tomorrow's miracles."

Deceptive Practices   Marketers are sometimes accused of deceptive practices that lead consumers to believe they will get more value than they actually do. Deceptive practices fall into three groups: pricing, promotion, and packaging. *Deceptive pricing* includes practices such as falsely advertising "factory" or "wholesale" prices or a large price reduction from a phony high retail list price. *Deceptive promotion* includes practices such as misrepresenting the product's features or performance or luring the customers to the store for a bargain that is out of stock. *Deceptive packaging* includes exaggerating package contents through subtle design, using misleading labelling, or describing size in misleading terms.

The Competition Bureau acts as a watchdog to prevent such practices. In 2009, for example, it brought criminal charges against individuals and companies who formed a cartel and conspired to fix gas prices in Victoriaville, Quebec. It charged The Brick with misleading advertising related to a mail-in rebate promotion. The company subsequently cancelled the campaign in response to these concerns. It also took action against Edmonton-based Bioenergy Wellness Inc. and its director after unsubstantiated claims were made online regarding products used to treat or prevent cancer.[5]

Deceptive practices have led to legislation and other consumer protection actions, but such regulations don't solve all the problems. Consider the glut of "environmental responsibility" claims marketers are now making:

Are you a victim of "greenwashing"? Biodegradable, eco-friendly, recycled, green, carbon neutral, carbon offsets, made from sustainable resources—such phrases are popping up more and more on products worldwide, leading many to question their validity. In 2008, in an attempt to ensure greater accuracy of such claims, the Competition Bureau in collaboration with the Canadian Standards Association issued guidelines to provide the business community with tools to ensure that green marketing claims are not misleading. Examples of best practices were also provided. "Environmental Claims: A Guide for Industry and Advertisers" can be found online at http://www.competitionbureau.gc.ca/eic/site/cb-bc.nsf/eng/02701.html.

The toughest problem is defining what is "deceptive." For instance, an advertiser's claim that its powerful laundry detergent "makes your washing machine 10 feet tall," showing a surprised homemaker watching her appliance burst through her laundry room ceiling, isn't intended

Exhibit 3.3   Deceptive practices: Despite plenty of regulation, some critics argue that deceptive claims are still the norm. Consider all of those "green marketing" claims.

Green-wash (green'wash', -wôsh') – verb: the act of misleading consumers regarding the environmental practices of a company or the environmental benefits of a product or service.

to be taken literally. Instead, the advertiser might claim, it is "puffery"—innocent exaggeration for effect. One noted marketing thinker, Theodore Levitt, once claimed that advertising puffery and alluring imagery are bound to occur—and that they may even be desirable: "There is hardly a company that would not go down in ruin if it refused to provide fluff, because nobody will buy pure functionality.... Worse, it denies ... people's honest needs and values. Without distortion, embellishment, and elaboration, life would be drab, dull, anguished, and at its existential worst."[6]

However, others claim that puffery and alluring imagery can harm consumers in subtle ways. Think about the popular and long-running MasterCard Priceless commercials that have painted pictures of consumers fulfilling their priceless dreams despite the costs. The ads suggest that your credit card can make it happen. But critics charge that such imagery by credit card companies encouraged a spend-now-pay-later attitude that caused many consumers to *over*use their cards. They point to statistics showing that Canadians are carrying record amounts of credit card debt—often more than they can repay. Canadians possess more than 50 million MasterCard and Visa cards alone, and nearly 40 percent fail to pay off their balance each month. Canadian household debt has risen to $1.3 trillion and those carrying credit card balances are paying off this debt at rates ranging from 17.5 to 24 percent.[7]

Marketers argue that most companies avoid deceptive practices. Because such practices harm a company's business in the long run, they simply aren't sustainable. Profitable customer relationships are built upon a foundation of value and trust. If consumers do not get what they expect, they will switch to more reliable products. In addition, consumers usually protect themselves from deception. Most consumers recognize a marketer's selling intent and are careful when they buy, sometimes even to the point of not believing completely true product claims.

High-Pressure Selling   Salespeople are sometimes accused of high-pressure selling that persuades people to buy goods they had no thought of buying. It is often said that insurance, real estate, and used cars are *sold*, not *bought*. Salespeople are trained to deliver smooth, canned talks to entice purchase. They sell hard because sales contests promise big prizes to those who sell the most. Similarly, TV infomercial pitchmen use "yell and sell" presentations that create a sense of consumer urgency that only those with the strongest willpower can resist.

But in most cases, marketers have little to gain from high-pressure selling. Such tactics may work in one-time selling situations for short-term gain. However, most selling involves building long-term relationships with valued customers. High-pressure or deceptive selling can do serious damage to such relationships. For example, imagine a P&G account manager trying to pressure a Wal-Mart buyer, or an IBM salesperson trying to browbeat a GE information technology manager. It simply wouldn't work.

Shoddy, Harmful, or Unsafe Products   Another criticism concerns poor product quality or function. One complaint is that, too often, products are not made well and services are not performed well. A second complaint is that many products deliver little benefit, or that they might even be harmful. Consider what happened to Leslie Alexander, a Vancouver-based folk singer. Being afraid that prescription sleeping pills were addictive, she began taking the "all-natural" product Sleepees. While the product helped her sleep "beautifully," she developed a rash around her eyes and other symptoms indicating an allergic reaction. She ignored these ailments since she soon found herself unable to sleep without the herbal medication and when she finally forced herself off the product, she fell into deep depression. She and her lawyer brought a class-action suit against the Canadian distributor of Sleepees, alleging "that hundreds of Canadians may have been harmed by the product and that some may not even be aware of the source of their health problems." These charges have yet to be proven, however.[8]

As suggested above, product safety is a major concern. Consider Toyota's massive recall in 2010, where the company recalled 270 000 cars in Canada and nearly 4.2 million worldwide because of problems related to braking and sudden acceleration. Toyota is now facing multiple class-action lawsuits and slumping sales, which could cost the company billions of dollars. More importantly, Toyota's once-stellar reputation of quality may be forever altered in the minds of consumers.[9]

Product safety has been a problem for several reasons, including company indifference, increased product complexity, and poor quality control. For years, Consumers Union—the non-profit testing and information organization that publishes the *Consumer Reports* magazine and website—has reported various hazards in tested products: electrical dangers in appliances, carbon monoxide poisoning from room heaters, injury risks from lawn mowers, and faulty automobile design, among many others. The organization's testing and other activities have helped consumers make better buying decisions and encouraged businesses to eliminate product flaws.

However, most manufacturers *want* to produce quality goods. The way a company deals with product quality and safety problems can damage or help its reputation. Companies selling poor-quality or unsafe products risk damaging conflicts with consumer groups and regulators. Unsafe products can result in product liability suits and large awards for damages. More fundamentally, consumers who are unhappy with a firm's products may avoid future purchases and talk other consumers into doing the same. Thus, quality missteps are not consistent with sustainable marketing. Today's marketers know that good quality results in customer value and satisfaction, which in turn creates sustainable customer relationships.

Planned Obsolescence   Critics also have charged that some companies practise planned obsolescence, causing their products to become obsolete before they actually should need replacement. They accuse some producers of using materials and components that will break, wear, rust, or rot sooner than they should. One analyst captures the concept this way: "Planned obsolescence, a diabolical manufacturing strategy that took root with the rise of mass production in the 1920s and 1930s, has now escalated from disposable lighters to major appliances. Its evil genius is this: Make the cost of repairs close to the item's replacement price and entice us to buy new." The analyst's 12-year-old stove needed a burner repaired—12 new screws. The price of the repair: $700, which was more than he'd paid for the stove new.[10]

Exhibit 3.4   Planned obsolescence: Almost everyone, it seems, has a "drawer filled with the detritus of yesterday's hottest product, now reduced to the status of fossils."

Other companies are charged with continually changing consumer concepts of acceptable styles to encourage more and earlier buying. An obvious example is constantly changing clothing fashions. Still others are accused of introducing planned streams of new products that make older models obsolete. Critics claim that this occurs in the consumer electronics and computer industries. For example, consider this writer's tale about an aging cellphone:[11]

Today, most people, myself included, are all agog at the wondrous outpouring of new technology, from cell phones to iPods, iPhones, laptops, BlackBerries, and on and on. I have a drawer filled with the detritus of yesterday's hottest product, now reduced to the status of fossils. I have video cameras that use tapes no longer available, laptops with programs incompatible with anything on today's market, portable CD players I no longer use, and more. But what really upsets me is how quickly some still-useful gadgets become obsolete, at least in the eyes of their makers.

I recently embarked on an epic search for a cord to plug into my wife's cell phone to recharge it. We were traveling and the poor phone kept bleating that it was running low and the battery needed recharging. So, we began a search—from big-box technology superstores to smaller suppliers and the cell phone companies themselves—all to no avail. Finally, a salesperson told my wife, "That's an old model, so we don't stock the charger any longer." "But I only bought it last year," she sputtered. "Yeah, like I said, that's an old model," he replied without a hint of irony or sympathy. The proliferation and sheer waste of this type of practice is mind-boggling.

Marketers respond that consumers *like* style changes; they get tired of the old goods and want a new look in fashion. Or they *want* the latest high-tech innovations, even if older models still work. No one has to buy the new product, and if too few people like it, it will simply fail. Finally, most companies do not design their products to break down earlier, because they do not want to lose customers to other brands. Instead, they seek constant improvement to ensure that products will consistently meet or exceed customer expectations. Much of the so-called planned obsolescence is the working of the competitive and technological forces in a free society—forces that lead to ever-improving goods and services.

Poor Service to Disadvantaged Consumers   Finally, the marketing system has been accused of serving disadvantaged consumers poorly. For example, critics claim that the urban poor often have to shop in smaller stores that carry inferior goods and charge higher prices. The presence of large national chain stores in low-income neighbour-hoods would help keep prices down. However, the critics accuse major chain retailers of "redlining," drawing a red line around disadvantaged neighbourhoods and avoiding placing stores there.

Similar redlining charges have been levelled at the insurance, consumer lending, banking, and health care industries. Most recently, consumer advocates charged that banks and mortgage lenders have practised "reverse-redlining." Instead of staying away from people in poor urban areas, they have targeted and exploited them, especially working-class consumers, by offering them risky subprime mortgages rather than safer mortgages with better terms. These subprime mortgages often featured adjustable inter-est rates that started out very low but quickly increased. Recently, when the interest rates went up, many owners could no longer afford their mortgage payments. And as housing prices dropped, these owners were trapped in debt and owed more than their houses were worth, leading to bankruptcies, foreclosures, and a subprime mortgage crisis.

Many critics charge that such subprime loans should be treated as bias crimes. A recent report issued by United for a Fair Economy claims that people of colour are three

Exhibit 3.5 Critics have accused mortgage lenders of "reverse redlining," targeting disadvantaged consumers with subprime mortgages that they couldn't afford.

Exhibit 3.6 Adbusters Media Foundation is a major critic of marketing's negative influence on our physical and cultural environments. It gets its message out through its website, *Adbusters* magazine, and worldwide campaigns such as Buy Nothing Day.

times more likely than other groups to have subprime loans. It estimates that the subprime mortgage crisis will drain US$213 billion in wealth from black Americans—the "greatest wealth loss in modern U.S. history." In response, the NAACP filed a racial discrimination suit against 18 mortgage providers, including GMAC, Wells Fargo, and HSBC.[12]

Clearly, better marketing systems must be built to service disadvantaged consumers. In fact, many marketers profitably target such consumers with legitimate goods and services that create real value. In cases in which marketers do not step in to fill the void, the government likely will. Action has been taken against sellers who advertise false values, wrongfully deny services, or charge disadvantaged customers too much.

MARKETING'S IMPACT ON SOCIETY AS A WHOLE

The marketing system has been accused of adding to several "evils" in society at large. Advertising has been a special target of many of these accusations.

False Wants and Too Much Materialism Critics, such as the organization Adbusters and environmental activist Annie Leonard, have charged that the marketing system urges too much interest in material possessions, and that North Americans' love affair with worldly possessions is not sustainable. Too often, people are judged by what they *own* rather than by who they *are*. The critics do not view this interest in material things as a natural state of mind but rather as a matter of false wants created by marketing. Marketers, they claim, stimulate people's desires for goods and create materialistic models of the good life. Thus, marketers have created an endless cycle of mass consumption based on a distorted interpretation of the "American Dream."

> What began in Vancouver, B.C. in the mid-eighties, Adbusters (www.adbusters.org) has evolved to a highly effective social-activist movement which spans the globe. The organization's magazine now reaches over 120,000 people in 40 countries around the globe, and its anti-consumption campaigns and spoof ads are getting noticed. For example, consider Buy Nothing Day, an Adbusters-sponsored campaign which began in 1992. This global event draws attention to the harmful effects of over-consumption and not only asks consumers to stop shopping for 24 hours, but also asks them to think about issues like where their products originate from, why they are making purchases, and what they do with their products after purchase. Usually held the Friday after American Thanksgiving, the day has been praised for drawing attention to issues such as how many resources consumers use in developed versus developing countries. However, with the economy in a tailspin and layoffs taking place daily, Buy Nothing Day has recently drawn criticism.[13]

Thus, marketing is seen as creating false wants that benefit industry more than they benefit consumers. "In the world of consumerism, marketing is there to promote consumption," says one marketing critic. It is "inevitable that marketing will promote over-consumption, and from this, a psychologically, as well as ecologically, unsustainable world."[14] This is the message that activist Annie Leonard has been promoting with the

Story of Stuff project. Founded in 2008, the project's mission is to build a strong, diverse, decentralized, cross-sector movement to transform systems of production and consumption to serve ecological sustainability and social well-being. Her 20-minute web film (www.storyofstuff.com) explores the hidden consequences of North America's love affair with stuff, and her 2010 book of the same name looks deeper into the issues described in the web film.

Marketers respond that such criticisms overstate the power of business to create needs. People have strong defences against advertising and other marketing tools. Marketers are most effective when they appeal to existing wants rather than when they attempt to create new ones. Furthermore, people seek information when making important purchases and often do not rely on single sources. Even minor purchases that may be affected by advertising messages lead to repeat purchases only if the product delivers the promised customer value. Finally, the high failure rate of new products shows that companies are not able to control demand.

On a deeper level, our wants and values are influenced not only by marketers but also by family, peer groups, religion, cultural background, and education. If North Americans are highly materialistic, these values arose out of basic socialization processes that go much deeper than business and mass media could produce alone.

Moreover, consumption patterns and attitudes are also subject to larger forces, such as the economy. As discussed in Chapter 1, the recent recession put a damper on materialism and conspicuous spending. In one consumer survey, 75 percent of respondents agreed that "the downturn is encouraging me to evaluate what is really important in life." Many observers predict a new age of consumer thrift. "The American dream is on pause," says one analyst. "The majority of Americans still believe they can achieve the dream in their lifetimes but, for [now], it's all about shoring up the foundations." As a result, far from encouraging today's more frugal consumers to overspend their means, marketers are working to help them find greater value with less. "The glib 'all your dreams will come true' approach to marketing will have to be re-evaluated," concludes another analyst.[15]

Too Few Social Goods   Business has been accused of overselling private goods at the expense of public goods. As private goods increase, they require more public services that are usually not forthcoming. For example, an increase in automobile ownership (private good) requires more highways, traffic control, parking spaces, and police services (public goods). The overselling of private goods results in "social costs." For cars, some of the social costs include traffic congestion, gasoline shortages, and air pollution. Millions of litres of fuel and hours of time are wasted in traffic jams.

A way must be found to restore a balance between private and public goods. One option is to make producers bear the full social costs of their operations. For example, the government is requiring automobile manufacturers to build cars with more efficient engines and better pollution-control systems. Automakers will then raise their prices to cover the extra costs. If buyers find the price of some cars too high, however, the producers of these cars will disappear. Demand will then move to those producers that can support the sum of the private and social costs.

A second option is to make consumers pay the social costs. For example, many cities around the world are now charging "congestion tolls" in an effort to reduce traffic congestion. To unclog its streets, the city of London levies a congestion charge of £8 per day per car to drive in an eight-square-mile area downtown. The charge has not only reduced traffic congestion within the zone by 21 percent (70 000 fewer vehicles per day) and increased bicycling by 43 percent, but has also raised money to shore up London's public transportation system.[16]

Exhibit 3.7   Balancing private and public goods: In response to lane-clogging traffic congestion like that to the left, London now levies a congestion charge. The charge has reduced congestion by 21 percent and raised money to shore up the city's public transportation system.

Cultural Pollution   Critics charge the marketing system with creating *cultural pollution*. Our senses are being constantly assaulted by marketing and advertising. Commercials interrupt serious programs; pages of ads obscure magazines; billboards mar beautiful scenery; spam fills our inboxes. These interruptions continually pollute people's minds with messages of materialism, sex, power, or status. A recent study found that more than half of North Americans feel constantly bombarded with too many marketing messages, and some critics call for sweeping changes.[17]

Marketers answer the charges of "commercial noise" with these arguments: First, they hope that their ads reach primarily the target audience. But because of mass-communication channels, some ads are bound to reach people who have no interest in the product and are therefore bored or annoyed. People who buy magazines addressed to their interests—such as *Vogue* or *Canadian Business*—rarely complain about the ads because the magazines advertise products of interest.

Second, ads make much of television and radio free to users and keep down the costs of magazines and newspapers. Many people think commercials are a small price to pay for these benefits. Consumers find many television commercials entertaining and seek them out—for example, ad viewership during the Super Bowl usually equals or exceeds game viewership. Finally, today's consumers have alternatives. For example, they can zip or zap TV commercials on recorded programs or avoid them altogether on many paid cable or satellite channels. Thus, to hold consumer attention, advertisers are making their ads more entertaining and informative.

MARKETING'S IMPACT ON OTHER BUSINESSES

Critics also charge that a company's marketing practices can harm other companies and reduce competition. Three problems are involved: acquisitions of competitors, marketing practices that create barriers to entry, and unfair competitive marketing practices.

Critics claim that firms are harmed and competition reduced when companies expand by acquiring competitors rather than by developing their own new products. The large number of acquisitions and the rapid pace of industry consolidation over the past several decades have caused concern that vigorous young competitors will be absorbed and that competition will be reduced. In virtually every major industry—retailing, entertainment, financial services, utilities, transportation, automobiles, telecommunications, health care—the number of major competitors is shrinking.

Acquisition is a complex subject. Acquisitions can sometimes be good for society. The acquiring company may gain economies of scale that lead to lower costs and lower prices. A well-managed company may take over a poorly managed company and improve its efficiency. An industry that was not very competitive might become more competitive after the acquisition. But acquisitions can also be harmful and, therefore, are closely regulated by the government.

Critics have also charged that marketing practices bar new companies from entering an industry. Large marketing companies can use patents and heavy promotion spending or tie up suppliers or dealers to keep out or drive out competitors. Those concerned with antitrust regulation recognize that some barriers are the natural result of the economic advantages of doing business on a large scale. Other barriers could be challenged by existing and new laws. For example, some critics have proposed a progressive tax on advertising spending to reduce the role of selling costs as a major barrier to entry.

Exhibit 3.8   Wal-Mart prescription pricing: Is it predatory pricing or just good business?

Finally, some firms have in fact used unfair competitive marketing practices with the intention of hurting or destroying other firms. They may set their prices below costs, threaten to cut off business with suppliers, or discourage the buying of a competitor's products. Various laws work to prevent such predatory competition. It is difficult, however, to prove that the intent or action was really predatory.

In recent years, Wal-Mart has been accused of using predatory pricing in selected market areas to drive smaller, mom-and-pop retailers out of business. Wal-Mart has become a lightning rod for protests by citizens in dozens of towns who worry that the mega-retailer's unfair practices will choke out local businesses. However, whereas critics charge that Wal-Mart's actions are predatory, others assert that its actions are just the healthy competition of a more efficient company against less efficient ones.

For instance, when Wal-Mart began a program to sell generic drugs at $4 a prescription, local pharmacists complained of predatory pricing. They charged that at those low prices, Wal-Mart must be selling under cost to drive them out of business. But Wal-Mart claimed that, given its substantial buying power and efficient operations, it could make a profit at those prices. The $4 pricing program was not aimed at putting competitors out of business. Rather, it was simply a good competitive move that served customers better and brought more of them in the door.[18]

CONSUMER ACTIONS TO PROMOTE SUSTAINABLE MARKETING (L03)

Sustainable marketing calls for more responsible actions by both businesses and consumers. Because some people view business as the cause of many economic and social ills, grassroots movements have arisen from time to time to keep business in line. The two major movements have been *consumerism* and *environmentalism*.

CONSUMERISM

North American business firms have been the target of organized consumer movements on three occasions. The first consumer movement took place in the early 1900s. It was fuelled by rising prices, by Upton Sinclair's writings on conditions in the meat industry, and by scandals in the drug industry. The second consumer movement, in the mid-1930s, was sparked by an upturn in consumer prices during the Great Depression and another drug scandal.

The third movement began in the 1960s. Consumers had become better educated, products had become more complex and potentially hazardous, and people were unhappy with institutions. Ralph Nader appeared on the scene to force many issues, and other well-known writers accused big business of wasteful and unethical practices. President John F. Kennedy declared that consumers had the right to safety and to be informed, to choose, and to be heard. Since then, many consumer groups have been organized and several consumer laws have been passed. The consumer movement has spread internationally and has become very strong in Europe.

Consumerism

An organized movement of citizens and government agencies to improve the rights and power of buyers in relation to sellers.

But what is the consumer movement? **Consumerism** is an organized movement of citizens and government agencies to improve the rights and power of buyers in relation to sellers. Traditional *sellers' rights* include the following:

☐ The right to introduce any product in any size and style, provided it is not hazardous to personal health or safety; or, if it is, to include proper warnings and controls

☐ The right to charge any price for the product, provided no discrimination exists among similar kinds of buyers

☐ The right to spend any amount to promote the product, provided it is not defined as unfair competition

☐ The right to use any product message, provided it is not misleading or dishonest in content or execution

☐ The right to use any buying incentive programs, provided they are not unfair or misleading

Traditional *buyers' rights* include the following:

☐ The right not to buy a product that is offered for sale

☐ The right to expect the product to be safe

☐ The right to expect the product to perform as claimed

Comparing these rights, many believe that the balance of power lies on the seller's side. True, the buyer can refuse to buy. But critics feel that the buyer has too little information, education, and protection to make wise decisions when facing sophisticated sellers. Consumer advocates call for the following additional consumer rights:

☐ The right to be well informed about important aspects of the product

☐ The right to be protected against questionable products and marketing practices

☐ The right to influence products and marketing practices in ways that will improve the "quality of life"

☐ The right to consume now in a way that will preserve the world for future generations of consumers

Each proposed right has led to more specific proposals by consumerists. The right to be informed includes the right to know the true interest on a loan (truth in lending), the true cost per unit of a brand (unit pricing), the ingredients in a product (ingredient labelling), the nutritional value of foods (nutritional labelling), product freshness (open dating), and the true benefits of a product (truth in advertising). Proposals related to consumer protection include strengthening consumer rights in cases of business fraud, requiring greater product safety, ensuring information privacy, and giving more power to government agencies. Proposals relating to quality of life include controlling the

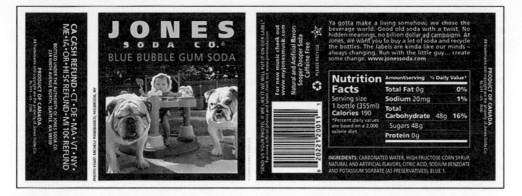

Exhibit 3.9   Today's labels contain much useful information, from ingredients and nutrition facts to recycling and country of origin information. Jones Soda even puts customer-submitted photos on its labels.

ingredients that go into certain products and packaging and reducing the level of advertising "noise." Proposals for preserving the world for future consumption include promoting the use of sustainable ingredients, recycling and reducing solid wastes, and managing energy consumption.

Sustainable marketing is up to consumers as well as to businesses and governments. Consumers have not only the *right* but also the *responsibility* to protect themselves instead of leaving this function to someone else. Consumers who believe they got a bad deal have several remedies available, including contacting the company or the media; contacting federal, provincial/territorial, or local agencies; and going to small-claims courts. Consumers should also make good consumption choices, rewarding companies that act responsibly, while punishing those that don't.

ENVIRONMENTALISM

Whereas consumerists consider whether the marketing system is efficiently serving consumer wants, environmentalists are concerned with marketing's effects on the environment and with the environmental costs of serving consumer needs and wants. **Environmentalism** is an organized movement of concerned citizens, businesses, and government agencies to protect and improve people's current and future living environment.

Environmentalists are not against marketing and consumption; they simply want people and organizations to operate with more care for the environment. The marketing system's goal, they assert, should not be to maximize consumption, consumer choice, or consumer satisfaction, but rather to maximize life quality. And "life quality" means not only the quantity and quality of consumer goods and services, but also the quality of the environment. Environmentalists want current and future environmental costs included in both producer and consumer decision-making.

The first wave of modern environmentalism in North America was driven by environmental groups and concerned consumers in the 1960s and 1970s. They were concerned with damage to the ecosystem caused by strip mining, forest depletion, acid rain, global warming, toxic and solid wastes, and litter. They were also concerned with the loss of recreational areas and with the increase in health problems caused by bad air, polluted water, and chemically treated food.

The second environmentalism wave was driven by government, which passed laws and regulations during the 1970s and 1980s governing industrial practices impacting the environment. This wave hit some industries hard. Steel companies and utilities had

Environmentalism
An organized movement of concerned citizens, businesses, and government agencies to protect and improve people's current and future living environment.

to invest billions of dollars in pollution-control equipment and costlier fuels. The auto industry had to introduce expensive emission controls in cars. The packaging industry had to find ways to improve recyclability and reduce solid wastes. These industries and others have often resented and resisted environmental regulations, especially when they have been imposed too rapidly to allow companies to make proper adjustments. Many of these companies claim they have had to absorb high costs that have made them less competitive.

The first two environmentalism waves have now merged into a third and stronger wave in which companies are accepting more responsibility for doing no harm to the environment. They are shifting from protest to prevention, and from regulation to responsibility. More and more companies are adopting policies of **environmental sustainability**. Simply put, environmental sustainability is about generating profits while helping to save the planet. Environmental sustainability is a crucial but difficult societal goal.

Environmental sustainability

A management approach that involves developing strategies that both sustain the environment and produce profits for the company.

Some companies have responded to consumer environmental concerns by doing only what is required to avert new regulations or to keep environmentalists quiet. Enlightened companies, however, are taking action not because someone is forcing them to, or to reap short-run profits, but because it is the right thing to do—for both the company and for the planet's environmental future.

Figure 3.2 shows a grid that companies can use to gauge their progress toward environmental sustainability. In includes both internal and external "greening" activities that will pay off for the firm and environment in the short run and "beyond greening" activities that will pay off in the longer term. At the most basic level, a company can practice *pollution* prevention. This involves more than pollution control—cleaning up waste after it has been created. Pollution prevention means eliminating or minimizing waste before it is created. Companies emphasizing prevention have responded with internal "green marketing" programs—designing and developing ecologically safer products, recyclable and biodegradable packaging, better pollution controls, and more energy-efficient operations.

For example, Nike produces PVC-free shoes, recycles old sneakers, and educates young people about conservation, reuse, and recycling. General Mills shaved off 20 percent of the paperboard packaging for Hamburger Helper, resulting in 500 fewer distribution trucks on the road each year. UPS has been developing its "green fleet," which now boasts more than 1600 low-carbon-emissions vehicles, including electric, hybrid-electric, compressed natural gas, liquefied natural gas, and propane trucks. Sun Microsystems created its Open Work program that gives employees the option to work from home, preventing nearly 29 000 tons of CO_2 emissions, while at the same time saving US$67.8 million in real-estate costs and increasing worker productivity by 34 percent.[19]

At the next level, companies can practise *product stewardship*—minimizing not just pollution from production and product design but all environmental impacts throughout the full product life cycle, and all the while reducing costs. Many companies are adopting *design for environment (DFE)* and *cradle-to-cradle* practices. This involves thinking ahead to design products that are easier to recover, reuse, recycle, or safely return to nature after usage, becoming part of the ecological cycle. Design for environment and cradle-to-cradle practices not only help sustain the environment but can also be highly profitable for the company.

FIGURE 3.2 The environmental sustainability portfolio

	Today: Greening	Tomorrow: Beyond Greening
Internal	**Pollution prevention** Eliminating or reducing waste before it is created	**New clean technology** Developing new sets of environmental skills and capabilities
External	**Product stewardship** Minimizing environmental impact throughout the entire product life cycle	**Sustainability vision** Creating a strategic framework for future sustainability

Sources: Stuart L. Hart, "Innovation, Creative Destruction, and Sustainability," *Research Technology Management,* September–October 2005, pp. 21–27.

For example, more than a decade ago, IBM started a business designed to reuse and recycle parts from its mainframe computers returned from lease. Today, IBM takes in 40 000 pieces of used IBM and other equipment per week, strips them down to their chips, and recovers valuable metals. "We find uses for more than 99 percent of what we take in, and have a return-to-landfill rate of [less than 1 percent]," says an IBM spokesperson. What started out as an environmental effort has now grown into a US$2 billion IBM business that profitably recycles electronic equipment at 22 sites worldwide.[20]

Today's "greening" activities focus on improving what companies already do to protect the environment. The "beyond greening" activities identified in Figure 3.2 look to the future. First, internally, companies can plan for *new clean technology*. Many organizations that have made good sustainability headway are still limited by existing technologies. To create fully sustainable strategies, they will need to develop innovative new technologies. For example, Coca-Cola is investing heavily in research addressing many sustainability issues:[21]

Exhibit 3.10 New clean technologies: Coca-Cola is investing heavily to develop new solutions to environmental issues. To reduce packaging waste problems, it's now testing new contour bottles made from corn, bioplastics, or— here—more easily recycled aluminum.

> From a sustainability viewpoint for Coca-Cola, an aluminum can is an ideal package. Aluminum can be recycled indefinitely. Put a Coke can in a recycling bin, and the aluminum finds its way back to a store shelf in about six weeks. The trouble is, people prefer clear plastic bottles with screw-on tops. Plastic bottles account for nearly 50 percent of Coke's global volume, three times more than aluminum cans. And they are not currently sustainable. They're made from oil, a finite resource. Most wind up in landfills or, worse, as roadside trash. They can't be recycled indefinitely because the plastic discFolours. To attack this waste problem, Coca-Cola will invest about US$44 million to build the world's largest state-of-the-art plastic-bottle-to-bottle recycling plant.
>
> As a more permanent solution, Coke is also investing in new clean technologies that address these and other environmental issues. For example, it's researching and testing new bottles made from aluminum, corn, or bioplastics. It's also designing more eco-friendly distribution alternatives. Currently, about ten million or so vending machines and refrigerated coolers gobble up energy and use potent greenhouse gases called HFCs to keep Cokes cold. To eliminate them, the company invested US$40 million in research and formed a refrigeration alliance with McDonald's and even competitor PepsiCo. It recently began installing a family of sleek new HFC-free coolers that use 30 to 40 percent less energy. Coca-Cola has also promised to become "water neutral" by researching ways to help its bottlers waste less water and ways to protect or replenish watersheds around the world.

Finally, companies can develop a *sustainability vision*, which serves as a guide to the future. It shows how the company's products and services, processes, and policies must evolve and what new technologies must be developed to get there. This vision of sustainability provides a framework for pollution control, product stewardship, and new environmental technology for the company and others to follow.

Most companies today focus on the upper-left quadrant of the grid in Figure 3.2, investing most heavily in pollution prevention. Some forward-looking companies practise product stewardship and are developing new environmental technologies. Few companies have well-defined sustainability visions. However, emphasizing only one or a few quadrants in the environmental sustainability grid can be short-sighted. Investing only in the left half of the grid puts a company in a good position today but leaves it vulnerable in the future. In contrast, a heavy emphasis on the right half suggests that a company has good environmental vision but lacks the skills needed to implement it. Thus, companies should work at developing all four dimensions of environmental sustainability.

Wal-Mart, for example, is doing just that. Through its own environmental sustainability actions and its impact on the actions of suppliers, Wal-Mart has emerged in recent years as the world's super "eco-nanny" (see Marketing@Work 3.1). Alcoa, the world's leading producer of aluminum, is also setting a high sustainability standard. For five years running it has been named one of the most sustainable corporations in the annual Global 100 Most Sustainable Corporations in the World ranking:

> Alcoa has distinguished itself as a leader through its sophisticated approach to identifying and managing the material sustainability risks that it faces as a company. From pollution prevention via greenhouse gas emissions reduction programs to engaging stakeholders over new environmental technology, such as controversial hydropower projects, Alcoa has the sustainability strategies in place needed to meld its profitability objectives with society's larger environmental protection goals.... Importantly, Alcoa's approach to sustainability is firmly rooted in the idea that sustainability programs can indeed add financial value. Perhaps the best evidence is the company's efforts to promote the use of aluminum in transportation, where aluminum—with its excellent strength-to-weight ratio—is making inroads as a material of choice that allows automakers to build low-weight, fuel-efficient vehicles that produce fewer tailpipe emissions. This kind of forward-thinking strategy of supplying the market with the products that will help solve pressing global environmental problems shows a company that sees the future, has plotted a course, and is aligning its business accordingly. Says CEO Alain Belda, "Our values require us to think and act not only on the present challenges, but also with the legacy in mind that we leave for those who will come after us ... as well as the commitments made by those that came before us."[22]

Environmentalism creates some special challenges for global marketers. As international trade barriers come down and global markets expand, environmental issues are having an ever-greater impact on international trade. Countries in North America, Western Europe, and other developed regions are generating strict environmental standards. A side accord to the North American Free Trade Agreement (NAFTA) set up the Commission for Environmental Cooperation for resolving environmental matters. The European Union (EU) has recently adopted a climate and energy package and legislation to reduce CO_2 emissions from new cars and transport fuels 20 percent below 1990 levels and to increase the share of renewable energy to 20 percent within one year. And the EU's Eco-Management and Audit Scheme (EMAS) provides guidelines for environmental self-regulation.[23]

However, environmental policies still vary widely from country to country. Countries such as Denmark, Germany, Japan, and the United States have fully developed environmental policies and high public expectations. But major countries such as China, India, Brazil, and Russia are in only the early stages of developing such policies. Moreover, environmental factors that motivate consumers in one country may have no impact on consumers in another. For example, PVC soft-drink bottles cannot be used in Switzerland or Germany. However, they are preferred in France, which has an extensive recycling process for them. Thus, international companies have found it difficult to develop standard environmental practices that work around the world. Instead, they are creating general policies and then translating these policies into tailored programs that meet local regulations and expectations.

PUBLIC ACTIONS TO REGULATE MARKETING

Citizen concerns about marketing practices will usually lead to public attention and legislative proposals. New bills will be debated—many will be defeated, others will be modified, and a few will become workable laws.

Many of the laws that affect marketing are listed in Chapter 4. The task is to translate these laws into the language that marketing executives understand as they make decisions about competitive relations, products, price, promotion, and channels of distribution. Figure 3.3 illustrates the major legal issues facing marketing management.

MARKETING@WORK 3.1

Wal-Mart: The World's Super Eco-Nanny

When you think of the corporate "good guys"—companies that are helping to save the world through sustainable actions—you probably think of names such as Patagonia, Timberland, Ben & Jerry's, Whole Foods Market, or Stonyfield Farm. But hold on to your seat. When it comes to sustainability, perhaps no company in the world is doing more good these days than Wal-Mart. That's right—big, bad Wal-Mart. Notes one incredulous reporter, "The company whose 2,300 supercenters take up at least 46,000 acres of earth, whose 117 square miles of asphalt parking lots add up to the size of Tampa, Florida, and who in 2004 faced fines for violating environmental laws in nine US states, has ... found green religion."

Critics have long bashed Wal-Mart for a broad range of alleged social misdeeds, from unfair labour practices to destroying small communities. So many consumers are surprised to learn that the world's largest company is also the world's biggest crusader for the cause of saving the world for future generations. When it comes to sustainability, Wal-Mart is rapidly emerging as the world's super "eco-nanny." In 2008, it was featured on the cover of *Strategy* magazine as Canada's top 'green' company. In the long run, Wal-Mart's stated environmental goals are to use 100 percent renewable energy, to create zero waste, and to sell only products that sustain the world's resources and environment. Toward that goal, not only is Wal-Mart greening up its own operations, it's also urging its vast network of suppliers to do the same.

Wal-Mart operates more than 7800 stores around the world, and its huge stores are gluttons for energy and other resources. So even small steps toward making stores more efficient can add up to huge environmental savings. But Wal-Mart isn't settling for small steps—it's moving in large leaps to develop new eco-technologies. In 2005, the giant retailer opened two experimental superstores designed to test dozens of environmentally friendly and energy-efficient technologies:

> A 43-metre-tall wind turbine stands outside a Wal-Mart Supercenter in Aurora, Colorado. Incongruous as it might seem, it is clearly a sign that something about this particular store is different. On the outside, the store's facade features row upon row of windows to allow in as much natural light as possible. The landscaping uses native, drought-tolerant plants well adapted to the hot, dry Colorado summers, cutting down on watering, mowing, and the amount of fertilizer and other chemicals needed. Inside the store, an efficient high-output linear fluorescent lighting system saves enough electricity annually from this store alone to supply the needs of 52 single-family homes. The store's heating system burns recovered cooking oil from the deli's fryers. The oil is collected, mixed with waste engine oil from the store's Tire and Lube Express, and burned in the waste-oil boiler. All organic waste, including produce, meats, and paper, is placed in an organic waste compactor, which is then hauled off to a company that turns it into mulch for the garden. These and dozens more technological touches make the supercenter a laboratory for efficient and Earth-friendly retail operations.

At the same time that Wal-Mart presses forward with its own sustainability initiatives, it's also affecting the environmental behaviours of its customers and suppliers. For example, it puts its marketing muscle behind eco-friendly products, regularly promoting brands such as SunChips, PUR water filters, and GE fluorescent bulbs. "If Wal-Mart can galvanize its regular shopper base into green purchasing and eco-friendly habits, it's succeeded in reducing the ecological footprint of 200 million people," says one analyst.

Wal-Mart is also laying down the eco-law to suppliers. To demonstrate its environmental leadership and determination, Wal-Mart recently outlined plans for holding its 61 000 suppliers accountable for reducing their "carbon footprints" and eliminating excessive packaging. And in a show of force few

Exhibit 3.11   For Wal-Mart, sustainability is about more than just doing the right thing. Above all, it makes good business sense—"driving out hidden costs, conserving our natural resources for future generations, and providing sustainable and affordable products for our customers so they can save money and live better."

governments could pull off, the company also "urged" 600 supplier executives to attend a Wal-Mart-sponsored seminar on sustainability. When imposing its environmental demands on suppliers, Wal-Mart "has morphed into ... a sort of privatized Environmental Protection Agency, only with a lot more clout," says an industry observer. "The EPA can levy [only] a seven-figure fine; Wal-Mart can wipe out more than a quarter of a business in one fell swoop."

With its immense buying power, Wal-Mart can humble even the mightiest supplier. Take, for example, the super-concentrated liquid laundry detergent market. Procter & Gamble and other detergent makers have long had the capability to formulate concentrated detergents. But it wasn't until Wal-Mart declared that it would sell nothing but super-concentrated detergents that P&G decided to invest US$100 million to make them, even in the face of uncertain financial returns. Wal-Mart's decision has resulted in smaller plastic detergent containers, conserving raw materials and eliminating millions and millions of tons of solid waste each year.

Because of Wal-Mart's size, even small supplier product and packaging changes have a substantial environmental impact. For example, to meet Wal-Mart's requests, P&G developed a mega roll technology for its Charmin brand, which combines the sheets of four regular toilet paper rolls into one small roll. The seemingly minor change saves 89.5 million cardboard rolls and 360 000 pounds of plastic packaging wrap a year. It also allows Wal-Mart to ship 42 percent more units on its trucks, saving about 54 000 gallons of fuel a year. Wal-Mart also pressured General Mills to straighten the once curly noodles in boxes of Hamburger Helper. This small change eliminated thousands of pounds of packaging.

Wal-Mart is working with the Carbon Disclosure Project, an independent not-for-profit environmental organization, to measure the amount of energy consumed in creating products throughout its supply chain. About 3400 suppliers of more than 13 000 products are participating in the project. Accordingly, Wal-Mart has developed a packaging scorecard that rates the vendors and will soon be used to guide Wal-Mart purchasing decisions. Wal-Mart has also established more than a dozen "sustainable value networks." These networks connect Wal-Mart people with suppliers, advocacy groups, academics, and independent experts who work together on "hot-button" environmental issues in various product categories, such as greenhouse gases, logistics, packaging, and alternative fuels.

So there you have it—Wal-Mart the eco-nanny. Wal-Mart's sustainability efforts have earned praise from even its harshest critics. As one skeptic begrudgingly admits, "Wal-Mart has more green clout than anyone." But for Wal-Mart, leading the eco-charge is about more than just doing the right thing. Above all, it also makes good business sense. More efficient operations and less wasteful products are not only good for the environment, they save Wal-Mart money. Lower costs, in turn, let Wal-Mart do more of what it has always done best—save customers money.

Says a Wal-Mart executive, "We've laid the foundation for a long-term effort that will transform our business by driving out hidden costs, conserving our natural resources for future generations, and providing sustainable and affordable products for our customers so they can save money and live better."

Sources: Quotes, adapted extract, and other information from Wal-Mart Canada website, http://www.walmart.ca/about-walmart, accessed June 2009; "Wal-Mart Says Latest High-Efficiency Store Cuts Energy Use 45%," *Environmental Leader,* March 18, 2008, accessed at www.environmentalleader.com; Jack Neff, "Why Wal-Mart Has More Green Clout than Anyone," *Advertising Age,* October 15, 2007, p. 1; Danielle Sacks, "Working with the Enemy," *Fast Company,* September 2007, pp. 74–81; Joseph Tarnowski, "Green Monster," *Progressive Grocer,* April 1, 2006, pp. 20–26; Ylan Q. Mui, "At Wal-Mart, 'Green' Has Various Shades," *Washington Post,* November 16, 2007, p. D1; Denise Lee Yohn, "A Big, Green, Reluctant Hug for Retailing's 800-lb. Gorilla," *Brandweek,* May 5, 2008, p. 61; and Connie Robbins Gentry, "Green Means Go," *Chain Store Age,* March 2009, pp. 47–48; and "Sustainable Value Networks," accessed at http://walmartstores.com/Sustainability/7672.aspx, November 2009.

BUSINESS ACTIONS TOWARD SUSTAINABLE MARKETING LO4

At first, many companies opposed consumerism, environmentalism, and other elements of sustainable marketing. They thought the criticisms were either unfair or unimportant. But by now, most companies have grown to embrace the new consumer rights, at least in principle. They might oppose certain pieces of legislation as inappropriate ways to solve specific consumer problems, but they recognize the consumer's right to information and protection. Many of these companies have responded positively to sustainable marketing as a way to create greater immediate and future customer value and to strengthen customer relationships.

SUSTAINABLE MARKETING PRINCIPLES

Under the sustainable marketing concept, a company's marketing should support the best long-run performance of the marketing system. It should be guided by five sustainable marketing principles: *consumer-oriented marketing, customer-value marketing, innovative marketing, sense-of-mission marketing,* and *societal marketing.*

FIGURE 3.3 Major marketing decision areas that may be called into question under the law

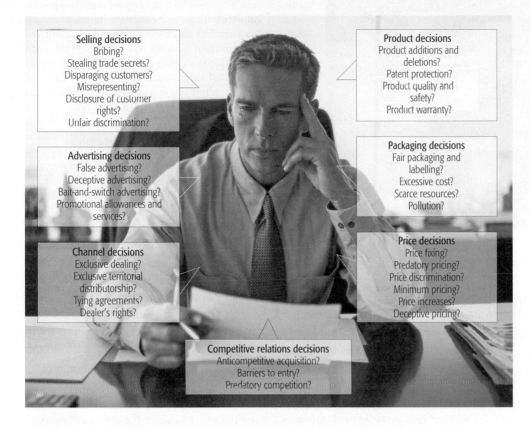

Selling decisions
Bribing?
Stealing trade secrets?
Disparaging customers?
Misrepresenting?
Disclosure of customer rights?
Unfair discrimination?

Product decisions
Product additions and deletions?
Patent protection?
Product quality and safety?
Product warranty?

Advertising decisions
False advertising?
Deceptive advertising?
Bait-and-switch advertising?
Promotional allowances and services?

Packaging decisions
Fair packaging and labelling?
Excessive cost?
Scarce resources?
Pollution?

Channel decisions
Exclusive dealing?
Exclusive territorial distributorship?
Tying agreements?
Dealer's rights?

Price decisions
Price fixing?
Predatory pricing?
Price discrimination?
Minimum pricing?
Price increases?
Deceptive pricing?

Competitive relations decisions
Anticompetitive acquisition?
Barriers to entry?
Predatory competition?

Consumer-Oriented Marketing   **Consumer-oriented marketing** means that the company should view and organize its marketing activities from the consumer's point of view. It should work hard to sense, serve, and satisfy the needs of a defined group of customers, both now and in the future. All of the good marketing companies that we've discussed in this text have had this in common: an all-consuming passion for delivering superior value to carefully chosen customers. Only by seeing the world through its customers' eyes can the company build lasting and profitable customer relationships.

Customer-Value Marketing   According to the principle of **customer-value marketing**, the company should put most of its resources into customer-value-building marketing investments. Many things marketers do—one-shot sales promotions, cosmetic packaging changes, direct-response advertising—may raise sales in the short run but add less *value* than would actual improvements in the product's quality, features, or convenience. Enlightened marketing calls for building long-run consumer loyalty and relationships by continually improving the value consumers receive from the firm's market offering. By creating value *for* consumers, the company can capture value *from* consumers in return.

Innovative Marketing   The principle of **innovative marketing** requires that the company continuously seek real product and marketing improvements. The company that overlooks new and better ways to do things will eventually lose customers to another company that has found a better way. An excellent example of an innovative marketer is Nintendo:[24]

> After Sony and Microsoft kicked the Mario out of Nintendo's GameCube in the Video Game War of 2001, the smallest of the three game platform makers needed a new plan. "Nintendo took a step back from the technology arms race and chose to focus on [customers and] the fun of playing, rather than cold tech specs," says the president of Nintendo of America. The resulting Wii system,

Consumer-oriented marketing
The philosophy of sustainable marketing that holds that the company should view and organize its marketing activities from the consumer's point of view.

Customer-value marketing
A principle of sustainable marketing that holds that a company should put most of its resources into customer-value-building marketing investments.

Innovative marketing
A principle of sustainable marketing that requires that a company seek real product and marketing improvements.

Exhibit 3.12 Innovative marketing: Nintendo's customer-focused innovation not only attracted new gamers and bruised competitors Sony and Microsoft, but also "opened doors of creativity throughout the video-game business."

Sense-of-mission marketing
A principle of sustainable marketing that holds that a company should define its mission in broad social terms rather than narrow product terms.

with its intuitive motion-sensitive controller and interactive games, appealed not only to teen boys typically targeted by the game industry but also to their sisters, moms, dads, and even grandparents. The result: the perpetually sold-out Wii system quickly outsold both the PlayStation 3 and Xbox 360. But get this: Unlike its competitors—which lose money on each console and earn it back on software—Nintendo actually turns a profit on its consoles, makes more selling games, then takes in still more in licensing fees. "Not to sound too obvious," says the Nintendo executive, "but it makes good business sense to make a profit on the products you sell." Nintendo's upset is doing more than attracting new gamers and bruising Sony and Microsoft. Says the president of competitor Sega of America, "It has opened doors of creativity throughout the video-game business."

Sense-of-Mission Marketing   **Sense-of-mission marketing** means that the company should define its mission in broad *social* terms rather than narrow *product* terms. When a company defines a social mission, employees feel better about their work and have a clearer sense of direction. Brands linked with broader missions can serve the best long-run interests of both the brand and the consumers. For example, Dove wants to do more than just sell its beauty care products. It's on a mission to discover "real beauty" and help women to be happy just the way they are:[25]

It all started with a Unilever study that examined the impact on women of images seen in entertainment, in advertising, and on fashion runways. The startling result: Only 2 percent of 3,300 women and girls surveyed in 10 countries around the world considered themselves beautiful. Unilever's conclusion: It's time to redefine beauty. So in 2004, Unilever launched the global Dove Campaign for Real Beauty, with ads that featured candid and confident images of real women of all types (not actresses or models) and headlines that made consumers ponder their perceptions of beauty. Among others, it featured full-bodied women ("Oversized or Outstanding?"), older women ("Gray or Gorgeous?"), and a heavily freckled woman ("Flawed or Flawless?"). The following year, as the campaign's popularity skyrocketed, Dove introduced six new "real beauties" of various proportions, in sizes ranging from 6 to 14. These women appeared in ads wearing nothing but their underwear and big smiles, with headlines proclaiming, "New Dove Firming: As Tested on Real Curves." "In Dove ads," says one advertising expert, "normal is the new beautiful."

The Dove Campaign for Real Beauty quickly went digital, with a www.campaignforrealbeauty. com Web site and award-winning viral videos with names such as "Evolution" and "Onslaught" that attacked damaging beauty stereotypes. As the campaign took off, so did sales of Dove products. But the people behind the Dove brand and the Campaign for Real Beauty have noble motives beyond sales and profits. According to a Unilever executive, Dove's bold and compelling mission to redefine beauty and reassure women ranks well above issues of dollars and cents. "You should see the faces of the people working on this brand now," he says. "There is a real love for the brand."

Some companies define their overall corporate missions in broad societal terms. For example, defined in narrow product terms, the mission of Unilever's Ben & Jerry's unit might be "to sell ice cream." However, the Ben & Jerry's brand states its mission more broadly, as one of "linked prosperity," including product, economic, and social missions. From its beginnings, Ben & Jerry's championed a host of social and environmental causes, and it donated a whopping 7.5 percent of pre-tax profits to support worthy causes each year. By the mid-1990s, Ben & Jerry's had become the number-two super-premium ice cream brand.

However, having a "double bottom line" of values and profits is no easy proposition. Throughout the 1990s, as competitors not shackled by "principles before profits" missions invaded its markets, Ben & Jerry's growth and profits flattened. In 2000, after several years of less-than-stellar financial returns, Ben & Jerry's was acquired by giant food producer Unilever. Looking back, the company appears to have focused too much on social issues at the expense of sound business management. Founder Ben Cohen once commented, "There came a time when I had to admit 'I'm a businessman.' And I had a hard time mouthing those words."[26]

Such experiences taught the socially responsible business movement some hard lessons. The result is a new generation of activist entrepreneurs—not social activists with big hearts who hate capitalism, but well-trained business managers and company builders with a passion for a cause. Founded by businesspeople who are proud of it, the new mission-driven companies are just as dedicated to building a viable, profitable business as to shaping the mission. They know that to "do good," they must first "do well" in terms of successful business operations. Jeff Swartz, CEO of outdoor shoe and apparel maker Timberland, refers to this as the beautiful—and profitable—nexus between "commerce and justice." Timberland's mission is to make profits while at the same time making a difference in the world (see Marketing@Work 3.2).

Societal Marketing   Following the principle of **societal marketing**, a company makes marketing decisions by considering consumers' wants and interests, the company's requirements, and society's long-run interests. The company is aware that neglecting consumer and societal long-run interests is a disservice to consumers and society. Alert companies view societal problems as opportunities.

Sustainable marketing calls for products that are not only pleasing but also beneficial. The difference is shown in Figure 3.4. Products can be classified according to their degree of immediate consumer satisfaction and long-run consumer benefit.

Deficient products, such as bad-tasting and ineffective medicine, have neither immediate appeal nor long-run benefits. **Pleasing products** give high immediate satisfaction but may hurt consumers in the long run. Examples include cigarettes and junk food. **Salutary products** have low immediate appeal but may benefit consumers in the long run; for instance, bicycle helmets or some insurance products. **Desirable products** give both high immediate satisfaction and high long-run benefits, such as a tasty *and* nutritious breakfast food.

Examples of desirable products abound. GE's Energy Smart compact fluorescent light bulb provides good lighting at the same time that it gives long life and energy savings. Toyota's hybrid Prius gives both a quiet ride and fuel efficiency. Maytag's front-loading Neptune washer provides superior cleaning along with water savings and energy efficiency.

Societal marketing
A principle of sustainable marketing that holds that a company should make marketing decisions by considering consumers' wants, the company's requirements, consumers' long-run interests, and society's long-run interests.

Deficient products
Products that have neither immediate appeal nor long-run benefits.

Pleasing products
Products that give high immediate satisfaction but may hurt consumers in the long run.

Salutary products
Products that have low appeal but may benefit consumers in the long run.

Desirable products
Products that give both high immediate satisfaction and high long-run benefits.

FIGURE 3.4 Societal classification of products

MARKETING@WORK 3.2

Timberland: Making a Difference in the World

Timberland is no ordinary for-profit company. Sure, it makes and sells rugged, high-quality boots, shoes, clothes, and other outdoor gear. But Timberland's corporate mission is about more than just making good products; it's about "trying to make a difference in the communities where we live and work."

Similarly, Timberland's Jeff Swartz is no ordinary CEO. He sees Timberland's place in the world as much bigger than the products it puts into it. He believes fervently that making money should go hand in hand with making the world a better place. Swartz is so passionate about this concept that he's sometimes referred to as a "prophet-CEO," as a messiah for a new age of social awareness. He's spreading the word about corporate citizenship to anyone who will listen, whether it's customers, suppliers, or employees.

For example, when Swartz recently met with McDonald's executives to pitch providing the fast-food giant with new uniforms, he didn't bring along any designs. In fact, he didn't even talk about clothing. Instead, he made an impassioned speech about how Timberland could help McDonald's create a more unified, motivated, purposeful workforce that would benefit both the company and the world at large. He preached the virtues of Timberland's corporate culture, which encourages employees to do volunteer work by giving them 40 hours of paid leave every year. He talked about Serv-a-palooza, Timberland's annual single-day volunteer-fest, which hosts hundreds of service projects in dozens of countries and provides tens of thousands of volunteer work hours.

Then, rather than trying to close the sale, Swartz left the McDonald's executives with the charge of truly helping every community in which it does business. In the end, Timberland didn't land the McDonald's uniform business,

but Swartz was elated all the same. "I told my team to find me 10 more places where I can have this conversation," he said. "No one believes in this more than we do, and that is our competitive advantage."

Founded by Jeff's grandfather, Nathan Swartz, in 1952, the now publicly traded company is out to show that it can both make profits and combat social ills, help the environment, and improve labour conditions around the world. Swartz isn't talking charity—he's an avowed capitalist. He's just passionately committed to the notion that a company can do well by doing good. Swartz refers to this as the beautiful—and profitable—nexus between "commerce and justice."

For years, Swartz's do-good philosophy paid off. Between 1992 and 2005, Timberland's market capitalization grew eightfold and annual sales hit US$1.6 billion. During that period, Swartz implemented social and environmental initiatives galore. He also implemented some of the toughest worker protection

standards in global manufacturing. The combination of financial performance and corporate responsibility won Swartz praise from both Wall Street and social activists alike.

But on the way to the awards ceremonies, Timberland stalled. In 2007, facing a weak retail economic environment, the company saw its first-ever revenue decline, an event that repeated in 2008. Timberland's stock price dropped dramatically and the company was forced to cut product lines and close stores. This left many analysts wondering—has Timberland put too much emphasis on justice and not enough on commerce? Is it possible for any company to serve a double bottom line of both values and profits?

In this time of company crisis, Swartz has learned some valuable lessons about the commerce side of the business. Especially during tough economic times, Swartz discovered, not all Timberland consumers place a high value on the "sustainability" part of the brand. All of the

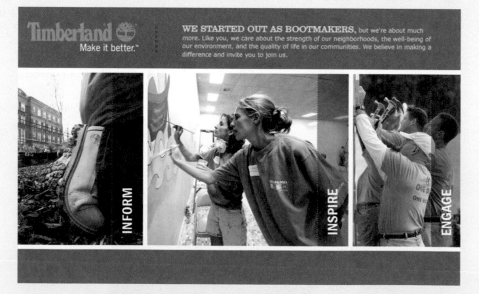

Exhibit 3.13   Timberland's corporate mission is about more than just making good products; it's about "trying to make a difference in the communities where we live and work."

"do good" works well in good times. But when things get tough, customers want a lot more. Swartz explains the following about today's more demanding customers:

> These days, customers are saying, "I'll have a conversation with you; [but] it will be all on my terms. Your product is going to have to be visually beautiful, technically perfect, and distinctive. And it has to be available where I shop at a price I'm willing to pay." Now, if it is all of those things, you gain the permission, in the one minute the consumer deals with your brand, to devote about 10 seconds to the issue of values. And if you miss any step along the way, you are talking to yourself, which is a terribly sad place to be.

Despite the challenging times, Swartz remains firmly committed to Timberland's mission of making a difference. Instead of backing off of Timberland's sustainable practices, he's ramping them up. He's more convinced than ever that doing so will help the profits side of the company. Looking beyond the world's current economic difficulties, Swartz insists that it is only a matter of time until consumers refuse to patronize companies that do not serve their communities. "I believe that there's a storm coming against the complacent who say good enough is good enough," he says.

To inspire consumers to make more sustainable decisions, Timberland now puts Green Index tags on its products. Modelled after the nutritional labels found on food products, the index provides a 0-to-10 rating of each product's ecological footprint in terms of climate impact, chemicals used, and resources consumed. The lower the score, the smaller the environmental footprint.

Timberland is doing everything it can to reduce the footprint of the products it makes and sells. But the company's sustainability efforts go far beyond environmental responsibility. Swartz recently commissioned a new long-term strategy for both environmental and social corporate responsibility. The plan lays out short- and long-term goals supported by key initiatives in line with four strategic pillars: *energy* (to become carbon neutral by 2010), *products* (to design environmentally responsible, recyclable products), *workplaces* (to establish fair, safe, and non-discriminatory workplaces), and *service* (to energize and engage Timberland's employees in service).

Timberland is moving along on these initiatives at a rapid pace. It has a solar-powered distribution centre in California and a wind-powered factory in the Dominican Republic. It's currently installing energy-efficient lighting and equipment retrofits in its facilities and educating workers about production efficiency. And it has launched two new footwear collections featuring outsoles made from recycled car tires. Timberland's new Earthkeeper line of boots, made from recycled and organic materials, has given rise to its Earthkeeper's campaign, an online social networking effort that seeks to inspire 1 million people to take actions to lighten their environmental footprints.

Thus, despite recent setbacks, Swartz and Timberland continue in their quest of "caring capitalism," doing well by doing good. Swartz has an advantage not held by many for-profit CEOs—although Timberland is a public company, the Swartz family controls 69 percent of shareholder voting rights. Therefore, Swartz can pursue his own corporate values while being less accountable to Wall Street. Still, he has no illusion that he's untouchable. For Timberland, "commerce" funds "justice." "No one's performance, especially in this age, will get supported through time if it's substandard," Swartz says. "Maybe I am self-indulgent, and if I am and our performance suffers, I will get fired. All I continue to say to shareholders is that I believe I am pursuing sustainable value."

Sources: Mark Borden and Anya Kamenetz, "The Prophet CEO," *Fast Company*, September 2008, p. 126; Jennifer Reingold, "Walking the Walk," *Fast Company*, November 2005, pp. 81–85; Elaine Wong, "Timberland Kicks Off Earth Day Effort," *Adweek*, March 24, 2009, accessed at www.adweek.com; "From the Power of One to the Effort of Many," *Business Wire*, April 19, 2009; and information from www.timberland.com, accessed November 2009.

Companies should try to turn all of their products into desirable products. The challenge posed by pleasing products is that they sell very well but may end up hurting the consumer. The product opportunity, therefore, is to add long-run benefits without reducing the product's pleasing qualities. The challenge posed by salutary products is to add some pleasing qualities so that they will become more desirable in consumers' minds.

MARKETING ETHICS

Good ethics are a cornerstone of sustainable marketing. In the long run, unethical marketing harms customers and society as a whole. Further, it eventually damages a company's reputation and effectiveness, jeopardizing the company's very survival. Thus, the sustainable marketing goals of long-term consumer and business welfare can be achieved only through ethical marketing conduct.

Conscientious marketers face many moral dilemmas. The best thing to do is often unclear. Because not all managers have fine moral sensitivity, companies need to develop *corporate marketing ethics policies*—broad guidelines that everyone in the organization must follow. These policies should cover distributor relations, advertising standards, customer service, pricing, product development, and general ethical standards.

The finest guidelines cannot resolve all the difficult ethical situations the marketer faces. Table 3.1 lists some difficult ethical issues marketers could face during their careers. If marketers choose immediate sales-producing actions in all these cases, their marketing behaviour might well be described as immoral or even amoral. If they refuse to go along with *any* of the actions, they might be ineffective as marketing managers and unhappy because of the constant moral tension. Managers need a set of principles that will help them figure out the moral importance of each situation and decide how far they can go in good conscience.

But *what* principle should guide companies and marketing managers on issues of ethics and social responsibility? One philosophy is that such issues are decided by the free-market and legal system. Under this principle, companies and their managers are not responsible for making moral judgments. Companies can in good conscience do whatever the market and legal systems allow.

A second philosophy puts responsibility not on the system but in the hands of individual companies and managers. This more enlightened philosophy suggests that a company should have a "social conscience." Companies and managers should apply high standards of ethics and morality when making corporate decisions, regardless of "what the system allows." History provides an endless list of examples of company actions that were legal but highly irresponsible.

TABLE 3.1 Some Morally Difficult Situations in Marketing

1. Your R&D department has changed one of your products slightly. It is not really "new and improved," but you know that putting this statement on the package and in advertising will increase sales. What would you do?

2. You have been asked to add a stripped-down model to your line that could be advertised to pull customers into the store. The product won't be very good, but salespeople will be able to switch buyers to higher-priced units. You are asked to give the green light for the stripped-down version. What would you do?

3. You are thinking of hiring a product manager who has just left a competitor's company. She would be more than happy to tell you all the competitor's plans for the coming year. What would you do?

4. One of your top dealers in an important territory recently has had family troubles, and his sales have slipped. It looks like it will take him a while to straighten out his family trouble. Meanwhile you are losing many sales. Legally, on performance grounds, you can terminate the dealer's franchise and replace him. What would you do?

5. You have a chance to win a big account that will mean a lot to you and your company. The purchasing agent hints that a "gift" would influence the decision. Your assistant recommends sending a large-screen television to the buyer's home. What would you do?

6. You have heard that a competitor has a new product feature that will make a big difference in sales. The competitor will demonstrate the feature in a private dealer meeting at the annual trade show. You can easily send a snooper to this meeting to learn about the new feature. What would you do?

7. You work for a cigarette company. Public policy debates over the past many years leave no doubt in your mind that cigarette smoking and cancer are closely linked. Although your company currently runs an "If you don't smoke, don't start" promotion campaign, you believe that other company promotions might encourage young (although legal age) non-smokers to pick up the habit. What would you do?

8. You have to choose between three ad campaigns outlined by your agency. The first (a) is a soft-sell, honest, straight-information campaign. The second (b) uses sex-loaded emotional appeals and exaggerates the product's benefits. The third (c) involves a noisy, somewhat irritating commercial that is sure to gain audience attention. Pretests show that the campaigns are effective in the following order: c, b, and a. What would you do?

9. You are interviewing a capable female applicant for a job as salesperson. She is better qualified than the men just interviewed. Nevertheless, you know that in your industry some important customers prefer dealing with men, and you will lose some sales if you hire her. What would you do?

Each company and marketing manager must work out a philosophy of socially responsible and ethical behaviour. Under the societal marketing concept, each manager must look beyond what is legal and allowed and develop standards based on personal integrity, corporate conscience, and long-run consumer welfare.

Dealing with issues of ethics and social responsibility in an open and forthright way helps to build strong customer relationships based on honesty and trust. In fact, many companies now routinely include consumers in the social responsibility process. Consider toy maker Mattel:[27]

In fall 2007, the discovery of lead paint on several of its best-selling products forced Mattel to make worldwide recalls on millions of toys. Threatening as this was, rather than hesitating or hiding the incident, the company's brand advisors were up to the challenge. Their quick, decisive response helped to maintain consumer confidence in the Mattel brand, even contributing to a 6 percent sales increase over the same period in the year before. Just who were these masterful "brand advisors"? They were the 400 moms with kids aged 3 to 10 comprising The Playground Community, a private online network launched by Mattel's worldwide consumer insights department in June 2007 to "listen to and gain insight from moms' lives and needs." Throughout the crisis, The Playground Community members kept in touch with Mattel regarding the product recalls and the company's forthright response plan, even helping to shape the post-recall promotional strategy for one of the affected product lines. Even in times of crisis, "brands that engage in a two-way conversation with their customers create stronger, more trusting relationships," says a Mattel executive.

Exhibit 3.14 Toy-maker Mattel's recent open and decisive product-recall response, based on input and help from its panel of brand advisors, helped to maintain customer confidence and create even more trusting customer relationships.

As with environmentalism, the issue of ethics presents special challenges for international marketers. Business standards and practices vary a great deal from one country to the next. For example, bribes and kickbacks are illegal for Canadian firms and a variety of treaties against bribery and corruption have been signed and ratified by more than 60 countries. Yet these are still standard business practices in many countries. The World Bank estimates that more than US$1 trillion per year worth of bribes are paid out worldwide. One studied showed that the most flagrant bribe-paying firms were from India, Russia, and China. Other countries where corruption is common include Iraq, Myanmar, and Haiti. The least corrupt companies were from Iceland, Finland, New Zealand, and Denmark.[28]

The question arises as to whether a company must lower its ethical standards to compete effectively in countries with lower standards. The answer is no. Companies should make a commitment to a common set of shared standards worldwide. For example, John Hancock Mutual Life Insurance Company operates successfully in Southeast Asia, an area that by Western standards has widespread questionable business and government practices. Despite warnings from locals that Hancock would have to bend its rules to succeed, the company set out strict guidelines. "We told our people that we had the same ethical standards, same procedures, and same policies in these countries that we have in the United States, and we do," said then-CEO Stephen Brown. "We just felt that things like payoffs were wrong—and if we had to do business that way, we'd rather not do business." Hancock employees feel good about the consistent levels of ethics. "There may be countries where you have to do that kind of thing," said Brown. "We haven't found that country yet, and if we do, we won't do business there."[29]

Many industrial and professional associations have suggested codes of ethics, and many companies are now adopting their own codes. For example, the Canadian Marketing Association developed the code of ethics shown in Table 3.2. Companies are

TABLE 3.2 Excerpts from Code of Ethics and Standards of Practice of the Canadian Marketing Association (CMA)

Mission of the CMA

To create an environment which fosters the responsible growth of marketing in Canada by:

☐ Representing the interests of our members on key issues;

   a) Taking a leadership role in identifying, planning for, and reacting to issues affecting marketing in Canada, and

   b) Influencing and shaping policy initiatives which impact marketing, through education of government, media, special interest groups, and the public;

☐ Establishing and promoting ethical standards of practice for marketing and taking an active role in ensuring compliance;

☐ Promoting integrity and high standards of business conduct among our members in the interests of consumers and each other;

☐ Being a major source of knowledge, marketing intelligence, and professional development; and

☐ Providing opportunities for members to meet, network, exchange information, and do business together.

Purpose of the CMA Code of Ethics and Standards of Practice

Marketers acknowledge that the establishment and maintenance of high standards of practice are a fundamental responsibility to the public, essential to winning and holding consumer confidence, and the foundation of a successful and independent marketing industry in Canada.

Definition of Marketing

Marketing is a set of business practices designed to plan for and present an organization's products or services in ways that build effective customer relationships.

Personal Information Practices

Marketers must promote responsible and transparent personal information management practices in a manner consistent with the provisions of the *Personal Information Protection and Electronic Documents Act* (Canada).

Truthfulness

Marketing communications must be clear and truthful. Marketers must not knowingly make a representation to a consumer or business that is false or misleading.

Campaign Limitations

Marketers must not participate in any campaign involving the disparagement or exploitation of any person or group on the grounds of race, colour, ethnicity, religion, national origin, gender, sexual orientation, marital status, or age.

Marketers must not knowingly exploit the credulity, lack of knowledge, or inexperience of any consumer, taking particular care when dealing with vulnerable consumers. The term "vulnerable consumer" includes, but is not limited to, children, teenagers, people with disabilities, the elderly, and those for whom English or French is not their first language.

Accuracy of Representation

Marketers must not misrepresent a product, service, or marketing program and must not mislead by statement or manner of demonstration or comparison.

Support for Claims

Test or survey data referred to in any marketing communication must be reliable, accurate, and current and must support the specific claim being made. Marketers must be able to substantiate the basis for any performance claim or comparison and must not imply a scientific, factual, or statistical basis where none exists.

Disguise

Marketers must not engage in marketing communications in the guise of one purpose when the intent is a different purpose.

Marketers must not claim to be carrying out a survey or research when their real purpose is to sell a product or service, or to raise funds.

Marketers must not mislead or deceive consumers or businesses into believing that a marketing communication is news, information, public service, or entertainment programming when its purpose is to sell products or services or to seek donations to causes or charities.

Disparagement

Marketers must not use inaccurate information to attack, degrade, discredit, or damage the reputation of competitors' products, services, advertisements, or organizations.

Protection of Personal Privacy

All consumer marketers must abide by the *Personal Information Protection and Electronic Documents Act* (PIPEDA), and/or applicable provincial privacy laws and the following ten Privacy Principles from the National Standard of Canada and five additional requirements as outlined in this section.

Ten Privacy Principles:

1. **Accountability:** An organization is responsible for personal information under its control and shall designate an individual or individuals who are accountable for the organization's compliance with the following principles.
2. **Identifying Purposes:** The purposes for which personal information is collected shall be identified by the organization at or before the time the information is collected.
3. **Consent:** The knowledge and consent of the individual are required for the collection, use, or disclosure of personal information, except where inappropriate.
4. **Limiting Collection:** The collection of personal information shall be limited to that which is necessary for the purposes identified by the organization. Information shall be collected by fair and lawful means.
5. **Limiting Use, Disclosure, and Retention:** Personal information shall not be used or disclosed for purposes other than those for which it was collected, except with the consent of the individual or as required by law. Personal information shall be retained only as long as necessary for the fulfillment of those purposes.
6. **Accuracy:** Personal information shall be as accurate, complete, and up-to-date as is necessary for the purposes for which it is being used.
7. **Safeguards:** Personal information shall be protected by security safeguards appropriate to the sensitivity of the information.
8. **Openness:** An organization shall make readily available to individuals specific information about its policies and practices relating to the management of personal information.
9. **Individual Access:** Upon request, an individual shall be informed of the existence, use and disclosure of his or her personal information and shall be given access to that information. An individual shall be able to challenge the accuracy and completeness of the information and have it amended as appropriate.
10. **Challenging Compliance:** An individual shall be able to address a challenge concerning compliance with the above principles to the designated individual or individuals accountable for the organization's compliance.

Use of CMA Do Not Contact Service

Marketers must use CMA's Do Not Contact Service when conducting a consumer mail campaign. In the absence of a government-mandated, national Do Not Call List, marketers must also use the CMA's Do Not Contact Service when conducting a consumer telephone and/or fax marketing campaign. The service must be used regardless of whether the campaign is being conducted in-house or through the use of an agency. This does not apply to B2B marketing, or to current customers, who can separately request that they be included on an organization's internal do not contact list.

also developing programs to teach managers about important ethics issues and to help them find the proper responses. They hold ethics workshops and seminars and set up ethics committees. Furthermore, most major North American companies have appointed high-level ethics officers to champion ethics issues and help resolve ethics problems and concerns facing employees.

PricewaterhouseCoopers (PwC) is a good example. In 2002, PwC established a global ethics office and comprehensive ethics program, headed by a high-level global ethics officer. The ethics program begins with a code of conduct called "The Way We Do Business." PwC employees learn about the code of conduct and about how to handle thorny ethics issues in comprehensive ethics training programs, which start when the employee joins the company and continue through the employee's career. The program also includes an ethics help line and regular communications at all levels. "It is obviously not enough to distribute a document," says PwC's global CEO, Samuel DiPiazza. "Ethics is in everything we say and do."[30]

Still, written codes and ethics programs do not ensure ethical behaviour. Ethics and social responsibility require a total corporate commitment. They must be a component of the overall corporate culture. According to PwC's DiPiazza, "I see ethics as a mission-critical issue ... deeply imbedded in who we are and what we do. It's just as important as our product development cycle or our distribution system.... It's about creating a culture based on integrity and respect, not a culture based on dealing with the crisis of the day.... We ask ourselves every day, 'Are we doing the right things?'"[31]

THE SUSTAINABLE COMPANY

At the foundation of marketing is the belief that companies that fulfill the needs and wants of customers will thrive. Companies that fail to meet customer needs or that intentionally or unintentionally harm customers, others in society, or future generations will decline. Sustainable companies are those that create value for customers through socially, environmentally, and ethically responsible actions.

Sustainable marketing goes beyond caring for the needs and wants of today's customers. It means having concern for tomorrow's customers in assuring the survival and success of the business, shareholders, employees, and the broader world in which they all live. Sustainable marketing provides the context in which companies can build profitable customer relationships by creating value *for* customers in order to capture value *from* customers in return, now and in the future.

RUFFLED FUR: KEEPING TRUE TO THE BRAND

Canada Goose's brand mantra is "Ask Anyone Who Knows™." The message is clear: If you understand the quality of fabric, down, and overall construction necessary to create an effective warm coat, you'll go with Canada Goose. However, in staying true to its message of value and utility, Canada Goose has faced some complex ethical choices.

For example, consider the fur-trimmed hood featured in many of its jacket designs. When investigating the best natural hood trim for its winter jackets, Canada Goose learned from Inuit experts that coyote fur was the most functional and practical way to keep people warm. However, in many of Canada Goose's markets, environmentalists and animal activists are against the use of fur under all circumstances. How could Canada Goose explain its decision to use real fur to these individuals?

For Canada Goose, the answer was to honour the "true users" segment of its customer makeup by providing the best cold-weather outerwear by using the most environmentally sustainable materials available. This meant rejecting the use of fake fur, which is a petroleum-based product and has little functional value for preserving warmth. Canada Goose delved deep into the science of fabrics and warmth and, with the aid of a researcher with a Ph.D., discovered that coyote fur has unique characteristics that lead to unparalleled efficacy at keeping the wearer's neck and face warm.

There was no doubt that if Canada Goose was to uphold its commitment to create the best cold-weather outdoor gear, then coyote fur was the best product. The company wanted, however, to assure its customers that the fur was not coming from "fur farms." Instead, it decided that it would purchase all fur through audited auctions.

"There will always be critics," said vice-president of marketing Kevin Spreekmeester. "But we felt that coyote fur was the right way to go. Coyote fur is more environmentally sustainable than a petroleum-based fake fur, coyote fur actually protects your face from frostbite and faux fur is not functional—it's simply an aesthetic, and we need to be loyal to our customers who expect us to provide the most effective cold weather materials."

To read more about Canada Goose's fur policy, visit the frequently asked questions section of its website at www.canada-goose.com/faq/.

QUESTIONS

1. Whether you agree or disagree with fur being used on the hoods, what do you think of the way Canada Goose has approached this issue?
2. Is "sustainability" simply a new marketing "flavour of the month," or does it have an ethical meaning for you? Discuss.
3. How closely related is corporate social responsibility to public relations? If public relations are about keeping good relations with the public and the public respects "socially responsible" organizations, can the two directives lead to the same point?

REVIEWING THE CONCEPTS

1. Define *sustainable marketing* and discuss its importance.

Sustainable marketing calls for meeting the present needs of consumers and businesses while still preserving or enhancing the ability of future generations to meet their needs. Whereas the marketing concept recognizes that companies thrive by fulfilling the day-to-day needs of customers, sustainable marketing calls for socially and environmentally responsible actions that meet both the immediate and future needs of customers and the company. Truly sustainable marketing requires a smooth-functioning marketing system in which consumers, companies, public policy–makers, and others work together to ensure responsible marketing actions.

2. Identify the major social criticisms of marketing.

Marketing's *impact on individual consumer welfare* has been criticized for its high prices, deceptive practices, high-pressure selling, shoddy or unsafe products, planned obsolescence, and poor service to disadvantaged consumers. Marketing's *impact on society* has been criticized for creating false wants and too much materialism, too few social goods, and cultural pollution. Critics have also criticized marketing's *impact on other businesses* for harming competitors and reducing competition through acquisitions, practices that create barriers to entry, and unfair competitive marketing practices. Some of these concerns are justified; some are not.

3. Define *consumerism* and *environmentalism*, and explain how they affect marketing strategies.

Concerns about the marketing system have led to *citizen action movements. Consumerism* is an organized social movement intended to strengthen the rights and power of consumers relative to sellers. Alert marketers view it as an opportunity to serve consumers better by providing more consumer information, education, and protection. *Environmentalism* is an organized social movement seeking to minimize the harm done to the environment and quality of life by marketing practices. The first wave of modern environmentalism was driven by environmental groups and concerned consumers; whereas the second wave was driven by government, which passed laws and regulations governing industrial practices impacting the environment. The first two environmentalism waves are now merging into a third and stronger wave in which companies are accepting responsibility for doing no environmental harm. Companies now are adopting policies of *environmental sustainability*—developing strategies that both sustain the environment and produce profits for the company. Both consumerism and environmentalism are important components of sustainable marketing.

4. Describe the principles of sustainable marketing.

Many companies originally opposed these social movements and laws, but most of them now recognize a need for positive consumer information, education, and protection. Under the sustainable marketing concept, a company's marketing should support the best long-run performance of the marketing system. It should be guided by five sustainable marketing principles: *consumer-oriented marketing, customer-value marketing, innovative marketing, sense-of-mission marketing*, and *societal marketing*.

5. Explain the role of ethics in marketing.

Increasingly, companies are responding to the need to provide company policies and guidelines to help their managers deal with questions of *marketing ethics*. Of course, even the best guidelines cannot resolve all the difficult ethical decisions that individuals and firms must make. But there are some principles that marketers can choose among. One principle states that such issues should be decided by the free market and legal system. A second, and more enlightened, principle puts responsibility not on the system but in the hands of individual companies and managers. Each firm and marketing manager must work out a philosophy of socially responsible and ethical behaviour. Under the sustainable marketing concept, managers must look beyond what is legal and allowable and develop standards based on personal integrity, corporate conscience, and long-term consumer welfare.

KEY TERMS

TALK ABOUT MARKETING

1. A bottle of Asacol, a drug for controlling intestinal inflammation, is more expensive than a bottle of the same drug as a generic product. Consumers accuse pharmaceutical manufacturers of unfair markups when the brand price is compared with the lower price of the generic product. As a marketer at a pharmaceutical company, how would you defend the higher prices for your company's branded products?

2. The Consumers' Association of Canada represents and informs consumers about issues affecting their quality of life. Visit www.consumer.ca to learn about this association. Select one of the issues or activities listed on its home page. Discuss how the information helped you become a more informed consumer.

3. Imagine that you work for a large consumer products company that makes soaps, detergents, and other products, such as shampoos, that ultimately end up being washed down the drain. How would you go about making sure that these products are not harming the environment?

4. Choose a company that you admire, shop at, or buy from—a company that you personally believe is a responsible social marketer. Investigate its website and find out what it does that you would consider "good" social marketing. What could it improve on?

5. If Kellogg's stops advertising to children, how should it change its marketing of products such as Froot Loops and Eggo waffles?

6. Consumer activist groups are beginning to raise awareness of the horrible wastefulness of bottled water. In Canada, no cities have unsafe drinking water, and since it was recently revealed that some branded bottled waters, such as Dasani, come from public sources (i.e., they are nothing more than bottled tap water), there is, logically, no reason for anyone to buy bottled water. What can consumer groups do to discourage or ban the sale of bottled water in Canada? Or should they?

THINK LIKE A MARKETING MANAGER

A forest full of trees has been spared thanks to a new paperless wine list being used at Aureole restaurants in Las Vegas and New York. The wine selection boasts an awe-inspiring 4000 different wine labels that would be impractical to print onto paper in the form of a manageable wine list. Instead of a paper wine list, customers are presented with a lightweight, wireless computer tablet. Pages are turned and selections are made by customers using either a stylus or their fingers. Aside from the positive environmental impact, there are other marketing applications for the electronic wine list. For example, the tablet can be used to display wine reviews and narratives about the winery, customers are allowed to bookmark favourite wine selections, and the tablet has the ability to let customers request that wine selection information and special offers be emailed to them at home.

QUESTIONS

1. What other businesses could benefit from using this sort of electronic device?
2. What sort of resistance do you think consumers may have to accessing printed material in an electronic format? How could such resistance be overcome?
3. What other typical paper documents do you commonly see when you go shopping, eat out, or purchase services that could be replaced with electronic devices?
4. List all the environmental benefits of such a system.

MARKETING ETHICS

K.G.O.Y. stands for "kids getting older younger," and marketers are getting much of the blame. Kids today see all types of messages, especially on the Internet, that they would never have seen in the past. Whereas boys may give up their G. I. Joes at an earlier age to play war games on their Xbox 360s, the greater controversy seems to surround claims of how girls have changed, or rather, how marketers have changed girls. Critics describe clothing designed for young girls aged 8 to 11 as "floozy" and sexual, with department stores selling thongs for youngsters and T-shirts that say "Naughty Girl!" Although Barbie's sexuality has never been subtle, she was originally targeted to girls 9 to 12 years old. Now, Barbie dolls target primarily 3- to 7-year-old girls.

QUESTIONS

1. Are marketers to blame for kids getting older younger? Give some examples other than those listed above.
2. Give an example of a company that is countering this trend by offering age-appropriate products for children.

MARKETING TECHNOLOGY

Does your computer have a floppy disk drive? Do you listen to music on a cassette deck or record movies on a VCR tape? Does your telephone handset have a cord? You probably answered no. All are examples of obsolete products. New products often provide greater value for customers, especially in fast-changing industries such as computers and electronics. But what happens to all the old products? This creates a growing concern over electronic waste, called *e-waste*. Although e-waste represents only 2 percent of the trash in our landfills, according to some analysts, it accounts for 70 percent of overall toxic waste. Recycling programs are increasing and are even required by law in some provinces. But the waste is often shipped for recycling or disposal to landfills in China, Kenya, India, and other developing countries, which have more lax standards concerning worker and environmental welfare.

QUESTIONS

1. Who should be responsible for properly disposing of discarded electronic products—consumers or manufacturers? Is it appropriate to ship e-waste to developing countries? Discuss alternative solutions.
2. Visit several electronics manufacturers' websites to learn whether they offer electronic recycling programs. Are manufacturers doing enough? Write a brief report on what you learned.

MARKETING BY THE NUMBERS

"High-low" pricing is popular with retailers but considered deceptive by some. Using this practice, retailers set initial prices very high for a short period and then discount the merchandise for the majority of the selling season. Critics complain that the supposed discounted price is in reality the regular price. For example, Canadian retailers such as Suzy Shier and The Bay were accused of double tagging—placing sale tags on goods right in the factory, so that the sale price was in fact the regular price.

QUESTIONS

1. Refer to Appendix 3, Marketing by the Numbers, to answer the following questions. If The Bay's cost for a piece of jewellery is $50 and it was marked up five times the cost, what is the "high" retail price? What is the "low" sales price if the price is reduced 60 percent off the "regular" price? What is The Bay's markup percentage on cost at this price? What is its markup percentage on the "low" selling price?
2. Judgments of some cases of high-low pricing have ruled that the retailer did not violate any laws and that one retailer cannot be singled out because most jewellery competitors promote sales prices in a similar way. Is it ethical for retailers to use this pricing tactic?

VIDEO CASE

Visit MyMarketingLab at www.pearsoned.ca/mymarketinglab to view the video for this chapter.

LAND ROVER

The automotive industry has seen better days. Many auto companies are now facing declining revenues and negative profits. Additionally, because of its primary dependence on products that consume petroleum, the auto industry has a big environmental black eye, especially companies that primarily make gas-guzzling trucks and SUVs.

During the past few years, however, Land Rover has experienced tremendous growth in revenues and profits. It is currently selling more vehicles than ever worldwide. How is this possible for a company that sells only SUVs? One of the biggest reasons is Land Rover's strategic focus on social responsibility and environmentalism. Land Rover believes that it can meet consumer needs for luxury all-terrain vehicles while at the same time providing a vehicle that is kinder to the environment. As a corporation, it is also working feverishly to reduce its carbon emissions, reduce waste, and reduce water consumption and pollution. With actions like this, Land Rover is successfully repositioning its brand away from the standard perceptions of SUVs as environmental enemies.

After viewing the video featuring Land Rover, answer the following questions about the company's efforts toward social responsibility.

QUESTIONS

1. Make a list of social criticisms of the automotive industry. Discuss all the ways that Land Rover is combating those criticisms.
2. By the textbook's definition, does Land Rover practise sustainable marketing?
3. Do you believe that Land Rover is sincere in its efforts to be environmentally friendly? Is it even possible for a large SUV to be environmentally friendly? Present support for both sides of these arguments.

END-OF-CHAPTER CASE

MARKETING FORTIFIED FOODS IN DEVELOPING COUNTRIES

Imagine teaching an elementary school class in which students are constantly inattentive and falling asleep—not because they are bored but because they are malnourished. In many countries, this problem is not unusual. Two billion people around the globe suffer from anemia, an iron deficiency. Iron deficiency leads to reduced resistance to disease, lowers learning ability in children, and contributes to the death of one out of five pregnant mothers. Two hundred million children do not get enough vitamin A. As a result, 250 000 of them go blind each year and 2.2 million children under the age of five die each year from diarrhea. Many malnourished children suffer from zinc deficiency, which leads to growth failure and infections. Close to two billion people do not get enough iodine, and iodine deficiency is the leading cause of preventable mental retardation in the world. If they only used the ordinary table salt found in homes and restaurants all across the Canada, this wouldn't happen.

Although estimates vary widely, it is clear that a substantial portion of the world's population suffers from malnutrition of some kind. Malnutrition exists everywhere, but one estimate places as many as 95 percent of the world's malnourished people in developing countries, where poverty levels are the highest. And although malnutrition is clearly a direct result of poverty, it also perpetuates poverty. Malnourished children are more likely to drop out of school, are less likely to benefit from schooling even if they remain enrolled, and end up having lower incomes as adults. According to Jean-Louis Sarbib, senior vice-president for human development at the World Bank, malnutrition costs developing countries up to 3 percent of their yearly GDP. "Put this in the context that the economies of many developing countries are growing at the rate of 2 to 3 percent annually, and improving nutrition could potentially double these rates," says Sarbib.

Today, many corporations, large and small, have social marketing initiatives of some kind, and two of the largest, Coca-Cola and Procter & Gamble, have made it part of their mission to fight global malnutrition. These two companies have invested millions of dollars in research of micronutrients and are learning how to fortify their products with additional minerals and vitamins in hopes of wiping out the deficiencies that prevent children around the world from being mentally prepared for school.

Fortifying foods is not new or unusual. Iodine has been added to ordinary table salt for decades; milk contains vitamin D and calcium; and most packaged cereals are fortified with micronutrients. A quick check of your pantry will likely reveal that many of the packaged foods and drinks you commonly consume have vitamins and minerals added to them. What's new is the growing social consciousness among major corporations, and their efforts to help the children of less fortunate nations. One example is a Coca-Cola beverage product called Vitango, which is marketed in Botswana.

Coca-Cola spent years developing a powdered beverage that, when mixed with water, looks and tastes like a sweeter version of Hi-C. The beverage is fortified with 12 vitamins and with minerals that are chronically lacking in the diets of people in developing countries. Coca-Cola tested this product in Botswana in Project Mission.

Every day for eight weeks, nurses visited schools where they mixed the beverage and passed out paper cups of the "new Hi-C." At the end of the test period, levels of iron and zinc in the children's blood levels had grown. Some parents noted that their children had become more attentive at school. After the Botswana tests, Coca-Cola also ran tests in Peru to determine how well the nutrients are absorbed into the bloodstream.

Although Vitango may seem like a miracle solution, Coca-Cola has faced challenges in distributing it. One issue is the fact that Vitango is produced as a powder to be mixed with water, but there is a lack of clean drinking water in much of Africa. Coca-Cola is working on developing a ready-to-drink formula. Meanwhile, competitor P&G is working on its own micronutrient-enriched drinks for distribution in developing countries.

In the 1990s, P&G developed its own proprietary iron, vitamin A, and iodine fortification technology, which it called GrowthPlus. GrowthPlus was the basic ingredient in a product called Nutridelight that P&G launched in the Philippines. Unfortunately, it didn't sell well—primarily because it was priced at 50 percent above the market price of other powdered drinks.

More recently, in Venezuela, P&G has launched another product, Nutristar, containing eight vitamins and five minerals. Sold at most food stores, it comes in flavours such as mango and passion fruit and promises to produce "taller, stronger, and smarter kids." To date, Nutristar is doing quite well. One reason is that it's available at McDonald's, where it is chosen by consumers with about half of all Happy Meals sold. P&G is also offering free samples in schools.

The major problem with both Coca-Cola's and P&G's nutritional products is price. These products were expensive to develop because of long lead times, the need to enlist the help of nutritional experts from around the world, and the need to develop products that appeal to the local population's tastes. If offered at "reasonable" prices, they would be out of the reach of the world's desperately poor, the group that needs them most. Consider P&G's Nutristar. The poor people in developing countries are not eating at McDonald's. They simply cannot afford to buy fortified sweetened drinks or, for that matter, any sweetened drinks.

How can P&G and Coca-Cola market such products without pricing them too high for the intended market? Learning its lesson in the Philippines, P&G priced Nutristar about 25 percent higher than other powdered drinks and 30 percent below carbonated soft drinks. Even so, that's still too high for the poverty-stricken. Coca-Cola originally planned to sell Vitango for about 20 cents for a 250-millilitre liquid serving but realizes that this price is too high. That's part of the reason for continuing developmental work on the product.

One solution to the pricing problem is to work with governments, but many of them are too poor to be able to afford the products. Many also lack the resources to educate their people on the merits of fortified foods. Additionally, some policy-makers fail to recognize the connection between malnutrition and the severe problems that it causes.

Enter GAIN—the Global Alliance for Improved Nutrition—an international consortium set up by the Bill and Melinda Gates Charitable Foundation. GAIN offers assistance to companies in order to profitably market fortified foods in developing countries. One $70 million GAIN program gives money to local governments in order to increase the demand for fortified foods, through means including large-scale public relations campaigns or a government "seal of approval." GAIN also actively lobbies for favourable tariffs and tax rates and for speedier regulatory review of new products in targeted countries. Of course, Coca-Cola and P&G can work with governments on their own, but their actions may be distrusted. After all, these are "for-profit" organizations whose motives may be suspect. GAIN has the advantage that it's a not-for-profit organization.

Another GAIN project provides $20 million to fortify salt, flour, and staple foods in developing countries by working directly with a network of more than a dozen manufacturers and retailers, as well as with governments. The idea is to motivate food-producing and food-distributing companies to make fortified foods available. After the initial funding period, the companies would then continue fortifying these foods without the need for additional aid money. Two such projects include GAIN-funded efforts that assist the government of Zambia in a three-year project to fortify maize meal and a project in China to produce and promote iron-fortified soy sauce.

In all, once fully implemented, GAIN projects will reach almost 700 million people with fortified food. "We are aiming for a realistic target of eliminating vitamin and mineral deficiencies in the next 10 years," said Marc Van Ameringen, executive director of GAIN. "Adding vitamins and minerals to the foods that people eat every day is a proven solution to a genuine health and development problem and it only costs around 25 cents per person per year."

Although GAIN seems like a wonderful resource for helping malnourished peoples, it does have critics. The critics point out that selling or giving away fortified foods does not solve the underlying problem of poverty. Nor does it teach people good nutritional habits. Moreover, in addition to vitamins and minerals, many of the "fortified" foods also contain overly large amounts of fat, sugar, and salt. So, for example, whereas the foods might help reduce iron deficiency, they could also lead to obesity. Some observers claim that it would be better to teach people how to grow fruits and vegetables. Finally, it's important to remember that a fortified beverage such as Vitango will help in dealing with malnutrition but can't eliminate it. People will still need to eat a variety of other foods, which makes education very important.

Given all these problems, why would Coca-Cola and P&G develop these products in the first place? One answer is future sales and profits. Products such as Vitango and Nutristar could create a basis from which to launch other Coca-Cola or P&G products, such as snack foods or juice drinks. As sales of carbonated beverages around the world have slowed, these fortified drinks pose a growth opportunity for the companies.

Sources: Shan Juan, "Iron-Fortified Soy Sauce for Every Kitchen," Chinadaily.com.cn, July 14, 2007; "Zambia Gains Support for Decision to Fortify Maize Meal with Vitamins, Minerals," *Times of Zambia*, September 28, 2006, accessed through LexisNexis; Sanjay Suri, "Development: Nutrient-Packed Food Headed for 200 Million," Inter Press Service, April 9, 2006; "World Bank: Malnutrition Causes Heavy Economic Losses," M2 Presswire, March 3, 2006; Jill Bruss, "Reaching the World," *Beverage Industry*, December 2001, p. 28; Rance Crain, "U.S. Marketers Must Develop Products to Help Third World," *Advertising Age*, December 3, 2001, p. 20; Betsy McKay, "Drinks for Developing Countries," *Wall Street Journal*, November 27, 2001; George Carpenter, "P&G and Sustainable Development—Finding Opportunity in Responsibility," April 1, 2003, accessed at www.eu.pg.com; "Hunger Kills Six Million Children Annually," *Advertiser*, November 22, 2005, p. 40; Betsy McKay, "Effort to Combat Malnutrition Cites Economic Impact," *Wall Street Journal*, March 3, 2006.

QUESTIONS

1. Which of the textbook's criticisms of marketing's impact on consumers, if any, are evident in the cases of Vitango and Nutristar?

2. Which of the criticisms of marketing's impact on society are evident in the Vitango and Nutristar cases?

3. Could Vitango and Nutristar be considered enlightened marketing efforts? Why or why not?

4. Are the development and marketing of such products as fortified foods and beverages ethical and socially responsible?

Visit the MyMarketingLab website at **www.pearsoned.ca/mymarketinglab**. This online homework and tutorial system puts you in control of your own learning with study and practice tools directly correlated to this chapter's content.

AFTER STUDYING THIS CHAPTER, YOU SHOULD BE ABLE TO

 describe the environmental forces that affect the company's ability to serve its customers

 explain how changes in the demographic and economic environments affect marketing decisions

3 identify the major trends in the firm's natural and technological environments

4 explain the key changes in the political and cultural environments

5 discuss how companies can react to the marketing environment

Analyzing the Marketing Environment

PREVIEWING THE CONCEPTS

In Part 1, you learned about the basic concepts of marketing, the steps in the marketing process for building profitable relationships with targeted consumers and the concepts of sustainable marketing. In Part 2, we'll look deeper into the first step of the marketing process—understanding the marketplace and customer needs and wants. In this chapter, you'll discover that marketing operates in a complex and changing environment. Other *actors* in this environment—suppliers, intermediaries, customers, competitors, publics, and others—may work with or against the company. Major environmental *forces*—demographic, economic, natural, technological, political, and cultural—shape marketing opportunities, pose threats, and affect the company's ability to build customer relationships. To develop effective marketing strategies, you must first understand the environment in which marketing operates.

Let's begin by having a look at how Loblaw Companies Limited, Canada's largest food distributor and one of Canada's largest private sector employers, responds to and also influences the social, cultural, and even the natural environment of the Canadian marketplace.

PRESIDENT'S CHOICE: THE BRAND OF CHOICE FOR CANADIAN GREEN CONSUMERS

"For product marketers, 'green' is the new 'low-fat,'" says William Smith, executive vice-president at the Academy for Educational Development in Washington. American marketers are jumping on the green bandwagon in droves, but to many Canadian consumers, the word green is synonymous with President's Choice. Loblaws began its GREEN program in 1989, and today it remains one of the most successful environmentally friendly product lines in the world.

Loblaw Companies Limited is the largest food distributor in Canada and operates retail stores under the banners Loblaws, Zehrs, Fortinos, and No Frills in Ontario; Provigo and Maxi in Quebec; and the Atlantic Superstore in the Maritimes. And one thing all those stores have in common is their selection of President's Choice products. The President's Choice brand made its debut in 1984 and quickly gained a devoted following among shoppers, who not only rave about the quality but can't wait for the next issue of the President's Choice *Insider's Report*. There's hardly a Canadian who doesn't know about, and hasn't enjoyed, President's Choice The Decadent Chocolate Chip Cookie, and today the brand makes its mark on everything from toasters to train sets, including banking, with the launch of PC Financial in 1998.

Today, the company's comprehensive, information-laden website at www. presidentschoice.ca educates Canadians about living green and explains how President's Choice GREEN products can help. For example, did you know that 80–90 percent of the energy we expend in washing our clothes is merely from heating the water? Washing laundry in hot water increases our reliance on Canada's coal-fired generating stations, which contribute to greenhouse gas emissions. PC GREEN 3× Coldwater Laundry Detergent is three times more powerful than regular detergent, which means you can do your laundry with less, and lower your water heating bills in the process. Not only that, but the product contains no perfumes or dyes that might harm the environment, and because it's concentrated, it comes in a smaller bottle, which uses less plastic.

President's Choice GREEN is about more than just marketing consumer products in the grocery store; it's a philosophy. Loblaws is no Home Depot, yet there's a section on the GREEN website about how to improve the energy efficiency of your home—advice about changing your furnace filter, testing your windows for their ability to keep out the cold and keep in the heat, and information about energy-efficient light bulbs.

In 2007, Loblaws launched its PC GREEN Reusable Shopping Bag program, selling cloth bags that hold twice as much as typical plastic grocery bags at each checkout for 99 cents. Loblaws estimates the program will save 1 billion plastic bags each year from ending up in Canada's landfills. The bags sold out the first day they were available, prompting Loblaws executive chairman Galen G. Weston to observe, "The sell-out of our PC GREEN Reusable Bag confirms it—when retailers make it simple for consumers to do their part, they will embrace the opportunity." Within a few months, four Loblaws stores in Milton, Ontario; Halifax, Nova Scotia; Sherbrooke, Quebec; and Langford, British Columbia, became the first major grocery stores in their respective markets to eliminate traditional plastic grocery bags at the checkouts.

The Milton Loblaws store was the first major grocery store in all of North America to eliminate traditional plastic shopping bags. At the Atlantic Superstore in Halifax, youth members of the HalifaxRegionalMunicipality's Adventure Earth Centre "H.E.A.T." (Helping the Earth by Acting Together) helped out at the store by providing assistance to customers, and the Sherbrooke Provigo store was the first major grocery store in the province of Quebec to go bagless. "With this bold decision to totally eliminate the use of plastic bags in this establishment—a first in Quebec—Provigo recognizes our city's place on the cutting edge of sustainable development. I am truly proud. Your initiative shows the willingness of Sherbrookers to change their habits in order to pass on to future generations a quality environment," stated Jean Perrault, mayor of Sherbrooke.

But Loblaws didn't stop there. It realized that, although it was doing what it could to encourage the use of reusable bags, there were still plastic bags out there, so in September 2007, it rolled out a PC GREEN Plastic Bag Recycling Program at Ontario stores located in municipalities where curbside plastic bag recycling is not available. The initiative is expected to divert more than 51 million plastic bags from Ontario landfills in year one of the program. Customers were encouraged to return plastic grocery bags to the store and deposit them in new recycling receptacles to be recycled into new usable plastic products.

In honour of Earth Day in April 2008, a new green product, PC GREEN Phosphate-Free Automatic Dishwashing Detergent, was launched as the first retail-branded phosphate-free and chlorine-free automatic dishwasher detergent. Currently, 5000 tonnes of phosphates attributed to automatic dishwasher detergents enter Canadian water bodies each year. The introduction of this product was ahead of the federal government's recent proposed limit on phosphates from dishwasher and laundry detergents to 0.5 percent by 2010.

As the green movement continues, President's Choice will continue to introduce new environmentally friendly products to the Canadian market, and consumers, it seems, will continue to look forward to them. For example, Loblaws introduced biodegradable eco-cornstarch dishware in 2010, which is durable as long as it is in use but breaks down within a year of being placed in a landfill. President's Choice GREEN products are not only friendly to the natural environment and in line with, even ahead of, the political and regulatory environment, but the ongoing popularity of the GREEN product line is a tribute to Canada's social and cultural environment.[1]

A COMPANY'S **marketing environment** consists of the actors and forces outside marketing that affect marketing management's ability to build and maintain successful relationships with target customers. Like Loblaws, companies constantly watch and adapt to the changing environment.

More than any other group in a company, marketers must be the environmental trend trackers and opportunity seekers. Although every manager in an organization needs to observe the outside environment, marketers have two special aptitudes. They have disciplined methods—marketing research and marketing intelligence—for collecting information about the marketing environment. They also spend more time in customer and competitor environments. By carefully studying the environment, marketers can adapt their strategies to meet new marketplace challenges and opportunities.

The marketing environment is made up of a *microenvironment* and a *macroenvironment*. The **microenvironment** consists of the actors close to the company that affect its ability to serve its customers—the company, suppliers, marketing intermediaries, customer markets, competitors, and publics. The **macroenvironment** consists of the larger societal forces that affect the microenvironment—demographic, economic, natural, technological, political, and cultural forces. We look first at the company's microenvironment.

THE COMPANY'S MICROENVIRONMENT LO1

Marketing management's job is to build relationships with customers by creating customer value and satisfaction. However, marketing managers cannot do this alone. Figure 4.1 shows the major actors in the marketer's microenvironment. Marketing success will require building relationships with other company departments, suppliers, marketing intermediaries, customers, competitors, and various publics, which combine to make up the company's value delivery network.

Marketing environment
The actors and forces outside marketing that affect marketing management's ability to build and maintain successful relationships with target customers.

Microenvironment
The actors close to the company that affect its ability to serve its customers—the company, suppliers, marketing intermediaries, customer markets, competitors, and publics.

Macroenvironment
The larger societal forces that affect the microenvironment—demographic, economic, natural, technological, political, and cultural forces.

FIGURE 4.1 Actors in the microenvironment

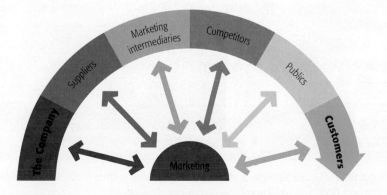

THE COMPANY

In designing marketing plans, marketing management takes other company groups into account—groups such as top management, finance, research and development (R&D), purchasing, operations, and accounting. All of these interrelated groups form the internal environment. Top management sets the company's mission, objectives, broad strategies, and policies. Marketing managers make decisions within the strategies and plans made by top management.

As we discussed in Chapter 2, marketing managers must work closely with other company departments. Other departments have an impact on the marketing department's plans and actions. And under the marketing concept, all of these functions must "think consumer." According to Xerox CEO Anne Mulcahy, to provide a great customer experience, Xerox must "find out what customers are facing—what their problems and opportunities are. Everyone at Xerox shares this responsibility. That includes people and departments that have not always been customer-facing, like finance, legal, and human resources."[2]

SUPPLIERS

Suppliers form an important link in the company's overall customer value delivery system. They provide the resources needed by the company to produce its goods and services. Supplier problems can seriously affect marketing. Marketing managers must watch supply availability and costs. Supply shortages or delays, labour strikes, and other events can cost sales in the short run and damage customer satisfaction in the long run. Rising supply costs may force price increases that can harm the company's sales volume.

Most marketers today treat their suppliers as partners in creating and delivering customer value. For example, Pratt & Whitney Canada (P&WC), based in Longueuil, Quebec, is a world leader in the design, manufacture and service of aircraft engines. P&WC knows the importance of building close relationships with its suppliers. The company was the first aircraft engine manufacturer to launch an e-business supplier portal to share information in real time with more than 1500 Canadian suppliers.

"This portal enables suppliers to instantly connect with P&WC and gain real-time responses to a wide range of questions and/or transactions," said P&WC's [former] vice-president procurement and logistics Mr. Danny Di Perna. "This e-business initiative reflects our commitment to continuously improve communication throughout our Supply Chain." The

Exhibit 4.1   Pratt & Whitney Canada partners with its 1500 Canadian suppliers to share vital business information. Creating satisfied suppliers helps P&WC improve its response to customer requirements.

fully customized portal provides registered suppliers with the necessary functionality to allow seamless collaboration with P&WC. It is also fully integrated with P&WC's back-end systems, to provide instantaneous information updates. "This high level of collaboration supports supplier capacity and raw material planning, reduces inventory, and improves on-time delivery," said Mr. Di Perna. "The final result is improved delivery visibility for P&WC production and its customers, which ultimately helps improve our response to customer requirements."[3]

MARKETING INTERMEDIARIES

Marketing intermediaries help the company to promote, sell, and distribute its products to final buyers. They include resellers, physical distribution firms, marketing services agencies, and financial intermediaries. *Resellers* are distribution channel firms that help the company find customers or make sales to them. These include wholesalers and retailers who buy and resell merchandise. Selecting and partnering with resellers is not easy. No longer do manufacturers have many small, independent resellers from which to choose. They now face large and growing reseller organizations such as Wal-Mart, Winners, Home Depot, Costco, and Future Shop. These organizations frequently have enough power to dictate terms or even shut smaller manufacturers out of large markets.

Physical distribution firms help the company to stock and move goods from their points of origin to their destinations. *Marketing services agencies* are the marketing research firms, advertising agencies, media firms, and marketing consulting firms that help the company target and promote its products to the right markets. *Financial intermediaries* include banks, credit companies, insurance companies, and other businesses that help finance transactions or insure against the risks associated with the buying and selling of goods.

Like suppliers, marketing intermediaries form an important component of the company's overall value delivery system. In its quest to create satisfying customer relationships, the company must do more than just optimize its own performance. It must partner effectively with marketing intermediaries to optimize the performance of the entire system.

Thus, today's marketers recognize the importance of working with their intermediaries as partners rather than simply as channels through which they sell their products. For example, when Coca-Cola signs on as the exclusive beverage provider for a fast-food chain, such as McDonald's, Wendy's, or Subway, it provides much more than just soft drinks. It also pledges powerful marketing support.

> Coke assigns cross-functional teams dedicated to understanding the finer points of each retail partner's business. It conducts a staggering amount of research on beverage consumers and shares these insights with its partners. It analyzes the demographics of U.S. zip code areas and helps partners to determine which Coke brands are preferred in their areas. Coca-Cola has even studied the design of drive-through menu boards to better understand which layouts, fonts, letter sizes, colors, and visuals induce consumers to order more food and drink. Based on such insights, the Coca-Cola Food Service group develops marketing programs and merchandising tools that help its retail partners to improve their beverage sales and profits. Coca-Cola Food Service's Web site, www.CokeSolutions.com, provides retailers with a wealth of information, business solutions, and merchandising tips. Such intense partnering efforts have made Coca-Cola a runaway leader in the U.S. fountain soft-drink market.[4]

COMPETITORS

The marketing concept states that to be successful, a company must provide greater customer value and satisfaction than its competitors do. Thus, marketers must do more than simply adapt to the needs of target consumers. They also must gain strategic advantage by positioning their offerings strongly against competitors' offerings in the minds of consumers.

Marketing intermediaries Firms that help the company to promote, sell, and distribute its goods to final buyers.

No single competitive marketing strategy is best for all companies. Each firm should consider its own size and industry position compared with those of its competitors. Large firms with dominant positions in an industry can use certain strategies that smaller firms cannot afford. But being large is not enough. There are winning strategies for large firms, but there are also losing ones. And small firms can develop strategies that give them better rates of return than large firms enjoy.

PUBLICS

Public
Any group that has an actual or potential interest in or impact on an organization's ability to achieve its objectives.

The company's marketing environment also includes various publics. A **public** is any group that has an actual or potential interest in or impact on an organization's ability to achieve its objectives. We can identify seven types of publics:

☐ *Financial publics.* This group influences the company's ability to obtain funds. Banks, investment houses, and stockholders are the major financial publics.

☐ *Media publics.* This group carries news, features, and editorial opinion. It includes newspapers, magazines, and radio and television stations.

☐ *Government publics.* Management must take government developments into account. Marketers must often consult the company's lawyers on issues of product safety, truth in advertising, and other matters.

☐ *Citizen-action publics.* A company's marketing decisions may be questioned by consumer organizations, environmental groups, minority groups, and others. Its public relations department can help it stay in touch with consumer and citizen groups.

☐ *Local publics.* This group includes neighbourhood residents and community organizations. Large companies usually appoint a community relations officer to deal with the community, attend meetings, answer questions, and contribute to worthwhile causes. For example, Ronald McDonald House Charities recognize the importance of community publics.

☐ *General public.* A company needs to be concerned about the general public's attitude toward its products and activities. The public's image of the company affects its buying.

Exhibit 4.2   Ronald McDonald House Charities® (RMHC®) of Canada recognizes the importance of community publics. At the cornerstone of RMHC is the Ronald McDonald House® program. The 12 Ronald McDonald Houses play a vital role in communities across Canada, providing a home-away-from-home for out-of-town families of children with serious illnesses being treated at a nearby children's hospital.

☐ *Internal publics.* This group includes workers, managers, volunteers, and the board of directors. Large companies use newsletters and other means to inform and motivate their internal publics. When employees feel good about their company, this positive attitude spills over to external publics.

A company can prepare marketing plans for these major publics as well as for its customer markets. Suppose the company wants a specific response from a particular public, such as goodwill, favourable word of mouth, or donations of time or money. The company would have to design an offer to this public that is attractive enough to produce the desired response.

CUSTOMERS

As we've emphasized throughout, customers are the most important actors in the company's microenvironment. The aim of the entire value delivery system is to serve target customers and create strong relationships with them. The company might target any or all of five types of customer markets. *Consumer markets* consist of individuals and households that buy goods and services for personal consumption. *Business markets* buy goods and services for further processing or for use in their production process, whereas *reseller markets* buy goods and services to resell at a profit. *Government markets* are made up of government agencies that buy goods and services to produce public services or transfer the goods and services to others who need them. Finally, *international markets* consist of these buyers in other countries, including consumers, producers, resellers, and governments. Each market type has special characteristics that call for careful study by the seller.

THE COMPANY'S MACROENVIRONMENT

The company and all of the other actors operate in a larger macroenvironment of forces that shape opportunities and pose threats to the company. Figure 4.2 shows the six major forces in the company's macroenvironment. In the remaining sections of this chapter, we examine these forces and show how they affect marketing plans.

DEMOGRAPHIC ENVIRONMENT LO2

Demography is the study of human populations in terms of size, density, location, age, gender, race, occupation, and other statistics. The demographic environment is of major interest to marketers because it involves people, and people make up markets. The world

Demography
The study of human populations in terms of size, density, location, age, gender, race, occupation, and other statistics.

FIGURE 4.2 Major forces in the company's macroenvironment

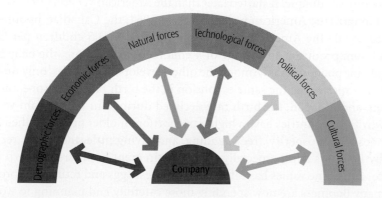

Exhibit 4.3 Demographics and markets: The growing Chinese "me generation" of only children—the "little emperors"—is affecting markets for everything from children's products to financial services, cellphone services, and luxury goods.

population is growing at an explosive rate. It now exceeds 6.8 billion people and will grow to more than 8 billion by the year 2030.[5] The world's large and highly diverse population poses both opportunities and challenges.

Changes in the world demographic environment have major implications for business. For example, consider China. Thirty years ago, to curb its skyrocketing population, the Chinese government passed regulations limiting families to one child each. As a result, China's youth born after 1980—called "balinghou" or the "me generation" by their elders—have been showered with attention and luxuries, resulting in what's known as the "little emperor" or "little empress" syndrome. As many as six adults, two parents and four doting grandparents, may be indulging the whims of each only child—all 600 million of them. Parents with only one child at home now spend about 40 percent of their income on their cherished child.[6]

China's me generation, now ranging in age from newborns to late-20s, is affecting markets for everything from children's products to financial services, cellphone services, and luxury goods. For example, Starbucks is targeting China's me generation, positioning itself as a new kind of informal but indulgent meeting place.[7]

China's one-child rule created a generation who have been pampered by parents and grandparents and have the means to make indulgent purchases. Instead of believing in traditional Chinese collective goals, these young people embrace individuality. "Their view of this world is very different," says the president of Starbucks Greater China. "They have never gone through the hardships of our generation." Starbucks is in sync with that, he says, given its customized drinks, personalized service, and original music compilations.

Thus, marketers keep close track of demographic trends and developments in their markets, both at home and abroad. They track changing age and family structures, geographic population shifts, educational characteristics, and population diversity. Here, we discuss the most important demographic trends in Canada.

Changing Age Structure of the Population   The Canadian population exceeded 33 million in 2009 and is expected to exceed 39 million by 2031. The single most important demographic trend in Canada is the changing age structure of the population. The Canadian population contains several generational groups. Here, we discuss the three largest groups—the Baby Boomers, Generation X, and the Millennials—and their impact on today's marketing strategies.

THE BABY BOOMERS   The post–World War II baby boom, which began in 1947 and ran through 1966, produced 9.8 million **Baby Boomers** in Canada. Although there was a baby boom in both Canada and the United States, Canadian marketers have to recognize that our baby boom was unique. It started later than the American version (1947 versus 1946) and lasted longer (the American boom ended in 1964; the Canadian boom continued until 1966). While the American baby boom resulted in 3.5 children per family, the Canadian boom produced an average of 4 children. Furthermore, the baby boom was not a worldwide phenomenon. Among the other developed countries, only Australia and New Zealand experienced the same expansion in the birth rate. In Europe, there was no baby boom, and in Japan, the birth rate declined during our baby boom years, which explains why these countries have a higher proportion of older people in their societies.[8]

After years of prosperity, free spending, and saving little, the recent recession hit many Baby Boomers hard, especially the pre-retirement boomers. A sharp decline in stock prices and home values has eaten into their nest eggs and retirement prospects. As a result, many Boomers are now spending more carefully and planning to work longer.

Baby Boomers
The 9.8 million Canadians born during the baby boom following World War II and lasting until the mid-1960s.

However, although they might now be feeling the pinch of the weakened economy, the Baby Boomers are still the wealthiest generation in Canadian history. Today's Baby Boomers account for about one-third of Canada's population and control over 50 percent of the country's wealth. As they reach their peak earning and spending years, the Boomers will continue to constitute a lucrative market for financial services, new housing and home remodelling, travel and entertainment, eating out, health and fitness products, and just about everything else.

It would be a mistake to think of the older Boomers as phasing out or slowing down. Today's Boomers think young no matter how old they are. Rather than viewing themselves as phasing out, they see themselves as entering new life phases. For example, Toyota recognizes these changing Boomer life phases. Ads for its Toyota Highlander show empty-nest Boomers and declare, "For your newfound freedom." Similarly, Curves fitness centres target Boomer women. Curves' older regulars "want to be strong and fit," says one expert. "They just don't want to go into Gold's Gym and be surrounded by spandex-clad Barbie dolls."[9]

GENERATION X   The baby boom was followed by a "birth dearth," creating another generation of 7 million Canadians born between 1967 and 1976. Author Douglas Coupland calls them **Generation X** because they lie in the shadow of the Boomers and lack obvious distinguishing characteristics.

The Generation Xers are defined as much by their shared experiences as by their age. Increasing parental divorce rates and higher employment for their mothers made them the first generation of latchkey kids. Although they seek success, they are less materialistic; they prize experience, not acquisition. For many of the Gen-Xers that are parents, family comes first—both children and their aging parents—and career second.[10] From a marketing standpoint, the Gen-Xers are a more skeptical bunch. They tend to research products before they consider a purchase, preferring quality over quantity, and they tend to be less receptive to overt marketing pitches.

Once labelled as "the MTV generation" and viewed as body-piercing slackers who whined about "McJobs," the Gen-Xers have grown up and are now taking over. They are increasingly displacing the lifestyles, culture, and values of the Baby Boomers. They are the most educated generation to date, and they possess hefty annual purchasing power. However, like the Baby Boomers, the Gen-Xers now face growing economic pressures. Most are woefully behind in saving for retirement—and they worry about it. Nearly half of Gen-Xers say they are so saddled with debt or live on such tight budgets that they can't even think about saving. Like almost everyone else these days, they are spending more carefully.[11]

Still, with so much potential, many companies are focusing on Gen-Xers as an important target segment. For example, Mountain Equipment Co-op (MEC), the largest retail co-operative in Canada appeals to the Gen X consumers—those who value family, life experience, and environmental sustainability. Founded in 1971, MEC has grown to service nearly 3 million members worldwide. With stores in 10 major Canadian cities and worldwide catalogue sales, the company has become Canada's leading supplier of quality outdoor gear, clothing, and camping equipment,

Generation X
The 7 million Canadians born between 1967 and 1976 in the "birth dearth" following the baby boom.

Exhibit 4.4   Targeting Gen-Xers: MFC has been highly successful in serving a segment of Gen-Xers who value family, life experiences, and environmental sustainability.

mec.ca | 1.800.663.2667 | SNOWSPORTS 08

I'VE SPENT HALF MY LIFE SKIING, AND THE OTHER HALF DREAMING ABOUT SKIING.
[DEAN, MEC MEMBER]

HOKKAIDO, JAPAN.

MOUNTAIN EQUIPMENT CO-OP

surpassing $200 million in annual sales. It promotes itself as an ethical company through its commitment to green building, community grants, ethical purchasing, product sustainability, and promotion of Canada-wide parks and protected areas.[12]

MILLENNIALS   Both the Baby Boomers and Gen-Xers will one day be passing the reins to the **Millennials** (also called **Generation Y** or the echo boomers). Born between 1977 and 2000, these children of the Baby Boomers number 10.4 million, dwarfing the Gen-Xers and larger even than the Baby Boomer segment. This group includes several age cohorts: *tweens* (aged 9–12), *teens* (13–18), and *young adults* (19–32). The Millennials make up a huge and attractive market.[13]

Millennials (or Generation Y)
The 10.4 million children of the Canadian Baby Boomers, born between 1977 and 2000.

One thing that all of the Millennials have in common is their utter fluency and comfort with digital technology. They don't just embrace technology; it's a way of life. The Millennials were the first generation to grow up in a world filled with computers, cellphones, satellite TV, iPods, and online social networks. A recent study found that 91 percent of Millennials are on the Web, making up 32 percent of all Internet users. According to another study, 77 percent of Millennials frequent social networking sites and 71 percent use instant messaging. "All generations are comfortable with technology, but this is the generation that's been formed by technology," says a Yahoo! executive. For them, "it's not something separate. It's just something they do."[14]

Marketers of all kinds now target the Millennials segment, from automakers to political campaigns. However, the Millennials are bombarded with marketing messages coming at them from all directions. And rather than having mass marketing messages pushed at them, they prefer to seek out information and engage in two-way brand conversations. Thus, reaching these message-saturated consumers effectively requires creative marketing approaches. Consider how 7-Eleven planned to reach the Millennials with this unique promotional campaign in the summer of 2010:[15]

Building on the growth of social media, 7-Eleven partnered with online social gaming leader Zynga in a cross-promotional effort to engage the Millennials. The retailer offered exclusive FarmVille-, Mafia Wars-, and YoVille-branded items on many of the convenience retailer's products in nearly 7000 stores in the United States and Canada. Consumers could purchase specially marked products to receive a redemption code that could be used for new, limited edition virtual goods in one of the three Zynga hit games. In conjunction with the launch of this promotion, 7-Eleven revamped its website with more content and graphics designed to appeal to the millennial crowd.

Exhibit 4.5   Reaching Millennials: 7-Eleven partnered with online social gaming leader Zynga in a cross-promotional effort to engage the Millennials.

Zynga has become the leading player in the fast-growing social gaming space, boasting more than 230 million active users. For 7-Eleven, Zynga's audience represents an attractive market to build loyalty and repeat visits from customers, particularly millennials, according to Stephanie Hoppe, senior director of marketing at 7-Eleven. "We know social networking and social gaming is something they're interested in," she said. "We want to give them experiences that they'll enjoy and will drive them back to 7-Eleven."

"7-Eleven's partnership with Zynga has launched one of the most unique campaigns in our company's history," said Rita Bargerhuff, 7-Eleven vice-president and chief marketing officer. "It gives millions of loyal fans, who regularly play Zynga games, access to incentives on more than 30 products in our stores. The Zynga universe of gamers is vast, and we knew we had to come up with a promotion fit for this demographic. Attracting millions of consumers to 7-Eleven stores with exclusive items for Zynga games creates an additional opportunity for them to try some of our newest products, like our proprietary 7-Select™ ice cream and candy, along with long-time favorites, such as Slurpee and coffee drinks."

GENERATIONAL MARKETING   Do marketers need to create separate products and marketing programs for each generation? Some experts warn that marketers need to be careful about turning off one generation each time they craft a product or message that appeals effectively to another. Others caution that each generation spans decades of time and many socio-economic levels. For example, marketers often split the Baby Boomers into three smaller groups—leading-edge boomers, core boomers, and trailing-edge boomers—each with its own beliefs and behaviours. Similarly, they split the Millennials into tweens, teens, and young adults.

Thus, marketers need to form more precise age-specific segments within each group. More important, defining people by their birth date may be less effective than segmenting them by their lifestyle, life stage, or the common values they seek in the products they buy. We will discuss many other ways to segment markets in Chapter 7.

The Changing Canadian Household   When one uses the term *household*, a stereotype of the typical family living in the suburbs with its two children may leap to mind. However, this stereotype is far from accurate. The 2006 census reveals some interesting trends. For example, there is a growing "crowded nest" syndrome. About 43.5 percent of young Canadians aged 20 to 29 now live with their parents. There are 8.9 million families in Canada, but fewer have children than in past years. In fact, the 2006 census marked the first time there were more census families without children than with children over the past 20 years. One-person households and couples without children grew more than twice as fast as the total population in private households, while households with children edged up only 0.4 percent. As a result, the average Canadian household shrank to 2.5 people in 2006. Two-thirds of Canada's children aged 14 and under lived with married parents in 2006, a decline from 81 percent in 1986. Lone-parent families headed by men increased almost 15 percent during the five years prior to 2006, more than twice the growth of lone-parent families headed by women.[16] Given these trends, marketers must increasingly consider the distinctive needs and buying habits of these non-traditional households, because they are now growing more rapidly than traditional ones.

Responsibility for household tasks and the care of children is also changing. There are now more dual-income families as more and more women enter the workforce. Today women account for 48 percent of the Canadian workforce. The employment rate of women with children has grown particularly sharply in the past two decades, especially for those with preschool-aged children. More than 68 percent of women with children under six were employed, more than double the figure of 1976.[17]

The significant number of women in the workforce has spawned the child daycare business and increased consumption of career-oriented women's clothing, financial services, and convenience foods and services. An example is Épicerie Direct, an Internet grocer that has served the greater Montreal area since 2007. By using www.epiceriedirect.com, instead of trekking to the grocery store, battling traffic, and waiting in line, busy working moms and dads can simply buy their groceries online. Épicerie Direct offers a virtual selection of products from more than 20 categories and delivers customers' orders to their doorsteps, providing a "grocery cart at your fingertips."[18]

Geographic Shifts in Population   The population of Canada grew by approximately 4.6 percent between 2005 and 2009. As Table 4.1 shows, however, growth rates across all provinces and territories are not uniform. The population of Alberta reached double-digit increases while that of Newfoundland and Labrador saw a slight decline during the 2005–2009 period. However, with the downturn in oil prices in 2008 and 2009, many people from the Atlantic provinces who moved to Alberta to work in the "oil patch" have returned home.

Canadians are a mobile people with itchy feet. For more than a century, Canadians have been moving from rural to urban areas. The urban areas show a faster pace of living, more commuting, higher incomes, and greater variety of goods and services than can be

TABLE 4.1 Canada's Population

	2005 (thousands)	2009 (thousands)	Change (%)
Canada	32 245.2	33 739.9	4.6
Newfoundland and Labrador	514.4	508.9	−1.1
Prince Edward Island	138.1	141.0	2.1
Nova Scotia	937.9	938.2	0
New Brunswick	748.0	749.5	0.2
Quebec	7581.9	7 828.9	3.3
Ontario	12 528.5	13 069.2	4.3
Manitoba	1 178.3	1 222.0	3.7
Saskatchewan	993.6	1 030.1	3.7
Alberta	3 322.2	3 687.7	11.0
British Columbia	4 196.8	4 455.2	6.2
Yukon	31.9	33.7	5.6
Northwest Territories	43.4	43.4	0
Nunavut	30.3	32.2	6.3

Source: "Population by year, by province and territory," http://www40.statcan.gc.ca/l01/cst01/demo02a-eng.htm, Statistics Canada, 2009. Reproduced with the permission of the Minister of Public Works and Government Services Canada, 2010.

found in the small towns and rural areas that dot Canada. In 2007, more than 370 800 Canadian residents changed provinces, a record number since 1981. Alberta and British Columbia are now the top two choices when it comes to interprovincial moves. Since 2003, Ontario has seen the largest net loss of residents from interprovincial moves of any province, but it maintains its growth in overall population through immigration from other countries. Recent research has shown that interprovincial moves and income are correlated. People who moved from one province to another tended to increase their earnings, especially if they moved away from a "have not" province. The effects were especially strong for men and younger people.[19]

Canada's cities are changing as well. Canadian cities are often surrounded by large suburban areas. Statistics Canada calls these combinations of urban and suburban populations "Census Metropolitan Areas" (CMAs). Over 50 percent of Canada's population lives in the top 10 CMAs. Marketers also track the relative growth of these markets to see which areas are expanding and which are contracting.

Population shifts interest marketers because people in different regions buy differently. For example, 46 percent of people classified as "serious technology users" reside in Ontario, compared with 18 percent who live in British Columbia and the 6 percent who live in Atlantic Canada.[20]

The shift in where people live has also caused a shift in where they work. For example, the migration toward metropolitan and suburban areas has resulted in a rapid increase in the number of people who telecommute—that is, work at home or in a remote office and conduct their business by phone, fax, modem, or the Internet.

This trend, in turn, has created a booming SOHO (small office/home office) market. Fifteen percent of Canadian households report that they have a home office. In addition to commuters, it is estimated that there were 618 000 home-based businesses in Canada. Typically, home-based business operators are male (60.3 percent) and between the ages of 25 and 54 (76.4 percent). Many (31 percent) are highly educated. The top five industries for home-based businesses are professional, scientific, and technical services (17.8 percent); agriculture (12.1 percent); trade (10.2 percent); health care and social assistance (9.2 percent); and construction (8.3 percent).[21]

Many marketers are actively courting the lucrative telecommuting market. For example, WebEx, the Web-conferencing division of Cisco, helps to overcome the isolation that often accompanies telecommuting. With WebEx, people can meet and collaborate online, no matter what their work location. "All you need to run effective online meetings is a browser and a phone," says the company. With WebEx, people working anywhere can interact with other individuals or small groups to make presentations, exchange documents, and share desktops, complete with audio and full-motion video. WebEx's Meet Me Now service can be launched from desktops, Microsoft Outlook and Office, and instant messaging clients such as Yahoo! Messenger and MSN Messenger. Meet Me Now automatically finds and configures users' webcams and lets meeting hosts switch among participants' video streams to form a virtual roundtable. More than 2.2 million people participate in WebEx sessions every day.[22]

Exhibit 4.6 Cisco targets the growing telecommuter market with WebEx, which lets people meet and collaborate online, no matter what their work location.

A Better-Educated, More White-Collar, More Professional Population   The Canadian population is becoming better educated. As of 2004, people with university degrees or post-secondary certificates equal 59.1 percent of the population. Eight percent have some post-secondary education. Those with a high-school education equal 20.1 percent. However, 12.9 percent of the population has less than a high-school education.[23] The rising number of educated people will increase the demand for quality products, books, magazines, travel, personal computers, and Internet services.

Increasing Diversity   Countries vary in their ethnic and racial makeup. At one extreme is Japan, where almost everyone is Japanese. At the other extreme are countries such as Canada and the United States, with people from virtually all nations. Anyone who has walked the streets of Vancouver, Montreal, Calgary, or Toronto will immediately understand that visible minorities in Canada are a force to be reckoned with. Over 5 million (16 percent) Canadians identified themselves as visible minorities in the 2006 census, and over 200 ethnic origins were reported. Between 2001 and 2006, the visible minority population increased five times faster than the population as a whole, mainly because of immigration. According to Statistics Canada's population projections, members of visible minority groups could account for roughly one-fifth of the total population by 2017.[24]

The purchasing power of visible minorities is huge, so it is not surprising that Sharifa Khan of Balmoral Marketing, an ethnic ad agency in Toronto, has seen a dramatic increase in spending directed at these markets. Many clients allocate as much as 15 percent of their total communications budget to ethnic marketing, up from 2 percent just a few years ago. Khan points out that once her clients realized that visible minorities are "real people with real desires to own a home, a nice car, and all the goods and services that complemented those things they desired it made the job of convincing [her clients] to embrace ethnic marketing a lot easier."[25] As the ethnic population continues to grow in Canada, large companies, from Sears, McDonald's, and Air Canada to Levi Strauss, Procter & Gamble, and General Mills, feature people from different backgrounds in their ads and can now target specially designed products and promotions to one or more of these groups. They can use a variety of media vehicles introduced to serve ethnic marketplaces. There are 18 television networks, 49 radio stations, and 190 newspapers and magazines available to reach various ethnic populations. Though there are approximately 200 different visible minorities living in Canada, only 12 groups are growing significantly and have well-developed media that target their communities: Chinese, Caribbean (predominantly Jamaican), South Asian (India, Pakistan, Tamil, Bangladesh), Korean, Hispanic, Italian, Greek, Portuguese, Ukrainian, Polish, Filipinos, and First Nations.[26] It must be remembered, however, that visible minorities often read the same media, such as daily newspapers, as other Canadians.

Targeting ethnic consumers involves far more than mere tokenism, as many ethnic marketing specialists warn. Merely placing a person from a visible minority in an advertisement is not sufficient evidence that one is an ethnic marketer. Communicating in the consumer's native language is often mandatory, but marketers must also face the challenge of not alienating sophisticated second-generation individuals. The TD Bank demonstrated the power of providing information in potential customers' native language. The bank launched a Chinese Green Info Line to target potential Chinese investors. More than 300 callers per month take advantage of the service, which has generated considerable investments. Wal-Mart now runs television spots targeting South Asian, Cantonese, Mandarin, Spanish, Portuguese, and Italian communities. TELUS and Nokia use print advertising to target consumers from various ethnic backgrounds in Toronto and Vancouver. Professor Ashwin Joshi of Schulich School of Business at York University in Toronto notes that IKEA is another marketer that is sensitive to the needs of consumers from different ethnic backgrounds. For example, through its extensive links with people of South Asian origins, it developed insights that it used to shape its marketing practices. IKEA learned that religion plays a key role for this community and that it is not uncommon for the different religious groups to have sacred places in their homes where they place their religious artifacts. This led IKEA to specifically design furniture to house these artifacts. IKEA also takes pride in participating in key festivals, such as Diwali and Id, by having the appropriate items (e.g., candle holders made of clay) on sale during the time of these events.[27]

The diversity in the Canadian marketplace isn't restricted to ethnic markets. The 2006 census enumerated 45 300 same-sex couples, up from 34 200 in 2001.[28] People's sexual orientation is another point of diversity, and there is growing tolerance of alternative lifestyles in Canada. For example, Toronto's Pride Week is the third largest outdoor festival in the world and attracts more than 1 million people each year. Since homosexual consumers tend to be cosmopolitan and professional, with high incomes, they are desirable target markets for everything from technology products and health and beauty products to travel, fashion, entertainment, and financial services. It is not surprising that the City of Toronto ran a campaign aimed at attracting more gay and lesbian tourists.

As a result of TV shows such as *Ugly Betty* and *The Ellen DeGeneres Show,* and Oscar-winning movies such as *Brokeback Mountain*, the LGBT (lesbian, gay, bisexual, and transgender) community has increasingly emerged into the public eye. A number of media now provide companies with access to this market. For example, Planet Out Inc. offers several successful

Exhibit 4.7 Firms such as TELUS know the importance of cultural sensitivity and building meaningful connections with people of different ethnic backgrounds.

magazines (*Out*, the *Advocate, Out Traveler*) and websites (Gay.com and www.daily.gay. com). Canada's only digital television channel specifically targeted at the gay and lesbian community, OUTtv, was launched nationally in 2001. By 2008, it became Canada's fastest-growing digital cable channel and had reached the half-million mark in subscribers.

Companies in a wide range of industries are now targeting the LGBT community with gay-specific marketing efforts. For example, Air Canada created a number of TV and print ads specifically targeting the LGBT community. The company also has a dedicated LGBT link on its corporate website and has been a sponsor of the LGBT community for over 25 years, donating air travel to such community initiatives as Fashion Cares.[29]

Diversity goes beyond ethnicity or sexual preferences. For example, 14.3 percent of the Canadian population (4.4 million) has some form of disability. This group has considerable spending power, as well as great need for tailored products and services. Not only do they value services that make daily life easier, but they are also a growing market for travel, sports, and other leisure-oriented products. The Canadian Abilities Foundation provides a wealth of information ranging from products and services to housing and travel advice on its EnableLink website.

How are companies trying to reach consumers with disabilities? Many marketers now recognize that the worlds of people with disabilities and those without disabilities are one and the same. Marketers such as McDonald's, Verizon Wireless, Sears, Nike, and Honda have featured people with disabilities in their mainstream advertising. For instance, Nike signs endorsement deals with Paralympian athletes.

Other companies use specially targeted media to reach this attractive segment. The new website Disaboom.com reaches people with disabilities through social networking features akin to Facebook combined with relevant information, everything from medical news to career advice, dating resources, and travel tips. Several large marketers, including Johnson & Johnson, Netflix, Avis, GM, and Ford have already signed on as Disaboom.com marketing partners.

As the population in Canada grows more diverse, successful marketers will continue to diversify their marketing programs to take advantage of opportunities in fast-growing segments.

ECONOMIC ENVIRONMENT

Markets require buying power as well as people. The **economic environment** consists of factors that affect consumer purchasing power and spending patterns. Marketers must pay close attention to major trends and consumer spending patterns both across and within their world markets. For example, the recent world economic meltdown had a dramatic impact on consumers spending and buying behaviour that will likely be felt for years to come.

Economic environment
Factors that affect consumer buying power and spending patterns.

Nations vary greatly in their levels and distribution of income. Some countries have *industrial economies*, which constitute rich markets for many different kinds of goods. At the other extreme are *subsistence economies*—they consume most of their own agricultural and industrial output and offer few market opportunities. In between are *developing economies*—which can offer outstanding marketing opportunities for the right kinds of products.

Consider India with its population of 1.1 billion people. In the past, only India's elite could afford to buy a car. In fact, only one in seven Indians now owns one. But recent dramatic changes in India's economy have produced a growing middle class and rapidly rising incomes. Now, to meet the new demand, European, North American, and Asian automakers are introducing smaller, more-affordable vehicles into India. But they'll have

Exhibit 4.8   Economic environment: To capture India's growing middle class, Tata Motors introduced the small, affordable Tata Nano, designed to be India's Model T—the car that puts the developing nation on wheels.

to find a way to compete with India's Tata Motors, which has unveiled the least expensive car ever in this market, the Tata Nano. Dubbed "the people's car," the Nano sells for only 100 000 rupees (about US$2500). It can seat four passengers, gets 50 miles per gallon (4.7L/100 km), and travels at a top speed of 60 miles (96 km) per hour. The ultra-low-cost car is designed to be India's Model T—the car that puts the developing nation on wheels. For starters, Tata hopes to sell 1 million of these vehicles a year.[30]

Following are some of the major economic trends in Canada.

Changes in Income and Spending   In recent years, North American consumers spent freely, fuelled by income growth, a boom in the stock market, rapid increases in housing values, and other economic good fortune. They bought and bought, seemingly without caution, amassing record levels of debt. However, the free spending and high expectations of those days were dashed by the recent worldwide economic crisis. Says one economist, "For a generation that has substituted rising home equity and stock prices for personal savings, the ... economic meltdown has been psychologically wrenching after a quarter century of unquestioned prosperity."[31]

As a result, people who over-consumed during the past decade have now adopted a back-to-basics frugality in their lifestyles and spending patterns. They are buying less, and they are looking for greater value in the things that they do buy. In turn, *value marketing* has become the watchword for many marketers. Rather than offering high quality at a high price, or lesser quality at very low prices, marketers in all industries are looking for ways to offer today's more financially cautious buyers greater value—just the right combination of product quality and good service at a fair price.

You'd expect value pitches from the makers of everyday products. For example, alongside milk moustache ads featuring glamorous celebrities such as Brooke Shields and Beyoncé Knowles, you now see one featuring celebrity financial advisor Suze Orman, telling consumers how to "Milk your budget." And discounter Winners offers "high fashion for low prices." However, these days, even luxury-brand marketers are emphasizing good value. For instance, upscale car brand Infiniti now promises to "make luxury affordable."

Marketers should pay attention to *income distribution* as well as income levels. Canadians in the top 5 percent of wage earners account for approximately 25 percent of the total income earned. According to the 2006 census, the median earnings among the top 20 percent of full-time workers increased over 16 percent, while the median earnings among those in the bottom one-fifth of the distribution fell by over 20 percent. In Canada, the rich are getting richer, the poor are getting poorer and the earnings of the middle class are stagnating. Aboriginal workers also earn significantly less than the average Canadian. In 2005, the median income across all Canadians was $41 400 while the Aboriginal worker earned $25 600. Poverty is widespread among Aboriginal reserves, where education rates are low, unemployment is high, and individual incomes may be as low as $4000 per year. One observer noted, "Reserves, especially in Western Canada, are somewhere between Mexico and Somalia in terms of standard of living. The disparity between the reserves and the rest of Canada is immense. It should be a major embarrassment."[32]

This distribution of income has created a tiered market. Many companies—such as Holt Renfrew and La Maison Simons department stores—aggressively target the affluent. Others—such as Buck or Two and Dollarama stores—target those with more modest means. In fact, such dollar stores are now the fastest-growing retailers in the nation. Still other companies tailor their marketing offers across a range of markets, from the affluent to the less affluent. For example, many high-end fashion designers whose designs sell at sky-high prices to those who can afford it now also sell merchandise at prices that the masses can manage.[33]

> Isaac Mizrahi, a high-end fashion designer, pioneered the "fashion for the masses" trend by offering a line of clothing and accessories at Target. Now, other designers such as Nicole Miller and Stella McCartney are offering less expensive lines at JCPenney and H&M, respectively. And Vera Wang, known for her US$10,000 wedding gowns found in boutiques and high-end retailers such as Bergdorf Goodman, offers a line called "Simply Vera—Vera Wang" at Kohl's. In one fall collection, a Vera Wang gold brocade skirt that is nearly identical to a skirt that fetches US$890 at a high-end department store will sell for US$68 at Kohl's.

Changing Consumer Spending Patterns Food, housing, and transportation use up the most household income. However, consumers at different income levels have different spending patterns. Some of these differences were noted more than a century ago by Ernst Engel, who studied how people shifted their spending as their income rose. He found that as family income rises, the percentage spent on food declines, the percentage spent on housing remains about constant (except for such utilities as gas, electricity, and public services, which decrease), and both the percentage spent on most other categories and that devoted to savings increase. **Engel's laws** generally have been supported by later studies.

Changes in major economic variables such as income, cost of living, interest rates, and savings and borrowing patterns have a large impact on the marketplace. Companies watch these variables by using economic forecasting. Businesses do not have to be wiped out by an economic downturn or caught short in a boom. With adequate warning, they can take advantage of changes in the economic environment.

Engel's laws
Differences noted more than a century ago by Ernst Engel in how people shift their spending across food, housing, transportation, health care, and other goods and services categories as family income rises.

NATURAL ENVIRONMENT (LO3)

The **natural environment** involves the natural resources that are needed as inputs by marketers or that are affected by marketing activities. Environmental concerns have grown steadily during the past three decades. In many cities around the world, air and water pollution have reached dangerous levels. World concern continues to mount about the possibilities of global warming, and many environmentalists fear that we soon will be buried in our own trash.

Marketers should be aware of several trends in the natural environment. The first involves growing *shortages of raw materials*. Air and water may seem to be infinite resources, but some groups see long-run dangers. Air pollution chokes many of the world's large cities; Great Lakes water levels are low, causing problems in many Canadian interior port cities; and water shortages are already a big problem in some parts of the United States and the world. By 2030, more than one in three of the world's human beings will not have enough water to drink.[34] Renewable resources, such as forests and food, also have to be used wisely. Non-renewable resources, such as oil, coal, and various minerals, pose a serious problem. Firms making products that require these scarce resources face large cost increases, even if the materials remain available.

Natural environment
Natural resources that are needed as inputs by marketers or that are affected by marketing activities.

A second environmental trend is *increased pollution*. Industry will almost always damage the quality of the natural environment. Consider the disposal of chemical and nuclear wastes; the dangerous mercury levels in the ocean; the quantity of chemical pollutants in the soil and food supply; and the littering of the environment with non-biodegradable bottles, plastics, and other packaging materials. Not to mention the devastating effects of accidents such as BP's oil spill in the Gulf of Mexico in 2010.

A third trend is *increased government intervention* in natural resource management. The governments of different countries vary in their concern and efforts to promote a clean environment. Some, such as the German government, vigorously pursue environmental quality. Others, especially many poorer nations, do little about pollution, largely because they lack the needed funds or political will. Even the richer nations lack the vast funds and political accord needed to mount a worldwide environmental effort. The general hope is that companies around the world will accept more social responsibility, and that less expensive devices can be found to control and reduce pollution.

The Canadian government passed the *Environmental Protection Act* in 1989. This act established stringent pollution-control measures as well as the means for their enforcement, including fines as high as $1 million if regulations are violated. In the United States, the Environmental Protection Agency (EPA) was created in 1970 to set and enforce pollution standards and to conduct pollution research. In the future, companies doing business in Canada and the United States can expect continued strong controls from government and pressure groups. Instead of opposing regulation, marketers should help develop solutions to the material and energy problems facing the world.

Concern for the natural environment has spawned the so-called green movement. In 2008, the Canadian Standards Association published guidelines for the business community to ensure that their environmental advertising and labelling was not false and misleading.[35] Today, enlightened companies go beyond what government regulations dictate. They are developing strategies and practices that support **environmental sustainability** —an effort to create a world economy that the planet can support indefinitely. They are responding to consumer demands with more environmentally responsible products.

Environmental sustainability
Developing strategies and practices that create a world economy that the planet can support indefinitely.

For example, General Electric is using its "ecomagination" to create products for a better world—cleaner aircraft engines, cleaner locomotives, cleaner fuel technologies. Taken together, for instance, all the GE Energy wind turbines in the world could produce enough power for 2.4 million homes. And in 2005, GE launched its Evolution series locomotives, diesel engines that cut fuel consumption by 5 percent and emissions by 40 percent compared with locomotives built just a year earlier. Up next is a triumph of sheer coolness: a GE hybrid diesel-electric locomotive that, just like a Prius, captures energy from braking and will improve mileage another 10 percent.[36]

Other companies are developing recyclable or biodegradable packaging, recycled materials and components, better pollution controls, and more energy-efficient operations. For example, PepsiCo—which owns businesses ranging from Frito Lay and Pepsi-Cola to Quaker, Gatorade, and Tropicana—is working to dramatically reduce its environmental footprint.

> PepsiCo markets hundreds of products that are grown, produced, and consumed worldwide. Making and distributing these products requires water, electricity, and fuel. In 2007, the company set as its goal to reduce water consumption by 20 percent, electricity consumption by 20 percent, and fuel consumption by 25 percent per unit of production by 2015. It's already well on its way to meeting these goals. For example, a solar-panel field now generates power for three-quarters of the heat used in Frito-Lay's Modesto, California, SunChips plant. A wind turbine now supplies more than two-thirds of the power at PepsiCo's beverage plant in Mamandur, India. On the packaging front, PepsiCo recently introduced new half-litre bottles of its Lipton iced tea, Tropicana juice, Aquafina FlavorSplash, and Aquafina Alive beverages that contain 20 percent less plastic than the original packaging. Aquafina has trimmed the amount of plastic used in its bottles by 35 percent since 2002, saving 50 million pounds of plastic annually.[37]

Companies today are looking to do more than just good deeds. More and more, they are recognizing the link between a healthy ecology and a healthy economy. They are learning that environmentally responsible actions can also be good business.

TECHNOLOGICAL ENVIRONMENT

The **technological environment** is perhaps the most dramatic force now shaping our destiny. Technology has released such wonders as antibiotics, robotic surgery, miniaturized electronics, laptop computers, and the Internet. It also has released such horrors as nuclear missiles, chemical weapons, and assault rifles. It has released such mixed blessings as the automobile, television, and credit cards.

Our attitude toward technology depends on whether we are more impressed with its wonders or its blunders. For example, what would you think about having tiny little transmitters implanted in all of the products you buy that would allow tracking products from their point of production through use and disposal? On the one hand, it would provide many advantages to both buyers and sellers. On the other hand, it could be a bit scary. Either way, it's already happening:[38]

Envision a world in which every product contains a tiny transmitter, loaded with information. As you stroll through the supermarket aisles, shelf sensors detect your selections and beam ads to your shopping cart screen, offering special deals on related products. As your cart fills, scanners detect that you might be buying for a dinner party; the screen suggests a wine to go with the meal you've planned. When you leave the store, exit scanners total up your purchases and automatically charge them to your credit card. At home, readers track what goes into and out of your pantry, updating your shopping list when stocks run low. For Sunday dinner, you pop a Butterball turkey into your "smart oven," which follows instructions from an embedded chip and cooks the bird to perfection.

Seem far-fetched? Not really. In fact, it might soon become a reality, thanks to radio-frequency identification (RFID) transmitters that can be embedded in the products you buy. Beyond benefits to consumers, RFID also gives producers and retailers an amazing new way to track their products electronically—anywhere in the world, anytime, automatically—from factories, to warehouses, to retail shelves, to recycling centers. Many large firms are adding fuel to the RFID fire. For example, Wal-Mart requires all suppliers shipping products to its Sam's Club's distribution centers to apply RFID tags to their pallets. If they don't, it charges $2 a pallet to do it for them. Sam's Club plans to use RFID tags on every pallet, case, and item by the fall of 2010. One study found that by using RFID, Wal-Mart can improve its inventory accuracy by 13 percent, saving millions and millions of dollars a year.

The technological environment changes rapidly. Think of all of today's common products that were not available 100 years ago, or even 30 years ago. John A. Macdonald did not know about automobiles, airplanes, radios, or the electric light. William Lyon Mackenzie King did not know about xerography, synthetic detergents, tape recorders, birth control pills, jet engines, or Earth satellites. John Diefenbaker did not know about personal computers, cellphones, the Internet, or googling.

New technologies create new markets and opportunities. However, every new technology replaces an older technology. Transistors hurt the vacuum-tube industry,

Exhibit 4.9 Environmental sustainability: PepsiCo is working to reduce its environmental footprint. For example, a solar-panel field now generates power for three-quarters of the heat used in Frito-Lay's Modesto, California, SunChips plant. "We're living up to our name."

Technological environment
Forces that create new technologies, creating new product and market opportunities.

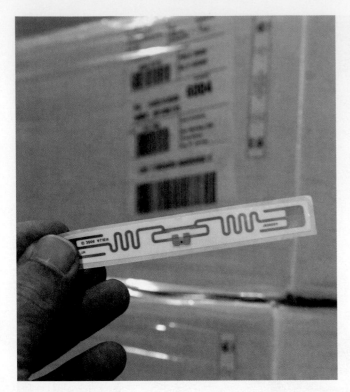

Exhibit 4.10 Technological environment: Envision a world in which every product contains a transmitter loaded with information. In fact, that's not so far-fetched, thanks to radio-frequency identification (RFID).

xerography hurt the carbon-paper business, CDs hurt phonograph records, and digital photography hurt the film business. When old industries fought or ignored new technologies, their businesses declined. Thus, marketers should watch the technological environment closely. Companies that do not keep up will soon find their products outdated. And they will miss new product and market opportunities.

The United States leads the world in R&D spending. Total U.S. R&D spending reached an estimated US$384 billion in 2008.[39] Canada, in comparison, spends approximately $29 billion per year on R&D.[40] Scientists today are researching a wide range of promising new products and services, ranging from practical solar energy, electric cars, paint-on computer and entertainment video displays, and powerful computers that you can wear or fold into your pocket to go-anywhere concentrators that produce drinkable water from the air.

Today's research usually is carried out by research teams rather than by lone inventors such as Thomas Edison or Alexander Graham Bell. Many companies are adding marketing people to R&D teams to try to obtain a stronger marketing orientation. Scientists also speculate on fantasy products, such as flying cars, 3-D televisions, and space colonies. The challenge in each case is not only technical but also commercial—to make *practical, affordable* versions of these products.

As products and technology become more complex, the public needs to know that these are safe. Canada has a complex web of departments and regulations devoted to issues associated with product safety. For example, Agriculture and Agri-Food Canada and the Canadian Food Inspection Agency monitor the safety of food products. The Department of Justice Canada oversees the *Consumer Packaging and Labelling Act*, the *Food and Drug Act*, and the *Hazardous Products Act*. Health Canada also has a food safety and product safety division. Transport Canada governs vehicle recalls. Such regulations have resulted in much higher research costs and in longer times between new-product ideas and their introduction. Marketers should be aware of these regulations when applying new technologies and developing new products.

POLITICAL AND SOCIAL ENVIRONMENT  **LO4**

Political environment

Laws, government agencies, and pressure groups that influence and limit various organizations and individuals in a given society.

Marketing decisions are strongly affected by developments in the political environment. The **political environment** consists of laws, government agencies, and pressure groups that influence or limit various organizations and individuals in a given society.

Legislation Regulating Business Even the most liberal advocates of free-market economies agree that the system works best with at least some regulation. Well-conceived regulation can encourage competition and ensure fair markets for goods and services. Thus, governments develop *public policy* to guide commerce—sets of laws and regulations that limit business for the good of society as a whole. Almost every marketing activity is subject to a wide range of laws and regulations.

INCREASING LEGISLATION Legislation affecting business around the world has increased steadily over the years. Canada has many laws covering issues such as competition, fair trade practices, environmental protection, product safety, truth in advertising, consumer privacy, packaging and labelling, pricing, and other important areas (see Table 4.2). The

TABLE 4.2 Major Federal Legislation Affecting Marketing

The *Competition Act* is a major legislative act affecting the marketing activities of companies in Canada. Specific sections and the relevant areas are as follows:

☐ Section 34: Pricing—Forbids suppliers to charge different prices to competitors purchasing like quantities of goods (price discrimination). Forbids price-cutting that lessens competition (predatory pricing).

☐ Section 36: Pricing and Advertising—Forbids advertising prices that misrepresent the "usual" selling price (misleading price advertising).

☐ Section 38: Pricing—Forbids suppliers to require subsequent resellers to offer products at a stipulated price (resale price maintenance).

☐ Section 33: Mergers—Forbids mergers by which competition is, or is likely to be, lessened to the detriment of the interests of the public.

Other selected acts that have an impact on marketing activities are the following:

☐ *National Trade Mark and True Labelling Act*—Established the term *Canada Standard,* or *CS,* as a national trademark; requires certain commodities to be properly labelled or described in advertising for the purpose of indicating material content or quality.

☐ *Consumer Packaging and Labelling Act*—Provides a set of rules to ensure that full information is disclosed by the manufacturer, packer, or distributor. Requires that all prepackaged products bear the quantity in French and English in metric as well as traditional Canadian standard units of weight, volume, or measure.

☐ *Motor Vehicle Safety Act*—Establishes mandatory safety standards for motor vehicles.

☐ *Food and Drug Act*—Prohibits the advertisement and sale of adulterated or misbranded foods, cosmetics, and drugs.

☐ *Personal Information Protection and Electronic Documents Act*—Establishes rules to govern the collection, use, and disclosure of personal information that recognize the right of privacy of individuals. The law recognizes the needs of organizations to collect, use, or disclose personal information for appropriate purposes. (For full details of the act, see http://laws.justice.gc.ca/en/P-8.6/.)

European Commission has been active in establishing a new framework of laws covering competitive behaviour, product standards, product liability, and commercial transactions for the nations of the European Union.

Understanding the public policy implications of a particular marketing activity is not a simple matter. For example, in Canada, many laws are created at the federal, provincial/territorial, and municipal levels, and these regulations often overlap. Moreover, regulations are constantly changing—what was allowed last year may now be prohibited, and what was prohibited may now be allowed. Marketers must work hard to keep up with changes in regulations and their interpretations.

Business legislation has been enacted for a number of reasons. The first is to *protect companies* from each other. Although business executives may praise competition, they sometimes try to neutralize it when it threatens them. So laws are passed to define and prevent unfair competition.

The second purpose of government regulation is to *protect consumers* from unfair business practices. Some firms, if left alone, would make shoddy products, invade consumer privacy, tell lies in their advertising, and deceive consumers through their packaging and pricing. Unfair business practices have been defined and are enforced by various agencies.

The third purpose of government regulation is to *protect the interests of society* against unrestrained business behaviour. Profitable business activity does not always create a better quality of life. Regulation arises to ensure that firms take responsibility for the social costs of their production or products.

CHANGING GOVERNMENT AGENCY ENFORCEMENT International marketers will encounter dozens, or even hundreds, of agencies set up to enforce trade policies and regulations. In Canada, several federal agencies, such as Health Canada, the Canadian Food Inspection

Agency, Industry Canada, and the Canadian Environmental Assessment Agency, have been established. Because such government agencies have some discretion in enforcing the laws, they can have a major impact on a company's marketing performance.

New laws and their enforcement will continue to increase. Business executives must watch these developments when planning their products and marketing programs. Marketers need to know about the major laws protecting competition, consumers, and society. They need to understand these laws at the local, provincial/territorial, national, and international levels.

INCREASED EMPHASIS ON ETHICS AND SOCIALLY RESPONSIBLE ACTIONS   Written regulations cannot possibly cover all potential marketing abuses, and existing laws are often difficult to enforce. However, beyond written laws and regulations, business is also governed by social codes and rules of professional ethics.

SOCIALLY RESPONSIBLE BEHAVIOUR   Enlightened companies encourage their managers to look beyond what the regulatory system allows and simply "do the right thing." These socially responsible firms actively seek out ways to protect the long-run interests of their consumers and the environment.

The recent rash of business scandals and increased concerns about the environment have created fresh interest in the issues of ethics and social responsibility. Almost every aspect of marketing involves such issues. Unfortunately, because these issues usually involve conflicting interests, well-meaning people can honestly disagree about the right course of action in a given situation. Thus, many industrial and professional trade associations have suggested codes of ethics. And more companies are now developing policies, guidelines, and other responses to complex social responsibility issues.

The boom in Internet marketing has created a new set of social and ethical issues. Critics worry most about online privacy issues. The amount of personal digital data available has exploded. Users, themselves, supply some of it. They voluntarily place highly private information on social networking sites such as Facebook or on genealogy sites, which are easily searched by anyone with a PC.

However, much of the information is systematically developed by businesses seeking to learn more about their customers, often without consumers realizing that they are under the microscope. Legitimate businesses plant cookies on consumers' PCs and collect, analyze, and share digital data from every mouse click consumers make at their websites. Critics are concerned that companies may now know *too* much, and that some companies might use digital data to take unfair advantage of consumers. Although most companies fully disclose their Internet privacy policies, and most work to use data to benefit their customers, abuses do occur. As a result, consumer advocates and policymakers are taking action to protect consumer privacy.

Throughout the text, we present "Marketing@Work" exhibits that summarize the main public policy and social responsibility issues surrounding major marketing decisions. These exhibits discuss the legal issues that marketers should understand and the common ethical and societal concerns that marketers face.

CAUSE-RELATED MARKETING   To exercise their social responsibility and build more positive images, many companies are now linking themselves to worthwhile causes. These days, every product seems to be tied to some cause. Buy a pink mixer from KitchenAid and support breast cancer research. Purchase Ethos water from Starbucks

Exhibit 4.11   Cause-related marketing: Signing up for Virgin Mobile Canada's Common Cents program proves how a few cents can add up to enormous change for worthwhile programs such as RE*Generation, a program developed with Virgin Unite that aims to help at-risk and homeless young people get back on their feet.

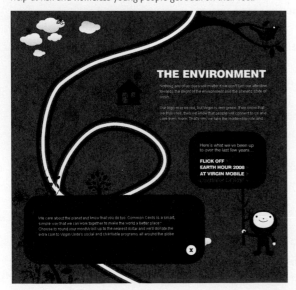

and help bring clean water to children around the world. For every Staples Easy Button you buy, the office supplies retailer will donate a portion to Special Olympics Canada. Sign up for a monthly cellphone package with Virgin Mobile Canada and you can enroll in the Common Cents program. This program rounds up your monthly bill to the nearest dollar and Virgin Mobile donates all proceeds to Virgin Unite, the non-profit foundation of the Virgin Group.

In fact, some companies are founded entirely on cause-related missions. Under the concept of "value-led business" or "caring capitalism," their mission is to use business to make the world a better place. For example, TOMS Shoes was founded as a for-profit company—it wants to make money selling shoes. But the company has an equally important not-for-profit mission—putting shoes on the feet of needy children around the world. For every pair of shoes you buy from TOMS, the company will give another pair to a child in need on your behalf (see Marketing@Work 4.1).

Cause-related marketing has become a primary form of corporate giving. It lets companies "do well by doing good" by linking purchases of the company's products or services with fundraising for worthwhile causes or charitable organizations. Companies now sponsor dozens of cause-related marketing campaigns each year. Many are backed by large budgets and a full complement of marketing activities. For example, consider P&G's "Pantene Beautiful Lengths" campaign, which last year received Cause Marketing Forum's Golden Halo Award for the best cause-related health campaign.[41]

The Pantene Beautiful Lengths campaign has involved a broad-based marketing effort, including a campaign website, public service TV and print ads, and promotional items and events. P&G kicked off the Pantene Beautiful Lengths with celebrity spokeswoman Diane Lane having her hair cut for donations on the *Today Show*. Since then the campaign has generated more than 700 million media impressions in major publications and on TV shows and websites. To date, the campaign has received more than 24 000 donated ponytails and more than 3000 free wigs have been distributed through the American Cancer Society's nationwide network of wig banks. Compare that to the 2000 wigs created over the past 10 years by charity Locks of Love. Pantene Beautiful Lengths has also contributed more than US$1 million to the EIF's Women's Cancer Research Fund, which raises funds and awareness for millions of women and their families affected by cancer.

Cause-related marketing has stirred some controversy. Critics worry that cause-related marketing is more a strategy for selling than a strategy for giving—that "cause-related" marketing is really "cause-exploitative" marketing. Thus, companies using cause-related marketing might find themselves walking a fine line between increased sales and an improved image, and facing charges of exploitation.

However, if handled well, cause-related marketing can greatly benefit both the company and the cause. The company gains an effective marketing tool while building a more positive public image. The charitable organization or cause gains greater visibility and important new sources of funding and support. Spending on cause-related marketing in the United States skyrocketed from only US$120 million in 1990 to more than US$1.57 billion by 2009.[42]

CULTURAL ENVIRONMENT

The **cultural environment** is made up of institutions and other forces that affect a society's basic values, perceptions, preferences, and behaviours. People grow up in a particular society that shapes their basic beliefs and values. They absorb a world view that defines their relationships with others. The following cultural characteristics can affect marketing decision-making.

Cultural environment
Institutions and other forces that affect society's basic values, perceptions, preferences, and behaviours.

MARKETING@WORK 4.1

TOMS Shoes: "*Be* the Change You Want to See in the World"

If the world were a village of 100 people, 14 of the 100 would be illiterate, 20 would be malnourished, 23 would drink polluted water, 25 would have no shelter, 33 would have no electricity, and 40 would have *no shoes*. In 2006, these stark facts, especially the last one, struck Blake Mycoskie up close and personally as he visited Argentina to learn how to play polo, practise his tango, and do some community service work. While there, the sight of barefooted children, too poor to have shoes, stunned him.

So in May 2006, Mycoskie launched TOMS Shoes with $300 000 of his own money. The founding concept was this: For every pair of TOMS shoes that customers bought, the company would donate another pair of shoes to a child in need around the world. Mycoskie had previously started five successful strictly for-profit businesses. "But I was ready to do something more meaningful," says Mycoskie. "I always knew I wanted to help

others. Now, it was time to do something that wasn't just for profit." Mycoskie remembered Mahatma Ghandi's saying: "*Be* the change you want to see in the world."

"Doing good" is an important part of TOMS' mission. But so is "doing well"—the company is very much a for-profit venture. However, at TOMS Shoes, the two missions go hand in hand. Beyond being socially admirable, the buy-one-give-one-away concept is also a good business proposition. In addition to scratching Mycoskie's itch to help people, "the timing was perfect for consumers, too," he says. "With the rise of social and eco-consciousness and the economy in a downturn, people were looking for innovative and affordable ways to make the world a better place."

With all of these "do good" and "do well" goals swirling in his head, Mycoskie returned home from his Argentina trip, hired an intern, and set about making 250

pairs of shoes in the loft of his Santa Monica, California, home. Stuffing the shoes into three duffel bags, he made the fledgling company's first "Shoe Drop" tour, returning to the Argentine village and giving one pair of shoes to each child. Mycoskie arrived back home to find an article about his project on the front page of the *Los Angeles Times* Calendar section. TOMS had been in business for only two weeks, but by that very afternoon, he had orders on his website for 2200 pairs of shoes.

By October 2006, TOMS had sold 10 000 pairs of shoes. True to the company's one-for-one promise, Mycoskie undertook a second TOMS Shoe Drop tour. Consistent with his new title, chief shoe giver of TOMS Shoes, Mycoskie led 15 employees and volunteers back to Argentina, where they went from school to school, village to village, and gave away another 10 000 pairs of shoes.

Exhibit 4.12   Cause-related marketing: TOMS pledges "No complicated formulas, it's simple ... you buy a pair of TOMS and we give a pair to a child on your behalf."

"We don't just drop the shoes off, as the name might imply," says Mycoskie. "We place the shoes on each child's feet so that we can establish a connection, which is such an important part of our brand. We want to give the children the feeling of love, and warmth, and experience. But *we* also get those feelings as we give the shoes."

The one-for-one idea caught fire. As word spread about TOMS, a non-profit organization called "Friends of Toms" formed to "create avenues for individuals to volunteer and experience [the TOMS] mission," participate in Shoe Drops, and "perform good works in their own communities and their own lives." *Vogue* magazine and other major publications ran stories on the company's philosophy and good works. In November 2007, 40 TOMS employees and volunteers embarked on the third Shoe Drop, travelling to South Africa to place shoes on the feet of 50 000 more children.

Next, TOMS Shoes turned its attention to Ethiopia, where 11 million people are at risk for podoconiosis, a disease often caused by silica in volcanic soils. Children's bare feet absorb the silica, which can cause elephantitis, severe swelling of the legs and feet. The disease progresses until surgery is required. The simple preventative cure? Shoes. As part of the Christmas season 2008, TOMS offered gift card packages, which included a certificate for a pair of shoes and a DVD telling the TOMS story. The goal was to give 30 000 pairs of shoes to Ethiopian children in 30 days.

TOMS has also focused on needy children in the United States, stepping in to help children whose families are still recovering from Hurricane Katrina in Louisiana. Also in the United States, TOMS started a grassroots marketing movement called "TOMS Vagabonds." These travelling groups of TOMS disciples hit the road in vans full of TOMS shoes and help to organize events on college and school campuses and in communities all around the country. The Vagabonds' goal is to raise awareness about TOMS, sell shoes, and inspire more people to get involved with the company's movement. The Vagabonds chronicle their travels on TOMS Facebook page (www.facebook.com/TOMSVagabonds), blog (www.tomsshoesblog.com), and Twitter site (http://twitter.com/tomsshoes).

With sales in excess of US$8 million, the company is profitable and growing exponentially. As of April 2010, TOMS had sold (and therefore given away) more than 600 000 pairs of shoes. Retailers such as Nordstrom, Urban Outfitters, and even Whole Foods are now offering TOMS in more than 400 U.S. outlets. In fact, Whole Foods is the company's biggest customer.

TOMS' rapid growth is the result of purchases by caring customers who then tell the TOMS story to their friends. Whereas the typical shoe company spends about 20 percent of sales on traditional advertising and promotion, TOMS hasn't spent a single dollar on it. It hasn't had to. "Ultimately, it is our customers who drive our success," says Mycoskie. "Giving not only makes you feel good, but it actually is

a very good business strategy, especially in this day and age. Your customers become your marketers."

Moreover, as TOMS' success shows, consumers like to feel good. A recent global study found that 71 percent of consumers said that despite the recession they had given just as much time and money to causes they deemed worthy. Fifty-five percent of respondents also indicated they would pay more for a brand if it supported a good cause.

TOMS Shoes is a great example of cause-related marketing—of "doing well by doing good." Mycoskie hopes that his company will inspire people to think differently about business. "My thinking was that TOMS would show that entrepreneurs no longer had to choose between earning money or making a difference in the world," he says. "Business and charity or public service don't have to be mutually exclusive. In fact, when they come together, they can be very powerful."

Sources: Quotes and other information from Stacy Perman, "Making a Do-Gooder's Business Model Work," *BusinessWeek Online*, January 26, 2009, accessed at www.businessweek.com/smallbiz/content/jan2009/sb20090123_264702.htm; Blake Mycoskie, "Shoes for a Better Tomorrow," presentation made March 13, 2009, accessed at www.clintonschoolspeakers.com/lecture/view/toms-shoes-better-tomorrow. Also see Michael Bush, "Consumers Continue to Stand by Their Causes During Downturn," *Advertising Age*, November 17, 2008, p. 4; "TOMS Shoes," *Obesity, Fitness & Wellness Week*, December 13, 2008, p. 2937; Patricia Sellers, "Be the Change You Want To See in the World," HuffingtonPost.com, October 11, 2008; and information found at www.tomsshoes.com and http://friendsoftoms.org/, accessed November 2009.

Persistence of Cultural Values   People in a given society hold many beliefs and values. Their core beliefs and values have a high degree of persistence. For example, many Canadians believe in cultural diversity (versus assimilation), respect for human rights, democracy, gender equality, stability of government, the rule of law, sustainable development, social support for the underprivileged, universal health care, a love of nature, hard work, getting married, giving to charity, and being honest.[43] These beliefs shape more specific attitudes and behaviours found in everyday life. *Core* beliefs and values are passed on from parents to children and are reinforced by schools, churches, business, and government.

Secondary beliefs and values are more open to change. Believing in marriage is a core belief; believing that people should get married early in life is a secondary belief. Marketers have some chance of changing secondary values but little chance of changing core values. For example, family-planning marketers could argue more effectively that people should get married later than not get married at all.

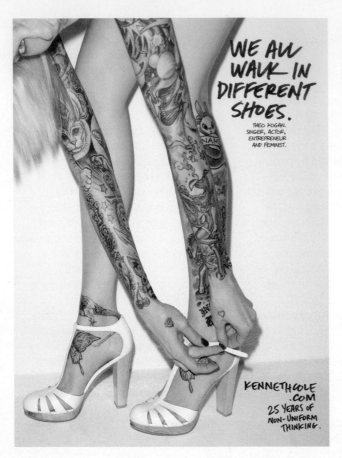

WE ALL
WALK IN
DIFFERENT
SHOES.
THEO KOGAN.
SINGER, ACTOR,
ENTREPRENEUR
AND FEMNIST.

KENNETHCOLE
.COM
25 YEARS OF
NON-UNIFORM
THINKING.

Exhibit 4.13 People's self-views: In its ads, Kenneth Cole targets fashion individualists. "25 years of non-uniform thinking."

Shifts in Secondary Cultural Values   Although core values are fairly persistent, cultural swings do take place. Consider the impact of popular music groups, movie personalities, and other celebrities on young people's hairstyling and clothing norms. Marketers want to predict cultural shifts to spot new opportunities or threats. Several firms offer "futures" forecasts in this connection. For example, the Yankelovich MONITOR has tracked consumer value trends for years. Its annual State of the Consumer report analyzes and interprets the forces that shape consumers' lifestyles and their marketplace interactions. The major cultural values of a society are expressed in people's views of themselves and others, as well as in their views of organizations, society, nature, and the universe.

PEOPLE'S VIEWS OF THEMSELVES   People vary in their emphasis on serving themselves versus serving others. Some people seek personal pleasure, wanting fun, change, and escape. Others seek self-realization through religion, recreation, or the avid pursuit of careers or other life goals. Some people see themselves as sharers and joiners; others see themselves as individualists. People use products, brands, and services as a means of self-expression, and they buy products and services that match their views of themselves.

Marketers can target their products and services based on such self-views. For example, TOMS Shoes appeals to people who see themselves as part of the broader world community. In contrast, Kenneth Cole shoes appeal to fashion individualists. In its ads, the company declares, "We all walk in different shoes," asserting that Kenneth Cole represents "25 years of non-uniform thinking."

PEOPLE'S VIEWS OF OTHERS   In past decades, observers have noted several shifts in people's attitudes toward others. Recently, for example, many trend trackers have seen a new wave of "cocooning" or "nesting." In part because of the downturn in the economy, people are going out less with others and are staying home more. One observer calls it "Cocooning 2.0," in which people are "newly intent on the simple pleasures of hearth and home." Says another, "The instability of the economy ... creates uncertainty for consumers, and this uncertainty tends to make them focus more on being home and finding ways to save money. It's a return to more traditional values, like home-cooked meals."[44]

The trend toward more cocooning suggests less demand for theatre-going, travel, eating out, and new cars but greater demand for homemade meals, home projects, and home entertainment products. For example, during the past holiday season, sales increased at craft stores such as Michaels as more people turned to saving money by making homemade holiday gifts. "Across the country, people are crafting more," says a spokesperson for the Craft & Hobby Association. "With the [recent] recession, people are looking for ways to save money, and doctors are recommending it as a major form of stress relief."[45]

The faltering economy and increased nesting also gave a boost to home appliances such as high-end coffee makers and big-screen TVs. Consumer electronics chain Best Buy even ran an ad that cast the purchase of a 60-inch flat-screen HDTV not as self-indulgence, but as an act of loving sacrifice and a practical alternative to other forms of entertainment.[46]

In the ad, after a man sells his football season tickets to pay for the wedding, his grateful bride surprises him with a huge set so he can still watch the big game. A kindly salesman sums it up this way: "Another love story at Best Buy with a 60-inch TV in the middle." Says a Samsung marketer, "People still have to live their lives. Even in a tough economy, people may not spring for that 61-inch [TV], but they may get a 42-inch HDTV because they're home and they're with their families and they'll spend $5 on a movie rental, versus $40 for the theatre and $80 for dinner."

PEOPLE'S VIEWS OF ORGANIZATIONS   People vary in their attitudes toward corporations, government agencies, trade unions, universities, and other organizations. By and large, people are willing to work for major organizations and expect them, in turn, to carry out society's work.

The past two decades have seen a sharp decrease in confidence in and loyalty toward business and political organizations and institutions. In the workplace, there has been an overall decline in organizational loyalty. Waves of company downsizings bred cynicism and distrust. In just the last decade, rounds of layoffs resulting from the recent recession; corporate scandals at Enron, WorldCom, and Tyco; the financial meltdown triggered by Wall Street bankers' greed and incompetence; and other unsettling activities have resulted in a further loss of confidence in big business. Many people today see work not as a source of satisfaction but as a required chore to earn money to enjoy their non-work hours. This trend suggests that organizations need to find new ways to win consumer and employee confidence.

PEOPLE'S VIEWS OF SOCIETY   People vary in their attitudes toward their society—nationalists defend it, reformers want to change it, malcontents want to leave it. People's orientation to their society influences their consumption patterns and attitudes toward the marketplace. For example, more and more Canadians have a sense of national pride. Some companies, such as Zellers, responded with "made-in-Canada" themes and promotions. Others, such as Petro-Canada, Clearly Canadian, Molson Canadian, and Upper Canada Brewing Company, made national identity part of their branding strategy.

Exhibit 4.14   Recent economic woes have contributed to a new wave of "cocooning" or "nesting." Best Buy ran an ad selling big-screen TVs as an alternative to more expensive forms of out-of-home entertainment.

Marketers respond with patriotic products and promotions, offering everything from floral bouquets to clothing with patriotic themes. Although most of these marketing efforts are tasteful and well received, waving the flag can prove tricky. Except in cases where companies tie product sales to charitable contributions, such flag-waving promotions can be viewed as attempts to cash in on triumph or tragedy. Marketers must take care when responding to such strong national emotions.

PEOPLE'S VIEWS OF NATURE   People vary in their attitudes toward the natural world— some feel ruled by it, others feel in harmony with it, and still others seek to master it. A long-term trend has been people's growing mastery over nature through technology and the belief that nature is bountiful. More recently, however, people have recognized that nature is finite and fragile, that it can be destroyed or spoiled by human activities.

This renewed love of things natural has created a 63-million-person "lifestyles of health and sustainability" (LOHAS) market, consumers who seek out everything from natural, organic, and nutritional products to fuel-efficient cars and alternative medicine. This segment spends nearly US$215 billion annually on such products. In the words of one such consumer,[47]

It's green.

even before it's green.

Our organic greens show their true colors long before they begin to peek through the soil. We raise our crops without harmful chemicals, in healthy soil that supports strong, nutrient-rich plants. Sure, organic farming can be more challenging in the short term, but the reward is delicious organic produce and a healthy planet. That's something we can all feel good about.

Get our new Pocket Guide to Choosing Organic at www.ebfarm.com.

Earthbound Farm. ORGANIC
Food to live by.

Exhibit 4.15   Riding the trend toward all things natural, Earthbound Farm has grown to become the world's largest producer of organic salads, fruits, and vegetables, with products in 75 percent of North America's supermarkets.

I am not an early adopter, a fast follower, or a mass-market stampeder. But I am a gas-conscious driver. So that's why I was standing in a Toyota dealership ... this week, the latest person to check out a hybrid car. Who needs $40 fill-ups? After tooling around in three different hybrid car brands— Toyota, Honda, and a Ford—I thought, How cool could this be? Saving gas money and doing well by the environment. Turns out there's a whole trend-watchers' classification for people who think like that: LOHAS. Lifestyles of Health and Sustainability. Buy a hybrid. Shop at places like Planet Organic Market. No skin off our noses. Conscientious shopping with no sacrifice or hippie stigma.

Many marketers are now tracking and responding to such cultural trends. For example, Wal-Mart recently developed a Live Better Index by which it tracks the attitudes of its more than 200 million annual shoppers. The Live Better Index tracks consumers' decisions regarding eco-friendly products such as compact fluorescent light bulbs, organic milk, and concentrated liquid laundry detergents in reduced packaging. The index shows that 11 percent of North Americans now consider themselves to be converts to more sustainable living and that 43 percent say they will be "extremely green" within the next five years.[48]

Food producers have also found fast-growing markets for natural and organic products. Consider Earthbound Farm, a company that grows and sells organic produce. It started in 1984 as a 2.5-acre raspberry farm in California's Carmel Valley. Founders Drew and Myra Goodman wanted to do the right thing by farming the land organically and producing food they'd feel good about serving to their family, friends, and neighbours. Today, Earthbound Farm has grown to become the world's largest producer of organic vegetables, with 33 000 acres under plow, annual sales of US$480 million, and products available in 75 percent of North America's supermarkets.[49]

In total, the North American organic-food market generated US$25 billion in sales last year, more than doubling over the past five years. Niche marketers, such as Planet Organic Market, have sprung up to serve this market, and traditional food chains such as Superstore and Sobeys have added separate natural and organic food sections. Even pet owners are joining the movement as they become more aware of what goes into Fido's food. Almost every major pet food brand now offers several types of natural foods.[50]

PEOPLE'S VIEWS OF THE UNIVERSE Finally, people vary in their beliefs about the origin of the universe and their place in it. Although many Canadians have religious beliefs, attendance at religious services has been dropping gradually through the years. A recent Statistics Canada survey shows Canadians' continuing slide out the doors of the country's churches, temples, and synagogues. In 1946, 67 percent of adult Canadians regularly attended religious services, but by 2001, the figure had dropped to 20 percent. Yann Martel, Canadian author of the acclaimed *Life of Pi*, noted in an interview that Canadians and Americans are going in opposite directions with regard to religion. "America is a very religious, almost puritanical country. In Canada, secularism is triumphant, and to talk noncynically, nonironically about religion is strange," he says. Only 30 percent of Canadians report that religion is very important to them, compared with 59 percent of Americans. The statistics would be even more skewed if it were not for the growing number of devout Muslim, Sikh, and Hindu immigrants now living in Canada. Canadian marketers have to use caution when picking up lifestyle ads from the United States. While showing people in religious settings may draw attention from American consumers, they may strike Canadians as inappropriate.[51]

RESPONDING TO THE MARKETING ENVIRONMENT **LO5**

Someone once observed, "There are three kinds of companies: those who make things happen, those who watch things happen, and those who wonder what's happened."[52] Many companies view the marketing environment as an uncontrollable element to which they must react and adapt. They passively accept the marketing environment and do not try to change it. They analyze the environmental forces and design strategies that will help the company avoid the threats and take advantage of the opportunities the environment provides.

Other companies take a *proactive* stance toward the marketing environment. Rather than simply watching and reacting, these firms take aggressive actions to affect the publics and forces in their marketing environment. Such companies hire lobbyists to influence legislation affecting their industries and stage media events to gain favourable press coverage. They run "advertorials" (ads expressing editorial points of view) to shape public opinion. They press lawsuits and file complaints with regulators to keep competitors in line, and they form contractual agreements to better control their distribution channels.

By taking action, companies can often overcome seemingly uncontrollable environmental events. For example, whereas some companies view the ceaseless online rumour mill as something over which they have no control, others work proactively to prevent or counter negative word of mouth. Tim Hortons had to deal with a persistent and potentially damaging rumour when it started to spread by email:[53]

> We've all heard the rumour—Tim Hortons coffee is so addictive it must contain nicotine (or MSG). This rumour began circulating via word of mouth several years ago, but it erupted in e-mail form in 2006. The bogus e-mail alleged that a man from Arkansas came up to Canada and suffered cardiac arrest. He was allergic to Nicotine. After asking Tim Hortons what was in their coffee and threatening legal action when they refused to divulge, the company supposedly admitted to adding nicotine to the coffee. The e-mail also alleged that a girl on a nicotine patch was diagnosed with nicotine overload because, even though she had quit smoking, she had not given up her daily coffee from Tim Hortons. The company was quick to respond to this false allegation and even addresses the question on the FAQ page of their corporate website, stating "Tim Hortons would like to clearly state that there is absolutely NO nicotine or MSG in our coffee. Tim Hortons coffee has NO ADDITIVES whatsoever." In fact, all their products must pass independent testing by the Canadian Food Inspection Agency, so additives of any kind in their coffee would just not be possible. Still, the rumour persists and Tim Hortons must continue to proactively manage this type of negative word of mouth.

Marketing management cannot always control environmental forces. In many cases, it must settle for simply watching and reacting to the environment. For example, a company would have little success trying to influence geographic population shifts, the economic environment, or major cultural values. But whenever possible, smart marketing managers will take a *proactive* rather than *reactive* approach to the marketing environment (see Marketing@Work 4.2).

MARKETING@WORK 4.2

YourCompanySucks.com

The Internet has been hailed by marketers as the great new relational medium. Companies use the Web to engage customers, gain insights into their needs, and create customer community. In turn, Web-empowered consumers share their brand experiences with companies and with each other. All of this back-and-forth helps both the company and its customers. But sometimes, the dialogue can get nasty. Consider the following examples:

MSN Money columnist Scott Burns accuses Home Depot of being a "consistent abuser" of customers' time. Within hours, MSN's servers are caving under the weight of 14,000 blistering e-mails and posts from angry Home Depot customers who storm the MSN comment room, taking the company to task for pretty much everything. It is the biggest response in MSN Money's history.

Blogger Jeff Jarvis posts a series of irate messages to his BuzzMachine blog about the many failings of his Dell computer and his struggles with Dell's customer support. The post quickly draws national attention, and an open letter posted by Jarvis to Dell founder Michael Dell becomes the third most linked-to post on the blogosphere the day after it appears. Jarvis's headline—Dell Hell—becomes shorthand for the ability of a lone blogger to deliver a body blow to an unsuspecting business.

Systems engineer Michael Whitford wakes up one morning to find that his favourite-ever laptop, an Apple Macbook, still under warranty, has "decided not to work." Whitford takes the machine to his local Apple store, where the counter person obligingly sends it off for repairs. However, Whitford later gets a call from an Apple Care representative, who claims that the laptop has "spill damage" not covered by the warranty and says that repairs will cost him $774. "I did not spill anything on my laptop," declares Whitford. "Too bad," says the Apple rep, and the Macbook is returned unrepaired. But that's not the end of the story—far from it. A short time later, Whitford posts a video on YouTube (www.youtube.com/watch?v=hHbrQqrgVgg). In the video, a seemingly rational Whitford calmly selects among a golf club, an axe, and a sword before finally deciding on a sledgehammer as his weapon of choice for bashing his nonfunctioning Macbook to smithereens. More than 475,000 people have viewed the smash-up on YouTube and the video has been passed along on countless blogs and other Web sites.

Extreme events? Not anymore. "Web 2.0" has turned the traditional power relationship between businesses and consumers upside-down. In the good old days, disgruntled consumers could do little more than bellow at a company service rep or shout out their complaints from a street corner. Now, armed with only a PC and a broadband connection, they can take it public, airing their gripes to millions on blogs, chats, online communities, or even hate sites devoted exclusively to their least-favourite corporations.

"I hate" and "sucks" sites are becoming almost commonplace. These sites target some highly respected companies with some highly *dis*respectful labels: PayPalSucks.com (a.k.a. NoPayPal); WalMart-blows.com; Microsucks.com; NorthWorstAir.org (Northwest Airlines); AmexSux.com (American Express); IHateStarbucks.com; DeltaREALLYsucks.com; and UnitedPackageSmashers.com (UPS), to name only a few.

Some of these sites and other Web attacks air legitimate complaints that should be addressed. Others, however, are little more than anonymous, vindictive slurs that unfairly ransack brands and corporate reputations. Some of the attacks are only a passing nuisance; others can draw serious attention and create real headaches.

How should companies react to Web attacks? The real quandary for targeted companies is figuring out how far they can go to protect their images without fuelling the already raging fire. One point upon which all experts seem to agree: Don't try to retaliate in kind. "It's rarely a good idea to lob bombs at the fire starters," says one analyst. "Preemption, engagement, and diplomacy are saner tools."

Some companies have tried to silence the critics through lawsuits but few have

Exhibit 4.16   Today, armed only with a PC and a broadband connection, the little guy can take it public against corporate America. By listening and proactively responding to such seemingly uncontrollable environmental events, companies can prevent the negatives from spiralling out of control or can even turn them into positives.

succeeded. The courts have tended to regard such criticism as opinion and therefore as protected speech. Given the difficulties of trying to sue consumer online criticisms out of existence, some companies have tried other strategies. For example, most big companies now routinely buy up Web addresses for their firm names preceded by the words "I hate" or followed by "sucks.com." But this approach is easily thwarted, as Wal-Mart learned when it registered IHateWalmart.com, only to find that someone else then registered IReallyHateWalmart.com.

In general, attempts to block, counterattack, or shut down consumer attacks may be short-sighted. Such criticisms are often based on real consumer concerns and unresolved anger. Hence, the best strategy might be to proactively monitor these sites and respond to the concerns they express. "The most obvious thing to do is talk to the customer and try to deal with the problem, instead of putting your fingers in your ears," advises one consultant.

For example, Home Depot CEO Francis Blake drew praise when he heeded the criticisms expressed in the MSN Money onslaught and responded positively. Blake posted a heartfelt letter in which he thanked critic Scott Burns, apologized to angry customers, and promised to make things better. And within a month of the YouTube video, Apple fessed up to its misdeeds and replaced Michael Whitford's laptop. "I'm very happy now," says Whitford. "Apple has regained my loyalty. I guess I finally got their attention."

Many companies have now set up teams of specialists that monitor Web conversations and engage disgruntled consumers. In the years since the Dell Hell incident, Dell has set up a 40-member "communities and conversation team," which does outreach on Twitter and communicates with bloggers. Southwest Airlines' social media team "includes a chief Twitter officer who tracks Twitter comments and monitors Facebook groups, an online representative who checks facts and interacts with bloggers, and another person who takes charge of the company's presence on sites such as YouTube, Flickr, and LinkedIn. So if someone posts a complaint in cyberspace, the company can respond in a personal way."

Thus, by listening and proactively responding to seemingly uncontrollable events in the environment, companies can prevent the negatives from spiralling out of control or can even turn them into positives. Who knows? With the right responses, WalMart-blows.com might even become WalMart-rules.com. Then again, probably not.

Sources: Quotes, excerpts, and other information from Michelle Conlin, "Web Attack," *BusinessWeek,* April 16, 2007, pp. 54–56; "Top 10 Service Complaint Sites," *Time Out New York,* March 8, 2007, accessed at www.timeout.com; Jena McGregor, "Consumer Vigilantes," *BusinessWeek,* March 3, 2008, p. 38; Christopher L. Martin and Nathan Bennett, "Corporate Reputation; What to Do About Online Attacks," *Wall Street Journal,* March 10, 2008, p. R6; Carolyn Y. Johnson, "Hurry Up, the Customer Has a Complaint," *Boston Globe,* July 7, 2008; and "Corporate Hate Sites," New Media Institute, at www.newmedia.org/categories/Hot-Topics-&-Issues/Corporate-Hate-Sites/, accessed April 2009.

WHEN THE ONLY ENVIRONMENT THAT MATTERS IS THE WEATHER

It might seem intuitive to many people that Canada Goose would see its sales decline during the recent recession; however, Canada Goose actually saw sales double in the two years following the economic downturn.

Economic forces in a recession often lead to losses in the manufacturing sector. Canadians, and particularly those in southwestern Ontario, are quite familiar with seeing manufacturing jobs go offshore. Perhaps because Canada Goose is the only Canadian outdoor gear manufacturer to manufacture domestically, the public has reacted favourably to its domestic, pro-Canada manufacturing agenda.

Canada's population is gradually aging, and the Baby Boomers are beginning to retire. Could this be creating a more favourable marketplace for Canada Goose? It is not perfectly clear. Canada Goose's core demographic was previously considered to be affluent adults ages 34 to 50, but now it is seeing its brand sported by many individuals outside of this demographic, particularly the age 16-to-34 segment.

One could surmise that the prevailing social and cultural trend of "investment clothing" is helping Canada Goose gain customers. Or perhaps increasing consumer concern about environmental causes is helping Canada Goose, as its brand is associated with social awareness and sustainability.

Today, many consumers have brand fatigue. They want authentic brands that deliver what they promise, brands that are not simply trying to encourage spending. Of course, no matter what happens in the environmental forces that surround the company marketplace, Canada Goose knows that it needs to remain vigilant in its marketing strategy.

QUESTIONS

1. What environmental forces do you think Canada Goose has been most responsive to?
2. What environmental forces do you think could hurt Canada Goose in the future?
3. Consider your generation: Do you think you view clothing brands differently than your parents did? Give examples.
4. What legal factors could affect Canada Goose's future sales? How so?

REVIEWING THE CONCEPTS

1. Describe the environmental forces that affect the company's ability to serve its customers.

The company's *microenvironment* consists of other actors close to the company that combine to form the company's value delivery network or that affect its ability to serve its customers. It includes the company's *internal environment*—its several departments and management levels—as it influences marketing decision-making. *Marketing channel firms*—suppliers and marketing intermediaries, including resellers, physical distribution firms, marketing services agencies, and financial intermediaries—co-operate to create customer value. Five types of customer *markets* include consumer, business, reseller, government, and international markets. *Competitors* vie with the company in an effort to serve customers better. Finally, various *publics* have an actual or potential interest in or impact on the company's ability to meet its objectives.

The *macroenvironment* consists of larger societal forces that affect the entire microenvironment. The six forces making up the company's macroenvironment include demographic, economic, natural, technological, political, and cultural forces. These forces shape opportunities and pose threats to the company.

2. Explain how changes in the demographic and economic environments affect marketing decisions.

Demography is the study of the characteristics of human populations. Today's *demographic environment* shows a changing age structure, shifting family profiles, geographic population shifts, a better-educated and more white-collar population, and increasing diversity. The *economic environment* consists of factors that affect buying power and patterns. The economic environment is characterized by more consumer concern for value and shifting consumer spending patterns. Today's squeezed consumers are seeking greater value—just the right combination of good quality and service at a fair price. The distribution of income also is shifting. The rich have grown richer, the middle class has shrunk, and the poor have remained poor, leading to a two-tiered market.

3. Identify the major trends in the firm's natural and technological environments.

The *natural environment* shows three major trends: shortages of certain raw materials, higher pollution levels, and more government intervention in natural resource management. Environmental concerns create marketing opportunities for alert companies. The *technological environment* creates both opportunities and challenges. Companies that fail to keep up with technological change will miss out on new product and marketing opportunities.

4. Explain the key changes in the political and cultural environments.

The *political environment* consists of laws, agencies, and groups that influence or limit marketing actions. The political environment has undergone three changes that affect marketing worldwide: increasing legislation regulating business, strong government agency enforcement, and greater emphasis on ethics and socially responsible actions. The *cultural environment* is made up of institutions and forces that affect a society's values, perceptions, preferences, and behaviours. The environment shows trends toward "cocooning," a lessening trust of institutions, increasing patriotism, greater appreciation for nature, a changing spiritualism, and the search for more meaningful and enduring values.

5. Discuss how companies can react to the marketing environment.

Companies can passively accept the marketing environment as an uncontrollable element to which they must as they arise. Or they can take a *proactive* stance, working to change the environment rather than simply reacting to it. Whenever possible, companies should try to be proactive rather than reactive.

KEY TERMS

TALK ABOUT MARKETING

1. An important macroenvironmental force on companies is the social/cultural environment, particularly in international markets. In a small group, select a country and discuss at least three elements of the cultural environment that differ from that in Canada and how they impact companies doing business in that culture.

2. The current economic crisis has been difficult for both consumers and companies. However, Tim Hortons has managed to pose record profits and sustainable growth over the past few years. Visit the company website at www.timhortons.com and review its latest annual report. What strategies have enabled Tim Hortons to continue to be successful?

3. What marketing strategies should the makers of luxury products use during tough economic times? Provide an example of one luxury brand that you think has handled the economic crisis well.

4. Are age cohorts (Millennials, Gen X, Baby Boomers) a good demographic variable to use when segmenting the marketplace? Why or why not? For what product categories might age be an important segmentation variable? For what product categories might age be less important?

5. In April 2009, the Canadian government introduced anti-spam legislation, the *Electronic Commerce Protection Act* (ECPA). Visit www.ic.gc.ca/eic/site/ic1.nsf/eng/04595.html and read about this new act. Discuss the implications for electronic commerce in Canada.

6. Cause-related marketing has grown considerably over the past 10 years. Visit www.causemarketingforum.com to learn about companies that have won Halo Awards for outstanding cause-related marketing programs. Present an award-winning case study to your class.

THINK LIKE A MARKETING MANAGER

Customer loyalty for online travel companies is low because the average consumer checks three different travel websites for the best prices on air travel, hotels, and rental cars before booking. With consumers highly motivated to make their selections based on price, online travel companies are trying to figure out other ways to differentiate themselves from the competition.

QUESTIONS

1. What current macroenvironmental forces do you think are having the greatest positive and negative impact on online travel companies?

2. How can online travel companies address the negative influences of the macroenvironment?

3. How can they take advantage of the positive influences of the macroenvironment?

4. What do you think will be the most significant environmental issues facing the online travel industry in the next five years?

MARKETING ETHICS

You've probably heard of heart procedures, such as angioplasty and stents, that are routinely performed on adults. But such heart procedures, devices, and related medications are not available for infants and children, despite the fact that almost 40 000 children a year are born in the United States with heart defects that oftentimes require repair. This is a life or death situation for many young patients, yet doctors must improvise by using devices designed and tested on adults. For instance, doctors use an adult kidney balloon on an infant's heart because it is the appropriate size for a newborn's aortic valve. However, this device is not approved for the procedure. Why are specific devices and medicines developed for the multibillion-dollar cardiovascular market not also designed for kids? It's a matter of economics—this segment of young consumers is just too small. One leading cardiologist attributed the discrepancy to a "profitability gap" between the children's market and the much more profitable adult market for treating heart disease. While not supplying this market might make good economic sense for companies, it is of little comfort to the parents of these small patients.

QUESTIONS

1. Discuss the environmental forces acting on medical devices and pharmaceuticals companies that are preventing them from meeting the needs of the infant and child market segment. Is it wrong for these companies to not address the needs of this segment?
2. Suggest some solutions to this problem.

MARKETING TECHNOLOGY

If you thought that getting 50 miles per gallon (4.7L/100 km) driving a Toyota Prius hybrid was good, how about 230 miles per gallon (1L/100 km)? Or 367 miles per gallon (0.64L/100 km)? Well, you are about to see a new breed of automobiles from big and small automakers touting this level of performance. In 2010, there was GM's Volt and Nissan's Leaf, but there will also be offerings from unknown start-ups such as V-Vehicle, a California-based electric car company backed by billionaire T. Boone Pickens. These automobiles range from hybrids—a combination of gas and electric—to all-electric vehicles. This level of performance comes at a high price, however. Although U.S. consumers will receive an expected US$7500 tax credit for purchasing one of these cars, the Volt's expected US$40 000 price tag will still cause sticker shock. Also, the lack of public recharging stations poses a significant challenge, especially for all-electric vehicles such as the Leaf, which needs recharging approximately every 100 miles (160 km). And some might question the efficiency claims, especially since the Environmental Protection Agency is still finalizing the methodology that factors in electricity used when making miles-per-gallon equivalency claims.

QUESTIONS

1. What factors in the marketing environment present opportunities or threats to automakers?
2. Will it be possible for a start-up automaker such as V-Vehicle to compete with big automakers such as Ford, GM, Chrysler, Toyota, Honda, Nissan, Volvo, Hyundai, BMW, and Mercedes? What factors in the marketing environment will enable or inhibit new competitors?

MARKETING BY THE NUMBERS

Many marketing decisions boil down to numbers. An important question is this: What is the market sales potential in a given segment? If the sales potential in a market is not large enough to warrant pursing that market, then companies will not offer products and services to that market, even though a need may exist. Consider the market segment of infants and children discussed in the preceding section on Marketing Ethics. Certainly there is a need for medical products to save children's lives. Still, companies are not pursuing this market.

QUESTIONS

1. Using the chain ratio method described in Appendix 3: Marketing by the Numbers, estimate the market sales potential for heart catheterization products to meet the needs of the infant and child segment. Assume that of the 40 000 children with heart defects each year, 60 percent will benefit from these types of products and that only 50 percent of their families have the financial resources to obtain such treatment. Also assume the average price for a device is $1000.

2. Research the medical devices market and compare the market potential you estimated to the sales of various devices. Are companies justified in not pursuing the infant and child segment?

VIDEO CASE

Visit MyMarketingLab at www.pearsoned.ca/mymarketinglab to view the video for this chapter.

TOMS SHOES

"Get involved: Changing a life begins with a single step." This sounds like a mandate from a non-profit volunteer organization. But in fact, this motto is for a for-profit shoe company located in Santa Monica, California. In 2006, Blake Mycoskie founded TOMS Shoes because he wanted to do something different. He wanted to run a company that would make a profit while at the same time helping the needy of the world.

Specifically, for every pair of shoes that TOMS sells, it gives a pair of shoes to a needy child somewhere in the world. So far, the company has given away tens of thousands of pairs of shoes and is on track to give away hundreds of thousands. Can TOMS succeed and thrive based on this idealistic concept? That all depends on how TOMS executes its strategy within the constantly changing marketing environment.

After viewing the video featuring TOMS Shoes, answer the following questions about the marketing environment.

QUESTIONS

1. What trends in the marketing environment have contributed to the success of TOMS Shoes?

2. Did TOMS Shoes first scan the marketing environment in creating its strategy, or did it create its strategy and fit the strategy to the environment? Does this matter?

3. Is TOMS' strategy more about serving needy children or creating value for customers? Explain.

END-OF-CHAPTER CASE

GLOBAL FACTORS THAT CAN CRIPPLE YOUR MARKETING PLAN

To hear all the talk about how effective or ineffective traditional media is compared with word-of-mouth, digital media, and other new media, you'd think all these marketing tactics are the only things driving the sales machine. Of course, they're important. But lost in the commotion is the dirty little secret that for many businesses, marketing affects just 9 percent to 15 percent of short-term sales. The rest of short-term revenue is attributed to non-marketing factors—all the external factors that affect a consumer's purchase decision, including weather, macroeconomic factors such as gas prices, operational practices, and competition—none of which a marketer can control.

It isn't that marketing doesn't matter, but growing a business is a highly complex undertaking, and marketing is just a piece of the puzzle. It's an important piece, certainly. But you can have the best marketing initiatives in the world to drive people into a store, and if cash registers are broken or there are other operational issues, sales may fall. In those situations, you can max out your marketing budget, but it won't move sales until the operational issues are fixed. Similarly, you can't market successfully unless you take into account environmental factors such as the economy. A home-improvements retailer, for example, might develop marketing messages that address budget concerns by appealing to the cost savings of "doing it yourself" rather than hiring a contractor.

Don't, however, think that doing everything we've said will dramatically move the needle. When it comes to marketing, judging outcomes is complicated. In fact, you can take every non-marketing factor into account, yet your marketing may not improve sales in the short term. But—and here's the rub—it may very well enhance the outcome over what would have happened had you stopped communicating with your market or, in marketing lingo, "gone dark." If you hadn't marketed, your sales may well have dropped. By continuing your marketing efforts, you at least have neutralized a fall-off.

Marketing Management Analytics (MMA) is a marketing analytics consulting firm that originated the commercial acceptance and use of marketing mix modelling to help companies plan, measure, validate, and optimize their marketing performance. The firm analyzed the performance of major brands during the recent recession, and discovered that many were able to limit the recession's impact, either by maintaining or increasing marketing spending, or by changing their message tactics.

In several studies, MMA found that by *not* marketing, companies end up hurting more than helping themselves by eroding what's known as base sales. The base is a proxy for your brand's value and accounts for sales you'd get whether or not you marketed. In fact, we've seen base sales for some brands erode in just three to four months of no marketing. One of the key drivers to this drop in base sales is an increased sensitivity to competitive advertising and pricing—non-marketing factors.

So what can a marketing manager learn from this? Above all, the influence of non-marketing factors on marketing teaches us the importance of understanding the relationship between the two so that your sales forecast more accurately reflects reality—including those factors you may not be able to control. To move from understanding the influence of non-marketing factors to implementation, MMA recommends a three-step process.

STEP ONE: EXPLAIN/QUANTIFY

Having the ability to explain the impact of non-marketing factors on your brand enables marketers to gain precise measures of their marketing investments. One big-box retailer, for example, took people off the selling floor and reduced the number of checkout attendants, replacing them with self-service checkout machines. The machines had high failure rates and people abandoned the goods because they couldn't check out. Not only can something like this reduce sales, it also can damage your brand. The poor in-store experience frustrated consumers and led them to migrate to a competitor. In this case, marketing was doing a good job driving consumers to the store, but the in-store experience and operational factors led to a reduction in sales.

Meanwhile, one consumer-products company made the decision to increase its marketing budget for the first quarter nearly 25 percent over the previous year. At the end of the first quarter, the business was flat year-over-year. Senior management's initial judgment was that the new campaign didn't work. Luckily, the marketing team had data that showed the marketing was very effective, and without the new marketing campaign, the business would have been significantly down because of non-marketing factors.

STEP TWO: PREDICT

When building a marketing plan, marketers need to predict the impact of investments in marketing on sales—and doing this without understanding the current and potential impact of non-marketing factors is nearly impossible. By developing conservative, moderate, and aggressive "what-if" scenarios during the annual planning processes, marketers can develop strategies for dealing with the impact of both marketing and non-marketing factors on their business.

For example, if your organization markets household decor, hardware, or construction materials, imagine the impact of a change in the demand for housing in your area: What if the housing market stays flat, what if it declines, and what if it grows? Now, think about how each of these scenarios would influence your marketing plan. This kind of strategic thinking will enable you to understand how the non-marketing factors could affect your business and how much you would need to invest in marketing to overcome their potential impact. And you'll be better able to answer this question: How much more will we need to spend on marketing to achieve our sales goals?

STEP THREE: RESPOND

Because environmental factors have such a significant impact on businesses, having the ability to quickly respond to unplanned events is critical to business success. One approach is to develop canned-response scenarios and keep them on the shelf, ready to deploy in case the scenario presents itself. Creating these response plans requires understanding in both how non-marketing factors will affect your business and, more important, which marketing tactics work best to respond to a particular change in a particular environmental factor. Consider the following scenarios as an example: What if gas prices rise (or fall) significantly? What if my major competitor suddenly increases its advertising? What if an unusually bad snowstorm (or heat wave) hits? Then, answer this question: How must my marketing plan change in response?

Without proper justification of marketing's impact on business results, marketing budgets will continue to fall victim to factors that are beyond marketing's control. Marketers need to gain greater insight into the levers they can't pull so they can quickly respond to them. For smart companies, that means developing a marketing plan that is aware of and sensitive to all the non-marketing factors of the business.

Source: Written by Ed See and Doug Brooks of Marketing Management Analytics.

QUESTIONS

1. List all consumer products and consumer shopping habits that would be affected by a significant increase in gas prices.

2. Which industries/products would benefit from a sustained colder-than-usual winter? Which would suffer?

3. Develop a marketing plan in response to three what-if economic scenarios.

4. What is the latest new technology development you are aware of? How might the widespread use of that new technology affect the marketing of other products and services?

If you had wanted a pair of **yellow pants,** you wouldn't have paid **$46 for these.**

TIDE WITH BLEACH ALTERNATIVE KEEPS WHITES WHITER, LONGER. SO THE LOOK YOU LOVE WILL LAST.

Tide BLEACH

knows fabrics best

AFTER STUDYING THIS CHAPTER, YOU SHOULD BE ABLE TO

1 explain the importance of information in gaining insights about the marketplace and customers

2 define the marketing information system and discuss its parts

3 outline the steps in the marketing research process

4 explain how companies analyze and use marketing information

5 discuss the special issues some marketing researchers face, including public policy and ethics issues

PREVIEWING THE CONCEPTS

In this chapter, we continue our exploration of how marketers gain insights into consumers and the marketplace. We look at how companies develop and manage information about important marketplace elements—customers, competitors, products, and marketing programs. To succeed in today's marketplace, companies must know how to turn mountains of marketing information into fresh customer insights that will help them deliver greater value to customers.

Let's start with a good story about marketing research and customer insights in action at Procter & Gamble, one of the world's largest and most respected marketing companies. P&G makes and markets a who's who list of consumer megabrands, including the likes of Tide, Crest, Bounty, Charmin, Puffs, Pampers, Pringles, Gillette, Dawn, Ivory, Febreze, Swiffer, Olay, CoverGirl, Pantene, Scope, NyQuil, Duracell, and a hundred others. P&G began its Canadian manufacturing in 1915 and was recently named as one of the top 100 employers in Canada. The company's stated purpose is to provide products that "improve the lives of the world's consumers." P&G's brands really do create value for consumers by solving their problems. But to build meaningful relationships with customers, you first have to understand them and how they connect with your brand. That's where marketing research comes in.

P&G: DEEP CUSTOMER INSIGHTS YIELD MEANINGFUL CUSTOMER RELATIONSHIPS

Creating customer value. Building meaningful customer relationships. All this sounds pretty lofty, especially for a company like P&G, which sells seemingly mundane, low-involvement consumer products such as detergents and shampoos, toothpastes and fabric softeners, and toilet paper and disposable diapers. Can you really develop a meaningful relationship between customers and a laundry detergent? For P&G, the resounding answer is *yes*. But first you have to get to know your customers well—really well.

Introduced in Canada in 1948, Tide revolutionized the industry as the first detergent to use synthetic compounds rather than soap chemicals for cleaning clothes. Tide really does get clothes clean. For decades, Tide's marketers have positioned the brand on superior functional performance, with hard-hitting ads showing before-and-after cleaning comparisons. But as it turns out, to consumers, Tide means a lot more than just getting grass stains out of that old pair of jeans.

So for several years, P&G has been on a consumer research mission: to unearth and cultivate the deep connections that customers have with its products. Behind this strategy lies the realization that competitors can quickly copy product benefits, such as cleaning power. However, they can't easily copy how consumers *feel* about a brand. Consequently, P&G's true strength lies in the relationships that it builds between its brands and customers.

Under this mandate, the Tide marketing team decided that it needed a new message for the brand. Tide's brand share, although large, had been stagnant for several years. Also, as a result of its hard-hitting functional advertising, consumers saw the Tide brand as arrogant, self-absorbed, and very male. The brand needed to recapture the hearts and minds of its core female consumers.

The team began by setting out to gain a deeper understanding of the emotional connections that women have with their laundry. Rather than just conducting the usual focus groups and marketing research surveys, however, marketing executives and strategists from P&G and its long-time ad agency, Saatchi & Saatchi, conducted research at a deeper level. They went into a two-week consumer immersion. They tagged along with women in North American cities as they worked, shopped, and ran errands, and they sat in on discussions to hear women talk about what's important to them.

"We got to an incredibly deep and personal level," says a Tide marketing executive. "We wanted to understand the role of laundry in their life." But "one of the great things," adds a Saatchi strategist about the research effort, "is we didn't talk [to consumers] about their laundry habits [and practices]. We talked about their lives, what their needs were, how they felt as women. And we got a lot of rich stuff that we hadn't tapped into before."

The immersion research produced some remarkable consumer insights. The Tide marketers learned that, although Tide and laundry aren't the most important things in customers' lives, women are very emotional about their clothing. For example, "there was the joy a plus-size, divorced woman described when she got a whistle from her boyfriend while wearing her "foolproof (sexiest) outfit." According to one P&G account, "Day-to-day fabrics in women's lives hold meaning and touch them in many ways. Women like taking care of their clothes and fabrics because they are filled with emotions, stories, feelings, and memories. The fabrics in their lives (anything from jeans to sheets) allow them to express their personalities, their multidimensions as women, their attitudes."

To share these research insights with members of the Tide team who couldn't join the two-week consumer odyssey, including Saatchi creative people, the agency videotaped the immersions, prepared scripts, and hired actresses to portray consumers in an hour-long play titled "Pieces of Her." "They were actually very good actresses who brought to life many dimensions of women," says the Saatchi executive. "It's difficult to inspire creatives sometimes. And [their reaction to the play] was incredible. There was crying and laughing. And you can see it in the [later] work. It's just very connected to women."

The marketing research impacted everything the brand did moving forward. Tide, the marketers decided, can do more than solve women's laundry problems. It can make a difference in something they truly care about—the fabrics that touch their lives.

Based on these insights, P&G and Saatchi developed an award-winning advertising campaign, built around the theme "Tide knows fabrics best." Rather than the mostly heartless demonstrations and side-by-side comparisons of past Tide advertising, the new campaign employed rich visual imagery and meaningful emotional connections. The "Tide knows fabrics best" slogan says little about cleaning. Instead, the message is that Tide lets women focus on life's important things. "One of our rallying cries was to get out of the laundry basket and into [your] life," says a Tide marketer.

Approximately 25 percent of Tide's advertising in North America is developed by Toronto-based Saatchi & Saatchi Canada. The Toronto agency developed the campaign for the launch of 2X Ultra Tide, featuring TV personality Kelly Ripa. This campaign has been among Tide's strongest and most unusual work in recent history, and Canadian consumers could relate to her and the values she personifies.

The initial "Tide knows fabrics best" ads had just the right mix of emotional connections and soft sell. In one TV commercial, a pregnant woman dribbled ice cream on the one last shirt that still fit her. It's Tide with Bleach to the rescue, so that "your clothes can outlast your cravings." Another ad showed touching scenes of a woman first holding a baby and then cuddling romantically with her husband, all to the tune of "Be My Baby." Tide with Febreze, said the ad, can mean "the difference between smelling like a mom and smelling like a woman."

In a third ad, a woman played with her daughter at a park, still in her white slacks from the office, thanks to her confidence in Tide with Bleach. "Your work clothes. Your play clothes. Yup, they're the same clothes," the ad concluded. "Tide with bleach: For looking great, it's child's play." In all, the "Tide knows fabrics best" campaign shows women that Tide really does make a difference in fabrics that touch their lives.

So ... back to that original question: *Can* you develop a relationship with a laundry detergent brand? Insights gained from P&G's deep-immersion consumer research showed that such relationships aren't just possible—they're inevitable. The key is to really understand the true nature of the relationship and to shape it by creating real value for customers. No brand is more successful at creating customer relationships than Tide. P&G's flagship brand captures an incredible 43 percent share of the cluttered and competitive laundry detergent market. That's right, 43 percent and growing—including a 7 percent increase in the year following the start of the "Tide knows fabrics best" campaign.

If you ask former P&G global marketing chief and consultant James Stengel, he'd say that kind of success comes from deeply understanding consumers and connecting the company's brands to their lives. Such understanding comes from marketing research, not just on a company's products and marketing programs, but on core customer needs and brand experiences. According to Stengel, "It's not about telling and selling. It's about bringing a [customer] relationship mindset to everything [you] do." A company needs to "think beyond consuming ... and to really directly understand the role and the meaning the brand [has in consumers'] lives."[1]

AS THE P&G Tide story highlights, good products and marketing programs begin with good customer information. Companies also need an abundance of information on competitors, resellers, and other actors and marketplace forces. But more than just gathering information, marketers must *use* the information to gain powerful *customer and market insights*.

MARKETING INFORMATION AND CUSTOMER INSIGHTS 🔴

To create value for customers and to build meaningful relationships with them, marketers must first gain fresh, deep insights into what customers need and want. Companies use such customer insights to develop competitive advantage. "In today's hypercompetitive world," states a marketing expert, "the race for competitive advantage is really a race for customer and market insights." Such insights come from good marketing information.[2]

Exhibit 5.1   Key customer insights, plus a dash of Apple's design and usability magic, have made the iPod a blockbuster. It now captures a more than 75 percent market share.

Consider Apple's phenomenally successful iPod. The iPod wasn't the first digital music player but Apple was the first to get it right. Apple's research uncovered a key insight about how people want to consume digital music—they want to take all their music with them but they want personal music players to be unobtrusive. This insight led to two key design goals—make it as small as a deck of cards and build it to hold 1,000 songs. Add a dash of Apple's design and usability magic to this insight, and you have a recipe for a blockbuster. Apple's expanded iPod line now captures a more than 75 percent market share.

Although customer and market insights are important for building customer value and relationships, these insights can be very difficult to obtain. Customer needs and buying motives are often anything but obvious—consumers themselves usually can't tell you exactly what they need and why they buy. To gain good customer insights, marketers must effectively manage marketing information from a wide range of sources.

Today's marketers have ready access to plenty of marketing information. With the recent explosion of information technologies, companies can now generate information in great quantities. In fact, most marketing managers—most people—are overloaded with data and often are overwhelmed by it. For example, consider these startling facts about the information environment:[3]

> It is estimated that a week's worth of the *New York Times* contains more information than a person was likely to come across in a lifetime in the 18th century. An estimated 4 exabytes (4.0 times 10 to the 19th) of unique information will be generated this year—more than in the previous 5000 years combined. The amount of new technical information is doubling every two years. For students now starting a four year technical degree, this means that half of what they learn in their first year of study will be outdated by their third year of study. Japanese communications giant NTT has successfully tested a fiber-optic cable that pushes 14 trillion bits per second down a single strand of fiber. That's the equivalent of 2660 CDs or 210 million phone calls every second. It is currently tripling that capacity every six months and is expected to do so for the next 20 years.

Despite this data glut, marketers frequently complain that they lack enough information of the right kind. They don't need *more* information, they need *better* information. And they need to make better *use* of the information they already have. Says another marketing information expert, "Transforming today's vast, ever-increasing volume of consumer information into actionable marketing insights ... is the number-one challenge for digital-age marketers."[4]

Thus, the real value of marketing research and marketing information lies in how it is used—in the **customer insights** that it provides. Says a marketing information expert, "Companies that gather, disseminate, and apply deep customer insights obtain powerful, profitable, sustainable competitive advantages for their brands."[5] Based on such thinking, many companies are now restructuring and renaming their marketing research and information functions. They are creating "customer insights teams," headed by a vice-president of customer insights and made up of representatives from all of the firm's functional areas. For example, the head of marketing research at Kraft Foods is called the director of consumer insights and strategy.

Customer insights groups collect customer and market information from a wide variety of sources—ranging from traditional marketing research studies to mingling with and observing consumers to monitoring consumer online conversations about the company and its products. Then, they *use* the marketing information to develop important customer insights from which the company can create more value for its customers. For example, Unilever's customer insights group states its mission simply as "getting better at understanding our consumers and meeting their needs."

Customer insights
Fresh understandings of customers and the marketplace derived from marketing information that become the basis for creating customer value and relationships.

In gathering and using customer insights, however, companies must be careful not to go too far and become *customer controlled*. The idea is not to give customers everything they request. Rather, it's to understand customers to the core and give them what they need—to create value for customers as a means of capturing value for the firm in return.[6]

Thus, companies must design effective marketing information systems that give managers the right information, in the right form, at the right time and help them to use this information to create customer value and stronger customer relationships. A **marketing information system (MIS)** consists of people and procedures for assessing information needs, developing the needed information, and helping decision makers to use the information to generate and validate actionable customer and market insights.

Figure 5.1 shows that the MIS begins and ends with information users—marketing managers, internal and external partners, and others who need marketing information. First, it interacts with these information users to *assess information needs*. Next, it interacts with the marketing environment to *develop needed information* through internal company databases, marketing intelligence activities, and marketing research. Finally, the MIS helps users to analyze and use the information to develop customer insights, make marketing decisions, and manage customer relationships.

Marketing information system (MIS)
People and procedures for assessing information needs, developing the needed information, and helping decision makers to use the information to generate and validate actionable customer and market insights.

ASSESSING MARKETING INFORMATION NEEDS

The marketing information system primarily serves the company's marketing and other managers. However, it may also provide information to external partners, such as suppliers, resellers, or marketing services agencies. For example, Wal-Mart's RetailLink system gives key suppliers access to information on customers' buying patterns and store inventory levels. And Dell creates tailored Premier Pages for large customers, giving them access to product design, order status, and product support and service information. In designing an information system, the company must consider the needs of all of these users.

A good MIS balances the information users would *like* to have against what they really *need* and what is *feasible* to offer. The company begins by interviewing managers to find out what information they would like. Some managers will ask for whatever

FIGURE 5.1 The marketing information system

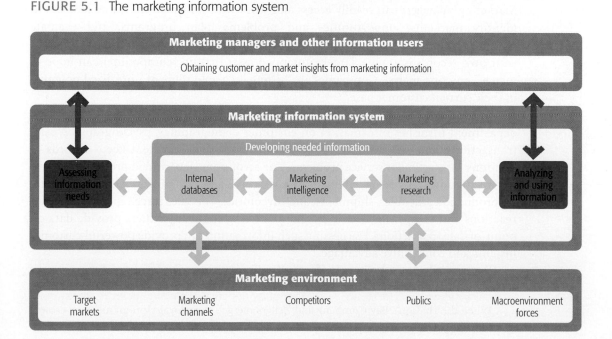

information they can get without thinking carefully about what they really need. Too much information can be as harmful as too little.

Other managers may omit things they ought to know, or they may not know to ask for some types of information they should have. For example, managers might need to know about surges in favourable or unfavourable consumer "word-of-Web" discussions about their brands on blogs or online social networks. Because they do not know about these discussions, they do not think to ask about them. The MIS must monitor the marketing environment to provide decision makers with information they should have in order to better understand customers and make key marketing decisions.

Sometimes the company cannot provide the needed information, either because it is not available or because of MIS limitations. For example, a brand manager might want to know how competitors will change their advertising budgets next year and how these changes will affect industry market shares. The information on planned budgets probably is not available. Even if it is, the company's MIS may not be advanced enough to forecast resulting changes in market shares.

Finally, the costs of obtaining, analyzing, storing, and delivering information can mount quickly. The company must decide whether the value of insights gained from additional information is worth the costs of providing it, and both value and cost are often hard to assess. By itself, information has no worth; its value comes from its *use*—from the customer insights it provides and their impact on decision-making. Rather, they should weigh carefully the costs of getting more information against the benefits resulting from it.

DEVELOPING MARKETING INFORMATION

Marketers can obtain the needed information from *internal data*, *marketing intelligence*, and *marketing research*.

INTERNAL DATA

Internal databases

Electronic collections of consumer and market information obtained from data sources within the company network.

Many companies build extensive **internal databases**, electronic collections of consumer and market information obtained from data sources within the company network. Marketing managers can readily access and work with information in the database to identify marketing opportunities and problems, plan programs, and evaluate performance. Internal data can provide strong competitive advantage. "Locked within your own records is a huge, largely untapped asset that no [competitor] can hope to match," says one analyst. Companies are "sitting on a gold mine of unrealized potential in their current customer base."[7]

Information in the database can come from many sources. The marketing department furnishes information on customer demographics, psychographics, sales transactions, and website visits. The customer service department keeps records of customer satisfaction or service problems. The accounting department prepares financial statements and keeps detailed records of sales, costs, and cash flows. Operations reports on production schedules, shipments, and inventories. The sales force reports on reseller reactions and competitor activities, and marketing channel partners provide data on point-of-sale transactions. Harnessing such information can provide powerful customer insights and competitive advantage.

For example, consider how Hudson's Bay Company uses internal databases to make better decisions:[8]

> When the Hudson's Bay Company and Zellers merged their loyalty programs, they created one of the most comprehensive and potentially far-reaching customer databases in Canada.

The database contains information on more than 8.5 million members, according to the database managers. As one VP noted, "When someone's buying kids' clothing at either the Bay or at Zellers, we now have the data to tell us that." In fact, the data is so detailed that by matching the stock keeping unit number (the SKU number) with the purchase information, the database managers and the marketers who depend on it can determine not only what size the child is, but also make an informed guess about the sex and age of the purchasers' children. And the information goes far beyond kids' clothes. The stores carry a massive array of merchandise that is purchased by the 85 percent of the Canadian population who comes through their doors every year.

Exhibit 5.2 Internal databases: HBC's database of over 8.5 million Canadian consumers makes it one of the most comprehensive customer databases in Canada.

Internal databases usually can be accessed more quickly and cheaply than other information sources, but they also present some problems. Because internal information was often collected for other purposes, it may be incomplete or in the wrong form for making marketing decisions. For example, sales and cost data used by the accounting department for preparing financial statements must be adapted for use in evaluating the value of a specific customer segment, sales force, or channel performance. Data also ages quickly; keeping the database current requires a major effort. In addition, a large company produces mountains of information, which must be well integrated and readily accessible so that managers can find it easily and use it effectively. Managing that much data requires highly sophisticated equipment and techniques.

COMPETITIVE MARKETING INTELLIGENCE

Competitive marketing intelligence is the systematic collection and analysis of publicly available information about consumers, competitors, and developments in the marketplace. The goal of competitive marketing intelligence is to improve strategic decision-making by understanding the consumer environment, assessing and tracking competitors' actions, and providing early warnings of opportunities and threats.

Competitive marketing intelligence The systematic collection and analysis of publicly available information about consumers, competitors, and developments in the marketing environment.

Marketing intelligence gathering has grown dramatically as more and more companies are now busily eavesdropping on the marketplace and snooping on their competitors. Techniques range from monitoring Internet buzz or observing consumers first-hand to quizzing the company's own employees, benchmarking competitors' products, researching on the Internet, lurking around industry trade shows, and even rooting through rivals' trash bins.

Good marketing intelligence can help marketers to gain insights into how consumers talk about and connect with their brands. Many companies send out teams of trained observers to mix and mingle with customers as they use and talk about the company's products. Other companies routinely monitor consumers' online chatter with the help of monitoring services such as Nielsen Online or Radian6. For example, Radian6 helps companies to keep track of almost any relevant online conversation:[9]

Social media make it easier than ever for people to share—to have conversations and express their opinions, needs, ideas, and complaints. And they're doing it with millions of blogs, tweets, videos, and comments daily. Companies face the difficult task of pinpointing all the conversations happening about their brands. Radian6 gives companies a Web-based platform that lets them listen to, share with, learn from, and engage customers across the entire social Web. Radian6's Web dashboard provides for real-time monitoring of consumer mentions of the company, its brands, relevant issues, and competitors on millions of blog posts, viral

Exhibit 5.3 Many companies routinely monitor consumers' online conversations with the help of monitoring services and platforms such as Radian6.

videos, reviews in forums, sharing of photos, and twitter updates. Dell's Customer Service group uses Radian6 to monitor and respond to what's being said online about its products and any problems after purchase. Lifestyle retailer PacSun uses Radian6 to track important trends and to better respond to customers in the online space.

Companies also need to actively monitor competitors' activities. Firms use competitive marketing intelligence to gain early warnings of competitor moves and strategies, new-product launches, new or changing markets, and potential competitive strengths and weaknesses. Much competitor intelligence can be collected from people inside the company—executives, engineers and scientists, purchasing agents, and the sales force. The company can also obtain important intelligence information from suppliers, resellers, and key customers. Or it can get good information by observing competitors and monitoring their published information.

Competitors often reveal intelligence information through their annual reports, business publications, trade show exhibits, press releases, advertisements, and webpages. The Web has become an invaluable source of competitive intelligence. By using Internet search engines, marketers can search specific competitor names, events, or trends and see what turns up. And tracking consumer conversations about competing brands is often as revealing as tracking conversations about the company's own brands. Moreover, most competitors now place volumes of information on their websites, providing details of interest to customers, partners, suppliers, investors, or franchisees. This can provide a wealth of useful information about competitors' strategies, markets, new products, facilities, and other happenings.

Intelligence seekers can also pore through any of thousands of online databases. Some are free. For example, you can search the System for Electronic Document Analysis and Retrieval (SEDAR) database for the documents and information filed by public companies and for investment funds with the Canadian Securities Administrators. The Howard Ross Library of Management at McGill University lists many resources for learning more about Canadian businesses, and Hoovers.com has a searchable website containing financial information on publicly traded Canadian and U.S. companies. And for a fee, companies can subscribe to any of more than 3000 online databases and information search services, such as Dialog, LCC; DataStar; LexisNexis; Dow Jones News/Retrieval; UMI ProQuest; and Dun & Bradstreet online access. Today's marketers have an almost overwhelming amount of competitor information only a few keystrokes away.

The intelligence game goes both ways. Facing determined competitive marketing intelligence efforts by competitors, most companies are now taking steps to protect their own information. For example, Unilever trains employees not just how to collect intelligence information but also how to protect company information from competitors. According to a former Unilever staffer, "We were even warned that spies from competitors could be posing as drivers at the minicab company we used." Unilever performs random checks on internal security. Says the former staffer, "At one [internal marketing] conference, we were set up when an actor was employed to infiltrate the group. The idea was to see who spoke to him, how much they told him, and how long it took to realize that no one knew him. He ended up being there for a long time."[10]

The growing use of marketing intelligence raises a number of ethical issues. Although most of the preceding techniques are legal, and some are considered to be shrewdly competitive, some may involve questionable ethics. Clearly, companies should take advantage of publicly available information. However, they should not stoop to snoop. With all the legitimate intelligence sources now available, a company does not need to break the law or accepted codes of ethics to get good intelligence.

MARKETING RESEARCH **LO3**

In addition to marketing intelligence information about general consumer, competitor, and marketplace happenings, marketers often need formal studies that provide customer and market insights for specific marketing situations and decisions. For example, Budweiser wants to know what appeals will be most effective in its Super Bowl advertising. Google wants to know how Web searchers will react to a proposed redesign of its site. Or Samsung wants to know how many and what kinds of people will buy its next-generation large-screen televisions. In such situations, marketing intelligence will not provide the detailed information needed. Managers will need marketing research.

Marketing research is the systematic design, collection, analysis, and reporting of data relevant to a specific marketing situation facing an organization. Companies use marketing research in a wide variety of situations. For example, marketing research gives marketers insights into customer motivations, purchase behaviour, and satisfaction. It can help them to assess market potential and market share or to measure the effectiveness of pricing, product, distribution, and promotion activities.

Some large companies have their own research departments that work with marketing managers on marketing research projects. This is how Procter & Gamble, GE, and many other corporate giants handle marketing research. In addition, these companies—like their smaller counterparts—frequently hire outside research specialists to consult with management on specific marketing problems and conduct marketing research studies. Sometimes firms simply purchase data collected by outside firms to aid in their decision-making.

The marketing research process has four steps (see Figure 5.2): defining the problem and research objectives, developing the research plan, implementing the research plan, and interpreting and reporting the findings.

Marketing research
The systematic design, collection, analysis, and reporting of data relevant to a specific marketing situation facing an organization.

DEFINING THE PROBLEM AND RESEARCH OBJECTIVES

Marketing managers and researchers must work closely together to define the problem and agree on research objectives. The manager best understands the decision for which information is needed; the researcher best understands marketing research and how to obtain the information. Defining the problem and research objectives is often the hardest

FIGURE 5.2 The marketing research process

Defining the problem and research objectives

Developing the research plan for collecting information

Implementing the research plan—collecting and analyzing the data

Interpreting and reporting the findings

Exploratory research
Marketing research to gather preliminary information that will help define the problem and suggest hypotheses.

Descriptive research
Marketing research to better describe marketing problems, situations, or markets, such as the market potential for a product or the demographics and attitudes of consumers.

Causal research
Marketing research to test hypotheses about cause-and-effect relationships.

step in the research process. The manager may know that something is wrong, without knowing the specific causes.

After the problem has been defined carefully, the manager and researcher must set the research objectives. A marketing research project might have one of three types of objectives. The objective of **exploratory research** is to gather preliminary information that will help define the problem and suggest hypotheses. The objective of **descriptive research** is to describe things, such as the market potential for a product or the demographics and attitudes of consumers who buy the product. The objective of **causal research** is to test hypotheses about cause-and-effect relationships. For example, would a 10 percent decrease in tuition at a university result in an enrolment increase sufficient to offset the reduced tuition? Managers often start with exploratory research and later follow with descriptive or causal research.

The statement of the problem and research objectives guides the entire research process. The manager and researcher should put the statement in writing to be certain that they agree on the purpose and expected results of the research.

DEVELOPING THE RESEARCH PLAN

Once the research problems and objectives have been defined, researchers must determine the exact information needed, develop a plan for gathering it efficiently, and present the plan to management. The research plan outlines sources of existing data and spells out the specific research approaches, contact methods, sampling plans, and instruments that researchers will use to gather new data.

Research objectives must be translated into specific information needs. For example, suppose that Red Bull wants to conduct research on how consumers would react to a proposed new vitamin-enhanced-water drink in several flavours sold under the Red Bull name. Red Bull currently dominates the worldwide energy drink market. However, in an effort to expand beyond its energy drink niche, the company recently introduced Red Bull Cola ("Why not?" asks the company—it's strong and natural, just like the original Red Bull energy drink). A new line of enhanced waters—akin to Glacéau's VitaminWater—

Exhibit 5.4 A decision by Red Bull to add a line of enhanced waters to its already successful mix of energy and cola drinks would call for marketing research that provides lots of specific information.

might help Red Bull to leverage its strong brand position even further. The proposed research might call for the following specific information:

☐ The demographic, economic, and lifestyle characteristics of current Red Bull customers. (Do current customers also consume enhanced-water products? Are such products consistent with their lifestyles? Or would Red Bull need to target a new segment of consumers?)

☐ The characteristics and usage patterns of the broader population of enhanced-water users: What do they need and expect from such products, where do they buy them, when and how do they use them, and what existing brands and price points are most popular? (The new Red Bull product would need strong, relevant positioning in the crowded enhanced-water market.)

☐ Retailer reactions to the proposed new product line: Would they stock and support it? Where would they display it? (Failure to get retailer support would hurt sales of the new drink.)

☐ Forecasts of sales of both the new and current Red Bull products. (Will the new enhanced-waters create new sales or simply take sales away from current Red Bull products? Will the new product increase Red Bull's overall profits?)

Red Bull's marketers will need these and many other types of information to decide whether and how to introduce the new product.

The research plan should be presented in a *written proposal*. A written proposal is especially important when the research project is large and complex or when an outside firm carries it out. The proposal should cover the management problems addressed and the research objectives, the information to be obtained, and how the results will help management decision-making. The proposal also should include research costs.

To meet the manager's information needs, the research plan can call for gathering secondary data, primary data, or both. **Secondary data** consist of information that already exists somewhere, having been collected for another purpose. **Primary data** consist of information collected for the specific purpose at hand.

Secondary data
Information that already exists somewhere, having been collected for another purpose.

Primary data
Information collected for the specific purpose at hand.

GATHERING SECONDARY DATA

Researchers usually start by gathering secondary data. The company's internal database provides a good starting point. However, the company can also tap into a wide assortment of external information sources, including commercial data services and government sources (see Table 5.1).

Companies can buy secondary data reports from outside suppliers. For example, Nielsen sells buyer data from a consumer panel of more than 250 000 households in 27 countries worldwide, with measures of trial and repeat purchasing, brand loyalty, and buyer demographics. Experian Consumer Research (Simmons) sells information on more than 8000 brands in 450 product categories, including detailed consumer profiles that assess everything from the products consumers buy and the brands they prefer to their lifestyles, attitudes, and media preferences. The MONITOR service by Yankelovich sells information on important social and lifestyle trends. These and other firms supply high-quality data to suit a wide variety of marketing information needs.[11]

By using **commercial online databases**, marketing researchers can conduct their own searches of secondary data sources. General database services such as ProQuest, LexisNexis, and Dialog, LCC, put an incredible wealth of information at the keyboards of marketing decision makers. Beyond commercial websites offering information for a fee, almost every industry association, government agency, business publication, and news

Commercial online databases
Computerized collections of information available from online commercial sources or via the Internet.

TABLE 5.1   Selected External Information Sources

For Business Data

ACNielsen Corporation (http://acnielsen.com) provides point-of-sale scanner data on sales, market share, and retail prices; data on household purchasing; and data on television audiences (a unit of VNU N.V.).

American Demographics (http://adage.com/americandemographics/) reports on demographic trends and their significance for businesses.

Arbitron (http://arbitron.com) provides local-market and Internet radio audience and advertising expenditure information, among other media and ad spending data.

Canadian Trade Index (www.ctidirectory.com) **and Fraser's Canadian Trade Directory** (www.frasers.com) provide information on manufacturers of different product categories, manufacturing equipment, and supplies.

Canoe (www.canoe.ca; Canadian Online Explorer) bills itself as Canada's leading news and information site.

CNN (http://cnn.com) reports U.S. and global news and covers the markets and news-making companies in detail.

comScore Networks (http://comscore.com) provides consumer behaviour information and geodemographic analysis of Internet and digital media users around the world.

Dialog, LCC (www.dialog.com) offers access to more than 900 databases containing publications, reports, newsletters, and directories covering dozens of industries.

For Government Data

Industry Canada's Strategis website (www.strategis.ic.gc.ca) provides resources for Canadian businesses.

Ontario Ministry for Economic Development and Trade (www.ontariocanada.com/ontcan/1medt/en/home_en.jsp) and other provincial governments, have sites that provide information for small business development.

Statistics Canada (www.statcan.gc.ca) provides summary data on demographic, economic, social, and other aspects of the Canadian economy and society.

Stat-USA (http://stat-usa.gov), a Department of Commerce site, highlights statistics on U.S. business and international trade.

U.S. Census (www.census.gov) provides detailed statistics and trends about the U.S. population.

Western Economic Diversification Canada (www.wd.gc.ca) provides information for people starting or operating a business in Western Canada.

For Internet Data

ClickZ (http://clickz.com) brings together a wealth of information about the Internet and its users, from consumers to e-commerce.

Forrester Research (www.forrester.com) monitors Web traffic and ranks the most popular sites.

Interactive Advertising Bureau (http://iab.net) covers statistics about advertising on the Internet.

Dun & Bradstreet (http://dnb.com) maintains a database containing information on more than 50 million individual companies around the globe.

Experian Consumer Research (Simmons) (http://smrb.com) provides detailed analysis of consumer patterns in 400 product categories in selected markets.

Factiva (http://factiva.com) specializes in in-depth financial, historical, and operational information on public and private companies.

Hoover's, Inc., (http://hoovers.com) provides business descriptions, financial overviews, and news about major companies around the world.

IMS Health (http://imshealth.com) tracks drug sales, monitors performance of pharmaceutical sales representatives, and offers pharmaceutical market forecasts.

Information Resources, Inc., (www.infores.com) provides supermarket scanner data for tracking grocery product movement and new product purchasing data.

J.D. Power and Associates (http://jdpower.com) provides information from independent consumer surveys of product and service quality, customer satisfaction, and buyer behaviour.

LexisNexis (http://lexisnexis.com) features articles from business, consumer, and marketing publications, plus tracking of firms, industries, trends, and promotion techniques.

Scott's Directories (www.scottsinfo.com) lists, on an annual basis, manufacturers, their products, and their North American Industry Classification (NAICS) codes, alphabetically as well as by city and region. The directory also provides the names and telephone and fax numbers of chief executives, as well as corporate information, such as annual sales. Directories come in four volumes: Ontario, Quebec, Atlantic Canada, and Western Canada.

SEDAR (www.sedar.com) has an extensive database that includes the financial filing information, annual reports, and company profiles for Canadian public companies.

Welcome to a new era in professional searching.

Dialog®, a leader in online information services for professional searchers, now offers ProQuest® products to corporate customers. The combination of precision search on Dialog with easy access to full text from ProQuest creates an unparalleled resource to support your organization's research needs. So whether you need research workflow tools like Professional ProQuest Central, ProQuest Pharma Collection, ProQuest Dissertations & Theses, Technology Research Database or RefWorks-COS, you can find them all in one place. **Start here.**

Discover

Validate

Innovate

Market

Dialog®
Authoritative answers enriched by ProQuest

To learn more about ProQuest products available through Dialog, visit **www.dialog.com/proquest**

Exhibit 5.5 Online database services, such as Dialog, LCC, put an incredible wealth of information at the keyboards of marketing decision makers. Dialog provides "authoritative answers enriched by ProQuest."

medium offers free information to those tenacious enough to find their websites. There are so many websites offering data that finding the right ones can become an almost overwhelming task.

Web search engines can also be a big help in locating relevant secondary information sources. However, they can also be very frustrating and inefficient. For example, a Red Bull marketer googling "enhanced water products" would come up with some 256 000 hits! Still, well-structured, well-designed Web searches can be a good starting point to any marketing research project.

Secondary data can usually be obtained more quickly and at a lower cost than primary data. Also, secondary sources can sometimes provide data an individual company cannot collect on its own— information that either is not directly available or would be too expensive to collect. For example, it would be too expensive for Red Bull's marketers to conduct a continuing retail store audit to find out about the market shares, prices, and displays of competitors' brands. But it can buy the InfoScan service from Information Resources, Inc., which provides this information based on scanner and other data from thousands of retail stores.[12]

Secondary data can also present problems. The needed information may not exist— researchers can rarely obtain all the data they need from secondary sources. For example, Red Bull will not find existing information about consumer reactions to a new enhanced-water line that it has not yet placed on the market. Even when data can be found, the information might not be very usable. The researcher must evaluate secondary information carefully to make certain it is *relevant* (fits research project needs), *accurate* (reliably collected and reported), *current* (up-to-date enough for current decisions), and *impartial* (objectively collected and reported).

PRIMARY DATA COLLECTION

Secondary data provide a good starting point for research and often help define research problems and objectives. In most cases, however, the company must also collect primary data. Just as researchers must carefully evaluate the quality of secondary information, they also must take great care when collecting primary data. They need to make sure that it will be relevant, accurate, current, and unbiased. Table 5.2 shows that designing a plan for primary data collection calls for a number of decisions on *research approaches, contact methods, sampling plan,* and *research instruments.*

Research Approaches   Research approaches for gathering primary data include observation, surveys, and experiments. Here, we discuss each one in turn.

OBSERVATIONAL RESEARCH   **Observational research** involves gathering primary data by observing relevant people, actions, and situations. For example, a bank might evaluate possible new branch locations by checking traffic patterns, neighbourhood conditions, and the location of competing branches.

Observational research
Gathering primary data by observing relevant people, actions, and situations.

TABLE 5.2 Planning Primary Data Collection			
Research Approaches	**Contact Methods**	**Sampling Plan**	**Research Instruments**
Observation	Mail	Sampling unit	Questionnaire
Survey	Telephone	Sample size	Mechanical instruments
Experiment	Personal	Sampling procedure	
	Online		

Researchers often observe consumer behaviour to glean customer insights they can't obtain by simply asking customers questions. For instance, Fisher-Price has set up an observation lab in which it can observe the reactions of little tots to new toys. The Fisher-Price PlayLab is a sunny, toy-strewn space where lucky kids get to test Fisher-Price prototypes, under the watchful eyes of designers who hope to learn what will get kids worked up into a new-toy frenzy. Similarly, in its research labs, using high-tech cameras and other equipment, Gillette observes women shaving and uses the insights to design new razors and shaving products.[13]

Kimberly-Clark's Huggies brand even had parents wear camera-equipped "glasses" at home so that it could "see what they saw" while changing babies' diapers. Among other things, the Huggies marketers learned that parents change their babies' diapers almost anywhere—on beds, floors, and on top of washing machines—often in awkward positions. The researchers could see they were struggling with wipe containers and lotions requiring two hands. So the company redesigned the wipe package with a push-button one-handed dispenser and designed lotion and shampoo bottles that can be grabbed and dispensed easily with one hand.[14]

Marketers not only observe what consumers do, they also observe what consumers are saying. As discussed earlier, marketers now routinely listen in on consumer conversations on blogs, social networks, and websites. Observing such naturally occurring feedback can provide inputs that simply can't be gained through more structured and formal research approaches.[15]

Observational research can obtain information that people are unwilling or unable to provide. In contrast, some things simply cannot be observed, such as feelings, attitudes, and motives, or private behaviour. Long-term or infrequent behaviour is also difficult to observe. Finally, observations can be very difficult to interpret. Because of these limitations, researchers often use observation along with other data collection methods.

A wide range of companies now use **ethnographic research**. Ethnographic research involves sending trained observers to watch and interact with consumers in their "natural habitat." Consider this example:[16]

Ethnographic research
A form of observational research that involves sending trained observers to watch and interact with consumers in their "natural habitat."

Mobile phone maker Nokia wants to add two billion new customers by the end of the decade. To do so, it has invested heavily in ethnographic research, focusing especially on emerging economies. Nokia deploys teams of anthropologists to study deeply the behaviour of mobile-phone owners in vast markets such as China, Brazil, and India. By "living with the locals," from the shanty towns of Soweto to the bedrooms of Seoul's painfully tech-savvy teens, Nokia gleans subtle insights into nuances of each local culture. For example, it knows first-hand that 50 percent of the world's women keep their phones in their handbags (and miss 20 percent of their calls) and that most Asian early adopters who watch mobile TV ignore the mobile part and tune in from home.

One of the biggest discoveries came from researchers studying how people in poor rural areas overcome some of the barriers to communication they face in their daily lives. Surprisingly, although usually considered a one-owner item, mobile phones in these areas are often used by entire families or even villages because of the cost. Based on this finding, Nokia designed its 1200 and 1208 phones, which make shared use the top priority. The

Exhibit 5.6   Ethnographic research: Teams of Nokia anthropologists "live with the locals" in emerging economies to glean subtle insights into each local culture. Such insights resulted in the robust Nokia 1200 phone, which makes shared use a top priority.

Survey research
Gathering primary data by asking people questions about their knowledge, attitudes, preferences, and buying behaviour.

Experimental research
Gathering primary data by selecting matched groups of subjects, giving them different treatments, controlling related factors, and checking for differences in group responses.

affordable phones offer many useful and durable features and are robust enough to accommodate many different people using them. For example, they contain a long-life battery and multiple phone books so each member of a family or village can keep his or her own contacts and numbers separately from others.

Observational and ethnographic research often yield the kinds of details that just don't emerge from traditional research questionnaires or focus groups. Whereas traditional quantitative research approaches seek to test known hypotheses and obtain answers to well-defined product or strategy questions, observational research can generate fresh customer and market insights. "The beauty of ethnography," says a research expert, is that it "allows companies to zero in on their customers' unarticulated desires." Agrees another researcher, "Classic market research doesn't go far enough. It can't grasp what people can't imagine or articulate. Think of the Henry Ford quote: 'If I had asked people what they wanted, they would have said faster horses.'"[17]

SURVEY RESEARCH   **Survey research**, the most widely used method for primary data collection, is the approach best suited for gathering *descriptive* information. A company that wants to know about people's knowledge, attitudes, preferences, or buying behaviour can often find out by asking them directly.

The major advantage of survey research is its flexibility—it can be used to obtain many different kinds of information in many different situations. Surveys addressing almost any marketing question or decision can be conducted by phone or mail, in person, or on the Web.

However, survey research also presents some problems. Sometimes people are unable to answer survey questions because they cannot remember or have never thought about what they do and why. People may be unwilling to respond to unknown interviewers or about things they consider private. Respondents may answer survey questions even when they do not know the answer in order to appear smarter or more informed. Or they may try to help the interviewer by giving pleasing answers. Finally, busy people may not take the time, or they might resent the intrusion into their privacy.

EXPERIMENTAL RESEARCH   Whereas observation is best suited for exploratory research and surveys for descriptive research, **experimental research** is best suited for gathering *causal* information. Experiments involve selecting matched groups of subjects, giving them different treatments, controlling unrelated factors, and checking for differences in group responses. Thus, experimental research tries to explain cause-and-effect relationships.

For example, before adding a new sandwich to its menu, McDonald's might use experiments to test the effects on sales of two different prices it might charge. It could introduce the new sandwich at one price in one city and at another price in another city. If the cities are similar, and if all other marketing efforts for the sandwich are the same, then differences in sales in the two cities could be related to the price charged.

Contact Methods   Information can be collected by mail, telephone, personal interview, or online. Table 5.3 shows the strengths and weaknesses of each of these contact methods.

MAIL, TELEPHONE, AND PERSONAL INTERVIEWING   *Mail questionnaires* can be used to collect large amounts of information at a low cost per respondent. Respondents may give more honest answers to more personal questions on a mail questionnaire than to an unknown interviewer in person or over the phone. Also, no interviewer is involved to bias the respondent's answers.

TABLE 5.3 Strengths and Weaknesses of Contact Methods				
	Mail	**Telephone**	**Personal**	**Online**
Flexibility	Poor	Good	Excellent	Good
Quantity of data that can be collected	Good	Fair	Excellent	Good
Control of interviewer effects	Excellent	Fair	Poor	Fair
Control of sample	Fair	Excellent	Good	Excellent
Speed of data collection	Poor	Excellent	Good	Excellent
Response rate	Poor	Poor	Good	Good
Cost	Good	Fair	Poor	Excellent

However, mail questionnaires are not very flexible—all respondents answer the same questions in a fixed order. Mail surveys usually take longer than other types of surveys to complete, and the response rate—the number of people returning completed questionnaires—is often very low. Finally, the researcher often has little control over the mail questionnaire sample. Even with a good mailing list, it is hard to control *who* at the mailing address fills out the questionnaire. As a result of the shortcomings, more and more marketers are now shifting to faster, more flexible, and lower-cost online surveys.

Telephone interviewing is one of the best methods for gathering information quickly, and it provides greater flexibility than mail questionnaires. Interviewers can explain difficult questions and, depending on the answers they receive, skip some questions or probe on others. Response rates tend to be higher than with mail questionnaires, and interviewers can ask to speak to respondents with the desired characteristics or even by name.

However, with telephone interviewing, the cost per respondent is higher than with mail or online questionnaires. Also, people may not want to discuss personal questions with an interviewer. The method introduces interviewer bias—the way interviewers talk, how they ask questions, and other differences may affect respondents' answers. Finally, in this age of do-not-call lists and promotion-harassed consumers, potential survey respondents are increasingly hanging up on telephone interviewers rather than talking with them. In fact, one poll revealed that 80 percent of Canadians who registered with Canada's National Do Not Call List, launched in September 2008 to cut down on unsolicited telemarketing, reported receiving fewer telemarketing calls and that awareness of and registration with this list continues to grow in this country.[18]

Personal interviewing takes two forms—individual and group interviewing. *Individual interviewing* involves talking with people in their homes or offices, on the street, or in shopping malls. Such interviewing is flexible. Trained interviewers can guide interviews, explain difficult questions, and explore issues as the situation requires. They can show subjects actual products, advertisements, or packages and observe reactions and behaviour. However, individual personal interviews may cost three to four times as much as telephone interviews.

Group interviewing consists of inviting six to ten people to meet with a trained moderator to talk about a product, service, or organization. Participants normally are paid a small sum for attending. The moderator encourages free and easy discussion, hoping that group interactions will bring out actual feelings and thoughts. At the same time, the moderator "focuses" the discussion—hence the name **focus group interviewing**.

Researchers and marketers watch the focus group discussions from behind one-way glass and record comments in writing or on video for later study. Today, focus group researchers can even use videoconferencing and Internet technology to connect marketers

Focus group interviewing
Personal interviewing that involves inviting six to ten people to gather for a few hours with a trained interviewer to talk about a product, service, or organization. The interviewer "focuses" the group discussion on important issues.

Exhibit 5.7   New focus group environments: To create a more congenial setting in which women could open up and share personal shaving and moisturizing stories, Schick sponsored "Slow Sip" sessions in local cafés.

in distant locations with live focus group action. By using cameras and two-way sound systems, marketing executives in a far-off boardroom can look in and listen, using remote controls to zoom in on faces and pan the focus group at will.

Along with observational research, focus group interviewing has become one of the major qualitative marketing research tools for gaining fresh insights into consumer thoughts and feelings. However, focus group studies present some challenges. They usually employ small samples to keep time and costs down, and it may be hard to generalize from the results. Moreover, consumers in focus groups are not always open and honest about their real feelings, behaviour, and intentions in front of other people.

Thus, although focus groups are still widely used, many researchers are tinkering with focus group design. For example, some companies prefer "immersion groups"—small groups of consumers who interact directly and informally with product designers without a focus group moderator present. Other researchers are combining focus groups with hypnosis in an effort to get deeper, more vivid insights. Consider this example:[19]

Volvo equals safety. In focus group after focus group, participants said the same thing. But to check these findings, Volvo called in a hypnotist. Members of Volvo focus groups were asked to test-drive a car. Immediately afterwards, they were hypnotized and asked their true feelings about the brand. It wasn't pretty: Many revealed that Volvo also equals being middle-aged. That idea "for some people was suffocating," says a Volvo researcher. "Hypnosis helped get past the clichés. We needed the conversation taken to a deeper, more emotional place."

Still other researchers are changing the environments in which they conduct focus groups. To help consumers relax and to elicit more authentic responses, they use settings that are more comfortable and more relevant to the products being researched. For example, to get a better understanding of how women shave their legs, Schick Canada created the "Slow Sip" sessions designed to be like a simple get-together with girlfriends.

In these Slow Sip sessions, participants gathered round at a local café to sip coffee or tea and munch on snacks together. The structure was loose, and the congenial setting helped the women to open up and share personal shaving and moisturizing stories on a subject that might have been sensitive in a more formal setting. The Slow Sip sessions produced a number of new customer insights. For example, researchers discovered that the message for their Schick Quattro for Women razor—that Quattro has four-blade technology—was too technical. Women don't care about the engineering behind a razor, they care about shaving results. So Schick Canada repositioned the Quattro as offering a smooth, long-lasting shave. As a side benefit, participants enjoyed the sessions so much that they wanted to stick around for more. They became a kind of ongoing advisory board for Schick's marketers and "brand ambassadors" for Schick's products.[20]

Thus, in recent years, many companies have been moving away from traditional, more formal, and numbers-oriented research approaches and contact methods. Instead, more and more, they are employing new ways of listening to consumers that don't involve traditional questionnaire formats. "Long known for crunching numbers and being statistical gatekeepers of the marketing industry," says one marketer, "market researchers need to shift their focus toward listening and developing ideas better on the front end and away from 'feeding the metrics monster.'" Beyond conducting surveys and tracking brand metrics, "researchers need to employ softer skills."[21]

ONLINE MARKETING RESEARCH   The growth of the Internet has had a dramatic impact on the conduct of marketing research. Increasingly, researchers are collecting primary data through **online marketing research** —*Internet surveys, online panels, experiments, and online focus groups.* By one estimate, U.S. online research spending reached an estimated US$2.1 billion in 2008 and is growing at 15 to 20 percent a year.[22]

Online research can take many forms. A company can use the Web as a survey medium. It can include a questionnaire on its website and offer incentives for completing it. It can use email, Web links, or Web pop-ups to invite people to answer questions. It can create online panels that provide regular feedback or conduct live discussions or online focus groups.

Beyond surveys, researchers can conduct experiments on the Web. They can experiment with different prices, headlines, or product features on different websites or at different times to learn the relative effectiveness of their offers. Or they can set up virtual shopping environments and use them to test new products and marketing programs. Finally, a company can learn about the behaviour of online customers by following their click streams as they visit the website and move to other sites.

The Internet is especially well suited to *quantitative* research—conducting marketing surveys and collecting data. Close to three-quarters of all North Americans now have access to the Web, making it a fertile channel for reaching a broad cross-section of consumers. As response rates for traditional survey approaches decline and costs increase, the Web is quickly replacing mail and the telephone as the dominant data collection methodology. Online research now accounts for about 50 percent of all survey research done in the United States and Canada.[23]

Web-based survey research offers some real advantages over traditional phone and mail approaches. The most obvious advantages are speed and low costs. By going online, researchers can quickly and easily distribute Internet surveys to thousands of respondents simultaneously via email or by posting them on selected websites. Responses can be almost instantaneous, and because respondents themselves enter the information, researchers can tabulate, review, and share research data as they arrive.

Online research usually costs much less than research conducted through mail, phone, or personal interviews. Using the Internet eliminates most of the postage, phone, interviewer, and data-handling costs associated with the other approaches. As a result, Internet surveys typically cost 15 to 20 percent less than mail surveys and 30 percent less than phone surveys. Moreover, sample size has little impact on costs. Once the questionnaire is set up, there's little difference in cost between 10 and 10 000 respondents on the Web.

Thus, online research is well within the reach of almost any business, large or small. In fact, with the Internet, "what was once the domain of the high-cost experts has now become available to practically anybody with a desire to use it," says a marketing research executive.[24] Even smaller, less sophisticated researchers can use online survey services such as Zoomerang (www.zoomerang.com) and SurveyMonkey (www.surveymonkey.com) to create, publish, and distribute their own custom surveys in minutes. However, tighter privacy legislation in several provinces, which was implemented in response to the *U.S.A. Patriot Act*, now require Canadian companies to store their customer data in Canada. As a result, Canadian-based survey tools, such as FluidSurveys (www.fluidsurveys.com), offer similar survey tools while storing consumer data on Canadian servers.

Beyond their speed and cost advantages, Web-based surveys also tend to be more interactive and engaging, easier to complete,

Online marketing research
Collecting primary data online through Internet surveys, online focus groups, Web-based experiments, or tracking consumers' online behaviour.

Exhibit 5.8 Online research: Thanks to survey services such as FluidSurveys, almost any business, large or small, can create, publish, and distribute its own custom surveys in minutes.

and less intrusive than traditional phone or mail surveys. As a result, they usually garner higher response rates. The Internet is an excellent medium for reaching the hard-to-reach—the often-elusive teen, single, affluent, and well-educated audiences. It's also good for reaching working mothers and other people who lead busy lives. Such people are well represented online, and they can respond in their own space and at their own convenience.

Just as marketing researchers have rushed to use the Internet for quantitative surveys and data collection, they are now also adopting *qualitative* Web-based research approaches—such as online depth interviews, focus groups, blogs, and social networks. The Internet can provide a fast, low-cost way to gain qualitative customer insights. For example, Anheuser-Busch uses the Web—both formally and informally—as a research "test-lab" for advertising ideas.[25]

> Anheuser-Busch is increasingly using the Web to spread and fine-tune its advertising. The Web allows it to test-drive edgy material that, in years past, would never have seen the light of day for fear of causing offense on TV. Witness the strange life of "Swear Jar," a commercial that portrays an effort to clean up office language by fining staffers 25 cent per profanity. The twist: the cash goes toward buying Bud Light—and the wholesome plan backfires spectacularly. Although the language was too raw for TV, A-B tested it out on the Internet. Someone sent it to YouTube, where it has since gotten more than 3.7 million hits, despite never appearing on television. "The digital space ... can be an incubator for ideas," says an Anheuser-Busch media executive. Using the Web to gauge fervour for offbeat ads promises broader and quicker insight than the traditional way—peeking through a one-way window as a test group watches new TV commercials. "The Web gives instant credibility or thumbs-down," says the executive.

Online focus groups
Gathering a small group of people online with a trained moderator to chat about a product, service, or organization and to gain qualitative insights about consumer attitudes and behaviour.

A primary qualitative Web-based research approach is **online focus groups**. Such focus groups offer many advantages over traditional focus groups. Participants can log in from anywhere—all they need is a laptop and a Web connection. Thus, the Internet works well for bringing together people from different parts of the country or the world, especially those in higher-income groups who can't spare the time to travel to a central site. Also, researchers can conduct and monitor online focus groups from just about anywhere, eliminating travel, lodging, and facility costs. Finally, although online focus groups require some advance scheduling, results are almost immediate.

Online focus groups can take any of several formats. Most occur in real time, in the form of online chat room discussions in which participants and a moderator sit around a virtual table exchanging comments. Alternatively, researchers might set up an online message board on which respondents interact over the course of several days or a few weeks. Participants log in daily and comment on focus group topics.

Although low in cost and easy to administer, online focus groups can lack the real-world dynamics of more personal approaches. The online world is devoid of the eye contact, body language, and direct personal interactions found in traditional focus group research. And the Internet format—running, typed commentary and online "emoticons" (punctuation marks that express emotion, such as :-) to signify happiness)—greatly restricts respondent expressiveness. The impersonal nature of the Internet can prevent people from interacting with each other in a normal way and getting excited about a concept.

To overcome these shortcomings, some researchers are now adding real-time audio and video to their online focus groups. For example, online research firm Channel M2 "puts the human touch back into online research" by assembling focus group participants in people-friendly "virtual interview rooms."[26]

> Participants are recruited using traditional methods and then sent a Web camera so that both their verbal and nonverbal reactions can be recorded. Participants then receive instructions via e-mail, including a link to the Channel M2 online interviewing room and a toll-free

teleconference number to call. At the appointed time, when they click on the link and phone in, participants sign on and see the Channel M2 interview room, complete with live video of the other participants, text chat, screen or slide sharing, and a whiteboard. Once the focus group is underway, questions and answers occur in "real time" in a remarkably lively setting. Participants comment spontaneously—verbally, via text messaging, or both. Researchers can "sit in" on the focus group from anywhere, seeing and hearing every respondent. Or they can review a recorded version at a later date.

Although the use of online marketing research is growing rapidly, both quantitative and qualitative Web-based research does have some drawbacks. One major problem is controlling who's in the online sample. Without seeing respondents, it's difficult to know who they really are. To overcome such sample and context problems, many online research firms use opt-in communities and respondent panels. For example, Zoomerang offers an online consumer and business panel profiled on more than 500 attributes.[27] Alternatively, many companies are now developing their own custom social networks and using them to gain customer inputs and insights (see Marketing@Work 5.1).

Exhibit 5.9   Some researchers have now added real-time audio and video to their online focus groups. For example, Channel M2 "puts the human touch back into online research" by assembling focus group participants in people-friendly "virtual interview rooms."

Perhaps the most explosive issue facing online researchers concerns consumer privacy. Some critics fear that unethical researchers will use the email addresses and confidential responses gathered through surveys to sell products after the research is completed. They are concerned about the use of technologies that collect personal information online without the respondents' consent. Failure to address such privacy issues could result in angry, less–co-operative consumers and increased government intervention. For example, Canada's *Personal Information Protection and Electronic Documents Act* and the *Electronic Commerce Protection Act* are designed to protect consumer privacy and personal security. Despite these concerns, most industry insiders predict healthy growth for online marketing research.[28]

Sampling Plan   Marketing researchers usually draw conclusions about large groups of consumers by studying a small sample of the total consumer population. A **sample** is a segment of the population selected for marketing research to represent the population as a whole. Ideally, the sample should be representative so that the researcher can make accurate estimates of the thoughts and behaviours of the larger population.

Designing the sample requires three decisions. First, *who* is to be studied (what *sampling unit*)? The answer to this question is not always obvious. For example, to learn about the decision-making process for a family automobile purchase, should the subject be the husband, wife, other family members, dealership salespeople, or all of these? The researcher must determine what information is needed and who is most likely to have it.

Second, *how many* people should be included (what *sample size*)? Large samples give more reliable results than small samples. However, larger samples usually cost more, and it is not necessary to sample the entire target market or even a large portion to get reliable results. If well chosen, samples of less than 1 percent of a population can often give good reliability.

Third, *how* should the people in the sample be *chosen* (what *sampling procedure*)? Table 5.4 describes different kinds of samples. Using *probability samples*, each population

Sample

A segment of the population selected for marketing research to represent the population as a whole.

MARKETING@WORK 5.1

Custom Social Networks: Del Monte Unleashes Dog-Lover Insights

When Del Monte Foods—maker of such well-known dog food brands as Kibbles 'n Bits, Gravy Train, and Milk-Bone—was considering a new breakfast treat for dogs, it sent out a note to an online community of dog owners, called "I Love My Dog," asking them what they most wanted to feed their pets in the morning. The consensus answer was something with a bacon-and-egg taste. The result: Del Monte introduced Snausages Breakfast Bites, born out of insights that a dedicated segment of dog owners love to share holiday events and mealtimes with their pets. The Snausages Breakfast Bites are flavoured like bacon and eggs and contain an extra dose of vitamins and minerals, which the dog owners said was also important to them.

The "I Love My Dog" online community isn't some random chat room or yet another website for dog enthusiasts—it's a custom social network created by Del Monte and research firm MarketTools. Its 400 members were hand-picked to join the private social network, which the company uses to help create products, test marketing campaigns, and stir up buzz. "The idea is to develop a relationship ... create ad hoc surveys and get feedback," says Del Monte senior customer insights manager Gala Amoroso. "If one of the brand managers has a new product idea or a different positioning, instead of just internal brainstorming within the company and before putting real research dollars behind it, we'll float it with the [online] community."

Such online networks are now rapidly spreading to companies ranging from Coca-Cola and P&G to Walt Disney's ABC Television Studios. They are often cheaper and more effective than phone surveys or traditional focus groups because companies can draw on the participants in a much broader and deeper way than they could in an offline setting.

Del Monte found that traditional market research techniques simply weren't providing enough depth of customer understanding. Traditional qualitative methods (such as ethnographies and focus groups) were either too time-consuming or too shallow. Surveys and other quantitative methods, although helpful in answering specific questions, did not allow for interactive exploration. In contrast, the custom dog-lover network lets Del Monte continuously observe and interact with important customers to obtain authentic, in-depth insights.

The "I Love My Dog" site and other custom networks bear a resemblance to other online social networking sites, where members create profile pages and post to discussion boards. Companies use them to administer polls, chat in real time with consumers, and even ask members to go to the store to try out specific products. The rapid back-and-forth between the company and the online community can help to

Exhibit 5.10   Del Monte's "I Love My Dog" custom social network lets the company continuously observe and interact with important customers to obtain authentic, in-depth insights.

substantially shorten the product-development cycle, a process that typically takes a year or more from the time a company comes up with a product idea until the item arrives in stores.

For Snausages Breakfast Bites, that process took only six months. During that time, Del Monte contacted "I Love My Dog" members dozens of times, both as a group and individually. The company has also tapped network members for pre-launch insights into other products, including its Pup-Peroni treat that recently landed on store shelves. "It is not just a focus group that you see for three hours; you are developing a relationship with these pet parents," says Amoroso.

As with any social-networking site, these private networks face the constant risk of member boredom and, ultimately, member dropout. There can be a fair amount of turnover on the private networks, and to keep members around, the companies that set them up have to constantly add games and other features,

along with incentives such as coupons, giveaways, and sneak peeks at new products. Properly tended, however, networks such as "I Love My Dog" help remove some of the guesswork for marketers by letting brands know exactly to whom they are talking and giving them more control over the discussions.

Based on the success of the "I Love My Dog" network, Del Monte has now worked with MarketTools to create another custom network, this one consisting of 10 200 moms. It plans to tap this Moms Insight Network for advice and collaboration on current brands as well as new product launches. One key insight already gleaned from the moms network is that moms trust experts less than ever and are more interested in hearing from other moms in similar situations. This finding lends even greater importance to the Moms Insight Network, which not only seeks in-depth inputs from mothers but connects them with each other in the context of Del Monte brands.

Amoroso has high hopes for Del Monte's custom social networks. "The online community Web sites give us a wealth of information about our target consumers' pains and needs and provides a platform for us to explore and understand their attitudes and behaviours," she says. "It helps us anticipate and identify opportunities, and it enables us to collaborate with our target market to develop new solutions that truly meet their needs. It's different than receiving a report from a study. It's about taking the time to go to the community and listen."

Sources: Portions adapted from Emily Steel, "The New Focus Groups: Online Networks," *Wall Street Journal,* January 14, 2008, p. B6; with quotes and other information from Abbey Klaassen, "Del Monte to Take Its Cues from Moms," *Advertising Age,* July 2, 2007; "Del Monte Foods Turns to Dog Owners to Unleash Innovation," MarketTools Case Study, May 2008, accessed at www.classmatandread.net/565media/DelMonte.pdf; Lisa Braziel, "Social Media Marketing Example #4: Del Monte Foods," October 20, 2008, accessed at www.ignitesocialmedia.com/social-media-marketing-example-4-del-monte-foods/; and Andrew McMains, "Customers Deliver Brand Insights Online," *Adweek,* April 20, 2009, accessed at www.adweek.com.

member has a known chance of being included in the sample, and researchers can calculate confidence limits for sampling error. But when probability sampling costs too much or takes too much time, marketing researchers often take *nonprobability samples*, even though their sampling error cannot be measured. These varied ways of drawing samples have different costs and time limitations as well as different accuracy and statistical properties. Which method is best depends on the needs of the research project.

Research Instruments In collecting primary data, marketing researchers have a choice of two main research instruments—the *questionnaire* and *mechanical instruments*.

TABLE 5.4 Types of Samples

Probability Sample

Simple random sample	Every member of the population has a known and equal chance of selection.
Stratified random sample	The population is divided into mutually exclusive groups (such as age groups), and random samples are drawn from each group.
Cluster (area) sample	The population is divided into mutually exclusive groups (such as blocks), and the researcher draws a sample of the groups to interview.

Nonprobability Sample

Convenience sample	The researcher selects the easiest population members from which to obtain information.
Judgment sample	The researcher uses his or her judgment to select population members who are good prospects for accurate information.
Quota sample	The researcher finds and interviews a prescribed number of people in each of several categories.

QUESTIONNAIRES   The *questionnaire* is by far the most common instrument, whether administered in person, by phone, or online. Questionnaires are very flexible—there are many ways to ask questions. *Closed-end questions* include all the possible answers, and subjects make choices among them. Examples include multiple-choice questions and scale questions. *Open-end questions* allow respondents to answer in their own words. In a survey of airline users, WestJet might simply ask, "What is your opinion of WestJet Airlines?" Or it might ask people to complete a sentence: "When I choose an airline, the most important consideration is...." These and other kinds of open-end questions often reveal more than closed-end questions because they do not limit respondents' answers.

Open-end questions are especially useful in exploratory research, when the researcher is trying to find out *what* people think but not measuring *how many* people think in a certain way. Closed-end questions, on the other hand, provide answers that are easier to interpret and tabulate.

Researchers should also use care in the *wording* and *ordering* of questions. They should use simple, direct, unbiased wording. Questions should be arranged in a logical order. The first question should create interest if possible, and difficult or personal questions should be asked last so that respondents do not become defensive.

MECHANICAL INSTRUMENTS   Although questionnaires are the most common research instrument, researchers also use *mechanical instruments* to monitor consumer behaviour. Nielsen Media Research attaches *people metres* to television sets, cable boxes, and satellite systems in selected homes to record who watches which programs. Retailers use *checkout scanners* to record shoppers' purchases.

Other mechanical devices measure subjects' physical responses. For example, advertisers use eye cameras to study viewers' eye movements while watching ads—at what points their eyes focus first and how long they linger on any given ad component. IBM's BlueEyes technology interprets human facial reactions by tracking pupil, eyebrow, and mouth movements. BlueEyes offers a host of potential marketing uses, such as marketing machines that "know how you feel" and react accordingly. An elderly man squints at a bank's ATM screen and the font size doubles almost instantly. A woman at a shopping centre kiosk smiles at a travel ad, prompting the device to print out a travel discount coupon.[29]

Still other researchers are applying "neuro marketing," measuring brain activity to learn how consumers feel and respond. Marketing scientists using MRI scans have learned that "strong brands trigger activity in parts of the brain associated with self-identification, positive emotions, and rewards." Several high-tech firms—such as EmSense, NeuroFocus, and Sands Research—now help firms peer into the inner workings of their customers' brains and emotions.

According to one observer, it "turns out the Nike's swoosh is more than just a feel-good brand logo. It actually lights up your brain." Similarly, when researchers strapped electrode-loaded caps on the noggins of test subjects during the recent Super Bowl to measure advertising engagement, they learned that brain activity soared for some ads but lagged for others.[30] In fact, Coca-Cola worked with EmSense before the Super Bowl to help it decide which ads would work best:

In the weeks leading up to the game, Coca-Cola produced about a dozen new ads for possible placement and asked EmSense to help it make the right choices.

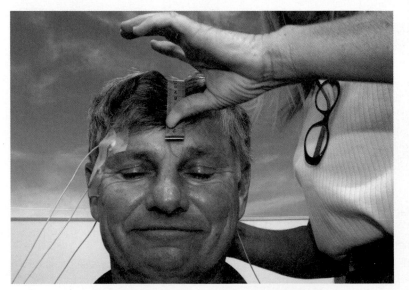

Exhibit 5.11 Mechanical measures of consumer response: Some marketers apply neuromarketing—peering into consumers' minds by measuring brain activity to discover how they respond to brands and marketing.

The EmSense device, shaped like a thin plastic headband, reads brain waves and monitors the breathing, heart rate, blinking, and skin temperatures of consumers who preview ads to measure their emotional and cognitive responses. The continuous measures help researchers to decipher consumer feelings and reactions at each moment of any given ad. According to Coca-Cola's North America CMO, the device not only helped whittle down the list of spots, it also aided in editing the two ads chosen to air, shoring up cognitive weak spots. For example, the music in one ad was adjusted in the days leading up to the game to build more of a crescendo than in the original version of the spot. Neuromarketing "provides you with more natural and unedited responses than you get when you force people through the cognitive loop of having to [remember and tell you] how they feel," says the Coca-Cola executive. "It's a great new tool."[31]

Although neuromarketing techniques can measure consumer involvement and emotional responses second by second, such brain responses can be difficult to interpret. Thus, neuromarketing is usually used in combination with other research approaches to gain a more complete picture of what goes on inside consumers' heads.

IMPLEMENTING THE RESEARCH PLAN

The researcher next puts the marketing research plan into action. This involves collecting, processing, and analyzing the information. Data collection can be carried out by the company's marketing research staff or by outside firms. Researchers should watch closely to make sure that the plan is implemented correctly. They must guard against problems with interacting with respondents, with the quality of participants' responses, and with interviewers who make mistakes or take shortcuts.

Researchers must also process and analyze the collected data to isolate important information and insight. They need to check data for accuracy and completeness and code it for analysis. The researchers then tabulate the results and compute statistical measures.

INTERPRETING AND REPORTING THE FINDINGS

The market researcher must now interpret the findings, draw conclusions, and report them to management. The researcher should not try to overwhelm managers with numbers and fancy statistical techniques. Rather, the researcher should present important findings and insights that are useful in the major decisions faced by management.

However, interpretation should not be left only to the researchers. They are often experts in research design and statistics, but the marketing manager knows more about the problem and the decisions that must be made. The best research means little if the manager blindly accepts faulty interpretations from the researcher. Similarly, managers may be biased—they might tend to accept research results that show what they expected and reject those that they did not expect or hope for. In many cases, findings can be interpreted in different ways, and discussions between researchers and managers will help point to the best interpretations. Thus, managers and researchers must work together closely when interpreting research results, and both must share responsibility for the research process and resulting decisions.

ANALYZING AND USING MARKETING INFORMATION 🄻🄾4

Information gathered in internal databases and through competitive marketing intelligence and marketing research usually requires additional analysis. And managers may need help applying the information to gain customer and market insights that will improve their marketing decisions. This help may include advanced statistical analysis to learn more about the relationships within a set of data. Information analysis might also involve the application of analytical models that will help marketers make better decisions.

Once the information has been processed and analyzed, it must be made available to the right decision makers at the right time. In the following sections, we look deeper into analyzing and using marketing information.

CUSTOMER RELATIONSHIP MANAGEMENT (CRM)

The question of how best to analyze and use individual customer data presents special problems. Most companies are awash in information about their customers. In fact, smart companies capture information at every possible customer *touch point*. These touch points include customer purchases, sales force contacts, service and support calls, website visits, satisfaction surveys, credit and payment interactions, market research studies—every contact between the customer and the company.

Customer relationship management (CRM)

Managing detailed information about individual customers and carefully managing customer "touch points" to maximize customer loyalty.

Unfortunately, this information is usually scattered widely across the organization. It is buried deep in the separate databases and records of different company departments. To overcome such problems, many companies are now turning to **customer relationship management (CRM)** to manage detailed information about individual customers and carefully manage customer touch points to maximize customer loyalty.

CRM first burst onto the scene in the early 2000s. Many companies rushed in, implementing overly ambitious CRM programs that produced disappointing results and many failures. More recently, however, companies are moving ahead more cautiously and implementing CRM systems that really work. Last year, companies worldwide spent US$7.8 billion on CRM systems from companies such as Oracle, Microsoft, Salesforce.com, and SAS, up 14.2 percent from the previous year. By 2012, they will spend an estimated US$13.3 billion on CRM systems.[32]

CRM consists of sophisticated software and analytical tools that integrate customer information from all sources, analyze it in depth, and apply the results to build stronger customer relationships. CRM integrates everything that a company's sales, service, and marketing teams know about individual customers to provide a 360-degree view of the customer relationship.

CRM analysts develop *data warehouses* and use sophisticated *data mining* techniques to unearth the riches hidden in customer data. A data warehouse is a company-wide electronic database of finely detailed customer information that needs to be sifted through for gems. The purpose of a data warehouse is not just to gather information, but to pull it together into a central, accessible location. Then, once the data warehouse brings the data together, the company uses high-powered data mining techniques to sift through the mounds of data and dig out interesting findings about customers.

These findings often lead to marketing opportunities. For example, Bell Canada, the largest provider of telecommunications services in Canada, was recognized for excellence in CRM Marketing Optimization. Fielding tens of thousands of customer calls each year, the company's CRM system automatically analyzes historical, personal, and contextual data to provide customized offers based on previous interactions, which helps the company improve the customer experience, increase revenue, and reduce customer churn. It identifies when customers are most receptive to its marketing initiatives and enables the company to upsell its services.[33]

Shoppers Drug Mart uses data mining techniques to dig deeply into data obtained from its Optimum customer loyalty card.

There's no fee to join the Shoppers Optimum Program. Members get a Shoppers Optimum Card, which they hand to the cashier, who swipes the card's magnetic strip through a reader.

When you sign up for the card, Shoppers Drug Mart collects your name, birth date, address, and the ages of your children, if you choose to fill out that information. Every time you use the card you collect points, and Shoppers collects data about the purchases you made that day and adds that information to your customer record. Once the company knows a little about you, they can begin marketing more effectively to you.

For example, if you are a 19-year-old unmarried female university student, with no children, you might appreciate getting special offers for cosmetics and hair care products but would have no use for coupons for diapers and other baby products. A 35-year-old woman with two small children, on the other hand, might appreciate getting both. When Gillette launches its latest men's shaving products, Shoppers might promote them to male Shoppers Optimum Card holders between the ages of 18 and 50, but not to its female members. Shoppers Drug Mart uses the data mining result to guide strategies for tailored promotions, pricing, placement, and even stocking variations from store to store. Consumer response to the loyalty program has been very popular. In fact, it is estimated that fifty percent of Canadian women are enrolled in what some have called the most generous loyalty program in Canada.[34]

Exhibit 5.12 Shoppers Drug Mart digs deeply into data obtained from its Optimum customer loyalty cards.

By using CRM to understand customers better, companies can provide higher levels of customer service and develop deeper customer relationships. They can use CRM to pinpoint high-value customers, target them more effectively, cross-sell the company's products, and create offers tailored to specific customer requirements.

CRM benefits don't come without costs or risk, either in collecting the original customer data or in maintaining and mining it. The most common CRM mistake is to view CRM only as a technology and software solution. But technology alone cannot build profitable customer relationships. "CRM is not a technology solution—you can't achieve ... improved customer relationships by simply slapping in some software," says a CRM expert. Instead, CRM is just one part of an effective overall *customer relationship management strategy*. "Focus on the *R*," advises the expert. "Remember, a relationship is what CRM is all about."[35]

When it works, the benefits of CRM can far outweigh the costs and risks. Based on a study by SAP, customers using its mySAP CRM software reported an average 10 percent increase in customer retention and a 30 percent increase in sales leads. Overall, 90 percent of the companies surveyed increased in value from use of the software and reported an attractive return on investment. The study's conclusion: "CRM pays off."[36]

DISTRIBUTING AND USING MARKETING INFORMATION

Marketing information has no value until it is used to gain customer insights and make better marketing decisions. Thus, the marketing information system must make the information readily available to the managers and others who need it. In some cases, this means providing managers with regular performance reports, intelligence updates, and reports on the results of research studies.

But marketing managers may also need non-routine information for special situations and on-the-spot decisions. For example, a sales manager having trouble with a large customer may want a summary of the account's sales and profitability over the past year. Or a retail store manager who has run out of a bestselling product may want to know the current inventory levels in the chain's other stores. These days, therefore, information distribution involves entering information into databases and making it available in a timely, user-friendly way.

Many firms use a company *intranet* to facilitate this process. The intranet provides ready access to research information, reports, shared work documents, contact information for employees and other stakeholders, and more. For example, iGo, a catalogue and Web retailer, integrates incoming customer service calls with up-to-date database information about customers' Web purchases and email inquiries. By accessing this information on the intranet while speaking with the customer, iGo's service representatives can get a well-rounded picture of each customer's purchasing history and previous contacts with the company.

In addition, companies are increasingly allowing key customers and value-network members to access account, product, and other data on demand through *extranets*. Suppliers, customers, resellers, and select other network members may access a company's extranet to update their accounts, arrange purchases, and check orders against inventories to improve customer service. For example, Penske Truck Leasing's extranet site, MyFleetAtPenske.com, lets Penske customers access all of the data about their fleets in one spot and provides an array of tools and applications designed to help fleet managers manage their Penske accounts and maximize efficiency. And Target's PartnersOnline extranet lets the retailer's supplier/partners review current sales, inventory, delivery, and forecasting data. Such information sharing helps Target, its suppliers, and its customers by elevating the performance of the supply chain.[37]

Thanks to modern technology, today's marketing managers can gain direct access to the information system at any time and from virtually any location. They can tap into the system while working at a home office, from a hotel room, or from the local Starbucks through a wireless network—anyplace where they can turn on a laptop or BlackBerry. Such systems allow managers to get the information they need directly and quickly and to tailor it to their own needs. From just about anywhere, they can obtain information from company or outside databases, analyze it by using statistical software, prepare reports and presentations, and communicate directly with others in the network.

OTHER MARKETING INFORMATION CONSIDERATIONS (L05)

This section discusses marketing information in two special contexts: marketing research in small businesses and non-profit organizations and international marketing research. Finally, we look at public policy and ethics issues in marketing research.

MARKETING RESEARCH IN SMALL BUSINESSES AND NON-PROFIT ORGANIZATIONS

Just like larger firms, small organizations need market information and the customer and market insights that it can provide. Start-up businesses need information about their potential customers, industries, competitors, unfilled needs, and reactions to new market offers. Existing small businesses must track changes in customer needs and wants, reactions to new products, and changes in the competitive environment.

Managers of small businesses and non-profit organizations often think that marketing research can be done only by experts in large companies with big research budgets. True, large-scale research studies are beyond the budgets of most small businesses. However, many of the marketing research techniques discussed in this chapter also can be used by smaller organizations in a less formal manner and at little or no expense. Consider how one small-business owner conducted market research on a shoestring before even opening his doors:[38]

Exhibit 5.13 Before opening Bibbentuckers dry cleaner, owner Robert Byerley conducted research to gain insights into what customers wanted. First on the list: quality.

> After a string of bad experiences with his local dry cleaner, Robert Byerley decided to open his own dry-cleaning business. But before jumping in, he conducted plenty of market research. He needed a key customer insight: How would he make his cleaners stand out? To start, Byerley spent an entire week in the library and online, researching the dry-cleaning industry. To get input from potential customers, using a marketing firm, Byerley held focus groups on the store's name, look, and brochure. He also took clothes to the 15 best competing cleaners in town and had focus group members critique their work. Based on his research, he made a list of features for his new business. First on his list: quality. His business would stand behind everything it did. Not on the list: cheap prices. Creating the perfect dry-cleaning establishment simply didn't fit with a discount operation.
>
> With his research complete, Byerley opened Bibbentuckers, a high-end dry cleaner positioned on high-quality service and convenience. It featured a bank-like drive-through area with curbside delivery. A computerized bar code system read customer cleaning preferences and tracked clothes all the way through the cleaning process. Byerley added other differentiators, such as decorative awnings, TV screens, and refreshments (even "candy for the kids and a doggy treat for your best friend"). "I wanted a place ... that paired five-star service and quality with an establishment that didn't look like a dry cleaner," he says. The market research yielded results. Today, Bibbentuckers is a thriving three-store operation.

"Too [few] small-business owners have a ... marketing mind-set," says a small-business consultant. "You have to think like Procter & Gamble. What would they do before launching a new product? They would find out who their customer is and who their competition is."[39]

Thus, small businesses and not-for-profit organizations can obtain good marketing insights through observation or informal surveys by using small convenience samples. Also, many associations, local media, and government agencies provide special help to small organizations. For example, the Conference Board of Canada and the Canadian Council for Small Business and Entrepreneurship offer dozens of free publications that give advice on topics ranging from preparing a business plan to ordering business signs. Other excellent Web resources for small businesses include Statistics Canada (www. statscan.gc.ca) and Industry Canada (www.ic.gc.ca). Finally, small businesses can collect a considerable amount of information at very little cost online. They can scour competitor and customer websites and use Internet search engines to research specific companies and issues.

In summary, secondary data collection, observation, surveys, and experiments can all be used effectively by small organizations with small budgets. However, although these informal research methods are less complex and less costly, they still must be conducted with care. Managers must think carefully about the objectives of the research, formulate questions in advance, recognize the biases introduced by smaller samples and less skilled researchers, and conduct the research systematically.[40]

INTERNATIONAL MARKETING RESEARCH

International marketing research has grown tremendously over the past decade. In 1995, the top 25 global marketing research organizations had total combined revenues of US$5.7 billion, with 45 percent of these revenues coming from outside companies' home countries. By 2007, total revenues for these organizations had grown to US$17.5 billion, and the out-of-home-country share had grown to more than 57 percent.[41]

International marketing researchers follow the same steps as domestic researchers, from defining the research problem and developing a research plan to interpreting and reporting the results. However, these researchers often face more and different problems. Whereas domestic researchers deal with fairly homogenous markets within a single country, international researchers deal with diverse markets in many different countries. These markets often vary greatly in their levels of economic development, cultures and customs, and buying patterns.

In many foreign markets, the international researcher may have a difficult time finding good secondary data. Whereas U.S. and Canadian marketing researchers can obtain reliable secondary data from dozens of domestic research services, many countries have almost no research services at all. Some of the largest international research services do operate in many countries. For example, The Nielsen Company (the world's largest marketing research company) has offices in more than 100 countries, from Schaumburg, Illinois, to Hong Kong, to Nicosia, Cyprus.[42] However, most research firms operate in only a relative handful of countries. Thus, even when secondary information is available, it usually must be obtained from many different sources on a country-by-country basis, making the information difficult to combine or compare.

Because of the scarcity of good secondary data, international researchers often must collect their own primary data. For example, they may find it difficult simply to develop good samples. U.S. and Canadian researchers can use current telephone directories, email lists, census tract data, and any of several sources of socio-economic data to construct samples. However, such information is largely lacking in many countries.

Once the sample is drawn, the U.S. and Canadian researcher usually can reach most respondents easily by telephone, by mail, on the Internet, or in person. Reaching respondents is often not so easy in other parts of the world. Researchers in Mexico cannot

Exhibit 5.14 Some of the largest research services firms have large international organizations. The Nielsen Company has offices in more than 100 countries, here Germany and Japan.

rely on telephone, Internet, and mail data collection—most data collection is door to door and concentrated in three or four of the largest cities. In some countries, few people have phones or personal computers. For example, whereas there are 75 Internet users per 100 people in Canada, there are only 22 Internet users per 100 people in Mexico. In Kenya, the numbers drop to 8 Internet users per 100 people. In some countries, the postal system is notoriously unreliable. In Brazil, for instance, an estimated 30 percent of the mail is never delivered. In many developing countries, poor roads and transportation systems make certain areas hard to reach, making personal interviews difficult and expensive.[43]

Cultural differences from country to country cause additional problems for international researchers. Language is the most obvious obstacle. For example, questionnaires must be prepared in one language and then translated into the languages of each country researched. Responses then must be translated back into the original language for analysis and interpretation. This adds to research costs and increases the risks of error.

Translating a questionnaire from one language to another is anything but easy. Many idioms, phrases, and statements mean different things in different cultures. For example, a Danish executive noted, "Check this out by having a different translator put back into English what you've translated from English. You'll get the shock of your life. I remember [an example in which] 'out of sight, out of mind' had become 'invisible things are insane.'"[44]

Consumers in different countries also vary in their attitudes toward marketing research. People in one country may be very willing to respond; in other countries, nonresponse can be a major problem. Customs in some countries may prohibit people from talking with strangers. In certain cultures, research questions often are considered too personal. For example, in many Latin American countries, people may feel embarrassed to talk with researchers about their choices of shampoo, deodorant, or other personal care products. Similarly, in many Muslim countries, mixed-gender focus groups are taboo, as is videotaping female-only focus groups. Even when respondents are *willing* to respond, they may not be *able* to because of high functional illiteracy rates.

Despite these problems, as global marketing grows, global companies have little choice but to conduct such international marketing research. Although the costs and problems associated with international research may be high, the costs of not doing it— in terms of missed opportunities and mistakes—might be even higher. Once recognized, many of the problems associated with international marketing research can be overcome or avoided.

PUBLIC POLICY AND ETHICS IN MARKETING RESEARCH

Most marketing research benefits both the sponsoring company and its consumers. Through marketing research, companies learn more about consumers' needs, resulting in more satisfying products and services and stronger customer relationships. However, the misuse of marketing research can also harm or annoy consumers. Two major public policy and ethics issues in marketing research are intrusions on consumer privacy and the misuse of research findings.

Intrusions on Consumer Privacy Many consumers feel positive about marketing research and believe that it serves a useful purpose. Some actually enjoy being interviewed and giving their opinions. However, others strongly resent or even mistrust marketing research. They don't like being interrupted by researchers. They worry that marketers are building huge databases full of personal information about customers. Or they fear that researchers might use sophisticated techniques to probe our deepest feelings, peek over our shoulders as we shop, or eavesdrop on our conversations and then use this knowledge to manipulate our buying.

There are no easy answers when it comes to marketing research and privacy. For example, is it a good or bad thing that marketers track and analyze consumers' Web clicks and target ads to individuals based on their browsing behaviour? (See Marketing@Work 5.2.) Should we applaud or resent companies that monitor consumer discussions on YouTube, Facebook, Twitter, or other public social networks in an effort to be more responsive? Remember the Radian6 and Dell example earlier in this chapter?

> Last spring, Canadian blogger Carman Pirie questioned Dell's decision to begin selling its computers through Wal-Mart and wrote about it on his blog. Given Dell's previously successful direct-only sales model, Pirie didn't think selling machines through Wal-Mart was a smart strategy and he wasn't shy about sharing his thoughts. What he didn't expect was a reply from a Dell representative in the form of a comment on his blog post, explaining in great detail why Dell was working with Wal-Mart. "Within a couple of hours of posting ... I got a response from Richard at Dell," said a duly impressed Pirie. "Here's Dell, based in Round Rock, Texas, interacting with a blogger in Halifax, Nova Scotia ... within a three-hour window," he said.
>
> Dell views tracking and responding to social media conversations as opportunities to engage consumers in helpful two-way conversations. However, some disconcerted consumers might see experiences such as Pirie's as an intrusion of privacy. Although Dell tracks only public forums, it does not inform consumers or obtain their consent. Interestingly, many consumers don't seem to mind. Consumers often moan that companies do not listen to them. Perhaps the monitoring of online discussions can provide an answer to that problem.[45]

Consumers may also have been taken in by previous "research surveys" that actually turned out to be attempts to sell them something. Still other consumers confuse legitimate marketing research studies with promotional efforts and say "no" before the interviewer can even begin. Most, however, simply resent the intrusion. They dislike mail, telephone, or Web surveys that are too long or too personal or that interrupt them at inconvenient times.

Increasing consumer resentment has become a major problem for the marketing research industry, leading to lower survey response rates in recent years. Just as companies face the challenge of unearthing valuable but potentially sensitive consumer data while also maintaining consumer trust, consumers wrestle with the trade-offs between personalization and privacy. Although many consumers willingly exchange personal information for free services, easy credit, discounts, upgrades, and all sorts of rewards, they also worry about the growth in online identity theft. A recent study by TRUSTe, an organization that monitors privacy practices of websites, found that more than 90 percent of respondents view online privacy as a "really" or "somewhat" important issue. More than 75 percent agreed with the statement, "The Internet is not well regulated, and naïve users can easily be taken advantage of." So it's no surprise that they are now less than willing to reveal personal information on websites.[46]

Banking is one industry where privacy has long been a concern, whether it is with regard to research or everyday transactions. RBC has been a leader in the area of privacy protection, believing that protecting confidentiality of personal and financial information is fundamental to the

Exhibit 5.15   RBC has a long history of respecting privacy and protecting financial information, which it sees as fundamental to the way it does business whether in person or online. It played an active role in developing Canadian privacy standards. Its website lists its Privacy Principles, which were designed to meet the needs and expectations of its clients.

MARKETING@WORK 5.2

Tracking Consumers on the Web: Smart Targeting or a Little Creepy?

On the Internet today, everybody knows who you are. In fact, legions of Internet companies also know your gender, your age, the neighbourhood you live in, that you like pickup trucks, and that you spent, say, three hours and 43 seconds on a website for pet lovers on a rainy day in January. All that data streams through myriad computer networks, where it's sorted, catalogued, analyzed, and then used to deliver ads aimed squarely at you, potentially anywhere you travel on the Web. It's called *behavioural targeting*—tracking consumers' online browsing behaviour and using it to target ads to them.

Information about what consumers do while they're trolling the vast expanse of the Internet—what searches they make, the sites they visit, what they buy—is pure gold to advertisers. And companies such as Google, Yahoo!, Microsoft's MSN, and AOL are busy mining that gold, helping advertisers to target ads based on just about every move you make on the Web. Online advertisers are now deploying a new breed of supersmart, supertargeted display ads geared to individual Web-browsing behaviour.

By using electronic markers on people's Web browsers called cookies, marketers have amassed a staggering amount of data about users. All that browsing data, blended with other online user information, can help marketers predict consumer behaviour and target their ads more precisely. Say you spent time at Yahoo! Autos sizing up cars based on fuel efficiency, then clicked over to Yahoo!'s Green Center to read about alternative fuels, and then looked at cars on eBay (which has a partnership with Yahoo!). Yahoo! can probably predict your next move. In fact, the company claims that it can tell with 75 percent certainty which of the 300 000 monthly visitors to Yahoo! Autos will actually purchase a car within the next three months. And the next time you visit Yahoo! Sports or

Finance, you'll likely see ads for hybrid cars.

Also moving quickly into online display advertising are a special breed of behavioural targeting advertising agencies, such as Audience Science (http://audiencescience.com) and the Yahoo! Network (http://advertising.yahoo.com/network). To get an even broader view of what consumers are thinking and doing online, such agencies track consumer behaviour across multiple websites. These companies "are, in effect, taking the trail of crumbs people leave behind as they move around the Internet, and then analyzing them to anticipate people's next steps," says an analyst.

This lets them merge audience data from one group of sites with ad placements on another. So if you surf home lawn and garden sites, don't be surprised to see ads for Scotts lawn products the next time you visit Weather.com. Or if you place a camera in an Amazon.ca shopping cart but don't buy it, expect to see some ads for that very type of camera the next time you visit

your favourite TSN site to catch up on the latest sports scores.

But what about consumer privacy? Yup. As you've no doubt already considered, that's the downside and the biggest danger to the rapidly expanding world of behavioural targeting. As the practice becomes more common, it faces growing consumer backlash. One observer calls it "the dark art of behavioural ad targeting"—eavesdropping on consumers without their knowledge or consent. "When you start to get into the details, it's scarier than you might suspect," says the director of a consumer privacy rights group. "We're recording preferences, hopes, worries, and fears."

In fact, the government has already stepped in to protect consumers from advertisers going too far. The U.S. Federal Trade Commission recently issued recommended voluntary guidelines, urging websites that apply behavioural advertising techniques to clearly and concisely spell out what they are doing and to give customers a simple way to opt out. The guidelines also suggested

Exhibit 5.16   Behavioural targeting: Wherever you go on the Internet, marketers are looking over your shoulder, and then targeting you with ads based on your Web browsing behaviour. Is it smart marketing or just "a little creepy"?

companies put limits on how long they store user information.

Most behavioural targeters have willingly complied with these guidelines. For example, Google labels ads so that people can click to find out more about how it places them. It also provides an online tool called the Ads Preferences Manager, which lets people view, delete, or add interest categories or opt out of ad-targeting cookies altogether. Yahoo! offers similar choices. And to protect consumer privacy further, both companies have agreed to limit the time they hold personally identifiable information to 90 days.

Despite privacy concerns, proponents claim that behavioural ad targeting benefits more than abuses consumers. Such targeting takes information from users' Web browsing behaviour and feeds back ads that are more relevant to their needs and interests. Yahoo! calls the practice "interest-matched advertising"; at

Google, it's "interest-based advertising." According to Google, people might even welcome more targeted ads. "We believe there is real value in seeing ads about the things that interest you," says a Google executive. "Most users prefer more relevant ads to less relevant ads. If, for example, you love adventure travel and therefore visited adventure travel sites, Google could show you more ads for activities like hiking trips to Patagonia or African safaris."

Although the practice may seem sinister to some consumers, advertisers sure like it. According to one estimate, by reaching the right person at the right time with the right ad, dollars spent on behavioural targeting yield a 37 percent return on investment. Still, it won't be easy to maintain consumer trust while at the same time walking the fine line between personalization and privacy. And as more and more companies enter the behavioural targeting ad space, the

chances of the tactic getting a bad name grow.

"We have something new and powerful," says an industry executive, "and there are likely to be people who abuse it." Abusive or beneficial, it'll be a hard sell to consumers. In a recent survey, when asked whether they were comfortable with behavioural targeting, only 28 percent of respondents said they were. More than half said they were not. As one analyst observes, following consumers online and stalking them with ads just "feels a little creepy."

Sources: Based on information found in Robert D. Hof, "Behavioral Targeting: Google Pulls out the Stops," *BusinessWeek*, March 12, 2009, accessed at www.businessweek.com; Brian Morissey, "Aim High: Ad Targeting Moves to the Next Level," *Adweek*, January 14, 2008, pp. 49–50; Brian Morissey, "Limits of Search Lead Some to Web Behavior," *Adweek*, March 27, 2006, p. 11; Steve Smith, "Behavioral Targeting Could Change the Game," *EContent*, January–February 2007, p. 22; Louise Story, "To Aim Ads, Web Is Keeping a Closer Eye on You," *New York Times*, March 10, 2008; and Stephanie Clifford, "Many See Privacy on the Web As Big Issue, Survey Says," *New York Times*, March 16, 2009.

way it does business. RBC's commitment has not changed with the arrival of new technologies, such as the Internet and online services.

Instead, it was extended to ensure that all clients' experiences with the bank were safe and secure. RBC was a strong supporter of industry privacy standards and related government regulation, playing an active role in the development of the Canadian Bankers Association's (CBA) Privacy Code of Conduct and the Canadian Standards Association's (CSA) Model for the Protection of Personal Privacy. These models were the foundation upon which RBC tailored its own privacy protection codes to meet the needs and expectations of its clients.[47]

Most major companies—including IBM, Facebook, Citigroup, American Express, and Microsoft—have now appointed a chief privacy officer (CPO), whose job is to safeguard the privacy of consumers who do business with the company. IBM's CPO claims that her job requires "multidisciplinary thinking and attitude." She needs to get all company departments, from technology, legal, and accounting to marketing and communications working together to safeguard customer privacy.[48]

American Express, which deals with a considerable volume of consumer information, has long taken privacy issues seriously. The company developed a set of formal privacy principles in 1991, and in 1998 it became one of the first companies to post privacy policies on its website. Its online Internet privacy statement tells customers in clear terms what information American Express collects and how it uses it, how it safeguards the information, and how it uses the information to market to its customers (with instructions on how to opt out).[49]

In the end, if researchers provide value in exchange for information, customers will gladly provide it. For example, Amazon.ca's customers do not mind if the firm builds a database of products they buy in order to provide future product recommendations. This saves time and provides value. Similarly, Bizrate users gladly complete surveys rating online seller sites because they can view the overall ratings of others when making purchase decisions. The best approach is for researchers to ask only for the information they need, to use it responsibly to provide customer value, and to avoid sharing information without the customer's permission.

Misuse of Research Findings Research studies can be powerful persuasion tools; companies often use study results as claims in their advertising and promotion. Today, however, many research studies appear to be little more than vehicles for pitching the sponsor's products. In fact, in some cases, the research surveys appear to have been designed just to produce the intended effect. Few advertisers openly rig their research designs or blatantly misrepresent the findings; most abuses tend to be subtle "stretches."

For example, the choice or wording in a survey can greatly affect the conclusions reached. One Black Flag survey asked, "A roach disk ... poisons a roach slowly. The dying roach returns to the nest and after it dies is eaten by other roaches. In turn these roaches become poisoned and die. How effective do you think this type of product would be in killing roaches?" Not surprisingly, 79 percent said effective.[50]

Recognizing that surveys can be abused, several associations—including the Marketing Research and Intelligence Association, the Canadian Marketing Association, and the American Marketing Association—have developed codes of research ethics and standards of conduct. In the end, however, unethical or inappropriate actions cannot simply be regulated away. Each company must accept responsibility for policing the conduct and reporting of its own marketing research to protect consumers' best interests and its own.

FOCUSING ON UNDERSTANDING YOUR CORE CUSTOMERS

Some companies have data banks bursting with information about their consumer bases. Skilled researchers and data miners then extract key information about their potential and existing customers. Marketers conduct this research to figure out who their core customers are and how they can better meet their customers' needs.

Canada Goose is a utility-first brand, and it aims to keep a steely-eyed focus on the utility of its coats and how its products match its customers. The company's core customers tend to be outdoors people, such as winter sport athletes and adventurers, ultra-marathoners, military personnel, police officers, and outdoor guides, However, you'll also see Canada Goose jackets on urban dwellers and celebrities who value the jackets for their style as much as their cold-weather protection.

To develop relationships with these different types of customers, Canada Goose has developed a number of unique corporate connections. The company has developed partnerships with organizations such as The Conservation Alliance and Polar Bears International (PBI) and has established two Canada Goose Resource Centres. These relationships are designed to help Canada Goose develop a community and keep in touch with its "true user" customer.

Collecting huge volumes of consumer data has not been the Canada Goose way, as it is a niche, not a mass-market, manufacturer. Instead, the company has formed relationships with Arctic climbers, northern Canadian Aboriginal peoples, and those in the know about cold weather. Close corporate partnerships and customer relationships have allowed Canada Goose to effectively determine which new products it should produce. Most importantly, Canada Goose listens to customers and retailers through a combination of both formal and informal channels. Every year, Canada Goose holds product development meetings where key retail partners are invited to provide feedback and discuss future design concepts. They also review online and in-store feedback from customers and fans who feel varying degrees of commitment and love for the brand.

QUESTIONS

1. What types of market research does Canada Goose conduct? What other areas of market research could the company explore?
2. Does Canada Goose create the product and pull the consumer to it or does it conduct research and adjust its product to the results of that research?
3. What would be some dangers of overreacting to changing findings from market research? How could Canada Goose avoid these pitfalls?
4. If you were doing observational research at a major retailer that carries Canada Goose, what might be some important information to seek out?

REVIEWING THE CONCEPTS

1. Explain the importance of information in gaining insights about the marketplace and customers.

The marketing process starts with a complete understanding of the marketplace and consumer needs and wants. Thus, the company needs sound information to produce superior value and satisfaction for customers. The company also requires information on competitors, resellers, and other actors and forces in the marketplace. Increasingly, marketers are viewing information not only as an input for making better decisions but also as an important strategic asset and marketing tool.

2. Define the marketing information system and discuss its parts.

The *marketing information system (MIS)* consists of people and procedures for assessing information needs, developing the needed information, and helping decision makers to use the information to generate and validate actionable customer and market insights. A well-designed information system begins and ends with users.

The MIS first assesses information needs. The MIS primarily serves the company's marketing and other managers, but it may also provide information to external partners. Then, the MIS develops information from internal databases, marketing intelligence activities, and marketing research. Internal databases provide information on the company's own operations and departments. Such data can be obtained quickly and cheaply but often needs to be adapted for marketing decisions. Marketing intelligence activities supply everyday information about developments in the external marketing environment. Market research consists of collecting information relevant to a specific marketing problem faced by the company. Lastly, the MIS helps users to analyze and use the information to develop customer insights, make marketing decisions, and manage customer relationships.

3. Outline the steps in the marketing research process.

The first step in the marketing research process involves *defining the problem and setting the research objectives*, which may be exploratory, descriptive, or causal research. The second step consists of *developing a research plan* for collecting data from primary and secondary sources. The third step calls for *implementing the marketing research plan* by gathering, processing, and analyzing the information. The fourth step consists of *interpreting and reporting the findings*. Additional information analysis helps marketing managers to apply the information and provides them with sophisticated statistical procedures and models from which to develop more rigorous findings.

Both *internal* and *external* secondary data sources often provide information more quickly and at a lower cost than primary data sources, and they can sometimes yield information that a company cannot collect by itself. However, needed information might not exist in secondary sources. Researchers must also evaluate secondary information to ensure that it is *relevant, accurate, current,* and *impartial.*

Primary research must also be evaluated for these features. Each primary data collection method—*observational, survey,* and *experimental*—has its own advantages and disadvantages. Similarly, each of the various research contact methods—mail, telephone, personal interview, and online—also has its own advantages and drawbacks.

4. Explain how companies analyze and use marketing information.

Information gathered in internal databases and through marketing intelligence and marketing research usually requires more analysis. This may include advanced statistical analysis or the application of analytical models that will help marketers to make better decisions. To analyze individual customer data, many companies have now acquired or developed special software and analysis techniques—called *customer relationship management (CRM)*—that integrate, analyze, and apply the mountains of individual customer data contained in their databases.

Marketing information has no value until it is used to make better marketing decisions. Thus, the MIS must make the information available to the managers and others who make marketing decisions or deal with customers. In some cases, this means providing regular reports and updates; in other cases it means making non-routine information available for special situations and on-the-spot decisions. Many firms use company intranets and extranets to facilitate this process. Thanks to modern technology, today's marketing managers can gain direct access to the MIS at any time and from virtually any location.

5. **Discuss the special issues some marketing researchers face, including public policy and ethics issues.**

Some marketers face special marketing research situations, such as those conducting research in small business, not-for-profit, or international situations. Marketing research can be conducted effectively by small businesses and non-profit organizations with limited budgets. International marketing researchers follow the same steps as domestic researchers but often face more and different problems. All organizations need to act responsibly to major public policy and ethical issues surrounding marketing research, including issues of intrusions on consumer privacy and misuse of research findings.

KEY TERMS

Causal research   166
Commercial online databases   167
Competitive marketing
   intelligence   163
Customer insights   160
Customer relationship management
   (CRM)   182
Descriptive research   166

Ethnographic research   171
Experimental research   172
Exploratory research   166
Focus group interviewing   173
Internal databases   162
Marketing information
   system (MIS)   161
Marketing research   165

Observational research   170
Online focus groups   176
Online marketing research   175
Primary data   167
Sample   177
Secondary data   167
Survey research   172

TALK ABOUT MARKETING

1. One source of competitive marketing intelligence is a company's website. Visit Apple's website (www.apple.com) to search for information that might be useful to competitors. Write a brief report of what you found.

2. Assume you are interested in opening a children's retail clothing store specializing in upscale children's fashions for newborns through 10-year-olds. You are unsure whether there is enough demand in your area to be profitable. In a small group, discuss what information you need before making this decision and decide on which secondary sources can provide that information. Furthermore, assume you plan to conduct a survey to better estimate demand for this product and describe the best primary data collection method for your needs.

3. Focus groups are commonly used during exploratory research. A focus group interview entails gathering a group of people to discuss a specific topic. In a small group, research how to conduct a focus group interview and then conduct one with six to ten other students to learn what services your university could offer to better meet student needs. Assign one person in your group to be the moderator while the others observe and interpret the responses from the focus group participants. Present a report of what you learned from this research.

4. Visit the website of Forrester Research at www.forrester.com. Browse the free sample research reports available on its site. Choose one that looks interesting, and read it. What kinds of companies could make use of this research report, and how?

5. Go to SRI Consulting's website (www.sric-bi.com), click on the VALS survey on the left side of the webpage, and complete the survey. What type of research is being conducted—exploratory, descriptive, or causal? How can marketers use this information?

THINK LIKE A MARKETING MANAGER

Outback Steakhouse currently operates restaurants in only two provinces, Ontario and Alberta. Outback's marketing department is working on a strategic plan to open five new restaurants in Canada in the next two years. They have come to you, the head of the marketing research department, to ask for your help in providing information that will assist them in deciding where to open these five restaurants.

QUESTIONS

1. Make a list of three questions you can find the answers to in secondary sources. Which secondary sources will you use to find the answers to these questions? Can you find the answers to all three questions just by using free Internet sources and your university's library databases? (Try!)

2. You're going to have to prepare a research plan to conduct some primary research. Which type or types of research will you use: observational, experimental, or causal? Think this through and make notes. What would you observe, and for what purpose? What kind of experiment might you conduct? What cause-and-effect relationships would you want to understand?

3. What type of research would you conduct to determine which markets in Canada are likely to respond most favourably to Outback's menu?

4. Assume that the marketing department has now made the decision about which five cities to enter. How can market research help make the next decision: Where exactly, in each city, should the restaurant be opened?

MARKETING ETHICS

You probably looked at a lot of information before selecting the college or university you are currently attending. Perhaps you even looked at *Maclean's* annual university ranking issue, which rates universities on a number of factors, including average entering grades, class size, calibre of faculty, and breadth and currency of its libraries. One survey suggests that 80 percent of first-year students used *Maclean's* rankings when deciding what school to attend. Since its inception nearly 20 years ago, the ranking has been fraught with controversy over the methods used. For example, Alberta universities once accused the Ontario education system of inflating high school grades, thus resulting in higher rankings for Ontario universities whose student body is primarily from that province. In one year, *Maclean's* admitted to using data from a previous year's survey when some universities refused to provide current data. Many universities have called the survey methodology "oversimplified and arbitrary" and have gone so far as to refuse to participate. Critics argue that since we do not have standardized high-school testing in Canada, such as the SAT in the United States, it is very difficult to compare the quality of incoming students province to province. Others have voiced concerns with how *Maclean's* handles missing or outdated information when generating a ranking.

QUESTIONS

1. Find the latest *Maclean's* annual university survey. Does the article explain how data are collected and what the values mean? Describe how data are collected and critique the information for usefulness.

2. Do you agree with the critics' assessment that this ranking is "oversimplified and arbitrary"? Why or why not? Cite specific examples to support your argument.

MARKETING TECHNOLOGY

If you've ever complained to friends about a bad product or service experience, the marketer probably never heard you. That is, until now. If you complain on a social networking site, you just might get a response. That's what Moosehead, Canada's oldest brewer, did. Moosehead learned of a customer who complained on a blog about purchasing spoiled beer that had not been stored properly at the retail level. The brewer's quick remedy resulted in the blogger posting a "glowing review" of the treatment he received. But how do companies monitor online communications among the millions of consumers worldwide by using social media such as blogs, video sharing (YouTube), photo sharing (Flickr), and microblogging (Twitter) sites? The key is that users of social media leave clues, such as social bookmarks, friends, followers, comments, favourites, votes, and so on. Companies could monitor these clues themselves, but most hire experts specializing in social media monitoring to track how people are talking about their brands.

QUESTIONS

1. Search "social media monitoring" on a search engine to find companies specializing in monitoring social media. Many of these sites discuss examples of how businesses use their service. Discuss two examples in which businesses used social media monitoring successfully.
2. Monitoring "tagging" is hailed as the way to keep tabs on the Internet. Explain what is meant by a "tag" and explain why monitoring such tags is beneficial for marketers.

MARKETING BY THE NUMBERS

"Company X has 34 percent market share," "Brand A is preferred by over 60 percent of consumers," "Prices are increasing at a rate of 44 percent," and "The average customer satisfaction rating is 4, satisfied, on a 1–5 scale." These are all conclusions based on statistics. Statistics lend credibility to conclusions and can be very persuasive. But are the conclusions legitimate? Many are survey-based claims, meaning that survey research is used to substantiate them. Claiming that 60 percent of consumers prefer a brand is powerful but can be misleading if only five consumers were sampled and three preferred that brand (that is, 60 percent). Interpretation of data can vary by who's interpreting it. For example, saying that your average customer is satisfied may not be accurate, as an average rating of 4 could result from half of respondents indicating 5 (extremely satisfied) and the other half rating 3 (neither satisfied nor dissatisfied), which paints a different picture. Market share is the ratio of the company's sales to total market sales, and a 34 percent market share is nice. But how is "market" defined? As you can see, numbers can say almost anything you want them to say. For more discussion of the financial and quantitative implications of marketing decisions, see Appendix 3, Marketing by the Numbers.

QUESTIONS

1. By using Statistics Canada data on education, training, and learning (available at www40.statcan.ca/l01/ind01/l2_1821-eng.htm?hili_none), develop statistics, such as percentages, to support the argument for tuition freezes for undergraduate education in Canada. Use any portion of the data you deem important to support your argument.
2. By using the same data on that website, develop different statistics to support the counter-argument to the one above. That is, interpret the data and present it in a way that supports the universities' position for the need to increase tuition fees. Again, use any portion of the data you deem important to support your argument.

VIDEO CASE

Visit MyMarketingLab at www.pearsoned.ca/ mymarketinglab to view the video for this chapter.

RADIAN6

As more and more consumers converse through digital media, companies are struggling to figure out how to "listen in" on the conversations. Traditional marketing research methods can't sift through the seemingly infinite number of words flying around cyberspace at any given moment. But one company is helping marketers get a handle on "word-of-Web" communication. Radian6 specializes in monitoring social media, tracking websites ranging from Facebook to Flickr. Radian6's unique software opens a door to an entirely different kind of research. Instead of using questionnaires, interviews, or focus groups, Radian6 scans online social media for whatever combination of keywords a marketer might specify. This gives companies valuable insights into what consumers are saying about their products and brands.

After viewing the video featuring Radian6, answer the following questions.

QUESTIONS

1. What benefits does Radian6 provide to marketers over more traditional market research methods? What are the shortcomings?

2. Classify Radian6's software with respect to research approaches, contact methods, sampling plan, and research instruments.

3. How is Radian6 helping companies develop stronger relationships with customers?

END-OF-CHAPTER CASE

RESEARCHING THE MARKET POTENTIAL FOR SLIM CAL IN CANADA

Canadians are obsessed with losing weight. Whether it's the Atkins diet, the latest Jenny Craig celebrity, or weight-loss potions being sold on The Shopping Channel, it seems like everyone is on a diet. For many years, one of the most popular trends in dieting has been the low-carb diet, and many consumer packaged-goods manufacturers, even beer companies, rushed to produce low-carb versions of their food. In 2004, a company called Symbiotics Ltd. developed a new product called the Slim Cal bar, and planned to market it across Canada. But first, they had a lot of research to do. Here is what they learned.

In November 2004, ACNielsen of Canada conducted its first annual weight-loss survey. The results indicated that more than half of Canadian adults went on a diet in the first half of 2004. The most popular methods for weight loss were eating smaller portions (26 percent of respondents), low-fat dieting (15 percent), and low-carb dieting (12 percent). The study further indicated that 92 percent of the respondents were "very" or "somewhat" concerned about the health risks of saturated fats and 91 percent were concerned about trans-fatty acids and obesity. Respondents to the survey were also asked what they were doing to alleviate these concerns. The results indicate that 56 percent were cutting back on fat consumption, 47 percent were cutting back on sugar, and 34 percent were cutting salt and sugar intake. Surprisingly, despite the popularity of the low-carb Atkins and related diet programs, the study found that only 26 percent of respondents were lowering their carbohydrate intake.

Major packaged-goods companies were responding to the weight-loss trend in a variety of ways. Unilever, the manufacturer of an old diet standby, Slim-Fast, was one of the first companies to commit to the low-carb trend in a major way by launching Carb Options. This comprehensive line of low-carb, low-fat products includes everything from peanut butter to chips to nutrition bars and shakes and condiments. Kraft Foods offers a "Healthy Living" section on its website that provides a carb-counter and ways to limit carbs while still enjoying many of Kraft's famous brands. The major soft-drink companies continue to offer diet versions of their most popular brands. And in the fall of 2004, General Mills announced that all its major cereal lines would be made with whole grains. The initiative included new packaging with bold, attention-getting "Whole Grain" labelling on every cereal box. Even venerable Snapple, best known for its bottled teas and fruit drinks, has launched a meal replacement beverage called Snapple-A-Day.

The Slim Cal bar was developed to compete in the meal replacement category. The product was formulated under the meal replacement regulations of Canada's *Food and Drugs Act*, legislation that requires that meal replacements provide the body with the equivalent of a complete, nutritionally balanced meal but with lower caloric content than most regular meals. A Slim Cal bar contains all the essential elements of a complete balanced meal but with less sugar and fat. Slim Cal uses a packaging format and materials that are similar to another Canadian product, Nutribar, but at 75 grams, Slim Cal offers 10 grams more per serving.

Working on the premise that lower caloric intake is a positive contributor to weight loss, Symbiotics decided to investigate the potential of Slim Cal in a test market.

But before reaching this decision, the company engaged in considerable consumer research by using an external research agency. Initially, the concept of the product and the name Slim Cal were tested in focus groups—the qualitative research method that brings together a small group of consumers to discuss the product and its attributes under the guidance of a trained interviewer. The results of this research were very positive, both in terms of the brand's concept and its proposed name. Management at Symbiotics concluded that, at a minimum, further research was warranted.

The next stage of research was a Pre Market Test (PMT). Personal interviews were conducted with consumers about usage behaviour and attitudes concerning meal replacement products such as bars and shakes. Respondents were exposed to the mock-ups of the product, the packaging, and some proposed print advertising that connected the use of Slim Cal with healthy weight loss. Then the survey respondents were given an opportunity to participate in the next stage of the research, which was actual in-home usage. Participants used two flavours of Slim Cal—a peanut butter flavour with a crunchy coating and a smooth, yogurt-coated "MultiBerry" flavour—for eight weeks. Respondents were then contacted by telephone and, via a questionnaire, asked about their attitudes toward the product, their usages of the product, and their intentions to purchase. This quantitative data was incorporated into computer models that included elements of Slim Cal's proposed marketing plan, including pricing, advertising, and distribution intensity. The final output from this stage provided estimates of household trial rates, repeat purchase rates, and average units purchased.

These figures in turn resulted in a first-year sales estimate that indicated the product had solid sales potential. And so, with favourable research results in hand, the decision was made to move Slim Cal into a test market.

Sources: Stephanie Thompson, "Unilever Hedges Bet on Low-Carb Craze," *Advertising Age*, July 1, 2004; and www.kraftcanada.com, http://nutribar.com, www.powerbar.com, http://carboptions.ca, and www.snapple.com.

QUESTIONS

1. What research approach, contact methods, and research instruments were used by Symbiotics in its primary data collection?

2. What secondary sources of data were used to compile the information presented in this case?

3. Choose a location, and draft a plan for the test market research.

4. Conduct a competitive analysis of the meal replacement/weight-loss bars and shakes currently available on the market. Begin by making a detailed list of every brand, product, flavour, and package size. Next, analyze your data. Which types of products are there the most of (in other words, which have the stiffest competition)? Which type of meal replacement/weight-loss bar/shake has the least direct competition? Where do you see the greatest opportunity for a new product to compete successfully?

AFTER STUDYING THIS CHAPTER, YOU SHOULD BE ABLE TO

 understand the consumer market and the major factors that influence consumer buyer behaviour

 identify and discuss the stages in the buyer decision process

 describe the adoption and diffusion process for new products

 define the business market and identify the major factors that influence business buyer behaviour

 list and define the steps in the business buying decision process

Understanding Consumer and Business Buyer Behaviour

PREVIEWING THE CONCEPTS

In the previous chapter, you studied how marketers obtain, analyze, and use marketing information to gain customer and market insights as a basis for creating customer value and relationships. In this chapter, you'll continue your marketing journey with a closer look at the most important element of the marketplace—customers. The aim of marketing is to affect how customers think about and behave toward the organization and its market offerings. But to affect the *whats*, *whens*, and *hows* of buying behaviour, marketers must first understand the *whys*. We look first at *final consumer* buying influences and processes and then at the buying behaviour of *business customers*. You'll see that understanding buying behaviour is an essential but very difficult task.

To get a better sense of the importance of understanding consumer behaviour, let's look first at Apple. What makes Apple users so fanatically loyal? Just what is it that makes them buy a Mac computer, an iPod, an iPhone, or all of these? Partly, it's the way the equipment works. But at the core, customers buy from Apple because the brand itself is a part of their own self-expression and lifestyle. It's a part of what the loyal Apple customer is.

APPLE: THE KEEPER OF ALL THINGS COOL

Few brands engender such intense loyalty as that found in the hearts of core Apple buyers. Whether they own a Mac computer, an iPod, or an iPhone, Apple devotees are granite-like in their devotion to the brand. At one end are the quietly satisfied Mac users, folks who own a Mac and use it for emailing, blogging, browsing, buying, and social networking. At the other extreme, however, are the Mac zealots—the so-called MacHeads or Macolytes. The Urban Dictionary defines a Macolyte as "one who is fanatically devoted to Apple products," as in "He's a Macolyte; don't even *think* of mentioning Microsoft within earshot."

The chances are good that you know one of these MacHeads. Maybe you *are* one. They're the diehards who buy all the latest Apple products and accessories to maximize their Mac lives. They virtually live in the local Apple store. Some have even been known to buy two iPhones—one for themselves and the other just to take apart, to see what it looks like on the inside, and maybe, just to marvel at Apple's ingenious ability to cram so much into a tight little elegant package.

There's at least a little MacHead in every Apple customer. Mac enthusiasts see Apple founder Steve Jobs as the Walt Disney of technology. Say the word "Apple" in front of Mac fans and they'll go into rhapsodies about the superiority of the brand. Put two MacHeads together and you'll never shut them up. Some MacHeads even tattoo the Apple logo on their bodies. According to one industry observer, a Mac or iPhone comes "not just as a machine in a box, it [comes] with a whole community" of fellow believers. The fanatically loyal core of Apple users is at the forefront of Apple's recent personal computer resurgence and its burgeoning iPod, iTunes, iPhone empire.

What is it that makes Apple buyers so loyal? Why do they buy a Mac instead of an HP or a Dell, or an iPhone instead of a Nokia or BlackBerry? Ask the true believers, and they'll tell you simply that Apple's products work better and do more, or that they're simpler to use. But Apple buyer behaviour has much deeper roots. Apple puts top priority on understanding its customers and what makes them tick deep down. It knows that, to Apple buyers, a Mac computer or an iPhone is much more than just a piece of electronics equipment. It's a part of buyers' own self-expression and lifestyle—a part of what they are. When you own a Mac, you are anything but mainstream. You're an independent thinker, an innovator, out ahead of the crowd.

Apple plays to these deep-seated customer buying needs and motives in everything it makes and sells. By one account,

> Apple is the epitome of cool—a company that has gained a cult-like following because it somehow manages to breathe new life into every category it touches. From sleek laptops to the even sleeker iPhone, Apple products are imaginative, irreverent, and pleasing to the eye. They're fun to use and have wreaked havoc on competitors. Apple has shown "a marketing and creative genius with a rare ability to get inside the imaginations of consumers and understand what will captivate them," says one analyst. Apple has been "obsessed with the Apple user's experience."

Apple's obsession with understanding customers and deepening their Apple experience shows in everything the company does. For example, a visit to an Apple retail store is a lot more than a simple shopping trip. Apple stores are very seductive places. The store design is clean, simple, and just oozing with style—much like an Apple iPod or iPhone. The stores invite shoppers to stay a while, use the equipment, and soak up all of the exciting new technology:

> It was 2 o'clock in the morning but in the subterranean retailing mecca in Midtown Manhattan, otherwise known as the Apple store, it might as well have been midafternoon. Late one night shortly before Christmas, parents pushed strollers, and tourists straight off the plane mingled with nocturnal New Yorkers, clicking through iPod playlists, cruising the Internet on MacBooks, and touch-padding their way around iPhones. And through the night, cheerful sales staff stayed busy, ringing up customers at the main checkout counter and on hand-held devices in an uninterrupted stream of brick-and-mortar commerce.
>
> Not only has the company made many of its stores feel like gathering places, but the bright lights and equally bright acoustics create a buzz that makes customers feel more like they are at an event than a retail store. Apple stores encourage a lot of purchasing, to be sure. But they also encourage lingering, with dozens of fully functioning computers, iPods, and iPhones for visitors to try—for hours on end. The policy has even given some stores, especially those in urban neighbourhoods, the feel of a community centre. You don't visit an Apple store, you experience it.

Apple's keen understanding of customers and their needs helped the brand to build a core segment of enthusiastic disciples. The most recent American Consumer Satisfaction Index gave

Apple a market-leading customer-satisfaction score of 85—the highest ever recorded for a company in the personal computer industry. Another survey showed that Apple commands the strongest repurchase intent of any personal computer brand—81 percent of households with an Apple as their primary home personal computer plan to repurchase an Apple. Apple also received the highest satisfaction scores among smartphone owners, according to a report released by J. D. Power and Associates.

In turn, the consumer love affair with Apple has produced stunning sales and profit results. Despite the 2008 economic meltdown, Apple's sales that year soared to a record US$32.5 billion, up 35 percent over the previous year and more than quadruple the sales just four years earlier. In 2009, despite the recession that crippled much of the electronics industry, Apple's iPod and iPhone sales continued to grow at a healthy rate. Last year alone, the company sold almost 12 million iPhones and 55 million iPods. Apple now claims a 14 percent share of the U.S. personal-computer market—third behind HP and Dell—and captures more than 70 percent of the iPod and iTunes markets that it created.

"To say Apple is hot just doesn't do the company justice," concludes one Apple watcher. "Apple is smoking, searing, blisteringly hot, not to mention hip, with a side order of funky. Gadget geeks around the world have crowned Apple the keeper of all things cool." Just ask your Macolyte friends. In fact, don't bother—they've probably already brought it up.[1]

Exhibit 6.1 The Urban Dictionary defines a Macolyte as "one who is fanatically devoted to Apple products," as in "He's a Macolyte; don't even think of mentioning Microsoft within earshot."

THE APPLE example shows that factors at many levels affect consumer buying behaviour. Buying behaviour is never simple, yet understanding it is the essential task of marketing management. First we explore the dynamics of the consumer market and consumer buyer behaviour. We then examine business markets and the business buyer process.

CONSUMER MARKETS AND CONSUMER BUYER BEHAVIOUR (LO1)

Consumer buyer behaviour refers to the buying behaviour of final consumers—individuals and households that buy goods and services for personal consumption. All of these final consumers combine to make up the **consumer market**. The North American consumer market includes more than 333 million people in Canada and the United States who consume more than US$14 trillion worth of goods and services each year, making it one of the most attractive consumer markets in the world. The world consumer market consists of more than 6.8 *billion* people who annually consume an estimated US$70 trillion worth of goods and services.[2]

Consumers around the world vary tremendously in age, income, education level, and tastes. They also buy an incredible variety of goods and services. How these diverse consumers relate with each other and other elements of the world around them impacts their choices among various products, services, and companies. Here we examine the fascinating array of factors that affect consumer behaviour.

Consumer buyer behaviour
The buying behaviour of final consumers—individuals and households that buy goods and services for personal consumption.

Consumer market
All the individuals and households that buy or acquire goods and services for personal consumption.

WHAT IS CONSUMER BEHAVIOUR?

Consumers make many purchase decisions and some are more complex than others. For example, a consumer buying a cup of coffee would go through a very different decision-making process than one buying his or her first house. Most large companies research consumer buying decisions in great detail to answer questions about what consumers

FIGURE 6.1 Some issues that arise during stages in the consumption process

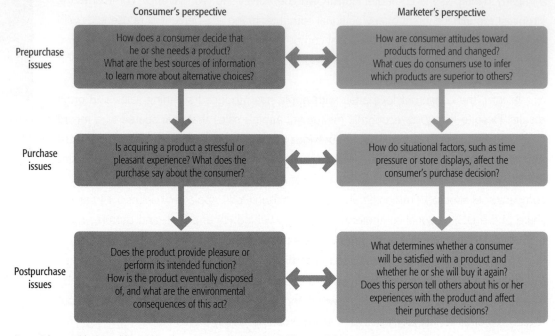

Source: Solomon, Michael R., Judith L. Zaichkowsky, and Rosemary Polegato (2011), "Consumer Behaviour: Buying, Having, and Being," 5th Canadian Edition, Pearson Education Canada, Toronto.

buy, where they buy, how and how much they buy, when they buy, and why they buy. Marketers can study actual consumer purchases to find out what they buy, where, and how much. But learning about the *whys* of consumer buying behaviour is not so easy—the answers are often locked deep within the consumer's mind.

Often, consumers themselves don't know exactly what influences their purchases. "The human mind doesn't work in a linear way," says one marketing expert. "The idea that the mind is a computer with storage compartments where brands or logos or recognizable packages are stored in clearly marked folders that can be accessed by cleverly written ads or commercials simply doesn't exist. Instead, the mind is a whirling, swirling, jumbled mass of neurons bouncing around, colliding and continuously creating new concepts and thoughts and relationships inside every single person's brain all over the world."[3]

The central question for marketers is as follows: Given all the characteristics (cultural, social, personal, and psychological) affecting consumer behaviour, how do we best design our marketing efforts to reach our consumers most effectively? Thus, the study of consumer behaviour begins and ends with the individual. In the past, the field was often referred to as *buyer behaviour*, reflecting an emphasis on the actual exchange of goods for money. Marketers now recognize the study of consumer behaviour is an ongoing process that starts long before the consumer purchases a product or service and continues long after he or she consumes it. This extended definition of consumer behaviour means that marketers must be aware of a number of issues before, during, and after purchase to build brand loyalty and lasting relationships with their customers. Figure 6.1 illustrates some issues that arise during each stage of the consumption process, but there are many more.

Consumers' responses, which can range from actual purchase to merely engaging in word-of-mouth communications about the product, is the ultimate test of whether or not a marketing strategy is successful. In the next section, we will examine each of the characteristics affecting consumer behaviour in more detail.

CHARACTERISTICS AFFECTING CONSUMER BEHAVIOUR

Consumer purchases are influenced strongly by cultural, social, personal, and psychological characteristics, shown in Figure 6.2. For the most part, marketers cannot control such factors, but they must take them into account.

Cultural Factors   Cultural factors exert a broad and deep influence on consumer behaviour. The marketer needs to understand the role played by the buyer's *culture*, *subculture*, and *social class*.

CULTURE Culture is the most basic cause of a person's wants and behaviour. Human behaviour is largely learned. Growing up in a society, a child learns basic values, perceptions, wants, and behaviours from the family and other important institutions. A child in the United States normally learns or is exposed to the following values: achievement and success, activity and involvement, efficiency and practicality, progress, hard work, material comfort, individualism, freedom, humanitarianism, youthfulness, and fitness and health. In contrast, *Maclean's* magazine annual poll of Canadian values suggests that the majority of Canadians treasure freedom; the beauty of our natural landscape; our beliefs in respect, equality, and fair treatment; our flag; our social safety net; our international role; and our multicultural and multiracial makeup. We see ourselves as unique and distinctly different from Americans. One commonality between our two cultures, however, for better or worse, is that we are a consumer culture, and marketing practices reinforce this as a way of life.[4]

Every group or society has a culture, and cultural influences on buying behaviour may vary greatly from country to country. Failure to adjust to these differences can result in ineffective marketing or embarrassing mistakes. It should not be assumed, however, that culture is a homogeneous system of shared meaning, way of life, or unifying values.[5] It is too broad a generalization to say, for example, that Canadians have one culture and the Japanese have another. In diverse societies, such as Canada, there is a multiplicity of overlapping cultural groupings. These in turn are influenced by the fact

Culture
The set of basic values, perceptions, wants, and behaviours learned by a member of society from family and other important institutions.

FIGURE 6.2 Factors influencing consumer behaviour

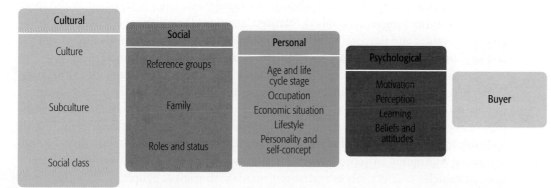

we are part of a global marketplace. Marketing practices and global media influence our values and consumption behaviours and even affect how we interpret and make sense of the world around us.

Marketers are always trying to spot *cultural shifts* in order to discover new products that might be wanted. For example, the cultural shift toward greater concern about health and fitness has created a huge industry for health-and-fitness services, exercise equipment and clothing, organic foods, and a variety of diets. The shift toward informality has resulted in more demand for casual clothing and simpler home furnishings.

Subculture

A group of people with shared value systems based on common life experiences and situations.

SUBCULTURE   Each culture contains smaller **subcultures**, or groups of people with shared value systems based on common life experiences and situations. Subcultures include nationalities, religions, racial groups, and geographic regions. Many subcultures make up important market segments, and marketers often design products and marketing programs tailored to their needs. Examples of four such important subculture groups in Canada include regional subcultures, founding nations, ethnic subcultures, and mature consumers.

Canada is a regional country, so marketers may develop distinctive programs for the Atlantic provinces, Quebec, Central Canada, the Prairies, and British Columbia. The sheer size of the country and its varied geographic features and climate have certainly shaped regional character and personality. For example, Atlantic Canada is largely defined by its proximity to and historical relationship with the sea. Equally, the isolation imposed by the mountain barrier, along with the abundance and grandeur of British Columbia's natural environment, shaped the outlook of that region's residents. Immigration has also had a differential effect on the different regions within Canada. The economy of each region furthers these differences. The fate of regions linked to the rise and fall of commodities, such as fish, timber, wheat, minerals, or oil, has affected regional mindsets as well as economies. Perceived disparities in political power have also increased regionalism, especially in Quebec, Newfoundland and Labrador, and Alberta.[6]

Canada had three founding nations: the English, French, and Aboriginal peoples. The unique history and language of each of these nations has driven many of the cultural differences that result in different buying behaviours across Canada. The most recent census results (2006) reported that people noting their English-language roots (anglophones) accounted for approximately 57 percent of the population, people whose mother tongue is French (francophones) made up approximately 22 percent of the population, and those reporting Aboriginal ancestry represented 3.7 percent of the total population.

Aboriginal Canadians are making their voices heard both in the political arena and in the marketplace. There are more than 1.17 million Aboriginal Canadians, including Métis and Inuit. Among Canada's Aboriginal population, Cree is reported as the most common mother tongue. Not only do Native Canadians have distinct cultures that influence their values and purchasing behaviour, but they also have profoundly influenced the rest of Canada through their art, love of nature, and concern for the environment.

Banks have been particularly responsive to the unique needs of Aboriginal Canadians.[7] Scotiabank, for example, has maintained its relationship with Aboriginal people through its three on-reserve branches and twenty-four Aboriginal banking centres. It also uses a lot of grassroots marketing and public relations efforts, including its sponsorship of the Aboriginal Achievement Awards and 10 annual scholarships of $2500 for young Aboriginal entrepreneurs. Publications, such as *Windspeaker* magazine, can be used as vehicles to effectively advertise to Canada's Aboriginal peoples.

According to Statistics Canada, roughly one out of every five people in Canada could be a member of a visible minority by 2017, when Canada celebrates its 150th anniversary.

Two hundred thousand new immigrants come to Canada each year.[8] Thus, being sensitive to their cultural values is important, because 70 percent of the visible minority population were born outside Canada. According to Balmoral Marketing, an ethnic ad agency in Toronto, many firms are now spending as much as 15 percent of their total communications budget on ethnic marketing.[9] People with a Chinese background are still the largest group among visible minorities in Canada. According to a 2006 *Marketing Magazine* report, 3.74 percent of Canada's population is Chinese, with 40 percent of this group residing in Toronto and 31 percent living in Vancouver. The average Chinese household spends $63 500 each year, slightly higher than the Canadian average of $58 500. People of South Asian origin (currently 23 percent of visible minorities) may represent as large a marketplace by 2017. According to a recent survey, 50 percent of South Asians say their opinion of a company would improve if they saw the ads on South Asian TV, and 62 percent stated that they would look more positively on companies that sponsored community events. When asked for advice on how to communicate to ethnic markets, Chris Bhang, vice-president group account director at Allard Johnson Direct, speaking at the 2005 Canadian Marketing Association's Diversity Conference said, "Be colloquial, be creative, but be relevant."

Canadian companies are realizing the importance of culturally relevant advertising that includes a multimedia approach to reach the Chinese Canadian market. A 2008 poll, conducted by Solutions Research Group, revealed that Internet use among Chinese

Exhibit 6.2 *Windspeaker* magazine is one tool promoted by the Aboriginal Multi-Media Society (AMMSA) to assist marketers who want to communicate with Canada's Aboriginal peoples effectively and efficiently.

Exhibit 6.3 Toronto-based 51.ca serves as a free market for information for Canada's Chinese community and has captured the attention of many Canadian advertisers.

Exhibit 6.4 Procter & Gamble's roots run deep in targeting black consumers. For example, its CoverGirl Queen Latifah line is specially formulated "to celebrate the beauty of women of color."

Canadians exceeds time spent listening to radio and watching TV combined. Internet portals such as Toronto-based 51.ca or Ottawa-based ComeFromChina .com, which serve as free markets for information for Canada's Chinese community, have captured the attention of many Canadian advertisers. Chinese Canadians appreciate advertising delivered in their native tongue. "There's a certain emotional connection a person makes when somebody speaks their own language," said Solutions Research Group president **Kaan** Yigit. "It speaks to the issue of showing respect or feeling like you're being acknowledged."[10]

People who identified themselves as "black" in the 2006 census are Canada's third largest visible minority.[11] While some members of this group trace their ancestry back to Africa, many others have more recently emigrated from the Caribbean. In recent years, many companies have developed special products, appeals, and marketing programs for black consumers. For example, P&G's roots run deep in this market. P&G currently spends six times more on media targeting black consumers than it did just five years ago. It has a long history of using black spokespeople in its ads, beginning in 1969 with entertainer Bill Cosby endorsing Crest. Today, you'll see Angela Bassett promoting the benefits of Olay body lotion for black skin and Queen Latifah in commercials promoting a CoverGirl line for black women. "The new Queen Collection was inspired by me to celebrate the beauty of women of color," says Latifah, "and it gives women the confidence they are looking for by accentuating our natural features."[12]

Though age is a demographic variable, some researchers also contend that different age cohorts have distinct cultures. As of July 2008, the median age in Canada was 39.4 years and higher than ever before (*median age* is defined as the point where exactly half of the population is older, and the other half is younger). According to the 2001 census, the median age was 37.6. To see how rapidly the Canadian population has aged, it is interesting to note that the median age in Canada in 1966 (the year when the last of the Baby Boomers was born) was 25.4 years. Thus, today Canada's working-age population is dominated by older individuals, but there are regional variations. Newfoundland and Labrador has the oldest population with a median age of 42.5. Alberta is the youngest, with a median age of 35.7. Because of high immigration rates, however, Canada's population is not aging as fast as the population of the United States.

As the Canadian population ages, *mature consumers* are becoming a very attractive market. By 2015, the entire baby boom generation, the largest and wealthiest demographic cohort in the country for more than half a century, will have moved into the 50-plus age bracket. They will control a larger proportion of wealth, income, and consumption than any current or previous generation. Despite some financial setbacks resulting from the recent economic crisis, mature consumers remain an attractive market for companies in all industries, from pharmaceuticals, groceries, beauty products, and clothing to consumer electronics, travel and entertainment, and financial services.[13]

Contrary to popular belief, mature consumers are not "stuck in their ways." To the contrary, a recent American Association of Retired Persons study showed that older consumers for products such as stereos, computers, and mobile phones are more willing to shop around and switch brands than their younger Generation-X counterparts. For example, notes one expert, "Some 25 percent of Apple's iPhones—the epitome of cool, cutting-edge product—have been bought by people over 50."[14]

The growing cadre of mature consumers creates an attractive market for convenient services. For example, Home Depot and Lowe's now target older consumers who are less enthusiastic about do-it-yourself chores than with "do-it-for-me" handyman services. And their desire to look as young as they feel also makes more-mature consumers good candidates for cosmetics and personal care products, health foods, fitness products, and other items that combat the effects of aging. The best strategy is to appeal to their active, multi-dimensional lives. For example, Dove's pro•age hair and skin care product line claims that "Beauty has no age limit." pro•age ads feature active and attractive, real women who seem to be benefiting from the product's promise. Says one ad, "Dove created pro•age to reflect the unique needs of women in their best years. This isn't anti-age, it's pro-age."[15]

SOCIAL CLASS Almost every society has some form of social class structure. **Social classes** are society's relatively permanent and ordered divisions whose members share similar values, interests, and behaviours. Social class is not determined by a single factor, such as income, but is measured as a combination of occupation, income, education, wealth, and other variables. In some social systems, members of different classes are reared for certain roles and cannot change their social positions. In North America, however, the lines between social classes are not fixed and rigid; people can move to a higher social class or drop into a lower one.

> **Social class**
> Relatively permanent and ordered divisions in a society whose members share similar values, interests, and behaviours.

Most Canadians see themselves as middle class, and we are less likely willing to think of ourselves in terms of social class than our neighbours south of the border. It is for this reason that the New Democratic Party no longer tries to appeal to "the working class" but to "ordinary Canadians." Marketers are interested in social class because people within a given social class tend to exhibit similar buying behaviour. Social classes show distinct product and brand preferences in areas such as clothing, home furnishings, leisure activity, and automobiles.

Social Factors A consumer's behaviour also is influenced by social factors, such as the consumer's *small groups*, *family*, and *social roles* and *status*.

GROUPS AND SOCIAL NETWORKS Many small **groups** influence a person's behaviour. Groups that have a direct influence and to which a person belongs are called membership groups. In contrast, reference groups serve as direct (face-to-face) or indirect points of comparison or reference in forming a person's attitudes or behaviour. People often are influenced by reference groups to which they do not belong. For example, an aspirational group is one to which the individual wishes to belong, as when a young hockey player hopes to someday emulate Sidney Crosby and play in the NHL.

> **Group**
> Two or more people who interact to accomplish individual or mutual goals.

Marketers try to identify the reference groups of their target markets. Reference groups expose a person to new behaviours and lifestyles, influence the person's attitudes and self-concept, and create pressures to conform that may affect the person's product and brand choices. The importance of group influence varies across products and brands. It tends to be strongest when the product is visible to others whom the buyer respects.

Marketers of brands subjected to strong group influence must figure out how to reach **opinion leaders**—people within a reference group who, because of special skills, knowledge, personality, or other characteristics, exert social influence on others. Some experts call this 10 percent of consumers the *influentials* or *leading adopters*. When influential friends talk, consumers listen. One survey found that nearly 78 percent of respondents trusted "recommendations from consumers," 15 percentage points higher than the second most-credible source, newspapers.[16]

> **Opinion leader**
> Person within a reference group who, because of special skills, knowledge, personality, or other characteristics, exerts social influence on others.

Marketers often try to identify opinion leaders for their products and direct marketing efforts toward them. They use *buzz marketing* by enlisting or even creating opinion leaders to serve as "brand ambassadors" who spread the word about their products. Many companies are now creating brand ambassador programs in an attempt to turn influential but everyday customers into brand evangelists.

P&G has created a huge word-of-mouth marketing arm—Vocalpoint—consisting of 350 000 moms. This army of natural-born buzzers uses the power of peer-to-peer communication to spread the word about brands. Vocalpoint recruits "connectors"—people with vast networks of friends and a gift for gab. They create buzz not just for

Exhibit 6.5 Buzz marketing: The Vocalpoint marketing arm of P&G has enlisted an army of buzzers to create word-of-mouth for brands. "We know that the most powerful form of marketing is a message from a trusted friend."

Online social networks
Online social communities—blogs, social networking websites, or even virtual worlds—where people socialize or exchange information and opinions.

P&G brands but for those of other client companies as well. P&G recently used the Vocalpoint network to help launch its new Pur Flavour Options filters—Pur faucet or pitcher filters that add fruit flavours as they filter water. P&G didn't pay the moms or coach them on what to say. It simply provided free samples and educated Vocalpointers about the product, and then asked them to share their "honest opinions with us and with other real women." In turn, the Vocalpoint moms created hundreds of thousands of personal recommendations for the new product.[17]

Over the past few years, a new type of social interaction has exploded onto the scene—online social networking. **Online social networks** are online communities where people socialize or exchange information and opinions. Social networking media range from blogs to social networking websites, such as Facebook and YouTube, to entire virtual worlds, such as Second Life and Gaia Online. This new form of high-tech buzz has big implications for marketers.

Personal connections—forged through words, pictures, video, and audio posted just for the [heck] of it—are the life of the new Web, bringing together the tens of millions of bloggers, more than 175 million active Facebook users, and millions more on single-use social networks where people share one category of stuff, like Flickr (photos), Del.icio.us (links), Digg (news stories), Wikipedia (encyclopedia articles), and YouTube (video).... It's hard to overstate the impact of these new network technologies on business: They hatch trends and build immense waves of interest in specific products. They serve up giant, targeted audiences to advertisers. They edge out old media with the loving labour of amateurs. They effortlessly provide hyperdetailed data to marketers. The new social networking technologies provide an authentic, peer-to-peer channel of communication that is far more credible than any corporate flackery.[18]

Marketers are working to harness the power of these new social networks to promote their products and build closer customer relationships. Instead of throwing more one-way commercial messages at ad-weary consumers, they hope to use social networks to *interact* with consumers and become a part of their conversations and lives. To see what's hot in the world of social networking for marketing, check out Marketing@Work 6.1.

Other companies regularly post ads or custom videos on video-sharing sites such as YouTube. For example, Toyota developed two YouTube channels to market its Corolla. One of these channels, Sketchies 11, hosted a competition offering cash and prizes worth US$40 000 for the best user-generated comedy sketches. The most-watched video received some 900 000 views. Similarly, small Blendtec has developed a kind of cult following for its flood of "Will It Blend?" videos, in which the seemingly indestructible Blendtec Total Blender grinds everything from a hockey puck and a golf club to an iPhone into dust. The low-cost, simple idea led to a fivefold increase in Blendtec's sales.[19]

But marketers must be careful when tapping into online social networks. Results are difficult to measure and control. Ultimately, the users control the content, so social network marketing attempts can easily backfire. We will dig deeper into online social networks as a marketing tool in Chapter 14.

FAMILY Family members can strongly influence buyer behaviour. The family is the most important consumer buying organization in society, and it has been researched extensively. Marketers are interested in the roles and influence of the husband, wife, and children on the purchase of different products and services.

MARKETING@WORK 6.1

Boom or Bust? Unravelling the Social Media Frenzy

It used to be that a person's social network consisted of the people he or she knew in real life—friends, family, co-workers. That's still true today, but now we have the ability to be members of virtual social networks in addition to our real-world ones. Online social networks are one kind of social media, the more general term that includes blogs, wikis, video sharing (YouTube), photo sharing (Flickr), and micro-blogging (Twitter). The use of social media worldwide is growing exponentially. For example, Facebook has experienced a 100 percent increase in usage from 2008–2009 and now has more than 400 million users. The growth in social networking has not gone unnoticed by advertisers. Approximately 20 percent of all online advertising is now done on social networking sites, representing about one in five ads viewed online. Forrester Research forecasts social-media budgets will on average grow 34 percent yearly from 2009 to 2014—faster than other kinds of digital advertising. But marketers realize that the true value of social media lies in the ability not only to advertise in these domains but also to connect with consumers in a more interactive and meaningful way.

In the world of marketing, social media is hot. However, marketers realize that what is hot today will not necessarily be so tomorrow. Take, for example, the excitement a few years ago over Second Life, a digital world where reportedly millions of people interact through their avatars. Some firms were quick to jump into this platform and create a brand presence in this virtual world, such as Adidas, which sold over 20 000 pairs of virtual shoes in Second Life. Despite promising predictions, however, Second Life did not live up to the hype. By late 2009, the number of concurrent Second Life users (the number of simultaneously logged in users) peaked at around 75 000. In terms of Web traffic, SecondLife.com currently ranks as approximately the 3800th most visited website worldwide and is visited by only about 0.04 percent of Internet users.

So what *is* hot in today's social media world? Facebook is by far the undisputed current king of social media. According to Alexa.com, a firm that tracks Internet site metrics, over 30 percent of global Internet users visit Facebook.com, making it the number two site in the world (behind Google.com) in Internet traffic. Several firms have been quick to create a presence on Facebook, such as Tim Hortons, which has almost 600 000 fans on its Facebook page.

Organizers and sponsors of the 2010 Vancouver Olympics alike made extensive use of social networking sites to promote the games and the sponsoring brands. Nearly 1.2 million people signed up as fans of Vancouver 2010 on Facebook and were able to follow athletes on Twitter. Sponsors also had a major presence in social media. For example, Coke created a virtual snowball fight for consumers to share and an iPhone app with the sounds of cheering, air horns, and a Coke being poured; and Coke-sponsored athletes tweeted on Twitter about their experiences. Visa posted six Olympic commercials on YouTube before they aired on TV. McDonald's created a virtual scavenger hunt called "How do you McNugget?" with a grand prize of a trip for two to the 2012 London Games. Bell Canada, a major sponsor of the Games, released its own free cowbell app geared toward event attendees, while Molson Canadian enabled Facebook users to create a personalized ice hockey jersey as their profile picture to show support for Team Canada.

So while interest in some social networking sites have dwindled (e.g., Second Life and MySpace), others, including Facebook, YouTube, and Twitter (currently 2nd, 4th, and 12th respectively in global Internet usage), have seen continued growth. But what new sites may be the next kings of social media? That has yet to be determined, but there are some interesting possibilities out there. For example,

Exhibit 6.6 During the Vancouver 2010 Olympics, Molson Canadian enabled Facebook users to create a personalized ice hockey jersey as their profile picture to show support for Team Canada.

Foursquare is a mobile app that allows people to "check in," telling the site their whereabouts.

Foursquare then tells your friends where they can find you and recommends places to go and things to do nearby. Users can check in to all kinds of places, including cafés, bars, restaurants, or offices. LinkedIn, a more business-oriented social networking site, offers users a wonderful tool for networking within the business community, such as facilitating connections between recruiters with job seekers. Bubbly, a new voice-based social network that works like an audio version of Twitter, is also gaining popularity in India thanks to Bollywood celebrities who are becoming early adopters. Whatever the popular platform is, the following fact remains: social networking is here to stay, and marketers must have a presence in this ever-evolving form of media.

Sources: Internet usage data from www.alexa.com and www.comscore.com, accessed March 16, 2010; Rupal Parekh, "**Is Voice-Based Bubbly the New Twitter?**" *Advertising Age*, **March 17, 2010, accessed at** http://adage.com/globalnews/article?article_id=142752; and Kunur Patel, "**You're using social media. But just who is overseeing it all?**" *Advertising Age*, February 22, 2010, p. 8.

Exhibit 6.7   Using online social networks: Blendtec has developed a kind of cult following for its flood of "Will It Blend?" videos on YouTube, resulting in a fivefold increase in Blendtec's sales.

Husband-wife involvement varies widely by product category and stage in the buying process. Buying roles change with evolving consumer lifestyles. In Canada and the United States, the wife traditionally has been the main purchasing agent for the family in the areas of food, household products, and clothing. But with 70 percent of women holding jobs outside the home and the willingness of husbands to do more of the family's purchasing, all this is changing. A recent study found that 65 percent of men grocery shop regularly and prepare at least one meal a week for others in the household. At the same time, women now influence 65 percent of all new car purchases, 91 percent of new home purchases, and 92 percent of vacation purchases. In all, women make almost 85 percent of all family purchases.[20]

Such changes suggest that marketers in industries that have sold their products to only men or only women are now courting the opposite sex. For example, women today account for 50 percent of all technology purchases. So consumer electronics are increasingly designing products that are easier to use and more appealing to female buyers.

As a growing number of women are embracing consumer electronics, engineers and designers are bringing a more feminine sensibility to products historically shaped by masculine tastes, habits, and requirements. Designs are more "feminine and softer," rather than masculine and angular. But many of the new touches are more subtle, like the wider spacing of the keys on a Sony ultraportable computer notebook. It accommodates the longer fingernails that women tend to have. Some of the latest cell phones made by LG Electronics have the cameras' automatic focus calibrated to arms' length. The company observed that young women are fond of taking pictures of themselves with a friend. Men, not so much. Nikon and Olympus recently introduced lines of lighter, more compact and easy-to-use digital single-lens-reflex cameras that were designed with women in mind because they tend to be a family's primary keeper of memories.[21]

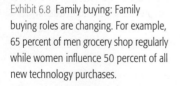

Exhibit 6.8 Family buying: Family buying roles are changing. For example, 65 percent of men grocery shop regularly while women influence 50 percent of all new technology purchases.

Children may also have a strong influence on family buying decisions. Canadian kids influence some $20 million in household spending each year and have memorized between 300 and 400 brand names by the age of 10.[22] One recent study found that kids significantly influence family decisions about everything from where they take vacations to what cars and cellphones they buy.[23] As a result, marketers of cars, full-service restaurants, cellphones, and travel destinations are now targeting kids as well as parents.

ROLES AND STATUS A person belongs to many groups—family, clubs, organizations. The person's position in each group can be defined in terms of both role and status. A role consists of the activities people are expected to perform according to the persons around them. Each role carries a status reflecting the general esteem given to it by society.

People usually choose products appropriate to their roles and status. Consider the various roles a working mother plays. In her company, she plays the role of a brand manager; in her family, she plays the role of wife and mother; at her favourite sporting events, she plays the role of avid fan. As a brand manager, she will buy the kind of clothing that reflects her role and status in her company.

Personal Factors A buyer's decisions also are influenced by personal characteristics such as the buyer's *age and life-cycle stage, occupation, economic situation, lifestyle,* and *personality and self-concept.*

AGE AND LIFE-CYCLE STAGE People change the goods and services they buy over their lifetimes. Tastes in food, clothes, furniture, and recreation are often age-related. Buying is also shaped by the stage of the family life cycle—the stages through which families might pass as they mature over time. Life-stage changes usually result from demographics and life-changing events—marriage, having children, purchasing a home, divorce, children going to college, changes in personal income, moving out of the house, and retirement. Marketers often define their target markets in terms of life-cycle stage and develop appropriate products and marketing plans for each stage.

Consumer information giant Acxiom's PersonicX life-stage segmentation system places households into one of 70 consumer segments and 21 life-stage groups, based on specific consumer behaviour and demographic characteristics. PersonicX includes life-stage groups with names such as *Beginnings, Taking Hold, Cash & Careers, Jumbo Families, Transition Blues, Our Turn, Golden Years,* and *Active Elders.* For example, the *Taking Hold* group consists of young, energetic, well-funded couples and young families who are busy with their careers, social lives, and interests, especially fitness and active recreation. *Transition Blues* are blue-collar, less-educated, mid-income consumers who are transitioning to stable lives and talking about marriage and children.

"Consumers experience many life-stage changes during their lifetimes," says Acxiom. "As their life stages change, so do their behaviour and purchasing preferences. Marketers who are armed with the data to understand the timing and makeup of life-stage changes among their customers will have a distinct advantage over their competitors."[24]

In line with today's tougher economic times, Acxiom has also developed a set of economic life-stage segments, including groups such as *Squeaking By, Eye on Essentials, Tight with a Purpose, It's My Life, Full Speed Ahead,* and *Potential Rebounders.* The *Potential Rebounders* are those more likely to loosen up on spending sooner. This group appears more likely than other segments to use online research before purchasing electronics, appliances, home decor, and jewellery. Thus, home improvement retailers appealing to this segment should have a strong online presence, providing pricing, features and benefits, and product availability.

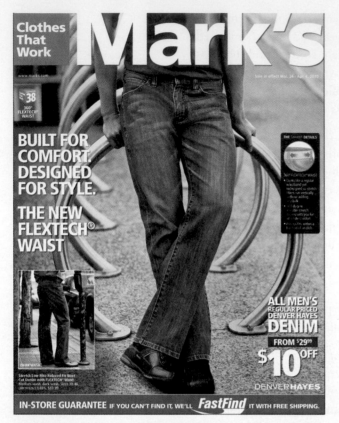

Exhibit 6.9 By using thorough research and powerful advertising, Mark's Work Wearhouse has transformed itself into a Canadian superbrand with the slogan "clothes that work."

OCCUPATION A person's occupation affects the goods and services bought. Blue-collar workers tend to buy more rugged work clothes, whereas executives buy more business suits. Marketers try to identify the occupational groups that have an above-average interest in their products and services. A company can even specialize in making products needed by a given occupational group.

Long known for its rugged workwear, Mark's Work Wearhouse faced the challenge of changing its image in the marketplace. By interviewing Canadian consumers, the marketing team soon found out that, while 95 percent of those interviewed were aware of the Mark's Work Wearhouse name, 66 percent thought of Mark's as primarily a blue-collar, work-wear store. Although workwear continues to make up a healthy 25 percent of sales, Mark's now carries a much larger selection of items and is focused on men's and women's casual clothing. Thus, marketing vice-president Michael Strachan's job was to convince consumers "that we aren't about blue-collar clothes, but about clothes that work." This has become its major brand proposition and a company mantra "that's on every single thing from the smallest indoor sign to the biggest billboard."[25]

ECONOMIC SITUATION A person's economic situation will affect his or her store and product choices. Marketers watch trends in personal income, savings, and interest rates. In the face of the recent recession, most companies are taking steps to redesign, reposition, and reprice their products. For example, at U.S.-based retailer Target, to counter the effects of the recession, "cheap has taken over chic." The discount retailer rolled out the "A new day. New ways to save." advertising campaign that focuses on value, with offers such as "the new barber shop—clippers $14.99," and "the new gym—gym ball $11.88." "This is the first time we've featured price points in our broadcast advertising," said a Target marketer at the start of the campaign. "As a whole we've increased our emphasis on value messaging. Our [tagline] is 'Expect more. Pay less.' We're putting more emphasis on the pay less promise."[26]

LIFESTYLE People coming from the same subculture, social class, and occupation may have quite different lifestyles. **Lifestyle** is a person's pattern of living as expressed in his or her psychographics. It involves measuring consumers' major AIO dimensions—activities (work, hobbies, shopping, sports, social events), interests (food, fashion, family, recreation), and opinions (about themselves, social issues, business, products). Lifestyle captures something more than the person's social class or personality. It profiles a person's whole pattern of acting and interacting in the world.

When used carefully, the lifestyle concept can help marketers understand changing consumer values and how they affect buying behaviour. Consumers don't just buy products, they buy the values and lifestyles those products represent. For example, BMW doesn't just sell convertibles, it sells the convertible lifestyle: "Skies never bluer. Knuckles never whiter." And Merrell sells more than just rugged footwear: It sells a "Let's Get Outside" lifestyle. Says one marketer, "People's product choices are becoming more and more like value choices. It's not, 'I like this water, the way it tastes.' It's 'I feel like this car, or this show, is more reflective of who I am.'"

For example, Pottery Barn, with locations in Toronto, Calgary, and Vancouver, sells more than just home furnishings. It sells a lifestyle to which its customers aspire. Pottery

Lifestyle

A person's pattern of living as expressed in his or her activities, interests, and opinions.

Barn Kids offers idyllic scenes of the perfect childhood, whereas PBteen offers a means of trendy, fashion-forward self-expression. The flagship Pottery Barn stores serve an upscale yet casual, family- and friend focused lifestyle—affluent but sensibly so.[27]

PERSONALITY AND SELF-CONCEPT   Each person's distinct personality influences his or her buying behaviour. **Personality** refers to the unique psychological characteristics that distinguish a person or group. Personality is usually described in terms of traits such as self-confidence, dominance, sociability, autonomy, defensiveness, adaptability, and aggressiveness. Personality can be useful in analyzing consumer behaviour for certain product or brand choices.

The idea is that brands also have personalities and that consumers are likely to choose brands with personalities that match their own. A *brand personality* is the specific mix of human traits that may be attributed to a particular brand. One researcher identified five brand personality traits: *sincerity* (down-to-earth, honest, wholesome, and cheerful); *excitement* (daring, spirited, imaginative, and up-to-date); *competence* (reliable, intelligent, and successful); *sophistication* (upper class and charming); and *ruggedness* (outdoorsy and tough).[28]

Most well-known brands are strongly associated with one particular trait: Jeep with "ruggedness," Apple with "excitement," CNN with "competence," and Dove with "sincerity." Hence, these brands will attract persons who are high on the same personality traits.

Exhibit 6.10   Lifestyle: Consumers don't just buy products, they buy the values and lifestyles those products represent. Merrell sells more than just rugged footwear, it sells a "Let's Get Outside" lifestyle.

Many marketers use a concept related to personality—a person's *self-concept* (also called *self-image*). The idea is that people's possessions contribute to and reflect their identities—that is, "we are what we have." Thus, to understand consumer behaviour, the marketer must first understand the relationship between consumer self-concept and possessions.

Apple applies these concepts in its long-running "Get a Mac" ad series that characterizes two people as computers—one guy plays the part of an Apple Mac and the other plays a personal computer (PC). The two have very different personalities and self-concepts. "Hello, I'm a Mac," says the guy on the right, who's younger and dressed in jeans. "And I'm a PC," says the one on the left, who's wearing dweeby glasses and a jacket and tie. The two men discuss the relative advantages of Macs versus PCs, with the Mac coming out on top. The ads present the Mac brand personality as young, laid-back, and cool. The PC is portrayed as buttoned-down, corporate, and a bit dorky. The message? If you see yourself as young and with it, you need a Mac.[29]

Psychological Factors   A person's buying choices are further influenced by four major psychological factors: *motivation, perception, learning,* and *beliefs and attitudes.*

MOTIVATION   A person has many needs at any given time. Some are biological, arising from states of tension such as hunger, thirst, or discomfort. Others are psychological, arising from the need for recognition, esteem, or belonging. A need becomes a motive when it is aroused to a sufficient level of intensity. A **motive** (or **drive**) is a need that is sufficiently pressing to direct the person to seek satisfaction. Psychologists have

Personality
The unique psychological characteristics that distinguish a person or group.

Motive (drive)
A need that is sufficiently pressing to direct the person to seek satisfaction of the need.

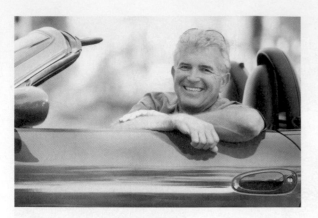

Exhibit 6.11 Motivation: An aging Baby Boomer who buys a sporty convertible might explain that he simply likes the feel of the wind in his thinning hair. At a deeper level, he may be buying the car to feel young and independent again.

developed theories of human motivation. Two of the most popular—the theories of Sigmund Freud and Abraham Maslow—have quite different meanings for consumer analysis and marketing.

Sigmund Freud assumed that people are largely unconscious about the real psychological forces shaping their behaviour. He saw the person as growing up and repressing many urges. These urges are never eliminated or under perfect control; they emerge in dreams, in slips of the tongue, in neurotic and obsessive behaviour, or ultimately in psychoses.

Freud's theory suggests that a person's buying decisions are affected by subconscious motives that even the buyer may not fully understand. Thus, an aging Baby Boomer who buys a sporty BMW 330Ci convertible might explain that he simply likes the feel of the wind in his thinning hair. At a deeper level, he may be trying to impress others with his success. At a still deeper level, he may be buying the car to feel young and independent again.

The term *motivation research* refers to qualitative research designed to probe consumers' hidden, subconscious motivations. Consumers often don't know or can't describe just why they act as they do. Thus, motivation researchers use a variety of probing techniques to uncover underlying emotions and attitudes toward brands and buying situations.

Many companies employ teams of psychologists, anthropologists, and other social scientists to carry out motivation research. One ad agency routinely conducts one-on-one, therapy-like interviews to delve into the inner workings of consumers. Another company asks consumers to describe their favourite brands as animals or cars (say, Cadillacs versus Chevrolets) in order to assess the prestige associated with various brands. Still others rely on hypnosis, dream therapy, or soft lights and mood music to plumb the murky depths of consumer psyches.

Such projective techniques seem pretty goofy, and some marketers dismiss such motivation research as mumbo-jumbo. But many marketers use such touchy-feely approaches, now sometimes called *interpretive consumer research*, to dig deeper into consumer psyches and develop better marketing strategies.

Abraham Maslow sought to explain why people are driven by particular needs at particular times. Why does one person spend much time and energy on personal safety and another on gaining the esteem of others? Maslow's answer is that human needs are arranged in a hierarchy, as shown in Figure 6.3, from the most pressing at the bottom to the least pressing at the top.[30] They include *physiological* needs, *safety* needs, *social* needs, *esteem* needs, and *self-actualization* needs.

A person tries to satisfy the most important need first. When that need is satisfied, it will stop being a motivator and the person will then try to satisfy the next most important need. For example, starving people (physiological need) will not take an interest in the latest happenings in the art world (self-actualization needs), nor in how they are seen or esteemed by others (social or esteem needs), nor even in whether they are breathing clean air (safety needs). But as each important need is satisfied, the next most important need will come into play. Critics of Maslow's Hierarchy argue that human motivation does not always follow this hierarchical structure. For example, consumers may often seek to satisfy esteem needs by purchasing a $400 pair of designer jeans, while ignoring lower-order safety needs by not paying the rent!

PERCEPTION A motivated person is ready to act. How the person acts is influenced by his or her perception of the situation. All of us learn by the flow of information through our five senses: sight, hearing, smell, touch, and taste. However, each of us receives,

FIGURE 6.3 Maslow's hierarchy of needs

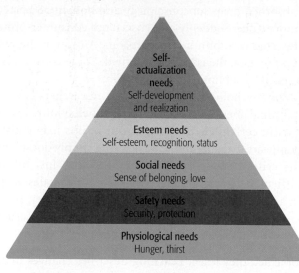

Self-actualization needs
Self-development and realization

Esteem needs
Self-esteem, recognition, status

Social needs
Sense of belonging, love

Safety needs
Security, protection

Physiological needs
Hunger, thirst

organizes, and interprets this sensory information in an individual way. **Perception** is the process by which people select, organize, and interpret information to form a meaningful picture of the world.

People can form different perceptions of the same stimulus because of three perceptual processes: selective attention, selective distortion, and selective retention. People are exposed to a great amount of stimuli every day. For example, people are exposed to an estimated 3000 to 5000 ad messages every day. It is impossible for a person to pay attention to all these stimuli. *Selective attention*—the tendency for people to screen out most of the information to which they are exposed—means that marketers must work especially hard to attract the consumer's attention.[31]

Even noticed stimuli do not always come across in the intended way. Each person fits incoming information into an existing mindset. *Selective distortion* describes the tendency of people to interpret information in a way that will support what they already believe. People also will forget much of what they learn. They tend to retain information that supports their attitudes and beliefs. *Selective retention* means that consumers are likely to remember good points made about a brand they favour and to forget good points made about competing brands. Because of selective attention, distortion, and retention, marketers must work hard to get their messages through.

Interestingly, although most marketers worry about whether their offers will be perceived at all, some consumers worry that they will be affected by marketing messages without even knowing it—through *subliminal advertising*. More than 50 years ago, a researcher announced that he had flashed the phrases "Eat popcorn" and "Drink Coca-Cola" on a screen in a New Jersey movie theatre every five seconds for

Perception
The process by which people select, organize, and interpret information to form a meaningful picture of the world.

Exhibit 6.12 Selective perception: It's impossible for people to pay attention to the thousands of ads they're exposed to every day, so they screen most of them out.

1/300th of a second. He reported that although viewers did not consciously recognize these messages, they absorbed them subconsciously and bought 58 percent more popcorn and 18 percent more Coke. Suddenly advertisers and consumer-protection groups became intensely interested in subliminal perception. Although the researcher later admitted to making up the data, the issue has not died. Some consumers still fear that they are being manipulated by subliminal messages.

Numerous studies by psychologists and consumer researchers have found little or no link between subliminal messages and consumer behaviour. Recent brainwave studies have found that in certain circumstances, our brains may register subliminal messages. However, it appears that subliminal advertising simply doesn't have the power attributed to it by its critics. Scoffs one industry insider, "Just between us, most [advertisers] have difficulty getting a 2 percent increase in sales with the help of $50 million in media and extremely *liminal* images of sex, money, power, and other [motivators] of human emotion. The very idea of [us] as puppeteers, cruelly pulling the strings of consumer marionettes, is almost too much to bear."[32]

LEARNING When people act, they learn. **Learning** describes changes in an individual's behaviour arising from experience. Learning theorists say that most human behaviour is learned. Learning occurs through the interplay of drives, stimuli, cues, responses, and reinforcement.

A *drive* is a strong internal stimulus that calls for action. A drive becomes a motive when it is directed toward a particular *stimulus object*. For example, a person's drive for self-actualization might motivate him or her to look into buying a camera. The consumer's response to the idea of buying a camera is conditioned by the surrounding cues. *Cues* are minor stimuli that determine when, where, and how the person responds. For example, the person might spot several camera brands in a shop window, hear of a special sale price, or discuss cameras with a friend. These are all cues that might influence a consumer's *response* to his or her interest in buying the product.

Suppose the consumer buys a Nikon camera. If the experience is rewarding, the consumer will probably use the camera more and more, and his or her response will be *reinforced*. Then, the next time the consumer shops for a camera, or for binoculars or some similar product, the probability is greater that he or she will buy a Nikon product. The practical significance of learning theory for marketers is that they can build up demand for a product by associating it with strong drives, by using motivating cues, and by providing positive reinforcement.

BELIEFS AND ATTITUDES Through doing and learning, people acquire beliefs and attitudes. These, in turn, influence their buying behaviour. A **belief** is a descriptive thought that a person has about something. Beliefs may be based on real knowledge, opinion, or faith and may or may not carry an emotional charge. Marketers are interested in the beliefs that people formulate about specific products and services, because these beliefs make up product and brand images that affect buying behaviour. If some of the beliefs are wrong and prevent purchase, the marketer will want to launch a campaign to correct them.

People have attitudes regarding religion, politics, clothes, music, food, and almost everything else. **Attitude** describes a person's relatively consistent evaluations, feelings, and tendencies toward an object or an idea. Attitudes put people into a frame of mind of liking or disliking things, of moving toward or away from them. Our camera buyer may hold attitudes such as "Buy the best," "The Japanese make the best electronics products in the world," and "Creativity and self-expression are among the most important things in life." If so, the Nikon camera would fit well into the consumer's existing attitudes.

Learning
Changes in an individual's behaviour arising from experience.

Belief
A descriptive thought that a person holds about something.

Attitude
A person's consistently favourable or unfavourable evaluations, feelings, and tendencies toward an object or an idea.

Attitudes are difficult to change. A person's attitudes fit into a pattern, and to change one attitude may require difficult adjustments in many others. Thus, a company should usually try to fit its products into existing attitudes rather than attempt to change attitudes. For example, today's beverage marketers now cater to people's new attitudes about health and well-being with drinks that do a lot more than just taste good or quench your thirst. Coca-Cola's Fuze brand, for example, offers a line of "healthy infusion" beverages packed with vitamins, minerals, and antioxidants but without artificial preservatives, sweeteners, or colours. Fuze promises drinks that are good-tasting (with flavours such as Blueberry Raspberry, Strawberry Melon, and Dragonfruit Lime) but also good for you—containing only natural ingredients that "help your metabolism work in your favour." By matching today's attitudes about life and healthful living, the Fuze brand has become a leader in the New Age beverage category.

Exhibit 6.13 Fuze fits well with people's attitudes about health and well-being: Its "healthy infusion" beverages promise drinks that are "good-tasting but also good for you."

We can now appreciate the many forces acting on consumer behaviour. The consumer's choice results from the complex interplay of cultural, social, personal, and psychological factors.

THE BUYER DECISION PROCESS **LO2**

Now that we have looked at the influences that affect buyers, we are ready to look at how consumers make buying decisions. Figure 6.4 shows that the buyer decision process consists of five stages: *need recognition, information search, evaluation of alternatives, purchase decision,* and *postpurchase behaviour.* Clearly, the buying process starts long before the actual purchase and continues long after. Marketers need to focus on the entire buying process rather than on just the purchase decision.

The figure suggests that consumers pass through all five stages with every purchase. But in more routine purchases, consumers often skip or reverse some of these stages. A woman buying her regular brand of toothpaste would recognize the need and go right to the purchase decision, skipping information search and evaluation. However, we use the model in Figure 6.4 because it shows all the considerations that arise when a consumer faces a new and complex purchase situation.

Need Recognition The buying process starts with *need recognition*—the buyer recognizes a problem or need. The need can be triggered by *internal stimuli* when one of the person's normal needs—hunger, thirst, sex—rises to a level high enough to become a drive. A need can also be triggered by *external stimuli*. For example, an advertisement or a discussion with a friend might get you thinking about buying a new car. At this stage, the marketer should research consumers to find out what kinds of needs or problems arise, what brought them about, and how they led the consumer to this particular product.

FIGURE 6.4 Buyer decision process

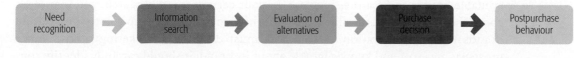

| Need recognition | → | Information search | → | Evaluation of alternatives | → | Purchase decision | → | Postpurchase behaviour |

Exhibit 6.14 Need recognition can be triggered by external stimuli: Time for a snack?

Information Search An interested consumer may or may not search for more information. If the consumer's drive is strong and a satisfying product is near at hand, the consumer is likely to buy it then. If not, the consumer may store the need in memory or undertake an *information search* related to the need. For example, once you've decided you need a new car, at the least, you will probably pay more attention to car ads, cars owned by friends, and car conversations. Or you may actively search the Web, talk with friends, and gather information in other ways.

Consumers can obtain information from any of several sources. These include *personal sources* (family, friends, neighbours, acquaintances), *commercial sources* (advertising, salespeople, dealer websites, packaging, displays), *public sources* (mass media, consumer rating organizations, Internet searches), and *experiential sources* (handling, examining, using the product). The relative influence of these information sources varies with the product and the buyer.

Generally, the consumer receives the most information about a product from commercial sources—those controlled by the marketer. The most effective sources, however, tend to be personal. Commercial sources normally *inform* the buyer, but personal sources *legitimize* or *evaluate* products for the buyer. As one marketer states, "It's rare that an advertising campaign can be as effective as a neighbour leaning over the fence and saying, 'This is a wonderful product.'" Increasingly, that "fence" is a digital one. A recent study revealed that consumers find sources of user-generated content—discussion forums, blogs, online review sites, and social networking sites—three times more influential when making a purchase decision than conventional marketing methods such as TV advertising.[33]

As more information is obtained, the consumer's awareness and knowledge of the available brands and features increase. In your car information search, you may learn about the several brands available. The information might also help you to drop certain brands from consideration. A company must design its marketing mix to make prospects aware of and knowledgeable about its brand. It should carefully identify consumers' sources of information and the importance of each source.

Evaluation of Alternatives We have seen how the consumer uses information to arrive at a set of final brand choices. How does the consumer choose among the alternative brands? The marketer needs to know about *alternative evaluation*—that is, how the consumer processes information to arrive at brand choices. Unfortunately, consumers do not use a simple and single evaluation process in all buying situations. Instead, several evaluation processes are at work.

The consumer arrives at attitudes toward different brands through some evaluation procedure. How consumers go about evaluating purchase alternatives depends on the individual consumer and the specific buying situation. In some cases, consumers use careful calculations and logical thinking. At other times, the same consumers do little or no evaluating; instead they buy on impulse and rely on intuition. Sometimes consumers make buying decisions on their own; sometimes they turn to friends, online reviews, or salespeople for buying advice.

Suppose you've narrowed your car choices to three brands. And suppose that you are primarily interested in four attributes—styling, operating economy, warranty, and price. By this time, you've probably formed beliefs about how each brand rates on each attribute. Clearly, if one car rated best on all the attributes, we could predict that you would choose it. However, the brands will no doubt vary in appeal. You might base your buying decision on only one attribute, and your choice would be easy to predict. If you wanted styling above everything else, you would buy the car that you think has the best styling. But most buyers consider several attributes, each with different importance. If we knew the importance that you assigned to each of the four attributes, we could predict your car choice more reliably.

Marketers should study buyers to find out how they actually evaluate brand alternatives. If they know what evaluative processes go on, marketers can take steps to influence the buyer's decision.

Purchase Decision In the evaluation stage, the consumer ranks brands and forms purchase intentions. Generally, the consumer's *purchase decision* will be to buy the most preferred brand, but two factors can come between the purchase *intention* and the purchase *decision*. The first factor is the *attitudes of others*. If someone important to you thinks that you should buy the lowest-priced car, then the chances of you buying a more expensive car are reduced.

The second factor is *unexpected situational factors*. The consumer may form a purchase intention based on factors such as expected income, expected price, and expected product benefits. However, unexpected events may change the purchase intention. For example, the economy might take a turn for the worse, a close competitor might drop its price, or a friend might report being disappointed in your preferred car. Thus, preferences and even purchase intentions do not always result in actual purchase choice.

Postpurchase Behaviour The marketer's job does not end when the product is bought. After purchasing the product, the consumer will be satisfied or dissatisfied and will engage in *postpurchase behaviour* of interest to the marketer. What determines whether the buyer is satisfied or dissatisfied with a purchase? The answer lies in the relationship between the *consumer's expectations* and the product's *perceived performance*. If the product falls short of expectations, the consumer is disappointed; if it meets expectations, the consumer is satisfied; if it exceeds expectations, the consumer is delighted. The larger the gap between expectations and performance, the greater the consumer's dissatisfaction. This suggests that sellers should promise only what their brands can deliver so that buyers are satisfied.

Almost all major purchases, however, result in **cognitive dissonance**, or discomfort caused by postpurchase conflict. After the purchase, consumers are satisfied with the

Cognitive dissonance
Buyer discomfort caused by postpurchase conflict.

benefits of the chosen brand and are glad to avoid the drawbacks of the brands not bought. However, every purchase involves compromise. So consumers feel uneasy about acquiring the drawbacks of the chosen brand and about losing the benefits of the brands not purchased. Thus, consumers feel at least some postpurchase dissonance for every purchase.[34]

Why is it so important to satisfy the customer? Customer satisfaction is a key to building profitable relationships with consumers—to keeping and growing consumers and reaping their customer lifetime value. Satisfied customers buy a product again, talk favourably to others about the product, pay less attention to competing brands and advertising, and buy other products from the company. Many marketers go beyond merely *meeting* the expectations of customers—they aim to *delight* the customer.

A dissatisfied consumer responds differently. Bad word of mouth often travels farther and faster than good word of mouth. It can quickly damage consumer attitudes about a company and its products. But companies cannot simply rely on dissatisfied customers to volunteer their complaints when they are dissatisfied. Most unhappy customers never tell the company about their problem. Therefore, a company should measure customer satisfaction regularly. It should set up systems that *encourage* customers to complain. In this way, the company can learn how well it is doing and how it can improve.

By studying the overall buyer decision, marketers may be able to find ways to help consumers move through it. For example, if consumers are not buying a new product because they do not perceive a need for it, marketing might launch advertising messages that trigger the need and show how the product solves customers' problems. If customers know about the product but are not buying because they hold unfavourable attitudes toward it, the marketer must find ways to change either the product or consumer perceptions.

THE BUYER DECISION PROCESS FOR NEW PRODUCTS LO3

We have looked at the stages buyers go through in trying to satisfy a need. Buyers may pass quickly or slowly through these stages, and some of the stages may even be reversed. Much depends on the nature of the buyer, the product, and the buying situation.

We now look at how buyers approach the purchase of new products. A **new product** is a good, service, or idea that is perceived by some potential customers as new. It may have been around for a while, but our interest is in how consumers learn about products for the first time and make decisions on whether to adopt them. We define the **adoption process** as "the mental process through which an individual passes from first learning about an innovation to final adoption," and *adoption* as the decision by an individual to become a regular user of the product.[35]

New product
A good, service, or idea that is perceived by some potential customers as new.

Adoption process
The mental process through which an individual passes from first hearing about an innovation to final adoption.

Stages in the Adoption Process Consumers go through five stages in the process of adopting a new product:

- ☐ *Awareness:* The consumer becomes aware of the new product, but lacks information about it.
- ☐ *Interest:* The consumer seeks information about the new product.
- ☐ *Evaluation:* The consumer considers whether trying the new product makes sense.
- ☐ *Trial:* The consumer tries the new product on a small scale to improve his or her estimate of its value.
- ☐ *Adoption:* The consumer decides to make full and regular use of the new product.

This model suggests that the new-product marketer should think about how to help consumers move through these stages. For example, as the recent recession set in, Hyundai discovered many potential customers were interested in buying new cars but refrained from doing so because of the uncertain economy. To help buyers pass this hurdle, the carmaker offered the Hyundai Assurance Program, promising to let buyers who financed or leased a new Hyundai return their vehicles at no cost and with no harm to their credit rating if they lost their jobs or incomes within a year. Sales of the Hyundai Sonata surged 85 percent in the month following the start of the campaign. Other carmakers soon followed with their own assurance plans.[36]

Individual Differences in Innovativeness People differ greatly in their readiness to try new products. In each product area, there are "consumption pioneers" and early adopters. Other individuals adopt new products much later. People can be classified into the adopter categories shown in Figure 6.5. After a slow start, an increasing number of people adopt the new product. The number of adopters reaches a peak and then drops off as fewer non-adopters remain. Innovators are defined as the first 2.5 percent of the buyers to adopt a new idea (those beyond two standard deviations from mean adoption time); the early adopters are the next 13.5 percent (between one and two standard deviations); and so forth.

The five adopter groups have differing values. *Innovators* are venturesome—they try new ideas at some risk. *Early adopters* are guided by respect—they are opinion leaders in their communities and adopt new ideas early but carefully. The *early majority* are deliberate—although they rarely are leaders, they adopt new ideas before the average person. The *late majority* are skeptical—they adopt an innovation only after a majority of people have tried it. Finally, *laggards* are tradition bound—they are suspicious of changes and adopt the innovation only when it has become something of a tradition itself.

This adopter classification suggests that an innovating firm should research the characteristics of innovators and early adopters in their product categories and should direct marketing efforts toward them.

Influence of Product Characteristics on Rate of Adoption The characteristics of the new product affect its rate of adoption. Some products catch on almost overnight—for example, the iPod and iPhone, both of which flew off retailers' shelves at an astounding rate from the day they were introduced. Others take a longer time to gain acceptance. For example, the first HDTVs were introduced in the North America in the 1990s, but by 2009 only about 25 percent of TV households owned a high-definition set.[37]

FIGURE 6.5 Adopter categorization on the basis of relative time of adoption of innovations

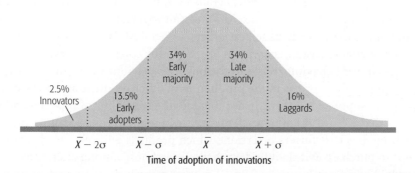

Source: Reprinted with permission of the Free Press, a Division of Simon & Schuster, from *Diffusion of Innovations*, Fifth Edition, by Everett M. Rogers. Copyright © 2003 by the Free Press.

Five characteristics are especially important in influencing an innovation's rate of adoption. For example, consider the characteristics of HDTV in relation to the rate of adoption:

☐ *Relative advantage:* the degree to which the innovation appears superior to existing products. HDTV offers substantially improved picture quality. This speeded up its rate of adoption.

☐ *Compatibility:* the degree to which the innovation fits the values and experiences of potential consumers. HDTV, for example, is highly compatible with the lifestyles of the TV-watching public. However, in the early years, HDTV was not yet compatible with programming and broadcasting systems, slowing adoption. Now, as more and more high-definition programs and channels have become available, the rate of HDTV adoption has increased. In fact, the number of HDTV-owning households has more than doubled in just the past two years.

☐ *Complexity:* the degree to which the innovation is difficult to understand or use. HDTVs are not very complex. Therefore, as more programming has become available and prices have fallen, the rate of HDTV adoption is increasing faster than that of more complex innovations.

☐ *Divisibility:* the degree to which the innovation may be tried on a limited basis. Early HDTVs and HD cable and satellite systems were very expensive, slowing the rate of adoption. As prices fall, adoption rates are increasing.

☐ *Communicability:* the degree to which the results of using the innovation can be observed or described to others. Because HDTV lends itself to demonstration and description, its use will spread faster among consumers.

Other characteristics influence the rate of adoption, such as initial and ongoing costs, risk and uncertainty, and social approval. The new-product marketer must research all these factors when developing the new product and its marketing program.

BUSINESS MARKETS AND BUSINESS BUYER BEHAVIOUR LO4

In one way or another, most large companies sell to other organizations. Companies such as DuPont, Bombardier, IBM, Caterpillar, and countless other firms sell *most* of their products to other businesses. Even large consumer-products companies, which make products used by final consumers, must first sell their products to other businesses. For example, General Mills makes many familiar consumer brands—Big G cereals (Cheerios, Wheaties, Trix, Chex), baking products (Pillsbury, Betty Crocker, Gold Medal flour), snacks (Nature Valley, Pop Secret, Chex Mix), Yoplait yogurt, Häagen-Dazs ice cream, and others. But to sell these products to consumers, General Mills must first sell them to its wholesaler and retailer customers, who in turn serve the consumer market.

Business buyer behaviour
The buying behaviour of the organizations that buy goods and services for use in the production of other products and services or to resell or rent them to others at a profit.

Business buyer behaviour refers to the buying behaviour of the organizations that buy goods and services for use in the production of other products and services that are sold, rented, or supplied to others. It also includes the behaviour of retailing and wholesaling firms that acquire goods to resell or rent them to others at a profit. In the *business buying process*, business buyers determine which products and services their organizations need to purchase and then find, evaluate, and choose among alternative suppliers and brands. *Business-to-business (B-to-B) marketers* must do their best to understand business markets and business buyer behaviour. Then, like businesses that sell to final buyers, they must build profitable relationships with business customers by creating superior customer value (see Marketing@Work 6.2).

MARKETING@WORK 6.2

GE: Building B-to-B Customer Partnerships

Few brands are more familiar than GE. For years, we've packed our homes with GE products—from good ol' GE light bulbs to refrigerators, ranges, clothes washers and dryers, microwave ovens, dishwashers, coffee makers, room air conditioners, and hundreds of other products bearing the familiar script GE logo. In fact, GE has operated in Canada for over 100 years and has major manufacturing facilities and sales and service locations across the country. The company's consumer finance unit—GE Money—helps finance these and other purchases through credit cards, loans, mortgages, and other financial services. GE even entertains us—its NBC Universal division serves up a diverse fare of network and cable television channels, movie entertainment, and even theme parks. In all, GE offers a huge assortment of consumer products and services.

But here's a fact that would startle most consumers. Did you know that GE's consumer products contribute less than one-third of the company's total US$183 billion in annual sales? To the surprise of many, most of GE's business comes not from final consumers but from commercial and industrial customers across a wide range of industries. Beyond light bulbs and electronics, GE sells everything from medical imaging technologies, water processing systems, and security solutions to power generation equipment, aircraft engines, and diesel locomotives.

At a general level, marketing medical imaging technology or diesel locomotives to business customers is like selling refrigerators to final buyers. It requires a deep-down understanding of customer needs and customer-driven marketing strategies that create superior customer value. But that's about where the similarities end. In its business markets, rather than selling to large numbers of small buyers, GE sells to a few very large buyers. Whereas it might be disappointing when a refrigerator buyer chooses a competing brand, losing a single sale to a large business customer can mean the loss of hundreds of millions of dollars in business.

Also, with GE's business customers, buying decisions are much more complex. An average consumer buying a refrigerator might do a little online research and then pop out to the local Future Shop to compare models before buying one. In contrast, buying a batch of jet engines involves a tortuously long buying process, dozens or even hundreds of decision makers from all levels of the buying organization, and layer upon layer of subtle and not-so-subtle buying influences.

To get an idea of the complexities involved in selling one of GE's industrial products, let's dig deeper into the company's GE Transportation division and one of its bread-and-butter products: diesel locomotives. GE locomotives might not seem glamorous to you, but they are beautiful brutes to those who buy and use them. One GE Evolution series locomotive can pull the equivalent of 170 Boeing 747 "Jumbo Jet" airliners. It's not difficult to identify potential buyers for a 207 ton, 4400 horsepower GE locomotive with an average estimated cost of US$2.2 million per unit. The real challenge is to win buyers' business by building day-in, day-out, year-in, year-out partnerships with them based on superior products and close collaboration.

In the buying decision, locomotive performance plays an important role. In such big-ticket purchases, buyers carefully scrutinize factors such as cost, fuel efficiency, and reliability. By most measures, GE's locomotives outperform competing engines on most of these dimensions. The company's innovative Evolution Series locomotives, part of a broader GE "ecomagination" initiative to build environmentally friendly products, are now the most technically advanced, fuel-efficient, and eco-friendly diesel-electric locomotives in history. Compared with their predecessors, they produce full power but cut fuel consumption by 5 percent and reduce particulate pollution by 40 percent. "If every freight locomotive in North America were as clean as GE's Evolution," notes one expert, "the annual reduction of emissions

would compare to removing 48 million cars from the road each year." GE's next-generation Evolution Hybrid diesel-electric engines will reduce fuel consumption by another 15 percent and emissions by as much as 50 percent.

But locomotive performance is only part of the buying equation. GE wins contracts by partnering with business customers to help them translate that performance into moving their passengers and freight more efficiently and reliably. CSX Transportation (CSXT), one of GE Transportation's largest customers, has purchased more than 300 GE Evolution locomotives since they were launched in 2005. According to a CSXT purchasing executive, the company "evaluates many cost factors before awarding ... a locomotive contract. Environmental impact, fuel consumption, reliability, serviceability [are] all key elements in this decision." But also important is "the value of our ongoing partnership with GE."

A recent high-stakes international deal involving hundreds of GE locomotives demonstrates the potential importance, scope, and complexity of some business-to-business decisions:

> GE Transportation recently landed a huge US$650 million contract to supply 310 Evolution locomotives to the Kazakhstan National Railway (KTZ)—the largest-ever order for locomotives delivered outside North America. Befitting its importance to not just the companies, but to their countries as well, the deal was inked at the Kazakhstan Embassy in Washington, DC. The signing was attended by high-level executives from both organizations, including the chief executive of GE Transportation and the president of KTZ.
>
> The buying decision was based on a host of factors. KTZ wanted the very best performance technology available, and GE's Evolution locomotives fit the bill nicely. But the deal also hinged on many factors that had little to do with the engine performance. For example, important matters of international economics and politics came into play as well. Whereas the first 10 locomotives were built at GE's U.S. plant, most of the remaining 300 locomotives will be assembled at a newly

built, state-owned plant in Pavlodar, Kazakhstan.

Finally, the current contract was anything but an impulsive, one-and-done deal. Rather, it represented the culmination of years of smaller steps between the two organizations—the latest episode in a long-running relationship between GE and KTZ that dates back to the mid-1990s. The relationship accelerated in 2003 when GE won the first of several contracts for modernization kits that updated older KTZ locomotives. "I am proud that KTZ and GE are extending our relationship," said the CEO of GE Transportation. "GE and Kazakhstan have a long and fruitful history of working together."

Thanks to stories like this one, GE Transportation dominates the worldwide rail locomotive industry, now capturing a phenomenal 80-percent market share. More broadly, people throughout the entire GE organization know that success in business-to-business markets involves more than just developing and selling superior products and technologies. Business customer buying decisions are made within the framework of a strategic, problem-solving partnership. "We love the challenge of a customer's problem," says

the company on its GE Transportation website. "Why? It's an opportunity for a true collaborative partnership. We enjoy the exchange of ideas, whether we're developing a brand new technology or applying existing technologies in innovative new ways. [We] go to great lengths to help our customers succeed."

"Customer partnerships are at the center of GE and Ecomagination," confirms GE chairman and CEO Jeffrey Immelt in a recent letter to shareholders. "We are viewed as a technical partner by customers around the world."

Exhibit 6.15 GE locomotives might not seem glamorous to you, but they are beautiful brutes to those who buy and use them. In this market, GE's real challenge is to win buyers' business by building day-in, day-out, year-in, year-out partnerships with them.

Sources: Quotes and other information from "GE Transportation Endorses New Tier 3 and 4 Emission Regulations," *Business Wire*, March 14, 2008; "General Electric Signs Contract to Supply 310 Evolution Series Locomotives to Kazakhstan," *Business Wire*, September 28, 2006; Jim Martin, "GE to Seal $650 Million Deal," *Knight Ridder Tribune Business News*, September 28, 2006, p. 1; Rick Stouffer, "GE Locomotives: 100 Years and Still Chuggin'," *Knight Ridder Tribune Business News*, September 23, 2007; David Lustig, "GE Unveils Hybrid Loco," *Railway Gazette International*, July 2007, p. 1; "GE Transportation Delivers 3,000th GE Evolution (R) Series Locomotive to Kazakstan Temir Zholy (KTZ), *Business Wire*, March 18, 2009; "Collaborating with Partners," at www.getransportation.com, accessed May 2009; and annual reports and various pages accessed at www.ge.com, accessed October 2009.

BUSINESS MARKETS

The business market is *huge*. In fact, business markets involve far more dollars and items than do consumer markets. For example, think about the large number of business transactions involved in the production and sale of a single set of Goodyear tires. Various suppliers sell Goodyear the rubber, steel, equipment, and other goods that it needs to produce tires. Goodyear then sells the finished tires to retailers, who in turn sell them to consumers. Thus, many sets of *business* purchases were made for only one set of *consumer* purchases. In addition, Goodyear sells tires as original equipment to manufacturers who install them on new vehicles, and as replacement tires to companies that maintain their own fleets of company cars, trucks, buses, or other vehicles.

In some ways, business markets are similar to consumer markets. Both involve people who assume buying roles and make purchase decisions to satisfy needs. However, business markets differ in many ways from consumer markets. The main differences are in *market structure and demand*, the *nature of the buying unit*, and the *types of decisions and the decision process* involved.

Market Structure and Demand   The business marketer normally deals with *far fewer but far larger buyers* than the consumer marketer does. Even in large business markets, a few buyers often account for most of the purchasing. For example, when Goodyear sells replacement tires to final consumers, its potential market includes the owners of the millions of cars currently in use around the world. But Goodyear's fate in the business market depends on getting orders from one of only a handful of large automakers.

Similarly, Black & Decker sells its power tools and outdoor equipment to tens of millions of consumers worldwide. However, it must sell these products through three huge retail customers—Home Depot, RONA, and Wal-Mart—which, combined, account for more than half its sales.

Further, business demand is **derived demand**—it ultimately comes from (derives from) the demand for consumer goods. Hewlett-Packard and Dell buy Intel microprocessor chips because consumers buy personal computers. If consumer demand for computers drops, so will the demand for microprocessors. Therefore, B-to-B marketers sometimes promote their products directly to final consumers to increase business demand. For example, Intel advertises heavily to personal computer buyers, selling them on the virtues of Intel and its microprocessors. Recent ads from Intel position its people as "Sponsors of Tomorrow"—just the folks you'd want making the chip in your computer. "Making microprocessors is a tricky business," says one ad. "This is why our clean rooms are 10,000 times cleaner than a hospital operating room. It's also why our workers must wear those silly-looking outfits." The increased demand for Intel chips boosts demand for the PCs containing them, and both Intel and its business partners win.

Many business markets have *inelastic demand*; that is, total demand for many business products is not affected much by price changes, especially in the short run. A drop in the price of leather will not cause shoe manufacturers to buy much more leather unless it results in lower shoe prices that, in turn, will increase consumer demand for shoes.

Finally, business markets have more *fluctuating demand*. The demand for many business goods and services tends to change more—and more quickly—than the demand for consumer goods and services does. A small percentage increase in consumer demand can cause large increases in business demand. Sometimes a rise of only 10 percent in consumer demand can cause as much as a 200 percent rise in business demand during the next period.

Nature of the Buying Unit Compared with consumer purchases, a business purchase usually involves *more decision participants* and a *more professional purchasing effort*. Often, business buying is done by trained purchasing agents who spend their working lives learning how to buy better. The more complex the purchase, the more likely it is that several people will participate in the decision-making process. Buying committees made up of technical experts and top management are common in the buying of major goods. Beyond this, B-to-B marketers now face a new breed of higher-level, better-trained supply managers. Therefore, companies must have well-trained marketers and salespeople to deal with these well-trained buyers.

Types of Decisions and the Decision Process

Business buyers usually face *more complex* buying decisions than do consumer buyers. Business purchases often involve large sums of money, complex technical and economic considerations, and interactions among many people at many levels of the buyer's organization. Because the purchases are more complex, business buyers may take longer to make their decisions. The business buying process also tends to be *more formalized* than the consumer buying process. Large business purchases usually call for detailed product specifications, written purchase orders, careful supplier searches, and formal approval.

Derived demand
Business demand that ultimately comes from (derives from) the demand for consumer goods.

Exhibit 6.16 Derived demand: Intel advertises heavily to sell users on the virtues of the company and its microprocessors. "Making microprocessors is tricky business," says this ad. "That's why our workers must wear those silly-looking outfits."

Finally, in the business buying process, the buyer and seller are often much *more dependent* on each other. B-to-B marketers may roll up their sleeves and work closely with their customers during all stages of the buying process—from helping customers define problems, to finding solutions, to supporting after-sale operation. They often customize their offerings to individual customer needs. In the short run, sales go to suppliers who meet buyers' immediate product and service needs. In the long run, however, business-to-business marketers keep a customer's sales and create customer value by meeting current needs *and* by partnering with customers to help them solve their problems.

In recent years, relationships between customers and suppliers have been changing from downright adversarial to close and chummy. In fact, many customer companies are now practising **supplier development**, systematically developing networks of supplier-partners to ensure an appropriate and dependable supply of products and materials that they will use in making their own products or resell to others. For example, Wal-Mart doesn't have a "Purchasing Department," it has a "Supplier Development Department." And giant Swedish furniture retailer IKEA doesn't just buy from its suppliers, it involves them deeply in the customer value–creation process.

> IKEA, the world's largest furniture retailer, is the quintessential global cult brand. Customers from Beijing to Moscow to Edmonton, AB, flock to the US$27 billion Scandinavian retailer's nearly 300 huge stores in 36 countries, drawn by IKEA's trendy but simple and practical furniture at affordable prices. But IKEA's biggest obstacle to growth isn't opening new stores and attracting customers. Rather, it's finding enough of the right kinds of *suppliers* to help design and produce the billions of dollars of affordable goods that those customers will carry out of its stores. IKEA currently relies on about 1,400 suppliers in 54 countries to stock its shelves. IKEA doesn't just rely on spot suppliers who might be available when needed. Instead, it has systematically developed a robust network of supplier-partners that reliably provide the more than 9,500 items it stocks. IKEA's designers start with a basic customer value proposition. Then, they find and work closely with key suppliers to bring that proposition to market. Thus, IKEA does more than just buy from suppliers; it also involves them deeply in the process of designing and making stylish but affordable products to keep IKEA's customers coming back.[38]

BUSINESS BUYER BEHAVIOUR

At the most basic level, marketers want to know how business buyers will respond to various marketing stimuli. Figure 6.6 shows a model of business buyer behaviour. In this model, marketing and other stimuli affect the buying organization and produce certain buyer responses. These stimuli enter the organization and are turned into buyer responses. To design good marketing strategies, the marketer must understand what happens within the organization to turn stimuli into purchase responses.

Within the organization, buying activity consists of two major parts: the buying centre, made up of all the people involved in the buying decision, and the buying decision process. The model shows that the buying centre and the buying decision process are influenced by internal organizational, interpersonal, and individual factors as well as by external environmental factors.

The model in Figure 6.6 suggests four questions about business buyer behaviour: What buying decisions do business buyers make? Who participates in the buying process? What are the major influences on buyers? How do business buyers make their buying decisions?

Major Types of Buying Situations There are three major types of buying situations.[39] In a **straight rebuy**, the buyer reorders something without any modifications. It is usually handled on a routine basis by the purchasing department. To keep the business, "in" suppliers try to maintain product and service quality. "Out" suppliers try to find new ways to add value or exploit dissatisfaction so that the buyer will consider them.

Supplier development

Systematic development of networks of supplier-partners to ensure an appropriate and dependable supply of products and materials for use in making products or reselling them to others.

Straight rebuy

A business buying situation in which the buyer routinely reorders something without any modifications.

FIGURE 6.6 The model of business buyer behaviour

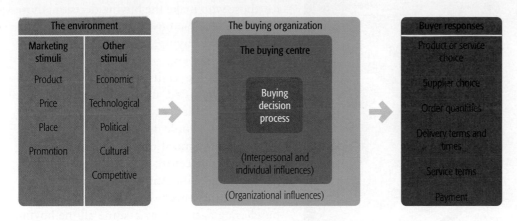

In a **modified rebuy**, the buyer wants to modify product specifications, prices, terms, or suppliers. The in suppliers may become nervous and feel pressured to put their best foot forward to protect an account. Out suppliers may see the modified rebuy situation as an opportunity to make a better offer and gain new business.

A company buying a product or service for the first time faces a **new-task** situation. In such cases, the greater the cost or risk, the larger the number of decision participants and the greater their efforts to collect information. The new-task situation is the marketer's greatest opportunity and challenge. The marketer not only tries to reach as many key buying influences as possible but also provides help and information. The buyer makes the fewest decisions in the straight rebuy and the most in the new-task decision.

Many business buyers prefer to buy a complete solution to a problem from a single seller instead of buying separate products and services from several suppliers and putting them together. The sale often goes to the firm that provides the most complete *system* for meeting the customer's needs and solving its problems. Such **systems selling (or solutions selling)** is often a key business marketing strategy for winning and holding accounts.

UPS does more than just ship packages for its business customers. It develops entire solutions to customers' transportation and logistics problems. For example, UPS bundles a complete system of services that support Nikon's consumer-products supply chain—including logistics, transportation, freight, and customs brokerage services—into one smooth-running system.[40]

> When Nikon entered the digital camera market, it decided that it needed an entirely new distribution strategy as well. So it asked transportation and logistics giant UPS to design a complete system for moving its entire electronics product line from its Asian factories to retail stores throughout the United States, Canada, Latin America, and the Caribbean. Now, products leave Nikon's Asian manufacturing centres and arrive on retailers' shelves in as few as two days, with UPS handling everything in between. UPS first manages air and ocean freight and related customs brokerage to bring Nikon products from Korea, Japan, and Indonesia to its Louisville, Kentucky, operations centre. There, UPS can either "kit" the Nikon merchandise with accessories such as batteries and chargers or repackage it for in-store display. Finally, UPS distributes the products to thousands of retailers across the United States or exports them to Canadian, Latin American or Caribbean retail outlets and distributors. Along the way, UPS tracks the goods and provides Nikon with a "snapshot" of the entire supply chain, letting Nikon keep retailers informed of delivery times and adjust them as needed.

Participants in the Business Buying Process Who does the buying of the trillions of dollars' worth of goods and services needed by business organizations? The decision-making unit of a buying organization is called its **buying centre**—all the individuals and units that play a role in the business purchase decision-making process. This group

Modified rebuy
A business buying situation in which the buyer wants to modify product specifications, prices, terms, or suppliers.

New task
A business buying situation in which the buyer purchases a product or service for the first time.

Systems selling (or solutions selling)
Buying a packaged solution to a problem from a single seller, thus avoiding all the separate decisions involved in a complex buying situation.

Buying centre
All the individuals and units that play a role in the purchase decision-making process.

Exhibit 6.17 Buying Centre: Cardinal Health deals with a wide range of buying influences, from purchasing executives and hospital administrators to the surgeons who actually use its products.

includes the actual users of the product or service, those who make the buying decision, those who influence the buying decision, those who do the actual buying, and those who control buying information.

The buying centre is not a fixed and formally identified unit within the buying organization. It is a set of buying roles assumed by different people for different purchases. Within the organization, the size and makeup of the buying centre will vary for different products and different buying situations. For some routine purchases, one person—say, a purchasing agent—may assume all the buying centre roles and serve as the only person involved in the buying decision. For more complex purchases, the buying centre may include 20 or 30 people from different levels and departments in the organization.

The buying centre concept presents a major marketing challenge. The business marketer must learn who participates in the decision, each participant's relative influence, and what evaluation criteria each decision participant uses. This can be difficult.

For instance, the medical products and services group of Cardinal Health sells disposable surgical gowns to hospitals. It identifies the hospital personnel involved in this buying decision as the vice-president of purchasing, the operating room administrator, and the surgeons. Each participant plays a different role. The vice-president of purchasing analyzes whether the hospital should buy disposable gowns or reusable gowns. If analysis favours disposable gowns, then the operating room administrator compares competing products and prices and makes a choice. This administrator considers the gowns' absorbency, antiseptic quality, design, and cost, and normally buys the brand that meets requirements at the lowest cost. Finally, surgeons affect the decision later by reporting their satisfaction or dissatisfaction with the brand.

The buying centre usually includes some obvious participants who are involved formally in the buying decision. For example, the decision to buy a corporate jet will probably involve the company's CEO, chief pilot, a purchasing agent, some legal staff, a member of top management, and others formally charged with the buying decision. It may also involve less obvious, informal participants, some of whom may actually make or strongly affect the buying decision. Sometimes, even the people in the buying centre are not aware of all the buying participants. For example, the decision about which corporate jet to buy may actually be made by a corporate board member who has an interest in flying and who knows a lot about airplanes. This board member may work behind the scenes to sway the decision. Many business buying decisions result from the complex interactions of ever-changing buying centre participants.

Major Influences on Business Buyers   Business buyers are subject to many influences when they make their buying decisions. Some marketers assume that the major influences are economic. They think buyers will favour the supplier who offers the lowest price or the best product or the most service. They concentrate on offering strong economic benefits to buyers. However, business buyers actually respond to both economic and personal factors. Far from being cold, calculating, and impersonal, business buyers are human and social as well. They react to both reason and emotion.

Today, most B-to-B marketers recognize that emotion plays an important role in business buying decisions. For example, you might expect that an advertisement promoting large trucks to corporate fleet buyers or independent owner-operators would stress objective technical, performance, and economic factors. For instance, befitting today's tougher economic times, premium heavy-duty truck maker Peterbilt does stress performance—its dealers and website provide plenty of information about factors such as manoeuvrability, productivity, reliability, comfort, and fuel efficiency. But Peterbilt ads appeal to buyers' emotions as well. They show the raw beauty of the trucks, and the Peterbilt slogan—"Class Pays"—suggests that owning a Peterbilt truck is a matter of pride as well as superior performance. Says the company, "On highways, construction sites, city streets, logging roads—everywhere customers earn their living—Peterbilt's red oval is a familiar symbol of performance, reliability, and pride."

Figure 6.7 lists various groups of influences on business buyers—environmental, organizational, interpersonal, and individual.[41] Business buyers are heavily influenced by *environmental factors*, such as economic, technological, political, competitive, and social and cultural developments. For example, in the wake of the recent economic downturn, just like final consumers, business buyers have tightened their budgets and spending. Like final consumers, they are looking for greater value in everything they buy. Now, more than ever, B-to-B marketers must sharpen their value propositions and help customers to find effective and efficient solutions. "Anyone who says the economy is not a challenge is totally in denial," says one B-to-B marketing expert. Companies "need to look at the needs of customers. It's customer, customer, and customer now."[42]

Organizational factors are also important. Each buying organization has its own objectives, policies, procedures, structure, and systems, and the business marketer must understand these factors well. Questions such as these arise: How many people are involved in the buying decision? Who are they? What are their evaluative criteria? What are the company's policies and limits on its buyers?

The buying centre usually includes many participants who influence one another, so *interpersonal factors* also influence the business buying process. However, it is often difficult to assess such interpersonal factors and group dynamics. Buying centre

TWO POWERFUL EXPRESSIONS OF FUEL EFFICIENCY.

PETERBILT MODELS 386 AND 387
FROM THE INNOVATIVE VERSATILITY OF THE MODEL 386 TO THE SPACIOUS AND ERGONOMIC MODEL 387. TWO CHOICES OF PREMIUM FUEL EFFICIENCY.

CLASS PAYS
WWW.PETERBILT.COM

Exhibit 6.18   Emotions play an important role in business buying: This Peterbilt ad stresses performance factors such as fuel efficiency. But it also stresses more emotional factors, such as the raw beauty of Peterbilt trucks and the pride of owning and driving one–"Class Pays."

FIGURE 6.7 Major influences on business buyer behaviour

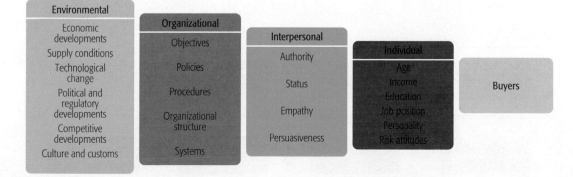

Environmental	Organizational	Interpersonal	Individual	
Economic developments	Objectives	Authority	Age	Buyers
Supply conditions	Policies	Status	Income	
Technological change	Procedures	Empathy	Education	
Political and regulatory developments	Organizational structure	Persuasiveness	Job position	
Competitive developments	Systems		Personality	
Culture and customs			Risk attitudes	

participants do not wear tags that label them as "key decision maker" or "not influential." Nor do buying centre participants with the highest rank always have the most influence. Interpersonal factors are often very subtle. Whenever possible, business marketers must try to understand these factors and design strategies that take them into account.

Finally, each participant in the business buying decision process brings in personal motives, perceptions, and preferences. These *individual factors* are affected by personal characteristics such as age, income, education, professional identification, personality, and attitudes toward risk. Also, buyers have different buying styles. Some may be technical types who make in-depth analyses of competitive proposals before choosing a supplier. Other buyers may be intuitive negotiators who are adept at pitting the sellers against one another for the best deal.

 The Business Buying Process   Figure 6.8 lists the eight stages of the business buying process.[43] Buyers who face a new-task buying situation usually go through all stages of the buying process. Buyers making modified or straight rebuys may skip some of the stages. We will examine these steps for the typical new-task buying situation.

The buying process begins with *problem recognition*—when someone in the company recognizes a problem or need that can be met by acquiring a specific product or service. Problem recognition can result from internal or external factors. Business marketers use their sales forces or advertising to alert customers to potential problems and then show how their products provide solutions. For example, a Sharp ad notes that a multi-function printer can present data security problems and asks, "Is your MFP a portal for identity theft?" The solution? Sharp's data security kits "help prevent sensitive information from falling into the wrong hands."

Having recognized a need, the buyer next prepares a *general need description* that describes the characteristics and quantity of the needed items or solutions. For standard purchases, this process presents few problems. For complex items, however, the buyer may need to work with others—engineers, users, consultants—to define what's needed.

Once the buying organization has defined the need, it develops the item's technical *product specifications*, often with the help of a value analysis engineering team. **Value analysis** is an approach to cost reduction in which the company carefully analyzes a product's or service's components to determine whether they can be redesigned and made more effectively and efficiently to provide greater value. The team decides on the best product or service characteristics and specifies them accordingly. Sellers, too, can use value analysis as a tool to help secure new accounts and keep old ones. Especially in a down economy, improving customer value and helping customers find more cost-effective solutions gives the business marketer an important edge in keeping current customers loyal and winning new business.

In the next buying process step, the buyer conducts a *supplier search* to find the best vendors. The buyer can locate qualified suppliers through trade directories, computer

Value analysis
Carefully analyzing a product's or service's components to determine whether they can be redesigned and made more effectively and efficiently to provide greater value.

FIGURE 6.8 Stages of the business buying process

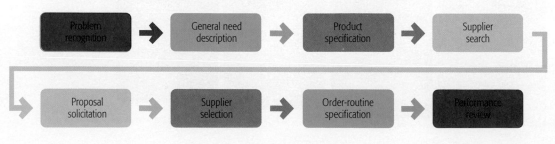

searches, or recommendations from others. Today, more and more companies are turning to the Internet to find suppliers. For marketers, this has levelled the playing field—the Internet gives smaller suppliers many of the same advantages as larger competitors. The supplier's task is to understand the search process and make certain that their firm is considered.

In the *proposal solicitation* stage of the business buying process, the buyer invites qualified suppliers to submit proposals. When the purchase is complex or expensive, the buyer will usually require detailed written proposals or formal presentations from each potential supplier. In response, business marketers must be skilled in researching, writing, and presenting proposals. The proposals should be marketing documents, not just technical documents. They should spell out how the seller's solution creates greater value for the customer than competing solutions.

The buyer next reviews the proposals and selects a supplier or suppliers. During *supplier selection*, the buyer will consider many supplier attributes and their relative importance. Such attributes include product and service quality, reputation, on-time delivery, ethical corporate behaviour, honest communication, and competitive prices. In the end, they may select a single supplier or a few suppliers. Today's supplier development managers often want to develop a full network of supplier-partners that can help the company bring more value to its customers.

Exhibit 6.19 Problem recognition: Sharp uses ads like this one to alert customers to potential problems and then provide solutions.

The buyer now prepares an *order-routine specification*. It includes the final order with the chosen supplier or suppliers and lists items such as technical specifications, quantity needed, expected time of delivery, return policies, and warranties. Many large buyers now practise *vendor-managed inventory*, in which they turn over ordering and inventory responsibilities to their suppliers. Under such systems, buyers share sales and inventory information directly with key suppliers. The suppliers then monitor inventories and replenish stock automatically as needed. For example, most major suppliers to large retailers such as Wal-Mart, Home Depot, and Lowe's assume vendor-managed inventory responsibilities.

The final stage of the business buying process is the supplier *performance review*, in which the buyer assesses the supplier's performance and provides feedback. For example, Home Depot has issued a set of supplier guidelines and policies and regularly evaluates each supplier in terms of quality, delivery, and other performance variables. It gives suppliers online performance scorecards that provide ongoing feedback that helps them to improve their performance.[44] The supplier performance review may lead the buyer to continue, modify, or drop the arrangement. The seller's job is to monitor the same factors used by the buyer to make sure that the seller is giving the expected satisfaction.

The eight-stage buying-process model provides a simple view of the business buying as it might occur in a new-task buying situation. The actual process is usually much more complex. In the modified rebuy or straight rebuy situation, some of these stages would be compressed or bypassed. Each organization buys in its own way, and each buying situation has unique requirements.

Different buying centre participants may be involved at different stages of the process. Although certain buying-process steps usually do occur, buyers do not always follow them in the same order, and they may add other steps. Often, buyers will repeat certain stages of the process. Finally, a customer relationship might involve many different types of purchases ongoing at a given time, all in different stages of the buying process. The seller must manage the total customer relationship, not just individual purchases.

E-Procurement: Buying on the Internet   Advances in information technology have changed the face of the B-to-B marketing process. Electronic purchasing, often called **e-procurement**, has grown rapidly in recent years. Virtually unknown less than a decade ago, online purchasing is standard procedure for most companies today. E-procurement gives buyers access to new suppliers, lowers purchasing costs, and hastens order processing and delivery. In turn, business marketers can connect with customers online to share marketing information, sell products and services, provide customer support services, and maintain ongoing customer relationships.

Companies can do e-procurement in any of several ways. They can conduct *reverse auctions*, in which they put their purchasing requests online and invite suppliers to bid for the business. Or they can engage in online *trading exchanges*, through which companies work collectively to facilitate the trading process. For example, Exostar is an online trading exchange that connects buyers and sellers in the aerospace and defence industry. The huge exchange has connected more than 300 procurement systems and 40 000 trading partners in 20 countries around the world.

Companies also can conduct e-procurement by setting up their own *company buying sites*. For example, GE operates a company trading site on which it posts its buying needs and invites bids, negotiates terms, and places orders. Or companies can create *extranet links* with key suppliers. For instance, they can create direct procurement accounts with suppliers such as Dell or Office Depot, through which company buyers can purchase equipment, materials, and supplies directly.

B-to-B marketers can help customers who wish to purchase online by creating well-designed, easy-to-use websites. For example, *BtoB* magazine rated the site of Cisco Systems—a market leader in Web networking hardware, software, and services—as one of its "10 great B-to-B Web sites":[45]

> To spur growth, Cisco Systems recently stepped up its focus on the small and midsize business segment (SMB). Its award-winning new SMB-specific Web site is simple, action-oriented, and engaging but gives SMB buyers deep access. At the most basic level, customers can find and download information about thousands of Cisco products and services. Dig deeper, and the site is loaded with useful video content—everything from testimonials to "how to" videos to informational and educational on-demand Webcasts.
>
> Cisco's SMB site gets customers interacting with the company and its partner resellers. For example, its live click-to-chat feature puts users in immediate touch with Cisco product experts. WebEx Web-conferencing software connects potential SMB customers with appropriate Cisco partner resellers, letting them share Web pages, PowerPoints, and other documents in a collaborative online space. Finally, the Cisco SMB site can actually personalize the online experience for users. For example, if it detects that someone from the legal industry is paying attention to wireless content, it might put together relevant pieces of content to create a page for that visitor. Such personalization really pays off. Customers visiting personalized pages stay two times longer than other visitors and go much deeper into the site.

Business-to-business e-procurement yields many benefits. First, it shaves transaction costs and results in more efficient purchasing for both buyers and suppliers. E-procurement reduces the time between order and delivery. And a Web-powered purchasing program eliminates the paperwork associated with traditional requisition and ordering procedures and helps an organization keep better track of all purchases.

E-procurement
Purchasing through electronic connections between buyers and sellers—usually online.

Finally, beyond the cost and time savings, e-procurement frees purchasing people from a lot of drudgery and paperwork. In turn, it frees them to focus on more-strategic issues, such as finding better supply sources and working with suppliers to reduce costs and develop new products.

To demonstrate these advantages, consider Kodak. When it recently remodelled its headquarters facilities in Rochester, N.Y., it used only e-procurement. From demolition to restoration, the massive project involved managing more than 1600 contract bids from 150 contractors. Throughout the project, e-procurement reduced paperwork and speeded up review and award times. In the end, the project was completed on time, and Kodak estimates that using e-procurement saved 15 percent on purchasing-process costs (including US$186 000 on photocopying expenses alone).[46]

The rapidly expanding use of e-procurement, however, also presents some problems. For example, at the same time that the Web makes it possible for suppliers and customers to share business data and even collaborate on product design, it can also erode decades-old customer–supplier relationships. Many buyers now use the power of the Web to pit suppliers against one another and to search out better deals, products, and turnaround times on a purchase-by-purchase basis.

Exhibit 6.20   Online buying: This Cisco Systems site helps customers who want to purchase online by providing deep access to information about thousands of Cisco products and services. The site can also personalize the online experience for users and connect them with appropriate Cisco partner resellers.

CANADA GOOSE® MINI CASE

OPINION LEADERS AND CONSUMER BEHAVIOUR

Canada Goose has made a point of targeting opinion leaders and experts in the ultra cold-weather user consumer segment. While Lance Mackey may not be well known to the average person, he is a dogsledding legend and the four-time winner of the Iditarod extreme dogsled race. His endorsement is highly credible and powerful for the "true user."

The film industry has also enjoyed a long-standing relationship with Canada Goose. In the early days, grips, best-boys, script assistants, and the likes wore Canada Goose parkas on long, cold overnight shoots. Soon wardrobe assistants learned that if they wanted a film set to look authentically cold, then they'd best outfit their talent in Canada Goose. As Hollywood caught on, so did celebrities. It wasn't long before Matt Damon, Sacha Baron-Cohen, Hillary Duff, Daniel Craig, Bill Clinton, and others began wearing Canada Goose. This endorsement, coupled with the brand's growing best-in-class status, has led to product collaborations with high-powered recording artists such as Drake.

Seeing celebrities sporting a Canada Goose jacket might inspire marketers to question how opinion leaders or well-known experts influence consumer behaviour. In addition, they might wonder how reference groups or aspirational groups (groups that people aspire to be in) affect Canada Goose's consumers' behaviour?

Experts say endorsements work only when the consumer has a credible belief that the expert or celebrity would be interested in buying and using a product or service despite being paid to do so. Canada Goose has taken special care to showcase true users who have purchased Canada Goose outerwear of their own volition. Perhaps this is why the company's true user endorsements seem so convincing to consumers of its gear.

Researchers have noted that premium brands, while seeking to appeal to a desire for status, also work more effectively when they can simultaneously create a sense of community around the brand. Appealing to community is not an attribute of premium brands, but an attribute of all brands. Companies such as Canada Goose use Facebook pages to help achieve this goal. They take care to gather, acknowledge, and use their community of users' opinions and thoughts in their product development and overall positioning.

Canada Goose does not see a contradiction in focusing on function first and having a high-status product. It believes that the focus on functionality has led to its reputation for quality, which has then led to the status and value of the brand.

QUESTIONS

1. Which stage of the consumer purchase decision process would you say that Canada Goose focuses on to influence its customers? Why?
2. How might you determine whether a consumer is responding to marketing stimuli or the core value of a Canada Goose jacket?
3. When you consider that Canada Goose coats were well received in Europe first and then the company used the cachet of that European success to achieve success in the North American market, what do you suppose might be different about the consumer behaviour of Europeans?
4. How valuable do you think a lifetime warranty is for consumers ages 16 to 24? How about those ages 24 to 45?

REVIEWING THE CONCEPTS

1. Understand the consumer market and the major factors that influence consumer buyer behaviour.

The *consumer market* consists of all the individuals and households who buy or acquire goods and services for personal consumption. Consumer behaviour should be viewed as an ongoing process that starts long before the consumer purchases a product or service and continues long after he or she consumes it. This extended definition of consumer behaviour means that marketers must be aware of a number of issues before, during, and after purchase to build brand loyalty and lasting relationships with their customers.

Consumer buyer behaviour is influenced by four key sets of buyer characteristics: cultural, social, personal, and psychological. Understanding these factors can help marketers to identify interested buyers and to shape products and appeals to serve consumer needs better. Each factor provides a different perspective for understanding the consumers' decision-making process.

2. Identify and discuss the stages in the buyer decision process.

When making a purchase, the buyer goes through a decision process consisting of need recognition, information search, evaluation of alternatives, purchase decision, and postpurchase behaviour. During *need recognition*, the consumer recognizes a problem or need that could be satisfied by a product or service. Once the need is recognized, the consumer moves into the *information search* stage. With information in hand, the consumer proceeds to *alternative evaluation* and assesses brands in the choice set. From there, the consumer makes a *purchase decision* and actually buys the product. In the final stage of the buyer decision process, *postpurchase behaviour*, the consumer takes action based on satisfaction or dissatisfaction. The marketer's job is to understand the buyer's behaviour at each stage and the influences that are operating.

3. Describe the adoption and diffusion process for new products.

The product *adoption process* is made up of five stages: awareness, interest, evaluation, trial, and adoption. New-product marketers must think about how to help consumers move through these stages. With regard to the *diffusion process* for new products, consumers respond at different rates, depending on consumer and product characteristics. Consumers may be innovators, early adopters, early majority, late majority, or laggards. Each group may require different marketing approaches. Marketers often try to bring their new products to the attention of potential early adopters, especially those who are opinion leaders.

4. Define the business market and identify the major factors that influence business buyer behaviour.

The *business market* comprises all organizations that buy goods and services for use in the production of other products and services or for the purpose of reselling or renting them to others at a profit. As compared to consumer markets, business markets usually have fewer, larger buyers. Business demand is derived demand, and the business buying decision usually involves more, and more-professional, buyers.

Business buyers make decisions that vary with the three types of *buying situations*: straight rebuys, modified rebuys, and new tasks. The decision-making unit of a buying organization—the *buying centre*—can consist of many different persons playing many different roles. The business marketer needs to know the following: Who are the major buying centre participants? In what decisions do they exercise influence and to what degree? What evaluation criteria does each decision participant use? The business marketer also needs to understand the major environmental, organizational, interpersonal, and individual influences on the buying process.

5. List and define the steps in the business buying decision process.

The *business buying decision process* itself can be quite involved, with eight basic stages: problem recognition, general need description, product specification, supplier search, proposal solicitation, supplier selection, order-routine specification, and performance review. Buyers who face a new-task buying situation usually go through all stages of the buying process. Buyers making modified or straight rebuys may skip some of the stages. Companies must manage the overall customer relationship, which often includes many different buying decisions in various stages of the buying decision process. Recent advances in information technology have given birth to "e-procurement," by which business buyers are purchasing all kinds of products and services online. Business marketers are increasingly connecting with customers online to share marketing information, sell products and services, provide customer support services, and maintain ongoing customer relationships.

KEY TERMS

Adoption process   222
Attitude   218
Belief   218
Business buyer behaviour   224
Buying centre   229
Cognitive dissonance   221
Consumer buyer behaviour   203
Consumer market   203
Culture   205
Derived demand   227

E-procurement   234
Group   209
Learning   218
Lifestyle   214
Modified rebuy   229
Motive (drive)   215
New product   222
New task   229
Online social networks   210
Opinion leader   209

Perception   217
Personality   215
Social class   209
Straight rebuy   228
Subculture   206
Supplier development   228
Systems selling
   (or solutions selling)   229
Value analysis   232

TALK ABOUT MARKETING

1. In designing the advertising for a soft drink, which would you find more helpful, information about consumer demographics or information about consumer lifestyles? Select a new soft drink on the market and give examples of how you would use each type of information.

2. Think of a product you've purchased recently that was not a routine purchase. Describe how you progressed through each of the five stages of the consumer buyer decision process. Did you experience any cognitive dissonance during your postpurchase behaviour?

3. Now, think about the product you discussed in #2 from the perspective of a marketer. What forms of marketing communications or programs could you use to influence a prospective buyer of the product you selected, at each of the five stages?

4. Marketers often target consumers before, during, or after a trigger event—an event in one's life that triggers change. For example, after having a child, new parents have an increased need for baby furniture, clothes, diapers, car seats, and lots of other baby-related goods. Consumers who never paid attention to marketing efforts for certain products may now be focused on those related to their life change. Discuss other trigger events that may provide opportunities to target the right buyer at the right time.

5. Choose a high-tech product that is commonly purchased by businesses. Under what circumstances should the business behave as an innovator? An early adopter? A laggard?

6. Imagine you work in the purchasing department at Canadian Tire. You are responsible for making all the purchase decisions about paint and related home decor items such as blinds and curtain rods. Which of the influences on business buyer behaviour would be your most important criteria? Are there any influences on consumer buyer behaviour that you would take into consideration when making your decisions?

THINK LIKE A MARKETING MANAGER

Performance review is one of the most critical stages in a business buying process. Perhaps nowhere is this more important than in the highly competitive aircraft manufacturing business. Whether the planes are large or small, once a purchase is made, the buyer is tied to the manufacturer for a long time for service and parts requirements. "Air wars" are currently being fought between Europe's Airbus Industrie and America's Boeing.

QUESTIONS

1. Refer to the model of business buyer behaviour (Figure 6.6). Which are the most critical influences on this business buying situation?
2. When and how should a performance review of the selected vendor be conducted?
3. What, exactly, should be studied in the performance review?
4. If the results of the performance review were negative, what are the next steps the buyers should take?

MARKETING ETHICS

Companies face many challenges when conducting business abroad. Cultural differences are particularly difficult. In several emerging markets, such as parts of Asia, Africa, the Middle East, the former Soviet Union, Eastern Europe, and South America, bribery is considered "standard operating procedure" in business buying. The World Bank estimates that bribery in international trade amounts to about $1 trillion annually.

Laws in both Canada and the United States prohibit North American companies from giving corrupt payments to obtain favour in business transactions, and now many more countries are joining the fight against corruption. In China, bribery is punishable by death, a sentence given to China's former director of the State Food and Drug Administration in 2007.

QUESTIONS

1. Is it right for Canadian companies to be penalized for going along with cultural norms in other countries? Is it right for Canada and other countries to demand that businesses in other countries follow our laws?
2. What are the consequences for Canadian companies of not going along with the cultural factors influencing foreign business customers?

MARKETING TECHNOLOGY

Comparison shopping has never been easier. Millions of bytes of information are just a click away. Are you shopping for a new high-definition television, and would you like to compare offerings? No problem! Just search "hdtv comparison guide" in an online search engine such as Google and more than a million results return. Google experimented with returning a greater number of results per page and found usage dropped off because it took a fraction of a second longer for results to appear—too long for today's consumers. Of course, buyers cannot go through all of the results, and it's human nature to start at the top. That spot is valuable real estate for online search results. The top result for TV comparisons was www.consumerreports.org. It was the same for most electronic products such as computers and digital cameras, as well as common household appliances such as washing machines and microwave ovens. Consumer Reports is not the only game in town, either. There's PriceCanada.com, PriceGrabber.ca, Shopbot.ca, and ShoptoIt.ca, to name just a few. All of these comparison-shopping websites assist buyers in selecting the right product and brand to suit their needs and desires.

QUESTIONS

1. Search for information regarding a product you are interested in purchasing. Using one or more online comparison-shopping websites, find the brand that is right for you. Discuss how long it took you to make this decision and what influenced your decision.

2. Discuss the benefits and drawbacks of using comparison-shopping websites in making buying decisions.

MARKETING BY THE NUMBERS

One way consumers can evaluate alternatives is to decide on important attributes and assess how purchase alternatives perform on those attributes. Consider the purchase of a notebook computer. Each attribute, such as computer memory, is given a weight to reflect its level of importance to that consumer. Then, the consumer evaluates each alternative on each attribute. For example, in the table below, memory (weighted at 0.5) is the most important computer purchase attribute for this consumer. The consumer believes that Brand C performs best on memory, rating it 7 (higher ratings indicate higher performance), Brand B rates worst on this attribute (rating of 3). Size and price are the consumer's next two most important attributes; warranty is least important.

A score for each brand can be calculated by multiplying the importance weight for each attribute by the brand's score on that attribute. These weighted scores are then summed to determine the score for that brand. For example, $Score_{Brand\ A} = (0.2 \times 4) + (0.5 \times 6) + (0.1 \times 5) + (0.2 \times 4) = 0.8 + 3.0 + 0.5 + 0.8 = 5.1$. This consumer will select the brand with the highest score.

QUESTIONS

1. Determine the scores for brands B and C. Which brand would this consumer likely choose?
2. Discuss some other "rules" consumers may use when evaluating alternatives in order to make a purchase decision.

| | | **Alternative Brands** | | |
Attributes	Importance Weight	A	B	C
Size	0.2	4	6	2
Memory	0.5	6	3	7
Warranty	0.1	5	5	4
Price	0.2	4	6	7

VIDEO CASE

Visit MyMarketingLab at www.pearsoned.ca/
mymarketinglab to view the video for this chapter.

RADIAN6

Social networking has had a huge impact on society. And
for marketers, online social communications are changing the way that consumers make purchase decisions.
Radian6 specializes in monitoring social media. It tracks a
wide array of websites at which consumers might "chat"
about companies, brands, and general market offerings.
Companies such as Dell and Microsoft obtain valuable
insights about what consumers are saying about their
products and about what factors or events are generating
the discussions. But more importantly, companies are
gaining a stronger understanding of how consumer
online conversations are affecting purchase decisions. In
this manner, Radian6 is on the cutting edge of getting a
grip on the ever-expanding scope of social networking
and "word-of-Web" communication.

After viewing the video featuring Radian6, answer
the following questions.

QUESTIONS

1. What cultural factors have led to the explosion of
   social networking?

2. How has Radian6 changed the way companies
   understand opinion leaders and buzz marketing?

3. How is Radian6 helping companies gain insights
   into the buying decision process?

END-OF-CHAPTER CASE

"TRADING UP" TO NEW LUXURY BRANDS

If you're like most Canadians, you probably don't consider yourself to be a consumer of luxury goods. There's no Jaguar in your driveway, no Rolex on your nightstand, and no beluga caviar in your refrigerator. Then again, it depends on how you define luxury goods. According to Michael Silverstein and Neil Fiske, authors of the book *Trading Up: Why Consumers* Want New Luxury Goods—and How Companies Create Them, a growing number of middle-class Canadian consumers are "trading up" for high-end, high-quality, expensive products, and forcing marketers to rethink their conception of the typical consumer of luxury goods. It might surprise you to know that right now the growing trend in consumer behaviour is trading up.

Trading up means being willing, even eager, to pay a premium price for high-end products in certain product categories—the ones that are important to you. It doesn't mean that everything you buy is high-end, only certain things. And in exchange for being able to afford those one or two luxuries, we are willing to "trade down" on other items, that is, to buy the lower-cost items in categories that are not important to us.

Before consumers can trade up in a product category, however, there must be high-end brands available for them to buy. Take Jake, for example. Jake is a construction worker who earns $50 000 per year. Jake owns a set of titanium-faced Callaway golf clubs, for which he paid more than $3000. Why is he willing to trade up on golf equipment? "The real reason I bought them is that they make me feel rich," he says. "You can run the biggest company in the world and be one of the richest guys in the world, but you can't buy any clubs better than these." Callaway golf clubs are just one of many New Luxury brands now available on the market for consumers who want to trade up.

Trading down is the behaviour of these same consumers when they choose the low-cost alternative in product categories that are of little importance to them. For marketers, that means it is important to offer products in those low-budget price ranges, because if there were no low-cost products available, consumers would not be able to trade up for the luxury products they desire. The end result is that for every product category into which a New Luxury brand enters, that market becomes polarized. Silverstein and Fiske advise marketers that, to be successful, a product must either be the New Luxury brand or the low-cost alternative—anything in the middle will struggle to succeed, and may not even survive.

Distinctive Appliances of Montreal, where a refrigerator can cost as much as $6300, wants to be the New Luxury brand in kitchen appliances. "Consumers are increasingly looking to turn their kitchens into pieces of art," says Michael Benoit, the company's president. "Instead of a white box sticking out of the wall, a consumer might choose a wood-panel fridge or something in stainless steel." Benoit understands the trading-up phenomenon in consumer behaviour. Traditional marketing wisdom would have said that no middle-class family with a household income of less than $100 000 would ever spend that much for a fridge, but Benoit has learned that the kitchen is emerging as a room to entertain guests, and as such it must be "decorated" just like the rest of the home.

Consumers of New Luxury brands are a diverse group, but like any market segment they have certain behaviours in common, and the marketer who understands the nature of this consumer group will be able to successfully design a marketing strategy and program to reach them. One of these behaviours is rocketing—spending a disproportionate amount of one's income on a single product category. The typical New Luxury consumer will "pay more" for at least one type of product that is important to them, and will have as many as 10 categories in which they will "rocket." New Luxury consumers are highly selective in their buying behaviour. When they make decisions about trading up they do it carefully and deliberately. Empty nesters—married couples whose children no longer live with them—are one segment of the New Luxury consumer. So are working singles in their 20s. Divorced women are another.

How does a New Luxury brand differ from an "old" luxury brand? According to Silverstein and Fiske, it's all about emotional involvement. BMW owners, for example, are emotionally attached to their cars. They wash them more frequently than owners of other car brands, and when they park them on the street they turn back to gaze lovingly at their car before they walk away. Old luxury brands such as Chanel and Cadillac, on the other hand, were not about emotion but about status.

When marketers fail to understand trends in consumer behaviour, the effects can be ravaging. Take Cadillac, for example. Once the epitome of old luxury brands, it provides marketers with a cautionary tale of what can happen when a company rests on its laurels. Up until the 1970s the name Cadillac was synonymous in America with status, achievement, and recognition. It was the car of choice for politicians, Hollywood celebrities, and the wealthy upper class. Believing that they had reached the top with this brand, General Motors reduced its investment in it. The result was that while new brands such as Toyota and Honda were entering the market with technical advances in their cars, Cadillac was suffering from increasingly out-of-date styling and only superficial improvements. Between 1975 and 2000, sales declined 2 percent each year, and the Cadillac brand eventually became the butt of jokes on late-night talk shows. Cadillac, it appears, cannot be the New Luxury brand in its category, and has fallen into the dangerous middle market zone.

"When the superpremium model fails to offer technical and functional benefits, it can coast for a while ... but not for very long," say Silverstein and Fiske. "And no matter how successful—even iconic—a product is, it can swiftly be dethroned by competitors who understand the escalating tastes of consumers.... In categories of durable goods, the dethroning can take less than a decade. In consumable goods, it can happen in two years or less."

Sources: Chris Daniels, "Almost Rich," *Marketing*, April 26, 2004; Michael J. Silverstein and Neil Fiske, Trading Up: Why Consumers Want New Luxury Goods—and How Companies Create Them (New York: Portfolio [Penguin Group], 2005).

QUESTIONS

1. Are you a consumer who "trades up" to New Luxury brands? Think of an item you own that is high end in its class. Do you consider this item to be a New Luxury brand? Explain why or why not.

2. Do you believe the authors of *Trading Up* when they suggest that more and more Canadian consumers engage in "trading up" behaviour? What items do you own that you have traded up for? What product categories do you "trade down" on?

3. The authors claim that modern consumers are emotionally attached to New Luxury brands. Think about some of the brands named in this case. Whether or not you own any products by those brands, are you "emotional" about any of them? What aspirational groups are associated with these New Luxury brands?

4. Think about the most luxurious item you own. Now, describe the buyer decision process you went through when you purchased it.

AFTER STUDYING THIS CHAPTER, YOU SHOULD BE ABLE TO

 define the major steps in designing a customer-driven marketing strategy: market segmentation, targeting, differentiation, and positioning

 list and discuss the major bases for segmenting consumer and business markets

 explain how companies identify attractive market segments and choose a market-targeting strategy

 discuss how companies differentiate and position their products for maximum competitive advantage

Segmentation, Targeting, and Positioning

7

PREVIEWING THE CONCEPTS

So far, you've learned what marketing is and about the importance of understanding consumers and the marketplace environment. With that as background, you're now ready to delve deeper into marketing strategy and tactics. This chapter looks further into key customer-driven marketing strategy decisions—how to divide up markets into meaningful customer groups (*segmentation*), choose which customer groups to serve (*targeting*), create market offerings that best serve targeted customers (*differentiation*), and position the offerings in the minds of consumers (*positioning*). Then, the chapters that follow explore the tactical marketing tools—the four *P*s—by which marketers bring these strategies to life.

At their most basic, target markets are simply groups of people with similar characteristics, and while those characteristics may have always been around for the targeting, it sometimes takes a new kind of thinking to decide to serve a particular group with a line of products that's new to them—in other words, to define a new market segment. Consider cosmetics and personal care products such as body wash and anti-aging creams. Every woman today regardless of age or culture has some knowledge of them, but until recently the same could not be said about men. During the last few years, however, several well-established women's cosmetics companies have begun to develop cosmetics for men. Let's look at one of these.

BIOTHERM HOMME: TARGETING A NEW MARKET SEGMENT

The male grooming industry has always been a tricky business. In ancient Greece, men reportedly used mudpacks and softened their skin with yogurt, but today's men seem to have left skin care behind with their togas. The classic image of the traditional Canadian man conjures up visions of ruggedness and the outdoors, not indulgence, and most men deliberately avoid anything feminine—like the cosmetics aisle of department and drug stores. "We actually know from studies that men do not feel at ease in the cosmetic section and that their heart rates go up," says a marketing manager at Biotherm Homme, a division of Montreal-based L'Oréal Canada.

In light of the lingering stigma surrounding the idea of men looking after their skin, a cosmetics firm would have to be crazy to launch a line of skin-care products targeting men, right?

As it turns out, it ain't necessarily so. Male grooming is a booming market, and developing and marketing new products that cater to this new segment has been a top trend for the last five years. There has been a huge increase not only in the level of acceptance of men's skin-care products but also in usage rates. The category has seen explosive growth, some 25 to 30 percent per year, reaching $2.7 billion in Canada in 2009. In the market for men's grooming products, which includes everything from shampoo to shaving cream, skin-care products is the fastest-growing category. Holt Renfrew stores in Montreal, Toronto, and Vancouver now have a large men's cosmetics area, designed with manly details such as dark hardwood floors. And many companies that traditionally marketed only to women, such as Dove, Clinique, Nivea, Lancôme, and L'Oréal, are launching complete lines of skin-care products for men.

There are many factors driving this change. The editor of *Cosmetics* magazine suggests, "Our society discriminates around age and I think guys as they get older still want to be seen in their careers as young, vibrant and energetic." Gender expert Michael Kaufman adds, "We are still bombarded every day with images of rugged men, but this idea that men don't care about themselves … it just doesn't work."

Welcome to the new era of heterosexual men who are manning up to the job of caring for their skin—and who are not afraid to admit it! It's been called the David Beckham effect, the new world in which women are demanding their partners look good, and men are rising to the challenge. The new attitude was captured in the award-winning "The Man Your Man Could Smell Like," campaign for Old Spice Red Zone body wash, starring former football star Isaiah Mustafa. British actor Clive Owen was the face of Lancôme Men, and now Chris Noth, the infamous Mr. Big from *Sex and the City*, is the face of Force Supreme from Biotherm Homme, a broad line of skin-care products for men, including cleansers, shaving gels, moisturizers, and anti-aging creams.

"Chris Noth is the perfect Biotherm Homme Ambassador," explains Marie-Josée Lamothe, vice-president and general manager for Biotherm, North America. "While always exuding a casual, suave and elegant attitude, Chris manages to create a bond with his audience remaining accessible and relatable to both men and women equally, values which are important to Biotherm. Charismatic and simple, Chris is a natural fit with the brand."

Founded in France in 1985, Biotherm Homme is the pioneer and world-leading men's skin-care brand, known for breaking barriers and eliminating taboos while standing by men and helping them feel comfortable about taking care of their skin to look and feel better. The Biotherm Homme brand strives to develop close relationships with men by communicating an in-depth understanding of their skin, and challenging men—in a friendly manner—to change their habits without challenging who they are.

Today, Biotherm Homme products are available in over 70 countries and include full lines of cleansers, moisturizers, anti-aging creams and eye creams. For example, there's Age Fitness Night Recharge, and Innovation Age Refirm, described on the company's website as "a skin firming wrinkle corrector with silicium and biopeptides." The price? A manly $54 for a 50-millilitre jar. There's also Age Refirm Eye Force, for "anti-slackening and anti-wrinkle eye care," at $45 for a 15-millilitre jar.

Slowing the signs of aging skin is a key element of Biotherm Homme's positioning. Recently the company launched Force Supreme Re-builder, an anti-aging "power tool" aimed at men over 30. "By age 30 men start to become aware that the shape of their face is changing.

Wrinkles are forming, facial features are beginning to sag, and the skin is losing its suppleness ... the need for effectiveness is even stronger.... It's time to get things under control," says the company.

Skin-care products have traditionally been marketed to women with claims of rejuvenation through moisturizing, but persuading men to use the same kind of product requires a different approach. Stereotypical masculine celebrities from film and sport are often used to break down the 'feminine' connotations associated with skin grooming products, and when talking about product benefits for men, it's best to focus on science and technology. Biotherm Homme does this by explaining that its products are developed by scientists working in the Biotherm laboratories, and contain the latest breakthroughs in anti-aging and skin-care technology. Many of the products include a substance called PETP—Pure Extract of Thermal Plankton, which is "acclaimed by scientists worldwide ... [is] rich in essential minerals and trace elements ... boosts cellular regeneration and helps the skin to stay beautifully healthy from within." The new product, Force Supreme Re-builder, combines the benefits of three anti-age ingredients (caffeine, soy protein, and kreatilane) that "diminish undereye bags ... visibly improve the appearance of the dreaded double chin ... tighten the epidermis ... and re-energize cellular activity." Manly talk, indeed.

Manly sensibilities are also taken into consideration by referring to the Force Supreme Re-builder applicator as a tool—and a power tool—with "an application method that is innately masculine and convenient ... Force Supreme Re-builder takes its shape from the sleek contours of the triple-headed electric razors men use every morning." Market research revealed that men don't like dipping their fingers into jars, so Force Supreme Re-builder is applied directly from the container, itself a high-tech precision instrument.

Though Biotherm Homme was a pioneering brand in men's skin care, nearly every major cosmetics brand has since entered the market. Unilever Canada recently launched a new line of products called Dove Men + Care. Nivea for Men offers a website called The Groom Room, an online resource for male personal care needs, featuring blog posts, grooming tips, dating and relationship advice, plus articles on sports, entertainment, career advice, and fashion. "Discover what men want and become part of it," exclaims the Nivea for Men website in both English and French. And it's not just the big brands jumping on the men's skin-care bandwagon. Sanofi-aventis recently acquired Canadian company Canderm, which commands approximately a 10 percent share of the country's non-prescription anti-aging skin-care market, and last year Toronto entrepreneur Brian Lau started a new skin-care venture called Bread & Butter Skincare, an online store that specializes in natural products that moisturize a man's skin.

AskMen.com, a Canadian men's lifestyle portal, reminds men that skin care "has come a long way from the days when your father washed his face with a withered bar of soap and covered up shaving nicks with bits of toilet paper." Indeed it has. At Biotherm Homme, the future of men's skin care is high-precision, high-tech instruments and formulations, dedicated to making men look good with minimum time wasted in front of the mirror.[1]

COMPANIES today recognize that they cannot appeal to all buyers in the marketplace, or at least not to all buyers in the same way. Buyers are too numerous, too widely scattered, and too varied in their needs and buying practices. Moreover, the companies themselves vary widely in their abilities to serve different segments of the market. Instead, a company must identify the parts of the market that it can serve best and most profitably. It must design customer-driven marketing strategies that build the *right* relationships with the *right* customers.

Companies are being choosier about the customers with whom they connect. Most have moved away from mass marketing and toward market segmentation and targeting—identifying market segments, selecting one or more of them as the most appropriate to serve, and developing products and marketing programs tailored to each.

Figure 7.1 shows the four major steps of designing a customer-driven marketing strategy. In the first two steps, the company selects the customers that it will serve. Market **segmentation** involves dividing a market into smaller groups of buyers with distinct needs, characteristics, or behaviours that might require separate marketing strategies or mixes. The company identifies different ways to segment the market and develops profiles of the resulting market segments. Market **targeting** consists of evaluating each market segment's attractiveness and selecting one or more market segments to enter. Next, the company decides on a value proposition—on how it will create value for target customers, and how it can stand out from its competition, or **differentiate** itself. When all these decisions have been made, the company positions its brand, or product, in the market. **Positioning** consists of arranging for a market offering to occupy a clear, distinctive, and desirable place relative to competing products in the minds of consumers. In this chapter, we'll look in detail at each of these four concepts.

MARKET SEGMENTATION **LO2**

Buyers in any market differ in their wants, resources, locations, buying attitudes, and buying practices. Through market segmentation, companies divide large, heterogeneous markets into smaller segments that can be reached more efficiently and effectively with products and services that match their unique needs. In this section, we discuss four important segmentation topics: segmenting consumer markets, segmenting business markets, segmenting international markets, and requirements for effective segmentation.

SEGMENTING CONSUMER MARKETS

There is no single way to segment a market. A marketer has to try different segmentation variables, alone and in combination, to find the best way to view the market structure. Table 7.1 outlines the major variables that might be used in segmenting consumer markets. Here we look at the major *geographic*, *demographic*, *psychographic*, and *behavioural* variables.

Geographic Segmentation **Geographic segmentation** calls for dividing a market into different geographical units, such as global regions, countries, regions within a country,

Segmentation

Dividing a market into distinct groups with distinct needs, characteristics, or behaviours that might require separate marketing strategies or mixes.

Targeting

The process of evaluating each market segment's attractiveness and selecting one or more segments to enter.

Differentiation

Actually differentiating the market offering to create superior customer value.

Positioning

Arranging for a market offering to occupy a clear, distinctive, and desirable place relative to competing products in the minds of target consumers.

Geographic segmentation

Dividing a market into different geographical units, such as global regions, countries, regions within a country, provinces, cities, or even neighbourhoods.

FIGURE 7.1 Designing a customer-driven marketing strategy

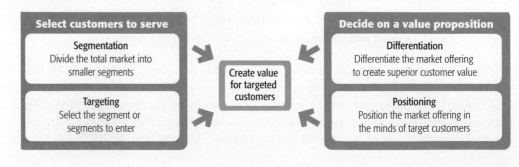

TABLE 7.1   Major Segmentation Variables for Consumer Markets

Geographic Segmentation

World region	North America, South America, Western Europe, Eastern Europe, the British Isles, the Middle East, the Pacific Rim, Asia, Southeast Asia, Africa, Australasia
Country	Canada, the United States, Brazil, England, China, etc.
Region of the country	The Maritimes, the prairie provinces, southern Ontario, Victoria and the Gulf Islands, Quebec
Population size	Under 5000; 5000–250 000; 250 000–500 000; 500 000–1 000 000; over 1 000 000, etc.
Type of region	Urban, suburban, rural, mountainous, far north, ocean/beaches, etc.

Demographic Segmentation

Age	Under 6, 6–12, 13–19, 20–34, 35–49, 50–64, 65+; or children, teens, young adults, middle-aged, seniors
Gender	Male, female
Family size	2, 3, 4, 5, more than 5
Life cycle	Young couple, young couple with children, single-parent family, older couple with grown children, divorced, etc.
Household income (HHI)	Under $20 000; $20 000–$50 000; $50 000–$100 000; over $100 000, etc.
Occupation	Professional, union worker, academic, small business owner, sales, farming/fishing, student, retired, homemaker, unemployed
Education	High school, college or trade school, university undergraduate, post-graduate
Ethnic or cultural group	African, Canadian, American, Chinese, Japanese, Korean, Caribbean/West Indies, East Indian, Filipino, Greek, Italian, German, Portuguese, Muslim, Jewish, Inuit, Métis, North American Indian
Generation	Baby Boomer, Generation X, Millennial

Psychographic Segmentation

Social class	Lower lowers, upper lowers, working class, middle class, upper middles, lower uppers, upper uppers
Lifestyle	Athletic/outdoors type, active suburban family, student, single urban professional, etc.
Personality	Highly organized and detail oriented; outgoing and adventurous; creative or artistic; quiet and solitary; ambitious, etc.

Behavioural Segmentation

Occasions	Regular occasion, special occasion, holiday, seasonal
Benefits	Quality, service, economy, convenience, speed
User status	Non-user, ex-user, potential user, first-time user, regular user
User rates	Light user, medium user, heavy user
Loyalty status	None, medium, strong, absolute
Readiness stage	Unaware, aware, informed, interested, desirous, intending to buy
Attitude toward product	Enthusiastic, positive, indifferent, negative, hostile

provinces, cities, or even neighbourhoods. A company may decide to operate in one or a few geographical areas or to operate in all areas but pay attention to geographical differences in needs and wants.

Many companies today are localizing their products, advertising, promotion, and sales efforts to fit the needs of individual regions, cities, and even neighbourhoods. For example, one consumer-products company ships additional cases of its low-calorie snack foods to stores in neighbourhoods near Weight Watchers clinics. Kraft developed Post's

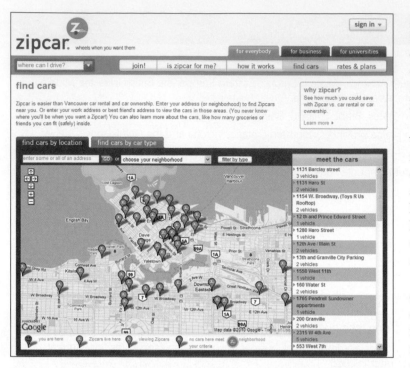

Exhibit 7.1   Geographic segmentation: Car-sharing service Zipcar targets markets by geography, focusing on large cities, especially those with university campuses, such as Vancouver.

Fiesta Fruity Pebbles cereal for areas high in Hispanics. Coca-Cola developed four ready-to-drink canned coffees for the Japanese market, each targeted to a specific geographic region. Procter & Gamble introduced Curry Pringles in England and Funky Soy Sauce Pringles in Asia.[2]

Other companies are seeking to cultivate as-yet untapped geographic territory. For example, many large companies are fleeing the fiercely competitive major cities and suburbs to set up shop in smaller towns. Four Points by Sheraton hotels has opened a chain of smaller-format hotels in places such as Kingston, Ontario, and Canmore, Alberta, that are too small for its standard-size, more upscale hotels.

Small businesses such as hair salons and dentists' offices typically focus their marketing efforts on a local region within a few kilometres from their location, while destination-type businesses, such as restaurants and sporting facilities, might market to a larger region. By contrast, car-sharing service Zipcar—which provides a network of self-service vehicles to members by the day or the hour—focuses only on densely populated metropolitan areas and congested college campuses, positioning itself as a low-cost, low-hassle alternative to owning or driving your own car.[3]

Demographic Segmentation **Demographic segmentation** divides the market into segments based on variables such as age, gender, family size, life cycle, household income (HHI), occupation, education, ethnic or cultural group, and generation. Demographic factors are the most popular bases for segmenting customer groups. One reason is that consumer needs, wants, and usage rates often vary closely with demographic variables. Another is that demographic variables are easier to measure than most other types of variables. Even when marketers first define segments by using other bases, such as benefits sought or behaviour, they must know segment demographic characteristics to assess the size of the target market and to reach it efficiently.

AGE AND LIFE-CYCLE SEGMENTATION   Consumer needs and wants change with age. Some companies segment the market based on age or, more specifically, family status, offering different products or using different marketing approaches for different groups. For example, for kids, Oscar Mayer offers Lunchables, full-of-fun, kid-appealing finger food. For older generations, it markets Deli Creations, everything these consumers need to create a "hot and melty fresh-baked sandwich in a microwave minute."

Other companies focus on marketing to groups that are in the same life-cycle stage. Some people get married and have children in their early 20s, some wait until they are 40; some people retire at age 50, some at 75, but retirement is a life-cycle stage. Companies that divide their markets by either age or life-cycle stage are using **age and life-cycle segmentation**. Disney Cruise Lines targets families with children, so most of its destinations and shipboard activities are designed with this life-cycle stage in mind. On board, Disney provides trained counsellors who help younger kids join in hands-on activities, teen-only spaces for older children, and family-time or individual-time options for parents and other adults. It's difficult to find a Disney Cruise Line advertisement or

Demographic segmentation
Dividing the market into segments based on variables such as age, gender, family size, life cycle, household income (HHI), occupation, education, ethnic or cultural group, and generation.

Age and life-cycle segmentation
Dividing a market into different age and life-cycle groups.

webpage that doesn't feature a family full of smiling faces. In contrast, Viking River Cruises, the deluxe smaller-boat cruise line that offers tours along the world's great rivers, primarily targets older adults, couples and singles. You won't find a single child in a Viking ad or webpage.

GENDER **Gender segmentation** has long been used in clothing, cosmetics, toiletries, and magazines. For example, P&G was among the first with Secret antiperspirant, a brand specially formulated for a woman's chemistry, packaged and advertised to reinforce the female image. Since women make 70 percent of shopping decisions, big-box stores such as home-improvement chain RONA are courting women consumers with trendy "paint cafés" and luxurious display kitchens. Owens Corning aimed a major advertising campaign for home insulation at women after a study showed that two-thirds of all women were involved in materials installation, with 13 percent doing it themselves. Half the women surveyed compared themselves to home improvement guru Bob Vila, whereas less than half compared themselves to Martha Stewart.[4] And, as we learned at the beginning of this chapter, many cosmetics makers have begun marketing men's lines.

> **Gender segmentation**
> Dividing a market into different segments based on gender.

A neglected gender segment can offer new opportunities in markets ranging from consumer electronics to motorcycles. For example, Harley-Davidson has traditionally targeted its product design and marketing to a bread-and-butter market of 35- to 55-year-old males. Women were more often just along for the ride—but no longer:[5]

Women are now among the fastest growing customer segments in the motorcycle business. The number of female Harley-Davidson owners has tripled in the past 20 years and female buyers now account for over 13 percent of new Harley-Davidson purchases. So the company is boosting its efforts to move more women from the back of the bike onto the driver's seat. It started by making its product more accessible to females, modifying motorcycles to fit women's smaller frames, and offering an instructional manual and courses to teach women how to handle their bikes. Ads and other marketing materials aimed at women play to the brand's established strengths but with a softer side.

Rather than indulging in female stereotypes, Harley-Davidson is appealing to "strong, independent women who enjoy taking on a challenge and a feeling of adventure," says the company's women's outreach manager. A recent ad sports the headline: "Not pictured: the weaker sex." A women's Web microsite encourages women to share inspirational riding stories with one another. And to kick off Women Riders Month, Harley-Davidson recently hosted special riding events designed to "celebrate the millions of women who have already grabbed life by the handlebars."

In marketing to women, Harley-Davidson is staying true to its tough, road tested image. "I don't think we're going to see any pink [Harley-Davidson motorcycles] on the road," says an analyst. And "they don't have to add bigger mirrors so women can do their cosmetics.... They want to sell Harleys to women, and they want to sell them to women who want to ride a *Harley*."

Exhibit 7.2   Gender segmentation: Women represent a significant market segment for Harley-Davidson motorcycles, so the company designs advertising campaigns specifically to reach them.

Household Income (HHI)
segmentation
Dividing a market into different income
segments.

HOUSEHOLD INCOME (HHI)   The marketers of products and services such as automobiles, clothing, cosmetics, financial services, and travel have long used **household income (HHI) segmentation**. Household income refers to the total income for the family, whether only one parent works or both parents work. Many companies target affluent consumers with luxury goods and convenience services. For example, for a price, luxury hotels provide amenities to attract specific groups of affluent travellers, such as families, expectant moms, and even pet owners.[6]

At the Four Seasons Hotel Chicago, guests can buy the Kids in the City package for $520 a night and, among other things, enjoy a visit in their room from the Ice Cream Man, who arrives with all the fixings to make any concoction they desire. At one spa in Scottsdale, Arizona, expectant parents can purchase the "Bundle of Joy" Babymoon package, which includes a 24-hour Cravings Chef service, a couples massage, and breakfast in bed. The Benjamin Hotel in New York City has the "Dream Dog" program, which provides dog beds in a variety of styles along with doggie bathrobes, canine room service, and DVDs for dogs, as well as access to pet spa treatments and a pet psychic. And if that isn't over the top enough, the Four Seasons Miami offers a Five Diamond package that includes a Graff diamond eternity band (or another diamond piece designed to your specifications) for $45,000, or a stay in the presidential suite with a bottle of 1990 Dom Pérignon Oenothéque champagne, caviar for two, and an 80-minute in-suite couples massage, using a lotion infused with real ground diamonds comes with a price tag: "From $50,000."

However, not all companies that use income segmentation target the affluent. For example, many retailers—such as No Frills, Giant Tiger, and the dollar-store chains—successfully target low- and middle-income groups. The core market for such stores is families with household incomes under $30 000.

Segmenting the market according to household income is one of the main ways car marketers divide the market, as each brand offers an economy car for the first-time buyer—the Toyota Yaris, for example—and a luxury model—like the much more expensive Lexus sedans and SUVs, which can reach nearly $100 000. A family that has a household income of $40 000 a year is not likely to purchase a car that costs twice as much as their income. The recent troubled economy has provided challenges for marketers targeting all income groups. Consumers at all income levels—including affluent consumers—are cutting back on their spending and seeking greater value from their purchases.

ETHNIC OR CULTURAL GROUP   Because of the multicultural makeup of Canada, and our two national languages (not to mention all the other languages spoken in our country), marketers often segment markets based on easy-to-define criteria such as race, ethnicity, and language. Statistics Canada, as we learned in Chapter 4, compiles census data about Canadians, and makes it available to marketers. It's not difficult, for example, to identify markets in Canada with high numbers of Chinese-speaking consumers, and place your advertising accordingly. Coast Capital Savings identifies a market segment of Cantonese- and Mandarin-speaking customers who have arrived in Canada in the last five years. To promote its free chequing account to this segment, it created ads featuring Jan Walls, a well-known retired Asian studies professor from Simon Fraser University.[7]

Exhibit 7.3   Income segmentation: Luxury hotels provide amenities to attract affluent travellers. The Benjamin Hotel in New York City offers a "Dream Dog" program that pampers not just guests, but also their dogs.

Quebec is a large market segment of its own, defined by geography, but more importantly by ethnicity and language. Hyundai created a French-only advertising campaign featuring Quebec actor Guillaume Lemay-Thivierge, who was chosen because the marketers felt his personality was similar to the brand personality of Hyundai—dynamic and exciting. The spots show Lemay-Thivierge bungee jumping and engaging in other thrilling pastimes, after which he yawns because those activities are boring compared with his Hyundai.[8]

Psychographic Segmentation **Psychographic segmentation** divides buyers into different segments based on social class, lifestyle, or personality characteristics. People in the same demographic group can have very different psychographic makeups.

The "new luxury" market in Canada is a fast-growing market segment, comprising approximately 250 000 individuals of high net worth. As a market segment, it is defined entirely by psychographics—in this case, lifestyle and social class. Denise Pickett, president of Amex Bank of Canada, says a company that wants to reach the "new luxury" market "has to include before they purchase, during the purchase, while they use the product, and even when they decide not to use your product—making sure that the whole experience is truly luxurious for the customer."[9]

Marketers also use *personality* variables to segment markets. For example, cruise line Royal Caribbean targets adventure seekers—high-energy couples and families—with hundreds of activities such as rock wall climbing and ice skating. Its commercials urge travellers to "declare your independence and become a citizen of our nation—Royal Caribbean, The Nation of Why Not." By contrast, Regent Seven Seas Cruises targets more serene and cerebral adventurers, mature couples seeking a more elegant ambiance and exotic destinations, such as the Orient. Regent invites them to come along as "luxury goes exploring."[10]

Behavioural Segmentation **Behavioural segmentation** divides buyers into segments based on their knowledge, attitudes, uses, or responses to a product. Many marketers believe that behaviour variables are the best starting point for building market segments.

OCCASIONS Buyers can be grouped according to occasions when they get the idea to buy, actually make their purchase, or use the purchased item. **Occasion segmentation** can help firms to build up product usage. For example, most consumers drink orange juice in the morning but orange growers have promoted drinking orange juice as a cool, healthful refresher at other times of the day. By contrast, Coca-Cola's "Good Morning" campaign attempts to increase Diet Coke consumption by promoting the soft drink as an early morning pick-me-up.

BENEFITS SOUGHT A powerful form of segmentation is to group buyers according to the different *benefits* that they seek from the product. **Benefit segmentation** requires finding the major benefits people look for in the product class, the kinds of people who look for each benefit, and the major brands that deliver each benefit.

Psychographic segmentation
Dividing a market into different segments based on social class, lifestyle, or personality characteristics.

Behavioural segmentation
Dividing a market into segments based on consumer knowledge, attitudes, uses, or responses to a product.

Occasion segmentation
Dividing the market into segments according to occasions when buyers get the idea to buy, actually make their purchase, or use the purchased item.

Benefit segmentation
Dividing the market into segments according to the different benefits that consumers seek from the product.

GOOD MORNING

Exhibit 7.4 Occasion segmentation: Coca-Cola's "Good Morning" campaign attempts to increase consumption by promoting the soft drink as an alternative to coffee.

Champion athletic wear segments its markets according to benefits that different consumers seek from their activewear. For example, "Fit and Polish" consumers seek a balance between function and style—they exercise for results but want to look good doing it. "Serious Sports Competitors" exercise heavily and live in and love their activewear—they seek performance and function. By contrast, "Value-Seeking Moms" have low sports interest and low activewear involvement—they buy for the family and seek durability and value. Thus, each segment seeks a different mix of benefits. Champion must target the benefit segment or segments that it can serve best and most profitably, using appeals that match each segment's benefit preferences.

USER STATUS   Markets can be segmented into non-users, ex-users, potential users, first-time users, and regular users of a product. Marketers want to reinforce and retain regular users, attract non-users, and reinvigorate relationships with ex-users.

Included in the potential user group are consumers facing life-stage changes—such as newlyweds and new parents—who can be turned into heavy users. For example, upscale kitchen and cookware retailer Williams-Sonoma actively targets newly engaged couples.[11]

> Eight-page Williams-Sonoma ad inserts in bridal magazines show a young couple strolling through a park or talking intimately in the kitchen over a glass of wine. The bride-to-be asks, "Now that I've found love, what else do I need?" Pictures of Williams-Sonoma knife sets, toasters, glassware, and pots and pans provide some strong clues. The retailer also offers a bridal registry, of course, but it takes its registry a step further. Through a program called "The Store Is Yours," it opens its stores after hours, by appointment, exclusively for individual couples to visit and make their wish lists. This segment is very important to Williams-Sonoma. About half the people who register are new to the brand—and they'll be buying a lot of kitchen and cookware in the future.

USAGE RATE   Markets can also be segmented into light, medium, and heavy product users. Heavy users are often a small percentage of the market but account for a high percentage of total consumption. For example, Burger King targets what it calls "Super Fans," young (age 18 to 34), Whopper-wolfing males and females who make up 18 percent of the chain's customers but account for almost half of all customer visits. They eat at Burger King an average of 16 times a month. Burger King targets these Super Fans openly with ads that exalt monster burgers containing meat, cheese, and more meat and cheese that can turn "innies into outies."[12]

LOYALTY STATUS   A market can also be segmented by consumer loyalty. Consumers can be loyal to brands, such as Apple; stores, such as Loblaws or Sobeys; and companies, such as Honda. Buyers can be divided into groups according to their degree of loyalty.

Some consumers are completely loyal—they buy one brand all the time. For example, Apple has an almost cult-like following of loyal users. Other consumers are somewhat loyal—they are loyal to two or three brands of a given product or favour one brand while sometimes buying others. Still other buyers show no loyalty to any brand. They either want something different each time they buy or they buy whatever's on sale.

A company can learn a lot by analyzing loyalty patterns in its market. It should start by studying its own loyal customers. For example, by studying Mac fanatics, Apple can better pinpoint its target market and develop marketing appeals. By studying its less-loyal buyers, the company can detect which brands are most competitive with its own. By looking at customers who are shifting away from its brand, the company can learn about its marketing weaknesses.

Using Multiple Segmentation Bases   Marketers rarely limit their segmentation analysis to only one or a few variables. Rather, they often use multiple segmentation bases in an effort to identify smaller, better-defined target groups. For example, Rockport Canada targets 18- to 34-year-old men, in different life-cycle stages—high school graduates, new careerists, and young marrieds. Jeff Roach, managing director at market research firm Youthography, explains, "The reason for that is what we call the prolonged pre-adult life stage. Young people have been getting more adult responsibilities younger, but they're not entering full adulthood until much later in life. We see very similar values across this group right up to age 34." What are those shared characteristics? They place a high value on personal relationships, media, and technology. They are relatively affluent. And they tend to delay marriage and having children until after age 35—which means they have more discretionary income to spend on lifestyle products.[13]

Several business information services—such as Nielsen Claritas, Acxiom, and Experian—provide multi-variable segmentation systems that merge geographic, demographic, lifestyle, and behavioural data to help companies segment their markets down to neighbourhoods, and even households. One of the leading segmentation systems is the PRIZM NE (New Evolution) system by Nielsen Claritas. PRIZM NE classifies households based on a host of demographic factors—such as age, educational level, income, occupation, family composition, ethnicity, and housing—and behavioural and lifestyle factors—such as purchases, free-time activities, and media preferences. It then classifies and names each segment, for example, Kids & Cul-de-Sacs, Gray Power, and Blue Blood Estates. The colourful names help bring the segments to life.[14]

An example of how geographic, demographic, and psychographic characteristics can all be brought to bear in describing a market segment is the LGBT (lesbian, gay, bisexual, and transgender) market.[15]

Exhibit 7.5 Multiple segmentation bases: The market segment comprising gay and lesbian couples is defined partly by gender and marital status (demographic segmentation), mainly by lifestyle (psychographic segmentation), but also by country, province, and city (geographic segmentation). The Ontario Tourism Marketing Partnership is just one organization that targets this segment through its advertising.

When gay marriage was pronounced legal in Canada it created a new market segment—which was exciting news to marketers of products such as formal wear, jewellery, hotels, and vacation packages. The new type of engaged couple includes both men and women, and is spawning segmentation of other areas, as well. Toronto magazine *Wedding Essentials* now publishes *Wedding Essentials for Same-Sex Couples*. Wedding trade shows and expos catering to the needs and tastes of same-sex couples are springing up all over the place, and so are specialized wedding planners. "For the gay community, weddings are as new to us as they are to the marketers," says Shane Wagg, owner of Wilde Marketing in Toronto, a gay consulting agency. For this new market segment, there is no such thing as a traditional wedding.

The new group is also an extremely desirable segment for marketers to target. Gay consumers earn on average 20 percent more than straight consumers, and spend approximately 10 percent more on their weddings. "With a projected $641 billion in purchasing power and higher discretionary spending patterns than mainstream consumers," states Harris

Interactive, a market research company, "the gay, lesbian, bisexual and transgender (GLBT) market segment has become an important target for some of the biggest brands." Not only that, but the new market segment is attracting American consumers—gays and lesbians who are increasingly choosing Canada as a travel destination and a place to get married—and American marketers, such as jeweller Cartier, which ran an ad in *Vanity Fair* that featured Melissa Etheridge and her partner wearing Cartier's handcuff bracelets.

Such segmentation provides a powerful tool for marketers of all kinds. It can help companies to identify and better understand key customer segments, target them more efficiently, and tailor market offerings and messages to their specific needs.

SEGMENTING BUSINESS MARKETS

Consumer and business marketers use many of the same variables to segment their markets. Business buyers can be segmented geographically, demographically (industry, company size), or by benefits sought, user status, usage rate, and loyalty status. Yet, business marketers also use some additional variables, such as customer *operating characteristics*, *purchasing approaches*, *situational factors*, and *personal characteristics*.

Almost every company serves at least some business markets. For example, American Express targets businesses in three segments—merchants, corporations, and small businesses. It has developed distinct marketing programs for each segment. In the merchants segment, American Express focuses on convincing new merchants to accept the card and on managing relationships with those that already do. For larger corporate customers, the company offers a corporate card program, which includes extensive employee expense and travel management services. It also offers this segment a wide range of asset management, retirement planning, and financial education services. For small business customers, American Express created OPEN: The Small Business Network, a system of small business cards and financial services. It includes credit cards and lines of credit, special usage rewards, financial monitoring and spending report features, and 24/7 customized financial support services. "OPEN is how we serve small business," says American Express.[16]

Many companies set up separate systems for dealing with larger or multiple-location customers. For example, Steelcase, a major producer of office furniture, first segments customers into seven industries, including banking, biosciences, health care, and higher education. Next, company salespeople work with independent Steelcase dealers to handle smaller, local, or regional Steelcase customers in each segment. But many national, multiple-location customers, such as ExxonMobil or IBM, have special needs that may reach beyond the scope of individual dealers. So Steelcase uses national account managers to help its dealer networks handle its national accounts.

Finally, a company need not choose between business and consumer market segments. Many companies, such as RIM and Dell successfully target both, and sometimes a company known for its business products decides to enter the consumer market. Cisco, for example, has long been known to large- and medium-sized businesses around the globe as a marketer of networking and teleconferencing hardware, but Cisco also competes in the consumer market with its Linksys home networking products and, more recently, with products for the home entertainment segment. Cisco's new Flip-branded products are attempting to bring high-quality videoconferencing technology to the home user.[17]

Within a given target industry and customer size, the company can segment by purchase approaches and criteria. As in consumer segmentation, many marketers believe that *buying behaviour* and *benefits* provide the best basis for segmenting business markets.

SEGMENTING INTERNATIONAL MARKETS

Few companies have either the resources or the will to operate in all, or even most, of the countries that dot the globe. Although some large companies, such as Coca-Cola and Sony, sell products in more than 200 countries, most international firms focus on a smaller set. Operating in many countries presents new challenges. Different countries, even those that are close together, can vary greatly in their economic, cultural, and political makeup. Thus, just as they do within their domestic markets, international firms need to group their world markets into segments with distinct buying needs and behaviours.

Companies can segment international markets by using one or a combination of several variables. They can segment by *geographic location*, grouping countries by regions such as Western Europe, the Pacific Rim, the Middle East, or Africa. Geographic segmentation assumes that nations close to one another will have many common traits and behaviours. Although this is often the case, there are many exceptions. For example, some U.S. marketers lump all Central and South American countries together, and assume they all speak Spanish, even though Brazilians speak Portuguese, and millions in other countries speak a variety of Indian dialects. And North America consists of three countries, though Mexico is usually ignored when marketers consider the North American market. Even Canada and the United States, though they have much in common, differ culturally, socially, and economically, and cannot be assumed to respond the same way to marketing offers.

World markets can also be segmented on the basis of *economic factors*. Countries might be grouped by population income levels or their overall level of economic development. A country's economic structure shapes its population's product and service needs and, therefore, the marketing opportunities it offers. For example, many companies are now targeting the BRIC countries—Brazil, Russia, India, and China—fast-growing developing economies with rapidly increasing buying power.

Countries can also be segmented by *political and legal factors* such as the type and stability of government, receptivity to foreign firms, monetary regulations, and amount of bureaucracy. *Cultural factors* can also be used, grouping markets according to common languages, religions, values and attitudes, customs, and behavioural patterns.

Segmenting international markets based on geographic, economic, political, cultural, and other factors assumes that segments should consist of clusters of countries. However, as new communications technologies, such as satellite TV and the Internet, connect consumers around the world, marketers can define and reach segments of like-minded consumers no matter where in the world they are. Using **intermarket segmentation** (also called *cross-market segmentation*), they form segments of consumers who have similar needs and buying behaviours even though they are located in different countries. For example, Lexus targets the world's well-to-do—the "global elite" segment—regardless of their country. Coca-Cola creates special programs to target teens, core consumers of its soft drinks the world over. And Swedish furniture giant IKEA targets the aspiring global middle class—it sells good-quality furniture that ordinary people worldwide can afford.

Intermarket segmentation
Forming segments of consumers who have similar needs and buying behaviour even though they are located in different countries.

Exhibit 7.6 Intermarket segmentation: Swedish furniture giant IKEA targets the aspiring global middle class—it sells good-quality furniture that ordinary people worldwide can afford.

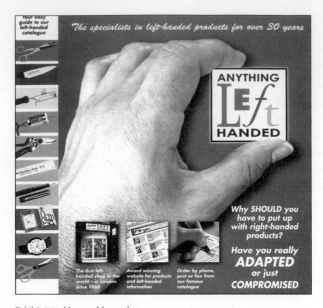

Exhibit 7.7 **Measurable market segments:** The "leftie" segment can be hard to identify and measure. As a result, few companies tailor their offers to left-handers. However, some nichers such as Anything Left-Handed in the United Kingdom target this segment.

REQUIREMENTS FOR EFFECTIVE SEGMENTATION

Clearly, there are many ways to segment a market, but not all segmentations are effective. For example, buyers of table salt could be divided into blond and brunette customers. But hair colour obviously does not affect the purchase of salt. Furthermore, if all salt buyers bought the same amount of salt each month, believed that all salt is the same, and wanted to pay the same price, the company would not benefit from segmenting this market.

To be useful, market segments must be the following:

☐ *Measurable:* The size, purchasing power, and profiles of the segments can be measured. Certain segmentation variables are difficult to measure. For example, although approximately 7 to 10 percent of adults are left-handed, there is no way to identify and target them. Perhaps this is why so few products are targeted toward this market segment.

☐ *Accessible:* The market segments can be effectively reached and served. Suppose a fragrance company finds that heavy users of its brand are single men and women who stay out late and socialize a lot. Unless this group lives or shops at certain places and is exposed to certain media, its members will be difficult to reach.

☐ *Substantial:* The market segments are large or profitable enough to serve. A segment should be the largest possible homogeneous group worth pursuing with a tailored marketing program. It would not pay, for example, for an automobile manufacturer to develop cars especially for people whose height is greater than seven feet (2.13 metres).

☐ *Differentiable:* The segments are conceptually distinguishable and respond differently to different marketing-mix elements and programs. If married and unmarried women respond similarly to a sale on perfume, they do not constitute separate segments.

☐ *Actionable:* Effective programs can be designed for attracting and serving the segments. For example, although one small airline identified seven market segments, its staff was too small to develop separate marketing programs for each segment.

MARKET TARGETING **L03**

Market segmentation reveals the firm's market segment opportunities. The firm now has to evaluate the various segments and decide how many and which segments it can serve best. We now look at how companies evaluate and select target segments.

EVALUATING MARKET SEGMENTS

In evaluating different market segments, a firm must look at three factors: segment size and growth, segment structural attractiveness, and company objectives and resources. The company must first collect and analyze data on current segment sales, growth rates, and expected profitability for various segments. It will be interested in segments that have the right size and growth characteristics.

But "right size and growth" is a relative matter. The largest, fastest-growing segments are not always the most attractive ones for every company. Smaller companies may lack the skills and resources needed to serve the larger segments. Or they may find these segments too competitive. Such companies may target segments that are smaller and less attractive, in an absolute sense, but that are potentially more profitable for them. And if a company identifies a segment as being unprofitable, they might take steps to encourage that group to shop at the competition instead. Best Buy in the United States, for example, identified its "demon" customers and implemented a segmentation strategy to discourage them (see Marketing@Work 7.1).

The company also needs to examine major structural factors that affect long-run segment attractiveness, such as the number and aggressiveness of *competitors*.[18] The existence of many actual or potential *substitute products* may limit prices and the profits that can be earned in a segment. For example, Finnish mobile phone manufacturer Nokia, though it holds 37 percent of the global market for handsets, has captured a meagre 8 percent market share in the United States, where it faces strong competition from RIM's BlackBerry and Apple's iPhone. Not only that, but there are many substitute products for a smartphone. The company recently partnered with AT&T in the United States to market its new smartphone, the E71x, which it touts as being the thinnest phone available, with all the features but at half the price of an iPhone.[19]

Exhibit 7.8 Evaluating market segments: Nokia partnered with AT&T in the United States to market its E71x thin smartphone, which sells for half the price of an iPhone.

The relative *power of buyers* also affects segment attractiveness. Buyers with strong bargaining power relative to sellers will try to force prices down, demand more services, and set competitors against one another—all at the expense of seller profitability. Finally, a segment may be less attractive if it contains *powerful suppliers* who can control prices or reduce the quality or quantity of ordered goods and services.

Even if a segment has the right size and growth and is structurally attractive, the company must consider its own objectives and resources. Some attractive segments can be dismissed quickly because they do not mesh with the company's long-run objectives. Or the company may lack the skills and resources needed to succeed in an attractive segment. For example, given current economic conditions, the economy segment of the automobile market is large and growing. But given its objectives and resources, it would make little sense for luxury-performance carmaker BMW to enter this segment. A company should enter only segments in which it can create superior customer value and gain advantages over competitors.

SELECTING TARGET MARKET SEGMENTS

After evaluating different segments, the company must decide which and how many segments it will target. A **target market** consists of a set of buyers who share common needs or characteristics that the company decides to serve. Market targeting can be carried out at several different levels. Figure 7.2 shows that companies can target very broadly (undifferentiated marketing), very narrowly (micromarketing), or somewhere in between (differentiated or concentrated marketing).

Target market
A set of buyers sharing common needs or characteristics that the company decides to serve.

FIGURE 7.2 Market targeting strategies

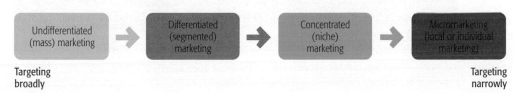

| Undifferentiated (mass) marketing | → | Differentiated (segmented) marketing | → | Concentrated (niche) marketing | → | Micromarketing (local or individual marketing) |

Targeting broadly

Targeting narrowly

MARKETING@WORK 7.1

Best Buy: Embracing the Angels and Ditching the Demons

There's no such thing as a bad customer. Right? And the more customers, the merrier. Makes sense? After all, more customers mean more money in the till. As it turns out, however, that's often not so. These days, many marketers are discovering a new truth: Some customers can be way, way wrong for the company—as in unprofitable. And trying to serve any and all customers can mean serving none of them well. Instead, companies need to make certain that they are serving the *right* customers, and serving them in the *right way*. They need to decide who their best potential customers are—and who they aren't.

Few companies do that better than consumer electronics retailer Best Buy. Five years ago, Best Buy in the United States embarked on a "customer-centricity" segmentation strategy, by which it set out to identify its best customers and win their loyalty by serving them better. At the same time, it identified less attractive customers and began to send them packing—off to Wal-Mart or some other competitor.

Best Buy began in 1966 as a small Minnesota home and car stereo chain. It has since blossomed into a profitable 925-store, $40-billion mega-retailer. Today's Best Buy stores are huge, warehouse-like emporiums featuring a treasure trove of goods—from consumer electronics, home office equipment, and appliances to software, CDs, and DVDs— all at low discount prices. A decade ago, however, Best Buy saw an influx of new competitors encroaching on its profitable consumer electronics turf. On one side was Wal-Mart, the world's largest retailer, which is now number two in store sales of consumer electronics. On the other side was a fast-growing cadre of online and direct retailers, ranging from computer-maker Dell to Web giant Amazon.com.

To better differentiate itself in this more crowded marketplace, Best Buy needed to stake out its own turf—to identify its best

customers and serve them in ways that no discount or online competitor could. Rather than trying to make all customers happy all of the time, Best Buy needed to segment its market, narrow its targeting, and sharpen its positioning. The answer: customer-centricity.

The customer-centricity strategy draws on the research of consultant Larry Selden, a Columbia University emeritus business professor. Selden argues that a company should see itself as a portfolio of *customers*, not product lines. His research has identified two basic types of customers: angels and demons. Angel customers are profitable, whereas demon customers may actually cost a company more to serve than it makes from them. In fact, Selden claims, serving the demons often wipes out the profits earned by serving the angels.

Following this logic, Best Buy assigned a task force to analyze its customers' purchasing habits. Sure enough, the analysts found both angels and demons.

The angels included the 20 percent of Best Buy customers who produced the bulk of its profits. They snapped up high-definition televisions, portable electronics, and newly released DVDs without waiting for markdowns or rebates. In contrast, the demons formed an "underground of bargain-hungry shoppers intent on wringing every nickel of savings out of the big retailer. They loaded up on loss leaders ... then flipped the goods at a profit on eBay. They slapped down rock-bottom price quotes from Web sites and demanded that Best Buy make good on its lowest-price pledge." According to Best Buy CEO Brad Anderson, these demon customers could account for up to 100 million of Best Buy's 500 million customer visits each year. "They can wreak enormous economic havoc," he says.

Further segmentation analysis revealed that the angels fall into eight groups of typical Best Buy shoppers, such as "Barrys," high-income men; "Jills,"

Exhibit 7.9   At Best Buy, customer-centricity means listening to customers and becoming "that trusted advisor capable of helping them use technology the way they dreamed."

suburban moms; "Buzzes," male technology enthusiasts; "Rays," young family men on a budget; or "Charlies and Helens," empty nesters with money to spend. Each group has unique needs and spending habits. Ray, for example, loves Best Buy, is a hardcore "techno-tainment" enthusiast, and is the company's bread-and-butter, accounting for over 20 percent of sales. And although "Helen" is by no means a Best Buy regular, she is rediscovering time for herself now that her children have left home and is open to being sold technology that will keep her connected to her community.

Based on these segmentation findings, Best Buy set out to embrace the angels and ditch the demons. To attract the angels, the retailer began stocking more merchandise and offering better service to them. For example, it set up digital photo centres and a "Geek Squad," which offers one-on-one in-store or at-home assistance to high-value buyers. It established a Reward Zone loyalty program, in which regular customers can earn points toward discounts on future purchases. To discourage the demons, Best Buy removed them from its marketing lists, reduced the promotions and other sales tactics that tended to attract them, and instituted a 15-percent restocking fee.

In line with its customer-centricity approach, Best Buy then combed through customer databases and began remodelling each store to align its product and service mix to reflect the store's makeup of core customer segments. At customer-centric stores, sales clerks now receive hours of training in identifying desirable customers according to their shopping preferences and behaviour.

At one store targeting upper-income Barrys, blue-shirted sales clerks prowl the DVD aisles looking for promising candidates. The goal is to steer them into the store's home theatre centre. Unlike the television sections, the home theatre centre has easy chairs, a leather couch, and a basket of popcorn. At stores popular with young Buzzes, Best Buy has set up video-game areas with leather chairs and game players hooked to mammoth, plasma-screen televisions. The games are conveniently stacked outside the playing area, the glitzy new TVs a short stroll away.

How is Best Buy's customer-centricity strategy working? Very well. Early customer-centricity stores clobbered Best Buy's traditional stores, with many posting sales gains more than triple those of stores with conventional formats. Since rolling out the new strategy five years ago, Best Buy's overall sales have nearly

doubled, as have profits. And despite the recently gloomy economy, Best Buy's share of U.S. retail consumer electronics sales jumped nearly 21 percent last year.

"We started this [customer-centricity] journey by learning how to see the differences in the desires of our customers, and then learning how to meet them," says CEO Anderson. Customer-centricity means "listening [in order] to understand how customers are going to deploy the stuff they buy from us and use it to enrich their lives, ... rather than worrying about selling the product." Best Buy wants to focus on customers' individual wants and needs—to become "that trusted advisor capable of helping customers use technology the way they dreamed," says Anderson. "That unlocks enormous horizons of growth opportunities for us."

Sources: "Connected World," Best Buy fiscal 2008 annual report," pp. 1–3, accessed at www.bestbuyinc.com; Jonathan Birchall, "Personal Approach to Expansion," *Financial Times*, May 13, 2008, p. 14; and Gary McWilliams, "Analyzing Customers, Best Buy Decides Not All Are Welcome," *Wall Street Journal*, November 8, 2004, p. A1. Other information from Laura Spinali and Jeff O'Heir, "Top 101," *Dealerscope*, March 2009, p. 38; "Consumer Survey: Best Buy, Wal-Mart Top CE Chains," *TWICE*, April 6, 2009, p. 6; Philippe Gohier, "Best Buy Isolates Its 'Demons,'" *Maclean's*, April 7, 2009, p. 40; and annual reports and other documents found at www.bestbuyinc.com, accessed September 2009.

By using an **undifferentiated marketing (or mass-marketing)** strategy, a firm might decide to ignore market segment differences and target the whole market with one offer. This mass-marketing strategy focuses on what is *common* in the needs of consumers rather than on what is *different*. The company designs a product and a marketing program that will appeal to the largest number of buyers.

As noted earlier in the chapter, most modern marketers have strong doubts about this strategy. Difficulties arise in developing a product or brand that will satisfy all consumers. Moreover, mass marketers often have trouble competing with more-focused firms that do a better job of satisfying the needs of specific segments and niches.

Differentiated Marketing By using a **differentiated marketing (or segmented-marketing)** strategy, a firm decides to target several market segments and designs separate offers for each. Toyota, for example, produces many different brands of cars, from Yaris to Lexus, each targeting a different group of car buyers—a different market segment. Procter & Gamble markets six different laundry detergent brands, which compete with each other on supermarket shelves. And VF Corporation offers a closet-full of more than 30 clothing brands, including Lee, Wrangler, and The North Face, each of which "taps into consumer aspirations to fashion, status, and well-being" in a well-defined segment."[20]

Undifferentiated (mass) marketing A market-coverage strategy in which a firm decides to ignore market segment differences and go after the whole market with one offer.

Differentiated (segmented) marketing A market-coverage strategy in which a firm decides to target several market segments and designs separate offers for each.

By offering product and marketing variations to segments, companies hope for higher sales and a stronger position within each market segment. Developing a stronger position within several segments creates more total sales than undifferentiated marketing across all segments. VF Corporation's combined brands give it a much greater, more stable market share than any single brand could. The company's jeans brands alone account for a quarter of all jeans sold in the United States. Similarly, P&G's multiple detergent brands capture four times the market share of nearest rival Unilever.

But differentiated marketing also increases the costs of doing business. A firm usually finds it more expensive to develop and produce, say, 10 units of 10 different products than 100 units of one product. Developing separate marketing plans for the separate segments requires extra marketing research, forecasting, sales analysis, promotion planning, and channel management. And trying to reach different market segments with different advertising campaigns increases promotion costs. Thus, the company must weigh increased sales against increased costs when deciding on a differentiated marketing strategy.

Concentrated (niche) marketing
A market-coverage strategy in which a firm goes after a large share of one or a few segments or niches.

Concentrated Marketing By using a **concentrated marketing (or niche marketing)** strategy, instead of going after a small share of a large market, the firm goes after a large share of one or a few smaller segments or niches. Through concentrated marketing, the firm achieves a strong market position because of its greater knowledge of consumer needs in the niches it serves and the special reputation it acquires. It can market more *effectively* by fine-tuning its products, prices, and programs to the needs of carefully defined segments. It can also market more *efficiently*, targeting its products or services, channels, and communications programs toward only consumers that it can serve best and most profitably. Consider Sabian, the second largest cymbal manufacturer in the world:[21]

> The village of Meductic, New Brunswick, has a population of only a few hundred people, and you've likely never heard of it—unless you're a musician. More specifically, a drummer. Neil Peart and Phil Collins, two of the most respected drummers in the world, have visited Meductic, because it's home to Sabian, a world-renowned cymbal maker. Sabian employs 130 people, sells its cymbals in 120 countries, and holds about half the market share.
>
> How big is the worldwide market for cymbals? In dollar terms, it's less than $100 million per year, which definitely qualifies it as a niche market. Sabian's only competitor to speak of is the company that holds the other half of this small market segment, the Avedis Zildjian Company of Boston. Sabian differentiates itself from Zildjian by projecting the idea that it is a creative, innovative company, whereas Zildjian is more traditional. Sabian invites the world's best drummers to New Brunswick to invent new cymbal sounds, which the company then markets as a signature line. One of these lines, called Paragon, was designed in collaboration with legendary Rush drummer Neil Peart, and featured an advertisement showing Canada's most famous drummer playing in a forest.

Powerful
Powerful sounds for dynamic drummers.

Exhibit 7.10   Niche marketing: Though the market for cymbals is small, New Brunswick cymbal manufacturer Sabian holds approximately half the market share. Their marketing strategy includes designing custom lines in collaboration with world-renowned drummers, such as Canada's Neil Peart.

Whereas most market segments are fairly large and normally attract several competitors, niche markets are smaller and may attract only one or two competitors. Niche marketing lets smaller companies focus their limited resources on serving very small groups of customers that may be unimportant to or overlooked by larger competitors. Many companies start as niche marketers to get a foothold against larger, more-resourceful competitors and then grow into broader competitors. For example, Enterprise Rent-A-Car began by building a network of neighbourhood offices that served the niche market of city dwellers who don't own a car, rather than competing with Hertz and Avis in airport locations, but is now one of the largest car rental companies.

In contrast, as markets change, some mega-marketers develop niche products to create sales growth. For example, in recent years, as consumers have grown more health conscious, the demand for carbonated soft drinks has declined while the market for energy drinks and juices has grown. Carbonated soft drink sales fell 2.3 percent last year; energy drink sales surged 26 percent. To meet this shifting demand, mainstream cola marketers PepsiCo and Coca-Cola have both developed or acquired their own niche products. PepsiCo developed Amp energy drink and purchased the SoBe and IZZE brands of enhanced waters and juices. Similarly, Coca-Cola developed Vault and acquired the VitaminWater and Odwalla brands. Says Pepsi-Cola North America's chief marketing officer, "The era of the mass brand has been over for a long time."[22]

Today, the low cost of setting up shop on the Internet plus the instant access to global markets makes it even more profitable to serve seemingly miniscule niches. Ostriches Online (Ostrich.com), for example, sells over 20 000 items such as feather boas, fans, and masks to retailers in more than 130 countries, and Edmonton's Kinnikinnick Foods reaches a worldwide market of consumers with its gluten-free baked goods.

Micromarketing Differentiated and concentrated marketers tailor their offers and marketing programs to meet the needs of market segments consisting of groups of people, however, they do not go so far as to customize their offers to each individual customer. **Micromarketing** is the practice of tailoring products and marketing programs to suit the tastes of specific individuals and locations. Micromarketing is an extreme form of market segmentation, where the market segment is so small it is contained within a small geographic area—*local marketing*—or so small that it consists of only one person—*individual marketing*.

LOCAL MARKETING **Local marketing** involves tailoring brands and promotions to the needs and wants of a small group of people who live in the same city, or neighbourhood, or who shop at the same store. Most convenience stores practise local marketing, stocking their shelves with the items they know the people in their neighbourhood are likely to want.

Advances in communications technology have given rise to a new high-tech version of location-based marketing. By coupling mobile phone services with GPS devices, many marketers are now targeting customers wherever they are with what they want.[23]

Location. Location. Location. This is the mantra of the real estate business. But it may not be long before marketers quote it, too. "Location-based technology allows [marketers] to reach people when they're mobile, near their stores, looking to make a decision," says one marketing expert. "When customers get information—even advertising information—linked to their location, research shows that's often perceived as value-added information, not as an advertisement." For example, Starbucks recently launched a store locator service for mobile devices, which allows people to use their phones and in-car GPS systems to search for the nearest Starbucks shop. A consumer sends a text message to "MYSBUX" (697289) including his or her zip code. Within 10 seconds, Starbucks replies with up to three nearby store locations. Starbucks plans to expand the service to include a wider range of text-messaging

Micromarketing
The practice of tailoring products and marketing programs to the needs and wants of specific individuals and local customer segments—includes *local marketing and individual marketing.*

Local marketing
A small group of people who live in the same city, or neighbourhood, or who shop at the same store.

Exhibit 7.11   Local marketing: By coupling mobile phone services with GPS devices, marketers such as Starbucks are now targeting customers wherever they are with what they want.

Individual marketing (mass customization)
Tailoring products and marketing programs to the needs and preferences of individual customers.

conversations with local customers that will "showcase Starbucks as a brand that truly listens." Such location-based marketing will grow astronomically as the sales of GPS devices skyrocket.

Local marketing has some drawbacks. It can drive up manufacturing and marketing costs by reducing economies of scale. It can also create logistics problems as companies try to meet the varied requirements of different regional and local markets. Further, a brand's overall image might be diluted if the product and message vary too much in different localities.

Still, as companies face increasingly fragmented markets, and as new supporting technologies develop, the advantages of local marketing often outweigh the drawbacks. Local marketing helps a company to market more effectively in the face of pronounced regional and local differences in demographics and lifestyles. It also meets the needs of the company's first-line customers—retailers—who prefer more finely tuned product assortments for their neighborhoods.

INDIVIDUAL MARKETING   In the extreme, micromarketing becomes **individual marketing** —tailoring products and marketing programs to the needs and preferences of individual customers. Individual marketing is also known as **mass customization**.

The modern custom of mass marketing has obscured the fact that for centuries consumers *were* served as individuals: The tailor custom-made a suit, the cobbler designed shoes for an individual, the cabinetmaker made furniture to order. So, in a sense we are returning to a time-honoured tradition, but employing contemporary technology to improve upon it. Computer databases, robotic production and flexible manufacturing, and interactive communication media have combined to foster mass customization. Today's marketers have the tools to interact on a one-to-one basis with masses of customers to produce products that are in some way customized to the individual. For example, Dell creates custom-configured computers, and hockey stick–maker Branches Hockey lets customers choose from more than two dozen options—including stick length, blade patterns, and blade curve—and turns out a customized stick in five days. Visitors to Nike's Nike ID website can personalize their sneakers by choosing from hundreds of colours and putting an embroidered word or phrase on the tongue. At www.myMMs. com, you can upload your photo and order a batch of M&Ms with your face and a personal message printed on each little candy. Toyota even lets Scion owners design their own personal "coat of arms" online, "a piece of owner-generated art that is meant to reflect their own job, hobbies, and—um, okay—Karma." Customers can download their designs and have them made into window decals or professionally airbrushed onto their cars.[24]

Marketers are also finding new ways to personalize promotional messages. For example, large screens placed in shopping malls around the country can now analyze shoppers' faces and place ads based on an individual shopper's gender, age, or ethnicity:[25]

> Watch an advertisement on a video screen in a mall, health club, or grocery store and there's a growing chance that the ad is watching you too. Small cameras can now be embedded in or around the screen, tracking who looks at the screen and for how long. With surprising accuracy, the system can determine the viewer's gender, approximate age range and, in some cases, ethnicity—and change the ads accordingly. That could mean razor ads for men, cosmetics ads for women, and videogame ads for teens. Or a video screen might show a motorcycle ad for a group of men, but switch to a minivan ad when women and children join them. "This is proactive merchandising," says a media executive. "You're targeting people with smart ads."

Business-to-business marketers are also finding new ways to customize their offerings. For example, John Deere manufactures seeding equipment that can be configured in more than two million versions to individual customer specifications. The seeders are produced one at a time, in any sequence, on a single production line. Mass customization provides a way to stand out against competitors.

Unlike mass production, which eliminates the need for human interaction, mass customization has made relationships with customers more important than ever. Just as mass production was the marketing principle of the past century, mass customization is becoming a marketing principle for the twenty-first century. The world appears to be coming full circle—from the good old days when customers were treated as individuals, to mass marketing when nobody knew your name, and back again.

Choosing a Targeting Strategy   Companies need to consider many factors when choosing a market-targeting strategy. Which strategy is best depends on *company resources*. When the firm's resources are limited, concentrated marketing makes the most sense. The best strategy also depends on the degree of *product variability*. Undifferentiated marketing is more suited for uniform products such as grapefruit or steel. Products that can vary in design, such as cameras and cars, are more suited to differentiation or concentration. The *product's life-cycle stage* also must be considered. When a firm introduces a new product, it may be practical to launch only one version, and undifferentiated marketing or concentrated marketing may make the most sense. In the mature stage of the product life cycle, however, differentiated marketing often makes more sense.

Exhibit 7.12   Individual marketing: Video screens in malls and stores can now determine who's watching them and change ads accordingly.

Another factor is *market variability*. If most buyers have the same tastes, buy the same amounts, and react the same way to marketing efforts, undifferentiated marketing is appropriate. Finally, *competitors' marketing strategies* are important. When competitors use differentiated or concentrated marketing, undifferentiated marketing can be suicidal. Conversely, when competitors use undifferentiated marketing, a firm can gain an advantage by using differentiated or concentrated marketing, focusing on the needs of buyers in specific segments.

SOCIALLY RESPONSIBLE TARGET MARKETING

Smart targeting helps companies to be more efficient and effective by focusing on the segments that they can satisfy best and most profitably. Targeting also benefits consumers—companies serve specific groups of consumers with offers carefully tailored to their needs. However, target marketing sometimes generates controversy and concern. The biggest issues usually involve the targeting of vulnerable or disadvantaged consumers with controversial or potentially harmful products.

For example, over the years, marketers in a wide range of industries—from cereal and toys to fast food and fashion—have been heavily criticized for their marketing efforts directed toward children. For example, Molson was criticized for using hockey icon Don Cherry in a campaign for its most popular beer, Molson Canadian, because young players

Exhibit 7.13   Socially responsible targeting: Victoria's Secret targets its Pink line of young, hip, and sexy clothing to young women 18 to 30 years old. However, critics charge that Pink is now all the rage among girls as young as 11.

look up to him. In Canada, advertising to children is carefully controlled by the CRTC's Broadcast Code for Advertising to Children, and closely monitored by organizations such as Concerned Children's Advertisers, and Advertising Standards Canada's Children's Clearance Committee.

Other problems arise when the marketing of adult products spills over into the kid segment—intentionally or unintentionally. For example, Victoria's Secret targets its Pink line of young, hip, and sexy clothing to young women 18 to 30 years old. In less than five years, Pink has generated more than $1 billion in sales. However, critics charge that Pink is now all the rage among girls as young as 11. Responding to Victoria's Secret's designs and marketing messages, tweens are flocking into stores and buying Pink, with or without their mothers. Other retailers, such as Abercrombie & Fitch and American Eagle Outfitters, have also jumped into the booming business of loungewear and intimate apparel for young buyers. More broadly, critics worry that marketers of everything from lingerie and cosmetics to Barbie dolls are directly or indirectly targeting young girls with provocative products, promoting a premature focus on sex and appearance.[26]

Ten-year-old girls can slide their low-cut jeans over "eye-candy" panties. French maid costumes, garter belt included, are available in preteen sizes. Barbie now comes in a "bling-bling" style, replete with halter top and go-go boots. And it's not unusual for girls under 12 to sing, "Don't cha wish your girlfriend was hot like me?" American girls, say experts, are increasingly being fed a cultural catnip of products and images that promote looking and acting sexy. "The message we're telling our girls is a simple one," laments one reporter about the Victoria's Secret Pink line. "You'll have a great life if people find you sexually attractive. Grown women struggle enough with this ridiculous standard. Do we really need to start worrying about it at 11?"

Not all attempts to target children, visible minorities, or other special segments draw such criticism. In fact, most provide benefits to targeted consumers. For example, Pantene markets Relaxed & Natural hair products to black women, Samsung markets the Jitterbug phone to seniors who need a simpler cellphone that is bigger and has a louder speaker, and Colgate makes a large selection of toothbrush shapes and toothpaste flavours for children—from Colgate Shrek Bubble Fruit Toothpaste to Colgate Bratz character toothbrushes. Such products help make tooth brushing more fun and get children to brush longer and more often.

Thus, in target marketing, the issue is not really *who* is targeted but rather *how* and for *what*. Controversies arise when marketers attempt to profit at the expense of targeted segments—when they unfairly target vulnerable segments or target them with questionable products or tactics. Socially responsible marketing calls for segmentation and targeting that serve not just the interests of the company but also the interests of those targeted.

DIFFERENTIATION AND POSITIONING LO4

Beyond deciding which segments of the market it will target, the company must decide on a *value proposition*—on how it will create differentiated value for targeted segments and what positions it wants to occupy in those segments. A **product position** is the way the product is *defined by consumers* on important attributes—the place the product occupies in consumers' minds relative to competing products. "Products are created in the factory, but brands are created in the mind," says a positioning expert.[27]

Most mobile devices, including smartphones, have similar features, so marketers attempt to position their brand in the mind of the consumer by using emotional appeals.

Product position
The way the product is defined by consumers on important attributes—the place the product occupies in consumers' minds relative to competing products.

For example, BlackBerry is positioned as a personal productivity aid, while iPhone is positioned as high tech with high style. One of the reasons Nokia has lost market share is due to its lack of positioning against these major competitors. "Americans don't think of Nokia as the cool, go-to company for advanced cell phones," says one expert.[28]

Tide is positioned through its advertising as a powerful, all-purpose family detergent, while Ivory Snow is positioned as the detergent for baby clothes. In the growing market for men's personal care products, Old Spice is positioned as being the choice for "manly men," Axe is the brand for young men who want to score with the opposite sex, and Dove is for the regular, everyday family man. Subway restaurants repositioned themselves with spectacular success as the healthy fast food. Beer is a relatively undifferentiated product, so beer brands position themselves on the basis of lifestyle: Corona is for when you're on vacation (or want to feel like you are); Molson Canadian is the hockey fan's beer, and Kokanee is for the outdoorsy type.

Consumers are overloaded with information about products and services. They cannot re-evaluate products every time they make a buying decision. To simplify the buying process, consumers organize products, services, and companies into categories and "position" them in their minds. A product's position is the complex set of perceptions, impressions, and feelings that consumers have for the product compared with competing products.

Consumers position products with or without the help of marketers. But marketers do not want to leave their products' positions to chance. They must *plan* positions that will give their products the greatest advantage in selected target markets, and they must design marketing mixes to create these planned positions.

POSITIONING MAPS

In planning their differentiation and positioning strategies, marketers often prepare *perceptual positioning maps,* which show consumer perceptions of their brands versus competing products on important buying dimensions. Figure 7.3 shows a positioning map for the U.S. large luxury sport utility vehicle market.[29] The position of each circle on the map indicates the brand's perceived positioning on two dimensions—price and orientation (luxury versus performance). The size of each circle indicates the brand's relative market share.

FIGURE 7.3   Positioning map: large luxury SUVs

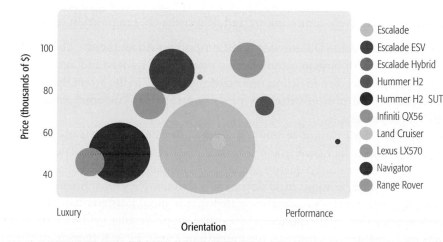

Source: Based on data provided by Ward's AutoInfoBank and Edmunds.com, 2009.

Exhibit 7.14 Positioning: Advertising for Toyota's Land Cruiser shows the vehicle performing in rough terrain, reinforcing its positioning as a rugged off-road vehicle.

Customers view the Hummer H2 as a higher-performance vehicle with some luxury thrown in. As the company's website puts it: "In a world where SUVs have begun to look like their owners, complete with love handles and mushy seats, the H2 SUV proves that there is still one out there that can drop and give you 20." The market-leading Cadillac Escalade is positioned as a moderately priced large luxury SUV with a balance of luxury and performance. The Escalade is positioned on urban luxury, and in its case, "performance" probably means power and safety performance. You'll find no mention of off-road adventuring in an Escalade ad.

By contrast, Range Rover and Land Cruiser are positioned on luxury with nuances of off-road performance. For example, the Toyota Land Cruiser began in 1951 as a four-wheel drive, Jeep-like vehicle designed to conquer the world's most gruelling terrains and climates. In recent years, Land Cruiser has retained this adventure and performance positioning but with luxury added. Its website brags of "legendary off-road capability," with off-road technologies such as downhill assist control and kinetic dynamic suspension systems. "In some parts of the world, it's an essential." Despite its ruggedness, however, the company notes that "its available Bluetooth hands-free technology, DVD entertainment, and a sumptuous interior have softened its edges."

CHOOSING A DIFFERENTIATION AND POSITIONING STRATEGY

Some firms find it easy to choose a differentiation and positioning strategy. For example, a firm well known for quality in certain segments will go for this position in a new segment if there are enough buyers seeking quality. But in many cases, two or more firms will go after the same position. Then, each will have to find other ways to set itself apart. Each firm must differentiate its offer by building a unique bundle of benefits that appeals to a substantial group within the segment. Above all else, a brand's positioning must serve the needs and preferences of well-defined target markets.

The differentiation and positioning task consists of three steps: identifying a set of differentiating competitive advantages upon which to build a position, choosing the right competitive advantages, and selecting an overall positioning strategy. The company must then effectively communicate and deliver the chosen position to the market.

Identifying Possible Value Differences and Competitive Advantages   To build profitable relationships with target customers, marketers must understand customer needs better than competitors do and deliver more customer value. To the extent that a company can differentiate and position itself as providing superior customer value, it gains **competitive advantage**.

But solid positions cannot be built on empty promises. If a company positions its product as *offering* the best quality and service, it must actually differentiate the product so that it *delivers* the promised quality and service. Companies must do much more than simply shout out their positions in ad slogans and taglines. They must first *live* the slogan. For example, when Staples's research revealed that it should differentiate itself on the basis of "an easier shopping experience," the office supply retailer held back its "Staples: That was easy" marketing campaign for more than a year. First, it remade its stores to actually deliver the promised positioning.[30]

Competitive advantage

An advantage over competitors gained by offering greater customer value, either through lower prices or by providing more benefits that justify higher prices.

Only a few years ago, things weren't so easy for Staples—or for its customers. The ratio of customer complaints to compliments was running a dreadful eight to one at Staples stores. Weeks of focus groups produced an answer: Customers wanted an easier shopping experience. That simple revelation has resulted in one of the most successful marketing campaigns in recent history, built around the now-familiar "Staples: That was easy" tagline. But Staples' positioning turnaround took a lot more than simply bombarding customers with a new slogan. Before it could promise customers a simplified shopping experience, Staples had to actually deliver one. First, it had to *live* the slogan.

So, for more than a year, Staples worked to revamp the customer experience. It remodeled its stores, streamlined its inventory, retrained employees, and even simplified customer communications. Only when all of the customer-experience pieces were in place did Staples begin communicating its new positioning to customers. The "Staples: That was easy" repositioning campaign has met with striking success, helping to make Staples the runaway leader in office retail. And the campaign's easy button has become a pop culture icon. No doubt about it, clever marketing helped. But marketing promises count for little if not backed by the reality of the customer experience. "What has happened at the store has done more to drive the Staples brand than all the marketing in the world," says Staples' vice president of marketing.

To find points of differentiation, marketers must think through the customer's entire experience with the company's product or service. An alert company can find ways to differentiate itself at every customer contact point. In what specific ways can a company differentiate itself or its market offer? It can differentiate along the lines of *product, services, channels, people,* or *image*.

Through *product differentiation* brands can be differentiated on features, performance, or style and design. For example, Maple Leaf Foods claims that its Maple Leaf Prime Naturally–branded chicken is fresher and more tender—and gets a price premium based on this differentiation. Whirlpool promotes its dishwashers on performance—they run more quietly—and Bose positions its speakers on their striking design characteristics. Similarly, companies can differentiate their products on attributes such as consistency, durability, reliability, or repairability.

Beyond differentiating its physical product, a firm can also differentiate the services that accompany the product. Some companies gain *services differentiation* through speedy, convenient, or careful delivery. For example, First Convenience Bank of Texas offers "Real Hours for Real People"—it remains open seven days a week, including evenings. Others differentiate their service based on high-quality customer care. Lexus makes fine cars but is perhaps even better known for the quality service that creates outstanding ownership experiences for Lexus owners.

Firms that practise *channel differentiation* gain competitive advantage through the way they design their channel's coverage, expertise, and performance. Caterpillar's success in the construction-equipment industry is based on superior channels and its dealers, such as Finning in Canada, are renowned for their first-rate service. ING Direct banking, Amazon.com, and Dell similarly distinguish themselves by their high-quality direct channels.

Exhibit 7.15   Positioning for competitive advantage: The "Staples: That was easy" marketing campaign has played a major role in repositioning Staples as the retailer that provides a simplified shopping experience.

Exhibit 7.16   Product differentiation: Maple Leaf differentiates its chicken breasts by branding them "Prime Naturally," and suggesting they are fresher and more tender than the competition's.

Companies can also gain a strong competitive advantage through *people differentiation*—hiring and training better people than their competitors do. Singapore Airlines enjoys an excellent reputation, largely because of the beauty and grace of its flight attendants, and WestJet staffers are known for their sense of humour. People differentiation requires that a company select its customer-contact people carefully and train them well.

Even when competing offers look the same, buyers may perceive a difference based on company or brand *image differentiation*. A company or brand image should convey the product's distinctive benefits and positioning. Developing a strong and distinctive image calls for creativity and hard work. A company cannot develop an image in the public's mind overnight by using only a few advertisements. If Ritz-Carlton means quality, this image must be supported by everything the company says and does.

Symbols—such as the McDonald's golden arches or the colourful animals in TELUS's advertising—can provide strong company or brand recognition and image differentiation. The company might build a brand around a famous person, as Nike did with its Air Jordan basketball shoes. Some companies even become associated with colours, such as IBM (blue), UPS (brown), or Coca-Cola (red). The chosen symbols, characters, and other image elements must be communicated through advertising that conveys the company's or brand's personality.

Choosing the Right Competitive Advantages   Suppose a company is fortunate enough to discover several potential differentiations that provide competitive advantages. It now must choose the ones on which it will build its positioning strategy. It must decide *how many* differences to promote and *which ones*.

HOW MANY DIFFERENCES TO PROMOTE   Many marketers think that companies should aggressively promote only one benefit to the target market. Adman Rosser Reeves, for example, said a company should develop a *unique selling proposition* (USP) for each brand and stick to it. Each brand should pick an attribute and tout itself as "number one" on that attribute. Buyers tend to remember number one better, especially in this over-communicated society. Thus, Wal-Mart promotes its unbeatable low prices and Burger King promotes personal choice—"Have it your way."

Other marketers think that companies should position themselves on more than one differentiator. This may be necessary if two or more firms are claiming to be best on the same attribute. Today, in a time when the mass market is fragmenting into many small segments, companies are trying to broaden their positioning strategies to appeal to more segments.

For example, SC Johnson recently introduced a new Pledge multi-surface cleaner. Known mainly as a brand for cleaning and dusting wood furniture, the new Pledge is positioned as a cleaner that works on wood, electronics, glass, marble, stainless steel, and other surfaces. Says its website, "No need to keep switching products—this multi-surface cleaner is perfect for a quick and easy cleanup of the whole room!" Clearly, many buyers want these multiple benefits. The challenge was to convince them that one brand can do it all. However, as companies increase the number of claims for their brands, they risk disbelief and a loss of clear positioning.

WHICH DIFFERENCES TO PROMOTE   Not all brand differences are meaningful or worthwhile; not every difference makes a good differentiator. Each difference has the potential to create company costs as well as customer benefits. A difference is worth establishing to the extent that it satisfies the following criteria:

- ☐ *Important:* The difference delivers a highly valued benefit to target buyers.
- ☐ *Distinctive:* Competitors do not offer the difference, or the company can offer it in a more distinctive way.

- ☐ *Superior:* The difference is superior to other ways that customers might obtain the same benefit.
- ☐ *Communicable:* The difference is communicable and visible to buyers.
- ☐ *Preemptive:* Competitors cannot easily copy the difference.
- ☐ *Affordable:* Buyers can afford to pay for the difference.
- ☐ *Profitable:* The company can introduce the difference profitably.

Many companies have introduced differentiations that failed one or more of these tests. When the Westin Stamford Hotel in Singapore once advertised that it is the world's tallest hotel, it was a distinction that was not important to most tourists—in fact, it turned many off. Polaroid's Polarvision, which produced instantly developed home movies, bombed too. Although Polarvision was distinctive and even preemptive, it was inferior to another way of capturing motion, namely, camcorders.

Choosing competitive advantages upon which to position a product or service can be difficult, yet such choices may be crucial to success. Choosing the right differentiators can help a brand to stand out from the pack of competitors. For example, when carmaker Nissan introduced its funky little Cube, it didn't position the car only on attributes shared with competing models, such as affordability and customization. Instead, it turned the Cube into something more—a "mobile device." (See Marketing@Work 7.2)

Selecting an Overall Positioning Strategy The full positioning of a brand is called the brand's **value proposition** —the full mix of benefits upon which the brand is differentiated and positioned. It is the answer to the customer's question "Why should I buy your brand?" Volvo's value proposition hinges on safety but also includes reliability, roominess, and styling, all for a price that is higher than average but seems fair for this mix of benefits.

Figure 7.4 shows possible value propositions upon which a company might position its products. In the figure, the five green cells represent winning value propositions—differentiation and positioning that gives the company competitive advantage. The red cells, however, represent losing value propositions. The centre yellow cell represents at best a marginal proposition. In the following sections, we discuss the five winning value propositions upon which companies can position their products: more for more, more for the same, the same for less, less for much less, and more for less.

Value proposition
The full positioning of a brand—the full mix of benefits upon which it is positioned.

FIGURE 7.4 Possible value propositions

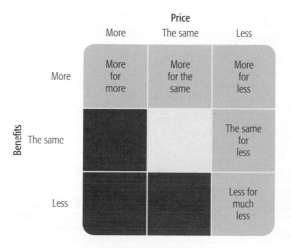

MARKETING@WORK 7.2

Nissan's Cube is Not Just a Car, It's a Mobile Device

You probably know about the Rubik's Cube, that 3-D puzzle that you solve by twisting, turning, and aligning the dozens of little coloured facets until each cube face is the same colour. Carmaker Nissan is now facing a different kind of cube puzzle. It recently introduced a new model—the Cube—a smallish, city car with a funky look. And as with the good-old Rubik's Cube, to be successful, Nissan will have to align all of the Cube's intricate marketing facets into a winning pattern that differentiates the car from competing models.

Solving this marketing puzzle would be difficult enough in normal times. But Nissan introduced the Cube in mid-2009, in the midst of a recession and plummeting auto sales, creating a challenge that makes a Rubik's Cube seem like child's play. What's more, although the Cube has been a huge hit in Japan for several years, Nissan was late to enter the American market with a small vehicle aimed at the 20-something first-car buyer. Honda and Toyota had already made their mark six years earlier with the boxy Honda Element (positioned as "a dorm room on wheels") and eccentric-

looking Toyota Scion (also known as "the toaster"). And by the time Nissan launched the Cube, the Canadian market was already crammed full of competing small cars such as the Toyota Yaris, Ford Focus, Kia Rio, and the startling, unique Smart Car marketed by Mercedes. Before introducing the Cube, Nissan needed to solve the puzzle of how to make its car distinctive. How could Nissan differentiate the Cube to make it stand out from the pack?

The Cube and its competitors primarily target Millennials, 18-to-25-year-old drivers for whom it would be their first car, or at least their first new car. Many of these buyers are in college or university, or are just starting their careers, so they often don't have much money. The young Millennials are an expressive, hypercreative bunch who are setting out to establish their independence. They value things built just for them, with lots of room for personalization. These younger buyers grew up with the Web, blogs, cellphones, text messaging, and social networks. They're a uniquely social group, with both the need and the technical savvy to stay in touch—

anywhere, anytime. They communicate constantly.

The Cube's young target buyers are looking for an affordable car, and for a car that lets them express their individuality. Cube has plenty of both qualities. The base model is priced at $17 400, and Nissan will help with the financing. Buyers can select from more than 40 accessories to customize the car. One writer describes the Cube as "an inspiring canvas for personalization." But many Cube competitors also offer these attributes. Many have base prices even lower than the Cube's, and others feature personalization as their main value proposition. For example, Toyota initially positioned its Scion with the slogan, "Personalization begins here—what moves you?"

So, to stand out from this crowded field, Nissan needed something more, something truly unique. The answer: Position the Cube not just as another small *car* but as a personal *mobile device*—as something that enhances young customers' individual, mobile, connected lifestyles. Nissan decided to present the Cube "as a part of a fun, busy life that can be customized and personalized as easily as a cellphone ring tone or a Web page," notes an analyst. "We decided we wouldn't think about it as a car," says the creative director at Nissan's advertising agency. Instead, Nissan designed the Cube "to bring young people together—like every mobile device they have."

The Cube, then, becomes a mobile space where young people can connect with friends. It's also a space that's their own, just like a Facebook page, where they can hang out and create. Nissan Canada created a blog (at CubeCommunity.ca) for Cube owners to post pictures and stories about their experiences with their Cubes, and launched it by giving away several Cubes.

With this novel positioning in mind, Nissan put together a marketing mix that

Exhibit 7.17 **Mark Orszulak**, one of the bloggers at CubeCommunity.ca, with his Nissan Cube.

delivers the desired value proposition. Advertising for the Cube reinforces the positioning, with messages such as "Say hello to a Cube that's extremely well-rounded. Personalize it. Share it. Connect with it." Promotion for the Cube supports and extends its targeting and innovative positioning. To reach the Millennials and draw them into Nissan's showrooms, the company has peppered its communications and product descriptions with terms such as *search engine*, *browse*, *storage capacity*, *add friends*, and *set preferences*. The company has avoided the usual ho-hum car advertising in favour of non-traditional media such as iPhone games, computer wallpaper, text messaging, a Facebook page, and MP3 downloads. Even ads in traditional media are designed as "all-screen videos," ready for viewing on everything from TVs and computers to cellphone and movie-theatre screens.

Then there's the car itself. As the name suggests, the Cube looks sort of like—you guessed it—a cube, but not an ordinary one. Its wrap-around rear window helps it to stand out visually. With its peppy 4-cylinder, 122-horsepower engine, the fun-to-drive Cube gets a combined 8.1 litres per 100 km. Although small, the Cube feels roomy inside, with comfortable seats and a high ceiling that gives passengers, especially those in the back seat, the sense that they are in a living room, not a car. In all, with its eye-catching but sensible design, the Cube is "more studio loft rather than economy car," says an analyst.

You don't just drive a Cube—it becomes a part of the mobile, connected you. The top-of-the-line Cube Krom (pronounced *chrome*), one of four Cube models, offers a Bluetooth hands-free phone system, an upgraded audio system with six speakers and Rockford Fosgate subwoofer, an interface for an iPod, titanium trim accents, automatic temperature control, an interior illumination system with 20 lights, and 16-inch aluminum-alloy wheels. Add in the abundance of customizing accessories and Nissan hopes you've got everything a young Millennial could want—a personalized, connected mobile device at an affordable price. Adding to the technological allure, rumour has it that Nissan will offer an electric Cube by 2012.

Has Nissan solved its Rubik's Cube marketing puzzle? Has it created important, distinctive, affordable—and profitable—differentiation? Only time will tell. Whatever the outcome, the Cube represents an innovative differentiation and positioning strategy in an otherwise me-too segment. The company thinks it has a winner, and many agree; in fact, *Automobile* magazine named the Cube its 2010 Design of the Year, calling the car "charming" and "funny-looking, but in an especially agreeable way."

Sources: Stuart Elliott, "With the Car Industry in Trouble, Nissan Rolls Out the Mobile Device," *New York Times*, April 6, 2009; Jeff Sabatini, "The Driver's Seat: Nissan's Compact: It's Fun Cubed," *Wall Street Journal*, March 28, 2009, p. W7; Jennifer Wells, "An Out-of-Box Campaign for a Square-Boned Newcomer," *The Globe and Mail*, March 20, 2009, p. B5; Dan Neil, "Nissan's Cube is Coolness in a Box," *Los Angeles Times*, March 6, 2009, p. 1; "Nissan North America, Inc.," *Science Letter*, February 24, 2009, p. 3836; Robert Cumberford, "2010 Design of the Year: 2010 Nissan Cube," *Automobile* magazine, November, 2009; www.nissan.ca and www.cubecommunity.ca, accessed May 2010.

MORE FOR MORE   "More-for-more" positioning involves providing the most upscale product or service and charging a higher price to cover the higher costs. Four Seasons hotels, Montblanc writing instruments, Mercedes automobiles, LG appliances—each claims superior quality, craftsmanship, durability, performance, or style and charges a price to match. Not only is the market offering high in quality, it also gives prestige to the buyer. It symbolizes status and a loftier lifestyle. Often, the price difference exceeds the actual increment in quality.

Sellers offering "only the best" can be found in every product and service category, from hotels, restaurants, food, and fashion to cars and household appliances. Consumers are sometimes surprised, even delighted, when a new competitor enters a category with an unusually high-priced brand. Starbucks coffee entered as a very expensive brand in a largely commodity category. When Apple premiered its iPhone, it offered higher-quality features than a traditional cellphone with a hefty price tag to match, and Häagen-Dazs entered the market as a premium ice cream brand at a price never before charged.

In general, companies should be on the lookout for opportunities to introduce a more-for-more brand in any underdeveloped product or service category. Yet more-for-more brands can be vulnerable. They often invite imitators who claim the same quality but at a lower price. For example, Starbucks now faces "gourmet" coffee competition from, surprisingly, McDonald's. Also, luxury goods that sell well during good times may be at

Before we knew it we were having Häagen-Dazs.

Fall deeply in Häagen-Dazs.

Exhibit 7.18   More-for-more positioning: Everything about Häagen-Dazs ice cream, from its price and packaging to its advertising, suggests luxury. Some marketers refer to this positioning as "*much* more for much more."

risk during economic downturns when buyers become more cautious in their spending. The recent gloomy economy hit premium brands, such as Starbucks, the hardest.

MORE FOR THE SAME   Companies can attack a competitor's more-for-more positioning by introducing a brand offering comparable quality but at a lower price. For example, Toyota introduced its Lexus line with a "more-for-the-same" value proposition versus Mercedes and BMW. Its first ad headline read "Perhaps the first time in history that trading a $72,000 car for a $36,000 car could be considered trading up." It communicated the high quality of its new Lexus through rave reviews in car magazines and through a widely distributed videotape showing side-by-side comparisons of Lexus and Mercedes automobiles. It published surveys showing that Lexus dealers were providing customers with better sales and service experiences than were Mercedes dealerships. Many Mercedes owners switched to Lexus, and the Lexus repurchase rate has been 60 percent, twice the industry average.

THE SAME FOR LESS   Offering "the same for less" can be a powerful value proposition—everyone likes a good deal. Discount stores such as Wal-Mart and "category killers" such as Best Buy, RONA hardware stores, and Chapters use this positioning. They don't claim to offer different or better products. Instead, they offer many of the same brands as department stores and specialty stores but at deep discounts based on superior purchasing power and lower-cost operations. Other companies develop imitative but lower-priced brands in an effort to lure customers away from the market leader. For example, AMD makes less-expensive versions of Intel's market-leading microprocessor chips.

LESS FOR MUCH LESS   A market almost always exists for products that offer less and therefore cost less. Few people need, want, or can afford "the very best" in everything they buy. In many cases, consumers will gladly settle for less than optimal performance or give up some of the bells and whistles in exchange for a lower price. For example, many travellers seeking lodgings prefer not to pay for what they consider unnecessary extras, such as a pool, attached restaurant, or mints on the pillow. Hotel chains such as Ramada Limited suspend some of these amenities and charge less accordingly.

"Less-for-much-less" positioning involves meeting consumers' lower performance or quality requirements at a much lower price. For example, Giant Tiger, Winners, and the many "dollar stores" offer more affordable goods at very low prices. Southwest Airlines, the most consistently profitable air carrier in the United States, also practises less-for-much-less positioning.

Exhibit 7.19   Less-for-much-less positioning: Southwest has positioned itself firmly as the no-frills, low-price airline. But no frills doesn't mean drudgery—Southwest's cheerful employees go out of their way to amuse, surprise, or somehow entertain passengers.

From the start, Southwest has positioned itself firmly as *the* no-frills, low-price airline. Southwest's passengers have learned to fly without the amenities. For example, the airline provides no meals—just pretzels. It offers no first-class section, only three-across seating in all of its planes. And there's no such thing as a reserved seat on a Southwest flight. Why, then, do so many passengers love Southwest? Perhaps most importantly, Southwest excels at the basics of getting passengers where they want to go on time, and with their luggage. Beyond the basics, however, Southwest offers shockingly low prices. In fact, prices are so low that when Southwest enters a market, it actually increases total air traffic by attracting customers who might otherwise travel by car or bus. No frills and low prices, however, don't mean drudgery. Southwest's cheerful employees go out of their way to amuse, surprise, or somehow entertain passengers. One analyst sums up Southwest's less-for-much-less positioning this way: "It is not luxurious, but it's cheap and it's fun."

MORE FOR LESS   Of course, the winning value proposition would be to offer "more for less." Many companies claim to do this. And, in the short run, some companies can actually achieve such lofty positions. For example, when it first opened for business, Home Depot had arguably the best product selection, the best service, *and* the lowest prices compared with local hardware stores and other home improvement chains, but today Home Depot is positioned more on selection than on price.

Yet in the long run, companies will find it very difficult to sustain such best-of-both positioning. Offering more usually costs more, making it difficult to deliver on the "for-less" promise. Companies that try to deliver both may lose out to more focused competitors. For example, facing determined competition from Canadian Tire and RONA stores, Home Depot must now decide whether it wants to compete primarily on superior service or on lower prices.

All said, each brand must adopt a positioning strategy designed to serve the needs and wants of its target markets. "More for more" will draw one target market, "less for much less" will draw another, and so on. Thus, in any market, there is usually room for many different companies, each successfully occupying different positions. The important thing is that each company must develop its own winning positioning strategy, one that makes it special to its target consumers.

Developing a Positioning Statement   Company and brand positioning should be summed up in a **positioning statement**. The statement should follow the form: To (target segment and need) our (brand) is (concept) that (point of difference).[31] For example, "To busy, mobile professionals who need to always be in the loop, BlackBerry is a wireless connectivity solution that gives you an easier, more reliable way to stay connected to data, people, and resources while on the go."

Note that the positioning first states the product's membership in a category (wireless connectivity solution) and then shows its point of difference from other members of the category (easier, more reliable connections to data, people, and resources). Placing a brand in a specific category suggests similarities that it might share with other products in the category. But the case for the brand's superiority is made on its points of difference.

Sometimes marketers put a brand in a surprisingly different category before indicating the points of difference. For example, Delissio frozen pizza is positioned in the delivered pizza category. All advertising for Delissio features the tagline "It's not delivery. It's Delissio!" and television commercials feature characters trying to trick each other into believing that they ordered takeout pizza when they really made Delissio at home.

Exhibit 7.20 Positioning by points of difference: Delissio positions its frozen pizza brand by suggesting it belongs in a different category altogether—home-delivered pizza.

Positioning statement
A statement that summarizes company or brand positioning—it takes this form: To (target segment and need) our (brand) is (concept) that (point of difference).

COMMUNICATING AND DELIVERING THE CHOSEN POSITION

Once it has chosen a position, the company must take strong steps to deliver and communicate the desired position to target consumers. All the company's marketing-mix efforts must support the positioning strategy.

Positioning the company calls for concrete action, not just talk. If the company decides to build a position on better quality and service, it must first *deliver* that position. Designing the marketing mix—product, price, place, and promotion—involves working out the tactical details of the positioning strategy. Thus, a firm that seizes on a more-for-more position knows that it must produce high-quality products, charge a high price, distribute through high-quality dealers, and advertise in high-quality media. It must hire and train more service people, find retailers who have a good reputation for service, and develop sales and advertising messages that broadcast its superior service. This is the only way to build a consistent and believable more-for-more position.

Companies often find it easier to come up with a good positioning strategy than to implement it. Establishing a position or changing one usually takes a long time. In contrast, positions that have taken years to build can quickly be lost. Once a company has built the desired position, it must take care to maintain the position through consistent performance and communication. It must closely monitor and adapt the position over time to match changes in consumer needs and competitors' strategies. However, the company should avoid abrupt changes that might confuse consumers. Instead, a product's position should evolve gradually as it adapts to the ever-changing marketing environment.

LEAVING DEMOGRAPHIC SEGMENTATION OUT IN THE COLD

Canada Goose is an international brand with growing markets in Canada, the United States, and over 40 other countries. The company has created distinct products for the Japanese market (geographic segmentation) and recently created a lighter coat for more active pursuits and for shoulder seasons when people don't need a full parka.

In addition to such geographic segmentation, Canada Goose has segmented its product mix based on benefits sought—with products ranging from a parka touted as the warmest on the planet to soft shell jackets, gloves, and vests.

Canada Goose initiates psychographic segmentation by building loyalty and community through the creation of brand ambassadors and by reaching out to those who value an authentic brand that is driven by a goal to make warm, comfortable, and attractive coats. Canada Goose marketers can further develop psychographic segmentation by observing the thoughts, attitudes, and values of their customers (as gathered through data collection) and by trying to figure out the most concentrated and profitable segments in that group.

President and CEO Dani Reiss stresses the idea that the company doesn't focus on demographic segmentation. "Our products have no demographic," he says. "We go by end use—in other words, urban fans, Arctic travellers, explorers, photographers and so on. We have far too broad an audience to narrow it down as a brand."

At the end of the day, Canada Goose's segmentation will engage both subjective and objective variables, but marketers need to realize that consumers always want to believe that their branded product is especially suited to them. The age of commodity products is waning; companies that are perceived as offering specialized services, products, and experiences will dominate. This is why Canada Goose is designing products that appeal to the true outdoors person and why it shows its products being worn by active subjects, not just attractive models.

QUESTIONS

1. If you had to segment by personality, how would you classify Canada Goose buyers?
2. Brainstorm examples of targeted segment clusters other than Canada Goose's North American market. Which countries might these be? What are their characteristics?
3. From generation to generation people change, but consumers can often be segmented based on life stage. Are there any particular life stages that might be relevant to Canada Goose? Why?
4. Try to create customer segment profiles based on the overall Canada Goose brand. Is it better to create profiles based on the brand or individual products? Why?
5. Who would be a demon customer for Canada Goose? Who would be an angel? Why?

REVIEWING THE CONCEPTS

1. **Define the major steps in designing a customer-driven marketing strategy: market segmentation, targeting, differentiation, and positioning.**

Customer-driven marketing strategy begins with selecting which customers to serve and with deciding on a value proposition that best serves the targeted customers. It consists of four steps. *Market segmentation* is the act of dividing a market into distinct segments of buyers with different needs, characteristics, or behaviours who might require separate products or marketing mixes. Once the groups have been identified, *market targeting* evaluates each market segment's attractiveness and selects one or more segments to serve. Market targeting consists of designing strategies to build the *right relationships* with the *right customers. Differentiation* involves actually differentiating the market offering to create superior customer value. *Positioning* consists of positioning the market offering in the minds of target customers.

2. **List and discuss the major bases for segmenting consumer and business markets.**

There is no single way to segment a market. Therefore, the marketer tries different variables to see which give the best segmentation opportunities. For consumer marketing, the major segmentation variables are geographic, demographic, psychographic, and behavioural. In *geographic segmentation*, the market is divided into different geographical units, such as nations, regions, states, counties, cities, or neighbourhoods. In *demographic segmentation*, the market is divided into groups based on demographic variables, including age, gender, family size, family life cycle, income, occupation, education, religion, race, generation, and nationality. In *psychographic* segmentation, the market is divided into different groups based on social class, lifestyle, or personality characteristics. In *behavioural segmentation*, the market is divided into groups based on consumers' knowledge, attitudes, uses, or responses to a product. Business marketers use many of the same variables to segment their markets. But business markets also can be segmented by business consumer *demographics* (industry, company size), *operating characteristics, purchasing approaches, situational factors,* and *personal characteristics.* The effectiveness of segmentation analysis depends on finding segments that are *measurable, accessible, substantial, differentiable,* and *actionable.*

3. **Explain how companies identify attractive market segments and choose a market-targeting strategy.**

To target the best market segments, the company first evaluates each segment's size and growth characteristics, structural attractiveness, and compatibility with company objectives and resources. It then chooses one of four market-targeting strategies—ranging from very broad to very narrow targeting. The seller can ignore segment differences and target broadly by using *undifferentiated (or mass) marketing.* This method involves mass producing, mass distributing, and mass promoting about the same product in about the same way to all consumers. Or the seller can adopt *differentiated marketing*—developing different market offers for several segments. *Concentrated marketing* (or *niche marketing)* involves focusing on only one or a few market segments. Finally, *micromarketing* is the practice of tailoring products and marketing programs to suit the tastes of specific individuals and locations. *Local marketing* refers to customizing marketing offers to a small group of people living in the same city, or neighbourhood, or who shop at the same store, and *individual marketing,* better known as *mass customization,* is the practice of customizing a marketing offer to an individual.

4. **Discuss how companies differentiate and position their products for maximum competitive advantage.**

Once a company has decided which segments to enter, it must decide on its *differentiation and positioning strategy.* The differentiation and positioning task consists of three steps: identifying a set of possible differentiations that create competitive advantage, choosing advantages upon which to build a position, and selecting an overall positioning strategy. The brand's full positioning is called its *value proposition*—the full mix of benefits upon which the brand is positioned. In general, companies can choose from one of five winning value propositions upon which to position their products: more for more, more for the same, the same for less, less for much less, or more for less. Company and brand positioning are summarized in positioning statements that state the target segment and need, positioning concept, and specific points of difference. The company must then effectively communicate and deliver the chosen position to the market.

KEY TERMS

TALK ABOUT MARKETING

1. Think of a product or a brand that you're familiar with that caters to a niche market. Describe the shared characteristics of consumers in that market, in terms of the four main bases of segmentation: geography, demographics, psychographics, and behaviour.

2. Geography, in terms of a basis of market segmentation, can refer to a country, region of a country, or region that is defined by its climate or its terrain, such as coastal areas, the far north, the prairies, or the Rockies. Describe three distinct geographic market segments in Canada. Then think of a product that could be successfully marketed to each of those segments but might not be as successful in another geographic market segment.

3. The George Foreman Grill is a compact cooking appliance with a double-sided cooking surface that is angled to allow fat to drip off the food and out of the grill. Describe a likely target market for this product in terms of its geographic, demographic, psychographic and behavioural characteristics. How does this target market rate with respect to size, growth, and structural attractiveness?

4. Find out what is the bestselling beer in Quebec and one other province. Describe each province as a market segment. Why do you think those particular beers have the most appeal in those provinces?

5. Think of an example of a hotel chain that falls into each of the five general value propositions. What does each hotel you selected do on the benefits dimension to offer more, the same, or less than competitors?

6. When A&W celebrated its 50th anniversary, it invited customers to write in about their favourite memories. Many customers, most of them Baby Boomers, reminisced about carhop service. Do you think that A&W should target Baby Boomers by reinstating carhops?

THINK LIKE A MARKETING MANAGER

A new trend in the market is men's group vacations, or, as they call them in Hollywood (in movies such as *Sideways*), "mancations." This is an example of creating a new market segment by virtue of behaviour with the product, something marketers refer to as behavioural segmentation. The size of this market indicates that it is worthwhile for marketers to target: According to one online survey, 34 percent of American male respondents said they had taken at least one trip with guy friends in the past year.

QUESTIONS

1. Imagine you are the marketing director at a hotel in Banff. What services could you offer that would appeal to this market segment? What forms of marketing communications would you use to reach this target market?

2. What tourist destinations in Canada, specifically, would appeal to this market? (For example, could Canada's Wonderland appeal to this group effectively?)

3. There are cruises that cater to families, cruises that cater to singles, and cruises that cater to gays and lesbians. Do you think it would be worthwhile for a cruise line to create a special cruise to cater to the mancationer market segment? How would you go about evaluating the potential value? Do you consider this a niche market? What ports of call would such a cruise visit, and what sorts of activities could the cruise company offer?

4. Choose a city or town in Canada that is near one of the tourist destinations you listed in #2 above. What local marketing could be done to attract mancationers?

MARKETING ETHICS

In 2009 Anheuser-Busch (A-B) launched the Bud Light "Fan Can," a promotion that included 27 different colour combinations of its cans in college team colours. For example, students at Louisiana State University could purchase purple-and-gold cans of Bud Light. Anheuser-Busch timed the campaign, called "Team Pride," to coincide with students returning to campus and with the kickoff of the football season. Several schools, such as Wisconsin, Michigan, Iowa State, University of Colorado, and others, objected strenuously. As a result, A-B halted the program in those markets. The promotion also caught the attention of the Federal Trade Commission (FTC). Both the FTC and college officials are concerned about the high rate of underage and binge drinking on college campuses. Some school officials also were concerned about trademark infringements, and about the appearance that they support Budweiser's activities. As criticism brewed around the country, A-B released a statement claiming that it did not mean to encourage underage drinking—it just wanted to create more fun for sports fans. Although the company halted the promotion in areas where college officials objected, controversy surrounding the promotion appeared in American news media.

QUESTIONS

1. What type of market-targeting strategy was Anheuser-Busch using with the Team Pride promotion?

2. In the United States, students typically attend college from the ages of 18–22, and the legal drinking age is 21 in all states. That means most students reach legal drinking age only during their last year at school. With that in mind, do you think the Team Pride promotion—or any other campus-based promotion by a beer marketer—is ethical?

MARKETING TECHNOLOGY

Today's micromarketing technology enables marketers to mass customize products ranging from clothing, skin-care products, and vitamin supplements to furniture, automobiles, and even postage stamps. And through behavioural targeting technologies, marketing communications also can be customized, based on Web surfing behaviour and television viewership, often without consumers being aware that their behaviour is being tracked.

QUESTIONS

1. At NikeID.com, consumers can design their own shoe. Go through the process on the website—design your own shoe and then price it. Do you feel the price is appropriate for the value you received from being able to customize your shoe? Find two other websites that allow consumers to similarly customize a product.

2. Online advertising technology has the ability to allow marketers to deliver Internet ads to individuals based on their Internet behaviour, for example, search terms they typed into a search engine, or how frequently they visit a particular website. As a marketer, how might you use this information to target a particular market?

MARKETING BY THE NUMBERS

Fisker Automotive of Finland shattered the stereotype of hybrids with its new luxury sports sedan, the Fisker Karma. In the increasingly crowded field of new-generation electric vehicles, Fisker Automotive wants to carve out a niche as a high-performance eco-car with lots of style. Prices range from $87 900 to $106 000, and the company already has orders from 1400 buyers. The company so far has raised $100 million of capital. But it needs more funding to develop the lower-priced model, so it is vying for a piece of the $25 billion available through the U.S. government's Advanced Technology Vehicles Manufacturing program. The company needs to estimate the market potential for this product before bringing it to market.

QUESTIONS

1. Discuss variables Fisker Automotive should consider when estimating the potential number of buyers for the high-performance Fisker Karma sports car.

2. Using the chain ratio method described in Appendix 3, Marketing by the Numbers, estimate the market potential for the Fisker Karma sports car. Search the Internet for reasonable numbers to represent the factors you identified in the previous question. Assume each buyer will purchase only one automobile and that the average purchase price is $100 000.

END-OF-CHAPTER CASE

SATURN: AN IMAGE MAKEOVER

Things are changing at Saturn. The General Motors (GM) brand had only three iterations of the same compact car for the entire decade of the 1990s. But over the last couple of years, Saturn has introduced an all-new lineup of vehicles that includes a mid-sized sport sedan, an eight-passenger crossover vehicle, a two-seat roadster, a new compact sport sedan, and a compact SUV. Having anticipated the brand's renaissance for years, Saturn executives, employees, and customers are beside themselves with joy.

But with all this change, industry observers wonder whether Saturn will be able to maintain the very characteristics that have distinguished the brand since its inception. Given that Saturn established itself based on a very narrow line of compact vehicles, many believe that the move from targeting one segment of customers to targeting multiple segments will be challenging. Will a newly positioned Saturn still meet the needs of one of the most loyal cadres of customers in the automotive world?

A NEW KIND OF CAR COMPANY

From its beginnings in 1985, Saturn set out to break through the GM bureaucracy and become "A different kind of car. A different kind of company." Saturn proclaimed that the single most defining characteristic of the new company would be people: customers, employees, and communities. The company's focus on employees included an unprecedented contract with the United Auto Workers (UAW) that focused on progressive work rules, benefits, work teams, and the concept of empowerment. It established a groundbreaking dealer network structure, reversing long-held customer perceptions of the dealer as a nemesis. Saturn also received awards and recognition for socially responsible policies that were beneficial to employees, communities, and the environment.

In addition to establishing an image as a people-oriented company, Saturn put significant resources into product development. The first Saturn cars were made "from scratch," without any allegiance to the GM parts bins or suppliers. The goal was to produce not only a high-quality vehicle but also one known for safety and innovative features that would wow the customer.

When the first Saturn vehicles rolled off the assembly line on July 30, 1990, the company offered a sedan, a coupe, and a wagon, all in two trim levels and all based on a single compact vehicle platform. Despite this minimalist approach, sales quickly exceeded expectations. By 1992, Saturn had sold 500 000 vehicles. That same year, the company achieved the highest new car sales per retail outlet, something that had not been done by a domestic car company for 15 years.

Indeed, customers were drawn to all the things that Saturn had hoped they would be. They loved the innovations, such as dent-resistant body panels; the high-tech paint job designed to resist oxidization and chipping longer than any other car in the industry; and safety features such as traction control, anti-lock brakes, and unparalleled body reinforcements. They were overwhelmed by the fresh sales approach that included no-haggle pricing, a 30-day return policy, and no hassle from the non-commissioned sales associates.

During Saturn's early years of operations, the accolades rolled in. The list included "Best Car" picks from numerous magazines and organizations, along with awards for quality, engineering, safety, and ease of maintenance. But the crowning achievement occurred in 1995 as the 1 millionth Saturn took to the road. That year, Saturn ranked number one out of all automotive nameplates on the J. D. Power and Associates Sales Satisfaction Index Study, achieving the highest score ever given by the organization. It would be the only company ever to achieve the highest marks in all three categories ranked by the satisfaction index (salesperson performance, delivery activities, and initial product quality). Saturn earned that honour for an astounding four consecutive years, and it was the only non-luxury brand to be at or near the top of J. D. Power's scores for the better part of a decade.

THE HONEYMOON ENDS

Looking back, Saturn unquestionably defied the odds. To launch an all-new automotive company in such a fiercely competitive and barrier-entrenched industry is one thing. To achieve the level of sales, the customer base, and the list of awards that Saturn achieved in such a short period of time is truly remarkable. But despite all of Saturn's initial successes, one thing was always missing from the GM division. Profit. As the new millennium dawned, GM had yet to earn a nickel of return on billions of dollars invested in the brand. Saturn sales peaked early in 1994 at 286 000 units and settled in at an average of about 250 000 units per year.

The lack of continued growth may have been partly because Saturn released no new models in the 1990s. GM finally introduced the mid-sized L-series and compact SUV Vue for 2000 and 2002, respectively. Saturn replaced the original S-series with the Ion in 2003. Although these new vehicles addressed the issue of a lack of model options, they brought with them a new concern: Saturn's history of high quality and its long-cherished J. D. Power ratings began to slide. In the early part of the new millennium, not only was Saturn's J. D. Power initial-quality rating far from the top, but it also fell to below the industry average.

Even with the new models, Saturn's sales did not improve. In fact, they declined. This decline was partly due to an industry-wide downturn in sales wrought by a recession. But Saturn's general manager, Jill Lajdziak, has conceded that for too long Saturn sold utilitarian vehicles. In 2005, Saturn sales fell to a record low of 213 000 units, only about 1 percent of the overall market. It seems that sales of the L-series and Vue were coming almost entirely from loyal Saturn customers who were trading up to something different, something bigger and, unfortunately, something not as good.

A NEW KIND OF SATURN

Given the troubles that Saturn was experiencing, it came as a surprise when, in 2008, GM executives announced expectations that Saturn would be its growth brand in the ensuing years. GM hoped to perform a makeover similar to the one it achieved with Cadillac earlier in the decade, infusing another $3 billion into its import-fighter nameplate. Given that GM had just posted a record loss of $38 billion, the world's biggest carmaker was clearly putting faith in one of its smallest brands to help turn the tide.

Lajdziak said, "Saturn's initial image as a smart innovation small-car company was blurred by bumps in quality and slow model turnover. We didn't grow the portfolio fast enough, and [now] we're growing it in a huge way." At the Vancouver International Auto Show in spring 2007, Lajdziak introduced one shiny new model after another: the 2007 Sky two-seat roadster, the 2007 Outlook crossover wagon, the completely redesigned 2008 Vue, the 2007 mid-sized Aura sedan, and the 2008 Astra. Not a single one of these models had been available in January 2006.

"By the end of this year, the oldest product in a Saturn showroom will be the Sky," said Lajdziak. Of GM's investment she remarked, "We've asked for beautifully designed products with a level of refinement, interiors, vehicle dynamics—we think we have it all. And we've got that married up with what consumers believe is the best industry experience in the marketplace." Commenting on the magnitude of the changes at Saturn, she said, "Nobody else has ever tried to grow the portfolio and turn it over as fast as we are, maintain industry-best customer satisfaction, and obviously deliver the [profit] results all at the same time."

At the heart of this makeover is something else new to Saturn: taking advantage of the GM family of vehicles and parts bins to achieve efficiencies of scale and to increase profit margins. In fact, the new Saturn models are largely rebranded Opels, GM's European division. In the future, new-product development will be carried out in a joint-venture fashion between the two divisions. For a company that in the past has been known as making the "car for people who hate cars," this is a 180-degree turnaround.

With a new lineup of European-engineered vehicles, Saturn is intent on repositioning its brand image with its "Rethink" campaign. The print and TV ads are designed to change consumers' perceptions of Saturn as a bland, functional economy car. Saturn may have the advantage of youth in this undertaking. Some industry analysts suggest it can reposition itself more easily than other brands because it is such a young company.

As for the new positioning, GM makes it clear that with Saturn, it's not trying to make another Chevrolet. Chevrolet will remain the only GM brand positioned as "all things to all people." Along with the other GM brands, Saturn will play a niche role and target a specific market segment. In fact, GM says it's just trying to help Saturn do more of what it has been doing all along—reaching the type of import-buying customer the company can't reach with any of its other brands. Indeed, top executives at GM acknowledge that many Saturn owners already believe their car is an Asian, not a domestic, brand. "Saturn has always been the one brand in the GM lineup suitable for attracting import-intenders," commented one GM executive.

SWIMMING OR SINKING?

GM set a lofty 2007 sales goal for Saturn of 400 000 vehicles, far more than the division had ever sold. However, it didn't even come close to that goal, selling only 240 000 vehicles. With so many new models, it is struggling to create brand awareness for each one. But although Saturn fell short of its goal, unit sales represented a 12 percent increase over the previous year. At a time when the entire industry was struggling, this increase was a notable achievement. Much more significant, however, was the fact that the average price of a Saturn transaction skyrocketed by a whopping US$7000. This translated into a huge 24 percent increase for dealer profitability.

"We're seeing more cross-shopping than ever," said Lajdziak. "Our retailers are seeing people they've never seen before in their showrooms, in terms of demographics and what they are trading in." And better yet, Saturn is not cannibalizing other GM brands. Saturn sales appear to be increasing at the expense of Honda, Nissan, and Toyota. In fact, not a single GM model ranks among the top 10 vehicles cross-shopped by potential Saturn buyers.

The new Saturn strategy is a big change: new positioning, new vehicles, and even a new advertising agency. But despite all this change, Saturn is remaining focused on the core elements that have always made Saturn a different kind of car company:

innovation, social responsibility, a focus on employees, and the creation and maintenance of strong customer relationships. This unique combination of change and consistency may just result in Saturn fulfilling GM's expectations of a growth brand.

Sources: Jamie LaReau, "Saturn Is Expected to Be GM's Growth Brand," *Automotive News*, February 18, 2008, p. 52; Frank Aukofer, "Resurgent Saturn Has Appealing Vue," *Washington Times*, April 18, 2008, p. G01; Gregory Solman, "Saturn Asks Americans to 'Rethink' Its Brand," *Adweek*, May 21, 2007, accessed at www.adweek.com; Jeremy Cato, "Saturn's Revival Shows What the 'New GM' Can Do," *Globe and Mail*, April 5, 2007, p. G10; Barbara Powell, "GM's Saturn Seeks to Shake Up Humdrum Image," *Ottawa Citizen*, April 12, 2006, p. F7; and "Our Story," at www.saturn.com, accessed November 2008.

QUESTIONS

1. Using the full spectrum of segmentation variables, describe how GM has segmented the automobile market.

2. What segment(s) is Saturn now targeting? How is GM now positioning Saturn? How do these strategies differ from those employed with the original Saturn S-series?

3. Describe the role that social responsibility plays in Saturn's targeting strategy.

4. Do you think that GM will accomplish its goals with the "new Saturn"? Why or why not?

5. What segmentation, targeting, and positioning recommendations would you make to GM for future Saturn models?

AFTER STUDYING THIS CHAPTER, YOU SHOULD BE ABLE TO

 define *product* and describe and classify different types of product offerings

 list and define the steps in the new-product development process and the major considerations in managing this process

 describe the stages of the product life cycle and how marketing strategies change during the product's life cycle

 describe the decisions companies make regarding their individual products and services, product lines, and product mixes

 identify the four characteristics that affect the marketing of services and the additional marketing considerations that services require

Developing and Managing Products and Services

PREVIEWING THE CONCEPTS

Now that you've had a good look at customer-driven marketing strategy, we'll take a deeper look at the marketing mix—the tactical tools that marketers use to implement their strategies and deliver superior customer value. In this chapter, we'll study how a product is defined, how companies develop new products, and how marketers manage products over time. You'll see that every product passes through several life-cycle stages and that each stage poses new challenges requiring different marketing strategies and tactics. We'll also consider the special challenges of marketing services—which are actually a type of product.

Developing new products requires innovation, so let's begin by looking at Google, one of the world's most innovative companies. Google seems to come up with an almost unending flow of knock-your-eye-out new technologies and services. If it has to do with finding, refining, or using information, there's probably an innovative Google solution for it. At Google, innovation isn't just a process, it's in the very spirit of the place.

GOOGLE: PRODUCT INNOVATION AT THE SPEED OF LIGHT

Google is wildly innovative. It recently topped *Fast Company* magazine's list of the world's most innovative companies, and it regularly ranks among everyone else's top two or three innovators. Google is also spectacularly successful. Despite formidable competition from giants such as Microsoft and Yahoo!, Google's share in its core business—online search—has climbed to a decisive 63 percent, twice the combined market share of its two closest competitors. The company also captures more than 70 percent of all search-related advertising revenues.

But Google has grown to become much more than just an Internet search and advertising company. Google's mission is "to organize the world's information and make it universally accessible and useful." In Google's view, information is a kind of natural resource, one to be mined and refined and universally distributed. That idea unifies what would otherwise appear to be a widely diverse set of Google projects, such as mapping the world, searching the Web on a cellphone screen, or even providing for early detection of flu epidemics. If it has to do with harnessing and using information, Google's got it covered in some new innovative way.

Google knows how to innovate. At many companies, new-product development is a cautious, step-by-step affair that might take a year or two to unfold. In contrast, Google's freewheeling new-product development process moves at the speed of light. The nimble innovator implements major new services in less time than it takes competitors to refine and approve an initial idea. For example, a Google senior project manager describes the lightning-quick development of iGoogle, Google's customizable home page:

> It was clear to Google that there were two groups [of Google users]: people who loved the site's clean, classic look and people who wanted tons of information there—e-mail, news, local weather. [For those who wanted a fuller home page,] iGoogle started out with me and three engineers. I was 22, and I thought, "This is awesome." Six weeks later, we launched the first version in May. The happiness metrics were good, there was healthy growth, and by September, we had [iGoogle fully operational with] a link on Google.com.

Such fast-paced innovation would boggle the minds of product developers at most other companies, but at Google its standard operating procedure. "That's what we do," says Google's vice-president for search products and user experience. "The hardest part about indoctrinating people into our culture is when engineers show me a prototype and I'm like, 'Great, let's go!' They'll say, 'Oh, no, it's not ready.' I tell them, 'The Googly thing is to launch it early on Google Labs [a site where users can try out experimental Google applications] and then to iterate, learning what the market wants—and making it great." Adds a Google engineering manager, "We set an operational tempo: When in doubt, do something. If you have two paths and you're not sure which is right, take the fastest path."

According to Google CEO Eric Schmidt, when it comes to new-product development at Google, there are no two-year plans. The company's new-product planning looks ahead only four to five months. Schmidt says that he would rather see projects fail quickly, than see a carefully planned, long drawn-out project fail.

Google's famously chaotic innovation process has unleashed a seemingly unending flurry of diverse products, ranging from an email service (Gmail), a blog search engine (Google Blog Search), an online payment service (Google Checkout), and a photo-sharing service (Google Picasa) to a universal platform for mobile-phone applications (Google Android), a cloud-friendly Web browser (Chrome), projects for mapping and exploring the world (Google Maps and Google Earth), and even an early-warning system for flu outbreaks in your area (FluTrends). Google claims that FluTrends has identified outbreaks two weeks sooner than has the U.S. Centers for Disease Control and Prevention.

Google is open to new-product ideas from about any source. What ties it all together is the company's passion for helping people to find and use information. Innovation is the responsibility of every Google employee. Google engineers are encouraged to spend 20 percent of their time developing their own new-product ideas. And all new Google ideas are quickly tested in beta form by the ultimate judges—those who will use them. According to one observer,

> Any time you cram some 20,000 of the world's smartest people into one company, you can expect to grow a garden of unrelated ideas. Especially when you give some of those geniuses one workday a week—Google's famous "20 percent time"—to work on whatever projects fan their passions. And especially when you create Google Labs (www.googlelabs.com), a Web site where the public can kick the tires on half-baked Google creations. Some Labs projects go on to become real Google services, and others are quietly snuffed out.

In the end, at Google, innovation is more than a process—it's part of the company's DNA. "Where does innovation happen at Google? It happens everywhere," says a Google research scientist.

Talk to Googlers at various levels and departments, and one powerful theme emerges: Whether they're designing search engines for the blind or preparing meals for their colleagues, these people feel that their work can change the world. The marvel of Google is its ability to continue to instill a sense of creative fearlessness and ambition in its employees. Prospective hires are often asked, "If you could change the world using Google's resources, what would you build?" But here, this isn't a goofy or even theoretical question: Google wants to know, because thinking—and building—on that scale is what Google does. This, after all, is the company that wants to make available online every page of every book ever published. Smaller-gauge ideas die of disinterest. When it comes to innovation, Google *is* different. But the difference isn't tangible. It's in the air, in the spirit of the place.[1]

AS THE Google story suggests, companies that excel at developing and managing new products reap big rewards. The name Google is both the name of the company, and the name of its flagship product, the Google search engine. Google is also a brand—one of the most valuable brands in the world—but that's the subject of our next chapter.

The product is usually the first and most basic marketing consideration. We'll start with a seemingly simple question: What *is* a product? As it turns out, however, the answer is not so simple.

WHAT IS A PRODUCT? (LO1)

We define a **product** as anything that can be offered to a market for attention, acquisition, use, or consumption that might satisfy a want or need. Products include more than just tangible objects, such as cars, computers, or cellphones. Broadly defined, "products" also include services, events, persons, places, organizations, ideas, or mixes of these. Throughout this text, we use the term *product* broadly to include any or all of these entities. Thus, an Apple iPhone, a Toyota Camry, and a box of Timbits at Tim Hortons are products; but so are a trip to Whistler, Scotiabank's or Bank of Montreal's investment services, and getting your car serviced.

Because of their importance in the world economy, we give special attention to services. **Services** are a form of product that consists of activities, benefits, or satisfactions offered for sale that are essentially intangible and do not result in the ownership of anything, for example, a day at an amusement park or a night in a hotel. We will look at services more closely later in this chapter.

Product
Anything that can be offered to a market for attention, acquisition, use, or consumption that might satisfy a want or need.

Service
An activity, benefit, or satisfaction offered for sale that is essentially intangible and does not result in the ownership of anything.

PRODUCTS, SERVICES, AND EXPERIENCES

Product is a key element in the overall *market offering*. Marketing-mix planning begins with building an offering that brings value to target customers. This offering becomes the basis upon which the company builds profitable customer relationships.

A company's market offering often includes both tangible goods and services. At one extreme, the offer may consist of a *pure tangible good*, such as soap, toothpaste, or salt—no services accompany the product. At the other extreme are *pure services*, for which the offer consists primarily of a service. Examples include a checkup at your dentist or an Air Canada flight. Between these two extremes, however, many goods-and-services combinations are possible.

Today, as products and services become more commoditized, many companies are moving to a new level in creating value for their customers. To differentiate their offers, beyond simply making products and delivering services, they are creating and managing customer *experiences* with their brands or their company.

NOT ALL KIDS WANT THE SAME
THING FOR CHRISTMAS.

COVENANT HOUSE 1-800-HELP-308

Exhibit 8.1 Organization marketing: Covenant House developed a hard-hitting advertising campaign to communicate the importance of the services it offers to homeless youth.

Experiences have always been an important part of marketing for some companies. Disney has long manufactured dreams and memories through its movies and theme parks. Today, however, all kinds of firms are recasting their traditional goods and services to create experiences. For example, Garnier, a division of L'Oréal Paris, used a contest to enhance customers' experiences with its products. It partnered with concert promoter House of Blues to offer Canadian consumers a chance to win the ultimate VIP Concert Experience. This promotion was designed as part of L'Oréal's entertainment marketing strategy, and "is a bull's-eye for its core psychographic segment," says one analyst. The winning concert-goer, along with three of her friends, also had the chance to participate in the "Green Room Experience" where they could all get a make-over backstage. This, combined with product placement at the concert, reinforced the brand's image among its young demographic.[2]

Companies that market experiences realize that customers are really buying much more than just products and services. They are buying what those offers will *do* for them. "A brand, product, or service is more than just a physical thing. Humans that connect with the brand add meaning and value to it," says one marketing executive. "Successfully managing the customer experience is the ultimate goal," adds another.[3]

ORGANIZATIONS, PERSONS, PLACES, AND IDEAS

In addition to tangible products and services, marketers have broadened the concept of a product to include other market offerings—organizations, persons, places, and ideas.

Organizations often carry out activities to "sell" the organization itself. *Organization marketing* consists of activities undertaken to create, maintain, or change the attitudes and behaviour of target consumers toward an organization. Both profit and not-for-profit organizations practise organization marketing. Business firms sponsor public relations or *corporate image advertising* campaigns to market themselves and polish their images. For example, Covenant House, Canada's largest youth shelter, must market itself so that both potential donors and young people who need its services are aware of the organization.

People can also be thought of as products. Person marketing consists of activities undertaken to create, maintain, or change attitudes or behaviour toward particular people. People ranging from politicians, entertainers, and sports figures to professionals such as real-estate agents, lawyers, and architects use person marketing to build their reputations.

Place marketing involves activities undertaken to create, maintain, or change attitudes or behaviour toward particular places. Cities and countries compete to attract tourists, new residents, conventions, and company offices and factories. For example, billboards advertising Cuba are commonly seen in Eastern Canada during the winter months. The government of China operates the China National Tourist Office (CNTO), with 15 overseas offices, including one in Toronto, for the purpose of promoting travel to China. Tourism in China has been booming as more and more travellers discover the treasures of China's ancient civilization alongside the towering skylines of modern cities such as Shanghai and Beijing (site of the 2008 Summer Olympics). At its website, the CNTO offers information about the country and its attractions, travel tips, lists of tour operators, and much more information that makes it easier to say yes to China travel.

Ideas can also be marketed. In one sense, all marketing is the marketing of an idea, whether it is the general idea of brushing your teeth or the specific idea that Crest toothpastes create "healthy, beautiful smiles for life." So we see that the line between hard products and pure services is not clear cut, but rather is a continuum, and today's marketing managers think about products and services in terms of levels.

Exhibit 8.2 Core, actual, and augmented product: People who buy a BlackBerry are buying more than a cellphone, email device, or organizer. They are buying the ability to stay connected while on the go.

LEVELS OF PRODUCTS AND SERVICES

Product marketers need to think about the product they manage as consisting of three levels (see Figure 8.1). Each level adds more customer value. The most basic level is the *core customer value*, which addresses the question *What is the buyer really buying?* When designing products, marketers must first define the core, problem-solving benefits or services that consumers seek. A woman buying lipstick buys more than lip colour. Charles Revson of Revlon saw this early: "In the factory, we make cosmetics; in the store, we sell hope." And people who buy a BlackBerry smartphone are buying more than a cellphone, email device, or personal organizer. They are buying freedom and on-the-go connectivity to people and resources.

At the second level, product planners must turn the core benefit into an *actual product*. They need to develop product and service features, design, a quality level, a brand name, and packaging. For example, the BlackBerry is an actual product. Its name, parts, styling, features, packaging, and other attributes have all been combined carefully to deliver the core customer value of staying connected.

FIGURE 8.1 Three levels of product

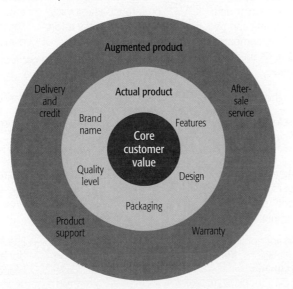

Finally, product planners must build an *augmented product* around the core benefit and actual product by offering additional consumer services and benefits. The BlackBerry offers more than just a communications device. It provides consumers with a complete solution to mobile connectivity problems. Thus, when consumers buy a BlackBerry, the company and its dealers also might give buyers a warranty on parts and workmanship, instructions on how to use the device, quick repair services when needed, and a toll-free telephone number and website to use if they have problems or questions.

Consumers see products as complex bundles of benefits that satisfy their needs. When developing products, marketers first must identify the *core customer value* that consumers seek from the product. They must then design the *actual* product and find ways to *augment* it to create this customer value and the most satisfying customer experience.

PRODUCT AND SERVICE CLASSIFICATIONS

Products and services fall into two broad classes based on the types of consumers that use them—*consumer products* and *industrial products*, and within each class there are several types of products.

Consumer product
A product bought by final consumers for personal consumption.

Convenience product
A consumer product that customers usually buy frequently, immediately, and with a minimum of comparison and buying effort.

Consumer Products   **Consumer products** are products and services bought by final consumers for personal consumption. Marketers usually classify these products and services further based on how consumers go about buying them. Consumer products include *convenience products, shopping products, specialty products,* and *unsought products*. These products differ in the ways consumers buy them and, therefore, in how they are marketed (see Table 8.1).

Convenience products are consumer products and services that customers usually buy frequently, immediately, and with a minimum of comparison and buying effort.

TABLE 8.1 Marketing Considerations for Consumer Products				
Marketing Considerations	**Type of Consumer Product**			
	Convenience	**Shopping**	**Specialty**	**Unsought**
Customer buying behaviour	Frequent purchase, little planning, little comparison or shopping effort, low customer involvement	Less frequent purchase, much planning and shopping effort, comparison of brands on price, quality, style	Strong brand preference and loyalty, special purchase effort, little comparison of brands, low price sensitivity	Little product awareness, knowledge (or, if aware, little or even negative interest)
Price	Low price	Higher price	High price	Varies
Distribution	Widespread distribution, convenient locations	Selective distribution in fewer outlets	Exclusive distribution in only one or a few outlets per market area	Varies
Promotion	Mass promotion by the producer	Advertising and personal selling by both producer and resellers	More carefully targeted promotion by both producer and resellers	Aggressive advertising and personal selling by producer and resellers
Examples	Toothpaste, magazines, laundry detergent	Major appliances, televisions, furniture, clothing	Luxury goods, such as Rolex watches or fine crystal	Life insurance, donations to Canadian Blood Services

Examples include laundry detergent, candy, magazines, and fast food. Convenience products are usually low priced, and marketers place them in many locations to make them readily available when customers need them.

Shopping products are less frequently purchased consumer products and services that customers compare carefully on suitability, quality, price, and style. When buying shopping products and services, consumers spend much time and effort in gathering information and making comparisons. Examples include furniture, clothing, used cars, major appliances, and hotel and airline services. Shopping products marketers usually distribute their products through fewer outlets but provide deeper sales support to help customers in their comparison efforts.

Specialty products are consumer products and services with unique characteristics or brand identification for which a significant group of buyers is willing to make a special purchase effort. Examples include specific brands of cars, high-priced photographic equipment, designer clothes, and the services of medical or legal specialists. A Lamborghini automobile, for example, is a specialty product because buyers are usually willing to travel great distances to buy one. Buyers normally do not compare specialty products. They invest only the time needed to reach dealers carrying the wanted products.

Unsought products are consumer products that the consumer either does not know about or knows about but does not normally think of buying. Most major new innovations are unsought until the consumer becomes aware of them through advertising. Classic examples of known but unsought products and services are life insurance, preplanned funeral services, and blood donations. By their very nature, unsought products require a lot of advertising, personal selling, and other marketing efforts.

Industrial Products   **Industrial products** are those purchased for further processing or for use in conducting a business. Thus, the distinction between a consumer product and an industrial product is based on the *purpose* for which the product is bought. If a consumer buys a lawn mower for use around home, the lawn mower is a consumer product. If the same consumer buys the same lawn mower for use in a landscaping business, the lawn mower is an industrial product.

The three groups of industrial products and services include materials and parts, capital items, and supplies and services. *Materials and parts* include raw materials and manufactured materials and parts. Raw materials consist of farm products (wheat, cotton, livestock, fruits, vegetables) and natural products (fish, lumber, crude petroleum, iron ore). Manufactured materials and parts consist of component materials (iron, yarn, cement, wires) and component parts (small motors, tires, castings). Most manufactured materials and parts are sold directly to industrial users. Price and service are the major marketing factors; branding and advertising tend to be less important.

Capital items are industrial products that aid in the buyer's production or operations, including installations and accessory equipment. Installations consist of major purchases such as buildings (factories, offices) and fixed equipment (generators, drill presses, large computer systems, elevators). Accessory equipment includes portable factory equipment and tools (hand tools, lift trucks) and office equipment (computers, scanners, desks). They have a shorter life than installations and simply aid in the production process.

The final group of industrial products is *supplies and services.* Supplies include operating supplies (lubricants, coal, paper, pencils) and repair and maintenance items (paint, nails, brooms). Supplies are the convenience products of the industrial field because they are usually purchased with a minimum of effort or comparison. Business services include maintenance and repair services (window cleaning, computer repair) and business advisory services (legal, management consulting, advertising). Such services are usually supplied under contract.

Shopping product
A consumer product that the customer, in the process of selection and purchase, usually compares on such bases as suitability, quality, price, and style.

Specialty product
A consumer product with unique characteristics or brand identification for which a significant group of buyers is willing to make a special purchase effort.

Unsought product
A consumer product that the consumer either does not know about or knows about but does not normally think of buying.

Industrial product
A product bought by individuals and organizations for further processing or for use in conducting a business.

NEW-PRODUCT DEVELOPMENT LO2

Now that we've learned that there's more to the first *P* of marketing, the product, than just hard goods, let's look at how new products are developed and managed.

Whether it's a new type of credit card from the Bank of Montreal or a new snowmobile from Bombardier, Canadians have a long history as inventors of new products. McIntosh apples, Pablum, frozen fish, and instant mashed potatoes are food products that all originated in Canada. Canadians are responsible for developing such sports and leisure activities as basketball, five-pin bowling, table hockey, and Trivial Pursuit. Many Canadian inventions spawned entire industries. Reginald Fessenden, born near Sherbrooke, Quebec, was known as the father of radio after he invented amplitude modulation (AM) radio and transmitted his first broadcast in 1900. In 1844, Nova Scotia's Charles Fenerty developed the product we now call newsprint, which is made from wood pulp. Modern air travel was made possible by another Canadian, Wallace Rupert Turnbull, who developed the variable-pitch propeller. Canadian marketers are leaders in technology, e-commerce, and especially telecommunications: from Bell Canada to Nortel to Research In Motion (RIM), creator of the BlackBerry.

Let's look at the formal process for developing, managing, and marketing new products.

NEW-PRODUCT DEVELOPMENT STRATEGY

A firm can obtain new products in two ways. One is through *acquisition*—by buying a whole company, a patent, or a license to produce someone else's product. The other is through the firm's own **new-product development** efforts. By *new products*, we mean original products, product improvements, product modifications, and new brands that the firm develops through its own research-and-development (R&D) efforts.

New products are important—to both customers and the marketers who serve them. For customers, they bring new solutions and variety to their lives. For companies, new products are a key source of growth. Even in a down economy, companies must continue to innovate. New products provide new ways to connect with customers as they adapt their buying to the changing economic times. Bad times are "when winners and losers get created," says Xerox CEO Anne Mulcahy. "The ability to reinforce great marketing and great brand is extraordinarily important." John Hayes, CEO of American Express, agrees: "The world will pass you by if you are not constantly innovating."[4]

Yet innovation can be very expensive and very risky. New products face tough odds. According to one estimate, 80 percent of all new products fail or dramatically underperform. Each year, companies lose an estimated $20 billion to $30 billion on failed food products alone.[5]

THE NEW-PRODUCT DEVELOPMENT PROCESS

Companies face a problem—they must develop new products, but the odds weigh heavily against success. In all, to create successful new products, a company must understand its consumers, markets, and competitors and develop products that deliver superior value to customers. It must carry out strong new-

New-product development
The development of original products, product improvements, product modifications, and new brands through the firm's own product-development efforts.

Exhibit 8.3   New products that failed: NewProductWorks of Ann Arbor, Michigan, manages a collection of failed products in a 687 square metre state-of-the-art facility.

product planning and set up a systematic, customer-driven *new-product development process* for finding and growing new products. This process consists of eight major stages (see Figure 8.2).

Idea Generation   New-product development starts with **idea generation**—the systematic search for new-product ideas. A company typically generates hundreds of ideas, even thousands, in order to find a few good ones. Major sources of new-product ideas include internal sources and external sources such as customers, competitors, distributors and suppliers, and others.

> **Idea generation**
> The systematic search for new-product ideas.

Companies can also obtain good new-product ideas from any of a number of external sources. For example, *distributors and suppliers* can contribute ideas. Distributors are close to the market and can pass along information about consumer problems and new-product possibilities. Suppliers can tell the company about new concepts, techniques, and materials that can be used to develop new products. *Competitors* are another important source. Companies watch competitors' ads to get clues about their new products. They buy competing new products, take them apart to see how they work, analyze their sales, and decide whether they should bring out a new product of their own. Other idea sources include trade magazines, shows, and seminars; government agencies; advertising agencies; marketing research firms; university and commercial laboratories; and inventors.

Perhaps the most important source of new-product ideas is *customers* themselves. The company can analyze customer questions and complaints to find new products that better solve consumer problems. For example, Staples developed its Easy Rebate program online in response to concerns expressed by small-business customers that lost paper rebates were one of their biggest frustrations.[6] Or a company can actively solicit ideas from customers. For example, Dell's IdeaStorm website asks consumers for insights on how to improve the company's product offering. Users post suggestions, the community votes, and the most popular ideas rise to the top. Since its launch in 2007, the site has received over 11 000 ideas and 650 000 votes.[7]

Idea Screening   The purpose of idea generation is to create a large number of ideas. The purpose of the succeeding stages is to *reduce* that number. The first idea-reducing stage is **idea screening**, which helps spot good ideas and drop poor ones as soon as possible. Product development costs rise greatly in later stages, so the company wants to go ahead only with the product ideas that will turn into profitable products.

> **Idea screening**
> Screening new-product ideas to spot good ideas and drop poor ones as soon as possible.

Many companies require their executives to write up new-product ideas in a standard format that can be reviewed by a new-product committee. The write-up describes the product or service, the proposed customer value proposition, the target market, and the competition. It makes some rough estimates of market size, product price, development time and costs, manufacturing costs, and rate of return. The committee then evaluates the idea against a set of general criteria.

FIGURE 8.2   Major stages in new-product development

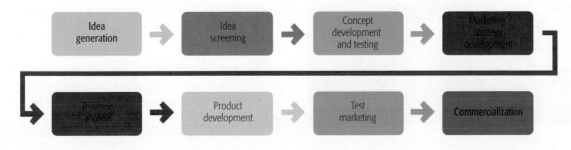

One marketing expert proposes an R-W-W ("real, win, worth it") new-product screening framework that asks three questions. First, *Is it real?* Is there a real need and desire for the product and will customers buy it? Is there a clear product concept and will the product satisfy the market? Second, *Can we win?* Does the product offer a sustainable competitive advantage? Does the company have the resources to make the product a success? Finally, *Is it worth doing?* Does the product fit the company's overall growth strategy? Does it offer sufficient profit potential? The company should be able to answer yes to all three R-W-W questions before developing the new-product idea further.[8]

Concept Development and Testing

Once the company has generated, and then screened, new-product ideas, the next step is to develop those ideas into a product concept. Whereas a product idea is an idea for a possible product that the company can potentially offer to the market, a **product concept** is a detailed description, drawing, or prototype of that idea that can be shown to potential customers. That product concept must then be developed and tested, that is, the new product idea is developed in various alternative forms, and tested with a group of potential customers.

Car manufacturers are well known for showing their concept cars at auto shows. Concept cars are real cars that can be driven; however, they are not yet in production, which means they are not yet available to the public. Concept cars are displayed at auto shows so that the automobile marketers can gauge the market's response to their product concept. For example, the Tesla Roadster, an electric car manufactured and marketed by Tesla Motors of California, spent years in the early stages of the new-product development process, and was advertised while still in the concept development stage.

For some concept tests, a word or picture description might be sufficient; however, a more concrete and physical presentation of the concept, such as a model, will increase the reliability of the concept test.

Marketing Strategy Development

After the product concept has been tested with members of the target market, and their opinions about the concept have been collected, the next step in the product development process is to design the marketing strategy. **Marketing strategy development** involves designing an initial marketing strategy for a new product based on the product concept. The strategy must answer questions about how, when, where, and to whom the product will be introduced.

The *marketing strategy statement* consists of three parts. The first part describes the target market; the planned value proposition; and the sales, market share, and profit goals for the first few years. Here is an example of the marketing strategy for the Tesla Roadster:

The target market is younger, well-educated, moderate- to high-income individuals, couples, or small families seeking practical, environmentally responsible transportation. The car will be positioned as more fun to drive and less polluting than today's internal combustion engine or hybrid cars. The company will aim to sell 100 000 cars in the first year, at a loss of not more than $15 million. In the second year, the company will aim for sales of 120 000 cars and a profit of $25 million.

The second part of the marketing strategy statement outlines the product's planned price, distribution, and marketing budget for the first year. For example,

Product concept
A detailed version of the new-product idea stated in meaningful consumer terms.

Marketing strategy development
Designing an initial marketing strategy for a new product based on the product concept.

Exhibit 8.4   Concept development and testing: Cars spend years in the concept development and testing phase, during which marketers use various means to gauge the market interest in the product. The Tesla electric car, for example, was advertised in magazines long before it was actually available on the market.

The Tesla Roadster will be offered in three colours—red, silver, and black—and will have a full set of accessories as standard features. It will sell at a retail price of $25 000—with 15 percent off the list price to dealers. Dealers who sell more than 10 cars per month will get an additional discount of 5 percent on each car sold that month. A marketing budget of $50 million will be split 50-50 between a national media campaign and local event marketing. Advertising and a website will emphasize the car's fun spirit and low emissions. During the first year, $100 000 will be spent on marketing research to find out who is buying the car and their satisfaction levels.

The third part of the marketing strategy statement describes the planned long-run sales, profit goals, and marketing mix strategy:

We hope the Tesla Roadster will capture a 3 percent long-run share of the total auto market and realize an after-tax return on investment of 15 percent. To achieve this, product quality will start high and be improved over time. Price will be raised in the second and third years if competition permits. The total marketing budget will be raised each year by about 10 percent. Marketing research will be reduced to $60 000 per year after the first year.

Business Analysis   Once management has decided on its product concept and marketing strategy, it can evaluate the business attractiveness of the proposal. **Business analysis** involves a review of the sales, costs, and profit projections for a new product to find out whether they satisfy the company's objectives. If they do, the product can move to the product development stage.

Business analysis
A review of the sales, costs, and profit projections for a new product to find out whether these factors satisfy the company's objectives.

To estimate sales, the company might look at the sales history of similar products and conduct market surveys. It can then estimate minimum and maximum sales to assess the range of risk. After preparing the sales forecast, management can estimate the expected costs and profits for the product, including marketing, R&D, operations, accounting, and finance costs. The company then uses the sales and costs figures to analyze the new product's financial attractiveness.

Product Development   So far, for many new-product concepts, the product may have existed only as a word description, a drawing, or perhaps a crude mock-up. If the product concept passes the business test, it moves into **product development**. Here, R&D or engineering develops the product concept into a physical product. The product development step, however, now calls for a large jump in investment. It will show whether the product idea can be turned into a workable product.

Product development
Developing the product concept into a physical product to ensure that the product idea can be turned into a workable market offering.

The R&D department will develop and test one or more physical versions of the product concept. R&D hopes to design a prototype that will satisfy and excite consumers and that can be produced quickly and at budgeted costs. Developing a successful prototype can take days, weeks, months, or even years depending on the product and prototype methods.

Often, products undergo rigorous tests to make sure that they perform safely and effectively, or that consumers will find value in them. Companies can do their own product testing or outsource testing to other firms that specialize in testing. For example, every working day at Gillette, 200 employees from various departments come to work unshaven, and act as test subjects to evaluate the company's newest razors, shaving cream, and aftershave.[9]

A new product must have the required functional features and also convey the intended psychological characteristics. The battery-powered electric car, for example, should strike consumers as being well built, comfortable, and safe. Management must learn what makes consumers decide that a car is well built. To some consumers, this means that the car has "solid-sounding" doors. To others, it means that the car is able to withstand heavy impact in crash tests. Consumer tests are conducted in which consumers test drive the car and rate its attributes.

Exhibit 8.5   Test-marketing: KFC test-marketed its new Kentucky Grilled Chicken product for three years before rolling it out to a larger market.

Test-marketing
The stage of new-product development in which the product and marketing program are tested in realistic market settings.

Commercialization
The full-scale introduction of the new product into the market.

Test-Marketing   If the product passes concept and product tests, the next step is **test-marketing**, the stage at which the product and marketing program are introduced into realistic market settings. Test-marketing gives the marketer experience with marketing the product before going to the great expense of full introduction. It lets the company test the product and its entire marketing program—targeting and positioning strategy, advertising, distribution, pricing, branding and packaging, and budget levels.

The amount of test-marketing needed varies with each new product. When the costs of developing and introducing the product are low, or when management is already confident about the new product, the company may do little or no test-marketing. Companies often do not test-market simple line extensions or copies of successful competitor products. However, when introducing a new product requires a big investment, when the risks are high, or when management is not sure of the product or the marketing program, a company may do a lot of test-marketing. For instance, KFC conducted more than three years of product and market testing before rolling out its major new Kentucky Grilled Chicken product. The fast-food chain built its legacy on serving crispy, seasoned fried chicken but hopes that the new product will lure back health-conscious consumers who dropped fried chicken from their diets. "This is transformational for our brand," says KFC's chief food innovation officer. Given the importance of the decision, "You might say, 'what took you so long,'" says the chain's president. "I've asked that question a couple of times myself. The answer is we had to get it right."[10]

Commercialization   The final step in the new-product development process is **commercialization**, or the full-scale introduction of the product into the market. If the company goes ahead with this stage, it will face high costs. For example, in the case of a major new consumer packaged-good, millions of dollars will be spent in advertising and

Exhibit 8.6   Commercialization: The first customers to take delivery of a Honda FCX Clarity were Ron Yerxa and Annette Ballester, at Honda of Santa Monica.

promotion. And in the case of a product as large and expensive as a car, entire distribution networks may need to be established. The Tesla electric car was finally commercialized in 2008, and today there are Tesla Stores opening all over the United States and in Europe, and one recently opened in the upscale Yorkville neighbourhood of Toronto.

The commercialization of the Honda FCX Clarity, the first hydrogen fuel cell–powered vehicle, began in 2008, and many of the first customers were Hollywood celebrities. Although the commercialization of the Honda FCX Clarity began on a small scale, it was not a test-market program. The owners of the cars, despite being celebrities, were real consumers, not test subjects. However, the car is very expensive, and requires a new type of fuelling station. Whether or not the car will be marketed outside California remains to be seen.

Thus, we see that the new-product development process is customer-centred, from idea generation to commercialization. Successful innovation boils down to finding fresh ways to meet the needs of customers—see Marketing@Work 8.1 for a great example of customer-centred new-product development.

MANAGING NEW-PRODUCT DEVELOPMENT

The new-product development process shown in Figure 8.2 highlights the important activities needed to find, develop, and introduce new products. However, new-product development involves more than just going through a set of steps. Companies must take a holistic approach to managing this process. Successful new-product development requires a *customer-centred*, *team-based*, and *systematic* effort.

Above all else, new-product development must be customer-centred. When looking for and developing new products, companies often rely too heavily on technical research in their R&D labs. But like everything else in marketing, successful new-product development begins with a thorough understanding of what consumers need and value.

One study found that the most successful new products are differentiated, solve major customer problems, and offer a compelling customer value proposition. Another study showed that companies that directly engage their customers in the new-product innovation process had twice the return on assets and triple the growth in operating income of firms that don't.[11]

Good new-product development also requires a total-company, cross-functional effort. Some companies organize their new-product development process into the orderly sequence of steps shown in Figure 8.2, starting with idea generation and ending with commercialization. Under this *sequential product development* approach, one company department works individually to complete its stage of the process before passing the new product along to the next department and stage. This orderly, step-by-step process can help bring control to complex and risky projects. But it can also be dangerously slow. In fast-changing, highly competitive markets, such slow-but-sure product development can result in product failures, lost sales and profits, and crumbling market positions.

To get their new products to market more quickly, many companies use a team-based new-product development approach. Under this approach, company departments work closely together in cross-functional teams, overlapping the steps in the product development process to save time and increase effectiveness. Instead of passing the new product from department to department, the company assembles a team of people from various departments that stays with the new product from start to finish. Such teams usually include people from the marketing, finance, design, manufacturing, and legal departments, and even supplier and customer companies. In the sequential process, a bottleneck at one phase can seriously slow the entire project. In the team-based approach, if one area hits snags, it works to resolve them while the team moves on. Samsung's Value Innovation Program (VIP) Center is an example of the team-based approach to new-product development.

MARKETING@WORK 8.1

IDEO's Design Approach: Putting Customers First

IDEO is a global industrial design firm that has won countless awards for innovative product design. Its roster of clients includes Apple, Microsoft, Marriott, Procter & Gamble, and Lufthansa. IDEO's design teams came up with the first laptop computer; the first Apple mouse; the industry-changing, sleek and elegant Palm V PDA; and even Crest's first standup toothpaste tube.

But it's not so much IDEO's innovative designs that make it stand out. It's IDEO's design *process*. In designing new products, IDEO doesn't start with engineers working in design labs. It starts with customers. And it doesn't just design products, it designs customer product *experiences*. At the start of every design project, IDEO's "human factors" teams conduct "deep dives" into consumer behaviour. The design teams shadow customers, get to know them deeply, and analyze the intricacies of their product-use experiences. "Tech companies design from the inside out," says an IDEO executive. "We design from the outside in so that we can put customers first."

IDEO's work with bicycle components maker Shimano illustrates its customer-centred design approach. Shimano sells bike parts—such as gears, crank arms, and derailleurs—to most of the world's major bicycle manufacturers. If you own a high-end bike, chances are good that it contains several Shimano parts. But in 2006, Shimano faced a problem. Bicycle manufacturers were selling fewer bikes, so Shimano was selling fewer parts. So Shimano turned to IDEO for help. IDEO's challenge? Design a premium bike that would get Baby Boomers and older Gen-Xers riding again. But IDEO didn't follow the usual industry design process—using computer models to turn out great-looking new high-tech marvels and then testing them out on bike-riding enthusiasts. Instead, IDEO began by sending its design team into the homes of people who *don't* ride bikes to look for insights. Here's what they learned:

> It wasn't so much that they were out of shape, or too busy or lazy. It was because cycling had become intimidating, something for hard-core athletes who love all the

technical minutiae. "Everything had changed in bicycling," says a senior Shimano marketing executive. "It had gone from fun to being a sport, and no one [in the industry] had noticed." For Boomers, bikes changed from the 10-speed rides on steel frame bikes to 30-speed carbon fiber and titanium machines. Costs rose from a few hundred dollars to thousands. Handlebars, pedals, tires, even seats came in so many varieties that consumers got overwhelmed. Expensive helmets, special shoes, and tight-fitting spandex clothes simply didn't appeal to recreational riders. And bike shops, filled with workers who fawned over gear, had little time for customers interested in just plain bikes.

Based on these customer insights, IDEO and Shimano came up with the concept of a "coasting" bike—a bicycle with a classic look that is simple, comfortable, and fun to use. Shimano built a prototype and sold the concept to three top bike manufacturers—Giant, Raleigh, and Trek. Coasting bikes are designed to create the ideal casual biking experience. They feature a traditional heads-up riding position, wide and comfortable seats, a chain guard to keep grease off the cyclist's pants, and old-fashioned coaster brakes that stop when you pedal backwards. The coasting bikes are high-tech—for example, they come equipped with computer-controlled automatic gear shifting. But the technology remains hidden behind soft and familiar contours.

Eventually, the manufacturers rolled out their first lines of coasting bikes, supported by a Shimano marketing campaign. The launch created more excitement than anything most industry insiders can remember. Surprised bicycle retailers soon found non-cyclists making their way into their stores, and the three manufacturers quickly sold out of their inventories. The new designs appear to have hit the high-end casual biking market spot-on. "The automatic shifting [has really resonated] with customers," says one bicycle shop owner. "Shimano is onto something."

Exhibit 8.7   Customer-centred new-product development: With the help of design firm IDEO, Shimano and bicycle makers such as Trek created coasting bikes that are simple, comfortable, and fun to use.

Despite their initial success, it remains to be seen whether coasting bikes will be real industry-changers or just a passing fad. But whatever happens, IDEO's customer-driven design ideas are opening eyes in the traditionally myopic bicycle industry. IDEO knows that bike riding has never really been about the bikes themselves. In the end, it's about customer biking experiences.

Sources: Extracts, quotes, and other information from Matt Wiebe, "Retailers Worry Over Future Coasting Sales," *Bicycle Retailer and Industry News*, March 15, 2008, pp. 1, 2; Jay Green, "Return of the Easy Rider," *BusinessWeek*, September 17, 2007, p. 78; Jessi Hempel, "Bringing Design to Blue Chips," *Fortune*, November 12, 2007, p. 32; Adam Voiland, "Slew of New Commuter Bikes Offer an Easier Ride," *U.S. News & World Report*, August 18, 2008, p. 62; Linda Tischler, "A Designer Takes on His Biggest Challenge Ever," *Fast Company*, February 2009, pp. 76–83; and *www.coasting.com*, accessed November 2009.

The VIP Center is the total opposite of Samsung's typical office facilities—which feature grey computers on grey desks inside grey walls—where workers adhere to strict Confucian traditions and would never dream of questioning a superior or making a wacky suggestion. Instead, the VIP Center features workrooms, dorm rooms, training rooms, a kitchen, and a basement filled with games, a gym, and sauna. Grass sprouts from the ceilings, doors are covered with funhouse mirrors, and walls are covered with chalk drawings of ideas. Inside, Samsung researchers, engineers, and designers sport Viking and bumblebee hats, play with Elmo toys and inflatable dolphins, and throw around ideas without regard to rank. Recent ideas sprouting from the VIP Center include a 102-inch plasma HDTV and a process to reduce material costs on a multi-function printer by 30 percent. The VIP Center has helped Samsung, once known as the maker of cheap knock-off products, become one of the world's most innovative and profitable consumer electronics companies.[12]

Exhibit 8.8 Team-based new-product development: Samsung's Value Innovation Program Center lets company researchers, engineers, and designers commingle to come up with creative new product ideas.

Finally, the new-product development process should be holistic and systematic rather than compartmentalized and haphazard. Otherwise, few new ideas will surface, and many good ideas will sputter and die.

THE PRODUCT LIFE CYCLE ⬤LO3

New-product success requires more than simply thinking up a few good ideas, turning them into products, and finding customers for them. It requires a holistic approach for finding new ways to create valued customer experiences, from generating and screening new-product ideas to creating and rolling out want-satisfying products to customers. And managing new products as they develop, are introduced to market, and grow requires an understanding of the "life cycle" of new products.

After launching the new product, a company wants the product to enjoy a long and happy life—and although it does not expect the product to sell forever, the company does expect the product to earn a profit sufficient to cover all the effort and risk that went into launching it. Marketing managers must understand that each product launched in the market will have a life cycle. The **product life cycle**, or PLC, is the course that a product's sales and profits take over its lifetime. The product life cycle has five distinct stages, as illustrated in Figure 8.3.

Product life cycle

The course of a product's sales and profits over its lifetime. It involves five distinct stages: product development, introduction, growth, maturity, and decline.

1. *Product development* begins when the company finds and develops a new-product idea. During product development, sales are zero and the company's investment costs mount.

2. *Introduction* is a period of slow sales growth as the product is introduced in the market. Profits are non-existent in this stage because of the heavy expenses of product introduction.

3. *Growth* is a period of rapid market acceptance and increasing profits.

4. *Maturity* is a period of slowdown in sales growth because the product has achieved acceptance by most potential buyers. Profits level off or decline because of increased marketing outlays to defend the product against competition.

5. *Decline* is the period when sales fall off and profits drop.

Not all products follow this product life cycle. Some products are introduced and die quickly; others stay in the mature stage for a long, long time. Some enter the decline stage and are then cycled back into the growth stage through strong promotion or repositioning. It seems that a well-managed brand could live forever. Such venerable brands as Coca-Cola, Gillette, and Tabasco, for instance, are still going strong after more than 100 years.

The PLC concept can describe a *product class* (gasoline-powered automobiles), a *product form* (SUVs), or a *brand* (the Ford Escape). The PLC concept applies differently in each case. Product classes have the longest life cycles—the sales of many product classes stay in the mature stage for a long time. Product forms, in contrast, tend to have the standard PLC shape. Product forms such as dial telephones and videotapes passed through a regular history of introduction, rapid growth, maturity, and decline.

A specific brand's life cycle can change quickly because of changing competitive attacks and responses. For example, although laundry soaps (product class) and powdered detergents (product form) have enjoyed fairly long life cycles, the life cycles of specific brands have tended to be much shorter. Today's leading brands of powdered laundry soap are Tide and Cheer; the leading brands almost 100 years ago were Fels-Naptha, Octagon, and Kirkman.

The PLC concept also can be applied to what are known as styles, fashions, and fads. Their special life cycles are shown in Figure 8.4. A **style** is a basic and distinctive mode of expression. For example, styles appear in homes (colonial, ranch, transitional), clothing (formal, casual), and art (realist, surrealist, abstract). Once a style is invented, it may last for generations, passing in and out of vogue. A style has a cycle showing several periods of renewed interest. A **fashion** is a currently accepted or popular style in a given field. For example, the more formal business attire of corporate dress of the 1980s and 1990s gave way to the business casual look of today. Fashions tend to grow slowly, remain popular for a while, and then decline slowly.

Style
A basic and distinctive mode of expression.

Fashion
A currently accepted or popular style in a given field.

FIGURE 8.3 Sales and profits over the product's life from inception to decline

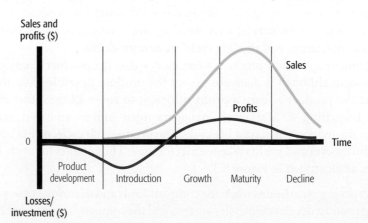

Fads are temporary periods of unusually high sales driven by consumer enthusiasm and immediate product or brand popularity.[13] A fad may be part of an otherwise normal life cycle, as in the case of recent surges in the sales of poker chips and accessories. Or the fad may comprise a brand's or product's entire life cycle. "Pet rocks" are a classic example. Upon hearing his friends complain about how expensive it was to care for their dogs, advertising copywriter Gary Dahl joked about his pet rock. He soon wrote a spoof of a dog-training manual for it, titled "The Care and Training of Your Pet Rock." Soon Dahl was selling some 1.5 million ordinary beach pebbles at $4 a pop. Yet the fad, which broke one October, had sunk like a stone by the next February. Dahl's advice to those who want to succeed with a fad: "Enjoy it while it lasts." Some fads of the 2000s include the Big Mouth Billy Bass, razor scooters, flash mobs, Sudoku puzzles, and Bratz dolls.[14]

Marketers can apply the PLC concept as a useful framework for describing how products and markets work. And when used carefully, the PLC concept can help in developing good marketing strategies for different stages of the product life cycle. But using the PLC concept for forecasting product performance or for developing marketing strategies presents some practical problems. For example, in practice, it is difficult to forecast the sales level at each PLC stage, the length of each stage, and the shape of the PLC curve. Using the PLC concept to develop marketing strategy also can be difficult because strategy is both a cause and a result of the product's life cycle. The product's current PLC position suggests the best marketing strategies, and the resulting marketing strategies affect product performance in later life-cycle stages.

Moreover, marketers should not blindly push products through the traditional stages of the product life cycle. Instead, marketers often defy the "rules" of the life cycle and position or reposition their products in unexpected ways. By doing this, they can rescue mature or declining products and return them to the growth phase of the life cycle. Or they can leapfrog obstacles to slow consumer acceptance and propel new products forward into the growth phase.

The moral of the product life cycle is that companies must continually innovate or they risk extinction. No matter how successful its current product lineup, for future success, a company must skilfully manage the life cycles of existing products. And to grow, it must develop a steady stream of new products that bring new value to customers.

STAGES OF THE PRODUCT LIFE CYCLE

We looked at the product-development stage of the product life cycle earlier in this chapter. We now look at strategies for each of the other life-cycle stages.

The **introduction stage** starts when the new product is first launched. Introduction takes time, and sales growth is apt to be slow. Well-known products such as instant coffee, frozen foods, and HDTVs lingered for many years before they entered a stage of more rapid growth.

Fad
A temporary period of unusually high sales driven by consumer enthusiasm and immediate product or brand popularity.

Introduction stage
The product life-cycle stage in which the new product is first distributed and made available for purchase.

FIGURE 8.4   Styles, fashions, and fads

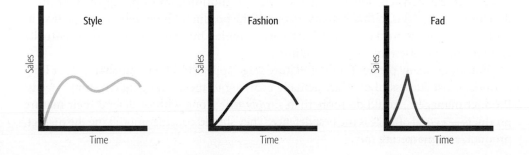

In this stage, as compared to other stages, profits are negative or low because of the low sales and high distribution and promotion expenses. Much money is needed to attract distributors and build their inventories. Promotion spending is relatively high to inform consumers of the new product and get them to try it. Because the market is not generally ready for product refinements at this stage, the company and its few competitors produce basic versions of the product. These firms focus their selling on those buyers who are the most ready to buy.

A company, especially the *market pioneer*, must choose a launch strategy that is consistent with the intended product positioning. It should realize that the initial strategy is just the first step in a grander marketing plan for the product's entire life cycle. If the pioneer chooses its launch strategy to make a "killing," it may be sacrificing long-run revenue for the sake of short-run gain. As the pioneer moves through later stages of the life cycle, it must continuously formulate new pricing, promotion, and other marketing strategies. It has the best chance of building and retaining market leadership if it plays its cards correctly from the start.

Growth stage
The product life-cycle stage in which a product's sales start climbing quickly.

If the new product satisfies the market, it will enter a **growth stage**, in which sales will start climbing quickly. The early adopters will continue to buy, and later buyers will start following their lead, especially if they hear favourable word of mouth. Attracted by the opportunities for profit, new competitors will enter the market. They will introduce new product features, and the market will expand. The increase in competitors leads to an increase in the number of distribution outlets, and sales jump just to build reseller inventories. Prices remain where they are or fall only slightly. Companies keep their promotion spending at the same or a slightly higher level. Educating the market remains a goal, but now the company must also meet the competition.

Profits increase during the growth stage as promotion costs are spread over a large volume and as unit manufacturing costs fall. The firm uses several strategies to sustain rapid market growth as long as possible. It improves product quality and adds new product features and models. It enters new market segments and new distribution channels. It shifts some advertising from building product awareness to building product conviction and purchase, and it lowers prices at the right time to attract more buyers.

In the growth stage, the firm faces a trade-off between high market share and high current profit. By spending a lot of money on product improvement, promotion, and distribution, the company can capture a dominant position. In doing so, however, it gives up maximum current profit, which it hopes to make up in the next stage.

Maturity stage
The product life-cycle stage in which sales growth slows or levels off.

At some point, a product's sales growth will slow down, and the product will enter a **maturity stage**. This maturity stage normally lasts longer than the previous stages, and it poses strong challenges to marketing management. Most products are in the maturity stage of the life cycle, and therefore most of marketing management deals with the mature product.

The slowdown in sales growth results in many producers with many products to sell. In turn, this overcapacity leads to greater competition. Competitors begin marking down prices, increasing their advertising and sales promotions, and upping their product development budgets to find better versions of the product. These steps lead to a drop in profit. Some of the weaker competitors start dropping out, and the industry eventually contains only well-established competitors.

Although many products in the mature stage appear to remain unchanged for long periods, most successful ones are actually evolving to meet changing consumer needs. Product managers should do more than simply ride along with or defend their mature products—a good offence is the best defence. They should consider modifying the market, product, and marketing mix.

In *modifying the market*, the company tries to increase consumption by finding new users and new market segments for its brands. For example, mature 101-year-old card maker American Greetings is now reaching younger consumers through social-networking widgets and instant-messaging channels.[15]

Women buy 80 percent of the greeting cards in the United States, and their median age is 47—not exactly the Facebook crowd. To younger buyers in this digital age, a snail-mail card is as antiquated as getting a $5 birthday check from your grandmother. So to make its brand more youthful, American Greetings created Kiwee.com, a repository for emoticons, video winks, postcards, graphics, widgets, and glitter text for all the major social-networking sites and instant-messaging services. A 47-year-old housewife may not be interested in the winking-turd emoticon that her 15-year-old son adores, but "we sell emotions," says AG Interactive's (AGI) chief technology officer. "Even younger people need help saying better what they want to say." Kiwee.com content is now being downloaded 1.2 million times per day, signaling American Greetings' adjustment to a segment where paper cards are passé. Young folks may not send paper anymore, but being remembered—that's universal.

The manager may also look for ways to increase usage among present customers. For example, Glad Products Company helps customers to find new uses for its Press'n Seal wrap, the plastic wrap that creates a Tupperware-like seal. As more and more customers contacted the company about alternative uses for the product, Glad set up a special "1000s of Uses. What's Yours?" website (www.1000uses.com) at which customers can swap usage tips. "We found out our heavy users use it for a lot more than just covering food," says a Glad brand manager. "And they all became heavy users when they had an 'aha' moment with Press'n Seal." Suggested uses for Press'n Seal range from protecting a computer keyboard from dirt and spills and keeping garden seeds fresh to soccer moms using it on damp benches before sitting down to watch their tykes play. "We just roll out the Glad Press'n Seal over the long benches," says the mom who shared the tip, "and everyone's bottom stays nice and dry."[16]

The company might also try *modifying the product*—changing characteristics such as quality, features, style, or packaging to attract new users and inspire more usage. It can improve the product's styling and attractiveness. It might improve the product's quality and performance—its durability, reliability, speed, and taste. Thus, makers of consumer food and household products introduce new flavours, colours, scents, ingredients, or packages to enhance performance and revitalize consumer buying.

Decline stage
The product life-cycle stage in which a product's sales decline.

Finally, the company can try *modifying the marketing mix*—improving sales by changing one or more marketing mix elements. The company can offer new or improved services to buyers. It can cut prices to attract new users and competitors' customers. It can launch a better advertising campaign or use aggressive sales promotions—trade deals, cents-off, premiums, and contests. In addition to pricing and promotion, the company can also move into new marketing channels to help serve new users.

The sales of most product forms and brands eventually dip. The decline may be slow, as in the case of oatmeal cereal, or rapid, as in the cases of cassette and VHS tapes. Sales may plunge to zero, or they may drop to a low level where they continue for many years. This is the **decline stage**.

Exhibit 8.9 Decline stage: Media storage products such as floppy disks and VHS tapes are in the decline stage of the product life cycle. They are being replaced with new media storage products such as flash drives and external hard drives, which will also grow, mature, and eventually decline.

Sales decline for many reasons, including technological advances, shifts in consumer tastes, and increased competition. As sales and profits decline, some firms withdraw from the market. Those remaining may prune their product offerings. They may drop smaller market segments and marginal trade channels, or they may cut the promotion budget and reduce their prices further.

Carrying a weak product can be very costly to a firm, and not just in profit terms. There are many hidden costs. A weak product may take up too much of management's time. It often requires frequent price and inventory adjustments. It requires advertising and sales-force attention that might be better used to make "healthy" products more profitable. A product's failing reputation can cause customer concerns about the company and its other products. The biggest cost may well lie in the future. Keeping weak products delays the search for replacements, creates a lopsided product mix, hurts current profits, and weakens the company's foothold on the future.

For these reasons, companies need to pay more attention to their aging products. A firm's first task is to identify those products in the decline stage by regularly reviewing sales, market shares, costs, and profit trends. Then, management must decide whether to maintain, harvest, or drop each of these declining products.

Management may decide to *maintain* its brand without change in the hope that competitors will leave the industry. For example, P&G made good profits by remaining in the declining liquid soap business as others withdrew. Another strategy for managing products as they decline is to reposition them and try to appeal to a new market segment. For example TAB, the original diet soda, had practically disappeared from the market before being repositioned as an energy drink for women; and Old Spice, known for years as your father's aftershave, recently launched a new marketing campaign in Canada to appeal to a younger generation of men.

Management may decide to *harvest* the product, which means reducing various costs (plant and equipment, maintenance, R&D, advertising, sales force) and hoping that sales hold up. If successful, harvesting will increase the company's profits in the short run. Or management may decide to *drop* the product from the line. It can sell it to another firm or simply liquidate it at salvage value. In recent years, P&G has sold off a number of lesser or declining brands such as Crisco oil, Comet cleanser, Sure deodorant, and Duncan Hines cake mixes. If the company plans to find a buyer, it will not want to run down the product through harvesting.

Table 8.2 summarizes the key characteristics of each stage of the product life cycle. The table also lists the marketing objectives and strategies for each stage.[17]

PRODUCT AND SERVICE DECISIONS (LO4)

Marketers make product and service decisions at three levels. At the first level, they make individual product decisions, which include decisions about product attributes such as *quality*, *features*, and *style and design*, as well as decisions about packaging, labelling, and product support services for each product. At the next level are decisions about product lines, or groups of products. Finally, marketers make decisions about the company's overall product portfolio, or product mix.

INDIVIDUAL PRODUCT AND SERVICE DECISIONS

The important decisions in the development and marketing of individual products and services include decisions about *product attributes*, *packaging*, *labelling*, and *product support* services.

TABLE 8.2   Summary of Product Life-Cycle Characteristics, Objectives, and Strategies

Characteristics	Introduction	Growth	Maturity	Decline
Sales	Low sales	Rapidly rising sales	Peak sales	Declining sales
Costs	High cost per customer	Average cost per customer	Low cost per customer	Low cost per customer
Profits	Negative	Rising profits	High profits	Declining profits
Customers	Innovators	Early adopters	Middle majority	Laggards
Competitors	Few	Growing number	Stable number beginning to decline	Declining number
Marketing Objectives				
	Create product awareness and trial	Maximize market share	Maximize profit while defending market share	Reduce expenditure and milk the brand
Strategies				
Product	Offer a basic product	Offer product extensions, service, warranty	Diversify brand and models	Phase out weak items
Price	Use cost-plus	Price to penetrate market	Price to match or beat competitors	Cut price
Distribution	Build selective distribution	Build intensive distribution	Build more intensive distribution	Go selective: phase out unprofitable outlets
Advertising	Build product awareness among early adopters and dealers	Build awareness and interest in the mass market	Stress brand differences and benefits	Reduce to level needed to retain hard-core loyals
Sales Promotion	Use heavy sales promotion to entice trial	Reduce to take advantage of heavy consumer demand	Increase to encourage brand switching	Reduce to minimal level

Source: Philip Kotler and Kevin Lane Keller, *Marketing Management,* 13th ed. (Upper Saddle River, NJ: Prentice Hall, 2009), p. 288.

Product and Service Attributes   Developing a product or service involves defining the benefits that it will offer. These benefits are communicated and delivered by product attributes such as *quality, features,* and *style and design.*

PRODUCT QUALITY   Product quality is one of the marketer's major positioning tools. Quality has a direct impact on product or service performance; thus, it is closely linked to customer value and satisfaction. In the narrowest sense, quality can be defined as "freedom from defects." But most customer-centred companies go beyond this narrow definition. Instead, they define quality in terms of creating customer value and satisfaction. Product quality is a serious matter for marketers, many of whom belong to the Society of Quality Assurance (SQA), an international professional membership organization that provides a forum for organizations to exchange information about research and regulations that govern quality assurance practices.

   Total quality management (TQM) is an approach in which all the company's people are involved in constantly improving the quality of products, services, and business processes. For most top companies, customer-driven quality has become a way of doing

Product quality

The characteristics of a product or a service that bear on its ability to satisfy stated or implied customer needs.

business. Today, companies are taking a "return on quality" approach, viewing quality as an investment and holding quality efforts accountable for bottom-line results.

Product quality has two dimensions—level and consistency. In developing a product, the marketer must first choose a *quality level* that will support the product's positioning. Here, product quality means *performance quality*—the ability of a product to perform its functions. For example, a Rolls-Royce provides higher performance quality than a Honda: It has a smoother ride, provides more "creature comforts," and lasts longer. Companies rarely try to offer the highest possible performance quality level—few customers want or can afford the high levels of quality offered in products such as a Rolls-Royce automobile, an LG refrigerator (with built-in computer screen), or a Rolex watch. Instead, companies choose a quality level that matches target market needs and the quality levels of competing products.

Beyond quality level, high quality also can mean high levels of quality consistency. Here, product quality means *conformance quality*—freedom from defects and *consistency* in delivering a targeted level of performance. All companies should strive for high levels of conformance quality. In this sense, a Honda Civic Sedan can have just as much quality as a Rolls-Royce Phantom. Although the Honda doesn't perform at the same level as the Rolls-Royce, it delivers the level of quality that customers pay for and expect.

PRODUCT FEATURES   A product can be offered with varying features. A stripped-down model, one without any extras, is the starting point. The company can create higher-level models by adding more features. Features are a competitive tool for differentiating the company's product from competitors' products. Being the first producer to introduce a valued new feature is one of the most effective ways to compete.

How can a company identify new features and decide which ones to add to its product? The company should periodically survey buyers who have used the product and ask these questions: How do you like the product? Which specific features of the product do you like most? Which features could we add to improve the product? The answers provide the company with a rich list of feature ideas. The company can then assess each feature's *value* to customers versus its *cost* to the company. Features that customers value highly in relation to costs should be added.

PRODUCT STYLE AND DESIGN   Another way to add customer value is through distinctive *product style and design*. Design is a larger concept than style. *Style* simply describes the appearance of a product. Styles can be eye-catching or yawn producing. A sensational style may grab attention and produce pleasing aesthetics, but it does not necessarily make the product *perform* better. Unlike style, *design* is more than skin deep—it goes to the very heart of a product. Good design contributes to a product's usefulness as well as to its looks.

Good design doesn't start with brainstorming new ideas and making prototypes. Design begins with observing customers and developing a deep understanding of their needs. More than simply creating product or service attributes, it involves shaping the customer's product-use experience. Product designers should think less about product attributes and technical specifications and more about how customers will use and benefit from the product. Consider OXO's outstanding design philosophy and process:[18]

> OXO's uniquely designed kitchen and gardening gadgets look pretty cool. But to OXO, good design means a lot more than good looks. It means that OXO tools work—*really* work—for anyone and everyone. "Oxo is practically the definition of 'good experience,'" notes one observer. For OXO, design means a salad spinner that can be used with one hand; tools with pressure-absorbing, nonslip handles that make them more efficient; or a watering can with a spout that rotates back toward the body, allowing for easier filling and storing. Ever since it came out with its supereffective Good Grips vegetable peeler in 1990, OXO has been known for clever designs that make everyday living easier.

Packaging   **Packaging** involves designing and producing the container or wrapper for a product. Traditionally, the primary function of the package was to hold and protect the product. In recent times, however, numerous factors have made packaging an important marketing tool as well. Increased competition and clutter on retail store shelves means that packages must now perform many sales tasks—from attracting attention, to describing the product, to making the sale.

Companies are realizing the power of good packaging to create immediate consumer recognition of a brand. For example, an average supermarket stocks 45 000 items; the typical shopper passes by some 300 items per minute, and more than 70 percent of all purchase decisions are made in stores. In this highly competitive environment, the package may be the seller's last and best chance to influence buyers. In fact, for some companies the package itself has become an important promotional medium.[19]

Poorly designed packages can cause headaches for consumers and lost sales for the company. Think about all those hard-to-open packages, such as DVD cases sealed with impossibly sticky labels, packaging with finger-splitting wire twist-ties, or sealed plastic clamshell containers that take the equivalent of the fire department's Jaws of Life to open. Such packaging causes what Amazon.com calls "'wrap rage'—the frustration we feel when trying to free a product from a nearly impenetrable package." Amazon.com recently launched a multi-year initiative to alleviate wrap rage. It's working with companies such as Fisher-Price, Mattel, Microsoft, and others to create "frustration-free packaging"—smaller, easy-to-open recyclable packages that use less packaging material and no frustrating plastic clamshells or wire ties. These new packages not only reduce customer frustration but also cut down on packaging waste and energy usage. "It will take many years," says the company, "but our vision is to offer our entire catalog of products in frustration-free packaging."[20]

Innovative packaging can give a company an advantage over competitors and boost sales. Sometimes even seemingly small packaging improvements can make a big difference. For example, Heinz revolutionized the 170-year-old condiments industry by inverting the good old ketchup bottle, letting customers quickly squeeze out even the last bit of ketchup. At the same time, it adopted a "fridge-door-fit" shape that not only slots into shelves more easily but also has a cap that is simpler for children to open. In the four months following the introduction of the new package, sales jumped 12 percent. What's more, the new package does double duty as a promotional tool. Says a packaging analyst, "When consumers see the Heinz logo on the fridge door every time they open it, it's taking marketing inside homes."[21]

Exhibit 8.10   Product design: OXO focuses on the desired end-user experience, and then translates its pie-cutter-in-the-sky notions into eminently usable gadgets.

Packaging
The activities of designing and producing the container or wrapper for a product.

Labelling   Labels range from simple tags attached to products to complex graphics that are part of the package. They perform several functions. At the very least, the label *identifies* the product or brand, such as the name Sunkist stamped on oranges. The label might also *describe* several things about the product—who made it, where it was made, when it was made, its contents, how it is to be used, and how to use it safely. For many companies, labels have become an important element in broader marketing campaigns.

amazon.com

Dear Customers,

"Wrap rage" describes the frustration we humans feel when trying to free a product from a nearly impenetrable package.

Some products are hermetically sealed inside plastic clamshell cases, while others (especially toys) use plastic-coated steel-wire ties. Without the right tools, wire ties can be painful and time-consuming to untwist.

Victim of wrap rage

Today, we're excited to announce the beginning of a multi-year initiative designed to alleviate wrap rage – Amazon "Frustration-Free Packaging."

Clamshell case

Amazon is working with leading manufacturers to deliver products inside smaller, easy-to-open, recyclable cardboard boxes with less packaging material (and no frustrating plastic clamshells or wire ties).

Steel-wire ties

One of the first products to launch with Frustration-Free Packaging is the Fisher-Price Imaginext Adventures Pirate Ship, which is now delivered in an easy-to-open, recyclable cardboard box.

The new packaging eliminates:

1,576.5 square inches of printed corrugated package inserts

175.25 square inches of PVC blisters

36.1 square inches of folding carton materials

36 inches of plastic-coated steel-wire ties

Two molded plastic fasteners

3.5 square inches of ABS molded styrene

Exhibit 8.11   Packaging: Amazon.com developed frustration-free packaging to eliminate "wrap rage."

In Canada, labelling decisions play a very important role in product marketing, because what must be, and what can be, included on a label is strictly regulated. Health Canada, a federal department responsible for helping Canadians maintain and improve their health, regulates labelling for all food products. To that end, nutrition labelling of all prepackaged foods became mandatory in Canada in 2007. Regulations governing the packaging of non-food items is defined in the *Consumer Packaging and Labelling Act*. Some forward-thinking packaged-food marketers benefited from these regulations by promoting the nutritious features of their products long before it became trendy to do so.

Product Support Services   Customer service is another element of product strategy. A company's offer usually includes some support services, which augment actual products.

Support services are an important part of the customer's overall product experience. For example, Lexus makes outstanding cars. But the company knows that good marketing doesn't stop with making the sale. Keeping customers happy *after* the sale is the key to building lasting relationships. Lexus's goal is to "create the most satisfying ownership experience the world has ever seen: The Lexus Covenant promises that its dealers will "treat each customer as we would a guest in our own home" and "go to any lengths to serve them better." So Lexus goes to great lengths to provide outstanding after-sale service. Sometimes, that means fulfilling even seemingly outrageous customer requests:[22]

Dave Wilson, owner of several Lexus dealerships in Southern California, tells of a letter he received from an angry Lexus owner who spent $374 to repair her car at his dealership. She'd owned four prior Lexus vehicles without a single problem. She said in her letter that she resented paying to fix her current one. Turns out, she thought they were maintenance free—as in get in and drive ... and drive and drive. "She didn't think she had to do anything to her Lexus," says Wilson. "She had 60,000 miles on it, and never had the oil changed." Wilson sent back her $374. Losing money on that single transaction meant keeping the customer for life.

Many companies use the Internet to provide support services that were not possible before. For example, HP offers a complete set of sales and after-sale services. It promises "HP Total Care—expert help for every stage of your computer's life. From choosing it, to configuring it, to protecting it, to tuning it up—all the way to recycling it." Customers can click onto the HP Total Care service portal that offers online resources for HP products and 24/7 tech support, which can be accessed via email, instant online chat, and telephone.[23]

PRODUCT LINE DECISIONS

Beyond decisions about individual products and services, product strategy also calls for building a product line. A **product line** is a group of products that are closely related because they function in a similar manner, are sold to the same customer groups, are marketed through the same types of outlets, or fall within given price ranges. For example, Nike produces several lines of athletic shoes and apparel, and Marriott offers several lines of hotels.

The major product line decision involves *product line length*—the number of items in the product line. The line is too short if the manager can increase profits by adding items; the line is too long if the manager can increase profits by dropping items.

Product line length is influenced by company objectives and resources. For example, one objective might be to allow for upselling. Thus, BMW wants to move customers up

Product line

A group of products that are closely related because they function in a similar manner, are sold to the same customer groups, are marketed through the same types of outlets, or fall within given price ranges.

from its 3-series models to 5- and 7-series models. Another objective might be to allow cross-selling: Hewlett-Packard sells printers as well as cartridges. Still another objective might be to protect against economic swings: Gap runs several clothing-store chains (Gap, Old Navy, and Banana Republic), covering different price points.

A company can expand its product line in two ways: by *line filling* or *line stretching*. *Product line filling* involves adding more items within the present range of the line. There are several reasons for product line filling: reaching for extra profits, satisfying dealers, using excess capacity, being the leading full-line company, and plugging holes to keep out competitors. However, line filling is overdone if it results in cannibalization and customer confusion. The company should ensure that new items are noticeably different from existing ones.

Product line stretching occurs when a company lengthens its product line beyond its current range. The company can stretch its line downward, upward, or both ways. Companies located at the upper end of the market can stretch their lines *downward*. A company may stretch downward to plug a market hole that otherwise would attract a new competitor or to respond to a competitor's attack on the upper end. Or it may add low-end products because it finds faster growth taking place in the low-end segments.

Companies can also stretch their product lines *upward*. Sometimes, companies stretch upward to add prestige to their current products. Or they may be attracted by a faster growth rate or higher margins at the higher end. For example, some years ago, each of the leading Japanese auto companies introduced an upmarket automobile: Honda launched Acura; Toyota launched Lexus; and Nissan launched Infiniti. They used entirely new names rather than their own names.

Companies in the middle range of the market may decide to stretch their lines in *both directions*. Marriott did this with its hotel product line. Along with regular Marriott hotels, it added eight new branded hotel lines to serve both the upper and lower ends of the market. For example, Renaissance Hotels & Resorts aims to attract and please top executives; Fairfield Inn by Marriott, vacationers and business travellers on a tight travel budget; and Courtyard by Marriott, salespeople and other "road warriors."[24] The major risk with this strategy is that some travellers will trade down after finding that the lower-price hotels in the Marriott chain give them pretty much everything they want. However, Marriott would rather capture its customers who move downward than lose them to competitors.

PRODUCT MIX DECISIONS

An organization with several product lines has a product mix. A **product mix (or product portfolio)** consists of all the product lines and items that a particular seller offers for sale. Some companies manage very complex product portfolios. For example, Sony's diverse portfolio consists of four primary product businesses worldwide: Sony Electronics, Sony Computer Entertainment (games), Sony Pictures Entertainment (movies, TV shows, music, DVDs), and Sony Financial Services (life insurance, banking, and other offerings).

Each major Sony business consists of several product lines. For example, Sony Electronics includes cameras and camcorders, computers, TV and home entertainment products, mobile electronics, and others. In turn, each of these lines contains many individual items. Sony's TV and home entertainment line includes TVs, DVD players, home audio components, digital home products, and more. Altogether, Sony's product mix includes a diverse collection of hundreds and hundreds of products.

A company's product mix has four important dimensions: width, length, depth, and consistency. Product mix *width* refers to the number of different product lines the company carries. Sony markets a wide range of consumer and industrial products around

Product mix (or product portfolio)
The set of all product lines and items that a particular seller offers for sale.

Exhibit 8.12   Product mix decisions: Sony has a large and diverse product portfolio, divided into four primary product businesses, each containing hundreds of products. "Welcome to the world of Sony."

the world, from TVs and PlayStation consoles to semiconductors. Product mix *length* refers to the total number of items the company carries within its product lines. Sony typically carries many products within each line. The camera and camcorder line, for instance, includes digital cameras, camcorders, photo printers, memory media, and tons of accessories.

Product mix *depth* refers to the number of versions offered of each product in the line. Sony has a very deep product mix. For example, it makes and markets about any kind of TV you'd ever want to buy—tube, flat panel, rear projection, front projection, HD or low resolution—each in almost any imaginable size. Finally, the *consistency* of the product mix refers to how closely related the various product lines are in end use, production requirements, distribution channels, or some other way. Within each major business, Sony's product lines are fairly consistent in that they perform similar functions for buyers and go through the same distribution channels. Company-wide, however, Sony markets a very diverse mix of products. Managing such a broad and diverse product portfolio requires much skill.

These product mix dimensions provide the handles for defining the company's product strategy. The company can increase its business in four ways. It can add new product lines, widening its product mix. In this way, its new lines build on the company's reputation in its other lines. The company can lengthen its existing product lines to become a more full-line company. Or it can add more versions of each product and thus deepen its product mix. Finally, the company can pursue more product line consistency—or less—depending on whether it wants to have a strong reputation in a single field or several fields.

SERVICES MARKETING (LO5)

Services are considered a type of product because they are a marketing offer, but marketing offers that are not tangible, hard goods, have special considerations when it comes to marketing.

The "service sector," as it is called, is bigger, in terms of dollar value, than the retail sector. Services constitute the single most important industry in Canada's economy, with 68 percent of total gross domestic product, 75 percent of employment and 53 percent of consumer spending. Service industries in Canada have grown faster than both goods-producing industries and the economy as a whole. The services sector is also a much larger employer than the goods-producing sector. Almost 12 million Canadians were employed in the service sector compared with the 4 million people working in the goods-producing sector. And the biggest service is the retail industry, with 132 000 workers.[25]

The service sector includes all government services, hospitals, the military, police and fire departments, Canada Post, schools, colleges, and universities. It also includes not-for-profit organizations such as museums, charities, and churches. The largest part of the service industry is the business services segment, that is, for-profit companies that market and sell services to either consumers or businesses, and develop and maintain profitable customer relationships. Business services include airlines, banks, hotels, insurance companies, consulting firms, law and accounting firms, entertainment companies, real-estate firms, and advertising agencies.

NATURE AND CHARACTERISTICS OF A SERVICE

A company must consider four special service characteristics when designing marketing programs: *intangibility, inseparability, variability,* and *perishability* (see Figure 8.5).

Service intangibility means that services cannot be seen, tasted, felt, heard, or smelled before they are bought. For example, people undergoing cosmetic surgery cannot see the result before the purchase. Airline passengers have nothing but a ticket and the promise that they and their luggage will arrive safely at the intended destination, ideally at the same time. To reduce uncertainty, buyers look for "signals" of service quality. They draw conclusions about quality from the place, people, price, equipment, and communications that they can see.

Therefore, the service provider's task is to make the service tangible in one or more ways and to send the right signals about quality. One analyst calls this *evidence management*, in which the service organization presents its customers with organized, honest evidence of its capabilities.

Physical goods are produced, then stored, later sold, and still later consumed. In contrast, services are first sold, then produced and consumed at the same time. In services marketing, the service provider is the product. **Service inseparability** means that services cannot be separated from their providers, whether the providers are people or machines. If a service employee provides the service, then the employee becomes a part of the service. Because the customer is also present as the service is produced, *provider–customer interaction* is a special feature of services marketing. Both the provider and the customer affect the service outcome.

Service variability means that the quality of services depends on who provides them as well as when, where, and how they are provided. For example, some hotels—say, Marriott—have reputations for providing better service than others. Still, within a given Marriott hotel, one registration-counter employee may be cheerful and efficient, whereas another standing just a metre away may be unpleasant and slow. Even the quality of a single Marriott employee's service varies according to his or her energy and frame of mind at the time of each customer encounter.

Service perishability means that services cannot be stored for later sale or use. Some salons charge customers for missed appointments because the service value existed only at that point and disappeared when the customer did not show up. The perishability of

Service intangibility
A major characteristic of services—they cannot be seen, tasted, felt, heard, or smelled before they are bought.

Service inseparability
A major characteristic of services—they are produced and consumed at the same time and cannot be separated from their providers.

Service variability
A major characteristic of services—their quality may vary greatly, depending on who provides them and when, where, and how.

Service perishability
A major characteristic of services—they cannot be stored for later sale or use.

FIGURE 8.5 Special characteristics of services

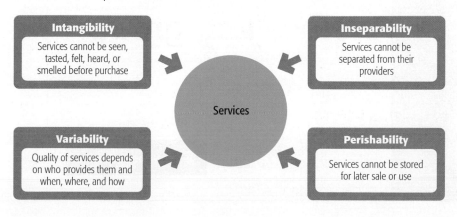

services is not a problem when demand is steady. However, when demand fluctuates, service firms often have difficult problems. For example, because of rush-hour demand, public transportation companies have to own much more equipment than they would if demand were even throughout the day. Thus, service firms often design strategies for producing a better match between demand and supply. Hotels and resorts charge lower prices in the off-season to attract more guests. And restaurants hire part-time employees to serve during peak periods.

MARKETING STRATEGIES FOR SERVICE FIRMS

Just like manufacturing businesses, good service firms use marketing to position themselves strongly in chosen target markets. For example, Scotiabank positions itself as the bank that helps you do more with your money, with its slogan, "You're richer than you think," while TD Canada Trust positions itself as the bank whose services are easy to use.

Because services differ from tangible products, they often require additional marketing approaches. These include understanding and managing the *service-profit chain*, *internal marketing*, and *interactive marketing*.

The Service-Profit Chain   In a service business, the customer and front-line service employee *interact* to create the service. Effective interaction, in turn, depends on the skills of front-line service employees and on the support processes backing these employees. Because of this, successful service companies must focus their attention on *both* their customers and their employees. They understand the **service-profit chain**, which links

Service-profit chain
The chain that links service firm profits with employee and customer satisfaction.

Exhibit 8.13   Positioning of service firms: Scotiabank's positioning as the bank that helps you do more with your money is reinforced with its slogan, "You're richer than you think," which appears on all the bank's marketing materials, from in-branch posters, to brochures, to the main bank website.

service firm profits with employee and customer satisfaction. This chain consists of five links (see Figure 8.6):[26]

- □ *Internal service quality:* superior employee selection and training, a quality work environment, and strong support for those dealing with customers, which results in ...
- □ *Satisfied and productive service employees:* more satisfied, loyal, and hard-working employees, which results in ...
- □ *Greater service value:* more effective and efficient customer value creation and service delivery, which results in ...
- □ *Satisfied and loyal customers:* satisfied customers who remain loyal, repeat purchase, and refer other customers, which results in ...
- □ *Healthy service profits and growth:* superior service firm performance.

Therefore, reaching service profits and growth goals begins with taking care of those who take care of customers. Four Seasons Hotels and Resorts, a chain legendary for its outstanding customer service, is also legendary for its motivated and satisfied employees (see Marketing@Work 8.2).

Internal Marketing   The marketing of pure services requires more than just traditional external marketing using the four *P*s. Services marketers understand the importance of **internal marketing** as well. A service firm must orient and motivate its customer-contact employees and supporting service people to work as a *team* to provide customer satisfaction. Marketers must get everyone in the organization to be customer centred. In fact, internal marketing must *precede* external marketing. For example, Four Seasons Hotels and Resorts starts by hiring the right people and carefully orienting and inspiring them to give unparalleled customer service.

Interactive Marketing   **Interactive marketing** means that service quality depends heavily on the quality of the buyer–seller interaction during the service encounter. In product marketing, product quality often depends little on how the product is obtained. But in services marketing, service quality depends on both the service deliverer and the quality of the delivery. Service marketers, therefore, have to master interactive marketing skills. Thus, Four Seasons selects only people with an innate "passion to serve" and instructs them carefully in the fine art of interacting with customers to satisfy their every need. All new hires complete a three-month training regimen, including improvisation exercises to help them improve their customer-interaction skills.

Internal marketing
Orienting and motivating customer-contact employees and supporting service people to work as a team to provide customer satisfaction.

Interactive marketing
Training service employees in the fine art of interacting with customers to satisfy their needs.

FIGURE 8.6   The service-profit chain

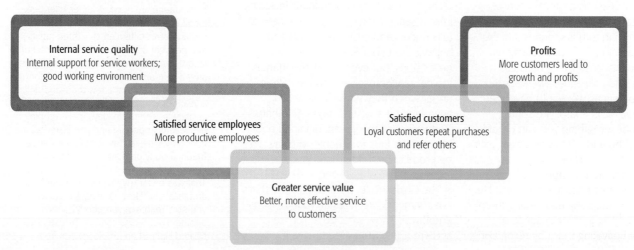

MARKETING@WORK 8.2

Four Seasons: Taking Care of Those Who Take Care of Customers

At a Four Seasons hotel, every guest is a somebody. Other exclusive resorts pamper their guests, but Four Seasons has perfected the art of high-touch, carefully crafted service. Guests paying $1000 or more a night expect to have their minds read, and this luxury hotel doesn't disappoint. Its mission is to perfect the travel experience through the highest standards of hospitality. "From elegant surroundings of the finest quality, to caring, highly personalized 24-hour service," says the company, "Four Seasons embodies a true home away from home for those who know and appreciate the best."

As a result, Four Seasons has a cult-like customer clientele. As one Four Seasons Maui guest recently told a manager, "If there's a heaven, I hope it's run by Four Seasons." But what makes Four Seasons so special? It's really no secret. Just ask anyone who works there. From the CEO to the doorman, they'll tell you—it's the Four Seasons staff. "What you see from the public point of view is a reflection of our people—they are the heart and soul of what makes this company succeed," says Four Seasons founder and CEO Isadore Sharp. "When we say people are our most important asset—it's not just talk." Just as it does for customers, Four Seasons respects and pampers its employees. It knows that happy, satisfied employees make for happy, satisfied customers.

The Four Seasons customer-service legacy is deeply rooted in the company's culture, which in turn is grounded in the Golden Rule. "In all of our interactions with our guests, customers, business associates, and colleagues, we seek to deal with others as we would have them deal with us," says Sharp. "Personal service is not something you can dictate as a policy," he adds. "How you treat your employees is a reflection of how you expect them to treat customers."

Four Seasons brings this culture to life by hiring the best people, orienting them carefully, instilling in them a sense of pride, and motivating them by recognizing

Exhibit 8.14 The service-profit chain: Happy employees make for happy customers. At Four Seasons, employees feel as important and pampered as the guests.

and rewarding outstanding service deeds. It all starts with hiring the right people—those who fit the Four Seasons culture. "Every job applicant, whether hoping to fold laundry or teach yoga, goes through at least four interviews," notes one reporter. "We look for employees who share that Golden Rule—people who, by nature, believe in treating others as they would have them treat us," says Sharp.

Once on board, all new employees receive three months of training, including improvisation exercises that help them to fully understand customer needs and behaviour. At Four Seasons, the training never stops. But even more important is the people themselves and the culture under which they work. "I can teach anyone to be a waiter," says CEO Sharp. "But you can't change an ingrained poor attitude. We look for people who say, 'I'd be proud to be a doorman.'" And the most important cultural guideline, restates Sharp, is "the Golden Rule: Do unto others.... That's not a gimmick." As a result, Four Seasons employees know what good service is and are highly motivated to give it.

Most importantly, once it has the right people in place, Four Seasons treats them as it would its most important guests. According to the reporter,

Compared with the competition, Four Seasons salaries are in the 75th to 90th percentile, with generous retirement and profit sharing plans. All employees—seamstresses, valets, the ski concierge, the general manager—eat together regularly, free, in the hotel cafeteria. It may not have white linen or a wine list, but the food and camaraderie are good. Another killer perk for all employees: free rooms. After six months, any staffer can stay three nights free per year at any Four Seasons hotel or resort. That number increases to six nights after a year and steadily thereafter. Although the benefit may cost a few thousand dollars a year per employee, the returns seem invaluable. The room stays make employees feel as important and pampered as the guests they serve. Says employee Kanoe Braun, a burly pool attendant at the Four Seasons Maui, "I've been to the one in Bali. That was by far my favorite. You walk in, and they say, 'How are you, Mr. Braun?' and you say, 'Yeah, I'm somebody!'" Adds another Four Season staffer, "You're never treated like just an employee. You're a guest. You come back from those trips on fire. You want to do so much for the guests."

As a result, the Four Seasons staff loves the hotel just as much as customers do. Although guests can check out anytime they like, employees never want to leave. The annual turnover for full-time employees is only 18 percent, half the industry average. Four Seasons has been included on *Fortune* magazine's list of 100 Best Companies to Work For every year since the list began in 1998. And that's the biggest secret to Four Seasons's success. Just as the service-profit chain suggests, taking good care of customers begins with taking good care of those who take care of customers.

Sources: Extract adapted from Jeffrey M. O'Brien, "A Perfect Season," *Fortune*, January 22, 2008, pp. 62–66. Other quotes and information obtained from Michael B. Baker, "Four Seasons Tops Ritz-Carlton in Deluxe Photo-Finish," *Business Travel News*, March 23, 2009, p, 10: Sean Drakes, "Keeping the Brand Sacred," *Black Enterprise*, April 2009, p. 47; and http://jobs.fourseasons.com and www.fourseasons.com/about_us/, accessed October 2009.

Today, as competition and costs increase, and as productivity and quality decrease, more service marketing sophistication is needed. Service companies face three major marketing tasks: They want to increase their *service differentiation*, *service quality*, and *service productivity*.

MANAGING SERVICE DIFFERENTIATION

In these days of intense price competition, service marketers often complain about the difficulty of differentiating their services from those of competitors. To the extent that customers view the services of different providers as similar, they care less about the provider than the price.

The solution to price competition is to develop a differentiated offer, delivery, and image. The offer can include innovative features that set one company's offer apart from competitors' offers.

Service companies can differentiate their service *delivery* by having more able and reliable customer-contact people, by developing a superior physical environment in which the service product is delivered, or by designing a superior delivery process. Service companies can also work on differentiating their *images*, which are often represented in their logos and advertising campaigns. Royal Bank's stylized "Leo the Lion" symbolizes strength and power—desirable qualities of a large bank. Other well-known service symbols include Canadian National Railway's CN symbol, Air Canada's maple leaf, TD Canada Trust's green armchair, and TELUS's colourful animals.

MANAGING SERVICE QUALITY

A service firm can differentiate itself by delivering consistently higher quality than its competitors provide. Like manufacturers before them, most service industries have now joined the customer-driven quality movement. And like product marketers, service providers need to identify what target customers expect in regards to service quality.

Exhibit 8.15   Service differentiation: British Airways positions itself as the airline that delivers the best service a customer can ask for, without having to ask.

Softer flat beds for a deeper sleep.

The best service anticipates your needs. To give you the best possible sleep, we used the latest in cushioning technology to create an even more comfortable flat bed. And to add to your comfort, we include plumper pillows and cozier blankets. Our goal is simple: to deliver the best service you could ask for, without you having to ask. So whether you're enjoying a gourmet meal, or an Arrivals Lounge that feels more like a spa, we think you'll find our business class like no other.

Visit ba.com/clubworld

Business class is different on **BRITISH AIRWAYS**

Unfortunately, service quality is harder to define and judge than product quality. For instance, it is harder to agree on the quality of a haircut than on the quality of a hair dryer. Customer retention is perhaps the best measure of quality—a service firm's ability to hang onto its customers depends on how consistently it delivers value to them.

Top service companies set high service-quality standards. They watch service performance closely, both their own and that of competitors. They do not settle for merely good service; they strive for 100 percent defect-free service. A 98 percent performance standard may sound good, but using this standard, 64 000 FedEx packages would be lost each day, 10 words would be misspelled on each printed page, 400 000 prescriptions would be misfiled daily, and drinking water would be unsafe eight days a year.[27]

MANAGING SERVICE PRODUCTIVITY

With their costs rising rapidly, service firms are under great pressure to increase service productivity. They can do so in several ways. They can train current employees better or hire new ones who will work harder or more skilfully. Or they can increase the quantity of their service by giving up some quality. The provider can "industrialize the service" by adding equipment and standardizing production, as in McDonald's assembly-line approach to fast-food retailing. Finally, the service provider can harness the power of technology. Although we often think of technology's power to save time and costs in manufacturing companies, it also has great—and often untapped—potential to make service workers more productive.

However, companies must avoid pushing productivity so hard that doing so reduces quality. Attempts to industrialize a service or cut costs can make a service company more efficient in the short run. But they can also reduce its longer-run ability to innovate, maintain service quality, or respond to consumer needs and desires. For example, some airlines have learned this lesson the hard way as they attempt to economize in the face of rising costs. They stopped offering even the little things for free—such as inflight snacks—and began charging extra for everything from curbside luggage check-in to aisle seats. The result is a plane full of resentful customers who avoid the airline whenever they can. In their attempts to improve productivity, these airlines mangled customer service.

Thus, in attempting to improve service productivity, companies must be mindful of how they create and deliver customer value. In short, they should be careful not to take the "service" out of service.

SEARCHING FOR NEW TECHNOLOGIES TO KEEP "TRUE USERS" WARM

New product development is important to Canada Goose. Canada Goose's new lightweight down collection of outerwear is a case in point. The collection was created to address shoulder seasons by using less, but still premium, down in lightweight fabrications. Down is the best insulator available, and Canada Goose uses its expertise in down insulation to adapt to changing and growing market needs.

With a complete sourcing and product development team that scours the globe looking for the best, most innovative fabric and trim technologies, Canada Goose has been able to selectively incorporate new fabric technologies into appropriate products.

This search for new technologies and enhanced product lines developed out of market feedback. When Canada Goose spoke to its customers, it recognized a need for a lightweight coat for people who were active outside (skiers, hikers, walkers). The company developed a new technology called Thermal Mapping™. Taking into consideration unique male and female heat conservation needs, it created a jacket line that strove to keep traditional soft shell lightness and flexibility.

When Canada Goose considered meeting customer need for a jacket that was more than a non-insulated coat and less than a full parka, it wanted to use lightweight down. The company knew that going from producing Arctic wear to a lightweight down product was a significant step. The lightweight down products provided a way to address shoulder seasons in traditional markets; enter new, less-extreme weather markets; and provide product for retailers that wanted Canada Goose products to have a year-round shelf life. It also answered a call from many Canada Goose fans for product they could wear when a parka was too warm.

In product development, Canada Goose looked at what was in the market and how it could improve on it. "Price was less of an issue as we are a premium brand," Reiss said. "This allowed us the latitude to create a better jacket that wouldn't necessarily be as price-sensitive as some other brands might. We could do the extras that people expect from Canada Goose, draw strings hidden in the pocket, full cuffs, synch cords at neck, extra layers of nylon ripstop fabric to make the jacket windproof where competition uses sew-through stitching that creates cold wind spots."

QUESTIONS

1. Canada Goose would be considered a specialty good as it limits its retail channel exposure. What do you think this designation does for the brand?
2. Canada Goose developed the Snow Mantra, the full winter parka for extreme cold-weather activities, in consultation with dog mushers, extreme athletes, and people who worked outdoors all day long. Would that approach pass the marketing expert who proposed the R-W-W strategy?
3. Considering the product life cycle, why is it important for Canada Goose to keep bringing in new products?

REVIEWING THE CONCEPTS

1. Define *product* and describe and classify different types of product offerings.

Broadly defined, a *product* is anything that can be offered to a market for attention, acquisition, use, or consumption that might satisfy a want or need. Products include physical objects but also services, events, persons, places, organizations, ideas, or mixes of these entities. *Services* are products that consist of activities, benefits, or satisfactions offered for sale that are essentially intangible, such as banking, hotel, tax preparation, and home-repair services.

A product is more than a simple set of tangible features. Each product or service offered to customers can be viewed on three levels. The *core customer value* consists of the core problem-solving benefits that consumers seek when they buy a product. The *actual product* exists around the core and includes the quality level, features, design, brand name, and packaging. The *augmented product* is the actual product plus the various services and benefits offered with it, such as a warranty, free delivery, installation, and maintenance.

Products and services fall into two broad classes based on the types of consumers that use them. *Consumer products*—those bought by final consumers—are usually classified according to consumer shopping habits (convenience products, shopping products, specialty products, and unsought products). *Industrial products*—purchased for further processing or for use in conducting a business—include materials and parts, capital items, and supplies and services. Other marketable entities—such as organizations, persons, places, and ideas—can also be thought of as products.

2. List and define the steps in the new-product development process and the major considerations in managing this process.

The new-product development process consists of eight sequential stages. The process starts with *idea generation*. Next comes *idea screening*, which reduces the number of ideas based on the company's own criteria. Ideas that pass the screening stage continue through *product concept development*, in which a detailed version of the new-product idea is stated in meaningful consumer terms. In the next stage, *concept testing*, new-product concepts are tested with a group of target consumers to determine whether the concepts have strong consumer appeal. Strong concepts proceed to *marketing strategy development*, in which an initial marketing strategy for the new product is developed from the product concept. In the *business-analysis* stage, a review of the sales, costs, and profit projections for a new product is conducted to determine whether the new product is likely to satisfy the company's objectives. With positive results here, the ideas become more concrete through *product development* and *test-marketing* and finally are launched during *commercialization*.

New-product development involves more than just going through a set of steps. Companies must take a systematic, holistic approach to managing this process. Successful new-product development requires a customer-centred, team-based, systematic effort.

3. Describe the stages of the product life cycle and how marketing strategies change during the product's life cycle.

Each product has a *life cycle* marked by a changing set of problems and opportunities. The sales of the typical product follow an S-shaped curve made up of five stages. The cycle begins with the *product development stage* in which the company finds and develops a new-product idea. The *introduction stage* is marked by slow growth and low profits as the product is distributed to the market. If successful, the product enters a *growth stage*, which offers rapid sales growth and increasing profits. Next comes a *maturity stage* in which sales growth slows down and profits stabilize. Finally, the product enters a *decline stage* in which sales and profits dwindle. The company's task during this stage is to recognize the decline and to decide whether it should maintain, harvest, or drop the product.

In the *introduction stage*, the company must choose a launch strategy consistent with its intended product positioning. Much money is needed to attract distributors and build their inventories and to inform consumers of the new product and achieve trial. In the *growth stage*, companies continue to educate potential consumers and distributors. In addition, the company works to stay ahead of the competition and sustain rapid market growth by improving product quality, adding new product features and models, entering new market segments and distribution channels, shifting advertising from building product awareness to building product conviction and purchase, and lowering prices at the right time to attract new buyers.

In the *maturity stage*, companies continue to invest in maturing products and consider modifying the market, the product, and the marketing mix. When *modifying the market*, the company attempts to increase the consumption of the current product. When *modifying the product*, the company changes some of the product's characteristics—such as quality, features, or style—to attract new users or inspire more usage. When *modifying the marketing mix*, the company works to improve sales by changing one or more of the marketing-mix elements. Once the company recognizes that a product has entered the *decline stage*, management must decide whether to *maintain* the brand without change, hoping that competitors will drop out of the market; *harvest* the product, reducing costs and trying to maintain sales; or *drop* the product, selling it to another firm or liquidating it at salvage value.

4. **Describe the decisions companies make regarding their individual products and services, product lines, and product mixes.**

Individual product decisions involve product attributes, packaging, labelling, and product support services. *Product attribute* decisions involve product quality, features, and style and design. *Packaging* provides many key benefits, such as protection, economy, convenience, and promotion. Package decisions often include designing *labels*, which identify, describe, and possibly promote the product. Companies also develop *product support services* that enhance customer service and satisfaction and safeguard against competitors.

Most companies produce a product line rather than a single product. A *product line* is a group of products that are related in function, customer-purchase needs, or distribution channels. *Line stretching* involves extending a line downward, upward, or in both directions to occupy a gap that might otherwise be filled by a competitor. In contrast, *line filling* involves adding items within the present range of the line. All product lines and items offered to customers by a particular seller make up the *product mix*. The mix can be described by four dimensions: width, length, depth, and consistency. These dimensions are the tools for developing the company's product strategy.

5. **Identify the four characteristics that affect the marketing of services and the additional marketing considerations that services require.**

Services are characterized by four key characteristics: they are *intangible*, *inseparable*, *variable*, and *perishable*. Each characteristic poses problems and marketing requirements. Marketers work to find ways to make the service more tangible, to increase the productivity of providers who are inseparable from their products, to standardize the quality in the face of variability, and to improve demand movements and supply capacities in the face of service perishability.

Good service companies focus attention on *both* customers and employees. They understand the *service-profit chain*, which links service firm profits with employee and customer satisfaction. Services marketing strategy calls not only for external marketing but also for *internal marketing* to motivate employees and *interactive marketing* to create service delivery skills among service providers. To succeed, service marketers must create *competitive differentiation*, offer high *service quality*, and find ways to increase *service productivity*.

KEY TERMS

Business analysis   297
Commercialization   298
Consumer product   292
Convenience product   292
Decline stage   305
Fad   303
Fashion   302
Growth stage   304
Idea generation   295
Idea screening   295
Industrial product   293
Interactive marketing   315

Internal marketing   315
Introduction stage   303
Marketing strategy development   296
Maturity stage   304
New-product development   294
Packaging   309
Product   289
Product concept   296
Product development   297
Product life cycle   301
Product line   310
Product mix (or product portfolio)   311

Product quality   307
Service   289
Service inseparability   313
Service intangibility   313
Service perishability   313
Service variability   313
Service-profit chain   314
Shopping product   293
Specialty product   293
Style   302
Test-marketing   298
Unsought product   293

TALK ABOUT MARKETING

1. Choose a company whose products you are familiar with. What specific sources might you turn to for new-product ideas? Assuming the company has a website, how might it be used to interact with the market to generate new-product ideas? Brainstorm your own new product ideas for this company.

2. Choose three of the products mentioned in this chapter. Which stage of the product life cycle is each of these products in? Explain how you were able to identify the stage. How long do you think it will be before each product enters the next stage of the life cycle?

3. Yoplait recently introduced a new product to the market called Go-GURT. Described as a "portable yogurt," its target market is children. Visit the Yoplait website and learn about this product. Now, assume the role of the product manager responsible for Go-GURT. You have been asked to modify the market for this product. Do you think this product can be adapted for the adult market? Devise a plan for testing the product

concept with 25- to 45-year-olds. What factors would be critical to your test? What questions would you ask the testers?

4. Visit a large department store, drug store, or grocery store and find a product you believe is an example of a fad. What evidence can you find—through online research or by asking people you know who have experience with the product—that supports your theory? Explain why you believe the product won't last in the market.

5. If you were a marketing manager at Tim Hortons's head office, what sort of internal and interactive marketing programs would you develop?

6. Discuss how the four characteristics of services—intangibility, inseparability, variability, and perishability—affect Air Canada. What marketing initiatives could Air Canada employ to try to mitigate the negative effects of these characteristics as much as possible?

THINK LIKE A MARKETING MANAGER

Dell revolutionized the personal computer industry in the 1990s by giving consumers what they wanted at the time: commodity components they needed without having to buy the ones they didn't need. The focus was on functionality, not on style. Now that all personal computers are functional, and prices have come down, and in light of the Apple revolution, computers, especially for younger consumers, are fashion accessories as well as tools. Dell's latest customer-focused new-product development strategy is to make its computers available in colours—the Dell Inspiron now comes in pink, blue, green, red, white, black, grey, and brown.

QUESTIONS

1. As a consumer, what do you value most in your personal computer? Talk to your friends and find out whether they value the same thing, or whether they name other features or benefits as most important. How could the marketers at Dell use this information to develop its next new personal computer?
2. Dell's colourful Inspirons have been available since 2006. Visit the Dell website, and find out whether they are still available. If not, were they just a fad?
3. What other computer manufacturers offer computers in different colours? How would you determine whether this option is one that consumers want or will continue to want in the future?
4. What else could Dell do to make its computers more stylish?

MARKETING ETHICS

You may be using a book you purchased or borrowed from another student. People sell or share books all the time, but not e-books! With the growth of electronic readers, such as Amazon.com's Kindle, buying electronic books is easy and growing in popularity. But purchasers of e-books don't have the same rights as those purchasing physical books. Some consumers found out that it is just as easy for sellers to take them back as it is for buyers to get them. For instance, Amazon.com realized it did not have the proper rights to sell certain books—such as George Orwell's *1984*—and used its wireless technology to delete them from its customers' Kindle e-readers. While purchases were refunded, some called the company an Orwellian "Big Brother" because the deletion was done without their knowledge. Imagine if you purchased *1984* and tried to read it right before the test only to learn it had disappeared from your Kindle. Owning an e-book is much like licensing software with digital rights management software embedded to prevent sharing and selling. Such digital rights management software also confuses consumers and limits the number of devices that can play a single e-book.

QUESTIONS

1. How would you classify e-books—a tangible good, an experience, or a service? Explain your choice.
2. Amazon.com had the legal right to delete e-books from the Kindle, but did the company do it the right way? Also, should consumers be able to do whatever they want with an e-book once they purchase it, just as they can with a tangible book?

MARKETING TECHNOLOGY

Today's advertisers are experimenting with new technologies in mobile video and how to use them to deliver advertising to consumers. In Canada, though mobile video technology is in use, the wireless carriers such as Rogers, Bell, and TELUS have not yet standardized their video capability, which makes it impossible for advertisers to develop an ad that can be viewed on all wireless devices. Marketers believe that when a cross-carrier video platform is developed, mobile video will take off and the platform will open all kinds of opportunities for entertainment, content, and advertising. A company called QuickPlay is already providing technology to Rogers Vision service that allows it to show video-on-demand from sources such as YouTube.

QUESTIONS

1. What factors in the marketing environment do you think are causing the delay in wireless carriers and wireless device manufacturers developing technology that will allow any consumer to access any video contact from any phone?

2. QuickPlay Media won the Best Video Service Provider award from *Mobile Entertainment* magazine. As a consumer, what features or functionality do you think make the "best" video service on a cellphone? Research the current status of QuickPlay's technology. Have you seen any video ads on your wireless device?

MARKETING BY THE NUMBERS

When introducing new products, it's usually not easy to determine at what price it should be offered. At the very least, however, a marketer must understand the costs associated with producing the product and set the price at some level above those costs. For example, suppose that a manufacturer of lawn mowers incurs a cost of $75 for each mower it produces and that it produces a total of 1 million mowers each year. Fixed costs for this company are $5 million.

QUESTIONS

1. What is the unit cost for each mower this company produces?

2. If the manufacturer desires a markup of 60 percent on sales, at what price should this product be sold to a reseller such as a wholesaler or a distributor?

END-OF-CHAPTER CASE

PRODUCT INNOVATION AT GILLETTE

Gillette is the most recognized brand in shaving. Whether you are male or female, if you are older than 16, you're a member of the target market for Gillette's shaving products. The Gillette brand has been in existence for over 100 years, but it doesn't rest on the laurels of its past successes. As you'll see, the company behind the brand owes much of its success to a passion for innovation and new-product development.

The Gillette Company was founded in 1901 and acquired by consumer-products giant Procter & Gamble in 2005 for US$57 billion. When Gillette reported its third-quarter results in October 2004, CEO James M. Kilts acknowledged the importance of new products to the company's success: "Our record third-quarter and nine-month results reflect the strong performance of our existing products plus the largest introduction of new products in recent years." That year the company launched several new products, including the M3Power razor for men, the Venus Divine razor for women, and two new electric toothbrushes, the ProfessionalCare 8000 and the Sonic Complete.

Since Gillette's founding, a deep commitment to innovation has kept the company razor sharp. Gillette is best known for its absolute dominance of the wet shaving, dry shaving, and personal grooming markets, but did you know the company also owns the Duracell brand, with its market-leading alkaline batteries, and the Oral-B brand of oral hygiene products? In fact, each division of the company is profitable, fast-growing, number one worldwide in its markets, and anchored by a steady flow of innovative new product offerings.

Every year sees new Gillette products introduced into the market. The year 2004 began with the introduction of the M3Power men's shaving system, "a revolutionary powered wet shaving system that delivers the world's best shave and a totally new shaving experience."

In December 2004, Gillette introduced two new women's razors under its highly popular Venus brand. In a company press release, blades and razors president Peter K. Hoffman said, "The introduction of Venus Vibrance and Venus Disposable reflects Gillette's commitment to product innovations that drive category growth. With Venus Vibrance, we are offering the world's best shaving performance through our power wet shaving technology, while Venus Disposable offers the category's best technology in a disposable razor. These new products reinforce Gillette's leadership position in female shaving."

New products don't just happen at Gillette. New-product success starts with a company-wide culture that supports innovation. Whereas many companies try to protect their successful existing products, Gillette encourages innovations that will cannibalize its established product hits. The company also accepts blunders and dead ends as a normal part of creativity and innovation. It knows that it must generate dozens of new product ideas to get just one success in the marketplace. Gillette strongly encourages its people to take creative risks in applying cutting-edge technologies to find substantial improvements that make life easier for customers.

New-product development is complex and expensive, but Gillette's mastery of the process has put the company in a class of its own. For example, Gillette spent $275 million on designing and developing its Sensor family of razors, garnering

29 patents along the way. And it spent an incredible $1.5 billion on the development of Sensor's successor, the triple-bladed Mach3, and applied for 35 more patents. Competing brands Bic and Wilkinson have managed to claim significant shares of the disposable-razor market, and Norelco and Remington compete effectively in electric razors with Gillette's Braun unit. But Gillette, with its stunning technological superiority, operates with virtually no competition worldwide in the burgeoning cartridge-razor sector. Backed by Gillette's biggest new-product launch up to that point, the Mach3 strengthened the company's stranglehold on this market. Within only a few months of its introduction, Mach3 razors and blades were number one sellers. The new M3Power system is the evolution of the Mach3 product line, and when it was introduced, Hoffman declared, "We expect this new system to substantially fuel the value of the blade and razor category, in the same way that Mach3Turbo has driven growth over the past two years."

At Gillette, it seems that almost everyone gets involved in one way or another with new-product development. Even people who don't participate directly in the product design and development are likely to be pressed into service-testing prototypes. Every working day at Gillette, 200 unshaven employees troop to the second floor of the company's gritty South Boston manufacturing and research plant to evaluate razors for sharpness of blade, smoothness of glide, and ease of handling. When finished, they enter their judgments into a computer.

Gillette simply excels at bringing new products to market. The company understands that, once introduced, fledgling products need generous manufacturing and marketing support to thrive in the hotly competitive consumer-products marketplace. To deliver the required support, Gillette has devised a formula that calls for R&D, capital investment, and advertising expenditures, which it refers to collectively as "growth drivers."

In addition to being an innovative product marketer, Gillette is a sports marketing pioneer. The company partners with NASCAR through its "Young Guns" program. The Gillette Company Young Guns are race-car drivers Kurt Busch, Dale Earnhardt, Jr., Kevin Harvick, Jimmie Johnson, Matt Kenseth, and Ryan Newman. The company's sponsorship of sporting events dates back to 1910, when baseball players were featured in advertisements for the original Gillette Safety Razor. And in Massachusetts, the home of the NFL's New England Patriots is called "Gillette Stadium." Gillette also maintains a close relationship with Major League Baseball, World Cup soccer, the PGA Tour, and the National Hockey League.

Thus, over the decades, superior new products combined with innovative marketing programs have been the cornerstone of Gillette's amazing success. In February 2005, the company reported record annual and fourth-quarter results with double-digit percentage increases in net sales. CEO James Kilts attributes the successful year to the company's new-product achievements:

Gillette posted excellent results across the board, fueled by our largest and most successful new products effort ever. Key successes included M3Power, the first battery powered wet shaving system; the Venus Divine premium system for women; the Oral B ProfessionalCare 8000 power rechargeable toothbrush; and the Sonic Complete, the Company's first entry in the sonic segment of brushing. We look forward to another very good year in 2005. It promises to again be our most active year for new products, with the ongoing international rollout of M3Power and several Oral Care products and the introduction of several major new trade-up products, including Venus Vibrance, our powered wet shaving system for women, and Venus Disposable, the most advanced women's disposable razor.

Success stories such as these made Gillette a desirable acquisition for Procter & Gamble. The deal to acquire Gillette is, to date, the largest acquisition in the history of P&G.

Sources: "P&G Signs Deal to Acquire The Gillette Company," at www.pg.com, accessed January 2005; press releases from The Gillette Company's website, www.gillettenews.com, accessed February 2005: "The Gillette Company: Over 100 Years of Shaving Innovation," "Gillette Introduces Two New High-Performance Venus Razors," "Gillette Reports Record Fourth-Quarter and Full-Year Results"; Lawrence Ingrassia, "Taming the Monster: How Big Companies Can Change," *Wall Street Journal*, December 10, 1992, pp. A1, A6; William H. Miller, "Gillette's Secret to Sharpness," *IndustryWeek*, January 3, 1994, pp. 24–30; Linda Grant, "Gillette Knows Shaving—And How to Turn Out Hot New Products," *Fortune*, October 14, 1996, pp. 207–210; and Dana Canedy, "Gillette's Strengths in Razors Undone by Troubles Abroad," *New York Times*, June 19, 1999, p. 3. Also see William C. Symonds, "Would You Spend $1.50 for a Razor Blade?" *BusinessWeek*, April 27, 1998, p. 46; James Heckman, "Razor Sharp: Adding Value, Making Noise with Mach3 Intro," *Marketing News*, March 29, 1999, pp. E4, E13; and William C. Symonds, "The Big Trim at Gillette," *BusinessWeek*, November 8, 1999, p. 42.

QUESTIONS

1. The Gillette brand is the most recognized name in wet shaving products: razors and razor blades. New products in this category have been developed since the acquisition of Gillette by Procter & Gamble. Research the most recent Gillette-branded shaving products. Does P&G market any other brands of shaving products? If so, how are these brands positioned in relation to Gillette?

2. A product marketing manager must be acutely aware of all the competing products on the market. Choose one product category, either men's wet shaving non-disposable razors or women's wet shaving non-disposable razors. Make a list of all the Gillette products (any and all variations, different sizes of packages, pricing, etc.) and at least three competitive products. Then, make a checklist or grid of all the product features, and check off which brand and product has which features. Write a competitive analysis report of how your products compare with those of the competition.

AFTER STUDYING THIS CHAPTER, YOU SHOULD BE ABLE TO

1. define *brand*, and explain how brand meaning is created and maintained

2. explain how brands are represented, and the role of brand personality and brand equity

3. list and describe the major strategic decisions marketers must make about brands

4. explain how brands are developed and managed, and describe the role of brand communications in the ongoing management of brands

Brand Strategy and Management

PREVIEWING THE CONCEPTS

In this chapter, we'll study how companies develop and manage products and brands. But what, exactly, is a brand? Sometimes the brand name is synonymous with the product or company name, but it's not only products that can be branded. Just as the definition of a product includes services, organizations, ideas, countries, and even people, so can all those things be branded.

Before starting into the chapter, let's look at an interesting brand story. Marketing is all about building brands that connect deeply with customers, and when it comes to branding beer, a product that is not highly differentiated, creating that connection with customers by developing brand relationships may be the most important part of the company's marketing strategy. One Canadian beer brand that has been developing relationships for more than a hundred years—that has become quite notorious, in fact—is Sleeman.

SLEEMAN: NOTORIOUSLY GOOD SINCE 1834

Brand managers strive to associate their brands with powerful emotions that bring the brand to life in the mind of the consumer, and establish a clear and unique positioning. That's particularly difficult to do for a product like beer, which, let's face it, is not highly differentiated. Coors associates its brand with the feeling of "cold"—they want to own that space in the beer consumer's mind. Molson is all about hockey and rock music. Corona is the beer for relaxing and feeling like you're on vacation. And Sleeman is, well, notorious.

As a brand positioning strategy, hanging your image on a word such as "notorious" is risky. *Notorious* means widely and publicly known, usually for a particular trait, but it has connotations of being dangerous. That's okay with John Sleeman, though, because he is an important part of the Sleeman brand story—and somewhat notorious himself. In the 1970s, he opened a pub in Oakville, Ontario, and started a company to import and distribute beers from abroad in Canada. In 1984, his aunt thought it was time he found out about his family heritage, since he was in the beer business anyway, and she encouraged him to restart the family brewery, which had closed in 1933. "They were told no one with the name Sleeman would get a liquor licence for 50 years," said Sleeman's aunt. "Now it's 51. Here you go." Then she handed him an old bottle and a leather-bound book filled with his grandfather's beer recipes, and the rest is history.

Sleeman traced the ownership of the dormant company to Nabisco, purchased the rights for just a few dollars, and opened the new brewery in Guelph, Ontario. Like any good notorious character, he's had his ups and downs. "There are few things that motivate me as much as somebody telling me I'm wrong or I'm going to fail," he said. But fail he did. When the bank called in a loan a year after the brewery relaunched, John Sleeman lost his family home. He didn't stay down for long, though. He sought refinancing from a U.S. bank and rose from the ashes to build Canada's largest microbrewery and create a brand based on the family's history. His grandfather's brewery had been called The Sleeman Brewing and Malting Company, but it went out of business after suffering the consequences of selling contraband liquor to the United States during Prohibition. "We haven't hidden the fact that my grandfather's brothers got caught smuggling," says Sleeman, though he adds that the family is not particularly proud of it.

Sleeman's beer bottles are notorious, too. The first product developed by the newly reopened brewery was a cream ale, painstakingly recreated from his grandfather's recipe and bottled in a re-creation of the original clear glass bottle, a move unique among beer brands in the 1980s. Unfortunately, it doubled packaging costs and increased quality control expenses, because clear bottles make the beer more susceptible to light. "We felt we needed to stay as close to the original as possible, and went over budget to get everything right," says Sleeman. In the days before the company could afford to advertise, the bottles got the beer noticed. Consumers liked the bottles so much that they kept them instead of returning them to the beer store. There was even a time in the 1990s when the company put out a call to consumers to please return them, as they were running out.

Beer sales in Canada have held steady for more than a decade, and many Canadian brands have made inroads into the much larger U.S. market. It's likely no surprise to any Canadian that we consume, by far, more beer than any other alcoholic beverage. According to Statistics Canada, the beer industry provides approximately 200 000 jobs and contributes $2 billion per year to the country's economy. Despite this, however, a few years ago Sleeman began experiencing intense competition from premium imports and discount brews, and again found itself struggling financially. In 2006, Sapporo Breweries purchased Sleeman, a match that seems to be built in brand heaven. Sapporo is one of Japan's oldest beers, dating back to 1876. It has a firmly established brand image, and its own unique packaging, the asymmetric top-heavy silver can.

Sapporo recognized the unique talent of John Sleeman, who managed to build the largest craft brewery in Canada, in a market dominated by two very large players, and invited him to stay on and run the company's operations in Canada. Sleeman agreed. "I explained to [Sapporo] that as consumers, Canadians are very proud of our beer and our heritage.... We still talk about the things that got us here: heritage, quality, caring about our customers, and putting money back into the community."

With this new financial support, Sleeman hired advertising agency Dentsu Canada for a brand positioning project, and after two years of working on it, the "Notorious" strategy was born. The creative genius behind the campaign was Glen Hunt, who is notorious himself in advertising circles as the writer behind the famous Molson Canadian "I Am Canadian" commercial, featuring a plaid-shirted "Joe" proclaiming his pride in being Canadian. "We went out and spoke to consumers who said, 'Where are you? [We] haven't heard from you in a while and we'd like to,'" said Hunt of Sleeman's return to TV. About the new campaign, Hunt jokes, "Notoriously good targets individuals 25 and older who are looking for a 'notoriously good evening.'"

The campaign features a 60-second spot that introduces viewers to a cast of real-life characters who inspired the brewery's beginnings, while the shorter ads focus on individual characters. Other marketing communications efforts include print ads, posters, in-bar elements such as specially designed pint glasses and tap handles, and coasters showing one of the characters on one side, and a little history of the individual on the other.

The five TV commercials are all done in the style of a vaudeville-era theatre. The first ad begins with a red velvet curtain under the title "Our History." The curtain opens to reveal a Sleeman beer case on the stage floor. The top opens, and the colourful, historical characters climb out: a pirate, a beer wench holding frosty mugs, dancing girls, a smuggler, and a philanderer. They gather on the stage in the manner of a cast assembling for their curtain call at the end of a play. Finally, a tuxedo-clad John Sleeman emerges from the box, holding the signature Sleeman clear bottle in one hand, and the famous black leather book in the other, as the announcer proclaims, "Five generations of infamous family brewing heritage. Sleeman: Notoriously good since 1834."

Subsequent executions tell stories about the brand: "Some of John Sleeman's early ancestors were pirates, philanderers, bootleggers, and smugglers," says one. Another shows a pirate climbing slyly out of the Sleeman beer case on the stage as the announcer tells us, "Our ancestors were pirates. The name was Slyman. On land they opened taverns. The name became Sleeman. Born of pirates. Brewed in Guelph." In another, we learn, "Prohibitionists wanted to run George Sleeman out of town. But George Sleeman ran for mayor, and ran *them* out of town." And finally, we are told of a particularly famous notorious character: "Sleeman beer was enjoyed by Al Capone. A man who did what he did, and took what he wanted."

The brand has always traded on its history. In 2005, the company announced the John Sleeman Presents series of beers, featuring an India Pale Ale designed "to recapture a piece of history of the British Empire" and described by John Sleeman as "inspired by page 46 in my grandfather's recipe book, [it] has an abundance of hops, a distinctive flavour, and a fascinating history." And behind each beer there's a story: India Pale Ale was originally developed in the 1700s, when breweries would send ale from England to British troops and expatriates in India. Because the voyage took months, the brewers came up with the idea of improving the beer's shelf life by adding extra hops, which acted as a natural preservative.

Five years after the merger with Sapporo, the Sleeman brand name is still going strong. Says John Sleeman, "I restarted a 100-and-something-year-old business thinking I was going to be this generation's custodian, and that someone in my family might be interested in taking over when I ended up in my pine box." With nearly two centuries of notorious history behind it, there seems to be no end to the potential for telling stories about this brand, even long after its founder is no longer part of the story.[1]

IN CHAPTER 8 we learned that when developing new product, marketers must make many important decisions about features, style, and design; level of quality; packaging; and labelling. In addition to these important decisions about how the product looks, feels, and works, marketers must make decisions about branding—which has more to do with how customers *perceive* the product. Brands have personality, brands have value, brands position the product in the mind of the consumer, and perform many other important functions in product marketing, yet a brand is not the same as a product. In this chapter, we'll look more closely at the abstract concepts of brands and branding, and how they are applied in marketing.

WHAT IS A BRAND? LO1

Perhaps the most distinctive skill of professional marketers is their ability to build and manage brands. A **brand** is a name, term, sign, symbol, or design, or a combination of these, that identifies the maker or seller of a product or a service. Consumers view a brand as an important part of a product, and branding can add value to a product.

The definition of a brand is far from simple. Says one advertising expert, "What's a brand? You realize that no two people, let alone two marketers, agree on the answer. It's a word, a metaphor, an analogy, a concept or some sort of thing with an existence and personality...."[2] A brand may identify one item, a family of items, or all items of that seller. If used for the firm as a whole, the preferred term is *trade name*—but a brand is much more than just a trade name. Brands are powerful. Brands have status and value. Brands have personality, and so they involve our emotions as consumers, and as human beings. But for all that, a brand is not real. It can't be touched, or even pointed at. A brand is nothing more than an idea. For the biggest brands in the world, it is precisely that idea that generates most of the company's revenue.

John Stewart, co-founder of Quaker Oats, once said, "If this business were split up, I would give you the land and bricks and mortar, and I would keep the brands and trademarks, and I would fare better than you." The CEO of McDonald's agrees: "A McDonald's board member who worked at Coca-Cola once talked to us about the value of our brand. He said if every asset we own, every building, and every piece of equipment were destroyed in a terrible natural disaster, we would be able to borrow all the money to replace it very quickly because of the value of our brand. And he's right. The brand is more valuable than the totality of all these assets."[3]

Branding has become so strong that today hardly anything goes unbranded. Salt is packaged in branded containers, common nuts and bolts are packaged with a distributor's label, and automobile parts—spark plugs, tires, filters—bear brand names that differ from those of the automakers. Even fruits, vegetables, dairy products, and poultry are branded—Sunkist oranges, B.C.–brand apples, Neilson Dairy Oh! milk, and Maple Leaf Prime chickens.

Branding helps buyers in many ways. Brand names help consumers to identify products that might benefit them. Brands also say something about product quality and consistency—buyers who always buy the same brand know that they will get the same features, benefits, and quality each time they buy. Branding also gives the seller several advantages. The brand name becomes the basis on which a whole story can be built about a product's special qualities. The seller's brand name and trademark provide legal protection for unique product features that otherwise might be copied by competitors. And branding helps the seller to segment markets. For example, Toyota Motor Corporation can offer the major Lexus, Toyota, and Scion brands, each with numerous sub-brands—such as Camry, Corolla, Prius, Matrix, Yaris, Tundra, Land Cruiser, and others—not just one general product for all consumers.

Exhibit 9.1 Anything can be branded: Apples are a fruit, Red Delicious is a name, but "B.C. Brand" is a trade name that differentiates this brand of apples from any other.

BRAND MEANING

In the beginning, products were just products, and they stayed that way for a long time. Then, someone came up with the idea of trademarks. Consumers came to trust trademarks, because they reassured them that the product they were getting had the attributes they wanted, and expected, from that maker. Today, trademarks can be names, symbols, even shapes, such as the Coca-Cola bottle, whose design was registered as a trademark in 1960.

Trademarks and logos often represent brands, yet the meaning of a brand encompasses much more than just a logo. Customers attach meanings to brands and develop brand relationships that go well beyond a product's physical attributes. For example, consider Coca-Cola:[4]

> In one interesting taste test of Coca-Cola versus Pepsi, 67 subjects were hooked up to brain-wave-monitoring machines while they consumed both products. When the soft drinks were unmarked, consumer preferences were split down the middle. But when the brands were identified, subjects choose Coke over Pepsi by a margin of 75 percent to 25 percent. When drinking the identified Coke brand, the brain areas that lit up most were those associated with cognitive control and memory—a place where culture concepts are stored. That didn't happen as much when drinking Pepsi. Why? According to one brand strategist, it's because of Coca-Cola's long-established brand imagery—the almost 100-year-old contour bottle and cursive font, and its association with iconic images ranging from Mean Joe Greene and the Polar Bears to Santa Claus. Pepsi's imagery isn't quite as deeply rooted. Although people might associate Pepsi with a hot celebrity or the "Pepsi generation" appeal, they probably don't link it to the strong and emotional American icons associated with Coke. The conclusion? Plain and simple: consumer preference isn't based on taste alone. Coke's iconic brand appears to make a difference.

Brand Relationships Brands are more than just names and symbols. They are a key element in the company's relationships with consumers. Brands represent consumers' perceptions and feelings about a product and its performance—everything that the product or service means to consumers. In the final analysis, brands exist in the heads of consumers. As one well-respected marketer once said, "Products are created in the factory, but brands are created in the mind."[5]

Today, there are so many different products competing in each category that many are at risk of becoming viewed as commodities. For example, the first automatic drip coffee maker for home use was Mr. Coffee, a trademark that commanded respect until every other appliance maker figured out how to make a similar device. Branding expert Kevin Roberts believes that marketers should strive to turn their brands into "lovemarks."[6]

> For anyone in business, the rapid cycling of their valued products into generic stuff is a dark and constant fear. Brands were developed to create differences for products that were in danger of becoming as hard to tell apart as chunks of gravel. The trademark symbol is good, but to be successful a marketer needs to make sure consumers know the *value* of what they are getting. "Brands do this brilliantly," say Roberts.
>
> Today, however, brands are in danger of becoming worn out from overuse. They're no longer mysterious. Today's consumer is better informed, more critical, less loyal, and harder to understand—and all of this adds up to bad news for brands.
>
> The solution, suggests Roberts, is Lovemarks—his term for a brand that inspires the kind of loyalty we exhibit toward those we love. Few of us are likely to disagree with the statement that love is the most powerful emotion of all. What makes us love Coke, not Pepsi, or Volkswagen, not Ford, is not something most of us can articulate, but marketers want to try to influence it. They want their brand to be more than just something we *like*; they want us to *love* it.
>
> To turn a brand into a Lovemark, a marketer has to think differently: Instead of providing information to customers, develop a relationship with them. Instead of striving for recognition, strive to be loved by consumers. Instead of making statements, tell a *story*. A brand must have a compelling, memorable story to tell, before it can be loved. Roberts offers this advice to marketers: Ask your friends if they can tell you a story about your brand. If they haven't got one, says Roberts, you have work to do.

Consumers sometimes bond *very* closely with specific brands. For example, one Michigan couple had such a passion for Black & Decker's DeWalt power tool brand that

Exhibit 9.2 Brand relationships: The DeWalt brand is so powerful it became a "lovemark" for one couple, who incorporated the brand into their wedding.

Brand advocates
Customers, employees, and others who willingly and voluntarily promote their favourite brands.

they designed their entire wedding around it. They wore trademark DeWalt black-and-yellow T-shirts, made their way to a wooden chapel that they'd built with their DeWalt gear, exchanged vows and power tools, and even cut cake with a power saw. Joked the wife about her husband (a carpenter by trade), "He loves DeWalt nearly as much as he loves me."[7]

Brand Advocacy   One of the jobs of brand marketers is to create and communicate stories about their brands; but today, with the rise in popularity of social media, consumers are telling—and spreading—stories about their favourite brands, too. While it's not possible for brand managers to control what consumers say about their brands, it is possible to encourage feedback and storytelling from those consumers who love the brand, and to create **brand advocates**—customers, employees, and others who willingly and voluntarily promote their favourite brands. Brand advocacy is a powerful marketing tool, but how can it be created and used effectively? Interbrand offers the following suggestions:[8]

☐ *Advocacy begins with trust:* Word of mouth, good or bad, has always influenced perceptions of brands. Online consumer opinions have also gained importance as new communications channels have emerged. Build trust with potential advocates by nurturing their recommendations and opinions.

☐ *Advocacy starts close to home:* Oprah telling the world she used her BlackBerry to write an article about First Lady Michelle Obama is a great brand story. But it is unlikely that a brand can capture Oprah's attention without first building a strong base of brand supporters. Brands must start by creating advocates in the world around them. If you gain the passionate support of customers and employees, their enthusiasm for the brand will spill over into words and actions.

☐ *Make customers and employees part of the brand story:* Transforming customers and employees into advocates puts them at the heart of the brand. Zappos, the online clothing and shoe retailer, has employees who are valued and empowered partners in creating and delivering the customer experience. Real customer-service calls were featured in television commercials; "I heart Zappos" stories are posted online; and CEO Tony Hsieh tells brand stories on his numerous speaking tours.

☐ *Deliver an experience that gets them talking:*Creating brand advocates requires persistence and effort. Loyalty is not enough, because loyalists can be quiet and passive, for example, such as Microsoft's customers. On the other hand, Apple's advocates go beyond loyalty to actively promote the brand.

☐ *Outperform where they care the most:* The secret to creating advocates is to outperform for brand participants when they most need it. Understanding and solving problems is universally one of the most effective ways to create brand advocates.

PEOPLE AS BRANDS

The skilful use of marketing can turn a person's name into a powerhouse brand. Carefully managed and well-known names such as Oprah Winfrey, Martha Stewart, and Donald Trump now adorn everything from sports apparel, housewares, and magazines to book clubs and casinos. Trump, who describes himself as "the hottest brand on the planet," has skilfully made his life a non-stop media event. Says a friend, "He's a skilful marketer, and what he markets is his name."[9]

Such well-known, well-marketed names hold substantial branding power. Consider Rachael Ray:

Rachael Ray has become a one-woman marketing phenomenon: In less than a decade, she's zipped from nobody to pop-culture icon. Beginning with her 30-Minute Meals cookbooks, followed later by a Food Network TV show, Ray won her way into the hearts of everyday cooks by demystifying cooking and dishing out a ton of energy. Thanks to her perky personality, Rachael Ray has moved far beyond quick meals. Bearing her name are more than a dozen best-selling cookbooks (the latest is *Yum-o! The Family Cookbook*), a monthly lifestyle magazine, three Food Network shows, a syndicated daytime talk show, a line of pet foods, and assorted licensing deals that have stamped her name on kitchen essentials from knives to her own "E.V.O.O." (extra-virgin olive oil for those not familiar with Rayisms). Ultimately, Ray's brand power derives from all that she has come to represent. Her brands "begin with food and move briskly on to the emotional, social, and cultural benefits that food gives us."[10]

Today, many athletes have become their own brands. Gone are the days when an athlete simply posed with sporting equipment or apparel. Today's athletes are brands in and of themselves, and with money, free time, and social media tools such as YouTube at their disposal, they're exerting more control over how, when, and where their image is marketed. Canadian basketball star Steve Nash promotes his brand in a variety of ways. He doesn't just appear in Nike commercials, he helps make them. He wrote the script for a viral video

Exhibit 9.3 People as brands: Steve Nash was featured on the cover of Canada's *Marketing* magazine as a leading example of how professional athletes can manage their personal brands.

called Training Day, which showed the basketball star practising on the court. Included in the spot was a new product Nash developed with Nike, a sneaker called Trash Talk that's made entirely from recycled materials.[11]

BRAND CHARACTERISTICS (LO2)

Most established brands are represented by a powerful name, a logo, or an icon, however, these symbols are only part of what makes up the brand. Brands also have *personality*, *status*, and value (*brand equity*).

BRAND REPRESENTATIONS

Logos can support the brand's positioning and add personality to the brand. For example, many companies are now redesigning their brand and company logos to make them more approachable, upbeat, and engaging. "The boxy, monochromatic look is out and soft fonts, lots of colors, and natural imagery is in," says one analyst. For instance, Kraft recently replaced its blocky red, white, and blue hexagon logo with a lower-case, multi-font, multi-colour one that includes a colourful starburst and the company's new slogan, "Make today delicious." Similarly, Wal-Mart swapped its blocky, single-colour logo for

Exhibit 9.4   Brand personality: Google Doodles are both a representation of the Google brand and an illustration of the brand's personality. Hundreds of Doodles have been designed to mark special occasions, including these for Canada Day, Google's fifth birthday, Chinese New Year, and the 2010 Winter Olympics in Vancouver.

Brand personality
The sum total of all the attributes of a brand, and the emotions it inspires in the minds of consumers.

one that has two colours and a sun icon. And Pepsi's recently updated packaging sports a new, more uplifting smiling logo. "It feels like the same Pepsi we know and love," says a brand expert, "but it's more adventurous, more youthful, with a bit more personality to it." It presents a "spirit of optimism and youth," says a Pepsi marketer.[12]

Logos are an important part of today's brand-centric universe, and wearing branded clothing, which was considered passé for a time, is now back in style. "We're seeing more of this kind of thing where people will adopt brand graphics as shorthand to express their affinity," says Gary Ludwig, creative director, Canada, for Interbrand.[13] Research shows that even subtle exposure to logos will, over time, influence consumers' brand choices. And many experts believe that the average consumer is exposed to as many as 3000 logos in a typical day!

Many of the most successful brands are those that have a distinctive *personality*. A **brand personality** is the sum total of all the attributes of a brand, and the emotions it inspires in the minds of consumers. Brand managers describe their brands by using the same kinds of adjectives we might use to describe people, and they use those attributes to establish the brand's positioning. For example, Coca-Cola is "traditional," while Pepsi is "youthful." Apple is "stylish," and Mac is "hip." Starbucks is "sophisticated," and Ford is "reliable," IBM is "conservative" and "practical," while Google is "quirky" and "fun-loving." In fact, Google is a brand that just oozes brand personality. Every April 1, Google's home page announces a new product, such as Google Custom Time or Google Surface Mail—which are not real products at all, but spoofs to celebrate April Fool's Day. And Google Doodles, the playful versions of Google's logo, are so well known as part of the Google personality, that today there are Google Doodle contests and fan-created logos. Says the company, "Having a little bit of fun with the corporate logo by redesigning it from time to time is unheard of at many companies but at Google, it is a part of the brand. While the doodle is primarily a fun way for the company to recognize events and notable people, it also illustrates the creative and innovative personality of the company itself."[14]

Finally, brands have *status*, that is, they occupy a level of social regard with respect to one another. Rolls-Royce and Bentley are higher-status car brands than Ford and Toyota; and Hyundai and Kia are lower-status brands. Within just about every product category there are high-status and low-status brands, however, status should not be confused with value or popularity. Many high-status brands, such as Chanel and Rolex, tend to be exclusive rather than popular, while lower-status brands, such as Canadian Tire and Keds, can still be highly popular.

BRAND EQUITY

A powerful brand has brand equity. **Brand equity** is the dollar amount attributed to the value of the brand, based on all the intangible qualities that create that value. A measure of a brand's equity is the extent to which people are willing to pay more for the brand. One study found that 72 percent of consumers would pay a 20 percent premium for their brand of choice relative to the closest competing brand; 40 percent said they would pay a 50 percent premium.[15] Tide and Heinz lovers are willing to pay a 100 percent premium. Loyal Coke drinkers will pay a 50 percent premium, and Volvo users a 40 percent premium.

Advertising agency Young & Rubicam's Brand Asset Valuator measures brand strength along four consumer perception dimensions: *differentiation* (what makes the brand stand out), *relevance* (how consumers feel it meets their needs), *knowledge* (how much consumers know about the brand), and *esteem* (how highly consumers regard and respect the brand). Brands with strong brand equity rate high on all of these dimensions. A brand must be distinct, or consumers will have no reason to choose it over other brands. But the fact that a brand is highly differentiated doesn't necessarily mean that consumers will buy it. The brand must stand out in ways that are relevant to consumers' needs. But even a differentiated, relevant brand is far from a shoo-in. Before consumers will respond to the brand, they must first know about and understand it. And that familiarity must lead to a strong, positive consumer-brand connection.[16]

Every two years, consulting firm Interbrand evaluates and ranks the top 100 global brands and the top 25 Canadian brands in terms of their value, or brand equity (see Table 9.1). To qualify for the global list, a brand must derive one-third of its earnings from outside its home country, be recognizable to people who are not customers, and have publicly available marketing and financial data. The ranking is then done through a complex procedure of calculating what percentage of the company's revenues can be credited to the brand. Interbrand then projects five years of earnings and sales for the brand, deducts operating costs and taxes, and strips out intangibles, such as patents and

Brand equity
The dollar amount attributed to the value of the brand, based on all the intangible qualities that create that value.

TABLE 9.1 Top 10 Global and Canadian Brands

Global rank	Brand	Value (US$ million)	Canadian rank	Brand	Value (CA$ million)
1	Coca-Cola	68 734	1	Thomson Reuters	9 413
2	IBM	60 211	2	TD	6 668
3	Microsoft	56 647	3	RBC	6 171
4	GE	47 777	4	BlackBerry	6 000
5	Nokia	34 864	5	Shoppers Drug Mart	3 425
6	McDonald's	32 275	6	Tim Hortons	2 654
7	Google	31 980	7	Bell	2 452
8	Toyota	31 330	8	Rogers	2 276
9	Intel	30 636	9	Scotiabank	2 159
10	Disney	28 447	10	BMO	1 972

Sources: "Best Canadian Brands 2010" and "Best Global Brands 2009" reports published by Interbrand and available on its website at www.interbrand.com; "Best Canadian Brands 2010" report published by Interbrand, p. 3; "IBM Expands Managed Wireless Services for BlackBerry," RIM press release, May 14, 2008; "In Depth: Research In Motion," from www.cbc.ca/news/background/rim, accessed June 2010; Canadian Press, "BlackBerry More Popular Than Expected," *Marketing*, February 22, 2008; Dave Scholz, "Earning a Reputation," *Marketing*, May 26, 2008, p. 24.

management. Interbrand believes this figure comes closest to representing a brand's true economic worth. How do Canadian brands stand up in the global market? "Our 2010 Best Canadian Brands study shows that Canadian brand values for the most part have been growing strongly," says Interbrand. "Despite challenging economic conditions, our top 25 have gained $14.9 billion in aggregate value, increasing by 35% since 2008. When contrasting that gain to the -2.5% drop in overall value of the top 25 brands in Interbrand's Best Global Brands from 2008 to 2009, we should feel both proud and relieved. The increase in brand value is making more Canadian brands comparable in value to those on Interbrand's global ranking."

BlackBerry is not only one of the most valuable brands in Canada, but it ranks #63 on the list of top global brands (see Marketing@Work 9.1). High brand equity provides a company with many competitive advantages. A powerful brand enjoys a high level of consumer brand awareness and loyalty. Because consumers expect stores to carry the brand, the company has more leverage in bargaining with resellers. Because the brand name carries high credibility, the company can more easily launch line and brand extensions. A powerful brand offers the company some defense against fierce price competition.

Above all, however, a powerful brand forms the basis for building strong and profitable customer relationships. The fundamental asset underlying brand equity is *customer equity*—the value of the customer relationships that the brand creates. A powerful brand is important, but what it really represents is a profitable set of loyal customers. The proper focus of marketing is building customer equity, with brand management serving as a major marketing tool. Companies need to think of themselves not as portfolios of products, but as portfolios of customers.

BRANDING STRATEGY LO3

Marketing managers responsible for brands must make high-level strategic decisions that govern the management of the brand and that guide the public and market perceptions about the brand. The main branding strategy decisions are *brand name selection*, *brand positioning*, and *brand sponsorship*.

BRAND NAME SELECTION

A good name can add greatly to a product's success. However, finding the best brand name is a difficult task. It begins with a careful review of the product and its benefits, the target market, and proposed marketing strategies. After that, naming a brand becomes part science, part art, and a measure of instinct. Here are what brand experts say are the things to consider when coming up with a new brand name:

- [ ] It should suggest something about the type of products it will brand, such as Beautyrest, Craftsman, Snuggle.
- [ ] It should be easy to pronounce, recognize, and remember, such as Tide, Crest, Ziploc.
- [ ] It should be distinctive, such as Google, Lexus, BlackBerry.
- [ ] It should be extendable, that is, not tied too closely to one product. Good names that illustrate this example are Oracle, Amazon.com, and Nike.
- [ ] It should be pronounceable in many languages, such as Kodak. Before changing its name to Exxon, Standard Oil of New Jersey rejected the name Enco, which it learned meant a stalled engine in Japanese.

MARKETING@WORK 9.1

Brand Equity: RIM, One of the Most Valuable Brands in the World

One of the most valuable brands in the world is owned by a Canadian company whose name few recognize: RIM. The brand is attached to a product that's carried by 14 million people in 135 countries around the world and whose name is known to millions more, whether they own one or not. It's appeared in movies, been talked about on late-night television, and been the punchline for stand-up comics. You probably recognize it from its photo, even if you have never owned one yourself. It's the BlackBerry.

Global market consulting firm Interbrand publishes an annual report on the most valuable brands in Canada and the world, and BlackBerry consistently ranks highly on both lists. BlackBerry was named the #1 Best Canadian Brand in 2008, and remains in the top five in terms of value. In 2010, it ranked #63 on the top 100 list of Best Global Brands. "BlackBerry is an example of what a brand can achieve if it thinks globally. Parent company Research In Motion (RIM) has taken its groundbreaking technology and capitalized on the explosive worldwide growth of mobile communications in both the business and consumer markets, catapulting it to the top of our rankings." According to RIM's 2008 annual report, about 92 percent of its revenues come from outside Canada, making it a truly global brand. In 2010, RIM continues to lead the U.S. smartphone market with the BlackBerry brand. It is first in smartphones globally, with around 16 million subscribers worldwide—double from the previous year.

Research In Motion was founded by two engineering students in Waterloo, Ontario, in 1984. The company became the first wireless data technology developer in North America. Their first product experiment, something they called a "two-way pager," was introduced in 1992 after CEO Jim Balsillie joined RIM. The company went public on the Toronto Stock Exchange in 1997 and in the United States on the NASDAQ exchange in 1999.

Exhibit 9.5 Canada's most valuable brand: RIM's corporate logo, and CEO Jim Balsillie, are two representations of the RIM brand. RIM also owns the BlackBerry brand, one of the most recognized brands in the world.

The first BlackBerry was introduced to the market in 1998 as a "wireless handheld computer." Product features included six lines of text display, which allowed for basic email communications, and two-way paging. There was limited Internet access; users could browse specially formatted web pages for basic information such as stock market data. A year later the BlackBerry 850 was released. The new feature on this brand extension was a traditional, though tiny, QWERTY keyboard. It's this feature that led to the explosive demand for the BlackBerry line of products. In 2002, BlackBerrys were first equipped with voice and data transmission capabilities, allowing consumers to get rid of their cellphones, which many carried in addition to their BlackBerrys. Now, the BlackBerry was truly the only device consumers needed. It was an organizer, a contact manager, a computer, an Internet device, and a telephone, all in one. Today, although BlackBerry faces stiff competition from the Apple iPhone, BlackBerry continues to be the business phone of choice.

When RIM announced that the BlackBerry would be sold in China, the news caused RIM shares to go up 8 percent, making it the most valuable *company* in Canada for a time. It seems the value of the BlackBerry brand is an integral part of the corporate reputation— and value—of RIM. "Brand equity is a part of corporate reputation, but it is not all that goes into corporate reputation," says Dave Scholz, vice-president at Leger Marketing in Toronto. "Beyond awareness and brand equity, a reputation is built on public perceptions of that company.... In this case, the corporate entity and the product brand seem to be two distinct identities, with the product having higher appeal than the corporation." That's because we've learned to use the word "BlackBerry" in conversation, but we rarely say, "the Research In Motion wireless device."

Though the BlackBerry has always been positioned as a brand for business professionals, more and more consumers are buying the devices every day, especially now that the product allows users to connect to their Facebook accounts, watch live television, and listen to music. Clearly, the BlackBerry is more than just a product; it's a brand that inspires extreme levels of loyalty and interest among consumers worldwide. People claim they are "addicted" to their BlackBerrys, and can't live without them, earning the product the nickname "Crackberry." It is ubiquitous, a part of global culture. Every new product introduction is discussed not only in the tech press, but also in mainstream media and blogs.

"The result is broad recognition and strong emotional bonds, verging on obsession with users around the world. What other Canadian brand could spawn an independent website that is devoted to spotting celebrities such as David Beckham using its products?" notes the Interbrand report.

"Canadian brands have historically seemed constrained by our geography and our demographics. We are a small country in population and exist in the shadow of our larger U.S. neighbour. Somewhat conservative by nature, we seem reluctant to make the investments and take the risks that would let us venture with our brands beyond our borders. We often do not communicate our brand stories aggressively and our

budgets for brand support can seem small compared to global brands with deep pockets. But brands such as BlackBerry give us a glimpse of possibilities regardless of size and budgets." The story of the BlackBerry will inspire Canadian marketers for years to come.

Sources:"Best Canadian Brands 2010" and "Best Global Brands 2009" reports published by Interbrand and available on its website at Interbrand.com; "IBM Expands Managed Wireless Services for BlackBerry," RIM press release, May 14, 2008; "In Depth: Research In Motion," at www.cbc.ca/news/background/rim, accessed June 5, 2010; Canadian Press, "BlackBerry More Popular Than Expected," *Marketing*, February 22, 2008; Dave Scholz, "Earning a Reputation," *Marketing*, May 26, 2008, p. 24.

☐ It should be capable of registration and protection as a trademark. A brand name cannot be registered if it infringes on existing brand names. Unique, "made up" names work best for this: Yahoo!, Novartis, Ugg.

Choosing a new brand name is hard work. After a decade of choosing quirky names (Yahoo!, Google) or trademark-proof made-up names (Novartis, Aventis, Lycos), today's style is to build brands around names that have real meaning. For example, names such as Silk (soy milk), Method (home products), Smartwater (beverages), and Blackboard (school software) are simple and make intuitive sense. But with trademark applications soaring, *available* new names can be hard to find. Try it yourself. Pick a product and see whether you can come up with a better name for it. How about Moonshot? Tickle? Vanilla? Treehugger? Simplicity? Do a quick online search and you'll find that they're already taken.

A great brand absolutely requires a good, strong, memorable name. When Google burst onto the scene in 1998, no one had to say the name twice. It was instantly memorable, and, only a few short years later, it had become synonymous with "Internet search." Perhaps the greatest example of how to choose a great brand name is the story of Kodak. The name was invented after researchers discovered that the K sound signals strength and as a result of testing its repetition in many popular languages.

Sometimes companies resurrect brand names from the past and give them a new life. Ford sold more than 7 million cars branded with the name Taurus but discontinued the brand in 2006. It didn't exactly stop making the car, it just changed the name to Ford Five Hundred. Even though it was essentially the same car, the Five Hundred flopped, because the name had no meaning to consumers. Consumer research conducted by Ford revealed that only 25 percent of people were aware of the Ford Five Hundred, but 80 percent of people recognized the name Taurus—in fact, it was the third strongest of all Ford's brand names (after F-150 and Mustang). So the company decided to switch the car's name back to Taurus.[17]

Once chosen, the brand name must be protected. Many firms try to build a brand name that will eventually become identified with the product category. Brand names such as Kleenex, Levi's, JELL-O, BAND-AID, Scotch Tape, Formica, and Ziploc have succeeded in this way. However, their very success may threaten the company's rights to the name. Many originally protected brand names—such as cellophane, aspirin, nylon, kerosene, linoleum, yo-yo, trampoline, escalator, thermos, and shredded wheat—are now generic words that any seller can use. To protect their brands, marketers present them by carefully using the word "brand" and the registered trademark symbol, as in "BAND-AID® Brand Adhesive Bandages." Even the long-standing "I am stuck on BAND-AID and BAND AID's stuck on me" jingle has now become "I am stuck on BAND AID *brand* and BAND AID's stuck on me."

BRAND POSITIONING

Marketers need to position their brands clearly in target customers' minds. They can position brands at any of three levels.[18] At the lowest level, they can position the brand on *product attributes*. For example, P&G invented the disposable diaper category with its Pampers brand. Early Pampers marketing focused on attributes such as fluid absorption, fit, and disposability. In general, however, attributes are the least desirable level for brand positioning. Competitors can easily copy attributes. More importantly, customers are not interested in attributes as such; they are interested in what the attributes will do for them.

A brand can be better positioned by associating its name with a desirable *benefit*. Thus, Pampers can go beyond technical product attributes and talk about the resulting containment and skin-health benefits from dryness. "There are fewer wet bottoms in the world because of us," says Jim Stengel, P&G's former global marketing officer. Some successful brands positioned on benefits are Volvo (safety), FedEx (guaranteed on-time delivery), Nike (performance), and Lexus (quality).

The strongest brands go beyond attribute or benefit positioning. They are positioned on strong *beliefs and values*. These brands pack an emotional wallop. Brands such as Godiva, Starbucks, Apple, and Victoria's Secret rely less on a product's tangible attributes and more on creating surprise, passion, and excitement surrounding a brand. Successful brands engage customers on a deep, emotional level. Thus, P&G knows that, to parents, Pampers mean much more than just containment and dryness. According to Stengel,[19]

> If you go back, we often thought of P&G's brands in terms of functional benefits. But when we began listening very closely to customers, they told us Pampers meant much more to them— Pampers are more about parent–child relationships and total baby care. So we started to say, "We want to be a brand experience; we want to be there to help support parents and babies as they grow and develop." In the initial days people thought we were nuts. How can a diaper help a baby's development? But babies wear diapers 24/7 for almost three years. It actually reorients R&D to ask a question like "How can we help babies sleep better?" Why are we concerned about babies sleeping better? Because sleep is important to brain development. It helps relationship skills. Thinking like that, we're able to help improve life for our consumers. The equity of great brands has to be something that a consumer finds inspirational and the organization finds inspirational. You know, our baby care business didn't start growing aggressively until we changed Pampers from being about dryness to being about helping mom with her baby's development.

When positioning a brand, the marketer should establish a mission for the brand and a vision of what the brand must be and do. A brand is the company's promise to deliver a specific set

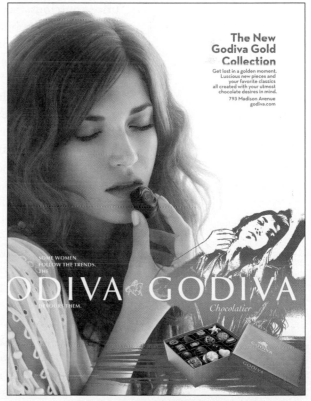

Exhibit 9.6 Brand positioning: The strongest brands go beyond attribute or benefits positioning, and strive for an emotional association. Godiva, for example, is positioned on beliefs and values, and packs an emotional wallop.

The New
Godiva Gold
Collection

Get lost in a golden moment. Luscious new pieces and your favorite classics all created with your utmost chocolate desires in mind.
793 Madison Avenue
godiva.com

of features, benefits, services, and experiences consistently to the buyers. The brand promise must be simple and honest. Motel 6, for example, offers clean rooms, low prices, and good service but does not promise expensive furniture or large bathrooms. In contrast, The Ritz-Carlton offers luxurious rooms and a truly memorable experience but does not promise low prices.

The brand's positioning will not take hold fully unless everyone in the company lives the brand. Therefore, the company needs to train its people to be customer centred. Even better, the company should carry on internal brand building to help employees to understand and be enthusiastic about the brand promise. Many companies go even further by training and encouraging their distributors and dealers to serve their customers well.

BRAND SPONSORSHIP

Brand sponsorship is an important branding strategy decision, and begins with the question, "To brand or not to brand?" Not all products are branded, but those that are may be *national brands* or *private brands*. Marketers may choose *licensing* as a method of branding a new product, or they may partner with another firm to *co-brand* a product.

National brand (or manufacturer's brand)
A brand created and owned by the manufacturer of the product.

Private brand (or store brand)
A brand created and owned by a reseller of a product or a service.

National Brands Versus Store Brands   A new product may be launched as a **national brand (or manufacturer's brand)**, as when Sony and Kellogg sell their output under their own brand names (Sony Bravia or Kellogg's Frosted Flakes). Or the manufacturer may sell to resellers who give the product a **private brand** (also called a **store brand**). National brands dominated the retail scene for many years, but today an increasing number of retailers and wholesalers have created their own **private brands** (see Marketing@Work 9.2). Although store brands have been gaining strength for more than a decade, recent tougher economic times have created a store-brand boom. "Bad times are good times for private labels," says a brand expert. "As consumers become more price-conscious, they also become less brand-conscious."[20]

In fact, store brands are growing much faster than national brands. In all, private label brands now capture some 22 percent of the unit sales of U.S. package-goods (things you'd find in a supermarket or drug store), and more than 17 percent of dollar sales. Private label apparel, such as Hollister, The Limited, Arizona Jean Company (a JCPenney store), and Xhilaration (a Target store brand), captures a 45 percent share of all U.S. apparel sales. Last year alone, store-brand sales grew 10 percent.[21] Many large retailers skilfully market a deep assortment of store-brand merchandise, spanning a broad range of categories. For example, Costco, the world's largest warehouse club, offers a staggering array of goods and services under its Kirkland Signature brand. Costco customers can buy anything from Kirkland Signature rotisserie chickens, to Kirkland brand apparel, to a $3439-per-person Kirkland Signature Tahitian cruise package.

In the grocery business, private brands are referred to as "private label," and private label is big business—it accounts for approximately 25 percent of Canadian grocery stores' and drug stores' revenues. Loblaws and Sobeys each have large buying departments where marketing managers work with vendors to develop private label products. Usually, store brands take a quiet back seat to well-known and heavily advertised national brands, but in the case of President's Choice, what was once a private label brand is now a national brand of its own. Loblaws' President's Choice The Decadent Chocolate Chip Cookies brand is now the leading cookie brand in Canada. Its private label President's Choice cola racks up 50 percent of Loblaws' canned cola sales. Based on this success, the private label powerhouse has expanded into a wide range of food and even non-food categories. For example, it now offers more than 3500 items under the President's Choice label, ranging from frozen desserts, paper, prepared foods, and boxed meats to pet foods, beauty care, and lawn-and-garden items. And the company launched PC Financial, a Web-based bank that offers no-fee bank accounts and mortgages. The President's Choice brand has become so popular that Loblaws now licenses it to retailers across the United States and 15 other countries where Loblaws has no stores of its own.[22]

Usually, private label products are manufactured by companies that also manufacture national brands, but sometimes a company can be *only* a manufacturer of private label products. Toronto's Cott Corp is the world's largest producer of store-branded private label soft drinks. It has operations in Canada, the United States, the United Kingdom, and Mexico, and manufactures soda, energy drinks, flavoured water, sports drinks, and juices for major retailers, including Wal-Mart.[23] In the so-called *battle of the brands* between national and private brands, retailers have many advantages. They control what products they stock, where they go on the shelf, what prices they charge, and which ones they will feature in local circulars. Retailers often price their store brands lower than comparable national brands, thereby appealing to the budget-conscious shopper in all of us. Although store brands can be hard to establish and costly to stock and promote, they also yield higher profit margins for the reseller. And they give resellers exclusive products that cannot be bought from competitors, resulting in greater store traffic and loyalty. Fast-growing American food retailer Trader Joe's, which carries 80 percent store brands, began creating its own brands so that "we could put our destiny in our own hands," says the company's president.[24]

Exhibit 9.7 Store brands: The most recognizable store brand or "private label" in Canada, by far, is President's Choice. It is so well known, in fact, that it has transformed into a national brand.

To compete with store brands, national brands must sharpen their value propositions, especially in low-margin product categories. In the long run, however, leading brand marketers must invest in R&D to bring out new brands, new features, and continuous quality improvements. They must design strong advertising programs to maintain high awareness and preference. And they must find ways to partner with major distributors in a search for distribution economies and improved joint performance.

Licensing Most manufacturers take years and spend millions to create their own brand names. However, some companies **license** names or symbols previously created by other manufacturers, names of well-known celebrities, or characters from popular movies and books. If you've ever bought a T-shirt, or a fridge magnet, or any other non-beverage product that's red and white and bears the Coca-Cola logo, you own an item made by a company that licensed the right to use that name from the Coca-Cola company. The value of a brand can be determined, in part, by the willingness of other companies to purchase the rights to use it.

Apparel and accessories sellers pay large licensing fees for the right to adorn their products—from blouses to ties, and linens to luggage—with the names or initials of well-known fashion innovators such as Calvin Klein, Tommy Hilfiger, Gucci, or Armani. Sellers of children's products attach an almost endless list of character names to clothing, toys, school supplies, linens, dolls, lunch boxes, cereals, and other items. Licensed character names range from classics such as Sesame Street, Disney, Star Wars, the Muppets, Scooby-Doo, Hello Kitty, and Dr. Seuss characters to the more recent Dora the Explorer, Go, Diego, Go!, Little Einsteins, Hannah Montana, and High School Musical

Licensing
Selling the rights to apply a brand name, logo, or image to another manufacturer.

MARKETING@WORK 9.2

Bad Times Are Good Times for Store Brands. But What's a National Brand to Do?

Most things in Michelle Moore's refrigerator, pantry, and laundry room are not name brands—national products with expensive advertising campaigns behind them. They are store-brand products, like Great Value milk fromWalmartor Private Selection or Kroger Value products from her local Kroger grocery store. "I'm weird, because I have always, always, with very few exceptions, bought the generic brands even when we are not in a recession," says Moore, a native ofFayetteville,Arkansas. She thinks that store brands are of pretty much the same quality as national brands. And her private-label grocery savings help her two children, 11 and 9, and husband do other things. "It might only be 50 cents, but 50 cents is 50 cents,"Moore says. The family saves their change in jars,then uses the money at the end of the month to see a movie or have a restaurant meal.

These days, more and more consumers are joining Moore's way of thinking. Already on the rise over the past decade, "the popularity of store brands has soared recently as the economy tanked, with shoppers looking to stretch their dollars," says one analyst. Notes another, "Bad times are good times for private labels ... as consumers become more price-conscious, they also become less brand conscious." From trying cheaper laundry detergents to slipping on a more affordable pair of jeans, consumers are changing their spending habits to save money. That often means abandoning brand name products in favour of store brands.

It seems that almost every retailer now carries its own store brands. Wal-Mart's private brands account for a whopping 40 percent of its sales: brands such as Great Value food products; Sam's Choice beverages; Equate pharmacy, health, and beauty products; White Cloud brand toilet tissue and diapers; Simple Elegance laundry products; and Canopy outdoor home products. Its private label brands alone generate nearly twice the sales of all P&G brands combined, and Great Value is the nation's largest single food brand. At the other end of the spectrum,

even upscale retailer Saks Fifth Avenue carries its own clothing line, which features $98 men's ties, $200 halter-tops, and $250 cotton dress shirts.

Once known as "generic" or "no-name" brands, today's store brands are shedding their image as cheap knock-offs of national brands. Store brands now offer much greater selection, and they are rapidly achieving name-brand quality. In fact, retailers such as Target and Trader Joe's are out-innovating many of their national-brand competitors. Rather than simply creating low-end generic brands that offer a low-price alternative to national brands, retailers are now moving toward higher-end private brands that boost both the store's revenues and its image.

As store brand selection and quality have improved, and as the recession put the brakes on spending, consumers have shown an ever-increasing openness to store brands. Some 40 percent of U.S. consumers now identify themselves as frequent store-brand buyers, up from just 12 percent in the early 1990s. And in a recent survey, 68 percent of consumers agreed that store brands "are usually extremely good value for the money." Some retail strategists predict that the slowdown in consumer spending could last for years. That fact, combined with increasingly

aggressive, more marketing-savvy retailers, could push the private label market to dizzying heights. The new consumer frugality could "lead to a 'downturn generation' that learns to scrimp and save permanently, including buying more private-label," says one strategist.

Does the surge in store brands spell doom for name-brand products? That's not likely. But what should national-brand marketers do to thwart the growing competition from store brands? For starters, they need to sharpen their value propositions in these tougher economic times.

Exhibit 9.8   The popularity of store brands has soared recently. Wal-Mart's store brands account for a whopping 40 percent of its sales.

So far, many national brands have been fighting back with a variety of value pitches. Procter & Gamble recently rolled out campaigns for Pantene and Gillette, among others, that stress the brand's bang for one's buck. Pantene positions itself as an affordable salon alternative. And Gillette Fusion claims that its pricey razor blades deliver "high-performance" shaves for "as little as a dollar a week." According to one P&G rep, that claim is meant to address an outdated notion about the brand. "Guys have consistently told us that they think our blades are costly, so reframing the true expense for them makes good sense." Faced with tighter-fisted consumers, other national brands have reacted by significantly repositioning themselves. For example, Unilever has integrated a value message into its recent campaign for Ragú. One print ad reads, "With Ragú and a pound of pasta, you can feed a family of four for less than four dollars. The perfect meal when your family is growing and the economy is shrinking."

Although such value pitches might work for now, long-term national-brand success requires continued investment in product innovation and brand marketing. In these lean times and beyond, rather than cheapening their products or lowering their prices, national brands need to distinguish themselves through superior customer value. For example, the Ragú value positioning emphasizes affordable quality rather than low prices. And when asked whether, in a weak economy, consumers aren't more concerned about lower prices (via store brands) than brand purpose (via national brands), marketing consultant and former P&G global marketing chief Jim Stengel replied,

> I don't think it's an either/or. I think great brands have a strong sense of their meaning, their ideals, their mission—and their ideas represent a tremendous value to consumers. [National brands] are very much in touch with consumers, and what's on their minds, and they communicate their value through that message. Those things done well actually create [both short-term value and long-term brand equity]. I think

great brands have to tell their stories. They have to do great things ... [bringing] joy, help, and service to people by making them laugh, giving them an idea, or solving a problem. If they do that, [more than survive in down times, national brands will thrive].

So, even when the economic pendulum swings downward, national brand marketers must remain true to their brand stories. "You can have a value proposition that accentuates good value, but you don't want to walk away from the core proposition of the brand," says one marketing executive. "That's the only thing you have to protect yourself" from private labels in the long run.

Even die-hard store brand buyers like Michelle Moore would agree. Despite her penchant for private labels and the savings they yield, there are some

national brands that she just has to buy. "Cheese is one of the things I have not switched. American cheese, I buy Borden," says Moore. She also buys Sunbeam bread—her family likes the soft texture that she hasn't been able to find in store-brand breads. Despite the tough times, Moore still finds many national brands well worth the higher price.

Sources: Excerpts adapted from Lana A. Flowers, "Consumers Turn to Private Labels in Down Economy," *Morning News (Arkansas)*, February 20, 2009, www.nwaonline.net; Elaine Wong, "Foods OK, but Some Can't Stomach More Increases," *Brandweek*, January 5, 2009, p. 7; Elaine Wong, "Stengel: Private Label, Digital Change Game," *Brandweek*, April 13, 2009, pp. 7, 37. Also see Matthew Boyle, "Generics: Making Gains in the Shelf War," *BusinessWeek*, November 10, 2008, p. 62; Sarah Skidmore, "Wal-Mart Revamping Own Brand," *Cincinnati Enquirer*, March 17, 2009, accessed at http://news.cincinnati.com/article/20090317/BIZ/903170336/-1/TODAY; Jack Neff, "Private Label Winning Battle of Brands," *Advertising Age*, February 23, 2009, p. 1; and **http://walmartstores.com/Video/?id=1305**, accessed November 2009.

---

characters. And currently a number of top-selling retail toys are products based on television shows and movies, such as the Hannah Montana Malibu Beach House and the Bob the Builder Interactive Construction Site.

Name and character licensing has grown rapidly in recent years. Annual retail sales of licensed products worldwide have grown from only $4 billion in 1977 to $55 billion in 1987 and more than $187 billion today. Licensing can be a highly profitable business for many companies. For example, U.S. television network Nickelodeon has developed a stable full of hugely popular characters, such as Dora the Explorer, Go, Diego, Go!, and SpongeBob SquarePants. Dora alone has generated more than $5.3 billion in retail sales in under five years. "When it comes to licensing its brands for consumer products, Nickelodeon has proved that it has the Midas touch," states a brand licensing expert.[25]

Co-branding   Although companies have been **co-branding** products for many years, there has been a recent resurgence in co-branding. Co-branding occurs when two established brand names of different companies are used on the same product. For example, financial services firms often partner with other companies to create co-branded credit cards, such as when CIBC and Air Canada joined forces to create the Aeroplan Visa card. Similarly, Costco teamed up with mattress maker Stearns & Foster to market a line of Kirkland Signature by Stearns & Foster mattress sets. And Nike and Apple co-branded the Nike+iPod Sport Kit, which lets runners link their Nike shoes with their iPod Nanos to track and enhance running performance in real time. "Thanks to a unique partnership between Nike and Apple, your iPod Nano [or iPod Touch] becomes your coach. Your personal trainer. Your favorite workout companion."[26]

Exhibit 9.9 Licensing: U.S. television network Nickelodeon owns the rights to the character SpongeBob SquarePants, which generates billions of dollars in revenue from licensing deals.

Most fashions only last a season. These pants never go out of style.

RECORD BREAKING

SpongeBob SquarePants has become an enduring, revolutionary pop icon, inspiring nautical nonsense in millions of people worldwide while generating record-breaking ratings and retail sales.

NICKELODEON SpongeBob SquarePants

Co-branding
The practice of using the established brand names of two different companies on the same product.

In most co-branding situations, one company licenses another company's well-known brand to use in combination with its own. Co-branding offers many advantages. Because each brand dominates in a different category, the combined brands create broader consumer appeal and greater brand equity. Co-branding also allows a company to expand its existing brand into a category it might otherwise have difficulty entering alone. For example, the Nike+iPod arrangement gives Apple a presence in the sports and fitness market. At the same time, it helps Nike to bring new value to its customers.

Co-branding also has limitations. Such relationships usually involve complex legal contracts and licenses. Co-branding partners must carefully coordinate their advertising, sales promotion, and other marketing efforts. Finally, when co-branding, each partner must trust that the other will take good care of its brand. For example, consider the marriage between Kmart and the Martha Stewart Everyday housewares brand. When Kmart declared bankruptcy before being acquired by Sears, it cast a shadow on the Martha Stewart brand. In turn, when Martha Stewart was convicted and jailed for illegal financial dealings, it created negative associations for Kmart. Finally, Kmart was further embarrassed when Martha Stewart Living Omnimedia struck major licensing agreements with Macy's and other U.S. department store chains, announcing that it would separate from Kmart when the contract ends. Thus, as one manager puts it, "Giving away your brand is a lot like giving away your child—you want to make sure everything is perfect."[27]

BRAND MANAGEMENT ⬤LO4

Brands are powerful, valuable assets that must be carefully developed and managed. An important part of the ongoing management of a brand is *brand communications*. Brand managers must also make decisions about *brand development*. In this section, we examine the strategic brand management decisions the firm must make to manage brands over the long term.

BRAND DEVELOPMENT

A company has four choices when it comes to developing brands (see Figure 9.1). It can introduce *line extensions*, *brand extensions*, *multibrands*, or *new brands*.

Line extensions
Extending an existing brand name to new forms, colours, sizes, ingredients, or flavours of an existing product category.

Line Extensions   Line extensions occur when a company extends existing brand names to new forms, colours, sizes, ingredients, or flavours of an existing product category. Thus, the Cheerios line of cereals was extended to include Honey Nut Cheerios, Yogurt Burst Cheerios, MultiGrain Cheerios, Banana Nut Cheerios, and several other variations.

FIGURE 9.1 Brand development strategies

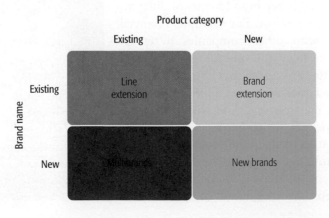

A company might use line extensions as a low-cost, low-risk way to introduce new products. Or it might want to meet consumer desires for variety, to use excess capacity, or simply to command more shelf space from resellers. However, line extensions involve some risks. An overextended brand name might lose its specific meaning. For example, you can now pick from an array of seven different Jeep SUV models—Commander, Grand Cherokee, Compass, Patriot, Liberty, Wrangler, and Wrangler Unlimited. It's unlikely that many customers will fully appreciate the differences across the many similar models, and such "Jeep creep" can cause consumer confusion or even frustration.

Another risk is that sales of an extension may come at the expense of other items in the line. For example, the original Doritos Tortilla Chips have now morphed into a full line of 20 different types and flavours of chips, including such high-decibel flavours as Jalapeno & Cheddar, Sweet Chili Heat, Spicy Nacho, and Scream Cheese. Although the line seems to be doing well, the original Doritos chips seem like just another flavour. A line extension works best when it takes sales away from competing brands, not when it "cannibalizes" the company's other items.

Exhibit 9.10 Brand extensions: P&G extended the Mr. Clean brand from its original household cleaning products to a new product category, auto cleaning kits.

Brand Extensions Brand extensions extend a current brand name to new or modified products in a new category. For example, Campbell Soup extended its V8 juice brand to a line of soups, creating "delicious ways to get your veggies while you please your palate." Victorinox extended its venerable Swiss Army brand from multi-tool knives to products ranging from cutlery and ballpoint pens to watches, luggage, and apparel. And P&G has leveraged the strength of its Mr. Clean household cleaner brand to launch several new lines: cleaning pads (Magic Eraser), bathroom cleaning tools (Magic Reach), and at-home auto cleaning kits (Mr. Clean AutoDry). It even launched Mr. Clean–branded car washes.

Brand extensions Extending an existing brand name to new product categories.

A brand extension gives a new product instant recognition and faster acceptance. It also saves the high advertising costs usually required to build a new brand name. At the same time, a brand extension strategy involves some risk. Brand extensions such as Cheetos lip balm, Heinz pet food, and Life Savers gum met early deaths. The extension may confuse the image of the main brand. And if a brand extension fails, it may harm consumer attitudes toward the other products carrying the same brand name. Furthermore, a brand name may not be appropriate to a particular new product, even if it is well made and satisfying—would you consider flying on Hooters Air or wearing an Evian water–filled padded bra? (Both failed.)

Each year, a survey by brand consultancy TippingSprung rates the year's best and worst brand extensions. The most recent poll gave a strong thumbs-up to extensions such as Coppertone sunglasses, Mr. Clean car washes, Zagat physician ratings, and Thin Mint Cookie Blizzard. Among the worst extensions—those that least fit the brand's core values—were Burger King men's apparel, Playboy energy drink, Allstate Green insurance, and Kellogg's hip-hop streetwear. "Marketers have come to learn that the potential harm inflicted on the brand can more than offset short-term revenue opportunities," says TippingSprung co-founder Robert Sprung. "But that doesn't seem to stop many from launching extensions that in retrospect seem questionable or even ludicrous." Thus, companies that are tempted to transfer a brand name must research how well the brand's associations fit the new product.[28]

Multibranding
A brand development strategy in which the same manufacturer produces many different brands in the same product category.

Multibrands **Multibranding** is a brand development strategy in which the same manfacturer produces many different brands in a given product category. For example, in the United States, P&G sells six brands of laundry detergent (Tide, Cheer, Gain, Era, Dreft, and Ivory), five brands of shampoo (Pantene, Head & Shoulders, Aussie, Herbal Essences, and Infusium 23); and four brands of dishwashing detergent (Dawn, Ivory, Joy, and Cascade). *Multibrands* area way to establish different features that appeal to different customer segments, lock up more reseller shelf space, and capture a larger market share. For example, P&G's six brands combined capture a whopping 62 percent of the U.S. laundry detergent market.

A major drawback of multibranding is that each brand might obtain only a small market share, and none may be very profitable. The company may end up spreading its resources over many brands instead of building a few brands to a highly profitable level. These companies should reduce the number of brands they sell in a given category and set up tighter screening procedures for new brands. This happened to General Motors, which cut numerous brands from its portfolio, including Saturn, Oldsmobile, Pontiac, Hummer, and Saab.

New Brands A company might believe that the power of its existing brand name is waning and a new brand name is needed. Or it may create a new brand name when it enters a new product category for which none of the company's current brand names are appropriate. For example, Toyota created the separate Scion brand, targeted toward Millennial consumers.

Grocery chain Sobeys recently launched a new group of stores under the banner of a new brand name, FreshCo. The new stores are positioned as high-quality products at low prices, with a focus on multicultural and ethnic foods, and were developed as a result of market research that described the changing consumer landscape, especially in the Greater Toronto Area. "In Brampton, the South Asian population has grown 250% in about 12 or 13 years, and there are varieties of produce that are important and relevant and required to satisfy that marketplace," says Sobeys president and CEO Bill McEwan.[29]

As with multibranding, offering too many new brands can result in a company spreading its resources too thin. And in some industries, such as consumer packaged-goods, consumers and retailers have become concerned that there are already too many brands, with too few differences between them. Thus, P&G, Frito Lay, Kraft, and other large consumer-product marketers are now pursuing *megabrand* strategies—weeding out weaker or slower-growing brands and focusing their marketing dollars only on brands that can achieve the number-one or number-two market share positions with good growth prospects in their categories.

Exhibit 9.11 New brands: Toyota created a new brand called *Scion* for a new line of vehicles that would target a new group of consumers, the generation born between 1980–1995, dubbed *Millennials*.

BRAND COMMUNICATIONS

Perhaps the most important task of the brand manager is the management of the many forms of brand communications. The brand's positioning must be continuously communicated to consumers. Major brand marketers often spend huge amounts on advertising to create brand awareness and build preference and loyalty. For example, U.S. mobile phone company Verizon spends more than $3.7 billion annually to promote its brand. McDonald's spends more than $1.2 billion.[30]

Brand Experiences and Touchpoints   Advertising campaigns can help to create name recognition, brand knowledge, and maybe even some brand preference. However, the fact is that brands are not maintained by advertising but by the customers' *brand experiences*. Today, customers come to know a brand through a wide range of contacts and **touchpoints**. These include advertising, but also personal experience with the brand, word of mouth, company webpages, and many others. The company must put as much care into managing these touchpoints as it does into producing its ads. "Managing each customer's experience is perhaps the most important ingredient in building [brand] loyalty," states one branding expert. "Every memorable interaction ... must be completed with excellence and ... must reinforce your brand essence." A former Disney executive agrees: "A brand is a living entity, and it is enriched or undermined cumulatively over time, the product of a thousand small gestures."[31]

The mandate of the Canadian Tourism Commission (CTC) is to promote Canada to the rest of the world, and central to their strategy for marketing Canada is communicating the attributes of Canada as a brand. The CTC is a Crown corporation based in Vancouver, with an annual budget of $75 million, $40 million of which is spent on marketing. The CTC provides its partners with a "brand toolkit" that includes a logo, a colour palette (Expressive Blue, Discovery Green, and Freedom Orange), a font, a description of appropriate tone, and lots and lots of pictures. Also in the toolkit are answers to the basic questions required for brand management:[32]

> **What is brand Canada?** A brand is a distinguishing symbol, mark, logo, name, word, sentence or combination of these that companies use to distinguish their product. In our case, Canada is the brand, and "Keep Exploring" is the tagline. The brand promise is what the consumer can expect from the brand. Ours is: When you come to Canada, you can create your own unique and extraordinary personal experiences. We call these "wow" experiences. The brand personality is confident, youthful, informal, warm, witty, intriguing, authentic (real) and open.

Touchpoints
Any and all points of contact a consumer has with a brand, including word of mouth, company webpages, points of purchase, and advertising.

Exhibit 9.12   Brand experiences: The Canadian Tourism Commission provides its marketing partners with a brand toolkit that helps them to develop "brand Canada" communications.

Who are we talking to? The curious traveller. We are talking to people who believe in participating in life, not sitting on the sidelines; people who are inquisitive, who want to learn about themselves and the world around them.

What tone of voice should be used in brand Canada communications? The tone of voice for brand Canada is personal. It must speak from the heart, and provide a launch pad for experience and imagination. "The tone of voice should be informal, personal, revealing and concise—like one traveller talking to another traveller. It should sound as though you are telling a good friend about your unique experience in Canada."

What is the message of the brand communications? The underlying message of brand Canada is freedom—freedom to explore, to be yourself, to experience Canada in a personal way. Canada is the blank canvas on which the traveller has the freedom to paint his/her own unprescribed experience.

The CTC was named one of Canada's Top Marketers by *Marketing* magazine for its brand campaign designed to attract more American tourists to Canada. Brand communications included a press release titled "Like the girl next door, Canada is tired of being taken for granted"; publicity stunts, such as wrapping Manhattan storefronts with images of Canada, taking over a park in New York with "Mountie Mondays"; and bringing Marilyn Monroe's bedroom slippers, which permanently reside in Toronto's Bata Shoe Museum, to an exhibit in Boston. Says Greg Klassen, CTC vice-president of marketing. "We had to improve our value proposition and create a sense of intrigue about what Canada is all about." The campaign proved to be a success when, despite the Canadian dollar being higher than the American dollar, travel to Canada from the United States increased 4.3 percent in just one month after the campaign ran.

Branded Entertainment   Brand marketers are continually experimenting with new ways to communicate their brand's attributes, messages, and positioning. One way to do this is to partner with filmmakers, musicians, and other artists to create branded content or branded entertainment. **Branded entertainment** is a form of entertainment, usually video, that is created with the co-operation or financial support of a marketer.

Branded entertainment
A form of entertainment, usually video, that is created with the co-operation or financial support of a marketer.

The first brand to create branded entertainment was BMW, with its series of short films called BMW Films. Each was written, acted, directed, and produced with the flair of a Hollywood movie, but the star of each film was a BMW car. The success of BMW Films led many marketers to produce their own films and music videos. Recently, Lady Gaga and Beyoncé produced a short film–music video called "Telephone," which clearly shows the main characters using a Virgin Mobile cellphone and a Polaroid camera; eating a Subway sandwich; logging into the dating site PlentyOfFish.com; and whipping up a poison-laced lunch with Wonder Bread and Miracle Whip. This type of long-form ad entertains, engages, and rewards the consumer, while simultaneously boosting visibility for the brands. "We've definitely seen an upswing in longer-form ads," says one branding expert. "While advertisers are looking for efficiencies in short-format/multiple platforms, they are also looking for new ways to engage consumers."[33]

Other recent examples of branded entertainment include fashion house Pringle of Scotland, which created a film starring Academy Award–

Exhibit 9.13   Branded entertainment: New forms of entertainment such as Lady Gaga's "Telephone" blend elements of music videos, short film, drama (or comedy), and advertising.

winning actor Tilda Swinton walking through the Scottish highlands wearing the brand's new spring line; Absolut Vodka, which produced a 15-minute documentary-style film featuring Jay-Z; and Kraft Foods, which produced a 27-minute branded movie for its Lacta chocolate brand, which is popular in Greece.

ONGOING BRAND MANAGEMENT

One of the most important marketing management roles is that of the brand manager. The brand manager's job, day in and day out, is to be responsible for, and to manage, a brand. Brand managers need to continually audit their brands' strengths and weaknesses, and ask (and answer) questions such as the following: Does our brand excel at delivering benefits that consumers truly value? Is the brand properly positioned? Do all of our consumer touchpoints support the brand's positioning? Do the brand's managers understand what the brand means to consumers? Does the brand receive proper, sustained support? The brand manager makes decisions about which brands need more support, which brands need to be dropped, and which brands should be rebranded or repositioned because of changing customer preferences or new competitors.

Another of the brand manager's ongoing tasks is to carefully manage the marketing communications and advertising that communicates the brand's attributes and positioning to the market. Brands must be maintained, not just by advertising but by the overall brand experience, points of purchase, word of mouth, websites, and, increasingly, social media.

Why is it so important to manage brands? Does it really matter whether Rachael Ray says "olive oil" or "EVOO," or whether Mickey Mouse has two buttons or five on his pants? To brand managers, it's everything. Brand images and logos must be consistent and exact to be recognizable, so the way Mickey Mouse looks—his white gloves, the two buttons on his pants, and the proportional size of his ears—must be carefully controlled and managed. In fact, it is illegal for a manufacturer to print Mickey Mouse T-shirts without Disney's permission. Disney actually polices the use of its brand images and goes after offenders with all its legal guns. If that seems harsh, consider what would happen if a company didn't carefully manage its brands. It wouldn't be long before Mickey would look ... odd ... and we wouldn't recognize him any more.

IT'S ABOUT AUTHENTICITY

"ASK ANYONE WHO KNOWS™"

This, of course, is Canada Goose's motto or tagline for its brand. In many ways, the motto is designed to succinctly capture Canada Goose's brand personality. Brand personality can be defined as "the set of human characteristics associated with a brand." This personality factor is crucial for brand success, as it helps differentiate brands, develop the emotional aspects of a brand, and give a personal meaning of a brand to the consumer.

Experts say that though we sometimes form interpretations of a particular brand personality directly from the brand's leadership (e.g., as in the case of Richard Branson and the Virgin Group), a consumer's sense of a product or service's brand personality is mainly developed from interaction with the product or service itself.

Personality traits can be associated with a brand by observing product-related attributes, product-category associations (e.g., the "sporting goods" product category), promotion, promotional style, brand name, symbol or logo, price, and distribution channel. With all these sources of brand personality, it is not easy for marketers to keep the brand focused.

Canada Goose is certainly aided by the singular strong leadership and vision of president and CEO Dani Reiss. His focus for the brand is authenticity. "Authentic, real brands and products are becoming increasingly important worldwide and people are taking more interest, not only in labour-friendly goods, but in iconic genuine brands with substance," says Reiss. "The truth is that until you've worn a Canada Goose jacket you really don't know; and once you've tried one, especially if it is in Arctic temperatures, you will have no doubt."

From the consumer perspective, brand personalities are not always seen the same way. But the important thing is that the consumer sees the brand as distinct, authentic, and positive.

According to Reiss, in the last 20 years, Canada Goose has always resolved being at a marketing crossroads by protecting and doing what is best for the brand. In 2000, when the company made the change from being called Snow Goose to being called Canada Goose, Snow Goose had a significant following, but the company was starting to see a sort of passion for the Canada Goose. "It was a big risk, but based on our intuition it was the right move," Reiss said.

QUESTIONS

1. What do you see as the Canada Goose brand personality? If you had to humanize the company, what type of person would you use?
2. How do you think Canada Goose is managing its brand?
3. List three ways in which the brand message of Canada Goose is constantly being reinforced.

REVIEWING THE CONCEPTS

1. Define *brand,* and explain how brand meaning is created and maintained.

A brand is a name, term, sign, symbol, design, or a combination of these that identifies the products or services of one seller or group of sellers and differentiates them from those of competitors. Brand names help consumers to identify products that might benefit them, and say something about product quality and consistency. Branding also gives the seller advantages, such as trademark protection and a method for segmenting the market for their products.

Brands are sometimes represented by trademarks, which reassure the consumer that the product they are getting has the attributes they want and expect from that maker. But brands are more than just names and symbols; they are a key element in the company's relationships with its customer. Brands have meaning to consumers, and represent their perceptions and feelings about a product and its performance. Consumers sometimes bond very closely with specific brands and may even become *brand advocates* who willingly and voluntarily promote their favourite brands. Finally, any product or service may be branded, and even people can become their own brands.

2. Explain how brands are represented, and the role of brand personality and brand equity.

Most established brands are represented by a powerful name, a logo, or an icon; however, these symbols are only part of what makes up the brand. Brands also have *personality*, *status*, and value (*brand equity*). Logos can support the brand's positioning and add personality to the brand. Logos are an important part of today's brand-centric universe, and recent research has shown exposure to logos will, over time, influence consumers' brand choices. Many of the most successful brands are those that have a distinctive *personality*. For example, Google is a brand that exhibits a modern, fun, and playful personality. A brand's personality is the sum total of all the attributes of a brand, and the emotions it inspires in the minds of consumers. Brands also have *status*, that is, they occupy a level of social regard with respect to one another.

Brand equity refers to the dollar amount that can be attributed to the value of the brand, based on all the intangible qualities that create that value. One measure of a brand's equity is the extent to which people are willing to pay more for the brand. The strength of a brand can be measured along four consumer perception dimensions: *differentiation* (what makes the brand stand out), *relevance* (how consumers feel it meets their needs), *knowledge* (how much consumers know about the brand), and *esteem* (how highly consumers regard and respect the brand). A powerful brand forms the basis for building strong and profitable customer relationships.

3. List and describe the major strategic decisions marketers must make about brands.

Marketing managers responsible for brands must make high-level strategic decisions that govern the management of the brand, and that guide the public and market perceptions about the brand. The main branding strategy decisions are *brand name selection, brand positioning,* and *brand sponsorship.* A good name can add greatly to a product's success. A good brand name should suggest something about the type of products it will brand, be easy to pronounce, recognize, and remember; be distinctive, extendable, pronounceable, and capable of protection as a trademark.

Another major strategic decision is how to position the brand. Marketers can position the brand on *product attributes*, by associating its name with a desirable *benefit*, or by positioning them on strong *beliefs and values*. The strongest brands usually engage customers on a deep, emotional level. A brand is the company's promise to deliver a specific set of features, benefits, services, and experiences consistently to the buyers. The *brand promise* must be simple and honest, and can take hold only if everyone in the company lives the brand.

Finally, marketers must make strategic decisions about *brand sponsorship*. Not all products are branded, but those that are may be *national brands* or *private brands*. Marketers may choose *licensing* as a method of branding a new product, or they may partner with another firm to *co-brand* a product.

4. Explain how brands are developed and managed, and describe the role of brand communications in the ongoing management of brands.

Brands are powerful, valuable assets that must be carefully developed and managed. Brand managers must make decisions about *brand development*. A company has four choices when it comes to developing brands. It can introduce *line extensions, brand extensions, multibrands,* or *new brands*. Line extensions occur when a company extends existing brand names to new forms, colours, sizes, ingredients, or flavours of an existing product category. Brand extensions extend a current brand name to new or modified products in a new category. Multi-branding is a brand development strategy in which the same manufacturer produces many different brands in the same product category. If a company believes that the power of its existing brand name is waning, it may choose to create a new brand name.

An important part of the ongoing management of a brand is *brand communications*, which are critical because the brand's positioning must be continuously communicated to consumers. Brand communications may focus on creating brand awareness or building loyalty and preference. Any time a customer comes into contact with a brand, through any form of communications, it is called a *touchpoint*. Brand communications, or touchpoints, include advertising, word of mouth, websites, and point of purchase. Personal experience is also an element of brand communications. A new form of brand communications in recent years is branded entertainment, a form of entertainment, usually video, that is created with the co-operation or financial support of a marketer.

Finally, the brand manager's job, day in and day out, is to be responsible for, and to manage, a brand. Brand managers need to continually audit their brands' strengths and weaknesses, and make decisions about which brands need more support, which brands need to be dropped, and which brands should be rebranded or repositioned because of changing customer preferences or new competitors.

KEY TERMS

Brand   332
Brand advocates   334
Brand equity   337
Brand extensions   347
Brand personality   336

Branded entertainment   350
Co-branding   346
Licensing   343
Line extensions   346
Multibrands   348

National brand (or manufacturer's brand)   342
Private brand (or store brand)   342
Touchpoints   349

TALK ABOUT MARKETING

1. Visit a TELUS retail store, and spend some time browsing the TELUS website. How would you describe TELUS's brand personality? What role does packaging play in TELUS's brand communications strategy?
2. Think of a specialty product you purchased in the past. How important was brand to your purchase decision? What other aspects of the product played important roles in your decision to purchase that brand of that particular product?
3. Choose a car manufacturer and brand that you are familiar with. How would you describe the brand's attributes, personality, and positioning? How do you feel about the brand? In other words, describe your emotions and beliefs about it.

4. Find or describe three TV commercials you remember seeing recently. Are these examples of brand communications? Explain why or why not.
5. Find an example of a brand extension and a line extension. Why do you think the marketers made these brand decisions for the products you've chosen? In other words, why do you think they decided on a brand extension instead of a line extension, and vice versa?
6. TippingSprung is a branding and marketing consulting firm. Visit its website, and learn about the services it offers its clients. How does it help clients to manage brands?

THINK LIKE A MARKETING MANAGER

General Mills owns, markets, and manages over 300 brands. On the company's website (www.generalmills.com), these brands are organized by food category: baking, breads, cereals, pasta, and so on. Visit the company's website, and choose one of the food categories to examine, and then answer the following questions about the brands in that category.

QUESTIONS

1. How many brands are in your food category? Are they line extensions, brand extensions, or new brand names? Briefly describe the positioning and brand personality for each.

2. Let's say General Mills wants to launch a new brand in your category. Would you recommend a line extension, brand extension, or new brand name? Briefly describe how the new brand should be positioned, for example, should it be a new flavour, or colour, and if so, what? Come up with a new brand name for your product.

MARKETING ETHICS

There are hundreds of different beer brands available to Canadian consumers, most of which are marketed to different segments based on lifestyle, and with advertising campaigns based on communicating brand personality. Yet alcohol is a controlled substance and cannot legally be promoted to underage drinkers. Visit the websites of Molson and Labatt, Canada's two largest brewers, and consider the following ethical questions.

QUESTIONS

1. Both companies on their websites encourage consumers to become a fan on Facebook, yet many Facebook users are underage. Visit the Facebook pages of both companies, and compare the fans on both. How many are there? Do most of them seem to be of legal drinking age? If you were a marketing manager at Molson or Labatt, what additional steps would you recommend to attempt to prevent children from becoming fans of the brewers on Facebook?

2. Look closely at the websites of both companies. Do they offer any communications that associate their brand with responsible drinking? Which brand do you think does the better job of positioning itself as "responsible?"

MARKETING TECHNOLOGY

BlackBerry and Apple are two of the most powerful technology brands. BlackBerry's smartphones compete directly against Apple's iPhone. The two brands are not highly differentiated in terms of features, functionality, or pricing, and brand communications from both companies tend to communicate brand personality and appeal to the consumer's emotions, rather than focusing on technical details.

QUESTIONS

1. Visit the two companies' websites, choose the latest smartphone product from each, and find the page that gives the technical specifications for each. If you were a marketing manager for BlackBerry, what technical details would you highlight in your brand communications to position your brand against the iPhone?
2. Describe the brand personality for both brands. Are technical qualities or attributes part of the personality for either of the brands? Which brand do you think does a better job of communicating its brand personality to the market?

MARKETING BY THE NUMBERS

Special K is the number one brand in the diet food category, and the Kellogg Company is planning to turn it into a megabrand. Brand extensions must be consistent with the brand's positioning as a weight-management food, and so the company will roll out Special K-branded protein waters and protein bars. Sales of Special K–branded cereals were $500 million worldwide last year, an increase of 16 percent from the previous year. The budget for advertising was $45 million. The worldwide market for bottled water is worth approximately $75 billion. Retail sales in the snack food category in Canada were approximately $500 million last year. The snack food category includes candy, gun, snacks, and bars. The natural snacks and bars segment of the market is approximately 10 percent of the larger snack category.

QUESTIONS

1. Kellogg hopes to capture 3 percent of the market with its new Special K protein water products by the end of next year. How much should the company spend on advertising in Canada to support this new product line?
2. How much should the company spend to advertise the new Special K protein bars in Canada? What percentage of the snack food market do you think they will be able to capture in the first year, and what is the value of that market?

END-OF-CHAPTER CASE

CLODHOPPERS: A BRAND MARKETING STORY

Sometimes, the most powerful brand story is the truth. Chris Emery and Larry Finnson founded Krave's Candy in Winnipeg in 1995 and began producing Clodhoppers—a crunchy treat made of graham wafers and fudge clusters, based on Emery's grandmother's recipe—in their basements. They started off small, sharing Clodhoppers with their friends and local merchants, and eventually saw Clodhoppers on the shelves of some of the biggest retailers in the United States.

As the company grew, Emery and Finnson hired a marketing agency to examine their candy, packaging, and brand, and were told to keep things pretty much as is. They were told to keep the dark-box packaging—which made some people think they were selling coffee—and not to touch the story on the back of the box! The original Clodhopper brand identity was built around the fictitious Krave family, which even has its own coat of arms. The first page of the original Krave's website claimed, "From their secluded castle high in the European Alps, secret recipes have been handed down from generation to generation." The family was used to help establish an image of quality for the Clodhopper product, which, according to the Krave family tradition, was made "using only the finest ingredients from around the world."

It was a great brand story, but then a funny thing happened. As the popularity of Clodhoppers grew, the true story became more interesting than the fictional one. Krave's Candy and its Clodhoppers were featured on an episode of *Venture*. It documented the unique story of best friends in high school who went into business by using Grandma's recipe and ended up competing with the likes of multinational giants such as Cadbury and Nestlé. "We got thousands of e-mails and phone calls from people who liked our story—a modern day David among the Goliaths. The support was there to help us build the brand; the consumers led us to water. So we thought we'd be more successful as Chris and Larry, and telling the real story," Finnson says.

Emery says the decision was finalized after visiting Bentonville, Arkansas, the birthplace of Wal-Mart, to sample Clodhoppers with candy buyers from across the country. "People kept saying to us we reminded them of Ben and Jerry. Well, I'm Chris and he's Larry," Emery says. "So we decided to change it and become cartoon characters to tell the real story on the box." Emery and Finnson revised the entire positioning of the brand. The entrepreneurs themselves replaced the fictitious Krave family as the trade characters for the product. The brand was renamed Chris and Larry's Clodhoppers, and both the retro-style packaging and the website feature Chris and Larry cartoon characters. The switch paid immediate dividends in new media coverage of the pair and amounted to an incalculable amount of free advertising, the likes of which they could never have afforded.

Their brand characters and story in place, Emery and Finnson turned their attention to packaging. Their original 300-gram plastic jar created shelving problems for retailers. Based on the packaging, retailers tended to place the product in the snack aisles, near the popcorn products. Since Clodhoppers were $6 a jar, the price was inconsistent with the lower-priced snacks. The plastic jar also made the product look cheap, and because the product settles over time, a 4-centimetre gap appeared at the top of the jar, making it look half-empty to consumers.

Emery and Finnson repackaged the product so that it fit into the upscale boxed chocolate product category, which includes the major players in the category, Black Magic and Pot of Gold. The quality image of the candy was reinforced by using a black package with gold and red trim. Consistent with the high-quality image, a gold-foil bag was used inside the package, which also helped establish the product as being appropriate as a gift. But even though the new packaging helped with product placement—retailers began to place it in the boxed chocolate section of stores—it did not do a good job of differentiating the product from its competitors.

The confectionery industry is highly concentrated in Canada—the leading eight companies constitute 87 percent of the value of total shipments. Further, 60 percent of industry shipments are done by foreign-controlled organizations such as Hershey Foods and Nestlé. The majority of chocolate operations in Canada are dedicated to three product categories: (1) boxed chocolates, (2) chocolate bars, and (3) seasonal novelties.

Boxed chocolates and novelty items are purchased primarily as gifts for birthdays, anniversaries, religious holidays, Valentine's Day, and Mother's Day. The chocolate bar market is highly fragmented: A 4 to 5 percent share of the market places a product in the top 10 brands. Firms in the chocolate industry compete on the basis of brand name, advertising, sales promotion, quality, and cost, depending on the market segment. The Baby Boomer segment, for example, is very quality oriented.

The Confectionery Manufacturers Association of Canada (CMAC) estimates that its members spend $55 million annually on advertising and sales promotion. From a consumption perspective, the CMAC estimates that the average Canadian consumes 10.3 kilograms of chocolate annually, with per capita annual spending on the category of $68. The total chocolate market is valued at approximately $1.4 billion per year and the boxed chocolate segment at between $160 million and $200 million.

A large part of Krave's success has been its ability to sell the brand to important retailers in Canada. Clodhoppers are available in Wal-Mart, Shoppers Drug Mart, Zellers, Loblaws, Sobeys, Safeway, and Save-On-Foods. However, one of the most important distribution arrangements for the future growth of Krave's is in the U.S. market. At a trade show in Toronto, Emery and Finnson met Wal-Mart U.S.A. president and CEO Lee Scott and secured a deal that expanded their distribution into Wal-Mart stores in the United States. Emery and Finnson are trying to achieve a large volume in the United States through aggressive pricing. The 212-gram box sells at U.S. Wal-Marts for US$1.97, compared with its Canadian retail price of $5.87 for a 300-gram box.

December is the most important time of the year for Krave's, with 85 percent of its sales occurring at this time. To reinforce the brand during the holidays, the company runs promotional sampling programs, giving free samples to consumers in stores. Emery and Finnson have relied on public relations more than advertising to create brand recognition and consumer positioning, partly because of their limited budget. However, recognizing the importance of consumer awareness for this product category, they have done some television advertising.

Consistent with the company's strategy to reduce its reliance on seasonal boxed chocolate sales, Emery and Finnson decided to launch Clodhoppers in a new line of small bags, targeted at consumers looking for a quick snack rather than a take-home product or a gift. The new line was launched in 45- and 225-gram packages, as well as in three flavours. By focusing on retailers with high-volume potential through consumers' impulse purchasing, the company has gained respectable distribution for the line.

Despite market complexities and large multinational competitors, Krave's Candy has had considerable success. Sales are already in the millions, and the company was named one of Canada's top 10 food companies by *Food in Canada* magazine. The key to maintaining that success will be effectively managing both the brand's identity and the company's growth through product line extensions and increased geographic distribution.

Sources: Geoff Kirbyson, "Krave's Sweet Success," December 15, 2003, accessed at www.brandchannel. com; Agriculture Canada, accessed at www.agr.gc.ca; Confectionery Manufacturers Association of Canada, accessed at www.confectioncanada.com; and Clodhoppers brand website at http:// clodhoppers.tv.

QUESTION

1. The Clodhoppers brand is now owned by Brookside Foods Ltd. of British Columbia. Brookside has its own brand story, with its own characters: founders Hugh Wiebe and Denis McGuire. Brookside manufactures and markets premium chocolates, similar to Clodhoppers, and, so far, still markets Clodhoppers under their original brand name. How would you recommend that the new company adapt, change, or use the Clodhopper brand story? Should the packaging of Clodhoppers and other Brookside products be the same? Which logo should be used? Should the characters of Chris and Larry still be included on the Clodhoppers package?

AFTER STUDYING THIS CHAPTER, YOU SHOULD BE ABLE TO

 identify the three major pricing strategies and discuss the importance of understanding customer-value perceptions, company costs, and competitor strategies when setting prices

 identify and define the other important external and internal factors affecting a firm's pricing decisions

 describe the major strategies for pricing new products

 explain how companies find a set of prices that maximizes the profits from the total product mix

 discuss how companies adjust their prices to take into account different types of customers and situations

discuss the key issues related to initiating and responding to price changes

Pricing: Understanding and Capturing Customer Value

PREVIEWING THE CONCEPTS

We continue your marketing journey with a look at another major marketing mix tool—pricing. If effective product development, promotion, and distribution sow the seeds of business success, effective pricing is the harvest. Firms successful at creating customer value with the other marketing mix activities must still capture some of this value in the prices they earn. Yet, despite its importance, many firms do not handle pricing well. In this chapter, we begin with the following question: What is a price? Next, we look at three major pricing strategies—customer value–based, cost-based, and competition-based pricing—and at other factors that affect pricing decisions. Finally, we examine strategies for new-product pricing, product mix pricing, price adjustments, and dealing with price changes.

Let's start with a look at Kodak and its revolutionary new pricing strategy for inkjet printers: Are you tired of buying a reasonably priced printer, and then paying scandalous prices for replacement ink cartridges? Kodak may have the answer. In a move that promises to turn the printer industry on its head, Kodak sells its EasyShare printers for more but charges you less for replacement ink.

KODAK: A WHOLE NEW CONCEPT IN PRINTER PRICING AND ECONOMICS

HP, Epson, Canon, and Lexmark have long dominated the US$50 billion printer industry with a maddening "razor-and-blades" pricing strategy (as in give away the razor, and then make profits on the blades). They sell printers at little or no profit. But once you own the printer, you're stuck buying their grossly overpriced, high-margin replacement ink cartridges.

For example, you can pick up a nifty little HP multi-function inkjet printer for only $69.99. But the HP tricolour inkjet cartridge that goes with it costs $24.99. And a 100-count pack of HP 4-by-6-inch photo paper costs another $14.49. The price per ounce of inkjet printer ink can exceed the per-ounce price of an expensive perfume, premium champagne, or even caviar. By one estimate, if you bought a gallon of the stuff at those prices, it would cost you a horrifying $4731.

The big manufacturers seem content with this captive-product pricing strategy. In fact, they pull in four times more revenues from ink cartridges and paper than from the printers themselves. Customers don't like being held hostage and having to pay through the nose for ink and paper—some are outraged by it. But what can they do? Only HP cartridges work with HP printers. Buying another brand isn't the answer, either—all of the manufacturers pursue the same pricing strategy. Besides, it's difficult to compare long-term per-print prices across manufacturers. Few of us know or go to the trouble to figure out in advance how many cartridges we'll use or what future ink prices will be.

Enter Kodak—with a unique solution. Kodak recently introduced its first line of printers— EasyShare All-in-One printers—with a revolutionary pricing strategy that threatens to turn the entire inkjet printer industry upside-down. In a twist on typical industry practice, Kodak sells its printers at premium prices with no discounts, and then sells the ink cartridges for less. EasyShare printers sell for $149.99 to $299.99, depending on features, about $50 higher than comparable printers sold by competitors. However, EasyShare black and colour ink cartridges go for just $9.99 and $14.99, respectively, about half the prevailing competitor prices. It's a whole new concept in printer pricing and economics.

To make the strategy work, Kodak first had to create a new kind of inkjet printer. It developed an innovative technology that uses tiny nozzles to squirt pigment ink drops that are just a few atoms in size. EasyShare printers take about 55 seconds to produce a 4-by-6-inch print, longer than some competitive printers that do it in 32 seconds. But the resulting photos take up to 90 years to fade versus dye-based inks that can begin to fade in as little as a year.

Moreover, Kodak found a way to contain all of the printing electronics within the EasyShare printer itself, whereas rivals include some of the electronics in the cartridges. This lets Kodak charge less for the cartridges. As a result, according to one independent lab study, Kodak's new printers "whomped" rival's printers in price per printout. The study showed that consumers using an EasyShare printer and buying specially priced packages of photo paper and an ink cartridge can print 4-by-6-inch photos for only 10 cents each, compared with about 29 cents each for typical home printers and 19 cents each at retail store photo services.

Thus, Kodak has the right printer and the right ink prices. Now, all it has to do is to re-educate consumers about printer pricing—about the benefits of paying more up front in order to reduce long-run printing costs. To do this, Kodak launched a "Think Ink" marketing campaign, built around the visual image "ThINK," with the first two letters in black and the last three in gold. The campaign asks the pivotal question "Is it smarter to save money on a printer or save money on ink? (Hint: You only buy the printer once.)"

The ThINK campaign began with online viral efforts, centred on a series of popular "Inkisit" videos, featuring two dorky guys, Nathan and Max, who love to print photos but who don't like ink's high cost. In the videos, they ask enthusiastically, "Have you ever thought about what life would be like if ink was cheaper?" Kodak posted the videos on YouTube and MySpace and set up an entertaining and informative microsite.

Then came the bread-and-butter "ThINK" media campaign, targeting budget-conscious consumers who want to print at home but have limited this activity because of high ink costs. Kodak's research showed that more than 70 percent of all families restrict their children's printing because of cost concerns. So the campaign targets "enterprising parents" who want to empower their kids' creativity and not have to worry about "silly economics."

The ThINK campaign tackles the very difficult task of shifting consumer value perceptions away from initial printer prices and toward prices per print. "Our strategy," says a Kodak marketing executive, "is to crystallize for consumers that they're not only buying a printer today but also buying into three to four years of ink purchases." The campaign sent shockwaves through the inkjet printer industry and its "razor-and-blades" pricing mentality. Says one analyst, Kodak is "plastering their costs per printed page all over the place. The most recent EasyShare ads even rant about a "$5 billion (ink) stain" on the economy caused by "overpaying" for other brands of inkjet printer ink. No one has ever done that before in this market. [The others] don't want to remind consumers how much it costs." Another analyst agrees:

This was not your usual printer introduction. Kodak completely changes the game ... and [these printers] will not be welcomed by competition. Competing openly on cost-per-print puts the profits of the printing industry in grave danger. To compete with Kodak, competitors will have to reveal their own printing costs and ultimately lower [their ink] prices. While this is great for consumers, it is bad for printer manufacturers' bottom lines. Kodak's [EasyShare printers] will take the market by storm.

It's still too soon to tell whether Kodak's revolutionary pricing strategy is working, but the early results are promising. The company exceeded its first-year sales forecasts in 2007 and sold 1.5 million EasyShare printers in 2008. Competitors are now scrambling to introduce their own lower-priced cartridges and longer-lasting inks. But Kodak claims that EasyShare printers will still save customers up to 50 percent on everything they print.

As one observer concludes, Kodak "has its priorities straight: Great-looking photos that last a lifetime," with affordable per-print prices in the bargain. "It makes a world-rocking point about the razor-blades model that's lined the coffers of the inkjet industry for years. If you're mad as hell, you don't have to take it anymore."[1]

Exhibit 10.1   Pricing: No matter what the state of the economy, companies should sell value, not price.

COMPANIES today face a fierce and fast-changing pricing environment. Value-seeking customers have put increased pricing pressure on many companies. Thanks to the weakened economy, the pricing power of the Internet, and value-driven retailers such as Wal-Mart, says one analyst. "These days, we're all cheapskates in search of a spend-less strategy." In response, it seems that almost every company is looking for ways to slash prices.[2]

Yet, cutting prices is often not the best answer. Reducing prices unnecessarily can lead to lost profits and damaging price wars. It can cheapen a brand by signalling to customers that the price is more important than the customer value a brand delivers. Instead, no matter what the state of the economy, companies should sell value, not price. In some cases, that means selling lesser products at rock-bottom prices. But in most cases, it means persuading customers that paying a higher price for the company's brand is justified by the greater value they gain.

WHAT IS A PRICE?

In the narrowest sense, **price** is the amount of money charged for a product or a service. More broadly, price is the sum of all the values that customers give up to gain the benefits of having or using a product or service. Historically, price has been the major factor affecting buyer choice. In recent decades, non-price factors have gained increasing importance. However, price still remains one of the most important elements determining a firm's market share and profitability.

Price is the only element in the marketing mix that produces revenue; all other elements represent costs. Price is also one of the most flexible marketing mix elements. Unlike product features and channel commitments, prices can be changed quickly. At the same time, pricing is the number one problem facing many marketing executives, and many companies do not handle pricing well. Some managers view pricing as a big headache, preferring instead to focus on the other marketing mix elements. However, smart managers treat pricing as a key strategic tool for creating and capturing customer value. Prices have a direct impact on a firm's bottom line. A small percentage improvement in price can generate a large percentage in profitability. More importantly, as a part of a company's overall value proposition, price plays a key role in creating customer value and building customer relationships. "Instead of running away from pricing," says the expert, "savvy marketers are embracing it."[3]

Price

The amount of money charged for a product or a service, or the sum of the values that customers exchange for the benefits of having or using the product or service.

MAJOR PRICING STRATEGIES LO1

The price the company charges will fall somewhere between one that is too high to produce any demand and one that is too low to produce a profit. Figure 10.1 summarizes the major considerations in setting price. Customer perceptions of the product's value set the ceiling for prices. If customers perceive that the price is greater than the product's value, they will not buy the product. Product costs set the floor for prices. If the company prices the product below its costs, company profits will suffer. In setting its price between these two extremes, the company must consider a number of other internal and external factors, including competitors' strategies and prices, the company's overall marketing strategy and mix, and the nature of the market and the demand.

The figure suggests three major pricing strategies: customer value–based pricing, cost-based pricing, and competition-based pricing.

CUSTOMER VALUE–BASED PRICING

In the end, the customer will decide whether a product's price is right. Pricing decisions, like other marketing mix decisions, must start with customer value. When customers buy a product, they exchange something of value (the price) to get something of value (the benefits of having or using the product). Effective, customer-oriented pricing involves understanding how much value consumers place on the benefits they receive from the product and setting a price that captures this value.

Customer value–based pricing
Setting price based on buyers' perceptions of value rather than on the seller's cost.

Customer value–based pricing uses buyers' perceptions of value, not the seller's cost, as the key to pricing. Value-based pricing means that the marketer cannot design a product and marketing program and then set the price. Price is considered along with the other marketing mix variables *before* the marketing program is set.

Figure 10.2 compares value-based pricing with cost-based pricing. Although costs are an important consideration in setting prices, cost-based pricing is often product driven. The company designs what it considers to be a good product, adds up the costs of making the product, and sets a price that covers costs plus a target profit. Marketing must then convince buyers that the product's value at that price justifies its purchase. If the price turns out to be too high, the company must settle for lower markups or lower sales, both resulting in disappointing profits.

Value-based pricing reverses this process. The company first assesses customer needs and value perceptions. It then sets its target price based on customer perceptions of value. The targeted value and price drive decisions about what costs can be incurred and the resulting product design. As a result, pricing begins with analyzing consumer needs and value perceptions, and price is set to match consumers' perceived value.

FIGURE 10.1 Considerations in setting price

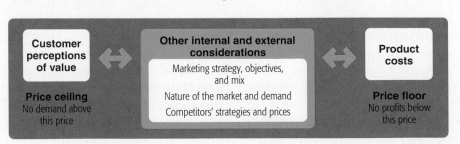

FIGURE 10.2 Value-based pricing versus cost-based pricing

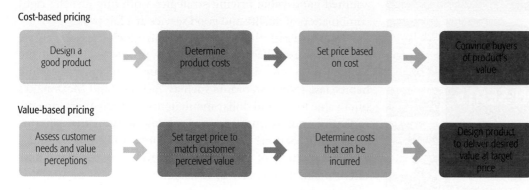

Cost-based pricing

Design a good product → Determine product costs → Set price based on cost → Convince buyers of product's value

Value-based pricing

Assess customer needs and value perceptions → Set target price to match customer perceived value → Determine costs that can be incurred → Design product to deliver desired value at target price

It's important to remember that "good value" is not the same as "low price." For example, a Steinway piano—any Steinway piano—costs a lot. But to those who own one, a Steinway is a great value:[4]

> A Steinway grand piano typically runs anywhere from US$40,000 to US$165,000. The most popular model sells for around US$72,000. But ask anyone who owns one and they'll tell you that, when it comes to Steinway, price is nothing, the Steinway experience is everything. Steinway makes very high quality pianos—handcrafting each Steinway requires up to one full year. But more important, owners get the Steinway mystique. The Steinway name evokes images of classical concert stages and the celebrities and performers who've owned and played Steinway pianos across more than 155 years.
>
> But Steinways aren't just for world-class pianists and the wealthy. Ninety-nine percent of all Steinway buyers are amateurs who perform only in their dens. To such customers, whatever a Steinway costs, it's a small price to pay for the value of owning one. As one Steinway owner puts it, "My friendship with the Steinway piano is one of the most important and beautiful things in my life." Who can put a price on such feelings?

Companies often find it hard to measure the value customers will attach to its product. For example, calculating the cost of ingredients in a meal at a fancy restaurant is relatively easy. But assigning a value to other satisfactions such as taste, environment, relaxation, conversation, and status is very hard. These values are subjective—they vary both for different consumers and different situations.

Still, consumers will use these perceived values to evaluate a product's price, so the company must work to measure them. Sometimes, companies ask consumers how much they would pay for a basic product and for each benefit added to the offer. Or a company might conduct experiments to test the perceived value of different product offers. According to an old Russian proverb, there are two fools in every market—one who asks too much and one who asks too little. If the seller charges more than the buyers' perceived value, the company's sales will suffer. If the seller charges less, its products sell very well but they produce less revenue than they would if they were priced at the level of perceived value.

We now examine two types of value-based pricing: *good-value pricing* and *value-added pricing*.

Good-Value Pricing Recent economic events have caused a fundamental shift in consumer attitudes toward price and quality. In response, many companies have changed their pricing approaches to bring them into line with changing economic conditions and

Exhibit 10.2 Perceived value: A Steinway piano—any Steinway piano—costs a lot. But to those who own one, a Steinway is a great value. "A Steinway takes you places you've never been."

Exhibit 10.3   Good-value pricing: Ryanair appears to have found a radical new pricing solution, one that customers are sure to love: Make flying free!

Good-value pricing
Offering just the right combination of quality and good service at a fair price.

consumer price perceptions. More and more, marketers have adopted **good-value pricing** strategies—offering just the right combination of quality and good service at a fair price.

In many cases, this has involved introducing less-expensive versions of established, brand-name products. To meet the tougher economic times and more frugal consumer spending habits, fast-food restaurants such as Taco Bell and McDonald's offer value meals and dollar menu items. Armani offers the less-expensive, more-casual Armani Exchange fashion line. Alberto-Culver's TRESemmé hair care line promises "A salon look and feel at a fraction of the price." And every car company now offers small, inexpensive models better suited to the strapped consumer's budget.

In other cases, good-value pricing has involved redesigning existing brands to offer more quality for a given price or the same quality for less. Some companies even succeed by offering less value but at rock-bottom prices. For example, passengers flying low-cost European airline Ryanair won't get much in the way of free amenities, but they'll like the airline's unbelievably low prices.[5]

Ireland's Ryanair, Europe's most profitable airline, appears to have found a radical new pricing solution: Make flying *free*! By the end of the decade, Ryanair promises, more than half of its passengers will pay nothing for their tickets. Remarkably, the airline already offers virtually free fares to a quarter of its customers. What's the secret? Ryanair's frugal cost structure makes even the most cost-conscious competitor look like a reckless spender. In addition, however, the airline charges for virtually everything except the seat itself, from baggage check-in to seat-back advertising space. Once in the air, flight attendants hawk everything from scratch-card games to perfume and digital cameras to their captive audience. Upon arrival at some out-of-the-way airport, Ryanair will sell you a bus or train ticket into town. The airline even gets commissions from sales of Hertz rental cars, hotel rooms, ski packages, and travel insurance. Despite Ryanair's sometimes pushy efforts to extract more revenue from each traveler, customers aren't complaining. Most of the additional purchases are discretionary, and you just can't beat those outrageously low prices.

An important type of good-value pricing at the retail level is *everyday low pricing (EDLP)*. EDLP involves charging a constant, everyday low price with few or no temporary price discounts. Retailers such as Costco and furniture seller Leon's, with its Integrity Pricing guarantee, practise EDLP. The king of EDLP is Wal-Mart, which practically defined the concept. Except for a few sale items every month, Wal-Mart promises everyday low prices on everything it sells. In contrast, *high-low pricing* involves charging higher prices on an everyday basis but running frequent promotions to lower prices temporarily on selected items. Department stores such as Sears and The Bay practise high-low pricing by having frequent sales days, early-bird savings, and bonus earnings for store credit-card holders.

Value-added pricing
Attaching value-added features and services to differentiate a company's offers and charging higher prices.

Value-Added Pricing   Value-based pricing doesn't mean simply charging what customers want to pay or setting low prices to meet the competition. Instead, many companies adopt **value-added pricing** strategies. Rather than cutting prices to match competitors, they attach value-added features and services to differentiate their offers and thus support higher prices. Consider this example:

The monsoon season in Mumbai, India, is three months of near-nonstop rain. For 147 years, most Mumbaikars protected themselves with a Stag umbrella from venerable Ebrahim Currim & Sons. Like Ford's Model T, the basic Stag was sturdy, affordable, and of any color, as long as it was black. By the end of the twentieth century, however, the Stag was threatened by cheaper imports from China. Stag responded by dropping prices and scrimping on quality. It was a bad move: For the first time since the 1940s, the brand began losing money.

Finally, however, Stag came to its senses. It abandoned the price war and started innovating. It launched designer umbrellas in funky designs and cool colors. Teenagers and young adults lapped them up. It then launched umbrellas with a built-in high-power flashlight for those who walk unlit roads at night, and models with prerecorded tunes for music lovers. For women who walk secluded streets after dark, there's Stag's Bodyguard model, armed with glare lights, emergency blinkers, and an alarm. Customers willingly pay up to a 100 percent premium for the new products. Under the new value-added strategy, the Stag brand has now returned to profitability. Come the monsoon in June, the grand old black Stags still reappear on the streets of Mumbai—but now priced 15 percent higher than the imports.[6]

Exhibit 10.4 Value-added pricing: Rather than dropping prices for its venerable Stag umbrella brand to match cheaper imports, Ebrahim Currim & Sons successfully launched umbrellas with funky designs, cool colours, and value-added features and sold them at even higher prices.

The Stag example illustrates once again that customers are motivated not by price, but by what they get for what they pay. "If consumers thought the best deal was simply a question of money saved, we'd all be shopping in one big discount store," says one pricing expert. "Customers want value and are willing to pay for it. Savvy marketers price their products accordingly."[7]

COST-BASED PRICING

Whereas customer-value perceptions set the price ceiling, costs set the floor for the price that the company can charge. **Cost-based pricing** involves setting prices based on the costs for producing, distributing, and selling the product plus a fair rate of return for its effort and risk. A company's costs may be an important element in its pricing strategy.

Some companies, such as Ryanair, Wal-Mart, and Dell, work to become the "low-cost producers" in their industries. Companies with lower costs can set lower prices that result in smaller margins but greater sales and profits. Other companies, however, intentionally pay higher costs so that they can claim higher prices and margins. For example, it costs more to make a "handcrafted" Steinway piano than a Yamaha production model. But the higher costs result in higher quality, justifying an eye-popping US$75 000 price. The key is to manage the spread between costs and prices—how much the company makes for the customer value it delivers.

Types of Costs A company's costs take two forms, fixed and variable. **Fixed costs** (also known as **overhead**) are costs that do not vary with production or sales level. For example, a company must pay each month's bills for rent, heat, interest, and executive salaries, whatever the company's output. **Variable costs** vary directly with the level of production. Each PC produced by HP involves a cost of computer chips, wires, plastic, packaging, and other inputs. These costs tend to be the same for each unit produced. They are called variable because their total varies with the number of units produced. **Total costs** are the sum of the fixed and variable costs for any given level of production. Management wants to charge a price that will at least cover the total production costs at a given level of production.

The company must watch its costs carefully. If it costs the company more than competitors to produce and sell a similar product, the company will need to charge a higher price or make less profit, putting it at a competitive disadvantage.

Cost-based pricing
Setting prices based on the costs for producing, distributing, and selling the product plus a fair rate of return for effort and risk.

Fixed costs (overhead)
Costs that do not vary with production or sales level.

Variable costs
Costs that vary directly with the level of production.

Total costs
The sum of the fixed and variable costs for any given level of production.

Cost-plus pricing (or markup pricing)
Adding a standard markup to the cost of the product.

Cost-Plus Pricing The simplest pricing method is **cost-plus pricing** (or **markup pricing**)—adding a standard markup to the cost of the product. For example, an electronics retailer might pay a manufacturer $20 for a flash drive and mark it up to sell at $30, a 50 percent markup on cost. The retailer's gross margin is $10. If the store's operating costs amount to $8 per flash drive sold, the retailer's profit margin will be $2. The manufacturer that made the flash drive probably used cost-plus pricing, too. If the manufacturer's standard cost of producing the flash drive was $16, it might have added a 25 percent markup, setting the price to the retailers at $20.

Does using standard markups to set prices make sense? Generally, no. Any pricing method that ignores consumer demand and competitor prices is not likely to lead to the best price. Still, markup pricing remains popular for many reasons. First, sellers are more certain about costs than about demand. By tying the price to cost, sellers simplify pricing. Second, when all firms in the industry use this pricing method, prices tend to be similar, minimizing price competition.

Break-even pricing (or target return pricing)
Setting price to break even on the costs of making and marketing a product, or setting price to make a target return.

Another cost-oriented pricing approach is **break-even pricing**, or a variation called **target return pricing**. The firm tries to determine the price at which it will break even or make the target return it is seeking. Target return pricing uses the concept of a *break-even chart*, which shows the total cost and total revenue expected at different sales volume levels. Figure 10.3 shows a break-even chart for the flash drive manufacturer discussed previously. Fixed costs are $6 million regardless of sales volume, and variable costs are $5 per unit. Variable costs are added to fixed costs to form total costs, which rise with volume. The slope of the total revenue curve reflects the price. Here, the price is $15 (for example, the company's revenue is $12 million on 800 000 units, or $15 per unit).

At the $15 price, the manufacturer must sell at least 600 000 units to *break even* (break-even volume = fixed costs ÷ (price − variable costs) = $6 000 000 ÷ ($15 − $5) = 600 000). That is, at this level, total revenues will equal total costs of $9 million, producing no profit. If the flash drive manufacturer wants a target return of $2 million, it must sell at least 800 000 units to obtain the $12 million of total revenue needed to cover the costs of $10 million plus the $2 million of target profits. In contrast, if the company charges a higher price, say $20, it will not need to sell as many units to break even or to achieve its target profit. In fact, the higher the price, the lower the manufacturer's break-even point will be.

FIGURE 10.3   Break-even chart for determining target return price and break-even volume

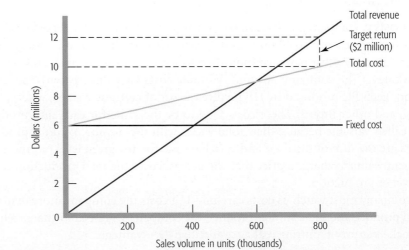

The major problem with this analysis, however, is that it fails to consider customer value and the relationship between price and demand. As the *price* increases, *demand* decreases, and the market may not buy even the lower volume needed to break even at the higher price. For example, suppose the flash drive manufacturer calculates that, given its current fixed and variable costs, it must charge a price of $30 for the product in order to earn its desired target profit. But marketing research shows that few consumers will pay more than $25. In this case, the company must trim its costs to lower the break-even point so that it can charge the lower price consumers expect.

Thus, although break-even analysis and target return pricing can help the company to determine minimum prices needed to cover expected costs and profits, they do not take the price–demand relationship into account. When using this method, the company must also consider the impact of price on sales volume needed to realize target profits and the likelihood that the needed volume will be achieved at each possible price.

COMPETITION-BASED PRICING

Competition-based pricing involves setting prices based on competitors' strategies, costs, prices, and market offerings. Consumers will base their judgments of a product's value on the prices that competitors charge for similar products.

Competition-based pricing
Setting prices based on competitors' strategies, prices, costs, and market offerings.

In assessing competitors' pricing strategies, the company should ask several questions. First, how does the company's market offering compare with competitors' offerings in terms of customer value? If consumers perceive that the company's product or service provides greater value, the company can charge a higher price. If consumers perceive less value relative to competing products, the company must either charge a lower price or change customer perceptions to justify a higher price.

Next, how strong are current competitors and what are their current pricing strategies? If the company faces a host of smaller competitors charging high prices relative to the value they deliver, it might charge lower prices to drive weaker competitors out of the market. If the market is dominated by larger, low-price competitors, the company may decide to target unserved market niches with value-added products at higher prices.

Exhibit 10.5 Pricing against larger, low-price competitors: Independent organic grocery store Pete's Frootique isn't likely to win a price war against Sobeys or Superstore. Instead, it relies on outstanding customer service, high-quality produce, and a cozy atmosphere to turn food lovers into loyal customers.

For example, Pete's Frootique, an independent organic grocery story in Halifax, Nova Scotia, isn't likely to win a price war against Sobeys or Superstore—it doesn't even try. Instead, the store relies on its personal approach, high-quality produce, cozy atmosphere, and friendly and knowledgeable staff to turn local food lovers into loyal patrons, even if they have to pay a little more. One customer writing on a consumer review website, The Coast, recently gave Pete's a five-star rating, supported by the following comments:[8]

> Whenever I visit one of Pete's locations I'm usually met by the same greeting ... wonderful displays of fresh produce, interesting potteries, or delicious (and intriguing!) foods. I try to go here as often as possible to purchase my produce—especially fruits and vegetables! Unlike the stuff I get from the grocery stores, my fruit is bruise free and always a fresh, wonderful colour. The staff are all kind and Pete himself (Can you believe I used to think he wasn't a real person?) is very knowledgeable and funny. But my absolute favourite thing here is the FOOD. Pete's "On the go" Deli/lunch stations are DELICIOUS ... I never cease to be impressed by the sheer freshness, taste and overall quality of the food. I find myself ordering a "grilled veggie" almost every time I go in there—simply wonderful! I also get a side salad, which is a VERY decent sized box stuffed to the brim with all of my favourite (and, again, fresh) fixings. The prices are very decent considering the food you're getting, I have yet to be disappointed.

What principle should guide decisions about what price to charge relative to those of competitors? The answer is simple in concept but often difficult in practice: No matter what price you charge—high, low, or in between—be certain to give customers superior value for that price.

OTHER INTERNAL AND EXTERNAL CONSIDERATIONS AFFECTING PRICING DECISIONS LO2

Beyond customer value perceptions, costs, and competitor strategies, the company must consider several additional internal and external factors. Internal factors affecting pricing include the company's overall marketing strategy, objectives, and marketing mix, as well as other organizational considerations. External factors include the nature of the market and the demand and other environmental factors.

OVERALL MARKETING STRATEGY, OBJECTIVES, AND MIX

Price is only one element of the company's broader marketing strategy. Thus, before setting price, the company must decide on its overall marketing strategy for the product or the service. If the company has selected its target market and positioning carefully, then its marketing mix strategy, including price, will be fairly straightforward. For example, when Honda developed its Acura brand to compete with European luxury-performance cars in the higher-income segment, this required charging a high price. In contrast, when it introduced the Honda Fit model—billed as "a pint-sized fuel miser with feisty giddy up"—this positioning required charging a low price. Thus, pricing strategy is largely determined by decisions on market positioning.

Pricing may play an important role in helping to accomplish company objectives at many levels. A firm can set prices to attract new customers or to profitably retain existing ones. It can set prices low to prevent competition from entering the market or set prices at competitors' levels to stabilize the market. It can price to keep the loyalty and support of resellers or to avoid government intervention. Prices can be reduced temporarily to create excitement for a brand. Or one product may be priced to help the sales of other products in the company's line.

Price is only one of the marketing mix tools that a company uses to achieve its marketing objectives. Pricing decisions must be coordinated with product design, distribution, and promotion decisions to form a consistent and effective integrated marketing program. Decisions made for other marketing mix variables may affect pricing decisions. For example, a decision to position the product on high-performance quality will mean that the seller must charge a higher price to cover higher costs. And producers whose resellers are expected to support and promote their products may have to build larger reseller margins into their prices.

Companies often position their products on price and then tailor other marketing mix decisions to the prices they want to charge. Here, price is a crucial product-positioning factor that defines the product's market, competition, and design. Many firms support such price-positioning strategies with a technique called **target costing**. Target costing reverses the usual process of first designing a new product, determining its cost, and then asking, "Can we sell it for that?" Instead, it starts with an ideal selling price based on customer-value considerations and then targets costs that will ensure that the price is met. For example, when Honda set out to design the Fit, it began with a US$13 950 starting price point and 33-miles-per-gallon operating efficiency firmly in mind. It then designed a stylish, peppy little car with costs that allowed it to give target customers those values.

Target costing
Pricing that starts with an ideal selling price, and then targets costs that will ensure that the price is met.

Other companies de-emphasize price and use other marketing mix tools to create *non-price* positions. Often, the best strategy is not to charge the lowest price but rather to differentiate the marketing offer to make it worth a higher price. For example, Bang & Olufsen—known for its cutting-edge consumer electronics—builds more value into its products and charges sky-high prices. For example, a B&O 50-inch BeoVision 4 HDTV will cost you US$7500; a 65-inch model runs US$13 500. A complete B&O sound system? Well, you don't really want to know. But target customers recognize Bang & Olufsen's very high quality and are willing to pay more to get it.

Some marketers even position their products on *high* prices, featuring high prices as part of their product's allure. For example, Grand Marnier offers a US$225 bottle of Cuvée du Cent Cinquantenaire that's marketed with the tagline "Hard to find, impossible to pronounce, and prohibitively expensive." And Titus Cycles, a premium bicycle manufacturer, features its high prices in its advertising. Ads humorously show people working unusual second jobs to earn the money to afford a Titus. Suggested retail price for a Titus Solera: US$7750. But "It's worth a second job," the ads confirm.

Thus, marketers must consider the total marketing strategy and mix when setting prices. But again, even when featuring price, marketers need to remember that customers rarely buy on price alone. Instead, they seek products that give them the best value in terms of benefits received for the prices paid.

Exhibit 10.6   Positioning on high price: Titus features its lofty prices in its advertising—"suggested retail price: US$7750."

ORGANIZATIONAL CONSIDERATIONS

Management must decide who within the organization should set prices. Companies handle pricing in a variety of ways. In small companies, prices are often set by top management rather than by the marketing or sales departments. In large companies, pricing is typically handled by divisional or product line managers. In industrial markets, salespeople may be allowed to negotiate with customers within certain price ranges. Even so, top management sets the pricing objectives and policies, and it often approves the prices proposed by lower-level management or salespeople.

In industries in which pricing is a key factor (airlines, aerospace, steel, railroads, oil companies), companies often have pricing departments to set the best prices or help others in setting them. These departments report to the marketing department or top management. Others who have an influence on pricing include sales managers, production managers, finance managers, and accountants.

THE MARKET AND DEMAND

As noted earlier, good pricing starts with an understanding of how customers' perceptions of value affect the prices they are willing to pay. Both consumer and industrial buyers balance the price of a product or a service against the benefits of owning it. Thus, before setting prices, the marketer must understand the relationship between price and demand for the company's product. In this section, we take a deeper look at the price–demand

Exhibit 10.7   Monopolistic competition: Toyota sets its Prius brand apart through strong branding and advertising, reducing the impact of price. The 3rd generation Prius takes you from "zero to sixty in 70% fewer emissions."

Demand curve
A curve that shows the number of units the market will buy in a given time period, at different prices that might be charged.

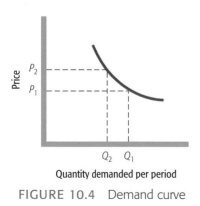

FIGURE 10.4   Demand curve

relationship and how it varies for different types of markets. We then discuss methods for analyzing the price–demand relationship.

Pricing in Different Types of Markets   The seller's pricing freedom varies with different types of markets. Economists recognize four types of markets, each presenting a different pricing challenge.

Under *pure competition*, the market consists of many buyers and sellers trading in a uniform commodity such as wheat, copper, or financial securities. No single buyer or seller has much effect on the going market price. In a purely competitive market, marketing research, product development, pricing, advertising, and sales promotion play little or no role. Thus, sellers in these markets do not spend much time on marketing strategy.

Under *monopolistic competition*, the market consists of many buyers and sellers who trade over a range of prices rather than a single market price. A range of prices occurs because sellers can differentiate their offers to buyers. Sellers try to develop differentiated offers for different customer segments and, in addition to price, freely use branding, advertising, and personal selling to set their offers apart. Thus, Toyota sets its Prius brand apart through strong branding and advertising, reducing the impact of price. It advertises that the 3rd generation Prius takes you from "zero to sixty in 70% fewer emissions." Because there are many competitors in such markets, each firm is less affected by competitors' pricing strategies than in oligopolistic markets.

Under *oligopolistic competition*, the market consists of a few sellers who are highly sensitive to each other's pricing and marketing strategies. Because there are few sellers, each seller is alert and responsive to competitors' pricing strategies and moves.

In a *pure monopoly*, the market consists of one seller. The seller may be a government monopoly (Canada Post), a private regulated monopoly (a power company), or a private non-regulated monopoly (DuPont when it introduced nylon). Pricing is handled differently in each case.

Analyzing the Price–Demand Relationship   Each price the company might charge will lead to a different level of demand. The relationship between the price charged and the resulting demand level is shown in the **demand curve** in Figure 10.4. The demand curve shows the number of units the market will buy in a given time period at different prices that might be charged. In the normal case, demand and price are inversely related; that is, the higher the price, the lower the demand. Thus, the company would sell less if it raised its price from P_1 to P_2. In short, consumers with limited budgets probably will buy less of something if its price is too high.

Understanding a brand's price–demand curve is crucial to good pricing decisions. ConAgra Foods learned this lesson when pricing its Banquet frozen dinners.[9]

ConAgra found out the hard way about the perils of pushing up the price of a Banquet frozen dinner. When it tried to recoup high commodity costs by hiking the list price last year, many retailers began charging up to $1.25 a meal. The response from shoppers used to paying $1? The cold shoulder. The resulting sales drop forced ConAgra to peddle excess dinners to discounters and contributed to a 40 percent drop in the company's stock price for the year. It turns out that "the key component for Banquet dinners—the key attribute— is you've got to be at $1," says ConAgra's CEO, Gary Rodkin. "Everything else pales in comparison to that." The price is now back to a buck a dinner. To make money at that price, ConAgra is doing a better job of managing costs. It tossed out pricey items such as barbecued chicken and country-fried pork in favour of grilled meat patties and rice and beans. It also shrank portion sizes while swapping in cheaper ingredients, such as mashed potatoes for brownies. Consumers are responding well to the brand's efforts to keep prices down. Where else can you find dinner for 99 cents?

Exhibit 10.8   The price–demand curve: When ConAgra raised prices on its Banquet frozen dinners, sales fell sharply. "You've got to be at $1," says CEO Gary Rodkin. "Everything else pales in comparison to that."

Most companies try to measure their demand curves by estimating demand at different prices. The type of market makes a difference. In a monopoly, the demand curve shows the total market demand resulting from different prices. If the company faces competition, its demand at different prices will depend on whether competitors' prices stay constant or change with the company's own prices.

Price Elasticity of Demand   Marketers also need to know **price elasticity**—how responsive demand will be to a change in price. If demand hardly changes with a small change in price, we say demand is *inelastic*. If demand changes greatly, we say the demand is *elastic*.

> Price elasticity
> A measure of the sensitivity of demand to changes in price.

If demand is elastic rather than inelastic, sellers will consider lowering their prices. A lower price will produce more total revenue. This practice makes sense as long as the extra costs of producing and selling more do not exceed the extra revenue. At the same time, most firms want to avoid pricing that turns their products into commodities. In recent years, forces such as deregulation and the instant price comparisons afforded by the Internet and other technologies have increased consumer price sensitivity, turning products ranging from telephones and computers to new automobiles into commodities in some consumers' eyes.

THE ECONOMY

Economic conditions can have a strong impact on the firm's pricing strategies. Economic factors such as a boom or a recession, inflation, and interest rates affect pricing decisions because they affect consumer spending, consumer perceptions of the product's price and value, and the company's costs of producing and selling a product.

In the aftermath of the recent recession, consumers have rethought the price–value equation. Many consumers have tightened their belts and become more value conscious. In the new, more-frugal economy, bemoans one marketer, "The frill is gone." As a result, many marketers have increased their emphasis on value-for-the-money pricing strategies. "Value is the magic word," says a P&G marketer. "In these economic times, people are ... being much more thoughtful before making purchases.... Now, we're going to be even more focused on helping consumers see value."[10]

The most obvious response to the new economic realities is to cut prices and offer deep discounts. And thousands of companies have done just that. Lower prices make products more affordable and help spur short-term sales. However, such price cuts can have undesirable long-term consequences. "Tempted to cut prices?" asks one pricing consultant. "You're not alone. With slumping sales, many businesses have been quick to

More saving. **More doing.**℠   THE HOME DEPOT

Exhibit 10.9   Pricing and the economy: Rather than just cutting prices, Home Depot shifted its marketing focus to more affordable items and projects under the tagline "More saving. More doing."

offer discounts. But price cuts raise some tough questions: Will deep discounts cheapen your brand? Once you cut prices, can you raise them again? How do you deal with narrower margins?"[11]

Rather than cutting prices, many companies are instead shifting their marketing focus to more affordable items in their product mixes. For example, whereas its previous promotions emphasized high-end products and pricey concepts such as creating dream kitchens, Home Depot's more recent advertising pushes items such as potting soil and hand tools under the tagline "More saving. More doing. That's the Power of Home Depot." Other companies are holding prices but redefining the "value" in their value propositions. For instance, Unilever has repositioned its higher-end Bertolli frozen meals as an eat-at-home brand that's more affordable than eating out. And Kraft's Velveeta cheese ads tell shoppers to "forget the cheddar, Velveeta is better," claiming that a package of Velveeta is "twice the size of cheddar, for the same price."[12]

Remember, even in tough economic times, consumers do not buy based on prices alone. They balance the price they pay against the value they receive. For example, according to a recent survey, despite selling its shoes for as much as $150 a pair, Nike commands the highest consumer loyalty of any brand in the footwear segment.[13] Customers perceive the value of Nike's products and the Nike ownership experience to be well worth the price. Thus, no matter what price they charge—low or high—companies need to offer great *value for the money*.

OTHER EXTERNAL FACTORS

When setting prices, beyond the market and the economy, the company must consider a number of other factors in its external environment. It must know what impact its prices will have on other parties in its environment. How will *resellers* react to various prices? The company should set prices that give resellers a fair profit, encourage their support, and help them to sell the product effectively. The *government* is another important external influence on pricing decisions. Finally, *social concerns* may need to be taken into account. In setting prices, a company's short-term sales, market share, and profit goals may need to be tempered by broader societal considerations. We will examine public policy issues in pricing later in the chapter.

We've now seen that pricing decisions are subject to a complex array of customer, company, competitive, and environmental forces. To make things even more complex, a company sets not a single price but rather a *pricing structure* that covers different items in its line. This pricing structure changes over time as products move through their life cycles. The company adjusts its prices to reflect changes in costs and demand and to account for variations in buyers and situations (see Marketing@Work 10.1 to see how the music industry adapted its pricing strategies in the digital age). As the competitive environment changes, the company considers when to initiate price changes and when to respond to them.

We now examine additional pricing approaches used in special pricing situations or to adjust prices to meet changing situations. We look in turn at *new-product pricing* for products in the introductory stage of the product life cycle, *product mix pricing* for related products in the product mix, *price adjustment tactics* that account for customer differences and changing situations, and strategies for initiating and responding to *price changes*.[14]

MARKETING@WORK 10.1

How Do You Compete with Free?

Even now that the music industry is in a state of flux, forget about peer-to-peer file sharing—the music industry has shown that even legitimate products can be free. Zero dollars was the price of Prince's 2007 CD *Planet Earth*, 3 million copies of which were given away via the U.K. *Daily Mail* newspaper to promote his latest European concert tour. Free—or "feels like free"—is an increasingly popular pricing strategy as the record industry tries to find new ways to reach fans and keep them paying for music one way or another. Experiments with alternative, advertising-supported revenue models, SpiralFrog for one, are cropping up.

Pricing was always touchy in the pre-digital era, but it reached a peak with the CD. Introduced in the early 1980s, consumers paid as much as $25 or even $30—roughly twice the usual price for vinyl albums or cassettes at the time. The price was based on the perceived value the CD offered: crystal clear sound after hundreds of plays, longer playing time, less storage space required, and no need to flip sides halfway through an album. Higher prices also underwrote development of the new technologies, with production limited to a few European plants with antiseptic "clean rooms" staffed by space-suited technicians. Further costs were incurred in shipping product overseas, in addition to designing and building new retail display fixtures and bins for the smaller discs.

Eventually North American CD production caught up with demand and vice versa. Major labels adopted multi-tiered pricing schemes, with a premium or "superstar" price point (about a dollar over most new releases) set for international marquee artists such as Madonna, Mariah Carey, or Bon Jovi; a "regular" price for front-line new releases or hit product by up-and-coming, mid-level acts; and one or two bargain pricing tiers for back catalogue releases, whether by current artists such as U2 or long-defunct bands such as the MC5 or The Velvet Underground. These mid- or budget-priced lines bore names such as Super Savers (WEA), Nice Price (BMG), and 20th Century Masters (Universal).

Classics by Van Morrison, Lou Reed, or The Who were discounted but labels also applied special low introductory prices (usually on a limited basis, for the first few thousand units sold) of new titles by "baby bands." For example, KT Tunstall's debut *Eye to the Telescope* could be found for as little as $7–$8 in some Canadian stores for the first few months of release until it gained market traction.

Such penetration pricing strategies were not always effective. Consumers may have associated lower prices with cut-outs (old, unpopular titles deleted from the labels' catalogues) or other dubious quality bargain bin product. Some argue that music was further devalued with the advent of "big box" mass-merchandise retailers such as Costco, Future Shop, and A&B Sound. In their rush to secure these lucrative accounts, labels often wrote massive orders for 3000 to 5000 pieces of a single Bryan Adams or Shania Twain title but took a beating on price. Substantial discounts, beyond the customary reductions for long-standing specialist music distributors (known as trade discounts, or "file" discounts in the United Kingdom) were conceded for order size and volume. Fans grew accustomed to buying current hit albums for only $12.99—great for consumers but bad for the industry.

Canadian CD prices came to be among the lowest in the world, in absolute and relative terms, thanks in part to favourable currency exchange rates and high CD production output. Low-cost exports reached foreign markets such as Japan, forcing products to be repackaged in deluxe containers or with exclusive bonus tracks to justify the higher Japanese domestic prices. Grey market imports also leaked into the United States, causing friction between NAFTA partners. Later, as the Napster era dawned, legal woes over price-fixing and Minimum Advertised Pricing (MAP) policies in the United States eroded any sympathy for the industry the consumers once had.

Exhibit 10.10   Recording artist KT Tunstall performs at a Barnes & Noble in New York City to promote the release of her U.S. debut album, Eye to the Telescope.

Now individual tracks are decoupled from the albums that were historically the labels' most profitable products, and they are sold for 99 cents on iTunes, so pricing remains a challenge. Radiohead, leaving its long-time major label (EMI), offered a flexible pricing model for the online release of its *In Rainbows* album, selling the MP3 download for whatever price fans were willing to pay. A minimum 50 cents covered bandwidth and transaction processing costs. The average price paid was said to be $5.00—about what it might cost for a vinyl LP by the Rolling Stones in the 1970s.

As today's consumers grow up surrounded by music, much of it free, some of it legally obtained, the industry struggles to find the magic pricing formula. It used to be that concert tours lost money but promoted album sales; in the iPod economy, the opposite may now be true.

Ken Ashdown is a 20-year veteran of the music and high-tech industries and head of the Entertainment Business Management department at VancouverFilmSchool. With an MA (Distinction) in Music Business Management from the University of Westminster, he is a member of the Music and Entertainment Industry Educators Association and MusicTank, a London-based music industry think tank.

NEW-PRODUCT PRICING LO3

Pricing strategies usually change as the product passes through its life cycle. The introductory stage is especially challenging. Companies bringing out a new product face the challenge of setting prices for the first time. They can choose between two broad strategies: *market-skimming pricing* and *market-penetration pricing*.

MARKET-SKIMMING PRICING

Market-skimming pricing (or price skimming)
Setting a high price for a new product to skim maximum revenues layer by layer from the segments willing to pay the high price; the company makes fewer but more profitable sales.

Many companies that invent new products set high initial prices to "skim" revenues layer by layer from the market. Sony frequently uses this strategy, called **market-skimming pricing** (or **price skimming**). When Apple first introduced the iPhone, it charged an initial price of as much as US$599 per phone. The phones were purchased only by customers who really wanted the sleek new gadget and could afford to pay a high price for it. Six months later, Apple dropped the price to US$399 for an 8 gigabyte model and US$499 for the 16 gigabyte model to attract new buyers. Within a year, it dropped prices again to US$199 and US$299. In this way, Apple skimmed the maximum amount of revenue from the various segments of the market.[15]

Market skimming makes sense only under certain conditions. First, the product's quality and image must support its higher price and enough buyers must want the product at that price. Second, the costs of producing a smaller volume cannot be so high that they cancel the advantage of charging more. Finally, competitors should not be able to enter the market easily and undercut the high price.

MARKET-PENETRATION PRICING

Market-penetration pricing
Setting a low initial price for a new product in order to attract a large number of buyers and a large market share.

Exhibit 10.11   Penetration pricing: To lure famously frugal Chinese customers, IKEA slashed its prices. The strategy worked. Weekend crowds at its cavernous Beijing store are so big that employees need to use megaphones to keep them in control.

Rather than setting a high initial price to skim off small but profitable market segments, some companies use **market-penetration pricing**. They set a low initial price in order to *penetrate* the market quickly and deeply—to attract a large number of buyers quickly and win a large market share. The high sales volume results in falling costs, allowing the companies to cut their prices even further. For example, giant Swedish retailer IKEA used penetration pricing to boost its success in the Chinese market:[16]

> When IKEA first opened stores in China in 2002, people crowded in, but not to buy home furnishings. Instead, they came to take advantage of the freebies—air conditioning, clean toilets, and even decorating ideas. Chinese consumers are famously frugal. When it came time to actually buy, they shopped instead at local stores just down the street that offered knockoffs of IKEA's designs at a fraction of the price. So to lure the finicky Chinese customers, IKEA slashed its prices in China to the lowest in the world, the opposite approach of many Western retailers there. By increasingly stocking its Chinese stores with China-made products, the retailer pushed prices on some items as low as 70 percent below prices in IKEA's outlets outside China. The penetration pricing strategy worked. IKEA now captures a 43 percent market share of China's fast-growing home wares market alone, and the sales of its six mammoth Chinese stores surged 25 percent last year. The cavernous Beijing store draws nearly 6 million visitors annually. Weekend crowds are so big that employees need to use megaphones to keep them in control.

Several conditions must be met for this low-price strategy to work. First, the market must be highly price sensitive so that a low price produces more market growth. Second, production and distribution costs must fall as sales volume increases. Finally, the low price must help keep out the competition, and the penetration pricer must maintain its low-price position—otherwise, the price advantage may be only temporary.

TABLE 10.1	Product Mix Pricing
Pricing Situation	**Description**
Product line pricing	Setting prices across an entire product line
Optional-product pricing	Pricing optional or accessory products sold with the main product
Captive-product pricing	Pricing products that must be used with the main product
By-product pricing	Pricing low-value by-products to get rid of them
Product bundle pricing	Pricing bundles of products sold together

PRODUCT MIX PRICING (LO4)

The strategy for setting a product's price often has to be changed when the product is part of a product mix. In this case, the firm looks for a set of prices that maximizes the profits on the total product mix. Pricing is difficult because the various products have related demand and costs, and face different degrees of competition. We now take a closer look at the five product mix pricing situations summarized in Table 10.1: *product line pricing, optional-product pricing, captive-product pricing, by-product pricing,* and *product bundle pricing.*

PRODUCT LINE PRICING

Companies usually develop product lines rather than single products. For example, Samsonite offers some 20 different collections of bags of all shapes and sizes, at prices that range from under US$50 for a Sammie's child's backpack to more than US$1250 for a bag from its Black Label Vintage Collection. **In product line pricing**, management must decide on the price steps to set between the various products in a line.

The price steps should take into account cost differences between the products in the line. More importantly, they should account for differences in customer perceptions of the value of different features. For example, QuickTax, the best-selling tax software in Canada, offers multiple versions of its personal tax software, including Basic, Standard, and Platinum, priced at $19.99, $39.99, and $69.99 respectively. Although it costs Intuit, the software company that developed QuickTax, no more to produce the CD and packaging containing the Platinum version than the CD containing the Basic version, many buyers happily pay more to obtain additional Platinum features. Intuit's task is to establish perceived value differences that support the price differences.

OPTIONAL-PRODUCT PRICING

Many companies use **optional-product pricing** —offering to sell optional or accessory products along with their main product. For example, a car buyer may choose to order a GPS navigation system and Bluetooth wireless communication. Refrigerators come with optional ice makers. And when you order a new PC, you can select from a bewildering array of hard drives, docking systems, software options, service plans, and carrying cases. Pricing these options is a sticky problem. Companies must decide which items to include in the base price and which to offer as options.

Product line pricing
Setting the price steps between various products in a product line based on cost differences between the products, customer evaluations of different features, and competitors' prices.

Optional-product pricing
The pricing of optional or accessory products along with a main product.

Exhibit 10.12   Product line pricing: Intuit offers an entire line of tax preparation software, including Basic, Standard, and Platinum versions priced at $19.99, $39.99, and $69.99.

Exhibit 10.13   Captive-product pricing: At Six Flags, you pay a daily-ticket or season-pass charge plus additional fees for food and other in-park features.

Captive-product pricing
Setting a price for products that must be used along with a main product, such as blades for a razor and games for a video-game console.

CAPTIVE-PRODUCT PRICING

Companies that make products that must be used along with a main product are using **captive-product pricing**. Examples of captive products are razor blade cartridges, video games, and printer cartridges. Producers of the main products (razors, video-game consoles, and printers) often price them low and set high markups on the supplies. For example, when Sony first introduced its PlayStation 3 video-game console, priced at US$499 and US$599 for the regular and premium versions, it lost as much as US$306 per unit sold. Sony hoped to recoup the losses through sales of more lucrative PS3 games.[17]

However, companies that use captive-product pricing must be careful. Finding the right balance between the main product and captive-product prices can be tricky. For example, despite industry-leading PS3 videogame sales, Sony has yet to earn back its losses on the PS3 console. What's more, consumers trapped into buying expensive captive products may come to resent the brand that ensnared them. This has happened in the printer and cartridges industry as we've seen in the chapter opening story.

In the case of services, this captive-product pricing is called *two-part pricing*. The price of the service is broken into a *fixed fee* plus a *variable usage rate*. Thus, at Six Flags and other amusement parks, you pay a daily-ticket or season-pass charge plus additional fees for food and other in-park features.

BY-PRODUCT PRICING

By-product pricing
Setting a price for by-products to make the main product's price more competitive.

Producing products and services often generates by-products. If the by-products have no value and if getting rid of them is costly, this will affect the pricing of the main product. Using **by-product pricing**, the company seeks a market for these by-products to help offset the costs of disposing of them and to help make the price of the main product more competitive. The by-products themselves can even turn out to be profitable—turning trash into cash. For example, MacTara Limited, Nova Scotia's largest sawmill, is the only one in Canada that uses all of the wood by-products. Wood chips are turned into paper, shavings are used to heat the company's kilns, and bark is turned into wood pellets used in old coal furnaces.[18]

PRODUCT BUNDLE PRICING

Product bundle pricing
Combining several products and offering the bundle at a reduced price.

By using **product bundle pricing**, sellers often combine several of their products and offer the bundle at a reduced price. For example, fast-food restaurants bundle a burger, fries, and a soft drink at a "combo" price. Bath & Body Works offers "three-fer" deals on its soaps and lotions (such as three antibacterial soaps for $10). And EastLink, Rogers Communications, and other telecommunications companies bundle TV service, phone service, and high-speed Internet connections at a low combined price. Price bundling can promote the sales of products consumers might not otherwise buy, but the combined price must be low enough to get them to buy the bundle.[19]

PRICE ADJUSTMENTS LO5

Companies usually adjust their basic prices to account for various customer differences and changing situations. Here we examine the seven price adjustment strategies summarized

TABLE 10.2	Price Adjustments
Strategy	**Description**
Discount and allowance pricing	Reducing prices to reward customer responses such as paying early or promoting the product
Segmented pricing	Adjusting prices to allow for differences in customers, products, or locations
Psychological pricing	Adjusting prices for psychological effect
Promotional pricing	Temporarily reducing prices to increase short-run sales
Geographical pricing	Adjusting prices to account for the geographic location of customers
Dynamic pricing	Adjusting prices continually to meet the characteristics and needs of individual customers and situations
International pricing	Adjusting prices for international markets

in Table 10.2: *discount and allowance pricing, segmented pricing, psychological pricing, promotional pricing, geographical pricing, dynamic pricing,* and *international pricing.*

DISCOUNT AND ALLOWANCE PRICING

Most companies adjust their basic price to reward customers for certain responses, such as early payment of bills, volume purchases, and off-season buying. These price adjustments—called *discounts* and *allowances*—can take many forms.

The many forms of **discounts** include a *cash discount*, a price reduction to buyers who pay their bills promptly. A typical example is "2/10, net 30," which means that although payment is due within 30 days, the buyer can deduct 2 percent if the bill is paid within 10 days. A *quantity discount* is a price reduction to buyers who buy large volumes. Under the provisions of the *Competition Act*, quantity discounts must be offered equally to all customers and must not exceed the seller's cost savings associated with selling large quantities. A *seasonal discount* is a price reduction to buyers who buy merchandise or services out of season.

Allowances are another type of reduction from the list price. For example, *trade in allowances* are price reductions given for turning in an old item when buying a new one. Trade-in allowances are most common in the automobile industry but are also given for other durable goods. *Promotional allowances* are payments or price reductions to reward dealers for participating in advertising and sales support programs.

SEGMENTED PRICING

Companies will often adjust their basic prices to allow for differences in customers, products, and locations. In **segmented pricing**, the company sells a product or service at two or more prices, even though the difference in prices is not based on differences in costs.

Segmented pricing takes several forms. Under *customer-segment pricing*, different customers pay different prices for the same product or service. Museums, for example, may charge a lower admission for students and senior citizens. Under *product-form pricing*, different versions of the product are priced differently but not according to differences in their costs. For instance, a 1 litre bottle of Evian mineral water may cost $1.59 at your local supermarket. But a 150 millilitre aerosol can of Evian Brumisateur Mineral Water Spray sells for a suggested retail price of $11.39 at beauty boutiques and spas. The water is all from the same source in the French Alps, and the aerosol packaging costs little more than the plastic bottles. Yet you pay about $0.16 per 100 millilitre for one form and $7.59 per 100 millilitre for the other.

Discount
A straight reduction in price on purchases during a stated period of time or of larger quantities.

Allowance
Promotional money paid by manufacturers to retailers in return for an agreement to feature the manufacturer's products in some way.

Segmented pricing
Selling a product or service at two or more prices, where the difference in prices is not based on differences in costs.

Exhibit 10.14   Product-form pricing: Evian water in a 1 litre bottle might cost you $0.16 per 100 millilitre at your local supermarket, whereas the same water might run $7.59 per 100 millilitre when sold in 150 millilitre aerosol cans as Evian Brumisateur Mineral Water Spray.

By using *location-based pricing*, a company charges different prices for different locations, even though the cost of offering each location is the same. For instance, theatres vary their seat prices because of audience preferences for certain locations and Canadian universities charge higher tuition for international students. Finally, by using *time-based pricing*, a firm varies its price by the season, the month, the day, and even the hour. Movie theatres charge matinee pricing during the daytime. Resorts give weekend and seasonal discounts.

For segmented pricing to be an effective strategy, certain conditions must exist. The market must be segmentable, and the segments must show different degrees of demand. The costs of segmenting and watching the market cannot exceed the extra revenue obtained from the price difference. Of course, the segmented pricing must also be legal.

Most importantly, segmented prices should reflect real differences in customers' perceived value. Consumers in higher price tiers must feel that they're getting their extra money's worth for the higher prices paid. By the same token, companies must be careful not to treat customers in lower price tiers as second-class citizens. Otherwise, in the long run, the practice will lead to customer resentment and ill will. For example, in recent years, the airlines have incurred the wrath of frustrated customers at both ends of the airplane. Passengers paying full fare for business or executive seats often feel that they are being gouged. At the same time, passengers in lower-priced economy seats feel that they're being ignored or abused. In all, the airlines today face many very difficult pricing issues (see Marketing@Work 10.2).

PSYCHOLOGICAL PRICING

Psychological pricing
Pricing that considers the psychology of prices and not simply the economics; the price is used to say something about the product.

Reference prices
Prices that buyers carry in their minds and refer to when they look at a given product.

Exhibit 10.15   Psychological pricing: What do the prices marked on this tag suggest about the product and buying situation?

Price says something about the product. For example, many consumers use price to judge quality. A $100 bottle of perfume may contain only $3 worth of scent, but some people are willing to pay the $100 because this price indicates something special.

In using **psychological pricing**, sellers consider the psychology of prices and not simply the economics. For example, consumers usually perceive higher-priced products as having higher quality. When they can judge the quality of a product by examining it or calling on past experience with it, they use price less to judge quality. But when they cannot judge quality because they lack the information or skill, price becomes an important quality signal. For example, who's the better lawyer, one who charges $50 per hour or one that charges $500 per hour? You'd have to do a lot of digging into the respective lawyers' credentials to answer this question objectively, and even then, you might not be able to judge accurately. Most of us would simply assume that the higher-priced lawyer is better.

Another aspect of psychological pricing is **reference prices** —prices that buyers carry in their minds and refer to when looking at a given product. The reference price might be formed by noting current prices, remembering past prices, or assessing the buying situation. Sellers can influence or use these consumers' reference prices when setting price. For example, a company could display its product next to more expensive ones to imply that it belongs in the same class, as when a grocery retailer shelves its store brand of bran flakes-and-raisins cereal priced at $2.99 next to Kellogg's Raisin Bran priced at $4.29.

For most purchases, consumers don't have all the skill or information they need to figure out whether they are paying a good price. They don't have the time, ability, or inclination to research different brands or stores, compare prices, and get the best deals. Instead, they may rely on certain cues that signal whether a price is high or low. Interestingly, such pricing cues are often provided by sellers, in the form of sales signs, price-matching guarantees, loss-leader pricing, and other helpful hints.[20]

MARKETING@WORK 10.2

Airline Pricing: Balancing the Price–Value Equation

It's the same plane going to the same place at exactly the same time. But these days, not all airline passengers are equal. Nor do they all pay equally. No matter where they sit, however, it seems that all passengers have one thing in common: Almost nobody's very happy with what they get for what they pay.

At the front of the plane, business or executive class passengers—who might pay as much as three to six times the fare paid by economy class passengers at the back of the plane—are wondering whether it's worth it. At the same time, back in economy, tempers are flaring over rising air travel prices coupled with fewer amenities and less attentive customer service. The American Customer Satisfaction Index rates the airline industry second-to-last among 44 industries in customer satisfaction, only a few points ahead of the perennial cellar-dweller, cable and satellite TV services.

Flying in economy has become an increasingly miserable experience. Legroom is practically non-existent. Passengers are more tightly packed together. Hot meals have been eliminated. Ditto pillows and blankets. And the next time that guy in front of you leans his seat back directly into your face, few of your fellow passengers are likely to blame you if you feel a brief, murderous urge to strike back.

Most of us have had experiences like those of Doug Fesler, an executive at a medical research group in Washington. He wasn't expecting much in the way of amenities on his American Airlines flight to Honolulu in September. In fact, knowing the airline no longer served free meals, he had packed his own lunch for the second leg of his flight from Dallas to Honolulu. But he said he was shocked at the lack of basic services and the overall condition of the cabin. On that flight, the audio for the movie was broken. The light that indicated when the bathroom was occupied was squirrelly, causing confusion and, in some cases, embarrassingly long waits for

Exhibit 10.16   The price–value equation: These days, when it comes to airline pricing, almost nobody's very happy with what they get for what they pay. Back in economy class, tempers are flaring over rising prices coupled with cattle-car service (or fewer amenities).

passengers in need of the lavatory. And though food was available for purchase, it ran out before the flight attendants could serve the entire cabin, leaving some fellow passengers looking longingly at the snack he had packed.

His return flight was just as disappointing. This time the audio for the movie worked—but only in Spanish—and his seat refused to stay in the upright position. "I was just appalled," said Fesler. "You pay $500 or $600 for a seat, and you expect it to be functional." He said he has considered refusing to fly airlines with such poor service, but added that "if you did that with every airline that made you mad, you'd never get anywhere in this country."

The story is much different in the front of the plane—and it's not just things like the four-course meal (served on china, with real utensils, and with a choice of four wines) that American Airlines now

serves its business-class passengers on overseas flights and the fact that, yes, a pillow and a blanket still await you. Passengers flying executive class on Air Canada from Montreal to Geneva, for example, are now offered lay-flat bed suites with personal seatback entertainment units. American and other airlines are also upgrading their upper-class cabins on international flights with such features as in-flight entertainment and new food options.

What with all these privileges and the impeccable service that comes with them, you'd think that upper-class passengers would be delighted, but that's often not so. Premium passengers *get* more. But, of course, they also *pay* a lot more—some think *too much* more. Many upper-class passengers complain that they're picking up an unfair share of the bill for those who fly cheaply in the back. And they may be right. United says just 8 percent of its customers—the ones paying a premium for first and business class—generate 36 percent of passenger revenue.

But it's the folks back in economy class who are grumbling the most. Why, they ask, has the quality of their flying experience degraded so quickly, even as prices have risen? The fact is that airlines, who flew so close to full capacity for many years, began to think that they really didn't have to cater to economy passengers—most of whom are booking on price alone and who increasingly have no real airline loyalty. However, times have changed with a downturn economy, and some airlines are taking a different route. Porter, for example, a new entrant into the Canadian marketplace, promises and delivers much more. It offers convenient departure points, like the

Island airport in Toronto, which sits right next to the downtown business core. Porter offers upscale amenities such as leather seats with more legroom than other airlines. It focuses on impeccable and innovative service that appeals to business and casual travellers alike. While other airlines believe pampering low-fare passengers would never be worth it in pure bottom-line terms, Porter is proving them wrong and is taking business away from its competitors.

In the short run, the restructured pricing scheme might help the airline industry's finances. However, continuing to haul plane loads of increasingly grumpy passengers can't be good for the airlines in the long run. Especially in an economic downdraft, airlines need all the lift they can get from customer goodwill. Any

airline that gets pricing right will surely reap the rewards.

More broadly, perhaps it's just a matter of adjusting passenger expectations. Some passengers seem to feel that the airlines should just acknowledge that the flying experience is no longer a glamorous or, at times, even tolerable one—especially back in coach—and that it's something passengers are going to have to accept. Low-cost carriers such as Southwest and WestJet have long managed to keep costs down while at the same time keeping customers delighted.

"I actually have more respect for Southwest Airlines in this area," says one experienced traveller, referring to that historically no-frills airline. "They've never pretended to have more than they do."

Even small differences in price can signal product differences. Consider a stereo receiver priced at $300 compared to one priced at $299.99. The actual price difference is only one cent, but the psychological difference can be much greater. For example, some consumers will see the $299.99 as a price in the $200 range rather than the $300 range. The $299.99 will more likely be seen as a bargain price, whereas the $300 price suggests more quality. Some psychologists argue that each digit has symbolic and visual qualities that should be considered in pricing. Thus, 8 is round and even and creates a soothing effect, whereas 7 is angular and creates a jarring effect.

PROMOTIONAL PRICING

Promotional pricing
Temporarily pricing products below the list price and sometimes even below cost to increase short-run sales.

With **promotional pricing**, companies will temporarily price their products below list price and sometimes even below cost to create buying excitement and urgency. Promotional pricing takes several forms. A seller may simply offer *discounts* from normal prices to increase sales and reduce inventories. Sellers also use *special-event pricing* in certain seasons to draw more customers. Thus, large-screen TVs and other consumer electronics are promotionally priced in November and December to attract Christmas shoppers into stores.

Manufacturers sometimes offer *cash rebates* to consumers who buy the product from dealers within a specified time; the manufacturer sends the rebate directly to the customer. Rebates have been popular with automakers and producers of cellphones and small appliances, but they are also used with consumer packaged-goods. Some manufacturers offer *low-interest financing*, *longer warranties*, or *free maintenance* to reduce the consumer's "price." This practice has become another favourite of the auto industry.

Promotional pricing, however, can have adverse effects. Used too frequently and copied by competitors, price promotions can create "deal-prone" customers who wait until brands go on sale before buying them. Or, constantly reduced prices can erode a brand's value in the eyes of customers. Marketers sometimes become addicted to promotional pricing, especially in difficult economic times. They use price promotions as a quick fix instead of sweating through the difficult process of developing effective longer-term strategies for building their brands. But companies must be careful to balance short-term sales incentives against long-term brand building. One analyst advises,[21]

> When times are tough, there's a tendency to panic. One of the first and most prevalent tactics that many companies try is an aggressive price cut. Price trumps all. At least, that's how it feels these days. 20% off. 30% off. 50% off. Buy one, get one free. Whatever it is you're selling, you're offering it at a discount just to get customers in the door. But aggressive pricing strategies can be risky business. Companies should be very wary of risking their brands' perceived quality by resorting to deep and frequent price cuts. Some discounting is unavoidable in a tough economy and consumers have come to expect it. But marketers have to find ways to shore up their brand identity and brand equity during times of discount mayhem.

The point is that promotional pricing can be an effective means of generating sales for some companies in certain circumstances. But it can be damaging for other companies or if taken as a steady diet.

GEOGRAPHICAL PRICING

A company also must decide how to price its products for customers located in different parts of the country or the world. Should the company risk losing the business of more-distant customers by charging them higher prices to cover the higher shipping costs? Or should the company charge all customers the same prices regardless of location? We will look at three **geographical pricing** strategies for the following hypothetical situation:

Geographical pricing
Setting prices for customers located in different parts of the country or the world.

> The Peerless Paper Company is located in Vancouver and sells paper products to customers all over Canada. The cost of freight is high and affects the companies from whom customers buy their paper. Peerless wants to establish a geographical pricing policy. It is trying to determine how to price a $10 000 order to three specific customers: Customer A (Vancouver), Customer B (Winnipeg), and Customer C (Halifax).

One option is for Peerless to ask each customer to pay the shipping cost from the Vancouver factory to the customer's location. All three customers would pay the same factory price of $10 000, with Customer A paying, say, $100 for shipping; Customer B, $150; and Customer C, $250. Called *FOB-origin pricing*, this practice means that the goods are placed *free on board* (hence, *FOB*) a carrier. At that point the title and responsibility pass to the customer, who pays the freight from the factory to the destination. Because each customer picks up its own cost, supporters of FOB pricing feel that this is the fairest way to assess freight charges. The disadvantage, however, is that Peerless will be a high-cost firm to distant customers.

Uniform-delivered pricing is the opposite of FOB pricing. Here, the company charges the same price plus freight to all customers, regardless of their location. The freight charge is set at the average freight cost. Suppose this is $150. Uniform-delivered pricing therefore results in a higher charge to the Vancouver customer (who pays $150 freight instead of $100) and a lower charge to the Halifax customer (who pays $150 instead of $250). Although the Vancouver customer would prefer to buy paper from another local paper company that uses FOB-origin pricing, Peerless has a better chance of winning over the Halifax customer.

Zone pricing falls between FOB-origin pricing and uniform-delivered pricing. The company sets up two or more zones. All customers within a given zone pay a single total price; the more distant the zone, the higher the price. For example, Peerless might set up a West Zone and charge $100 freight to all customers in this zone, a Central Zone in which it charges $150, and an East Zone in which it charges $250. In this way, the customers within a given price zone receive no price advantage from the company. For example, customers in Vancouver and Calgary pay the same total price to Peerless. The complaint, however, is that the Vancouver customer is paying part of the Calgary customer's freight cost.

DYNAMIC PRICING

Throughout most of history, prices were set by negotiation between buyers and sellers. *Fixed price* policies—setting one price for all buyers—is a relatively modern idea that arose with the development of large-scale retailing at the end of the nineteenth century. Today, most prices are set this way. However, some companies are now reversing the fixed pricing trend. They are using **dynamic pricing** —adjusting prices continually to meet the characteristics and needs of individual customers and situations.

Dynamic pricing
Adjusting prices continually to meet the characteristics and needs of individual customers and situations.

For example, think about how the Internet has affected pricing. From the mostly fixed pricing practices of the past century, the Web seems now to be taking us back—into a new age of fluid pricing. The flexibility of the Internet allows Web sellers to instantly and constantly adjust prices on a wide range of goods based on demand dynamics (sometimes called *real-time* pricing). In other cases, customers control pricing by bidding on auction sites such as eBay or negotiating on sites such as Priceline. Still other companies customize their offers based on the characteristics and behaviours of specific customers. For example, airlines are increasingly able to create unique prices and advertisements for people as they surf the Web.[22]

Dynamic pricing offers many advantages for marketers. For example, Internet sellers such as Amazon.ca can mine their databases to gauge a specific shopper's desires, measure his or her means, instantaneously tailor products to fit that shopper's behaviour, and price products accordingly. Catalogue retailers such as L.L.Bean or Tilley Endurables can change prices on the fly according to changes in demand or costs, changing prices for specific items on a day-by-day or even hour-by-hour basis. And many direct marketers monitor inventories, costs, and demand at any given moment and adjust prices instantly.

Consumers also benefit from the Web and dynamic pricing. A wealth of price comparison sites—such as Shopbot.ca, PriceCanada.com, PriceGrabber.ca, and Pricenetwork.ca—offer instant product and price comparisons from thousands of vendors. Shopbot.ca, for instance, lets shoppers browse by category or search for specific products and brands in either English or French. It lists only products available from reliable Canadian retailers, allows users to compare prices from various sellers, and enables shoppers to order them right on the site.

In addition, consumers can negotiate prices at online auction sites and exchanges. Suddenly the centuries-old art of haggling is back in vogue. Want to sell that antique pickle jar that's been collecting dust for generations? Post it on eBay, the world's biggest online flea market. Want to name your own price for a hotel room or a rental car? Visit Priceline.com or another reverse auction site. Want to bid on a ticket to a Coldplay show? Check out Ticketmaster.com, which now offers an online auction service for concert tickets.

Dynamic pricing makes sense in many contexts—it adjusts prices according to market forces, and it often works to the benefit of the customer. But marketers need to be careful not to use dynamic pricing to take advantage of certain customer groups, damaging important customer relationships.

INTERNATIONAL PRICING

Companies that market their products internationally must decide what prices to charge in the different countries in which they operate. In some cases, a company can set a uniform worldwide price. For example, Bombardier sells its jetliners at about the same price everywhere, whether Canada, Europe, or a developing country. However, most companies adjust their prices to reflect local market conditions and cost considerations.

The price that a company should charge in a specific country depends on many factors, including economic conditions, competitive situations, laws and regulations, and development of the wholesaling and retailing system. Consumer perceptions and preferences also may vary from country to country, calling for different prices. Or the company may have different marketing objectives in various world markets, which require changes in pricing strategy. For example, Samsung might introduce a new product into mature markets in highly developed countries with the goal of quickly gaining mass-market share—this would call for a penetration-pricing strategy. In contrast, it might enter a less-developed market by targeting smaller, less price-sensitive segments; in this case, market-skimming pricing makes sense.

Costs play an important role in setting international prices. Travellers abroad are often surprised to find that goods that are relatively inexpensive at home may carry outrageously higher price tags in other countries. A pair of Levi's selling for $30 in North America might go for $63 in Tokyo and $88 in Paris. A McDonald's Big Mac selling for a modest $3.50 here might cost $7.50 in Reykjavik, Iceland, and an Oral-B toothbrush selling for $2.49 at home may cost $10 in China. Conversely, a Gucci handbag going for only $140 in Milan, Italy, might fetch $240 in Canada. In some cases, such *price escalation* may result from differences in selling strategies or market conditions. In most instances, however, it is simply a result of the higher costs of selling in another country—the additional costs of product modifications, shipping and insurance, import tariffs and taxes, exchange-rate fluctuations, and physical distribution.

Price has become a key element in the international marketing strategies of companies attempting to enter emerging markets, such as China, India, and Brazil. Consider Unilever's pricing strategy for developing countries:

> There used to be one way to sell a product in developing markets, if you bothered to sell there at all: Slap on a local label and market at premium prices to the elite. Unilever—maker of such brands as Dove, Lipton, and Vaseline—changed that. Instead, it built a following among the world's poorest consumers by shrinking packages to set a price even consumers living on $2 a day could afford. The strategy was forged about 25 years ago when Unilever's Indian subsidiary found its products out of reach for millions of Indians. To lower the price while making a profit, Unilever developed single-use packets for everything from shampoo to laundry detergent, costing just pennies a pack. The small, affordable packages put the company's premier brands within reach of the world's poor. Today, Unilever continues to woo cash-strapped customers with great success. For example, its approachable pricing helps explain why Unilever now captures 70 percent of the Brazil detergent market.[23]

PRICE CHANGES (LO6)

After developing their pricing structures and strategies, companies often face situations in which they must initiate price changes or respond to price changes by competitors.

INITIATING PRICE CHANGES

In some cases, the company may find it desirable to initiate either a price cut or a price increase. In both cases, it must anticipate possible buyer and competitor reactions.

Initiating Price Cuts Several situations may lead a firm to consider cutting its price. One such circumstance is excess capacity. Another is falling demand in the face of strong price competition or a weakened economy. In such cases, the firm may aggressively cut prices to boost sales and share. But as the airline, fast-food, automobile, and other industries have learned in recent years, cutting prices in an industry loaded with excess capacity may lead to price wars as competitors try to hold on to market share.

Exhibit 10.17   Initiating price increases: When gasoline prices rise rapidly, angry consumers often accuse the major oil companies of enriching themselves by gouging customers.

A company may also cut prices in a drive to dominate the market through lower costs. Either the company starts with lower costs than its competitors, or it cuts prices in the hope of gaining market share that will further cut costs through larger volume. Bausch & Lomb used an aggressive low-cost, low-price strategy to become an early leader in the competitive soft contact lens market. Costco used this strategy to become the world's largest warehouse retailer.

Initiating Price Increases   A successful price increase can greatly improve profits. For example, if the company's profit margin is 3 percent of sales, a 1 percent price increase will boost profits by 33 percent if sales volume is unaffected. A major factor in price increases is cost inflation. Rising costs squeeze profit margins and lead companies to pass cost increases along to customers. Another factor leading to price increases is overdemand: When a company cannot supply all that its customers need, it may raise its prices, ration products to customers, or both. Consider today's worldwide oil and gas industry.

When raising prices, the company must avoid being perceived as a *price gouger*. For example, when gasoline prices rise rapidly, angry customers often accuse the major oil companies of enriching themselves at the expense of consumers. Customers have long memories, and they will eventually turn away from companies or even whole industries that they perceive as charging excessive prices. In the extreme, claims of price gouging may even bring about increased government regulation.

There are some techniques for avoiding these problems. One is to maintain a sense of fairness surrounding any price increase. Price increases should be supported by company communications that tell customers why prices are being raised.

Wherever possible, the company should consider ways to meet higher costs or demand without raising prices. For example, it can consider more cost-effective ways to produce or distribute its products. It can shrink the product or substitute less-expensive ingredients instead of raising the price, as ConAgra did in an effort to hold its Banquet frozen dinner prices at $1. Or it can "unbundle" its market offering, removing features, packaging, or services and separately pricing elements that were formerly part of the offer.

Buyer Reactions to Price Changes   Customers do not always interpret price changes in a straightforward way. A price *increase*, which would normally lower sales, may have some positive meanings for buyers. For example, what would you think if Rolex *raised* the price of its latest watch model? On the one hand, you might think that the watch is even more exclusive or better made. On the other hand, you might think that Rolex is simply being greedy by charging what the traffic will bear.

Similarly, consumers may view a price *cut* in several ways. For example, what would you think if Rolex were to suddenly cut its prices? You might think that you are getting a better deal on an exclusive product. More likely, however, you'd think that quality had been reduced, and the brand's luxury image might be tarnished.

A brand's price and image are often closely linked. A price change, especially a drop in price, can adversely affect how consumers view the brand. Tiffany found this out when it attempted to broaden its appeal by offering a line of more affordable jewellery:[24]

Tiffany is all about luxury and the cachet of its blue boxes. However, in the late 1990s, the high-end jeweller responded to the "affordable luxuries" craze with a new "Return to Tiffany" line of less expensive silver jewellery. The "Return to Tiffany" silver charm bracelet quickly became a must-have item, as teens jammed Tiffany's hushed stores clamouring for the $110 silver bauble. Sales skyrocketed. But despite this early success, the bracelet fad appeared to alienate the firm's older, wealthier, and more conservative clientele, damaging Tiffany's reputation for luxury. So, in 2002, the firm began reemphasizing its pricier jewellery collections. Although high-end jewellery has once again replaced silver as Tiffany's fastest growing business, the company has yet to fully regain its exclusivity. Say's one well-heeled customer: "You used to aspire to be able to buy something at Tiffany, but now it's not that special anymore."

Exhibit 10.18   Price changes: A brand's price and image are often closely linked. Tiffany found this out when it attempted to broaden its appeal by offering a line of more affordable jewellery.

Competitor Reactions to Price Changes   A firm considering a price change must worry about the reactions of its competitors as well as those of its customers. Competitors are most likely to react when the number of firms involved is small, when the product is uniform, and when the buyers are well informed about products and prices.

How can the firm anticipate the likely reactions of its competitors? The problem is complex because, like the customer, the competitor can interpret a company price cut in many ways. It might think the company is trying to grab a larger market share, or that it's doing poorly and trying to boost its sales. Or it might think that the company wants the whole industry to cut prices to increase total demand.

The company must guess each competitor's likely reaction. If all competitors behave alike, this amounts to analyzing only a typical competitor. In contrast, if the competitors do not behave alike—perhaps because of differences in size, market shares, or policies—then separate analyses are necessary. However, if some competitors will match the price change, there is good reason to expect that the rest will also match it.

RESPONDING TO PRICE CHANGES

Here we reverse the question and ask how a firm should respond to a price change by a competitor. The firm needs to consider several issues: Why did the competitor change the price? Is the price change temporary or permanent? What will happen to the company's market share and profits if it does not respond? Are other competitors going to respond? Besides these issues, the company must also consider its own situation and strategy and possible customer reactions to price changes.

Figure 10.5 shows the ways a company might assess and respond to a competitor's price cut. Suppose the company learns that a competitor has cut its price and decides that this price cut is likely to harm company sales and profits. It might simply decide to hold its current price and profit margin. The company might believe that it will not lose too much market share or that it would lose too much profit if it reduced its own price. Or it might decide that it should wait and respond when it has more information on the effects of the competitor's price change. However, waiting too long to act might let the competitor get stronger and more confident as its sales increase.

If the company decides that effective action can and should be taken, it might make any of four responses. First, it could *reduce its price* to match the competitor's price. It may decide that the market is price sensitive and that it would lose too much market share to the lower-priced competitor. Cutting the price will reduce the company's profits in the short run. Some companies might also reduce their product quality, services, and marketing communications to retain profit margins, but this will ultimately hurt long-run market share. The company should try to maintain its quality as it cuts prices.

Alternatively, the company might maintain its price but *raise the perceived value* of its offer. It could improve its communications, stressing the relative value of its product over that of the lower-price competitor. The firm may find it cheaper to maintain price and

FIGURE 10.5   Assessing and responding to competitor price changes

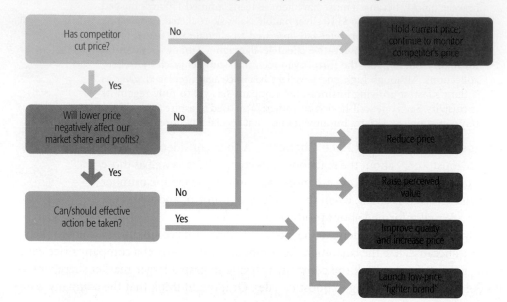

spend money to improve its perceived value than to cut price and operate at a lower margin. Or, the company might *improve quality and increase price*, moving its brand into a higher price–value position. The higher quality creates greater customer value, which justifies the higher price. In turn, the higher price preserves the company's higher margins.

Finally, the company might *launch a low-price "fighter brand"*—adding a lower-price item to the line or creating a separate lower-price brand. This is necessary if the particular market segment being lost is price sensitive and will not respond to arguments of higher quality. Thus, to compete with low-price airlines Southwest and JetBlue, Virgin Group (an owner of Virgin Atlantic Airways) invested in Virgin America airline, which offers amenities such as Wi-Fi, movies, and food on demand, "all for a radically low fare."[25]

To counter store brands and other low-price entrants, Procter & Gamble turned a number of its brands into fighter brands. Luvs disposable diapers give parents "premium leakage protection for less than pricier brands." And P&G offers popular budget-priced Basic versions of several of its major brands. For example, Charmin Basic is "the quality toilet tissue at a price you'll love." And Bounty Basic is "practical, not pricey."

It offers "great strength at a great price—the paper towel that can take care of business without costing a bundle." In all, the Bounty brand claims an astounding 44 percent share of the paper towel market, and Bounty Basic has accounted for much of the brand's recent growth.[26]

Exhibit 10.19   Fighter brands: P&G offers popular budget-priced Basic versions of several of its major brands. For example, Bounty Basic is "practical, not pricey."

PUBLIC POLICY AND PRICING

Price competition is a core element of our free-market economy. In setting prices, companies usually are not free to charge whatever prices they wish. Several laws restrict pricing practices and companies must also consider broader societal pricing concerns.

Legal issues surrounding pricing are outlined in Part VI: Offences in Relation to Competition and Part VII.1: Deceptive Marketing Practices of the *Competition Act*. Canadian pricing legislation was designed with two goals in mind: to foster a competitive environment and to protect consumers.[27] Although pricing decisions made by firms do not generally require regulatory approval, Canadian marketers should be aware of the major public policy issues in pricing outlined in Figure 10.6. These include potentially damaging pricing practices within a given level of the channel (price-fixing and predatory pricing) and across levels of the channel (retail price maintenance, discriminatory pricing, and deceptive pricing).[28]

PRICING WITHIN CHANNEL LEVELS

Federal legislation on *price-fixing* states that sellers must set prices without talking to competitors. Otherwise, price collusion is suspected. Price-fixing is illegal per se—that is, the government does not accept any excuses for price-fixing. Under the *Competition Act*, the legal charge for offences of this nature is *conspiracy*. Companies found guilty of such practices can receive heavy fines. In fact, 2009 changes to the *Competition Act* increased potential fines by as much as $25 million and increased jail sentences for breaching new conspiracy provisions to 14 years.[29]

Section 47 of the Act also identifies bid rigging, where one party agrees not to submit a bid or tender in response to a call or agrees to withdraw a bid or tender submitted at the request of another party, as another indictable offense pertaining to price-fixing. Under section 78 (Abuse of Dominant Position) of the *Competition Act*, sellers are prohibited from using *predatory pricing*—selling below cost with the intention of punishing a competitor or gaining higher long-run profits by putting competitors out of business. This protects small sellers from larger ones who might sell items below cost temporarily or in a specific locale to drive them out of business. The biggest problem is determining just what constitutes predatory pricing behaviour. Selling below cost to unload excess inventory is not considered predatory; selling below cost to drive out competitors is. Thus, the same action may or may not be predatory depending on intent, and intent can be very difficult to determine or prove.

In recent years, several large and powerful companies have been accused of predatory pricing. For example, Wal-Mart has been sued by dozens of small competitors charging that it lowered prices in their specific geographic areas or on specific products—such as gasoline and generic drugs—to drive them out of business.

PRICING ACROSS CHANNEL LEVELS

The *Competition Act* seeks to prevent unfair *price discrimination* by ensuring that sellers offer the same price terms to customers at a given level of trade. For example, every retailer

FIGURE 10.6 Public policy issues in pricing

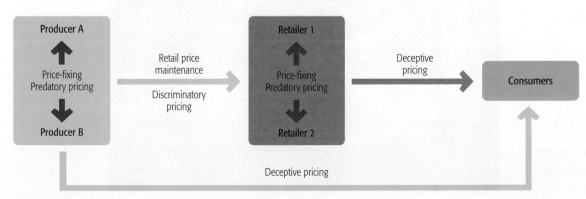

is entitled to the same price terms from a given manufacturer, whether the retailer is Sears or your local bicycle shop. However, price discrimination is allowed if the seller can prove that its costs are different when selling to different retailers—for example, that it costs less per unit to sell a large volume of bicycles to Sears than to sell a few bicycles to the local dealer. In other words, quantity or volume discounts are not prohibited. However, discriminatory promotional allowances (those not offered on proportional terms to all other competing customers) are illegal. Thus, large competitors cannot negotiate special discounts, rebates, and price concessions that are not made proportionally available to smaller competitors. For example, a small customer purchasing one-third as much as a larger competitor must receive a promotional allowance equal to one-third of what the large competitor was offered.

Although functional discounts (offering a larger discount to wholesalers than to retailers) are legal in the United States, they are illegal in Canada. In Canada, retailers and wholesalers are considered competing customers who must receive proportionally equal promotional allowances. Often, Canadian marketers who work for multinational firms must explain the differences in the law to their U.S. counterparts. Canadian marketers must also keep in mind that it is illegal for a buyer to knowingly benefit from any form of price discrimination. Price differentials may be used to "match competition" in "good faith," provided the firm is trying to meet competitors at its own level of competition and the price discrimination is temporary, localized, and defensive rather than offensive.

Canadian marketers are allowed to offer price breaks for one-shot deals, such as store-opening specials, anniversary specials, and stock clearance sales. However, regional price differentials that limit competition are illegal. Canadian firms cannot price products unreasonably low in one part of the country with the intent of driving out the competition.

Laws also prohibit *retail (or resale) price maintenance*—a manufacturer cannot require dealers to charge a specified retail price for its product. Although the seller can propose a manufacturer's *suggested* retail price to dealers, it cannot refuse to sell to a dealer who takes independent pricing action, nor can it punish the dealer by shipping late or denying advertising allowances.

Deceptive pricing practices are outlined in section 74 of the *Competition Act*. For example, firms cannot advertise a product at a low price, carry very limited stock, and then tell consumers they are out of the product so that they can entice them to switch to a higher-priced item. This "bait and switch" advertising is illegal in Canada. Firms must

Exhibit 10.20   Deceptive pricing concerns: The widespread use of checkout scanners has led to increasing complaints of retailers overcharging their customers.

offer their customers "rain checks" to avoid legal sanctions if advertised items are not stocked in sufficient quantities to cover expected demand.

Deceptive pricing occurs when a seller states prices or price savings that are not actually available to consumers. Some deceptions are difficult for consumers to discern, such as when an airline advertises a low one-way fare that is available only with the purchase of a round-trip ticket, or when a retailer sets artificially high "regular" prices, and then announces "sale" prices close to its previous everyday prices.

Other deceptive pricing issues include *scanner fraud* and price confusion. The widespread use of scanner-based computer checkouts has led to increasing complaints of retailers overcharging their customers. Most of these overcharges result from poor management—from a failure to enter current or sale prices into the system. Other cases, however, involve intentional overcharges. Price confusion results when firms employ pricing methods that make it difficult for consumers to understand just what price they are really paying. Canadian law requires firms to charge consumers the lesser price in cases where more than one price is supplied by the seller either through its advertising, packaging, or in-store display.

VALUE PRICING: IT'S ABOUT A LOT MORE THAN JUST MONEY

Conventional wisdom about a recession assumes that when people have less discretionary income they simply spend less on premium goods. However, as is often the case with "conventional wisdom," this is not really true. Some premium products do better, and some do worse; how the goods fare is always a complex matter of perceived value and not just price sensitivity.

For a company that retails expensive products, such as Canada Goose jackets, a recession might have presented some difficult pricing challenges. However, during the most recent recession, Canada Goose didn't drop its prices at all. Instead, it increased them and sales doubled. Why?

Price sensitivity is more difficult to calculate than simply comparing the thickness of your billfold yesterday, today, and tomorrow. Profit potential can be strongly influenced by the overall emotional value of a product, which is based on brand and image, quality, and design. In a market economy where people do have discretionary income (albeit perhaps less than in pre-recession days), consumer purchases depend on the value consumers give to the brand and their willingness (not necessarily ability) to pay. This means that perceived value is what matters.

Canada Goose jackets, which range in price from approximately $450 to more than $1500, would be considered expensive by most consumers. However, the jackets also come with a lifetime warranty. What does this do to the price/value combination of a Canada Goose coat? Conceivably, whether or not Canada Goose owners end up wearing their coats until they start a-knocking on heaven's door, this warranty changes the value perception for Canada Goose parkas. For example, if consumers were to buy an inexpensive coat costing $150 every three years starting at age 25, assuming they live until age 80, they will end up spending $2750 on coats. Thus, a $600 coat that lasts a lifetime, or even 15 years, doesn't seem like such a bad deal.

President and CEO Dani Reiss echoes this thought, deeming a Canada Goose coat "investment clothing." The fact that consumers responded so positively to Canada Goose products during a difficult economic climate suggests that even in a recession a valuable product with a high price point can have significant consumer appeal.

QUESTIONS

1. Canada Goose does not encourage discounting. Why might this be an effective strategy?
2. Look at your own price sensitivity. Is there anything that you purchase regularly that some might consider a premium product? If so, why do you buy it?
3. Sometimes a perception of value is driven by price (usually when people have a hard time discerning quality). Do you think this is the case in much of the high-end winter outerwear market?

REVIEWING THE CONCEPTS

1. **Identify the three major pricing strategies and discuss the importance of understanding customer-value perceptions, company costs, and competitor strategies when setting prices.**

A price is the sum of all the values that customers give up to gain the benefits of having or using a product or service. The three major pricing strategies include customer value–based pricing, cost-based pricing, and competition-based pricing. Good pricing begins with a complete understanding of the value that a product or service creates for customers and setting a price that captures that value. The price the company charges will fall somewhere between one that is too high to produce any demand and one that is too low to produce a profit.

Customer perceptions of the product's value set the ceiling for prices. If customers perceive that the price is greater than the product's value, they will not buy the product. At the other extreme, company and product costs set the floor for prices. If the company prices the product below its costs, its profits will suffer. Between these two extremes, consumers will base their judgments of a product's value on the prices that competitors charge for similar products. Thus, in setting prices, companies need to consider all three factors: customer perceived value, costs, and competitor's pricing strategies.

2. **Identify and define the other important external and internal factors affecting a firm's pricing decisions.**

Other *internal* factors that influence pricing decisions include the company's overall marketing strategy, objectives, and marketing mix, as well as organizational considerations. Price is only one element of the company's broader marketing strategy. If the company has selected its target market and positioning carefully, then its marketing mix strategy, including price, will be fairly straightforward. Some companies position their products on price and then tailor other marketing mix decisions to the prices they want to charge. Other companies de-emphasize price and use other marketing mix tools to create *non-price* positions.

Other *external* pricing considerations include the nature of the market and the demand and environmental factors such as the economy, reseller needs, and government actions. The seller's pricing freedom varies with different types of markets. Ultimately, the customer decides whether the company has set the right price. The customer weighs the price against the perceived values of using the product—if the price exceeds the sum of the values, consumers will not buy. So the company must understand concepts such as demand curves (the price–demand relationship) and price elasticity (consumer sensitivity to prices).

Economic conditions can also have a major impact on pricing decisions. The recent recession caused consumers to rethink the price–value equation. Marketers have responded by increasing their emphasis on value-for-the-money pricing strategies. Even in tough economic times, however, consumers do not buy based on prices alone. Thus, no matter what price they charge—low or high—companies need to offer superior value for the money.

3. **Describe the major strategies for pricing new products.**

Pricing is a dynamic process. Companies design a *pricing structure* that covers all their products. They change this structure over time and adjust it to account for different customers and situations. Pricing strategies usually change as a product passes through its life cycle. The company can decide on one of several price–quality strategies for introducing an imitative product, including premium pricing, economy pricing, good value, or overcharging. In pricing innovative new products, it can use *market-skimming pricing* by initially setting high prices to "skim" the maximum amount of revenue from various segments of the market. Or it can use *market-penetrating pricing* by setting a low initial price to penetrate the market deeply and win a large market share.

4. **Explain how companies find a set of prices that maximizes the profits from the total product mix.**

When the product is part of a product mix, the firm searches for a set of prices that will maximize the profits from the total mix. In *product line pricing*, the company decides on price steps for the entire set of products it offers. In addition, the company must set prices for *optional products* (optional or accessory products included with the main product), *captive products* (products that are required for use of the main product), *by-products* (waste or residual products produced when making the main product), and *product bundles* (combinations of products at a reduced price).

5. **Discuss how companies adjust their prices to take into account different types of customers and situations.**

Companies apply a variety of *price adjustment strategies* to account for differences in consumer segments and situations. One is *discount and allowance pricing*, whereby the company establishes cash, quantity, functional, or seasonal discounts, or varying types of allowances. A second strategy is *segmented pricing*, where the company sells a product at two or more prices to accommodate different customers, product forms, locations, or times. Sometimes companies consider more than economics in their pricing decisions, using *psychological pricing* to better communicate a product's intended position. In *promotional* pricing, a company offers discounts or temporarily sells a product below list price as a special event, sometimes even selling below cost as a loss leader. Another approach is *geographical pricing*, whereby the company decides how to price to distant customers, choosing from such alternatives as FOB-origin pricing, uniform-delivered pricing, and zone pricing. Finally, *international pricing* means that the company adjusts its price to meet different conditions and expectations in different world markets.

6. **Discuss the key issues related to initiating and responding to price changes.**

When a firm considers initiating a *price change*, it must consider customers' and competitors' reactions. There are different implications to *initiating price cuts* and *initiating price increases*. Buyer reactions to price changes are influenced by the meaning customers see in the price change. Competitors' reactions flow from a set reaction policy or a fresh analysis of each situation.

There are also many factors to consider in responding to a competitor's price changes. The company that faces a price change initiated by a competitor must try to understand the competitor's intent as well as the likely duration and impact of the change. If a swift reaction is desirable, the firm should preplan its reactions to different possible price actions by competitors. When facing a competitor's price change, the company might sit tight, reduce its own price, raise perceived quality, improve quality and raise price, or launch a fighting brand.

KEY TERMS

TALK ABOUT MARKETING

1. Identify three price-comparison shopping websites, and shop for an MP3 player of your choice. Compare the price ranges given at these three websites.
2. You are an owner of a small independent chain of coffeehouses competing head-to-head with Starbucks. The retail price your customers pay for coffee is exactly the same as at Starbucks. The wholesale price you pay for roasted coffee beans has increased by 25 percent. You know that you cannot absorb this increase and that you must pass it on to your customers. However, you are concerned about the consequences of an open price increase. Discuss three alternative price-increase strategies that address these concerns.
3. Why do marketers charge customers different prices for the same product or service? Explain how this type of pricing is implemented and the conditions under which it is effective.
4. Explain market-skimming and market-penetration pricing strategies. Why would a marketer of innovative high-tech products choose market-skimming pricing rather than market-penetration pricing when launching a new product?
5. What does the following positioning statement suggest about the firm's marketing objectives, marketing-mix strategy, and costs? "No one beats our prices. We crush the competition."
6. Retailers often use psychological pricing as a price-adjustment strategy. Explain this pricing strategy. How do reference prices affect psychological pricing decisions?

THINK LIKE A MARKETING MANAGER

As you read in the chapter opening story, the printer industry is intensively competitive with respect to pricing. The first home printers, marketed by companies such as Epson and Hewlett-Packard, were almost as expensive as computers themselves. But like most technology products, as technology improves and features are added, the price is forced down. Today, consumers can choose from a wide range of desktop printers for home use. Printers come with a variety of features and can be purchased from many different vendors.

QUESTIONS

1. What role does price play in a consumer's selection of a home printer? What about a business buyer making a purchase decision about an office printer? What about a business person selecting a portable printer to take on business trips?
2. List all the different features a printer can have. Which of these do you think are most important to consumers, and how much extra are they willing to pay for them? Which do you think are most important to business buyers?
3. Do some online research and find three different marketers that sell printers that are suitable for home use. Are the prices of the three brands the same or very different? If they are different, what accounts for the difference? What pricing strategy do you think each marketer is using?
4. How is Kodak's pricing strategy of expensive printers/cheap ink cartridges likely to impact the pricing decisions of its major competitors?

MARKETING ETHICS

Businesses often charge different prices to different customers. For example, movie theatres charge less to students and senior citizens, and prices vary across times of the day. Women are charged more for dry cleaning and haircuts. Business flyers pay more than leisure travellers. And that person sitting next to you on the airplane may have paid more or less than you did—the same goes for hotel rooms. Consumers with arthritis pay more per milligram of pain relief when they buy the Tylenol Arthritis product than when they buy regular Tylenol, even though the active ingredient, acetaminophen, and dosage over an eight-hour period are identical. Technology offers marketers the ability to price-discriminate in various ways. For example, Coca-Cola once experimented with vending machines that raised prices as outdoor temperatures went higher. Electronic shelf labels allow retailers to change prices based on supply and demand. Moreover, the Internet provides the capability for businesses to charge different prices on their websites to different customers of the same product.

QUESTIONS

1. Is it fair for businesses to charge different prices to different customers?
2. Go to www.answers.com/topic/price-discrimination?cat=biz-fin and research the "three degrees of price discrimination." Does this discussion impact your opinion stated in #1 regarding the fairness of this practice? Explain.

MARKETING TECHNOLOGY

You know what an auction is, but what about a *reverse auction*? In a typical auction, a seller offers a good or service for sale and buyers bid on it, with the highest bidder winning the auction. In a reverse auction, however, buyer and seller roles are reversed. A buyer wants to purchase a good or service and solicits sellers to make an offer, with the lowest bidder winning the sale. Like traditional auctions that take place on websites such as eBay, the Internet is facilitating reverse auctions that drive down a company's procurement costs as much as 25 percent to 50 percent. The key to reverse auctions is that they take place quickly and sellers see the lowest bid, which drives down price for the host buyer. Basically, sellers are bidding for how low they are willing to sell a product or service to the buyer. Reverse auctions became popular in the 1990s, and one researcher estimates that almost half of all corporate expenditures will soon be done through reverse auctions.

Reverse auctions aren't just for business-to-business purchases anymore, either. They are now used in the business-to-consumer and consumer-to-consumer marketspace as well. Because of technology, businesses and consumers are now able to set the price they are willing to pay and have sellers compete for their business from anywhere in the world.

QUESTIONS

1. Search the Internet for reverse auction sites. Learn how these sites operate, and explain how they work and the costs associated with conducting a reverse auction.
2. Search for articles about reverse auctions. What are the advantages and disadvantages of using reverse auctions to purchase products and services for businesses? For consumers?

MARKETING BY THE NUMBERS

When introducing new products, some manufacturers use a price-skimming strategy by setting a high initial price and then reducing the price later. However, reducing price also reduces contribution margins, which in turn impacts profitability. To be profitable, the reduced price must sufficiently increase sales. For example, a company with a contribution margin of 30 percent on sales of $60 million realizes a total contribution to fixed costs and profits of $18 million ($60 million × 0.30 = $18 million). If this company decreases price, the contribution margin will also decrease. So to maintain or increase profitability, the price reduction must increase sales considerably.

QUESTIONS

1. Refer to Appendix 3, Marketing by the Numbers, and calculate the new contribution margin for the company discussed above if it reduces price by 10 percent. Assume that unit variable costs are $70 and the original price was $100.
2. What total sales must the company capture at the new price to maintain the same level of total contribution (that is, total contribution = $18 million)?

VIDEO CASE

Visit MyMarketingLab at www.pearsoned.ca/mymarketinglab to view the video for this chapter.

IKEA

Lots of companies have idealistic missions. But IKEA's vision, "To create a better everyday life for the many people," seems somewhat implausible. How can a company that makes furniture improve everyday life for the masses? Interestingly, the most important part of that strategy is price. For every product that it designs, from leather sofas to plastic mugs, IKEA starts with a target price. The target price is one that's deemed affordable, making the product accessible to the masses.

Only then does IKEA begin the gruelling process of creating a high-quality, stylish, and innovative product that can be delivered to the customer for that target price. As IKEA points out, anyone can make high-quality goods for a high price or poor-quality goods for a low price. The real challenge is making high-quality products at a low price. To do so requires a relentless focus on costs combined with a thirst for innovation. That has been IKEA's quest for more than 65 years.

After viewing the video featuring IKEA, answer the following questions about the company's pricing strategy.

QUESTIONS

1. What is IKEA's promise of value?
2. Referring to the Klippan sofa, illustrate how IKEA delivers its promise of value to consumers.
3. Based on the concepts from the text, does IKEA employ a value-based pricing approach or a cost-based pricing approach? Support your answer.

END-OF-CHAPTER CASE

PAYLESS SHOESOURCE: PAYING LESS FOR FASHION

When you think of New York's Fifth Avenue, what retailers come to mind? Tiffany? Gucci? Armani? One name that probably doesn't come to mind is Payless ShoeSource. But for the past few years, Payless has been operating one of its low-priced shoe stores on this avenue of luxury retailing. In fact, Payless is now well on its way to placing stores in more than 100 higher-end malls around North America.

Although the discount shoe peddler still focuses on selling inexpensive shoes to the masses, Payless is now moving upscale. It's on a mission to "democratize fashion"—to make truly fashionable products more accessible by applying its cost-effective model to a product portfolio infused with well-known brand labels and some of the hottest high-end designers in the business. Sound like a hare-brained scheme? Well, you might change your mind after hearing the whole story.

Founded in 1956 in Topeka, Kansas, Payless grew rapidly, based on what was then a revolutionary idea: selling shoes in a self-service environment. Fifty years later, Payless had become the largest shoe retailer in the Western hemisphere, with over 4500 stores throughout the Americas. Targeting budget-minded families, Payless was serving up more than 150 million pairs of shoes each year, roughly 1 in every 10 pairs of shoes purchased in America.

Although all seemed rosy for the choose-it-yourself shoe store, by 2005, Payless was losing market share and closing stores. The retail landscape had changed, and giant discount one-stop shops such as Wal-Mart, Target, and Kohl's had become the vendors of choice for budget-conscious shoppers buying shoes. Said one industry insider, "You can no longer produce the same boring shoes year after year and hope that price alone will get customers to your door." With thrift as its only positioning point, Payless had lost its edge.

NEW IMAGE, HIGHER PRICES

So in June 2005, Payless made its first move to turn things around. It hired a new CEO, Matt Rubel. Rubel knew that to regain its market leadership, Payless would have to design shoes that *Sex in the City*'s Carrie Bradshaw would drool over but at prices that Roseanne could afford. It had to change its image from the dusty dungeon of cheap footwear into the fun, hip merchant of fashion. "We have the ability to make shoes at the most affordable prices anywhere in the world, and we want to marry that with the greatest creativity," Rubel said in a statement reflecting the company's new strategy.

Rubel wasted no time in making big changes. To reflect the new image and communicate change to consumers, Payless redesigned its logo for the first time in 20 years. It then launched new "Fashion Lab" and "Hot Zone" store formats. Both were a drastic improvement, making the stores more open, light, and airy, with a more satisfying consumer experience built around style and design rather than price. Of the new store atmosphere, Rubel said, "It makes the $12 shoe look like a $20 shoe." Rubel hopes not only that the new formats will attract more customers, but also that customers will be willing to pay a little bit more than they have in the past. All new Payless stores now have one of the two new formats, and old stores are being progressively remodelled.

A FASHION REVOLUTION

Beyond these changes in presentation, Rubel focused on the ultimate product. He implemented a "House of Brands" strategy, shifting the Payless product line from one made up of almost entirely store brands to one dominated by well-known national brands. Payless now sells shoes under numerous brand names that it either owns or licenses, including Airwalk, Champion, Spalding, Dexter, Shaquille O'Neal–endorsed Dunkman, and various Disney brands. Rubel also acquired the Stride Rite chain and all its associated brands. To organize the new corporate structure and keep track of all the brands, he created a holding company (Collective Brands) as an umbrella over Payless, Stride Rite, and all the licensing activities for the company's brands.

To develop products that would resonate better with consumers, Payless stepped up its emphasis on fashion. The Payless Design Team, an in-house design group, dedicated itself to developing original footwear and accessory designs to keep new styles on target with changing fashion trends. Top designers from Kenneth Cole and Michael Kors were hired as full-time employees to head the new team.

But in perhaps the biggest move to raise the cachet of the brand, Rubel started "Designer Collections." Aiming for the highest levels of haute couture, Payless has forged relationships with four top New York–based designers: Laura Poretzky, Lela Rose, Stacey Bendet, and Patricia Field. The four are designing everything from pumps to boots to handbags for Payless under the brands Abaeté, Lela Rose, alice + olivia, and Patricia Field.

To support this design effort and the new Fashion Lab store format, Payless has done something really out of character. After signing its first designer, Laura Poretzky, Payless took its designs to the runway of New York's Fashion Week, the invitation-only event where designers debut fall fashions for the industry. In another first, Payless began running full-page ads in *Elle*, *Vogue*, and *W*, featuring the tagline "Look Again."

Can Payless's luxury-meets-low-price strategy work? Or will this go down as a disaster of two drastically different worlds that collided, crashed, and burned? "There's nothing cool about shopping at Payless," says skeptic Marian Salzman, a trends forecaster at a major ad firm. "It gets the cash strapped working girl." But Rubel refutes this view, quickly pointing out that Payless shoppers have median household incomes that are higher than those of both Wal-Mart and Target. "All we've done is bring Payless into the twenty-first century. We're ... speaking with greater clarity to who our customer already is."

Maxine Clark, former president of Payless and now CEO of Build-A-Bear Workshop, also recognizes the potential of the new strategy. "The customer who wants to buy Prada will not come to Payless. But this will energize the old customers who they lost and attract new ones." Mardi Larson, head of public relations for Payless, claims that the trendy new image is perfect for existing customers. "We target the 24-year-old demographic, because women in their 40s who shop for their family are nostalgic about that time in their lives, while [at the same time] teenagers aspire to that age group."

But what about that potential new customer? Does this risky venture into high fashion stand a chance of appealing to those who have never crossed the threshold of a Payless store? Rubel admits to going after new customers. The "cheap chic" approach is attempting to lure 20- to 30-year-old women who are looking for something trendy. Given that such fashion-conscious females buy 50 percent more shoes than most current Payless customers, going after new customers make sense.

Perhaps Lela Rose's experience in 2007 best illustrates why Payless might just succeed in attracting this previously out-of-reach customer: When actresses Sophia Bush (*One Tree Hill*) and Brittany Snow (*Hairspray*) landed backstage in Lela Rose's showroom at New York Fashion Week, they swooned over the designer's new shoe collection that was about to debut on the runway. Rose, best known for US$1500 frocks, happily handed pairs of navy peep-toe pumps and polka-dot round-toe pumps over to the young celebs, who would soon be flaunting them on the sidelines of the catwalk. "Did they know they were Payless shoes?" says Rose, who's now designing her fifth exclusive line for the discounter. "Absolutely. They didn't care. They looked cute to them and that's all that mattered."

Additionally, Payless is not the first to try this new direction. In fact, co-branded designer lines for retailers date back decades. But in recent years, the trend is proliferating. Karl Lagerfeld has designed for Britain's H&M, Vera Wang has teamed up with Kohl's, Ralph Lauren has put store brands on JCPenney's shelves, and Todd Oldham has stepped out with Old Navy, to name just a few.

Although many ventures such as these have failed miserably, some have been wildly successful. Lela Rose claims that she would never have considered her arrangement with Payless if it hadn't been for the success of Target's alliance with Isaac Mizrahi. Mizrahi's couture career was pretty much on the rocks. Then he started designing preppy cashmere sweaters, cheerful jersey dresses, and trendy trench coats for Target, all priced at under US$40. With the low-rent strategy, Mizrahi became more popular and famous than ever. After that, he once again had high-end retailers knocking on his door. Since Mizrahi's successful entry to the mainstream in 2003, more than two dozen designers have co-branded with mass retailers.

PAYING LESS OR PAYING MORE?

There's more in it for Payless than just making the brand more attractive to both old and new customers. The company is looking to move its average price point up a notch or two. Whereas "higher price" is a relative term when most of a store's product line is priced below US$15, higher margins are higher margins. Rubel has suggested that in many cases, price increases may be as little as 50 cents per pair of shoes. But the expansion of its brand portfolio to include famous labels will certainly give Payless greater pricing flexibility. And the designer collections will allow for some of the highest priced products that have ever graced its shelves—think US$25 for pumps and up to US$45 for boots. Whereas that is a substantial price increase from Payless's average, it's a bargain for fashion-conscious consumers.

One industry insider declares, "Fashion isn't a luxury, it's a right." With Rubel's mission to democratize fashion, it seems that this right is becoming a reality in the shoe world. The benefits of such democracy are plentiful. The designers get tremendous exposure, a large customer base, and the power and budget of a mass retailer. Payless gets brand cachet that is almost certain to transform its outdated image. And consumers get runway styles they can afford. Payless is banking that making everyone happy will ring up the sales and profits it needs.

Sources: Danielle Sacks, "The Fast 50 Companies," *Fast Company*, March 2008, p. 112; Maria Puente, "Top Designers Go Down-Market," *USA Today*, September 26, 2007, p. 11B; Eric Wilson, "The Big Brand Theory," *New York Times Magazine*, September 9, 2007, p. 74; Bruce Horovitz, "Payless Is Determined to Put a Fashionably Shod Foot Forward," *USA Today*, July 28, 2006, p. 1B; Nicole Zerillo, "Payless Launches 'I Love Shoes,'" *PR Week*, March 10, 2008, p. 3; and www.paylessinfo.com, accessed September 2008.

QUESTIONS

1. Which of the different product mix pricing strategies discussed in the text applies best to Payless's new strategy? Discuss this in detail.

2. How do concepts such as psychological pricing and reference pricing apply to the Payless strategy? In what ways does Payless's strategy deviate from these concepts?

3. Discuss the benefits and risks of the new Payless strategy for both Payless and the designers. Which of these two stands to lose the most?

4. Consider the scale on which Payless operates. How much of a price increase does Payless need to achieve to make this venture worthwhile?

AFTER STUDYING THIS CHAPTER, YOU SHOULD BE ABLE TO

 explain why companies use marketing channels, and describe the functions channels perform

 explain how channels are organized, designed, and managed

 define retailing and the major types of retailers, and explain the role of retailers in the distribution channel

 describe the major types of wholesalers and their marketing decisions

 discuss the nature and importance of marketing logistics and integrated supply chain management

Marketing Channels: Retailing and Wholesaling

PREVIEWING THE CONCEPTS

We now arrive at the third marketing mix tool—distribution. Firms rarely work alone in creating value for customers and building profitable customer relationships. Instead, most are only a single link in a larger supply chain and marketing channel. As such, an individual firm's success depends not only on how well *it* performs but also on how well its *entire marketing channel* competes with competitors' channels. To be good at customer relationship management, a company must also be good at partner relationship management. The first part of this chapter explores the nature of marketing channels and the marketer's channel design and management decisions. We then look closely at two of the most common and most important channels, retailing and wholesaling. Finally, we examine physical distribution—or logistics—an area that is growing dramatically in importance and sophistication. We'll start with a look at a company whose groundbreaking, customer-centred distribution strategy took it to the top of its industry.

ENTERPRISE: LEAVING CAR RENTAL COMPETITORS IN THE REAR-VIEW MIRROR

Quick, which rental-car company is number one? Chances are good that you said Hertz. Okay, who's number two? That must be Avis, you say. After all, for years Avis advertising said, "We're #2, so we try harder!" But if you said Hertz or Avis, you're about to be surprised. By any measure—most locations, revenues, profits, or number of cars—the number-one rental-car company in the United States is Enterprise Rent-A-Car. What's more, this is no recent development. Enterprise left number-two Hertz in its rear-view mirror in the late 1990s and has never looked back.

What may have fooled you is that for a long time, Hertz was number one in airport car rentals. However, with revenues of $13 billion and growing, Enterprise is now more than 50 percent bigger than Hertz. What's more, by all estimates, the privately owned Enterprise is much more profitable as well.

How did Enterprise become such a dominating industry leader? The company might argue that it was through better prices or better marketing. But what contributed most to Enterprise taking the lead was an industry-changing, customer-driven distribution strategy. While competitors such as Hertz and Avis focused on serving travellers at airports, Enterprise developed a new distribution doorway to a large and untapped segment. It opened off-airport, neighbourhood locations that provided short-term car-replacement rentals for people whose cars were wrecked, stolen, or being serviced, or for people who simply wanted a different car for a short trip or a special occasion.

It all started more than half a century ago when Enterprise founder Jack Taylor discovered an unmet customer need. He was working at a St. Louis auto dealership, and customers often asked him where they could get a replacement car when theirs was in the shop for repairs or body work. To meet this need, Taylor opened a car-leasing business. But rather than competing head-on with the likes of Hertz and Avis, serving travellers at airports, Taylor located his rental offices in centre-city and neighbourhood areas, closer to his replacement-car target customers. These locations also gave Taylor a cost advantage—property rents were lower and he didn't have to pay airport taxes and fees.

Taylor's groundbreaking distribution strategy worked and the business grew quickly. As he opened multiple locations in St. Louis and other cities, he renamed his business Enterprise Rent-A-Car after the U.S. Navy aircraft carrier on which he had served as a naval aviator. Enterprise continued to focus steadfastly on what it called the "home-city" market, primarily serving customers who'd been in wrecks or whose cars were being serviced. Enterprise branch managers developed strong relationships with local auto insurance adjusters, dealership sales and service personnel, and body shops and service garages, making Enterprise their preferred neighbourhood rental-car provider.

Customers in the home-city market had special needs. Often, they were at the scene of a wreck or at a repair shop and had no way to get to an Enterprise office to pick up a rental car. So the company came up with another game-changing idea—picking customers up wherever they happened to be and bringing them back to the rental office. Hence, the tagline: "Pick Enterprise. We'll Pick You Up," which remains the company's main value proposition to this day.

By the late 1980s, Enterprise had a large nationwide network of company-owned off-airport locations and a virtual lock on the home-city market. From this strong base, in the mid-1990s Enterprise began expanding its distribution system by directly challenging Hertz and Avis in the on-airport market. A decade later, it had set up operations in 230 airports in North America and Europe. Then, in late 2007, Enterprise purchased the Vanguard Car Rental Group, which owned the National and Alamo brands. National focused on the corporate-negotiated rental market while Alamo served primarily the leisure traveller airport market.

With the Vanguard acquisition, Enterprise now captures a 27.4 percent share of the airport market, putting it neck-and-neck with Hertz at 28.5 percent and jointly owned Avis/Budget at 30.1 percent. That, combined with its more than 55 percent share of the off-airport market, makes Enterprise the runaway leader in overall car rental. It now operates 8000 locations in the United States and four other countries.

Another secret to Enterprise's success is its passion for creating customer satisfaction. To measure satisfaction, Enterprise has developed what it calls its ESQi (Enterprise Service Quality index). The company calls some 2 million customers a year and asks two simple questions: "Were you completely satisfied with the service?" and "Are you coming back?" Enterprise managers don't get promoted unless they keep customers satisfied. It's as simple as that. If customer feedback is bad, "we call it going to ESQi jail," says an Enterprise human resources manager. "Until the numbers start to improve, you're going nowhere."

Looking ahead, rather than resting on its laurels, Enterprise continues to seek better ways to keep customers happy by getting cars where they want them. The enterprising company has now motored into yet another innovative distribution venue—"car sharing" and hourly rentals. Car-sharing was pioneered in the late 1990s by Zipcar, which operates on parking-starved college campuses and in congested urban areas, where it rents cars on an hourly or daily basis to people who want to run errands or make short trips.

Enterprise is now revving up its own car-sharing program, WeCar. This operation will park automobiles at convenient locations in densely populated urban areas, where residents often don't own cars and where business commuters would like to have occasional car access. Enterprise is first targeting businesses that want to have WeCar vehicles available in their parking lots for commuting employees to use. WeCar members pay a $35 annual membership fee. They can then rent conveniently located, fuel-efficient cars (mostly Toyota Prius hybrids) for $10 per hour or $30 overnight—the rate includes gas and a 320-kilometre allotment.

Renting a WeCar vehicle is a simple get-in-and-go operation. Just pass your member key fob over a sensor to unlock the car, and then open the glove box and enter a PIN to release the car key. Although the car sharing market now belongs to tiny Zipcar, a $100-million company that has cars on more than 70 college campuses in several large metropolitan areas, look for giant Enterprise to perfect and expand the new distribution concept.

Thus, Enterprise continues to move ahead aggressively with its winning distribution strategy. Says Andy Taylor, founder Jack's son and now long-time Enterprise CEO, "We own the high ground in this business and we aren't going to give it up. As the dynamics of our industry continue to evolve, it's clear to us that the future belongs to the service providers who offer the broadest array of services for anyone who needs or wants to rent a car." The company intends to make cars available wherever, whenever, and however customers want them.[1]

AS THE Enterprise story shows, good distribution strategies can contribute strongly to customer value and create competitive advantage for both a firm and its channel partners. It demonstrates that firms cannot bring value to customers by themselves. Instead, they must work closely with other firms in a larger value delivery network.

In this chapter, we consider marketing channels, or channels of distribution; why they are important, and the major marketing decisions companies make in managing their channels. We look closely at the major marketing channels of retailing and wholesaling. Finally, we define logistics and examine the challenges for marketers of managing and moving inventory.

MARKETING CHANNELS AND THE SUPPLY CHAIN [L01]

Producing a product or service and making it available to buyers requires building relationships not just with customers, but also with key suppliers and resellers in the company's *supply chain*. This supply chain consists of "upstream" and "downstream" partners. Upstream from the company is the set of firms that supply the raw materials, components, parts, information, finances, and expertise needed to create a product or service. Marketers, however, have traditionally focused on the "downstream" side of the supply chain—on the *marketing channels* (or *distribution channels*) that look toward the customer. Downstream marketing channel partners, such as wholesalers and retailers, form a vital connection between the firm and its customers.

The term *supply chain* may be too limited—it takes a *make-and-sell* view of the business. It suggests that raw materials, productive inputs, and factory capacity should serve as the starting point for market planning. A better term would be *demand chain* because it suggests a *sense-and-respond* view of the market. Under this view, planning starts with the needs of target customers, to which the company responds by organizing a chain of resources and activities with the goal of creating customer value.

Even a demand chain view of a business may be too limited, because it takes a step-by-step, linear view of purchase-production-consumption activities. With the advent of the Internet and other technologies, however, companies are forming more numerous and complex relationships with other firms. For example, Ford manages numerous supply chains—think about all of the parts it takes to create a vehicle, from radios to catalytic converters to tires. Ford also sponsors or transacts on many B-to-B websites and online purchasing exchanges as needs arise. Like Ford, most large companies today are engaged in building and managing a continuously evolving *value delivery network.*

Value delivery network

The network made up of the company, suppliers, distributors, and ultimately customers who "partner" with each other to improve the performance of the entire system in delivering customer value.

A firm's **value delivery network** is made up of the company, suppliers, distributors, and ultimately customers who "partner" with each other to improve the performance of the entire system. For example, in making and marketing its iPod Touch products, Apple manages an entire network of people within Apple plus suppliers and resellers outside the company who work together effectively to give final customers the take-anything-anywhere iPod that's "So much to touch."

THE NATURE AND IMPORTANCE OF MARKETING CHANNELS

Marketing channel (or distribution channel)

A set of interdependent organizations that help make a product or service available for use or consumption by the consumer or business user.

Few producers sell their goods directly to the final users. Instead, most use intermediaries to bring their products to market. They try to forge a **marketing channel (or distribution channel)** —a set of interdependent organizations that help make a product or service available for use or consumption by the consumer or business user.

A company's channel decisions directly affect every other marketing decision. Pricing depends on whether the company works with national discount chains, uses high-quality specialty stores, or sells directly to consumers via the Web. The firm's sales force and communications decisions depend on how much persuasion, training, motivation, and support its channel partners need. Whether a company develops or acquires certain new products may depend on how well those products fit the capabilities of its channel members. For example, Kodak initially sold its EasyShare printers only in Best Buy stores to take advantage of the retailer's on-the-floor sales staff and their ability to educate buyers on the economics of paying higher initial prices for the printer but lower long-term ink costs.

Companies often pay too little attention to their distribution channels, sometimes with damaging results. In contrast, many companies have used imaginative distribution systems to *gain* a competitive advantage. FedEx's creative and imposing distribution system made it a leader in express delivery. Enterprise revolutionized the car-rental business by setting up off-airport rental offices. And Apple turned the retail music business on its head by selling music for the iPod via the Internet on iTunes.

Exhibit 11.1   Innovative marketing channels: FedEx revolutionized express package delivery with its creative and imposing distribution system.

Distribution channel decisions often involve long-term commitments to other firms. For example, companies such as Ford, HP, or McDonald's can easily change their advertising, pricing, or promotion programs. They can scrap old products and introduce new ones as market tastes demand. But when they set up distribution channels through contracts with franchisees, independent dealers, or large retailers, they cannot readily replace these channels with company-owned stores or websites if conditions change. Therefore, management must design its channels carefully, with an eye on tomorrow's likely selling environment as well as today's.

HOW CHANNEL MEMBERS ADD VALUE

Why do producers give some of the selling job to channel partners? After all, doing so means giving up some control over how and to whom they sell their products. Producers use intermediaries because they create greater efficiency in making goods available to target markets. Through their contacts, experience, specialization, and scale of operation, intermediaries usually offer the firm more than it can achieve on its own.

Figure 11.1 shows how using intermediaries can provide economies. Figure 11.1A shows three manufacturers, which each use direct marketing to reach three customers. This system requires nine different contacts. Figure 11.1B shows the three manufacturers working through one distributor, which contacts the three customers. This system requires only six contacts. In this way, intermediaries reduce the amount of work that must be done by both producers and consumers.

From the economic system's point of view, the role of marketing intermediaries is to transform the assortments of products made by producers into the assortments wanted by consumers. Producers make narrow assortments of products in large quantities, but consumers want broad assortments of products in small quantities. Marketing channel members buy large quantities from many producers and break them down into the smaller quantities and broader assortments wanted by consumers.

For example, Unilever makes millions of bars of Lever 2000 hand soap each day, but you want to buy only a few bars at a time. So big food, drug, and discount retailers, such as Shoppers Drug Mart, London Drugs, and Safeway buy Lever 2000 by the truckload and stock it on their stores' shelves. In turn, you can buy a single bar of Lever 2000, along with a shopping cart full of small quantities of toothpaste, shampoo, and other related products as you need them. Thus, intermediaries play an important role in matching supply and demand.

In making products and services available to consumers, channel members add value by bridging the major time, place, and possession gaps that separate goods and services from those who would use them. Members of the marketing channel perform many key functions. Some help to complete transactions:

☐ *Information:* Gathering and distributing marketing research and intelligence information about actors and forces in the marketing environment needed for planning and aiding exchange.

☐ *Promotion:* Developing and spreading persuasive communications about an offer

☐ *Contact:* Finding and communicating with prospective buyers

FIGURE 11.1 How adding a distributor reduces the number of channel transactions

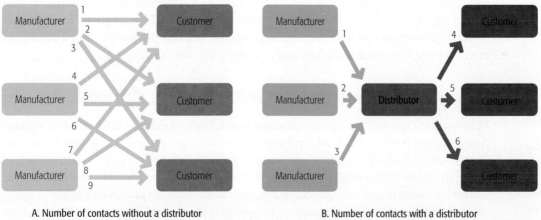

A. Number of contacts without a distributor
M × C = 3 × 3 = 9

B. Number of contacts with a distributor
M + C = 3 + 3 = 6

□ *Matching:* Shaping and fitting the offer to the buyer's needs, including activities such as manufacturing, grading, assembling, and packaging.

□ *Negotiation:* Reaching an agreement on price and other terms of the offer so that ownership or possession can be transferred.

Others help to fulfill the completed transactions:

□ *Physical distribution:* Transporting and storing goods.

□ *Financing:* Acquiring and using funds to cover the costs of the channel work.

□ *Risk taking:* Assuming the risks of carrying out the channel work.

The question is not *whether* these functions need to be performed—they must be—but rather *who* will perform them. To the extent that the manufacturer performs these functions, its costs go up and its prices must be higher. When some of these functions are shifted to intermediaries, the producer's costs and prices may be lower, but the intermediaries must charge more to cover the costs of their work. In dividing the work of the channel, the various functions should be assigned to the channel members who can add the most value for the cost.

CHANNEL LEVELS

Channel level
A layer of intermediaries that performs some work in bringing the product and its ownership closer to the final buyer.

Direct marketing channel
A marketing channel that has no intermediary levels.

Indirect marketing channel
A marketing channel that includes one or more intermediaries.

Companies can design their distribution channels to make products and services available to customers in different ways. Each layer of marketing intermediaries that performs some work in bringing the product and its ownership closer to the final buyer is a **channel level**. Because the producer and the final consumer both perform some work, they are part of every channel.

The *number of intermediary levels* indicates the *length* of a channel. Figure 11.2A shows several consumer distribution channels of different lengths. Channel 1, called a **direct marketing channel**, has no intermediary levels; the company sells directly to consumers. For example, Mary Kay and The Pampered Chef sell their products door-to-door, through home and office sales parties, and on the Web; many insurance companies sell insurance directly via the telephone and the Internet. The remaining channels shown in Figure 11.2A are **indirect marketing channels**, containing one or more intermediaries.

Figure 11.2B shows some common business distribution channels. The business marketer can use its own sales force to sell directly to business customers. Or it can sell to various types of intermediaries, who in turn sell to these customers. Consumer and business marketing channels with even more levels can sometimes be found, but less often. From the producer's point of view, a greater number of levels means less control and greater channel complexity. Moreover, all of the institutions in the channel are connected by several types of *flows*. These include the *physical flow* of products, the *flow of ownership*, the *payment flow*, the *information flow*, and the *promotion flow*. These flows can make even channels with only one or a few levels very complex.

CHANNEL BEHAVIOUR AND ORGANIZATION **LO2**

Distribution channels are more than simple collections of firms tied together by various flows. They are complex behavioural systems in which people and companies interact to accomplish individual, company, and channel goals. Some channel systems consist only of informal interactions among loosely organized firms. Others consist of formal interactions guided by strong organizational structures. Moreover, channel systems do not stand still—new types of intermediaries emerge and whole new channel systems evolve. Here we look at channel behaviour and at how members organize to do the work of the channel.

FIGURE 11.2 Consumer and business marketing channels

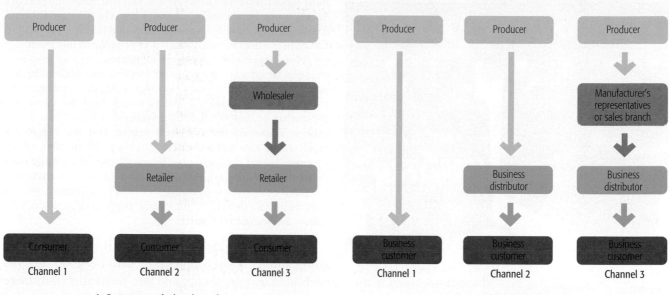

A. Customer marketing channels   B. Business marketing channels

Channel Behaviour A marketing channel consists of firms that have partnered for their common good. Each channel member depends on the others. For example, a Honda dealer depends on Honda to design cars that meet consumer needs. In turn, Honda depends on the dealer to attract consumers, persuade them to buy Honda cars, and service cars after the sale. Each Honda dealer also depends on other dealers to provide good sales and service that will uphold the brand's reputation. In fact, the success of individual Honda dealers depends on how well the entire Honda marketing channel competes with the channels of other auto manufacturers.

Each channel member plays a specialized role in the channel. For example, consumer electronics maker Samsung's role is to produce electronics products that consumers will like and to create demand through national advertising. Best Buy's role is to display these Samsung products in convenient locations, to answer buyers' questions, and to complete sales. The channel will be most effective when each member assumes the tasks it can do best.

Ideally, because the success of individual channel members depends on overall channel success, all channel firms should work together smoothly. They should understand and accept their roles, coordinate their activities, and co-operate to attain overall channel goals. However, individual channel members rarely take such a broad view. Co-operating to achieve overall channel goals sometimes means giving up individual company goals. Although channel members depend on one another, they often act alone in their own short-run best interests. They often disagree on who should do what and for what rewards. Such disagreements over goals, roles, and rewards generate **channel conflict**.

Channel conflict may occur among firms at the same level of the channel. For instance, a Honda dealer in a large city such as Vancouver might complain that the other dealers in the city steal sales from them by pricing too low or by advertising outside their assigned territories. Or conflicts may occur between different levels of the same channel. For example, Goodyear created hard feelings and conflict with its premier independent-dealer channel when it began selling through mass-merchant retailers:[2]

> For more than 60 years, Goodyear sold replacement tires exclusively through its premier network of independent Goodyear dealers. Then, in the 1990s, Goodyear shattered tradition and jolted its dealers by agreeing to sell its tires through mass-merchants such as Sears and

Channel conflict
Disagreement among marketing channel members on goals, roles, and rewards—who should do what and for what rewards.

Exhibit 11.2   Channel conflict: Goodyear created conflict with its premiere independent-dealer channel when it began selling through mass-merchant retailers. Fractured dealer relations weakened the Goodyear name and dropped the company into a more than decade-long profit funk.

Conventional distribution channel
A channel consisting of one or more independent producers, wholesalers, and retailers, each a separate business seeking to maximize its own profits, even at the expense of profits for the system as a whole.

Vertical marketing system (VMS)
A distribution channel structure in which producers, wholesalers, and retailers act as a unified system. One channel member owns the others, has contracts with them, or has so much power that they all co-operate.

Corporate VMS
A vertical marketing system that combines successive stages of production and distribution under single ownership—channel leadership is established through common ownership.

Wal-Mart, placing dealers in direct competition with the nation's most potent retailers. Goodyear claimed that value-minded tire buyers were increasingly buying from cheaper, multibrand discount outlets and department stores, and that it simply had to put its tires where many consumers were going to buy them.

Not surprisingly, Goodyear's aggressive moves into new channels set off a surge of channel conflict, and dealer relations deteriorated rapidly. Some of Goodyear's best dealers defected to competitors. Other angry dealers struck back by taking on competing brands of cheaper private-label tires. Such dealer actions weakened the Goodyear name, and the company's replacement tire sales—which make up 73 percent of its revenues—went flat, dropping the company into a more than decade-long profit funk. Although Goodyear has since repaired fractured dealer relations, it still has not fully recovered. "We lost sight of the fact that it's in our interest that our dealers succeed," admits a Goodyear executive.

Some conflict in the channel takes the form of healthy competition. Such competition can be good for the channel—without it, the channel could become passive and non-innovative. But severe or prolonged conflict, as in the case of Goodyear, can disrupt channel effectiveness and cause lasting harm to channel relationships. Companies should manage channel conflict to keep it from getting out of hand.

Vertical Marketing Systems   For the channel as a whole to perform well, each channel member's role must be specified and channel conflict must be managed. The channel will perform better if it includes a firm, agency, or mechanism that provides leadership and has the power to assign roles and manage conflict.

Historically, *conventional distribution channels* have lacked such leadership and power, often resulting in damaging conflict and poor performance. One of the biggest channel developments over the years has been the emergence of *vertical marketing systems* that provide channel leadership. Figure 11.3 contrasts the two types of channel arrangements.

A **conventional distribution channel** consists of one or more independent producers, wholesalers, and retailers. Each is a separate business seeking to maximize its own profits, perhaps even at the expense of the system as a whole. No channel member has much control over the other members, and no formal means exists for assigning roles and resolving channel conflict.

In contrast, a **vertical marketing system (VMS)** consists of producers, wholesalers, and retailers acting as a unified system. One channel member owns the others, has contracts with them, or wields so much power that they must all co-operate. The VMS can be dominated by the producer, wholesaler, or retailer. Three types of VMSs are *corporate*, *contractual*, and *administered*.

CORPORATE VMS   A **corporate VMS** integrates successive stages of production and distribution under single ownership. Coordination and conflict management are attained through regular organizational channels. For example, U.S. grocery giant Kroger owns and operates 40 plants—18 dairies, 10 deli and bakery plants, five grocery product plants, three beverage plants, two meat plants, and two cheese plants—that crank out 40 percent of the more than 14 400 private label items found on its store shelves. And little-known Italian eyewear maker Luxottica produces many famous eyewear brands—including its own Ray-Ban brand and licensed brands such as Polo Ralph Lauren, Dolce & Gabbana, Prada, Versace, and Bvlgari. It then sells these brands through two of the world's largest optical chains, LensCrafters and Sunglass Hut, which it also owns.[3] And controlling the

FIGURE 11.3 Comparison of conventional distribution channel with vertical marketing system

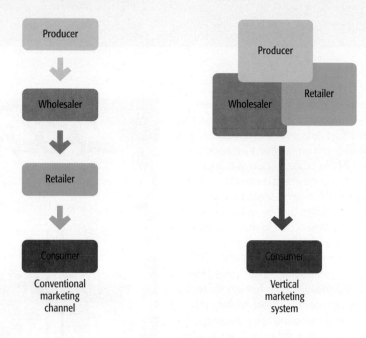

Conventional marketing channel

Vertical marketing system

entire distribution chain has turned Spanish clothing chain Zara into the world's fastest-growing fashion retailer (see Marketing@Work 11.1).

CONTRACTUAL VMS A **contractual VMS** consists of independent firms at different levels of production and distribution who join together through contracts to obtain more economies or sales impact than each could achieve alone. Channel members coordinate their activities and manage conflict through contractual agreements.

The **franchise organization** is the most common type of contractual relationship—a channel member called a *franchisor* links several stages in the production-distribution process. In the United States, some 1500 franchise businesses and 865 000 franchise outlets account for more than $839 billion of economic output. Industry analysts estimate that a new franchise outlet opens somewhere in the United States every eight minutes and that about one out of every 12 retail business outlets is a franchised business.[4] Almost every kind of business has been franchised—from motels and fast-food restaurants to dental centres and dating services, from wedding consultants and maid services to fitness centres and funeral homes.

There are three types of franchises. The first type is the *manufacturer-sponsored retailer franchise system*—for example, Ford and its network of independent franchised dealers. The second type is the *manufacturer-sponsored wholesaler franchise system*—Coca-Cola licenses bottlers (wholesalers) in various markets who buy Coca-Cola syrup concentrate and then bottle and sell the finished product to retailers in local markets. The third type is the *service-firm sponsored retailer franchise system*—for example, Edmonton-based Boston Pizza, which boasts more than 325 independent franchises across the country, plus 50 locations in the United States and one in Mexico.[5] Other types of service franchises are auto-rental firms, motels, fast-food, and, more recently, health care:

> Let's face it: Canadians are getting older. And with the aging population comes a greater need for quality senior home health care. Enter Ken Sim and John DeHart, founders of Nurse Next Door Home Healthcare Services, who sought to "provide high quality services that could help improve the lives of those struggling with sick or aging family members." Established in 2001,

Contractual VMS
A vertical marketing system in which independent firms at different levels of production and distribution join together through contracts to obtain more economies or sales impact than they could achieve alone.

Franchise organization
A contractual vertical marketing system in which a channel member, called a franchisor, links several stages in the production-distribution process.

MARKETING@WORK 11.1

Zara: Fast Fashions—*Really* Fast

Fashion retailer Zara is on a tear. It sells "cheap chic"—stylish designs that resemble those of big-name fashion houses but at moderate prices. Zara is the prototype for a new breed of "fast-fashion" retailers, companies that recognize and respond to the latest fashion trends quickly and nimbly. While competing retailers are still working out their designs, Zara has already put the latest fashion into its stores and is moving on to the next big thing.

Zara has attracted a near cult-like clientele in recent years. Following the recent economic slide, even upscale shoppers are swarming to buy Zara's stylish but affordable offerings. Thanks to Zara's torrid growth, the sales, profits, and store presence of its parent company, Spain-based Inditex, have more than quadrupled since 2000. Despite the poor economy, Inditex's sales grew 10 percent last year. By comparison, Gap's sales *fell* in 2008 by almost 10 percent. As a result, Inditex sprinted past Gap to become the world's largest clothing retailer. Its 4264 stores in 71 countries sewed up $14.2 billion in sales. And Inditex planned to open as many as 450 new stores in 2009, compared with Gap's plans for 50 new stores.

Zara clearly sells the right goods for these times. But its amazing success comes not just from *what* it sells. Perhaps more important, success comes from how and how fast Zara's cutting-edge distribution system *delivers* what it sells to eagerly awaiting customers. Zara delivers fast fashion—*really* fast fashion. Through vertical integration, Zara controls all phases of the fashion process, from design and manufacturing to distribution through its own managed stores. The company's integrated supply system makes Zara faster, more flexible, and more efficient than international competitors such as Gap, Benetton, and H&M. Zara can take a new fashion concept through design, manufacturing, and store-shelf placement in as little as

two weeks, whereas competitors often take six months or more. And the resulting low costs let Zara offer the very latest midmarket chic at downmarket prices.

The whole process starts with input about what consumers want. Zara store managers act as trend-spotters. They patrol store aisles, and by using handheld computers, they report in real time what's selling and what's not. They talk with customers to learn what they're looking for but not yet finding. At the same time, Zara trend-seekers roam fashion shows in Paris and concerts in Tokyo, looking for young people who might be wearing something new or different. Then, they're on the phone to company headquarters in tiny La Coruña, Spain, reporting on what they've seen and heard. Back home, based on this and other feedback, the company's team of 300 designers conjures up a prolific flow of hot new fashions.

Once the designers have done their work, production begins. But rather than relying on a hodgepodge of slow-moving suppliers in Asia, as most competitors do, Zara makes 40 percent of its own fabrics and produces more than half of its own clothes. Even farmed-out manufacturing goes primarily to local contractors. Almost all clothes sold in Zara's stores worldwide are made quickly and efficiently at or near company headquarters in the remote northwest corner of Spain.

Finished goods then feed into Zara's modern distribution centres, which ship finished products immediately and directly to stores around the world, saving time, eliminating the need for warehouses, and keeping inventories low. The highly automated centres can sort, pack, label, and allocate up to 80 000 items an hour.

Again, the keyword describing Zara's distribution system is *fast*. The time between receiving an order at the distribution centre to the delivery of goods to a store averages 24 hours for European stores and a maximum of 48 hours for American or Asian stores. Zara stores

Exhibit 11.3 Effective vertical integration makes Zara more flexible and more efficient—a virtual blur compared with competitors. It can take a new line from design to production to worldwide distribution in its own stores in less than a month (versus an industry average of nine months).

receive small shipments of new merchandise two to three times each week, compared with competing chains' outlets, which get large shipments seasonally, usually just four to six times per year.

Speedy design and distribution allows Zara to introduce a copious supply of new fashions—some 30 000 items last year, compared with a competitor average of less than 10 000. The combination of a large number of new fashions delivered in frequent small batches gives Zara stores a continually updated merchandise mix that brings customers back more often. Zara customers visit the store an average of 17 times per year, compared with less than five customer visits at competing stores. Fast turnover also results in less outdated and discounted merchandise. Because Zara makes what consumers already want or are now wearing, it doesn't have to guess what will be hot six months out.

In all, Zara's carefully integrated design and distribution process gives the fast-moving retailer a tremendous competitive advantage. Its turbocharged system gets out the goods customers want, when they want them—maybe even before:

A couple of summers ago, Zara managed to latch onto one of the season's hottest trends in just four weeks. The process started when trend-spotters spread the word back to headquarters: White eyelet—cotton with tiny holes in it—was set to become white-hot. A quick telephone survey of Zara store managers confirmed

that the fabric could be a winner, so in-house designers got down to work. They zapped patterns electronically to Zara's factory across the street, and the fabric was cut. Local subcontractors stitched white-eyelet V-neck belted dresses—think Jackie Kennedy, circa 1960—and finished them in less than a week. The $129 dresses were inspected, tagged, and transported through a tunnel under the street to a distribution center. From there, they were quickly dispatched to Zara stores from New York to Tokyo—where they were flying off the racks just two days later.

Sources: "Cecilie Rohwedder, "Zara Grows as Retail Rivals Struggle," *Wall Street Journal*, March 26, 2009, p. B1; "Inditex Outperforms with Growth in All Its Markets," *Retail Week*, March 27, 2009, accessed at www.retail-week.com; Kerry Capell, "Fashion Conquistador," *BusinessWeek*, September 4, 2006, pp. 38–39; Cecilie Rohwedder, "Turbocharged Supply Chain May Speed Zara Past Gap as Top Clothing Retailer," *The Globe and Mail*, March 26, 2009, p. B12; and information from the Inditex Press Dossier, at www.inditex.com/en/press/information/press_kit, accessed October 2009.

the company began franchising in 2007. By 2009, Nurse Next Door had 30 franchises across Canada and continues to expand at a rate of two franchises per month across North America—a staggering 3400 percent growth rate since 2001! The company's success has largely been attributed to the way it supports its franchise operators. For example, client calls are handled through a centralized call centre in Vancouver, freeing franchisees from the time-consuming task of fielding urgent calls around the clock. Nurse Next Door is highly selective about which franchisee applicants it takes on, and those that are successful receive the highest level of support and training possible. The company has earned a number of awards, including being named the sixth best midsize franchise system in North America by *Franchise Business Review* in 2009. As it looks toward the future, Nurse Next Door's goal is to generate $1 billion in sales and have 500 franchisees worldwide by 2021. Given its explosive growth and the aging world population, this goal seems very achievable.[6]

Exhibit 11.4 Franchise organization: Vancouver-based Nurse Next Door has more than 30 franchises across Canada, and is highly selective about which franchisee applicants it takes on.

ADMINISTERED VMS In an **administered VMS**, leadership is assumed not through common ownership or contractual ties but through the size and power of one or a few dominant channel members. Manufacturers of a top brand can obtain strong trade co-operation and support from resellers. For example, General Electric, P&G, and Kraft can command unusual co-operation from resellers regarding displays, shelf space, promotions, and price policies. In turn, large retailers can exert strong influence on the many manufacturers that supply the products they sell.

Horizontal Marketing Systems Another channel development is the **horizontal marketing system**, in which two or more companies at one level join together to follow a new marketing opportunity. By working together, companies can combine their financial, production, or marketing resources to accomplish more than any one company could alone.

Companies might join forces with competitors or non-competitors. They might work with each other on a temporary or permanent basis, or they may create a separate company. For example, Tim Hortons set up express versions of their stores at Esso gas stations, so

---

Administered VMS
A vertical marketing system that coordinates successive stages of production and distribution, not through common ownership or contractual ties, but through the size and power of one of the parties.

Horizontal marketing system
A channel arrangement in which two or more companies at one level join together to follow a new marketing opportunity.

commuters can fill up and get a coffee on the way to work without making two stops. Similarly, some Home Depot stores in Canada have a self-contained Harvey's restaurant. Each business is run by its own corporate management, but the companies join forces to reach the same market—hungry shoppers. In a different sort of horizontal marketing system, Loblaw's joined forces with CIBC to create President's Choice Financial, a separate company under the Loblaw umbrella.

Multichannel Distribution Systems   In the past, many companies used a single channel to sell to a single market or market segment. Today, with the proliferation of customer segments and channel possibilities, more and more companies have adopted **multichannel distribution systems**—often called *hybrid marketing channels*. Such multi-channel marketing occurs when a single firm sets up two or more marketing channels to reach one or more customer segments. The use of multichannel systems has increased greatly in recent years.

Figure 11.4 shows a multichannel marketing system. In the figure, the producer sells directly to consumer segment 1 by using catalogues, telemarketing, and the Internet, and reaches consumer segment 2 through retailers. It sells indirectly to business segment 1 through distributors and dealers, and to business segment 2 through its own sales force.

These days, almost every large company and many small ones distribute through multiple channels. Multichannel distribution systems offer many advantages to companies facing large and complex markets. With each new channel, the company expands its sales and market coverage and gains opportunities to tailor its products and services to the specific needs of diverse customer segments. But such multichannel systems are harder to control, and they generate conflict as more channels compete for customers and sales.

Changing Channel Organization   Changes in technology and the explosive growth of direct and online marketing are having a profound impact on the nature and design of marketing channels. One major trend is toward **disintermediation**—a big term with a clear message and important consequences. Disintermediation occurs when product or service producers cut out intermediaries and go directly to final buyers, or when radically new types of channel intermediaries displace traditional ones.

Thus, in many industries, traditional intermediaries are dropping by the wayside. For example, airlines sell tickets directly to consumers, cutting travel agents from their

Multichannel distribution system
A distribution system in which a single firm sets up two or more marketing channels to reach one or more customer segments.

Disintermediation
The cutting out of marketing channel intermediaries by product or service producers, or the displacement of traditional resellers by radical new types of intermediaries.

FIGURE 11.4   Multichannel distribution system

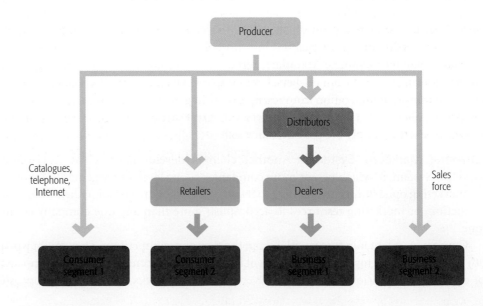

marketing channels altogether. In other cases, new forms of resellers are displacing traditional intermediaries. For example, online marketers have taken business from traditional brick-and-mortar retailers. Consumers can buy hotel rooms and airline tickets from Travelocity and Hotels.com, and just about every other form of consumer product from a variety of online merchants, or direct from the manufacturer. Online music download services such as iTunes and Amazon.com are threatening the very existence of traditional music-store retailers.

Disintermediation presents both opportunities and problems for producers and resellers. Channel innovators who find new ways to add value in the channel can sweep aside traditional resellers and reap the rewards. In turn, traditional intermediaries must continue to innovate in order to avoid being swept aside. In the United States, Netflix pioneered online video rentals, but very quickly Blockbuster developed its own online DVD-rental service. Now, both Netflix and Blockbuster face disintermediation threats from an even hotter channel—digital video downloads and video on demand. But instead of simply watching digital video distribution developments, Netflix intends to lead them:[7]

Exhibit 11.5   Disintermediation: In the entertainment content delivery business, Netflix "disintermediated" the traditional video rental store, but now faces disintermediation by new forms of entertainment delivery.

> Netflix has already added a "watch instantly" feature to its Web site that allows subscribers to instantly stream near-DVD quality video for a limited but growing list of movie titles and TV programs. "Our intention," says Netflix founder and CEO Reed Hasting, "is to get [our watch instantly] service to every Internet-connected screen, from cellphones to laptops to Wi-Fi-enabled plasma screens." In this way, Netflix plans to disintermediate its own distribution model before others can do it. To Hastings, the key to the future is all in how Netflix defines itself. "If [you] think of Netflix as a DVD rental business, [you're] right to be scared," he says. But "if [you] think of Netflix as an online movie service with multiple different delivery models, then [you're] a lot less scared. We're only now starting to deliver [on] that second vision."

Similarly, to remain competitive, product and service producers must develop new channel opportunities, such as the Internet and other direct channels. However, developing these new channels often brings them into direct competition with their established channels, resulting in conflict.

To ease this problem, companies often look for ways to make going direct a plus for the entire channel. For example, guitar and amp maker Fender knows that many customers would prefer to buy its guitars, amps, and accessories online. But selling directly through its website would create conflicts with retail partners—music and guitar stores all over the world. So Fender's website provides detailed information about the company's products but you can't buy a new Fender Stratocaster there. Instead, the Fender website refers you to resellers' websites and stores. Thus, Fender's direct marketing helps both the company and its channel partners.

CHANNEL DESIGN DECISIONS

In designing marketing channels, manufacturers struggle between what is ideal and what is practical. A new firm with limited capital usually starts by selling in a limited market area. Deciding on the best channels might not be a problem: The problem might simply be how to convince one or a few good intermediaries to handle the line.

If successful, the new firm can branch out to new markets through the existing intermediaries. In smaller markets, the firm might sell directly to retailers; in larger markets, it might sell through distributors. In one part of the country, it might grant exclusive franchises; in another, it might sell through all available outlets. Then, it might add a Web store that sells directly to hard-to-reach customers. In this way, channel systems often evolve to meet market opportunities and conditions.

For maximum effectiveness, however, channel analysis and decision-making should be more purposeful. **Marketing channel design** calls for analyzing customer needs, setting channel objectives, making decisions about type and number of intermediaries, and evaluating the alternatives.

Marketing channel design
Designing effective marketing channels by analyzing consumer needs, setting channel objectives, identifying major channel alternatives, and evaluating them.

Analyzing Customer Needs
As noted previously, marketing channels are part of the overall *customer-value delivery network*. Each channel member and level adds value for the customer—whether that customer is a business or an individual consumer. Thus, designing the marketing channel starts with finding out what the target market wants from the channel. Do customers want to buy from nearby locations or are they willing to travel to more distant centralized locations? Would they rather buy in person, by phone, or online? Do they value breadth of assortment or do they prefer specialization? Do they want services such as delivery, repairs, and installation, or will they obtain these elsewhere? The faster the delivery, the greater the assortment provided, and the more add-on services supplied, the greater the channel's service level.

Providing the fastest delivery, greatest assortment, and most services may not be possible or practical. The company and its channel members may not have the resources or skills needed to provide all the desired services. Also, providing higher levels of service results in higher costs for the channel and therefore higher prices for the customer.

Setting Channel Objectives
Companies should state their marketing channel objectives in terms of targeted levels of customer service. Usually, a company can identify several segments wanting different levels of service, and for each segment, the company wants to minimize the total channel cost of meeting customer-service requirements.

The company's channel objectives are also influenced by the nature of the company, its products, its marketing intermediaries, its competitors, and the environment. For example, the company's size and financial situation determine which marketing functions it can handle itself and which it must give to intermediaries. Companies selling perishable products may require more direct marketing to avoid delays and too much handling.

In some cases, a company may want to compete in or near the same outlets that carry competitors' products. For example, Maytag wants its appliances displayed alongside competing brands to facilitate comparison shopping. In other cases, companies may avoid the channels used by competitors. Mary Kay Cosmetics, for example, sells direct to consumers through its corps of 1.8 million independent beauty consultants in more than 35 markets worldwide rather than going head-to-head with other cosmetics makers for scarce positions in retail stores.

Finally, environmental factors such as economic conditions and legal constraints may affect channel objectives and design. For example, in a depressed economy, producers want to distribute their goods in the most economical way, using shorter channels and dropping unneeded services that add to the final price of the goods.

Types and Number of Intermediaries
A firm should identify the types of channel members available to carry out its channel work. Most companies face many channel member choices. For example, until recently, Dell sold directly to final consumers and business buyers only through its sophisticated phone and Internet marketing channel. It

also sold directly to large corporate, institutional, and government buyers by using its direct sales force. However, to reach more consumers and to match competitors such as HP, Dell now sells indirectly through retailers such as Best Buy, Staples, and Wal-Mart. It also sells indirectly through "value-added resellers," independent distributors and dealers who develop computer systems and applications tailored to the special needs of small- and medium-sized business customers.

Companies must also determine the number of channel members to use at each level. Three strategies are available: intensive distribution, exclusive distribution, and selective distribution. Producers of convenience products and common raw materials typically seek **intensive distribution**—a strategy in which they stock their products in as many outlets as possible. These products must be available where and when consumers want them. For example, toothpaste, candy, and other similar items are sold in millions of outlets to provide maximum brand exposure and consumer convenience. Kraft, Coca-Cola, Kimberly-Clark, and other consumer-goods companies distribute their products in this way.

By contrast, some producers purposely limit the number of intermediaries handling their products. The extreme form of this practice is **exclusive distribution**, in which the producer gives only a limited number of dealers the exclusive right to distribute its products in their territories. Exclusive distribution is often found in the distribution of luxury brands. For example, Rolex watches are typically sold by only a handful of authorized dealers in any given market. By granting exclusive distribution, Rolex gains stronger dealer selling support and more control over dealer prices, promotion, and services. Exclusive distribution also enhances the brand's image and allows for higher markups.

Exhibit 11.6 Exclusive distribution: Rolex sells its watches exclusively through only a handful of authorized dealers in any given market. Such limited distribution enhances the brand's image and generates stronger retailer support.

Between intensive and exclusive distribution lies **selective distribution**—the use of more than one, but fewer than all, of the intermediaries who are willing to carry a company's products. Most television, furniture, and home appliance brands are distributed in this manner. For example, Whirlpool and General Electric sell their major appliances through dealer networks and selected large retailers. By using selective distribution, they can develop good working relationships with selected channel members and expect a better-than-average selling effort. Selective distribution gives producers good market coverage with more control and less cost than does intensive distribution.

Intensive distribution
Stocking the product in as many outlets as possible.

Exclusive distribution
Giving a limited number of dealers the exclusive right to distribute the company's products in their territories.

Selective distribution
The use of more than one, but fewer than all, of the intermediaries who are willing to carry the company's products.

Evaluating Channel Alternatives Suppose a company has identified several channel alternatives and wants to select the one that will best satisfy its long-run objectives. Each alternative should be evaluated against economic, control, and adaptability criteria.

Using *economic criteria*, a company compares the likely sales, costs, and profitability of different channel alternatives. What will be the investment required by each channel alternative, and what returns will result? The company must also consider *control issues*. Using intermediaries usually means giving them some control over the marketing of the product, and some intermediaries take more control than others. Other things being equal, the company prefers to keep as much control as possible. Finally, the company must apply *adaptability criteria*. Channels often involve long-term commitments, yet the company wants to keep the channel flexible so that it can adapt to environmental changes. Thus, to be considered, a channel involving long-term commitments should be greatly superior on economic and control grounds.

CHANNEL MANAGEMENT DECISIONS

Once the company has decided on the best channel design, it must implement and manage the channels. **Marketing channel management** calls for selecting, managing, and motivating individual channel members and evaluating their performance over time.

Marketing channel management
Selecting, managing, and motivating individual channel members and evaluating their performance over time.

Selecting Channel Members   Producers vary in their ability to attract qualified marketing intermediaries. Some producers have no trouble signing up channel members, but some have to work hard to line up enough qualified intermediaries. For example, when Timex first tried to sell its inexpensive watches through regular jewellery stores, most refused to carry them. The company then managed to get its watches into mass-merchandise outlets. This turned out to be a wise decision because of the rapid growth of mass-merchandising.

When selecting intermediaries, the company should determine what characteristics distinguish the better ones. It will want to evaluate each channel member's years in business, other lines carried, growth and profit record, co-operativeness, and reputation. If the intermediaries are sales agents, the company will want to evaluate the number and character of other lines carried and the size and quality of the sales force. If the intermediary is a retail store that wants exclusive or selective distribution, the company will want to evaluate the store's customers, location, and future growth potential.

Managing Channel Members   Once selected, channel members must be continuously managed and motivated to do their best. The company must sell not only *through* the intermediaries but *to* and *with* them. Most companies see their intermediaries as first-line customers and partners. They practise strong *partner relationship management* to forge long-term partnerships with channel members. This creates a value delivery system that meets the needs of both the company *and* its marketing partners.

In managing its channels, a company must convince distributors that they can succeed better by working together as a part of a cohesive value delivery system. Thus, P&G works closely with Wal-Mart to create superior value for consumers. The two jointly plan merchandising goals and strategies, inventory levels, and advertising and promotion programs.

Similarly, heavy-equipment manufacturer Caterpillar and its worldwide network of independent dealers work in close harmony to find better ways to bring value to industrial customers.[8]

Exhibit 11.7   Managing channel partners: Caterpillar works closely with its worldwide network of independent dealers to find better ways to bring value to customers.

Caterpillar produces innovative, high-quality products. Yet the most important reason for Caterpillar's dominance is its distribution network of 181 outstanding independent dealers worldwide. Caterpillar and its dealers work as partners. According to a former Caterpillar CEO: "After the product leaves our door, the dealers take over. They are the ones on the front line. They're the ones who live with the product for its lifetime. They're the ones customers see." When a big piece of Caterpillar equipment breaks down, customers know that they can count on Caterpillar and its outstanding dealer network for support. Dealers play a vital role in almost every aspect of Caterpillar's operations, from product design and delivery to product service and support.

Caterpillar really knows its dealers and cares about their success. It closely monitors each dealership's sales, market position, service capability, and financial situation. When it sees a problem, it jumps in to help. In addition to more formal business ties, Cat forms close personal ties with dealers in a kind of family relationship. Caterpillar and its dealers feel a deep pride in what they are accomplishing together. As the former

CEO puts it, "There's a camaraderie among our dealers around the world that really makes it more than just a financial arrangement. They feel that what they're doing is good for the world because they are part of an organization that makes, sells, and tends to the machines that make the world work."

As a result of its partnership with dealers, Caterpillar dominates the world's markets for heavy construction, mining, and logging equipment. Its familiar yellow tractors, crawlers, loaders, bulldozers, and trucks capture some 40 percent of the worldwide heavy-equipment business, twice that of number-two Komatsu.

Many companies are now installing integrated high-tech partner relationship management (PRM) systems to coordinate their whole-channel marketing efforts. Just as they use customer relationship management (CRM) software systems to help manage relationships with important customers, companies can now use PRM and supply chain management (SCM) software to help recruit, train, organize, manage, motivate, and evaluate relationships with channel partners.

Finally, the company must regularly check channel member performance against standards such as sales quotas, average inventory levels, customer delivery time, treatment of damaged and lost goods, co-operation in company promotion and training programs, and services to the customer. The company should recognize and reward intermediaries who are performing well and adding good value for consumers. Those who are performing poorly should be assisted or, as a last resort, replaced.

RETAILING AND WHOLESALING LO3

Now that we've learned about the importance of marketing channels, and the structure of business-to-consumer and business-to-business channels, let's look more closely at the two largest and most important channel members: the retailer and the wholesaler. In the first section, we look at the nature and importance of retailing, major types of store and non-store retailers, the decisions retailers make, and the future of retailing. In the second section, we discuss the function of wholesalers, the major types of wholesalers, and the marketing decisions wholesalers make.

RETAILING

What is retailing? We all know that Canadian Tire, The Bay, and Tim Hortons are retailers, but so are Avon representatives, Amazon.com, Holiday Inn, and your local gas station. **Retailing** includes all the activities involved in selling products and services directly to consumers for their personal, non-business use. Many institutions—manufacturers, wholesalers, and retailers—do retailing. But most retailing is done by **retailers**: businesses whose sales come *primarily* from retailing.

The most recent information from Statistics Canada and the Retail Council of Canada identifies 227 200 retail establishments across the country. Of those, 18 percent are food and beverage stores (see Figure 11.5). All together Canadian retailers generate more than $350 billion in annual sales, with the largest category being food, generating just over $73 billion in annual sales. The next largest categories are new cars ($40 billion); automobile fuels and oils ($38 billion); drugs, vitamins, and supplements ($26 billion); hardware and home renovations ($23 billion); and alcoholic beverages ($20 billion).[9]

Retailing provides 2 million jobs, or more than 12 percent of all jobs in every community across the country, and represents Canada's second-largest labour force. Many of these jobs lead to a career in retailing. For example, almost half a million of the jobs generated represent positions in managerial, business, finance, and administration occupations—offering Canadians the ability to develop their skills and advance through the trade.[10]

Retailing
All activities involved in selling goods or services directly to final consumers for their personal, non-business use.

Retailer
A business whose sales come *primarily* from retailing.

FIGURE 11.5   Canadian retail market share by type of store

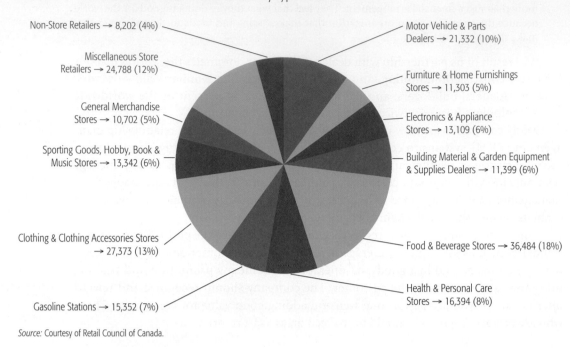

Non-Store Retailers → 8,202 (4%)

Miscellaneous Store
Retailers → 24,788 (12%)

General Merchandise
Stores → 10,702 (5%)

Sporting Goods, Hobby, Book &
Music Stores → 13,342 (6%)

Clothing & Clothing Accessories Stores
→ 27,373 (13%)

Gasoline Stations → 15,352 (7%)

Motor Vehicle & Parts
Dealers → 21,332 (10%)

Furniture & Home Furnishings
Stores → 11,303 (5%)

Electronics & Appliance
Stores → 13,109 (6%)

Building Material & Garden Equipment
& Supplies Dealers → 11,399 (6%)

Food & Beverage Stores → 36,484 (18%)

Health & Personal Care
Stores → 16,394 (8%)

Source: Courtesy of Retail Council of Canada.

Retailing plays a very important role in most marketing channels. They connect brands to consumers in what marketing agency OgilvyAction calls "the last mile"—the final stop in the consumer's path to purchase. It's the "distance a consumer travels between an attitude and an action," explains OgilvyAction's CEO. At least 40 percent of all consumer decisions are made in or near the store. Thus, retailers "reach consumers at key moments of truth, ultimately [influencing] their actions at the point of purchase."[11]

Types of Retailers   Retail stores come in all shapes and sizes—from your local hairstyling salon or family-owned restaurant to national department stores and restaurant chains. The major types of store retailers are *specialty stores, department stores, supermarkets, convenience stores, discount stores, off-price retailers,* and *superstores.* They can be classified in terms of the *amount of service* they offer, the breadth and depth of their *product lines,* the *relative prices* they charge, and how they are *organized.*

AMOUNT OF SERVICE   *Self-service retailers* serve customers who are willing to perform their own "locate-compare-select" process to save time or money. Self-service is the basis of all discount operations and is typically used by retailers selling convenience goods and fast-moving shopping goods, such as grocery stores and drug stores. *Limited-service retailers,* such as Home Depot and Canadian Tire, provide more sales assistance because they carry more shopping goods about which customers need information. In *full-service retailers,* such as high-end specialty stores—for example, Tiffany and Williams-Sonoma—and first-class department stores—for example, Holt Renfrew—salespeople assist customers in every phase of the shopping process. Full-service stores usually carry more specialty goods for which customers need or want assistance or advice. They provide more services, resulting in much higher operating costs, which are passed along to customers as higher prices.

PRODUCT LINE   Some retailers, such as **specialty stores,** carry narrow product lines with deep assortments within those lines. In contrast, **department stores** carry a wide variety of product lines. **Supermarkets** are the most frequently shopped type of retail

Specialty store
A retail store that carries a narrow product line with a deep assortment within that line.

Department store
A retail organization that carries a wide variety of product lines—each line is operated as a separate department managed by specialist buyers or merchandisers.

Supermarket
A large, low-cost, low-margin, high-volume, self-service store that carries a wide variety of grocery and household products.

store, however, in recent years they have faced stiff competition as general merchandise retailers such as Zellers and Wal-Mart, and many drug stores, have begun to carry grocery items. **Convenience stores** are small stores that carry a limited line of high-turnover convenience goods, while **superstores** are much larger than regular supermarkets and offer a large assortment of routinely purchased food products, non-food items, and services. Very large specialty stores that carry thousands of products in a particular category, such as Home Depot and Best Buy, are sometimes referred to as *category killers*.

Finally, for some retailers the product line is actually a service; for example, hotels, banks, airlines, movie theatres, and restaurants are *service retailers*.

RELATIVE PRICES Retailers can also be classified according to the prices they charge. Most retailers charge regular prices and offer normal-quality goods and customer service. Others offer higher-quality goods and service at higher prices. There are several types of retailers, however, that position themselves as always offering low prices. **Discount stores**, such as Zellers and Giant Tiger, sell standard merchandise at lower prices by accepting lower margins and selling higher volume. **Off-price retailers**, such as Winners, buy end-of-season or overstock goods at less than regular wholesale prices and charge consumers less than retail. **Factory outlets** are manufacturer-owned and operated stores by firms such as J. Crew, Gap, and Levi Strauss, and are usually grouped together in malls. Finally, **warehouse clubs** such as Costco operate in huge, drafty, warehouse-like facilities and offer few frills. Customers themselves must wrestle furniture, heavy appliances, and other large items to the checkout line. Such clubs make no home deliveries and often accept no credit cards. However, they do offer ultralow prices and surprise deals on selected branded merchandise.

ORGANIZATION Although many retail stores are independently owned, others band together under some form of corporate or contractual organization. The major types of retail organizations are *corporate chains*, *voluntary chains*, *retailer co-operatives*, and *franchise organizations*.

Chain stores are two or more stores or retail outlets that are commonly owned and controlled. Functions such as purchasing, merchandising, advertising, and inventory control are typically done from a central location. The great success of corporate chains caused many independents to band together in one of two forms of contractual associations. One is the *voluntary chain*—a wholesaler-sponsored group of independent retailers that engages in group buying and common merchandising, such as the Independent Grocers Alliance (IGA). The other type of contractual association is the *retailer co-operative*—a group of independent retailers that band together to set up a jointly owned, central wholesale operation and conduct joint merchandising and promotion efforts. Today, many chain stores have learned to apply the principles of experiential marketing, epitomized by retailers such as Ikea, Hard Rock Cafe, and even Home Depot. A store is no longer just a store but a destination packed with experiences (see Marketing@Work 11.2).

Another form of contractual retail organization is the franchise, which we defined earlier in this chapter. The main difference between retail franchise organizations and other contractual systems such as voluntary chains and retail co-operatives is that franchises are normally based on some unique product or service; on a method of doing business; or on the trade name, goodwill, or patent that the franchisor has developed. Retail franchises include any type of retail outlet, from stores, to restaurants, to fitness clubs.

Retailing Trends and Developments Retailers operate in a harsh and fast-changing environment, which offers threats as well as opportunities. New retail forms continue to emerge to meet new situations and consumer needs, but the life cycle of new retail forms is getting shorter. Department stores took about 100 years to reach the mature stage of

Convenience store
A small store, located near a residential area, that is open long hours seven days a week and carries a limited line of high-turnover convenience goods.

Superstore
A store much larger than a regular supermarket that offers a large assortment of routinely purchased food products, non-food items, and services.

Discount store
A retail operation that sells standard merchandise at lower prices by accepting lower margins and selling at higher volume.

Off-price retailer
A retailer that buys at less-than-regular wholesale prices and sells at less than retail. Examples are factory outlets, independents, and warehouse clubs.

Factory outlet
An off-price retailing operation that is owned and operated by a manufacturer and that normally carries the manufacturer's surplus, discontinued, or irregular goods.

Warehouse club
An off-price retailer that sells a limited selection of brand name grocery items, appliances, clothing, and a hodgepodge of other goods at deep discounts to members who pay annual membership fees.

Chain store
Two or more outlets that are commonly owned and controlled.

MARKETING@WORK 11.2

Cabela's: Creating a Sense of Wonder for People Who Hate to Shop

At first glance, outdoor-products retailer Cabela's seems to break all the rules of retailing. First, it locates its stores in tiny, off-the-beaten-path locations—places such as Sidney, Nebraska; Prairie du Chien, Wisconsin; Dundee, Michigan; Owatonna, Minnesota; and Gonzales, Louisiana. Then, to make matters worse, it targets customers who hate to shop! The typical Cabela's customer is a reclusive male outdoorsman who yearns for the great outdoors, someone who detests jostling crowds and shopping.

So how do you explain Cabela's success? Over the past decade, Cabela's has evolved from a mail-order catalogue business into a popular $2.5 billion multichannel retailer. Despite Cabela's often remote locations, customers flock to its 28 superstores to buy hunting, fishing, and outdoor gear. A typical Cabela's store draws 4.4 million customers a year—an average of 40 000 customers on a Saturday and 50 000 to 100 000 on a holiday weekend. Half of Cabela's customers drive 160 kilometres or more to get there, and many travel up to 560 kilometres. Schools even send busloads of kids.

Cabela's isn't just a store chain, it's a name with star power. According to reporters' accounts,

When a store opened in Scottsdale, Arizona, two news helicopters hovered overhead as if covering some celebrity wedding. In other cities, customers pitched tents and camped out to be the first in the store. Some 3,500 eager customers showed up for the recent opening of a new Billings, Montana, Cabela's. Most arrived three or more hours early and it took nearly 20 minutes for the crowd, pouring constantly through the door shoulder-to-shoulder, to get in the store. Cars with license plates from all over the state were parked outside in the lot. One Canadian couple even drove down from Alberta just to see the store.

In fact, Cabela's stores have become tourist destinations. Its store in Michigan is the state's largest tourist attraction, drawing more than 6 million people a year. The Minnesota store trails only the Mall of America in the number of annual visitors. And the Cabela's in Sidney, Nebraska, a town of only 6000 people located 240 kilometres from the nearest city (Denver), attracts 1.2 million visitors a year, making it Nebraska's second-largest tourist attraction behind The Omaha Zoo. In all, Cabela's captures an astonishing 37 cents of every retail dollar spent by hunters.

Just what is it that attracts these hordes of otherwise reluctant shoppers to Cabela's remote stores? Part of the answer lies in all the stuff the stores sell. Cabela's huge superstores (as much as one and one-half times larger than a typical Wal-Mart supercentre) house a vast assortment of quality merchandise at reasonable prices. Cabela's competes on price with discounters, but carries a selection that's six to ten times deeper— more than 200 000 kinds of items for hunting, fishing, boating, camping, and archery.

Cabela's also sells lines of branded clothing and gifts that appeal to customers' wives and children, making it a popular stop for the whole family. And to top things off, Cabela's offers first-class service. It staffs its departments with a generous supply of employees, all of whom must pass a 100-question test on the products they sell. For customers who stop by during hunting trips, Cabela's even offers use of outdoor kennels and corrals to house their hunting dogs or horses while they shop. Hunters with rifles are welcomed.

But deep product assortments and good service don't explain the huge crowds that show up at Cabela's. The retailer's real magic lies in the *experiences* it creates for those who visit. "This is more than a place to go get fishhooks," says a Cabela's spokesperson. "The Cabelas"— Nebraska brothers Dick and Jim—"wanted to create a sense of wonder." Mission accomplished! In each of its stores, Cabela's has created what amounts to a natural history theme park for outdoor enthusiasts.

Take the store near Fort Worth, Texas, for example. Dominating the centre of the

Exhibit 11.8   Store atmosphere: Cabela's real magic lies in the experiences it creates for those who visit. "This is more than a place to go get fishhooks ... we wanted to create a sense of wonder."

store is Conservation Mountain, a two-storey mountain replica with two waterfalls and cascading streams. The mountain is divided into four ecosystems and five bioregions: a Texas prairie, an Alaskan habitat, an Arctic icecap, an American woodlands, and an Alpine mountaintop. Each bioregion is populated by life-like, museum-quality taxidermy animals in action poses—everything from prairie dogs, deer, elk, and caribou to brown bears, polar bears, musk oxen, and mountain goats.

Elsewhere in the store, Cabela's has created an African diorama, complete with African animals depicted in their natural habitats—an elephant, a rhinoceros, a Cape buffalo, and lions downing their prey. Other store attractions include a trophy deer museum and three walk-through aquariums, where visitors can view trophy-quality freshwater fish and learn to identify them. Getting hungry? Drop by the Mesquite Grill café for an elk, ostrich, or wild boar sandwich—no Big Macs here! The nearby General Store offers old-fashioned candy and snacks.

Cabela's spares no expense in developing this sportsman's paradise. A stuffed polar bear can cost up to $10 000. The Fort Worth store presents 800 such animals, right down to a Texas rattlesnake.

Cabela's even created a new post—Taxidermy Purchasing Specialist—an executive who seeks out stuffed animals and mounts them in authentic scenes—two grizzly bears locked in battle, a leopard leaping for a monkey—even the droppings are real. "The muscle tone of the animal, the eyes, the posture—everything must be just right," says the executive. The taxidermy collection at Cabela's Fort Worth store is twice as large as the one at the Fort Worth Museum of Science and History. Cabela's shoppers typically spend an hour or more touring the wildlife displays before they start shopping.

So, if you scratch a little deeper, you find that far from breaking the rules, Cabela's is doing all the right things. It's creating total experiences that delight the senses as well as the wallets of carefully targeted customers. Put it all together and you've got a powerful magnet for outdoorsmen and their families. Just ask one of the millions of anything-but-reluctant Cabela's customers:

> Mike and Jolene Lande brought their 4-year-old son, Isaiah, to the Billings grand opening just to browse. Jolene says she's been to six other Cabela's stores—it's a family tradition to stop at them while on road trips. "It's just awesome in there," says Mike.

"I'll do just about anything to avoid shopping," says John Brown, a small-business owner in Cheyenne, Wyoming. In 35 years of marriage, his wife says she's persuaded him to go shopping only twice. Yet one day last month he invited her to drive 100 miles with him for a day of shopping at Cabela's. "I'm like a kid in a candy store here," he said, dropping a new tackle box into his cart.

The trick is appealing to the family member who is usually the most reluctant to shop: Dad. One recent morning, Lara Miller was trying to round up her husband and three kids, as their morning trip to Cabela's stretched into afternoon. Mrs. Miller—normally the only family member who likes to shop—now was the one most ready to leave. "We haven't had breakfast yet," she moaned. Her husband, Darren Miller, a farmer in Jerome, Idaho, said, "I love this place."

Sources: "Extracts, quotes, and other information from Zach Benoit, "New Cabela's Packs them In," *McClatchy-Tribune Business News*, May 15, 2009; Heather Landy, "Plenty in Store," *Knight Ridder Tribune Business News*, May 22, 2005, p. 1; Kevin Helliker, "Hunter Gatherer: Rare Retailer Scores by Targeting Men Who Hate to Shop," *The Wall Street Journal*, December 17, 2002, p. A1; Bud Kennedy, "Bud Kennedy Column," *Fort Worth Star-Telegram*, May 26, 2005, p. 1; "Bargain Hunting," *Fortune*, November 24, 2008, p. 16; Jan Falstad, "Outdoor Retailer Adds New Dynamic to Local Marketplace," *McClatchy-Tribune Business News*, May 10, 2009; and information from www.cabelas.com, accessed October 2009.

the life cycle; more recent forms, such as warehouse stores, reached maturity in about 10 years. In such an environment, seemingly solid retail positions can crumble quickly. Of the top 10 discount retailers in the United States in 1962 (the year that Wal-Mart and Kmart began), not one still exists today. Even the most successful retailers can't sit back with a winning formula. To remain successful, they must keep adapting.

Many retailing innovations are partially explained by the **wheel of retailing** concept (see Figure 11.6). According to this concept, many new types of retailing forms begin as low-margin, low-price, low-status operations. They challenge established retailers that have become "fat" by letting their costs and margins increase. The new retailers' success leads them to upgrade their facilities and offer more services. In turn, their costs increase, forcing them to increase their prices. Eventually, the new retailers become like the conventional retailers they replaced. The cycle begins again when still newer types of retailers evolve with lower costs and prices. The wheel-of-retailing concept seems to explain the initial success and later troubles of department stores, supermarkets, and discount stores, and the recent success of off-price retailers.

Following years of good economic times for retailers, the recent recession turned many retailers' fortunes from boom to bust. According to one observer,[12]

> It was great to be in retailing during the past 15 years. Inflated home values, freely available credit, and low interest rates fueled unprecedented levels of consumer spending. Retailers

Wheel of retailing

A concept that states that new types of retailers usually begin as low-margin, low-price, low-status operations but later evolve into higher-priced, higher-service operations, eventually becoming like the conventional retailers they replaced.

FIGURE 11.6   The wheel of retailing

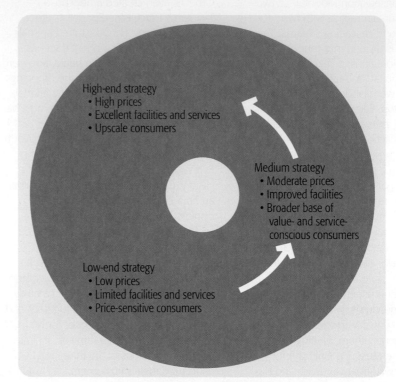

responded by aggressively adding new stores, launching new concepts, building an online presence, and expanding internationally. While the U.S. economy grew 5 percent annually from 1996 to 2006 ... the retail sector grew at more than double that rate—an eye-popping 12 percent. Revenues rose sharply, profits ballooned, and share prices soared. But that's all gone now. Even before the [recent] financial crisis and recession began, retailers were hitting the wall. Same-store sales ... have dropped by double digits for many chains, store closures have accelerated, store openings are slowed, and share-holder-value destruction has been massive.

Some retailers actually benefit from a down economy. For example, as consumers cut back and look for ways to spend less on what they buy, big discounters such as Wal-Mart scoop up new business from bargain-hungry shoppers. "Consumers will continue to trade down to the lowest-cost retailer, and Wal-Mart is it," says one analyst.[13] Similarly, lower-priced fast-food retailers, such as McDonald's, have taken business from their pricier eat-out competitors.

ONLINE RETAILING   Canadians have always been leaders in communications technologies, Internet usage, and e-commerce, and today more than 80 percent of Canadians over the age of 16 say they use the Internet for personal reasons. According to Statistics Canada, regular home use is now commonplace. As for online shopping, 65 percent of Canadians say they use the Internet for "window shopping"—browsing for goods or services but not placing an order—and 50 percent use it to order personal goods or services, spending a total of more than $13 billion.[14]

Retailers' websites also influence a large amount of in-store buying. In the United States, 80 percent of shoppers said they research products online before going to a store to make a purchase, and 62 percent say that they spend at least 30 minutes online every week to help them decide whether and what to buy.[15] A whopping 92 percent said they had more confidence in information they seek out online than anything coming from a salesclerk or other source. So shoppers are devoting time and energy to ferreting out detailed info before they buy. Whether it's cars, homes, or electronics, nearly four in five shoppers say they gather information on their own from the Web before buying. Customers appear at the car dealership with the wholesale price and the model already picked out. Now this trend is spreading down the product chain. In the survey, 24 percent of shoppers said they are doing online research before buying shampoo. And they have questions: How does this shampoo work on different hair types, thicknesses, and colours? Are the bottles recyclable? Has the product been tested on animals?[16]

Exhibit 11.9   Retail technology: Bloom supermarkets in the United States give shoppers a scanner to help record their purchases as they move through the store.

RETAIL TECHNOLOGY   Retail technologies have become critically important as competitive tools. Progressive retailers are using advanced information technology and software systems to produce better forecasts, control inventory costs, interact electronically with suppliers, send information between stores, and even sell to customers within stores. They have adopted sophisticated systems for checkout scanning, RFID inventory tracking, merchandise handling, information sharing, and interacting with customers.

Perhaps the most startling advances in retail technology concern the ways in which retailers are connecting with consumers. Today's customers have gotten used to the speed and convenience of buying online and to the control that the Internet gives them over the buying process. "The Web provides shopping when you like it, where you like it, with access to gobs of research—from a product's attributes to where it's cheapest," says one retail technology expert. "No real-world store can replicate all that."

But increasingly, retailers are attempting to meet these new consumer expectations by bringing Web-style technologies into their stores. Many retailers now routinely use technologies ranging from touch-screen kiosks, hand-held shopping assistants, customer-loyalty cards, and self-scanning checkout systems, to in-store access, to store inventory databases. Consider the following example:[17]

> Bloom supermarkets, a grocery chain in the southeastern United States, have poured money into a sophisticated system that allows shoppers to pick up a scanner and grocery bag at the front of the store, keep track of the bill as they shop, download the scanner and grocery bag at the self-service checkout, and pay. Voilà—the weekly food run with fewer hassles, in Internet time. Along the way, a computerized kiosk in the wine section lets shoppers scan a bottle and get serving suggestions. The kiosk, and a second one in the meat section, lets them print recipes off the screen. And if shoppers drop off a prescription, the pharmacy can send a message to the scanner when their order is ready. Visitors to Shopbloom.com can even key in a shopping list before going to the store to get a printout of aisles they need to hit.

Many Canadian retailers, such as Canadian Tire, Home Depot, and Loblaws have added self-checkout aisles—and more are sure to follow.

WHOLESALING LO4

Wholesaling includes all activities involved in selling goods and services to those buying for resale or business use. We call **wholesalers** those firms engaged *primarily* in wholesaling activities. Wholesalers buy mostly from producers and sell mostly to retailers, business customers, and other wholesalers. As a result, many of the largest and most important wholesalers are largely unknown to consumers. For example, you may never

Wholesaling
All activities involved in selling goods and services to those buying for resale or business use.

Wholesaler
A firm engaged *primarily* in wholesaling activities.

have heard of Grainger, even though it's very well known and much valued by its more than 1.8 million business and institutional customers across North America, India, China, and Panama.[18]

Grainger may be the biggest market leader you've never heard of. It's a $6.9 billion business that offers more than 900,000 maintenance, repair, and operating (MRO) products to more than 1.8 million customers. Through its branch network, service centers, sales reps, catalog, and Web site, Grainger links customers with the supplies they need to keep their facilities running smoothly—everything from light bulbs, cleaners, and display cases to nuts and bolts, motors, valves, power tools, test equipment, and safety supplies. Grainger's 617 branches, 18 strategically located distribution centers, more than 18,000 employees, and innovative Web site handle more than 115,000 transactions a day. Its customers include organizations ranging from factories, garages, and grocers to schools and military bases. Customers include Abbott Laboratories, General Motors, Campbell Soup, American Airlines, Chrysler, and the U.S. Postal Service.

Grainger operates on a simple value proposition: to make it easier and less costly for customers to find and buy MRO supplies. It starts by acting as a one-stop shop for products needed to maintain facilities. On a broader level, it builds lasting relationships with customers by helping them find *solutions* to their overall MRO problems. Acting as consultants, Grainger sales reps help buyers with everything from improving their supply chain management to reducing inventories and streamlining warehousing operations.

Functions of Wholesalers   Why would a producer use wholesalers rather than selling directly to retailers or consumers? Wholesalers add value to the distribution channel by performing a variety of functions. For example, because the wholesaler usually has more local contacts, they may provide valuable *market information* to the manufacturer. They may also be responsible for local *sales and promotions*, reaching many small customers at a low cost. Wholesalers can select items and build assortments needed by their customers, thereby saving the consumers much work. They save their customers money by buying in carload lots and *breaking bulk* (breaking large lots into small quantities.

Wholesalers provide *warehousing* functions. They hold inventories, thereby reducing the inventory costs and risks of suppliers and customers. They also absorb *risk* by taking title and bearing the cost of theft, damage, spoilage, and obsolescence. Because they are closer to the customer, wholesalers may provide *transportation* and *delivery* functions. They may also provide *financing* services and *management* services.

Types of Wholesalers   Wholesalers fall into three major groups: merchant wholesalers, agents and brokers, and manufacturers' sales branches and offices.

Merchant wholesalers are the largest single group of wholesalers, accounting for roughly 50 percent of all wholesaling. They are typically independently owned businesses that take title to the merchandise they handle. Merchant wholesalers include two broad types: full-service wholesalers and limited-service wholesalers. *Full-service wholesalers* provide a full set of services from carrying stock and maintaining a sales force to making deliveries and providing financing; whereas the various *limited-service wholesalers* offer fewer services to their suppliers and customers.

The several different types of limited-service wholesalers perform varied specialized functions in the distribution channel. *Drop shippers* do not carry inventory or handle the product. On

Merchant wholesaler
An independently owned wholesaler business that takes title to the merchandise it handles.

"Service Delivered"

Exhibit 11.10   Wholesalers: Many of the largest wholesalers are unknown to consumers. Grainger sells supplies and equipment to customers such as General Motors and Campbell Soup.

receiving an order, they select a manufacturer, who ships the merchandise directly to the customer. The drop shipper assumes title and risk from the time the order is accepted to its delivery to the customer. They operate in bulk industries, such as coal, lumber, and heavy equipment. *Rack jobbers* serve grocery and drug retailers, mostly in non-food items. They send delivery trucks to stores, where the delivery people set up toys, paperbacks, hardware items, health and beauty aids, or other items. They price the goods, keep them fresh, set up point-of-purchase displays, and keep inventory records. Rack jobbers retain title to the goods and bill the retailers only for the goods sold to consumers.

Brokers and *agents* differ from merchant wholesalers in two ways: They do not take title to goods, and they perform only a few functions. Like merchant wholesalers, they generally specialize by product line or customer type. A **broker** brings buyers and sellers together and assists in negotiation, but does not carry inventory, get involved in financing, or assume risk. **Agents** represent buyers or sellers on a more permanent basis.

Manufacturers' agents (also called manufacturers' representatives) are the most common type of agent wholesaler. They may represent two or more manufacturers of complementary lines, and operate under a formal written agreement with each manufacturer that covers pricing, territories, order handling, delivery service and warranties, and commission rates. Manufacturers' agents are often used in such lines as apparel, furniture, and electrical goods. Most manufacturers' agents are small businesses with only a few skilled salespeople as employees. They are hired by small manufacturers who cannot afford their own field sales forces and by large manufacturers who use agents to open new territories or cover territories that cannot support full-time salespeople.

Finally, wholesaling may be done in manufacturers' sales branches and offices by sellers or buyers themselves rather than through independent wholesalers.

Wholesaler Marketing Decisions   Wholesalers must make many important marketing decisions, just as retailers and product and services marketers do. They make strategic decisions about segmentation and targeting, differentiation and positioning, and the marketing mix—product and service assortments, price, promotion, and distribution.

Wholesalers must segment and define their target markets and differentiate and position themselves effectively—they cannot serve everyone. They can choose a target group by size of customer (only large retailers), type of customer (convenience stores only), need for service (customers who need credit), or other factors. Within the target group, they can identify the more profitable customers, design stronger offers, and build better relationships with them. They can propose automatic reordering systems, set up management-training and advising systems, or even sponsor a voluntary chain. They can discourage less-profitable customers by requiring larger orders or adding service charges to smaller ones.

Wholesalers must decide on product and service assortments, prices, promotion, and place. Wholesalers add customer value though the *products and services* they offer. They are often under great pressure to carry a full line and to stock enough for immediate delivery. But this practice can damage profits. Wholesalers today are cutting down on the number of lines they carry, choosing to carry only the more-profitable ones. They are also rethinking which services count most in building strong customer relationships and which should be dropped or paid for by the customer. The key is to find the mix of services most valued by their target customers.

Price is also an important wholesaler decision. Wholesalers usually mark up the cost of goods by a standard percentage—say, 20 percent. Expenses may run 17 percent of the gross margin, leaving a profit margin of 3 percent. In grocery wholesaling, the average profit margin is often less than 2 percent. Wholesalers are trying new pricing approaches. The recent economic downturn put heavy pressure on wholesalers to cut their costs and prices. As their retail and industrial customers face sales and margin

Broker
A wholesaler who does not take title to goods and whose function is to bring buyers and sellers together and assist in negotiation.

Agent
A wholesaler who represents buyers or sellers on a relatively permanent basis, performs only a few functions, and does not take title to goods.

declines, the customers turn to wholesalers looking for lower prices. Wholesalers may cut their margins on some lines to keep important customers. They may ask suppliers for special price breaks, when they can turn them into an increase in the supplier's sales.

Although *promotion* can be critical to wholesaler success, most wholesalers are not promotion minded. They use largely scattered and unplanned trade advertising, sales promotion, personal selling, and public relations. Many are behind the times in personal selling—they still see selling as a single salesperson talking to a single customer instead of as a team effort to sell, build, and service major accounts. Wholesalers also need to adopt some of the non-personal promotion techniques used by retailers. They need to develop an overall promotion strategy and make greater use of supplier promotion materials and programs.

Finally, *distribution* (location) is important—wholesalers must choose their locations, facilities, and Web locations carefully. There was a time when wholesalers could locate in low-rent, low-tax areas and invest little money in their buildings, equipment, and systems. Today, however, as technology zooms forward, such behaviour results in outdated materials-handling, order-processing, and delivery systems. Instead, today's large and progressive wholesalers have reacted to rising costs by investing in automated warehouses and information technology systems. Orders are fed from the retailer's information system directly into the wholesaler's, and the items are picked up by mechanical devices and automatically taken to a shipping platform where they are assembled. Most large wholesalers are using technology to carry out accounting, billing, inventory control, and forecasting. Modern wholesalers are adapting their services to the needs of target customers and finding cost-reducing methods of doing business. They are also transacting more business online. For example, e-commerce is Grainger's fastest growing sales channel. Online purchasing now accounts for 24 percent of the wholesaler's U.S. sales.[19]

MARKETING LOGISTICS AND SUPPLY CHAIN MANAGEMENT (LO5)

In today's global marketplace, selling a product is sometimes easier than getting it to customers. Companies must decide on the best way to store, handle, and move their products and services so that they are available to customers in the right assortments, at the right time, and in the right place. Effective logistics management and supply chain management have a major impact on both customer satisfaction and company costs.

NATURE AND IMPORTANCE OF MARKETING LOGISTICS

Marketing logistics (or physical distribution)
Planning, implementing, and controlling the physical flow of materials, final goods, and related information from points of origin to points of consumption to meet customer requirements at a profit.

To some managers, marketing logistics means only trucks and warehouses. But modern logistics is much more than this. **Marketing logistics**—also called **physical distribution**—involves planning, implementing, and controlling the physical flow of goods, services, and related information from points of origin to points of consumption to meet customer requirements at a profit. In short, it involves getting the right product to the right customer in the right place at the right time.

In the past, physical distribution planners typically started with products at the plant and then tried to find low-cost solutions to get them to customers. However, today's marketers prefer *customer-centred* logistics thinking, which starts with the marketplace and works backward to the factory, or even to sources of supply. Marketing logistics involves not only *outbound distribution* (moving products from the factory to resellers and ultimately to customers) but also *inbound distribution* (moving products and materials from suppliers to the factory) and *reverse distribution* (moving broken, unwanted, or excess products returned by consumers or resellers). That is, it involves entire **supply chain management**—managing upstream and downstream value-added flows of materials, final goods, and related information among suppliers, the company, resellers, and final consumers, as shown in Figure 11.7.

The logistics manager's task is to coordinate activities of suppliers, purchasing agents, marketers, channel members, and customers. These activities include forecasting, information systems, purchasing, production planning, order processing, inventory, warehousing, and transportation planning.

Companies today are placing greater emphasis on logistics for several reasons. First, companies can gain a powerful competitive advantage by using improved logistics to give customers better service or lower prices. Second, improved logistics can yield tremendous cost savings to both the company and its customers. As much as 20 percent of an average product's price is accounted for by shipping and transport alone. This far exceeds the cost of advertising and many other marketing costs.

To give you an idea of the amount of money spent moving goods, in 2008, commercial transportation services accounted for 4.1 percent of Canada's GDP. Canadian railways carried 355 million tonnes of freight, and approximately $340 billion was spent in cross-border road transportation. The total value of Canadian exports—goods transported to other countries—was $483 billion. Trucking accounted for 54 percent of our $375 billion in trade with the United States, followed by pipeline at 18 percent, rail at 16 percent, and marine and air at six percent each.[20]

Third, the explosion in product variety has created a need for improved logistics management. For example, in 1911, the typical A&P grocery store carried only 270 items. The store manager could keep track of this inventory on about 10 pages of notebook paper stuffed in a shirt pocket. Today, the average A&P carries a bewildering stock of more than 25 000 items. A Wal-Mart Supercentre store carries more than 100 000 products, 30 000 of which are grocery products.[21] Ordering, shipping, stocking, and controlling such a variety of products presents a sizable logistics challenge.

Improvements in information technology have also created opportunities for major gains in distribution efficiency. Today's companies are using sophisticated supply chain management software, Web-based logistics systems, point-of-sale scanners, RFID tags, satellite tracking, and electronic transfer of order and payment data. Such technology lets them quickly and efficiently manage the flow of goods, information, and finances through the supply chain.

Finally, more than almost any other marketing function, logistics affects the environment and a firm's environmental sustainability efforts. Transportation, warehousing, packaging, and other logistics functions are typically the biggest supply chain contributors to the company's environmental footprint. At the same time, they also provide one of the most fertile areas for cost savings. So developing a *green supply chain* is not only

Supply chain management
Managing upstream and downstream value-added flows of materials, final goods, and related information among suppliers, the company, resellers, and final consumers.

FIGURE 11.7 Supply chain management

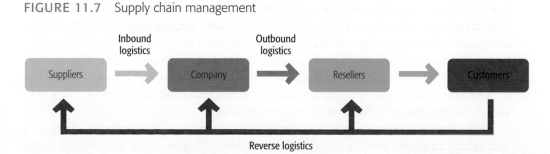

Exhibit 11.11 Logistics: Approximately 90 percent of the world's non-bulk cargo is transported by intermodal containers, which can be loaded onto ships for long voyages, and then transferred to trucks for ground transportation.

Distribution centre
A large, highly automated warehouse designed to receive goods from various plants and suppliers, take orders, fill them efficiently, and deliver goods to customers as quickly as possible.

environmentally responsible, it can also be profitable. "Your CO_2 footprint of transportation and your cost of fuel are permanently linked," says one logistics manager. "The good news is if you can reduce logistics costs you can write an environmental story about it."[22]

GOALS AND FUNCTIONS OF LOGISTICS

Some companies state their logistics objective as providing maximum customer service at the least cost. Unfortunately, no logistics system can *both* maximize customer service *and* minimize distribution costs. Maximum customer service implies rapid delivery, large inventories, flexible assortments, liberal returns policies, and other services—all of which raise distribution costs. In contrast, minimum distribution costs imply slower delivery, smaller inventories, and larger shipping lots— which represent a lower level of overall customer service.

The goal of marketing logistics should be to provide a *targeted* level of customer service at the least cost. A company must first research the importance of various distribution services to customers and then set desired service levels for each segment. The objective is to maximize *profits*, not sales. Therefore, the company must weigh the benefits of providing higher levels of service against the costs. Some companies offer less service than their competitors and charge a lower price. Other companies offer more service and charge higher prices to cover higher costs.

Given a set of logistics objectives, the company is ready to design a logistics system that will minimize the cost of attaining these objectives. The major logistics functions include *warehousing, inventory management, transportation,* and *logistics information management.*

Warehousing   Production and consumption cycles rarely match, so most companies must store their goods while they wait to be sold. For example, Snapper, Toro, and other lawn mower manufacturers run their factories all year long and store up products for the heavy spring and summer buying seasons. The storage function overcomes differences in needed quantities and timing, ensuring that products are available when customers are ready to buy them.

A company must decide on *how many* and *what types* of warehouses it needs and *where* they will be located. The company might use either *storage warehouses* or *distribution centres*. Storage warehouses store goods for moderate to long periods. **Distribution centres** are designed to move goods rather than just store them. They are large and highly automated warehouses designed to receive goods from various plants and suppliers, take orders, fill them efficiently, and deliver goods to customers as quickly as possible.

For example, Wal-Mart operates a network of 147 huge distribution centres. A single centre, serving the daily needs of 75 to 100 Wal-Mart stores, typically contains some 93 000 square metres of space (about 20 football fields) under a single roof. At a typical centre, laser scanners route as many as 190 000 cases of goods per day along eight kilometres of conveyer belts, and the centre's 500 to 1000 workers load or unload some 500 trucks daily. Wal-Mart's Monroe, Georgia, distribution centre contains a 11 800-square-metre freezer (that's about two and a half football fields) that can hold 10 000 pallets—room enough for 58 million Popsicles.[23]

Like almost everything else these days, warehousing has seen dramatic changes in technology in recent years. Outdated materials-handling methods are steadily being replaced by newer, computer-controlled systems requiring few employees. Computers and scanners read orders and direct lift trucks, electric hoists, or robots to gather goods, move them to loading docks, and issue invoices. For example, office supplies retailer Staples now employs "a team of super-retrievers—in day-glo orange—that keep its warehouse humming".[24]

Exhibit 11.12   High-tech distribution centres: Staples employs "a team of super-retrievers–in day-glo orange–to keep its warehouse humming."

Imagine a team of employees that works 16 hours a day, seven days a week. They never call in sick or show up late, because they never leave the building. They demand no benefits, require no health insurance, and receive no pay checks. And they never complain. Sounds like a bunch of robots, huh? They are, in fact, robots—and they're dramatically changing the way Staples delivers notepads, pens, and paper clips to its customers. Every day, Staples' huge Chambersburg, Pennsylvania, distribution center receives thousands of customer orders, each containing a wide range of office supply items. Having people run around a warehouse looking for those items is expensive, especially when the company has promised to delight customers by delivering orders the next day.

Enter the robots. On the distribution center floor, the 150 robots most resemble a well-trained breed of working dogs, say, golden retrievers. When orders come in, a centralized computer tells the robots where to find racks with the appropriate items. The robots retrieve the racks and carry them to picking stations, then wait patiently as humans pull the correct products and place them in boxes. When orders are filled, the robots neatly park the racks back among the rest. The robots pretty much take care of themselves. When they run low on power, they head to battery-charging terminals, or, as warehouse personnel say, "They get themselves a drink of water." The robots now run 50 percent of the Chambersburg facility, where average daily output is up 60 percent since they arrived on the scene.

Inventory Management   Inventory management requires managers to maintain the delicate balance between carrying too little inventory and carrying too much. Many companies have greatly reduced their inventories and related costs through **just-in-time logistics systems**. With such systems, producers and retailers carry only small inventories of parts or merchandise, often only enough for a few days of operations. New stock arrives exactly when needed, rather than being stored in inventory until being used. Just-in-time systems require accurate forecasting and can result in substantial savings in inventory-carrying and handling costs.

Just-in-time logistics system
A type of inventory management system in which only small inventories of parts or merchandise are held, and new stock arrives "just in time" when it is needed.

Today, new technologies such as RFID or "smart tags," by which small transmitter chips are embedded in or placed on products and packaging, on everything from flowers and razors to tires, are helping to make inventory management more efficient. "Smart" products could make the entire supply chain—which accounts for nearly 75 percent of a product's cost—intelligent and automated. Companies using RFID would know, at any time, exactly where a product is located physically within the supply chain. "Smart shelves" would not only tell them when it's time to reorder but would also place the order automatically with their suppliers. Such exciting new information technology applications will revolutionize distribution as we know it. Many large and resourceful marketing companies, such as Wal-Mart, P&G, Kraft, IBM, HP, and Best Buy, are investing heavily to make the full use of RFID technology a reality.[25]

Transportation The choice of transportation carriers affects the pricing of products, delivery performance, and condition of the goods when they arrive—all of which will affect customer satisfaction. Logistics managers may use truck, rail, water, pipeline, or air transportation to move physical goods, or they may use **intermodal transportation**—combining two or more modes of transportation.

Intermodal transportation
Combining two or more modes of transportation.

Trucks are highly flexible in their routing and time schedules, and they can usually offer faster service than railroads. They are efficient for short hauls of high-value merchandise. *Railroads* are one of the most cost-effective modes for shipping large amounts of bulk products—coal, sand, minerals, and farm and forest products—over long distances. Canada has one of the largest rail networks in the world, with 48 000 kilometres of track.[26] *Water transportation* is less expensive but slower, and is best for shipping bulky, low-value, non-perishable products such as sand, coal, grain, oil, and metallic ores. *Air transportation* is the most expensive method and is typically used for perishables (fresh fish, cut flowers) and high-value, low-bulk items (technical instruments, jewellery).

The *Internet* is the fastest and lowest-cost method of transporting digital products from producer to customer. Software firms, the media, music companies, and education all make use of the Internet to transport digital products.

Logistics Information Management

Companies manage their supply chains through information. Channel partners often link up to share information and make better joint logistics decisions. From a logistics perspective, flows of information, such as customer transactions, billing, shipment and inventory levels, and even customer data, are closely linked to channel performance. Companies need simple, accessible, fast, and accurate processes for capturing, processing, and sharing channel information.

Information can be shared and managed in many ways but most sharing takes place through traditional or Internet-based *electronic data interchange (EDI)*, the computerized exchange of data between organizations, which primarily is transmitted via the Internet. Wal-Mart, for example, requires EDI links with its more than 90 000 suppliers. If new suppliers don't have EDI capability, Wal-Mart will work with them to find and implement the needed software. "EDI has proven to be the most efficient way of conducting business with our product suppliers," says Wal-Mart. "This system of exchanging information ... allows us to improve customer service, lower expenses, and increase productivity."[27]

In some cases, suppliers might actually be asked to generate orders and arrange deliveries for their customers. Many large retailers—such as Wal-Mart and Home Depot—work closely with major suppliers such as P&G or Black & Decker to set up *vendor-managed inventory* (VMI) systems or *continuous inventory replenishment* systems. By using VMI, the customer shares real-time data on sales and current inventory levels with the supplier. The supplier then takes full responsibility for managing inventories and deliveries. Some retailers even go so far as to shift inventory and delivery costs to the supplier. Such systems require close co-operation between the buyer and the seller.

Integrated Logistics and Supply Chain Management

Today, more and more companies are adopting the concept of **integrated logistics management**. This concept recognizes that providing better customer service and trimming distribution costs require *teamwork*, both inside the company and among all the marketing channel organizations. Inside, the company's various departments must work closely together to maximize the company's own logistics performance. Outside, the company must integrate its logistics system with those of its suppliers and customers to maximize the performance of the entire distribution network.

Integrated logistics management
The logistics concept that emphasizes teamwork, both inside the company and among all the marketing channel organizations, to maximize the performance of the entire distribution system.

Most companies assign responsibility for various logistics activities to many different departments—marketing, sales, finance, operations, and purchasing. Too often, each function tries to optimize its own logistics performance without regard for the activities of the other functions. However, transportation, inventory, warehousing, and information management activities interact, often in an inverse way. Lower inventory levels reduce inventory-carrying costs. But they may also reduce customer service and increase costs from stockouts, back orders, special production runs, and costly fast-freight shipments. Because distribution activities involve strong trade-offs, decisions by different functions must be coordinated to achieve better overall logistics performance.

The goal of integrated supply chain management is to harmonize all of the company's logistics decisions. Close working relationships among departments can be achieved in several ways. Some companies have created permanent logistics committees made up of managers responsible for different physical distribution activities. Companies can also create supply chain manager positions that link the logistics activities of functional areas. For example, P&G has created supply managers, who manage all of the supply chain activities for each of its product categories. Many companies have a vice-president of logistics with cross-functional authority.

Finally, companies can employ sophisticated, system-wide supply chain management software, now available from a wide range of software enterprises large and small, from SAP and Oracle to Infor

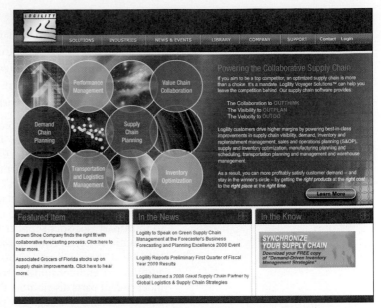

Exhibit 11.13   Integrated logistics management: Many companies now employ sophisticated, system-wide supply chain management software, available from companies such as Logility.

and Logility. The worldwide market for supply chain management software topped $6.4 billion last year and will reach an estimated $11.6 billion by 2013.[28] The important thing is that the company must coordinate its logistics and marketing activities to create high market satisfaction at a reasonable cost.

Building Logistics Partnerships   Companies must do more than improve their own logistics. They must also work with other channel partners to improve whole-channel distribution. The members of a marketing channel are linked closely in creating customer value and building customer relationships. One company's distribution system is another company's supply system. The success of each channel member depends on the performance of the entire supply chain. For example, IKEA can create its stylish but affordable furniture and deliver the "IKEA lifestyle" only if its entire supply chain—consisting of thousands of merchandise designers and suppliers, transport companies, warehouses, and service providers—operates at maximum efficiency and customer-focused effectiveness.

Smart companies coordinate their logistics strategies and forge strong partnerships with suppliers and customers to improve customer service and reduce channel costs. Many companies have created *cross-functional, cross-company teams*. For example, P&G has a team of more than 200 people working in Bentonville, Arkansas, home of Wal-Mart. The P&Gers work jointly with their counterparts at Wal-Mart to find ways to squeeze costs out of their distribution system. Working together benefits not only P&G and Wal-Mart but also their shared, final consumers.

Other companies partner through *shared projects*. For example, many large retailers conduct joint in-store programs with suppliers. Home Depot allows key suppliers to use its stores as a testing ground for new merchandising programs. The suppliers spend time at Home Depot stores watching how their product sells and how customers relate to it. They then create programs specially tailored to Home Depot and its customers. Clearly, both the supplier and the customer benefit from such partnerships. The point is that all supply chain members must work together in the cause of bringing value to final consumers.

Third-Party Logistics   Most big companies love to make and sell their products. But many loathe the associated logistics "grunt work." They detest the bundling, loading, unloading, sorting, storing, reloading, transporting, customs clearing, and tracking required to supply their factories and get products out to customers. They hate it so much that a growing number of firms now outsource some or all of their logistics to **third-party logistics (3PL) providers**. Here's an example:[29]

Third-party logistics (3PL) provider
An independent logistics provider that performs any or all of the functions required to get its client's product to market.

> Whirlpool's ultimate goal is to create loyal customers who continue to buy its brands over their lifetimes. One key loyalty factor is good repair service, which in turn depends on fast and reliable parts distribution. Only a few years ago, however, Whirlpool's replacement parts distribution system was fragmented and ineffective, often causing frustrating customer service delays. "Whirlpool is the world's largest manufacturer and marketer of appliances, but we're not necessarily experts in parts warehousing and distribution," says Whirlpool's national director of parts operations. So to help fix the problem, Whirlpool turned the entire job over to third-party logistics supplier Ryder, which quickly streamlined Whirlpool's service parts distribution system. Ryder now provides order fulfillment and worldwide distribution of Whirlpool's service parts across six continents to hundreds of customers that include, in addition to end-consumers, the Sears service network, authorized repair centers, and independent parts distributors that in turn ship parts out to a network of service companies and technicians. "Through our partnership with Ryder, we are now operating at our highest service level ever," says the Whirlpool executive. "We've ... dramatically reduced [our parts distribution] costs. Our order cycle time has improved, and our customers are getting their parts more quickly."

The "3PLs"—companies such as Ryder, UPS Supply Chain Solutions, Penske Logistics, BAX Global, DHL Logistics, and FedEx Logistics—help clients to tighten up sluggish, overstuffed supply chains, slash inventories, and get products to customers more quickly and reliably. According to a survey of chief logistics executives at *Fortune* 500 companies, 82 percent of these companies use third-party logistics (also called *3PL, outsourced logistics,* or *contract logistics*) services. In just the past 10 years, the revenues for 3PL companies in the United States has more than tripled in size to $128 billion, and they are expected to reach nearly $650 billion by 2014.[30]

Companies use 3PL providers for several reasons. First, because getting the product to market is their main focus, these providers can often do it more efficiently and at lower cost. Outsourcing typically results in 15 percent to 30 percent cost savings. Second, outsourcing logistics frees a company to focus more intensely on its core business. Finally, integrated logistics companies understand increasingly complex logistics environments.

Third-party logistics partners can be especially helpful to companies attempting to expand their global market coverage. For example, companies distributing their products across Europe face a bewildering array of environmental restrictions that affect logistics, including packaging standards, truck size and weight limits, and noise and emissions pollution controls. By outsourcing its logistics, a company can gain a complete pan-European distribution system without incurring the costs, delays, and risks associated with setting up its own system.

Exhibit 11.14   Third-party logistics (3PL): Companies such as Ryder help clients to tighten up sluggish, overstuffed supply chains, slash inventories, and get products to customers more quickly and reliably.

NOT JUST ANY RETAILER WILL DO

Canada Goose does not want to open up distribution channels full throttle even if it means more sales. The company has not started up its own branded retail store, and it carefully selects its retailers. Canada Goose restricts its retail channel to the best retailers in its category that are currently positioned upmarket and that are not active discounters (although legally Canada Goose cannot and does not command a retailer not to discount). The company wants retailers with an overall market position that supports the Canada Goose brand and a reputation of offering strong sales and service. The retail channel, in short, needs to be properly aligned with the brand itself.

Canada Goose sells its products at Harry Rosen, Holt Renfrew, Sporting Life in Toronto, Envy on the east coast, Henry Singer in Calgary, Simons in Quebec, and Harrods in London, England, and Bloomingdale's in New York, as well as at numerous other retailers around the world. The company breaks down its retail channels as follows, with specific objectives applied to each channel:

- Hunting/Fishing: stores that cater to hunters and fishers, including soft goods and hard goods, such as rifles and fishing rods
- Sporting Goods/Big Box: larger-format stores that could include some hunting, fishing, or active outdoor, but also carry a broader assortment of soft goods and hard goods, and, most importantly, the best brands in their respective categories
- Active Outdoor: climbing, paddling, ski/snowboard, hiking, biking types of outdoor stores
- Hybrid Lifestyle: retailers that sell mostly soft goods and reach across multiple segments of apparel, including fashion and outdoor; that tend to sell the best brands in their categories; and that are often global premium powerhouse brands
- Contemporary Fashion: smaller fashion boutiques or urban streetwear stores that will often be denim- and/or footwear-centric as well as retailers of select outerwear collections
- Department Stores/Majors: large-format stores that focus on high-end mainstream fashion

QUESTIONS

1. What would be some positives and some negatives of Canada Goose opening a branded store in the manner of Nike, Apple, Abercrombie & Fitch, The North Face, and others?
2. What could Canada Goose do if retailers demand exclusive selling agreements?
3. How should Canada Goose handle the issue of prominence of its coats within the retail space? Should it demand a distinct selling area, signage, or close proximity to high-traffic areas of the store? What are the advantages and disadvantages of this type of strategy?

REVIEWING THE CONCEPTS

1. Explain why companies use marketing channels, and describe the functions channels perform.

Most producers use intermediaries to bring their products to market. They try to forge a *marketing channel* (or *distribution channel*)—a set of interdependent organizations involved in the process of making a product or service available for use or consumption by the consumer or business user. Through their contacts, experience, specialization, and scale of operation, intermediaries usually offer the firm more than it can achieve on its own.

Marketing channels perform many key functions. Some help *complete* transactions by gathering and distributing *information* needed for planning and aiding exchange; by developing and spreading persuasive *communications* about an offer; by performing *contact* work—finding and communicating with prospective buyers; by *matching*—shaping and fitting the offer to the buyer's needs; and by entering into *negotiation* to reach an agreement on price and other terms of the offer so that ownership can be transferred. Other functions help to *fulfill* the completed transactions by offering *physical distribution*—transporting and storing goods; *financing*—acquiring and using funds to cover the costs of the channel work; and *risk taking*—assuming the risks of carrying out the channel work.

2. Explain how channels are organized, designed, and managed.

The channel will be most effective when each member is assigned the tasks it can do best. Each producer must organize and design its channels of distribution in the most efficient and effective way to reach its customers. Available means vary from direct selling to using one, two, three, or more intermediary *channel levels*. Marketing channels face continuous and sometimes dramatic change. Three of the most important trends are the growth of *vertical, horizontal,* and *multichannel marketing systems*. These trends affect channel co-operation, conflict, and competition.

Channel design begins with assessing customer channel service needs and company channel objectives and constraints. The company then identifies the major channel alternatives in terms of the *types* of intermediaries, the *number* of intermediaries, and the *channel responsibilities* of each. Each channel alternative must be evaluated according to economic, control, and adaptive criteria.

Channel management calls for selecting qualified intermediaries and motivating them. Individual channel members must be evaluated regularly.

3. Define retailing and the major types of retailers, and explain the role of retailers in the distribution channel.

Retailing includes all activities involved in selling goods or services directly to final consumers for their personal, non-business use. Retail stores come in all shapes and sizes, and new retail types keep emerging. Store retailers can be classified by the *amount of service* they provide (self-service, limited service, or full service), *product line sold* (specialty stores, department stores, supermarkets, convenience stores, superstores, and service businesses), and *relative prices* (discount stores and off-price retailers). Today, many retailers are banding together in corporate and contractual *retail organizations* (corporate chains, voluntary chains, retailer co-operatives, and franchise organizations).

The role of the retailer in the distribution channel is much more than simply providing an assortment of goods: Beyond the products and services they offer, today's successful retailers carefully orchestrate virtually every aspect of the consumer store experience. A retailer's price policy must fit its target market and positioning, products and services assortment, and competition, and retailers use any or all of the promotion tools—advertising, personal selling, sales promotion, public relations, and direct marketing—to reach consumers.

4. Describe the major types of wholesalers and their marketing decisions.

Wholesaling includes all the activities involved in selling goods or services to those who are buying for the purpose of resale or for business use. Wholesalers fall into three groups. First, *merchant wholesalers* take possession of the goods. They include *full-service wholesalers* (wholesale merchants, industrial distributors) and *limited-service wholesalers* (cash-and-carry wholesalers, truck wholesalers, drop shippers, rack jobbers, producers' co-operatives, and mail-order wholesalers). Second, *brokers* and *agents* do not take possession of the goods but are paid a commission for aiding buying and selling. Finally, *manufacturers' sales branches and offices* are wholesaling operations conducted by non-wholesalers to bypass the wholesalers.

Like retailers, wholesalers must decide on product and service assortments, prices, promotion, and place. Progressive wholesalers constantly watch for better ways to meet the changing needs of their suppliers and target customers. They recognize that, in the long run, their only reason for existence comes from adding value by increasing the efficiency and effectiveness of the entire marketing channel. As with other types of marketers, the goal was to build value-adding customer relationships.

5. Discuss the nature and importance of marketing logistics and integrated supply chain management.

Just as firms are giving the marketing concept increased recognition, more business firms are paying attention to *marketing logistics* (or *physical distribution*). Logistics is an area of potentially high cost savings and improved customer satisfaction. Marketing logistics addresses not only *outbound distribution* but also *inbound distribution* and *reverse distribution*. That is, it involves entire *supply* chain management—managing value-added flows between suppliers, the company, resellers, and final users. No logistics system can both maximize customer service and minimize distribution costs. Instead, the goal of logistics management is to provide a *targeted* level of service at the least cost. The major logistics functions include *warehousing, inventory management, transportation,* and *logistics information management.*

The *integrated supply chain management* concept recognizes that improved logistics requires teamwork in the form of close working relationships across functional areas inside the company and across various organizations in the supply chain. Companies can achieve logistics harmony among functions by creating cross-functional logistics teams, integrative supply manager positions, and senior-level logistics executives with cross-functional authority. Channel partnerships can take the form of cross-company teams, shared projects, and information-sharing systems. Today, some companies are outsourcing their logistics functions to *third-party logistics (3PL)* providers to save costs, increase efficiency, and gain faster and more effective access to global markets.

KEY TERMS

TALK ABOUT MARKETING

1. Describe the marketing channel, and all the intermediaries, that would be involved in moving apples produced in British Columbia's Okanagan Valley to a grocery store in Kingston, Ontario, and for moving T-shirts manufactured in Montreal, Quebec, to an independent clothing retailer in Saskatoon, Saskatchewan.

2. What is *disintermediation*? Think of an example (other than those given in the chapter) of a company that has been disintermediated and one that has disintermediated another type of company. Do you think that traditional retailers will ever be completely disintermediated?

3. Which distribution strategy—intensive, selective, or exclusive—is used for the following products and why? (a) Piaget watches, (b) Acura automobiles, and (c) Snickers chocolate bars.

4. Why do you think a company would choose to use an intermediary to distribute its products rather than handling the distribution itself? What are the benefits and risks of using a marketing intermediary for this function?

5. Coca-Cola markets an astonishing 2800 different beverages. Not all these beverages are available for sale in all areas, and certainly there is no retailer that offers all 2800. What marketing decisions does the retailer need to make when deciding which of those 2800 to stock on its shelves? How can the distributor (the bottler) help the retailer with this decision?

6. List all the services you can think of that can be delivered from the producer to the customer via the Internet (that is, with no physical distribution required). Can you think of any other levels of the marketing channel that could be conducted online or electronically, rather than physically?

THINK LIKE A MARKETING MANAGER

A group of 50 Coca-Cola bottlers in the United States sued the Coca-Cola Company when it announced a plan to ship its Powerade sports drink directly to Wal-Mart warehouses, thus upsetting the established chain of distribution. Coca-Cola uses a distribution system called "direct-to-store delivery" that relies on the licensed bottlers to package and deliver Coca-Cola products to retailers. Bottlers also set up retail displays and stock the shelves. Rival Pepsi-Cola, which markets Gatorade, the competitor to Powerade, ships its products directly to retailers' warehouses. Coca-Cola says forcing them to distribute their products through bottlers will make them less competitive. From Wal-Mart's perspective, cutting the bottlers out of the channel of distribution could reduce their operating costs and therefore increase their profits. Wal-Mart's margin on Gatorade is 30 percent, but on Powerade it is only 20 percent.

QUESTIONS

1. Not all retailers have warehouses. Convenience stores and smaller independent grocery stores don't have them. Assuming that the Coca-Cola bottlers deliver to these stores as well as Wal-Mart, why were they so upset about the possibility of losing just one customer?

2. Wal-Mart makes more profit on each bottle of Gatorade that it sells than on a bottle of Powerade. List all the things a Wal-Mart store manager could do to encourage consumers to choose Gatorade over Powerade.

3. If it wants to be more competitive with Pepsi, why doesn't Coca-Cola simply increase Wal-Mart's margin on Powerade?

4. If Pepsi has been shipping direct to Wal-Mart's warehouse all along, why aren't its bottlers upset?

MARKETING ETHICS

If not for a stroke of luck, consumers might never have enjoyed some of the best tortilla products sold in retail stores—the Tam-x-ico's and Wrap-itz brands. In 2008, La Bonita Olé, maker of these brands (www.tamxicos.com), was named "Tortilla Manufacturer of the Year" by *Snack & Wholesale Bakery* magazine and one of the "100 Best Packaged Foods for Women" by *Women's Health* magazine. But back in 1992, founder Tammy Young couldn't afford the slotting fees required to get her brands into large retail stores or to get good shelf placement in available stores. The stroke of luck came when a high school friend's wealthy husband became her benefactor in 1996. Now, with both brands available in major retail stores in the eastern United States—10 stockkeeping units (SKUs) of Tam-x-ico's and 12 SKUs of Wrap-itz—La Bonita Olé is a $20 million a year company.

Slotting fees, also called listing fees, are fees that retailers charge manufacturers to place their products on retail shelves (or to "list" them). In their early days, small manufacturers such as La Bonita Olé usually couldn't ante up these fees, which in the United States average $10 000 per chain for each new product according to the Federal Trade Commission. Big consumer-goods makers report total slotting fees in the $1 million to $2 million range per new brand. Young was lucky—she had a wealthy friend who helped her get started. But you have to wonder how many small manufacturers of outstanding products are denied entry into retail stores.

QUESTIONS

1. Find out whether slotting fees are legal in Canada, and, if they are, whether they are controlled by any government body.
2. Do you think slotting fees are ethical? Should they be more strictly regulated? If retailers were prohibited from charging slotting fees, how else might they control or limit the products and brands they stock? Or shouldn't they?

MARKETING TECHNOLOGY

Brewing craft beer is both an art and a science, and Sonia Collin, a Belgian researcher, is trying to devise a way for this highly perishable beer to have a longer shelf life. If successful, brewers can ship more for longer distances. Hoping to boost exports of homegrown products, the Belgian government is investing $7 million for research, with $1.7 million of that allocated to Collin's research. The $250 000 tasting machine in her laboratory identifies the chemical compounds in a sample of beer, which allowed researchers to recommend using organic ingredients, adjusting the oxygen and yeast levels, and reducing the time the beer spends at high temperatures in the brewing process. While pasteurization and bottling methods allow giants such as Heineken and Molson to export their brews, aficionados prefer the more delicate flavour of craft beers. But craft brews don't travel well—sunlight is their worst enemy, and most craft beers lose flavour in less than three months.

QUESTIONS

1. Describe the channel of distribution for a craft beer from Belgium to your city or town. How many channel levels will be involved?
2. Is there a small brewer in your area whose distribution is limited to the local market? List all the marketing decisions that brewer would have to make if brewing technology improves to the point where it would be possible to increase its distribution.

MARKETING BY THE NUMBERS

One external factor manufacturers must consider when setting prices is reseller margins. Manufacturers do not have the final say concerning the price to consumers—retailers do. So, manufacturers must start with their suggested retail prices and work back, subtracting out the markups required by resellers that sell the product to consumers. Once that is considered, manufacturers know at what price to sell their products to resellers, and they can determine what volume they must sell to break even at that price and cost combination. To answer the following questions, refer to Appendix 3, Marketing by the Numbers.

QUESTIONS

1. A consumer purchases a flat iron to straighten her hair for $150 from a salon at which she gets her hair cut. If the salon's markup is 40 percent and the wholesaler's markup is 15 percent, both based on their selling prices, for what price does the manufacturer sell the product to the wholesaler?

2. If the unit variable costs for each flat iron are $40 and the manufacturer has fixed costs totalling $200 000, how many flat irons must this manufacturer sell to break even? How many must it sell to realize a profit of $800 000?

END-OF-CHAPTER CASE

WHOLE FOODS: A WHOLE-ISTIC STRATEGY

It's tough to compete in the grocery business these days. What was once a landscape littered with hundreds of local and regional players has now become an industry dominated by the mega-chains. Wal-Mart, Sobeys, and Loblaw have each taken their own approach to expanding as far and wide as possible with one goal: sell massive amounts of groceries to mainstream consumers at the lowest possible prices. Sure, there are still some small, regional grocers. But they exist mostly because some segment of customers wants to support local businesses. It's getting harder and harder for such grocers to stay alive or avoid getting gobbled up by the big dogs on the block.

So how does a smaller chain not only survive but thrive in such a dog-eat-dog environment? Perhaps the worst strategy is trying to out-Wal-Mart Wal-Mart. Instead of competing head-to-head, smart competitors choose their turf carefully. Rather than competing directly with the volume and price leaders, some have succeeded by reducing emphasis on price and focusing instead on providing something that the low-price, high-volume competitors simply can't supply.

The grocer that's doing the best job of this is Whole Foods Market. Growing from a single store in 1980, Whole Foods has gone far beyond the status of "regional player." It now operates more than 270 stores in 36 states, Canada, and the United Kingdom. Although that's tiny compared with Sobeys' 1300 stores or Wal-Mart's 7300, Whole Foods is thriving and expanding.

How does Whole Foods do it? Through careful positioning—specifically, by positioning away from the industry giants. Rather than pursuing mass-market sales volume and razor-thin margins, Whole Foods targets a select group of upscale customers and offers them "organic, natural, and gourmet foods, all swaddled in Earth Day politics." As one analyst puts it, "While other grocers are looking over their shoulder, watching and worrying about Wal-Mart, Whole Foods is going about business as usual. The tofu is still selling; the organic eggs are fresh in the back dairy cooler; and meats are still hormone free." The value package that Whole Foods offers to its unique customers is best summed up in its motto: "Whole Foods, Whole People, Whole Planet."

WHOLE FOODS

Customers that enter Whole Foods' doors are looking for the highest quality, least processed, most flavourful, and naturally preserved foods. Whole Foods claims that "Food in its purest state is the best tasting and most nutritious food available."

The Whole Foods website reinforces the company's positioning. The site offers up recipes for healthy and gourmet eating, such as "Sweet Potato Pancakes with Creamy Dill Sauce," "Baked Basmati & Currant Stuffed Trout," and "Beginner's Tips for Tofu, Tempeh, and Other Soy Foods."

One aspect of Whole Foods' strategy that allows it to deliver products that foodies love might seem like a step back in time in the supply chain–driven grocery industry. The bigger chains are centralized, sourcing their products from all over the world in identical batches through various distribution centres. But Whole Foods uses a more local approach. Each geographic division, headed by its own president, handles its own store network. Thus, in addition to gathering some foods globally, Whole Foods obtains a significant portion of its goods locally, often from small, uniquely dedicated food artisans. The company backs its talk with action on this issue. Its Local Producer Loan Program doles out US$10 million annually in long-term, low-interest loans to local suppliers.

WHOLE PEOPLE

Whole Foods' customers appreciate the fact that the store's quality commitment reaches far beyond what's on its shelves. In its "Declaration of Interdependence," the company recognizes that living up to its "Whole Foods, Whole People, Whole Planet" motto means doing more than simply selling food. It means caring about the well-being and quality of life of everyone associated with the business, from customers and employees to suppliers to the broader communities in which it operates.

Nowhere is this more evident than in the way that Whole Foods treats its employees. For 11 consecutive years, Whole Foods has been listed among *Fortune* magazine's "Top 100 Companies to Work for in America." Ranked as high as fifth, it is one of only 14 companies ranked every year since the list's inception. Said Whole Foods CEO and cofounder, John Mackey:

> To be among only 14 companies in the nation to be named as one of the Best Companies to Work for since the listing began is an amazing achievement and a validation that we are honoring our core value of "Supporting Team Member Excellence and Happiness" by creating an empowering work environment.

"Empowering work environment," "self-directed teams," and "self-responsibility" all sound like corporate catch phrases that get tossed around by management without permeating the culture. But at Whole Foods, employees believe in these pillars of the company's mission. In fact, two-thirds of Fortune's ranking is based on survey responses from randomly selected employees. Just ask Shateema Dillard, who after two years as an employee is a supervisor and proud owner of two stock option grants. Even though these grants are worth less than $200, Dillard feels "well-paid and confident that opportunities for growth are phenomenal."

Whole Foods is one of a shrinking number of companies that still pay 100 percent of their employees' health care premiums. It also ranks very high on the diversity of its employee team. Out of a sense of teamwork and fairness, it caps the salaries of its highest-paid team members at 19 times the average total compensation of all full-time team members in the company.

WHOLE PLANET

"We believe companies, like individuals, must assume their share of responsibility as tenants of Planet Earth," professes the company's value statement. While this might seem simple, the extensiveness of Whole Foods' environmental program illustrates just how complex a genuine "Earth first" philosophy can be.

For starters, Whole Foods actively supports organic farming on a global basis. This, it believes, is the best way to promote sustainable agriculture and protect both the environment and farm workers. This policy supports Whole Foods' core product offering, but it's just the tip of the company's sustainability iceberg.

In January 2006, Whole Foods became the first Fortune 500 company to offset 100 percent of its electricity use with the purchase of wind energy credits. The credits cover its stores, bakehouses, distribution centres, offices, and every other facility. Beyond energy conservation, Whole Foods has committed to completely eliminating disposable plastic grocery bags, not only conserving resources but also reducing non-biodegradable wastes. No other U.S. grocer has made this commitment.

Such efforts represent a tremendous corporate-wide commitment to environmental protection. However, the Whole Planet culture reaches right down to the store level. Each and every store has a Green Mission Team, a task force composed of team members who meet often to improve environmental actions for their stores. This has led many Whole Foods stores to serve as collection points for plastic bag recycling. Most stores also participate in composting programs for food waste and compostable paper goods. One store in Berkeley, California, even gets most of its electrical power from roof-top solar panels.

Under the Whole Planet mantra, Whole Foods also supports the local communities in which it operates. It believes that local efforts will create healthier and more productive societies at the micro-level, resulting in less need to ship products and waste long distances. This, in turn, lowers pollution and carbon emissions. Whole Foods supports food banks, sponsors neighbourhood events, and even provides financial support for employees doing voluntary community service. Perhaps most telling of Whole Foods' community commitment: It donates 5 percent of its after-tax profits to not-for-profit organizations.

A WHOLE LOT OF CUSTOMERS

Each element of the three-part philosophy underlying the Whole Foods strategy just happens to appeal strongly to a carefully targeted segment of consumers. Whole Foods is not for everyone—intentionally. Whole Foods' customers are affluent, liberal, educated people living in university towns. Their median annual household income exceeds the U.S. average by almost US$8000. Whole Foods' customers live a health-conscious lifestyle, care about the food they eat, and worry about the environment. They tend to be social do-gooders who abhor soulless corporate greed. Whole Foods doesn't really need to compete with mass merchandisers such as Wal-Mart for these customers. In fact, a Whole Foods customer is more likely to boycott the local Wal-Mart than to shop at it.

But something beyond great food, environmental conscience, and human rights draws these people to Whole Foods. A store visit is more than just a shopping trip—it's an experience. And the experience is anything but what you'd find at Wal-Mart. "We create store environments that are inviting, fun, unique, informal, comfortable, attractive, nurturing, and educational," the company claims. "We want our stores to become community meeting places where our customers come to join their friends and to make new ones." Whole Foods' concern for customers runs deep. "We go to extraordinary lengths to satisfy and delight our customers," says a company spokesperson. "We want to meet or exceed their expectations on every shopping trip."

Such commitment, along with strong targeting and positioning, have made Whole Foods one of the nation's fastest-growing and most profitable food retailers. After acquiring nearly 100 stores in its 2007 merger with Wild Oats, a growing chain with a similar positioning strategy, Whole Foods is now the world's number-one natural food chain. Its upscale stores ring up an average of $689 in sales per square foot (0.09 square metres), almost twice that of a traditional grocer. And the chain reaps 35 percent gross margins, which are much larger than those of its traditional competitors. Whereas other grocers have faced limited sales and profit growth or even declines in the face of the withering Wal-Mart assault, Whole Foods' sales and profits have more than doubled over the past four years.

So, Whole Foods can't compete directly with the Wal-Marts of the world. It can't match Wal-Mart's massive economies of scale, incredible volume purchasing power, ultra-efficient logistics, wide selection, and hard-to-beat prices. But then again, it doesn't even try. Instead, it targets customers that Wal-Mart can't serve, offering them value that Wal-Mart can't deliver. And while Whole Foods' future is not without challenges, it has found its own very profitable place in the world by positioning away from the grocery behemoths. Says Whole Foods' chief executive, "Not everyone is concerned with getting mediocre food at the lowest price."

Sources: David Kesmodel, "Whole Foods Net Falls," *Wall Street Journal*, May 14, 2008, p. B5; "The Fast 50 Companies," *Fast Company*, March 2008, p. 111; Diane Brady, "Eating Too Fast at Whole Foods," *Business Week*, October 24, 2005, p. 82; Samantha Thompson Smith, "Grocer's Success Seems Entirely Natural," *News & Observer*, May 21, 2004, p. D1; Marianne Wilson, "Retail as Theater, Naturally," *Chain Store Age*, May 25, 2005, p. 182; Carl Gutierrez, "Court Frees Whole Foods to Swallow Wild Oats," *Forbes*, August 23, 2007, accessed at www.forbes.com; and information from www.wholefoodsmarket.com.

QUESTIONS

1. Define Whole Foods' "product." How does it deliver value to customers?

2. Organic foods are becoming very popular. Many chains, including Wal-Mart, have begun offering and expanding their selection of organics. Does this pose a competitive threat to Whole Foods?

3. With respect to Whole Foods' targeting and positioning strategies, what challenges will the company face in the future as it continues to grow and expand?

4. In some places, Whole Foods is commonly known as "Whole Paycheque." While the firm has clearly positioned itself away from pricing issues, can it avoid this element of the marketing mix forever? Why or why not?

5. What other trends in the future of retailing do you think will have an impact on Whole Foods?

AFTER STUDYING THIS CHAPTER, YOU SHOULD BE ABLE TO

 define the five promotion mix tools for communicating customer value

2 discuss the changing communications landscape and the need for integrated marketing communications

3 describe how advertising objectives are set and how advertising strategy zis developed

4 explain how advertising effectiveness is evaluated and the role of the advertising agency

5 explain how companies use public relations to communicate with their publics

Communicating Customer Value: Advertising and Public Relations

PREVIEWING THE CONCEPTS

We'll forge ahead now into the last of the marketing mix tools—promotion. Companies must do more than just create customer value. They must also use promotion to clearly and persuasively communicate that value. You'll find that promotion is not a single tool but rather a mix of several tools. Ideally, under the concept of *integrated marketing communications,* the company will carefully coordinate these promotion elements to deliver a clear, consistent, and compelling message about the organization and its products. We'll begin by introducing you to the various promotion mix tools. Next, we'll examine the rapidly changing communications environment and the need for integrated marketing communications. Finally, we'll look more closely at two of the promotion tools—advertising and public relations. In the next chapter, we'll visit two other promotion mix tools—sales promotion and personal selling. Then, in Chapter 14, we'll explore direct and online marketing.

To start this chapter, let's look at one of the world's biggest marketers—Unilever—and at one of today's biggest marketing communication issues—the impact of the digital revolution on how marketers communicate with customers. More than most other companies, Unilever has mastered the digital marketing space. However, Unilever's marketers will tell you that they don't really do "digital campaigns" as such. Instead, they do *integrated* marketing communications campaigns that include digital.

UNILEVER: CROSSING THE DIVIDE BETWEEN DIGITAL AND TRADITIONAL MEDIA

These days, most advertisers are scrambling to make sense of the Web and other digital media, everything from websites and social networks to blogs, viral video, webisodes, and branded entertainment. The digital revolution has created a kind of media divide, pitting traditional media such as television and magazines against the new-age digital media. Consumer-goods giant Unilever, however, appears to have mastered the new digital space. In fact, Unilever was recently anointed Digital Marketer of the Year by *Advertising Age.*

But here's the funny thing about Unilever being Digital Marketer of the Year: The company doesn't really do "digital campaigns" as such. For Unilever, it's not an either-or proposition—that is, either traditional media or digital media. Instead, Unilever has made Web and digital tactics just another important part of its mainstream marketing, seamlessly blending the old and the new into fully integrated communications campaigns.

Sure, Unilever does plenty of stand-out digital. It creates innovative websites for its bevy of familiar brands, ranging from Dove, Suave, Axe, Lever 2000, and Vaseline to Hellmann's, Knorr, Lipton, Ragú, Slim-Fast, Bertolli, Breyers, and Ben & Jerry's. And Unilever has made headlines for numerous Web and viral video successes. For example, its Dove brand won a cyber Grand Prix award at the Cannes Lions International Advertising Festival for its spectacularly successful "Evolution" viral video, created by Unilever's advertising agency, Ogilvy & Mather Toronto. And Suave developed a series of "In the Motherhood" webisodes—the Web's version of TV soap operas—that drew more than 5.5 million viewers per episode.

It seems that every Unilever brand has something big going digitally. At one extreme, Axe launches an online hair "Crisis Relief Effort," stating that most women think that guys' hair just doesn't cut it and inviting viewers to create ads showing how Axe's new Hair Crisis products will give them "girl-approved hair." At the other extreme, comparatively stodgy Hellmann's produces an online "Real Food Summer School" program, which features recipes and cooking demos by celebrity chefs such as the Food Network's Bobby Flay. During its first season, about a million unique visitors clicked onto the Real Food site, and more than 5000 visitors signed up to be a part of the Real Food online community. After Hellmann's aired the show, Web searches for "Hellmann's" and related words jumped 50 percent on Yahoo!

Although these and other Unilever digital efforts were highly successful in their own right, none were purely digital campaigns. Instead, each digital effort was carefully integrated with other media and marketing tactics, such as TV and print ads and broader public relations initiatives. "Digital is [not] done in isolation," says Rob Master, Unilever's North American media director. "It's part of a broader campaign. In many cases now it's the centerpiece of a broader campaign. I think that's become a real integral part of how we use the Web, moving beyond just promoting Web addresses in TV spots or print ads to really making them a critical part of the storytelling for the brands."

Unilever certainly has not abandoned traditional media in favour of digital—anything but. The world's number-two advertiser (behind only Procter & Gamble) still devotes a sizable majority of its huge $5.3 billion global advertising and promotion spending to television and print media. But whereas Unilever is actually cutting back on traditional advertising, such as the 30-second spot, its overall promotion budget is increasing, with most of the extra dollars pouring into online and digital. In recent years, spending on digital media has surged from 2 or 3 percent to 15 percent of Unilever's overall marketing budget.

The real secret behind Unilever's digital success is its skilful blending of new media with old to build and extend customer involvement and the brand experience. For example, Suave's "In the Motherhood" webisodes were only a small part of a much larger integrated communications campaign for the brand. It started with television spots featuring real, funny, frenzied mothers sharing their experiences, including beauty experiences. "Is motherhood messing with your hair?" the commercials asked. "Say yes to beautiful without paying the price."

The TV ads pulled customers onto two related websites: www.suave.com confirmed that "Motherhood Isn't Always Pretty" and let visitors dig more deeply into the lives and trials of mothers featured in the TV ads. And www.inthemotherhood.com presented entertaining and engaging webisodes created "For Moms. By Moms. About Moms" based on true-life experiences of motherhood. Each site was loaded with links to other Suave-related content.

Public relations has also played a role in the Suave campaign. When "In the Motherhood" was just starting, clips or even whole five-minute episodes aired on *The Ellen DeGeneres*

Show, whose host called on moms to submit their real-life stories and vote on the best entries. Thus, the entire Suave campaign—television, digital, and public relations—was all wonderfully integrated to create a "sisterhood" of moms and to deliver the brand's "Say yes to beauty" positioning. The webisodes became so popular that—much to the dismay of many Web viewers—ABC picked up *In the Motherhood* as a network TV sitcom, ending the Web series.

The degree to which digital is integrated into the mainstream of Unilever's marketing is clear in how the efforts are managed. "We don't have a digital-media person in the media organization," Master says. "But all of us are very fluent in digital." Unlike many other advertisers today, Unilever doesn't hand its online promotional efforts off to digital shops. Instead, online efforts are handled by Unilever's mainstream advertising agencies, further helping to integrate digital with more traditional promotional tactics.

One powerful result of integrating digital with traditional media is what Unilever calls "superdistribution," the idea of getting Web programs, most often video, picked up by other media—most often for free. One of the best examples is Dove's "Evolution" video created as part of its "Real Beauty" campaign. "Evolution" shows an ordinary young woman being transformed into a beautiful poster model with a lot of help from a makeup artist and photo-editing software. The end line: "It's no wonder our perception of beauty is distorted." "Evolution" has racked up an impressive 20 million views on YouTube and other video sites. But throw in viewership via everything from TV news and talk shows to classrooms and general word-of-Web, and global viewership has exceeded *400* million. To put that in perspective, the video—which cost just $50,000 to make—has created the equivalent of $200 million worth of free media coverage.

But, again, this isn't just about "digital," it's about "communication," says Unilever's global communications planning director. "The right answer for any particular Unilever brand might not be digital. It could be placement in a film or on TV, or some form of content creation, a campaign site or a wiki." But "it so happens that so much of what consumers are doing now is in the digital space." Adds another Unilever marketer: "Our media landscape isn't changing—it's changed. We're in the new world, and there's a new marketing paradigm." Again, we're talking about *integrated* marketing communications.

In all, Unilever—Digital Marketer of the Year and all—understands that the growing shift to digital doesn't really change the fundamentals much. If anything, says Master, it means brand managers have to be more firmly grounded in what their brands are about in order to clearly and consistently define the brands across an exploding array of old and new media. But "almost inherent in what we do, I think, is the importance of storytelling for our brands," he says. "A 30-second ad is a story we pull together for consumers on TV. Digital is an extension of that storytelling in a typically longer format." The richness of the story and the resulting brand experience depend on everything communicating well together.[1]

BUILDING good customer relationships calls for more than just developing a good product, pricing it attractively, and making it available to target customers. Companies must also *communicate* their value propositions to customers, and what they communicate should not be left to chance. All of their communications must be planned and blended into carefully integrated marketing communications programs. Just as good communication is important in building and maintaining any kind of relationship, it is a crucial element in a company's efforts to build profitable customer relationships.

THE PROMOTION MIX 🔴L01

A company's total **promotion mix**—also called its **marketing communications mix**—consists of the specific blend of advertising, public relations, personal selling, sales promotion, and direct-marketing tools that the company uses to persuasively communicate customer value and build customer relationships. Definitions of the five major promotion tools follow:[2]

Promotion mix (or marketing communications mix)
The specific blend of promotion tools that the company uses to persuasively communicate customer value and build customer relationships.

☐ **Advertising**: Any paid form of non-personal presentation and promotion of ideas, goods, or services by an identified sponsor.

☐ **Sales promotion**: Short-term incentives to encourage the purchase or sale of a product or a service.

☐ **Personal selling**: Personal presentation by the firm's sales force for the purpose of making sales and building customer relationships.

☐ **Public relations (PR)**: Building good relations with the company's various publics by obtaining favourable publicity, building up a good corporate image, and handling or heading off unfavourable rumours, stories, and events.

☐ **Direct marketing**: Direct connections with carefully targeted individual consumers to both obtain an immediate response and cultivate lasting customer relationships.

Each category involves specific promotional tools used to communicate with consumers. For example, advertising uses mass media—broadcast (television and radio), print (newspapers and magazines), the Internet, and out-of-home. Sales promotions use discounts, rebates, coupons, contests, displays, and demonstrations. Personal selling uses sales presentations, trade shows, and incentive programs. Public relations uses press releases, sponsorships, special events, and websites. And direct marketing uses websites, catalogues, direct mail, direct response television, and mobile marketing.

At the same time, marketing communication goes beyond these specific promotion tools. The product's design, its price, the shape and colour of its package, and the stores that sell it *all* communicate something to buyers. Thus, although the promotion mix is the company's primary communication activity, the entire marketing mix—promotion *and* product, price, and place—must be coordinated for greatest communication impact.

Advertising
Any paid form of non-personal presentation and promotion of ideas, goods, or services by an identified sponsor.

Sales promotion
Short-term incentives to encourage the purchase or sale of a product or a service.

Personal selling
Personal presentation by the firm's sales force for the purpose of making sales and building customer relationships.

Public relations (PR)
Building good relations with the company's various publics by obtaining favourable publicity, building up a good corporate image, and handling or heading off unfavourable rumours, stories, and events.

Direct marketing
Direct connections with carefully targeted individual consumers to both obtain an immediate response and cultivate lasting customer relationships.

INTEGRATED MARKETING COMMUNICATIONS 🔴L02

In past decades, marketers perfected the art of mass marketing—selling highly standardized products to masses of customers. In the process, they developed effective mass-media communications techniques to support these strategies. Large companies now routinely invest millions of dollars in television, magazine, Internet, and other mass-media advertising, reaching tens of millions of consumers with a single ad. Today, however, marketing managers face some new marketing communications realities. Perhaps no other area of marketing is changing so profoundly as marketing communications, creating both exciting and scary times for marketing communicators.

THE NEW MARKETING COMMUNICATIONS LANDSCAPE

Several major factors are changing the face of today's marketing communications. First, *consumers* are changing. In this digital, wireless age, they are better informed and more communications empowered. Rather than relying on marketer-supplied information, they can use the Internet and other technologies to seek out information on their own. More than that, they can more easily connect with other consumers to exchange brand-related information or even to create their own marketing messages.

Second, *marketing strategies* are changing. As mass markets have fragmented, marketers are shifting away from mass marketing. More and more, they are developing focused marketing programs designed to build closer relationships with customers in more narrowly defined micromarkets. Vast improvements in information technology are speeding the movement toward segmented marketing. Today's marketers can amass detailed customer information, keep closer track of customer needs, and tailor their offerings to narrowly defined target groups.

Finally, sweeping changes in *communications technology* are causing remarkable changes in the ways in which companies and customers communicate with each other. The digital age has spawned a host of new information and communication tools—on-demand television, satellite radio, downloadable music and video, wireless and cellular networks, smartphones, social networking, the Kindle, and the iPad. The new communications technologies give companies exciting new media for interacting with consumers. At the same time, they give consumers more control over the nature and timing of messages they choose to send and receive.

THE SHIFTING MARKETING COMMUNICATIONS MODEL

The explosive developments in communications technology and changes in marketer and customer communication strategies have had a dramatic impact on marketing communications. Just as mass marketing once gave rise to a new generation of mass-media communications, the new digital media have given birth to a new marketing communications model.

Although television, magazines, and other mass media remain very important, their dominance is declining. In their place, advertisers are now adding a broad selection of more-specialized and highly targeted media to reach smaller market segments with more-personalized, interactive messages. The new media range from Facebook, Twitter, and other social networking tools to mobile marketing (advertising delivered to mobile phones and other personal electronic devices) and RSS feeds. In all, companies are doing less *broadcasting* and more *narrowcasting*.

Some advertising industry experts even predict a doom-and-gloom "chaos scenario," in which the old mass-media communications model will collapse entirely. They note that mass-media costs are rising, audiences are shrinking, ad clutter is increasing, and viewers are gaining control of message exposure through technologies such as digital video recorders (DVRs) that let them skip past disruptive television commercials. As a result, marketers are rushing to abandon traditional media in favour of new digital technologies. Many skeptics even predict the demise of the old mass-media mainstays—30-second television commercials and glossy magazine advertisements.[3]

In the new marketing communications world, rather than the old approaches that interrupt customers and force-feed them mass messages, the new technologies will let marketers reach smaller groups of consumers in more interactive, engaging ways. For example, just think about what's happening to television viewing these days. Consumers can now watch their favourite programs on just about anything with a screen—on TV but also on laptops, smartphones, and iPods. And they can choose to watch programs whenever and wherever they wish, often with or without commercials. Moreover, increasingly, some "TV" programs and videos are being produced just for Internet viewing.

Thus, like Unilever in our chapter-opening story, many large advertisers are now shifting their advertising budgets away from network television in favour of more targeted, cost-effective, interactive, and engaging media—especially digital media.

Rather than a "chaos scenario," however, other industry insiders see a more gradual shift to the new marketing communications model. They note that broadcast television and other mass media still capture a lion's share of the promotion budgets of most major marketing firms, a fact that isn't likely to change quickly. For example, Procter & Gamble, a leading proponent of digital media, still spends most of its huge advertising budget on mass media. Although P&G's digital outlay more than doubled last year, digital still accounts for only about 5 percent of the company's total advertising spending.[4]

At a broader level, although some may question the future of the 30-second spot, it's still very much in use today. Last year, more than 43 percent of U.S. advertising dollars was spent on national and local television commercials versus 7.6 percent on Internet advertising. "So if you think that TV is an aging dinosaur," says one media expert, "maybe you should think again." Another expert agrees: "Does TV work? Of course it does. It's just not the only game in town anymore."[5]

Thus, it seems likely that the new marketing communications model will consist of a shifting mix of both traditional mass media and a wide array of exciting, new, more-targeted, more-personalized media. The challenge for traditional advertisers is to bridge the "media divide" that too often separates traditional creative and media approaches from new interactive and digital ones. Many established agencies are struggling with this transition (see Marketing@Work 12.1).

In the end, however, regardless of whether it's traditional or digital, the key is to find the mix of media that best communicates the brand message and enhances the customer's brand experience. Says one analyst, "advertisers need to look at old media and new media as just plain media." Says another, "The whole landscape has changed.... Marketers have to be savvy enough [to understand] what to do with all this stuff."[6]

THE NEED FOR *INTEGRATED* MARKETING COMMUNICATIONS

The shift toward a richer mix of media and communication approaches poses a problem for marketers. Consumers today are bombarded by commercial messages from a broad range of sources. But consumers don't distinguish between message sources the way marketers do. In the consumer's mind, messages from different media and promotional approaches all become part of a single message about the company. Conflicting messages from these different sources can result in confused company images, brand positions, and customer relationships.

All too often, companies fail to integrate their various communications channels. The result is a hodgepodge of communications to consumers. Mass-media advertisements say one thing, while a price promotion sends a different signal, and a product label creates still another message. Company sales literature says something altogether different, and the company's website seems out of sync with everything else.

The problem is that these communications often come from different parts of the company. Advertising messages are planned and implemented by the advertising department or an advertising agency. Personal-selling communications are developed by sales management. Other company specialists are responsible for public relations, sales promotion events, Internet marketing, and other forms of marketing communications. However, whereas these companies have separated their communications tools, customers won't. Mixed communications from these sources will result in blurred consumer brand perceptions.

Integrated marketing communications (IMC)

Carefully integrating and coordinating the company's many communications channels to deliver a clear, consistent, and compelling message about the organization and its products.

Today, more companies are adopting the concept of **integrated marketing communications (IMC)**. Under this concept, as illustrated in Figure 12.1, the company carefully integrates its many communications channels to deliver a clear, consistent, and compelling message about the organization and its brands.

Integrated marketing communications calls for recognizing all touchpoints where the public may encounter the company and its brands. Each *brand contact* will deliver a message, whether good, bad, or indifferent. The company wants to deliver a consistent and

MARKETING@WORK 12.1

Staying Relevant in a Shifting Advertising Universe: The Old versus the New

In today's splintering advertising universe, advertising agency Saatchi & Saatchi understands the importance—and difficulty—of staying relevant. From its roots as a start-up agency in London in 1970, Saatchi & Saatchi grew to a major international player, with 140 offices in 80 countries. Today, it's still signing up blue-chip clients at an impressive rate and scooping up awards for its creative work. Yet Saatchi CEO Kevin Roberts worries that at a time when there are more new places than ever to stick ads—online, on mobile phones, in all places digital and interactive—Saatchi may not be ready for this new universe.

Saatchi & Saatchi cut its teeth on developing creative ads for big-budget—mostly television and magazine—campaigns. But the ad landscape is now shifting. Here is the universe as CEO Roberts sees it:

> TV viewers are using DVRs to blast through the very commercials that are Saatchi's bread and butter. Marketers are stampeding online, where Saatchi lacks the tools and talent to compete. Digital boutiques are proliferating, staffed with tech vets and Gen Y video artists dedicated to making ads for video-sharing and social-networking sites and whatever comes after them.

These days, Saatchi often finds itself outmanoeuvred by nimbler new-age rivals. Traditional agencies like Saatchi still have a long way to go to match the new-media prowess of today's specialized digital, interactive, and media agencies. The traditional agencies didn't predict how dramatically the industry would go digital, and they must now struggle to catch up.

> For most of the twentieth century the so-called creatives ruled the industry. They didn't worry about where or how an ad ran. They were about Big Ideas that would connect a brand emotionally with millions of consumers. Today, you might say, the Small Idea is on the rise. Ads are targeted at individuals or communities of consumers rather than to the masses. The media universe is now so fragmented—into blogs, social networks, television, magazines, and

Exhibit 12.1   In today's splintered advertising universe, Saatchi & Saatchi Worldwide's CEO Kevin Roberts is scrambling to keep his advertising agency relevant. To become a Web-era player, "We've got to reinvent and transform the way we work."

so on—that finding the right medium is fast becoming more important than the creative message itself.

> And the people best equipped to deal with this new world are not the big creative agencies. Instead, it is the direct marketers who are now perfect for the Web—the folks who've always interacted directly with individual consumers. And as the media fragment and reform, media buyers—once consigned by the creative agencies to back-office obscurity—are playing a much bigger role in helping clients figure out where they should spend their advertising budgets. More and more, these media buyers are steering advertisers into new digital and direct media, a powerful threat to the venerable 30-second TV spot that has always been at the heart and soul of traditional creative agencies like Saatchi.

Saatchi's CEO Roberts still believes in the power of creative—the emotional connection to the customer. But the truth is that creative and media feed off of one another, and media is shifting into a new realm that Saatchi has yet to master. Most clients still believe in creating an emotional bond with consumers. But in today's fragmented media universe, advertisers are looking for agencies that can help them create an integrated customer experience across multiple media, including both the traditional mass media that Saatchi knows so well and the new digital and direct media that remain a bit beyond Saatchi's comfort zone.

To fill the widening gap between traditional and digital, Saatchi is now hiring its own corps of Web ad makers, direct marketers, and digital media specialists. In fact, a while back, Saatchi tried to buy an existing digital agency, Blast Radius, known for building websites and creating passionate online communities for with-it companies such as Nike and game maker Electronic Arts. However, in a deeply troubling development, Blast Radius declined Saatchi's proposal. Instead, it merged with Wunderman, one of the world's largest direct-marketing agencies. Said Blast Radius's CEO at the time, "As an interactive agency, ... we saw a big chasm between us ... versus the more traditional agencies. The traditional agencies were still very much about [messages and creativity]."

Interestingly, Publicis Groupe, the mammoth holding company that owns Saatchi & Saatchi along with dozens of other communications agencies, appears not to be counting on Saatchi and its other traditional agencies to lead the

digital transformation. Instead, Publicis invested heavily to purchase an existing interactive agency, Digitas, and to bankroll the creation of another, Droga5. Publicis's CEO sees these interactive agencies as defining the very future of both his company and the entire advertising industry. His goal is to make Publicis the industry's premier digital-marketing outfit— to create a blueprint of the agency of the future. "It's not about cosmetic changes," he says, "it's about profound and unsettling changes."

Such actions and thinking have created an undercurrent of near-panic at some traditional creative agencies, including large and successful ones such as Saatchi & Saatchi. The question is clear: With

digital and direct agencies muscling onto Saatchi's turf, is it "too late for an old-school creative shop to transform itself into a Web-era player"? CEO Roberts doesn't think so. But it won't be an easy transition for Saatchi and the other traditional agencies. "We've got to reinvent and transform the way we work," he says.

Sources: Excerpts and quotes adapted from Burt Helm, "Struggles of a Mad Man," *BusinessWeek*, December 3, 2007, pp. 44–49; and Linda Tischler, "A Mad Man Gets His Head Together," *Fast Company*, January 2008, pp. 90–97. Also see Michael Learmonth, "Agencies Need to Think More Facebook, Twitter, Less TV," *Advertising Age*, April 7, 2009, accessed at http://adage.com/print?article_id=135837; and Brian Steinberg, "Advertisers Need Patience to Tap into Web's Potential," *Boston Globe*, February 24, 2009, p. B5.

FIGURE 12.1   Integrated marketing communications

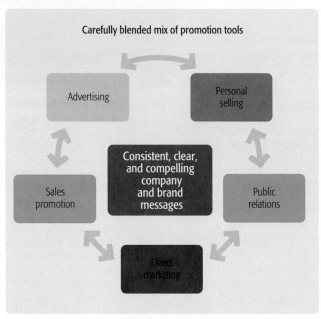

positive message with each contact. Integrated marketing communications leads to a total marketing communication strategy aimed at building strong customer relationships.

Integrated marketing communications ties together all of the company's messages and images. The company's television and print advertisements have the same message, look, and feel as its email and personal-selling communications. And its public relations materials project the same image as its website or social network presence. Often, different media play unique roles in attracting, informing, and persuading consumers, and these roles must be carefully coordinated under the overall marketing communications plan.

A great example of the power of a well-integrated marketing communications effort is Burger King's Whopper Freakout campaign:[7]

> To celebrate the 50th anniversary of the iconic Whopper, Burger King launched a campaign to show what would happen if it suddenly removed the sandwich from its menu "forever." It dropped the Whopper in selected restaurants and used hidden cameras to capture the real-time reactions of stricken customers. It then shared the results in a carefully integrated, multipronged promotional campaign. The campaign began with coordinated TV, print, and radio spots announcing that "We stopped selling the Whopper for one day to see what would happen.... What happened was, people freaked!" The ads drove consumers to *www.whopperfreakout.com*, which featured a video documentary outlining the entire experiment. The documentary was also uploaded to YouTube. At the Web site, visitors could view Freakout ads showing the disbelieving, often angry reactions of a dozen or more customers. Burger King also promoted the campaign through rich media ad banners on several other popular Web sites. Customers themselves extended the campaign with spoofs and parodies posted on YouTube. The richly integrated Whopper Freakout campaign was a smashing success. The ads became the most recalled campaign in Burger King's history, and the whopperfreakout.com Web site received 4 million views in only the first three months. In all, the IMC campaign drove store traffic and sales of the Whopper up a whopping 29 percent.

In the past, no one person or department was responsible for thinking through the communication roles of the various promotion tools and coordinating the promotion mix. To help implement integrated marketing communications, some companies appoint a marketing communications director who has overall responsibility for the company's communications efforts. This helps to produce better communications consistency and greater sales impact. It places the responsibility in someone's hands—where none existed before—to unify the company's image as it is shaped by thousands of company activities.

Exhibit 12.2   Integrated marketing communications: Burger King's richly integrated, multi-pronged Whopper Freakout campaign, which employed a carefully coordinated mix—everything from TV and radio ads to rich media ad banners, YouTube videos, and a Freakout website—boosted store traffic and Whopper sales by 29 percent.

SHAPING THE OVERALL PROMOTION MIX

The concept of integrated marketing communications suggests that the company must blend the promotion tools carefully into a coordinated *promotion mix*. But how does the company determine what mix of promotion tools it will use? Companies within the same industry differ greatly in the design of their promotion mixes. For example, Mary Kay spends most of its promotion funds on personal selling and direct marketing, whereas competitor CoverGirl spends heavily on mass media advertising. We now look at factors that influence the marketer's choice of promotion tools.

THE NATURE OF EACH PROMOTION TOOL

Each promotion tool has unique characteristics and costs. Marketers must understand these characteristics in shaping the promotion mix.

Advertising   Advertising can reach masses of geographically dispersed buyers at a low cost per exposure, and it enables the seller to repeat a message many times. Of all the mass media used for advertising, television reaches the largest audiences. For example, an estimated 99 million Americans tuned in to watch Super Bowl XLIII, about 36 million people watched at least part of the 81st Academy Awards broadcast, and 30 million fans tuned in to watch the debut episode of the eighth season of *American Idol*. For companies that want to reach a mass audience, TV is the place to be.[8]

Beyond its reach, large-scale advertising says something positive about the seller's size, popularity, and success. Because of advertising's public nature, consumers tend to view advertised products as more legitimate. Advertising is also very expressive—it allows the company to dramatize its products through the artful use of visuals, print, sound, and colour. On the one hand, advertising can be used to build up a long-term image for a brand—ads for new models of cars, for example. On the other hand, advertising can trigger quick sales, for example, when car dealerships advertise special financing or clearance sales.

Advertising also has some shortcomings. Although it reaches many people quickly, advertising is impersonal and cannot be as directly persuasive as can company salespeople. For the most part, advertising can carry on only a one-way communication with the audience, and the audience does not feel that it has to pay attention or respond. In addition, advertising can be very costly. Although some advertising forms, such as newspaper and radio advertising, can be done on smaller budgets, other forms, such as network TV advertising, require very large budgets.

Personal Selling   Personal selling is the most effective tool at certain stages of the buying process, particularly in building up buyers' preferences, convictions, and actions. It is the most common promotional tool for business-to-business marketers, such as software companies and business services, and involves long-term personal interaction between decision makers from the customer organization and sales representatives from the vendor. Personal selling focuses on developing relationships with the customer, and an effective salesperson always keeps the customers' interests at heart, listens to their needs, and attempts to solve their problems. Finally, with personal selling, the buyer usually feels a greater need to listen and respond, even if the response is a polite "No thank you."

Exhibit 12.3   Sales promotion: Leon's "Honey! They Shrunk the Prices!" sales promotion offers strong incentives to purchase, but always for a limited time, to encourage consumers to purchase now rather than wait until later.

These unique qualities come at a cost, however. A sales force requires a longer-term commitment than does advertising—advertising can be turned up or down, but sales force size is harder to change. Personal selling is also the company's most expensive promotion tool, costing companies as much as $452 on average per sales call, depending on the industry.[9] Most business-to-business firms spend up to three times as much on personal selling as they do on advertising.

Sales Promotion   Sales promotion includes a wide assortment of tools—coupons, rebates, contests, discounts or "sales," "buy one get one free" offers, and other limited time offers. Sales promotions are designed to achieve one or more of the following goals: attract consumer attention, offer strong incentives to purchase, dramatize product offers, encourage trial, or boost sagging sales. For example, furniture retailer Leon's offers regular but different sales promotions, each typically lasting one month. Sometimes sales promotions may be combined, such as the "Honey! They Shrunk the Prices!" sale combined with a special financing offer, "Don't pay for 16 months!"

Sales promotions invite and reward quick response—whereas advertising says, "Buy our product," sales promotion says, "Buy it now." Sales promotion effects are often short-lived, however, and often are not as effective as advertising or personal selling in building long-run brand preference and customer relationships.

Public Relations   Public relations (PR) is very believable—news stories, features, sponsorships, and events seem more real and believable to readers than ads do. Public relations can also reach many prospects who avoid salespeople and advertisements—the message gets to the buyers as "news" rather than as a sales-directed communication. And, as with advertising, PR can dramatize a company or product. Marketers tend to underuse PR or to use it as an afterthought. Yet a well-thought-out PR campaign used with other promotion mix elements can be very effective and economical.

For example, Edelman, the largest PR agency in the world, worked with the American Heart Association to expand the "Go Red" campaign for the American Heart Association, designed to educate women about how to prevent heart disease. Company president Richard Edelman believes that PR should lead the communications mix because it engages consumers in a conversation that is timely, relevant, and credible.

Exhibit 12.4   Public relations (PR): The "Go Red" campaign for the American Heart Association was designed and executed by PR agency Edelman, and won the 2009 Nonprofit Campaign of the Year award from *PRWeek* magazine.

Direct Marketing   Although there are many forms of direct marketing—direct mail and catalogues, online marketing, telephone marketing, and others—they all share four distinctive characteristics. Direct marketing is *less public*: The message is normally directed to an individual. Direct marketing is *immediate* and *customized*: Messages can be prepared very quickly and can be tailored to appeal to specific consumers. Finally, direct marketing is *interactive*: It allows a dialogue between the marketing team and the consumer, and messages can be altered depending on the consumer's response. Thus, direct marketing is well suited to highly targeted marketing efforts and to building one-to-one customer relationships.

PROMOTION MIX STRATEGIES

Marketers can choose from two basic promotion mix strategies—*push* promotion or *pull* promotion. Figure 12.2 contrasts the two strategies. The relative emphasis given to the specific promotion tools differs for push and pull strategies. A **push strategy** involves "pushing" the product through marketing channels to final consumers. The producer directs its marketing activities (primarily personal selling and trade promotion) toward channel members to induce them to carry the product and promote it to final consumers.

Push strategy
A promotion strategy that calls for using the sales force and trade promotion to push the product through channels. The producer promotes the product to channel members who in turn promote it to final consumers.

FIGURE 12.2 Push versus pull promotion strategy

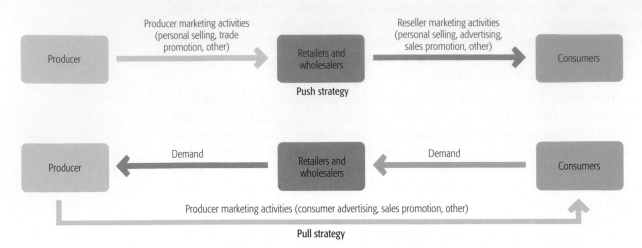

Pull strategy

A promotion strategy that calls for spending a lot on advertising and consumer promotion to induce final consumers to buy the product, creating a demand vacuum that "pulls" the product through the channel.

Using a **pull strategy**, the producer directs its marketing activities (primarily advertising and consumer promotion) toward final consumers to induce them to buy the product. For example, Unilever promotes its Axe grooming products directly to its young male target market by using TV and print ads, a brand website, its YouTube channel, and other marketing channels. If the pull strategy is effective, consumers will then demand the brand from retailers, who will in turn demand it from Unilever. Thus, under a pull strategy, consumer demand "pulls" the product through the channels.

Some business-to-business marketers use only push strategies; some consumer-products companies use only pull. However, most large companies use some combination of both. For example, Unilever spends $2.2 billion on U.S. media advertising and consumer sales promotions to create brand preference and pull customers into stores that carry its products. At the same time, it uses its own and distributors' sales forces and trade promotions to push its brands through the channels, so that they'll be available on store shelves when consumers come calling. In recent years, facing a tight economy and slumping sales, many consumer-goods companies have been decreasing the brand-building pull portions of their mixes in favour of more push. This has caused concern that they may be driving short-run sales at the expense of long-term brand equity.

Companies consider many factors when designing their promotion mix strategies, including *type of product/market* and the *product life-cycle stage*. For example, the importance of different promotion tools varies between consumer and business markets. Business-to-consumer companies usually "pull" more, putting more of their funds into advertising, followed by sales promotion, personal selling, and then PR. In contrast, business-to-business marketers tend to "push" more, putting more of their funds into personal selling, followed by sales promotion, advertising, and PR. In general, personal selling is used more heavily with expensive and risky goods and in markets with fewer and larger sellers.

Now that we've examined the concept of integrated marketing communications and the factors that firms consider when shaping their promotion mixes, let's look more closely at each of the five major marketing communications tools.

ADVERTISING (LO3)

Advertising can be traced back to the very beginnings of recorded history. Archaeologists working in the countries around the Mediterranean Sea have dug up signs announcing various events and offers. The Romans painted walls to announce gladiator fights, and the Phoenicians painted pictures promoting their wares on large rocks along parade routes. During the golden age in Greece, town criers announced the sale of cattle, crafted items, and even cosmetics. An early "singing commercial" went as follows: "For eyes that are shining, for cheeks like the dawn / For beauty that lasts after girlhood is gone / For prices in reason, the woman who knows / Will buy her cosmetics from Aesclyptos."

Modern advertising, however, is a far cry from these early efforts. Today, worldwide ad spending exceeds $600 billion, and nearly half of that is spent in the United States. Procter & Gamble, the world's largest advertiser, last year spent $4.8 billion on U.S. advertising and $8.5 billion worldwide.[10] According to the Canadian Marketing Association (CMA), every dollar spent on advertising in Canada results in $9 of economic activity. Advertising spending in Canadian media is expected to reach $23 billion in 2011.[11]

Most mass-media advertising is created by consumer-products companies, however, a wide range of not-for-profit organizations, professionals, and social agencies also use advertising to promote their causes to various audiences. Advertising is a good way to inform and persuade, whether the purpose is to sell Coca-Cola worldwide or to get consumers in a developing nation to use birth control.

Marketing management must make four important decisions when developing an advertising program (see Figure 12.3): *setting advertising objectives, setting the advertising budget, developing advertising strategy (message decisions and media decisions), and evaluating advertising campaigns.*

SETTING ADVERTISING OBJECTIVES

The first step is to set *advertising objectives*. These objectives should be based on past decisions about the target market, positioning, and the marketing mix, which define the job that advertising must do in the total marketing program. The overall advertising objective is to help build customer relationships by communicating customer value. Here, we discuss specific advertising objectives.

An **advertising objective** is a specific communication *task* to be accomplished with a specific *target* audience during a specific period of *time*. Advertising objectives can be classified by primary purpose—whether the aim is to *inform, persuade,* or *remind.* Table 12.1 lists examples of each of these specific objectives.

Advertising objective
A specific communication *task* to be accomplished with a specific *target* audience during a specific period of *time.* The overall advertising goal is to help build customer relationships by communicating customer value.

FIGURE 12.3 Major advertising decisions

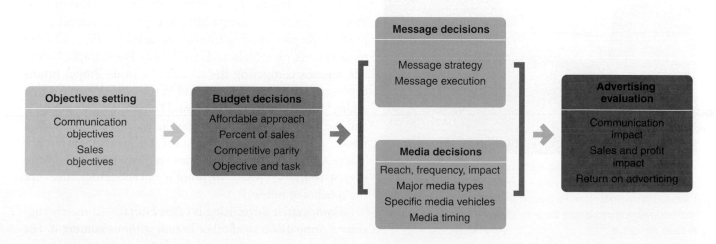

TABLE 12.1 Possible Advertising Objectives

Informative Advertising

Communicating customer value	Suggesting new uses for a product
Building a brand and company image	Informing the market of a price change
Telling the market about a new product	Describing available services and support
Explaining how a product works	Correcting false impressions

Persuasive Advertising

Building brand preference	Persuading customers to purchase now
Encouraging switching to a brand	Persuading customers to receive a sales call
Changing customer's perception of product value	Convincing customers to tell others about the brand

Reminder Advertising

Maintaining customer relationships	Reminding consumers that the product may be needed in the near future
Reminding consumers where to buy the product	Keeping the brand in the consumer's mind during off-seasons

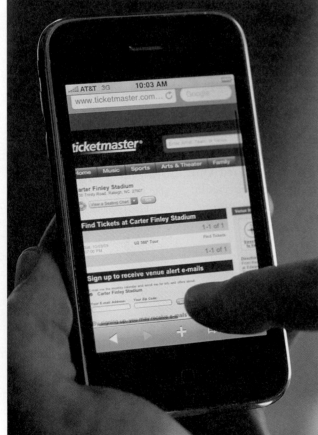

Exhibit 12.5   Informative advertising: Ads for new products typically take the approach of informing consumers that the product is available, and they sometimes demonstrate its use. For example, the first ads for the Apple iPhone showed close-ups of people using the device's revolutionary new touch screen to access the Internet.

Informative advertising is used heavily when introducing a new product or brand to the market. In this case, the objective is to build primary demand by communicating the benefits of the product. Informative advertising may also have an educational purpose, for example, when the iPhone was first introduced to the market, Apple's advertising objectives focused on communicating how the product worked, and demonstrating the use of the touch screen. *Persuasive advertising* becomes more important as competition in the product category increases. Here, the company's advertising objective is to build selective demand, in other words, to persuade the consumer that the company's product has more benefits than the competitor's. For example, when the Motorola Droid and the Palm Pre were launched, their advertising attempted to persuade the consumer that their brands were superior, in some way, to the iPhone.

Some persuasive advertising has become *comparative advertising* (or *attack advertising*), in which a company directly or indirectly compares its brand with one or more other brands. You see examples of comparative advertising in almost every product category, ranging from sports drinks, coffee, and soup to computers, car rentals, and credit cards. For example, Gatorade ran ads comparing the 25 calories in its Propel fitness beverage to the 125 calories found in Glacéau's VitaminWater, asking "How Fit Is Your Water?" And Dunkin' Donuts ran a TV and Web campaign comparing the chain's coffee to Starbucks's brews. "In a recent national blind taste test," proclaimed the ads, "more Americans preferred the taste of Dunkin' Donuts coffee over Starbucks. It's just more proof it's all about the coffee (not the couches or music)."

Comparative advertising is often indirect—it merely suggests a comparison to another brand, without naming it. For example, advertising for the Palm Pre claims it is "Smarter. Simpler. And way more fun," suggesting that it is more fun than an iPhone, but without directly saying so. Indirect comparative advertising is less risky than direct comparative advertising, which may result in a counterattack from the named competitor. For example, Sara Lee recently sued Kraft over ad claims that taste tests showed that Kraft's Oscar Mayer brand hot dogs taste better than Sara Lee's Ball Park Franks. Similarly, PepsiCo sued Coca-Cola, asserting that ads for Coca-Cola's Powerade sports drink made inaccurate claims that Powerade was more "complete" than PepsiCo's Gatorade.[12]

Reminder advertising is important for mature products—it helps to maintain customer relationships and keep consumers thinking about the product. Advertising for mature products such as Tide laundry detergent and Crest toothpaste primarily build and maintain the brand relationship rather than inform or persuade consumers to buy in the short run.

Advertising's goal is to help move consumers through the buying process. Some advertising is designed to move people to immediate action. For example, a direct-response television ad by Weight Watchers urges consumers to pick up the phone and sign up right away, and a Best Buy newspaper insert for a weekend sale encourages immediate store visits. However, many of the other ads focus on building or strengthening long-term customer relationships. For example, a Nike television ad in which well-known athletes work through extreme challenges in their Nike gear never directly asks for a sale. Instead, the goal is to somehow change the way the people think or feel about the brand.

SETTING THE ADVERTISING BUDGET

After determining its advertising objectives, the company next sets its **advertising budget** for each product. Here, we look at four common methods used to set the total budget for advertising: the *affordable method*, the *percentage-of-sales method*, the *competitive-parity method*, and the *objective-and-task method*.[13]

Affordable Method   Some companies use the **affordable method**: They set the advertising budget at the level they think the company can afford. Small businesses often use this method, reasoning that the company cannot spend more on advertising than it has. They start with total revenues, deduct operating expenses and capital outlays, and then devote some portion of the remaining funds to advertising.

Unfortunately, this method of setting budgets completely ignores the effects of advertising on sales. It tends to place promotion last among spending priorities, even in situations in which advertising is critical to the firm's success. It leads to an uncertain annual promotion budget, which makes long-range market planning difficult. Although the affordable method can result in overspending on advertising, it more often results in underspending.

Percentage-of-Sales Method   Other companies use the **percentage-of-sales method**, setting the promotion budget at a certain percentage of current or forecasted sales. Or they budget a percentage of the unit sales price. The percentage-of-sales method has advantages. It is simple to use and helps management to think about the relationships among promotion spending, selling price, and profit per unit.

Despite these claimed advantages, however, the percentage-of-sales method has little to justify it. It wrongly views sales as the *cause* of promotion rather than as the *result*. Although studies have found a positive correlation between promotional spending and brand strength, this relationship often turns out to be effect and cause, not cause and effect. Stronger brands with higher sales can afford the biggest ad budgets.

Thus, the percentage-of-sales budget is based on availability of funds rather than on opportunities. It may prevent the increased spending sometimes needed to turn around

Advertising budget
The dollars and other resources allocated to a product or company advertising program.

Affordable method
Setting the advertising budget at the level management thinks the company can afford.

Percentage-of-sales method
Setting the promotion budget at a certain percentage of current or forecasted sales, or as a percentage of the unit sales price.

falling sales. Because the budget varies with year-to-year sales, long-range planning is difficult. Finally, the method does not provide any basis for choosing a *specific* percentage, except what has been done in the past or what competitors are doing.

Competitive-Parity Method   Still other companies use the **competitive-parity method**, setting their promotion budgets to match competitors' outlays. They monitor competitors' advertising or get industry promotion spending estimates from publications or trade associations, and then set their budgets based on the industry average.

Two arguments support this method. First, competitors' budgets represent the collective wisdom of the industry. Second, spending what competitors spend helps prevent promotion wars. Unfortunately, neither argument is valid. There are no grounds for believing that the competition has a better idea of what a company should be spending on promotion than does the company itself. Companies differ greatly, and each has its own special promotion needs. Finally, there is no evidence that budgets based on competitive parity prevent promotion wars.

Objective-and-Task Method   The most logical budget-setting method is the **objective-and-task method**, whereby the company sets its advertising budget based on what it wants to accomplish with promotion. This budgeting method entails (1) defining specific promotion objectives, (2) determining the tasks needed to achieve these objectives, and (3) estimating the costs of performing these tasks. The sum of these costs is the proposed advertising budget.

The advantage of the objective-and-task method is that it forces management to spell out its assumptions about the relationship between dollars spent and promotion results. But it is also the most difficult method to use. Often, it is hard to figure out which specific tasks will achieve stated objectives. For example, suppose Sony wants 95 percent awareness for its latest Blu-ray player during the six-month introductory period. What specific advertising messages and media schedules should Sony use to attain this objective? How much would these messages and media schedules cost? Sony management must consider such questions, even though they are hard to answer.

No matter what method is used, setting the advertising budget is no easy task. John Wanamaker, the department store magnate, once said, "I know that half of my advertising is wasted, but I don't know which half. I spent $2 million for advertising, and I don't know if that is half enough or twice too much."

As a result of such thinking, advertising is one of the easiest budget items to cut when economic times get tough. Cuts in brand-building advertising appear to do little short-term harm to sales. For example, in the wake of the 2008 recession, U.S. advertising expenditures plummeted 12 percent. In the long run, however, slashing ad spending risks long-term damage to a brand's image and market share. In fact, companies that can maintain or even increase their advertising spending while competitors are decreasing theirs can gain competitive advantage. Consider carmaker Audi:[14]

Competitive-parity method
Setting the promotion budget to match competitors' outlays.

Objective-and-task method
Developing the advertising budget by (1) defining specific objectives, (2) determining the tasks that must be performed to achieve these objectives, and (3) estimating the costs of performing these tasks. The sum of these costs is the proposed advertising budget.

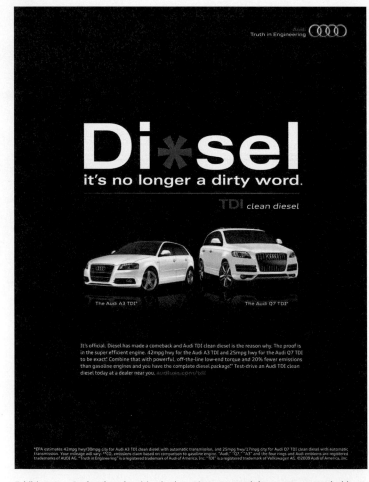

Exhibit 12.6   Setting the advertising budget: It's no easy task for a company to decide how much is the right amount to spend on advertising. Audi spent heavily during a time when competitors BMW, Mercedes, and Lexus cut back severely on advertising—and benefited from the decision.

Although Audi's U.S. sales slipped last year, they fell far less than those of competitors amid a calamitous year for the auto industry. What's more, Audi's brand awareness and buyer consideration reached record levels by the end of the year, with gains outstripping those of BMW, Mercedes, and Lexus. In short: Audi might be the hottest auto brand on the market right now. And it's strongly positioned for the future when the economy recovers. What's Audi's advantage? The brand is spending heavily on advertising and marketing at a time when rivals are retrenching. During the past two years, despite the harsh economy, Audi has increased its ad presence, including high-profile placements such as the last two Super Bowls, the Academy Awards, the NCAA basketball tournament, and Sunday Night Football. Audi "has kept its foot on the pedal while everyone else is pulling back," says an Audi ad executive. "Why would we go backwards now when the industry is generally locking the brakes and cutting spending?" adds Audi's chief marketing executive. The acceleration has paid off. "In a world of bad news and fear, confidence is contagious," says an industry consultant.

DEVELOPING ADVERTISING STRATEGY

Advertising strategy consists of two major elements: creating advertising *messages* and selecting advertising *media*. In the past, companies often viewed media planning as secondary to the message-creation process. The creative department first created good advertisements, and then the media department selected and purchased the best media for carrying these advertisements to desired target audiences. This often caused friction between creatives and media planners.

Today, however, soaring media costs, more-focused target marketing strategies, and the blizzard of new media have promoted the importance of the media-planning function. The decision about which media to use for an ad campaign—television, magazines, mobile devices, banner ads—is now sometimes more critical than the creative elements of the campaign. As a result, more and more, advertisers are orchestrating a closer harmony between their messages and the media that deliver them. In fact, in a really good ad campaign, you often have to ask, "Is that a media idea or a creative idea?"[15]

Creating the Advertising Message   No matter how big the budget, advertising can succeed only if advertisements gain attention and communicate well. Good advertising messages are especially important in today's costly and cluttered advertising environment. In the early days of television there were only a few channels, and the broadcasting day ended at midnight. Today, cable television services deliver hundreds of channels—and that's just one form of mass media. Most urban areas offer more than a dozen radio stations for the consumer to choose from, thousands of magazines are available no matter where you live, and the Internet is a virtually unlimited source of advertising. As a result, consumers are exposed to as many as 3000 to 5000 commercial messages every day.[16]

BREAKING THROUGH THE CLUTTER   If all this advertising clutter bothers some consumers, it also causes huge headaches for advertisers. Take the situation facing network television advertisers. They pay an average of $381 000 to make a single 30-second commercial. Then, each time they show it, they regularly pay $250 000 or more for 30 seconds of advertising time during a popular prime-time program. They pay even more if it's an especially popular program such as *American Idol* (up to $700 000), or a mega-event such as the Super Bowl ($3 million per 30 seconds!).[17]

Then, their ads are sandwiched in with a clutter of other commercials, announcements, and network promotions, totalling nearly 20 minutes of non-program material per prime-time hour with commercial breaks coming every six minutes on average. Such clutter in television and other ad media has created an increasingly hostile advertising environment. According to recent studies, 63 percent of television viewers believe there are too many ads, and 47 percent say ads spoil their viewing enjoyment.[18]

Advertising strategy
The strategy by which the company accomplishes its advertising objectives. It consists of two major elements: creating advertising messages and selecting advertising media.

It used to be that television viewers were pretty much a captive audience for advertisers, but today's new media technology has given consumers a rich new set of information and entertainment choices. Most television networks in Canada and the United States offer some of their programs for viewing on their websites. Cable companies offer video on demand and DVR services, and many television programs can be downloaded from online services such as Amazon.com and iTunes. While some of these program delivery systems still include advertising, the technology makes it easier for viewers to skip the ads. One ad agency executive calls DVR services "electronic weedwhackers." Research shows that 85 percent of DVR owners skip at least three-quarters of all ads. In one study, about 20 percent of brands experienced lower sales in ad-skipping households. At the same time, the number of viewers who watch video on demand, rather than scheduled broadcast television, is expected to quadruple during the next five years. These viewers will be able to watch programming on their own time terms, with or without commercials.[19]

Thus, advertisers can no longer force-feed the same old cookie-cutter ad messages to captive consumers through traditional media. Just to gain and hold attention, today's advertising messages must be better planned, more imaginative, more entertaining, and more emotionally engaging. "Interruption or disruption as the fundamental premise of marketing" no longer works, says one advertising executive. Instead, "you have to create content that is interesting, useful, or entertaining enough to invite [consumers]." According to another, "Everything is about control. If an ad is interesting to you, you'll have a conversation with the brand. If it's not, it's a waste of time."[20]

MERGING ADVERTISING AND ENTERTAINMENT   To break through the clutter, many marketers are now experimenting with forms of advertising that are in some way merged with entertainment. *Advertising Age* magazine refers to this as "Madison & Vine," from Madison Avenue, the New York City street that houses the headquarters of many large advertising agencies, and Hollywood & Vine, the Hollywood intersection that symbolizes the heart of the movie industry.

This merging of advertising and entertainment began as product placements within movies and television shows, but in recent years has developed into longer-form videos that are sponsored by one brand, yet are themselves entertainment. For example, Dove's "Evolution" video wasn't technically an ad, but it drew more—and more meaningful—views than many TV ads do, and the views were initiated by consumers. A range of new brand messaging platforms—from webisodes and viral videos to sponsored music videos—are now blurring the line between ads and entertainment.

Product placements involve imbedding brands as props within other programming. It might be a brief glimpse of the latest LG phone on *Grey's Anatomy* or the men on *How I Met Your Mother* lingering around the Victoria's Secret Fashion Show. The product placement might even be scripted into the theme of the program. For example, in one episode of *30 Rock*, network boss Jack Donaghy blatantly extols the virtues of his Verizon wireless service. Liz Lemon agrees: "Well sure, that Verizon wireless service is just unbeatable." She then turns to the camera and deadpans, "Can we have our money now?"[21]

Originally created with TV in mind, product placement has spread quickly into other sectors of the entertainment industry. It's widely used in movies (remember all those GM vehicles in *Transformers* or the prominence of Purina Puppy Chow in *Marley & Me*?). If you look carefully, you'll also see product placements in video games, comic books, Broadway musicals, and even pop music. The distinction between advertising and programming becomes even more blurred when an advertiser works with the network to produce the program. Take Frito Lay, for example:[22]

> One of Frito Lay Canada's signature marketing initiatives was the Juno Fan Choice Award, sponsored by Doritos. It debuted in 2003 as a product placement and interactive TV initiative

during a time when CTV and CARAS (Canadian Academy of Recording Arts and Sciences) were trying to attract a younger audience for the Juno Awards—which corresponded with the target market for Doritos, one of Frito Lay's most popular brands. Marc Guay, president of Frito Lay Canada, explains the decision to go beyond traditional television advertising: "[It's] when the art meets the science—you build your brand plan and your budgets, and you're going to have equity advertising and event-specific advertising whether it's innovation or promotional.... So we collectively built a program that would allow consumers to participate in the show—vote for a winner—and have a 'money can't buy experience' for the ultimate fan."

Does product placement work? A recent study by media agency Mediaedge: CIA and Canadian broadcast network CTV tested audience reaction to different levels of product placement in an entertainment news show with four test brands. The results showed that viewer enjoyment actually increased for versions with product placement and where products were an integral part of the script. Almost half the respondents said they would be more likely to buy products featured. Awareness levels also rose, by more than 16 percent for product placement over a 30 second spot, and by 24 percent when the product was finally integrated into the script.

For Frito Lay Canada and CTV, the goals were achieved. The audience for the Junos has gotten younger, fan participation has quadrupled in four years and the winner in year four (Simple Plan) was the first artist not to have the number-one-selling album of the year. And it continues to grow. Frito Lay was the first brand to support the CTV two-screen program where consumers could play along with the show on the Internet.

So, advertising as entertainment seems to be working, both for advertisers and for consumers. The goal is for brand messages to become a part of the entertainment rather than interrupting it. As advertising agency JWT puts it, "We believe advertising needs to stop interrupting what people are interested in and be what people are interested in."

Exhibit 12.7 Merging advertising and entertainment: Members of Canadian band Simple Plan are shown here accepting their Fan Choice Award, sponsored by Doritos in conjunction with CTV.

MESSAGE STRATEGY The first step in creating effective advertising messages is to plan a *message strategy*—to decide what general message will be communicated to the audience. The purpose of advertising is to get consumers to think about or react to the product or the company in a certain way. People will react only if they believe that they will benefit from doing so. Thus, developing an effective message strategy begins with identifying customer *benefits* that can be used as advertising appeals.

Ideally, advertising message strategy will follow directly from the company's broader positioning and customer value strategies. Message strategy statements tend to be plain, straightforward outlines of benefits and positioning points that the advertiser wants to stress. The advertiser must next develop a compelling **creative concept**—or *"big idea"*—that will bring the message strategy to life in a distinctive and memorable way. At this stage, simple message ideas become great ad campaigns. Usually, a copywriter and art director will team up to generate many creative concepts, hoping that one of these concepts will turn out to be the big idea. The creative concept may emerge as a visualization, a phrase, or a combination of the two.

The creative concept will guide the choice of specific appeals to be used in an advertising campaign. *Advertising appeals* should have three characteristics. First, they should be *meaningful*, pointing out benefits that make the product more desirable or interesting to consumers. Second, appeals must be *believable*—consumers must believe

Creative concept
The compelling "big idea" that will bring the advertising message strategy to life in a distinctive and memorable way.

Exhibit 12.8   Message strategy and creative concept: The creative concept behind all of TELUS's advertising is to use friendly, colourful animals to communicate brand personality and represent a feature of the company's products or services. Here the hippo tells consumers in British Columbia that TELUS's network is big. (The rabbits are reprised from a previous campaign in which they communicated messages about family plans.)

that the product or service will deliver the promised benefits. For example, TELUS's advertising for years has been based on the creative concept of using colourful animals to represent aspects of the company's services. Rabbits—and "rabbit ears"—were featured when TELUS mobile devices began offering television services, and recently the hippo was featured to communicate that TELUS's network is BIG.

Advertising appeals should also be *distinctive*—they should tell how the product is better than the competing brands. For example, the most meaningful benefit of owning a wristwatch is that it keeps accurate time, yet few watch ads feature this benefit. Instead, based on the distinctive benefits they offer, watch advertisers might select any of a number of advertising themes. For years, Timex has been the affordable watch. Last Father's Day, for example, Timex ads suggested, "Tell Dad more than time this Father's Day. Tell him that you've learned the value of a dollar." Similarly, Rolex ads never talk at all about keeping time. Instead, they talk about the brand's "obsession with perfection" and the fact that "Rolex has been the preeminent symbol of performance and prestige for more than a century."

MESSAGE EXECUTION   The advertiser now has to turn the big idea into an actual ad execution that will capture the target market's attention and interest. The creative team must find the best approach, style, tone, words, and format for executing the message. Any message can be presented in different **execution styles**, such as the following:

Execution style
The approach, style, tone, words, and format used for executing an advertising message.

□ *Slice of life:* This style shows one or more "typical" people using the product in a normal setting. For example, a Silk Soymilk "Rise and Shine" ad shows a young professional starting the day with a healthier breakfast and high hopes.

□ *Lifestyle:* This style shows how a product fits in with a particular lifestyle. For example, an ad for Athleta activewear shows a woman in a complex yoga pose and states, "If your body is your temple, build it one piece at a time."

□ *Fantasy:* This style creates a fantasy around the product or its use. For example, a recent Travelers Insurance ad features a gentleman carrying a giant red umbrella (the company's brand symbol). The man helps people by using the umbrella to protect them from the rain, sail them across a flooded river, and fly home. The ad closes with "Travelers Insurance. There when you need it."

□ *Mood or image:* This style builds a mood or image around the product or service, such as beauty, love, intrigue, or serenity. Few claims are made about the product except through suggestion. For example, ads by India's Ministry of Tourism feature images of inspiring experiences and vibrant local landscapes in "Incredible !ndia."

▢ *Musical:* This style shows people or cartoon characters singing about the product. For example, FreeCreditReport.com tells its story exclusively through a set of popular singing commercials such as "Dreamgirl" and "Pirate." Similarly Oscar Mayer's long-running ads show children singing its now-classic "I wish I were an Oscar Mayer wiener ..." jingle.

▢ *Personality symbol:* This style creates a character that represents the product. The character might be *animated* (Mr. Clean, Tony the Tiger, the Pillsbury Doughboy) or *real* (the Maytag repairman, the E*TRADE baby).

▢ *Technical expertise:* This style shows the company's expertise in making the product. Thus, natural-foods maker Kashi shows its buyers carefully selecting ingredients for its products, and Jim Koch of the Boston Beer Company tells about his many years of experience in brewing Samuel Adams beer.

▢ *Scientific evidence:* This style presents survey or scientific evidence that the brand is better or better liked than one or more other brands. For years, Crest toothpaste has used scientific evidence to convince buyers that Crest is better than other brands at fighting cavities.

▢ *Testimonial evidence or endorsement:* This style features a highly believable or likable source endorsing the product. It could be ordinary people saying how much they like a given product. For example, Subway uses spokesman Jared, a customer who lost 245 pounds on a diet of Subway heroes. Or it might be a celebrity presenting the product, such as Sidney Crosby speaking for Reebok.

Escape the yard.
And all the work that goes with it. Let a new Red Haus Salzburg condo take care of everything — inside and out.

Red Haus
redhausliving.com

Exhibit 12.9   Message execution: This ad for condominiums in Calgary uses slice-of-life, fantasy, humour, and a compelling image that draws the consumer's attention. The headline reads, "Escape the yard," but the message is "Condominiums are better than houses."

The advertiser also must choose a *tone* for the ad. Procter & Gamble always uses a positive tone: Its ads say something very positive about its products. Other advertisers now use edgy humour to break through the commercial clutter. Bud Light commercials are famous for this.

The advertiser must use memorable and attention-getting *words* in the ad. For example, rather than claiming simply that the Toyota Tundra is a "well-designed pickup truck," Toyota uses higher-impact phrasing: It's "The truck that's changing it all. Power and efficiency. Like steak and eggs." Similarly, Flip Video's stylish and innovative little Mino isn't just a "video camcorder." It's "designable, simple, shareable, adaptable, remarkable. Meet the Mino. Now Playing: You."

Finally, *format* elements make a difference in an ad's impact as well as in its cost. A small change in ad design can make a big difference in its effect. In a print ad, the *illustration* is the first thing the reader notices—it must be strong enough to draw attention. Next, the *headline* must effectively entice the right people to read the copy. Finally, the *copy*—the main block of text in the ad—must be simple but strong and convincing. Moreover, these three elements must effectively work *together* to persuasively present customer value.

CONSUMER-GENERATED MESSAGES   Taking advantage of today's interactive technologies, many companies are now tapping consumers for message ideas or actual ads. They

Exhibit 12.10   Consumer-generated advertising: Doritos' "Crash the Super Bowl" challenge, which invites consumers to create their own videos, has become an annual event.

are searching existing video sites, setting up their own sites, and sponsoring ad-creation contests and other promotions.

Sometimes, marketers capitalize on consumer videos that are already posted on YouTube. For example, one of the most viewed amateur videos on the Web a couple years ago showed two men in lab coats mixing Diet Coke with Mentos candies to produce shooting fountains of soda. The video produced a windfall of free buzz for Coca-Cola. To gain even more mileage, Coca-Cola hired the amateur videographers—a professional juggler and a lawyer—to create another video and to star in a 30-second Coke ad.[23]

Many other brands hold contests or develop brand websites of their own that invite consumers to submit ad message ideas and videos. For example, PepsiCo's Doritos brand holds its annual "Crash the Super Bowl Challenge" contest that invites consumers to create their own video ads about the tasty triangular corn chips. Last year, Doritos received 2700 user-generated videos and posted the top five on the contest website, where consumers could view the ads and vote for a winner. The five finalists received a $25 000 prize, and PepsiCo revealed and aired the winning ad during the Super Bowl. The consumer-generated Doritos ads have been a smashing success. Last year's consumer-generated ad, "Snow Globe-Free Doritos," placed first in *USA Today* Ad Meter's most popular Super Bowl ad ratings, earning the winner a massive $1 million bonus from PepsiCo. Both the contests and the user-created ads themselves have earned Doritos a heap of pre– and post–Super Bowl buzz.[24]

Not all consumer-generated advertising efforts are so successful. In fact, it can be downright dangerous to give consumers too much creative freedom and control. In one case, when Chevrolet ran a promotion for its Tahoe SUV allowing consumers to write their own text for video clips of the vehicle, it got some unexpected negative results. Many of the user-created ads contained critical gibes about the big SUV's poor gas mileage, high operating costs, and harmful environmental impact. Thus, marketers should be cautious when inviting consumer creative inputs.[25]

If used carefully, however, consumer-generated advertising efforts can produce big benefits. First, for relatively little expense, companies can collect new creative ideas, as well as fresh perspectives on the brand and what it actually means to consumers who experience it. Second, consumer-generated message campaigns can boost consumer involvement and get consumers talking and thinking about a brand and its value to them. Says one marketer, "Engage a satisfied customer in a dialogue about a product— and give them a forum to express their creative aspirations for that product—and you will have a brand advocate who speaks from the heart."[26]

Advertising media

The types of media and media vehicles through which advertising messages are delivered to their intended audiences.

Selecting Advertising Media   The major steps in **advertising media** selection are (1) deciding on *reach*, *frequency*, and *impact*; (2) choosing among major *media types*; (3) selecting specific *media vehicles*; and (4) deciding on *media timing*.

DECIDING ON REACH, FREQUENCY, AND IMPACT   To select media, the advertiser must decide on the reach and frequency needed to achieve advertising objectives. *Reach* is a measure of the *percentage* of people in the target market who are exposed to the ad campaign during a given period of time. For example, the advertiser might try to reach 70 percent of the target market during the first three months of the campaign. *Frequency* is a measure of how many *times* the average person in the target market is exposed to the message. For example, the advertiser might want an average exposure frequency of three.

But advertisers want to do more than just reach a given number of consumers a specific number of times. The advertiser also must decide on the desired *media impact*—the *qualitative value* of a message exposure through a given medium. For example, the same message in one magazine (say, *Newsweek*) may be more believable than in another (say, the *National Enquirer*). For products that need to be demonstrated, messages on television may have more impact than messages on radio because television uses sight *and* sound. Products for which consumers want to select colours and features (cars, for example) might be better promoted by using banner ads that invite consumers to build their own car on the company's website, and when a direct response is desired, such as encouraging consumers to come to the opening of a new Best Buy store, direct mail is often the best media choice.

More generally, the advertiser wants to choose media that will *engage* consumers rather than simply reach them. For example, for television advertising, how relevant an ad is for its audience is often much more important than how many people it reaches. "This is about 'lean to' TV rather than 'lean back,'" says one expert. According to Unilever's director of global communications, advertising is "moving away from interruption and towards engagement. We have this term: 'penetrate the culture.' It's about getting into what people are interested in, what they are engaged in."[27]

Although Nielsen is beginning to measure levels of television *media engagement*, such measures are hard to come by for most media. "All the measurements we have now are media metrics: ratings, readership, listenership, click-through rates," says an executive of the Advertising Research Foundation, but engagement "happens inside the consumer, not inside the medium. What we need is a way to determine how the targeted prospect connected with, got engaged with, the brand idea. With engagement, you're on your way to a relationship."[28]

CHOOSING AMONG MEDIA TYPES   The media planner has to know the reach, frequency, and impact of each of the major media types. As summarized in Table 12.2, the major media types are television, the Internet, newspapers, direct mail, magazines, radio, and out-of-home. Each medium has advantages and limitations. Media planners consider many factors when making their media choices. They want to choose media that will effectively and efficiently present the advertising message to target customers. Thus, they must consider each medium's impact, message effectiveness, and cost. Typically, it's not a question of which one medium to use. Rather, the advertiser selects a mix of media and blends them into a fully integrated marketing communications campaign. Each medium plays a specific role.

Today, advertisers have many options beyond traditional media. As mass-media costs rise, audiences shrink, and exciting new digital media emerge, many advertisers are finding new ways to reach consumers. They are supplementing the traditional mass media with more-specialized and highly targeted media that cost less, target more effectively, and engage consumers more fully, such as *digital media*, *alternative media*, and *new media*. Digital media includes any form of media delivered on a screen and operated by a computer, for example, electronic signs and video screens in airports, elevators, retail environments, and gas stations. Alternative media is any form of non-traditional out-of-home media, such as ads on pool tables, in public washrooms, or on top of taxicabs. New media is a general term applied to whatever forms of media are still in the early stages of being used for advertising, for example, the "third screen" of personal mobile devices and, most recently, the iPad:[29]

> The latest personal electronic device from Apple, the iPad, was launched into the market in 2010 and was an instant success, selling more than three million units in less than three

TABLE 12.2	Profiles of Major Media Types	
Medium	**Advantages**	**Limitations**
Television	Good mass-marketing coverage; low cost per exposure; combines sight, sound, and motion; appealing to the senses	High absolute costs; high clutter; fleeting exposure; less audience selectivity
The Internet	High selectivity; low cost; immediacy; interactive capabilities	Relatively low impact; the audience controls exposure
Newspapers	Flexibility; timeliness; good local market coverage; broad acceptability; high believability	Short life; poor reproduction quality; small pass-along audience
Direct mail	High audience selectivity; flexibility; no ad competition within the same medium; allows personalization	Relatively high cost per exposure; "junk mail" image
Magazines	High geographic and demographic selectivity; credibility and prestige; high-quality reproduction; long life and good pass-along readership	Long ad purchase lead time; high cost; no guarantee of position
Radio	Good local acceptance; high geographic and demographic selectivity; low cost	Audio only, fleeting exposure; low attention ("the half-heard" medium); fragmented audiences
Out-of-home	Flexibility; high repeat exposure; low cost; low message competition; good positional selectivity	Little audience selectivity; creative limitations

months. Consumers are not the only ones clamouring for the iPad, however—advertisers are scrambling to get their messages onto the hot new device. A new advertising technology company called Pointroll placed advertising campaigns for Ford, Unilever, Marriott, and Target on iPods sold in the U.S. So far, click-through rates (a measure of how many people are interacting with the ads) have been six times higher than usual. "Much of [this] can probably be explained by the fact that the iPad's early adopters find just about everything on the device—including the ads—a curiosity," says one observer.

Pioneering advertisers like Ford are eager to proceed, but are doing so with caution. "We're approaching it as a trial," says Scott Kelly, digital marketing manager at Ford Motor Co. "This is all new territory and we are in experimentation mode." Meanwhile, the VP of advertising and marketing at Pointroll says the company is encouraging marketers like Ford to think of the iPad as another form of media in their marketing plans.

Finally, an important trend affecting media selection is the rapid growth in the number of "media multitaskers," people who absorb more than one medium at a time. One survey found that three-fourths of TV viewers read the newspaper while they watch TV, and two-thirds of them go online during their TV time. According to another study, consumers aged 8 to 18 are managing to cram an average 8.5 hours of media consumption into 6.5 hours. These days, says one analyst, "it's not uncommon to find a teenage boy chasing down photos of Keira Knightley on Google, IMing several friends at once, listening to a mix of music on iTunes, and talking on the mobile phone to a friend—all while, in the midst of the multimedia chaos, trying to complete an essay he's got open in a Word file a few layers down on his desktop."[30] Media planners need to take such media interactions into account when selecting the types of media they will use.

Exhibit 12.11   New media advertising: The latest electronic device to provide a platform for advertisers is the iPad, a tablet computer with a large, high-quality viewing screen. Major advertisers such as Ford, Unilever, and Marriott are already experimenting with forms of advertising on the iPad.

SELECTING MEDIA VEHICLES The media planner now must choose the best **media vehicles**—specific media within each general media type. Television is a media type, but CTV and *Hockey Night in Canada* are media vehicles. Similarly magazines are a media type, but *Maclean's* and *Chatelaine* are media vehicles.

Media planners buy media space in CPMs—units of 1000 impressions, that is, 1000 viewings of the ad. CPM stands for cost per thousand impressions (M is the Roman numeral for one thousand). CPM is a way for media planners to compare the cost of reaching their target audience across different forms of media. For example, if a full-page, four-colour advertisement in *Newsweek* costs $226 590 and *Newsweek's* readership is 2.6 million people, the CPM (cost of reaching each group of 1000 persons) is about $87. Television audiences are much larger than magazine audiences, but they are less targeted, therefore the CPM is lower, in the range of $10-$20, depending on the program.

The media planner must also consider the costs of producing ads for different media. Whereas radio ads may cost only a few hundred dollars to produce, flashy television ads can be very costly. For example, a typical car commercial can cost from $500 000 to $1 million or more to produce. Guinness recently filmed a 90-second commercial titled "Tipping Point" in a tiny town of just 2000 people high in the mountains of northern Argentina, where you can't even get a pint of the stout. Some billed it as the best beer commercial ever. But the cost to create the ad? An almost unimaginable $20 million.[31]

In choosing media types and selecting media vehicles, the media planner must balance media costs against several media effectiveness factors. While CPM is a method of pricing advertising media, it is up to the media planner to determine the *value* of the audience. First, the planner should evaluate the media vehicle's *audience quality*. For a Huggies disposable diapers advertisement, for example, *Parenting* magazine would have a high exposure value; *Maxim* would have a low exposure value. Second, the media planner should consider *audience engagement*. Readers of *Vogue*, for example, typically pay more attention to ads than do *Newsweek* readers. Third, the planner should assess the vehicle's *editorial quality*— *Time* and *The Wall Street Journal* are more believable and prestigious than *Star* or the *National Enquirer*.

DECIDING ON MEDIA TIMING The advertiser must also decide how to schedule the advertising over the course of a year. Suppose sales of a product peak in December and drop in March (for winter sports gear, for instance). The firm can vary its advertising to follow the seasonal pattern, oppose the seasonal pattern, or be the same all year. Most firms do some seasonal advertising. For example, The Picture People, a chain of portraits studios in the United States, advertises more heavily before major holidays such as Christmas, Easter, and Valentine's Day. Some marketers do *only* seasonal advertising: For instance, P&G advertises its Vicks NyQuil only during the cold and flu season.

Finally, the advertiser has to choose the pattern of the advertising schedule. *Continuity* means scheduling ads evenly within a given period. *Pulsing* means scheduling ads unevenly over a given time period. Thus, 52 ads could either be scheduled at one per week during the year or pulsed in several bursts. The idea behind pulsing is to

Media vehicle
The specific media (publication or program) within a general media type (magazine, radio, television).

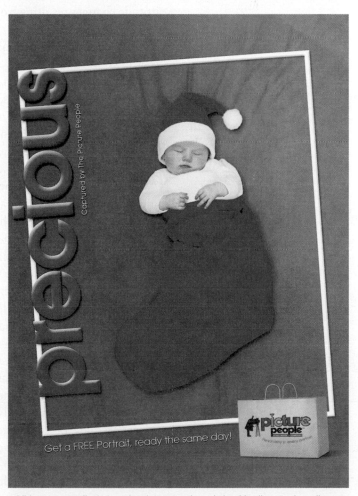

Exhibit 12.12   Media timing: The Picture People, a chain of family portrait studios, advertises more heavily before special holidays.

advertise heavily for a short period to build awareness that carries over to the next advertising period. Those who favour pulsing feel that it can be used to achieve the same impact as a steady schedule but at a much lower cost. However, some media planners believe that although pulsing achieves minimal awareness, it sacrifices depth of advertising communications.

EVALUATING ADVERTISING EFFECTIVENESS AND RETURN ON ADVERTISING INVESTMENT LO4

Return on advertising investment
The net return on advertising investment divided by the costs of the advertising investment.

Measuring advertising effectiveness and **return on advertising investment** has become a hot issue for most companies, especially since the recent economic recession. Two separate studies show that advertising effectiveness has fallen 40 percent over the past decade and that 37.3 percent of advertising budgets are wasted. This leaves top management and many companies asking their marketing managers, "How do we know that we're spending the right amount on advertising?" and "What return are we getting on our advertising investment?"[32]

Advertisers should regularly evaluate two types of advertising results: the communication effects and the sales and profit effects. Measuring the *communication effects* of an ad or ad campaign tells whether the ads and media are communicating the ad message well. Individual ads can be tested before or after they are run. Before an ad is placed, the advertiser can show it to consumers, ask how they like it, and measure message recall or attitude changes resulting from it. After an ad is run, the advertiser can measure how the ad affected consumer recall or product awareness, knowledge, and preference. Pre- and post-evaluations of communication effects can be made for entire advertising campaigns as well.

Advertisers have gotten pretty good at measuring the communication effects of their ads and ad campaigns. However, *sales and profit* effects of advertising are often much harder to measure. For example, what sales and profits are produced by an ad campaign that increases brand awareness by 20 percent and brand preference by 10 percent? Sales and profits are affected by many factors other than advertising—such as product features, price, and availability.

One way to measure the sales and profit effects of advertising is to compare past sales and profits with past advertising expenditures. Another way is through experiments. For example, to test the effects of different advertising spending levels, Coca-Cola could vary the amount it spends on advertising in different market areas and measure the differences in the resulting sales and profit levels. More complex experiments could be designed to include other variables, such as differences in the ads or media used.

However, because so many factors affect advertising effectiveness, some controllable and others not, measuring the results of advertising spending remains an inexact science. For example, many major brands spend lavishly on high-profile Super Bowl ads each year. Although they sense that the returns are worth the sizable investment, few can actually measure or prove it (see Marketing@Work 12.2). A recent survey of marketing and advertising agency executives concluded that over 80 percent of marketers don't measure return on investment because it's just too difficult to measure.[33] The ANA study cited earlier asked advertising managers if they would be able to "forecast the impact on sales" of a 10 percent cut in advertising spending—63 percent said no.

"Marketers are tracking all kinds of data and they still can't answer basic questions" about advertising accountability, says a marketing analyst, "because they don't have real models and metrics by which to make sense of it." Advertisers are measuring "everything they can, and that ranges from how many people respond to an ad to how many sales are closed and then trying to hook up those two end pieces," says another analyst. "The

MARKETING@WORK 12.2

The Super Bowl: The Mother of All Advertising Events—But Is It Worth It?

The Super Bowl is the mother of all advertising events. Each year, dozens of blue-chip advertisers showcase some of their best work to huge audiences around the world. But all this doesn't come cheap. Last year, major advertisers plunked down an average of $3 million per 30-second spot—that's $100 000 per second! But that's just for the air time. Throw in ad production costs—which average $2 million per showcase commercial—and running even a single Super Bowl ad becomes a super-expensive proposition. Anheuser-Busch ran *seven* spots last year.

So every year, as the Super Bowl season nears, up pops the BIG QUESTION: Is Super Bowl advertising worth all that money? Does it deliver a high advertising ROI? As it turns out, there's no easy answer to the question, especially when the economy's hurting. These days, in the wake of a recession that has companies watching every penny, spending such big bucks on a single event raises more questions than ever.

Advertiser and industry expert opinion varies widely. Super Bowl stalwarts such as Anheuser-Busch, E*TRADE, Bridgestone, CareerBuilder, and PepsiCo's Frito-Lay, Gatorade, and Pepsi-Cola divisions must think it's a good investment—they come back year after year. But what about savvy marketers such as Unilever and FedEx, who opted out last year? In a survey of board members of the National Sports Marketing Network, 31 percent said they would recommend Super Bowl ads. But 41 percent said no— Super Bowl ads just aren't worth the money. What's more, in these down economic times, advertisers worry the Super Bowl advertising might send the wrong message. In pulling out after 12 straight previous Super Bowls, FedEx expressed concerns that such lavish spending at a time when it was asking employees to do more with less might look just plain wrong.

The naysayers make some pretty good arguments. Super Bowl advertising is outrageously expensive. Advertisers pay 85 percent more per viewer than they'd pay by using prime-time network programming. And that $3 million would buy a lot of alternative media—for example, 50 different product placements in movies, TV shows, and video games; or two massive billboards in New York's Times Square that would be seen by a million people each day for a year. Beyond the cost, the competition for attention during the Super Bowl is fierce. Every single ad represents the best efforts of a major marketer trying to design a knock-your-socks-off spectacular that will reap high ratings from both critics and consumers. Many advertisers feel they can get more for their advertising dollar in venues that aren't so crowded with bigger-than-life commercials.

Then there's the question of strategic fit. Whereas the Super Bowl might be a perfect advertising event for companies selling beer, snacks, soft drinks, or sporting goods, it simply doesn't fit the creative strategies of many other brands. Consider Unilever's Dove.

Four years ago, the company ran a sentimental 45-second commercial from the Dove "Campaign for Real Beauty." The ad was highly rated by consumers, and it created considerable buzz—some 400 million impressions of the ad before and after its single appearance on the Super Bowl. But much of that buzz came from publicity surrounding the issue of girls' self-esteem rather than the product. And research showed that the ad produced low levels of involvement with the brand message.

Dove got almost equal exposure numbers and more engagement for a lot less money from an outdoor campaign that it ran that same year, and it got a much larger online response from its viral "Dove Evolution" and "Onslaught" films, which incurred no media cost at all. "The

Exhibit 12.13 Advertising ROI: The Super Bowl plays to a huge and receptive audience—almost 100 million viewers put away their DVR remotes and watch it live, glued to their screens, ads and all. But is the advertising worth the huge cost?

Super Bowl really isn't the right environment for Dove," says a Unilever executive. The past three years, instead, Dove opted to run consumer-generated ads during the more-female-oriented Academy Awards, an event where beauty brands thrive.

Still, the Super Bowl has a lot to offer to the right advertisers. It's the most-watched TV event of the year. It plays to a huge and receptive audience—almost 100 million viewers who put away their DVR remotes and watch it live, glued to their screens, ads and all. In fact, to many viewers, the Super Bowl ads are more important than what happens on the gridiron. Last year, the game itself drew an average rating (the percent of TV-owning households watching) of 41.6; the ads drew 41.22.

"There is no other platform quite like the Super Bowl," says the chief creative officer at Anheuser-Busch. "It's worth it. When you can touch that many households [with that kind of impact] in one sitting, it's actually efficient." In terms of dollars and cents, a study by one research firm found that consumer package-goods firms get a return of $1.25 to $2.74 for every dollar invested in Super Bowl advertising and one Super Bowl ad is as effective as 250 regular TV spots.

What's more, for most advertisers, the Super Bowl ad itself is only the centrepiece of something much bigger. Long after the game is over, ad critics, media pundits, and consumers are still reviewing, rehashing, and rating the commercials. Advertisers don't usually sit back and just hope that consumers will talk about their ads. They build events that help boost the buzz. For example, as noted previously, Doritos's annual "Crash the Super Bowl" contest produced more than 2700 entries last year, and the winning ad—"Free Doritos"—was voted best ad by the USA Today Ad Meter. And consumers were still buzzing about the ad days and weeks following the event.

For example, YouTube viewers gave the consumer-generated Doritos ad top honours in YouTube's Ad Blitz, a special YouTube section created to showcase Super Bowl commercials. The Doritos ad drew more than 800 000 views and more than 1200 comments in just three days. A second Doritos contest ad finished in the top 5 in both the USA Today and YouTube ratings. That's the kind of buzz that money just can't buy.

Similarly, the Super Bowl's largest advertiser, Anheuser-Busch, extends the festivities far beyond game day. It follows up with a post-game email campaign to keep the fires burning. It also hosts a designated website, where consumers can view all of the company's Super Bowl ads and vote for their favourites via the website or text messages.

So—back to the original question: Is the Super Bowl advertising really worth the huge investment? It seems that there's no definitive answer—for some

advertisers it's "yes"; for others, "no." The real trick is in trying to measure the returns. As the title of one recent article asserts, "Measuring Bowl Return? Good Luck!" The writer's conclusion: "For all the time, energy, and angst marketers spend crafting the perfect Super Bowl spot, [that's] a relative breeze compared to trying to prove its return on investment."

Sources: Quotes and other information from Bruce Horovitz, "$2 Million Average Production Cost + $3 Million Average Cost of a Commercial = Pressure," USA Today, January 30, 2009, p. B1; Claire Atkinson, "Measuring Bowl ROI? Good Luck," Advertising Age, January 29, 2007, p. 9; Jack Neff, "P&G, Unilever Sit Out the Super Bowl," Advertising Age, January 29, 2007, pp. 1, 36; Suzanne Vranica, "Tough Times Complicate Case for Buying Super Bowl Ads," Wall Street Journal, November 11, 2008, accessed at www.wsj.com; Scott Collins, "Take II: Super Bowl Was Most Watched," Los Angeles Times, February 4, 2009, p. D8; Brian Morressey, "YouTube Viewers Crown Doritos SB Champ" Adweek, February 5, 2009, accessed at www.adweek.com; Paul Thomasch and Ben Kalyman, "Recession Raises Stakes for Super Bowl Advertising," Reuters, January 6, 2009, accessed at www.reuters.com; and Tim Calkins and Derek D. Rucker, "Does a $3M Super Bowl Ad Make Sense In a Recession?" Advertising Age, January 12, 2009, p. 17.

tough part is, my goodness, we've got so much data. How do we sift through it?"[34] Thus, although the situation is improving as marketers seek more answers, managers often must rely on large doses of judgment along with quantitative analysis when assessing advertising performance.

OTHER ADVERTISING CONSIDERATIONS

In developing advertising strategies and programs, the company must address two additional questions. First, how will the company organize its advertising function—who will perform which advertising tasks? Second, how will the company adapt its advertising strategies and programs to the complexities of international markets?

Organizing for Advertising   Different companies organize in a variety of ways to handle advertising. In small companies, advertising might be handled by someone in the sales department. Large companies set up advertising departments whose job it is to set the advertising budget, work with the advertising agency, and handle other advertising not done by the agency. Most large companies use outside advertising agencies because they offer several advantages.

Advertising agency

A marketing services firm that assists companies in planning, preparing, implementing, and evaluating all or portions of their advertising programs.

How does an **advertising agency** work? Advertising agencies were started in the mid- to late-1800s by salespeople and brokers who worked for the media and received a commission for selling advertising space in newspapers and magazines to companies. Later, as radio and television, and eventually the Internet, emerged as advertising media, agencies began to handle all aspects of advertising, from strategic development, to creative production, to media buying.

Today's agencies employ specialists who can often perform advertising tasks better than the company's own staff can. Agencies also bring an outside point of view to solving the company's problems, along with lots of experience from working with different clients and situations. So, today, even companies with strong advertising departments of their own use advertising agencies.

Some ad agencies are huge—the largest U.S. agency, BBDO Worldwide, has annual gross U.S. revenues of more than $635 million. In recent years, many agencies have grown by gobbling up other agencies, thus creating huge agency holding companies. The largest of these agency "megagroups," WPP, includes several large advertising, public relations, and promotion agencies with combined worldwide revenues of $13.6 billion.[35] Most large advertising agencies have the staff and resources to handle all phases of an advertising campaign for their clients, from creating a marketing plan to developing ad campaigns and preparing, placing, and evaluating ads.

Exhibit 12.14 Advertising agencies: Cossette Communications, one of the largest advertising agencies in Canada, created this integrated, interactive campaign for GM's new line of small cars, targeting 18–34 year olds.

In Canada, Cossette Communications is one of the largest agencies, handling advertising for Bell Canada, BMO Financial Group, Procter & Gamble, Canada Post, and General Motors of Canada:[36]

> When General Motors of Canada launched its new series of Pontiac and Chevrolet small cars targetting the 18–34 market, GM turned to Cossette Communications to develop an original, interactive advertising campaign to encourage consumers to discover the features and advantages of the new cars.
>
> Realizing that the Internet is the main source of information for this target group of consumers, Cossette designed a national advertising campaign that pushed the boundaries of Internet advertising. An "interactive showroom" was built on the Web, simulating the experience of visiting a dealership, but in an environment that corresponded more closely to the lifestyle of the typical 18–34 year old. Visitors to the site could learn about the cars with the guidance of a virtual salesperson. The site also included more than 650 video sequences showing young owners interacting with the cars, each of which could be clicked on by the site visitor.
>
> The advertising campaign ran for the summer season, reaching more than 11.4 million consumers for an average of three minutes and ten seconds each.

Most large agencies, such as BBDO, Saatchi & Saatchi, and Ogilvy & Mather, have offices in every major city in the world, and advertising for each country is normally created by the agency in that country—even for global brands such as McDonald's and Coca-Cola. Advertising must be "localized" to fit with the country's culture and to abide by its rules. For example, China has restrictive censorship rules for TV and radio advertising—the words *the best* are banned, as are ads that "violate social customs" or present women in "improper ways." McDonald's once avoided government sanctions by publicly apologizing for an ad that crossed cultural norms by showing a customer begging for a discount. Similarly, Coca-Cola's Indian subsidiary was forced to end a promotion that offered prizes, such as a trip to Hollywood, because it violated India's established trade practices by encouraging customers to buy in order to "gamble." Thus, although advertisers may develop global strategies to guide their overall advertising efforts, specific advertising programs must usually be adapted to meet local cultures and customs, media characteristics, and advertising regulations.

PUBLIC RELATIONS L05

Another major mass-promotion tool is public relations (PR)—building good relations with the company's various publics by obtaining favourable publicity, building up a good corporate image, and handling or heading off unfavourable rumours, stories, and events. Public relations departments may perform any or all of the following functions:[37]

☐ *Press relations or press agency:* Creating and placing newsworthy information in the news media to attract attention to a person, a product, or a service.

☐ *Product publicity:* Publicizing specific products.

☐ *Public affairs:* Building and maintaining national or local community relations.

☐ *Lobbying:* Building and maintaining relations with legislators and government officials to influence legislation and regulation.

☐ *Investor relations:* Maintaining relationships with shareholders and others in the financial community.

☐ *Development:* Using public relations with donors or members of non-profit organizations to gain financial or volunteer support.

Public relations is used to promote products, people, places, ideas, activities, organizations, and even nations. Companies use PR to build good relations with consumers, investors, the media, and their communities. Public relations often works hand in hand with advertising to communicate a consistent message to the public, but whereas advertising uses paid media placement, public relations strives to get publicity through the news media—which cannot be paid for. For example, the state of New York turned its image around when its "I ♥ New York!" publicity and advertising campaign took root, bringing in millions more tourists. Trade associations have used PR to rebuild interest in declining commodities such as eggs, apples, potatoes, and milk. For example, the milk industry's popular "Got Milk?" public relations campaign, featuring celebrities with milk moustaches, reversed a long-standing decline in milk consumption.[38]

Public relations is an important part of any successful integrated marketing communications. For example, Gatorade and its advertising agency, TBWA\Chiat\Day (Los Angeles) generated millions of dollars in free publicity with their "Replay" publicity campaign. The event reunited two high school football teams to "replay" an important 1993 high school game that had resulted in a tie. Gatorade recruited the original players—now in their mid-30s—and coached them for eight weeks, while organizing and promoting the game which, when played before 15 000 fans, was covered by CNN and Fox, eventually reaching 90 million households. Gatorade's advertising agency spent US$225 000 on paid advertising media, but estimates the event generated more than US$3 billion in actual media time—most of it free. The campaign won the Grand Prix award at the Cannes Lions International Advertising Festival in the PR category, and also won awards in the promotions category and the direct-marketing category.[39]

THE ROLE AND IMPACT OF PUBLIC RELATIONS

Public relations can have a strong impact on public awareness at a much lower cost than advertising can. The company does not pay for the space or time in the media. Rather, it pays for a staff to develop and circulate information and to manage events. If the company develops an interesting story or event, it could be picked up by several different media, having the same effect as advertising that would cost millions of dollars. And it would have more credibility than advertising.

Public relations results can sometimes be spectacular. Consider the launch of Nintendo's Wii game console:[40]

By 2006, once-dominant Nintendo had dropped to third place in the video-game industry behind Sony and Microsoft. To get back on top, Nintendo's newest offering, the amazing Wii, needed to soar. The Wii's motion-sensitive controller makes it fun for almost anyone to play. This let Nintendo target the core gaming audience but also "dabblers," "lapsed gamers," and "nongamers," including girls, women, and seniors. But rather than investing millions in media advertising, Nintendo took advantage of Wii's natural appeal to create a results-producing

PR campaign. Prelaunch, Nintendo held preview events at which industry analysts and the media spent time with the Wii. The company targeted consumers on MySpace, where the "How Wii Play" profile made more than 60,000 friends. Nintendo also launched an ambassador program that got the game into the hands of gamers, moms, and large intergenerational families, who spread information about the system through blogs and word of mouth.

On launch day, Nintendo midnight events, held in New York and Los Angeles, were attended by thousands of consumers, with coverage by media ranging from AP to MTV and *Good Morning America*. In the end, the Wii PR campaign earned an incredible 10 billion audience impressions over just three months, including 14 *Today Show* appearances and a stint on *South Park*. Despite early surveys showing that only 11 percent of consumers intended to buy it, Wii sales sizzled. Stores experienced two years of non-stop stock-outs, and the Wii outsold the Xbox 360 by two to one and the newly introduced Playstation 3 by three to one. As a result, the Wii PR effort was named *PRWeek's* 2008 Consumer Launch Campaign of the Year.

Exhibit 12.15   Public relations results can sometimes be spectacular. Starting with preview events like this one, Nintendo's award-winning PR campaign for its new Wii game produced non-stop stock-outs for more than two years.

Despite its potential strengths, public relations is sometimes described as a marketing stepchild because of its often limited and scattered use. The PR department is often located at corporate headquarters or handled by a third-party agency. Its staff is so busy dealing with various publics—stockholders, employees, legislators, the press—that PR programs to support product marketing objectives may be ignored. Moreover, marketing managers and PR practitioners do not always speak the same language. Whereas many PR practitioners see their jobs as simply communicating, marketing managers tend to be much more interested in how advertising and PR affect brand building, sales and profits, and customer relationships.

This situation is changing, however. Although public relations still captures only a small portion of the overall marketing budgets of most firms, PR can be a powerful brand-building tool. And in this digital age, more and more, the lines between advertising and PR are blurring. For example, are brand websites, blogs, and viral brand videos advertising efforts or PR efforts? All are both. The point is advertising, and PR should work hand in hand within an integrated marketing communications program to build brands and customer relationships.[41]

MAJOR PUBLIC RELATIONS TOOLS

Public relations uses several tools. One of the major tools is *news*. Public relations professionals find or create favourable news about the company and its products or people. Sometimes news stories occur naturally, and sometimes the PR person can suggest events or activities that would create news. *Speeches* can also create product and company publicity. Increasingly, company executives must field questions from the media or give talks at trade associations or sales meetings, and these events can either build or hurt the company's image. Another common PR tool is *special events*, ranging from news conferences, press tours, grand openings, and fireworks displays to laser shows, hot air balloon releases, multi-media presentations, or educational programs designed to reach and interest target publics.

Exhibit 12.16   Public relations tools: Aveeno used buzz marketing and social networking to get consumers to spread the word about its new product line. This YouTube video was viewed more than 1.5 million times.

Public relations people also prepare *written materials* to reach and influence their target markets. These materials include annual reports, brochures, articles, and company newsletters and magazines. *Audiovisual materials,* such as slide-and-sound programs, DVDs, and online videos are being used increasingly as communication tools. *Corporate identity materials* can also help create a corporate identity that the public immediately recognizes. Logos, stationery, brochures, signs, business forms, business cards, buildings, uniforms, and company cars and trucks—all become marketing tools when they are attractive, distinctive, and memorable. Finally, companies can improve public goodwill by contributing money and time to *public service activities.*

Many marketers are now also designing *buzz marketing* campaigns to generate excitement and favourable word of mouth for their brands. Buzz marketing takes advantage of social media such as YouTube, Facebook, and Twitter by getting consumers themselves to spread information about a product or a service to others in their communities. For example, to build buzz for its new Aveeno Positively Ageless product line, Johnson & Johnson employed street artist Julian Beever—the "Pavement Picasso"—to create a 3-D "Fountain of Youth" chalk drawing on a sidewalk in the heart of New York City. Although the drawing captivated thousands of passersby, Aveeno turned "Fountain of Youth" into an online event via a four-minute, time-lapse video of the artist at work posted on YouTube. In addition, the brand distributed the video to more than 50 blogs, with 21 responding by promoting the YouTube posting. With a soft "Aveeno Presents" slate at the beginning of the video and a close-up of the Fountain of Youth artwork showing the Aveeno logo at the end, the spot was well branded but without appearing to be commercial. The video reverberated through video sites and the blogosphere via strong word of mouth and was viewed more than 1.5 million times.[42]

A company's website is another important public relations tool. Consumers and members of other publics often visit websites for information or entertainment. Such sites can be extremely popular. Consider My.BarackObama.com, President Barack Obama's community-based, interactive campaign website. Created by Obama's campaign committee as a new way to spread the word, by the time the campaign ended successfully, site users had created more than 2 million profiles, planned 200 000 offline events, formed 35 000 groups, posted 400 000 blogs, and raised $30 million on 70 000 personal fundraising pages.[43] Websites can also be ideal for handling crisis situations.

CRISIS COMMUNICATIONS

Perhaps the most important job of public relations professionals—though one they don't look forward to—is handling communications during times of crisis. Many companies have learned the importance of carefully conceived and well-executed corporate communications after an event that casts the company in a negative light, and companies that have never experienced a crisis nevertheless learn from observing how others in difficult situations manage their communications. The best example of how to handle crisis communications well is the Tylenol scare of the 1980s, when several bottles of the painkiller were tampered with while on the store shelves. Not only did Johnson & Johnson, the makers of Tylenol, immediately step up and take responsibility for the problem, but they worked to find a solution—today's tamper-proof bottles—and kept the public informed every step of the way. The best example of how not to respond to a crisis is the Exxon Valdez oil spill. The company also responded quickly, but denied all responsibility.

Public relations experts warn that it is important to be authentic in crisis communications. If managed correctly, the crisis can sometimes be turned into an opportunity. For example, in 2007 when several popular brands of pet food, all produced in China, were found to be contaminated, it presented an opportunity for smaller, local producers of organic pet food. And when several bottles of Odwalla apple juice sold in California were found to contain *E. coli* bacteria, Odwalla initiated a massive product recall. Within only three hours, it set up a website laden with information about the crisis and Odwalla's response. Company staffers also combed the Internet looking for newsgroups discussing Odwalla and posted links to the site. In all, in this age where "it's easier to disseminate information through e-mail marketing, blogs, and online chat," notes an analyst, "public relations is becoming a valuable part of doing business in a digital world."[44]

As with the other promotion tools, in considering when and how to use product public relations, management should set PR objectives, choose the PR messages and vehicles, implement the PR plan, and evaluate the results. The firm's PR should be blended smoothly with other promotion activities within the company's overall integrated marketing communications effort.

PROUD TO BE CANADIAN

Promotion, like all of the Ps, needs to remain consistent with the brand. Canada Goose is an exclusive brand; some might consider it a premium brand. For this reason, Canada Goose has not pursued a mass-media or traditional promotional strategy. So what overall promotional or integrated marketing communications strategy has Canada Goose chosen to pursue?

PRODUCT PLACEMENT

Canada Goose is worn by brand opinion leaders such as Laurie Skreslet, the first Canadian to summit Mount Everest, and Ray Zahab, extreme athlete. According to researchers, a key part of brand development is making a brand instantly accessible in memory, and that's what product placement does. A person can think of maybe one to three brands instantly. So, when people reach into their memories for a product, just as when they reach for a word, those that come to mind quickly (often stored as images, not words) are at the top of the mental agenda. The companies that own these brands have a distinct advantage over the companies whose brands emerge only after extensive dredging. Having a brand that is instantly recalled in consumers' memories is like being part of the top 10 hits on a Google search!

PUBLICITY

Canada Goose sponsors charities that focus on Arctic conservation, and it has built partnerships with successful Canadian organizations such as First Air airline (a northern Canadian airline), Maple Leaf Sports & Entertainment, Gap Adventures, Fairmont Hotels & Resorts, and The North West Company. It's not difficult to see familiar threads running through these organizations. There is an attempt to associate the Canada Goose brand with Canada, in particular with the authentic Canadian North, true (not weekend-warrior) athletes, extreme northern activities, and success (with a Canadian flavour).

Canada Goose focuses on tactical marketing. The brand took root in Europe partly because of its concerted effort to get its jackets on bouncers and doormen at popular clubs. The jackets were worn by people who stood in the cold all night in front of a captive and engaged audience.

COMMUNITY BUILDING THROUGH SOCIAL MEDIA

On Canada Day, Canada Goose runs a contest where entrants post "Why I'm proud to be a Canadian" stories on Canada Goose's Facebook wall. Again, Canada Goose aims to leverage its brand by connecting it with the Canada associated with the "true north." This reputation (perhaps helped by the recent Vancouver Winter Olympics) helps build the company's brand. You can read more about this contest on Canada Goose's Facebook page at www.facebook.com/CanadaGoose?v=info.

QUESTIONS

1. Why are more and more companies pursuing unconventional promotional strategies?
2. Can you think of any unconventional promotional strategies that might work well for Canada Goose?
3. When there is no "call to action" in a promotion, can you identify any difference between brand building and promotion?
4. Can you think of any well-known celebrities or events that would suit the Canada Goose brand?

REVIEWING THE CONCEPTS

1. Define the five promotion mix tools for communicating customer value.

A company's total *promotion mix*—also called its *marketing communications mix*—consists of the specific blend of *advertising, personal selling, sales promotion, public relations (PR)*, and *direct-marketing* tools that the company uses to persuasively communicate customer value and build customer relationships. Advertising includes any paid form of non-personal presentation and promotion of ideas, goods, or services by an identified sponsor. In contrast, public relations focuses on building good relations with the company's various publics. Personal selling is any form of personal presentation by the firm's sales force for the purpose of making sales and building customer relationships. Firms use sales promotion to provide short-term incentives to encourage the purchase or sale of a product or a service. Finally, firms seeking immediate response from targeted individual customers use direct-marketing tools to communicate with customers and cultivate relationships with them.

2. Discuss the changing communications landscape and the need for integrated marketing communication.

The explosive developments in communications technology and changes in marketer and customer communication strategies have had a dramatic impact on marketing communications. Advertisers are now adding a broad selection of more-specialized and highly targeted media—including digital media—to reach smaller customer segments with more-personalized, interactive messages. As they adopt richer but more fragmented media and promotion mixes to reach their diverse markets, they risk creating a communications hodgepodge for consumers. To prevent this, more companies are adopting the concept of *integrated marketing communications (IMC)*. Guided by an overall IMC strategy, the company works out the roles that the various promotional tools will play and the extent to which each will be used. It carefully coordinates the promotional activities and the timing of when major campaigns take place.

3. Describe how advertising objectives are set and how advertising strategy is developed.

Advertising—the use of paid media by a seller to inform, persuade, and remind about its products or organization—is a strong promotion tool that takes many forms and has many uses. *Advertising decision-making* involves decisions about the objectives, the budget, the message, and the media. Advertisers begin by setting a clear *objective* as to whether the advertising is supposed to inform, persuade, or remind buyers. The advertising *budget* can be based on what is affordable, on sales, on competitors' spending, or on the objectives and tasks. Developing the *advertising strategy* begins by determining what *message* the advertising must send to the target audience, and then developing a compelling *creative concept* to communicate the message. Message *execution* refers to the style, tone, words, and format of the ad. Finally, the *media decision* involves defining reach, frequency, and impact goals; choosing major media types; selecting media vehicles; and deciding on media timing. Message and media decisions must be closely coordinated for maximum campaign effectiveness.

4. Explain how advertising effectiveness is evaluated and the role of the advertising agency.

Evaluating advertising calls for evaluating the communication and sales effects of advertising before, during, and after the advertising is placed and measuring advertising return on investment. Companies must measure the effectiveness of their advertising, and specifically try to measure the *return on advertising investment*. Advertising must be measured in terms of its *communication effects*, as well as its sales and profit effects. Measuring return on advertising is difficult; however, most companies today recognize its importance and are constantly looking for new methods. Advertising *agencies* work with the company (i.e., the advertiser) to develop, produce, plan, and execute advertising campaigns. Most large companies use agencies, which employ specialists in design, production, and media planning.

5. Explain how companies use public relations to communicate with their publics.

Public relations (PR) involves building good relations with the company's various publics. Its functions include *press agentry, product publicity, public affairs, lobbying, investor relations*, and *development*. Public relations can have a strong impact on public awareness at a much lower cost than advertising can, and PR results can sometimes be spectacular. Despite its potential strengths, however, PR sometimes sees only limited and scattered use. Public relations tools include *news, speeches, special events, buzz marketing,* *written materials,* *audiovisual materials,* *corporate identity materials,* and *public service activities.* A company's website can be a good PR vehicle. In considering when and how to use product PR, management should set PR objectives, choose the PR messages and vehicles, implement the PR plan, and evaluate the results. PR should be blended smoothly with other promotion activities within the company's overall IMC effort.

KEY TERMS

Advertising   450
Advertising agency   474
Advertising budget   461
Advertising media   468
Advertising objective   459
Advertising strategy   463
Affordable method   461
Competitive-parity method   462

Creative concept   465
Direct marketing   450
Execution style   466
Integrated marketing communications (IMC)   452
Media vehicle   471
Objective-and-task method   462
Percentage-of-sales method   461

Personal selling   450
Promotion mix (or marketing communications mix)   450
Public relations (PR)   450
Pull strategy   458
Push strategy   457
Return on advertising investment   472
Sales promotion   450

TALK ABOUT MARKETING

1. The shift from mass marketing to targeted marketing and the corresponding use of a richer mix of marketing communications tools pose challenges for many marketers. If you were responsible for promoting your college or university, which of the five major forms of marketing communications would you use? How would you make sure they were integrated? Who are your publics and target audience, and how can you best reach them with your communications?

2. Imagine that you are the marketing communications manager for a small local brewery (pick one that you know about). Make a list of your top five competitors. Which method of setting the advertising budget do you think each of your competitors uses? Which method will you use?

3. Refer to the section in the chapter that discusses creative execution and some of the most common forms of advertising messages (slice of life, testimonial, and so on). Provide an example of each type of advertising message that you've seen recently.

4. Go to the website of your favourite magazine, and look for the advertising sales kit or media kit. Download it or open it, and examine it. What is the price of a full-page, four-colour ad, if it is run only once? What is the price if it is run six times?

5. In a small group, discuss the major public relations tools and develop three public relations items for each of the following: (a) a charity, (b) a bank, (c) a brand of beer, (d) a health club.

6. Press releases are one of the tools of the public relations manager. Go to the website of Canada Newswire, and read some of today's press releases. If you were a business journalist, which of the press releases would you choose to write a story about? Explain why you picked that one over all the others.

THINK LIKE A MARKETING MANAGER

In Germany, it's "*Ich liebe es*"; in France, "*C'est tout ce que j'aime.*" In China, it translates into "I like it," because one doesn't say "love" lightly in that culture. The McDonald's "I'm lovin' it" campaign was launched simultaneously in more than 100 countries. It was unprecedented in McDonald's history because it was the first time an international campaign was consistent in flavour and brand message in every country McDonald's serves. "It's much more than just a new tagline or commercials—it's a new way of thinking about and expressing our worldwide brand appeal to the consumer," said Larry Light, McDonald's executive vice-president and global chief marketing officer, and the man behind the campaign. The McDonald's website at McDonalds.com features an international welcome page with a drop-down selection for each country's site. Here the online marketing is localized, the campaign adapted, the words translated, but even while capturing the spirit, music, and flavour of each country the brand message remains consistent.

QUESTIONS

1. List all the publics and audiences that McDonald's' main corporate website communicates with.
2. Go to the McDonald's site, choose a country, and explore that country's site. How is the "I'm lovin' it" message translated and adapted? What are the signs that local culture, language, and customs have been incorporated into the campaign?
3. Find out what the most recent new menu item available at your local McDonald's is. Is it being promoted through advertising? What other forms of marketing communications are being used to promote it, and how are they integrated?
4. In response to public pressure and claims that fast food makes children obese, McDonald's geared up a major public relations campaign on the theme "It's what I eat and what I do ... I'm lovin' it." Describe how this new public relations initiative could be integrated with each of the other four major elements of marketing communications for McDonald's.

MARKETING ETHICS

Legally, companies are not allowed to make untrue claims in their advertising, however, most advertising tries to push the limits of what is "true" through implication and other subtle methods of persuasion. Ethically speaking, the line between truthful advertising claims and outright lies is not an easy one to define clearly. For example, Kentucky Fried Chicken has been trying for years to reposition its brand as "healthy," yet its efforts are repeatedly being met with criticism from the advertising community and cynicism from consumers. Most recently it was accused of jumping on the wagon to align its brand with the movement to find a cure for breast cancer. It built a website called "Buckets For The Cure," designed pink buckets, and donated a portion of every bucket purchased to the cause. Advertising expert Bob Garfield scorned, "That sort of dishonesty is just so pathetic."

QUESTIONS

1. Most people would agree that fast food is not healthy, no matter what the advertising claims. Choose another fast-food restaurant and examine its advertising. Is it making any claims about offering healthy food? Do you find the claims believable?
2. KFC is prohibited by law from claiming in its advertising that its fried chicken is healthy (because it's not), which leaves the company only two choices: change its menu completely, so that it can honestly claim in its advertising that its food is healthy, or keep its fried chicken and change its advertising objectives. Which would you recommend?

MARKETING TECHNOLOGY

Marketers today are constantly experimenting with new technologies, most of them online, to help them promote their products—but the technologies come and go so quickly, what's a marketer to do? MySpace was the first social networking site and was once highly desired by advertisers, but within a few short years it was overshadowed by Facebook to the point where MySpace is now struggling to survive. When virtual world Second Life launched in 2003, it quickly grew to more than 9 million inhabitants, who created online digital alter egos called *avatars*, to speak to each other. Marketers such as IBM, Sony, Adidas, Pontiac, Kraft, Coca-Cola, and even Canada Post, set up virtual presences in Second Life—much like product placement in other forms of media. Yet by 2010 Second Life was declared lifeless. Today, Twitter is in the experimental stages, marketing-wise. It's extremely popular with celebrities such as Ashton Kutcher and his millions of followers—consumers—but advertisers have yet to figure out how to make money by using it.

QUESTIONS

1. If you haven't already done so, sign up on Twitter and search for your favourite brand or company. Are they represented? Follow them on Twitter and observe how they are using this social media tool for promotion.

2. How much does it cost to advertise on Facebook, and what different forms of advertising does it offer? If you were the marketing communications manager for Axe or Mac, would you recommend they purchase advertising on Facebook? Why or why not?

MARKETING BY THE NUMBERS

AARP The Magazine and *Reader's Digest* are the top 2 magazines with regard to circulation. They also attract similar audiences. Although consumers aged 50+ are plugged in online like younger consumers, they still like print media, making these two magazines valuable for reaching seniors with advertising. Advertisers use cost per thousand (CPM) to compare the efficiency of different media vehicles. CPM is calculated by taking the cost of the ad times 1000 and dividing by the number of potential readers or viewers. For example, for a magazine, the CPM would be calculated as follows: CPM = (ad cost × 1000)/circulation.

QUESTIONS

1. Using advertising rate information for *AARP The Magazine* and *Reader's Digest* (look up the information on each magazine's website), determine the cost per thousand of a full-page, four-colour advertisement in each. Which magazine is more cost effective for advertisers?

2. Suppose a manufacturer of a diabetes testing monitor wants to advertise in *AARP The Magazine*. Refer to Appendix 3, Marketing by the Numbers, to determine by how much the manufacturer's sales must increase to break even on the purchase of 10 full-page, four-colour advertisements in *AARP The Magazine*. Assume that the company has a 40 percent contribution margin. Should the advertiser purchase this advertising space?

END-OF-CHAPTER CASE

LOVING YOUR BATHROOM: AN INTEGRATED MARKETING COMMUNICATIONS CAMPAIGN

You probably haven't thought much about your bathroom—it's not something that most of us get very inspired about. But you probably have a relationship with your bathroom unlike that with any other room in your house. It's where you start and end your day, primp and preen and admire yourself, escape from the rigours of everyday life, and do some of your best thinking. The marketers at American Standard, the plumbing fixtures giant, understand this often-overlooked but special little room. And that understanding led to the creation of a successful integrated marketing communications strategy.

Working with its ad agency, Carmichael Lynch, American Standard created a wonderfully warm and highly effective marketing campaign called "We want you to love your bathroom." The communications targeted men and women aged 25 to 54 from households planning to remodel bathrooms or replace fixtures. The campaign employed a carefully integrated mix of brand-image and direct-response media ads, direct mailings, and personal contacts to create a customer database, generate sales leads, gently coax customers into its retail showrooms, and build sales and market share.

The campaign began with a series of humorous, soft-sell brand-image ads in magazines such as *Home*, *House Beautiful*, and *Country Living*, which are typically read by homeowners who are considering undertaking remodelling projects. Featuring simple but artistic shots of ordinary bathroom fixtures and scenes, the ads positioned American Standard as a company that understands the special relationships we have with our bathrooms. For example, one ad showed a white toilet and a partially unwound roll of toilet paper, artfully arranged in a corner against plain blue-grey walls. "We're not in this business for the glory," proclaimed the headline. "Designing a toilet or sink may not be as glamorous as, say, designing a Maserati. But to us, it's every bit as important. After all, more people will be sitting on our seats than theirs."

Another ad showed the feet of a man standing on a white tile bathroom floor wearing his goofy-looking floppy-eared dog slippers. "The rest of the world thinks you're a genius," noted the ad. But "after a long day of being brilliant, witty, and charming, it's nice just to be comfortable. The right bathroom understands. And accepts you unconditionally." Each simple but engaging ad included a toll-free phone number and urged readers to call for a free guidebook "overflowing with products, ideas, and inspiration."

The communications goal of these brand-image ads was to position American Standard and its products, but when it came to generating responses, the company turned to coupon-like direct response ads that ran in the same magazines. One such ad noted, "You will spend seven years of your life in the bathroom. You will need a good book." Readers could obtain the free guidebook by mailing in the coupon or calling the toll-free number listed in the ad—and, of course, American Standard could measure the response.

Consumers who responded found that they'd taken the first step in a carefully orchestrated relationship-building venture. First, they received the entertaining, highly informative, picture-filled 30-page guidebook *We Want You to Love Your Bathroom*, along with a folksy letter thanking them for their interest and noting the locations of nearby American Standard dealers. The guidebook's purpose was straightforward:

"Walk into your bathroom, turn the knob and suddenly, for a moment or an hour, the world stops turning. You should love the place. If you don't, well, American Standard wants to further your relationship. Thumb through this book. In the bathroom, perhaps...." The guidebook was full of helpful tips on bathroom design, starting with answers to some simple questions: What kind of lavatory—what colour? The bathtub—how big? Big enough for two? The toilet—sleek one-piece or familiar two-piece? The faucet? "You'll fumble for it every morning, so be particular about how it operates." To spice things up, the guidebook also contained loads of entertaining facts and trivia. An example: Did you know that "you will spend seven years in your bathroom ... here's hoping your spouse doesn't sneak in first!" Another example: "During the Middle Ages, Christianity preached that to uncover your skin, even to bathe it, was an invitation to sin. Thank heavens for perfume. These days, we average about 4 baths or 7.5 showers a week." And, of course, the booklet contained plenty of information on American Standard products, along with a tear-out card that prospective customers could return to obtain more detailed guides and product catalogues.

Other marketing communications sent to the consumer, by request, from American Standard included a series of "Bathroom Reading" bulletins, each containing information on specific bathroom design issues. For example, one issue contained information and tips on how to make a bathroom safer; another offered "10 neat ways to save water."

The "call to action" in all these integrated marketing communications elements was either to telephone a toll-free number to request more information or to return a coupon or fill in a form to request more information. Every time a prospective customer requested more information from American Standard, that person's contact details went into American Standard's customer database. This data was then sorted and organized into "leads"—lists of interested customers—which were given to American Standard's sales representatives, their distributors, and kitchen and bath dealers, to follow up on.

The key was to get customers who'd made inquiries to come into the showroom. Not long after making their inquiries, prospective customers would receive either a postcard in the mail or a phone call from a local dealer's showroom consultant, who extended a personal invitation to visit, see American Standard products first-hand, and discuss bathroom designs. Thus, the integrated marketing communications program built relationships not just with buyers but with dealers as well.

American Standard's "We want you to love your bathroom" campaign also did wonders for the company's positioning and performance. After the campaign began, American Standard's plumbing division experienced steady increases in sales and earnings. The campaign generated tens of thousands of qualified leads for local showrooms. Market research conducted by the company after the campaign showed that consumer perceptions of American Standard and its products shifted from "boring and institutional" to well designed and loaded with "personal spirit." According to Bob Srenaski, group vice-president of marketing at American Standard, the campaign "totally repositioned our company and established a momentum and winning spirit that is extraordinary." Says Joe Summary, an account manager at Carmichael Lynch, "the campaign was incredible. It gave American Standard and its products a more personal face, one that's helped us to build closer relationships with customers and dealers. From the first ad to the last contact with our dealers, the campaign was designed to help customers create bathrooms they'd love."

QUESTIONS

1. Which method of setting the marketing communications budget do you think American Standard uscd? Explain why you think so.

2. American Standard products are available in Canada. If you were a media planner, which Canadian media vehicles would you choose for the print advertising? Justify your choices in terms of the target market.

3. Which forms of direct response marketing were used in this campaign? What was the desired response, and how would American Standard measure it? What pieces of data would American Standard have in its database as a result of this campaign?

4. If the "We want you to love your bathroom" campaign were to be re-created today, what forms of new media would you recommend for the marketing communications?

Visit the MyMarketingLab website at **www.pearsoned.ca/mymarketinglab**. This online homework and tutorial system puts you in control of your own learning with study and practice tools directly correlated to this chapter's content.

AFTER STUDYING THIS CHAPTER, YOU SHOULD BE ABLE TO

 discuss the role of a company's salespeople in creating value for customers and building customer relationships

 identify and explain the six major sales force management steps and the role of sales force automation

 discuss the personal selling process, distinguishing between transaction-oriented marketing and relationship marketing

 define sales promotion and list the major consumer sales promotion tools

 distinguish between consumer and trade promotions

Personal Selling and Sales Promotion

PREVIEWING THE CONCEPTS

In the previous chapter, you learned about communicating customer value through integrated marketing communications (IMC) and about two elements of the promotion mix—advertising and public relations. In this chapter, we'll look at two more IMC elements—personal selling and sales promotion. Personal selling is the interpersonal arm of marketing communications, in which the sales force interacts with customers and prospects to build relationships and make sales. Sales promotion consists of short-term incentives to encourage purchase or sale of a product or a service. As you read on, remember that although this chapter examines personal selling and sales promotion as separate tools, they must be carefully integrated with other elements of the promotion mix.

When you think of salespeople, perhaps you think of pushy retail sales clerks, "yell and sell" TV pitchmen, or the stereotypical "used-car salesman." But such stereotypes simply don't fit the reality of most of today's salespeople—well-trained, well-educated, dedicated sales professionals who succeed not by taking advantage of customers but by listening to their needs and forging solutions to their problems. For most companies, personal selling plays an important role in building profitable customer relationships. Consider CDW Corporation, whose customer-focused sales strategy has helped it grow rapidly while competitors have faltered.

CDW CORPORATION: CUSTOMER-FOCUSED SELLING

CDW Corporation, a leading provider of multibrand technology products and services, is thriving. In the 25 years since founder Michael Krasny started the business at his kitchen table, CDW has grown to an $8 billion high-tech heavyweight in its highly volatile and competitive industry. The company owes its success to good old-fashioned high-touch personal selling that builds lasting one-to-one customer relationships. The strategy is fuelled by a genuine passion for solving customer problems. Under CDW's "Circle of Service" philosophy, "everything revolves around the customer."

CDW sells a complex assortment of more than 100 000 technology products and advanced technology services—computers, software, accessories, and networking products. Many of CDW's competitors chase after a relative handful of very large customers. However, although CDW serves customers of all sizes, one of the company's core customer segments is small and mid-size businesses (SMBs). These smaller customers often need lots of advice and support. "Many of our clients don't have IT departments," says one CDW executive, "so they look to us for expertise."

That's where CDW's sales force comes in. The major responsibility for building and managing customer relationships falls to CDW's sales force of more than 2500 account managers. Each customer is assigned an account manager, who helps the customer select the right products and technologies to keep his or her company running smoothly. "The server room can be a cold and lonely place," notes one CDW advertisement. "We can definitely help with the lonely part. At CDW, we provide you with a personal account manager who knows your business and the IT challenges you face."

Account managers orchestrate the efforts of a team of CDW specialists who help customers to select the best mix of products, services, and support. But they do more than just sell technology products and services. They work closely with customers to find solutions to their technology problems. "This is a big deal to us," says a senior CDW sales executive. "We want to go beyond fulfilling the order and become the trusted adviser for them. We [want to] talk ... about what a customer is trying to accomplish and really add value to the sale, as opposed to just sending out a box."

To become trusted advisers and effective customer relationship builders, CDW account managers really have to know their stuff. And CDW boasts some of the most knowledgeable salespeople in the industry. Before they make a single sales call, new account managers complete a six-week orientation and then a six-month training program on the company's products and in the art of consultative selling. But that's just the beginning—the training never ends. Each year, CDW's sales force completes a whopping 339 000 hours of sales-specific training. John Edwardson, chairman and CEO of CDW and former head of United Airlines, likes to point out that CDW reps get more training than some pilots.

Customers who want to access CDW's products and expertise without going through their account manager can do so easily at any of several CDW websites. Better yet, CDW will create a free personalized CDW@work extranet site that reflects a given customer's pricing, order status, account history, and special considerations. The extranet site serves as a 24-hour extension of the customer's account manager. But even here, the ever-present account managers are likely to add personal guidance. Account managers receive immediate notification of their customers' online activities. So if a blurry-eyed SMB manager makes a mistake on an emergency order placed in the middle of the night, chances are good that the account manager will find and correct the error first thing in the morning.

At this point, you're probably envisioning CDW's army of account managers suiting up and visiting customers face to face in the field. How else could they develop such close consultative relationships? But what's perhaps most amazing about CDW's salespeople is they do all this by telephone. That's right, they're "telemarketers." Despite the lack of face time, however, CDW account managers forge very close ties with customers. Take CDW account manager Ron Kelly, for example. If you're one of his regular customers, you probably know that he's 35 and has a wife named Michelle, a 9-year-old son named Andrew, and a German shepherd named Bones. You know that he majored in journalism and political science at Southern Illinois University, and that he bleeds red and black for the Chicago Blackhawks. You also know that he knows as much, if not more, about you. Kelly, an affable account manager, is a master at relationship-based selling, CDW's specialty. Customers love it. "He's my sales rep, but he's also my friend," says Todd Greenwald, director of operations for Heartland Computers, which sells barcode scanners. "Most of the time we don't even talk about price. I trust Ron."

What's particularly impressive is that, for the most part, the customer interaction occurs over the phone and the Internet. Still, it's far from the arm's-length, impersonal relationships that the term *telemarketing* often conjures up. For example, one customer invited his CDW contact to his wedding. Kelly and Greenwald share Blackhawks season tickets. It's not uncommon to find customers and reps whose partnership has outlasted job changes, budget cuts, and marriages. Of course, the relationships aren't based solely on being likable. They're grounded in helping customers succeed. Account managers think like the customer and try to anticipate problems. For instance, before storms rocked Florida one summer, some account managers called or emailed clients there with battery and backup-storage solutions. "Instead of just sending a purchase order, we want to ask, 'Why are you buying [that product]?' says a CDW executive. "That's how you identify customers' needs." In this way, to their customers, CDW account managers are much more than just telemarketing peddlers. When asked whether she thinks of her CDW rep as a salesperson anymore, one customer replied, "Never. He's my business partner."

CDW's sales force instills loyalty in what are traditionally very price-conscious SMB customers. The company wants to create customer satisfaction at every touchpoint. Says a former CDW marketing executive, "We're competitively priced, but what's most important is the service and the customers' relationships with their account managers. It's how we actually touch people that creates our most long-lasting [success]."[1]

IN THIS chapter, we examine two more promotion mix tools—*personal selling* and *sales promotion*. Personal selling consists of interpersonal interactions with customers and prospects to make sales and maintain customer relationships. Sales promotion involves using short-term incentives to encourage customer purchasing, reseller support, and sales force efforts.

PERSONAL SELLING 🔵

Robert Louis Stevenson once noted, "Everyone lives by selling something." Companies all around the world use sales forces to sell products and services to business customers and consumers, but sales forces are also found in many other kinds of organizations. For example, colleges and universities use recruiters to attract new students, and museums use fundraisers to contact donors and raise money. In the first part of this chapter, we examine personal selling's role in the organization, sales force management decisions, and the personal selling process.

THE NATURE OF PERSONAL SELLING

Personal selling is one of the oldest professions in the world. The people who do the selling go by many names: salespeople, sales representatives, district managers, account executives, sales consultants, sales engineers, agents, and account development reps to name just a few.

People hold many stereotypes of salespeople—including some unfavourable ones. "Salesman" may bring to mind the image of Arthur Miller's pitiable Willy Loman in *Death of a Salesman* or Dwight Schrute, the opinionated Dunder Mifflin paper salesman from the TV show *The Office*, who lacks both common sense and social skills. And then there are the real-life "yell-and-sell" "pitchmen," who hawk everything from OxiClean, Kaboom, and ShamWow to the Awesome Auger and Samurai Shark sharpener in TV infomercials. However, the majority of salespeople are a far cry from these unfortunate stereotypes.

Personal selling
Personal presentation by the firm's sales force for the purpose of making sales and building customer relationships.

Exhibit 13.1 Professional selling: It takes more than fast talk and a warm smile to sell high-tech aircraft, where a single big sale can easily run into billions of dollars. Success depends on building solid, long-term relationships with customers.

Salesperson
An individual representing a company to customers by performing one or more of the following activities: prospecting, communicating, selling, servicing, information gathering, and relationship building.

Most salespeople are well-educated, well-trained professionals who add value for customers and maintain long-term customer relationships. They listen to their customers, assess customer needs, and organize the company's efforts to solve customer problems.[2]

Some assumptions about what makes someone a good salesperson are dead wrong. There's this idea that the classic sales personality is overbearing, pushy, and outgoing, the kind of people who walk in and suck all the air out of the room. But the best salespeople are good at one-on-one contact. They create loyalty and customers because people trust them and want to work with them. It's a matter of putting the client's interests first—which is the antithesis of how most people view salespeople. The most successful salespeople are successful for one simple reason: They know how to build relationships. You can go in with a big personality and convince people to do what you want them to do, but that isn't really selling. It's manipulation, and it works only in the short term. A good salesperson can read customer emotions without exploiting them, because the bottom line is that he or she wants what's best for the customer.

Consider Boeing, the aerospace giant competing in the rough-and-tumble worldwide commercial aircraft market. It takes more than fast talk and a warm smile to sell expensive high-tech aircraft. A single big sale can easily run into billions of dollars. Boeing salespeople head up an extensive team of company specialists—sales and service technicians, financial analysts, planners, engineers—all dedicated to finding ways to satisfy airline customer needs. The selling process is nerve-rackingly slow—it can take two or three years from the first sales presentation to the day the sale is announced. After getting the order, salespeople then must stay in almost constant touch to make certain the customer stays satisfied. Success depends on building solid, long-term relationships with customers, based on performance and trust.

The term **salesperson** covers a wide range of positions. At one extreme, a salesperson might be largely an *order taker*, such as the department store salesperson standing behind the counter. At the other extreme are *order getters*, whose positions demand *creative selling* and *relationship building* for products and services ranging from appliances, industrial equipment, and airplanes to insurance and information technology services. Here, we focus on the more creative types of selling and on the process of building and managing an effective sales force.

THE ROLE OF THE SALES FORCE

Personal selling is the interpersonal arm of the promotion mix. Advertising consists largely of non-personal communication with mass audiences. In contrast, personal selling involves interpersonal interactions between salespeople and individual customers—whether face to face, by telephone, via email, through video or Web conferences, or by other means. Personal selling can be more effective than advertising in more complex selling situations. Salespeople can probe customers to learn more about their problems and then adjust the marketing offer and presentation to fit the special needs of each customer.

The role of personal selling varies from company to company. Some firms have no salespeople at all—for example, companies that sell only online or through catalogues, or companies that sell through manufacturer's reps, sales agents, or brokers. In most firms, however, the sales force plays a major role. In companies that sell business products and services, such as IBM, DuPont, or Boeing, the company's salespeople work directly with customers. In consumer-products companies such as P&G and Nike, the sales force plays an important behind-the-scenes role. It works with wholesalers and retailers to gain their support and help them be more effective in selling the company's products.

Exhibit 13.2   Linking the company with its customers: Building a relationship with the customer is the goal of every salesperson. To many customers, the salesperson *is* the company.

Linking the Company with Its Customers   The sales force serves as a critical link between a company and its customers. In many cases, salespeople serve both masters—the seller and the buyer. First, they *represent the company to customers*. They find and develop new customers and communicate information about the company's products and services. They sell products by approaching customers, presenting their offerings, answering objections, negotiating prices and terms, and closing sales. In addition, salespeople provide customer service and carry out market research and intelligence work.

At the same time, salespeople *represent customers to the company*, acting inside the firm as "champions" of customers' interests and managing the buyer–seller relationship. Salespeople relay customer concerns about company products and actions back inside to those who can handle them. They learn about customer needs and work with other marketing and non-marketing people in the company to develop greater customer value.

In fact, to many customers, the salesperson *is* the company—the only tangible manifestation of the company that they see. Hence, customers may become loyal to salespeople as well as to the companies and products they represent. This concept of "salesperson-owned loyalty" lends even more importance to the salesperson's customer relationship building abilities. Strong relationships with the salesperson will result in strong relationships with the company and its products. Conversely, poor salesperson relationships will probably result in poor company and product relationships.[3]

Given its role in linking the company with its customers, the sales force must be strongly customer-solutions focused. In fact, such a customer-solutions focus is a must not just for the sales force, but also for the entire organization. Just ask someone who knows, like Anne Mulcahy, who started her career in sales and then rose to the top at Xerox and saved the company from bankruptcy (see Marketing@Work 13.1).

Coordinating Marketing and Sales   Ideally, the sales force and the firm's other marketing functions should work together closely to jointly create value for both customers and the company. Unfortunately, however, some companies still treat marketing and sales as separate functions. When this happens, the separated marketing and sales functions often don't get along well. When things go wrong, the marketers (marketing planners, brand managers, and researchers) blame the sales force for its poor execution of an otherwise splendid strategy. In turn, the sales team blames the marketers for being out of touch with what's really going on with customers. The marketers sometimes feel that salespeople have their "feet stuck in the mud" whereas salespeople feel that the marketers have their "heads stuck in the clouds." Neither group fully values the other's contributions. If not

MARKETING@WORK 13.1

The Role of the Sales Force—and the Entire Company: Putting Customers First

When someone says "salesperson," what image comes to mind? Perhaps you think about a stereotypical glad-hander who's out to lighten customers' wallets by selling them something they don't really need. Think again. Today, for most companies, personal selling plays an important role in building profitable customer relationships. In turn, those relationships contribute greatly to overall company success.

Just ask Anne Mulcahy, the recently retired CEO and current chairman of the board at Xerox. She's the person who took the reins of the then-nearly-bankrupt copier company in early 2001 and transformed it into a successful modern-day digital technology and services enterprise. Mulcahy has received much praise from analysts, investors, and others as a transformative leader at Xerox. In 2007, *Fortune* magazine named her the second-most-powerful woman in business, and *Forbes* ranked her as the 13th-most-powerful woman in the world. In 2008, she became the first female CEO selected by her peers as *Chief Executive* magazine's Chief Executive of the Year.

But the roots of Mulcahy's success go back to the lessons she learned and the skills she honed in sales. The one-time undergraduate English and journalism major began her career in 1976 as a Xerox sales rep in Boston. From there, she worked her way up the sales ladder to become Xerox's vice-president of global sales in the late 1990s. Then, 25 years after first knocking on customer doors in New England, she was appointed CEO of Xerox.

As CEO, Mulcahy brought with her a sales and marketing mentality that now permeates the entire Xerox organization. The company's transformation started with a new focus on solving customer problems. Mulcahy believes that understanding customers is just as important as understanding technology. "Having spent so much time in sales,... I knew you have to keep customers in the forefront." But looking back, Mulcahy

Exhibit 13.3   Putting the customer first: Transformative former Xerox CEO and current chairman Anne Mulcahy, who started her career in sales, emphasizes the importance of staying focused on the customer.

recalls, Xerox had lost touch with its markets. To turn things around at Xerox, the company needed to focus on customers. "In a crisis, that is what really matters."

"Sales helps you understand what drives the business and that customers are a critical part of the business," Mulcahy says. "This will be important in any business function, but you learn it [best] in sales management where it is critical, the jewel in the crown." Implementing this customer-first sales philosophy, one of Mulcahy's first actions as CEO was to put on her old sales hat and hit the road to visit customers. She has stayed in direct touch with customers ever since—she still spends a part of every day responding to customer emails.

Mulcahy knows that putting customers first isn't just a sales force responsibility—it's an emphasis for everyone in the company. To stress that point at all levels, she quickly set up a rotating Customer Officer of the Day program at Xerox, which requires a top executive to answer customer calls that get through to corporate headquarters. As Customer Officer of the Day, the executive has three

responsibilities: listen to the customer, resolve the problem, and take responsibility for fixing the underlying cause. That sounds a lot like sales.

So if you're still thinking of salespeople as fast-talking, ever-smiling peddlers who foist their wares off on reluctant customers, you're probably working with an out-of-date stereotype. Good salespeople succeed not by taking customers in, but by helping them out—by assessing customer needs and solving customer problems. At Xerox, salespeople are well-trained professionals who listen to customers and win their business by doing what's right for them. In fact, that isn't just good sales thinking—it applies to the entire organization. According to Mulcahy, that "has to be the center of your universe, the heartland of how you run your company."

Sources: Henry Canaday, "Sales Rep to CEO: Anne Mulcahy and the Xerox Revolution," *Selling Power,* November/December 2008, pp. 53–57; "2008 Chief Executive of the Year," *Chief Executive,* September/October 2008, p. 68; Andrea Deckert, "Mulcahy Describes the Keys to Xerox Turnaround," November 2, 2007, p. 3; "Women CEOs, Xerox," *Financial Times,* December 31, 2008, p. 10; and "Anne Mulcahy to Retire as Xerox CEO," *Wireless News,* May 27, 2009.

repaired, such disconnects between marketing and sales can damage customer relationships and company performance.

A company can take several actions to help bring its marketing and sales functions closer together. At the most basic level, it can *increase communications* between the two groups by arranging joint meetings and spelling out when and with whom each group should communicate. The company can create *joint assignments*[4]—opportunities for marketers and salespeople to work together. This will make them more familiar with each other's ways of thinking and acting. It's useful for marketers, particularly brand managers and researchers, to occasionally go along on sales calls. They should also sit in on important account-planning sessions. Salespeople, in turn, should help develop marketing plans. They should sit in on product-planning reviews and share their deep knowledge about customers' purchasing habits. They should preview ad and sales-promotion campaigns. Jointly, marketers and salespeople should generate a playbook for expanding business with the top 10 accounts in each market segment. They should also plan events and conferences together.

A company can also create *joint objectives and reward systems* for sales and marketing or appoint *marketing-sales liaisons*—people from marketing who "live with the sales force" and help coordinate marketing and sales force programs and efforts. Finally, the firm can appoint a *chief revenue officer* (or *chief customer officer*)—a high-level marketing executive who oversees both marketing and sales. Such a person can help infuse marketing and sales with the common goal of creating value for customers in order to capture value in return.

MANAGING THE SALES FORCE (LO2)

We define **sales force management** as the analysis, planning, implementation, and control of sales force activities. It includes designing sales force strategy and structure and recruiting, selecting, training, compensating, supervising, and evaluating the firm's salespeople. These major sales force management decisions are shown in Figure 13.1 and are discussed in the following sections.

> **Sales force management**
> The analysis, planning, implementation, and control of sales force activities. It includes designing sales force strategy and structure and recruiting, selecting, training, compensating, supervising, and evaluating the firm's salespeople.

DESIGNING SALES FORCE STRATEGY AND STRUCTURE

Marketing managers face several sales force strategy and design questions. How should salespeople and their tasks be structured? How big should the sales force be? Should salespeople sell alone or work in teams with other people in the company? Should they sell in the field or by telephone or on the Web? We address these issues next.

Sales Force Structure   A company can divide sales responsibilities along any of several lines. The structure decision is simple if the company sells only one product line to one industry with customers in many locations. In that case the company would use a *territorial sales force structure*. However, if the company sells many products to many types of customers, it might need either a *product sales force structure* or a *customer sales force structure*, or a combination of the two.

FIGURE 13.1   Major steps in sales force management

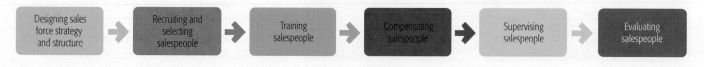

Territorial sales force structure
A sales force organization that assigns each salesperson to an exclusive geographic territory in which that salesperson sells the company's full line.

TERRITORIAL SALES FORCE STRUCTURE   In the **territorial sales force structure**, each salesperson is assigned to an exclusive geographic area and sells the company's full line of products or services to all customers in that territory. This organization clearly defines each salesperson's job and fixes accountability. It also increases the salesperson's desire to build local customer relationships that, in turn, improve selling effectiveness. Finally, because each salesperson travels within a limited geographic area, travel expenses are relatively low.

A territorial sales organization is often supported by many levels of sales management positions. For example, Black & Decker uses a territorial structure in which each salesperson is responsible for selling all of the company's products—from hand tools to lawn and garden equipment—in assigned territories. Starting at the bottom of the organization are entry-level *territory sales representatives* who report to *territory managers*. Territory sales representatives cover smaller areas, such as one city or part of a larger city, and the territory managers cover larger areas such as the province. Territory managers, in turn, report to *regional managers*, who cover regions of the country. The regional managers, in turn, report to a *director of sales*.

Product sales force structure
A sales force organization under which salespeople specialize in selling only a portion of the company's products or lines.

Customer (or market) sales force structure
A sales force organization under which salespeople specialize in selling only to certain customers or industries.

PRODUCT SALES FORCE STRUCTURE   Salespeople must know their products—especially when the products are numerous and complex. This need, together with the growth of product management, has led many companies to adopt a **product sales force structure**, in which the sales force sells along product lines. For example, GE employs different sales forces within different product and service divisions of its major businesses. Within GE Infrastructure, for instance, the company has separate sales forces for aviation, energy, transportation, and water processing products and technologies. Within GE Healthcare, it employs different sales forces for diagnostic imaging, life sciences, and integrated IT solutions products and services. In all, a company as large and complex as GE might have dozens of separate sales forces serving its diverse product and service portfolio.

The product structure can lead to problems, however, if a single large customer buys many different company products. For example, several different GE salespeople might end up calling on the same large healthcare customer in a given period. This means that they travel over the same routes and wait to see the same customer's purchasing agents. These extra costs must be compared with the benefits of better product knowledge and attention to individual products.

Exhibit 13.4   Customer sales force structure: Leading medical-equipment supplier Hill-Rom changed to a customer-based sales force structure, which helped it to focus more intensely on the needs of large key customers. In the two years following the sales force redesign, sales growth doubled.

CUSTOMER SALES FORCE STRUCTURE   More and more companies are now using a **customer (or market) sales force structure**, in which they organize the sales force along customer or industry lines. Separate sales forces may be set up for different industries, for serving current customers versus finding new ones, and for major accounts versus regular accounts. Many companies even have special sales forces set up to handle the needs of individual large customers. For example, above its territory structure, Black & Decker has a Home Depot sales organization and a Canadian Tire sales organization.

Organizing the sales force around customers can help a company to build closer relationships with important customers. Consider Hill-Rom, a leading supplier of medical equipment, such as hospital beds, stretchers, and nurse communication systems, which recently restructured its product-based sales force into a customer-based one:[5]

Hill-Rom has divided its sales force into two customer-based teams. One sales force focuses on "key" customers—large accounts that purchase high-end equipment and demand high levels of sales force collaboration. The second sales force focuses on "prime" customers—smaller accounts that are generally more concerned about getting the features and functions they need for the best possible price. Assigning the separate sales forces helps Hill-Rom to better understand what the different types of customers need. It also lets the company track how much attention the sales force devotes to each customer group.

For example, prior to restructuring the sales force, Hill-Rom had been treating both key and prime customers the same way. As a result, it was trying to sell smaller prime customers a level of service and innovation that they did not value or could not afford. So the cost of sales for prime customers was four to five times higher than for key customers. Now, a single account manager and team focuses intensely on all the areas of each key customer's business, working together to find product and service solutions. Such intensive collaboration would have been difficult under the old product-based sales structure, in which multiple Hill-Rom sales reps serviced the different specialty areas within a single key account. In the two years following the sales force redesign, Hill-Rom's sales growth doubled.

COMPLEX SALES FORCE STRUCTURES   When a company sells a wide variety of products to many types of customers over a broad geographic area, it often combines several types of sales force structures. Salespeople can be specialized by customer and territory, by product and territory, by product and customer, or by territory, product, and customer. For example, Black & Decker specializes its sales force by customer (with different sales forces calling on Home Depot, Canadian Tire, and smaller independent retailers) *and* by territory for each key customer group (territory representatives, territory managers, regional managers, and so on). No single structure is best for all companies and situations. Each company should select a sales force structure that best serves the needs of its customers and fits its overall marketing strategy.

A good sales structure can mean the difference between success and failure. Over time, sales force structures can grow complex, inefficient, and unresponsive to customers' needs. Companies should periodically review their sales force organizations to be certain that they serve the needs of the company and its customers.

Sales Force Size   Once the company has set its structure, it is ready to consider *sales force size*. Sales forces may range in size from only a few salespeople to tens of thousands. Some sales forces are huge—for example, PepsiCo employs 36 000 salespeople; American Express, 23 400; GE, 16 400; and Xerox, 15 000.[6] Salespeople constitute one of the company's most productive—and most expensive—assets. Therefore, increasing their number will increase both sales and costs.

Many companies use some form of *workload approach* to set sales force size. When using this approach, a company first groups accounts into different classes according to size, account status, or other factors related to the amount of effort required to maintain them. It then determines the number of salespeople needed to call on each class of accounts the desired number of times.

The company might think as follows: Suppose we have 1000 Type-A accounts and 2000 Type-B accounts. Type-A accounts require 36 calls

Exhibit 13.5   Sales force size: Some sales forces are huge. For example, Xerox employs 15 000 salespeople; GE, 16 400; American Express, 23 400; and PepsiCo, 36 000.

a year and Type-B accounts require 12 calls a year. In this case, the sales force's *workload*—the number of calls it must make per year—is 60 000 calls $[(1000 \times 36) + (2000 \times 12) = 36\ 000 + 24\ 000 = 60\ 000]$. Suppose our average salesperson can make 1000 calls a year. Thus, we need 60 salespeople $(60\ 000 \div 1000)$.[7]

Other Sales Force Strategy and Structure Issues   Sales management must also decide who will be involved in the selling effort and how various sales and sales support people will work together.

Outside sales force (or field sales force)
Outside salespeople who travel to call on customers in the field.

Inside sales force
Inside salespeople who conduct business from their offices via telephone, the Internet, or visits from prospective buyers.

OUTSIDE AND INSIDE SALES FORCES   The company may have an **outside sales force (or field sales force)**, an **inside sales force**, or both. Outside salespeople travel to call on customers in the field. Inside salespeople conduct business from their offices via telephone, the Internet, or visits from buyers.

Some inside salespeople provide support for the outside sales force, freeing them to spend more time selling to major accounts and finding new prospects. For example, *technical sales support people* provide technical information and answers to customers' questions. *Sales assistants* provide administrative backup for outside salespeople. They call ahead and confirm appointments, follow up on deliveries, and answer customers' questions when outside salespeople cannot be reached. Using such combinations of inside and outside salespeople can help to serve important customers better. The inside rep provides daily access and support; the outside rep provides face-to-face collaboration and relationship building.

Other inside salespeople do more than just provide support. *Telemarketers* and *Web sellers* use the phone and Internet to find new leads and qualify prospects or to sell and service accounts directly. Telemarketing and Web selling can be very effective, less costly ways to sell to smaller, harder-to-reach customers. Depending on the complexity of the product and the customer, for example, a telemarketer can make from 20 to 33 decision-maker contacts a day, compared with the average of four that an outside salesperson can make. And whereas an average business-to-business field sales call costs $329 or more, a routine industrial telemarketing call costs only about $5 and a complex call about $20.[8]

Although the federal government's Do Not Call Registry put a dent in telephone sales to consumers, telemarketing remains a vital tool for many business-to-business marketers. For some smaller companies, telephone and Web selling may be the primary sales approaches. However, larger companies also use these tactics, either to sell directly to small and mid-size customers or to help out with larger ones. Especially in the leaner times following the recent recession, many companies are cutting back on in-person customer visits in favour of more telephone, email, and Internet selling.[9]

For many types of products and selling situations, phone or Web selling can be as effective as a personal sales call. Notes a DuPont telemarketer, "I'm more effective on the phone. [When you're in the field], if some guy's not in his office, you lose an hour. On the phone, you lose 15 seconds.... Through my phone calls, I'm in the field as much as the rep is." There are other advantages. "Customers can't throw things at you," quips the rep, "and you don't have to outrun dogs."[10]

What's more, although they may seem impersonal, the phone and Internet can be surprisingly personal when it comes to building customer relationships. For example, remember the chapter-opening story about technology products and services company CDW, which sells only by phone and the Web? CDW account managers such as Ron Kelly develop strong personal relationships with customers large and small.

Team selling
Using teams of people from sales, marketing, engineering, finance, technical support, and even upper management to service large, complex accounts.

TEAM SELLING   As products become more complex, and as customers grow larger and more demanding, a single salesperson simply can't handle all of a large customer's needs. Instead, most companies now use **team selling** to service large, complex accounts. Sales teams can unearth problems, solutions, and sales opportunities that no individual salesperson could. Such teams might include experts from any area or level of the selling firm—sales, marketing, technical and support services, R&D, engineering, operations, finance, and others. In team selling situations, the salesperson shifts from "soloist" to "orchestrator."

In many cases, the move to team selling mirrors similar changes in customers' buying organizations. "Buyers implementing team-based purchasing decisions have necessitated the equal and opposite creation of team-based selling—a completely new way of doing business for many independent, self-motivated salespeople," says a sales force analyst. "Today, we're calling on teams of buying people, and that requires more firepower on our side," agrees one sales vice-president. "One salesperson just can't do it all—can't be an expert in everything we're bringing to the customer. We have strategic account teams, led by customer business managers, who basically are our quarterbacks."[11]

Exhibit 13.6   Inside sales: For many types of selling situations, phone or Web selling can be as effective as a personal sales call. Phone reps can build surprisingly strong and personal customer relationships.

Some companies, such as IBM, Xerox, and P&G, have used teams for a long time. P&G sales reps are organized into "customer business development (CBD) teams." Each CBD team is assigned to a major P&G customer, such as Wal-Mart, Safeway, or Shoppers Drug Mart. Teams consist of a customer business development manager, several account executives (each responsible for a specific category of P&G products), and specialists in marketing strategy, operations, information systems, logistics, and finance. This organization places the focus on serving the complete needs of each important customer. It lets P&G "grow business by working as a 'strategic partner' with our accounts, not just as a supplier. Our goal: to grow their business, which also results in growing ours."[12]

Team selling does have some pitfalls. For example, salespeople are by nature competitive and have often been trained and rewarded for outstanding individual performance. Salespeople who are used to having customers all to themselves may have trouble learning to work with and trust others on a team. In addition, selling teams can confuse or overwhelm customers who are used to working with only one salesperson. Finally, difficulties in evaluating individual contributions to the team selling effort can create some sticky compensation issues.

RECRUITING, SELECTING, AND TRAINING SALESPEOPLE

At the heart of any successful sales force operation is the recruitment and selection of good salespeople. Once selected, the new members of the sales team must be trained—they must learn about the company and its products, and how those products can benefit customers. The performance difference between an average salesperson and a top salesperson can be substantial. In a typical sales force, the top 30 percent of the salespeople might bring in 60 percent of the sales. Beyond the differences in sales performance, poor selection results in costly turnover. When a salesperson quits, the costs of finding and training a new salesperson—plus the costs of lost sales—can be very high. Also, a sales force with many new people is less productive, and turnover disrupts important customer relationships.

What sets great salespeople apart from all the rest? In an effort to profile top sales performers, Gallup Management Consulting Group, a division of the well-known Gallup polling organization, has interviewed hundreds of thousands of salespeople. Its

Exhibit 13.7   Selecting salespeople: The best salespeople, such as Jennifer Hansen of 3M, possess intrinsic motivation, disciplined work style, the ability to close a sale, and, perhaps most important, the ability to build relationships with customers.

research suggests that the best salespeople possess four key talents: intrinsic motivation, disciplined work style, the ability to close a sale, and, perhaps most important, the ability to build relationships with customers.[13]

Super salespeople are motivated from within—they have an unrelenting drive to excel. Some salespeople are driven by money, a desire for recognition, or the satisfaction of competing and winning. Others are driven by the desire to provide service and build relationships. The best salespeople possess some of each of these motivations. They also have a disciplined work style. They lay out detailed, organized plans and then follow through in a timely way.

But motivation and discipline mean little unless they result in closing more sales and building better customer relationships. Super salespeople build the skills and knowledge they need to get the job done. Perhaps most important, top salespeople are excellent customer problem solvers and relationship builders. They understand their customers' needs. Talk to sales executives and they'll describe top performers in these terms: empathetic, patient, caring, responsive, good listeners. Top performers can put themselves on the buyer's side of the desk and see the world through their customers' eyes. They don't want just to be liked, they want to add value for their customers.

New salespeople may spend anywhere from a few weeks or months to a year or more in training. Then, most companies provide continuing sales training via seminars, sales meetings, and Web e-learning throughout the salesperson's career. Although training can be expensive, it can also yield dramatic returns. For example, U.S. technology companies invest 29 percent of their training budgets on sales training, and one recent study showed that sales training conducted by administrative services firm ADP resulted in a return on investment of nearly percent in only 90 days.[14] The Canadian Professional Sales Association (CPSA) offers sales training and certification, and reports that two-thirds of graduates from its Certified Sales Professional training program increased their sales by 15 percent or more.[15]

Training programs have several goals. First, salespeople need to know about customers and how to build relationships with them. So the training program must teach them about different types of customers and their needs, buying motives, and buying habits. And it must teach them how to sell effectively and train them in the basics of the selling process. Salespeople also need to know and identify with the company, its products, and its competitors. So an effective training program teaches them about the company's objectives, organization, chief products and markets, and about the strategies of major competitors.

Many companies are now using imaginative and sophisticated e-learning techniques to make sales training more efficient—and sometimes even more fun. For example, Bayer Healthcare Pharmaceuticals worked with healthcare marketing agency Concentric Rx to create a role-playing simulation video game to train its sales force on a new drug marketing program:[16]

You don't usually associate fast-paced rock music and flashy graphics with online sales training tools. But Concentric Rx's innovative role-playing video game—Rep Race: The Battle for Office Supremacy—has all that and a lot more. Rep Race gives Bayer sales reps far more entertainment than the staid old multiple-choice skills tests it replaces. The game was created to help breathe new life into a mature Bayer product—Betaseron, a 17-year-old multiple sclerosis (MS) therapy treatment. The aim was to find a fresh, more active way to help Bayer sales reps apply the in-depth information they learned about Betaseron to actual selling and objections-handling situations. Bayer also wanted to increase rep engagement through interactive learning and feedback through real-time results. Bayer reps liked Rep Race from the start. According to Bayer, when the game was first launched, reps played it as many as 30 times. In addition to its educational and motivational value, Rep Race allowed Bayer to measure sales reps' individual and collective performance. In the end, Bayer calculates that the Rep Race simulation helped improve the Betaseron sales team's effectiveness by 20 percent.

COMPENSATING, SUPERVISING, AND MOTIVATING SALESPEOPLE

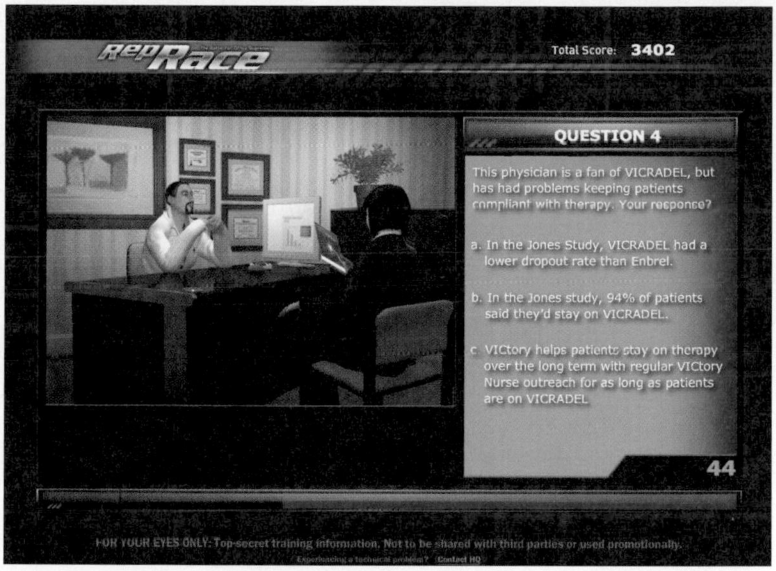

Exhibit 13.8   Training salespeople: E-training can make sales training more efficient—and more fun. Bayer Healthcare Pharmaceuticals's role-playing video game—Rep Race—helped improve sales rep effectiveness by 20 percent.

To attract good salespeople, a company must have an appealing compensation plan. Compensation is made up of several elements—a fixed amount, a variable amount, expenses, and fringe benefits. The fixed amount, usually a salary, gives the salesperson some stable income. The variable amount, which might be commissions or bonuses based on sales performance, rewards the salesperson for greater effort and success. Different combinations of fixed and variable compensation give rise to four basic types of compensation plans—straight salary, straight commission, salary plus bonus, and salary plus commission. A study of sales force compensation showed that the average salesperson's pay consists of about 67 percent salary and 33 percent incentive pay.[17]

The sales force compensation plan can both motivate salespeople and direct their activities. Compensation should direct salespeople toward activities that are consistent with overall sales force and marketing objectives. For example, if the strategy is to acquire new business, grow rapidly, and gain market share, the compensation plan might include a larger commission component, coupled with a new-account bonus to encourage high sales performance and new-account development. In contrast, if the goal is to maximize current account profitability, the compensation plan might contain a larger base-salary component with additional incentives for current account sales or customer satisfaction.

New salespeople need more than a territory, compensation, and training—they need supervision and motivation. The goal of *supervision* is to help salespeople "work smart" by doing the right things in the right ways. The goal of *motivation* is to encourage salespeople to "work hard" and energetically toward sales force goals. If salespeople work smart and work hard, they will realize their full potential, to their own and the company's benefit.

Companies vary in how closely they supervise their salespeople. Many help salespeople to identify target customers and set call norms. Some may also specify how much time the sales force should spend prospecting for new accounts and set other time management priorities. One tool is the weekly, monthly, or annual *call plan* that shows which customers and prospects to call on and which activities to carry out. Another tool is *time-and-duty analysis*. In addition to time spent selling, the salesperson spends time travelling, waiting, taking breaks, and doing administrative chores.

Figure 13.2 shows how salespeople spend their time. On average, active selling time accounts for only 10 percent of total working time! If selling time could be raised from 10 percent to 30 percent, this would triple the time spent selling.[18] Companies always are

FIGURE 13.2   How salespeople spend their time

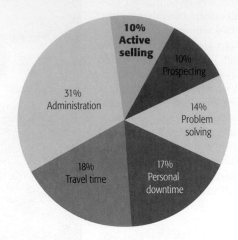

Source: Proudfoot Consulting. Data used with permission.

looking for ways to save time—simplifying administrative duties, developing better sales-call and routing plans, supplying more and better customer information, and using phones, email, or video conferencing instead of travelling. Consider the changes GE made to increase its sales force's face-to-face selling time.[19]

> When Jeff Immelt became General Electric's new chairman, he was dismayed to find that members of the sales team were spending far more time on deskbound administrative chores than in face-to-face meetings with customers and prospects. "He said we needed to turn that around," recalls Venki Rao, an IT leader in global sales and marketing at GE Power Systems, a division focused on energy systems and products. "[We need] to spend four days a week in front of the customer and one day for all the admin stuff." GE Power's salespeople spent much of their time at their desks because they had to go to many sources for the information needed to sell multimillion-dollar turbines, turbine parts, and services to energy companies worldwide. To fix the problem, GE created a new sales portal, a kind of "one-stop shop" for just about everything they need. The sales portal connects the vast array of existing GE databases, providing everything from sales tracking and customer data to parts pricing and information on planned outages. GE also added external data, such as news feeds. "Before, you were randomly searching for things," says Bill Snook, a GE sales manager. Now, he says, "I have the sales portal as my home page, and I use it as the gateway to all the applications that I have." The sales portal has freed Snook and 2,500 other users around the globe from once time-consuming administrative tasks, greatly increasing their face time with customers.

Beyond directing salespeople, sales managers must also motivate them. Some salespeople will do their best without any special urging from management. To them, selling may be the most fascinating job in the world. But selling can also be frustrating. Salespeople often work alone and they must sometimes travel away from home. They may face aggressive competing salespeople and difficult customers. Therefore, salespeople often need special encouragement to do their best.

Many companies motivate their salespeople by setting **sales quotas**—standards stating the amount they should sell and how sales should be divided among the company's products. Compensation is often related to how well salespeople meet their quotas. Companies also use various *positive incentives* to increase sales force effort. *Sales meetings* provide social occasions, breaks from routine, chances to meet and talk with "company brass," and opportunities to air feelings and identify with a larger group. Companies also sponsor *sales contests* to spur the sales force to make a selling effort above what would normally be expected. Other incentives include honours, merchandise and cash awards, trips, and profit-sharing plans.

Sales quota

A standard that states the amount a salesperson should sell and how sales should be divided among the company's products.

EVALUATING SALESPEOPLE AND SALES FORCE PERFORMANCE

The last step in managing the sales force is evaluating individual salespeople and overall sales force performance. Management gets information about its salespeople in several ways. The most important source is *sales reports*, including weekly or monthly work plans and longer-term territory marketing plans. Salespeople also write up their completed activities on *call reports* and turn in *expense reports* for which they are partly or wholly repaid. The company can also monitor the sales and profit performance data in the salesperson's territory. Additional information comes from personal observation, customer surveys, and talks with other salespeople.

By using various sales force reports and other information, sales management evaluates members of the sales force. It evaluates salespeople on their ability to "plan their work and work their plan." Formal evaluation forces management to develop and communicate clear standards for judging performance. It also provides salespeople with constructive feedback and motivates them to perform well.

On a broader level, management should evaluate the performance of the sales force as a whole. Is the sales force accomplishing its customer relationship, sales, and profit objectives? Is it working well with other areas of the marketing and company organization? Are sales force costs in line with outcomes? As with other marketing activities, the company wants to measure its *return on sales investment*.

SALES FORCE AUTOMATION

Many firms have adopted *sales force automation systems*—computerized, digitized sales force operations that let salespeople work more effectively anytime, anywhere. Companies now routinely equip their salespeople with technologies such as laptops, smartphones and other personal digital devices, wireless Internet, webcams for videoconferencing, and customer-contact and relationship management software. Armed with these technologies, salespeople can more effectively and efficiently profile customers and prospects, analyze and forecast sales, schedule sales calls, make presentations, prepare sales and expense reports, and manage account relationships. The result is better time management, improved customer service, lower sales costs, and higher sales performance.[20]

Today, the Internet offers every organization, regardless of the size of its sales force, the ability to connect quickly and easily with its customers—whether they are next door or on the other side of the world. The latest development in sales force automation is the merging of sales processes with Web 2.0 trends, such as social networking—some call it "Sales 2.0."[21]

Web 2.0 enables a new way of interacting, collaborating, and information sharing. With the Internet as a new business platform, now all stakeholders—prospects, customers, salespeople, and marketers—can connect, learn, plan, analyze, engage, collaborate, and conduct business in ways that were not even imaginable a few years ago. Such innovations as Wikipedia, online conferencing, i-reports, user ratings, blogs, Twitter, and social networking have elevated the potential for human collaboration to a higher level. In turn, Sales 2.0 brings together customer-focused methodologies and productivity-enhancing technologies that transform selling from an art to an interactive science. Sales 2.0 has forever changed the process by which people buy and companies sell.

Exhibit 13.9   Sales force automation: Today's technology offers a host of advanced, interactive tools for the sales force. Some refer to it as "Sales 2.0."

Web-based technologies can produce big organizational benefits for sales forces. They help conserve salespeople's valuable time, save travel dollars, and give salespeople a new vehicle for selling and servicing accounts. Over the past decade, customer buying patterns have changed. In today's Web 2.0 world, customers often know almost as much about a company's products as salespeople do. This gives customers more control over the sales process than they had in the days when brochures and pricing were available only from a sales rep. Sales 2.0 recognizes and takes advantage of these buying process changes, creating new avenues for connecting with customers in the Internet age.

For example, sales organizations can now generate lists of prospective customers from online databases and networking sites such as Hoovers and Linked In. They create dialogues when prospective customers visit their websites through live chats with the sales team. They can use Web conferencing tools such as WebEx or GoToMeeting to talk live with customers about products and services. Other Sales 2.0 tools allow salespeople to monitor Internet interactions between customers about how they would like to buy, how they feel about a vendor, and what it would take to make a sale. Ultimately, "Sales 2.0 technologies are delivering instant information that builds relationships and enables sale to be more efficient and cost-effective and more productive.... Just as the Internet allowed buyers to literally let their fingers do the walking, these new Sales 2.0 technologies are allowing the customer's online behavior to dictate the communication—before sales does the talking."[22]

But the technologies also have some drawbacks. For starters, they're not cheap. And such systems can intimidate low-tech salespeople or clients. What's more, there are some things you just can't present or teach via the Web, things that require personal interactions. For these reasons, some high-tech experts recommend that sales executives use Web technologies to supplement training, sales meetings, and preliminary client sales presentations, but resort to old-fashioned, face-to-face meetings when the time draws near to close the deal.

THE PERSONAL SELLING PROCESS (L03)

We now turn from designing and managing a sales force to the actual personal selling process. The **selling process** consists of several steps that salespeople must master. These steps focus on the goal of getting new customers and obtaining orders from them. However, most salespeople spend much of their time maintaining existing accounts and building long-term customer *relationships*. We discuss the relationship aspect of the personal selling process in a later section.

STEPS IN THE SELLING PROCESS

As shown in Figure 13.3, the selling process consists of seven steps: prospecting and qualifying, preapproach, approach, presentation and demonstration, handling objections, closing, and follow-up.

Prospecting and Qualifying   The first step in the selling process is **prospecting**— identifying qualified potential customers. Approaching the right potential customers is crucial to the selling success. As one sales expert puts it, "If the sales force starts chasing anyone who is breathing and seems to have a budget, you risk accumulating a roster of expensive-to-serve, hard-to-satisfy customers who never respond to whatever value proposition you have." He continues, "The solution to this isn't rocket science. [You must] train salespeople to actively scout the right prospects." Another expert concludes, "Increasing your prospecting effectiveness is the fastest single way to boost your sales."[23]

Selling process
The steps that salespeople follow when selling, which include prospecting and qualifying, preapproach, approach, presentation and demonstration, handling objections, closing, and follow-up.

Prospecting
The step in the selling process in which the salesperson or company identifies qualified potential customers.

FIGURE 13.3   Steps in the selling process

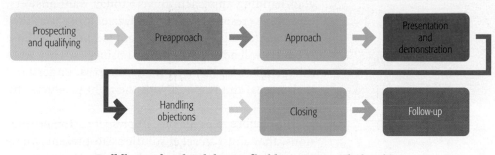

Building and maintaining profitable customer relationships

The salesperson must often approach many prospects to get just a few sales. Although the company supplies some leads, salespeople need skill in finding their own. The best source is referrals. Salespeople can ask current customers for referrals and cultivate other referral sources, such as suppliers, dealers, non-competing salespeople, and Web or other social networks. They can also search for prospects in directories or on the Web and track down leads by using the telephone and email. Or they can drop in unannounced on various offices—a practice known as *cold calling*.

Salespeople also need to know how to *qualify* leads—that is, how to identify the good ones and screen out the poor ones. Prospects can be qualified by looking at their financial ability, volume of business, special needs, location, and possibilities for growth.

Preapproach   Before calling on a prospect, the salesperson should learn as much as possible about the organization (what it needs, who is involved in the buying) and its buyers (their characteristics and buying styles). This step is known as the **preapproach.** "Revving up your sales starts with your preparation," says one sales consultant. "A successful sale begins long before you set foot in the prospect's office." Preapproach begins with good research. The salesperson can consult standard industry and online sources, acquaintances, and others to learn about the company. Then, the salesperson must apply the research to develop a customer strategy. "Being able to recite the prospect's product line in your sleep isn't enough," says the consultant. "You need to translate the data into something useful for your client."[24]

The salesperson should set *call objectives*, which may be to qualify the prospect, gather information, or make an immediate sale. Another task is to decide on the best approach, which might be a personal visit, a phone call, or a letter or email. The best timing should be considered carefully because many prospects are busiest at certain times. Finally, the salesperson should give thought to an overall sales strategy for the account.

Approach   During the **approach** step, the salesperson should know how to meet and greet the buyer and get the relationship off to a good start. This step involves the salesperson's appearance, opening lines, and the follow-up remarks. The opening lines should be positive to build goodwill from the beginning of the relationship. This opening might be followed by some key questions to learn more about the customer's needs or by showing a display or sample to attract the buyer's attention and curiosity. As in all stages of the selling process, listening to the customer is crucial.

Presentation and Demonstration   During the **presentation** step of the selling process, the salesperson tells the "value story" to the buyer, showing how the company's offer solves the customer's problems. The *customer-solution approach* fits better with today's

Preapproach
The step in the selling process in which the salesperson learns as much as possible about a prospective customer before making a sales call.

Approach
The step in the selling process in which the salesperson meets the customer for the first time.

Presentation
The step in the selling process in which the salesperson tells the "value story" to the buyer, showing how the company's offer solves the customer's problems.

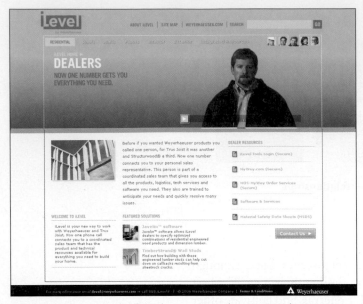

Exhibit 13.10   Communicating the "value story:" Weyerhaeuser created a customer-solutions-focused sales organization called iLevel. It promises customers "a coordinated sales team that gives you access to all the products, logistics, tech services, and software you need [to] quickly resolve issues."

relationship marketing focus than does a hard-sell or glad-handing approach. Buyers today want answers, not smiles; results, not razzle-dazzle. Moreover, they don't want just products, they want to know how those products will add value to their businesses. They want salespeople who listen to their concerns, understand their needs, and respond with the right products and services.

But before salespeople can *present* customer solutions, they must *develop* solutions to present. Many companies now train their salespeople to go beyond "product thinking." Weyerhaeuser, the $8 billion U.S. forest products company, reorganized its entire sales force around customer-solutions selling:

Weyerhaeuser, long a product-driven company, undertook an extreme makeover, creating a customer-solutions-focused sales organization called iLevel. Rather than selling wood products piecemeal, Weyerhaeuser wants to be considered the one-stop location for all of the innovation and products required to construct residential home frames—joists, beams, floors, and all. The new iLevel organization assigns a single salesperson to each major builder or dealer. The sales rep leads a coordinated sales team that serves all of the customer's needs. To implement iLevel, Weyerhaeuser retrained its 250 salespeople to present customers with solutions, not products. "It is a consultative selling approach," says a Weyerhaeuser executive. Never again will salespeople merely sell orders of lumber. "What we want [our sales reps] to do is help our customers find solutions that make them [and us] money."[25]

The solutions approach calls for good listening and problem-solving skills. One study revealed that 74 percent of 200 purchasers surveyed at companies nationwide said they would be much more likely to buy from a salesperson if the seller would simply listen to them. Says one experienced salesperson, "That typecast chatty character may be the kind of person who's most often drawn to sales, but it's not often the one who's most successful at it. Unless you listen to what your customer is saying, you won't understand his deeper wants and needs. And you'll find that the more you listen to others, the more they'll listen to you. As the old saying goes, 'God gave us two ears and only one mouth, to use in that proportion.'"[26]

The qualities that buyers *dislike most* in salespeople include being pushy, late, deceitful, unprepared, or disorganized. The qualities they *value most* include good listening, empathy, honesty, dependability, thoroughness, and follow-through. Great salespeople know how to sell, but more importantly they know how to listen and build strong customer relationships. Says one professional, "Everything starts with listening. I think the magic of these days is we've got so many more ways to listen."[27]

Salespeople must also plan their presentation methods. Good interpersonal communication skills count when it comes to making effective sales presentations. However, today's media-rich and cluttered communications environment presents many new challenges for sales presenters:[28]

The goal of a sales presentation is to deliver a clear, concise, and consistent message to your prospects about your product and your brand, as well as why you are better than the competition. Doing that and keeping your audience's attention for longer than 30 minutes is the real challenge. Today's information-overloaded prospects demand a richer presentation experience. And sales presenters must now overcome multiple distractions from cell phones, text messaging, and portable Internet viewers during a presentation.

Sales presentations today take creativity, careful planning, and the application of the hottest technologies available. You can't fill your prospects' heads with unnecessary, useless information, and you have to capture their interest fast or risk losing them forever. So you must deliver your message in a more engaging and compelling way than your competition does, and you must deliver more information in less time.

Today's salespeople are employing advanced presentation technologies that allow for full multi-media presentations to only one or a few people. The venerable old flip chart has been replaced by DVDs, online presentation technologies, interactive white boards, and hand-held and laptop computers with sophisticated presentation software.

Exhibit 13.11   Presentation technology: Today's media-rich communications environment presents many new opportunities for sales presenters.

Handling Objections   Customers almost always have objections during the presentation or when asked to place an order. The problem can be either logical or psychological, and objections are often unspoken. In **handling objections**, the salesperson should use a positive approach, seek out hidden objections, ask the buyer to clarify any objections, take objections as opportunities to provide more information, and turn the objections into reasons for buying. Every salesperson needs training in the skills of handling objections.

Handling objections
The step in the selling process in which the salesperson seeks out, clarifies, and overcomes customer objections to buying.

Closing   After handling the prospect's objections, the salesperson now tries to close the sale. Some salespeople do not get around to **closing** or do not handle it well. They may lack confidence, feel guilty about asking for the order, or fail to recognize the right moment to close the sale. Salespeople should know how to recognize closing signals from the buyer, including physical actions, comments, and questions. For example, the customer might sit forward and nod approvingly or ask about prices and credit terms.

Salespeople can use one of several closing techniques. They can ask for the order, review points of agreement, offer to help write up the order, ask whether the buyer wants this model or that one, or note that the buyer will lose out if the order is not placed now. The salesperson may offer the buyer special reasons to close, such as a lower price or an extra quantity at no charge.

Closing
The step in the selling process in which the salesperson asks the customer for an order.

Follow-Up   The last step in the selling process—**follow-up**—is necessary if the salesperson wants to ensure customer satisfaction and repeat business. Right after closing, the salesperson should complete any details on delivery time, purchase terms, and other matters. The salesperson then should schedule a follow-up call when the initial order is received to make sure there is proper installation, instruction, and servicing. This visit would reveal any problems, assure the buyer of the salesperson's interest, and reduce any buyer concerns that might have arisen since the sale.

Follow-up
The last step in the selling process in which the salesperson follows up after the sale to ensure customer satisfaction and repeat business.

Finally, the selling process must be understood in the context of building and maintaining profitable customer relationships—the essence of our definition of marketing. The steps in the selling process as just described are *transaction oriented*—their aim is to help salespeople to close a specific sale with a customer. But in most cases, the company is not simply seeking a sale. Rather, it wants to serve the customer over the long haul in a mutually profitable relationship—and today's modern sales forces have an important role to play.

SALES PROMOTION 〔LO4〕

Sales promotion
Short-term incentives to encourage the purchase or sale of a product or a service.

Personal selling and advertising often work closely with another promotion tool, sales promotion. **Sales promotion** consists of short-term incentives to encourage purchase or sales of a product or a service. Whereas advertising offers reasons to buy a product or service, sales promotion offers reasons to buy *now*.

Examples of sales promotions are found everywhere. A free-standing insert in the *Globe and Mail* alerts you to the special offers available from Dell next week. An email from Ticketmaster offers you a discount on tickets if you order before a certain date. A display in convenience stores during hockey season features a life-size Sidney Crosby to attract your attention, and explain how you can win seats to a game by purchasing a Pepsi product. A Bed Bath & Beyond flyer arrives in your mailbox, offering you 20 percent off if you bring it into the store. An executive buys a new HP laptop and gets a free carrying case, or a family buys a new Ford Escape and receives a factory rebate of $1000. A hardware store chain receives a 10 percent discount on Black & Decker portable power tools if it agrees to advertise them in local newspapers. Sales promotion includes a wide variety of promotion tools designed to stimulate earlier or stronger market response.

Because sales promotions are typically time-sensitive, they must be planned well in advance, and often correspond to seasons or holidays. For example, Canadian Tire's "Get Ready For Canada Day" event takes place the week of July 1 and includes a flyer advertising the specific products that will be on sale that week, plus special offers for extra Canadian Tire money with certain purchases. Sales promotions are often used in conjunction with other forms of marketing communications; for example, retailers such as Bed Bath & Beyond and Best Buy regularly send postcard-sized flyers to consumers in a targeted geographic area, inviting them to bring the flyer into a particular store on a certain day to receive 20 percent off. These limited time promotions may also be advertised in newspapers, in magazines, on television, or on radio. Increasingly, marketers are using social media tools such as Facebook and Twitter to conduct sales promotions, giving the added advantage of allowing the consumer to interact with the brand (see Marketing@Work 13.2).

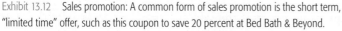

Exhibit 13.12   Sales promotion: A common form of sales promotion is the short term, "limited time" offer, such as this coupon to save 20 percent at Bed Bath & Beyond.

RAPID GROWTH OF SALES PROMOTION

Sales promotion tools are used by most organizations, including manufacturers, distributors, retailers, and not-for-profit institutions. They are targeted toward consumers (*consumer promotions*), retailers and wholesalers (*trade promotions*), business customers (*business promotions*), and members of the sales force (*sales force promotions*). Today, in the average consumer packaged-goods company, sales promotion accounts for 74 percent of all marketing expenditures.[29]

Marketing Gets Social: Fast-Fooders and Retailers Get Personal Online, and Consumers Can't Get Enough

Marketers today are scrambling to get on board the social media train—especially for sales promotions. Facebook has 400 million members who spend over 500 billion minutes per month on the site; and every day 300 000 new users start tweeting on Twitter. That's a lot of consumers primed to engage with content and information, and wherever large numbers of consumers congregate, marketing needs to be there.

Just about every major brand has a Facebook site, and large companies, such as Nike, have several. When Facebook users search for their favourite brand on the social networking site, they have the option of clicking the "Like" button, which instantly connects them to the brand. A recent study revealed that the main reason consumers choose to "like" a brand on Facebook is for the coupons and discounts. "Coupons remain a leading driver of brand interactions in social networks," says one market research analyst, who goes on to recommend that marketers who use social media must make sure that the discount offer can be printed or easily downloaded, and that it must work as promised. Furthermore, it's critical to integrate communications with retailers, so that they are prepared for increased demand.

Harvey's ran a promotion last summer to name their new burger. Advertisements on radio and television encouraged listeners to log onto Facebook and submit a name suggestion, along with a 250-word explanation of their idea, for a chance to win $10 000. Three finalists, all of whom won free burgers for a year (a value of $2000) were chosen by judges, and their submissions posted on Facebook for the entire community to vote on. Online consumers could also sign up for "Harvey's mail" to have coupons—for example, for free fries or a free drink that week—emailed to them. The coupons were personalized, and could be used only by the person who requested them,

Exhibit 13.13   Sales promotion using social media: Guess the TELUS hippo's location was a summer-long contest that consumers could enter daily—via Facebook and Twitter—to win prizes.

however, each email coupon came with a link to forward the offer to friends so they could sign up to receive their own coupons. More than 70 000 Facebook users signed up for the Harvey's promotion, the first time the fast-food chain had participated in social media to this extent. "This is a new approach for Harvey's ... we're all about a customized, personalized experience," noted the chain's brand manager.

Over at competitor Wendy's, a summer "Great After 8" promotion included a Facebook site and microsite at GreatAfter8.ca, where consumers could play games and win a code to get a free Frosty after 8 p.m. And all summer long the TELUS Hippo was "on vacation," sending daily tweets on Twitter and posting videos and photos on Facebook, where social media users could guess the Hippo's location and win prizes. Toronto's

Mill Street Brewery ran a summer promotion called "The Mill Street Lemon Tea Beer Challenge," to launch its new lemon tea–flavoured beer. Consumers could stand in front of a camera at participating bars and events and talk about why they like the new beer. The videos were uploaded to a website that was linked to Facebook and Twitter, where friends could vote for their favourite video by using either (or both) of the social networking tools. The Mill Street fans in the video and their friends were encouraged to share news about the promotion and vote for the videos, because the video with the most votes would win a party for 10 friends at the Mill Street Brewpub.

"Marketing has traditionally focused on the four Ps: product, price, place, and promotion. Social media has morphed into the fifth, and possibly most important

P: people," says one social marketing expert. People are at the centre of Best Buy's forays into social media. Customers can "follow" Best Buy and Best Buy Canada on Twitter, get nearly daily tweets about door-crasher sales and other special offers, and follow the retailer's Twelpforce—live help force on Twitter—to ask questions of Best Buy employees.

Shoppers Drug Mart Optimum members can sign up to receive email promotions: Each email comes with colourful coupons and a "Follow us on Twitter" link to receive "tweets" of the weekly flyer, customizable by postal code. Twitter restricts tweets to 140 characters, so the Shoppers offers are short: "FREE $10 Quickpay Tim Card when you spend $50 or more on a l most anything in the store," and "Get a $20 Esso Gift Card when you spend $75 or more at Shoppers Drug Mart."—but you have to hurry. Like most sales promotions, these are limited time offers. If you don't click within a few days, the link will take you to a "Sorry, we are unable to find the page you requested" message. Conducting an effective sales promotion requires keen day-to-day management.

One expert recommends marketers merge their followers list from Twitter and fans list from Facebook with their marketing database. "You can start by direct messaging all of your followers or placing the special offers on your Facebook page. When you send a direct communication (in email or direct mail), make sure that your fans and followers get it first by using direct messaging and posting to Facebook. For those followers and fans also opted in to your email program, consider (or better yet, *test*) tempering your email contact strategy with social communications. Finally, always use the forward-to social features within email and highlight your social media presence within your creative and on your website."

And if that's not enough to manage, new social networking sites are springing up all the time: Foursquare is covered with sponsored "badges" and coupon discounts from local marketers. Location-based social networking site Gowalla inked promotional deals with Nike and Lance Armstrong in conjunction with the Tour de France that included a "chalkbot" machine painting user-submitted messages of encouragement on the roads for cyclists to see. Another promotion, with Chicago-based T-shirt retailer Threadless, saw a marketing team travel across the United States in an Airstream trailer, documenting the trip on Gowalla.

The importance of integrating social media into the marketing mix has never been greater. A recent Infogroup study emphasized the need for marketers to tune in: "For every customer who complains, there are 26 other customers who've had similar problems and six of these people have had serious problems. Ninety-six percent of customers who've had a bad experience will not complain, 90 percent of these customers will not return." It seems social media is a conversation that marketers can't afford to miss hearing and participating in.

Sources: "Coupons Drive Sales on Social Media," Adweek online (Adweek.com), June 9, 2010; Hank Wasiak, "How Social Media Has Radically Altered Advertising," published on Mashable.com, July 7, 2010; Caroline McCarthy, "Gowalla: We're Still in the Location Race," published on C|Net News (News.Cnet.com), July 8, 2010; Jeff Hassemer, "Mixing and Measuring Social Media," published on iMedia Connection (iMediaConnection.com), July 7, 2010; Melita Kubaras, "Harvey's Flips No-name Burger," *Strategy* (StrategyOnline.ca), June 16, 2010.

Several factors have contributed to the rapid growth of sales promotion, particularly in consumer markets. First, inside the company, product managers face greater pressures to increase their current sales, and promotion is viewed as an effective short-run sales tool. Second, externally, the company faces more competition and competing brands are less differentiated. Increasingly, competitors are using sales promotion to help differentiate their offers. Third, advertising efficiency has declined because of rising costs, media clutter, and legal restraints. Finally, consumers have become more deal oriented, demanding lower prices and better deals. Sales promotions can help attract today's more frugal consumers.

The growing use of sales promotion has resulted in *promotion clutter*, similar to advertising clutter. A given promotion runs the risk of being lost in a sea of other promotions, weakening its ability to trigger immediate purchase. Manufacturers are now searching for ways to rise above the clutter, such as offering larger coupon values, creating more dramatic point-of-purchase displays, or delivering promotions through new interactive media, such as the Internet or cellphones.

In developing a sales promotion program, a company must first set sales promotion objectives and then select the best tools for accomplishing these objectives.

SALES PROMOTION OBJECTIVES

Sales promotion objectives vary widely. Marketers may use *consumer promotions* to urge short-term customer buying or enhance customer brand involvement. Objectives for *trade promotions* include getting retailers to carry new items and more inventory, buy

Exhibit 13.14   Sales promotion objectives: Some sales promotions are designed to encourage customers to purchase during slow sales periods. Coffee consumption tends to drop when the weather gets warmer, so Tim Hortons begins its annual "Roll Up The Rim To Win" promotion in March.

ahead, or promote the company's products and give them more shelf space. For the *sales force*, objectives include getting more sales force support for current or new products or getting salespeople to sign up new accounts.

Sales promotions are usually used together with advertising, personal selling, direct marketing, or other promotion mix tools as part of an integrated marketing campaign. Consumer promotions must usually be advertised and can add excitement and pulling power to ads. Trade and sales force promotions support the firm's personal selling process.

During slow sales periods, or off-seasons, marketers may use sales promotion to encourage customers to purchase. For example, the annual, and very popular, "Roll Up The Rim To Win" promotion from Tim Hortons happens every spring when the weather gets warmer and people tend to drink less coffee. It's easy, and often tempting, to simply offer discounts to spur consumer spending. In general, however, rather than creating only short-term sales or temporary brand switching, sales promotions should help to reinforce the product's position and build long-term *customer relationships*. If properly designed, every sales promotion tool has the potential to build both short-term excitement and long-term consumer relationships. Marketers should avoid "quick fix," price-only promotions in favour of promotions designed to build brand equity.

One way to build relationships is through frequency marketing programs or loyalty programs, such as Shoppers Drug Mart's Optimum program, or the Air Miles rewards card. Most hotels, airlines, and rental car companies offer *loyalty programs* that reward regular customers and keep them coming back. Loyal customers—customers who voluntarily join frequency marketing programs—spend more than casual customers. Shoppers Drug Mart, Canada's largest drug store chain, is the most successful loyalty program offered by any Canadian retailer. Members of the Optimum program spend 60 percent more on their purchases than non-members, and overall Shoppers generates two-thirds of its non-prescription sales from Optimum cardholders.[30]

Today many coffee shops, from your local store to national chains, have also created loyalty programs. For example, a few years ago Starbucks suffered sales setbacks as a result of increased competition from fast-food competitors such as McDonald's, which introduced gourmet coffee. In response, Starbucks could have lowered its prices or offered promotional discounts. But deep discounts might have damaged the chain's long-term premium positioning. So instead, Starbucks dropped its prices only slightly and ran ads

Exhibit 13.15   Loyalty programs: Rather than offering promotional discounts that might damage its premium positioning, Starbucks ran ads telling customers why its coffee is worth the higher price. Then, to build loyalty, the company promoted the Starbucks Card Rewards program.

telling customers why its coffee is worth a higher price. With headlines such as "Beware of a cheaper cup of coffee. It comes with a price," the ads laid out what separates Starbucks from the competition, such as its practices of buying fair-trade beans. At the same time, to build loyalty, Starbucks promoted its Starbucks Card Rewards program:[31]

In 1981, when American Airlines was struggling to differentiate itself in a newly deregulated industry, it invented the frequent flyer mile. Ten years later, American Express responded to its own competitive crisis by introducing what we now know as Membership Rewards. So it shouldn't come as any big surprise that Starbucks, facing its own troubled times, would also turn to a loyalty program, Starbucks Card Rewards. In order to fight off lower-priced competitors such as Dunkin' Donuts and McDonald's and keep its loyal customers, well, loyal, Starbucks unveiled a rewards card. Cardholders benefit from perks such as free in-store refills on coffee, complementary in-store Wi-Fi for up to 2 hours per day, and a free coffee with a purchase of a pound of coffee beans. Such perks increase customer value without big discounts or price reductions. "There is a need for Starbucks to win back customers," says a loyalty marketing consultancy. "The [loyalty] card is a vehicle for doing that."

Another objective of sales promotion is to engage the consumer with the brand—in other words, to develop a *relationship* with existing customers and new customers. General Motors of Canada ran a promotion during hockey season that aimed to tie the Chevrolet brand to hockey in the minds of consumers. A television ad showed hockey legend Bobby Orr taking a young boy's hockey gear from the trunk of a Chevy, and invited consumers to share their hockey memories at a website, LetsGoChevrolet.ca. The promotion ran for several weeks, and at the end a winner was selected to receive a trip for four to the World Junior Hockey Championship in Ottawa. "It's built out of our overall Chevy hockey strategy," said Fred Lautenschlager, manager of sponsorships for General Motors of Canada, "If you think about your own hockey moments and memories, probably somewhere along the line you think about the vehicles that take you to the rink."[32]

MAJOR SALES PROMOTION TOOLS

Many tools can be used to accomplish sales promotion objectives, however, the decision about which form of sales promotion should be employed depends on whether it is a consumer, trade, or business promotion.

Consumer promotions

Sales promotion tools used to boost short-term customer buying and involvement or to enhance long-term customer relationships.

Consumer Promotions   **Consumer promotions** include a wide range of tools—from samples, coupons, rebates, premiums, and point-of-purchase displays to contests, sweepstakes, and event marketing. Here we describe the major forms of sales promotion.

SAMPLES   Samples are offers of a trial amount of a product. Sampling is the most effective—but most expensive—way to introduce a new product or create new excitement for an existing one. Some samples are free; for others, the company charges a small amount to offset its cost. The sample might be delivered door-to-door, sent by mail, handed out in a store or a kiosk, attached to another product, or featured in an ad. Sometimes, samples are combined into sample packs, which can then be used to promote other products and services. Sampling can be a powerful promotional tool.

COUPONS   Coupons are certificates that give buyers a saving when they purchase specified products. Most consumers love coupons. Major packaged-goods companies distributed more than 317 billion coupons last year with an average face value of $1.44, and consumers redeemed more than 2.6 billion of them for a total savings of about

$3.7 billion.[33] Coupons can promote early trial of a new brand or stimulate sales of a mature brand. However, as a result of coupon clutter, redemption rates have been declining in recent years. Thus, most major consumer-goods companies are issuing fewer coupons and targeting them more carefully.

Marketers are also cultivating new outlets for distributing coupons, such as supermarket shelf dispensers, electronic point-of-sale coupon printers, email and online media, and even mobile text-messaging systems. Mobile couponing is very popular in Europe, India, and Japan and is now gaining popularity in the United States. For example, consider Cellfire, a mobile couponing company in California:[34]

> Cellfire distributes digital coupons to the cell phones of consumers who sign up for its free service. Cellfire's growing list of clients ranges from Domino's Pizza, T.G.I. Friday's, Sears, and Hardee's and Carl's Jr. restaurants to Kimberly-Clark, Supercuts, Hollywood Video, 1-800-FLOWERS.COM, and Enterprise Rent-A-Car. Cellfire sends an ever-changing assortment of digital coupons to users' cell phones. To use the coupons, users simply call up the stored coupon list, navigate to the coupon they want, press the "Use Now" button, and show the digital coupon to the store cashier. Domino's even permits consumers holding the mobile coupons to simply click on a link to have their cell phones dial the nearest Domino's store to place an order. To date, Cellfire users have redeemed more than $29 million in coupon savings.
>
> Coupons distributed through Cellfire offer distinct advantages to both consumers and marketers. Consumers don't have to find and clip paper coupons or print out Web coupons and bring them along when they shop. They always have their cell phone coupons with them. For marketers, mobile coupons allow more careful targeting and eliminate the costs of printing and distributing paper coupons. "We don't pay for distribution of digital coupons," says one client. "We pay on redemptions." And the redemption rates can be dazzling. Redemption rates are as high as [20] percent, while the industry average paper response is ... less than 1 percent.

Exhibit 13.16   Coupons: New media such as the Internet and mobile phones present new ways for marketers to distribute coupons, and new opportunities for distribution companies such as Cellfire.

REBATES   Rebates, or cash refunds, are like coupons except that the price reduction occurs after the purchase rather than at the retail outlet. The consumer sends a "proof of purchase" to the manufacturer, who then refunds part of the purchase price by mail. For example, Toro ran a clever pre-season promotion on some of its snow blower models, offering a rebate if the snowfall in the buyer's market area turned out to be below average. Competitors were not able to match this offer on such short notice, and the promotion was very successful. Canadian Tire money is another form of rebate, the cash refund, where consumers who pay with cash for their purchases at the store receive a small percentage back in the form of Canadian Tire money. Rebates are most often used by retailers selling big ticket items, such as appliances. "Rebates boost sales by allowing retailers to feature items at lower prices than their manufacturer partners could otherwise afford," says one marketing expert. Advertising the rebates also attracts more consumers, providing opportunities for additional sales.[35]

PRICE PACKS   Price packs (also called *cents-off deals*) offer consumers savings off the regular price of a product. The producer marks the reduced prices directly on the label or the package. Price packs can be single packages sold at a reduced price (such as two for the price of one) or two related products banded together (such as a toothbrush and toothpaste). Price packs are very effective—even more so than coupons—in stimulating short-term sales.

PREMIUMS   Premiums are goods offered either free or at low cost as an incentive to buy a product, ranging from toys included with kids' products to phone cards and DVDs. A premium may come inside the package (in-pack), outside the package (on-pack), or through the mail. For example, over the years, McDonald's has offered a variety of premiums in its Happy Meals—from Teeny Beanie Babies to Speed Racers to *Monsters vs. Aliens* toy characters. The Happy Meal promotions are now integrated with online media, and kids can go to HappyMeal.com and play games associated with the current Happy Meal sponsor.[36]

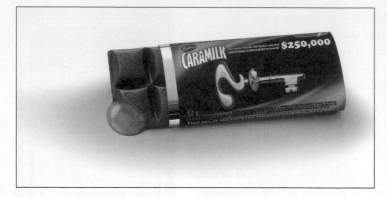

Exhibit 13.17   Contests: Most sales promotions employ several forms of marketing communications, all working together to accomplish the same goal. The Cadbury "Key to the Secret" sales promotion, for example, included a contest, public relations activities, advertising, social media, and even specially marked product packaging.

Advertising specialties, also called *promotional products,* are useful articles imprinted with an advertiser's name, logo, or message that are given as gifts to consumers. Typical items include T-shirts and other apparel, pens, coffee mugs, calendars, key rings, mouse pads, matches, tote bags, coolers, golf balls, and caps. U.S. marketers spent over $19 billion on advertising specialties last year. Such items can be very effective. The "best of them stick around for months, subtly burning a brand name into a user's brain," notes a promotional products expert.[37]

POINT-OF-PURCHASE (POP)   Point-of-purchase (POP) promotions include displays and demonstrations that take place at the point of sale. Think of your last visit to your local convenience store, grocery store, liquor store, or drug store. Chances are good that you were tripping over aisle displays, promotional signs, "shelf talkers," or demonstrators offering free tastes of featured food products. Unfortunately, many retailers do not like to handle the hundreds of displays, signs, and posters they receive from manufacturers each year, and some end up unused or discarded. Manufacturers have responded by offering better POP materials, offering to set them up, and tying them in with television, print, or online messages.

CONTESTS AND SWEEPSTAKES   Contests, sweepstakes, and games give consumers the chance to win something, such as cash, trips, or goods, by luck or through extra effort. A contest calls for consumers to submit an entry—a jingle, guess, suggestion—to be judged by a panel that will select the best entries. A sweepstakes calls for consumers to submit their names for a draw. A game presents consumers with something—bingo numbers, missing letters—every time they buy, which may or may not help them win a prize. Such promotions can create considerable brand attention and consumer involvement. For example, Cadbury's "Key to the Secret" promotion engaged consumers with a well-known brand attribute:[38]

> Canadian chocolate brand Caramilk has based over 40 years of advertising on "The Secret" of how they get the caramel inside the Caramilk bar, and in a 2010 promotion, the company gave consumers the first-ever chance to guard the secret—and win up to $250,000.
>
> The promotion, called "Key to the Secret," awarded one lucky consumer the opportunity to get up close and personal with "The Secret" for the first time in history. To be eligible for the grand prize, consumers had to first find one of 10 golden keys randomly hidden inside Caramilk bars across Canada. At the end of the contest period, each of the 10 key finders tried to unlock the vault that holds "The Secret" at the Cadbury Chocolate Factory in Toronto. The person whose key unlocked the vault became the "Protector of the Secret" for six months. They were given a sealed envelope that holds "The Secret" and a cheque for $125,000—half the prize money. The winner would receive the second half, another $125,000, only if the envelope was returned unopened at the end of the six months.
>
> Advertising, public relations, and social media were employed, and during the course of the promotion and as keys were discovered, Cadbury posted updates via Facebook and Twitter.

Event marketing
Creating a brand-marketing event or serving as a sole or participating sponsor of events created by others.

EVENT MARKETING   Marketers can promote their brands through **event marketing** (or *event sponsorships*), either by creating their own brand marketing events or by serving as a sponsor of events created by others. The events might include anything from mobile brand tours to festivals, reunions, marathons, concerts, or other sponsored gatherings. Event marketing is huge, and it may be the fastest-growing area of promotion, especially in tough economic times. Consumer event-marketing spending in the United States exceeded $19 billion last year, up 12 percent from a year earlier.[39]

Procter & Gamble creates numerous events for its major brands. Consider this example:

> For the past few years, P&G has sponsored a holiday event promotion for its Charmin brand in New York's Times Square, where it can be very difficult to find a public restroom. P&G sets up 20 free, sparkling clean Charmin-themed mini-bathrooms, each with its own sink and a bountiful supply of Charmin. The event is the ultimate in experiential marketing—touching people in places advertising wouldn't dare to go. Over the past three holiday seasons, more than one million people have gratefully used the facilities.[40]

Event marketing can provide a less costly alternative to expensive TV commercials. When it comes to event marketing, sports are in a league of their own. Marketers spent more than $7.6 billion last year to associate their brands with sporting events. For example, events at Citi Field, the New York Mets stadium, include The Pepsi Party Patrol—brand reps that run contests and give away T-shirts—and the Pepsi Porch, a 1284-seat area in right field that extends over the playing field, identified by a Pepsi sign above it.[41]

Exhibit 13.18   Event marketing: Charmin's promotional (but functional) bathrooms in Times Square were designed to look like a powder room you might have in your home, making them inviting to grateful users.

Event sponsorship can take many different forms. For example, the Indy car race in Toronto was sponsored for years by Molson and was called the Molson Indy, but recently the sponsorship changed and now the annual summer race through the streets of Toronto is called the Honda Indy. Event sponsorship may take the form of sponsoring the building in which the event takes place. For example, the Vancouver Canucks play at General Motors Place, the Toronto Blue Jays play at the Rogers Centre, and the Edmonton Oilers play in Rexall Place. When multiple sponsors are involved in an event, the event cannot take all their names; instead, the sponsors will have signs in the venues, or logos on event advertising. For example, Lotto Québec and Vidéotron sponsor the Just For Laughs (Juste Pour Rire) annual comedy festival in Montreal.

Trade Promotions   Manufacturers direct more sales promotion dollars toward retailers and wholesalers (81 percent) than to final consumers (19 percent).[42] **Trade promotions** can persuade resellers to carry a brand, give it shelf space, promote it in advertising, and push it to consumers. Shelf space is so scarce these days that manufacturers often have to offer price-offs, allowances, buy-back guarantees, or free goods to retailers and wholesalers to get products on the shelf and, once there, to keep them on it.

Trade promotions
Sales promotion tools used to persuade resellers to carry a brand, give it shelf space, promote it in advertising, and push it to consumers.

Manufacturers use several trade promotion tools. Many of the tools used for consumer promotions—contests, premiums, displays—can also be used as trade promotions. Or the manufacturer may offer a straight *discount* off the list price on each case purchased during a stated period of time (also called a *price-off*, *off-invoice*, or *off-list*). Manufacturers also may offer an *allowance* (usually so much off per case) in return for the retailer's agreement to feature the manufacturer's products in some way. An advertising allowance compensates retailers for advertising the product. A display allowance compensates them for using special displays.

Manufacturers may offer *free goods*, which are extra cases of merchandise, to resellers who buy a certain quantity or who feature a certain flavour or size. They may offer *push money*—cash or gifts to dealers or their sales forces to "push" the manufacturer's goods. Manufacturers may give retailers free *specialty advertising items* that carry the company's name, such as pens, pencils, calendars, paperweights, matchbooks, memo pads, and yardsticks.

Business Promotions   Companies spend billions of dollars each year on promotion to industrial customers. **Business promotions** are used to generate business leads, stimulate

Business promotions
Sales promotion tools used to generate business leads, stimulate purchases, reward customers, and motivate salespeople.

Exhibit 13.19   Business promotions: Some trade shows are huge. The annual International Consumer Electronics Show in Las Vegas attracts 3000 exhibitors and 110 000 professional visitors.

purchases, reward customers, and motivate salespeople. Business promotions include many of the same tools used for consumer or trade promotions. Here, we focus on two additional major business promotion tools—conventions and trade shows, and sales contests.

Many companies and trade associations organize *conventions and trade shows* to promote their products. Firms selling to the industry show their products at the trade show. Vendors receive many benefits, such as opportunities to find new sales leads, contact customers, introduce new products, meet new customers, sell more to present customers, and educate customers with publications and audiovisual materials. Trade shows also help companies to reach many prospects not reached through their sales forces.

Some trade shows are huge. For example, at a recent International Consumer Electronics Show in Las Vegas, 3000 exhibitors attracted more than 110 000 professional visitors. Even more impressive, at the Bauma mining and construction equipment trade show in Munich, Germany, more than 3000 exhibitors from 49 countries presented their latest product innovations to more than 500 000 attendees from 191 countries.[43]

A *sales contest* is a contest for salespeople or dealers to motivate them to increase their sales performance over a given period. Sales contests motivate and recognize good company performers, who may receive trips, cash prizes, or other gifts. Some companies award points for performance, which the receiver can turn in for any of a variety of prizes. Sales contests work best when they are tied to measurable and achievable sales objectives (such as finding new accounts, reviving old accounts, or increasing account profitability).

DEVELOPING THE SALES PROMOTION PROGRAM

Beyond selecting the types of promotions to use, marketers must make several other decisions in designing the full sales promotion program. First, they must decide on the *size of the incentive.* A certain minimum incentive is necessary if the promotion is to succeed; a larger incentive will produce more sales response. The marketer also must set *conditions for participation.* Incentives might be offered to everyone or only to select groups.

Marketers must decide how to *promote and distribute the promotion* program itself. A $2-off coupon could be given out in a package, at the store, via the Internet, or in an advertisement. Each distribution method involves a different level of reach and cost. Increasingly, marketers are blending several media into a total campaign concept. The *length of the promotion* is also important. If the sales promotion period is too short, many prospects (who may not be buying during that time) will miss it. If the promotion runs too long, the deal will lose some of its "act now" force.

Evaluation is also very important. Many companies fail to evaluate their sales promotion programs, and others evaluate them only superficially. Yet marketers should work to measure the returns on their sales promotion investments, just as they should seek to assess the returns on other marketing activities. The most common evaluation method is to compare sales before, during, and after a promotion. Marketers should ask: Did the promotion attract new customers or more purchasing from current customers? Can we hold onto these new customers and purchases? Will the long-run customer relationship and sales gains from the promotion justify its costs?

Clearly, sales promotion plays an important role in the total promotion mix. To use it well, the marketer must define the sales promotion objectives, select the best tools, design the sales promotion program, implement the program, and evaluate the results. Moreover, sales promotion must be coordinated carefully with other promotion mix elements within the overall integrated marketing communications program.

FROM ADVERSITY TO PROSPERITY

In the early 1980s, a major client of Metro Sportswear Ltd. (the corporate predecessor of Canada Goose) had gone bankrupt, and the company was going through a difficult time, so David Reiss (father of current president and CEO Dani Reiss) began approaching new clients. Dani Reiss says, "My father was a great salesman and he called on companies he wanted to sell to."

Eventually, shoe leather and perspiration prevailed, and David Reiss had brought on accounts such as Eddie Bauer, L.L.Bean, Lands' End, Browning, and Orvis.

David Reiss recalls that period: "It was a very challenging time in our existence. At first I got orders for vests for minimal profit from small discount department stores, just to keep the operation running. I then worked to recruit salesmen in Canada and the U.S. and started bidding for government contracts. Eventually we came out on top, but it wasn't without many sleepless nights."

Today, Canada Goose is soaring. The company faces a unique and happy problem: the temptation to oversell its product. It has North American sales representatives who represent designated territories; it has a corporate office in Stockholm, with a European general manager who oversees sales representatives in Sweden, Denmark, Norway, Germany, and Iceland. While eschewing a formal market research structure, Canada Goose relies on its representatives, distributors, and brand fans to give it product feedback.

"We are not big enough to buy markets or buy our way out of challenges," says vice-president of marketing Kevin Spreekmeester. "We have to be smarter."

Canada Goose uses a number of sales metrics, including retail support and channel control, and making sure the right product gets to the right stores. Retail co-operation is key to Canada Goose.

"Retail stores need to understand our growth objectives," says Dani Reiss. "They need to understand the role they play within these objectives. They need to focus on how they can support the global growth of the brand as opposed to their personal growth. They need patience. Their victories will come along with those of the company."

QUESTIONS

1. What would team selling represent in the case of Canada Goose?
2. Canada Goose has not bought into sales force automation. Why do you think the company is not pursuing this strategy?
3. Thus far, the Canada Goose cases have not mentioned sales promotion. Can you explain why Canada Goose does not pursue sales promotion strategies?

REVIEWING THE CONCEPTS

1. **Discuss the role of a company's salespeople in creating value for customers and building customer relationships.**

Most companies use salespeople, and many companies assign them an important role in the marketing mix. For companies selling business products, the firm's salespeople work directly with customers. Often, the sales force is the customer's only direct contact with the company and therefore may be viewed by customers as representing the company itself. In contrast, for consumer-product companies that sell through intermediaries, consumers usually do not meet salespeople or even know about them. The sales force works behind the scenes, dealing with wholesalers and retailers to obtain their support and helping them become effective in selling the firm's products.

As an element of the promotion mix, the sales force is very effective in achieving certain marketing objectives and carrying out such activities as prospecting, communicating, selling and servicing, and information gathering. But with companies becoming more market oriented, a customer-focused sales force also works to produce both *customer satisfaction* and *company profit*. The sales force plays a key role in developing and managing profitable *customer relationships*.

2. **Identify and explain the six major sales force management steps and the role of sales force automation.**

High sales force costs necessitate an effective sales management process consisting of six steps: designing sales force strategy and structure, recruiting and selecting, training, compensating, supervising, and evaluating salespeople and sales force performance. In designing a sales force, sales management must address strategy issues such as what type of sales force structure will work best (*territorial*, *product*, *customer*, or *complex* structure), how large the sales force should be, who will be involved in the selling effort, and how its various salespeople and sales-support people will work together (inside or outside sales forces and team selling).

In recruiting salespeople, a company may look to job duties and the characteristics of its most successful salespeople to suggest the traits it wants in its salespeople. After the selection process is complete, training programs familiarize new salespeople not only with the art of selling but also with the company's history, its products and policies, and the characteristics of its market and competitors. The sales force compensation system helps to reward, motivate, and direct salespeople. In addition to compensation, all salespeople need supervision, and periodically, the company must evaluate their performance to help them do a better job. Many firms today use *sales force automation systems* to aid in the management of the sales force. Sales force automation includes technologies such as laptops, smartphones and other personal digital devices, wireless Internet, webcams for videoconferencing, and customer-contact and relationship management software.

3. **Discuss the personal selling process, distinguishing between transaction-oriented marketing and relationship marketing.**

The art of selling involves a seven-step selling process: *prospecting* and *qualifying*, *preapproach*, *approach*, *presentation* and *demonstration*, *handling objections*, *closing*, and *follow-up*. These steps help marketers to close a specific sale and as such are transaction oriented. However, a seller's dealings with customers should be guided by the larger concept of relationship marketing. The company's sales force should help to orchestrate a whole-company effort to develop profitable long-term relationships with key customers based on superior customer value and satisfaction.

4. **Define sales promotion and list the major consumer sales promotion tools.**

Sales promotions are short-term incentives designed to encourage the purchase or sale of a product or a service. Sales promotions encourage consumers to act now, rather than wait until later to purchase, by providing the consumer with an incentive. However, the most effective sales promotions also aim to build relationships with consumers. Sales promotion campaigns call for setting sales promotions objectives. The marketer must decide on the *size* of the incentive. A certain minimum incentive is necessary if the promotion is to succeed; a larger incentive will produce more sales response. The marketer also must set *conditions for participation*. Incentives might be offered to everyone or only to select groups. Marketers must decide how to *promote and distribute the promotion* program itself. Each distribution method involves a different level of reach and cost.

The major tools of consumer sales promotions are coupons, refunds, premiums, point-of-purchase promotions, contests, sweepstakes, and events.

5. Distinguish between consumer and trade promotions.

Trade promotions are incentives offered to retailers, distributors, or sales agents in order to encourage them to promote immediate sales. The major *trade promotion tools* are discounts, allowances, free goods, and push money. *Business promotions* are sales promotion tools used to generate business leads, stimulate purchases, reward customers, and motivate salespeople, using tools such as conventions, trade shows, and sales contests.

KEY TERMS

Approach   505
Business promotions   515
Closing   507
Consumer promotions   512
Customer (or market) sales force
   structure   496
Event marketing   514
Follow-up   507
Handling objections   507

Inside sales force   498
Outside sales force (or field sales
   force)   498
Personal selling   491
Preapproach   505
Presentation   505
Product sales force structure   496
Prospecting   504
Sales force management   495

Sales promotion   508
Sales quota   502
Salesperson   492
Selling process   504
Team selling   498
Territorial sales force structure   496
Trade promotions   515

TALK ABOUT MARKETING

1. For what kinds of products and services, and what kind of situations, is personal selling a more effective marketing communications tool than advertising?

2. Cellphone companies such as Rogers, Bell, and TELUS have both inside and outside sales forces. List all the tasks that each performs. Where might you encounter these sales forces as a consumer?

3. If you've ever worked in retail, you know something about personal selling. Which of the seven steps in the personal selling process do you think is the most difficult? Which step is the most critical to successful selling?

4. Sales promotions are sometimes used to encourage use of seasonal facilities (sports arenas, ski hills, amusement parks, etc.) during the off-season. Choose a seasonal facility near you that is currently in the off-season. Visit the facility's website. Are there any offers designed to encourage immediate purchase during the off-season?

5. Which of the sales promotion tools described in the chapter would be best for stimulating sales of the following products or services? (a) a dry cleaner wanting to emphasize low prices on washed and pressed dress shirts, (b) Gummy Bears new black cherry flavour, (c) Procter & Gamble's efforts to bundle laundry detergent and fabric softener together in a combined marketing effort, and (d) a company that wants its customers to aid in developing a new jingle.

6. Sales promotions frequently include an online and an offline component. If you were designing a sales promotion for your favourite car brand, how would you use Facebook, Twitter, or other social media tools to engage your target market and provide them with an incentive to purchase your cars?

THINK LIKE A MARKETING MANAGER

After riding high for so many years, Starbucks's steamy-hot growth has gone cold. The coffee house's sales, profits, and stock price have plummeted, resulting in layoffs and store closures. Much of the blame goes to increased consumer frugality brought on by tough economic times. Newly intensified competition hasn't helped Starbucks either, especially from companies now selling premium brews at much lower prices. Starbucks has tried various tactics to convince customers that its products offer high value for the price. It has also tenaciously avoided reducing prices, doing everything possible to maintain its premium image. Instead, Starbucks is putting efforts into things like its Starbucks Card Rewards, a major sales promotion initiative designed to generate customer loyalty. The rewards program offers incentives such as free add-ins to coffee drinks, free in-store refills on drip coffee, complimentary in-store Wi-Fi, and free coffee with the purchase of a pound of coffee beans. The company hopes that such incentives will entice customers to visit more often and to spend more when they visit. Starbucks asserts that, as it gains experience in using the program to gather customer information and track customer purchases, Starbucks Card Rewards will become more effective in achieving its goals.

QUESTIONS

1. Find out what other forms of marketing communications Starbucks uses in Canada and the United States. Does it advertise? Use public relations? What about social media? Is the Starbucks loyalty card program well integrated with these other forms of marketing communications?
2. Starbucks's baristas are sales representatives. What other forms of personal selling does—or could—Starbucks use?
3. Does the Starbucks Card Rewards program go far enough in providing incentives to increase customer spending in the wake of the economic downturn? What else could Starbucks do with the program?
4. What other forms of sales promotion could Starbucks use that might provide a sufficient incentive to increase sales, yet stay true to its premium brand image?

MARKETING ETHICS

Free samples, gifts, expensive trips, dinners, and entertainment—these tools have been, and sometimes still are, widely used by pharmaceutical companies to influence doctors' prescribing behaviour. Physicians control the majority of healthcare expenditures through the prescriptions they write. Although direct-to-consumer advertising is common in the United States, it is heavily restricted in Canada, and so most promotion of new and branded drugs is done through pharmaceutical sales representatives who vie for healthcare professionals' attention to pitch their drugs. Research has shown that pharmaceutical company marketing tactics do influence physicians, causing them to prescribe more-expensive drugs over less-expensive alternatives. Critics claim that such tactics are unethical. However, the pharmaceutical companies claim that their sales representatives keep healthcare professionals well informed in this rapidly changing industry.

QUESTIONS

1. Is it ethical for pharmaceutical sales representatives to influence physician prescribing behaviour through the use of free samples and promotional gifts?
2. National and international pharmaceuticals trade associations publish codes of conduct regarding interactions with healthcare professionals. Visit the websites of the International Federation of Pharmaceutical Manufacturers Association (IFPMA). Examine their codes of ethics regarding sales activities. Write a brief report of what you learn.

MARKETING TECHNOLOGY

Want to improve your business's operations? Hold a contest and get some of the best and brightest minds in the world working on it! That's what Netflix did. Netflix, the DVD rental company, held a three-year, $1 million contest with the goal of improving its movie-recommendation system by 10 percent. The company wanted to improve its system for predicting what customers might like to rent based on their ratings of previous movies rented. The contest garnered more than 51 000 contestants from almost 200 countries. The contest attracted entries from scientists, researchers, and engineers, and the winning team consisted of one-time competitors who joined forces to submit the best solution within a few minutes of the contest's deadline. Netflix is not done with contests, though. The sequel—Netflix Prize 2—aims to improve the movie-recommendation system for Netflix customers who do not regularly rate movies on Netflix.

QUESTIONS

1. When marketers organize contests as sales promotions, one of the goals is to conduct market research—to better understand customers in order to better serve them. Make a list of all the data Netflix would have collected during this contest (e.g., names, ages). The data can be converted into statistics and percentages by using a computer, but it takes a human being to analyze the results and make decisions based on them. What do you think you might be able to learn from the data gathered from this contest? How might you use that analysis to make improvements to the Netflix service?

2. Other than collecting data, what benefits would Netflix gain by running this contest? What were the benefits to the Netflix customer?

MARKETING BY THE NUMBERS

Salespeople do more than just sell products and services—they manage relationships with customers to deliver value to both the customer and their company. Companies must ensure that they have enough salespeople to do the job.

QUESTIONS

1. Refer to Appendix 3, Marketing by the Numbers, to determine the number of salespeople a company needs if it has 3000 customers who must be called on 10 times per year. Each sales call lasts approximately two and a half hours, and each sales rep has approximately 1250 hours per year to devote to customers.

2. If each sales representative earns a salary of $60 000 per year, what sales are necessary to break even on sales force costs if the company has a contribution margin of 40 percent? What effect will adding each additional sales rep have on the break-even sales?

END-OF-CHAPTER CASE

PROCTER & GAMBLE: SELLING THROUGH CUSTOMER BUSINESS DEVELOPMENT

It seems that when it comes to personal selling, the term *win–win* gets thrown around so much that it has become a cliché. But, at Procter & Gamble, the sales concept that the company benefits only as much as the customer benefits is a way of life. Since William Procter and James Gamble formed a family-operated soap and candle company in 1837, P&G has understood that if the customer doesn't do well, neither will the company.

That's why even though P&G boasts a massive sales force of more than 12 000 employees worldwide, P&G people rarely utter the term *sales*. At P&G, it's called *customer business development*, or CBD. The title alone pretty much says it all. Rather than just selling detergent or toothpaste, P&G's philosophy is to grow its own business by growing the business of its customers. In this case, customers are the thousands of retailers and wholesalers that distribute P&G's brands throughout the world. P&G isn't just a supplier, it's a strategic business partner with its customers. "We depend on them as much as they depend on us," says Jeff Weedman, a CBD manager.

THE CORE COMPETENCY OF CUSTOMER BUSINESS DEVELOPMENT

As the big-box retailers get bigger and bigger, they also grow more complex. Take companies such as Wal-Mart or Loblaw Companies Limited. How can a vendor like P&G ever fully understand such a customer? These complex organizations have so many arms and legs that it becomes nearly impossible to get a full grasp of their operations and needs.

To deal with such customer complexities, P&G organizes its sales representatives into customer business development teams. Rather than assigning reps to specific geographic regions or products, it assigns each CBD team to a P&G customer. For the company's biggest customer, Wal-Mart (which accounts for a massive 20 percent of all P&G sales), the CBD team consists of some 350 employees. For smaller customers, the CBD team may have as few as 30 employees. Regardless of the team's size, the strength of the CBD concept derives from the fact that each team, in and of itself, is a complete customer service unit, containing at least one support specialist for every important business function. In addition to a general CBD manager and several sales account executives (each responsible for a specific category of P&G products), each CBD team includes a marketing strategy, operations, information systems, logistics, finance, and human resources specialist. This multi-functional structure enables each team to meet the multiple and vast needs of its customer, whether the needs revolve around those of a chief financial officer or an entire IT department.

A real strength of the CBD teams is that team members function as a collaborative whole rather than as individuals performing their own tasks in isolation. Team members share information, organizational capabilities, and technologies. "I have all the resources I need right here," says Amy Fuschino, a health care and cosmetics account executive. "If I need to, I can go right down the hall and talk with someone in marketing about doing some kind of promotional deal. It's that simple."

But the multi-functional nature of the CBD team also means that collaboration extends far beyond internal interactions. Each time a CBD team member contacts the customer, he or she represents the entire team. For example, if during a customer call a CBD account executive receives a question about a promotional, logistical, or financial matter, the account executive acts as the liaison with the appropriate CBD specialist. So although each CBD member doesn't have specialized knowledge in every area, the CBD team as a unit does.

Competitors have attempted to implement some aspects of P&G's multi-functional approach. However, P&G pioneered the CBD structure. And it has built in some unique characteristics that have allowed it to leverage more power from its team structure than its rivals can.

THE TRUE ADVANTAGE

For starters, P&G's CBD structure is broader and more comprehensive, making it more multi-functional than similar team structures employed by other companies. But perhaps most important, P&G's structure is designed to accomplish four key objectives that are referred to internally as the "core work" of CBD:

- ☐ Align Strategy—to create opportunities for both P&G and the customer to benefit by collaborating in strategy development
- ☐ Create Demand—to build profitable sales volume for P&G and the customer through consumer value and shopper satisfaction
- ☐ Optimize Supply—to maximize the efficiency of the supply chain from P&G to the point of purchase to optimize cost and responsiveness
- ☐ Enable the Organization—to develop capabilities to maximize business results by creating the capacity for frequent breakthrough

More than just corporate catchphrases jotted down in an employee handbook, for CBD employees, these are words to live by. P&G trains sales employees in methods of achieving each objective and evaluates their effectiveness in meeting the objectives.

In fact, the CBD concept came about through the recognition that to develop true win–win relationships with each customer, P&G would need to accomplish the first objective. According to Bill Warren, a CBD senior account executive, "The true competitive advantage is achieved by taking a multifunctional approach from basic selling to strategic customer collaboration!"

Strategic collaboration starts with annual joint business planning. Both the P&G team and the customer come to the table focused on the most important thing: How can each best provide value for the final consumer? The team and customer give much attention during this planning phase to how products can best be presented and placed in the retail setting. This is because P&G and its customers know that the end consumer assesses value within the first three to seven seconds of seeing that product on the shelf. At P&G, this is known as "winning the first moment of truth." If customers quickly perceive that a product will meet their needs, they will likely purchase it.

CBD team members are very good at demonstrating to the retailer that the best way to win the first moment of truth is most often with a P&G product. But P&G is so committed to the principle of developing the customer's business as a means of developing its own, it is open to the possibility that the best way to serve the customer may be through a competitor's product. The CBD team's primary goal is to help the customer win in each product category. Sometimes, analysis shows that the best solution for the customer is "the other guy's product." For P&G, that's okay. P&G knows that creating the best situation for the retailer ultimately brings in more customer traffic, which in turn will likely result in increased sales for other P&G products in the same category. Because most of P&G's brands are market leaders, it stands to benefit more from the increased traffic than competitors. Again, it's a win–win situation. This type of honesty also helps build trust and strengthen the company–customer relationship.

The collaborative efforts between P&G and each of its customers do not involve only planning and the sharing of information. They may also involve co-operative efforts to share the costs of different activities. "We'll help customers run these commercials or do those merchandising events, but there has to be a return on investment," explains Amy Fuschino. "Maybe it's helping us with a new distribution or increasing space for fabric care. We're very willing if the effort creates value for us in addition to creating value for the customer and the consumer."

An example of such a joint effort is the recent rollout of PRISM. P&G partnered with Wal-Mart to implement this system of infrared sensors that counts the number of times shoppers are exposed to product displays, banners, and video monitors. The goal with PRISM is to improve the effectiveness of in-store marketing, making consumers more aware of the value provided by P&G's products.

If the CBD team can effectively accomplish the first objective of aligning strategy and collaborating on strategic development, accomplishing the other three objectives will follow more easily. For example, if strategic planning leads to winning the first moment of truth, not only does the consumer benefit, but both the retailer and P&G achieve higher revenues and profits as well. Through proper strategic planning it is also more likely that both P&G and the customer will create greater efficiencies in the supply chain.

IT'S BETTER TO GIVE ... THAN TO RECEIVE

As a result of collaborating with customers, P&G receives as much as or more than it gives. Among other things, P&G receives information that helps in achieving the fourth CBD objective: enabling the organization to achieve innovation. Where the R&D process is concerned, this means creating better products. This objective is one reason why, at the 2007 Product of the Year Awards held in London, P&G cleaned up, winning 10 of the 32 categories and taking home a special prize for "most innovative company." P&G's dominance in innovation is not a one-time fluke. Gianni Ciserani, vice-president and managing director of P&G UK & Ireland, claims that some of P&G's strongest innovations are yet to come. "We have shared this portfolio with the key retailers and got strong collaboration on how we can drive these ideas forward."

In the five years leading up to 2008, P&G's profits doubled, revenues nearly doubled, and stock price increased by more than 50 percent. Not only is P&G the world's largest consumer products firm with US$76 billion in revenues, it ranks 23rd among all U.S. companies in the most recent *Fortune* 500 ranking. P&G manages a whopping 23 brands that each bring in over US$1 billion every year. Last year, Pampers sales exceeded US$7 billion, a figure that would have placed the leading diaper brand all by itself as number 350 on *Fortune*'s prestigious list.

Many factors have contributed to P&G's growth and success. But the role that CBD plays can't be overestimated. And as P&G moves forward, Jeff Weedman's words that "We depend on them as much as they depend on us" ring ever truer. As P&G's megacustomers grow in size and power, developing P&G's business means first developing its customers' business. And the CBD sales organization lies at the heart of that effort.

Sources: Officials at Procter & Gamble contributed to and supported the development of this case; other information from www.pg.com, accessed July 2008. See also Craig Smith, "P&G Tops List for Innovation," *Marketing*, January 31, 2007, p. 6; and "Will She, Won't She?—Procter & Gamble," *Economist* at www.economist.com, accessed August 2007.

QUESTIONS

1. Which of the sales force structures discussed in the text best describes P&G's CBD structure?

2. From the perspective of team selling, discuss the positive as well as some possible negative aspects to the customer business development sales organization.

3. Visit www.mypgcareer.com, and click on the Customer Business Development link at the bottom of the page to learn more about the P&G CBD organization. Based on information from this website and on information in this case, discuss the importance of recruiting, training, and compensation in making the CBD structure more effective.

4. Discuss some ways that the CBD structure may be more effective than a single sales rep for each step in the personal-selling process.

5. It seems that P&G has the most-effective sales force structure of any company in its industry. Why have competitors not been able to match it?

AFTER STUDYING THIS CHAPTER, YOU SHOULD BE ABLE TO

 define direct marketing and discuss its benefits to customers and companies

 explain the use of a database in direct marketing

 identify and discuss the major forms of direct marketing

 explain how companies have responded to the Internet and other new technologies with online marketing strategies

discuss how companies go about conducting online marketing to profitably deliver more value to customers

Direct and Online Marketing

PREVIEWING THE CONCEPTS

In the previous two chapters, you learned about communicating customer value through integrated marketing communication (IMC) and about four specific elements of the marketing communications mix—advertising, publicity, personal selling, and sales promotion. In this chapter, we'll look at the final IMC element, direct marketing, and at its fastest-growing form, online marketing. Actually, direct marketing can be viewed as more than just a communications tool. In many ways it constitutes an overall marketing approach—a blend of communication and distribution channels all rolled into one. As you read on, remember that although this chapter examines direct marketing as a separate tool, it must be carefully integrated with other elements of the promotion mix.

For starters, let's look at Amazon.com. In 15 years, Amazon.com has blossomed from an obscure dot-com upstart into one of the best-known names on the Internet. According to one estimate, 52 percent of people who shopped the Internet last year started at Amazon.com. How has Amazon.com become such an incredibly successful direct and online marketer in such a short time? It's all about creating direct, personal, satisfying customer experiences. Few direct marketers do that as well as Amazon.com.

AMAZON.COM: WHERE DIRECT AND ONLINE MARKETING MEET

When you think of shopping on the Web, chances are good that you think first of Amazon.com. Amazon.com first opened its virtual doors in 1995, selling books out of founder Jeff Bezos's garage in suburban Seattle. The online pioneer still sells books—*lots and lots* of books. But now its U.S. site sells just about everything else as well, from music, videos, electronics, tools, housewares, apparel, shoes, groceries, and kids' products to loose diamonds and Maine lobsters. And it's no longer just Amazon.com (United States); it's Amazon.ca (Canada), Amazon.co.uk (United Kingdom), Amazon.co.jp (Japan), Amazon.de (Germany), Amazon.fr (France), and Amazon.cn (China). "We have the Earth's Biggest Selection," declares the company's website, and 50 percent of Amazon.com's sales come from outside the United States.

In only a decade and a half, Amazon.com has become one of the best-known names on the Web. In perfecting the art of online selling, it has also rewritten the rules of marketing. Many analysts view Amazon.com as *the* model for businesses in the digital age.

From the start, Amazon.com has grown explosively. Its annual sales have rocketed from a modest $150 million in 1997 to more than $19 *billion* today. In only the past five years its sales have more than tripled. Although it took Amazon.com eight years to turn its first full-year profit in 2003, profits have since surged more than 18-fold. Last year alone, sales grew 29 percent; profits popped 36 percent. This past holiday season, the online store's more than 88 million active customers purchased 72.9 items per second on its site. One study estimates that 52 percent of all consumers who went to the Internet to shop last year started at Amazon.com.

What has made Amazon.com one of the world's premier direct marketers? To its core, the company is relentlessly customer driven. "The thing that drives everything is creating genuine value for customers," says founder Jeff Bezos. "If you focus on what customers want and build a relationship, they will allow you to make money." In one promotion in Japan, for example, Bezos donned a delivery driver's uniform and went house to house with packages. His point: Everything at Amazon—from top to bottom—begins and ends with the customer.

Anyone at Amazon.com will tell you that the company wants to do much more than just sell books or DVDs or digital cameras. It wants to deliver a special *experience* to every customer. "The customer experience really matters," says Bezos. "We've focused on just having a better store, where it's easier to shop, where you can learn more about the products, where you have a bigger selection, and where you have the lowest prices. You combine all of that stuff together and people say, 'Hey, these guys really get it.'"

And customers get it, too. Most Amazon.com regulars feel a surprisingly strong relationship with the company, especially given the almost complete lack of actual human interaction. Amazon.com obsesses over making each customer's experience uniquely personal. For example, the Amazon.com website greets customers with their very own personalized home pages, and the site's "Recommended for you" feature prepares personalized product recommendations. Amazon.com was first to use "collaborative filtering" technology, which sifts through each customer's past purchases and the purchasing patterns of customers with similar profiles to come up with personalized site content. "We want Amazon.com to be the right store for you as an individual," says Bezos. "If we have 88 million customers, we should have 88 million stores."

Visitors to Amazon.com's website receive a unique blend of benefits: huge selection, good value, convenience, and what the company calls "discovery." In books alone, for example, Amazon.com offers an easily searchable virtual selection of more than 3 million titles, 15 times more than in any physical bookstore. Good value comes in the form of reasonable prices, plus free delivery on orders over $25. And at Amazon.com, it's irresistibly convenient to buy. You can log on, find anything and everything you want, and order with a single mouse click, all in less time than it takes to find a parking space at the local mall.

But it's the "discovery" factor that makes the Amazon.com buying experience really special. Once on the website, you're compelled to stay for a while—looking, learning, and discovering. Amazon.com has become a kind of online community, in which customers can browse for products, research purchase alternatives, share opinions and reviews with other visitors, and chat online with authors and experts. In this way, Amazon.com does much more than just sell goods on the Web. It creates direct, personalized customer relationships and satisfying online experiences. Year after year, Amazon.com comes in number one or number two on the American Customer Satisfaction Index, regardless of industry.

In fact, Amazon.com has become so good at managing online relationships that many traditional brick-and-mortar retailers are turning to Amazon for help in adding more "clicks" to their "bricks." For example, Amazon.com now partners with well-known retailers such as Target and Bebe to help them run their Web interfaces. And to create even greater selection and convenience for customers, Amazon.com allows competing retailers—from mom-and-pop operations to Marks & Spencer—to offer their products on its website, creating a virtual shopping mall of incredible proportions. It even encourages customers to sell used items on the site.

Amazon.com is constantly on the lookout for innovative new ways to use the power of the Web and direct marketing to create more shopping selection, value, convenience, and discovery. For example, it started Amazon Prime, a program by which members pay $79 per year and get free two-day shipping on all orders and next-day shipping for $3.99 on any order. Amazon.com now offers music downloading, with the music files not restricted by digital rights management software (DRM), which means that, unlike iTunes, you can freely and conveniently copy the songs. All four major music labels promptly signed on. The Web merchant also launched an Amazon.com application for the iPhone, which allows consumers to shop on the go.

And two years ago, Amazon.com took another bold customer-convenience and personalization step. It introduced the Kindle, a wireless reading device for downloading books, blogs, magazines, newspapers, and other matter. Lighter and thinner than a typical paperback book, the Kindle wireless reader connects like a cellphone, letting customers buy and download content of personal interest—from the *Wall* Street Journal or *Time* magazine to the latest *New York Times* bestsellers—from home or on the go in less than 60 seconds. The Kindle has a paper-like electronic-ink display that's easy to read even in bright daylight. Now available in two models, Kindles are flying off the Web seller's virtual shelves.

So, what do you think? Will Amazon.com become the Wal-Mart of the Web? That remains to be seen. But whatever its fate, the direct and online pioneer has forever changed the face of marketing. Most importantly, Amazon.com has set a very high bar for the online customer experience. "The reason I'm so obsessed with ... the customer experience is that I believe [that our success] has been driven exclusively by that experience," says Jeff Bezos. "We are not great advertisers. So we start with customers, figure out what they want, and figure out how to get it to them."[1]

MANY of the marketing and promotion tools that we've examined in previous chapters were developed in the context of *mass marketing*: targeting broad markets with standardized messages and offers distributed through intermediaries. Today, however, with the trend toward more narrowly targeted marketing, many companies are adopting *direct marketing*, either as a primary marketing approach, as in Amazon.com's case, or as a supplement to other approaches. In this section, we explore the exploding world of direct marketing.

Direct marketing consists of connecting directly with carefully targeted individual consumers to both obtain an immediate response and cultivate lasting customer relationships. Direct marketers communicate directly with customers, often on a one-to-

Direct marketing
Connecting directly with carefully targeted individual consumers to both obtain an immediate response and cultivate lasting customer relationships.

one, interactive basis. By using detailed databases, they tailor their marketing offers and communications to the needs of narrowly defined segments or even individual buyers.

Beyond brand and relationship building, direct marketers usually seek a direct, immediate, and measurable consumer response. For example, as we learned in the chapter-opening story, Amazon.com interacts directly with customers on its website to help them to discover and buy almost anything and everything on the Internet, with only a few clicks of the mouse button. Similarly, Dell interacts directly with customers, by telephone, through its website, on its Facebook page, and through several Twitter accounts to answer customer questions, and give information about special offers.

THE NEW DIRECT MARKETING MODEL

Early direct marketers—catalogue companies, direct mailers, and telemarketers—gathered customer names and sold goods mainly by mail and telephone. Today, however, fired by rapid advances in database technologies and new marketing media—especially the Internet—direct marketing has undergone a dramatic transformation.

In previous chapters, we've discussed direct marketing as direct distribution—as marketing channels that contain no intermediaries. We also include direct marketing as one element of the promotion mix—as an approach for communicating directly with consumers. In actuality, direct marketing is both of these things and more.

Most companies still use direct marketing as a supplementary channel or medium. Thus, Lexus markets mostly through mass-media advertising and its high-quality dealer network but also supplements these channels with direct marketing. Its direct marketing includes promotional DVDs and other materials mailed directly to prospective buyers and a website that provides consumers with information about various models, competitive comparisons, financing, and dealer locations. Similarly, many retailers, in addition to selling merchandise off their store shelves, market their products and services through various direct and online channels. For example, Canadian Tire uses its website to deliver electronic versions of its weekly flyer to consumers who subscribe to receive it, and the Canadian Tire website serves as an online catalogue, allowing consumers to view the details of all its products, then check inventory at their local store. The weekly flyer is also delivered in paper format through other direct channels, such as newspaper inserts and unaddressed direct mail.

Exhibit 14.1 New models of direct marketing: Consumers anywhere in Canada can view the entire catalogue of products on the Canadian Tire website or enter their postal code and view the flyer for their local store.

However, for many companies today, direct marketing is more than just a supplementary channel or advertising medium. For these companies, direct marketing—especially in its most recent transformation, online marketing—constitutes a complete model for doing business. Rather than using direct marketing and the Internet only as supplemental approaches, firms employing this new *direct model* use it as the *only* approach. Companies such as Amazon.com and eBay have built their entire approach to the marketplace around direct marketing. The direct model is rapidly changing the way that companies think about building relationships with customers.

GROWTH AND BENEFITS OF DIRECT MARKETING

Direct marketing has become the fastest-growing form of marketing. According to the Direct Marketing Association (DMA), U.S. companies spent $176.9 billion on direct marketing last year, which is 52 percent of total dollars spent on advertising. In 2008, an investment of $1 in direct marketing advertising expenditures returned, on average, an estimated $11.63 in incremental revenue across all industries. Put another way, these expenditures generated an estimated $2.1 trillion in direct marketing sales, or about 10 percent of total sales in the U.S. economy. The DMA estimates that direct marketing sales will grow 5.3 percent annually through 2013, compared with a projected 4.1 percent annual growth for total U.S. sales.[2] In Canada, direct marketing is an important contributor to the economy. The Canadian Marketing Association (CMA) estimates the sales impact of direct mail will reach $25 billion by 2011.[3]

Direct marketing continues to become more Web-oriented, and Internet marketing is claiming a fast-growing share of direct marketing spending and sales. The Internet now accounts for only about 23 percent of direct marketing–driven sales. However, the DMA predicts that over the next five years, Internet marketing expenditures will grow at a blistering 13 percent a year, about three times faster than expenditures in other direct marketing media. Internet-driven sales will also grow by 13 percent.

Whether employed as a complete business model or as a supplement to a broader integrated marketing mix, direct marketing brings many benefits to both buyers and sellers.

BENEFITS TO BUYERS

For buyers, direct marketing is convenient, easy, and private. Direct marketers never close their doors, and customers don't have to battle traffic, find parking spaces, and trek through stores to find products. From the comfort of their homes and offices they can flip through catalogues and flyers, or browse websites at any time of the day or night. Business buyers can learn about products and services without tying up time with salespeople. Direct marketing gives consumers and business buyers a greater measure of control— they decide which catalogues they will browse and which websites they will visit.

Direct marketing gives buyers ready access to a virtually unlimited assortment of products that would be physically impossible to contain in a brick-and-mortar store. For instance, log onto Bulbs.com, "the Web's number-one light bulb superstore," and you'll have instant access to every imaginable kind of light bulb or lamp—incandescent bulbs, fluorescent bulbs, projection bulbs, surgical bulbs, automotive bulbs— you name it. Similarly, Web shoes and accessories retailer Zappos.com stocks more than 2.7 million shoes, handbags, clothing items, and accessories from more than 1300 brands. No physical store could offer handy access to such vast selections.

Unrestrained by physical boundaries, direct marketers can offer their products to consumers in remote locations who would otherwise be unable to get them. For example, people who live near the Atlantic Ocean are used to having easy access to lobsters, but today, with direct marketing and the Internet, consumers in Kansas and Alberta can order fresh lobsters from the Clearwater Seafoods in Nova Scotia through their website at Clearwater.ca.

Exhibit 14.2 Benefits of direct marketing: Buyers anywhere in Canada and the United States can purchase live lobsters online, directly from Clearwater Seafoods in Nova Scotia.

Direct marketing channels also give buyers access to a wealth of comparative information about companies, products, and competitors. Today, most companies' websites often provide more information in more useful forms than even the most helpful retail salesperson can. For example, the Amazon.com site offers more information than most of us can digest, ranging from top-10 product lists, extensive product descriptions, and expert and user product reviews to recommendations based on customers' previous purchases. And at Volkswagen.com you can choose your country—any country in the world where Volkswagens are available—then build your own virtual car—any model, in any colour, with any available options. That's something no dealership can possibly provide.

Finally, direct marketing is interactive and immediate—buyers can interact with sellers by phone or online, create exactly the configuration of information, products, or services they desire, and then order them on the spot. For example, consumers can watch The Shopping Channel at home and immediately call about any product that interests them, from Tiffany-style lamps to cosmetics. Or, they can visit TSC.ca at any time of the day, and interact with customer-service representatives online.

BENEFITS TO SELLERS

For sellers, direct marketing is a powerful tool for building customer relationships. By using database marketing, today's marketers can target small groups or individual consumers and promote their offers through personalized communications. Because of the one-to-one nature of direct marketing, companies can interact with customers by phone or online, learn more about their needs, and tailor products and services to specific customer tastes. In turn, customers can ask questions and volunteer feedback.

Direct marketing also offers sellers a low-cost, efficient, speedy alternative for reaching their markets. Direct marketing has grown rapidly in business-to-business marketing, partly in response to the ever-increasing costs of marketing through the sales force. When personal sales calls cost an average of more than $400 per contact, they should be made only when necessary and only to high-potential customers and prospects.[4] Lower-cost-per-contact media—such as business-to-business telemarketing, direct mail, and company websites—often prove more cost effective.

Similarly, online direct marketing results in lower costs, improved efficiencies, and speedier handling of channel and logistics functions, such as order processing, inventory handling, and delivery. Direct marketers such as Amazon.com or Netflix also avoid the expense of maintaining a store and the related costs of rent, insurance, and utilities, passing the savings along to customers.

Direct marketing can also offer greater flexibility. It allows marketers to make ongoing adjustments to its prices and programs, or to make immediate, timely, and personal announcements and offers. For example, Heritage Education Funds, a provider of Registered Education Savings Plans (RESPs), used direct marketing to personalize its offerings through a direct mail campaign:[5]

> Every fall, Heritage Education Funds sends direct mail to its approximately 50,000 customers, reminding them to contribute to their child's education fund. In the past, the colourful brochure was personalized only with the name of the recipient's child, but last fall the company challenged its marketing department to improve on the lackluster results of the campaign. In the most recent direct mail brochure, not only was the child's name included but the images in the brochure were customized to reflect the child's age and ethnicity. Printing technology from Xerox allowed Heritage to customize each brochure as it was printed.
>
> "Ethnicity is relevant to our business because the number one reason new immigrants come to Canada is to provide their children with better opportunities," said Heritage's vice

president of marketing. The results were astonishing. Not only did Heritage measure a 76% increase in the number of RESP units sold, but the new piece also convinced clients to increase their monthly payments by, on average, $40.

Finally, direct marketing gives sellers access to buyers that they could not reach through other channels. Smaller firms can mail catalogues to customers outside their local markets and offer toll-free telephone numbers to handle orders and inquiries. Internet marketing is a truly global medium that allows buyers and sellers to click from one country to another in seconds. A Web user from Paris or Istanbul can access an online L.L.Bean catalogue as easily as someone living in Freeport, Maine, the direct retailer's hometown. Even small marketers find that they have ready access to global markets.

CUSTOMER DATABASES AND DIRECT MARKETING L02

Effective direct marketing begins with a good customer database. A **customer database** is an organized collection of comprehensive data about individual customers or prospects, including geographic, demographic, psychographic, and behavioural data. A good customer database can be a potent relationship-building tool. The database gives companies a 360-degree view of their customers and how they behave. A company is no better than what it knows about its customers.

In consumer marketing, the customer database might contain a customer's demographics (age, income, family members, birthdays), psychographics (activities, interests, and opinions), and buying behaviour (buying preferences and the recency, frequency, and monetary value—RFM—of past purchases). In business-to-business marketing, the customer profile might contain the products and services the customer has bought, past volumes and prices, key contacts at the customer's organization (and their ages, birthdays, hobbies, and favourite foods), competing suppliers, status of current contracts, estimated customer spending for the next few years, and assessments of competitive strengths and weaknesses in selling and servicing the account.

Some of these databases are huge. For example, casino operator Harrah's Entertainment has built a customer database containing 700 terabytes worth of customer information. It uses this data to create special customer experiences. Similarly, Wal-Mart captures data on every item, for every customer, for every store, every day. Its database contains more than 2.5 petabytes of data—that's equivalent to 50 million four-drawer filing cabinets full of text. Google processes an astonishing 20 petabytes (one petabyte = 1000 terabytes) of data a day.[6]

Companies use their databases in many ways. They use databases to locate good potential customers and generate sales leads. They can mine their databases to learn about customers in detail, and then fine-tune their market offerings and communications to the special preferences and behaviours of target segments or individuals. In all, a company's database can be an important tool for building stronger long-term customer relationships.

For example, financial services provider USAA uses its database to find ways to serve the long-term needs of customers, regardless of immediate sales impact, creating an incredibly loyal customer base:

> USAA provides financial services to U.S. military personnel and their families, largely through direct marketing via the telephone and Internet. It maintains a customer database built from customer purchasing histories and from information collected directly from customers. To keep the database fresh, the organization regularly surveys its more than 7 million customers worldwide to learn such things as whether they have children (and if so, how old they are), if they have moved recently, and when they plan to retire. USAA uses the database to tailor direct

Customer database
An organized collection of comprehensive data about individual customers or prospects, including geographic, demographic, psychographic, and behavioural data.

Exhibit 14.3   Customer databases: Financial services provider USAA uses its extensive database to tailor its services to the specific needs of individual customers, creating incredible customer loyalty.

marketing offers to the specific needs of individual customers. For example, for customers looking toward retirement, it sends information on estate planning. If the family has college-age children, USAA sends those children information on how to manage their credit cards. If the family has younger children, it sends booklets on things such as financing a child's education.

One delighted reporter, a USAA customer, recounts how USAA even helped him teach his 16-year-old daughter to drive. Just before her birthday, but before she received her driver's license, USAA mailed a "package of materials, backed by research, to help me teach my daughter how to drive, help her practice, and help us find ways to agree on what constitutes safe driving later on, when she gets her license." What's more, marvels the reporter, "USAA didn't try to sell me a thing. My take-away: that USAA is investing in me for the long term, that it defines profitability not just by what it sells today." Through such skillful use of its database, USAA serves each customer uniquely, resulting in high levels of customer loyalty and sales growth. The average customer household owns almost five USAA products, and the $13.4 billion company retains 97 percent of its customers. For four years running, USAA has received the top score of any insurance company in Forrester Research, Inc.'s respected customer advocacy survey. And it ranked number 1 among companies from all industries on last year's MSN Money Customer Service Hall of Fame survey, ahead of such well-regarded companies as Amazon.com, Southwest Airlines, Nordstrom, and Apple.[7]

Like many other marketing tools, database marketing requires a special investment. Companies must invest in computer hardware, database software, analytical programs, communication links, and skilled personnel. The database system must be user-friendly and available to various marketing groups, including those in product and brand management, new-product development, advertising and promotion, direct mail, telemarketing, Web marketing, field sales, order fulfillment, and customer service. However, a well-managed database should lead to sales and customer-relationship gains that will more than cover its costs.

FORMS OF DIRECT MARKETING ●LO3

The major forms of direct marketing—as shown in Figure 14.1—include personal selling, direct-mail marketing, catalogue marketing, telephone marketing, direct-response television marketing, kiosk marketing, new digital direct marketing technologies, and online marketing. We examined personal selling in depth in Chapter 13. Here, we examine the other direct-marketing forms.

DIRECT-MAIL MARKETING

Direct-mail marketing
Direct marketing by sending an offer, announcement, reminder, or other item to a person at a particular physical or virtual address.

Direct-mail marketing involves sending an offer, announcement, reminder, or other item to a person at a particular physical or virtual address. Using highly selective mailing lists, direct marketers send out millions of mail pieces each year—letters, catalogues, ads, brochures, samples, DVDs, and other "salespeople with wings." Direct mail is by far the largest direct marketing medium. The Direct Marketing Association reports that direct mail (including both catalogue and non-catalogue mail) accounts for 34 percent of all U.S. direct marketing spending and drives 29 percent of direct marketing sales, and Canada Post estimates that $1.4 billion of the approximately $24 billion spent on advertising in Canada last year was spent on direct-mail marketing.[8]

Direct mail is well suited to direct, one-to-one communication. It permits high target-market selectivity, can be personalized, is flexible, and allows easy measurement

FIGURE 14.1 Forms of direct marketing

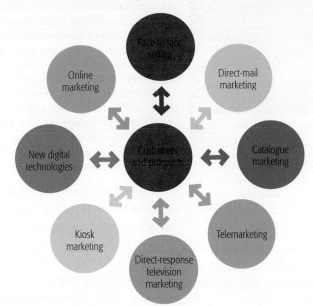

of results. Although direct mail costs more per thousand people reached than mass media such as television or magazines, the people it reaches are much better prospects. Direct mail has proved successful in promoting all kinds of products, from books, music, DVDs, and magazine subscriptions to insurance, gift items, clothing, gourmet foods, and industrial products. Charities also use direct mail heavily to raise billions of dollars each year.

Some analysts predict a decline in the use of traditional forms of direct mail in coming years, as marketers switch to newer digital forms, such as email and mobile (cellphone) marketing. Email, in particular, is booming as a direct marketing tool. Today's new breed of email ads use animation, interactive links, streaming video, and personalized audio messages to reach out and grab attention. Email, mobile, and other newer forms of direct mail deliver direct messages at incredible speeds and lower costs compared with the post office's "snail mail" pace. We will discuss email and mobile marketing in more detail later in the chapter.

However, even though the new digital forms of direct mail are gaining popularity, the traditional form is still by far the most widely used. Mail marketing offers some distinct advantages. "Mail advertising provides a tangible piece to hold and keep," says one analyst. "E-mail is trashed too easily." Says another, "Mail is real, tactile, and shows you care more than a blanket e-mail."[9]

Traditional direct mail and email can be used effectively in combination with other media, such as temporary, personalized websites or microsites. For example, some marketers now send out direct mail featuring personalized URLs (PURLs)—Web addresses such as www.intel.comJohnDoe—that invite intrigued prospects to individualized websites. Consider this example:[10]

For companies that had their heads in the clouds when it came time to upgrade their computers, JDA Software Group decided it was time for some skywriting. It teamed with HP, Intel, and marketing agency The Mahoney Company to send out personalized direct mail pieces that featured a man with his arms spread upward, experiencing an epiphany in the form of fluffy words forming above his head: "Bruce Schwartz, The Moment Has Arrived." In reality, the direct mail piece didn't come from out of the blue. Based on customers' upgrade schedules, JDA targeted carefully selected decision makers who were considering buying $500,000 to $1.5 million software suites. These high-value prospects received personalized

Exhibit 14.4   Direct mail: Combining traditional direct mail with online marketing in the form of personalized URLs (PURLs) cost JDA only $50 000 but yielded a high response rate and $13 million in sales.

direct mailings and e-mails, complete with personalized URLs (PURLs) that led them to individualized Web pages. Once there, prospects learned all about how hardware from HP and Intel would support software from JDA. Customers revealed more information about themselves each time they visited the PURL, which allowed JDA, HP, and Intel to work with them throughout the buying process. The result? The $50,000 campaign yielded a 9.2 percent response rate and $13 million in sales. "Sending specific [information] to specific people does make a huge difference," says Intel's strategic relationships manager.

Direct mail, whether traditional or digital may be resented as junk mail or spam if sent to people who are not carefully selected. For this reason, smart marketers are targeting their direct mail carefully—usually to existing customers or prospects, or interested consumers who have requested information through the company's website—so as not to waste their money and the recipients' time. They are designing permission-based programs, sending email and mobile ads only to those who want to receive them.

CATALOGUE MARKETING

Catalogue marketing

Direct marketing through print, video, or digital catalogues that are mailed to select customers, made available in stores, or presented online.

Advances in technology, along with the move toward personalized, one-to-one marketing have resulted in exciting changes in **catalogue marketing**. *Catalog Age* magazine used to define a *catalogue* as "a printed, bound piece of at least eight pages, selling multiple products, and offering a direct ordering mechanism." Today, only a few years later, this definition is sadly out of date.

In the age of the Internet, more and more catalogues are going digital. A variety of Web-only cataloguers have emerged, and most print cataloguers have added Web-based catalogues to their marketing mixes. For example, Mountain Equipment Co-op, the famous Canadian camping and sporting gear supplier, has an e-catalogue but also offers its clients the option of ordering a printed catalogue. Online catalogues eliminate production, printing, and mailing costs, and whereas print-catalogue space is limited, online catalogues can offer an almost unlimited amount of merchandise. Finally, online catalogues allow real-time merchandising—products and features can be added or removed as needed and prices can be adjusted instantly to match demand.

However, despite the advantages of online catalogues, printed catalogues are still thriving. Why aren't companies ditching their old-fashioned paper catalogues in this new digital era? It turns out that printed catalogues are one of the best ways to drive online sales. "Our catalogue is itself an advertising vehicle, and it is an effective way to drive traffic to our Web site," says an L.L.Bean marketer. A recent study found that 70 percent of Web purchases are driven by catalogues. Even online-only retailers, such as eBay and UncommonGoods, have started producing catalogues in the hopes of driving online sales. The retailers said that 13 percent of new online customers in one year resulted from catalogue mailings, and about 43 percent of catalogue customers also buy online.[11]

In addition, paper catalogues can create emotional connections with customers that Web-based sales spaces simply can't. For example, Sears recently brought back its holiday

Wish Book after a 14-year hiatus. According to Sears' chief marketing officer, many customers were nostalgic for the catalogue, reminiscing about the days when they would fold over pages and hope that Santa would notice.[12]

In all, catalogue marketing—printed and online—has grown explosively during the past 25 years. According to one study, there are 8000 to 10 000 unique catalogue titles in the United States that collectively send out over 19 billion catalogues a year, 6 million more than a decade ago. Annual catalogue sales in the United States amounted to about $155 billion last year and are expected to top $182 billion by 2013.[13]

These days, consumers can buy just about anything from a catalogue. Each year Lillian Vernon sends out 17 editions of its three catalogues with total circulation of 80 million copies to its 20-million-person database, selling more than 700 products in each catalogue, ranging from shoes to decorative lawn birds and monogrammed oven mitts.[14] High-end American department stores, such as Neiman Marcus, Bloomingdale's, and Saks Fifth Avenue, use catalogues to c ultivate upper-middle-class markets for high-priced, often exotic, merchandise. Want Jack Nicklaus to design a three-hole golf course for your backyard? It was featured in a Neiman Marcus Christmas catalogue for only $1 million (not including construction and site preparation costs).

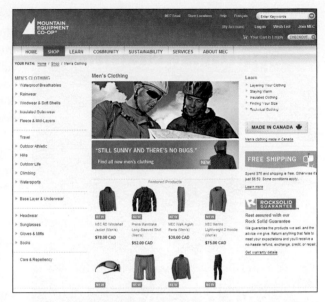

Exhibit 14.5 Catalogue marketing: Most retailers who once sold merchandise via printed catalogues have long since moved their catalogues online. Some companies, such as Mountain Equipment Co-op, still offer their customers the option of receiving a printed catalogue.

TELEPHONE MARKETING

Telephone marketing, or telemarketing, involves using the telephone to sell directly to consumers and business customers. Telephone marketing now accounts for more than 17 percent of all direct marketing–driven sales. We're all familiar with telephone marketing directed toward consumers, but business-to-business marketers also use telephone marketing extensively, accounting for more than 56 percent of all telephone marketing sales.[15]

Marketers use *outbound* telemarketing to sell directly to consumers and businesses. They use *inbound* toll-free 800 numbers to receive orders from television and print ads, direct mail, or catalogues. The use of 800 numbers has taken off in recent years as more and more companies have begun using them, and as current users have added new features such as toll-free fax numbers. To accommodate this rapid growth, new toll-free area codes, such as 888, 877, and 866, have been added.

Properly designed and targeted telemarketing provides many benefits, including purchasing convenience and increased product and service information. However, the explosion in unsolicited outbound telephone marketing over the years annoyed many consumers, who objected to the almost daily "junk phone calls" that pulled them away from the dinner table or filled the answering machine.

In Canada, telephone marketing is controlled by a National Do Not Call List. Canadian consumers can reduce the number of telemarketing calls they receive by registering their residential, wireless, fax, or VoIP telephone number through the website at DNCL.gc.ca. The website is maintained by the CRTC, the Canadian Radio-television and Telecommunications Commission, and it also provides online forms for consumers to register complaints against telemarketers. Canadian marketers must register with the National DNCL, and are required by law to periodically verify that any consumer on the DNCL list is removed from their telemarketing database. Marketers who violate the rules

Careful...you might sprain a taste bud.

Don't wait another day! Call now to place an order or request a catalog. Also, go on line at **www.carolinacookie.com** to place an order, request a catalog or view our entire selection of products.

1-800-447-5797

CAROLINA COOKIE
JUST BAKED
COMPANY

Exhibit 14.6   Telephone marketing: Marketers use inbound toll-free 800 numbers to receive orders from television and print ads, direct mail, or catalogues. Here, the Carolina Cookie Company boldly displays its toll-free number and urges customers to call.

are investigated by the CRTC and can face fines of up to $15 000 per violation. And even when marketers abide by the DNCL rules, they must follow certain procedures when making legal telemarketing calls. For example, at the beginning of a call telemarketers must tell you why they're calling, they must identify on whose behalf the call is being made, and calls may be made only within certain calling hours.

Do-not-call legislation has changed telemarketing for the better—it's easier for consumers to judge the legitimacy of the organizations that call them, and marketers are better able to reach and communicate with prospective customers who are interested in their services. Two major forms of telemarketing—inbound consumer telemarketing and outbound business-to-business telemarketing—remain strong and growing. Telemarketing also remains a major fundraising tool for non-profit and political groups. However, many telemarketers are shifting to alternative methods for capturing new customers and sales, from direct mail, direct-response TV, and live-chat Web technology to sweepstakes that prompt customers to call in.

For example, ServiceMaster's TruGreen lawn-care service used to generate about 90 percent of its sales through telemarketing. It now uses more direct mail, as well as having employees go door-to-door in neighbourhoods where it already has customers. The new approach appears to be working even better than the old cold-calling one. The company's sales have grown under the new methods, and less than 50 percent of sales come from telemarketing. "We were nervous, but were thrilled with what we've accomplished," says ServiceMaster's chief executive.[16]

In fact, do-not-call appears to be helping most direct marketers more than it's hurting them. Many are shifting their call-centre activity from making cold calls on often resentful customers to managing existing customer relationships. They are developing "opt-in" calling systems, in which they provide useful information and offers to customers who have invited the company to contact them by phone or email. These "sales tactics have [produced] results as good—or even better—than telemarketing," declares one analyst. "The opt-in model is proving [more] valuable for marketers [than] the old invasive one."[17]

Meanwhile, marketers who violate do-not-call regulations have themselves increasingly become the targets of crusading consumer activist groups, who return the favour by flooding the violating company's phone system with return calls and messages.[18]

DIRECT-RESPONSE TELEVISION MARKETING

Direct-response television marketing
Direct marketing via television, including direct-response television advertising (or infomercials) and home shopping channels.

Direct-response television marketing takes one of two major forms. The first is *direct-response television advertising* (DRTV). Direct marketers air television spots, often 60 or 120 seconds long, which persuasively describe a product and give customers a toll-free number or website for ordering. Television viewers also often encounter full 30-minute or longer advertising programs, or *infomercials*, for a single product.

Successful direct-response television campaigns can ring up big sales. For example, Bowflex has grossed more than $1.3 billion in infomercial sales. And little-known infomercial maker Guthy-Renker has helped to propel Proactiv Solution acne treatment into a power brand that pulls in $850 million in sales annually to 5 million active customers. Proactiv's incredible success derives from powerful, formulaic infomercials in which celebrities and average Joes gush about how Proactiv cleared their skin. "My skin is now clear and beautiful," says Serena Williams. "Yours can be too!"[19]

DRTV ads are most often associated with somewhat loud or questionable pitches for cleaners and stain removers, kitchen gadgets, and nifty ways to stay in shape without working very hard at it. For example, over the past few years yell-and-sell TV pitchmen such as Anthony Sullivan (Swivel Sweeper, Awesome Auger) and smooth-talking peddlers such as Vince Offer (ShamWow chamois cloths) have racked up billions of dollars in sales of "as seen on TV" products. Brands such as OxiClean, ShamWow, and the Snuggie (a blanket with sleeves), have become DRTV cult classics.[20]

In recent years, however, a number of large companies—from P&G, Dell, Sears, Disney, Bose, Ford, and Revlon to Apple, Coca-Cola, and Anheuser-Busch— have begun using infomercials to sell their wares, refer customers to retailers, send out product information,

Exhibit 14.7   Direct-response TV advertising: The Snuggie, a fuzzy blanket with sleeves, became a huge success through direct-response advertising. Happy Snuggie owners held parties in bars and picnics in parks, and participants came dressed in their favourite Snuggie.

recruit members, or attract buyers to their websites. For example, Coca-Cola has used DRTV to promote its "My Coke Rewards" program. An estimated 20 percent of all new infomercials now come to you courtesy of *Fortune* 1000 companies.[21]

The recent trend toward consumer bargain-hunting has given DRTV a boost. Whereas overall advertising spending fell 2009, DRTV spending increased by more than 9 percent. Moreover, unlike most media campaigns, direct-response ads always include a 1-800 number, Web address, or SMS number (Short Message Service number for mobile phones), making it easier for marketers to track the impact of their pitches. "In a business environment where marketers are obsessed with return on investment," notes one expert, "direct response is tailor-made—[marketers can] track phone calls and Web-site hits generated by the ads. [They can] use DRTV to build brand awareness while simultaneously generating leads and sales."[22]

Home shopping channels such as The Shopping Channel in Canada, and QVC and HSN in the United States, are another form of direct-response television marketing. These television channels tend to be perceived as cheesy, but make no mistake—they are highly sophisticated, very successful marketing operations. Long gone are the days of the Ginsu knives. Today's shopping channels feature Lexmark printers, Dell and HP computers, high-end DeLonghi coffee machines, and fashion brands such as Bugatti, Roots, Marc Jacobs, and Diesel.

Want to learn how to whip up chef Wolfgang Puck's soy-steamed salmon fillets with shiitakes and brown rice? Check out the two-minute video on HSN.com and TSC.ca, where Puck prepares it by using his 5-Cup Rice Cooker. The appliance sells for $49.93 through TSC's round-the-clock TV channel and Web outlet. "You don't have to turn your oven on," coos Puck in the Web demonstration. What is notable on both media is the new, toned-down approach to infomercials. Abandoning the yell-and-sell it helped pioneer 31 years ago, HSN now has hosts not so pushy and goods not so schlocky. HSN has replaced the cheesy baubles and generic electronics once featured on HSN with mainstream brands such as Sephora cosmetics and 7 For All Mankind jeans. Celebrities and entrepreneurs, including Puck, interior designer Colin Cowie, and Joy Mangano, inventor of HSN's curiously popular Huggable Hangers, often get as much airtime as HSN's TV and Web hosts. They chit-chat with shoppers who call in to rave about products—the effervescent Mangano often refers to callers as "my darling"—more often

Exhibit 14.8   Kiosk marketing: Redbox operates more than 15 000 DVD rental kiosks in supermarkets and fast-food outlets in the United States.

than they push merchandise. HSN wants to be its female audience's "best girlfriend" says HSN's CEO: "It's not just a transactional relationship. It becomes an emotional relationship."[23]

KIOSK MARKETING

As consumers become more and more comfortable with computer and digital technologies, many companies are placing information and ordering machines—called *kiosks* (in contrast to vending machines, which dispense actual products)—in stores, airports, and other locations. Kiosks are popping up everywhere these days, from self-service hotel and airline check-in devices to in-store ordering kiosks that let you order merchandise not carried in the store.

In-store Kodak, Fuji, and HP kiosks let customers transfer pictures from memory sticks, mobile phones, and other digital storage devices, edit them, and make high-quality colour prints. Kiosks in Hilton hotel lobbies let guests view their reservations, get room keys, view pre-arrival messages, check in and out, and even change seat assignments and print boarding passes for flights on any of 18 airlines. At JetBlue's Terminal Five at New York's JFK airport, more than 200 screens throughout the terminal allow travellers to order food and beverages to be delivered to their gate. And Redbox operates more than 15 000 DVD rental kiosks in McDonald's, Wal-Marts, Walgreens drug stores, and other retail outlets in the United States. Customers make their selections on a touch screen, and then swipe a credit or debit card to rent DVDs at $1 a day. Customers can even pre-reserve DVDs online to ensure that their trip to the kiosk will not be a wasted one.[24]

Business marketers also use kiosks. For example, Dow Plastics places kiosks at trade shows to collect sales leads and provide information on its 700 products. The kiosk system reads customer data from encoded registration badges and produces technical data sheets that can be printed at the kiosk or faxed or mailed to the customer. The system has resulted in a 400 percent increase in qualified sales leads.[25]

NEW DIGITAL DIRECT MARKETING TECHNOLOGIES **LO4**

Today, thanks to a wealth of new digital technologies, direct marketers can reach and interact with consumers just about anywhere, at anytime, about almost anything. Here, we look into several exciting new digital direct marketing technologies: mobile phone marketing, podcasts and vodcasts, and interactive TV (iTV).

Mobile Phone Marketing   More than 270 million Americans and 20 million Canadians carry mobile electronic devices, and today's digital marketers view mobile phones—sometimes referred to as "the third screen"—as the next big direct marketing medium. About 60 percent of mobile phone users also use their devices to send and receive text messages, and approximately 20 percent use their phones to access the Web, a number that is expected to rise to 40 percent within the next five years. Some 23 percent of cellphone users have seen advertising on their phones in the last 30 days and about half of them responded to the ads.[26]

The Interactive Advertising Bureau of Canada reports that mobile advertising revenue in Canada exceeds $12 million annually and is growing at a phenomenal rate of nearly

50 percent per year. Most mobile advertising is in the form of mobile content, display or sponsorship advertising, and mobile messaging (SMS), and more than half of the mobile advertising in Canada is created by telecommunications companies, followed by packaged goods, automobiles, and entertainment. It seems marketers of all kinds are now integrating mobile phones into their direct marketing. Cellphone promotions include everything from ring-tone giveaways, mobile games, text-in contests, and ad-supported content to retailer announcements of discounts, brand coupons, gift suggestions, and shopper information apps (see Marketing@Work 14.1).

When used properly, mobile marketing can greatly enrich the buyer's experience. For example, Fresh Encounter, a Findlay, Ohio, grocery store, uses text messaging to help customers plan their meals:[27]

> Like many food retailers, Fresh Encounter tries to help shoppers resolve their daily dilemma: What to have for dinner? But this 32-store chain has come up with a unique strategy: texting suggestions to the cell phones of shoppers who've opted into its Text-N-Save mobile advertising program. Last month, for example, Fresh Encounter sent text messages at 2 p.m. on a Thursday and Friday offering a deal on a whole rotisserie chickens to shoppers who came in after 5 p.m. on those days. "We asked them, 'What's for dinner?' and if they don't know, then how about this for $3.99?" says Fresh Encounter executive Eric Anderson.
>
> Shoppers in the program receive new text offers each Sunday, ranging from free items (such as milk and soft drinks) to 5 percent off a total purchase of $50 or more. The offers can be customized by store. To cash in, shoppers present their cell phone to the cashier, showing a PLU number in the text message. The redemption rates are "unbelievable," Anderson says—20 percent or more. Takers inevitably buy complementary items as well. When Fresh Encounter sends out a more urgent same-day offer, as in the chicken promotion, redemptions can exceed 30 percent.

Exhibit 14.9   Mobile marketing: Grocery store Fresh Encounter uses text messaging to help customers plan their meals. Offer redemptions can exceed 30 percent.

As with other forms of direct marketing, however, companies must use mobile marketing responsibly or risk angering already ad-weary consumers. "If you were interrupted every two minutes by advertising, not many people want that," says a mobile marketing expert. "The industry needs to work out smart and clever ways to engage people on mobiles." The key is to provide genuinely useful information and offers that will make consumers want to opt in or call in. One study found that 42 percent of cellphone users are open to mobile advertising if it's relevant.[28]

Podcasts   Podcasting is the latest on-the-go, on-demand technology. The name **podcast** derives from Apple's iPod. With podcasting, consumers can download audio files (podcasts) or video files (vodcasts) via the Internet to an iPod or any other personal electronic device and then listen to or view them whenever and wherever they wish. These days, you can download podcasts or vodcasts on an exploding array of topics, everything from your favourite CBC radio program to a recent sitcom episode, sports features, or music video.

One recent study predicts that the U.S. podcast audience will reach 38 million by 2013, up from 6 million in 2005.[29] As a result, this new medium is drawing much attention from marketers. Many are now integrating podcasts and vodcasts into their direct marketing programs in the form of ad-supported podcasts, downloadable ads and informational features, and other promotions.

For example, The Walt Disney World Resort offers weekly podcasts on a mix of topics, including behind-the-scenes tours, interviews, upcoming events, and news about new attractions. New podcasts automatically download to subscribers' computers, where they can transfer them to portable media players to enjoy and share them. And Nestlé Purina publishes "Petcasts" on animal training and behavioural issues. It invites customers to

Podcast

An audio or video file, such as a radio or television program, sports feature, or music video, that can be downloaded from the Internet and viewed or listened to on an iPod or other personal electronic device.

MARKETING@WORK 14.1

Mobile Marketing: *Do* Call Me, Please—or I'll Call You!

You're at the local Best Buy checking out portable GPS navigation systems. You've narrowed it down to a Garmin nüvi 350 versus a less-expensive competing model, but you're not certain that Best Buy has the best prices. Also, you'd love to know how other consumers rate the two brands. No problem. Just pull out your iPhone and launch Amazon.com's iPhone application, which lets you browse the brands you're considering, read consumer reviews, and compare prices of portable GPS systems sold by Amazon.com and its retail partners. The application even lets you snap a photo of an item by using your phone's camera, and Amazon.com employees will try to find similar items for sale on their website. If Amazon.com offers a better deal, you can make the purchase directly from the application.

Welcome to the new world of mobile marketing. Today's new smartphones are changing the way we live—including the way we shop. And as they change how we shop, they also change how marketers sell to us.

A growing number of consumers—especially younger ones—are using their cellphones as a "third screen" for text messaging, surfing the wireless Web, watching downloaded videos and shows, and checking email. According to one expert, "the cell phone ... is morphing into a content device, a kind of digital Swiss Army knife with the capability of filling its owner's every spare minute with games, music, live and on-demand TV, Web browsing, and, oh yes, advertising." Says the president of the Mobile Marketing Association, "It's only a matter of time before mobile is the 'first screen.'" According to another industry insider,

Mobile phones and wireless devices have quietly become the hottest new frontier for marketers, especially those targeting the coveted 18- to 34-year-old set. TV networks are prodding viewers to send text messages to vote for their favorite reality TV character. Wireless websites are lacing sports scores and news digests with banner ads for Lexus, Burger King, and Sheraton. A few companies

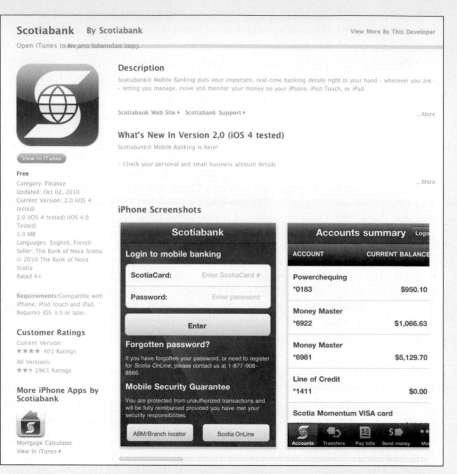

Exhibit 14.10   More than just advertising: Mobile marketing applications deliver content, information, and services to users on the go. For example, Scotiabank customers can use their smartphones to locate branches and ABMs, check their account balances, and conduct transfers.

are even customizing 10-second video ads for short, TV-style episodes that are edging their way onto mobile phones. For advertisers, the young audience is just one selling point. Wireless gadgets are always-on, ever-present accessories. The fact that a phone is tethered to an individual means that ads can be targeted. And users can respond instantly to time-sensitive offers. The mobile phone is very personal and it's always with you.

Marketers large and small are weaving mobile marketing into their direct marketing mixes. Wal-Mart uses text message alerts to spread the news about sales—you can click on links within the

messages to go to the retailer's mobile website and check on details. Unilever phones out mobile coupons for Ragú pasta sauce, Dove body wash, Breyers ice cream, and its other brands—just hold up your cellphone at the checkout and the cashier will scan the barcode off the screen. Target's "Gift Globe" iPhone app gives you gift recommendations based on the age and gender of recipients—enter the data and shake your phone, and recommended gift items pop up on the screen. You can also use the app to link to Target's website to buy the item or find the nearest store.

Beyond helping you buy, other mobile marketing applications provide helpful services, useful information, and even entertainment. Scotiabank's mobile services include a BlackBerry app, a Branch & ABM iPhone app, a Mortgage iPhone app, and ScotiaInfoAlerts, which send you text messages or email alerts to your mobile device to keep you up to date on account balances, transactions, account limits, and account activities. REI's The Snow and Ski Report app gives ski slope information for locations throughout the United States and Canada, such as snow depth, snow conditions, and number of open lifts. The app also links you to "Shop REI," for times "when you decide you can't live without a new set of K2 skis or a two-man Hoo-Doo tent." For entertainment, carmaker Audi offers The Audi A4 Driving Challenge game, which features a tiny A4 that manoeuvres its way through different driving courses—to steer, you tilt your phone right or left. Audi claims that the app has been downloaded nearly 3 million times since it was introduced, resulting in 400 000 visitors to the Audi A4 iPhone website.

One of the most effective mobile marketing applications is Kraft's iFood Assistant, which provides easy-to-prepare recipes for food shoppers on the go. It supplies advice on how to prepare some 7000 simple but satisfying meals—at three meals a day, that's almost 20 years worth of recipes. The iFood Assistant will even give you directions to local stores. Of course, most of the meals call for ingredients that just happen to be Kraft brands. The iFood Assistant app cost Kraft less than $100 000 to create but has engaged millions of shoppers, providing great marketing opportunities for Kraft and its brands.

Most consumers are initially skeptical about receiving mobile ad messages. Their first reaction is likely to be "Don't call me. I'll call you (yeah, right)." But they often change their minds if the ads deliver value in the form of useful brand and shopping information, entertaining content, or discounted prices and coupons for their favourite products and services. Most mobile marketing efforts target only consumers who voluntarily opt in or who download applications. In the increasingly cluttered mobile marketing space, customers just won't do that unless they see real value in it. The challenge for marketers: Develop useful and engaging mobile marketing applications that make customers say, "*Do* call me, please. Or, I *will* call you."

Sources: Adapted extract, quotes, and other information from Joseph De Avila, "Please Hold, My Cell Phone Is Buying a Gift," *Wall Street Journal*, December 9, 2008, p. D1; Todd Wasserman, "I'm on the Phone!" *Adweek*, February 23, 2009, pp. 6–7; Alice Z. Cuneo, "Scramble for Content Drives Mobile," *Advertising Age*, October 24, 2005, p. S6; Jen Arnoff, "Wising Up to Smart Phones," *News & Observer* (Raleigh), April 22, 2009, p. 5B; and Carol Angrisani, "Priced to Cell," *Supermarket News*, June 1, 2009, p. 28.

"Take these shows on the road—from serious discussions with veterinarians about pet health to wacky animal videos featuring dogs and cats, Purina has a podcast (or two) for you."[30]

Interactive TV (iTV)   Interactive TV (iTV) lets viewers interact with television programming and advertising by using their remote controls. In the past, iTV has been slow to catch on. However, the technology now appears poised to take off as a direct marketing medium. Research shows that the level of viewer engagement with interactive TV is much higher than with 30-second spots. A recent poll indicated that 66 percent of viewers would be "very interested" in interacting with commercials that piqued their interest. And satellite broadcasting systems such as DIRECTV, EchoStar, and Time Warner are now offering iTV capabilities.[31]

Interactive TV gives marketers an opportunity to reach targeted audiences in an interactive, more involving way. For example, shopping channel HSN developed a "Shop by Remote" interactive TV service that allows viewers to immediately purchase any item on HSN by using their remote. TiVo and Domino's Pizza partnered to launch a service that lets consumers order pizza directly via their set-top TiVo box—during Domino's commercials, TiVo flashes pop-up ads asking whether users want to order a pizza, and then directs them to a Domino's ordering screen.[32]

Nike's "Quick Is Deadly" campaign for its Zoom training-shoe line included more than 20 minutes of interactive content accessible to Dish Network subscribers with DVRs. The campaign let Dish DVR users click into 30- and 60-second TV spots starring San Diego Chargers running back LaDainian Tomlinson and other fleet-footed Nike athletes. They could then opt to view interview footage of the football star discussing his exhaustive training regimen, footage of Tomlinson's signature spin move in different speeds, a Nike-branded game designed to test viewers' remote-control reflexes, and a 3-D demo of the

Zoom shoe. Nike made similar interactive content available in ads featuring several other Nike endorsers, including basketball's Steve Nash, runner Lauren Fleshman, Olympic sprinters Asafa Powell and Sanya Richards, and tennis player Rafael Nadal. Using zip-code information in each Dish unit, users could also find stores carrying the shoe at the click of a button. The campaign stopped short of actually letting viewers buy the shoes directly from their sets, although the technology enables that function. "We've gotten to the point where all media needs to be interactive," says a creative director at Nike's advertising agency.

Mobile phone marketing, podcasts and vodcasts, and interactive TV offer exciting direct marketing opportunities. But marketers must be careful to use these new direct marketing approaches wisely. As with other direct marketing forms, marketers who use them risk backlash from consumers who may resent such marketing as an invasion of their privacy. Marketers must target their direct marketing offers carefully, bringing real value to customers rather than making unwanted intrusions into their lives.

ONLINE MARKETING LO5

Online marketing
Company efforts to market products and services and build customer relationships over the Internet.

As noted earlier, **online marketing** is the fastest-growing form of direct marketing. Recent technological advances have created a digital age. Widespread use of the Internet is having a dramatic impact on both buyers and the marketers who serve them. In this section, we examine how marketing strategy and practice are changing to take advantage of today's Internet technologies.

MARKETING AND THE INTERNET

Much of the world's business today is carried out over the Internet, which connects consumers, companies, and other organizations to each other and to an amazingly large information repository—the World Wide Web. The Internet and the Web have fundamentally changed customers' notions of convenience, speed, price, product information, and service. As a result, it has given marketers a whole new way to create value for customers and build relationships with them.

Internet usage and impact continues to grow steadily. In 2009, 80 percent of Canadians aged 16 and older, or 21.7 million people, used the Internet for personal reasons, up from 73 percent in 2007. In cities with a population of 10 000 or more, the rate is 83 percent, and Calgary and Saskatoon tie for the top spot in Canadian Internet usage, at a whopping 89 percent each! Most online consumers today access the Internet from home, with high-speed connections, and are online for five hours or more during a typical week.[33]

With all those consumers online, companies today must include the Internet in their marketing activities, whether they are click-only companies that operate *only* on the Internet (Amazon.com, Expedia), or traditional brick-and-mortar marketers. As the Internet grew, the success of the dot-coms caused existing manufacturers and retailers to re-examine how they served their markets. Now, almost all of these traditional companies have set up their own online sales and communications channels, becoming click-and-mortar organizations. It's hard to find a company today that doesn't have a substantial Web presence.

In fact, many companies that operate both online and through traditional channels are now having more online success than their click-only competitors. In a recent ranking of the top 10 online retail sites, only two were click-only retailers. All of the others were multichannel retailers.[34] For example, Office Depot's more than 1000 office-supply superstores rack up annual sales of $14.5 billion in more than 48 countries. But you might be surprised to learn that Office Depot's fastest recent growth has come not from its traditional brick-and-mortar channels, but from the Internet.[35]

Office Depot's online sales have soared in recent years, now accounting for 33 percent of total sales. Selling on the Web lets Office Depot build deeper, more personalized relationships with customers large and small. For example, a large customer such as GE or P&G can create lists of approved office products at discount prices and then let company departments or even individuals do their own online purchasing. This reduces ordering costs, cuts through the red tape, and speeds up the ordering process for customers. At the same time, it encourages companies to use Office Depot as a sole source for office supplies. Even the smallest companies find 24-hour-a-day online ordering easier and more efficient. Importantly, Office Depot's Web operations don't steal from store sales. Instead, the OfficeDepot.com site actually builds store traffic by helping customers find a local store and check stock. In return, the local store promotes the website through in-store kiosks. If customers don't find what they need on the shelves, they can quickly order it via the Web from the kiosk. Thus, Office Depot now offers a full range of contact points and delivery modes—online, by phone or fax, and in the store. No click-only or brick-only seller can match the call, click, or visit convenience and support afforded by Office Depot's click-and-mortar model.

Exhibit 14.11   Online marketing: No click-only or brick-only seller can match the call, click, or visit convenience and support afforded by Office Depot's "4 easy ways to shop."

ONLINE MARKETING DOMAINS

The four major online marketing domains are shown in Figure 14.2. They include B2C (business-to-consumer), B2B (business-to-business), C2C (consumer-to-consumer), and C2B (consumer-to-business).

Business-to-Consumer (B2C)   The popular press has paid the most attention to **business-to-consumer (B2C) online marketing**—businesses selling goods and services online to individual consumers for their personal needs. Today's consumers can buy almost anything online—from clothing, kitchen gadgets, and airline tickets to computers and cars. More than 50 percent of Canadians have ordered goods or services online.[36]

Perhaps more importantly, the Internet now influences 35 percent of total retail sales—sales transacted online plus those carried out offline but encouraged by online research. Some 81 percent of Web-goers now use the Internet to research a product before purchase, and by some estimates the Internet influences a staggering 50 percent

Business-to-consumer (B2C) online marketing
Businesses selling goods and services online to individual consumers for their personal needs.

FIGURE 14.2   Online marketing domains

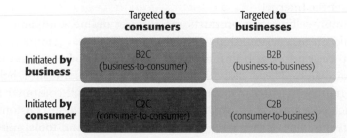

	Targeted **to** consumers	Targeted **to** businesses
Initiated **by** business	B2C (business-to-consumer)	B2B (business-to-business)
Initiated **by** consumer	C2C (consumer-to-consumer)	C2B (consumer-to-business)

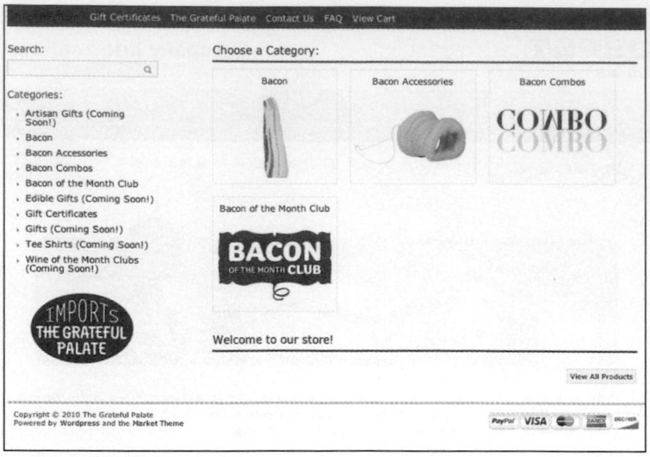

Exhibit 14.12   B2C online marketing: The Web makes it easy for niche marketers such as The Grateful Palate, a company that sells only bacon products, to reach a very large audience.

of total retail sales.[37] Thus, smart marketers are employing integrated multichannel strategies that use the Web to drive sales to other marketing channels.

Internet buyers differ from traditional offline consumers in their approaches to buying and in their responses to marketing. In the Internet exchange process, customers initiate and control the contact. Traditional marketing targets a somewhat passive audience. In contrast, online marketing targets people who actively select which websites they will visit and what marketing information they will receive about which products and under what conditions. Thus, online marketing requires new marketing approaches.

People now go online to order a wide range of goods—clothing from Gap or L.L.Bean, books and music from Amazon.com, major appliances from Sears, and lobsters from Clearwater.ca. And where else but the Web could you find a place that specializes in anything and everything bacon?[38]

Americans have a guilty relationship with food, and perhaps no food is more guilt-inducing than bacon—forbidden by religions, disdained by dietitians and doctors. Loving bacon is like shoving a middle finger in the face of all that is healthy and holy. There is something comfortingly unambiguous about a thick slab of bacon. It's bad for you. It tastes fantastic. Any questions? As Dan Philips says, "Bacon is the ultimate expression of freedom." Philips is the founder of The Grateful Palate (online at GratefulPalate.com), a company whose products have probably done more for the bacon chic movement than anything else. At The Grateful Palate, bacon enthusiasts can find everything bacon. It offers a bacon of the month club—Iron Chef Bobby Flay's a member—that includes artisanal bacon from farms across North America cured in a variety of delicious ways, from applewood smoked to hickory smoked with cinnamon sugar. The Grateful Palate also sells bacon-related gifts for people who can't get enough bacon in their day, such as bacon soap, bacon Christmas tree ornaments, bacon toilet paper, bacon air freshener, and even BLT candles—a set of bacon, lettuce, and tomato votives. Says one fan, "You can light them individually, maybe just tomato and lettuce if your vegetarian friends are visiting."

Business-to-Business (B2B)   Although the popular press has given the most attention to B2C websites, **business-to-business (B2B) online marketing** is also flourishing. Business-to-business marketers use B2B websites, email, online product catalogues, online trading networks, and other online resources to reach new business customers, serve current customers more effectively, and obtain buying efficiencies and better prices.

Most major B2B marketers now offer product information, customer purchasing, and customer-support services online. For example, corporate buyers can visit networking equipment and software maker Cisco Systems's website (www.cisco.com), select detailed descriptions of Cisco's products and service solutions, request sales and service information, attend events and training seminars, view videos on a wide range of topics, have live chats with Cisco staff, and place orders. Some major companies conduct almost all of their business on the Web. For example, Cisco Systems takes more than 80 percent of its orders over the Internet.

Beyond simply selling their products and services online, companies can use the Internet to build stronger relationships with important business customers. For example, Dell has set up customized websites for more than 113 000 business and institutional customers worldwide. These individualized Premier.Dell.com sites help business customers to more efficiently manage all phases of their Dell computer buying and ownership. Each customer's Premier.Dell.com website can include a customized online computer store, purchasing and asset management reports and tools, system-specific

Business-to-business (B2B) online marketing

Businesses using B2B websites, email, online catalogues, online trading networks, and other online resources to reach new business customers, serve current customers more effectively, and obtain buying efficiencies and better prices.

technical information, links to useful information throughout Dell's extensive website, and more. The site makes all the information a customer needs to do business with Dell available in one place, 24 hours a day, seven days a week.[39]

Consumer-to-Consumer (C2C) Much **consumer-to-consumer (C2C) online marketing** and communication occurs on the Web between interested parties over a wide range of products and subjects. In some cases, the Internet provides an excellent means by which consumers can buy or exchange goods or information directly with one another. For example, eBay and craigslist offer popular market spaces for displaying and selling almost anything, from art and antiques, computers and consumer electronics to cars.

eBay's C2C online trading community of more than 81 million unique monthly visitors worldwide facilitated some $60 billion in trades 2009. At any given time, the company's website lists more than 113 million items up for auction in more than 50 000 categories. Such C2C sites give people access to much larger audiences than the local flea market or newspaper classifieds. Interestingly, based on its huge success in the C2C market, eBay has now attracted more than 500 000 B2C sellers, ranging from small businesses peddling their regular wares to large businesses liquidating excess inventory at auction.[40]

In other cases, C2C involves interchanges of information through Internet forums that appeal to specific special-interest groups. Such activities may be organized for commercial or non-commercial purposes. One example of this type of forum is a **blog**, a personal website in journal or diary format, where people post their thoughts, usually on a narrowly defined topic. Many journalists, such as CNN's Anderson Cooper, have their own blogs, as do some corporate executives, such as Richard Edelman, the president and CEO of the world's largest independent public relations firm. Some companies encourage their employees to write blogs and provide them with the tools to do so. For example, Microsoft and Oracle dedicate sections of their corporate websites to blogs written by employees. These types of blogs allow customers and other interested people to read and comment on the companies' activities. There are also millions of blogs written by individuals, using free software such as Google's Blogger. These personal blogs can be about anything, from politics or baseball to haiku, car repair, or the latest television series. Since 2002, 133 million blogs have been "keyed" in 81 different languages. Currently, 47 percent of online consumers read them. Such numbers give blogs—especially those with large and devoted followings—substantial influence.[41]

Many marketers are now tapping into blogs as a medium for reaching carefully targeted consumers. For example, Wal-Mart created the ElevenMoms network (www.elevenmoms.com), a community of influential mommy-bloggers—women who write about their lives as mothers—who were already blogging about money-saving ideas. The blog provides a community in which customers can receive tips and share views on money-saving practices and products. The site also provides a platform for programs by brands such as Kimberly-Clark's Huggies, Unilever's Suave, P&G's Pantene, and others.[42]

Companies can also advertise on existing blogs or influence content there. For example, they might encourage "sponsored conversations" by influential bloggers:[43]

As part of its "Living in High Definition" push, Panasonic wanted to build buzz about its brand at the recent Consumer Electronics Show (CES) in Las Vegas. But rather than relying on the usual tech journalists attending the show, Panasonic recruited five influential bloggers—including popular Internet figures Chris Brogan and Steve Garfield—to travel to CES at its expense. It footed the bill for their travel and passes to the event while also

Consumer-to-consumer (C2C) online marketing
Online exchanges of goods and information between individual consumers.

Blog
A personal website in journal or diary format, where people post their thoughts, usually on a narrowly defined topic.

Exhibit 14.13 Blogs: Many companies set up their own blogs, such as Wal-Mart's Check Out blog, on which Wal-Mart buyers and merchandise managers such as Alex Cook speak candidly, even critically, about the products the chain carries.

loaning them digital video and still cameras. In return, the bloggers agreed to share their impressions of the show, including Panasonic product previews, with their own powerful distribution networks, in the form of blog posts, Twitter updates, and YouTube videos. The catch: Panasonic had no say on what their guests posted. To maintain credibility, Panasonic kept its distance and the bloggers fully disclosed the brand's sponsorship. Still, even though Panasonic didn't dictate content—and didn't want to—the "sponsored conversations" allowed the brand to tap into the groundswell of Internet buzz. "When you give [bloggers] equipment and they love it, just like any other consumer they'll evangelize it," says a Panasonic spokesperson. "We're not looking for them to hit message points and in effect shill." Panasonic just wants to be a catalyst for conversations about its brand.

Other companies set up their own blogs. For example, Southwest Airline's Nuts About Southwest blog (www.nutsaboutsouthwest.com) gives visitors a behind-the-scenes look at Southwest and a chance to interact with Southwest insiders. Similarly, at Wal-Mart's Check Out blog (www.checkoutblog.com), with the company's blessing, Wal-Mart buyers and merchandise managers speak candidly, even critically, about the products the chain carries. Says one analyst, the employee-fed blog "has become a forum for [everything from] unvarnished rants about gadgets [and] raves about new video games [to] advice on selecting environmentally sustainable food." The blog also provides a glimpse into the personal lives of posters. According to Wal-Mart, Check Out helps buyers to obtain quick feedback on merchandise from consumers, and it shows a softer side of the giant company.[44]

As a marketing tool, blogs offer some advantages. They can offer a fresh, original, personal, and cheap way to enter into consumers' online conversations. However, the "blogosphere" is cluttered and difficult for marketers to control. Although companies can sometimes leverage blogs to engage in meaningful customer relationships, consumers remain largely in control.

Consumer-to-business (C2B) online marketing
Online exchanges in which consumers search out sellers, learn about their offers, and initiate purchases, sometimes even driving transaction terms.

Whether or not they actively participate in the blogosphere, companies should show up, monitor, and listen to them. For example, Starbucks sponsors its own blog (www.mystarbucksidea.com) but also closely follows consumer dialogue on the 30 or more other third-party online sites devoted to the brand. It then uses the customer insights it gains from all of these proprietary and third-party blogs to adjust its marketing programs.[45]

In all, C2C means that online buyers don't just consume product information—increasingly, they create it. As a result, "word of Web" is joining "word of mouth" as an important buying influence.

Consumer to Business (C2B) The final online marketing domain is **consumer-to-business (C2B) online marketing.** Thanks to the Internet, today's consumers are finding it easier to communicate with companies. Most companies now invite prospects and customers to send in suggestions and questions via company websites. Beyond this, rather than waiting for an invitation, consumers can search out sellers on the Web, learn about their offers, initiate purchases, and give feedback. By using the Web, consumers can even drive transactions with businesses, rather than the other way around. For example, by using Priceline.com, would-be buyers can bid for airline tickets, hotel rooms, rental cars, cruises, and vacation packages, leaving the sellers to decide whether to accept their offers.

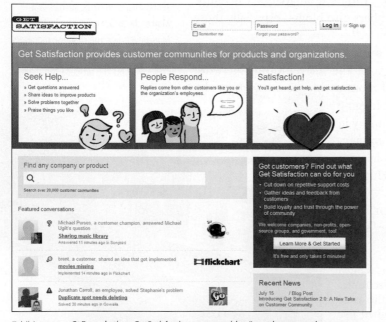

Exhibit 14.14   C2B marketing: GetSatisfaction.com provides "people-powered customer service" by creating a user-driven customer-service community where customers discuss product and service problems.

Consumers can also use public websites such as GetSatisfaction.com, Complaints.com, and PlanetFeedback.com to ask questions, offer suggestions, lodge complaints, or deliver compliments to companies. GetSatisfaction.com provides "people-powered customer service" by creating a user-driven customer-service community. The site provides forums where customers discuss problems they're having with the products and services of 2500 companies—from Apple to Zappos.com—whether the company participates or not. GetSatisfaction.com also provides tools by which companies can adopt GetSatisfaction.com as an official customer-service resource. Since launching in 2007, the site has drawn more than a million unique visitors.[46]

SETTING UP AN ONLINE MARKETING PRESENCE

In one way or another, most companies have now moved online. Companies conduct online marketing in any of the four ways shown in Figure 14.3: creating a website, placing ads and promotions online, setting up or participating in online social networks, or using email.

Creating a Website   For most companies, the first step in conducting online marketing is to create a website. However, beyond simply creating a website, marketers must design an attractive site and find ways to get consumers to visit the site, stay around, and come back often.

TYPES OF WEBSITES   Websites vary greatly in purpose and content. The most basic type is a **corporate (or brand) website**. These sites are designed to build customer goodwill, collect customer feedback, and supplement other sales channels, rather than to sell the company's products directly. They typically offer a rich variety of information and other features in an effort to answer customer questions, build closer customer relationships, and generate excitement about the company or the brand.

For example, you can't buy anything at P&G's Old Spice brand site, but you can learn about the different Old Spice products, watch recent ads, enter the latest contest, and post comments on the Old Spice blog. At the other extreme, GE's corporate website serves as a global public face for the huge company. It presents a massive amount of product, service, and company information to a diverse audience of customers, investors, journalists, and employees. It's both a B2B site and a portal for consumers, and it serves as a link to more than 65 other corporate country sites. Whether it's a Canadian consumer researching a microwave, an Indonesian business buyer checking into eco-friendly locomotives, or a German investor looking for shareholder information, "we have to get every different user to their destination," says a GE Web executive. "For such an extensive corporate site, the overall experience is elegantly simple," says a Web design consultant.[47]

Corporate (or brand) website
A website designed to build customer goodwill, collect customer feedback, and supplement other sales channels, rather than to sell the company's products directly.

FIGURE 14.3   Setting up for online marketing

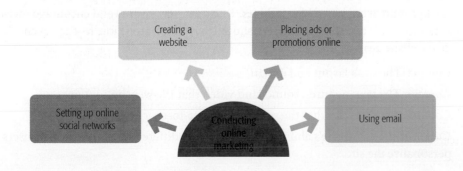

Exhibit 14.15   Corporate websites: You can't buy anything at GE's corporate site. Instead, it serves as a public face for the huge company, presenting a massive amount of information to a diverse global audience.

Marketing website

A website that engages consumers in interactions that will move them closer to a direct purchase or other marketing outcome.

Other companies create a **marketing website**. These sites engage consumers in an interaction that will move them closer to a direct purchase or other marketing outcome. For example, visitors to www.sonystyle.com can search through dozens of categories of Sony products, learn more about specific items, and read expert product reviews. They can check out the latest hot deals and place orders online.

MINI operates country-specific marketing websites at MINIUSA.com (for American consumers) and MINI.ca (for Canadians—in English and French). The first time a potential customer visits the sites, the carmaker wastes no time trying to turn the inquiry into a sale, and then into a long-term relationship. The sites offer a garage-full of useful information and interactive selling features, including detailed and fun descriptions of current MINI models, tools for designing your very own MINI, information on dealer locations and services, fun MINI accessories, and even tools for tracking your new MINI from factory to delivery.

Before Angela DiFabio bought her MINI Cooper last September, she spent untold hours on the company's website, playing with dozens of possibilities before coming up with the perfect combination: a chili-pepper-red exterior, white racing stripes on the hood, and a "custom rally badge bar" on the grill. When DiFabio placed her order with her dealer, the same build-your-own tool—and all the price and product details it provided—left her feeling like she was getting a fair deal. "He even used the site to order my car," she says. While she waited for her MINI to arrive, DiFabio logged on to MINI's website every day, this time using its "Where's My Baby?" tracking tool to follow her car, like an expensive FedEx package, from the factory in Britain to its delivery. The website does more than just provide information or sell products or services. It makes an impact on the customer experience: It's fun, it's individual, it makes users feel like part of the clan.[48]

DESIGNING EFFECTIVE WEBSITES   Creating a website is one thing; getting people to *visit* the site is another. To attract visitors, companies aggressively promote their websites in offline print and broadcast advertising and through ads and links on other sites. But today's savvy Internet consumers are quick to abandon any website that doesn't measure up. The key is to create enough value and excitement to get consumers who come to the site to stick around and come back again. This means that companies must constantly update their sites to keep them current, fresh, and useful.

A key challenge is designing a website that is attractive on first view and interesting enough to encourage repeat visits. Many marketers create colourful, graphically sophisticated sites that combine text, sound, and animation to capture and hold attention—for example, Pepsi's website at Pepsi.com, which features games and activities on a background of animated blue bubbles. To attract new visitors and encourage revisits, suggests one expert, online marketers should pay close attention to the seven *C*s of effective website design:[49]

- ☐ *Context:* The site's layout and design.
- ☐ *Content:* The text, pictures, sound, and video that the website contains.
- ☐ *Community:* The ways that the site enables user-to-user communication.
- ☐ *Customization:* The site's ability to tailor itself to different users or to allow users to personalize the site.

☐ *Communication:* The ways the site enables site-to-user, user-to-site, or two-way communication.

☐ *Connection:* The degree that the site is linked to other sites.

☐ *Commerce:* The site's capabilities to enable commercial transactions.

And to keep customers coming back to the site, companies need to embrace yet another *C*—constant change. Maintaining a top website is a complex and ongoing task. For example, The Walt Disney Company recently overhauled its marquee Disney.com site for the second time in only two years:[50]

Exhibit 14.16 Marketing website: To be effective, marketing websites must target their markets carefully. For example, MINI cars are marketed through country-specific websites, and in Canada there are separate websites for the English- and French-speaking markets.

> The changes to Disney.com will introduce more free videos (including full-length movies like *Finding Nemo*) as well as more games and things for visitors to do with their mobile phones. For instance, little girls (or bigger ones) who create fairy avatars in a virtual world called Pixie Hollow will be able to use their phones to create pet butterflies for their fairies. With the changes, Disney is trying to position its website more as a place that entertains and less of one that exists to promote Disney wares. No longer will the site ask youngsters to navigate through categories like "Movies," "TV," and "Live Events." New options will include "Games," "Videos" and "Characters" and will emphasize how to find immediate entertainment. "It's a repositioning of our digital front door," says a Disney Online executive. The constant changes reflect the whiplash-fast pace at which online is evolving. The previous site overhaul increased unique visitors to Disney.com by about 40 percent to nearly 30 million a month, making it the number-one Web destination for children and family-oriented websites. The average user spends 45 minutes per visit. But refreshing the site is an ongoing process.

At the very least, a website should be easy to use, professional looking, and physically attractive. Ultimately, however, websites must also be *useful*. When it comes to Web searching, browsing, and shopping, most people prefer substance over style and function over flash. A recent survey of 12 000 Canadians rated Canada's top 10 consumer websites, and found that even the best site in terms of overall experience, Amazon.ca, ranked 5.00 out of a possible 7.00. The Canadian version of the online bookseller also ranked highest for ease of use, but didn't score as well on look—the winner in that category was Honda Canada's website. And it's not just a matter of including the seven *C*s, it's a matter of finding the right balance between them. "Too many sites are a hodgepodge that are far too heavy with content," says a professor of marketing at HEC Montreal.

Effective websites, therefore, contain deep and useful information, interactive tools that help buyers to find and evaluate products of interest, links to other related sites, changing promotional offers, and entertaining features that lend relevant excitement—all carefully balanced.

Placing Ads and Promotions Online As consumers spend more and more time on the Internet, companies are shifting more of their marketing

Exhibit 14.17 Banner ads: The most common form of online advertising is the banner ad, a square or rectangular graphical advertisement that typically appears at the top of a webpage, such as the banner ad for ING Direct shown here.

Online advertising

Advertising that appears on websites that sell advertising space, including display ads (also called graphic ads and banner ads), search ads, text links, online classifieds, and full-screen animated or video ads (interstitials).

Banner ad

A square or rectangular graphical advertisement that typically appears at the top or along the side of a webpage.

Interstitial

A type of online advertising that appears between screen changes, usually as you navigate from one site to another, and resembles a very short television commercial that takes over the full browser screen before disappearing to reveal the website underneath.

Exhibit 14.18   Rich media ads: Today's Web design tools allow advertisers to create interactive "rich media" ads, such as this ad for RBC Royal Bank which, when clicked on, allows students to enter a contest (and apply for a student banking account) without leaving the advertiser's space.

dollars to **online advertising** to build their brands or to attract visitors to their sites. The Web has become a major advertising medium. According to the Interactive Advertising Bureau (IAB) of Canada, online advertising revenue exceeded $1.8 billion in 2009. The rate of spending on online advertising has more than quadrupled in Canada over the past five years, and the IAB predicts Canadian marketers will spend more than $2 billion next year—and this, despite the recent economic recession. IAB Canada president Paula Gignac says, "It seems incredible that after passing the $1 billion revenue mark just two years ago—and after the worst recession in history—Internet advertising in Canada is poised to break through to the $2 billion mark in 2010."[51] Of all forms of major mass-media advertising (TV, newspapers, Internet, radio, magazines, and out-of-home), online now ranks third in terms of spending by advertisers. Here, we discuss forms of online advertising and promotion and their future.

FORMS OF ONLINE ADVERTISING   The major forms of online advertising are search ads (text ads that appear on a search site in response to the requested search), display ads (any form of graphic or banner ad), and online classifieds. Online display ads might appear anywhere on a webpage once the user has navigated to a site that sells advertising. The most common form of display advertising is the **banner ad,** a square or rectangular graphical advertisement that typically appears at the top or along the side of a webpage. For example, while checking the hockey scores on NHL.com, you might see a banner ad promoting business banking services at Scotiabank, or while catching up on the news on CBC.ca, you might see a banner ad promoting banking services at ING Direct.

Interstitials are display ads that appear between screen changes, usually as you navigate from one site to another. An interstitial ad resembles a very short television commercial that takes over the full browser screen before disappearing to reveal the website underneath. Interstitial ads are always relevant to the website that displays them. For example, you might visit Marketwatch.com, a stock information website, and see a short interstitial ad for Visa credit cards for small business. *Pop-up*s and *pop-under*s are display ads that appear in a separate, small, browser window, either on top of or underneath the website that sold the advertising space. For example, if you visit movie information site IMDB.com, you might see a pop-up ad for Netflix, the movie rental service.

Today, most Internet users have broadband or high-speed service, which means web-pages and all their associated graphic files can load quite quickly. This has led advertisers to create *rich media* online display ads, which incorporate animation, video, sound, and interactivity. Rich media ads attract and hold consumer attention better than traditional banner ads, which were either static or had only simple animation. Rich media ads employ techniques such as float, fly, and snapback—animations that jump out and sail over the webpage before retreating to their original space.

Many rich media ads do more than create a little bit of jumping animation—they also create interactivity. They can provide consumers with product information, local or online buying options, a brand experience, or an opportunity to enter a contest without taking them away from the site they are viewing. For example, Verizon ads touting the LG Versa phone as a gaming device on Yahoo! Games interacted with the site's contents—as the Versa tilted, the site's elements tilted as well. Intel banner ads on information technology sites such as CIO Today, CINET, and Computerworld.com even connected interested users directly into live chats with Intel technology experts.[52] And a sales promotion from the Royal Bank, targeting students, included a rich media ad on various entertainment websites that announced, "Students win $1000 every day!" by opening a student banking account or credit card account. The rich media ad linked directly to a form where students could apply for an account and automatically be entered into the contest.

Another hot growth area for online advertising is *search-related ads* (or *contextual advertising*), in which text-based ads and links appear alongside search engine results on sites such as Google and Yahoo! For example, search Google for "LCD TVs." At the top and side of the resulting search list, you'll see inconspicuous ads for 10 or more advertisers, ranging from Samsung and Dell to Best Buy, Sears, and Amazon.com, Walmart.com, and Nextag.com. Nearly all of Google's $22 billion in revenues come from ad sales. An advertiser buys search terms from the search site and pays only if consumers click through to its site. Search is an always-on kind of medium. And importantly for marketers, the results—and therefore the return on advertising investment—are easily measured. Search-related ads account for some 45 percent of all online advertising expenditures, more than any other category of online advertising.[53]

In the early days of the Internet only technology products companies advertised on search engines, but today search-related advertising has grown increasingly popular with consumer package good firms:[54]

> Type "Coke" or "Coca-Cola" or even just "soft drinks" or "rewards" into your Google or Yahoo! search engine and without fail "My Coke Rewards" comes up as one of the top options. Coincidence? Definitely not. Since the popular online loyalty program began, the cola giant has been supporting it largely through search buys. When Coke first launched My Coke Rewards three years ago, it started with traditional TV and print advertising. But it quickly learned that search was the most effective and efficient way to bring consumers to the www.mycokerewards.com website to register. Now, any of dozens of purchased search terms will return MyCokeRewards.com at or near the top of the search list.
>
> Coca-Cola is not alone—most companies now do search-related advertising. For example, search is the primary driver for ConAgra's recipe site, www.simpleanddelicious.com. The company has purchased a comprehensive list of search terms, everything from "easy-to-prepare" to "great tasting recipe." ConAgra's interactive marketing director likens search advertising to securing virtual shelf space. "When someone looks for your brand online, what do they see?" he asks. "Do you own those results ... can you influence those results if other websites are coming up and competing against your brand?" Search advertising is 24/7 kind of medium. "That speaks to a dial-tone level of search. Like the electricity in your house, it should always be on."

OTHER FORMS OF ONLINE PROMOTION   Other forms of online promotions include content sponsorships, affiliate programs, and viral advertising.

By using *content sponsorships*, companies gain name exposure on the Internet by sponsoring special content on various websites, such as news or financial information or special-interest topics. For example, Scotts, the lawn-and-garden products company, sponsors the Local Forecast section on WeatherChannel.com, and Marriott sponsors "Summer to the Rescue!" microsite at Travelocity.com. Sponsorships are best placed in carefully targeted sites where they can offer relevant information or service to the audience. Internet companies can also develop **affiliate programs**, in which they work with other companies, online and offline, to "promote each other." For example, through its Amazon Associates Program, Amazon.com has more than 900 000 affiliates who link to specific books or pages on Amazon.com from their websites. If a visitor to the affiliate's website clicks through to Amazon.com and makes a purchase, the affiliate receives a small commission.

Finally, online marketers use **viral marketing**, the Internet version of word-of-mouth marketing. Viral marketing involves creating a website, video, email message, cellphone message, advertisement, or other marketing event that is so infectious that customers will want to pass it along to their friends. Because customers pass the message or promotion along to others, viral marketing can be very inexpensive. And when the information comes from a friend, the recipient is much more likely to view or read it.

Affiliate program
A type of co-marketing arrangement in which one website links to another and can receive small commissions or other benefits when visitors click through and make purchases.

Viral marketing
The Internet version of word-of-mouth marketing—websites, videos, email messages, cellphone messages, or other marketing events that are so infectious that customers will want to pass them along to friends.

Exhibit 14.19   Viral marketing: OfficeMax's ElfYourself.com viral website has propelled itself into the digital record books. With no promotion at all, the site logged more than 193 million visits between late November and early January. One-third of those visiting the site were influenced to shop at OfficeMax.

Sometimes a well-made regular ad can go viral with little help from the company. For example, McDonald's clever "Gimme back the Filet-O-Fish" ad, featuring a mechanized singing fish mounted on a wall, grabbed 780 000 YouTube views and a 5-star rating in little more than three months. It also inspired a rash of consumer-generated spots posted on YouTube featuring people singing the song while ordering. However, leaving viral efforts to chance rarely works. "It's one of those things you never really know until it's out there," says a McDonald's marketer.[55]

Although marketers usually have little control over where their viral messages end up, a well-concocted viral campaign can gain vast exposure. Consider OfficeMax's wacky ElfYourself.com seasonal viral website, which for the past three years has let visitors paste images of their own faces onto dancing elves, along with a personal message.[56]

OfficeMax's holiday ElfYourself.com viral website has propelled itself into the digital record books, all with no hint of promotion. Between late November 2007 and early January 2008, ElfYourself.com logged more than 193 million site visits and a whopping 123 million elves were created, with 53 percent of visitors returning for additional visits. The elves were publicity magnets for OfficeMax, drawing heavy coverage from media ranging from *Good Morning America* to CNN to the *New York* Times. Popular in more than 50 countries, the elves even popped up dancing on the Jumbo Tron overlooking Times Square in New York City. OfficeMax executives joke about the elves replacing Frosty and Rudolph as holiday icons for this generation. More important, one-third of those who visited the ElfYourself.com site were influenced to shop at OfficeMax, and another one-third said the holiday treat improved their perception of the retailer.

However, achieving such success isn't as easy as it might seem. In its first season, ElfYourself.com was just one of 20 holiday-themed viral websites developed by OfficeMax, which hoped that at least one would catch fire among bored office workers looking for things to share online over the holidays. (All 20 sites were built at less than the cost of producing just one television commercial—generally about $350 000.) ElfYourself.com was the only one that blossomed. "There's a lot of luck to this stuff," says one of the site's creators. Companies "don't make things viral, consumers do. We were lucky enough to land on something that worked very well."

Creating or Participating in Social Networks   The newest form of online communication available to both consumers and marketers is social networking. **Social networks** are online communities where individuals and organizations can create mini websites; post blogs, photos, and videos; and exchange information and opinions. Countless independent and commercial websites such as MySpace, Facebook, Twitter, YouTube, Digg, StumbleUpon, Flickr, and Foursquare have arisen that give consumers online places to congregate, socialize, and exchange views and information. And, of course, wherever consumers congregate, marketers will surely follow. More and more marketers are now riding the huge social networking wave.

Marketers can engage in social networks in two ways: They can participate in existing communities—by creating a YouTube channel, a Facebook group, or a Twitter account—or they can create their own online community. Joining existing networks seems easiest. Harley-Davidson, Volkswagen, Victoria's Secret, and MuchMusic have their own YouTube channels. GM and other companies have posted visual content on Flickr. The Apple

Social networks
Online communities where individuals and organizations can create mini websites; post blogs, photos, and videos; and exchange information and opinions.

Students group on Facebook, which offers information and deals on Apple products, has more than 1.3 million members. Coca-Cola's Facebook page has 3.5 million fans, and Mars recently transformed its Skittles home page into an online portal that links its core teenage customers—who spend a lot of time using social media—directly to its Twitter feed, Facebook page, and YouTube channel. All of these destinations contain unfiltered consumer-generated conversations and content about the Skittles brand. The new site resulted in a more than 1300 percent jump in Web traffic for the brand.[57]

Although the large online social networks such as Facebook, YouTube, and Twitter have grabbed most of the headlines, a new breed of more focused niche networks has recently emerged. These more focused networks cater to the needs of smaller communities of like-minded people, making them ideal vehicles for marketers who want to target special interest groups (see Marketing@Work 14.2).

Exhibit 14.20 Marketing by participating in social networks: Marketers can create their own "channels" on YouTube to distribute content and/or advertising. For example, MuchMusic's official YouTube channel offers video clips and other content, broadcast information, and links to MuchMusic's website.

But participating in social marketing presents challenges. First, online social networks are new and results are hard to measure. Most companies are still experimenting with how to use them effectively. Second, such Web communities are largely user controlled. The company's goal is to make the brand a part of consumers' conversations and their lives. However, marketers can't simply muscle their way into consumers' online interactions—they need to earn the right to be there. "You're talking about conversations between groups of friends," says one analyst. "And in those conversations a brand has no right to be there, unless the conversation is already about that brand." Rather than intruding, marketers must learn to become a valued part of the online experience. "The only appropriate way to insert a brand into social media is to give some kind of benefit to people," says another analyst. "You don't trick people into sharing your brand."[58]

To avoid the mysteries and challenges of building a presence on existing social networking sites, many companies are now launching their own targeted Web communities. For example, on Nike's Nike Plus website, more than 500 000 runners upload, track, and compare their performances. More than half visit the site at least four times a week, and Nike plans eventually to have 15 percent or more of the world's 100 million runners actively participating in the Nike Plus online community.

Email Marketing Email is an important and growing online marketing tool. Over 90 percent of Canadian marketers are doing some form of email marketing. According to the Canadian Marketing Association (CMA), email marketing is extremely cost-efficient, has the lowest cost per response, and the highest ROI effectiveness of any direct marketing medium.[59] **Email marketing** is any form of promotional message sent by a marketer to a group of consumers, usually existing customers or subscribers. Email marketing is used for a variety of purposes, such as welcoming new customers, qualifying leads, announcing events, cross-selling and upselling, promoting new products, and assisting in customer relationship management.

Marketers who use email to communicate with targeted customers should proceed carefully, so as not to have their messages viewed as "spam"—unsolicited junk email—by recipients. Email marketers walk a fine line between adding value for consumers and being intrusive. To address these concerns, most legitimate marketers now practise *permission-based email marketing,* sending email pitches only to customers who opt in—that is, who actively choose, usually through customer registration on a website, to receive this type of communications. Amazon.com, for example, includes long lists of opt-in boxes for different categories of marketing material and sends helpful "we thought you'd

Email marketing
Any form of promotional message sent by a marketer to a group of consumers, usually existing customers or subscribers.

MARKETING@WORK 14.2

Online Social Networks: Targeting Niches of Like-Minded People

Marketers who think bigger is better may want to reconsider, at least when it comes to online social networks. Although giant networks such as Facebook and Twitter get all the attention these days, social networks focused on topics as remote as knitting or birdwatching can present marketers with strong targeting opportunities.

When jet-setters began flocking to an exclusive social networking website reserved for the rich, they got the attention of an online community's most valuable ally: advertisers. The invitation-only site, ASmallWorld.net, has 300 000 select members who have become a magnet for companies that make luxury goods and are trying to reach people who can afford them. The site's biggest advertisers include Burberry, Cartier, and Land Rover. Cognac maker Rémy Martin last month threw a tasting party for the site's elite members, at which its top-shelf, $1800-a-bottle liquor flowed freely.

Thousands of social-networking sites have popped up to cater to specific interests, backgrounds, professions, and age groups. Nightclub frequenters can converge at DontStayIn.com. Wine connoisseurs have formed Snooth.com, and people going through divorce can commiserate at Divorce360.com.

More and more, marketers are taking a chance on smaller sites that could be more relevant to their products. AT&T, for example, recently promoted one of its global cellphones on WAYN.com (short for "Where are you now?"), a social network for international travellers. While AT&T advertises on the bigger sites such as MySpace to reach a large audience quickly, the wireless carrier is also turning to niche networks, "where your ads are more meaningful—those are the real gems," says a social networking expert.

There's at least one social network for just about every interest or hobby. Yub.com is for shopaholics, Fuzzster.com is for pet lovers, Ravelry.com sews up the knitting and crocheting community,

Exhibit 14.21 Niche social networks: Thousands of social-networking sites have popped up to cater to specific interests, backgrounds, professions, and age groups. Yub.com connects a community of shopaholics.

Jango.com lets music fans find others with similar tastes, and PassportStamp.com is one of several sites for avid travellers.

Some cater to the obscure. Passions Network is an "online dating niche social network" with 600 000 members and 110 groups for specific interests, including *Star Trek* fans, truckers, atheists, and people who are shy. The most popular group is a dating site for the overweight. A new social networking site called LinkExpats.com allows people living in foreign countries to find and connect with people from their home country. Membership on niche networking sites varies greatly, ranging from a few hundred to a few million. Flixster.com, for example, has 40 million members who rate movies and gossip about actors.

According to eMarketer, by 2011, half of all adults in the United States and 84 percent of online teens will use social networks. A running tally of emerging social networks, now upward of 7000 by

one estimate, suggests an explosive market. That's both a golden opportunity and a colossal headache for brands trying to nail down the best new network for their campaigns.

Although the niche sites have many fewer members than mega-sites such as Facebook (200 million worldwide), they contain dedicated communities of like-minded people. And as on the bigger networks, members can build personalized pages and use them to share information, photos, and news with friends. That makes the niche sites ideal vehicles for marketers who want to target special interest groups.

The niche sites often provide a better marketing message environment. "Because members of niche social networks share common interests and experiences, they tend to spend more time on the site and contribute to the group by chatting and posting comments," notes an online consultant. On bigger sites, "members tend to be less involved ... and are therefore less appealing to advertisers." Also, "the bigger sites have become so cluttered and overrun with advertisers that members are used to tuning stuff out, even personalized ads.... But on networking sites that have a self-selecting demographic, people tend to trust the content, including ads."

Not all niche networks welcome marketers. Sermo.com—a social-networking site at which some 65 000 licensed physicians consult with colleagues specializing in areas ranging from dermatology to psychiatry—allows no marketing. However, for a fee, companies can gain access to Sermo.com data and member discussions. "They can monitor online discussions, with the doctors' names omitted, or see a tally of topics being discussed at the site to determine what's rising or falling in popularity," notes an American healthcare industry analyst.

The more focused audiences offered by niche networks are increasingly popular with brands because "relevance," says the consultant, "trumps size." But how brands execute social-networking campaigns is as important as where they do it. Marketers must be careful not to become too commercial or too intrusive. Keeping sites hip and unencumbered by advertising is a balancing act for both the brands and the social networks. The best approach is not to *market* to network members but to *interact* with them on topics of mutual interest. Says one online marketer, "The real way of getting into social media is you don't advertise, you participate in the community."

Sources: Portions adapted from Betsey Cummings, "Why Marketers Love Small Social Networks," *Brandweek,* April 27, 2008, accessed at www.brandweek.com; with adapted extracts, quotes, and other information from Kim Hart, "Online Networking Goes Small, and Sponsors Follow," *Washington Post,* December 29, 2007, p. D1; and Jessica E. Vascellaro, "Social Networking Goes Professional," *Wall Street Journal,* August 28, 2007, p. D1. Also see Paula Lehman, "Social Networks That Break a Sweat," *BusinessWeek,* February 4, 2008, p. 68; and Tim Parry, "Social Climbing," *Multichannel Merchant,* June 2009, p. 32.

like to know" messages based on customers' expressed preferences and previous purchases. Few customers object and many actually welcome such promotional messages. On the Kraft Canada website, consumers can sign up to receive a monthly email called Kraft Kitchens—full of recipes and other helpful food-related information.

When used properly, email can be the ultimate direct marketing medium. Many marketers such as Indigo Books & Music, Fairmont Hotels & Resorts, and L'Oréal Canada, use it regularly, and with great success. Email lets these marketers send highly targeted, tightly personalized, relationship-building messages to consumers who actually *want* to receive them. Consider StubHub, a website that allows people to buy and sell concert tickets:

> As a start-up almost a decade ago, online ticket merchant StubHub ran "batch-and-blast" e-mail campaigns focused on building awareness. For years, sheer volume far outweighed e-mail relevancy. But StubHub has now learned the value of carefully targeted, relevant e-mail messages. It now lets customers opt in for e-mail at registration, during purchases, and at sign-up modules throughout the StubHub site. Using opt-in customer data, StubHub targets designated consumer segments with ticket and event information aligned closely with their interests. Incorporating customer data produced immediate and stunning results. E-mail clickthrough rates quickly jumped 30 percent, and the company saw a 79 percent year-over-year increase in ticket sales despite having sent fewer e-mails. The more targeted campaigns have "enabled us to test and deliver the type of high-impact marketing that is needed in these times," says a StubHub marketer. "The results speak for themselves—these [new targeted campaigns] are driving 2,500 percent more revenue per e-mail than [our] average marketing campaigns."[60]

RULES OF EMAIL MARKETING When marketers use email to deliver legitimate marketing messages, they must take great care to follow the rules of etiquette for email marketing so that their messages are not perceived as spam. The Canadian Marketing Association (CMA) prohibits its members from sending unsolicited commercial email. The organization, with over 800 Canadian companies as members, explains the difference between email marketing and spam this way: "If you asked for it, it's not spam." For example, if a consumer

Exhibit 14.22   Rules of email marketing: Air Canada sends permission-based email marketing messages to Aeroplan members who opt in to receive them. Does this email message follow all the rules?

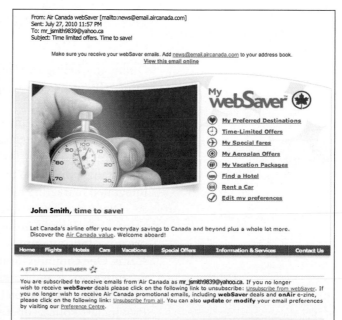

signed up for a newsletter and no longer wishes to receive it, he or she can simply unsubscribe—any legitimate organization will provide an easy way for you to be taken off its subscription list. However, be cautious when unsubscribing to an email message from an unknown organization—it could be spam, and attempting to unsubscribe can serve to confirm that your email is valid and cause you to receive even more spam.

Thus, professional Internet marketers must take care to follow certain rules of etiquette when it comes to email marketing:[61]

☐ *Send email only by permission.* The ethical email marketer never buys a list of email addresses and sends email messages only to those consumers who have subscribed to receive them.

☐ *Clearly identify the sender.* The name of the company must appear on the "from" line when the subscriber receives the email message.

☐ *Remind recipients why they're receiving the message.* Every marketing message sent via email should include a brief note to remind the customer where and how they subscribed to receive it.

☐ *Provide an easy way to unsubscribe.* Ethical email marketers use complex software systems to manage the delivery and tracking of email campaigns sent to subscribers. Thousands, if not tens or hundreds of thousands of messages are sent simultaneously by the email management system. These systems also manage the subscribe/ unsubscribe function automatically.

☐ *The default is always opt-in, never opt-out.* Subscribing to receive email offers typically involves checking a box on a Web form. If the box is pre-checked and the user is forced to uncheck it in order to *not* receive email, that is called opting out. The smart Internet marketer knows that it's better to have the conscious permission of 100 consumers than to have tricked 1000 consumers; therefore, ethical email marketers always leave the box unchecked and allow consumers to opt in to receive email.

Given its targeting effectiveness and low costs, email can be an outstanding marketing investment. According to the Direct Marketing Association, email marketing produces a return on investment 40 to 50 percent higher than other forms of direct-marketing media.[62]

THE PROMISE AND CHALLENGES OF DIRECT AND ONLINE MARKETING

Online marketing continues to offer both great promise and many challenges for the future. Its most ardent apostles still envision a time when the Internet and online marketing will replace magazines, newspapers, and even stores as sources for information and buying. Most marketers, however, hold a more realistic view. To be sure, online marketing has become a successful business model for some Internet-only companies, however, for most companies, online marketing will remain just one important approach to the marketplace that works alongside other approaches in a fully integrated marketing mix.

Direct marketers and their customers usually enjoy mutually rewarding relationships. Occasionally, however, a darker side emerges, as unscrupulous individuals and organizations attempt to use email and other online communications to perpetrate scams. One common form of Internet fraud is *phishing*, a type of identity theft that uses deceptive emails and fraudulent websites to fool users into divulging their personal data. The RCMP, in conjunction with Competition Bureau Canada and the Ontario Provincial Police, operates a public information website called PhoneBusters (Phonebusters.com), which educates consumers about how to avoid phishing and other types of online scams, and Industry Canada's Task Force on Spam publishes a site called StopSpamHere.ca, which advises consumers about how to combat email spam.

Many consumers also worry about *online security*. They fear that unscrupulous snoopers will eavesdrop on their online transactions, picking up personal information or intercepting credit and debit card numbers. Another Internet marketing concern is that of access by vulnerable or unauthorized groups. For example, marketers of adult-oriented materials have found it difficult to restrict access by minors. A case in point: 13 percent of the respondents in a *Consumer Reports* survey had children in their household registered as MySpace users who were under the online community's official minimum age of 14. The survey also indicated that many parents haven't prepared their children for potential online risks.[63]

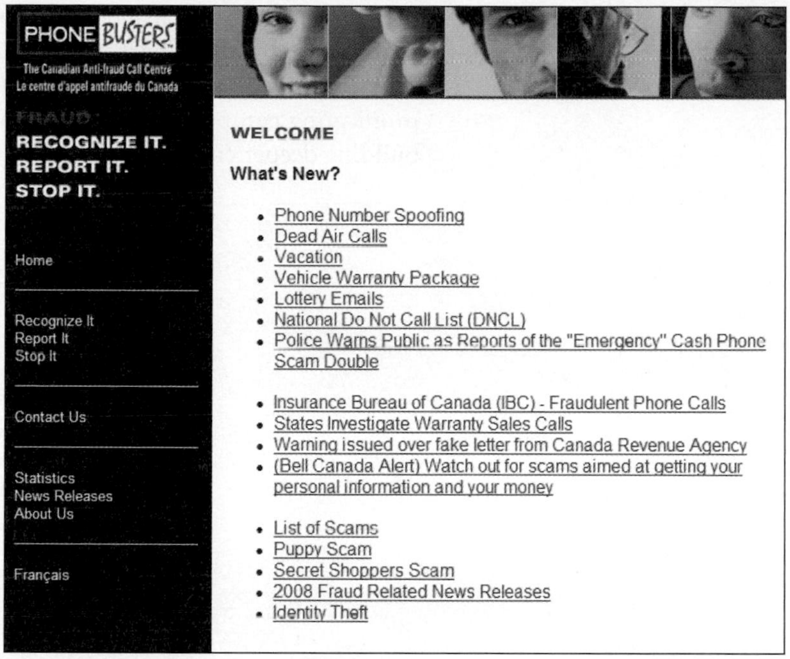

PHONE BUSTERS
The Canadian Anti-fraud Call Centre
Le centre d'appel antifraude du Canada

FRAUD
RECOGNIZE IT.
REPORT IT.
STOP IT.

Home

Recognize It
Report It
Stop It

Contact Us

Statistics
News Releases
About Us

Français

WELCOME

What's New?

- Phone Number Spoofing
- Dead Air Calls
- Vacation
- Vehicle Warranty Package
- Lottery Emails
- National Do Not Call List (DNCL)
- Police Warns Public as Reports of the "Emergency" Cash Phone Scam Double

- Insurance Bureau of Canada (IBC) - Fraudulent Phone Calls
- States Investigate Warranty Sales Calls
- Warning issued over fake letter from Canada Revenue Agency
- (Bell Canada Alert) Watch out for scams aimed at getting your personal information and your money

- List of Scams
- Puppy Scam
- Secret Shoppers Scam
- 2008 Fraud Related News Releases
- Identity Theft

Exhibit 14.23   The RCMP, Competition Bureau, and OPP are behind PhoneBusters, a website that informs Canadians about how to protect themselves from telemarking and Internet scams.

Invasion of privacy is perhaps the toughest public policy issue now confronting the direct-marketing industry. Consumers often benefit from database marketing—they receive more offers that are closely matched to their interests. However, many critics worry that marketers may know *too* much about consumers' lives and that they may use this knowledge to take unfair advantage of consumers. At some point, they claim, the extensive use of databases intrudes on consumer privacy.

Many companies have responded to consumer privacy and security concerns with actions of their own. Still others are taking an industry-wide approach. For example, TRUSTe, a non-profit self-regulatory organization, works with many large corporate sponsors, including Microsoft, AT&T, and Intuit, to audit companies' privacy and security measures and help consumers to navigate the Web safely. According to the company's website, "TRUSTe believes that an environment of mutual trust and openness will help make and keep the Internet a free, comfortable, and richly diverse community for everyone." To reassure consumers, the company lends its "trustmark" stamp of approval to websites that meet its privacy and security standards.[64]

The direct-marketing industry as a whole is also addressing public policy issues. For example, both the Direct Marketing Association and the Canadian Marketing Association require that members adhere to a carefully developed set of consumer privacy rules. Members must agree to notify customers when any personal information is rented, sold, or exchanged with others. They must also honour consumer requests to opt out of receiving further solicitations or having their contact information transferred to other marketers. Finally, they must abide by the DMA's Preference Service and the CMA's Do Not Call List by removing the names of consumers who do not wish to receive mail, telephone, or email offers.

Direct marketers know that, left untended, such direct-marketing abuses will lead to increasingly negative consumer attitudes, lower response rates, and calls for more restrictive provincial/territorial and federal legislation. Most direct marketers want the same things that consumers want: honest and well-designed marketing offers targeted only toward consumers who will appreciate and respond to them. Direct marketing is just too expensive to waste on consumers who don't want it.

Despite the many challenges, companies large and small have now integrated online marketing into their marketing strategies and mixes. As it continues to grow, online marketing will prove to be a powerful direct-marketing tool for improving sales, communicating company and product information, delivering products and services, and building deeper customer relationships.

DIRECT AND ONLINE MARKETING: TWEETING ABOUT GEESE

When Canada Goose developed its social networking strategy, its focus was on cultivating long-lasting customer relations rather than on getting an immediate buying response from its base. On Canada Goose's Facebook page, customers are able to give direct feedback to the company about its product design. Canada Goose fans can also see videos of famous people sporting Canada Goose apparel and get information on product availability.

Through social networking sites such as Facebook and Twitter, Canada Goose has worked to establish and grow a grass roots community of outdoor enthusiasts and adventurers. The Canada Goose Facebook page allows fans of the company's products to share stories, ask questions, and explore the company's involvement in charitable causes. Twitter updates and Facebook contests such as the patriotic Canada Day "Why I'm proud to be a Canadian" contest keep followers connected and create a club atmosphere in which athletes, explorers, and Canada Goose fans from around the world can exchange advice and share adventures.

The blog page, which links from the Canada Goose home page, focuses on numerous areas that impact the Canada Goose community. From postings by an Arctic researcher on his experiences in the Far North to announcements on the results of a design contest that allowed Canada Goose aficionados to vote on their favourite parka, the variety is large and the topic changes are frequent.

QUESTIONS

1. What aspects of the brand do you see being reinforced in the Canada Goose's social media and blogging efforts?
2. How might Canada Goose use mobile marketing in the future?
3. When a company is focused on creating value partially through the creation of community, what other efforts might it try?
4. Direct marketing usually employs a "call to action," whereby it gets the consumer to do something (e.g., to purchase the product, sample the product, sign up for a contest). Because Canada Goose is not a direct retailer, it cannot use price-driven calls to action. What other calls to action can it employ to engage the consumer?

REVIEWING THE CONCEPTS

1. Define direct marketing and discuss its benefits to customers and companies.

Direct marketing consists of direct connections with carefully targeted individual consumers to both obtain an immediate response and cultivate lasting customer relationships. By using detailed databases, direct marketers tailor their offers and communications to the needs of narrowly defined segments or even individual buyers.

For buyers, direct marketing is convenient, easy to use, and private. It gives buyers ready access to a wealth of products and information, at home and around the globe. Direct marketing is also immediate and interactive, allowing buyers to create exactly the configuration of information, products, or services they desire, then to order them on the spot. For sellers, direct marketing is a powerful tool for building customer relationships. By using database marketing, today's marketers can target small groups or individual consumers, tailor offers to individual needs, and promote these offers through personalized communications. It also offers them a low-cost, efficient alternative for reaching their markets. As a result of these advantages to both buyers and sellers, direct marketing has become the fastest-growing form of marketing.

2. Explain the use of a database in direct marketing.

Effective direct marketing requires a customer database, an organized collection of comprehensive data about individual customers or prospects, including geographic, demographic, psychographic, and behavioural data. Databases are used for consumer marketing, where the database might contain data about an individual's age, income, interests, buying preferences and the recency, frequency, and monetary value of past purchases. In business-to-business marketing, the customer database contains information such as key contacts at the customer's organization, order statuses, and past purchases. Most databases are very large, containing terabytes worth of customer information. Companies use databases to locate good potential customers and to generate sales leads. They can mine their databases to learn about customers in detail, and then fine-tune their market offerings and communications to the special preferences and behaviours of target segments or individuals. In all, a company's database can be an important tool for building stronger long-term customer relationships.

3. Identify and discuss the major forms of direct marketing.

Direct-mail marketing, the largest form of direct marketing, consists of the company sending an offer, announcement, reminder, or other item to a person at a specific address. Recently, new forms of "mail delivery" have become popular, such as email and *mobile marketing*. Some marketers rely on *catalogue marketing*—selling through catalogues mailed to a select list of customers, made available in stores, or accessed on the Web. *Telephone marketing* consists of using the telephone to sell directly to consumers. *Direct-response television marketing* has two forms: direct-response advertising (or infomercials) and home shopping channels. *Kiosks* are information and ordering machines that direct marketers place in stores, airports, and other locations. In recent years, a number of new digital direct-marketing technologies have emerged, including mobile marketing, podcasts, and interactive TV. Online marketing involves online channels that digitally link sellers with consumers.

4. Explain how companies have responded to the Internet and other new technologies with online marketing strategies.

Online marketing is the fastest-growing form of direct marketing. The Internet enables consumers and companies to access and share huge amounts of information with just a few mouse clicks. In turn, the Internet has given marketers a whole new way to create value for customers and build customer relationships. It's hard to find a company today that doesn't have a substantial Web marketing presence. Online consumer buying continues to grow at a healthy rate, as more and more online users consider the Internet a place to shop. Perhaps more importantly, the Internet influences offline shopping. Thus, smart marketers are employing integrated multichannel strategies that use the Web to drive sales to other marketing channels.

5. Discuss how companies go about conducting online marketing to profitably deliver more value to customers.

Companies of all types are now engaged in online marketing. The Internet gave birth to the click-only dot-coms, which operate only online. In addition, many traditional brick-and-mortar companies have now added online marketing operations, transforming themselves into click-and-mortar competitors. Many click-and-mortar companies are now having more online success than their click-only competitors.

Companies can conduct online marketing in any of four ways: creating a website, placing ads and promotions online, setting up or participating in Web communities or social networks, or using email. The first step typically is to set up a website. Beyond simply setting up a site, however, companies must make their sites engaging, easy to use, and useful in order to attract visitors, hold them, and bring them back again.

Online marketers can use various forms of online advertising and promotion to build their Internet brands or attract visitors to their websites. Forms of online promotion include online display advertising (banner ads and interstitials), search-related advertising, content sponsorships, affiliate programs, and viral marketing, the Internet version of word-of-mouth marketing. Online marketers can also participate in social networking and other Web communities, which take advantage of the C2C properties of the Web, and use permission-based email marketing to communicate and develop relationships with customers.

Online marketers face growing concerns about invasion-of-privacy and Internet security issues. In the end, most direct marketers want the same things that consumers want: honest and well-designed marketing offers targeted only toward consumers who will appreciate and respond to them.

KEY TERMS

Affiliate program   553
Banner ad   552
Blog   547
Business-to-business (B2B) online marketing   546
Business-to-consumer (B2C) online marketing   545
Catalogue marketing   536
Consumer-to-business (C2B) online marketing   548

Consumer-to-consumer (C2C) online marketing   547
Corporate (or brand) website   549
Customer database   533
Direct marketing   529
Direct-mail marketing   534
Direct-response television marketing   538
Email marketing   555
Interstitial   552

Marketing website   550
Online advertising   552
Online marketing   544
Podcast   541
Social networks   554
Viral marketing   553

TALK ABOUT MARKETING

1. Collect all the direct mail that arrives at your home during a one-week period. Look through the collection and identify the "call to action" in each piece. If the direct-mail piece was addressed to you by name, it means that you are in the sending organization's customer database. Do you remember how you got there? Some pieces of direct mail are not addressed, but are delivered by Canada Post as "unaddressed ad mail." If you have any pieces of unaddressed ad mail in your collection, why do you think the marketers chose to deliver that particular piece to your mailbox?

2. Have you ever seen any kind of advertising on your mobile phone? Who was the advertiser, and what was the promotion? Did you take advantage of the offer? What kinds of marketing promotions or offers would you be willing to receive on your phone?

3. Visit the Canada Goose website. How many of the seven Cs of effective Web design are evident on the site? Explain how each C is used. If there are any Cs that have not been used, can you think of a way for them to be incorporated?

4. Choose your favourite news or information website and explore its various sections. What forms of online advertising are sold on the site?

5. Describe the differences between a B2B marketer such as Cisco Systems and a B2C marketer such as La Senza. Dell is a company that markets its products both to businesses and consumers. How does its website serve these two separate markets? In which ways (if any) does Dell also incorporate C2C or C2B marketing?

6. Write a short email marketing message for RONA, the hardware retailer. Be sure to follow the rules of email marketing etiquette. If you were the online marketing manager at RONA, to whom would you send this message?

THINK LIKE A MARKETING MANAGER

Maestro S.V.P. is an upscale seafood restaurant and oyster bar on trendy St. Laurent Boulevard in Montreal. The clientele of the restaurant is mainly tourists, especially during the summer season, but there are also many regular customers who return again and again because they enjoy the food and the atmosphere, and because they have an oyster shell with their name on it installed on the oyster wall of fame. The chef is famous for his unique and flavourful seafood sauces, and customers often ask whether they can purchase these sauces to take home. Responding to market demand, the owner has recently begun packaging and retailing a line of Maestro sauces, such as Havane sauce for tuna, and Porto & Raspberry sauce, which is excellent with mussels. So far, sauces have been sold only from within the restaurant. Lately, the owner has been wondering which forms of Internet marketing might help grow her business.

QUESTIONS

1. If Maestro began the task of creating a customer database, what forms of direct marketing would you recommend it employ to promote its business?
2. Visit the restaurant's website at MaestroSVP.com. Would you recommend that the owner include e-commerce capabilities on the site? Explain why or why not.
3. Maestro is a small business and doesn't have a budget for mass-media advertising. Investigate possible opportunities for inexpensive online advertising for Maestro.
4. How might Maestro use social networking to promote its business? Be specific—which social networks would you recommend it participate in, and how? Are there any niche social network sites that would be appropriate for Maestro?

MARKETING ETHICS

The World Wide Web is often referred to as the "Wild West." Unlike advertising, which openly identifies the sponsor, most of the product and brand information seen on the Internet does not reveal sponsorship. You might read about a product in a blog, see it in a YouTube video, or follow it in Twitter, often unaware that the person was paid or was provided free merchandise or other goodies to say positive things about a product or a service. These undercover company shills are difficult to detect. Kmart, Sony Pictures, Hewlett-Packard, and other marketers use companies such as IZEA to develop "sponsored conversations" by using its network of bloggers. Sponsored conversations generated by IZEA disclose sponsorships; many others do not. But that is about to change. The U.S. Federal Trade Commission recently updated its endorsement guidelines requiring disclosure of sponsorship by

bloggers. Violators could be slapped with an $11 000 fine per violation, but with almost 30 million bloggers out there—80 percent of whom occasionally or frequently post product or brand reviews—it will be difficult, if not impossible, to enforce this rule.

QUESTIONS

1. Find examples of product information posted in blogs. Did the blogger indicate in the post that he or she was paid or received free products? Should the government enact laws to require bloggers and others on the Internet to disclose sponsorship from marketers? Explain.
2. Visit the Word of Mouth Marketing Association's website (WOMMA.org) and IZEA's website (IZEA.com). Write a set of recommendations on how marketers can effectively use sponsored conversations.

MARKETING TECHNOLOGY

The iPad is shaping up to be the electronic device that will propel catalogue shopping into the twenty-first century. For years marketers have been experimenting with e-commerce applications for the iPhone and other smartphones, but have found that the tiny screens with their limited visual displays have shortchanged the efforts. Consumers might use their smartphones to locate a retail store, but they're not inclined to actually shop by using the device. Enter the iPad, Apple's latest gadget with a screen the size of a magazine. It seems like a natural fit for catalogues, and retailers agree—they're scrambling to develop touch-to-buy applications to reach the more than 3 million consumers who already own iPads. Amazon, Gap, and eBay have already created online shopping applications specifically designed for the iPad, and Sears is considering putting its next Christmas Wish book on the iPad.

QUESTIONS

1. The goal of every direct-marketing campaign is to move the customer as close to the sale as possible. How does the new technology of the iPad move customers even closer to the sale?
2. Fashion retailer Gilt Groupe describes building its iPad app as "throwing out the mouse and keyboard and starting over with the way users want to interact with products and images." List all the ways in which the consumer experience of catalogue shopping is different from traditional and online shopping.

MARKETING BY THE NUMBERS

Many companies are realizing the efficiency of telemarketing in the face of soaring sales force costs. Whereas an average cost of a business-to-business sales call by an outside salesperson costs more than $300, the cost of a telemarketing sales call can be as little as $5 to $20. And telemarketers can make 20 to 33 decision-maker contacts per day to a salesperson's four per day. This has gotten the attention of many business-to-business marketers—where telemarketing can be very effective.

QUESTIONS

1. Refer to Appendix 3, Marketing by the Numbers, to determine the marketing return on sales (marketing ROS) and return on marketing investment (marketing ROI) for Company A and Company B in the chart at right. Which company is performing better? Explain.

2. Should all companies consider reducing their sales forces in favour of telemarketing? Discuss the pros and cons of this action.

	Company A (sales force only)	Company B (telemarketing only)
Net sales	$1,000,000	$850,000
Cost of goods sold	$500,000	$425,000
Sales expenses	$300,000	$100,000

END-OF-CHAPTER CASE

STUBHUB: TICKET SCALPING, A RESPECTABLE ENDEAVOUR?

When the rock band KISS returned to the United States for the final performances of its Alive/35 tour in the summer of 2008, Roger felt like reliving some old memories. Just because he was in his 50s didn't mean he was too old to rock. After all, he was an original KISS fan dating back to the 70s. It had been years since he had gone to a concert by any band. On the day the KISS tickets went on sale, he grabbed a lawn chair and headed to his local Ticketmaster outlet to "camp out" in line. Roger knew that the terminal, located inside a large chain music store, wouldn't open until 10 a.m. when tickets went on sale. He got to the store at 6 a.m. to find only three people ahead of him. "Fantastic," Roger thought. With so few people in front of him, getting good seats would be a snap. Maybe he would even score something close to the stage.

By the time the three people in front of him had their tickets it was 10:13. As the clerk typed away on the Ticketmaster computer terminal, Roger couldn't believe what he heard. No tickets were available. The show at the Palms Resort in Las Vegas was sold out. Dejected, Roger turned to leave. As he made his way out the door, another customer said, "You can always try StubHub." As the fellow KISS fan explained what StubHub was, it occurred to Roger that the world had become a very different place with respect to buying concert tickets.

Indeed, in this Internet age, buying tickets for live events has changed dramatically since Roger's concert-going days. Originators such as Ticketmaster now sell tickets online for everything from Broadway shows to sporting events. Increasingly, however, event tickets are resold through websites such as eBay, Razorgator, TicketsNow, craigslist, and StubHub, the fastest-growing company in the business. Various industry observers estimate that as many as 30 percent of all event tickets are resold. This secondary market for online sports and entertainment tickets has grown to billions of dollars in annual revenues.

And although prices are all over the map, tickets for sold-out hot events routinely sell for double or triple their face value. In some cases, the markup is astronomical. The nationwide average price for kids to see Miley Cyrus was $249, up from about $50 for the highest face-value seat. A pair of tickets to see Bruce Springsteen at the Washington, D.C., Verizon Center set some back as much as $2000. Prices for a seat at Super Bowl XLII in Phoenix, one of the hottest ticket-resale events of all time, were as high as $13 000. And one U.K. Led Zeppelin fan with obviously far too much money on his hands paid over $160 000 for a pair of Led Zeppelin tickets close enough to the stage to see a geriatric Robert Plant perspire. Extreme cases? Yes. But not uncommon.

When most people think of buying a ticket from a reseller, they probably envision a seedy scalper standing in the shadows near an event venue. But scalping is moving mainstream. While the Internet and other technologies have allowed professional ticket agents to purchase event tickets in larger numbers, anyone with a computer and a broadband connection can instantly become a scalper. And regular folks, even fans, are routinely doing so. "Because we allowed people to buy four [tickets], if they only need two they put the other two up for sale," said Dave Holmes, manager for Coldplay. This dynamic, occurring for events across the board, has dramatically increased the number of ticket resellers.

STUBHUB ENTERS THE GAME

With the ticket-resale market booming, StubHub started operations in 2000 as Liquid Seats. It all began with an idea by two first-year students at the Stanford Graduate School of Business. Eric Baker and Jeff Fluhr had been observing the hysteria on the ticket-resale market. In their opinion, the market was highly fragmented and rampant with fraud and distorted pricing. Two buyers sitting side by side at the same event might find they'd paid wildly different prices for essentially the same product. Even with heavy hitter eBay as the biggest ticket reseller at the time, Baker and Fluhr saw an opportunity to create a system that would bring buyers and sellers together in a more efficient manner.

They entered their proposal in a new–business plan competition. Fluhr was utterly convinced the concept would work—so much so that he withdrew the proposal from the competition and dropped out of school to launch the business. At a time when dot-coms were dropping like flies, this action might have seemed like a very poor decision. But Fluhr ultimately became CEO of StubHub, the leader and fastest-growing company of a $10 billion-a-year industry.

Home to over 300 employees, StubHub uses 1860 square metres of prime office space in San Francisco's pricey financial district, seven satellite offices, and two call centres. Even more telling is the company's growth. In November 2006, a little over six years after starting, StubHub sold its 5 millionth ticket. Just over one year later it sold its 10 millionth ticket. And six months after that, in June 2008, StubHub rewarded the buyer and seller of the 15 millionth ticket sold with a pair of $5000 gift certificates for its website. In its first few years of operations, StubHub posted a staggering growth rate of more than 3200 percent. According to comScore Inc., a firm that tracks Web traffic, StubHub.com is the leading site among more than a dozen competitors in the ticket-resale category.

THE DEVIL IS IN THE DETAILS

StubHub's model is showing that buying a ticket on the aftermarket doesn't have to mean paying a huge price premium. Sharing his own experience, a *New York Times* writer provides his own StubHub experience:

> To test the system I started with the New York Yankees. A series with the Seattle Mariners was coming up, just before the Yankees left town for a long road trip. Good tickets would be scarce. I went to StubHub. Lots of tickets there, many priced stratospherically. I settled on two Main Box seats in Section 313, Row G. They were in the right-field corner, just one section above field level. The price was $35 each, or face price for a season ticketholder. This was tremendous value for a sold-out game. I registered with StubHub, creating a user name and password, ordered the tickets, then sealed the deal by providing my credit card number. An email message arrived soon after, confirming the order and informing me that StubHub was contacting the seller to arrange for shipment. My card would not be charged until the seller had confirmed to StubHub the time and method of delivery. A second email message arrived a day later giving the delivery details. The tickets arrived on the Thursday before the game, and the seller was paid by StubHub on confirmation of delivery. On Saturday, under a clear, sunny sky, the Yankees were sending a steady stream of screaming line drives into the right-field corner.

From the beginning, Baker and Fluhr set out to provide better options for both buyers and sellers by making StubHub different. Like eBay, StubHub has no ticket inventory of its own, reducing its risk. It simply provides the venue that gives buyers and sellers the opportunity to come together. But it's the differences, perhaps, that have allowed StubHub to achieve such success in such a short period of time.

One of the first differences noticed by buyers and sellers is StubHub's ticket-listing procedure. Sellers can list tickets by auction or at a fixed price, a price that declines as the event gets closer. Whereas some sites charge fees just to list tickets, StubHub lists them for free. Thus, initially, the seller has no risk whatsoever. StubHub's system is simpler than most, splitting the fee burden between buyer and seller. It charges sellers a 15 percent commission and buyers a 10 percent fee.

StubHub's website structure also creates a marketplace that comes closer to pure competition than any other reseller's website. All sellers are equal on StubHub, as ticket listings are identical in appearance and seller identity is kept anonymous. StubHub even holds the shipping method constant, via FedEx. This makes the purchase process much more transparent for buyers. They can browse tickets by event, venue, and section. Comparison shopping is very easy as shoppers can simultaneously view different pairs of tickets in the same section, even in the same row.

Although prices still vary, this system makes tickets more of a commodity and allows market forces to narrow the gap considerably from one seller to another. In fact, while tickets often sell for high prices, this reselling model can also have the effect of pushing ticket prices below face value. Many experts believe that the emergence of Internet resellers such as StubHub is having an equalizing effect, often resulting in fair prices determined by market forces.

Unlike eBay, StubHub provides around-the-clock customer service via a toll-free number. But perhaps the biggest and most important difference between StubHub and competitors is the company's 100 percent FanProtect guarantee. Initially, it might seem more risky buying from a seller whose identity is unknown. But StubHub puts the burden of responsibility on the seller, remaining involved after the purchase, where competing sites bow out. Buyers aren't charged until they confirm receipt of the tickets. "If you open the package and it contains two squares of toilet paper instead of the tickets," Baker explains, "then we debit the seller's credit card for the amount of the purchase." StubHub will also revoke site privileges for fraudulent or unreliable sellers. In contrast, the eBay system is largely self-policing and does not monitor the shipment or verification of the purchased items.

WHAT THE FUTURE HOLDS

When StubHub was formed, it targeted professional ticket brokers and ordinary consumers. In examining individuals as sellers, Baker and Fluhr capitalized on the underexploited assets of sports team season ticketholders. "If you have season tickets to the Yankees, that's 81 games," Baker said. "Unless you're unemployed or especially passionate, there's no way you're going to attend every game." StubHub entered the equation, not only giving ticketholders a way to recoup some of their investment, but allowing them to have complete control over the process rather than selling to a ticket agent.

It quickly became apparent to StubHub's founders that the benefits of season ticketholders selling off unused tickets extended to the sports franchises as well. Being able to sell unwanted tickets encourages season ticketholders to buy again. It also puts customers in seats that would otherwise go empty—customers who buy hot dogs, souvenirs, and programs. Thus, StubHub began entering into signed agreements with professional sports teams. The company has signed agreements with numerous NFL, NBA, and NHL teams to be their official secondary marketplace for season ticketholders.

But most recently, StubHub scored a huge breakthrough deal by becoming the official online ticket reseller for the MBA and its 30 teams. Given that an estimated US$10 billion worth of baseball tickets are resold each year, this single move will likely bring tremendous growth to StubHub. "This is the final vindication for the secondary ticketing market," StubHub spokesman Sean Pate said. "That really puts the final stamp of approval on StubHub."

Revenues from sporting events account for more than half of all StubHub sales. So it's not surprising that the company continues to pursue new partnerships with collegiate sports organizations and even media organizations, such as AOL, Sporting News, and CBS SportsLine. However, it has arranged similar contractual agreements with big-name performers such as Madonna, Coldplay, the Dixie Chicks, Justin Timberlake, Jessica Simpson, and country music's rising star, Bobby Pinson. Arrangements allow StubHub to offer exclusive event packages with a portion of the proceeds supporting charities designated by the performer.

The reselling of event tickets is here to stay. With the rise of safe and legal reseller websites and the repeal of long-standing anti-scalping laws, aftermarket ticket reselling continues to gain legitimacy. There are numerous hands in the fast-growing cookie jar that is the secondary ticket market. StubHub founder Eric Baker left the company and formed viagogo, a European ticket-reseller site that is entering the U.S. market. Even Ticketmaster—the long-established dominant force in primary ticket sales—has jumped into the act. Not only has the ticket powerhouse turned to auctioning a certain portion of premium tickets to the highest bidders, but it has its own resale arm, TicketExchange.

Although there is more than one channel to buy or sell, StubHub's future looks bright. The company's model of entering into partnerships with event-producing organizations is establishing it as "the official" ticket reseller. In fact, in an "if you can't beat 'em, join 'em," move, rival reseller eBay bought StubHub last year for over US$300 million, allowing it to continue to function as its own entity. At this point, there is no end in sight to StubHub's growth curve. Who knows, at some point ticket-seeking consumers may even think of StubHub before thinking of Ticketmaster.

Sources: Ethan Smith, "StubHub Enlisted in Resale of Madonna Concert Tickets," *Wall Street Journal,* May 9, 2008, p. B6; Neil Best, "Want Super Bowl Tickets? Sell or Rent the House," *Newsday,* January 25, 2008, p. A70; Joe Nocera, "Internet Puts a Sugarcoat on Scalping," *New York Times,* January 19, 2008, p. C1; Amy Feldman, "Hot Tickets," *Fast Company,* September 1, 2007, p. 44; "Ticket Reseller StubHub Hits a Home Run," Reuters, August 2, 2007; William Grimes, "That Invisible Hand Guides the Game of Ticket Hunting," *New York Times,* June 18, 2004, p. E1; Steve Stecklow, "Can't Get No ... Tickets?" *Wall Street Journal,* January 7, 2006, p. P1; Steve Stecklow, "StubHub's Ticket to Ride," *Wall Street Journal,* January 17, 2006, p. B1; and information from www.stubhub.com, accessed November 2008.

QUESTIONS

1. Conduct a brief analysis of the marketing environment and the forces shaping the development of StubHub.

2. Discuss StubHub's business model. What general benefits does it afford buyers and sellers? Which benefits are most important in terms of creating value for buyers and sellers?

3. Discuss StubHub as a new intermediary. What effects has this new type of intermediary had on the ticket industry?

4. Apply the text's e-marketing domains framework to StubHub's business model. How has each domain played a role in the company's success?

5. What recommendations can you make for improving StubHub's future growth and success?

6. What are the legal or ethical issues, if any, for ticket-reselling websites?

Appendix 1
General Company Information: Canada Goose

INTRODUCTION

Canada Goose Inc. is a privately held premium outerwear manufacturer based in Toronto, Canada. Its outdoor gear is branded with a distinctive Arctic disc and is considered by many to be among the warmest and most fashionable cold weather outerwear produced anywhere in the world. (The Canada Goose Arctic Program disc shows an inverted image of the North Pole, accompanied by lines of longitude and latitude, to approximate the look and feel of a traditional Arctic map.) The outerwear is sold at high-end Canadian retailers, ranging from Sporting Life in Toronto to Envy on the west coast and Henry Singer in Calgary. Canada Goose is also sold in many international locations, including Bloomingdales in New York, Harrods in London, England, and Collette in Paris.

Canada Goose manufactures and markets premium parkas, snow pants, hats, and gloves, with prices ranging from $100 to more than $1500. The company's Snow Mantra jacket is regarded by many as the warmest parka in the world, and its Lance Mackay Constable jacket has been modified for the "world's toughest athlete" and four-time Iditarod champion Lance Mackey.

Canada Goose also sells a broad range of lightweight down coats and bomber jackets, targeting the user who does not experience extreme winter cold. Its clothing is sold in over 40 countries and is particularly popular in Scandinavian countries and Japan. Canada Goose's parkas are specifically geared toward a "true user" segment: those who live, work, and play in the coldest places on Earth. This segment includes people such as police officers, travel guides, dogsled drivers, and military personnel.

Canada Goose's mantra is authenticity, and its brand personality is represented in the strong, independent-spirited northerner facing down a -70°C snowstorm in Rankin Inlet, Nunavut, and still persevering onward.

In 2007, Canada Goose celebrated its 50-year anniversary by creating a high-quality hard cover book called *Goose People*. *Goose People traces* the company's history and gives sketches of its community—made up of "goose people." Brand aficionados range from Laurie Skreslet, the first Canadian to summit Mount Everest; to Lance Mackey, four-time Iditarod champion; Ray Zahab, endurance athlete; to Chandra Crawford, Olympic gold medalist; to Chantal Kreviazuk, singer; and Walter Gretzky, father of Wayne Gretzky.

THE CANADA GOOSE STORY

Canada Goose's story begins with Sam Tick, a determined immigrant from Poland, who founded Canada Goose, originally called Metro Sportswear Ltd., in 1957. The original premises were in a converted Victorian house on Spadina Avenue in Toronto. Metro had a third-floor room and just enough space for a cutting table and several sewers. Among Metro's early accounts were Kresge's, Woolworths, and Arrow Shirts, for which they produced vests and wool jackets. In the early years, Metro even made specialty clothing for the employees of lumber companies.

"Mr. Tick was a real gentleman from the old school," says Mimi Kujak, a German immigrant who began working at Metro as a sewing machine operator in 1962. "He was very polite and quiet—he'd never say a bad word. Everybody liked him and the atmosphere at Metro was like a big family. He was such a good, honest businessman."

A turning point came for Metro in the early 1970s when the company began making down-filled garments for the Woods bag and canvas company. David found that the down-filling machinery on the market was difficult to work with, time-consuming, and ineffective, so he designed his own machine. (He still owns patents on the technology, and his machine is used to this day.)

David remarks, "At first we used a gravity feed down-filling machine, which was frustratingly slow and inaccurate. I had to find a solution to this problem and so I embarked on the challenge of inventing a superior machine which brought the down into the weighing chamber using air instead of gravity. This was a huge step forward for us."

From 1972 to 1982, Metro's business was largely orders from private label manufacturers as well as custom ordered down-filled coats for the Canadian Rangers, various city police departments, the Ontario Provincial Police, the Ministry of the Environment, the Ministry of Correctional Services, and municipal workers.

In 1982, David and his wife Malca, Sam's daughter, bought Metro from Tick. In his early years, David was a jack-of-all-trades, buying material, serving as chief salesman and head designer, negotiating prices, and cutting material. However, in the early 1980s, a major customer went bankrupt, an event that proved to be a significant setback for Metro. Ultimately, however, Metro prevailed and eventually added accounts such as Eddie Bauer, L.L.Bean, Browning, and Orvis.

THE DEVELOPMENT OF CANADA GOOSE

In late 1983, Metro expanded to 50 workers when it landed Sears as a major account. In the early 1980s, Reiss registered Snow Goose as the name for Metro's down-filled coats. Later, in the mid-1990s, when Metro began selling small quantities of product in Europe, it was discovered that the Snow Goose name was already registered there. The company registered the European products under the name Canada Goose.

The company grew slowly, and the modern era of Canada Goose began only in 1997, when current President and CEO Dani Reiss, son of David Reiss and grandson of Sam Tick, joined the company. At age 24, Dani had no expectation of staying around, but he soon changed his mind.

"The more I learned about our product," Dani explains, "and the more testimonials I heard from people thanking us for making their lives easier by producing our Canada Goose parkas the more inspired I became."

In Dani's early years at Canada Goose, the factory routinely closed for months at a time when work was scarce because of the effects of globalization. The private label business that had once thrived was becoming more and more challenging.

Metro shifted its focus from the private label business to work exclusively on building Canada Goose and, at the time, Snow Goose. A few years later, with business on the upswing, the decision was made to produce under only the Canada Goose name. These changes helped build momentum and fueled the growth that followed.

Current vice-president global marketing Kevin Spreekmeester explains further: "David Reiss was a manufacturer, Dani is a marketer. He took us from selling a commodity to transcending commodity and turning an iconic product into a real brand."

Dani Reiss formally took over running the company in 2001, bringing with him tools that would eventually include a Canada's Top 40 Under 40 award, a YPO network, and the first-hand experience of having worked in every facet of the business. He would also bring his considerable skills and influence to bear as chairman of the board of

Polar Bears International, a global charity committed to preserving the habitat of the polar bear.

According to Dani, the brand really took off in 2000. At this point, the company received positive reaction to its products at a trade show in Germany. For the next few years, Dani spent a lot of time with the European vice-president of sales adding international distribution partners. After the first trade show, Dani travelled to Sweden with Joe Sudow, Canada Goose's distribution and branding partner in Scandinavia. Through Sudow, Dani came to realize how important being made in Canada was to Canada Goose.

So Canada Goose's growth was initially export led. The brand was built in Europe and that success led to emerging growth in North America. In the 14 years since Dani joined Canada Goose, the company has grown substantially. The company's sales have increased over 2000 percent under Dani's guidance. Canada Goose now sells in more than 40 countries and has an international office in Stockholm, Sweden.

A CUSTOMER-DRIVEN MARKETING STRATEGY

When it comes to marketing, Canada Goose pursues unconventional strategies. Many people associate marketing strategies with promotional strategies, but if the essence of marketing is found at the core of the brand—with product, placement, pricing, and promotion working together—then Canada Goose is a brand-focused company.

While Canada Goose does not disclose or overtly focus on a demographic analysis of its customer base, it is generally considered to cater to affluent and active outdoor types, ages 18 to 35.

Canada Goose is careful to cater to its brand leaders (influential persons who have either conventional celebrity status or scientific- or northern Canada–related achievement status). It makes sure that its outerwear is represented and photographed (with material being made available for its own Facebook fan base as well as the fashion and outdoor press).

When looking back at a successful brand formation, people often assume that a company's path was clearly mapped out before the beginning. However, brand formation did not happen this way for Canada Goose. Its initial success in Europe (its parkas were worn by the Swedish royal family and quickly became the most popular outerwear brand in Sweden) taught Canada Goose the value of the "Canada" brand and label, and helped Canada Goose develop its convictions that the market wanted authentic outerwear that went back to the core value of outerwear itself—that of keeping the wearer warm and comfortable.

The European perspective on outerwear placed a greater emphasis on quality over superficial aesthetics and bargain pricing. In hindsight, one might say that the brand value of Canada Goose is a fallback to the original role of branding: to act as a guarantor of quality. Today, Canada Goose continues to focus almost fanatically on quality and improvement.

THE MARKETING PROGRAM

1. LEVERAGE "MADE IN CANADA"

Canada Goose discovered that outside Canada and, in particular, in Scandinavian countries, Canada is perceived to be an authentic cold weather country. Outerwear that is manufactured in Canada is thus also perceived to be authentic. The fact that Canada Goose is the only Canadian outerwear company still manufacturing in country also lends authenticity to the brand name. Add to this the leadership role Canada Goose's

Dani Reiss has taken in bringing manufacturing back to Canada and making "made in Canada" cool, and consumers become excited about the authentic story.

The impact of Canada Goose's "made in Canada" strategy has caught the attention of Canadian retailers and politicians, including James M. Flaherty, Minister of Finance, who referenced president and CEO Dani Reiss in a 2010 Standing Senate Committee on National Finance meeting:

> When combined with other Canadian advantages, such as the lowest overall tax rate on new business investment in the G7, Canada will be on an even more attractive scale for business investment. This will complement our government's efforts at diversifying trade relationships such as the recently concluded free trade agreements. Since the initial unveiling of the tariff-free zone for manufacturing initiative in early March, we have heard very positive feedback from Canadian entrepreneurs.
>
> For example, Canada Goose CEO Dani Reiss, the manufacturer of the world renowned Arctic coats, said:
>
>> This is a great move ... tariffs only made it more expensive to be a Canadian manufacturer.... I think this move by the government will make 'Made in Canada' viable for more apparel companies.
>
> Our tariff elimination will help to ensure that more and more Canadian manufacturers can showcase their products in the global marketplace and succeed. (Courtesy of the Senate of Canada)

Clearly, Canada Goose's choice to manufacture in Canada has differentiated the company in the marketplace and enhanced the trend of valuing products that are made in Canada.

2. FOCUS AND LISTEN TO THE TRUE USER CATEGORY

Canada Goose's motto is "Ask Anyone Who Knows™" and the key message is that the core customers are driven by functionality, not by fashion. The company focuses on the true user, who may make up only a small component of the overall customer base but who, nevertheless, lends authenticity and legitimacy to the brand. Canada Goose has worked to move its products beyond commodity status by showing the product actually being used in cold weather outdoor experiences.

The follow up to the "Ask Anyone Who Knows™" motto is "and listen."
According to president and CEO Dani Reiss,

> Members of our product development team have spent more time in airports than they'd like to speak about while they scour the world for the best technologies and stay on top of the latest innovations in outerwear. Our production facility is outfitted with the best and newest equipment and we use nothing but top-flight materials. There are no compromises on quality because Canada Goose wearers expect the best quality, and respect our attention to detail.

3. LET FASHIONABILITY COME TO YOU

Many companies who strive to be perceived as fashionable are driven by aesthetics and promotion. Canada Goose realizes that its niche in the outerwear market is to create outerwear that puts function on a higher ranking than being in fashion. This understanding has led to the creation of a true user segment, and the appeal of that segment pulls in many others who might otherwise be attracted by traditional fashion outerwear brands. Canada Goose believes that function pushed far enough becomes fashion.

4. BUILD COMMUNITY THROUGH TRUE USERS

Canada Goose has substituted traditional promotion with initiatives to build relationships with prominent true users—that is, people involved in cold weather activities or research, and traditional celebrities who have become fans of the Canada Goose brand.

Furthermore, Canada Goose actively uses social media (Twitter and Facebook) to help build community with its brand fans. In addition, Canada Goose uses its community to gather valuable feedback on its product and brand.

5. DON'T OVERSELL; KEEP A TIGHT REIN ON THE RETAIL CHANNEL

Canada Goose knows that retail channels are its customers' main contact with the Canada Goose brand. The company wants to make sure that the retail stores it chooses are aligned well with the Canada Goose brand and also wants to make sure the stores focus on service, providing sound information, acting ethically, and not overselling the product lines.

QUESTIONS

1. Visit Canada Goose's website (www.canada-goose.com) and review the information available on the company, including its product lines, products, and product availability. Compare this information with information on Canada Goose's competitors, Moncler (www.moncler.com) and The North Face (www.theNorthFace.com). What is Canada Goose's competitive advantage?
2. Look at Canada Goose's distribution strategy. Does it make sense that the company is very particular in choosing its retail partners? What would you do if you had to find a new retailer for Canada Goose? What criteria would you base your decision on?
3. Given what you know of Canada Goose, what would you recommend as the next product line to be launched? Support your answer.
4. Canada Goose does not use traditional promotional vehicles but rather focuses on community building and "true user" endorsements. Do you think that large, branded outerwear companies should try and pursue the same strategy? Why or why not?

Appendix 2
The Marketing Plan: An Introduction

As a marketer, you'll need a good marketing plan to provide direction and focus for your brand, product, or company. With a detailed plan, any business will be better prepared to launch a new product or build sales for existing products. Non-profit organizations also use marketing plans to guide their fundraising and outreach efforts. Even government agencies put together marketing plans for initiatives such as building public awareness of proper nutrition and stimulating area tourism.

THE PURPOSE AND CONTENT OF A MARKETING PLAN

Unlike a business plan, which offers a broad overview of the entire organization's mission, objectives, strategy, and resource allocation, a marketing plan has a more limited scope. It serves to document how the organization's strategic objectives will be achieved through specific marketing strategies and tactics, with the customer as the starting point. It is also linked to the plans of other departments within the organization. Suppose a marketing plan calls for selling 200 000 units annually. The production department must gear up to make that many units; the finance department must arrange funding to cover the expenses; the human resources department must be ready to hire and train staff; and so on. Without the appropriate level of organizational support and resources, no marketing plan can succeed.

Although the exact length and layout will vary from company to company, a marketing plan usually contains the sections described in Chapter 2. Smaller businesses may create shorter or less formal marketing plans, whereas corporations frequently require highly structured marketing plans. To guide implementation effectively, every part of the plan must be described in considerable detail. Sometimes a company will post its marketing plan on an internal website, which allows managers and employees in different locations to consult specific sections and collaborate on additions or changes.

THE ROLE OF RESEARCH

Marketing plans are not created in a vacuum. To develop successful strategies and action programs, marketers need up-to-date information about the environment, the competition, and the market segments to be served. Often, analysis of internal data is the starting point for assessing the current marketing situation, supplemented by marketing intelligence and research investigating the overall market, the competition, key issues, and threats and opportunities. As the plan is put into effect, marketers use a variety of research techniques to measure progress toward objectives and to identify areas for improvement if results fall short of projections.

Finally, marketing research helps marketers learn more about their customers' requirements, expectations, perceptions, and satisfaction levels. This deeper understanding provides a foundation for building competitive advantage through well-informed segmenting, targeting, differentiating, and positioning decisions. Thus, the marketing plan should outline what marketing research will be conducted and how the findings will be applied.

THE ROLE OF RELATIONSHIPS

The marketing plan shows how the company will establish and maintain profitable customer relationships. In the process, however, it also shapes a number of internal and external relationships. First, it affects how marketing personnel work with each other and with other departments to deliver value and satisfy customers. Second, it affects how the company works with suppliers, distributors, and strategic alliance partners to achieve the objectives listed in the plan. Third, it influences the company's dealings with other stakeholders, including government regulators, the media, and the community at large. All of these relationships are important to the organization's success, and so they should be considered when a marketing plan is being developed.

FROM MARKETING PLAN TO MARKETING ACTION

Companies generally create yearly marketing plans, although some plans cover a longer period. Marketers start planning well in advance of the implementation date to allow time for marketing research, thorough analysis, management review, and coordination between departments. Then, after each action program begins, marketers monitor ongoing results, compare them with projections, analyze any differences, and take corrective steps as needed. Some marketers also prepare contingency plans for implementation if certain conditions emerge. Because of inevitable and sometimes unpredictable environmental changes, marketers must be ready to update and adapt marketing plans at any time.

For effective implementation and control, the marketing plan should define how progress toward objectives will be measured. Managers typically use budgets, schedules, and performance standards for monitoring and evaluating results. With budgets, they can compare planned expenditures with actual expenditures for a given week, month, or other period. Schedules allow management to see when tasks were supposed to be completed—and when they were actually completed. Performance standards track the outcomes of marketing programs to see whether the company is moving toward its objectives. Some examples of performance standards are market share, sales volume, product profitability, and customer satisfaction.

SAMPLE MARKETING PLAN FOR CANADA GOOSE

EXECUTIVE SUMMARY

Executive summary
This section summarizes the main goals, recommendations, and points. It serves as an overview for senior managers who will read and approve the marketing plan. For management convenience, a table of contents generally follows this section.

Canada Goose is currently a market leader in the high-end, extreme weather outerwear market. The company's focus is on core users who value Canada Goose products for use in genuine cold weather conditions. The company continues to innovate the design and features of its outerwear so it can produce the warmest and most practical outdoor gear on the planet. The Canada Goose brand is also very centred on being Canadian and on the mystique and allure of the Canadian North. This image is supported by the company's decision and determination to manufacture in Canada.

As Canada Goose moves forward, the company will continue to leverage the vision of CEO Dani Reiss and focus on new-product development, especially for users involved in very active outdoor pursuits or who want a coat for late fall and early spring conditions. Canada Goose will continue to develop its exclusive retail channels in North America, Western Europe, and more than 40 other countries around the world.

CURRENT MARKETING SITUATION

Canada Goose is prospering. Its products are moving extremely well in the market and sales have seen healthy increases in each of the last two years. Its outerwear is now adopted by a broad range of audiences that include celebrities, urban dwellers, and core users. Today, strong growth allows Canada Goose to focus its resources on the corporate infrastructure needs of tomorrow.

Its products, such as the Snow Mantra parka and the Lance Mackey Constable Parka, have traditionally focused on being able to keep a wearer warm in an arctic climate. However, Canada Goose is now moving into outdoor wear that focuses more on people who want Canada Goose products for their more active lifestyle and for the shoulder seasons of late fall and early spring. This latest suite of outerwear uses new technology such as the innovations seen in the Hybridge line, which employs Thermal Mapping™ technology and incorporates both fleece and lightweight down. These new products are well positioned to contribute to Canada Goose's future growth.

Market Description

Just over 10 years ago, when it discovered a European appetite for Canadian quality and authenticity, Canada Goose set out to reinforce its brand with an emphasis on psychographic, behavioural, and geographic segmentation. The psychographic elements of distinct customer thoughts and attitudes were reflected in a core customer base that had an appreciation for authenticity and a commitment to the northern environment. The behavioural segmentation targeted users who stayed long periods of time in extreme cold climates.

Stories about the hearty people in northern Canada and their rugged ability to survive in a difficult environment are key components of Canada Goose's image, especially in its European markets. The company has experienced considerable successes leveraging authentic stories of Canadian survival and of adventure and often requires little additional marketing to sell its products. This strategy illustrates that there is a distinct attitude, perception, and value in the Canada Goose image that customers are buying into. Canada Goose will continue to leverage these stories through "Goose People" ads.

While Canada Goose does not compile traditional demographic numbers on its customer base, conduct traditional focus groups, or engage in traditional market research, it does have a strong sense of its core users that comes from informal studies and discussions with a variety of key customers. The company's market is expanding beyond the extreme cold true users by providing high-technology lightweight-down and polar fleece outerwear for less extreme winters or for fall and spring seasons.

Product Review

One of the many ways the products are displayed is by showing "core users" and celebrities in an experiential context as opposed to a traditional fashion context. This distinction emphasizes product functionality over product looks.

Canada Goose products are divided according to functionality and benefits. The main product lines are Arctic Line, Multizone, Accessories, Youth, and Special Collections.

Current marketing situation
In this section, marketing managers discuss the overall market, identify the market segments they will target, and provide information about the company's current situation.

Market description
Describing the targeted segments in detail provides context for the marketing strategies and detailed action programs discussed later in the plan.

Product review
The product review summarizes the main features for all the company's products, organized by product line, type of customer, market, or order of product introduction.

The trek across Lake Baikal was daunting. It was frozen over and windswept, exposing treacherous black ice. The humidity was high, yet the temperature was well below -30, which can be a dangerous cocktail when it comes to wilderness survival. I tried hauling my way across but each gust of wind was so ridiculously strong that I was completely doubled over and unable to run. Our sleds were continuously getting flipped over, making every step an unbearable struggle forward. Every muscle in my body was telling me to give up. What had I gotten myself into? There are always moments when I want to turn back but I have to remind myself that I had chosen to be there and the rewards would far exceed my pain. I know that within all of us is the ability to do something extraordinary.

Ray Zahab, endurance athlete, on his expedition across Siberia

Ray depends on Canada Goose outerwear for all of his expeditions

ASK ANYONE WHO KNOWS™

PROUDLY MADE IN CANADA
WWW.CANADA-GOOSE.COM

Exhibit A2.1 "Goose People" are individuals who appreciate the sanctity of the Northern climes and who are dedicated to the preservation of its climate and ecosystem. Goose People are not content to sit on the sidelines of life: They cherish nature and look for outdoor gear that is dedicated to keeping them warm and that will last for many seasons.

Product Line	Strategic Goal and Target Market
Arctic Line	Designed to meet the needs of the classic true user with an overarching focus on providing warmth for the user who is out in the cold for extended periods of time. Some users could be arctic guides, northern military personnel, and upscale outdoor club workers.
Multizone	Designed for those who are not exposed to the same extent of northern temperature plumbs as above but who still want a coat that uses technology (down, fabric, zippers, treatments) to maximize warmth conservation and freedom of motion. Some users could be persons in less frigid climates, cross-country skiers, and others.
Accessories	Cold weather accessories made in the same spirit as the other Canada Goose gear. High-quality gloves, hats, and snow pants designed to last and to maximize both warmth, ease of movement, and functionality (the company knows that people in the cold still have work to do and need to be free to move around and perform necessary functions without unnecessary constriction by fabric and material). It is focused on a broad market, for those who want quality accessories that last more than a season.
Youth	Youth, especially the very young, have been shown to lose more heat due to transpiration from exposed skin. Canada Goose has devoted products that cross lines (but focus on the arctic line), designed to keep children warm (from newborns to tweens).
Special Collections	As the name implies, these are special collections designed around the needs of a single user (e.g., the Lance Mackey Constable Jacket) or focused on the vision of a singular designer. This product line is featured in a very limited run and changes every year.

Competitive Review

Competitive review
The purpose of a competitive review is to identify key competitors, describe their market positions, and briefly discuss their strategies.

The outerwear market is very large. Canada Goose sits between brands in the fashion and the high-utility outdoor markets, and sells to a variety of retailers, including fashion stores, women's stores, men's stores, sporting goods stores, ski shops, industrial shops, and streetwear stores.

Canada Goose considers two companies to be direct competitors. On the utility or practical side, Canada Goose's main competition is from The North Face Inc. The North Face is also a user-focused outerwear company, although it focuses on a more price-sensitive consumer. On the fashion side, Canada Goose's main competitor is Moncler. However, Moncler is priced higher than Canada Goose gear and the company is focused on meeting the needs of individuals who are ultimately more concerned about fashion and image than utility.

Canada Goose has managed to create brand authenticity that supports itself on both the fashion and utility side, and the company is continuing to maintain this balance. The company will not compromise between the two sectors even though its heritage comes from the utility side.

Distribution (Channel) Review

Distribution (channel) review
In this section, marketers list the most important channels, provide an overview of each channel arrangement, and identify developing issues in channels.

Canada Goose products are distributed in retail stores, ranging from Sporting Life to Harrods of London. Canada Goose has retail partnerships in over 40 countries around the world. In Toronto, for example, there are 27 retailers, including Sporting Life, Over the Rainbow, Harry Rosen, Holt Renfrew, Uncle Otis Clothing, etc. Across Canada, Canada Goose products are sold in Envy on the west coast, Henry Singer in Calgary, and Simons in Quebec.

The retail channel is tightly controlled and Canada Goose management will continue to pay close attention to ensure that the Canada Goose brand is reinforced by partnering only with the best retailers within each retail category. While most are brick-and-mortar retailers with supporting e-commerce websites, some retailer partners are strictly online retailers.

SWOT ANALYSIS

Strengths

- ☐ *Brand:* The brand is very popular as it has become iconic and consumers recognize it as authentic. Even in the summer, winter coats are selling out quickly.

- ☐ *Core user:* Canada Goose has established a "core user" base with loyal brand fans.

- ☐ *Management:* Canada Goose has a strong management with private ownership allowing them to tightly manage the brand.

- ☐ *Loyalty:* A large social media and Facebook community indicates a high degree of customer loyalty.

- ☐ *Product diversity:* Canada Goose has a broad selection of outerwear, ranging from lightweight down to Arctic parkas and hats, gloves, and pants.

- ☐ *Quality:* The company's Snow Mantra jacket is the warmest coat on the market. Canada Goose's Canadian manufacturing enables it to keep high controls on quality.

- ☐ *Innovation expertise:* Canada Goose is working with textile technology companies around the world. These companies provide fabrics that facilitate superior wind/rain resistance, heat retention, and/or heat venting.

- ☐ *Expansionary competency:* Canada Goose gained brand momentum in Europe and has expanded to more than 40 countries. It has a proven ability to develop new markets.

- ☐ *True Canadian:* Canada Goose is the only outwear manufacturer to manufacture 100 percent of its jackets in Canada.

- ☐ *Blue Ocean space:* Canada Goose has found a niche market with a broad appeal across different markets, including fashion, outdoor, and among consumers who work outdoors and need extreme protection against the cold. (The "blue ocean" metaphor means the wide blue ocean where customers do not perceive much competition.)

Weaknesses

- ☐ *Capital access:* Private companies cannot issue publicly traded shares and thus have to depend on debt financing when they need money to expand.

- ☐ *Over-stretched human resources:* Canada Goose is a small company growing very quickly. The demands of this high growth could take senior management resources away from their core function of managing brand management and research and development.

- ☐ *Small company:* Small companies tend to have a narrower product scope and thus can be more susceptible to negative events and temporary downturns.

Opportunities

- ☐ *New products:* Canada Goose can leverage its very strong brand and move into other areas within the outerwear or outdoor gear market.

☐ *Riding the crest:* Canada Goose is riding the crest of a growing market and a growing desire for authenticity in its brands.

☐ *Geographic expansion:* Canada Goose has a proven expertise in developing new markets.

☐ *Product diversification:* Canada Goose is building today's product development infrastructure to meet future goals. It has established relationships with the world's leading companies in textile innovations.

☐ *Commercial sales:* Canada Goose could develop an exclusive line for military, police, SWAT teams, etc.

Threats

Threats
Threats are current or emerging external elements that could potentially challenge the company's performance.

☐ *Manufacturing costs:* Competition can undercut the company on price because of Canada Goose's higher domestic manufacturing cost.

☐ *Competitors:* Competitive threat from existing European and U.S.-based manufacturers: They could move aggressively into Canada Goose's market niche.

☐ *Excessive demand for its products:* In the face of strong demand, Canada Goose could have difficulty or be unable to meet market demand.

☐ *Increasing value of the Canadian dollar:* When the Canadian dollar rises in value against foreign currencies, foreign companies must pay more in their own currency to purchase Canada Goose products. They must pass this cost on to their customers.

☐ *Manufacturing limitations:* A lack of skilled workers for manufacturing in Canada combined with limited Canadian manufacturing infrastructure could make it difficult for Canada Goose to meet global demand.

☐ *Future leadership potential:* While the existing management team is young, with Dani Reiss still in his 30s, potential new leaders need to be groomed in the event of a planned or an unexpected need for a corporate successor to Reiss.

☐ *Economic downturn:* Declining consumer confidence index set off by continued poor economic news in the United States could lead to people delaying Canada Goose coat purchases.

OBJECTIVES AND ISSUES

Objectives

Objectives and Issues
Objectives and Issues should be defined in specific terms so management can measure progress and plan corrective action if needed to stay on track. This section describes any major issues that might affect the company's marketing strategy and implementation.

Canada Goose has set out the following aggressive and optimistic objectives for 2010–2011.

☐ Increase brand awareness.

☐ Expand into shoulder seasons. Canada Goose will expand its product range to include the shoulder seasons of spring and fall.

☐ Continue to position Canada Goose as the gold standard for the "core user." The core user or the "true user" is the person who, because of his or her work or activities, absolutely needs a coat of Canada Goose's warmth-providing capabilities.

☐ Increase community base. Canada Goose will continue to grow its community, which includes all those who wear its products, love its brand, and typically keep in touch with Canadian Goose through social media and through participating in Canadian Goose contests and/or events.

□ Increase relationships with environmental organizations/associations with similar objectives to Canada Goose. An example of such an organization would be the World Wildlife Foundation, a charity that finances scientific research on the condition of the Canadian polar bear's ecosystem and environment.

Issues

□ Can Canada Goose increase sales and not sacrifice the exclusivity of the brand?

□ Can Canada Goose continue to enjoy success using non-traditional marketing?

MARKETING STRATEGY

Canada Goose's marketing strategy has four tiers.

A. Brand development

□ Continue to build Canada Goose's reputation

□ Develop public relations initiatives with a focus on Canada, the United States, and key European markets

□ Develop website in French and German

□ Build up social media presence

□ Extend media buy in outdoor and niche environmental magazines

□ Enhance trade show presence

□ Increase co-op buys with retailers

□ Develop more point-of-purchase materials

Exhibit A2.2 This image shows the original Canada Goose–sponsored coat check at Air Canada Centre in Toronto, Ontario.

B. Product specific

□ Support Lance Mackey outfit in 2010–2011
  • Use hang tangs, POP, PR, social media, work through Lance Mackey website

□ Support Canada Goose active pursuits and shoulder seasons with Hybridge/Soft Shells
  • Use hang tangs, POP, PR, social media, work through Lance Mackey website

□ Thermal Mapping
  • Focus on trade magazines; use hang tangs, POP, PR, social media

C. Retail support

□ Ensure growth of partnerships and sell through of increased buys

□ Develop structured co-op program with clear communication for North America

D. Guerilla marketing: "Taking it to the streets"

□ Continue to bring the Canada Goose product suite directly in contact with its core potential customer segments (not only via retailers) by innovative ideas such as the Canada Goose Coat Checks at Air Canada Centre in Toronto, Bell Centre in Montreal, and Rexall Place in Edmonton. In these arenas, as a service to the best season seats in the building, Canada Goose hosts a free coat check. Within the coat check are new Canada Goose magazines, samples of coats, and a well-trained staff who can direct patrons to the nearest Canada Goose retailer should they ask.

Positioning

Canada Goose will continue to position itself as a market-leading provider of authentic outerwear while continuing to develop the stylistic aspects of its products that are popular in the lifestyle and high-end fashion markets.

The Canada Goose design team will continue to reinforce Canada Goose's reputation as the best-quality gear that is authentic, functional, and inherently Canadian. It is the only Canadian outdoor gear manufacturer that still manufactures in Canada. This allows it to keep tight reins on quality and production and is a key component of the authentic "Canada" part of the brand. However, one part of its product line—its gloves—is not manufactured in Canada. To address this exception to its overall manufacturing strategy, Canada Goose came up with a message that is included on the tags for all of its gloves.

Canada Goose's brand is about being authentic and authentically Canadian. For Canada Goose, an important aspect of this Canadian authenticity is manufacturing its products in Canada. When Canada Goose was not able to find Canadian factories that could manufacture its gloves and accessories, it was forced to manufacture in China. Rather than hide this fact and possibly look less than authentic, Canada Goose decided to be upfront and used the situation as an opportunity to connect with its customers, asking for their help in finding domestic manufacturing opportunities for this particular line of clothing.

Product Strategy

Canada Goose will develop beyond the extreme cold weather market and offer soft shell, lightweight down jackets. It will also continue to support its strong Arctic line.

To fulfill the brand mandate of having the warmest and most functional outerwear, Canada Goose has product partners so that it can leverage technical expertise outside of Canada Goose and ensure that world-leading textile/fastener/coating technologies are employed, whether or not they have been developed in-house.

Pricing Strategy

Canada Goose will maintain its premium pricing points. See below for typical men's product pricing.* Product selection and pricing for women is similar. Canada Goose's kids' pricing line runs from $150 to $275.

1. Men's Freestyle Vest: $225
2. Men's Banff Parka: $595
3. Men's Chateau Parka: $575
4. Men's Lance Mackey Constable Parka: not for sale
5. Snow Mantra Parka: $995
6. Lodge Down Vest: $295
7. Tremblant Pullover: $300
8. Tremblant Jacket: $300
9. Down Mitts: $150
10. Calgary Jacket: $625
11. Montreal Vest: not for sale
12. Corduroy Down Vest: not for sale
13. Pearson Field Jacket: not for sale

Positioning

A positioning built on meaningful differentiation, supported by appropriate strategy and implementation, can help the company build competitive advantage.

Exhibit A2.3

14. Expedition Parka: $650
15. Polar Bear International Expedition Jacket: $700
16. Constable Parka: $475
17. Chilliwack Parka: $495
18. Heli-Arctic Parka: $695
19. Arctic Rigger Coverall: $650

*All prices in Canadian dollars. Prices as of December 2010.

Distribution Strategy

Canada Goose will continue its cautious retail growth with both brick-and-mortar and online retailers by developing relationships with sporting goods, fashion, hybrid/lifestyle, and outdoor stores that are a strong fit with the brand.

Marketing tools
These sections summarize the brand logic that will guide decisions made about the marketing tools to be used during the period covered by this plan.

Marketing Communications Strategy

☐ Support retailers with co-op dollars (often in the form of point-of-purchase displays that the retailer and the manufacture pay for jointly).

☐ Create new French- and German-language versions of its Canada Goose website. New sources for print advertising will be explored with magazines such as *Explore* and *Canadian Geographic*.

☐ Canada Goose will expand the scope of its Canada Goose Coat Checks at major Canadian hockey arenas. By offering a free coat check service and displaying its gear and Canada Goose magazines, Canada Goose builds goodwill with potential customers and spreads the Canada Goose brand message.

Marketing Research

Canada Goose will continue to gather information from its core user segment, social media community, and retail and trade partners.

Marketing research
This section shows how marketing research will be used to support development, implementation, and evaluation of strategies and action programs.

Marketing Organization

Dani Reiss and Kevin Spreekmeester will continue to lead the marketing initiatives.

Marketing organization
The marketing department may be organized by function, geography, product, or customer.

ACTION PROGRAMS

Canada Goose does not release any listing of planned action programs for publication in order to protect its strategy and competitive advantage.

Action programs
Action programs should be coordinated with the resources and activities of other departments, including production, finance, operations, and purchasing.

Partnerships

Canada Goose has a clear positioning strategy where it wants to be perceived as a socially conscious and environmentally concerned company. This "ethical/brand DNA" is supported by partnerships with various organizations, which are listed below:

☐ *Polar Bear International:* PBI is a not-for-profit organization devoted to preserving the habitat of polar bears around the world.

☐ *Conservation Alliance:* The Conservation Alliance is an environmental group dedicated to environmental preservation.

☐ *Maple Leaf Sports and Entertainment Ltd.:* Maple Leaf Sports and Entertainment Ltd. is the parent company of numerous professional sports teams, including the

Toronto Maple Leafs, Toronto Raptors, Toronto Football Club (TFC), and the Toronto Marlies.

☐ *Gap Adventure:* This adventure company offers northern trips and expeditions.

☐ *Fairmont:* Fairmont is a world leader in the global hospitality industry with a large portfolio of well-known hotels, such as Chateau Lake Louise.

Budgets
Managers use budgets to project profitability and plan for each marketing program's expenditures, scheduling, and operations.

BUDGETS

Budgets (or after-the-fact financial statements) for publicly traded companies (companies that sell shares that trade on the stock market) are, by law, accessible by shareholders. A privately owned company such as Canada Goose does not offer shares to the general public and, thus, is under no obligation to post budgets or financial statements. Therefore, its budgets are confidential.

Marketing controls
Controls help management assess results after their plan has been implemented, identify any problems or performance variations, and initiate corrective action.

Marketing Controls

Canada Goose uses the following measurement systems to monitor and control its marketing efforts:

☐ *Market share analysis:* It gathers information from its retailers on how the Canada Goose line is selling within their stores.

☐ *Returns:* Canada Goose measures the rate of product returns and complaints against industry norms. Canada Goose has among the lowest return rate in the industry.

☐ *Quality control:* Canada Goose gathers feedback from customers and employees through a quality control department that conducts annual formal surveys and monitors defect rates.

☐ *Sales:* Canada Goose tracks sales through its retail partners—the metric is officially called "sell through."

☐ *Collaborative marketing with retailers (e.g., a window display and an accompanying display unit):* Canada Goose has set agreements with retailers that are monitored to see how well the retailer complies with the agreement and to measure the success of the collaborative marketing initiative in increasing store traffic, consumer awareness, etc.

Appendix 3
Marketing by the Numbers

Marketing managers are facing increased accountability for the financial implications of their actions. This appendix provides a basic introduction to measuring marketing financial performance. Such financial analysis guides marketers in making sound marketing decisions and in assessing the outcomes of those decisions.

The appendix is built around a hypothetical manufacturer of consumer electronics products—ConnectPhone. In the past, ConnectPhone has concentrated on making Internet modems. However, the company is now introducing a new type of product—a *media phone* that replaces a household's telephone and provides "always-on" Internet connectivity and wireless phone access through VoIP (Voice over Internet Protocol) technology. In this appendix, we will analyze the various decisions ConnectPhone's marketing managers must make before and after the new-product launch.

The appendix is organized into *three sections*. The *first section* introduces pricing, break-even, and margin analysis assessments that will guide the introduction of ConnectPhone's new product. The *second section* discusses demand estimates, the marketing budget, and marketing performance measures. It begins with a discussion of estimating market potential and company sales. It then introduces the marketing budget, as illustrated through a *pro forma* profit-and-loss statement followed by the actual profit-and-loss statement. Next, we discuss marketing performance measures, with a focus on helping marketing managers to better defend their decisions from a financial perspective. In the *third section*, we analyze the financial implications of various marketing tactics.

Each of the three sections ends with a set of quantitative exercises that provide you with an opportunity to apply the concepts you learned to situations beyond ConnectPhone.

PRICING, BREAK-EVEN, AND MARGIN ANALYSIS

PRICING CONSIDERATIONS

Determining price is one of the most important marketing-mix decisions. The limiting factors are demand and costs. Demand factors, such as buyer-perceived value, set the price ceiling. The company's costs set the price floor. In between these two factors, marketers must consider competitors' prices and other factors such as reseller requirements, government regulations, and company objectives.

Current competing media phone products in this relatively new product category were introduced in 2009 and sell at retail prices between $500 and $1,000. ConnectPhone plans to introduce its new product at a lower price in order to expand the market and gain market share rapidly. We first consider ConnectPhone's pricing decision from a cost perspective. Then, we consider consumer value, the competitive environment, and reseller requirements.

Determining Costs Recall from Chapter 10 that there are different types of costs. **Fixed costs** do not vary with production or sales level and include costs such as rent, interest, depreciation, and clerical and management salaries. Regardless of the level of output, the company must pay these costs. Whereas total fixed costs remain constant

> Fixed costs
>
> Costs that do not vary with production or sales level.

585

Variable costs
Costs that vary directly with the level of production.

as output increases, the fixed cost per unit (or average fixed cost) will decrease as output increases because the total fixed costs are spread across more units of output. **Variable costs** vary directly with the level of production and include costs related to the direct production of the product (such as costs of goods sold—COGS) and many of the marketing costs associated with selling it. Although these costs tend to be uniform for each unit produced, they are called *variable* because their total varies with the number of units produced. **Total costs** are the sum of the fixed and variable costs for any given level of production.

Total costs
The sum of the fixed and variable costs for any given level of production.

ConnectPhone has invested $10 million in refurbishing an existing facility to manufacture the new media phone product. Once production begins, the company estimates that it will incur fixed costs of $20 million per year. The variable cost to produce each device is estimated to be $250 and is expected to remain at that level for the output capacity of the facility.

SETTING PRICE BASED ON COSTS

Cost-plus pricing (or markup pricing)
A standard markup to the cost of the product.

ConnectPhone starts with the cost-based approach to pricing discussed in Chapter 10. Recall that the simplest method, **cost-plus pricing (or markup pricing)**, simply adds a standard markup to the cost of the product. To use this method, however, ConnectPhone must specify expected unit sales so that total unit costs can be determined. Unit variable costs will remain constant regardless of the output, but *average unit fixed costs* will decrease as output increases.

To illustrate this method, suppose ConnectPhone has fixed costs of $20 million, variable costs of $250 per unit, and expects unit sales of 1 million media phones. Thus, the cost per unit is given by

$$\text{Unit cost} = \text{variable cost} + \frac{\text{fixed costs}}{\text{unit sales}} = \$250 + \frac{\$20,000,000}{1,000,000} = \$270$$

Relevant costs
Costs that will occur in the future and that will vary across the alternatives being considered.

Note that we do *not* include the initial investment of $10 million in the total fixed cost figure. It is not considered a fixed cost because it is not a *relevant* cost. **Relevant costs** are those that will occur in the future and that will vary across the alternatives being considered. ConnectPhone's investment to refurbish the manufacturing facility was a one-time cost that will not reoccur in the future. Such past costs are *sunk costs* and should not be considered in future analyses.

Also notice that if ConnectPhone sells its product for $270, the price is equal to the total cost per unit. This is the **break-even price**—the price at which unit revenue (price) equals unit cost and profit is zero.

Break-even price
The price at which total revenue equals total cost and profit is zero.

Suppose ConnectPhone does not want to merely break even but rather wants to earn a 25 percent markup on sales. ConnectPhone's markup price is[1]

$$\text{Markup price} = \frac{\text{unit cost}}{(1 - \text{desired return on sales})} = \frac{\$270}{1 - 0.25} = \$360$$

This is the price at which ConnectPhone would sell the product to resellers such as wholesalers or retailers to earn a 25 percent profit on sales.

Return on investment (ROI) pricing (or target-return pricing)
A cost-based pricing method that determines price based on a specified rate of return on investment.

Another approach ConnectPhone could use is called **return on investment (ROI) pricing (or target-return pricing)**. In this case, the company *would* consider the initial $10 million investment, but only to determine the dollar profit goal. Suppose the company wants a 30 percent return on its investment. The price necessary to satisfy this requirement can be determined by

$$\text{ROI price} = \text{unit cost} = \frac{\text{ROI} \times \text{investment}}{\text{unit sales}} = \$270 + \frac{0.3 \times \$10,000,000}{1,000,000} = \$273$$

That is, if ConnectPhone sells its product for $273, it will realize a 30 percent return on its initial investment of $10 million.

In these pricing calculations, unit cost is a function of the expected sales, which were estimated to be 1 million units. But what if actual sales were lower? Then the unit cost would be higher because the fixed costs would be spread over fewer units, and the realized percentage markup on sales or ROI would be lower. Alternatively, if sales are higher than the estimated 1 million units, unit cost would be lower than $270, so a lower price would produce the desired markup on sales or ROI. It's important to note that these cost-based pricing methods are *internally* focused and do not consider demand, competitors' prices, or reseller requirements. Because ConnectPhone will be selling this product to consumers through wholesalers and retailers offering competing brands, the company must consider markup pricing from this perspective.

SETTING PRICE BASED ON EXTERNAL FACTORS

Whereas costs determine the price floor, ConnectPhone also must consider external factors when setting price. ConnectPhone does not have the final say concerning the final price of its media phones to consumers—retailers do. So it must start with its suggested retail price and work back. In doing so, ConnectPhone must consider the markups required by resellers that sell the product to consumers.

In general, a dollar **markup** is the difference between a company's selling price for a product and its cost to manufacture or purchase it. For a retailer, then, the markup is the difference between the price it charges consumers and the cost the retailer must pay for the product. Thus, for any level of reseller,

$$\text{Dollar markup} = \text{selling price} - \text{cost}$$

Markups are usually expressed as a percentage, and there are two different ways to compute markups—on *cost* or *selling price*:

$$\text{Markup percentage on cost} = \frac{\text{dollar markup}}{\text{cost}}$$

$$\text{Markup percentage on selling price} = \frac{\text{dollar markup}}{\text{selling price}}$$

To apply reseller margin analysis, ConnectPhone must first set the suggested retail price and then work back to the price at which it must sell the product to a wholesaler. Suppose retailers expect a 30 percent margin and wholesalers want a 20 percent margin based on their respective selling prices. And suppose that ConnectPhone sets a manufacturer's suggested retail price (MSRP) of $599.99 for its product.

Recall that ConnectPhone wants to expand the market by pricing low and generating market share quickly. ConnectPhone selected the $599.99 MSRP because it is lower than most competitors' prices, which can be as high as $1,000. And the company's research shows that it is below the threshold at which more consumers are willing to purchase the product. By using buyers' perceptions of value and not the seller's cost to determine the MSRP, ConnectPhone is using **value-based pricing**. For simplicity, we will use an MSRP of $600 in further analyses.

To determine the price ConnectPhone will charge wholesalers, we must first subtract the retailer's margin from the retail price to determine the retailer's cost ($600 − [$600 × 0.30] = $420). The retailer's cost is the wholesaler's price, so ConnectPhone next subtracts the wholesaler's margin ($420 − [$420 × 0.20] = $336). Thus, the **markup chain**

Markup
The difference between a company's selling price for a product and its cost to manufacture or purchase it.

Value-based pricing
Offering just the right combination of quality and good service at a fair price.

Markup chain
The sequence of markups used by firms at each level in a channel.

representing the sequence of markups used by firms at each level in a channel for ConnectPhone's new product is

Suggested retail price:	$600
minus retail margin (30%):	− $180
Retailer's cost/wholesaler's price:	$420
minus wholesaler's margin (20%):	− $ 84
Wholesaler's cost/ConnectPhone's price:	$336

By deducting the markups for each level in the markup chain, ConnectPhone arrives at a price for the product to wholesalers of $336.

BREAK-EVEN AND MARGIN ANALYSIS

The previous analyses derived a value-based price of $336 for ConnectPhone's product. Although this price is higher than the break-even price of $270 and covers costs, that price assumed a demand of 1 million units. But how many units and what level of dollar sales must ConnectPhone achieve to break even at the $336 price? And what level of sales must be achieved to realize various profit goals? These questions can be answered through break-even and margin analysis.

Determining Break-Even Unit Volume and Dollar Sales Based on an understanding of costs, consumer value, the competitive environment, and reseller requirements, ConnectPhone has decided to set its price to wholesalers at $336. At that price, what sales level will be needed for ConnectPhone to break even or make a profit on its media phones? **Break-even analysis** determines the unit volume and dollar sales needed to be profitable given a particular price and cost structure. At the break-even point, total revenue equals total costs and profit is zero. Above this point, the company will make a profit; below it, the company will lose money. ConnectPhone can calculate break-even volume by using the following formula:

$$\text{Break-even volume} = \frac{\text{fixed costs}}{\text{price} - \text{unit variable cost}}$$

The denominator (price − unit variable cost) is called **unit contribution** (sometimes called *contribution margin*). It represents the amount that each unit contributes to covering fixed costs. Break-even volume represents the level of output at which all (variable and fixed) costs are covered. In ConnectPhone's case, break-even unit volume is

$$\text{Break-even volume} = \frac{\text{fixed costs}}{\text{price} - \text{unit variable cost}} = \frac{\$20,000,000}{\$336 - \$250} = 232,558.1 \text{ units}$$

Thus, at the given cost and pricing structure, ConnectPhone will break even at 232,559 units.

To determine the break-even dollar sales, simply multiply unit break-even volume by the selling price:

$$\text{BE}_{\text{sales}} = \text{BE}_{\text{vol}} \times \text{price} = 232,559 \times \$336 = \$78,139,824$$

Another way to calculate dollar break-even sales is to use the percentage contribution margin (hereafter referred to as **contribution margin**), which is the unit contribution divided by the selling price:

$$\text{Contribution margin} = \frac{\text{price} - \text{unit variable cost}}{\text{price}} = \frac{\$336 - \$250}{\$336} = 0.256 \text{ or } 25.6\%$$

Then,

$$\text{Break-even sales} = \frac{\text{fixed costs}}{\text{contribution margin}} = \frac{\$20,000,000}{0.256} = \$78,125,000$$

Note that the difference between the two break-even sales calculations is due to rounding.

Break-even analysis
Analysis to determine the unit volume and dollar sales needed to be profitable given a particular price and cost structure.

Unit contribution
The amount that each unit contributes to covering fixed costs—the difference between price and variable costs.

Contribution margin
The unit contribution divided by the selling price.

Such break-even analysis helps ConnectPhone by showing the unit volume needed to cover costs. If production capacity cannot attain this level of output, then the company should not launch this product. However, the unit break-even volume is well within ConnectPhone's capacity. Of course, the bigger question concerns whether ConnectPhone can sell this volume at the $336 price. We'll address that issue a little later.

Understanding contribution margin is useful in other types of analyses as well, particularly if unit prices and unit variable costs are unknown or if a company (say, a retailer) sells many products at different prices and knows the percentage of total sales variable costs represent. Whereas unit contribution is the difference between unit price and unit variable costs, total contribution is the difference between total sales and total variable costs. The overall contribution margin can be calculated by

$$\text{Contribution margin} = \frac{\text{total sales} - \text{total variable costs}}{\text{total sales}}$$

Regardless of the actual level of sales, if the company knows what percentage of sales is represented by variable costs, it can calculate contribution margin. For example, ConnectPhone's unit variable cost is $250, or 74 percent of the selling price ($250 ÷ $336 = 0.74). That means for every $1 of sales revenue for ConnectPhone, $0.74 represents variable costs, and the difference ($0.26) represents contribution to fixed costs. But even if the company doesn't know its unit price and unit variable cost, it can calculate the contribution margin from total sales and total variable costs or from knowledge of the total cost structure. It can set total sales equal to 100 percent regardless of the actual absolute amount and determine the contribution margin:

$$\text{Contribution margin} = \frac{100\% - 74\%}{100\%} = \frac{1 - 0.74}{1} = 1 - 0.74 = 0.26 \text{ or } 26\%$$

Note that this matches the percentage calculated from the unit price and unit variable cost information. This alternative calculation will be very useful later when analyzing various marketing decisions.

DETERMINING "BREAKEVEN" FOR PROFIT GOALS

Although it is useful to know the break-even point, most companies are more interested in making a profit. Assume ConnectPhone would like to realize a $5 million profit in the first year. How many must it sell at the $336 price to cover fixed costs and produce this profit? To determine this, ConnectPhone can simply add the profit figure to fixed costs and again divide by the unit contribution to determine unit sales:

$$\text{Unit volume} = \frac{\text{fixed cost} - \text{profit goal}}{\text{price} - \text{variable cost}} = \frac{\$20,000,000 + \$5,000,000}{\$336 - \$250} = 290,697.7 \text{ units}$$

Thus, to earn a $5 million profit, ConnectPhone must sell 290,698 units. Multiply by price to determine dollar sales needed to achieve a $5 million profit:

$$\text{Dollar sales} = 290,698 \text{ units} \times \$336 = \$97,674,528$$

Or use the contribution margin:

$$\text{Sales} = \frac{\text{fixed cost} + \text{profit goal}}{\text{contribution margin}} = \frac{\$20,000,000 + \$5,000,000}{0.256} = \$97,656,250$$

Again, note that the difference between the two break-even sales calculations is due to rounding.

As we saw previously, a profit goal can also be stated as a return on investment goal. For example, recall that ConnectPhone wants a 30 percent return on its $10 million investment. Thus, its absolute profit goal is $3 million ($10,000,000 × 0.30). This profit goal is treated the same way as in the previous example:[2]

$$\text{Unit volume} = \frac{\text{fixed cost} + \text{profit goal}}{\text{price} - \text{variable cost}} = \frac{\$20,000,000 + \$3,000,000}{\$336 - \$250} = 267,442 \text{ units}$$

$$\text{Dollar sales} = 267,442 \text{ units} \times \$336 = \$89,860,512$$

Or

$$\text{Dollar sales} = \frac{\text{fixed cost} + \text{profit goal}}{\text{contribution margin}} = \frac{\$20,000,000 + \$3,000,000}{0.256} = \$89,843,750$$

Finally, ConnectPhone can express its profit goal as a percentage of sales, which we also saw in previous pricing analyses. Assume ConnectPhone desires a 25 percent return on sales. To determine the unit and sales volume necessary to achieve this goal, the calculation is a little different from the previous two examples. In this case, we incorporate the profit goal into the unit contribution as an additional variable cost. Look at it this way: If 25 percent of each sale must go toward profits, that leaves only 75 percent of the selling price to cover fixed costs. Thus, the equation becomes

$$\text{Unit volume} = \frac{\text{fixed cost}}{\text{price} - \text{variable cost} - (0.25 \times \text{price})} \text{ or } \frac{\text{fixed cost}}{(0.75 \times \text{price}) - \text{variable cost}}$$

So,

$$\text{Unit volume} = \frac{\$20,000,000}{(0.75 \times \$336)} = 10,000,000 \text{ units}$$

$$\text{Dollar sales necessary} = 10,000,000 \text{ units} \times \$336 = \$3,360,000,000$$

Thus, ConnectPhone would need more than $3 billion in sales to realize a 25 percent return on sales given its current price and cost structure! Could it possibly achieve this level of sales? The major point is this: Although break-even analysis can be useful in determining the level of sales needed to cover costs or to achieve a stated profit goal, it does not tell the company whether it is *possible* to achieve that level of sales at the specified price. To address this issue, ConnectPhone needs to estimate demand for this product.

Before moving on, however, let's stop here and practise applying the concepts covered so far. Now that you have seen pricing and break-even concepts in action as they related to ConnectPhone's new product, here are several exercises for you to apply what you have learned in other contexts.

MARKETING BY THE NUMBERS EXERCISE SET ONE

Now that you've studied pricing, break-even, and margin analysis as they relate to ConnectPhone's new-product launch, use the following exercises to apply these concepts in other contexts.

1.1 Sanborn, a manufacturer of electric roof vents, realizes a cost of $55 for every unit it produces. Its total fixed costs equal $2 million. If the company manufactures 500,000 units, compute the following:
   a. unit cost
   b. markup price if the company desires a 10 percent return on sales
   c. ROI price if the company desires a 25 percent return on an investment of $1 million
1.2 An interior decorator purchases items to sell in her store. She purchases a lamp for $125 and sells it for $225. Determine the following:
   a. dollar markup
   b. markup percentage on cost
   c. markup percentage on selling price

1.3 A consumer purchases a toaster from a retailer for $60. The retailer's markup is 20 percent, and the wholesaler's markup is 15 percent, both based on selling price. For what price does the manufacturer sell the product to the wholesaler?

1.4 A vacuum manufacturer has a unit cost of $50 and wishes to achieve a margin of 30 percent based on selling price. If the manufacturer sells directly to a retailer who then adds a set margin of 40 percent based on selling price, determine the retail price charged to consumers.

1.5 Advanced Electronics manufactures DVDs and sells them directly to retailers who typically sell them for $20. Retailers take a 40 percent margin based on the retail selling price. Advanced's cost information is as follows:

DVD package and disc	$2.50/DVD
Royalties	$2.25/DVD
Advertising and promotion	$500,000
Overhead	$200,000

Calculate the following:

a. contribution per unit and contribution margin

b. break-even volume in DVD units and dollars

c. volume in DVD units and dollar sales necessary if Advanced's profit goal is 20 percent profit on sales

d. net profit if 5 million DVDs are sold

DEMAND ESTIMATES, THE MARKETING BUDGET, AND MARKETING PERFORMANCE MEASURES

MARKET POTENTIAL AND SALES ESTIMATES

ConnectPhone has now calculated the sales needed to break even and to attain various profit goals on its new product. However, the company needs more information regarding demand to assess the feasibility of attaining the needed sales levels. This information is also needed for production and other decisions. For example, production schedules need to be developed and marketing tactics need to be planned.

The **total market demand** for a product or a service is the total volume that would be bought by a defined consumer group in a defined geographic area in a defined time period in a defined marketing environment under a defined level and mix of industry marketing effort. Total market demand is not a fixed number but a function of the stated conditions. For example, next year's total market demand for media phones will depend on how much other producers spend on marketing their brands. It also depends on many environmental factors, such as government regulations, economic conditions, and the level of consumer confidence in a given market. The upper limit of market demand is called **market potential**.

One general but practical method that ConnectPhone might use for estimating total market demand uses three variables: (1) the number of prospective buyers, (2) the quantity purchased by an average buyer per year, and (3) the price of an average unit. Using these numbers, ConnectPhone can estimate total market demand as follows:

$$Q = n \times q \times p$$

Where

Q = total market demand

n = number of buyers in the market

q = quantity purchased by an average buyer per year

p = price of an average unit

Total market demand
The total volume that would be bought by a defined consumer group in a defined geo-graphic area in a defined time period in a defined marketing environment under a defined level and mix of industry marketing effort.

Market potential
The upper limit of market demand.

Chain ratio method
Estimating market demand by multiplying a base number by a chain of adjusting percentages.

A variation of this approach is the **chain ratio method**. This method involves multiplying a base number by a chain of adjusting percentages. For example, ConnectPhone's product is designed to replace a household's telephone as well as provide "always on" Internet access. Thus, only households with broadband Internet access will be able to use the product. Finally, not all Internet households will be willing and able to purchase the new product. ConnectPhone can estimate U.S. demand by using a chain of calculations like the following:

Total number of U.S. households

$\times$ The percentage of U.S. households with broadband Internet access

$\times$ The percentage of these households willing and able to buy this device

The U.S. Census Bureau estimates that there are approximately 113 million households in the United States.[3] Research also indicates that 50 percent of U.S. households have broadband Internet access.[4] Finally, ConnectPhone's own research indicates that 33.1 percent of households possess the discretionary income needed and are willing to buy a device such as this. Then, the total number of households willing and able to purchase this product is

113 million households $\times$ 0.50 $\times$ 0.331 = 18.7 million households

Households will need only one media phone. Assuming the average retail price across all brands is $750 for this product, the estimate of total market demand is as follows:

18.7 million households $\times$ 1 device per household $\times$ $750 = $14 billion

This simple chain of calculations gives ConnectPhone only a rough estimate of potential demand. However, more detailed chains involving additional segments and other qualifying factors would yield more accurate and refined estimates. Still, these are only *estimates* of market potential. They rely heavily on assumptions regarding adjusting percentages, average quantity, and average price. Thus, ConnectPhone must make certain that its assumptions are reasonable and defendable. As can be seen, the overall market potential in dollar sales can vary widely given the average price used. For this reason, ConnectPhone will use unit sales potential to determine its sales estimate for next year. Market potential in terms of units is 18.7 million (18.7 million households $\times$ 1 device per household).

Assuming that ConnectPhone wants to attain 2 percent market share (comparable to its share of the Internet modem market) in the first year after launching this product, then it can forecast unit sales at 18.7 million units $\times$ 0.02 = 374,000 units. At a selling price of $336 per unit, this translates into sales of $125,664,000 (374,000 units $\times$ $336 per unit). For simplicity, further analyses will use forecasted sales of $125 million.

This unit volume estimate is well within ConnectPhone's production capacity and exceeds not only the break-even estimate (232,559 units) calculated earlier but also the volume necessary to realize a $5 million profit (290,698 units) or a 30 percent return on investment (267,442 units). However, this forecast falls well short of the volume necessary to realize a 25 percent return on sales (10 million units!) and may require that ConnectPhone revise expectations.

To assess expected profits, we must now look at the budgeted expenses for launching this product. To do this, we will construct a pro forma profit-and-loss statement.

THE PROFIT-AND-LOSS STATEMENT AND MARKETING BUDGET

Pro forma (or projected) profit-and-loss statement (or income statement or operating statement)
A statement that shows projected revenues less budgeted expenses and estimates the projected net profit for an organization, a product, or a brand during a specific planning period, typically a year.

All marketing managers must account for the profit impact of their marketing strategies. A major tool for projecting such profit impact is a **pro forma (or projected) profit-and-**

loss statement (also called an **income statement or operating statement**). A pro forma statement shows projected revenues less budgeted expenses and estimates the projected net profit for an organization, a product, or a brand during a specific planning period, typically a year. It includes direct product production costs, marketing expenses budgeted to attain a given sales forecast, and overhead expenses assigned to the organization or the product. A profit-and-loss statement typically consists of several major components (see Table A3.1):

☐ *Net sales*—gross sales revenue minus returns and allowances (e.g., trade, cash, quantity, and promotion allowances). ConnectPhone's net sales for 2010 are estimated to be $125 million, as determined in the previous analysis.

☐ *Cost of goods sold*—(sometimes called cost of sales)—the actual cost of the merchandise sold by a manufacturer or a reseller. It includes the cost of inventory, purchases, and other costs associated with making the goods. ConnectPhone's cost of goods sold is estimated to be 50 percent of net sales, or $62.5 million.

☐ *Gross margin (or gross profit)*—the difference between net sales and cost of goods sold. ConnectPhone's gross margin is estimated to be $62.5 million.

☐ *Operating expenses*—the expenses incurred while doing business. These include all other expenses beyond the cost of goods sold that are necessary to conduct business. Operating expenses can be presented in total or broken down in detail. Here, ConnectPhone's estimated operating expenses include marketing expenses and general and administrative expenses.

Marketing expenses include sales expenses, promotion expenses, and distribution expenses. The new product will be sold through ConnectPhone's sales force, so the company budgets $5 million for sales salaries. However, because sales representatives earn a 10 percent commission on sales, ConnectPhone must also add a variable component to sales expenses of $12.5 million (10 percent of $125 million net sales), for a total budgeted sales expense of $17.5 million. ConnectPhone sets its advertising and promotion to launch this product at $10 million. However, the company also budgets 4 percent of sales, or $5 million, for co-operative advertising allowances to retailers who promote ConnectPhone's new product in their advertising. Thus, the total budgeted advertising and promotion expenses are $15 million ($10 million for advertising plus $5 million in co-op allowances). Finally, ConnectPhone budgets 10 percent of net sales, or $12.5 million, for freight and delivery charges. In all, total

TABLE A3.1 Pro Forma Profit-and-Loss Statement for the 12-Month Period Ended December 31, 2010

			% of Sales
Net Sales		$125,000,000	100%
Cost of Goods Sold		62,500,000	50%
Gross Margin		$ 62,500,000	50%
Marketing Expenses			
Sales expenses	$17,500,000		
Promotion expenses	15,000,000		
Freight	12,500,000	45,000,000	36%
General and Administrative Expenses			
Managerial salaries and expenses	$2,000,000		
Indirect overhead	3,000,000	5,000,000	4%
Net Profit Before Income Tax		$12,500,000	10%

marketing expenses are estimated to be $17.5 million + $15 million + $12.5 million = $45 million.

General and administrative expenses are estimated at $5 million, broken down into $2 million for managerial salaries and expenses for the marketing function, and $3 million of indirect overhead allocated to this product by the corporate accountants (such as depreciation, interest, maintenance, and insurance). Total expenses for the year, then, are estimated to be $50 million ($45 million marketing expenses + $5 million in general and administrative expenses).

☐ *Net profit before taxes*—profit earned after all costs are deducted. ConnectPhone's estimated net profit before taxes is $12.5 million.

In all, as Table A3.1 shows, ConnectPhone expects to earn a profit on its new product of $12.5 million in 2010. Also note that the percentage of sales that each component of the profit-and-loss statement represents is given in the right-hand column. These percentages are determined by dividing the cost figure by net sales (i.e., marketing expenses represent 36 percent of net sales determined by $45 million ÷ $125 million). As can be seen, ConnectPhone projects a net profit return on sales of 10 percent in the first year after launching this product.

MARKETING PERFORMANCE MEASURES

Profit-and-loss statement (or income statement or operating statement)
A statement that shows actual revenues less expenses and net profit for an organization, product, or brand during a specific planning period, typically a year.

Now let's fast-forward a year. ConnectPhone's product has been on the market for one year and management wants to assess its sales and profit performance. One way to assess this performance is to compute performance ratios derived from ConnectPhone's **profit-and-loss statement (or income statement or operating statement)**.

Whereas the pro forma profit-and-loss statement shows *projected* financial performance, the statement given in Table A3.2 shows ConnectPhone's *actual* financial performance based on actual sales, cost of goods sold, and expenses during the past year. By comparing the profit-and-loss statement from one period to the next, ConnectPhone can gauge performance against goals, spot favourable or unfavourable trends, and take appropriate corrective action.

The profit-and-loss statement shows that ConnectPhone lost $1 million rather than making the $12.5 million profit projected in the pro forma statement. Why? One obvious reason is that net sales fell $25 million short of estimated sales. Lower sales translated

TABLE A3.2 Profit-and-Loss Statement for the 12-Month Period Ended December 31, 2010

			% of Sales
Net Sales		$100,000,000	100%
Cost of Goods Sold		55,000,000	55%
Gross Margin		$ 45,000,000	45%
Marketing Expenses			
Sales expenses	$15,000,000		
Promotion expenses	14,000,000		
Freight	10,000,000	39,000,000	39%
General and Administrative Expenses			
Managerial salaries and expenses	$2,000,000		
Indirect overhead	5,000,000	7,000,000	7%
Net Profit Before Income Tax		($1,000,000)	(1%)

into lower variable costs associated with marketing the product. However, both fixed costs and the cost of goods sold as a percentage of sales exceeded expectations. Hence, the product's contribution margin was 21 percent rather than the estimated 26 percent. That is, variable costs represented 79 percent of sales (55 percent for cost of goods sold, 10 percent for sales commissions, 10 percent for freight, and 4 percent for co-op allowances). Recall that contribution margin can be calculated by subtracting that fraction from one $(1 - 0.79 = 0.21)$. Total fixed costs were $22 million, $2 million more than estimated. Thus, the sales that ConnectPhone needed to break even given this cost structure can be calculated as

$$\text{Break-even sales} = \frac{\text{fixed costs}}{\text{contribution margin}} = \frac{\$22,000,000}{0.21} = \$104,761,905$$

If ConnectPhone had achieved another $5 million in sales, it would have earned a profit.

Although ConnectPhone's sales fell short of the forecasted sales, so did overall industry sales for this product. Overall industry sales were only $2.5 billion. That means that ConnectPhone's **market share** was 4 percent ($100 million ÷ $2.5 billion = 0.04 = 4%), which was higher than forecasted. Thus, ConnectPhone attained a higher-than-expected market share but the overall market sales were not as high as estimated.

Market share
Company sales divided by market sales.

ANALYTIC RATIOS

The profit-and-loss statement provides the figures needed to compute some crucial **operating ratios**—the ratios of selected operating statement items to net sales. These ratios let marketers compare the firm's performance in one year to that in previous years (or with industry standards and competitors' performance in that year). The most commonly used operating ratios are the gross margin percentage, the net profit percentage, and the operating expense percentage. The inventory turnover rate and return on investment (ROI) are often used to measure managerial effectiveness and efficiency.

Operating ratios
The ratios of selected operating statement items to net sales.

The **gross margin percentage** indicates the percentage of net sales remaining after cost of goods sold that can contribute to operating expenses and net profit before taxes. The higher this ratio, the more a firm has left to cover expenses and generate profit. ConnectPhone's gross margin ratio was 45 percent:

Gross margin percentage
The percentage of net sales remaining after cost of goods sold—calculated by dividing gross margin by net sales.

$$\text{Gross margin percentage} = \frac{\text{gross margin}}{\text{net sales}} = \frac{\$45,000,000}{\$100,000,000} = 0.45 = 45\%$$

Note that this percentage is lower than estimated, and this ratio is seen easily in the percentage of sales column in Table A3.2. Stating items in the profit-and-loss statement as a percent of sales allows managers to quickly spot abnormal changes in costs over time. If there was previous history for this product and this ratio was declining, management should examine it more closely to determine why it has decreased (i.e., because of a decrease in sales volume or price, an increase in costs, or a combination of these). In ConnectPhone's case, net sales were $25 million lower than estimated, and cost of goods sold was higher than estimated (55 percent rather than the estimated 50 percent).

The **net profit percentage** shows the percentage of each sales dollar going to profit. It is calculated by dividing net profits by net sales:

Net profit percentage
The percentage of each sales dollar going to profit—calculated by dividing net profits by net sales.

$$\text{Net profit percentage} = \frac{\text{net profit}}{\text{net sales}} = \frac{-\$1,000,000}{\$100,000,000} = -0.01 = -1.0\%$$

This ratio is easily seen in the percent of sales column. ConnectPhone's new product generated negative profits in the first year, not a good situation given that before the product launch net profits before taxes were estimated at more than $12 million. Later in this appendix, we will discuss further analyses the marketing manager should conduct to defend the product.

Operating expense percentage
The portion of net sales going to operating expenses—calculated by dividing total expenses by net sales.

The **operating expense percentage** indicates the portion of net sales going to operating expenses. Operating expenses include marketing and other expenses not directly related to marketing the product, such as indirect overhead assigned to this product. It is calculated by

$$\text{Operating expense percentage} = \frac{\text{total expenses}}{\text{net sales}} = \frac{\$46{,}000{,}000}{\$100{,}000{,}000} = 0.46 = 46\%$$

This ratio can also be quickly determined from the percent of sales column in the profit-and-loss statement by adding the percentages for marketing expenses and general and administrative expenses (39% + 7%). Thus, 46 cents of every sales dollar went for operations. Although ConnectPhone wants this ratio to be as low as possible, and 46 percent is not an alarming amount, it is of concern if it is increasing over time or if a loss is realized.

Inventory turnover rate
(or stock-turn rate)
The number of times an inventory turns over or is sold during a specified time period (often one year)—calculated based on costs, selling price, or units.

Another useful ratio is the **inventory turnover rate** (also called **stockturn rate** for resellers). The inventory turnover rate is the number of times an inventory turns over or is sold during a specified time period (often one year). This rate tells how quickly a business is moving inventory through the organization. Higher rates indicate that lower investments in inventory are made, thus freeing up funds for other investments. It may be computed on a cost, selling price, or unit basis. The formula based on cost is

$$\text{Inventory turnover rate} = \frac{\text{cost of goods sold}}{\text{average inventory at cost}}$$

Assuming ConnectPhone's beginning and ending inventories were $30 million and $20 million, respectively, the inventory turnover rate is

$$\text{Inventory turnover rate} = \frac{\$55{,}000{,}000}{(\$30{,}000{,}000 + \$20{,}000{,}000)/2} = \frac{\$55{,}000{,}000}{\$25{,}000{,}000} = 2.2$$

That is, ConnectPhone's inventory turned over 2.2 times in 2010. Normally, the higher the turnover rate, the higher the management efficiency and company profitability. However, this rate should be compared with industry averages, competitors' rates, and past performance to determine whether ConnectPhone is doing well. A competitor with similar sales but a higher inventory turnover rate will have fewer resources tied up in inventory, allowing it to invest in other areas of the business.

Return on investment (ROI)
A measure of managerial effectiveness and efficiency—net profit before taxes divided by total investment.

Companies frequently use **return on investment (ROI)** to measure managerial effectiveness and efficiency. For ConnectPhone, ROI is the ratio of net profits to total investment required to manufacture the new product. This investment includes capital investments in land, buildings, and equipment (here, the initial $10 million to refurbish the manufacturing facility) plus inventory costs (ConnectPhone's average inventory totalled $25 million), for a total of $35 million. Thus, ConnectPhone's ROI for this product is

$$\text{Return on investment} = \frac{\text{net profit before taxes}}{\text{investment}} = \frac{\$1{,}000{,}000}{\$35{,}000{,}000} = -0.0286 = -2.86\%$$

ROI is often used to compare alternatives, and a positive ROI is desired. The alternative with the highest ROI is preferred to other alternatives. ConnectPhone needs to be concerned with the ROI realized. One obvious way ConnectPhone can increase ROI is to increase net profit by reducing expenses. Another way is to reduce its investment, perhaps by investing less in inventory and turning it over more frequently.

MARKETING PROFITABILITY METRICS

Given the above financial results, you may be thinking that ConnectPhone should drop this new product. But what arguments can marketers make for keeping or dropping this product? The obvious arguments for dropping the product are that first-year sales were well below expected levels and the product lost money, resulting in a negative return on investment.

So what would happen if ConnectPhone did drop this product? Surprisingly, if the company drops the product, the profits for the total organization will decrease by $4 million! How can that be? Marketing managers need to look closely at the numbers in the profit-and-loss statement to determine the *net marketing contribution* for this product. In ConnectPhone's case, the net marketing contribution for the product is $4 million, and if the company drops this product, that contribution will disappear as well. Let's look more closely at this concept to illustrate how marketing managers can better assess and defend their marketing strategies and programs.

Net Marketing Contribution   **Net marketing contribution (NMC)**, along with other marketing metrics derived from it, measures *marketing* profitability. It includes only components of profitability that are controlled by marketing. Whereas the previous calculation of net profit before taxes from the profit-and-loss statement includes operating expenses not under marketing's control, NMC does not. Referring back to ConnectPhone's profit-and-loss statement given in Table A3.2, we can calculate net marketing contribution for the product as

> **Net marketing contribution (NMC)**
> A measure of marketing profitability that includes only components of profitability controlled by marketing.

$$\text{NMC} = \text{net sales} - \text{cost of goods sold} - \text{marketing expenses}$$
$$= \$100 \text{ million} - \$55 \text{ million} - \$41 \text{ million} = \$4 \text{ million}$$

The marketing expenses include sales expenses ($15 million), promotion expenses ($14 million), freight expenses ($10 million), and the managerial salaries and expenses of the marketing function ($2 million), which total $41 million.

Thus, the product actually contributed $4 million to ConnectPhone's profits. It was the $5 million of indirect overhead allocated to this product that caused the negative profit. Further, the amount allocated was $2 million more than estimated in the pro forma profit-and-loss statement. Indeed, if only the estimated amount had been allocated, the product would have earned a *profit* of $1 million rather than losing $1 million. If ConnectPhone drops the product, the $5 million in fixed overhead expenses will not disappear—it will simply have to be allocated elsewhere. However, the $4 million in net marketing contribution *will* disappear.

Marketing Return on Sales and Investment   To get an even deeper understanding of the profit impact of marketing strategy, we'll now examine two measures of marketing efficiency—*marketing return on sales* (marketing ROS) and *marketing return on investment* (marketing ROI).[5]

Marketing return on sales (or marketing ROS) shows the percent of net sales attributable to the net marketing contribution. For our product, ROS is

> **Marketing return on sales (or marketing ROS)**
> The percent of net sales attributable to the net marketing contribution—calculated by dividing net marketing contribution by net sales.

$$\text{Marketing ROS} = \frac{\text{net marketing contribution}}{\text{net sales}} = \frac{\$4,000,000}{\$100,000,000} = 0.04 = 4\%$$

Thus, out of every $100 of sales, the product returns $4 to ConnectPhone's bottom line. A high marketing ROS is desirable. But to assess whether this is a good level of performance, ConnectPhone must compare this figure to previous marketing ROS levels for the product, the ROSs of other products in the company's portfolio, and the ROSs of competing products.

Marketing return on investment (or marketing ROI) measures the marketing productivity of a marketing investment. In ConnectPhone's case, the marketing investment is represented by $41 million of the total expenses. Thus, marketing ROI is

> **Marketing return on investment (or marketing ROI)**
> A measure of the marketing productivity of a marketing investment—calculated by dividing net marketing contribution by marketing expenses.

$$\text{Marketing ROI} = \frac{\text{net marketing contribution}}{\text{marketing expenses}} = \frac{\$4,000,000}{\$41,000,000} = 0.0976 = 9.76\%$$

As with marketing ROS, a high value is desirable, but this figure should be compared with previous levels for the given product and with the marketing ROIs of competitors' products. Note from this equation that marketing ROI could be greater than 100 percent. This can be achieved by attaining a higher net marketing contribution and/or a lower total marketing expense.

In this section, we estimated market potential and sales, developed profit-and-loss statements, and examined financial measures of performance. In the next section, we discuss methods for analyzing the impact of various marketing tactics. However, before moving on to those analyses, here's another set of quantitative exercises to help you apply what you've learned to other situations.

MARKETING BY THE NUMBERS EXERCISE SET TWO

2.1 Determine the market potential for a product that has 50 million prospective buyers who purchase an average of three per year and price averages $25. How many units must a company sell if it desires a 10 percent share of this market?

2.2 Develop a profit-and-loss statement for the Westgate division of North Industries. This division manufactures light fixtures sold to consumers through home improvement and hardware stores. Cost of goods sold represents 40 percent of net sales. Marketing expenses include selling expenses, promotion expenses, and freight. Selling expenses include sales salaries totalling $3 million per year and sales commissions (5 percent of sales). The company spent $3 million on advertising last year, and freight costs were 10 percent of sales. Other costs include $2 million for managerial salaries and expenses for the marketing function, and another $3 million for indirect overhead allocated to the division.

    a. Develop the profit-and-loss statement if net sales were $20 million last year.

    b. Develop the profit-and-loss statement if net sales were $40 million last year.

    c. Calculate Westgate's break-even sales.

2.3 Using the profit-and-loss statement you developed in question 2.2b, and assuming that Westgate's beginning inventory was $11 million, ending inventory was $7 million, and total investment was $20 million, including inventory, determine the following:

    a. gross margin percentage

    b. net profit percentage

    c. operating expense percentage

    d. inventory turnover rate

    e. return on investment (ROI)

    f. net marketing contribution

    g. marketing return on sales (marketing ROS)

    h. marketing return on investment (marketing ROI)

    i. Is the Westgate division doing well? Explain your answer.

FINANCIAL ANALYSIS OF MARKETING TACTICS

Although the first-year profit performance for ConnectPhone's new product was less than desired, management feels that this attractive market has excellent growth opportunities. Although the sales of ConnectPhone's product were lower than initially projected, they were not unreasonable given the size of the current market. Thus, ConnectPhone wants to explore new marketing tactics to help grow the market for this product and increase sales for the company.

For example, the company could increase advertising to promote more awareness of the new product and its category. It could add salespeople to secure greater product distribution. ConnectPhone could decrease prices so that more consumers could afford its product. Finally, to expand the market, ConnectPhone could introduce a lower-priced model in addition to the higher-priced original offering. Before pursuing any of these tactics, ConnectPhone must analyze the financial implications of each.

INCREASE ADVERTISING EXPENDITURES

Although most consumers understand the Internet and telephones, they may not be aware of media phones. Thus, ConnectPhone is considering boosting its advertising to make more people aware of the benefits of this device in general and of its own brand in particular.

What if ConnectPhone's marketers recommend increasing national advertising by 50 percent to $15 million (assume no change in the variable co-operative component of promotional expenditures)? This represents an increase in fixed costs of $5 million. What increase in sales will be needed to break even on this $5 million increase in fixed costs?

A quick way to answer this question is to divide the increase in fixed cost by the contribution margin, which we found in a previous analysis to be 21 percent:

$$\text{Increase in sales} = \frac{\text{increase in fixed cost}}{\text{contribution margin}} = \frac{\$5,000,000}{0.21} = \$23,809,524$$

Thus, a 50 percent increase in advertising expenditures must produce a sales increase of almost $24 million to just break even. That $24 million sales increase translates into an almost 1 percentage point increase in market share (1 percent of the $2.5 billion overall market equals $25 million). That is, to break even on the increased advertising expenditure, ConnectPhone would have to increase its market share from 4 percent to 4.95 percent ($123,809,524 ÷ $2.5 billion = 0.0495 or 4.95% market share). All of this assumes that the total market will not grow, which might or might not be a reasonable assumption.

INCREASE DISTRIBUTION COVERAGE

ConnectPhone also wants to consider hiring more salespeople in order to call on new retailer accounts and increase distribution through more outlets. Even though ConnectPhone sells directly to wholesalers, its sales representatives call on retail accounts to perform other functions in addition to selling, such as training retail salespeople. Currently, ConnectPhone employs 60 sales reps who earn an average of $50,000 in salary plus 10 percent commission on sales. The product is currently sold to consumers through 1,875 retail outlets. Suppose ConnectPhone wants to increase that number of outlets to 2,500, an increase of 625 retail outlets. How many additional salespeople will ConnectPhone need, and what sales will be necessary to break even on the increased cost?

One method for determining what size sales force ConnectPhone will need is the **workload method**. The workload method uses the following formula to determine the sales force size:

$$NS = \frac{NC \times FC \times LC}{TA}$$

where

    NS = number of salespeople

    NC = number of customers

    FC = average frequency of customer calls per customer

    LC = average length of customer call

    TA = time an average salesperson has available for selling per year

Workload method
An approach to determining sales force size based on the workload required and the time available for selling.

ConnectPhone's sales reps typically call on accounts an average of 20 times per year for about 2 hours per call. Although each sales rep works 2,000 hours per year (50 weeks per year × 40 hours per week), they spent about 15 hours per week on nonselling activities, such as administrative duties and travel. Thus, the average annual available selling time per sales rep per year is 1,250 hours (50 weeks × 25 hours per week). We can now calculate how many sales reps ConnectPhone will need to cover the anticipated 2,500 retail outlets:

$$NS = \frac{2,500 \times 20 \times 2}{1,250} = 80 \text{ salespeople}$$

Therefore, ConnectPhone will need to hire 20 more salespeople. The cost to hire these reps will be $1 million (20 salespeople × $50,000 salary per sales person).

What increase in sales will be required to break even on this increase in fixed costs? The 10 percent commission is already accounted for in the contribution margin, so the contribution margin remains unchanged at 21 percent. Thus, the increase in sales needed to cover this increase in fixed costs can be calculated by

$$\text{Increase in sales} = \frac{\text{increase in fixed cost}}{\text{contribution margin}} = \frac{\$1,000,000}{0.21} = \$4,761,905$$

That is, ConnectPhone's sales must increase almost $5 million to break even on this tactic. So, how many new retail outlets will the company need to secure to achieve this sales increase? The average revenue generated per current outlet is $53,333 ($100 million in sales divided by 1,875 outlets). To achieve the nearly $5 million sales increase needed to break even, ConnectPhone would need about 90 new outlets ($4,761,905 ÷ $53,333 = 89.3 outlets), or about 4.5 outlets per new rep. Given that current reps cover about 31 outlets apiece (1,875 outlets ÷ 60 reps), this seems very reasonable.

DECREASE PRICE

ConnectPhone is also considering lowering its price to increase sales revenue through increased volume. The company's research has shown that demand for most types of consumer electronics products is elastic—that is, the percentage increase in the quantity demanded is greater than the percentage decrease in price.

What increase in sales would be necessary to break even on a 10 percent decrease in price? That is, what increase in sales will be needed to maintain the total contribution that ConnectPhone realized at the higher price? The current total contribution can be determined by multiplying the contribution margin by total sales:[6]

$$\text{Current total contribution} = \text{contribution margin} \times \text{sales} =$$
$$0.21 \times \$100 \text{ million} = \$21 \text{ million}$$

Price changes result in changes in unit contribution and contribution margin. Recall that the contribution margin of 21 percent was based on variable costs representing 79 percent of sales. Therefore, unit variable costs can be determined by multiplying the original price by this percentage: $336 × 0.79 = $265.44 per unit. If price is decreased by 10 percent, the new price is $302.40. However, variable costs do not change just because price decreased, so the contribution and contribution margin decrease as follows:

	Old	New (reduced 10%)
Price	$336	$302.40
− Unit variable cost	$265.44	$265.44
= Unit contribution	$70.56	$36.96
Contribution margin	$70.56/$336 = 0.21 or 21%	$36.96/$302.40 = 0.12 or 12%

So a 10 percent reduction in price results in a decrease in the contribution margin from 21 percent to 12 percent.[7] To determine the sales level needed to break even on this price reduction, we calculate the level of sales that must be attained at the new contribution margin to achieve the original total contribution of $21 million:

New contribution margin × new sales level = original total contribution

So,

$$\text{New sales level} = \frac{\text{original contribution}}{\text{new contribution margin}} = \frac{\$21,000,000}{0.21} = \$175,000,000$$

Thus, sales must increase by $75 million ($175 million – $100 million) just to break even on a 10 percent price reduction. This means that ConnectPhone must increase market share to 7 percent ($175 million ÷ $2.5 billion) to achieve the current level of profits (assuming no increase in the total market sales). The marketing manager must assess whether or not this is a reasonable goal.

EXTEND THE PRODUCT LINE

As a final option, ConnectPhone is considering extending its product line by offering a lower-priced model. Of course, the new, lower-priced product would steal some sales from the higher-priced model. This is called **cannibalization**—the situation in which one product sold by a company takes a portion of its sales from other company products. If the new product has a lower contribution than the original product, the company's total contribution will decrease on the cannibalized sales. However, if the new product can generate enough new volume, it is worth considering.

Cannibalization
The situation in which one product sold by a company takes a portion of its sales from other company products.

To assess cannibalization, ConnectPhone must look at the incremental contribution gained by having both products available. Recall in the previous analysis we determined that unit variable costs were $265.44 and unit contribution was just over $70. Assuming costs remain the same next year, ConnectPhone can expect to realize a contribution per unit of approximately $70 for every unit of the original product sold.

Assume that the first model offered by ConnectPhone is called MP1 and the new, lower-priced model is called MP2. MP2 will retail for $400, and resellers will take the same markup percentages on price as they do with the higher-priced model. Therefore, MP2's price to wholesalers will be $224 as follows:

Retail price:	$400
minus retail margin (30%):	– $120
Retailer's cost/wholesaler's price:	$280
minus wholesaler's margin (20%):	– $ 56
Wholesaler's cost/ConnectPhone's price	$224

If MP2's variable costs are estimated to be $174, then its contribution per unit will equal $50 ($224 – $174 = $50). That means for every unit that MP2 cannibalizes from MP1, ConnectPhone will *lose* $20 in contribution toward fixed costs and profit (i.e., contributionMP2 – contributionMP1 = $50 – $70 = –$20). You might conclude that ConnectPhone should not pursue this tactic because it appears as though the company will be worse off if it introduces the lower-priced model. However, if MP2 captures enough *additional* sales, ConnectPhone will be better off even though some MP1 sales are cannibalized. The company must examine what will happen to *total* contribution, which requires estimates of unit volume for both products.

Originally, ConnectPhone estimated that next year's sales of MP1 would be 600,000 units. However, with the introduction of MP2, it now estimates that 200,000 of those sales will be cannibalized by the new model. If ConnectPhone sells only 200,000 units of the new MP2 model (all cannibalized from MP1), the company would lose $4 million in total contribution (200,000 units × −$20 per cannibalized unit = −$4 million)—not a good outcome. However, ConnectPhone estimates that MP2 will generate the 200,000 of cannibalized sales plus an *additional* 500,000 unit sales. Thus, the contribution on these additional MP2 units will be $25 million (i.e., 500,000 units × $50 per unit = $25 million). The net effect is that ConnectPhone will gain $21 million in total contribution by introducing MP2.

The following table compares ConnectPhone's total contribution with and without the introduction of MP2:

	MP1 only	MP1 and MP2
MP1 contribution	600,000 units × $70 = $42,000,000	400,000 units × $70 = $28,000,000
MP2 contribution	0	700,000 units × $50 = $35,000,000
Total contribution	$42,000,000	$63,000,000

The difference in the total contribution is a net gain of $21 million ($63 million − $42 million). Based on this analysis, ConnectPhone should introduce the MP2 model because it results in a positive incremental contribution. However, if fixed costs will increase by more than $21 million as a result of adding this model, then the net effect will be negative and ConnectPhone should not pursue this tactic.

Now that you have seen these marketing tactic analysis concepts in action as they related to ConnectPhone's new product, here are several exercises for you to apply what you have learned in this section in other contexts.

MARKETING BY THE NUMBERS EXERCISE SET THREE

3.1 Kingsford Inc. sells small plumbing components to consumers through retail outlets. Total industry sales for Kingsford's relevant market last year were $80 million, with Kingsford's sales representing 10 percent of that total. Contribution margin is 25 percent. Kingsford's sales force calls on retail outlets and each sales rep earns $45,000 per year plus 1 percent commission on all sales. Retailers receive a 40 percent margin on selling price and generate average revenue of $10,000 per outlet for Kingsford.

   a. The marketing manager has suggested increasing consumer advertising by $300,000. By how much would dollar sales need to increase to break even on this expenditure? What increase in overall market share does this represent?

   b. Another suggestion is to hire three more sales representatives to gain new consumer retail accounts. How many new retail outlets would be necessary to break even on the increased cost of adding three sales reps?

   c. A final suggestion is to make a 20 percent across-the-board price reduction. By how much would dollar sales need to increase to maintain Kingsford's current contribution? (See endnote 7 to calculate the new contribution margin.)

   d. Which suggestion do you think Kingsford should implement? Explain your recommendation.

3.2 PepsiCo sells its soft drinks in approximately 400,000 retail establishments, such as supermarkets, discount stores, and convenience stores. Sales representatives call on each retail account weekly, which means each account is called on by a sales rep 52 times per year. The average length of a sales call is 75 minutes (or 1.25 hours). An average salesperson works 2,000 hours per year (50 weeks per year × 40 hours per week), but each spends 10 hours a week on non-selling activities, such as administrative tasks and travel. How many sales people does PepsiCo need?

3.3 Hair Zone manufactures a brand of hair-styling gel. It is considering adding a modified version of the product—a foam that provides stronger hold. Hair Zone's variable costs and prices to wholesalers are as follows:

	Current Hair Gel	New Foam Product
Unit selling price	2.00	2.25
Unit variable costs	0.85	1.25

Hair Zone expects to sell 1 million units of the new styling foam in the first year after introduction, but it expects that 60 percent of those sales will come from buyers who normally purchase Hair Zone's styling gel. Hair Zone estimates that it would sell 1.5 million units of the gel if it did not introduce the foam. If the fixed cost of launching the new foam will be $100,000 during the first year, should Hair Zone add the new product to its line? Why or why not?

Endnotes

CHAPTER 1

1. Norma Ramage, "Slowing down," *Marketing*, May 2005, p. 9; Jason Kirby, "The Marathon Man," *Maclean's*, August 6, 2007, p. 44; *The Globe and Mail* online at http://www.theglobeandmail.com/life/health/running/ask-a-running-expert-john-stanton-takes-your-questions/article1589817/, accessed June 2010; information obtained from The Running Room website at http://www.runningroom.com/hm/, accessed June 2010; Yana Doyle, "Writer makes tracks at marathon," *Calgary Herald*, June 10, 2010, at http://www.calgaryherald.com/Writer+makes+tracks+marathon/3135672/story.html, accessed June 2010; Laura Young, "Stoughton takes down Boston Marathon," *The Sudbury Star*, at http://www.thesudburystar.com/ArticleDisplay.aspx?e=2601158, accessed June 2010; Pat O'Brien, "Butt out, grab your sneakers and hit the road," *Times&Transcript*, June 14, 2010, at http://timestranscript.canadaeast.com/lifetimes/article/1093234, accessed June 2010; Keith B., "Q&A with Running Room founder John Stanton," *Calgary Herald*, May 16, 2010, at http://communities.canada.com/calgaryherald/blogs/calgaryrunner/archive/2010/05/16/q-amp-a-with-running-room-founder-john-stanton.aspx, accessed May 2010; Press Release, "Scotiabank Toronto Waterfront Marathon gears up for biggest year yet as the marathon marks its 2,500th year," at http://www.digitaljournal.com/pr/60080, accessed June 2010; Press release, "More than 7,000 Canadians Together Log Thousands of Kilometers in National Walking Event Highlighting the Benefits of Physical Activity," at http://www.newswire.ca/en/releases/archive/June2010/24/c7851.html, accessed June 2010.

2. Adam Morgan, "Three Rules for Thriving in 2009," *AdweekMedia*, January 5, 2009, p. 11.

3. See Adam L. Penenberg, "All Eyes on Apple," *Fast Company*, December 2007–January 2008, pp. 83–91; and "Apple Reports First Quarter Results; iPod Sales Set New Record," *PR Newswire*, January 21, 2009.

4. As quoted in John J. Burnett, *Nonprofit Marketing Best Practices* (New York: John Wiley & Sons, 2008), p. 21.

5. The American Marketing Association offers the following definition: "Marketing is an organizational function and a set of processes for creating, communicating, and delivering value to customers and for managing customer relationships in ways that benefit the organization and its stakeholders." Accessed at http://www.marketingpower.com/_layouts/Dictionary.aspx?dLetter=M, November 2009. Also see, Lisa M. Keefe, "Marketing Defined," *Marketing News*, January 15, 2008, pp. 28–29.

6. http://www.theglobeandmail.com/life/health/running/ask-a-running-expert-john-stanton-takes-your-questions/article1589817/, accessed June 2010.

7. See Theodore Levitt's classic article, "Marketing Myopia," *Harvard Business Review*, July–August 1960, pp. 45–56. For more recent discussions, see Yves Doz, Jose Santos, and Peter J. Williamson, "Marketing Myopia Re-Visited: Why Every Company Needs to Learn from the World," *Ivey Business Journal*, January–February 2004, p. 1; "What Business Are You In?" *Harvard Business Review*, October 2006, pp. 127–137; and Lance A. Bettencourt, "Debunking Myths about Customer Needs," *Marketing Management*, January/February 2009, pp. 46–51.

8. Information from a recent "The Computer Is Personal Again" advertisement and www.hp.com/personal, November 2009.

9. See "The Campaign to Turn on the Tap and Ditch the Bottle," *Canada NewsWire*, December 12, 2008; and "Green PR Campaign," *PR News*, March 2, 2009.

10. See Larry Edwards et al., "75 Years of Ideas," *Advertising Age*, February 14, 2005, p. 14; Harris Interactive, "The 9th Annual RQ: Reputations of the 60 Most Visible Companies, A Survey of the U.S. General Public," 2008, accessed at http://www.harrisinteractive.com/news/mediaaccess/2008/HI_BSC_REPORT_AnnualRQ_USA Summary07-08.pdf and www.jnj.com/our_company/our_credo/index.htm, accessed December 2009.

11. See David Kiley, "How to Sell Luxury to Penny-Pinchers," *BusinessWeek*, November 10, 2008, p. 60.

12. For more on how to measure customer satisfaction, see D. Randall Brandt, "For Good Measure," *Marketing Management*, January–February 2007, pp. 21–25.

13. Portions adapted from Julie Barker, "Power to the People," *Incentive*, February 2008, p. 34 and Carmine Gallo, "Employee Motivation the Ritz-Carlton Way," *BusinessWeek*, February 29, 2008, accessed at www.businessweek.com. Also see "The World's Best Hotels—Where Luxury Lives," *Institutional Investor*, November 2007, p. 1; and http://corporate.ritzcarlton.com/en/About/Awards.htm#Hotel, accessed November 2009.

14. Information about the Harley Owners Group accessed at www.harley-davidson.com/wcm/Content/Pages/HOG/HOG.jsp?locale= en_US, accessed November 2009.

15. Elizabeth A. Sullivan, "Just Say No," *Marketing News*, April 15, 2008, p. 17.

16. Sullivan, "Just Say No," p. 17.

17. Quotes from Andrew Walmsley, "The Year of Consumer Empowerment," *Marketing*, December 20, 2006, p. 9; and Jeff Heilman, "Rules of Engagement: During a Recession, Marketers Need to Have Their Keenest Listening-to-Customers Strategy in Place," *The Magazine of Branded Content*, Winter 2009, p. 7.

18. See Jefferson Graham, "Twitter Took off from Simple to 'Tweet' success," *USA Today*, July 21, 2008, p. B1; Elizabeth A. Sullivan, "We Were Right!" *Marketing News*, December 15, 2008, p. 16; James Rainey, "On the Media: Twitter's Charms Sort of Grow on You,"

Los Angeles Times, February 18, 2009, p. A1; and B. L. Ochman, "Debunking Six Social Media Myths," *BusinessWeek,* February 19, 2009, accessed at www.businessweek.com.

19. David Kenny and Jack Klues, "The Art of Friending: How to Move from Conversation to Conversion in Social Media, the Communications Platform of the Future," *AdWeek.com,* November 18, 2008, accessed at www.adweek.com.

20. Sullivan, "We Were Right!" p. 17; and Brian Morrissey, "Kraft Gives Facebook Users Reason to Share," *AdWeek.com,* December 30, 2008, accessed at www.adweek.com.

21. "Frito-Lay, Doritos Fan Trumps Advertising Professionals and Wins $1 Million Super Bowl Advertising Challenge," *Marketing Weekly News,* February 21, 2009, p. 51.

22. For more examples, see Karen E. Klein, "Should Your Customers Make Your Ads?" *BusinessWeek,* January 2, 2008, www.businessweek.com; and Max Chafkin, "The Customer Is the Company," *Inc.,* June 2008, p. 88.

23. Philip Kotler and Kevin Lane Keller, *Marketing Management,* 13th ed. (Upper Saddle River, NJ: Prentice Hall, 2009), p. 11.

24. Michael Bush, "Marketers Put Emphasis on Loyalty," *Advertising Age,* July 9, 2008, accessed at http://adage.com/print?article_id =129501; and Stanley F. Slater, Jakki J. Mohr, and Sanjit Sengupta, "Know Your Customers," *Marketing Management,* February 2009, pp. 37–44.

25. "Customer Loyalty: You Can't Put a Price on True Loyalty," *Precision Marketing,* January 19, 2009, p. 12. Also see Victoria Colliver, "Customer Loyalties Shifting with Prices," *Fort Wayne Journal-Gazette,* January 26, 2009, p. C5.

26. "Stew Leonard's," *Hoover's Company Records,* July 15, 2009, pp. 104–226; and www.stew-leonards.com/html/about.cfm, accessed November 2009.

27. Graham Brown, "MobileYouth Key Statistics," March 28, 2008, www.mobileyouth.org. For interesting discussions on assessing and using customer lifetime value, see Sunil Gupta et al., "Modeling Customer Lifetime Value," *Journal of Service Research,* November 2006, pp. 139–146; Detlef Schoder, "The Flaw in Customer Lifetime Value," *Harvard Business Review,* December 2007, p. 26; Lynette Ryals, "Determining the Indirect Value of a Customer," *Journal of Marketing Management,* September 2008, p. 847; and Nicolas Glady, Bart Baesens, and Christophe Croux, "Modeling Churn Using Customer Lifetime Value," *European Journal of Operational Research,* August 16, 2009, p. 402.

28. Erick Schonfeld, "Click Here for the Upsell," *Business 2.0,* July 11, 2007, accessed at http://cnnmoney.com; "Getting Shoppers to Crave More," *Fortune Small Business,* August 24, 2007, p. 85; and Heather Green, "How Amazon Aims to Keep You Clicking," *BusinessWeek,* March 2, 2009, pp. 34–40.

29. Don Peppers and Martha Rogers, "Customers Don't Grow on Trees," *Fast Company,* July 2005, pp. 26.

30. See Roland T. Rust, Valerie A. Zeithaml, and Katherine A. Lemon, *Driving Customer Equity* (New York: Free Press, 2000); Rust, Lemon, and Zeithaml, "Return on Marketing: Using Customer Equity to Focus Marketing Strategy," *Journal of Marketing,* January 2004, pp. 109–127; Roland T. Rust, "Seeking

Higher ROI? Base Strategy on Customer Equity," *Advertising Age,* September 10, 2007, pp. 26–27; Dominique M. Hanssens, Daniel Thorpe, and Carl Finkbeiner, "Marketing When Customer Equity Matters," *Harvard Business Review,* May 2008, pp. 117–124; Verena Vogel, Heiner Evanschitzky, and B. Ramaseshan, "Customer Equity Drivers and Future Sales," *Journal of Marketing,* November 2008, pp. 98–108; and Thorsten Wiesel, Bernd Skieram, and Julián Villanueva, "Customer Equity: An Integral Part of Financial Reporting," *Journal of Marketing,* March 8, 2008, pp. 1–14.

31. This example is adapted from information in Rust, Lemon, and Zeithaml, "Where Should the Next Marketing Dollar Go?" *Marketing Management,* September–October 2001, pp. 24–28. Also see David Welch and David Kiley, "Can Caddy's Driver Make GM Cool?" *BusinessWeek,* September 20, 2004, pp. 105–106; Jean Halliday, "Comeback Kid Cadillac Stalls after Shop Swap," *Advertising Age,* September 24, 2007, p. 1; and "A Caddy Not Just for Granddaddy," *The Review,* February 11, 2009, p. 17.

32. Werner Reinartz and V. Kumar, "The Mismanagement of Customer Loyalty," *Harvard Business Review,* July 2002, pp. 86–94. Also see Stanley F. Slater, Jakki J. Mohr, and Sanjit Sengupta, "Know Your Customer," *Marketing Management,* February 2009, pp. 37–44.

33. Noreen O'Leary, "Riders on the Storm: How Marketers Are Navigating a Downturn that Hit Consumers Hard," *Adweek,* July 28–August 4, 2008, p. 20.

34. Dan Sewell, "New Frugality Emerges," *Washington Times,* December 1, 2008; and Noreen O'Leary, "Squeeze Play," *Adweek,* January 12, 2009, pp. 8–9.

35. Layura Petrecca, "Marketers Try to Promote Value without Cheapening Image," *USA Today,* November 17, 2008, p. B1. Also see Kenneth Hein, "Why Price Isn't Everything," *Brandweek,* March 2, 2009, p. 6.

36. Emily Thornton, "The New Rules," *BusinessWeek,* January 19, 2009, pp. 30–34.

37. CMO Council, "Marketing Outlook 2009: Setting the Course for Marketing Strategy and Spend," accessed at www.cmocouncil. org/resources. Also see John A. Quelch and Katherine E. Jocz, "How to Market in a Downturn," *Harvard Business Review,* April 2009, pp. 52–62.

38. "Let Them Eat Big Macs," *BusinessWeek,* February 9, 2009, p. 8; and O'Leary, "Squeeze Play," p. 9.

39. Internet usage stats from www.internetworldstats.com/stats. htm, accessed March 2009; James Lewin, "People Now Spend Twice as Much Time on the Internet as Watching TV," *Podcasting News,* February 25, 2008, accessed at www.podcastingnews.com/2008/02/ 25/podcasting-statistics-television/; "Pew Internet and the American Life Project: Latest Trends" at www.pewinternet.org/ trends.asp, accessed January 2009; and Pew/Internet, "The Future of the Internet III," December 14, 2008, accessed at www.pewinternet. org/PPF/r/270/report_display.asp.

40. "Research and Markets: Semantic Wave Report: Industry Roadmap to Web 3.0 and Multibillion Market Opportunities," *M2 Presswire,* January 20, 2009.

41. Laurie Rowell, "In Search of Web 3.0," *netWorker,* September 2008, pp. 18–24. Also see "Research and Markets: Web 3.0

Manifesto," *Business Wire*, January 21, 2009; and Jessi Hempel, "Web 2.0 Is So Over. Welcome to Web 3.0," *Fortune*, January 19, 2009, p. 36.

42. "Internet World Stats: Usage and Population Statistics" at http://www.internetworldstats.com/am/ca.htm, accessed April 10, 2010.

43. Adapted from information in Don Frischmann, "Nothing Is Insignificant When It Comes to Brand Fulfillment," *Advertising Age*, January 21, 2008, p. 16.

44. Quotes and information found at www.patagonia.com/web/us/contribution/patagonia.go?assetid=2329, accessed September 2009.

45. For examples, and for a good review of non-profit marketing, see Philip Kotler and Alan R. Andreasen, *Strategic Marketing for Nonprofit Organizations*, 6th ed. (Upper Saddle River, NJ: Prentice Hall, 2003); Philip Kotler and Karen Fox, *Strategic Marketing for Educational Institutions* (Upper Saddle River, NJ: Prentice Hall, 1995); Philip Kotler, John Bowen, and James Makens, *Marketing for Hospitality and Tourism*, 3rd ed. (Upper Saddle River, NJ: Prentice Hall, 2003); and Philip Kotler and Nancy Lee, *Marketing in the Public Sector: A Roadmap for Improved Performance* (Philadelphia: Wharton School Publishing, 2007).

46. Adapted from information in Stephanie Strom, "Ad Featuring Singer Proves Bonanza for A.S.P.C.A.," *New York Times*, December 26, 2008, p. 20.

47. "Media in Canada," *Strategy*, November 15, 2005. For other examples, and for a good review of non-profit marketing, see Kotler and Andreasen, *Strategic Marketing for Nonprofit Organizations*, 2003.

CHAPTER 2

1. Quotes and other information from Barbara Lippert, "Game Changers," *Adweek*, November 17–24, 2008, p. 20; Jay Greene, "This Social Network Is Up and Running," *Business Week*, November 17, 2008; Jeremy Mullman, "Nike," *Advertising Age*, October 20, 2008, p. 34; Gene Marcial, "Nike: Set for Two Great Leaps," *BusinessWeek*, April 14, 2008, p. 78; Mark Borden, "Nike," *Fast Company*, March 2008, p. 93; "Nike, Inc.," *Computer Business Week*, April 14, 2008; Michael McCarthy, "Nike's Swoosh Is Under Wraps," *USA Today*, January 7, 2009; Jonathon Birchall, "Nike Seeks 'Opportunities' in Turmoil," *Financial Times*, March 16, 2009, p. 20; and annual reports and other sources at www.nikebiz.com, accessed November 2009.

2. Mission statements are from Amazon.com at http://phx.corporate-ir.net/phoenix.zhtml?c=97664&p =irol-faq#14296, accessed September 2009; and Under Armour at http://www.uabiz.com/company/mission.cfm, accessed September 2010.

3. Jack and Suzy Welch, "State Your Business; Too Many Mission Statements Are Loaded with Fatheaded Jargon. Play It Straight," *BusinessWeek*, January 14, 2008, p. 80. Also see Leia Fransisco, "A Good Mission Statement Can Lead a Business," *McClatchy-Tribune Business News*, November 8, 2008.

4. See "Kohler Mulls Possible Expansion," *Chemical Business Newsbase*, November 30, 2008; "Kohler Waters Spa Opened in Chicago-Area," April 2008 at www.destinationkohler.com/pr/presshospitality.html, and "Kohler Acquires Hospitality Furniture Leader Mark David," May 2008 at www.kohler.com/corp/pr/newscurrent.html. Also see the Kohler Press Room, "IBS Press Kit,"

www.us.kohler.com/pr/presskit.jsp?aid=1194383270995, accessed January 2009.

5. The following discussion is based in part on information found at www.bcg.com/publications/files/Experience_Curve_IV_Growth_Share_Matrix_1973.pdf, accessed December 2009.

6. Matthew Garrahan, "Disney Profits Fall as Recession Hits," *Financial Times*, February 4, 2009, p. 25; and Richard Siklos, "Bob Iger Rocks Disney," *Fortune*, January 19, 2009, pp. 80–86.

7. For an interesting discussion on managing growth, see Matthew S. Olson, Derek van Bever, and Seth Verry, "When Growth Stalls," *Harvard Business Review*, March 2008, pp. 51–61.

8. H. Igor Ansoff, "Strategies for Diversification," *Harvard Business Review*, September–October 1957, pp. 113–124.

9. Information about Under Armour in this section is from Stephanie N. Metha, "Under Armour Reboots," *Fortune*, February 2, 2009, pp. 29–34; Elaine Wong, "Under Armour Makes Long-Run Calculation," *Brandweek*, January 19, 2009, p. 28; Liz Farmer, "Baltimore-Based Under Armour Says Revenue Will Be Lower," *Daily Record* (Baltimore), January 15, 2009; Farmer, "This Super Bowl Weekend, Baltimore-Based Under Armour Taking Grass Roots Marketing Approach," *Daily Record* (Baltimore), January 30, 2009; "Under Armour Reports 20% Top-Line Growth for the Full Year with 3% Growth for the Fourth Quarter," Under Armour press release, January 29, 2009, at http://investor.underarmour.com; and Under Armour annual reports and other documents at www.underarmour.com, accessed April 2009.

10. See Michael E. Porter, *Competitive Advantage: Creating and Sustaining Superior Performance* (New York: Free Press, 1985); and Michel E. Porter, "What Is Strategy?" *Harvard Business Review*, November–December 1996, pp. 61–78; Also see "The Value Chain" at www.quickmba.com/strategy/value-chain, accessed July 2008; and Philip Kotler and Kevin Lane Keller, *Marketing Management* (Upper Saddle River, NJ: Prentice Hall, 2009), pp. 35–36 and pp. 252–253.

11. Nirmalya Kumar, "The CEO's Marketing Manifesto," *Marketing Management*, November–December 2008, pp. 24–29.

12. Rebecca Ellinor, "Crowd Pleaser," *Supply Management*, December 13, 2007, pp. 26–29; and information from www.loreal.com/_en/_ww/html/suppliers/index.aspx, accessed August 2009.

13. See www.nikebiz.com/company_overview/, accessed April 2009.

14. Jack Trout, "Branding Can't Exist Without Positioning," *Advertising Age*, March 14, 2005, p. 28.

15. "100 Leading National Advertisers," special issue of *Advertising Age*, June 23, 2008, p. 10.

16. The four *P*s classification was first suggested by E. Jerome McCarthy, *Basic Marketing: A Managerial Approach* (Homewood, IL: Irwin, 1960). For the four *C*s, other proposed classifications, and more discussion, see Robert Lauterborn, "New Marketing Litany: 4P's Passé C-Words Take Over," *Advertising Age*, October 1, 1990, p. 26; Don E. Schultz, "New Definition of Marketing Reinforces Idea of Integration," *Marketing News*, January 15, 2005, p. 8; Phillip Kotler, "Alphabet Soup," *Marketing Management*, March–April 2006, p. 51; and Nirmalya Kumer, "The CEO's Marketing

Manifesto," *Marketing Management,* November/December 2008, pp. 24–29.

17. For more discussion of the CMO position, see Pravin Nath and Vijay Mahajan, "Chief Marketing Officers: A Study of Their Presence in Firms' Top Management Teams," *Journal of Marketing,* January 2008, pp. 65–81; Philip Kotler and Kevin Lane Keller, *Marketing Management* (Upper Saddle River, NJ: Prentice Hall, 2009), pp. 11–12.

18. Adapted from information found in Diane Brady, "Making Marketing Measure Up," *BusinessWeek,* December 13, 2004, pp. 112–113; and Gray Hammond, "You Gotta Be Accountable," *Strategy,* December 2008, p. 48.

19. See Kenneth Hein, "CMOs Pressured to Show ROI," *Brandweek,* December 12, 2008, p. 6; and Hammond, "You Gotta Be Accountable," p. 48. Also see CMO Council, "Marketing Outlook 2009: Setting the Course for Marketing Strategy and Spend," March 2009, accessed at www.cmocouncil.org/resources.

20. Mark McMaster, "ROI: More Vital than Ever," *Sales & Marketing Management,* January 2002, pp. 51–52. Also see Steven H. Seggie, Erin Cavusgil, and Steven Phelan, "Measurement of Return on Marketing Investment: A Conceptual Framework and the Future of Marketing Metrics," *Industrial Marketing Management,* August 2007, pp. 834–841; and David Armano, "The New Focus Group: The Collective," *BusinessWeek Online,* January 8, 2009, accessed at www.businessweek.com.

21. See Hein, "CMOs Pressured to Show ROI," p. 6; and Hammond, "You Gotta Be Accountable," p. 48.

22. For more discussion, see Bruce H. Clark, Andrew V. Abela, and Tim Ambler, "Behind the Wheel," *Marketing Management,* May–June 2006, pp. 19–23; Christopher Hosford, "Driving Business with Dashboards," *BtoB,* December 11, 2006, p. 18; Allison Enwright, "Measure Up: Create a ROMI Dashboard That Shows Current and Future Value," *Marketing News,* August 15, 2007, pp. 12–13; and Lawrence A. Crosby, Bruce A. Corner, and Cheryl G. Rieger, "Breaking Up Should Be Hard to Do," *Marketing Management,* January/February 2009, pp. 14–16.

23. For a full discussion of this model and details on customer-centred measures of return on marketing investment, see Roland T. Rust, Katherine N. Lemon, and Valerie A. Zeithaml, "Return on Marketing: Using Customer Equity to Focus Marketing Strategy," *Journal of Marketing,* January 2004, pp. 109–127; Roland T. Rust, Katherine N. Lemon, and Das Narayandas, *Customer Equity Management* (Upper Saddle River, NJ: Prentice Hall, 2005); David Tiltman, "Everything You Know Is Wrong," *Marketing,* June 13, 2007, pp. 28–29; Roland T. Rust, "Seeking Higher ROI? Base Strategy on Customer Equity," *Advertising Age,* September 10, 2007, pp. 26–27; and Thorsen Wiesel, Bernd Skiera, and Julián Villanueva, "Customer Equity: An Integral Part of Financial Reporting," *Journal of Marketing,* March 2008, pp. 1–14.

24. Bob Liodice, "Marketers, Get Serious about Accountability," *Advertising Age,* September 8, 2008, p. 22; and Hammond, "You Gotta Be Accountable," p. 48.

CHAPTER 3

1. Information from Bullfrog Power website, www.bullfrogpower. com, accessed October 2009; Michelle Warren, "The Best of '08

Marketers: Bullfrog Power," *Marketing,* November 24, 2008; Peter Gorrie, "Tiny Bullfrog Power Making a Mark," thestar.com, www.thestar.com/article/429893, accessed October 2009.

2. For lots of information on SUV safety and environmental performance, see www.citizen.org/autosafety/suvsafety, accessed September 2009.

3. The figure and the discussion in this section are adapted from Philip Kotler, Gary Armstrong, Veronica Wong, and John Saunders, *Principles of Marketing: European Edition,* 5th ed. (London: Pearson Publishing, 2009), Chapter 2.

4. McDonald's financial information and other facts from www.mcdonalds.com/corp/invest.html and www.mcdonalds.com/ corp/about/factsheets.html, accessed September 2009. Also see "Dow Jones Sustainability United States 40 Index," May 2009, accessed at www.sustainability-index.com/07_htmle/publications/ factsheets.html.

5. The actions described in this section and others undertaken each year by the Competition Bureau are outlined on its "Announcements" webpage at http://www.cb-bc.gc.ca/eic/site/ cb-bc.nsf/eng/h_02705.html, accessed June 2009.

6. Theodore Levitt, "The Morality (?) of Advertising," *Harvard Business Review,* July–August 1970, pp. 84–92. For counterpoints, see Heckman, "Don't Shoot the Messenger," *Marketing News,* May 24, 1999, pp. 1, 9; and Marc Fetscherin and Mark Toncar, "Visual Puffery in Advertising," *International Journal of Market Research,* 51(2), 2009, pp. 147–148.

7. "Canadian Households $1.3 Trillion in Debt," The Canadian Press, May 26, 2009, at http://cnews.canoe.ca/CNEWS/Canada/2009/05/ 26/9574516-cp.html, accessed June 2009; "Credit Card Debt Measures an 'Insult,'" TheStar.com, January 29, 2009, at http:// www.thestar.com/business/article/578881, accessed June 2009; Tom McFeat, "Credit Cards—Convenience at a Price," CBC News Online, September 20, 2004, at http://www.cbc.ca/news/ background/personalfinance/creditcards.html, accessed June 2009.

8. André Picard, "Losing Sleep over 'Natural' Aides," *Globe and Mail,* August 14, 2007.

9. Daryl-Lynn Carlson, "Toyota Recalls Class-Action Boon," *The Financial Post,* May 5, 2010, at http://www.financialpost.com/ news-sectors/legal/story.html?id=2987056, accessed May 5, 2010; Scott Deveau, "Toyota Sales Fall as Ford, Hyundai Surge," *Ottawa Citizen,* May 3, 2010, at http://www.ottawacitizen.com/opinion/ Toyota+sales+fall+Ford+Hyundai+surge/2980421/story.html, accessed May 5, 2010.

10. See Gerri Hirshey, "Time to Buy a New Stove. Again." *New York Times,* December 14, 2008, p. LI 4.

11. Adapted from David Suzuki, "We All Pay for Technology," *Niagara Falls Review,* March 15, 2007, p. A4. For more discussion, see Joseph Guiltinan, "Creative Destruction and Destructive Creations: Environmental Ethics and Planned Obsolescence," *Journal of Business Ethics,* May 2009, pp. 19–28.

12. Harry Alford, "Subprime Scandal—The Largest Hate Crime in History," *New York Beacon,* April 3–9, 2008, p. 12; Edward R. Culvert, "Sub-Prime Loans Should Be Treated as Bias Crimes," *Culvert Chronicles,* March 13–19, 2008, p. 1; Kenneth R. Harney,

"Lawsuit Paints Loan Crisis in Black, White, and Brown," *Washington Post*, November 29, 2008, p. F01; and "NAACP Files Landmark Lawsuit Today Against Wells Fargo and HSBC," March 13, 2009, www.naacp.org/ news/press/2009-03-13/index.htm.

13. "Buy Nothing Day spawns debate," *Vancouver Courier*, November 28, 2008.

14. The quote is from Oliver James, "It's More Than Enough to Make You Sick," *Marketing*, January 23, 2008, pp. 26–28.

15. "Consumerism: New Era of Frugality Dawns," *Marketing Week*, December 18, 2008, p. 12; and "The American Dream Has Been Revised Not Reversed," *Business Wire*, March 9, 2009.

16. See www.tfl.gov.uk/roadusers/congestioncharging/6710.aspx, accessed September 2009.

17. See Allison Linn, "Ads Inundate Public Places," *MSNBC.com*, January 22, 2007; and Bob Garfield, "The Chaos Scenario 2.0: The Post-Advertising Age," *Advertising Age*, March 26, 2007, pp. 1, 12–13.

18. See Martin Sipkoff, "Four-Dollar Pricing Considered Boom or Bust," *Drug Topics*, August 2008, p. 4S; and Sarah Bruyn Jones, "Economic Survival Guide: Drug Discounts Common Now," *McClatchy-Tribune Business News*, February 23, 2009.

19. For these and other examples, see "Strong Growth in Green Logistics," *World Trade*, December 28, 2008, p. 13; Mark Borden et al., "50 Ways to Green Your Business," *Fast Company*, November 2007; and Jack Neff, "Green-Marketing Revolution Defies Economic Downturn," *Advertising Age*, April 20, 2009, accessed at http://adage.com/print?article_id=136091.

20. See Brown, "The Many Shades of Green," *M. E. Magazine*, accessed at http://memagazine.asme.org/Articles/2009/January/Many_Shades_Green.cfm.

21. Based on information from Marc Gunther, "Coca-Cola's Green Crusader," *Fortune*, April 28, 2008, p. 150; "Cold Test Markets Aluminum Bottles," February 20, 2008, accessed at www.bevnet.com/news/2008/02-20-2008-Coke.asp; Jessie Scanlon, "The Shape of a New Coke," *BusinessWeek*, September 2008, p. 72; and "Coca-Cola to Install 1800 CO_2 Coolers in North America," April 30, 2009, accessed at www.r744.com/articles/2009-04-30-coca-cola-to-install-1800-co2-coolers-in-north-america.php.

22. Adapted from "The Top 3 in 2005," *Global 100*, accessed at www.global100.org, July 2005. See also "Alcoa Again Named One of the World's Most Sustainable Companies at Davos," January 29, 2009, accessed at www.alcoa.com; and information from www.global100.org, accessed August 2009. For further information on Alcoa's sustainability program, see Alcoa's Sustainability Report, found at www.alcoa.com.

23. See Geoffrey Garver and Aranka Podhora, "Transboundary Environmental Impact Assessment as Part of the North American Agreement on Environmental Cooperation," *Impact Assessment & Project Appraisal*, December 2008, pp. 253–263; http://ec.europa.eu/environment/index_en.htm, accessed May 2009; and "What is EMAS?" at http://ec.europa.eu/environment/emas/index_en.htm, accessed October 2009.

24. Based on information found in Chuck Salter, "Fast 50: The World's Most Innovative Companies," *Fast Company*, March 2008, pp. 73+. Also see Yukari Iwatani Kane and Daisuke Wakabayashi,

"Nintendo Looks Outside the Box," *Wall Street Journal*, May 27, 2009, p. B5.

25. See Laurel Wentz, "'Evolution' Win Marks Dawn of New Cannes Era," *Advertising Age*, June 25, 2007, p. 1; Theresa Howard, "Ad Campaign Tells Women to Celebrate How They Are," *USA Today*, August 7, 2005, accessed at www.usatoday.com; "Cause: Conscience Marketing. You Stand for Something. Shouldn't Your Brand?" *Strategy*, June 2007, p. 22; and information found at www.campaignforrealbeauty.com, accessed September 2009. For a thorough case study on the brand, see Jennifer Millard, "Performed Beauty: Dove's 'Real Beauty' Campaign" *Symbolic Interaction*, Spring 2009, pp. 146–168.

26. Information from Mike Hofman, "Ben Cohen: Ben & Jerry's Homemade, Established in 1978," *Inc.*, April 30, 2001, p. 68; and the Ben & Jerry's website at www.benjerrys.com, accessed October 2009.

27. Adapted from material found in Jeff Heilman, "Rules of Engagement," *The Magazine of Branded Engagement*, Winter 2009, pp. 7–8.

28. See The World Bank, "The Costs of Corruption," April 8, 2004, accessed at www.worldbank.org; Joseph A. McKinney and Carlos W. Moore, "International Bribery: Does a Written Code of Ethics Make a Difference in Perceptions of Business Professionals," *Journal of Business Ethics*, April 2008, pp. 103–111; and *Global Corruption Report 2009*, Transparency International, accessed at www.transparency.org/publications/gcr/download_gcr#download.

29. John F. McGee and P. Tanganath Nayak, "Leaders' Perspectives on Business Ethics," *Prizm*, first quarter, 1994, pp. 71–72. Also see Adrian Henriques, "Good Decision—Bad Business?" *International Journal of Management & Decision Making*, 2005, p. 273; and Marylyn Carrigan, Svetla Marinova, and Isabelle Szmigin, "Ethics and International Marketing: Research Background and Challenges," *International Marketing Review*, 2005, pp. 481–494.

30. See Samuel A. DiPiazza, "Ethics in Action," *Executive Excellence*, January 2002, pp. 15–16; Samuel A. DiPiazza, Jr., "It's All Down to Personal Values," at www.pwcglobal.com, accessed August 2003; and "Code of Conduct: The Way We Do Business," www.pwc.com/ethics, accessed December 2009.

31. DiPiazza, "Ethics in Action," p. 15.

CHAPTER 4

1. Danny Sinopoli, "Spotted: Eco-cornstarch dishware," *The Globe and Mail*, April 23, 2010, accessed at http://www.theglobeandmail.com/life/style/design-snapshot-eco-cornstarch-dishware/article1544452/; "Going Green," *Marketing News*, a publication of the American Marketing Association, February 1, 2008, pp. 15–19; and Loblaw Companies Limited press releases: "Loblaw Business Grows with the President's Choice GREEN Brand," April 21, 2008, and "Loblaw Launches Plastic Bag Recycling Program," September 11, 2007.

2. "Copy This Advice: Xerox's CEO Says 'Let's Get Personal,'" *Marketing News*, October 15, 2008, pp. 18–19.

3. Company press release, "Pratt & Whitney Canada Launches eBusiness Supplier Portal," November 14, 2002, accessed at http://www.pwc.ca/en/news-events/press/details/394205.

4. Information from Robert J. Benes, Abbie Jarman, and Ashley Williams, "2007 NRA Sets Records," at www.chefmagazine.com/nra.htm, accessed September 2007; and www.thecoca-colacompany.com/presscenter/presskit_fs.html and www.cokesolutions.com, accessed November 2009.

5. World POPClock, U.S. Census Bureau, at www.census.gov, accessed September 2009. This website provides continuously updated projections of the U.S. and world populations.

6. See Clay Chandler, "Little Emperors," *Fortune,* October 4, 2004, pp. 138–150; "China's 'Little Emperors,'" *Financial Times,* May 5, 2007, p. 1; "Me Generation Finally Focuses on US," Chinadaily.com.cn, August 27, 2008; Melinda Varley, "China: Chasing the Dragon," *Brand Strategy,* October 6, 2008, p. 26; and Clifford Coonan, "New Rules to Enforce Chain's One-Child Policy," *Irish Times,* January 14, 2009, p. 12.

7. Adapted from information in Janet Adamy, "Different Brew: Eyeing a Billion Tea Drinkers, Starbucks Pours It On in China," *Wall Street Journal,* November 29, 2006, p. A1. Also see "Where the Money Is," *Financial Times,* May 12, 2007, p. 8; and Melissa Allison, "Starbucks Thrives in China," *McClatchy-Tribune Business News,* January 14, 2009.

8. Daniel Stoffman, "Completely Predictable People," *Report on Business,* November 1990, pp. 78–84; David Foot and Daniel Stoffman, *Boom, Bust and Echo* (Toronto: Macfarlane Walter & Ross, 1996), pp. 18–22.

9. Dee Depass, "Designed with a Wink, Nod at Boomers," *Minneapolis-St. Paul Star Tribune,* April 1, 2006, p. 1. Also see Linda Stern, "It's Not All Downhill," *Newsweek,* December 1, 2008, at www.newsweek.com.

10. "NAS Insights: Getting to Know Generation X," 2006, www.nasrecruitment.com/TalentTips/NASinsights/GettingtoKnowGenerationX.pdf; and Marshall Lager, "The Slackers' X-cellent Adventure," *CRM Magazine,* November 1, 2008, pp. 30–33.

11. For more discussion, see R. K. Miller and Kelli Washington, *Consumer Behavior 2009,* (Atlanta, GA: Richard K. Miller & Associates, 2009), Chapter 27.

12. Information from www.mec.ca, accessed April 28, 2010.

13. Julie Liesse, "Getting to Know the Millennials," *Advertising Age,* July 9, 2007, pp. A1–A6; and "The Millennials," *Time,* Spring 2008, p. 55.

14 Jessica Tsai, "Who, What, Where, When, Y," *Customer Relationship Management,* November 2008, pp. 24–28; and John Austin, "Automakers Try to Reach Gen Y: Carmakers Look for New Marketing Approaches, Technological Advances to Attract Millennials," *McClatchy-Tribune Business News,* February 1, 2009.

15 Brian Morrissey, "Zynga, 7-Eleven Link Virtual, Real Goods," *Adweek,* May 23, 2010, accessed at http://www.adweek.com/aw/content_display/news/agency/e3i4a68f0689d02bf9eb1d308a5ea40a771; and "7-Eleven and Zynga Offer Exclusive Farmville, Mafia Wars, and Yoville Products In-store and Virtual Gifts In-game," press release, May 24, 2010, accessed at http://www.7-eleven.com/NewsRoom/2010NewsReleases/ZYNGA/tabid/425/Default.aspx.

16 Statistics Canada, "2006 Census: Family portrait: Continuity and Change in Canadian Families and Households in 2006: Highlights,"

at http://www12.statcan.ca/census-recensement/2006/as-sa/97-553/p1-eng.cfm, accessed May 20, 2010.

17 Statistics Canada, "The Canadian Labour Market at a Glance," accessed at http://www12.statcan.ca/census-recensement/2006/as-sa/97-553/p1-eng.cfm.

18. Information from https://www.epiceriedirect.com/index.php, accessed May 22, 2010.

19. Statistics Canada, "Report on the Demographic Situation in Canada," http://www.statcan.gc.ca/bsolc/olc-cel/olc-cel?catno=91-209-x&lang=eng, accessed April 23, 2009; and Ross Finnie, "The Effects of Inter-Provincial Mobility on Individuals' Earnings: Panel Model Estimates for Canada," Analytical Studies Branch Research Paper Series, Report 163, Catalogue No. 11F0019MIE2001163, October 2001, http://collection.nlc-bnc.ca/100/200/301/statcan/research_paper_analytical_11f0019-e/no163/11F0019MIE01163.pdf.

20. Canadian Consumer Demographics, Industry Canada, Retail Interactive, at http://strategis.ic.gc.ca/SSG/ri00140e.html, accessed May 6, 2003.

21. "Who Works from Home," GDSourcing, *The Business Researcher Newsletter Archives,* 5(3), March 22, 2002; and Kate Lorenz, "What's the Advantage to Telecommuting," at www.cnn.com, accessed April 27, 2007. Also see "Number of Worldwide Mobile Workers Increasing," *Workspan,* March 2008, p. 19; Sue Shellenbarger, "Some Companies Rethink That Telecommuting Trend," *Wall Street Journal,* February 28, 2008, p. D1.

22. See Ryan Underwood, "OK, Everybody, Let's Do This!" *Inc.,* July 2008, pp. 40–42; "WebEx Communications, Inc.," *Hoover's Company Records,* March 15, 2009, p. 99024; and "About WebEx," at www.webex.com/companyinfo/company-overview.html, accessed July 2009.

23. Adapted from "A Profile of Education in Canada," Canadian Council on Social Development, 2004, www.ccsd.ca/factsheets/education; and "Educational Attainment," U.S. Census Bureau, January 2008, accessed at www.census.gov/population/www/socdemo/educ-attn.html.

24. Statistics Canada, "2006 Census: Ethnic Origin, Visible Minorities, Place of Work and Mode of Transportation," http://www.statcan.gc.ca/daily-quotidien/080402/dq080402a-eng.htm, accessed May 1, 2009.

25. Hamlin Grange and Don Miller, "How to Leverage Diversity," *Marketing Magazine,* August 29, 2005.

26. Grange and Miller, "How to Leverage Diversity."

27. Ashwin W. Joshi, "The Visible Majority," *Marketing Magazine,* August 29, 2005.

28. Statistics Canada, "2006 Census: Family Portrait: Continuity and Change in Canadian Families and Households in 2006: Highlights," at http://www12.statcan.ca/census-recensement/2006/as-sa/97-553/p1-eng.cfm, accessed April 20, 2009.

29. Information from Air Canada's website, at http://www.aircanadavacations.com/en/ideas/activities/our_promise/interests/Gay-and-lesbian-travel, accessed May 25, 2010.

30. Gavin Rabinowitz, "India's Tata Motors Unveils $2,500 Car, Bringing Car Ownership Within Reach of Millions," *Associated*

Press, January 10, 2008; Ray Hutton, "Indian Car Firm Plans to Take a Domestic Drive," *Sunday Times* (London), December 28, 2008, p. 6; and Jessica Scanlon, "What Can Tata's Nano Teach Detroit?" *BusinessWeek Online*, March 19, 2009, accessed at www.BusinessWeek.com.

31. Noreen O'Leary, "Squeeze Play," *Adweek*, January 12, 2009, pp. 8–9. Also see Alessandra Stanley, "For Hard Times, Softer Sells," *New York Times*, February 6, 2009; and Kenneth Hein, "Why Price Isn't Everything," *Brandweek,* March 2, 2009, p. 6.

32. Statistics Canada, "Study: High Income Canadians," September 2007, at http://www.statcan.gc.ca/daily-quotidien/070924/dq070924a-eng.htm, "2006 Census: Earnings, Income, and Shelter Costs," accessed May 2008, http://www.statcan.gc.ca/daily-quotidien/080501/dq080501a-eng.htm, and "Census Release Topics," http://www12.statcan.ca/census-recensement/2006/rt-td/index-eng.cfm, accessed April 29, 2009; Mark MacKinnon, "High-Income Neighbourhoods," *Globe and Mail,* March 1, 1999, p. B1; and Mark MacKinnon, "The Lowest Incomes in Canada Are Found on Native Reserves," *Globe and Mail*, March 1, 1999, p. B2.

33. Kelly Nolan, "Mass Movement of High Fashion," *Retailing Today*, January 8, 2007, pp. 4–6; Eric Wilson and Michael Barbaro, "Can You Be Too Fashionable?" *New York Times*, June 17, 2007, p. 1; Elizabeth Wellington, "Mirror, Mirror: Discounted to Distraction," *Philadelphia Inquirer*, November 4, 2007, p. M1; and Yelena Moroz, "Mass Fashion in Focus: Cheap Chic Fever Quickly Catching On," *Retailing Today*, February 11, 2008, p. 1.

34. Andrew Zolli, "Business 3.0," *Fast Company*, March 2007, pp. 64–70.

35. Canadian Standards Association, "PLUS 14021 - Environmental Claims: A Guide for Industry and Advertisers," June 2008, at http://www.csa.ca/Default.asp?language=english, accessed April 29, 2009.

36. "GE Transportation's Evolution Hybrid Debuts at RSA Railway Technology Exhibition," *Wireless News,* September 21, 2008; Steve Bronstein, *Fast Company*, November 2007, pp. 90–99; and various pages at www.ge.com, accessed July 2009.

37. Facts from www.pepsico.com/Purpose/Environment.aspx, accessed April 2009.

38. See "Wal-Mart Expands RFID Requirements," *McClatchy-Tribune Business News*, January 30, 2008; David Blanchard, "Wal-Mart Lays Down the Law on RFID," *Industry Week*, May 2008, p. 72; David Blanchard, "The Five Stages of RFID," *Industry Week,* January 2009, p. 50; and information at www.autoidlabs.org, accessed April 2009.

39. See Lori Vallgra, "US to Spend Less on R&D in 2009," *Science Business*, January 22, 2009, at http://bulletin.sciencebusiness.net/ebulletins/showissue.php3?page=/548/art/12638/.

40. Statistics Canada, "Domestic Spending on Research and Development (GERD)," at www40.statcan.ca/l01/cst01/scte01a.htm, accessed April 29, 2009.

41. See Jack Neff, "Unilever, P&G War Over Which Is Most Ethical," *Advertising Age*, March 3, 2008, p. 1; and information at www.beautifullengths.com, accessed August 2009.

42. See "The Growth of Cause Marketing," at www.causemarketingforum.com/page.asp?ID=188, accessed August 2009.

43. For one discussion of Canadian values, see "Projecting Canadian Values and Culture," Foreign Affairs Canada, February 17, 2003; and www.dfait-maeci.gc.ca/foreign_policy/cnd-world/chap5_en.asp.

44. Karen Von Hahn, "Plus ça Change: Get Set for Cocooning 2.0," *Globe and Mail*, January 3, 2008, p. L1; and Liza N. Burby, "Tips for Making Your Home a Cozy Nest, or 'Hive,'" *Newsday*, January 23, 2009, www.newsday.com/services/newspaper/printedition/exploreli/ny-hocov6007466jan23,0,2603167.story.

45. Mike Duff, "Consumer Return to the Cocoon Could Help Retailers," *BNET Retail Blog*, December 19, 2008, at http://industry.bnet.com/retail/1000343/consumer-return-to-the-cocoon-could-help-retailers/; and Claire Cain Miller, "For Craft Sales, the Recession Is a Help," *New York Times*, December 23, 2008, p. B1.

46. Based on information from Beth Snyder Bulik, "Stay-at-Home Trend Feathers Samsung Nest," *Advertising Age*, November 3, 2008, p. 18; and Alessandra Stanley, "For Hard Times, Softer Sells," *New York Times*, February 6, 2009.

47. L. A. Chung, "New Greetings of Hybrid Fans: Aloha, LOHAS," *Mercury News*, April 29, 2005, at www.mercurynews.com/mld/mercurynews/news/columnists/la_chung/11520890.htm; with information from www.lohas.com, accessed November 2009.

48. See www.livebetterindex.com/sustainability.html, accessed November 2009.

49. "Earthbound Farm Facts," at www.earthboundfarm.com, accessed September 2009.

50. See Nigel Hunt and Brad Dorfman, "Organic Food Growth Slows Amid Downturn," *Reuters*, January 28, 2009, accessed at http://uk.reuters.com.

51. Michael Valpy, "Religious Observance Continues To Decline," *Globe and Mail*, March 19, 2003, p. A18; and Clifford Krauss, "In God We Trust. . . Canadians Aren't So Sure," *New York Times*, at www.nytimes.com, March 26, 2003.

52. See Philip Kotler, *Kotler on Marketing* (New York: Free Press, 1999), p. 3; and Kotler, *Marketing Insights from A to Z* (Hoboken, NJ: John Wiley & Sons, 2003), pp. 23–24.

53. Based on information found at http://urbanlegends.about.com/library/bl_tim_hortons_coffee.htm, http://www.snopes.com/food/ingredient/timhortons.asp, and http://www.timhortons.com/ca/en/about/faq.html, accessed May 3, 2009.

CHAPTER 5

1. Quotes and other information from Jonah Bloom, "Stengel Exhorts 4As: It's Not About Telling and Selling," *Advertising Age*, March 1, 2007, accessed at http://adage.com/4asmedia07/article?article_id=115259; Robert Berner, "Detergent Can Be So Much More," *BusinessWeek*, May 1, 2006, pp. 66–67; Jack Neff, "New Tide Campaign Goes Beyond Stains," *Advertising Age*, February 13, 2006, p. 16; "For P&G, Success Lies in More than Merely a Dryer Diaper," *Advertising Age*, October 15, 2007, p. 30;

"Case Study: Tide Knows Fabrics Best," at www.thearf.org/awards/ogilvy-current-winners.html, accessed April 2008; Roger O. Crockett, "The Soapy Path to Power at P&G," *BusinessWeek,* March 16, 2009, p. 49; "P&G: Our Purpose, Values, and Principles," at www.pg.com/company/who_we_are/ppv.jhtml, accessed December 2009; and Lucy Saddleton, "Tide Rolls On," *Strategy Magazine,* October 2008, http://www.strategymag.com/articles/magazine/20081001/tributetide.html?__s=yes&print=yes, accessed May 1, 2009.

2. Unless otherwise noted, quotes in this section are from the excellent discussion of customer insights found in Mohanbir Sawhney, "Insights into Customer Insights," at www.redmond.nl/hro/upload/Insights_into_Customer_Insights.pdf, accessed April 2009. The Apple iPod example is also adapted from this article.

3. Facts obtained from "Did You Know," video presentation, June 2008, accessed at www.flixxy.com/technology-and-education-2008.htm.

4. Michael Fassnacht, "Beyond Spreadsheets," *Advertising Age,* February 19, 2007, p. 15.

5. Robert Scheiffer and Eric Leininger, "Customers at the Core," *Marketing Management,* January/February 2008, pp. 31–37.

6. For more discussion, see Schieffer and Leininger, "Customers at the Core," pp. 31–37.

7. Ian C. MacMillan and Larry Seldon, "The Incumbent's Advantage," *Harvard Business Review,* October 2008, pp. 111–121.

8. Scott Gardiner, "A Truly Awesome Database," *Marketing Magazine,* April 29, 2002.

9. Example based on information from "PacSun to Surf the Social Web with Radian6," Radian6 press release, March 24, 2009, accessed at www.radian6.com; Don Macpherson, "Radian6 Has Ears of Big Business," *Daily Gleaner,* September 25, 2008, p. D1; and www.Radian6.com, accessed November 2009.

10. James Curtis, "Behind Enemy Lines," *Marketing,* May 21, 2001, pp. 28–29. Also see Jim Middlemiss, "Firms Look to Intelligence to Gain a Competitive Edge," *Law Times,* March 5, 2007, accessed at www.lawtimesnews.com; and "Outwards Insights; Competitive Intelligence Drives More Corporate Decisions, New Survey Shows," *Marketing Business Weekly,* October 19, 2008, p. 385.

11. For more on research firms that supply marketing information, see Jack Honomichl, "Honomichl Top 50," special section, *Marketing News,* June 15, 2008, pp. H1–H67. Other information from www.smrb.com, www.nielsen.com, and www.yakelovich.com, accessed August 2009.

12. See http://us.infores.com/page/solutions/market_content/infoscan, accessed April 5, 2008.

13. See Jenn Abelson, "Gillette Sharpens Its Focus on Women," *Boston Globe,* January 4, 2009.

14. See David Kiley, "Shoot the Focus Group," *BusinessWeek,* November 14, 2005, pp. 120–121; Richard G. Starr and Karen V. Fernandez, "The Mindcam Methodology: Perceiving Through the Native's Eye," *Quantitative Market Research,* Spring 2007, pp. 168+; and Todd Wasserman, "Thinking by Design," *Brandweek,* November 3, 2008, pp. 18–21.

15. See Jack Neff, "Marketing Execs: Researchers Could Use a Softer Touch," *Advertising Age,* January 27, 2009, accessed at http://adage.com/article?article_id=134144; and Neff, "The End of Consumer Surveys?" *Advertising Age,* p. 4.

16. Example adapted from information in Rhys Blakely, "You Know When It Feels Like Somebody's Watching You..." *Times,* May 14, 2007, p. 46; and Nandini Lakshman, "Nokia: It Takes a Village to Design a Phone for Emerging Markets," *BusinessWeek,* September 10, 2007, p. 12. See also Sara Corbett, "Can the Cellphone Help End Global Poverty?" *New York Times Magazine,* April 13, 2008, p. 34; and Todd Wasserman, "Thinking by Design," *Brandweek,* November 3, 2008, pp. 18–21.

17. Spencer E. Ante, "The Science of Desire," *BusinessWeek,* June 5, 2006, p. 100; Rhys Blakely, "You Know When It Feels Like Somebody's Watching You..." *Times,* May 14, 2007, p. 46; and Jack Neff, "Marketing Execs: Researchers Could Use a Softer Touch," *Advertising Age,* January 27, 2009, accessed at http://adage.com/article?article_id=134144.

18. "National Do Not Call List effective, but challenges remain, VoxPop survey finds," Marketing Research and Intelligence Association, press release, March 9, 2009, accessed at www.mria-arim.ca/DNCL/NEWS/PDF/VoxPopdnclv8Mar4_2009.pdf.

19. Adapted from information in Kenneth Hein, "Hypnosis Brings Groups into Focus," *Brandweek,* May 23, 2008, p. 4.

20. Emily Spensieri, "A Slow, Soft Touch," *Marketing,* June 5, 2006, pp. 15–16.

21. Jack Neff, "Marketing Execs: Researchers Could Use a Softer Touch," *Advertising Age,* January 27, 2009, accessed at http://adage.com/article?article_id=134144.

22. "E-Rewards Rakes in $60M in New Funding," October 17, 2008, accessed at http://dallas.bizjournals.com/dallas/stories/2008/10/20/story5.html.

23. See "E-Rewards Rakes in $60M in New Funding," p. 1; and Internet penetration statistics found at www.internetworldstats.com/stats14.htm, accessed July 2009.

24. Nikki Hopewell, "Surveys by Design," *Marketing News,* December 15, 2008, p. 12.

25. Based on information found in Jeremiah McWilliams, "A-B Sees Web As Fertile Ground for Advertising Efforts," *St. Louis Post-Dispatch,* December 19, 2007; and www.youtube.com/watch?v=EJJL5dxgVaM, accessed December 2009.

26. Based on information found www.channelm2.com/HowOnlineQualitativeResearch.html, accessed December 2009.

27. See "Company Survey Respondents," at www.zoomerang.com, accessed December 2009.

28. For more on Internet privacy, see Jessica E. Vascellaro, "They've Got Your Number (and a Lot More)," *Wall Street Journal,* March 13, 2007, pp. D1–D2; Jim Puzzanghera, "Internet; Tough Cookies for Web Surfers Seeking Privacy," *Los Angeles Times,* April 19, 2008, p. C1; and "What Would You Reveal on the Internet?" *Privacy Journal,* January 2009, p. 1.

29. See "Creating Computers That Know How You Feel," at www.almaden.ibm.com/cs/BlueEyes/index.html, accessed November 2009.

30. See Josh Goldstein, "Branding on the Brain," *News & Observer*, December 6, 2006, p. 9E; Jack Neff, "This Is Your Brain on Super Bowl Spots," *Advertising Age*, February 11, 2008, pp. 1, 21; and "Super Bowl Ad Analysis," at www.sandsresearch.com, accessed April 2009.

31. Adapted from Steve McClennan, New Tool Puts Brands in Touch with Feelings," *Adweek*, February 18, 2008, pp. 16–17. Also see Elizabeth A. Sullivan, "Pick Your Brain," *Marketing News*, March 15, 2009, pp. 10–12.

32. See Barney Beal, "Gartner: CRM Spending Looking Up," SearchCRM.com, April 29, 2008, at http://searchcrm.techtarget.com/news/article/0,289142,sid11_gci1311658,00.html; and David White, "CRM Magazine Announces Winners of 2009 CRM Service Awards," *Business Wire*, April 1, 2009.

33. "Infor CRM Customer Bell Canada Wins Marketing Optimization Award," *Marketing Business Weekly* (Atlanta), October 5, 2008, p. 109.

34. "Loyalty Cards: Getting to Know You," *Marketplace*, broadcast on CBC, October 24, 2004; and information accessed at www.canadaloyalty.com.

35. Michael Krauss, "At Many Firms, Technology Obscures CRM," *Marketing News*, March 18, 2002, p. 5. Also see William Boulding et al., "A Customer Relationship Management Roadmap: What Is Known, Potential Pitfalls, and Where to Go," *Journal of Marketing*, October 2005, pp. 155–166; "Study: Marketers Stink When It Comes to CRM," *Brandweek*, April 14, 2008, p. 7; and Robert Kane, "Straight Talk: Advice from the Trenches of SaaS CRM," *Customer Relationship Management*, January 2009, p. S3.

36. See "Value Added with mySAP CRM: Benchmarking Study," at www.sap.com/solutions/business-suite/crm/pdf/Misc_CRM_Study.pdf, accessed June 2008.

37. See "Penske Launches Improved Extranet," *Refrigerated Transporter*, March 2009, p. 47; and information found at www.partnersonline.com, accessed September 2009.

38. Adapted from information in Ann Zimmerman, "Small Business; Do the Research," *Wall Street Journal*, May 9, 2005, p. R3; with information from www.bibbentuckers.com, accessed July 2009.

39. Zimmerman, "Small Business; Do the Research," *Wall Street Journal*, p. R3.

40. For some good advice on conducting market research in a small business, see "Marketing Research... Basics 101," at www.sba.gov/smallbusinessplanner/index.html, accessed August 2009; and "Researching Your Market," U.S. Small Business Administration, at www.sba.gov/idc/groups/public/documents/sba_homepage/pub_mt8.pdf, accessed November 2009.

41. See Jack Honomichl, "Top Firms Consolidated Grip on Industry," *Marketing News*, August 15, 2008, p. H1.

42. See http://en-us.nielsen.com/main/about/Profile, accessed July 2009.

43. Phone and Internet stats are from http://www.worldbank.org, accessed July 2009. See also www.iwcp.hpg.ig.com.br/communications.html, accessed February 2009, and www.internetworldstats.com, accessed June 2010.

44. Subhash C. Jain, *International Marketing Management*, 3rd ed. (Boston: PWS-Kent, 1990), p. 338. For more discussion on international marketing research issues and solutions, see Michael Fielding, "Shift the Focus: Ethnography Proves Fruitful in Emerging Economies," *Marketing News*, September 1, 2006, pp. 18, 20; Robert B. Young and Rajshekhar G. Javalgi, "International Marketing Research: A Global Project Management Perspective," *Business Horizons*, March–April 2007, pp. 113–122; and Julia Lin, "By the Numbers: How to Avoid Language Problems in International IT Research," *Quirk's Marketing Research Review*, November 2008, accessed at www.quirks.com.

45. Adapted from David Shipley, "Can Firm Monitor the Word on the Web," *Daily Gleaner*, August 14, 2008, p. D1; Sean McDonald, "Dell and Radian6: It All Starts with Listening," Direct2Dell, August 19, 2008, accessed at http://en.community.dell.com/blogs/direct2dell/archive/2008/08/19/dell-and-radian6-it-all-starts-with-listening.aspx.

46. Stephanie Clifford, "Many See Privacy on the Web as Big Issue, Survey Says," *New York Times*, March 16, 2009. Also see "What Was Privacy?" *Harvard Business Review*, October 2008, pp. 123–131.

47. "RBC Privacy Policy Statement," at http://www.rbc.com/privacysecurity/ca/our-privacy-policy.html, accessed June 3, 2010.

48. Jaikumar Vijayan, "Disclosure Laws Driving Data Privacy Efforts, Says IBM Exec," *Computerworld*, May 8, 2006, p. 26; and "Facebook Chief Privacy Officer—Interview," *Analyst Wire*, February 18, 2009.

49. Information at www10.americanexpress.com/sif/cda/page/0,1641,14271,00.asp, accessed July 2009.

50. Cynthia Crossen, "Studies Galore Support Products and Positions, But Are They Reliable?" *Wall Street Journal*, November 14, 1991, pp. A1, A9. Also see Allan J. Kimmel, "Deception in Marketing Research and Practice: An Introduction," *Psychology and Marketing*, July 2001, pp. 657–661; Jack Neff, "Who's No. 1? Depends on Who's Analyzing the Data," *Advertising Age*, June 12, 2006, p. 8; and Carl Bialik, "In Ads, 1 Out of 5 Stats Is Bogus," *Wall Street Journal*, March 11, 2009.

CHAPTER 6

1. Extracts, quotes, and other information adapted from or found in Peter Burrows, "The World's Most Influential Companies: Apple," *BusinessWeek*, December 22, 2008, p. 46; Katie Hafner, "Inside Apple Stores, a Certain Aura Enchants the Faithful," *New York Times*, December 27, 2007; Terry Semel, "Steve Jobs: Perpetual Innovation Machine," *Time*, April 18, 2005, p. 78; Steve Maich, "Nowhere to Go But Down," *Maclean's*, May 9, 2005, p. 32; Stephen Withers, "Apple Tops for Brand Loyalty: Report," *iTWire*, September 12, 2008, accessed at www.itwire.com/content/view/20603/1151/l; Chris Nuttall, "Credit Crunch Passes Apple by as iPod Popularity Keeps on Growing," *Financial Times*, January 22, 2009, p. 15; "Macolyte," *Urban Dictionary*, at www.urbandictionary.com, accessed May 2009; and financial information found at www.apple.com, accessed May 2009.

2. GDP figures from *The World Fact Book,* April 2, 2009, accessed at www.cia.gov/cia/publications/factbook/. Population figures from the World POPClock, U.S. Census Bureau, at www.census.gov, accessed May 2009. This website provides continually updated projections of the U.S. and world populations.

3. Don E. Schultz, "Lines or Circles" *Marketing News,* November 5, 2007, p. 21; and Elizabeth A. Sullivan, "Pick Your Brain," *Marketing News,* March 15, 2009, pp. 10–13.

4. Allan R. Gregg, "Strains Across the Border," *Maclean's,* December 30, 2002, accessed at www.macleans.ca; and "Maclean's Annual Poll," *Maclean's,* November 21, 2007, accessed at www.macleans.ca.

5. For a deeper discussion of consumer culture theory, see Eric J. Arnold and Craig J. Thompson, "Consumer Culture Theory (CCT): Twenty Years of Research," *Journal of Consumer Research,* 31(4), 2005, pp. 868–883.

6. *The Political Voice of Canadian Regional Identities,* The Centre for Canadian Studies, 2001, at http://culturescope.ca/even.php?ID=9417201&ID2=DO_TOPIC, accessed September 2006.

7. Sara Minogue, "Reaching New Canadians: Multicultural Experts Offer Their Best Practice Advice to Niche Marketers," *Strategy Magazine,* September 22, 2003, at www.strategymag.com, accessed July 13, 2004.

8. Statistics Canada, "Study: Canada's Visible Minority Population in 2017," *The Daily,* March 22, 2005.

9. Hamlin Grange and Don Miller, "How to Leverage Diversity," *Marketing Magazine,* August 29, 2005.

10. Huixia Sun, "Chinese Websites Beat Economic Blues," *The Vancouver Sun,* May 15, 2009; and Chris Powell, "New Chinese Canadians Prefer Internet to TV: Diversity Study," *Marketing Magazine,* April 2008.

11. Statistics Canada, "2006 Census Data Products," at http://www12.statcan.ca/census-recensement/2006/dp-pd/index-eng.cfm, accessed May 15, 2009.

12. "About the Queen Collection," at www.covergirl.com/products/collections/queen/, accessed April 2009. Facts from Cliff Peale, "P&G Showed the Way: Company's Ads Targeted to Blacks Paid Off," *Cincinnati Enquirer,* February 25, 2007, accessed at www.cincinnati.com; and "Top 10 Advertisers across All African American Media," *Adweek,* February 9, 2009, p. 16.

13. See Noreen O'Leary, "Squeeze Play," *Adweek,* January 12, 2009, pp. 8–9; and Emily Brandon, "Planning to Retire: 10 Things You Didn't Know About Baby Boomers," USNews.com, January 15, 2009, accessed at www.usnews.com.

14. "Boom Time of America's New Retirees Feel Entitled to Relax—and Intend to Spend," *Financial Times,* December 6, 2007, p. 9.

15. See www.dove.us/#/products/collections/proage.aspx, accessed November 2009.

16. For a discussion of influencers, see Clive Thompson, "Is the Tipping Point Toast?" *Fast Company,* February 2008, pp. 75–105; and Edward Keller and Jonathan Berry, *The Influentials* (New York:

The Free Press, 2003). The study results reported in Holly Shaw, "Buzzing Influencers," *National Post,* March 13, 2009, p. 12.

17. See Rob Walker, "Tap Dance," *New York Times,* January 6, 2009; and facts about Vocalpoint at www.vocalpoint.com, accessed July 2009.

18. Adapted from Anya Kamenetz, "The Network Unbound," *Fast Company,* June 2006, pp. 69–73. Also see Brad Stone, "Social Networking's Next Phase," *New York Times,* March 3, 2007, accessed at www.nytimes.com; Chuck Brymer, "The Birds and the Bees," *Adweek,* January 7, 2008, p. 16; and Facebook statistics, at www.facebook.com/press/info.php?statistics, accessed April 2009.

19. Beth Krietsch, "YouTube Channel for Congress Builds Dialogue, Transparency," *PR Week,* January 19, 2009, p. 9; "Death of TV Advertising," *Business and Finance,* June 24, 2008; and Samir Balwani, "Presenting: 10 of the Smartest Big Brands in Social Media," *Mashable,* February 6, 2009, accessed at http://mashable.com/2009/02/06/social-media-smartest-brands/.

20. See Scott Hidebrink, "Women and the Automotive Aftermarket," *Motor Age,* September 2007, pp. 60+; Andrew Adam Newman, "The Man of the House," *Adweek,* August 11–18, 2008, pp. 16–19; Eleftheria Parpis, "She's in Charge," *Adweek,* October 6–13, 2008, p. 38; and Abigail Posner, "Why Package-Goods Companies Should Market to Men," *Advertising Age,* February 9, 2009, accessed at http://adage.com/print?article_id=134473.

21. Adapted from Michel Marriott, "Gadget Designers Take Aim at Women," *New York Times,* June 7, 2007, p. C7. Also see Dean Takahashi, "Philips Focuses on TVs Women Buyers," *McClatchy-Tribune Business News,* January 6, 2008.

22. Chris Powell, "Under the Influence," *Marketing,* February 16, 2004, p. 9.

23. R. K. Miller and Kelli Washington, *Consumer Behavior 2009* (Atlanta, GA: Richard K. Miller & Associates, 2009), Chapter 27.

24. For this quote and other information on Acxiom's PersonicX segmentation system, see "Acxiom Study Reveals Inside an Evolving Consumer Shopping Behaviors in Trying Economic Times," *Reuters,* January 13, 2009, accessed at www.reuters.com/article/pressRelease/idUS180299+13-Jan-2009+BW20090113; and "Acxiom PersonicX" and "Intelligent Solutions for the Travel Industry: Life-Stage Marketing," at www.acxiom.com, accessed April 2009.

25. Norma Ramage, "Mark's Super Brand Ambition," *Marketing,* March 29, 2004.

26. Kenneth Hein, "Target Tries Price Point Play," *Adweek.com,* January 15, 2009, accessed at www.adweek.com/aw/content_display/creative/news/e3i0b84325122066ed9830db4ccb41e7ecf.

27. Portions adapted from Linda Tischler, "How Pottery Barn Wins with Style," *Fast Company,* June 2003, pp. 106–113; and Carole Sloan, "Lifestyle Specialists Enjoy Strong Year," *Furniture Today,* August 28, 2006, p. 28; with information from www.potterybarn.com, www.potterybarnkids.com, and www.pbteen.com, accessed October 2008.

28. See Jennifer Aaker, "Dimensions of Measuring Brand Personality," *Journal of Marketing Research,* August 1997, pp. 347–356; and Vanitha Swaminathan, Karen M. Stilley, and Rohini Ahluwalla, "When Brand Personality Matters: The Moderating Role of Attachment Styles," *Journal of Consumer Research,* April 2009, pp. 985–1002.

29. See www.apple.com/getamac/ads/, accessed May 2009.

30. See Abraham. H. Maslow, "A Theory of Human Motivation," *Psychological Review,* 50 (1943), pp. 370–396. Also see Maslow, *Motivation and Personality,* 3rd ed. (New York: HarperCollins Publishers, 1987); and Barbara Marx Hubbard, "Seeking Our Future Potentials," *Futurist,* May 1998, pp. 29–32.

31. See Louise Story, "Anywhere the Eye Can See, It's Now Likely to See an Ad," *New York Times,* January 15, 2007, accessed at www.nytimes.com; Matthew Creamer, "Caught in the Clutter Crossfire: Your Brand," *Advertising Age,* April 1, 2007, p. 35; and Ruth Mortimer, "Consumer Awareness: Getting the Right Attention," *Brand Strategy,* December 10, 2008, p. 55.

32. Bob Garfield, "'Subliminal' Seduction and Other Urban Myths," *Advertising Age,* September 18, 2000, pp. 4, 105; and Lewis Smith, "Subliminal Advertising May Work, but Only If You're Paying Attention," *Times,* March 9, 2007. For more on subliminal advertising, see Alastair Goode, "The Implicit and Explicit Role of Ad Memory in Ad Persuasion: Rethinking the Hidden Persuaders," *International Journal of Marketing Research,* 49(2), 2007, pp. 95–116; Cynthia Crossen, "For a time in the 50s, a Huckster Fanned Fears of an Ad 'Hypnosis,'" *Wall Street Journal,* November 5, 2007, p. B1; and Beth Snyder Bulik, "This Brand Makes You More Creative," *Advertising Age,* March 24, 2008, p. 4.

33. Quotes and information from Yubo Chen and Jinhong Xie, "Online Consumer Review: Word-of-Mouth as a New Element of Marketing Communication Mix," *Management Science,* March 2008, pp. 477–491; Douglas Pruden and Terry G. Vavra, "Controlling the Grapevine," *Marketing Management,* July–August 2004, pp. 25–30; and "Leo J. Shapiro & Associates: User-Generated Content Three Times More Influential Than TV Advertising on Consumer Purchase Decisions," *Marketing Business Weekly,* December 28, 2008, p. 34.

34. See Leon Festinger, *A Theory of Cognitive Dissonance* (Stanford, CA: Stanford University Press, 1957); Cynthia Crossen, "'Cognitive Dissonance' Became a Milestone in the 1950s Psychology," *Wall Street Journal,* December 12, 2006, p. B1; and Anupam Bawa and Purva Kansal, "Cognitive Dissonance and the Marketing of Services: Some Issues," *Journal of Services Research,* October 2008–March 2009, p. 31.

35. The following discussion draws from the work of Everett M. Rogers. See his *Diffusion of Innovations,* 5th ed. (New York: Free Press, 2003).

36. Nick Bunkley, "Hyundai, Using a Safety Net, Wins Market Share," *New York Times,* February 5, 2009; and Chris Woodyard and Bruce Horvitz, "GM, Ford Are Latest Offering Help to Those Hit by Job Loss," *USA Today,* April 1, 2009, accessed at www.usatoday.com/money/advertising/2009-03-30-consumers-retail-job-loss_N.htm.

37. See "U.S. HDTV Penetration Nears 25%" *NielsenWire,* December 11, 2008.

38. See Theresa Ooi, "Amazing Key to IKEA Success," *Australian,* September 22, 2008; Kerry Capell, "How the Swedish Retailer Became a Global Cult Brand," *BusinessWeek,* November 14, 2005, p. 103; IKEA, *Hoover's Company Records,* April 1, 2009, p. 42925; "IKEA Group Stores," at www.ikea-group.ikea.com/?ID=11, accessed April 2009; and information from www.ikea.com, accessed September 2009.

39. This classic categorization was first introduced in Patrick J. Robinson, Charles W. Faris, and Yoram Wind, *Industrial Buying Behavior and Creative Marketing* (Boston: Allyn & Bacon, 1967). Also see James C. Anderson and James A. Narus, *Business Market Management,* 2nd ed. (Upper Saddle River, NJ: Prentice Hall, 2004), Chapter 3; James C. Anderson, James A. Narus, and Wouter van Rossum, "Customer Value Propositions in Business Markets," *Harvard Business Review,* March 2006, pp. 91–99; and Philip Kotler and Kevin Lane Keller, *Marketing Management,* 13th ed. (Upper Saddle River, NJ: Prentice Hall, 2009), Chapter 7.

40. Example adapted from information found in "Nikon Focuses on Supply Chain Innovation—and Makes New Product Distribution a Snap," UPS case study, at www.pressroom.ups.com/about/cs_nikon.pdf, accessed July 2009.

41. See Frederick E. Webster, Jr., and Yoram Wind, *Organizational Buying Behavior,* pp. 33–37.

42. Henry Canaday, "What Recession?" *Selling Power,* January–February 2009, pp. 44–49.

43. Robinson, Faris, and Wind, *Industrial Buying Behavior,* p. 14.

44. See https://suppliercenter.homedepot.com/wps/portal, accessed May 2009.

45. For this and other examples, see "10 Great Web Sites," *BtoB Online,* September 15, 2008, accessed at www.btobonline.com. Other information from www.cisco.com/cisco/web/solutions/small_business/index.html, accessed November 2009.

46. See William J. Angelo, "e-Procurement Process Delivers Best Value for Kodak," *Engineering News-Record,* March 17, 2008, p. 22.

CHAPTER 7

1. Chris Daniels, "The Softer, Smoother Man," *Marketing,* February 7, 2005, pp. 12–13; Hollie Shaw, "Coming Clean on Men's Skin Care Products," *The Vancouver Sun,* March 23, 2010; Katie Nichol, "Sanofi-aventis to Acquire Canadian Skin Care Company," published on the website CosmeticsDesign.com, accessed June 15, 2010; "Chris Noth Becomes the New Face of Biotherm Homme in North America," press release issued by L'Oréal Canada, August 14, 2009; "Force Supreme Re-builder Press Dossier 2010," provided by L'Oréal Canada.

2. For these and other examples, see Darell K. Rigby and Vijay Vishwanath, "Localization: The Revolution in Consumer Markets," *Harvard Business Review,* April 2006, pp. 82–92.

3. For these and other examples, see Rupal Parekh, "Zipcar Finds a Niche in a Turbulent Economy," *Advertising Age,* January 26, 2009, p. 15; and Philip Kotler and Kevin Lane Keller, *Marketing Management,* 13th ed. (Upper Saddle River, NJ: Prentice Hall, 2009), pp. 210–211.

4. See Hillary Chura, "Marketing Messages for Women Fall Short," *Advertising Age*, September 23, 2002, pp. 1, 14–15; Alice Z. Cuneo, "Advertisers Target Women, but Market Remains Elusive," *Advertising Age*, November 10, 1997, pp. 1, 24; and Bruce Upbin, "Merchant Princes," *Forbes*, January 20, 2003, pp. 52–56.

5. Adapted from information found in Elizabeth A. Sullivan, "H.O.G.: Harley-Davidson Shows Brand Strength as It Navigates Down New Roads—and Picks Up More Female Riders Along the Way," November 1, 2008, p. 8: and "Harley-Davidson Hosts Special Rides to Kick Off Women Riders Month," *PR Newswire*, March 23, 2009.

6. Adapted from information found in Laura Koss-Feder, "At Your Service," *Time*, June 11, 2007, p. 1; and "Guide to Hotel Packages," *Travel + Leisure*, at www.travelandleisure.com/articles/the-suspicious-package/sidebar/1, accessed February 2009.

7. Eve Lazarus, "Coast Capital Singing a Chinese Song," *Marketing Daily,* July 24, 2007, accessed at www.marketingmag.ca.

8. Kristin Laird, "Hyundai Harnesses Star Power in Quebec," *Marketing Daily*, March 28, 2008, accessed at www.marketingmag.ca.

9. Rebecca Harris, "Rich Rewards," *Marketing*, June 25, 2007, p. 17.

10. Information from the websites of Regent Seven Seas, www.rssc.com, and Royal Caribbean International, at www.royalcaribbean.com, accessed July 2010.

11. See Louise Story, "Finding Love and the Right Linens," *New York Times*, December 13, 2006, accessed at www.nytimes.com; and www.williams-sonoma.com/cust/storeevents/index.cfm, accessed September 2009.

12. Janet Adamy, "Man Behind the Burger King Turnaround: Chidsey Says Identifying His Restaurant's Superfan Helped Beef Up Its Offerings," *Wall Street Journal*, April 2, 2008, p. B1; and Blair Chancey, "King, Meet the World," *QSR Magazine*, February 2009, accessed at www.qsrmagazine.com/articles/interview/112/shaufelberger-3.phtml.

13. Matt Semansky, "The 'ME' Years," *Marketing*, November 12, 2007, pp. 34–35.

14. For more on the PRIZM NE Lifestyle Segmentation System, see the Neilsen website, www.nielsen.com.

15. "The Legalization of Gay Marriage in California Offers New Opportunity for the Jewelry Industry," a press release issued by Platinum Guild International USA, July 14, 2008; "The Impact of Extending Marriage to Same-Sex Couples on the California Budget," published by the Williams Institute, June 2008; Andrea Zoe Aster, "... and the Grooms Wore Pink," *Marketing*, May 10, 2004, pp. 11–12; Michelle Halpern, "Gay Getaways: Canada is a popular vacation spot for gay Americans," *Marketing*, May 22/29, 2006, p. 4.

16. Information from American Express's website, www201.americanexpress.com/business-credit-cards, accessed July 2010.

17. Stephen H. Wildstrom, "Meet Cisco, the Consumer Company," *Businessweek*, May 4, 2009, pp. 73–74.

18. See Michael Porter, *Competitive Advantage* (New York: Free Press, 1985), pp. 4–8, 234–236. For more recent discussions, see Stanley Slater and Eric Olson, "A Fresh Look at Industry and Market Analysis," *Business Horizons*, January–February 2002, pp. 15–22; Kenneth Sawka and Bill Fiora, "The Four Analytical Techniques Every Analyst Must Know: 2. Porter's Five Forces Analysis," *Competitive Intelligence Magazine*, May–June 2003, p. 57; and Philip Kotler and Kevin Lane Keller, *Marketing Management*, 13th ed. (Upper Saddle River, NJ: Prentice Hall, 2009), pp. 342–343.

19. Olga Kharif and Jack Ewing, "A Bid to Reconnect with America," *Businessweek*, April 13, 2009, p. 22.

20. See Suzanne Kapner, "How Fashion's VF Supercharges Its Brands," *Fortune*, April 14, 2008, pp. 108–110; and www.vfc.com, accessed October 2009.

21. Kathleen Martin, "Global Cymbals," *Marketing*, March 22, 2004, p. 13; Sabian website at www.sabian.com.

22. See Gerry Khermouch, "Call It the Pepsi Blue Generation," *BusinessWeek*, February 3, 2003, p. 96; and Martinne Geller, "U.S. Soft Drink Sales Volume Falls More in '07," *Reuters*, March 12, 2008; and Sarah Theodore, "Energy Drinks: New Concepts Keep Category Charged," *Beverage Industry*, August 2008, pp. 14–16.

23. See Arundhati Parmar, "On the Map," *Marketing News*, February 15, 2008, pp. 13–15; and information from www.mysbuxinteractive.com, accessed July 2009. For more examples see Nitasha Tiku, "We See You: Want a List of Nearby Stores?" *Inc.*, October 2008, p. 55; and Stephen Baker, "The Next Net," *BusinessWeek*, March 9, 2009, p. 42.

24. For these and other examples see Lynnley Browning, "Do-It-Yourself Logos for Proud Scion Owners," *New York Times*, March 24, 2008, accessed at www.nytimes.com; and Mike Beirne, "Mars Gives M&M's a Face," *Brandweek*, May 22, 2008, accessed at www.brandweek.com.

25. Adapted from information found in "When You Watch These Ads, the Ads Check You Out," *New York Times*, January 31, 2009, accessed at www.nytimes.com.

26. Adapted from portions of Fae Goodman, "Lingerie Is Luscious and Lovely," *Chicago Sun-Times*, February 19, 2006, p. B2; and Stacy Weiner, "Goodbye to Girlhood," *Washington Post*, February 20, 2007, p. HE01. Also see Suzanne C. Ryan, "Would Hannah Montana Wear It?" *Boston Globe*, January 10, 2008, www.boston.com; and Betsy Cummings, "Tickled Pink," *Brandweek*, September 8, 2008, pp. MO26–MO28.

27. Jack Trout, "Branding Can't Exist Without Positioning," *Advertising Age*, March 14, 2005, p. 28.

28. Kharif and Ewing, "A Bid to Reconnect with America," p. 22.

29. Adapted from a positioning map initially prepared by students Brian May, Josh Payne, Meredith Schakel, and Bryana Sterns, University of North Carolina, April 2003. SUV sales data furnished by www.WardsAuto.com, accessed June 2008. Price data from www.edmunds.com, accessed June 2008.

30. Based on information found in Michael Myser, "Marketing Made Easy," *Business 2.0*, June 2006, pp. 43–44; Steve Smith, "Staples' Sales Rise While Office Depot's Drop," *Twice*, March 10, 2008, p. 62; Alan Wolf, "Staples Sales Rose, Profits Fell in Q3," *Twice*, December 15, 2008, p. 89; and "Staples, Inc." *Hoover's Company*

Records, at http://www.premium.hoovers.com/subscribe/co/ factsheet.xhtml?ID=14790, accessed April 2009.

31. See Bobby J. Calder and Steven J. Reagan, "Brand Design," in Dawn Iacobucci, ed., *Kellogg on Marketing* (New York: John Wiley & Sons, 2001) p. 61. For more discussion, see Philip Kotler and Kevin Lane Keller, *Marketing Management*, 13th ed. (Upper Saddle River, NJ: Prentice Hall, 2009), pp. 315–316.

CHAPTER 8

1. Extracts and quotes from or adapted from information found in Chuck Salter, "Google: The Faces and Voices of the World's Most Innovative Company," *Fast Company*, March 2008, pp. 74–88; "The World's Most Innovative Companies," *Fast Company*, March 2009, p. 52; "Google Shines a Light on Innovation," *Computer Weekly*, September 9–September 15, 2008, p. 3; Jessica Guynn, "Internet; Google's Results Defy Downturn," *Los Angeles Times*, October 17, 2008, p. C1; David Pogue, "Geniuses at Play, On the Job," *New York Times*, February 26, 2009, p. B1; and www.google.com and www.googlelabs.com, accessed June 2009.

2. Joel Parent, "Top Three Contests," *Strategy*, August 2005, p. 9.

3. Calvin Hodock, "Winning the New-Products Game," *Advertising Age*, November 12, 2007, p. 35; Neale Martin, "Force of Habit," *Brandweek*, October 13, 2008, pp. 18–20; and "How P&G Plans to Clean up," *BusinessWeek*, April 13, 2009, pp. 44–45.

4. "In a Tough Economy, Innovation Is King," *Marketing News*, April 15, 2009, p. 14.

5. Hodock, "Winning the New-Products Game," p. 35; Martin, "Force of Habit," pp. 18–20; and "How P&G Plans to Clean up," *BusinessWeek*, pp. 44–45.

6. Paul Gillin, "Get Customers Involved in Innovations," *BtoB*, March 12, 2007, p. 111. See also Patricia B. Seybold, *Outside Innovation: How Your Customers Will Co-Design Your Company's Future* (New York: Collins, 2006); and Patricia B. Seybold's blog at http://outsideinnovation.blogs.com, accessed April 2007.

7. "Bill Invites Customers to Share Ideas and Original Video via Dell IdeaStorm and StudioDell," February 16, 2007, accessed at www.dell.com; and Jon Fortt, "Michael Dell 'Friends' His Customers," *Fortune*, September 15, 2008, p. 35. Also see www.ideastorm.com, accessed November 2009.

8. See George S. Day, "Is It Real? Can We Win? Is It Worth Doing?" *Harvard Business Review*, December 2007, pp. 110–120.

9. Example adapted from information found in Linda Grant, "Gillette Knows Shaving—and How to Turn Out Hot New Products," *Fortune*, October 14, 1996, pp. 207–210; and Jenn Abelson, "Gillett Sharpens Its Focus on Women," *Boston Globe*, January 4, 2009.

10. "KFC Fires Up Grilled Chicken," March 23, 2008, accessed at www.money.cnn.com; and "KFC Serves Up a Second Secret Recipe: Kentucky Grilled Chicken," *PR Newswire*, April 14, 2009.

11. Robert G. Cooper, "Formula for Success," *Marketing Management*, March–April 2006, pp. 19–23; and Barry Jaruzelski and Kevin Dehoff, "The Global Innovation of 1000," *Strategy + Business*, Issue 49, fourth quarter, 2007, pp. 68–83.

12. Based on material from Anna Fifield, "Samsung Sows for the Future with Its Garden of Delights," *Financial Times*, January 4, 2008, p. 13; and Peter Lewis, "A Perpetual Crisis Machine," *Fortune*, September 19, 2005, pp. 58–67. Also see "Camp Samsung," *BusinessWeek Online*, July 3, 2006, accessed at www.businessweek. com.

13. This definition is based on one found in Bryan Lilly and Tammy R. Nelson, "Fads: Segmenting the Fad-Buyer Market," *Journal of Consumer Marketing*, 20(3), 2003, pp. 252–265.

14. See Katya Kazakina and Robert Johnson, "A Fad's Father Seeks a Sequel," *New York Times*, May 30, 2004, p. 3.2; John Schwartz, "The Joy of Silly," *New York Times*, January 20, 2008, p. 5; and www.crazyfads.com, accessed August 2010.

15. "American Greetings Introduces New 'Ideas' Online," *PR News wire*, November 28, 2008.

16. See Constantine von Hoffman, "Glad Gives Seal of Approval to Alternate Wrap Uses," *Brandweek*, November 27, 2006, p. 10; and www.1000uses.com, accessed August 2010.

17. For a more comprehensive discussion of marketing strategies over the course of the product life cycle, see Philip Kotler and Kevin Lane Keller, *Marketing Management*, 13th ed. (Upper Saddle River, NJ: Prentice Hall, 2009), pp. 278–290.

18. Quotes and other information from Regina Schrambling, "Tool Department; The Sharpest Knives in the Drawer," *Los Angeles Times*, March 8, 2006, p. F1; Arricca Elin SanSone, "OXO: Universal Design Innovator," *Cooking Light*, April 2007, p. 118; "Alex Lee at Gel 2008," video and commentary at http://vimeo.com/3200945, accessed June 2009; and www.oxo.com/about.jsp, accessed November 2009.

19. See "Supermarket Facts," on the website of the Food Marketing Institute, at www.fmi.org, accessed April 2009; and "Wal-Mart Facts," at walmartstores.com/pressroom, accessed August 2010.

20. See "Amazon Frustration-Free Packaging," at www.amazon. com, accessed June 2009; and Brennon Slattery, "Amazon Offers Easy-to-Open Packaging," *PC World*, January 2009, p. 36.

21. Sonja Reyes, "Ad Blitz, Bottle Design Fuel Debate over Heinz's Sales," *Brandweek*, February 12, 2007, accessed at www.brandweek. com.

22. Example from Steve Finlay, "At Least She Puts Fuel in It," *WARD'S Dealer Business*, August 1, 2003. Other information from www.lexus.com, accessed November 2009.

23. See "HP Total Care," a section of the HP website at www.hp. com, accessed August 2010.

24. Information from the "Our Brands" section of the Marriott website, www.marriott.com, accessed August 2010.

25. Information from the Statistics Canada website, www.statcan. gc.ca, accessed March 2010.

26. See James L. Heskett, W. Earl Sasser Jr., and Leonard A. Schlesinger, *The Service Profit Chain: How Leading Companies Link Profit and Growth to Loyalty, Satisfaction, and Value* (New York: Free Press, 1997); Heskett, Sasser, and Schlesinger, *The Value Profit Chain: Treat Employees Like Customers and Customers Like*

Employees (New York: Free Press, 2003); John F. Milliman, Jeffrey M. Ferguson, and Andrew J. Czaplewski, "Breaking the Cycle," *Marketing Management*, March–April 2008, pp. 14–17; and Christian Homburg, Jan Wieseke, and Wayne D. Hoyer, "Social Identity and the Service-Profit Chain," *Journal of Marketing*, March 2009, pp. 38–54.

27. See James L. Heskett, W. Earl Sasser Jr., and Christopher W.L. Hart, *Service Breakthroughs* (New York: Free Press, 1990).

CHAPTER 9

1. Sleeman Breweries Ltd. website, www.sleeman.com, accessed August 2010; Sapporo's website, www.sapporobeer.ca, accessed August 2010; Kristin Laird, "Dentsu Launches Sapporo's First National Canadian Campaign, *Marketing*, June 7, 2010, accessed at marketingmag.ca; Kristin Laird, "Sleeman Puts Its Notorious History on TV," *Marketing*, May 7, 2010, accessed at marketingmag.ca; "Sleeman Brews Up a Crafty Takeover of Established Quebec-based Beermaker," *Canadian Packaging*, May 2004, *57*(5), p. 7; Andy Holloway, "John Sleeman," *Canadian Business*, Summer 2004, *77*(10), pp. 204–205; "Sleeman Swallows Up Maritime Beer Producer," *Canadian Packaging*, October 2000, *53*(10), p. 7; Interview with John Sleeman in "Ask the Legends," *Profit*, November 2008, pp. 112–113; Colin Campbell, "Our Beer Sure Goes Down Smooth," *Maclean's*, September 4, 2006, pp. 38–39; Alicia Clegg, "Old Brands in New Bottles," *Financial Times*, June 1, 2006, p. 12; "Sleeman Brews Up Another Holiday Treat with Historic Recipe and Classy Packaging," *Canadian Packaging*, November 2005, p. 7.

2. Jonathan Salem Baskin, "Our Measurement Problem Begins With Definitions," AdAge.com, May 17, 2010.

3. See "McAtlas Shrugged," *Foreign Policy*, May–June 2001, pp. 26–37; and Philip Kotler, *Marketing Management*, 11th ed. (Upper Saddle River, NJ: Prentice Hall, 2003), p. 423.

4. Andy Goldsmith, "Coke vs. Pepsi: The Taste They Don't Want You to Know About," *The 60-Second Marketer*, at www.60secondmarketer.com/60SecondArticles/Branding/cokevs.pepsitast.html, accessed May 2009.

5. See Jack Trout, "'Branding' Simplified," *Forbes*, April 19, 2007, accessed at www.forbes.com.

6. Kevin Roberts, Lovemarks: The Future Beyond Brands (New York: powerHouse Books, 2004).

7. Al Ehrbar, "Breakaway Brands," *Fortune*, October 31, 2005, pp. 153–170. Also see "DeWalt Named Breakaway Brand," *Snips*, January 2006, p. 66.

8. "Best Canadian Brands 2010" report published by Interbrand.

9. See Diane Brady, "It's All Donald, All the Time," *BusinessWeek*, January 22, 2007, p. 51; and Liz Wolgemuth, "Build Your Own Brand," *U.S. News & World Report*, December 29, 2008, p. 62.

10. Based on information from Sonia Reyes, "Faster Than a Ray of Light," *Brandweek*, October 9, 2006, pp. M28–M31; "Food Network Orders More Helpings of Rachael Ray," *McClatchy-Tribune Business News*, December 17, 2007; Rachael Ray, "10 Questions," *Time*, April 28, 2008, p. 6; and "'Ray' Hits 500th Show," *TelevisionWeek*, March 30–April 6, 2009, p. 8.

11. Matt Semansky, "Brand Nash," September 14, 2009, p. 11.

12. Natalie Zmuda, "What Went into the Updated Pepsi Logo," *Advertising Age*, October 27, 2008, p. 6; Natalie Zmuda, "Pepsi, Coke Tried to Outdo Each Other with Rays of Sunshine," *Advertising Age*, January 19, 2009, p. 6; and Todd Wasserman, "Grim Times Prompt More Upbeat Logos," *Brandweek*, February 23, 2009, p. 9.

13. Lisa Hannam, "Instantly Recognizable," *Marketing*, January 26, 2009.

14. "Google Doodle History," in "About Google" at www.google.com/doodle4google/history.html, accessed June 1, 2010.

15. David C. Bello and Morris B. Holbrook, "Does an Absence of Brand Equity Generalize Across Product Classes?" *Journal of Business Research*, October 1995, p. 125; Scott Davis, *Brand Asset Management: Driving Profitable Growth through Your Brands* (San Francisco: Jossey-Bass, 2000). Also see Kevin Lane Keller, *Building, Measuring, and Managing Brand Equity*, 2nd ed. (Upper Saddle River, NJ: Prentice Hall, 2003), Chapter 2.

16. For more on Young & Rubicam's Brand Asset Valuator, see "Brand Asset Valuator," Value Based Management.net, at www.valuebasedmanagement.net/methods_brand_asset_valuator.html, accessed May 2009; W. Ronald Lane, Karen Whitehill King, and J. Thomas Russell, *Kleppner's Advertising Procedure*, 17th ed. (Upper Saddle River, NJ: Prentice Hall, 2008), p. 105; and www.brandassetconsulting.com/, accessed May 2009.

17. Jean Halliday, "Ford Resurrects Taurus Name," *Advertising Age*, February 7, 2007, accessed at adage.com.

18. See Scott Davis, *Brand Asset Management*, 2nd ed. (San Francisco: Jossey-Bass, 2002). For more on brand positioning, see Philip Kotler and Kevin Lane Keller, *Marketing Management*, 13th ed. (Upper Saddle River, NJ: Prentice Hall, 2009), Chapter 10.

19. Adapted from information found in Geoff Colvin, "Selling P&G," *Fortune*, September 17, 2007, pp. 163–169; "For P& G, Success Lies in More Than Merely a Dryer Diaper," *Advertising Age*, October 15, 2007, p. 20; Jack Neff, "Stengel Discusses Transition at P&G," *Advertising Age*, July 21, 2008, p. 17; and Elaine Wong, "Stengel: Private Label, Digital Change Game," *Brandweek*, March 13, 2009, p. 7.

20. Susan Wong, "Foods OK, but Some Can't Stomach More Ad Increases," *Brandweek*, January 5, 2009, p. 7.

21. See Vanessa L. Facenda, "A Swift Kick to the Privates," *Brandweek*, September 3, 2007, pp. 24+; Jack Neff, "Private Label Winning Battle of Brands," *Advertising Age*, February 23, 2009, p. 1; Chris Burritt and Carol Wolf, "Wal-Mart's Store-Brand Groceries to Get New Emphasis," *Bloomberg.com*, February 19, 2009; and Lana F. Flowers, "Consumers Turn to Private Labels In Down Economy," *Morning News (Arkansas)*, February 20, 2009, at www.nwaonline.net.

22. Warren Thayer, "Loblaws Exec Predicts: Private Labels to Surge," *Frozen Food Age*, May 1996, p. 1; "President's Choice Continues Brisk Pace," *Frozen Food Age*, March 1998, pp. 17–18; David Dunne and Chakravarthi Narasimhan, "The New Appeal of Private Labels," *Harvard Business Review*, May–June 1999, pp. 41–52; "New Private Label Alternatives Bring Changes to Supercenters, Clubs," *DSN Retailing Today*, February 5, 2001, p. 66; and "The PC

Story" on the President's Choice website, www.presidentschoice.ca, accessed August 2010.

23. Canadian Press, "Cott Focuses on Private Brands," *Marketing*, June 19, 2008.

24. Nirmalya Kumar and Jan-Benedict E. M. Steenkamp, *Private Label Strategy* (Boston, MA: Harvard Business School Press, 2007), p. 5.

25. "Dora the Explorer Takes the Lead as Sales Growth Elevates Property to Megabrand Status as Number-One Toy License in 2006," *PR Newswire*, February 8, 2007; Clint Cantwell, "$187 Billion Global Licensing Industry Comes to Life at Licensing International Expo 2008," *Business Wire*, June 6, 2008; "Nickelodeon Expands Product Offerings and Debuts New Properties for Kids and Teens at Licensing 2008 International Show," June 10, 2008, accessed at http://biz.yahoo.com/prnews/080610/nytu056.html?.v=101; and "SpongeBob SquarePants Swims to the Cricut," *Business Wire*, January 28, 2009.

26. Quote from www.apple.com/ipod/nike, accessed August 2009.

27. Gabrielle Solomon, "Cobranding Alliances: Arranged Marriages Made by Marketers," *Fortune*, October 12, 1998, p. 188; Gene Marcial, "Martha Cozies Up to Wal-Mart," *BusinessWeek*, August 4, 2008, p. 72; "Country Living's Vibrancy Grows with Sears/Kmart Partnership," *Media Industry Newsletter*, April 13, 2009, accessed at www.minonline.com/min/10629.html.

28. The quote and the best/worst examples are from "TippingSprung Publishes Results from Fifth Annual Brand-Extensions Survey," January 6, 2009, accessed at www.tippingsprung.com/index.php?/knowledge/knowledge_article/tippingsprung_publishes_results_from_fifth_annual_brand-extension_survey/.

29. Canadian Press, "Sobeys Inc. Launches FreshCo Brand in Ontario," Marketingmag.ca, May 12, 2010.

30. "Leading National Advertisers," *Advertising Age*, June 22, 2009, p. 12.

31. Quotes from Stephen Cole, "Value of the Brand," *CA Magazine*, May 2005, pp. 39–40; and Lawrence A. Crosby and Sheree L. Johnson, "Experience Required," *Marketing Management*, July/August 2007, pp. 21–27.

32. Eve Lazarus, "Canada's Top Marketers 2007: Canadian Tourism Commission," *Marketing*, November 26, 2007, p. 24; Canadian Tourism Commission website, www.corporate.canada.travel.

33. Rupal Parekh, "Why Long-Form Ads Are the Wave of the Future," *Advertising Age*, at AdAge.com, accessed May 3, 2010.

CHAPTER 10

1. Quotes and other information from Beth Snyder Bulik, "Kodak Develops New Model: Inexpensive Printer, Cheap Ink," *Advertising Age*, March 12, 2007, p. 4; Clive Akass, "Kodak Inkjets Shake Industry," *Personal Computer World*, April 2007, accessed at www.pcw.co.uk/personal-computer-world/news/2174253/kodak-halves-cost-photo-prints; Stephen H. Wildstrom, "Kodak Moments for Less," *BusinessWeek*, May 14, 2007, p. 24; William M. Bulkeley, "Kodak's Strategy for First Printer—Cheaper Cartridges," *Wall Street Journal*, February 6, 2007, p. B1; "Consumer Launch Campaign of the Year 2008," *PRweek*, March 10, 2008, p. S11; Lonnie Brown, "Database: Why Cartridge Companies Are in the Black," *Ledger* (Lakeland, FL), January 23, 2009, p. C7; Stuart Elliott, "Are You Fed Up? This Ad's for You," *News and Observer* (Raleigh), May 15, 2009, p. 1; and www.kodak.com, accessed November 2009.

2. George Mannes, "The Urge to Unbundle," *Fast Company*, February 27, 2005, pp. 23–24. Also see Stuart Elliott, "Creative Spots, Courtesy of a Stalled Economy," *New York Times*, April 11, 2008; and Elliott, "Nevermind What It Costs. Can I Get 70 Percent Off?" *New York Times*, April 27, 2009.

3. For more on the importance of sound pricing strategy, see Thomas T. Nagle and John Hogan, *The Strategy and Tactics of Pricing: A Guide to Growing More Profitably* (Upper Saddle River, NJ: Prentice Hall, 2007), Chapter 1.

4. Based on information from Anne Marie Chaker, "For a Steinway, I Did It My Way," *Wall Street Journal*, May 22, 2008; and www.steinway.com/steinway and www.steinway.com/steinway/quotes.shtml, accessed November 2009.

5. See Kevin Done, "Runway Success—Ryanair," *Financial Times*, March 20, 2009, accessed at www.ft.com; Matthew Maier, "A Radical Fix for Airlines: Make Flying Free," *Business 2.0*, April 2006, pp. 32–34; Kerry Capell, "Fasten Your Seatbelt, Ryanair," *BusinessWeek*, February 18, 2008, p. 16; and www.ryanair.com, accessed July 2009.

6. Example adapted from Anupam Mukerji, "Monsoon Marketing," *Fast Company*, April 2007, p. 22.

7. Elizabeth A. Sullivan, "Value Pricing: Smart Marketers Know Cost-Plus Can Be Costly," *Marketing News*, January 15, 2008, p. 8. Also see Venkatesh Bala and Jason Green, "Charge What Your Products Are Worth," *Harvard Business Review*, September 2007, p. 22; and Peter J. Williamson and Ming Zeng, "Value-for-the-Money Strategies," *Harvard Business Review*, March 2009, pp. 66–74.

8. Comments from www.thecoast.ca/halifax/pete_s_frootique/Location?oid=978244, accessed June 2010.

9. Adapted from information found in Joseph Weber, "Over a Buck for Dinner? Outrageous," *BusinessWeek*, March 9, 2009, p. 57.

10. Susan Mires, "The New Economy of Frugality: Cost-Seating Skills Going up in Value," *McClatchy-Tribune Business News*, March 19, 2009; Laura Petrecca, "Marketers Try to Promote Value without Cheapening Image," *USA Today*, November 17, 2008, p. B1; and Anne D'Innocenzio, "Butter, Kool-Aid in Limelight in Advertising Shift," April 21, 2009, accessed at www.azcentral.com/business/articles/2009/04/21/20090421biz-NewFrugality0421.html.

11. Ryan McCarthy, "Pricing: How Low Can You Go?" *Inc.*, March 2009, pp. 91–92.

12. Petrecca, "Marketers Try to Promote Value without Cheapening Image," *USA Today*, November 17, 2008, p. B1; and D'Innocenzio, "Butter, Kool-Aid in Limelight in Advertising Shift," April 21, 2009, accessed at www.azcentral.com/business/articles/2009/04/21/20090421biz-NewFrugality0421.html.

13. Hein, "Study: Trumps Price among Shoppers," *Brandweek*, March 2, 2009, p. 6.

14. For comprehensive discussions of pricing strategies, see Nagle and Hogan, *The Strategy and Tactics of Pricing*, 4th ed. (Upper Saddle River, NJ: Prentice Hall, 2007).

15. See Brian Chen, "WWDC: Apple Slashes Prices with iPhone 3G, Shipping in July," June 9, 2008, accessed at www.macworld.com/article/133838/2008/06/iphone3g.html; and Olga Kharif, "Can Apple Keep a Shine on the iPhone?" *BusinessWeek (Online)*, March 18, 2009, accessed at www.businessweek.com.

16. Adapted from information found in Mei Fong, "IKEA Hits Home in China; The Swedish Design Giant, Unlike Other Retailers, Slashes Prices for the Chinese," *Wall Street Journal*, March 3, 2006, p. B1; and "IKEA China to Boost Sales by Slashing Prices," *China Knowledge*, March 9, 2009, accessed at www.chinaknowledge.com.

17. Paul Miller, "Sony Losing Mad Loot on Each PS3," *Engadet*, November 16, 2006, accessed at www.engadget.com/2006/11/16/sony-losing-mad-loot-on-each-ps3/; and Sam Kennedy, "Sony Has Lost More on the PS3 than It Made on PS2," *1UP News*, August 19, 2008, accessed at www.1up.com/do/newsStory?cId=3169439.

18. Information from "Pollution Prevention Success Stories: MacTara Limited," Environment Canada, accessed at www.atl.ec.gc.ca/epb/pollprev/mactara.html; "MacTara Jobs May Be Safe After Deal with Creditors," *CBC News*, March 11, 2008, www.cbc.ca/canada/nova-scotia/story/2008/03/11/lumber-yard.html, Monique Chiasson, "Deal in the Works for MacTara," *Truro Daily News*, March 13, 2008, at www.atlanticfarmfocus.ca/index.cfm?sid=124503&sc=586, accessed July 2009.

19. See Nagle and Hogan, *The Strategy and Tactics of Pricing*, 4th ed. (Upper Saddle River, NJ: Prentice Hall, 2007), pp. 244–247; Bram Foubert and Els Gijsbrechts, "Shopper Response to Bundle Promotions for Packaged Goods," *Journal of Marketing Research*, November 2007, pp. 647–662; Roger M. Heeler et al., "Bundles = Discount? Revisiting Complex Theories of Bundle Effects," *Journal of Product & Brand Management*, 16(7), 2007, pp. 492–500; and Timothy J. Gilbride et al., "Framing Effects in Mixed Price Bundling," *Marketing Letters*, June 2008, pp. 125–140.

20. Based on information from Eric Anderson and Duncan Simester, "Mind Your Pricing Cues," *Harvard Business Review*, September 2003, pp. 96–103. Also see Monika Kukar-Kinney et al., "Consumer Responses to Characteristics of Price-Matching Guarantees," *Journal of Retailing*, April 2007, p. 211; and Peter J. Boyle and E. Scott Lathrop, "Are Consumers' Perceptions of Price-Quality Relationships Well Calibrated?" *International Journal of Consumer Studies*, January 2009, p. 58.

21. Adapted from information found in Elizabeth A. Sullivan, "Stay on Course," *Marketing News*, February 15, 2009, pp. 11–13. Also see Stuart Elliott, "Never Mind What It Costs. Can I Get It 70 Percent Off?" *New York Times*, April 27, 2009, accessed at www.nytimes.com.

22. Example adapted from Louise Story, "Online Pitches Made Just for You," *New York Times*, March 6, 2008.

23. Based on information found in "The World's Most Influential Companies: Unilever," *BusinessWeek*, December 22, 2008, p. 47; and www.unilever.com/sustainability/people/consumers/affordability/, accessed June 2009.

24. Example adapted from information found in Ellen Byron, "Fashion Victim: To Refurbish Its Image, Tiffany Risks Profits," *Wall Street Journal*, January 10, 2007, p. A1; and Aliza Rosenbaum and John Christy, "Financial Insight: Tiffany's Boutique Risk; By Breaking Mall Fast, High-End Exclusivity May Gain Touch of Common," *Wall Street Journal*, October 20, 2007, p. B14. Also see Bernadette Morra, "Tiffany Seeks to Break Down Some Barriers," *Toronto Star*, April 23, 2009, p. L3.

25. "Virgin America Launches 'Flydealism' Campaign," *PR Newswire*, March 10, 2009; and www.virginamerica.com/va/vaDifference.do, accessed June 2009.

26. Jack Neff, "Viva Viva! K-C Boosts Brand's marketing," *Advertising Age*, June 11, 2007, p. 4; and Jack Neff, "Bounty," *Advertising Age*, November 17, 2008, p. S-18.

27. See the *Competition Act*, Sections 34–38, http://laws.justice.gc.ca/en/C-34/.

28. For discussions of these issues, see Dhruv Grewel and Larry D. Compeau, "Pricing and Public Policy: A Research Agenda and Overview of Special Issue," *Journal of Public Policy and Marketing*, Spring 1999, pp. 3–10; and Michael V. Marn, Eric V. Roegner, and Craig C. Zawada, *The Price Advantage* (Hoboken, NJ: John Wiley & Sons, 2004), Appendix 2.

29. Jim Middlemiss, "Don't Get Caught Offside in Rule Changes," *Financial Post*, March 23, 2009.

CHAPTER 11

1. The "e" logo, Enterprise, and "We'll Pick You Up" are registered trademarks of Enterprise Rent-A-Car Company. Quotes and other information from "Enter Enterprise," *Business Travel News*, April 23, 2007; Carol J. Loomis, "Enterprise Pulls Up at the Airport," *Fortune*, July 23, 2007, p. 50; Darren Everson, "Car-Rental Companies Learn to Share," *Wall Street Journal*, February 7, 2008, p. D1; Stephan Stern, "Revealed: the Secret to Survival in 2009 (Pass It On)," *Financial Times*, December 23, 2008, p. 12; David LaGesse, "A 'Stealth Company' No Longer; Family-Run Enterprise Becomes an Auto Rental Giant," *U.S. News & World Report*, October 27, 2008, p. 79; and www.hertz.com and http://aboutus.enterprise.com/press_room/fact_sheets.html, accessed October 2009.

2. See Kevin Kelleher, "Giving Dealers a Raw Deal," *Business 2.0*, December 2004, pp. 82–84; Jim MacKinnon, "Goodyear Boasts of Bright Future," *McClatchy-Tribune Business News*, April 9, 2008; Andrea Doyle, "Forging Ahead," *Successful Meetings*, May 2009, pp. 36–42; and information at www.goodyear.com, accessed September 2009.

3. Information at www.kroger.com and www.luxottica.com/english/profilo_aziendale/index_keyfacts.html, accessed October 2008.

4. Franchising facts from *2009 Franchise Business Economic Outlook*, January 7, 2009, at www.franchise.org/uploadedFiles/2009 Economic Outlook Factsheet.pdf; and www.azfranchises.com/franchisefacts.htm, accessed March 2009.

5. Press Info section, Boston Pizza website, www.bostonpizza.com.

6. Tony Martin, "Love Thy Franchisees," *Profit*, May 2008, p. 62; and information at www.nursenextdoor.com, accessed June 2009.

7. Quotes and other information from Matthew Boyle, "Reed Hastings," *Fortune*, May 28, 2007, p. 30; Nick Wingfield, "Netflix vs. Naysayers," *Wall Street Journal*, March 27, 2007, p. B1; Michael V. Copeland, "Netflix Lives!" *Fortune*, April 28, 2008, p. 40; and www.netflix.com, accessed June 2009.

8. Quotes and other information from Alex Taylor III, "Caterpillar," *Fortune*, August 20, 2007, pp. 48–54; Donald V. Fites, "Make Your Dealers Your Partners," *Harvard Business Review*, March–April 1996, pp. 84–95; and information at www.caterpillar.com, accessed August 2009.

9. Retail Fast Facts, April 2010, published by the Retail Council of Canada.

10. Information published on the website of the Retail Council of Canada, www.retailcouncil.org.

11. Quotes and other information on OgilvyAction from Katy Bachman, "Suit Your Shelf," *AdweekMedia*, January 19, 2009, pp. 10–12; "OgilvyAction Takes Regional Marketers to the Last Mile," January 23, 2008, accessed at www.entrepreneur.com/tradejournals/article/173710015.html, and Jack Neff, "Trouble in Store for Shopper Marketing," *Advertising Age*, March 2, 2009, pp. 3–4. Retail sales statistics from "Annual Revision of Monthly Retail and Food Services: Sales and Inventories—January 1992–2008," U.S. Census Bureau, March 2009, p. 3.

12. Ken Favaro, Tim Romberger, and David Meer, "Five Rules for Retailing in a Recession," *Harvard Business Review*, April 2009, pp. 64–72.

13. Elizabeth Ody, "Six Retailers that Are Thriving," February 17, 2009, accessed at www.kiplinger.com/printstory.php?pid+15397.

14. Canadian Internet Use Survey 2009 and "The Daily" November 17, 2008, published by Statistics Canada.

15. Mark Penn, "New Info Shoppers," *Wall Street Journal*, January 8, 2009, accessed at http://online.wsj.com/article/SB123144483005365353.html.

16. The online shopper statistics and extract example are from or adapted from Mark Penn, "New Info Shoppers," *Wall Street Journal*, January 8, 2009, accessed at http://online.wsj.com/article/SB123144483005365353.html.

17. See www.shopbloom.com, accessed November 2009.

18. Based on 2008 sales data. See the *Grainger 2009 Fact Book* and other information accessed at www.grainger.com.

19. *Grainger 2009 Fact Book*, at www.grainger.com, accessed July 2009.

20. *Transportation in Canada 2008: An Overview.* Published by Transport Canada.

21. Shlomo Maital, "The Last Frontier of Cost Reduction," *Across the Board*, February 1994, pp. 51–52; and information at www.walmartstores.com, accessed June 2009.

22. William Hoffman, "Supplying Sustainability," *Traffic World*, April 7, 2008.

23. Gail Braccidiferro, "One Town's Rejection Is Another's 'Let's Do Business,'" *New York Times*, June 15, 2003, p. 2; Dan Scheraga, "Wal Smart," *Chain Store Age*, January 2006 supplement, pp. 16A–21A; and facts from www.walmart.com, accessed June 2009.

24. Example adapted from Evan West, "These Robots Play Fetch," *Fast Company*, July/August 2007, pp. 49–50. Also see John Teresko, "Getting Lean with Armless Robots," *Industry Week*, September 2008, p. 26.

25. See "A Worldwide Look at RFID," *Supply Chain Management Review*, April 2007, pp. 48–55; "Wal-Mart Says Use RFID Tags or Pay Up," *Logistics Today*, March 2008, p. 4; and David Blanchard, "The Five Stages of RFID," *Industry Week*, January 1, 2009, p. 50.

26. Website of Transport Canada, at www.tc.gc.ca, accessed June 2010.

27. See Wal-Mart's supplier requirements at http://walmartstores.com/Suppliers/248.aspx, accessed June 2009. Also see Sriram Narayanan, Ann S. Marucheck, and Robert B. Handfield, "Electronic Data Interchange: Research Review and Future Directions," *Decision Sciences*, February 2009, p. 121.

28. See Bob Trebilcock, "Top 20 Supply Chain Management Software Suppliers," *Modern Material Handling*, July 1, 2008, accessed at www.mmh.com/article/CA6574264.html; and "The 2009 Supply & Demand Chain Executive 100," *Supply & Demand Chain Executive*, June–July 2009, accessed at www.sdcexec.com.

29. "Whirlpool: Outsourcing Its National Service Parts Operation Provides Immediate Benefits," at www.ryder.com/pdf/MCC633_Whirlpool_single.pdf, accessed October 2008.

30. See Alan Field, "Outsourced Logistics Growing," *Journal of Commerce*, March 10, 2009; and Alan Field, "3PL Revenue Drops 6.7 Percent," *Journal of Commerce*, April 3, 2009.

CHAPTER 12

1. Portions adapted from Jack Neff, "Digital Marketer of the Year: Unilever," *Advertising Age*, March 17, 2008, p. 50. Also see Stephanie Kang, "Media & Marketing: Hellmann's Spreads Message with Flay," *Wall Street Journal*, May 23, 2008, p. B9; Adam Woods, "Dragging Unilever into the Digital Age," *Revolution*, December 2008, p. 38; Karl Greenberg, "Unilever's DiComo on 'TV & Everything Video,'" *MediaPostNews*, February 12, 2009, accessed at www.mediapost.com; Todd Wasserman, "Unilever Seeks Reviewer-Created Current TV Ads," *Brandweek*, May 28, 2009, accessed at www.brandweek.com; and Brian Stelter, "'Motherhood' Viewers: Hold the Ideas," *New York Times*, March 24, 2009, p. C4.

2. For other definitions, see www.marketingpower.com/_layouts/Dictionary.aspx, accessed December 2009.

3. For more on this "chaos scenario," see Bob Garfield, "The Chaos Scenario," *Advertising Age*, April 4, 2005, pp. 1, 57+; Garfield, "The Chaos Scenario 2.0: The Post-Advertising Age," *Advertising Age*, March 26, 2007, pp. 1, 12–13; and Garfield, "Future May Be Brighter but It's Apocalypse Now," *Advertising Age*, March 23, 2009, pp. 1, 14.

4. Jack Neff, "'Passion for Digital' Pumps P&G's Spending," *Advertising Age*, June 8, 2009, accessed at http://adage.com/print?article_id-137134.

5. TV advertising stats at http://adage.com/datacenter/article?article_id=127791, accessed June 2009. Quotes from Mike Shaw, "Direct Your Advertising Dollars Away from TV at Your Own Risk," *Advertising Age*, February 27, 2006, p. 29; Bob Liodice, "TV Make Strides While Marketers Experiment Widely, *Advertising Age*,

March 24, 2008, pp. 16–17; and Jack Neff, "Future of Advertising? Print, TV, Online Ads," *Advertising Age*, June 1, 2009, accessed at http://adage.com/datacenter/article?article_ id=136993.

6. Adam Armbruster, "TV Central in Mixology of Multimedia," *TelevisionWeek*, March 3–March 10, 2008, p. 30; Liodice, "TV Make Strides While Marketers Experiment Widely," pp. 16–17; and Ed Castillo, "The Song Remains the Same: Media Platforms Are Exploding, but Human Nature Stays Right Where It's Always Been," *Adweek*, February 16, 2009, p. AM5.

7. "Integrated Campaigns," Advertising Annual 2008, *Communication Arts*, pp. 72–73.

8. See Jonah Bloom, "Turn the Oscars from Boring Twaddle to a Marketing Tool," *Advertising Age*, March 2, 2009, p. 11; Scott Collins, "Take II: Super Bowl Was Most Watched," *Los Angeles Times*, February 4, 2009, p. D8; and Collins, "Viewers Just Weren't That Curious," *Los Angeles Times*, January 15, 2009, p. E13.

9. Garry Duncan, "Every Sales Call Requires an Objective and Decision," *Denver Business Journal*, October 13, 2006, accessed at http://denver.bizjournals.com/denver/stories/2006/10/16/smallb8.html.

10. Data on U.S. and global advertising spending obtained at "Leading National Advertisers," *Advertising Age*, June 22, 2009, pp. 12–13; and http://adage.com/datacenter/#top_marketers;_adspend_stats, accessed September 2009.

11. "Canadian ad spend across all media signals strong growth to 2011: CMA," a press release issued by the Canadian Marketing Association, November 12, 2007.

12. For these and other examples of comparative advertising, see Emily Bryson York, "The Gloves Are Off: More Marketers Opt for Attack Ads," *Advertising Age*, May 25, 2009, accessed at http://adage.com/article?article_id=136841; Bryon York, "Brand vs. Brand: Attack Ads on the Rise," *Advertising Age*, October 27, 2008, p. 1; Kenneth Hein, "Domino's Burns Subway," January 22, 2009, accessed at www.brandweek.com; and "Pepsi Suing Coca-Cola Over Powerade Ads," *New York Times*, April 13, 2009, accessed at www.nyt.com.

13. For more on setting promotion budgets, see W. Ronald Lane, Karen Whitehill King, and J. Thomas Russell, *Kleppner's Advertising Procedure*, 17th ed. (Upper Saddle River, NJ: Prentice Hall, 2008), Chapter 6.

14. Example adapted from Jean Halliday, "Thinking Big Takes Audi from Obscure to Awesome," *Advertising Age*, February 2, 2009, accessed at http://adage.com/print?article_id=134234. Also see Jack Neff, "Study: Cutting Spending Hurts Brands in Long-Term: Following Boom/Bust Cycle Flirts with Danger," *Advertising Age*, April 6, 2009, accessed at http://adage.com/print?article_id135790; and Joe Mandese, "Nielsen: U.S. Ad Spending Plummets $3.8 Billion," *MediaPost News*, June 8, 2009, accessed at www.mediapost.com.

15. For more discussion, see John Consoli, "Heavy Lifting," *MediaWeek*, March 3, 2008.

16. Louise Story, "Anywhere the Eye Can See, It's Likely to See an Ad," *New York Times*, January 15, 2007, p. A12, accessed at www.nytimes.com; and Matthew Creamer, "Caught in the Clutter Crossfire: Your Brand," *Advertising Age*, April 1, 2007, pp. 1, 35.

17. See Brian Steinberg, "'Sunday Night Football' Beats 'Grey's Anatomy,'" *Advertising Age*, October 6, 2008, p. 10; Tim Arango, "Broadcast TV Faces Struggle to Stay Viable," *New York Times*, February 28, 2009, p. 1; and Louis Llovio, "Breaking Down the Super Bowl Ads," *McClatchy-Tribune Business News*, February 5, 2009.

18. Ken Krimstein, "Tips for the Ad World," *Forbes*, October 16, 2006, p. 34; and Bob Garfield, "The Chaos Scenario 2.0: The Post-Advertising Age," *Advertising Age*, March 26, 2007, pp. 1, 12–13.

19. Brain Steinberg, "Ad Skipping? Just Wait, It's Going to Get Worse," *Advertising Age*, August 11, 2008, p. 1; Daisy Whitney, "DVR, Broadband Users Take Control," *Television Week*, October 29, 2007, p. 10; Steinberg, "Ad Nauseum: Repetition of TV Spots Risks Driving Consumers Away," *Advertising Age*, December 1, 2008, p. 1; Anthony Crupi, "Report: Ad Execs Stymied by DVR Ad Skipping," *Mediaweek*, June 29, 2009, accessed at www.mediaweek.com; and Steinberg, "Ad Skippers Beware: Ask.com Going After You with TV Crawl," *Advertising Age*, March 2, 2009, pp. 4–5.

20. See Steve McKee, Advertising: Less Is Much More," *BusinessWeek Online*, May 10, 2006, accessed at www.businessweek.com; Stuart Elliott, "Now, the Clicking Is to Watch the Ads, Not Skip Them," *New York Times*, August 17, 2007, accessed at www.nytimes.com; and Elliott, "Slow Those Fast-Forwarders, Study Says, with Emotion," *New York Times*, March 31, 2009, accessed at www.nytimes.com.

21. See Alessandra Stanley, "Commercials You Can't Zap," *New York Times*, June 7, 2009, p. MT1.

22. Lisa D'Innocenzo, "Frito Lay Canada: Potato Chips ... for Dinner? With Innovation as a Core DNA Strand, Frito Lay Will Continue to Reinvent Its Products. But the Foodco Also Wants Canadians to Think of Chips in a Whole New Way," *Strategy*, January 2007, p. 11; Alexandra Jardine, "Product Placement: The Potential," *Promotions & Incentives*, Nov/Dec 2006, pp. 17–18.

23. For this and other examples, see Wendy Tanaka, "D.I.Y Ads," *Red Herring*, January 29, 2007, accessed at www.redherring.com/Home/20955; Lee Gomes, "Tips from Web Greats on Becoming a Legend in Your Spare Time," *Wall Street Journal*, November 14, 2007, p. B1; and Brian Boyko, "Feature: The Diet Coke & Mentos Saga of the EepyBirds," March 18, 2009, accessed at www.geeksaresexy.net/2009/03/18/feature-the-diet-coke-mentos-saga-of-the-eepybirds/.

24. "MultiVu Video Feed: Doritos Reveals Final Five Consumer-Created Commercials Vying...," *Reuters.com*, January 23, 2009, www.reuters.com/article/pressRelease/idUS169640+23-Jan-2009+PRN20090123; www.crashthesuperbowl.com, accessed July 2009, and "*USA Today* 2009 Ad Meter: Best Super Bowl Commercials," at www.usatoday.com/money/advertising/admeter/2009admeter.htm, accessed July 2009.

25. See Tanaka, "D.I.Y. Ads," accessed at www.redherring.com/Home/20955; Laura Petrecca, "Madison Avenue Wants You! (Or at Least Your Videos)," *USA Today*, June 21, 2007, p. 1B; and Michael Learmonth, "Brands Team Up for User-Generated-Ad Contests," *Advertising Age*, March 23, 2009, p. 8.

26. Allision Enright, "Let Them Decide," June 1, 2006, pp. 10–11; and "Who's in Control?" *Advertising Age*, January 28, 2008, p. C1.

27. Woods, "Dragging Unilever into the Digital Age," p. 38.

28. Betsy Cummings, "Marketers Size Up New Metric System," *Brandweek*, April 6, 2008, accessed at www.brandweek.com; and Castillo, "The Song Remains the Same, p. AM5.

29. Michael Learmonth, "IPad's Early Adopters Are Gazing at the Ads—for Now," *Advertising Age* online (AdAge.com), June 15, 2010.

30. See Claudia Wallis, "The Multitasking Generation," *Time*, March 27, 2006, accessed at www.time.com; Tanya Irwin, "Study: Kids Are Master Multitaskers on TV, Web, Mobile," *MediaPost Publications*, March 10, 2008, accessed at www.mediapostpublications.com; and Jon Lafayette, "Integrated Campaigns Worth Overcoming Hurdles," April 29, 2009, accessed at www.tvweek.com.

31. See "Pounds 10M Domino Effect Cheers Up Guinness," *Daily Record*, February 15, 2008; and www.youtube.com/watch?v=JinnnukLCbM; and Suzanne Vranica, "Payments Drag Out TV Spots," *Wall Street Journal*, February 23, 2008, p. B6.

32. See Stuart Elliott, "How Effective Is This Ad, in Real Numbers? Beats Me," *New York Times*, July 20, 2005, p. C8; Jack Neff, "Half Your Advertising Isn't Wasted—Just 37.3 Percent," *Advertising Age*, August 7, 2006, pp. 1, 32; Ben Richards and Faris Yakob, "The New Quid pro Quo," *Adweek*, March 19, 2007, p. 17; Kate Maddox, "ROI Takes Center Stage at CMO Summit," *BtoB*, February 11, 2008, p. 3; and Elizabeth A. Sullivan, "Measure Up," *Marketing News*, May 30, 2009, p. 8.

33. David Tiltman, "Everything You Know Is Wrong," *Marketing*, June 13, 2008, pp. 28+.

34. Elliott, "How Effective Is This Ad, in Real Numbers? Beats Me," p. C8; and "Taking Measure of Which Metrics Matter," *BtoB*, May 5, 2008.

35. Information on advertising agency revenues from "Agency Report 2009," *Advertising Age*, accessed at http://adage.com/datacenter/ article?article_id=136094.

36. Cossette Communications case study.

37. Adapted from Scott Cutlip, Allen Center, and Glen Broom, *Effective Public Relations*, 10th ed. (Upper Saddle River, NJ: Prentice Hall, 2009), Chapter 1.

38. See Jeff Manning and Kevin Lane Keller, "Got Advertising That Works?" *Marketing Management*, January–February 2004, pp. 16–20; Alice Z. Cuneo, "Now Even Cellphones Have Milk Mustaches," *Advertising Age*, February 26, 2007, p. 8; "Got Milk? Campaign Searches for America's First-Ever 'Chief Health Officer,'" *Business Wire*, May 6, 2008; "Local Man to Tell Got Milk? Ads Story," *McClatchy-Tribune Business News*, May 7, 2009; and information from www.bodybymilk.com and www.whymilk.com, accessed September 2009.

39. Winners of the 2010 Cannes Lions International Advertising Festival, Cannes Lions website, at www.canneslions.com, accessed June 2010.

40. "Consumer Launch Campaign of the Year 2008," *PRWeek*, March 6, 2008, accessed at www.prweekus.com/Consumer-Launch-Campaign-of-the-Year-2008/article/100570.

41. See David Robinson. "Public Relations Comes of Age," *Business Horizons*, May–June 2006, pp. 247+; Noelle Weaver, "Why Advertising and PR Can't Be Separated," *Advertising Age*, May 14, 2007, accessed at www.adage.com; and Jennifer Jones, "PR, Marketing Must Blend Together," *PRWeek*, June 30, 2008, p. 8.

42. "Aveeno Case Study," at www.ogilvypr.com/case-studies/aveeno.cfm, accessed October 2008; and see www.youtube.com/watch?v=hfn8Dz_13Ms.

43. Ellen McGirt, "How Chris Hughes Helped Launch Facebook and the Barack Obama Campaign," *Fast Company*, March 17, 2009, accessed at www.fastcompany.com.

44. Paul Holmes, "Senior Marketers Are Sharply Divided about the Role of PR in the Overall Mix," *Advertising Age*, January 24, 2005, pp. C1–C2.

CHAPTER 13

1. Quotes, adapted extract example, and other information from "*Fortune* Ranks CDW First in Wholesalers: Electronics on America's Most Admired Company List," *Business Wire*, March 10, 2008; Chuck Salter, "The Soft Sell," *Fast Company*, January 2005, pp. 72–73; Paolo Del Nibletto, "CDW Goes to Class," *Computer Dealer News*, May 25, 2007, p. 20; "CDW Reports Full-Year 2008 Sales," CDW press release, March 12, 2009, accessed at http://newsroom.cdw.com/news-releases/news-release-03-12-09.html; and "Our Values," at www.cdw.com/content/about/our-values.asp, accessed September 2009.

2. Adapted from information in Kim Wright Wiley, "For the Love of Sales," *Selling Power*, October 2008, pp. 70–73.

3. For more on "salesperson-owned loyalty," see Robert W. Palmatier et al., "Customer Loyalty to Whom? Managing the Benefits and Risks of Salesperson-Owned Loyalty," *Journal of Marketing Research*, May 2007, pp. 185–199. Also see Norm Brodsky, "It Takes a Company," *Inc.*, August 2008, pp. 63–64.

4. This extract and strategies that follow are based on Philip Kotler, Neil Rackham, and Suj Krishnaswamy, "Ending the War Between Sales and Marketing," *Harvard Business Review*, July–August 2006, pp. 68–78. Also see Timothy Smith, Srinath Gopalakrishna, and Rabikar Chatterjee, "A Three-Stage Model of Integrated Marketing Communications at the Marketing-Sales Interface," *Journal of Marketing Research*, November 2006, pp. 564–579; and Christian Homburg, Ove Jensen, and Harley Krohmer, "Configurations of Marketing and Sales: A Taxonomy," *Journal of Marketing*, March 2008, pp. 133–154.

5. Example based on Ernest Waaser et al., "How You Slice It: Smarter Segmentation for Your Sales Force," *Harvard Business Review*, March 2004, pp. 105–111.

6. "Selling Power 500," at www.sellingpower.com/sp500/index.asp, accessed October 2009.

7. For more on this and other methods for determining sales force size, see Mark W. Johnston and Greg W. Marshall, *Sales Force Management*, 9th ed. (Boston: McGraw-Hill Irwin, 2009), pp. 152–156.

8. Roy Chitwood, "Making the Most out of Each Outside Sales Call," February 4, 2005, accessed at http://seattle.bizjournals.com/seattle/stories/2005/02/07/smallb3.html; and "The Cost of the Average Sales Call Today Is More Than $400," *Business Wire*, February 28, 2006.

9. Michael A. Brown, "You Make the Call," *Target Marketing*, October 2008, pp. 81–82.

10. See Martin Everett, "It's Jerry Hale on the Line," *Sales & Marketing Management*, December 1993, pp. 75–79. Also see Irene Cherkassky, "Target Marketing," *BtoB*, October 2006, pp. 22–24.

11. Jennifer J. Salopek, "Bye, Bye, Used Car Guy," *T+D*, April 2007, pp. 22–25; and William F. Kendy, "No More Lone Rangers," *Selling Power*, April 2004, pp. 70–74; Michelle Nichols, "Pull Together—Or Fall Apart," *BusinessWeek* Online, December 2, 2005, accessed at www.businessweek.com; Theodore Kinni, "The Team Solution," *Selling Power*, April 2007, pp. 27–29; and John Boe, "Cross-Selling Takes Teamwork," *American Salesman*, March 2009, pp. 14–16.

12. "Customer Business Development," at www.pg.com/jobs/jobs_us/cac/f_cbd_home.shtml, accessed June 2009.

13. For more information and discussion, see Benson Smith, *Discover Your Strengths: How the World's Greatest Salespeople Develop Winning Careers* (New York: Warner Business Books, 2003); Tom Reilly, "Planning for Success," *Industrial Distribution*, May 2007, p. 25; Dave Kahle, "The Four Characteristics of Successful Salespeople," *Industrial Distribution*, April 2008, p. 54; Wright Wiley, "For the Love of Sales," pp. 70–73; and www.gallup.com/consulting/1477/Sales-Force-Effectiveness.aspx, accessed October 2009.

14. "2008 Corporate Learning Factbook Values U.S. Training at $58.5B," *Business Wire*, January 29, 2008; and "ADP Case Study," Corporate Visions, Inc., at www.corporatevisions.com/client_result.html, accessed August 2009.

15. Website of the Canadian Professional Sales Association, www.cpsa.com.

16. Based on information found in Sara Donnelly, "Staying in the Game," *Pharmaceutical Executive*, May 2008, pp. 158–159; "Improving Sales Force Effectiveness: Bayer's Experiment with New Technology," Bayer Healthcare Pharmaceutical, 2008, accessed at www.icmrindia.org/casestudies/catalogue/Marketing/MKTG200.htm; and Tanya Lewis, "Concentric," *Medical Marketing and Media*, July 2008, p. 59.

17. Joseph Kornak, "'07 Compensation Survey: What's It All Worth?" *Sales & Marketing Management*, May 2007, pp. 28–39.

18. See Henry Canady, "How to Increase the Times Reps Spend Selling," *Selling Power*, March 2005, p. 112; David J. Cichelli, "Plugging Sales 'Time Leaks,'" *Sales & Marketing Management*, April 2006, p. 23; and Rebecca Aronauer, "Time Well Spent," *Sales & Marketing Management*, January–February 2007, p. 7.

19. See Gary H. Anthes, "Portal Powers GE Sales," *Computerworld*, June 2, 2003, pp. 31–32. Also see Cichelli, "Plugging Sales 'Time Leaks,'" p. 23; Henry Canaday, "How to Boost Sales Productivity and Save Valuable Time," *Agency Sales*, November 2007, p. 20; and "According to IDC, One-Third of Potential Selling Time Is Wasted Due to Poor Sales Enhancement," *Business Wire*, November 13, 2008.

20. For extensive discussions of sales force automation, see the May 2005 issue of *Industrial Marketing Management*, which is devoted to the subject; Anupam Agarwal, "Bringing Science to Sales," *Customer Relationship Management*, March 2008, p. 16; and, Robert M. Barker, Stephen F. Gohmann, Jian Guan, and David J. Faulds, "Why Is My Sales Force Automation System Failing?" *Harvard Business Review*, May/June 2009, p. 233.

21. Adapted from information found in Pelin Wood Thorogood, "Sales 2.0: How Soon Will It Improve Your Business?" *Selling Power*, November/December 2008, pp. 58–61.

22. See "What Does Sales 2.0 Mean for You?" *Selling Power Sales Management Newsletter*, March 3, 2008; "Why Sales 2.0 Is Fundamentally Different from CRM," *Selling Power Sales Management Newsletter*, November 11, 2008; David Thompson, "Embracing the Future: A Step by Step Overview of Sales 2.0," *Sales and Marketing Management*, July/August 2008, p. 21; and Geoffrey James, "Sales Success through CRM," *Selling Power Source Book*," 2009, pp. 36–38.

23. Quotes from Bob Donath, "Delivering Value Starts with Proper Prospecting," *Marketing News*, November 10, 1997, p. 5; and Bill Brooks, "Power-Packed Prospecting Pointers," *Agency Sales*, March 2004, p. 37. Also see Maureen Hrehocik, "Why Prospecting Gets No Respect," *Sales & Marketing Management*, October 2007, p. 7; and "Referrals," *Partner's Report*, January 2009, p. 8.

24. Quotes in this paragraph from Lain Ehmann, "Prepare to Win," *Selling Power*, April 2008, pp. 27–29.

25. Adapted from Charlotte Huff, "EXTREME Makeover," *Workforce Management*, May 8, 2006, p. 1. Also see "iLevel Performance Home Educates Homebuyers on What to Look for in a Home's Structural Framing," *PR Newswire*, April 29, 2008; and www.ilevel.com, accessed November 2009.

26. Phil Sasso, "Listening in for More Sales," *Professional Distributor*, December 2007, pp. 18–19. Also see Gerhard Gschwandtner, "The Basics of Successful Selling," *Selling Power*, 25th anniversary issue, 2007, pp. 22–26; and Robert L. Bailey, "Story of Two Salespeople," *Rough Notes*, April 2008, p. 142.

27. "For B-to-B, Engagement, Retention Are Key," *Marketing News*, April 15, 2009, p. 9.

28. Adapted from Izabella Iizuka, "Not Your Father's Presentation," *Sales & Marketing Management*, March/April 2008, pp. 33–35.

29. *Shopper-Centric Trade: The Future of Trade Promotion* (Wilton, CT: Cannondale Associates, October 2007), p. 15.

30. "Shoppers Drug Mart Tightens Up Optimum Rewards," Canadian Press, June 18, 2010.

31. Based on information and quotes from Richard H. Levey, "A Slip Between Cup and Lip," *Direct*, May 1, 2008, accessed at http://directmag.com/roi/0508-starbucks-loyalty-program/index.html; Ron Lieber, "The Card-Carrying Starbucks Fan," *New York Times*, June 7, 2008, p. C1; and Emily Bryson York, "Starbucks: Don't Be Seduced by Lower Prices," *Advertising Age*, April 30, 2009, accessed at http://adage.com/print?article_id=136389.

32. Matt Semansky, "Sharing Hockey Memories for Chevrolet," *Marketing Daily*, November 12, 2007.

33. See "Consumers Turn to Coupons in Tough Economic Times," September 4, 2008, accessed at www.pmalink.org/press_ releases/ default.asp?p=pr_09042008; and "Renewed Consumer Interest Drives Fourth Quarter Surge in Coupon Use," at www.couponinfonow.com, accessed February 2009.

34. Quotes and other information from Alan J. Liddle, "Hardee's Connects with Mobile Device Users, Offers Discounts," *Nation's Restaurant News*, May 14, 2007, p. 16; Alice Z. Cuneo, "Package-Goods Giants Roll Out Mobile Coupons," *Advertising Age*, March 10, 2008, p. 3; Alex Palmer, "Cellular Savings," *Incentive*, April 2008, p. 69; and www.cellfire.com, accessed October 2009.

35. Wayne Mouland, "Rebates Rule!" *Marketing*, October 18, 2004, p. 35.

36. See www.happymeal.com, accessed April 2009.

37. See "Promotion Products Fact Sheet," at Promotion Products Association International website, www.ppai.org, accessed April 2009.

38. Kristin Laird, "Protecting Caramilk Secret is Key to Big Rewards," *Marketing* (online version), June 10, 2010.

39. "Exclusive PQ Media Research: Branded Entertainment Defies Slowing Economy," February 12, 2008, accessed at www.pqmedia. com/about-press-20080212-bemf.html; "Direct Impact," *Promo*, October 1, 2008, accessed at http://promomagazine.com/1001-eventmarketing-impact/index.html; and Richard Tedesco, "2009 Promo Event Marketing Survey: Marketers Are Still Staging Events," *Promo*, January 1, 2009, accessed at http://promomagazine. com/eventmarketing/0109-marketers-staging-events/.

40. "Charmin Restrooms Offers Luxurious Relief to Millions in Times Square on New Year's Eve," *PR Newswire*, January 1, 2009.

41. "Pepsi Porch Opens at New York Mets New Home," *Promo*, March 31, 2009, accessed at http://promomagazine.com/ eventmarketing/news/pepsi-porch-opens-stadium-0331/index.html.

42. *Shopper-Centric Trade: The Future of Trade Promotion*, p. 15.

43. See "CES 2009 Attendance Lower than Expected," January 13, 2009, accessed at http://news.softpedia.com; "Economy Does Not Worry Bauma Show Officials," *Roads & Bridges*, February 4, 2009, accessed at www.roadsbridges.com; and the Bauma website, www.bauma.de, accessed October 2009.

CHAPTER 14

1. Quotes and other information from Heather Green, "How Amazon Aims to Keep You Clicking," *BusinessWeek*, March 2, 2009, pp. 34–40; Josh Quittner, "The Charmed Life of Amazon's Jeff Bezos," *CNNMoney.com*, April 15, 2008, accessed at www.cnnmoney.com; Joe Nocera, "Putting Buyers First? What a Concept," *New York Times*, January 5, 2008; Jena McGregor, "Bezos: How Frugality Drives Innovation," *BusinessWeek*, April 28, 2008, p. 64; Jeffrey M. O'Brien, "Amazon's Next Revolution," *Fortune*, June 8, 2009, p. 68; and annual reports and other information at www.amazon.com, accessed September 2009.

2. For these and other direct-marketing statistics in this section, see Direct Marketing Association, *The DMA 2009 Statistical Fact Book, 31st edition*, February 2009; and Direct Marketing Association, *The Power of Direct Marketing: 2008–2009 Edition*, June 2009;

"Direct Marketing to Account for 53% of US Ad Spend in 2009," at www.marketingcharts.com, accessed November 24, 2008; and a wealth of other information at www.the-dma.org, accessed November 2009.

3. Marketing's Contribution to the Canadian Economy 2007, published by the Canadian Marketing Association.

4. Roy Chitwood, "Making the Most Out of Each Outside Sales Call," February 4, 2005, accessed at http://seattle.bizjournals.com/seattle/ stories/2005/02/07/smallb3.html; and "The Cost of the Average Sales Call Today Is More than $400," *Business Wire*, February 28, 2006.

5. Chris Daniels, "Customized copying," *Marketing*, July 4, 2005, p. 15.

6. Mike Freeman, "Data Company Helps Wal-Mart, Casinos, Airlines Analyze Data," *Knight Ridder Business Tribune News*, February 24, 2006, p. 1; and Eric Lai, "Teradata Creates Elite Club for Petabyte-Plus Data Warehouse Customers," *Computer World*, accessed at October 14, 2008, www.computerworld.com/action/ article.do?command= viewArticleBasic&articleId=9117159.

7. Quotes from Scott Horstein, "Use Care with That Database," *Sales & Marketing Management*, May 2006, p. 22; with information from Travis E. Poling, "*BusinessWeek* Says USAA Is Best in Nation When It Comes to Customer Service," *Knight Ridder Tribune Business News*, April 9, 2007, p. 1; *Hoover's Company Records*, June 15, 2009, p. 40508; Karen Aho, "10 Companies That Treat You Right," *MSN Money*, June 10, 2009, accessed at http://articles. moneycentral.www.msn.com; and www.usaa.com, accessed October 2009.

8 See DMA, *The Power of Direct Marketing*, June 2009; and "Integrated Marketing Media Mix Study: More Digital with the Stay Traditional," at www.marketingcharts.com, accessed June 2009; and Canada Post website, canadapost.ca.

9. Julie Liesse, "When Times Are Hard, Mail Works," *Advertising Age*, March 30, 2009, p. 14. For counterpoints, see Gavin O'Malley, "Direct-Mail Doomed, Long Live E-Mail," *MediaPost News*, May 20, 2009, accessed at www.mediapost.com.

10. Based on information from "JDA, HP, and Intel Team Up with Mahoney to Yield Outstanding Quantifiable Results," The Mahoney Company, accessed at www.mahoneyprint.com/caseStudies/jda. pdf; and Heather Fletcher, "PURLs of Wisdom," *Target Marketing*, January 2009, pp. 27–29.

11. Emily Bryson York, "This Isn't the Holiday Catalog You Remember," *Advertising Age*, October 29, 2007; and Jenny Kincaid Boone, "Catalogs Change Roles During Holiday Season," *Roanoke Times*, November 30, 2008, accessed at www.roanoke.com.

12. Ylan Q. Mui, "Paging Through the Holidays," *Washington Post*, December 1, 2007, p. D1.

13. See Karen E. Kleing, "Making It with Mail-Order," *BusinessWeek*, January 23, 2006, accessed at www.businessweek. com; Paul Wenske, "Retailers Join Movement to Curb the Cascade of Catalogs," *McClatchy-Tribune Business News*, December 5, 2007; and DMA, *The Power of Direct Marketing*, August 2009.

14. See "About Lillian Vernon," at www.lillianvernon.com, accessed September 2009.

15. DMA, *The Power of Direct Marketing*, August 2009.

16. Ira Teinowitz, "'Do Not Call' Does Not Hurt Direct Marketing," *Advertising Age*, April 11, 2005, pp. 3, 95. Also see Brendan B. Read, "Do Not Call, Five Years Later," *Customer Inter@ction Solutions*, October 2008, pp. 34–35.

17. Teinowitz, "'Do Not Call' Does Not Hurt Direct Marketing," p. 3.

18. See Jeffrey A. Fowler, "Peeved at Auto Warranty Calls, a Web Posse Strikes Back," *Wall Street Journal*, May 15, 2009, p. A1.

19. See Brian Steinberg, "Read This Now! But Wait! There's More! The Infomercial King Explains," *Wall Street Journal*, March 9, 2005, p. 1; Natasha Singer, "Why Kids Have All the Acne," *New York Times*, October 18, 2007, p. G1; and "Guthy-Renker Celebrates Top Honors at Annual Awards Ceremony," *PR Newswire*, September 26, 2008.

20. Brian O'Keefe, "Secrets of the TV Pitchmen," *Fortune*, April 13, 2009, pp. 82–90; and Andrew Adam Newman, "Snuggie Rode Silly Ads to Stardom Over Rivals," *New York Times*, February 26, 2009.

21. Steve McClellan, "New Clients Embrace DRTV as Sales Soar," *Adweek*, August 25–September 1, 2008, p. 9; and Stephanie Clifford, "As Seen on TV (and Increasingly on Prime Time)," *New York Times*, January 26, 2009, p. B7.

22. "Analysis: Can DRTV Really Build Brands Better than Image Ads?" *Precision Marketing*, February 9, 2007, p. 11; McClellan, "New Clients Embrace DRTV as Sales Soar," p. 9; and O'Keefe, "Secrets of the TV Pitchmen," pp. 82–90.

23. Adapted from Allison Fass, "Extreme Makeover," *Forbes*, September 1, 2008, pp. 64–66. Also see Eric J. Savitz, "Writing on the Wall for HSN and John Malone," *Barron's*, May 25, 2009, p. 32.

24. Beth Snyder Bulik, "Redbox Rakes in Green in Tough Times," *Advertising Age*, February 23, 2009, p. 6; Jessica Mintz, "Redbox's Machines Take on Netflix's Red Envelopes," *USA Today*, June 22, 2009, accessed at www.usatoday.com/tech/news/2009-06-22-redbox_N.htm; and www.redbox.com, accessed August 2009.

25. "Interactive: Ad Age Names Finalists," *Advertising Age*, February 27, 1995, pp. 12–14.

26. Daniel B. Honigman, "On the Verge: Mobile Marketing Will Make Strides," *Marketing News*, January 15, 2008, pp. 18–21; "Nielsen Says Mobile Ads Growing, Consumers Respond," *Reuters*, March 5, 2008, accessed at www.reuters.com; "Mobile Search Ads to Grow 130% by 2013," *TechWeb*, February 25, 2009; and "Wireless Quick Facts," at www.ctia.org, accessed July 2009.

27. Cyril Altmeyer, "Smartphones, Social Networks to Boost Mobile Advertising," *Reuters*, June 29, 2009, accessed at www.reuters.com.

28. See Emily Burg, "Acceptance of Mobile Ads on the Rise," *MediaPost Publications*, March 16, 2007, accessed at http://publications.mediapost.com; Steve Miller and Mike Beirne, "The iPhone Effect," *Adweek.com*, April 28, 2008; and Altmeyer, "Smart Phones, Social Networks to Boost Mobile Advertising," June 29, 2009.

29. "Marketing News' Digital Handbook," *Marketing News*, April 3, 2009, pp. 9–18.

30. For these and other examples, see Karyn Strauss and Derek Gale, *Hotels*, March 2006, p. 22; Kate Calder, "Hot Topic Cranks Its Music Biz," *Kidscreen*, May 2007, p. 22; and "Official Disneyland Resort Podcasts," http://disneyland.disney.go.com/disneyland/en_US/ podcast/index?name=PodcastListingPage, accessed December 2008.

31. Shahnaz Mahmud, "Survey: Viewers Crave TV Ad Fusion," *Adweek.com*, January 25, 2008; and Andrew Hampp, "Addressable Ads Are Here; Who's Ready?" *Advertising Age*, April 13, 2009, p. 9.

32. See Alice Z. Cuneo, "Nike Setting the Pace in Interactive-TV Race" *Advertising Age*, August 13, 2007, p. 3; and Alana Semuels, "Pizza at the Click of a TiVo Button," *Los Angeles Times*, November 18, 2008, p. C1.

33. For these and other statistics on Internet usage, see "Nielsen Online Reports Topline U.S. Data for February 2009," *Nielsen Online*, March 11, 2009, accessed at www.nielsen-online.com/pr/pr_090311.pdf; "Global Index Chart," at www.nielsen-online.com/press_fd.jsp?section=pr_netv&nav=3, accessed April 2009; and www.InternetWorldStats.com, accessed July 2009.

34. Statistics Canada, Canadian Internet Use Survey 2009, published May 10, 2010, accessed at statcan.gc.ca.

35. See Tom Sullivan, "A Lot More Than Paper Clips," *Barron's*, April 16, 2007, pp. 23–25; and information from www.officedepot.com, accessed September 2009.

36. See Shop.org, Forrester Research Inc., *The State of Retailing Online 2008*, accessed at www.forrester.com/SORO; and Rachel Metz, "Report: Online Retail Could Reach $156B in 2009," *Associated Press*, January 29, 2009, accessed at www.thestandard.com/news/2009/01/29/report-online-retail-could-reach-156b-2009.

37. Statistics Canada, Canadian Internet Use Survey 2009.

38. Information for this example from Sarah Hepola, "A Divine Cut of Swine," *National Post* (Canada), July 14, 2008, p. AL4; Laura Giovanelli, "Silly Stuff for the Season," *McClatchy-Tribune Business News*, December 11, 2008; and www.gratefulpalate.com, accessed November 2009.

39. Information for this example from www.dell.com/html/us/segments/pub/premier/tutorial/users_guide.html, accessed August 2009.

40. See "eBay Inc.," *Hoover's Company* Records, April 19, 2009, p. 56307; and facts from eBay annual reports and other information at www.ebay.com, accessed July 2009.

41. Beth Snyder Bulik, "Who Blogs?" *Advertising Age*, June 4, 2007, p. 20; Nigel Hollis, "Going Global? Better Think Local Instead," *Brandweek*, December 1, 2008 p. 14; and Jeff Vandam, "Blogs Find Favor as Buying Guides," *New York Times*, December 22, 2008, p. B3.

42. Jack Neff, "Owning the Concept of Value Online," *Advertising Age*, March 30, 2009, p. 22; and www.elevenmoms.com, accessed July 2009.

43. Adapted from information found in Brian Morrissey, "Brands Tap into Web Elite for Advertorial 2.0: Well-Connected Bloggers Are Creating Content on Behalf of Sponsors Thirsty for Buzz," *Adweek*, January 12, 2009, p. 9. Also see Josh Bernoff, "Be More

Than an Ad, Get in the Conversation," *Marketing News*, March 15, 2009.

44. Michael Barbaro, "Wal-Mart Tastemakers Write Unfiltered Blog," *New York Times*, March 3, 2008, accessed at www.nytimes.com/2008/ 03/03/business/03walmart.html?hp; and Jack Neff, "Owning the Concept of Value Online," *Advertising Age*, March 30, 2009, p. 22.

45. See Michael Bush, "Starbucks Gets Web 2.0 Religion, But Can It Convert Nonbelievers?" *Advertising Age*, March 24, 2008, p. 1.

46 .Carolyn Kepcher, "Bad Service? Point, Click, Complain," *New York Daily News*, May 12, 2008; and Kermit Pattison, "Does a New Website Hold the Secret to Great Customer Service?" *Fast Company*, April 2008, accessed at www.fastcompany.com/articles/2008/04/interview-muller.html.

47. "GE Corporate Website," *Communication Arts* Interactive Annual, 2008, pp. 134–135; and www.ge.com, accessed August 2009.

48. Adapted from Jena McGregor, "High-Tech Achiever: MINI USA," *Fast Company*, October 2004, p. 86, with information from www.miniusa.com, accessed September 2009.

49. Jeffrey F. Rayport and Bernard J. Jaworski, *e-Commerce* (New York: McGraw-Hill, 2001), p. 116. Also see "Looks Are Everything," *Marketing Management*, March/April 2006, p. 7; Benjamin Palmer, "Rethinking the User Experience," *Adweek*, August 25–September 1, 2008, p. 10; and Elizabeth A. Sullivan, "Virtually Satisfied," *Marketing News*, October 15, 2008, p. 26.

50. Adapted from Brooks Barnes, "In Overhaul, Disney.com Seeks a Path to More Fun," *New York Times*, June 25, 2008.

51. Jeff Beer, "Canadian Online Ad Spend Goes Up in Down Year," *Marketing*, August 10, 2010, accessed at marketingmag.ca.

52. Abbey Klaassen, "Breathing New Life into Online Creative," *Advertising Age*, March 30, 2009, p. 6; and Karlene Lukovitz, "Intel Live-Chat Banner Ads Engage End Users," *MediaPost News*, April 2, 2009, accessed at www.mediapost.com.

53. Internet Advertising Bureau, *IAB Internet* Advertising *Revenue Report*, March 2009.

54. Adapted from information in Elaine Wong, "Coke, ConAgra, Kellogg Cozy Up with Search Buys," *Brandweek*, October 12, 2008, accessed at www.brandweek.com.

55. Leftheria Parpis, "Behind McD's Flashy New Spot: Mounted Musical Mouthpiece Makes a Splash on the Net," *Adweek*, March 10, 2009, accessed at www.adweek.com.

56. Adapted from information found in Jeff Gordon, "Good Cheer: OfficeMax's Viral Campaign Revels in Its Elfin Glory and Returns Happy Results," *Marketing News*, March 15, 2008, pp. 24–28; and Jon Fine, "Bargain-Rate Buzz," *BusinessWeek*, February 9, 2009, p. 65.

57. See Emily Steele, "Skittles Cozies Up to Social Media," *Wall Street Journal*, March 3, 2009, p. B4; and Laura McKay, "Skittles: A Rainbow of Social Media Marketing," *Customer Relationship Management*, May 2009, p. 18.

58. Chaddus Bruce, "Big Biz Buddies Up to Gen Y," *Wired*, December 20, 2006, accessed at www.wired.com; and Brian Morrissey, "Kraft Gives Facebook Users Reason to Share," *Adweek*, December 30, 2008, accessed at www.adweek.com.

59. *CMA Guide to E-mail Marketing*, 2007.

60. Jessica Tsai, "How Much Marketing Is Too Much?" *DestinationCRM.com*, October 1, 2008, accessed at www.destinationcrm.com/Articles/PrintArticle.aspx?ArticleID=50752; and "StubHub Increases Revenue Per E-mail by Over 2,500 Percent with Responsys Interact and Omniture Recommendations," February 18, 2009, accessed at www.responsys.com/company/press/2009_02_18.php.

61. Adapted from the Canadian Marketing Association's guidelines for Internet marketing.

62. William Hupp, "E-Mail," *Advertising Age*, March 17, 2008, p. 48; and Jessica Tsai, "Email: What's Inside?" *Customer Relationship Management*, January 2009, pp. 32–38.

63. "Net Threats," *Consumer Reports*, September 2007, p. 28.

64. Information on TRUSTe, at www.truste.com, accessed October 2009.

APPENDIX 3

1. This is derived by rearranging the following equation and solving for price: Percentage markup = (price - cost) ÷ price.

2. Again, using the basic profit equation, we set profit equal to ROI × I: ROI × I = (P × Q) – TFC – (Q × UVC). Solving for Q gives Q = (TFC + (ROI × I)) ÷ (P – UVC).

3. U.S. Census Bureau, at www.census.gov/prod/1/pop/p25-1129.pdf, accessed October 26, 2009.

4 ."Broadband Internet to Reach 77 Percent of Households by 2012," at www.tmcnet.com/voip/ip communications/articles/35393-gartner-broadband-internet-reach-77-percent-households-2012.htm, accessed August 25, 2008.

5. See Roger J. Best, *Market-Based Management*, 4th ed. (Upper Saddle River, NJ: Prentice Hall, 2005).

6. Total contribution can also be determined from the unit contribution and unit volume: Total contribution = unit contribution × unit sales. Total units sold were 297,619 units, which can be determined by dividing total sales by price per unit ($100 million ÷ $336). Total contribution = $70 contribution per unit × 297,619 units = $20,833,330 (difference due to rounding).

7. Recall that the contribution margin of 21 percent was based on variable costs representing 79 percent of sales. Therefore, if we do not know price, we can set it equal to $1.00. If price equals $1.00, 79 cents represents variable costs and 21 cents represents unit contribution. If price is decreased by 10 percent, the new price is $0.90. However, variable costs do not change just because price decreased, so the unit contribution and contribution margin decrease as follows:

	Old	New (reduced 10%)
Price	$1.00	$0.90
– Unit variable cost	$0.79	$0.79
= Unit contribution	$0.21	$0.11
Contribution margin	$0.21/$1.00 = 0.21 or 21%	$0.11/$0.90 = 0.12 or 12%

Glossary

Action programs Action programs should be coordinated with the resources and activities of other departments, including production, finance, operations, and purchasing.

Administered VMS A vertical marketing system that coordinates successive stages of production and distribution, not through common ownership or contractual ties, but through the size and power of one of the parties.

Adoption process The mental process through which an individual passes from first hearing about an innovation to final adoption.

Advertising Any paid form of non-personal presentation and promotion of ideas, goods, or services by an identified sponsor.

Advertising agency A marketing services firm that assists companies in planning, preparing, implementing, and evaluating all or portions of their advertising programs.

Advertising budget The dollars and other resources allocated to a product or company advertising program.

Advertising media The types of media and media vehicles through which advertising messages are delivered to their intended audiences.

Advertising objective A specific communication *task* to be accomplished with a specific *target* audience during a specific period of *time*. The overall advertising goal is to help build customer relationships by communicating customer value.

Advertising strategy The strategy by which the company accomplishes its advertising objectives. It consists of two major elements: creating advertising messages and selecting advertising media.

Affiliate program A type of co-marketing arrangement in which one website links to another and can receive small commissions or other benefits when visitors click through and make purchases.

Affordable method Setting the advertising budget at the level management thinks the company can afford.

Age and life-cycle segmentation Dividing a market into different age and life-cycle groups.

Agent A wholesaler who represents buyers or sellers on a relatively permanent basis, performs only a few functions, and does not take title to goods.

Allowance Promotional money paid by manufacturers to retailers in return for an agreement to feature the manufacturer's products in some way.

Approach The step in the selling process in which the salesperson meets the customer for the first time.

Attitude A person's consistently favourable or unfavourable evaluations, feelings, and tendencies toward an object or an idea.

Baby Boomers The 9.8 million Canadians born during the baby boom following World War II and lasting until the mid-1960s.

Banner ad A square or rectangular graphical advertisement that typically appears at the top or along the side of a webpage.

Behavioural segmentation Dividing a market into segments based on consumer knowledge, attitudes, uses, or responses to a product.

Belief A descriptive thought that a person holds about something.

Benefit segmentation Dividing the market into segments according to the different benefits that consumers seek from the product.

Blog A personal website in journal or diary format, where people post their thoughts, usually on a narrowly defined topic.

Brand A name, term, sign, symbol, or design, or a combination of these, that identifies the products or services of one seller or group of sellers and differentiates them from those of competitors.

Brand advocates Customers, employees, and others who willingly and voluntarily promote their favourite brands.

Brand equity The dollar amount attributed to the value of the brand, based on all the intangible qualities that create that value.

Brand extensions Extending an existing brand name to new product categories.

Brand personality The sum total of all the attributes of a brand, and the emotions it inspires in the minds of consumers.

Branded entertainment A form of entertainment, usually video, that is created with the co-operation or financial support of a marketer.

Break-even analysis Analysis to determine the unit volume and dollar sales needed to be profitable given a particular price and cost structure.

Break-even price The price at which total revenue equals total cost and profit is zero.

Break-even pricing (or target return pricing) Setting price to break even on the costs of making and marketing a product, or setting price to make a target return.

Broker A wholesaler who does not take title to goods and whose function is to bring buyers and sellers together and assist in negotiation.

Budgets Managers use budgets to project profitability and plan for each marketing program's expenditures, scheduling, and operations.

Business analysis A review of the sales, costs, and profit projections for a new product to find out whether these factors satisfy the company's objectives.

Business buyer behaviour The buying behaviour of the organizations that buy goods and services for use in the production of other products and services or to resell or rent them to others at a profit.

Business portfolio The collection of businesses and products that make up the company.

Business promotions Sales promotion tools used to generate business leads, stimulate purchases, reward customers, and motivate salespeople.

Business-to-business (B2B) online marketing Businesses using B2B websites, email, online catalogues, online trading networks, and other online resources to reach new business customers, serve current customers more effectively, and obtain buying efficiencies and better prices.

Business-to-consumer (B2C) online marketing Businesses selling goods and services online to individual consumers for their personal needs.

Buying centre All the individuals and units that play a role in the purchase decision-making process.

By-product pricing Setting a price for by-products to make the main product's price more competitive.

Cannibalization The situation in which one product sold by a company takes a portion of its sales from other company products.

Captive-product pricing Setting a price for products that must be used along with a main product, such as blades for a razor and games for a video-game console.

Catalogue marketing Direct marketing through print, video, or digital catalogues that are mailed to select customers, made available in stores, or presented online.

Causal research Marketing research to test hypotheses about cause-and-effect relationships.

Chain ratio method Estimating market demand by multiplying a base number by a chain of adjusting percentages.

Chain store Two or more outlets that are commonly owned and controlled.

Channel conflict Disagreement among marketing channel members on goals, roles, and rewards—who should do what and for what rewards.

Channel level A layer of intermediaries that performs some work in bringing the product and its ownership closer to the final buyer.

Closing The step in the selling process in which the salesperson asks the customer for an order.

Co-branding The practice of using the established brand names of two different companies on the same product.

Cognitive dissonance Buyer discomfort caused by postpurchase conflict.

Commercial online databases Computerized collections of information available from online commercial sources or via the Internet.

Commercialization The full-scale introduction of the new product into the market.

Competition-based pricing Setting prices based on competitors' strategies, prices, costs, and market offerings.

Competitive advantage An advantage over competitors gained by offering greater customer value, either through lower prices or by providing more benefits that justify higher prices.

Competitive marketing intelligence The systematic collection and analysis of publicly available information about consumers, competitors, and developments in the marketing environment.

Competitive review The purpose of a competitive review section in a marketing plan is to identify key competitors, describe their market positions, and briefly discuss their strategies.

Competitive-parity method Setting the promotion budget to match competitors' outlays.

Concentrated (niche) marketing A market-coverage strategy in which a firm goes after a large share of one or a few segments or niches.

Consumer buyer behaviour The buying behaviour of final consumers—individuals and households that buy goods and services for personal consumption.

Consumer market All the individuals and households that buy or acquire goods and services for personal consumption.

Consumer product A product bought by final consumers for personal consumption.

Consumer promotions Sales promotion tools used to boost short-term customer buying and involvement or to enhance long-term customer relationships.

Consumer-generated marketing Brand exchanges created by consumers themselves—both invited and uninvited—by which consumers are playing an increasing role in shaping their own brand experiences and those of other consumers.

Consumer-oriented marketing The philosophy of sustainable marketing that holds that the company should view and organize its marketing activities from the consumer's point of view.

Consumer-to-business (C2B) online marketing Online exchanges in which consumers search out sellers, learn about their offers, and initiate purchases, sometimes even driving transaction terms.

Consumer-to-consumer (C2C) online marketing Online exchanges of goods and information between individual consumers.

Consumerism An organized movement of citizens and government agencies to improve the rights and power of buyers in relation to sellers.

Contractual VMS A vertical marketing system in which independent firms at different levels of production and distribution join together through contracts to obtain more economies or sales impact than they could achieve alone.

Contribution margin The unit contribution divided by the selling price.

Convenience product A consumer product that customers usually buy frequently, immediately, and with a minimum of comparison and buying effort.

Convenience store A small store, located near a residential area, that is open long hours seven days a week and carries a limited line of high-turnover convenience goods.

Conventional distribution channel A channel consisting of one or more independent producers, wholesalers, and retailers, each a separate business seeking to maximize its own profits, even at the expense of profits for the system as a whole.

Corporate (or brand) website A website designed to build customer goodwill, collect customer feedback, and supplement other sales channels, rather than to sell the company's products directly.

Corporate VMS A vertical marketing system that combines successive stages of production and distribution under single ownership—channel leadership is established through common ownership.

Cost-based pricing Setting prices based on the costs for producing, distributing, and selling the product plus a fair rate of return for effort and risk.

Cost-plus pricing (or markup pricing) Adding a standard markup to the cost of the product.

Creative concept The compelling "big idea" that will bring the advertising message strategy to life in a distinctive and memorable way.

Cultural environment Institutions and other forces that affect society's basic values, perceptions, preferences, and behaviours.

Culture The set of basic values, perceptions, wants, and behaviours learned by a member of society from family and other important institutions.

Current marketing situation In this section of a marketing plan, marketing managers discuss the overall market, identify the market segments they will target, and provide information about the company's current situation.

Customer (or market) sales force structure A sales force organization under which salespeople specialize in selling only to certain customers or industries.

Customer database An organized collection of comprehensive data about individual customers or prospects, including geographic, demographic, psychographic, and behavioural data.

Customer equity The total combined customer lifetime values of all of the company's customers.

Customer insights Fresh understandings of customers and the marketplace derived from marketing information that become the basis for creating customer value and relationships.

Customer lifetime value The value of the entire stream of purchases that the customer would make over a lifetime of patronage.

Customer relationship management (CRM) Managing detailed information about individual customers and carefully managing customer "touch points" to maximize customer loyalty; the overall process of building and maintaining profitable customer relationships by delivering superior customer value and satisfaction.

Customer satisfaction The extent to which a product's perceived performance matches a buyer's expectations.

Customer value–based pricing Setting price based on buyers' perceptions of value rather than on the seller's cost.

Customer-managed relationships Marketing relationships in which customers, empowered by today's new digital technologies, interact with companies and with each other to shape their relationships with brands.

Customer-perceived value The customer's evaluation of the difference between all the benefits and all the costs of a market offering relative to those of competing offers.

Customer-value marketing A principle of sustainable marketing that holds that a company should put most of its resources into customer-value-building marketing investments.

Decline stage The product life-cycle stage in which a product's sales decline.

Deficient products Products that have neither immediate appeal nor long-run benefits.

Demand curve A curve that shows the number of units the market will buy in a given time period, at different prices that might be charged.

Demands Human wants that are backed by buying power.

Demographic segmentation Dividing the market into segments based on variables such as age, gender, family size, life cycle, household income (HHI), occupation, education, ethnic or cultural group, and generation.

Demography The study of human populations in terms of size, density, location, age, gender, race, occupation, and other statistics.

Department store A retail organization that carries a wide variety of product lines—each line is operated as a separate department managed by specialist buyers or merchandisers.

Derived demand Business demand that ultimately comes from (derives from) the demand for consumer goods.

Descriptive research Marketing research to better describe marketing problems, situations, or markets, such as the market potential for a product or the demographics and attitudes of consumers.

Desirable products Products that give both high immediate satisfaction and high long-run benefits.

Differentiated (segmented) marketing A market-coverage strategy in which a firm decides to target several market segments and designs separate offers for each.

Differentiation Actually differentiating the market offering to create superior customer value.

Direct marketing Connecting directly with carefully targeted individual consumers to both obtain an immediate response and cultivate lasting customer relationships.

Direct marketing channel A marketing channel that has no intermediary levels.

Direct-mail marketing Direct marketing by sending an offer, announcement, reminder, or other item to a person at a particular physical or virtual address.

Direct-response television marketing Direct marketing via television, including direct-response television advertising (or infomercials) and home shopping channels.

Discount A straight reduction in price on purchases during a stated period of time or of larger quantities.

Discount store A retail operation that sells standard merchandise at lower prices by accepting lower margins and selling at higher volume.

Disintermediation The cutting out of marketing channel intermediaries by product or service producers, or the displacement of traditional resellers by radical new types of intermediaries.

Distribution (channel) review In this section of a marketing plan, marketers list the most important channels, provide an overview of each channel arrangement, and identify developing issues in channels.

Distribution centre A large, highly automated warehouse designed to receive goods from various plants and suppliers, take orders, fill them efficiently, and deliver goods to customers as quickly as possible.

Diversification A strategy for company growth through starting up or acquiring businesses outside the company's current products and markets.

Downsizing Reducing the business portfolio by eliminating products or business units that are not profitable or that no longer fit the company's overall strategy.

Dynamic pricing Adjusting prices continually to meet the characteristics and needs of individual customers and situations.

E-procurement Purchasing through electronic connections between buyers and sellers—usually online.

Economic environment Factors that affect consumer buying power and spending patterns.

Email marketing Any form of promotional message sent by a marketer to a group of consumers, usually existing customers or subscribers.

Engel's laws Differences noted more than a century ago by Ernst Engel in how people shift their spending across food, housing, transportation, health care, and other goods and services categories as family income rises.

Environmental sustainability A management approach that involves developing strategies that both sustain the environment and produce profits for the company; developing strategies and practices that create a world economy that the planet can support indefinitely.

Environmentalism An organized movement of concerned citizens, businesses, and government agencies to protect and improve people's current and future living environment.

Ethnographic research A form of observational research that involves sending trained observers to watch and interact with consumers in their "natural habitat."

Event marketing Creating a brand-marketing event or serving as a sole or participating sponsor of events created by others.

Exchange The act of obtaining a desired object from someone by offering something in return.

Exclusive distribution Giving a limited number of dealers the exclusive right to distribute the company's products in their territories.

Execution style The approach, style, tone, words, and format used for executing an advertising message.

Executive summary The section of a marketing plan that summarizes the main goals, recommendations, and points. It serves as an overview for senior managers who will read and approve the marketing plan. For management convenience, a table of contents generally follows this section.

Experimental research Gathering primary data by selecting matched groups of subjects, giving them different treatments, controlling related factors, and checking for differences in group responses.

Exploratory research Marketing research to gather preliminary information that will help define the problem and suggest hypotheses.

Factory outlet An off-price retailing operation that is owned and operated by a manufacturer and that normally carries the manufacturer's surplus, discontinued, or irregular goods.

Fad A temporary period of unusually high sales driven by consumer enthusiasm and immediate product or brand popularity.

Fashion A currently accepted or popular style in a given field.

Fixed costs (overhead) Costs that do not vary with production or sales level.

Focus group interviewing Personal interviewing that involves inviting six to ten people to gather for a few hours with a trained interviewer to talk about a product, service, or organization. The interviewer "focuses" the group discussion on important issues.

Follow-up The last step in the selling process in which the salesperson follows up after the sale to ensure customer satisfaction and repeat business.

Franchise organization A contractual vertical marketing system in which a channel member, called a franchisor, links several stages in the production-distribution process.

Gender segmentation Dividing a market into different segments based on gender.

Generation X The 7 million Canadians born between 1967 and 1976 in the "birth dearth" following the baby boom.

Geographic segmentation Dividing a market into different geographical units, such as global regions, countries, regions within a country, provinces, cities, or even neighbourhoods.

Geographical pricing Setting prices for customers located in different parts of the country or the world.

Good-value pricing Offering just the right combination of quality and good service at a fair price.

Gross margin percentage The percentage of net sales remaining after cost of goods sold—calculated by dividing gross margin by net sales.

Group Two or more people who interact to accomplish individual or mutual goals.

Growth stage The product life-cycle stage in which a product's sales start climbing quickly.

Growth-share matrix A portfolio-planning method that evaluates a company's strategic business units (SBUs) in terms of its market growth rate and relative market share. SBUs are classified as stars, cash cows, question marks, or dogs.

Handling objections The step in the selling process in which the salesperson seeks out, clarifies, and overcomes customer objections to buying.

Horizontal marketing system A channel arrangement in which two or more companies at one level join together to follow a new marketing opportunity.

Household Income (HHI) segmentation Dividing a market into different income segments.

Idea generation The systematic search for new-product ideas.

Idea screening Screening new-product ideas to spot good ideas and drop poor ones as soon as possible.

Indirect marketing channel A marketing channel that includes one or more intermediaries.

Individual marketing (mass customization) Tailoring products and marketing programs to the needs and preferences of individual customers.

Industrial product A product bought by individuals and organizations for further processing or for use in conducting a business.

Innovative marketing A principle of sustainable marketing that requires that a company seek real product and marketing improvements.

Inside sales force Inside salespeople who conduct business from their offices via telephone, the Internet, or visits from prospective buyers.

Integrated logistics management The logistics concept that emphasizes teamwork, both inside the company and among all the marketing channel organizations, to maximize the performance of the entire distribution system.

Integrated marketing communications (IMC) Carefully integrating and coordinating the company's many communications channels to deliver a clear, consistent, and compelling message about the organization and its products.

Intensive distribution Stocking the product in as many outlets as possible.

Interactive marketing Training service employees in the fine art of interacting with customers to satisfy their needs.

Intermarket segmentation Forming segments of consumers who have similar needs and buying behaviour even though they are located in different countries.

Intermodal transportation Combining two or more modes of transportation.

Internal databases Electronic collections of consumer and market information obtained from data sources within the company network.

Internal marketing Orienting and motivating customer-contact employees and supporting service people to work as a team to provide customer satisfaction.

Interstitial A type of online advertising that appears between screen changes, usually as you navigate from one site to another, and resembles a very short television commercial that takes over the full browser screen before disappearing to reveal the website underneath.

Introduction stage The product life-cycle stage in which the new product is first distributed and made available for purchase.

Inventory turnover rate (or stock-turn rate) The number of times an inventory turns over or is sold during a specified time period (often one year)—calculated based on costs, selling price, or units.

Just-in-time logistics system A type of inventory management system in which only small inventories of parts or merchandise are held, and new stock arrives "just in time" when it is needed.

Learning Changes in an individual's behaviour arising from experience.

Licensing Selling the rights to apply a brand name, logo, or image to another manufacturer.

Lifestyle A person's pattern of living as expressed in his or her activities, interests, and opinions.

Line extensions Extending an existing brand name to new forms, colours, sizes, ingredients, or flavours of an existing product category.

Local marketing A small group of people who live in the same city, or neighbourhood, or who shop at the same store.

Macroenvironment The larger societal forces that affect the microenvironment—demographic, economic, natural, technological, political, and cultural forces.

Market The set of all actual and potential buyers of a product or a service.

Market description Describing the targeted segments in detail provides context for the marketing strategies and detailed action programs discussed later in a marketing plan.

Market development A strategy for company growth by identifying and developing new market segments for current company products.

Market offerings Some combination of products, services, information, or experiences offered to a market to satisfy a need or want.

Market penetration A strategy for company growth by increasing sales of current products to current market segments without changing the product.

Market potential The upper limit of market demand.

Market segment A group of consumers who respond in a similar way to a given set of marketing efforts.

Market segmentation Dividing a market into distinct groups of buyers who have different needs, characteristics, or behaviours, and who might require separate products or marketing programs.

Market share Company sales divided by market sales.

Market targeting The process of evaluating each market segment's attractiveness and selecting one or more segments to enter.

Marketing The process by which companies create value for customers and build strong customer relationships in order to capture value from customers in return.

Marketing channel (or distribution channel) A set of interdependent organizations that help make a product or service available for use or consumption by the consumer or business user.

Marketing channel design Designing effective marketing channels by analyzing consumer needs, setting channel objectives, identifying major channel alternatives, and evaluating them.

Marketing channel management Selecting, managing, and motivating individual channel members and evaluating their performance over time.

Marketing concept The marketing management philosophy that holds that achieving organizational goals depends on knowing the needs and wants of target markets and delivering the desired satisfactions better than competitors do.

Marketing control The process of measuring and evaluating the results of marketing strategies and plans and taking corrective action to ensure that objectives are achieved.

Marketing controls Controls help management assess results after their plan has been implemented, identify any problems or performance variations, and initiate corrective action.

Marketing environment The actors and forces outside marketing that affect marketing management's ability to build and maintain successful relationships with target customers.

Marketing implementation The process that turns marketing strategies and plans into marketing actions to accomplish strategic marketing objectives.

Marketing information system (MIS) People and procedures for assessing information needs, developing the needed information, and helping decision makers to use the information to generate and validate actionable customer and market insights.

Marketing intermediaries Firms that help the company to promote, sell, and distribute its goods to final buyers.

Marketing logistics (or physical distribution) Planning, implementing, and controlling the physical flow of materials, final goods, and related information from points of origin to points of consumption to meet customer requirements at a profit.

Marketing management The art and science of choosing target markets and building profitable relationships with them.

Marketing mix The set of controllable, tactical marketing tools—product, price, place, and promotion—that the firm blends to produce the response it wants in the target market.

Marketing myopia The mistake of paying more attention to the specific products a company offers than to the benefits and experiences produced by these products.

Marketing organization The marketing department may be organized by function, geography, product, or customer.

Marketing research The systematic design, collection, analysis, and reporting of data relevant to a specific marketing situation facing an organization; the section of a marketing plan that shows how marketing research will be used to support development, implementation, and evaluation of strategies and action programs.

Marketing return on investment (or marketing ROI) A measure of the marketing productivity of a marketing investment—calculated by dividing net marketing contribution by marketing expenses.

Marketing return on sales (or marketing ROS) The percent of net sales attributable to the net marketing contribution—calculated by dividing net marketing contribution by net sales.

Marketing strategy The marketing logic by which the company hopes to create customer value and achieve profitable customer relationships.

Marketing strategy development Designing an initial marketing strategy for a new product based on the product concept.

Marketing tools These sections of a marketing plan summarize the brand logic that will guide decisions made about the marketing tools to be used during the period covered by the plan.

Marketing website A website that engages consumers in interactions that will move them closer to a direct purchase or other marketing outcome.

Market-penetration pricing Setting a low initial price for a new product in order to attract a large number of buyers and a large market share.

Market-skimming pricing (or price skimming) Setting a high price for a new product to skim maximum revenues layer by layer from the segments willing to pay the high price; the company makes fewer but more profitable sales.

Markup The difference between a company's selling price for a product and its cost to manufacture or purchase it.

Markup chain The sequence of markups used by firms at each level in a channel.

Maturity stage The product life-cycle stage in which sales growth slows or levels off.

Media vehicle The specific media (publication or program) within a general media type (magazine, radio, television).

Merchant wholesaler An independently owned wholesaler business that takes title to the merchandise it handles.

Microenvironment The actors close to the company that affect its ability to serve its customers—the company, suppliers, marketing intermediaries, customer markets, competitors, and publics.

Micromarketing The practice of tailoring products and marketing programs to the needs and wants of specific individuals and local customer segments—includes *local marketing and individual marketing.*

Millennials (or Generation Y) The 10.4 million children of the Canadian Baby Boomers, born between 1977 and 2000.

Mission statement A statement of the organization's purpose—what it wants to accomplish in the larger environment.

Modified rebuy A business buying situation in which the buyer wants to modify product specifications, prices, terms, or suppliers.

Motive (drive) A need that is sufficiently pressing to direct the person to seek satisfaction of the need.

Multibranding A brand development strategy in which the same manufacturer produces many different brands in the same product category.

Multichannel distribution system A distribution system in which a single firm sets up two or more marketing channels to reach one or more customer segments.

National brand (or manufacturer's brand) A brand created and owned by the manufacturer of the product.

Natural environment Natural resources that are needed as inputs by marketers or that are affected by marketing activities.

Needs States of felt deprivation.

Net marketing contribution (NMC) A measure of marketing profitability that includes only components of profitability controlled by marketing.

Net profit percentage The percentage of each sales dollar going to profit—calculated by dividing net profits by net sales.

New product A good, service, or idea that is perceived by some potential customers as new.

New task A business buying situation in which the buyer purchases a product or service for the first time.

New-product development The development of original products, product improvements, product modifications, and new brands through the firm's own product-development efforts.

Objective-and-task method Developing the advertising budget by (1) defining specific objectives, (2) determining the tasks that must be performed to achieve these objectives, and (3) estimating the costs of performing these tasks. The sum of these costs is the proposed advertising budget.

Objectives and Issues Objectives and Issues should be defined in specific terms so management can measure progress and plan corrective action if needed to stay on track. This section of a marketing plan describes any major issues that might affect the company's marketing strategy and implementation.

Observational research Gathering primary data by observing relevant people, actions, and situations.

Occasion segmentation Dividing the market into segments according to occasions when buyers get the idea to buy, actually make their purchase, or use the purchased item.

Off-price retailer A retailer that buys at less-than-regular wholesale prices and sells at less than retail. Examples are factory outlets, independents, and warehouse clubs.

Online advertising Advertising that appears on websites that sell advertising space, including display ads (also called graphic ads and banner ads), search ads, text links, online classifieds, and full-screen animated or video ads (interstitials).

Online focus groups Gathering a small group of people online with a trained moderator to chat about a product, service, or organization and to gain qualitative insights about consumer attitudes and behaviour.

Online marketing Company efforts to market products and services and build customer relationships over the Internet.

Online marketing research Collecting primary data online through Internet surveys, online focus groups, Web-based experiments, or tracking consumers' online behaviour.

Online social networks Online social communities—blogs, social networking websites, or even virtual worlds—where people socialize or exchange information and opinions.

Operating expense percentage The portion of net sales going to operating expenses—calculated by dividing total expenses by net sales.

Operating ratios The ratios of selected operating statement items to net sales.

Opinion leader Person within a reference group who, because of special skills, knowledge, personality, or other characteristics, exerts social influence on others.

Opportunities Opportunities are external elements that the company may be able to exploit to its advantage.

Optional-product pricing The pricing of optional or accessory products along with a main product.

Outside sales force (or field sales force) Outside salespeople who travel to call on customers in the field.

Packaging The activities of designing and producing the container or wrapper for a product.

Partner relationship management Working closely with partners in other company departments and outside the company to jointly bring greater value to customers.

Percentage-of-sales method Setting the promotion budget at a certain percentage of current or forecasted sales, or as a percentage of the unit sales price.

Perception The process by which people select, organize, and interpret information to form a meaningful picture of the world.

Personal selling Personal presentation by the firm's sales force for the purpose of making sales and building customer relationships.

Personality The unique psychological characteristics that distinguish a person or group.

Pleasing products Products that give high immediate satisfaction but may hurt consumers in the long run.

Podcast An audio or video file, such as a radio or television program, sports feature, or music video, that can be downloaded from the Internet and viewed or listened to on an iPod or other personal electronic device.

Political environment Laws, government agencies, and pressure groups that influence and limit various organizations and individuals in a given society.

Portfolio analysis The process by which management evaluates the products and businesses that make up the company.

Positioning A positioning built on meaningful differentiation, supported by appropriate strategy and implementation, can help the company build competitive advantage; arranging for a product (market offering) to occupy a clear, distinctive, and desirable place relative to competing products in the minds of target consumers.

Positioning statement A statement that summarizes company or brand positioning—it takes this form: To (target segment and need) our (brand) is (concept) that (point of difference).

Preapproach The step in the selling process in which the salesperson learns as much as possible about a prospective customer before making a sales call.

Presentation The step in the selling process in which the salesperson tells the "value story" to the buyer, showing how the company's offer solves the customer's problems.

Price The amount of money charged for a product or a service, or the sum of the values that customers exchange for the benefits of having or using the product or service.

Price elasticity A measure of the sensitivity of demand to changes in price.

Primary data Information collected for the specific purpose at hand.

Private brand (or store brand) A brand created and owned by a reseller of a product or a service.

Pro forma (or projected) profit-and-loss statement (or income statement or operating statement) A statement that shows projected revenues less budgeted expenses and estimates the projected net profit for an organization, a product, or a brand during a specific planning period, typically a year.

Product Anything that can be offered to a market for attention, acquisition, use, or consumption that might satisfy a want or need.

Product bundle pricing Combining several products and offering the bundle at a reduced price.

Product concept A detailed version of the new-product idea stated in meaningful consumer terms; the idea that consumers will favour products that offer the most quality, performance, and features and that the organization should therefore devote its energy to making continuous product improvements.

Product development A strategy for company growth by offering modified or new products to current market segments; developing the product concept into a physical product to ensure that the

product idea can be turned into a workable market offering.

Product life cycle The course of a product's sales and profits over its lifetime. It involves five distinct stages: product development, introduction, growth, maturity, and decline.

Product line A group of products that are closely related because they function in a similar manner, are sold to the same customer groups, are marketed through the same types of outlets, or fall within given price ranges.

Product line pricing Setting the price steps between various products in a product line based on cost differences between the products, customer evaluations of different features, and competitors' prices.

Product mix (or product portfolio) The set of all product lines and items that a particular seller offers for sale.

Product position The way the product is defined by consumers on important attributes—the place the product occupies in consumers' minds relative to competing products.

Product quality The characteristics of a product or a service that bear on its ability to satisfy stated or implied customer needs.

Product review The product review section of a marketing plan summarizes the main features for all the company's products, organized by product line, type of customer, market, or order of product introduction.

Product sales force structure A sales force organization under which salespeople specialize in selling only a portion of the company's products or lines.

Product/market expansion grid A portfolio planning tool for identifying company growth opportunities through market penetration, market development, product development, or diversification.

Production concept The idea that consumers will favour products that are available and highly affordable and that the organization should therefore focus on improving production and distribution efficiency.

Profit-and-loss statement (or income statement or operating statement) A statement that shows actual revenues less expenses and net profit for an organization, product, or brand during a specific planning period, typically a year.

Promotion mix (or marketing communications mix) The specific blend of promotion tools that the

company uses to persuasively communicate customer value and build customer relationships.

Promotional pricing Temporarily pricing products below the list price and sometimes even below cost to increase short-run sales.

Prospecting The step in the selling process in which the salesperson or company identifies qualified potential customers.

Psychographic segmentation Dividing a market into different segments based on social class, lifestyle, or personality characteristics.

Psychological pricing Pricing that considers the psychology of prices and not simply the economics; the price is used to say something about the product.

Public Any group that has an actual or potential interest in or impact on an organization's ability to achieve its objectives.

Public relations (PR) Building good relations with the company's various publics by obtaining favourable publicity, building up a good corporate image, and handling or heading off unfavourable rumours, stories, and events.

Pull strategy A promotion strategy that calls for spending a lot on advertising and consumer promotion to induce final consumers to buy the product, creating a demand vacuum that "pulls" the product through the channel.

Push strategy A promotion strategy that calls for using the sales force and trade promotion to push the product through channels. The producer promotes the product to channel members who in turn promote it to final consumers.

Reference prices Prices that buyers carry in their minds and refer to when they look at a given product.

Relevant costs Costs that will occur in the future and that will vary across the alternatives being considered.

Retailer A business whose sales come *primarily* from retailing.

Retailing All activities involved in selling goods or services directly to final consumers for their personal, non-business use.

Return on advertising investment The net return on advertising investment divided by the costs of the advertising investment.

Return on investment (ROI) A measure of managerial effectiveness and efficiency—net profit before taxes divided by total investment.

Return on investment (ROI) pricing (or target-return pricing) A cost-based pricing method that determines price based on a specified rate of return on investment.

Return on marketing investment (or marketing ROI) The net return from a marketing investment divided by the costs of the marketing investment.

Sales force management The analysis, planning, implementation, and control of sales force activities. It includes designing sales force strategy and structure and recruiting, selecting, training, compensating, supervising, and evaluating the firm's salespeople.

Sales promotion Short-term incentives to encourage the purchase or sale of a product or a service.

Sales quota A standard that states the amount a salesperson should sell and how sales should be divided among the company's products.

Salesperson An individual representing a company to customers by performing one or more of the following activities: prospecting, communicating, selling, servicing, information gathering, and relationship building.

Salutary products Products that have low appeal but may benefit consumers in the long run.

Sample A segment of the population selected for marketing research to represent the population as a whole.

Secondary data Information that already exists somewhere, having been collected for another purpose.

Segmentation Dividing a market into distinct groups with distinct needs, characteristics, or behaviours that might require separate marketing strategies or mixes.

Segmented pricing Selling a product or service at two or more prices, where the difference in prices is not based on differences in costs.

Selective distribution The use of more than one, but fewer than all, of the intermediaries who are willing to carry the company's products.

Selling concept The idea that consumers will not buy enough of the firm's products unless it undertakes a large-scale selling and promotion effort.

Selling process The steps that salespeople follow when selling, which include prospecting and qualifying, preapproach, approach, presentation and demonstration, handling objections, closing, and follow-up.

Sense-of-mission marketing A principle of sustainable marketing that holds that a company should define its mission in broad social terms rather than narrow product terms.

Service An activity, benefit, or satisfaction offered for sale that is essentially intangible and does not result in the ownership of anything.

Service inseparability A major characteristic of services—they are produced and consumed at the same time and cannot be separated from their providers.

Service intangibility A major characteristic of services—they cannot be seen, tasted, felt, heard, or smelled before they are bought.

Service perishability A major characteristic of services—they cannot be stored for later sale or use.

Service variability A major characteristic of services—their quality may vary greatly, depending on who provides them and when, where, and how.

Service-profit chain The chain that links service firm profits with employee and customer satisfaction.

Share of customer The portion of the customer's purchasing that a company gets in its product categories.

Shopping product A consumer product that the customer, in the process of selection and purchase, usually compares on such bases as suitability, quality, price, and style.

Social class Relatively permanent and ordered divisions in a society whose members share similar values, interests, and behaviours.

Social networks Online communities where individuals and organizations can create mini websites; post blogs, photos, and videos; and exchange information and opinions.

Societal marketing A principle of sustainable marketing that holds that a company should make marketing decisions by considering consumers' wants, the company's requirements, consumers' long-run interests, and society's long-run interests.

Societal marketing concept The idea that a company's marketing decisions should consider consumers' wants, the company's requirements, consumers' long-run interests, and society's long-run interests.

Specialty product A consumer product with unique characteristics or brand identification for which a significant group of buyers is willing to make a special purchase effort.

Specialty store A retail store that carries a narrow product line with a deep assortment within that line.

Straight rebuy A business buying situation in which the buyer routinely reorders something without any modifications.

Strategic planning The process of developing and maintaining a strategic fit between the organization's goals and capabilities and its changing marketing opportunities.

Strengths Strengths are internal capabilities that can help the company reach its objectives.

Style A basic and distinctive mode of expression.

Subculture A group of people with shared value systems based on common life experiences and situations.

Supermarket A large, low-cost, low-margin, high-volume, self-service store that carries a wide variety of grocery and household products.

Superstore A store much larger than a regular supermarket that offers a large assortment of routinely purchased food products, non-food items, and services.

Supplier development Systematic development of networks of supplier-partners to ensure an appropriate and dependable supply of products and materials for use in making products or reselling them to others.

Supply chain management Managing upstream and downstream value-added flows of materials, final goods, and related information among suppliers, the company, resellers, and final consumers.

Survey research Gathering primary data by asking people questions about their knowledge, attitudes, preferences, and buying behaviour.

Sustainable marketing Socially and environmentally responsible marketing that meets the present needs of consumers and businesses while also preserving or enhancing the ability of future generations to meet their needs.

SWOT analysis An overall evaluation of the company's strengths (S), weaknesses (W), opportunities (O), and threats (T).

Systems selling (or solutions selling) Buying a packaged solution to a problem from a single seller, thus avoiding all the separate decisions involved in a complex buying situation.

Target costing Pricing that starts with an ideal selling price, and then targets costs that will ensure that the price is met.

Target market A set of buyers sharing common needs or characteristics that the company decides to serve.

Targeting The process of evaluating each market segment's attractiveness and selecting one or more segments to enter.

Team selling Using teams of people from sales, marketing, engineering, finance, technical support, and even upper management to service large, complex accounts.

Technological environment Forces that create new technologies, creating new product and market opportunities.

Territorial sales force structure A sales force organization that assigns each salesperson to an exclusive geographic territory in which that salesperson sells the company's full line.

Test-marketing The stage of new-product development in which the product and marketing program are tested in realistic market settings.

Third-party logistics (3PL) provider An independent logistics provider that performs any or all of the functions required to get its client's product to market.

Threats Threats are current or emerging external elements that could potentially challenge the company's performance.

Total costs The sum of the fixed and variable costs for any given level of production.

Total market demand The total volume that would be bought by a defined consumer group in a defined geographic area in a defined time period in a defined marketing environment under a defined level and mix of industry marketing effort.

Touchpoints Any and all points of contact a consumer has with a brand, including word of mouth, company webpages, points of purchase, and advertising.

Trade promotions Sales promotion tools used to persuade resellers to carry a brand, give it shelf space, promote it in advertising, and push it to consumers.

Undifferentiated (mass) marketing A market-coverage strategy in which a firm decides to ignore market segment differences and go after the whole market with one offer.

Unit contribution The amount that each unit contributes to covering fixed costs—the difference between price and variable costs.

Unsought product A consumer product that the consumer either does not know about or knows about but does not normally think of buying.

Value analysis Carefully analyzing a product's or service's components to determine whether they can be redesigned and made more effectively and efficiently to provide greater value.

Value chain The series of internal departments that carry out value-creating activities to design, produce, market, deliver, and support a firm's products.

Value delivery network The network made up of the company, suppliers, distributors, and ultimately customers who "partner" with each other to improve the performance of the entire system in delivering customer value.

Value proposition The full positioning of a brand—the full mix of benefits upon which it is positioned.

Value-added pricing Attaching value-added features and services to differentiate a company's offers and charging higher prices.

Value-based pricing Offering just the right combination of quality and good service at a fair price.

Variable costs Costs that vary directly with the level of production.

Vertical marketing system (VMS) A distribution channel structure in which producers, wholesalers, and retailers act as a unified system. One channel member owns the others, has contracts with them, or has so much power that they all co-operate.

Viral marketing The Internet version of word-of-mouth marketing—websites, videos, email messages, cellphone messages, or other marketing events that are so infectious that customers will want to pass them along to friends.

Wants The form human needs take as shaped by culture and individual personality.

Warehouse club An off-price retailer that sells a limited selection of brand name grocery items, appliances, clothing, and a hodgepodge of other goods at deep discounts to members who pay annual membership fees.

Weaknesses Weaknesses are internal elements that may interfere with the company's ability to achieve its objectives.

Wheel of retailing A concept that states that new types of retailers usually begin as low-margin, low-price, low-status operations but later evolve into higher-priced, higher-service operations, eventually becoming like the conventional retailers they replaced.

Wholesaler A firm engaged *primarily* in wholesaling activities.

Wholesaling All activities involved in selling goods and services to those buying for resale or business use.

Workload method An approach to determining sales force size based on the workload required and the time available for selling.

Photo Credits

CHAPTER 1

2: Courtesy of the Running Room Canada Inc. **9:** Courtesy of EarthShare. **11:** Courtesy of Daimler. **13:** Getty Images, Inc. **14:** Courtesy of Johnson & Johnson. Reprinted with permission. **15:** Courtesy of General Electric Company. **16:** Courtesy of myRoomBud. Used with permission. **17:** Courtesy of the Ritz-Carleton. **18:** © Jeff Greenberg/Alamy. **19:** Clemson/Flickr.com. **20:** Tourism PEI. **21:** © AJ Mast/The New York Times/ Redux. **23:** Courtesy of Stew Leonard's. Reprinted with permission. **24:** Courtesy of Corbis. **27:** Courtesy of the DeBeers Family of Companies. **29 (from top):** Getty Images; BlackBerry®, RIM®, Research In Motion®, SureType®, SurePress™ and related trademarks, names and logos are the property of Research In Motion Limited and are registered and/or used in the U.S. and countries around the world. **31:** Courtesy of the ASPCA, Sarah McLachlan, and Eagle-Com. **34 (from top):** Images and artwork courtesy of Canada Goose Inc.; Images and artwork courtesy of Canada Goose Inc., Photos courtesy of i2P.

CHAPTER 2

42: Courtesy of Riza Ayson. **45:** Courtesy of Getty. **46:** Reprinted with permission from Indigo Books & Music Inc. **48:** AP Wide World. **49:** Courtesy of Kohler Co. **52:** © Beth A. Keiser/Corbis. **53:** © 2008 UNDER ARMOUR INC. **55:** Gary Armstrong. **56:** Courtesy of Alamy. **58:** © 2009 Logitech. All rights reserved. Image used with permission from Logitech. **60:** The BURGER KING® trademarks and advertisements are used with permission from Burger King Corporation. **65:** Courtesy of Getty. **67:** © 2009 MarketingNPV LLC. All rights reserved. Used with permission. **69 (from top):** Images and artwork courtesy of Canada Goose Inc.; Images and artwork courtesy of Canada Goose Inc., Photos courtesy of i2P.

CHAPTER 3

76: Courtesy of Bullfrog Power. **80:** Courtesy of Redux. **81:** Pearson Education/PH College. **82:** Courtesy of TerraChoice, www.terrachoice.com. **84:** Courtesy of CORBIS. **85:** © Andy Dean/iStock. **86:** Courtesy of Adbusters Media Foundation. **88: (from left)** The Image Works; PA/Topham/The Image Works. **89:** AP Wide Work Photos. **91:** © 2009 Jones Soda Seattle. All rights reserved. Used with permission. **93:** Getty Images. **95:** Jeff Mitchell/Reuters Limited. **98:** © Aaron Harris/AP Wide World. **100:** © 2009 The Timberland Company. Used with permission. **103:** Courtesy of Redux. **107 (from top):** Images and artwork courtesy of Canada Goose Inc.; Images and artwork courtesy of Canada Goose Inc., Photos courtesy of i2P.

CHAPTER 4

116: David Vandenheede. **120:** Courtesy of Pratt & Whitney Canada. **122:** RMHC Canada. **124:** Mark Ralston Getty Images, Inc. **125:** Courtesy of Mountain Equipment Co-op. **126:** Courtesy of 7-Eleven, Inc. **129:** © 2009 Cisco Systems, Inc. **130:** Courtesy of TELUS. **132:** © Desmond Boylan/Reuters. **135:** Courtesy of Frito-Lay, Inc. **136:** AP Wide World. **138:** Courtesy of Virgin Mobile Canada. **140:** AP Wide World. **142:** Courtesy of Kenneth Cole. **143:** Courtesy of Getty. **144:** © 2009 Earthbound Farm. All rights reserved. Used with permission. **146:** Courtesy of Michael Whitford. Used with permission. **148 (from top):** Images and artwork courtesy of Canada Goose Inc.; Images and artwork courtesy of Canada Goose Inc., Photos courtesy of i2P.

CHAPTER 5

156: Copyright © 2009 The Procter & Gamble Company. All rights reserved. Reprinted with permission. **160:** AP Wide World. **163:** THE CANADIAN PRESS/Jonathan Hayward. **164:** Courtesy of Radian6 Technologies Inc. **166:** Courtesy of Red Bull North America. **170:** With permission of Dialog, LLC. **174:** Thinkstock/Corbis RF. **175:** Courtesy of fluidsurveys.com. **177:** © 2009 Channel M2, LLC. All rights reserved. Used with permission. **178:** © Lauren Burkes/Taxi/Getty Images. **180:** Bill Alkofer/The New York Times/Redux Pictures. **183:** Courtesy of Shoppers Drug Mart. **185:** Copyright © 2009 Bibbentuckers. All rights reserved. Reprinted with permission. **186:** Copyright © 2009 The Nielsen Company. All rights reserved. Reprinted with permission. **188:** Reproduced with permission of Royal Bank of Canada. **189:** Courtesy of Getty Images. **192 (from top):** Images and artwork courtesy of Canada Goose Inc.; Images and artwork courtesy of Canada Goose Inc., Photos courtesy of i2P.

CHAPTER 6

200: Getty Images, Inc. **203:** Reprinted courtesy of Doug Hardman, www.hardman.org. **207 (from left):** Courtesy of Windspeaker/AMMSA; Courtesy of 51.ca. **208:** Product photographer: Olof Wahlund. Beauty photographer: Patrick Demarchelier. Copyright © 2009 The Procter & Gamble Company. All rights reserved. Reprinted with permission. **210:** Copyright © 2008 The Procter & Gamble Company. All rights reserved. Reprinted with permission. Photograph © Kevin Dodge/Corbis. **211:** Photo courtesy of Molson Coors Canada. **212 (from top):** Courtesy of Blendtec; © Randy Faris/CORBIS; Jochen Sand/Digital Vision/Getty Images. **214:** Courtesy of Mark's Work Wearhouse. **215:** Courtesy of Merrell. **216:** © Kevin Dodge/Comet/CORBIS. All rights reserved. **217:** Courtesy of CORBIS. **219:** Amanda Kamen. **220:** BeaverTails® pastry image Courtesy of BeaverTails Brands Inc. **226:** Courtesy of General Electric Company. **227:** Courtesy of Intel Corporation.

Index

COMPANIES AND ORGANIZATIONS INDEX

SUBJECT INDEX